ACHIEVA/CALAIS/GRAND AM/SKYLARK/SOMERSET
1985-95 REPAIR MANUAL

CHILTON'S

Senior Vice President	Ronald A. Hoxter
Publisher and Editor-In-Chief	Kerry A. Freeman, S.A.E.
Executive Editors	Dean F. Morgantini, S.A.E., W. Calvin Settle, Jr., S.A.E.
Managing Editor	Nick D'Andrea
Special Products Manager	Ken Grabowski, A.S.E., S.A.E.
Senior Editors	Jacques Gordon, Michael L. Grady, Debra McCall, Kevin M. G. Maher, Richard J. Rivele, S.A.E., Richard T. Smith, Jim Taylor, Ron Webb
Project Managers	Martin J. Gunther, Will Kessler, A.S.E., Richard Schwartz
Production Manager	Andrea Steiger
Product Systems Manager	Robert Maxey
Director of Manufacturing	Mike D'Imperio
Editor	Christine L. Nuckowski

CHILTON BOOK COMPANY

Manufactured in USA
© 1995 Chilton Book Company
Chilton Way, Radnor, PA 19089
ISBN 0-8019-8688-5
Library of Congress Catalog Card No. 94-069429
3456789012 6543210987

Contents

1 GENERAL INFORMATION AND MAINTENANCE

1-2	HOW TO USE THIS BOOK	1-16	ROUTINE MAINTENANCE
1-3	TOOLS AND EQUIPMENT	1-32	FLUIDS AND LUBRICANTS
1-5	SERVICING YOUR VEHICLE SAFELY	1-46	JACKING
		1-50	SPECIFICATIONS CHARTS

2 ENGINE PERFORMANCE AND TUNE-UP

2-12	FIRING ORDERS	2-39	C³I IGNITION SYSTEM
2-13	HEI SYSTEM	2-56	IGNITION TIMING
2-23	IDI SYSTEM	2-57	VALVE LASH & IDLE
2-33	DIRECT IGNITION	2-58	SPECIFICATIONS CHARTS

3 ENGINE AND ENGINE OVERHAUL

3-2	BASIC ELECTRICITY	3-117	EXHAUST SYSTEM
3-4	ENGINE ELECTRICAL	3-122	BASIC MECHANICAL TROUBLESHOOTING
3-12	ENGINE MECHANICAL		
3-15	SPECIFICATIONS CHARTS		

4 EMISSION CONTROLS

4-2	AIR POLLUTION	4-24	SELF-DIAGNOSTICS
4-3	AUTOMOTIVE EMISSIONS	4-27	TROUBLE CODES AND CHARTS
4-6	EMISSION CONTROLS		
4-16	ENGINE CONTROLS	4-117	VACUUM DIAGRAMS

5 FUEL SYSTEM

5-2	BASIC FUEL SYSTEM DIAGNOSIS	5-9	MULTI-PORT FUEL INJECTION
5-2	THROTTLE BODY FUEL INJECTION	5-28	SEQUENTIAL FUEL INJECTION
		5-38	FUEL LINE FITTINGS

6 CHASSIS ELECTRICAL

6-2	UNDERSTANDING ELECTRICAL SYSTEMS	6-43	WIPERS
6-10	SIR/AIR BAG	6-49	INSTRUMENTS
6-14	HEAT & A/C	6-56	LIGHTING
		6-69	WIRING DIAGRAMS

Contents

7-2 MANUAL TRANSAXLE
7-22 CLUTCH
7-29 AUTOMATIC TRANSAXLE

DRIVE TRAIN 7

8-2 WHEELS
8-3 FRONT SUSPENSION
8-14 SPECIFICATIONS CHARTS
8-16 REAR SUSPENSION
8-21 STEERING

SUSPENSION AND STEERING 8

9-2 BRAKE OPERATING SYSTEM
9-12 FRONT DISC BRAKES
9-18 REAR DRUM BRAKES
9-25 PARKING BRAKE
9-28 ANTI-LOCK BRAKE SYSTEM (ABS)
9-49 SPECIFICATIONS CHARTS

BRAKES 9

10-2 EXTERIOR
10-18 INTERIOR
10-50 SPECIFICATIONS CHARTS

BODY 10

10-52 GLOSSARY

GLOSSARY

10-57 MASTER INDEX

MASTER INDEX

SAFETY NOTICE

Proper service and repair procedures are vital to the safe, reliable operation of all motor vehicles, as well as the personal safety of those performing repairs. This manual outlines procedures for servicing and repairing vehicles using safe, effective methods. The procedures contain many NOTES, CAUTIONS, and WARNINGS which should be followed along with standard procedures to eliminate the possibility of personal injury or improper service which could damage the vehicle or compromise its safety.

It is important to note that the repair procedures and techniques, tools and parts for servicing motor vehicles, as well as the skill and experience of the individual performing the work vary widely. It is not possible to anticipate all of the conceivable ways or conditions under which vehicles may be serviced, or to provide cautions as to all of the possible hazards that may result. Standard and accepted safety precautions and equipment should be used when handling toxic or flammable fluids, and safety goggles or other protection should be used during cutting, grinding, chiseling, prying, or any other process that can cause material removal or projectiles.

Some procedures require the use of tools specially designed for a specific purpose. Before substituting another tool or procedure, you must be completely satisfied that neither your personal safety, nor the performance of the vehicle will be endangered.

Although information in this manual is based on industry sources and is complete as possible at the time of publication, the possibility exists that some car manufacturers made later changes which could not be included here. While striving for total accuracy, Chilton Book Company cannot assume responsibility for any errors, changes or omissions that may occur in the compilation of this data.

PART NUMBERS

Part numbers listed in this reference are not recommendation by Chilton for any product by brand name. They are references that can be used with interchange manuals and aftermarket supplier catalogs to locate each brand supplier's discrete part number.

SPECIAL TOOLS

Special tools are recommended by the vehicle manufacturer to perform their specific job. Use has been kept to a minimum, but where absolutely necessary, they are referred to in the text by the part number of the tool manufacturer. These tools can be purchased, under the appropriate part number, from your local dealer or regional distributor, or an equivalent tool can be purchased locally from a tool supplier or parts outlet. Before substituting any tool for the one recommended, read the SAFETY NOTICE at the top of this page.

ACKNOWLEDGMENTS

Portions of materials contained herein have been reprinted with permission of General Motors Corporation, Service Technology Group.

FLUIDS AND LUBRICANTS
  AUTOMATIC TRANSAXLE 1-35
  BODY LUBRICATION AND
    MAINTENANCE 1-44
  BRAKE MASTER CYLINDER 1-42
  CHASSIS GREASING 1-44
  CLUTCH MASTER CYLINDER 1-43
  COOLING SYSTEM 1-39
  ENGINE 1-33
  FLUID DISPOSAL 1-32
  FUEL AND ENGINE OIL
    RECOMMENDATIONS 1-32
  MANUAL TRANSAXLE 1-35
  POWER STEERING 1-43
  REAR WHEEL BEARINGS 1-45
HOW TO USE THIS BOOK 1-2
JACKING
  CHANGING A FLAT TIRE 1-46
JUMP STARTING 1-48
MODEL IDENTIFICATION 1-7
ROUTINE MAINTENANCE
  AIR CLEANER 1-16
  AIR CONDITIONING SYSTEM 1-25
  BATTERY 1-18
  BELTS 1-22
  CV-BOOT 1-25
  EVAPORATIVE CANISTER 1-18
  FUEL FILTER 1-17
  HOSES 1-24
  PCV VALVE 1-17
  TIMING BELT 1-24
  TIRES AND WHEELS 1-27
  WINDSHIELD WIPERS 1-26
SERIAL NUMBER IDENTIFICATION
  ENGINE 1-7
  TRANSAXLE 1-7
  VEHICLE 1-7
SERVICING YOUR VEHICLE SAFELY
  DO'S 1-5
  DON'TS 1-6
SPECIFICATIONS CHARTS
  CAPACITIES 1-48
  ENGINE IDENFICATION 1-7
  MAINTENANCE INTERVALS 1-48
  VEHICLE IDENTIFICATION 1-7
TOOLS AND EQUIPMENT
  SPECIAL TOOLS 1-5
TOWING THE VEHICLE 1-46
TRAILER TOWING
  GENERAL RECOMMENDATIONS 1-45
  HITCH WEIGHT 1-45
  TRAILER WEIGHT 1-45
  WIRING 1-45

1

GENERAL INFORMATION AND MAINTENANCE

FLUIDS AND LUBRICANTS 1-32
HOW TO USE THIS BOOK 1-2
JACKING 1-46
JUMP STARTING 1-48
MODEL IDENTIFICATION 1-7
ROUTINE MAINTENANCE 1-16
SERIAL NUMBER IDENTIFICATION 1-7
SERVICING YOUR VEHICLE
SAFELY 1-5
SPECIFICATIONS CHARTS 1-7
TOOLS AND EQUIPMENT 1-3
TOWING THE VEHICLE 1-46
TRAILER TOWING 1-45

HOW TO USE THIS BOOK

Chilton's Total Car Care manual for Buick Skylark, Buick Somerset, Oldsmobile Calais, Oldsmobile Achieva and Pontiac Grand Am is intended to teach you more about the inner workings of your car and save you money on its upkeep. The first two sections will be used the most, since they contain maintenance and tune-up information and procedures. The following sections concern themselves with the more complex systems. Operating systems from engine through brakes are covered to the extent that we feel the average do-it-yourselfer should get involved as well as more complex procedures that will benefit both the advanced do-it-yourselfer mechanic as well as the professional.

A secondary purpose of this book is as a reference for owners who want to understand their car and/or their mechanics better. In this case, no tools at all are required.

Before attempting any repairs or service on your car, read through the entire procedure outlined in the appropriate section. This will give you the overall view of what tools and supplies will be required. There is nothing more frustrating than having to walk to the bus stop on Monday morning because you were short one gasket on Sunday afternoon. So read ahead and plan ahead. Each operation should be approached logically and all procedures thoroughly understood before attempting any work. Some special tools that may be required can often be rented from local automotive jobbers or places specializing in renting tools and equipment. Check the yellow pages of your phone book.

All sections contain adjustments, maintenance, removal and installation procedures, and overhaul procedures. When overhaul is not considered practical, we tell you how to remove the failed part and then how to install the new or rebuilt replacement. In this way, you at least save the labor costs. Backyard overhaul of some components is just not practical, but the removal and installation procedure is often simple and well within the capabilities of the average car owner.

Two basic mechanic's rules should be mentioned here. First, whenever the LEFT side of the car or engine is referred to, it is meant to specify the DRIVER'S side of the car. Conversely, the RIGHT side of the car means the PASSENGER'S side. Second, all screws and bolts are removed by turning counterclockwise, and tightened by turning clockwise, unless otherwise noted.

Safety is always the most important rule. Constantly be aware of the dangers involved in working on or around an automobile and take proper precautions to avoid the risk of personal injury or damage to the vehicle. See the section in this section, Servicing Your Vehicle Safely, and the SAFETY NOTICE on the acknowledgment page before attempting any service procedures and pay attention to the instructions provided. There are 3 common mistakes in mechanical work:

1. Incorrect order of assembly, disassembly or adjustment. When taking something apart or putting it together, doing things in the wrong order usually just costs you extra time; however it CAN break something. Read the entire procedure before beginning disassembly. Do everything in the order in which the instructions say you should do it, even if you can't immediately see a reason for it. When you're taking apart something that is very intricate, you might want to draw a picture of how it looks when assembled at one point in order to make sure you get everything back in its proper position. We will supply exploded views whenever possible, but sometimes the job requires more attention to detail than an illustration provides. When making adjustments (especially tune-up adjustments), do them in order. One adjustment often affects another and you cannot expect satisfactory results unless each adjustment is made only when it cannot be changed by any other.

2. Overtorquing (or undertorquing) nuts and bolts. While it is more common for overtorquing to cause damage, undertorquing can cause a fastener to vibrate loose and cause serious damage, especially when dealing with aluminum parts. Pay attention to torque specifications and utilize a torque wrench in assembly. If a torque figure is not available remember that, if you are using the right tool to do the job, you will probably not have to strain yourself to get a fastener tight enough. The pitch of most threads is so slight that the tension you put on the wrench will be multiplied many times in actual force on what you are tightening. A good example of how critical torque is can be seen in the case of spark plug installation, especially where you are putting the plug into an aluminum cylinder head. Too little torque can fail to crush the gasket, causing leakage of combustion gases and consequent overheating of the plug and engine parts. Too much torque can damage the threads or distort the plug, which cha nges the spark gap at the electrode. Since more and more manufacturers are using aluminum in their engine and chassis parts to save weight, a torque wrench should be in any serious do-it-yourselfer's tool box.

➡**There are many commercial chemical products available for ensuring that fasteners won't come loose, even if they are not torqued just right (a very common brand is Loctite®). If you're worried about getting something together tight enough to hold, but loose enough to avoid mechanical damage during assembly, one of these products might offer substantial insurance. Read the label on the package and make sure the product is compatible with the materials, fluids, etc. involved before choosing one.**

3. Crossthreading. This occurs when a part such as a bolt is screwed into a nut or casting at the wrong angle and forced, causing the threads to become damaged. Crossthreading is more likely to occur if access is difficult. It helps to clean and lubricate fasteners, and to start threading with the part to be installed going straight in, using your fingers. If you encounter resistance, unscrew the part and start over again at a different angle until it can be inserted and turned several times without much effort. Keep in mind that many parts, especially spark plugs, use tapered threads so that gentle turning will automatically bring the part you're threading to the proper angle if you don't force it or resist a change in angle. Don't put a wrench on the part until it's been turned in a couple of times by hand. If you suddenly encounter resistance, and the part has not seated fully, don't force it. Pull it back out and make sure it's clean and threading properly.

Always take your time and be patient; once you have some experience, working on your car will become an enjoyable hobby.

TOOLS AND EQUIPMENT

♦ **See Figures 1, 2, 3, 4, 5, 6, 7, 8, 9 and 10**

Naturally, without the proper tools and equipment it is impossible to properly service your vehicle. It would be impossible to catalog each tool that you would need to perform each or every operation in this book. It would also be unwise for the amateur to rush out and buy an expensive set of tools an the theory that he/she may need one or more of them at sometime.

The best approach is to proceed slowly, gathering together a good quality set of those tools that are used most frequently. Don't be misled by the low cost of bargain tools. It is far better to spend a little more for better quality. Forged wrenches, 6- or 12-point sockets and fine tooth ratchets are by far preferable to their less expensive counterparts. As any good mechanic can tell you, there are few worse experiences than trying to work on a truck with bad tools. Your monetary savings will be far outweighed by frustration and mangled knuckles.

Certain tools, plus a basic ability to handle tools, are required to get started. A basic mechanics tool set, a torque wrench, and a Torx bits set. Torx bits are hexlobular drivers which fit both inside and outside on special Torx head fasteners used in various places on your vehicle.

Begin accumulating those tools that are used most frequently; those associated with routine maintenance and tune-up. In addition to the normal assortment of screwdrivers and pliers you should have the following tools for routine maintenance jobs (your vehicle, depending on the model year, uses both SAE and metric fasteners):

• SAE/Metric wrenches, sockets and combination open end/box end wrenches in sizes from ⅛ in. (3mm) to ¾ in. (19mm); and a spark plug socket ¹³/₁₆ in. or ⅝ in.

➡If possible, buy various length socket drive extensions. One break in this department is that the metric sockets available in the U.S. will all fit the ratchet handles and extensions you may already have (¼ in., ⅜ in., and ½ in. drive).

- Jackstands for support
- Oil filter wrench
- Oil filter spout for pouring oil
- Grease gun for chassis lubrication
- Hydrometer for checking the battery
- A container for draining oil
- Many rags for wiping up the inevitable mess
- A quality floor jack

In addition to the above items there are several others that are not absolutely necessary, but handy to have around. These include oil-dry (cat box litter works just as well and may be cheaper), a transmission funnel and the usual supply of lubricants, antifreeze and fluids, although these can be purchased as needed. This is a basic list for routine maintenance, but only your personal needs and desires can accurately determine your list of necessary tools.

The second list of tools is for tune-ups. While the tools involved here are slightly more sophisticated, they need not be

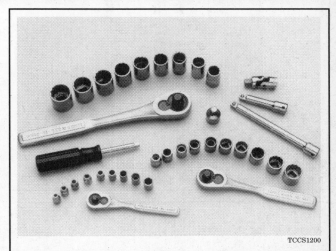

TCCS1200

Fig. 1 All but the most basic procedure will require an assortment of ratchets and sockets

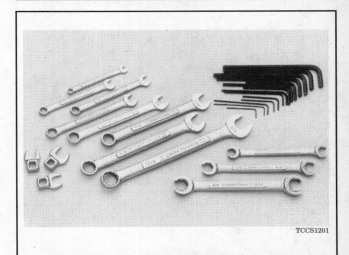

TCCS1201

Fig. 2 In addition to ratchets, a good set of wrenches and hex keys will be necessary

outrageously expensive. There are several inexpensive tach/dwell meters on the market that are every bit as good for the average mechanic as a professional model. Just be sure that it goes to at least 1,200-1,500 rpm on the tach scale and that it works on 4, 6 and 8 cylinder engines. A basic list of tune-up equipment could include:

- Tach-dwell meter
- Spark plug wrench
- Timing light (a DC light that works from the vehicle's battery is best, although an AC light that plugs into 110V house current will suffice at some sacrifice in brightness)
- Wire spark plug gauge/adjusting tools
- A set of feeler gauges

Fig. 3 A hydraulic floor jack and a set of jackstands are essential for lifting and supporting the vehicle

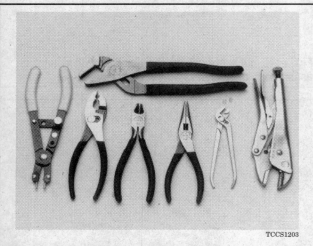

Fig. 4 An assortment of pliers will be handy, especially for old rusted parts and stripped bolt heads

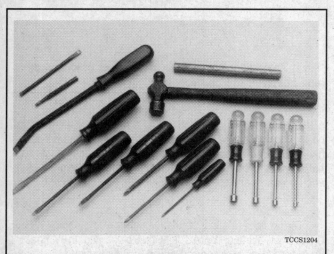

Fig. 5 You should have various screwdrivers, a hammer, chisels and prybars in your toolbox

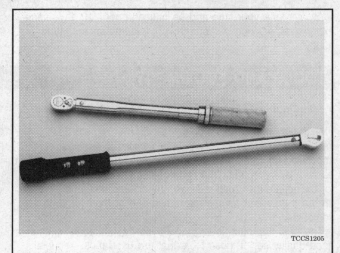

Fig. 6 Many repairs will require the use of a torque wrench to assure the components are properly fastened

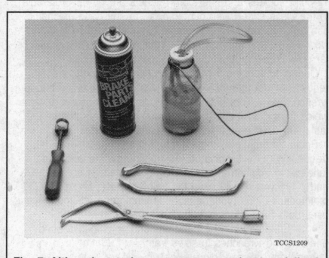

Fig. 7 Although not always necessary, using specialized brake tools will save time

In addition to these basic tools, there are several other tools and gauges you may find useful. These include:

• A compression gauge. The screw-in type is slower to use, but eliminates the possibility of a faulty reading due to escaping pressure
• A manifold vacuum gauge
• A test light
• An induction meter. This is used for determining whether or not there is current in a wire. These are handy for use if a wire is broken somewhere in a wiring harness.

As a final note, you will probably find a torque wrench necessary for all but the most basic work. The beam type models are perfectly adequate, although the newer click type are more precise.

Torque specification for each fastener will be given in the procedure in any case that a specific torque value is required. If no torque specifications are given, use the following values as a guide, based upon fastener size:

Bolts marked 6T
- 6mm bolt/nut — 5-7 ft. lbs. (7-9 Nm)
- 8mm bolt/nut — 12-17 ft. lbs. (16-23 Nm)
- 10mm bolt/nut — 23-34 ft. lbs. (31-46 Nm)
- 12mm bolt/nut — 41-59 ft. lbs. (56-80 Nm)
- 14mm bolt/nut — 56-76 ft. lbs. (76-103 Nm)

Bolts marked 8T
- 6mm bolt/nut — 6-9 ft. lbs. (8-12 Nm)
- 8mm bolt/nut — 13-20 ft. lbs. (18-27 Nm)
- 10mm bolt/nut — 27-40 ft. lbs. (37-54 Nm)
- 12mm bolt/nut — 46-69 ft. lbs. (62-93 Nm)
- 14mm bolt/nut — 75-101 ft. lbs. (102-137 Nm)

Special Tools

Normally, the use of special factory tools is avoided for repair procedures, since these are not readily available for the do-it-yourself mechanic. When it is possible to perform the job with more commonly available tools, it will be pointed out, but occasionally, a special tool was designed to perform a specific function and should be used. Before substituting another tool, you should be convinced that neither your safety nor the performance of the vehicle will be compromised.

When a special tool is indicated, it will be referred to by the manufacturer's part number. Some special tools are available commercially from major tool manufacturers. Others for your car can be purchased from your GM dealer.

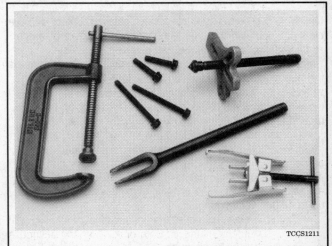

Fig. 9 Various pullers, clamps and separator tools are needed for the repair of many components

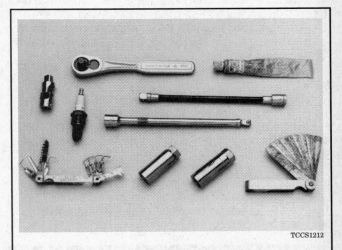

Fig. 10 A variety of tools and gauges are needed for spark plug service

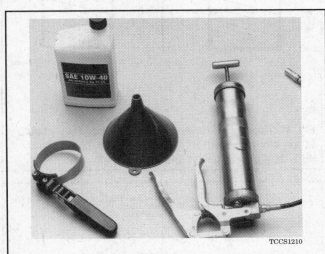

Fig. 8 A few inexpensive lubrication tools will make regular service easier

SERVICING YOUR VEHICLE SAFELY

▶ **See Figures 11 and 12**

It is virtually impossible to anticipate all of the hazards involved with automotive maintenance and service but care and common sense will prevent most accidents.

The rules of safety for mechanics range from "don't smoke around gasoline," to "use the proper tool for the job." The trick to avoid injuries is to develop safe work habits and take every possible precaution.

Do's

- Do keep a fire extinguisher and first aid kit within easy reach.
- Do wear safety glasses or goggles when cutting, drilling, grinding or prying, even if you have 20/20 vision. If you wear glasses for the sake of vision, wear safety goggles over your regular glasses.

• Do shield you eyes whenever you work around the battery. Batteries contain sulfuric acid. In case of contact with the eyes or skin, flush the area with water or a mixture of water and baking soda and get medical attention immediately.

• Do use safety stands for any under-car service. Jacks are for raising vehicles; safety stands are for making sure the vehicle stays raised until you want it to come down. Whenever the vehicle is raised, block the wheels remaining on the ground and set the parking brake.

• Do use adequate ventilation when working with any chemicals. Asbestos dust resulting from brake lining wear can cause cancer.

• Do disconnect the negative battery cable when working on the electrical system. The primary ignition system can contain up to 40,000 volts.

• Do follow manufacturer's directions whenever working with potentially hazardous materials. Both brake fluid and antifreeze are poisonous if taken internally.

• Do properly maintain your tools. Loose hammerheads, mushroomed punches and chisels, frayed or poorly grounded electrical cords, excessively worn screwdriver, spread wrenches (open end), cracked sockets can cause accidents.

• Likewise, keep your tools clean; a greasy wrench can slip off a bolt head, ruining the bolt and often ruining your knuckles in the process.

• Do use the proper size and type of tool for the job being done.

• Do when possible, pull on a wrench handle rather than push on it, and adjust your stance to prevent a fall.

• Do be sure that adjustable wrenches are tightly adjusted on the nut or bolt and pulled so that the face is on the side of the fixed jaw.

• Do select a wrench or socket that fits the nut or bolt. The wrench or socket should sit straight, not cocked.

• Do strike squarely with a hammer to avoid glancing blows.

• Do set the parking brake and block the drive wheels if the work requires a running engine.

Don'ts

• Don't run an engine in a garage or anywhere else without proper ventilation — EVER! Carbon monoxide is poisonous. It is absorbed by the body 400 times faster than oxygen. It takes a long time to leave the human body and you can build up a deadly supply of it in you system by simply breathing in a little every day. You may not realize you are slowly poisoning yourself. Always use power vents, windows, fans or open the garage doors.

• Don't work around moving parts while wearing a necktie or other loose clothing. Short sleeves are much safer than long, loose sleeves. Hard-toed shoes with neoprene soles protect your toes and give a better grip on slippery surfaces. Jewelry such as watches, fancy belt buckles, beads or body adornment of any kind is not safe working around a car. Long hair should be tied back under a hat or cap.

• Don't use pockets for tool boxes. A fall or bump can drive a screwdriver deep into you body. Even a wiping cloth hanging from the back pocket can wrap around a spinning shaft or fan.

• Don't smoke when working around gasoline, cleaning solvent or other flammable material.

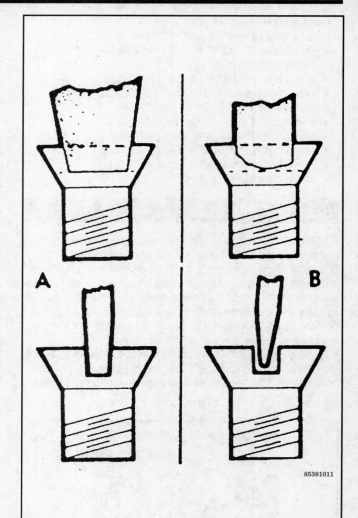

Fig. 11 Keep screwdrivers in good shape. They should fit the slot as shown in "A". If they look like those in "B", they should be ground or replaced.

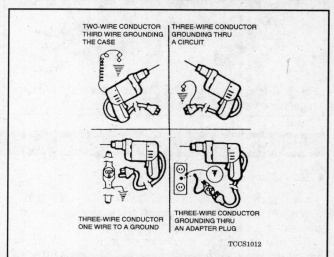

Fig. 12 When using electric tools, make sure they are properly grounded

- Don't smoke when working around the battery. When the battery is being charged, it gives off explosive hydrogen gas.
- Don't use gasoline to wash your hands. There are excellent soaps available. Gasoline contains certain compounds which are hazardous to your health, and can enter the body through a cut, accumulating in the body until you are very ill. Gasoline also removes all the natural oils from the skin so that bone dry hands will suck up oil and grease.
- Don't service the air conditioning system unless you are equipped with the necessary tools and training. The refrigerant R-12 or R-134a is extremely cold when compressed, and when released into the air, will instantly freeze any surface it comes in contact with, including your eyes. Although the refrigerant is normally nontoxic, R-12 becomes a deadly poisonous gas in the presence of an open flame. One good whiff of the vapors from burning refrigerant can be fatal.

- Don't release refrigerant into the atmosphere. In most states it is now illegal to discharge refrigerant into the atmosphere due to the harmful effects Freon® (R-12) has on the ozone layer. Check with local authorities about the laws in your state.
- Don't use screwdrivers for anything other than driving screws! A screwdriver used as a prying tool can snap when you least expect it, causing injuries. At the very least, you ruin a good screwdriver.
- Don't use a bumper jack (that little ratchet, scissors or pantograph jack supplied with the car) for anything other than changing a flat! These jacks are only intended for emergency use out on the road; they are NOT designed as a maintenance tool. If you are serious about maintaining your vehicle yourself, invest in a hydraulic floor jack of at least 1½ ton capacity, and at least two sturdy jackstands.

MODEL IDENTIFICATION

General Motors introduced the N body line of vehicles in 1985 to three of its divisions: Buick, Oldsmobile and Pontiac. The Buick models included the Somerset and Skylark. The Somerset was discontinued after 1987. The Oldsmobile version was the Cutlass Calais until 1992 and the Pontiac model remains the Grand Am. General Motors did a body redesign for all three N body vehicles in 1992, with the Oldsmobile model changing its name from Cutlass Calais to Achieva.

SERIAL NUMBER IDENTIFICATION

Vehicle

▶ See Figures 13 and 14

The Vehicle Identification Number (VIN) plate which contains the Vehicle Identification Number (VIN) is located at the top and back of the instrument panel on the left side and is visible from outside the vehicle on the lower left (driver's) side of the windshield. The VIN consists of 17 characters which represent codes supplying important information about your vehicle. Refer to the illustration of an example of VIN interpretation.

Engine

▶ See Figures 15, 16, 17, 18, 19, 20, 21 and 22

The engine code is represented by the eighth character in the VIN and identifies the engine type, displacement, fuel system type and manufacturing division.

The engine identification code is either stamped onto the engine block or found on a label affixed to the engine. This code supplies information about the manufacturing plant location and time of manufacture. The location for a particular engine is shown in the accompanying illustrations.

86881014

Fig. 13 The VIN is made up of 17 characters which represent codes supplying important information about your vehicle

Transaxle

▶ See Figures 23, 24, 25, 26, 27 and 28

Similar to the engine identification code, the transaxle identification code supplies information about the transaxle such as manufacturing plant, Julian date of manufacture, shift number and model. The location for the transaxle code is shown in the accompanying illustrations.

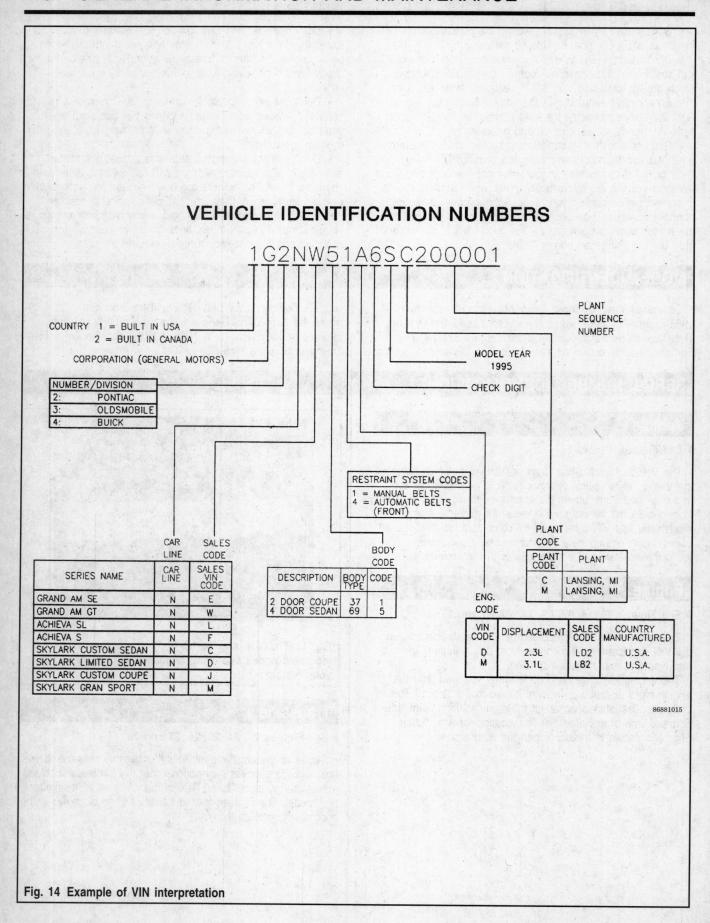

VEHICLE IDENTIFICATION NUMBERS

1G2NW51A6SC200001

COUNTRY 1 = BUILT IN USA
         2 = BUILT IN CANADA

CORPORATION (GENERAL MOTORS)

NUMBER/DIVISION	
2:	PONTIAC
3:	OLDSMOBILE
4:	BUICK

PLANT SEQUENCE NUMBER

MODEL YEAR 1995

CHECK DIGIT

RESTRAINT SYSTEM CODES
1 = MANUAL BELTS
4 = AUTOMATIC BELTS (FRONT)

CAR LINE

SALES CODE

SERIES NAME	CAR LINE	SALES VIN CODE
GRAND AM SE	N	E
GRAND AM GT	N	W
ACHIEVA SL	N	L
ACHIEVA S	N	F
SKYLARK CUSTOM SEDAN	N	C
SKYLARK LIMITED SEDAN	N	D
SKYLARK CUSTOM COUPE	N	J
SKYLARK GRAN SPORT	N	M

BODY CODE

DESCRIPTION	BODY TYPE	CODE
2 DOOR COUPE	37	1
4 DOOR SEDAN	69	5

ENG. CODE

PLANT CODE

PLANT CODE	PLANT
C	LANSING, MI
M	LANSING, MI

VIN CODE	DISPLACEMENT	SALES CODE	COUNTRY MANUFACTURED
D	2.3L	LD2	U.S.A.
M	3.1L	L82	U.S.A.

86881015

Fig. 14 Example of VIN interpretation

VEHICLE IDENTIFICATION CHART

Engine Code							Model Year	
Code	Liters	Cu. In. (cc)	Cyl.	Fuel Sys.	Eng. Mfg.		Code	Year
M [1]	2.0	121 (1983)	4	MFI-Turbo	Pontiac		F	1985
A	2.3	138 (2261)	4	MFI	Pontiac/Olds.		G	1986
D	2.3	138 (2261)	4	MFI	Pont./Olds./Buick		H	1987
3	2.3	138 (2261)	4	MFI	Pont./Olds./Buick		J	1988
U	2.5	151 (2474)	4	TFI	Pont./Olds./Buick		K	1989
L	3.0	183 (2999)	6	MFI	Pont./Olds./Buick		L	1990
M	3.1	191 (3130)	6	MFI	Pont./Olds./Buick		M	1991
N	3.3	204 (3342)	6	MFI	Pont./Olds./Buick		N	1992
							P	1993
							R	1994
							S	1995

TFI - Throttle body fuel injection

MFI - Multiport fuel injection

BOC - Buick/Oldsmobile/Cadillac

1 Turbocharged

86881500

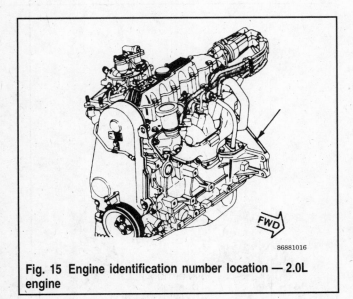

Fig. 15 Engine identification number location — 2.0L engine

86881016

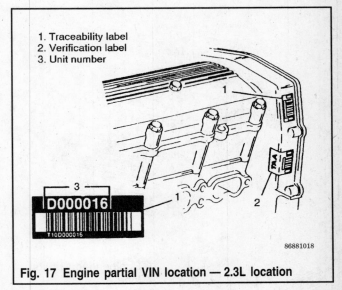

1. Traceability label
2. Verification label
3. Unit number

3

D000016

T10D000016

86881018

Fig. 17 Engine partial VIN location — 2.3L location

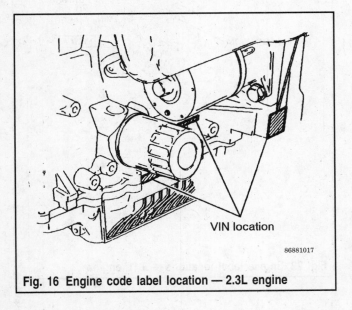

VIN location

86881017

Fig. 16 Engine code label location — 2.3L engine

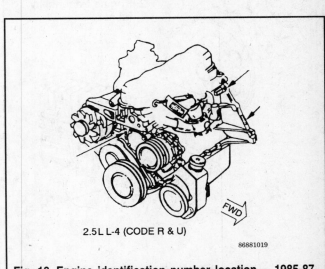

2.5L L-4 (CODE R & U)

86881019

Fig. 18 Engine identification number location — 1985-87 2.5L engine

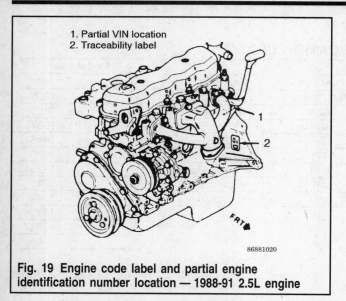

1. Partial VIN location
2. Traceability label

86881020

Fig. 19 Engine code label and partial engine identification number location — 1988-91 2.5L engine

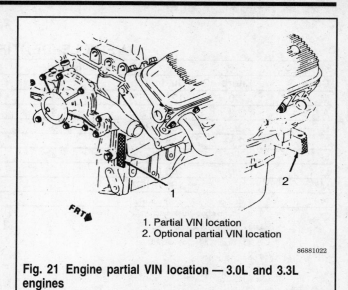

1. Partial VIN location
2. Optional partial VIN location

86881022

Fig. 21 Engine partial VIN location — 3.0L and 3.3L engines

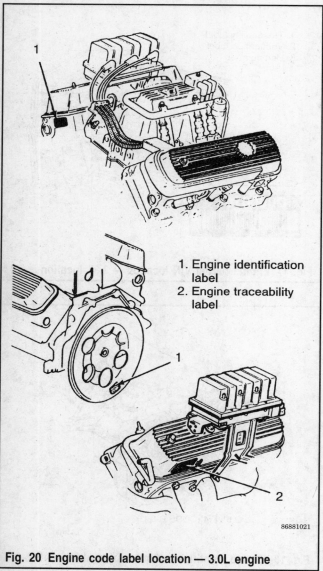

1. Engine identification label
2. Engine traceability label

86881021

Fig. 20 Engine code label location — 3.0L engine

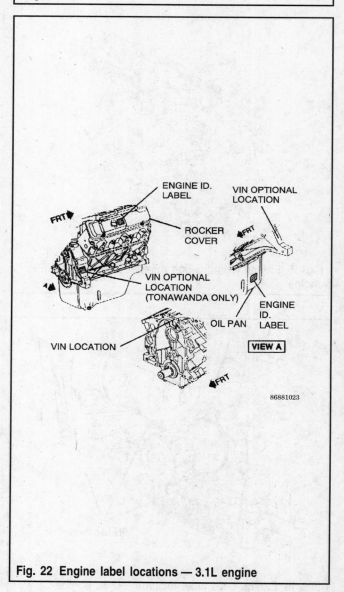

86881023

Fig. 22 Engine label locations — 3.1L engine

ENGINE IDENTIFICATION

Year	Model	Engine Displacement Liters (cc)	Engine Series (ID/VIN)	Fuel System	No. of Cylinders	Engine Type
1985	Grand Am	2.5 (2475)	U	TBI	4	OHV
	Grand Am	3.0 (2998)	L	MFI	6	OHV
	Calais	2.5 (2474)	U	TBI	4	OHV
	Calais	3.0 (2999)	L	MFI	6	OHV
	Somerset Regal	2.5 (2474)	U	TBI	4	OHV
	Somerset Regal	3.0 (2999)	L	MFI	6	OHV
1986	Grand Am	2.5 (2475)	U	TBI	4	OHV
	Grand Am	3.0 (2998)	L	MFI	6	OHV
	Calais	2.5 (2474)	U	TBI	4	OHV
	Calais	3.0 (2999)	L	MFI	6	OHV
	Somerset Regal	2.5 (2474)	U	TBI	4	OHV
	Somerset Regal	3.0 (2999)	L	MFI	6	OHV
1987	Grand Am	2.0 (1998)	M	MFI-Turbo	4	SOHC
	Grand Am	2.5 (2475)	U	TBI	4	OHV
	Grand Am	3.0 (2998)	L	MFI	6	OHV
	Calais	2.5 (2474)	U	TBI	4	OHV
	Calais	3.0 (2999)	L	MFI	6	OHV
	Somerset Regal	2.5 (2474)	U	TBI	4	OHV
	Somerset Regal	3.0 (2999)	L	MFI	6	OHV
1988	Grand Am	2.0 (1998)	M	MFI-Turbo	4	SOHC
	Grand Am	2.3 (2262)	D	MFI	4	DOHC
	Grand Am	2.5 (2475)	U	TBI	4	OHV
	Cutlass Calais	2.3 (2261)	D	MFI	4	DOHC
	Cutlass Calais	2.5 (2474)	U	TBI	4	OHV
	Cutlass Calais	3.0 (2999)	L	MFI	6	OHV
	Skylark	2.3 (2261)	D	MFI	4	DOHC
	Skylark	2.5 (2474)	U	TBI	4	OHV
	Skylark	3.0 (2999)	L	MFI	6	OHV
1989	Grand Am	2.0 (1998)	M	MFI-Turbo	4	SOHC
	Grand Am	2.3 (2262)	A	MFI	4	DOHC
	Grand Am	2.3 (2262)	D	MFI	4	DOHC
	Grand Am	2.5 (2475)	U	TBI	4	OHV
	Cutlass Calais	2.3 (2261)	A	MFI	4	DOHC
	Cutlass Calais	2.3 (2261)	D	MFI	4	DOHC
	Cutlass Calais	2.5 (2474)	U	TBI	4	OHV
	Cutlass Calais	3.3 (3342)	N	MFI	6	OHV
	Skylark	2.3 (2261)	D	MFI	4	DOHC
	Skylark	2.5 (2474)	U	TBI	4	OHV
	Skylark	3.3 (3342)	N	MFI	6	OHV
1990	Grand Am	2.3 (2262)	A	MFI	4	DOHC
	Grand Am	2.3 (2262)	D	MFI	4	DOHC
	Grand Am	2.5 (2475)	U	TBI	4	OHV
	Cutlass Calais	2.3 (2261)	A	MFI	4	DOHC
	Cutlass Calais	2.3 (2261)	D	MFI	4	DOHC
	Cutlass Calais	2.5 (2474)	U	TBI	4	OHV
	Cutlass Calais	3.3 (3342)	N	MFI	6	OHV
	Skylark	2.3 (2261)	D	MFI	4	DOHC
	Skylark	2.5 (2474)	U	TBI	4	OHV
	Skylark	3.3 (3342)	N	MFI	6	OHV

86881501

ENGINE IDENTIFICATION

Year	Model	Engine Displacement Liters (cc)	Engine Series (ID/VIN)	Fuel System	No. of Cylinders	Engine Type
1991	Grand Am	2.3 (2262)	A	MFI	4	DOHC
	Grand Am	2.3 (2262)	D	MFI	4	DOHC
	Grand Am	2.5 (2475)	U	TBI	4	OHV
	Cutlass Calais	2.3 (2261)	A	MFI	4	DOHC
	Cutlass Calais	2.3 (2261)	D	MFI	4	DOHC
	Cutlass Calais	2.5 (2474)	U	TBI	4	OHV
	Cutlass Calais	3.3 (3342)	N	MFI	6	OHV
	Skylark	2.3 (2261)	D	MFI	4	DOHC
	Skylark	2.5 (2474)	U	TBI	4	OHV
	Skylark	3.3 (3342)	N	MFI	6	OHV
1992	Grand Am	2.3 (2262)	A	MFI	4	DOHC
	Grand Am	2.3 (2262)	D	MFI	4	DOHC
	Grand Am	2.3 (2262)	3	MFI	4	SOHC
	Grand Am	3.3 (3344)	N	MFI	6	OHV
	Achieva	2.3 (2262)	A	MFI	4	DOHC
	Achieva	2.3 (2262)	D	MFI	4	DOHC
	Achieva	2.3 (2262)	3	MFI	4	SOHC
	Achieva	3.3 (3344)	N	MFI	6	OHV
	Skylark	2.3 (2262)	3	MFI	4	SOHC
	Skylark	3.3 (3344)	N	MFI	6	OHV
1993	Grand Am	2.3 (2262)	A	MFI	4	DOHC
	Grand Am	2.3 (2262)	D	MFI	4	DOHC
	Grand Am	2.3 (2262)	3	MFI	4	SOHC
	Grand Am	3.3 (3344)	N	MFI	6	OHV
	Achieva	2.3 (2262)	A	MFI	4	DOHC
	Achieva	2.3 (2262)	D	MFI	4	DOHC
	Achieva	2.3 (2262)	3	MFI	4	SOHC
	Achieva	3.3 (3344)	N	MFI	6	OHV
	Skylark	2.3 (2262)	3	MFI	4	SOHC
	Skylark	3.3 (3344)	N	MFI	6	OHV
1994	Grand Am	2.3 (2262)	A	MFI	4	DOHC
	Grand Am	2.3 (2262)	D	MFI	4	DOHC
	Grand Am	2.3 (2262)	3	MFI	4	SOHC
	Grand Am	3.1 (3136)	M	SFI	6	OHV
	Achieva	2.3 (2262)	A	MFI	4	DOHC
	Achieva	2.3 (2262)	D	MFI	4	DOHC
	Achieva	2.3 (2262)	3	MFI	4	SOHC
	Achieva	3.3 (3344)	N	MFI	6	OHV
	Skylark	2.3 (2262)	3	MFI	4	SOHC
	Skylark	3.1 (3130)	M	SFI	6	OHV
1995	Grand Am	2.3 (2262)	D	MFI	4	DOHC
	Grand Am	3.1 (3136)	M	SFI	6	OHV
	Achieva	2.3 (2261)	D	MFI	4	DOHC
	Achieva	3.1 (3130)	M	SFI	6	OHV
	Skylark	2.3 (2261)	D	MFI	4	DOHC
	Skylark	3.1 (3130)	M	SFI	6	OHV

TBI - Throttle Body fuel Injection
MFI - Multi-port Fuel Injection
SFI - Sequential Fuel Injection
OHV - Overhead Valve
SOHC - Single Overhead Camshaft
DOHC - Double overhead camshaft

86881502

ENGINE IDENTIFICATION

Year	Model	Engine Displacement Liters (cc)	Engine Series (ID/VIN)	Fuel System	No. of Cylinders	Engine Type
1995	Achieva	3.1 (3130)	M	MFI	6	OHV
	Skylark	2.3 (2261)	D	MFI	4	DOHC
	Skylark	3.1 (3130)	M	MFI	6	OHV

TFI - Throttle body fuel injection
MFI - Multi-port fuel injection
SOHC - Single overhead camshaft
OHV - Overhead valve
DOHC - Double overhead camshaft

86881503

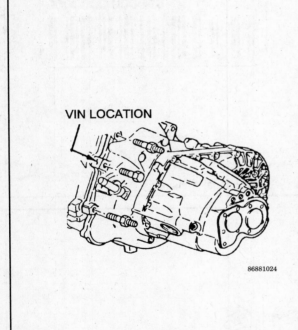

Fig. 23 Manual transaxle identification number location — HM-282 manual transaxle

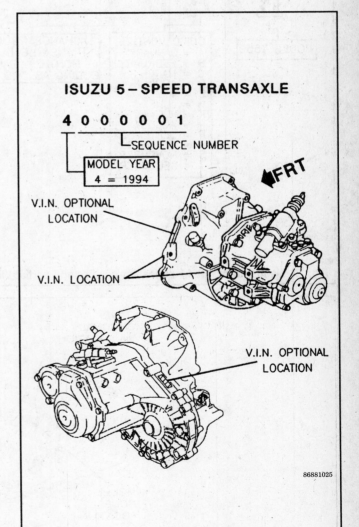

Fig. 24 Manual transaxle identification number and partial VIN location — Isuzu 76mm manual transaxle

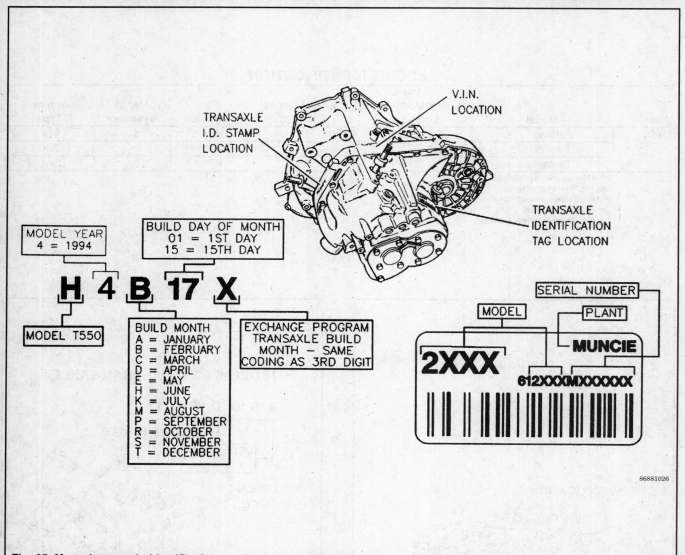

Fig. 25 Manual transaxle identification number and partial VIN location — 5T40 manual transaxle

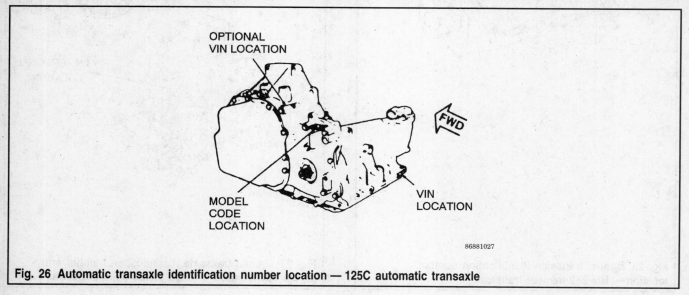

Fig. 26 Automatic transaxle identification number location — 125C automatic transaxle

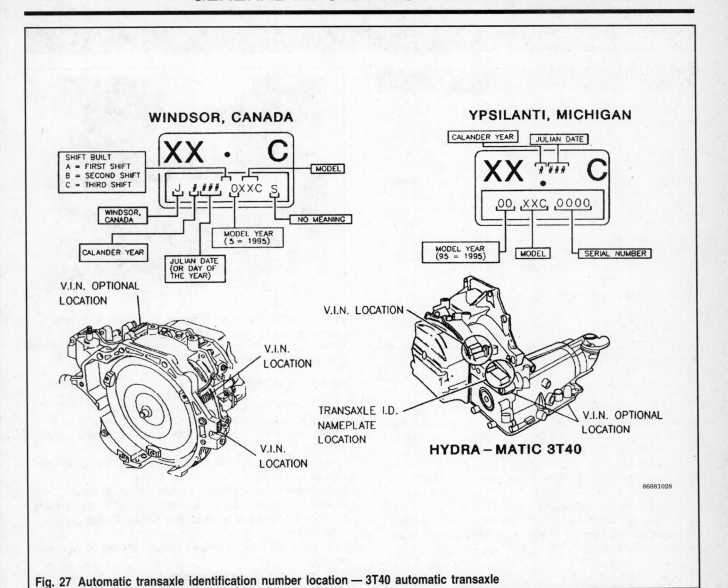

Fig. 27 Automatic transaxle identification number location — 3T40 automatic transaxle

Fig. 28 Automatic transaxle identification number location — 4T60E automatic transaxle

ROUTINE MAINTENANCE

Air Cleaner °

The air cleaner keeps airborne dust and dirt from flowing into the engine. If allowed to enter the engine, dust and dirt combine with engine oil to create an abrasive compound which can drastically shorten engine life. Accordingly, the engine should never be run for a prolonged period without the air cleaner in place. A dirty air cleaner blocks the flow of air into the engine and can artificially richen the air/fuel mixture adversely affecting fuel economy and can even lead to damage to the catalytic converter.

The air cleaner should be checked periodically and replaced at least every 30,000 miles, more frequently in dusty driving conditions. Be sure the replacement air cleaner provides a proper fit and is not loose so that air is able to flow around the air cleaner instead of through it.

REMOVAL & INSTALLATION

♦ See Figures 29 and 30

2.0L (VIN M) and 2.5L (VIN U)

1. Remove the air cleaner cover by removing the wing nut(s). For some early model 2.5L engines, it will be necessary to first remove the top of the cleaner assembly by releasing the fastener clip(s) to access the wing nut(s).
2. Remove the old air cleaner element.
3. Wipe remaining dirt from the air cleaner housing.
   To install:
4. Install the new air cleaner element
5. Install the air cleaner cover, then install the wing nut(s). If applicable, install the top of the air cleaner assembly fastening the retaining clip(s).

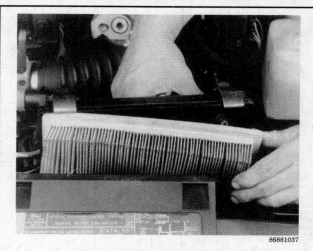

Fig. 30 After the cover is pulled away, the air cleaner element can be removed from the housing

2.3L (VIN D, A and 3)

1988-91 VEHICLES

1. Remove the upper and lower duct clamps.
2. Disconnect the intake duct-to-oil/air separator hose.
3. Remove the air duct from the throttle body and air filter housing.
4. Remove the 2 air filter housing-to-cover hold-down clips, then separate.
5. Remove the air cleaner element and clean the air cleaner housing to remove any remaining dirt. Inspect the element for dirt, dust and/or water, and replace if necessary.
   To install:
6. Install the new air cleaner element into the air cleaner housing.
7. Install the air cleaner housing cover.
8. Install the 2 hold-down clips to the cover.
9. Connect the upper air filter duct with clamps to the air filter housing inlet and throttle body.
10. Connect the intake duct-to-oil/air separator hose.
11. Install the upper and lower duct clamps.

1992-95 VEHICLES

1. Depending upon application, unfasten the air cleaner clamp, or disconnect the air cleaner screws.
2. Remove the upper air cleaner, then remove the filter from the upper air cleaner. Inspect the air cleaner element/filter for dust, dirt and/or water and replace if necessary.
   To install:
3. Place the air cleaner element/filter in the upper air cleaner.
4. Install the upper air cleaner to the lower air cleaner.
5. Install the retaining screws, or fasten the clamp.

3.0L (VIN L) and 3.3L (VIN N)

1. Remove the air cleaner cover, by unlatching the retaining clamp(s).
2. Remove the air cleaner element.

Fig. 29 Remove the air cleaner cover by unlatching the retaining clamps as applicable

3. Wipe the inside of the air cleaner housing to remove dirt. Inspect the element for dust, dirt and/or water and replace if necessary.

To install:

4. Install the air cleaner element.

5. Install the air cleaner cover by fastening the retaining clamp(s).

3.1L (VIN M)

1. Disconnect and remove the air cleaner retaining screws, then remove the upper air cleaner assembly and position is aside.

2. Remove the air cleaner filter/element. Inspect the filter/element for dust, dirt, or other contaminants, and replace if necessary.

To install:

3. Position the filter/element to the upper air cleaner.

4. Install the upper air cleaner to the lower air cleaner, then install the retaining screws.

Fuel Filter

The fuel filter is located near the rear of the vehicle, forward or rearward of the fuel tank, depending upon application.

REMOVAL & INSTALLATION

▶ See Figures 31 and 32

1. Relieve the fuel system pressure. For details regarding this procedure, please refer to Section 5 of this manual.

2. If not done already, disconnect the negative battery cable.

3. Raise and safely support the vehicle.

4. Clean both fuel feed pipe connections and the surrounding areas at the in-line fuel filter with a clean rag to avoid possible contamination of the fuel system.

5. Using a backup wrench, remove the fuel line fittings from the fuel filter.

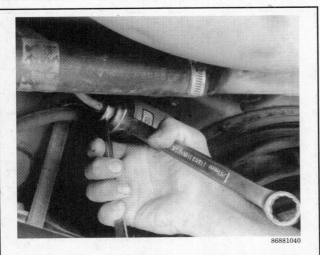

Fig. 31 Always use a backup wrench to avoid twisting the lines

6. Either disconnect the quick-connect fittings or remove the fuel filter mounting screws, then remove the filter from the vehicle.

7. Discard the fuel line O-rings and replace with new ones during installation.

To install:

8. Install new O-rings to the fuel line fittings.

9. Connect the fuel lines to the fuel filter.

10. Position the filter in the same position it was during removal. Using a backup wrench, tighten the fuel lines to 20-22 ft. lbs. (27-30 Nm).

11. Install the fuel filter mounting screws.

12. Lower the vehicle. Install or tighten the fuel filler cap, then connect the negative battery cable.

13. Start the engine and check for leaks.

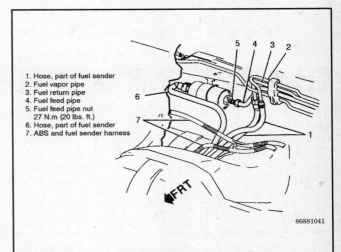

1. Hose, part of fuel sender
2. Fuel vapor pipe
3. Fuel return pipe
4. Fuel feed pipe
5. Fuel feed pipe nut 27 N.m (20 lbs. ft.)
6. Hose, part of fuel sender
7. ABS and fuel sender harness

Fig. 32 View of the in-line fuel filter and related components

PCV Valve

Vehicles equipped with 2.3L engines (VIN D, A and 3) for all years or the 2.5L engine (VIN U) for 1991 use a crankcase breather system that does not use a PCV valve. The 2.3L engines (VIN D and A) are equipped with an oil/air separator that does not require service. Should the oil/air separator become clogged, the unit must be replaced. In the 2.5L engine (VIN U) in 1991 the standard PCV valve is replaced with a constant bleed orifice. If the orifice becomes clogged, clear if possible or replace.

REMOVAL & INSTALLATION

▶ See Figure 33

1. Remove the PCV valve from the grommet in the valve cover.

2. Remove the PCV valve from the breather hose.

To install:

3. Install the new PCV valve into the breather hose.

4. Install the PCV valve into the grommet in the valve cover.

Fig. 33 Removing the PCV valve — 1986 3.0L Grand Am shown

Evaporative Canister

This system is designed to limit gasoline vapor, which normally escapes from the fuel tank and the intake manifold, from discharging into the atmosphere. Vapor absorption is accomplished through the use of the charcoal canister and stores them until they can be removed and burned in the combustion process.

REMOVAL & INSTALLATION

1. Disconnect the negative battery cable.
2. Label and disconnect the hoses from the canister.
3. Remove the charcoal canister retaining nuts, then remove the canister from the vehicle.
4. Installation is the reverse of the removal procedure. Refer to the Vehicle Emission Control Information (VECI) label, located in the engine compartment, for proper routing of the vacuum hoses.

Battery

GENERAL MAINTENANCE

▶ See Figures 34, 35 and 36

Loose, dirty, or corroded battery terminals are a major cause of "no-start" conditions. Every 3 months or so, remove the battery terminals and clean them. This will help to retard corrosion.

Check the battery cables for signs of wear or chafing and replace any cable or terminal that looks marginal. Battery terminals can be easily cleaned and inexpensive terminal cleaning tools are an excellent investment that will pay for themselves many times over. They can usually be purchased from any well-equipped auto store or parts department. Side terminal batteries require a different tool to clean the threads in the battery case. The accumulated white powder and corrosion can

be cleaned from the top of the battery with an old toothbrush and a solution of baking soda and water.

Unless you have a maintenance-free battery, check the electrolyte level and the specific gravity of each cell. Be sure that the vent holes in each cell cap are not blocked by grease or dirt. The vent holes allow hydrogen gas, formed by the chemical reaction in the battery, to escape safely.

FLUID LEVEL (EXCEPT MAINTENANCE-FREE BATTERIES)

▶ See Figure 37

Check the battery electrolyte level at least once a month, or more often in hot weather or during periods of extended car operation. The level can be checked through the case on translucent polypropylene batteries; the cell caps must be removed on other models. The electrolyte level in each cell should be kept filled to the split ring inside, or the line marked on the outside of the case.

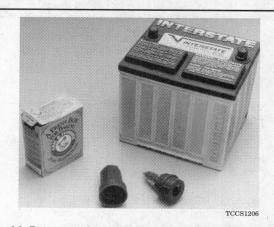

Fig. 34 Battery maintenance may be accomplished with household items (such as baking soda to neutralize spilled acid) or with special tools such as this post and terminal cleaner

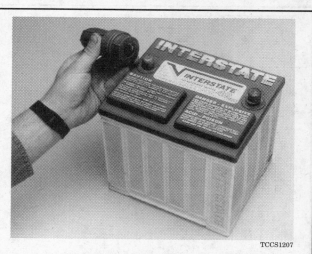

Fig. 35 The underside of this special battery tool has a wire brush to clean post terminals

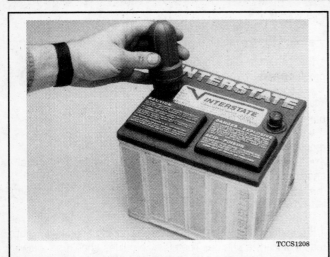

Fig. 36 Place the tool over the terminals and twist to clean the post

If the level is low, add only distilled water, or colorless, odorless drinking water, through the opening until the level is correct. Each cell is completely separate from the others, so each must be checked and filled individually.

If water is added in freezing weather, the car should be driven several miles to allow the water to mix with the electrolyte. Otherwise, the battery could freeze.

SPECIFIC GRAVITY (EXCEPT MAINTENANCE-FREE BATTERIES)

At least once a year, check the specific gravity of the battery using a hydrometer.

A hydrometer, is an inexpensive instrument available from many sources, including auto parts stores. The hydrometer has a squeeze bulb at one end and a nozzle at the other. Battery electrolyte is sucked into the hydrometer until the float is lifted from its seat. The specific gravity is then read by noting the position of the float. Generally, if after charging, the specific

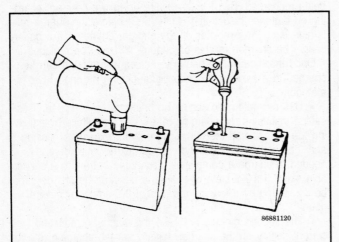

Fig. 37 Two devices used to maintain electrolyte level: A self-leveling filler which fills to a predetermined level and a syringe-type filler

gravity between any two cells varies more than 50 points (0.50), the battery is bad and should be replaced.

It is not possible to check the specific gravity in this manner on sealed (maintenance-free) batteries. Instead, the indicator built into the top of the case must be relied on to display any signs of battery deterioration. If the indicator is dark, the battery can be assumed to be OK. If the indicator is light, the specific gravity is low, and the battery should be charged or replaced.

CABLES

Once every 6 months, the battery terminals and the cable clamps should be cleaned. Loosen the clamps and remove the cables, negative cable first. On batteries with posts on top, the use of a puller specially made for this purpose is recommended. Damage may occur to the battery if proper terminal pullers are not used. These are inexpensive, and available in auto parts stores. Side terminal battery cables are secured with a bolt, and do not require a puller.

Clean the cable clamps and the battery terminal with a wire brush, until all corrosion, grease, etc. is removed and the metal is shiny. It is especially important to clean the inside of the clamp thoroughly, since a small deposit of foreign material or oxidation there can prevent a sound electrical connection and inhibit starting and/or charging. Special tools are available for cleaning these parts, one type for conventional batteries and another type for side terminal batteries.

Before installing the cable, loosen the battery hold-down clamp or strap, remove the battery and check the battery tray. Clear it of any debris, and check it for soundness. Rust should be wire brushed away, and the metal given a coat of anti-rust paint. Before replacing the battery, wash it with soap and water to remove any dirt. Replace the battery and tighten the hold-down clamp or strap securely, but be careful not to overtighten, which will crack the battery case.

After the clamps and terminals are clean, reinstall the cables, negative cable last; do not hammer on the clamps to install. Tighten the clamps securely, but do not distort them. Give the clamps and terminals a thin external coat of grease after installation, to retard corrosion.

Check the cables at the same time that the terminals are cleaned. If the cable insulation is cracked or broken, or if the ends are frayed, the cable should be replaced with a new cable of the same length and gauge.

✳✳CAUTION

Keep flames and sparks away from the battery; it gives off explosive hydrogen gas. Battery electrolyte contains sulfuric acid. If you should splash any on your skin or in your eyes, flush the affected areas with plenty of clear water; if it lands in your eyes, get medical help immediately.

TESTING

▶ See Figure 38

Some maintenance-free batteries are equipped with a built-in hydrometer. To check the condition of the battery, observe the "eye" on the top of the battery case for the following conditions:

1. If the indicator is dark, the battery has enough fluid. If the eye is light, the electrolyte level is low and the battery must be replaced.

2. If the indicator is green, the battery is sufficiently charged. Proceed to Step 3. If the green dot is not visible, charge the battery.

➡**Do not charge the battery for more than 50 amp-hours. If the green dot appears or if the electrolyte squirts out of the vent hole, stop the charge and proceed to Step 4. It may be necessary to tip the battery from side-to-side in order to get the green dot to appear after charging.**

✳✳WARNING

When charging the battery, the electrical system and control unit can be quickly damaged by improper connections, high output battery chargers or incorrect service procedures.

3. Connect a battery load tester and a voltmeter across the battery terminals (the battery cable should be disconnected from the battery). Apply a 300 amp load to the battery for 15 seconds to remove the surface charge. Remove the load.

4. Wait 15 seconds to allow the battery to recover. Apply the appropriate test load for 15 seconds while reading the voltage. Disconnect the load.

5. Check the results against specifications. If the voltage is at or above the specified voltage for the temperature listed, the battery is good. If the voltage falls below specification, the battery should be replace.

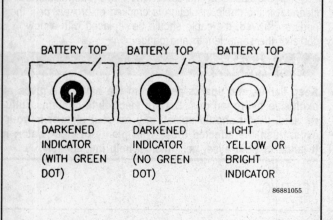

BATTERY TOP — DARKENED INDICATOR (WITH GREEN DOT)

BATTERY TOP — DARKENED INDICATOR (NO GREEN DOT)

BATTERY TOP — LIGHT YELLOW OR BRIGHT INDICATOR

86881055

Fig. 38 Some maintenance-free batteries are equipped with a built-in hydrometer

CHARGING

Before recharging a battery, see if any of the following problems exist:
- Loose alternator belt
- Pinched or grounded alternator/voltage regulator wiring harness
- Loose wiring connection at the alternator and/or voltage regulator
- Loose or corroded connections at the battery and/or the engine ground
- Excessive battery drain due to any accessories or lighting left on.

If any of these exist, remedy the problem, then check to see if the battery still needs to be charged. Cold batteries will not readily accept a charge. Therefore, batteries should be allowed to warm up to approximately 41°F (5°C) before charging. This may require allowing the battery to warm up at room temperature for four to eight hours, depending on the initial temperature and the size of the battery. A battery which has been completely discharged may be slow to accept a charge initially, and in some cases may not accept a charge at the normal charger setting. When batteries are in this condition, charging can be started by using a dead battery switch, on chargers equipped with one.

Completely discharged batteries, which have been discharged for a prolonged period of time (over one month) or which have an open circuit voltage of less than two volts, may not indicate accepting a charge even when the dead battery switch is used. The initial charge rate accepted by batteries in this condition is so low, that the ammeter on some charges will not show any indication of charge for up to 10 minutes. To determine whether a battery is accepting a charge, follow the charger manufacturer's instructions for the use of the dead battery switch. If the dead battery switch is the spring-loaded type, it should be held in the ON position for up to three minutes.

After releasing the dead battery switch and with the charger still on, measure the battery voltage. If it shows 12 volts or higher, the battery is accepting a charge and is capable of being recharged. But, it may require up to two hours of charging on batteries colder than 41°F (5°C) before the charge rate is high enough to register on the charger ammeter. If a battery cannot be charged by this procedure, it should be replaced.

Once the battery has begun to accept a charge, it can be charged to a serviceable state or full charge by one of two methods:
- Use the automatic setting on chargers so equipped. This setting maintains the charging rate within safe limits by adjusting the voltage and the current to prevent excessive gassing and the spewing of electrolyte. About two to four hours is needed to charge a completely discharged battery to a serviceable state. If a full state of charge is desired, the charge can be completed by a low current rate of 3-5 amps for several hours.
- The second method is to use the manual or constant current setting on the charger. Initially set the charging rate for 30-40 amps and maintain this setting for about 30 minutes or as long as there is not excessive gassing and electrolyte spewing. If gassing results, the charge rate must be reduced to a level where gassing will stop. This is especially true for

maintenance-free batteries, in which excessive gassing will result in non-replaceable loss of electrolyte, shortening the battery life.

The total charge necessary will vary with battery size and its initial state of charge. In general, to bring a discharged battery to a serviceable state of charge, the amount of charging current multiplied by the charging time should equal the battery amp-hour capacity. For example, a 45 AH battery will need 15 amps of charge for three hours, or 9 amps of charge for five hours. If a full state of charge is desired, the charge can be completed by a low constant current of 3-5 amps for several hours.

REPLACEMENT

▶ **See Figures 39 and 40**

The cold power rating of a battery measures battery starting performance and provides an approximate relationship between battery size and engine size. As a general rule, the cold power rating of a replacement battery should match or exceed your engine size in cubic inches.

❄❄WARNING

Always turn off the ignition switch when connecting or disconnecting the battery cables or a battery charger. Failure to do so could damage the computer control module (ECM/PCM) or other electronic components. Disconnecting the battery cable may interfere with the functions of the on board computer systems and may require the computer to undergo a complete relearning process once the negative battery cable is connected.

❄❄CAUTION

Batteries normally produce explosive gases which can cause personal injury. DO NOT allow flames, sparks or lighted substances to come near the battery. When charging or working near a battery, always shield your face and protect your eyes. Also, always provide adequate ventilation.

1. Carefully disconnect the negative battery cable from the battery terminal, and position it aside.
2. Remove any brackets or braces that are in the way.
3. Carefully disconnect the positive cable from the battery terminal, and position it aside.
4. Clean the cable terminals using an acid neutralizing solution and a terminal cleaning brush.
5. Remove the retainer bolt, then remove the retainer.
6. Remove the battery from the vehicle. Some vehicles covered by this manual have a battery insulator around the battery. To remove the insulator, simply slide it off the top of the battery.
   To install:
7. Clean the battery tray and hold-down clamp(s) with a wire brush and scraper. Replace any components that are worn.

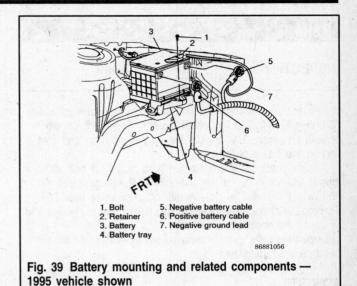

1. Bolt
2. Retainer
3. Battery
4. Battery tray
5. Negative battery cable
6. Positive battery cable
7. Negative ground lead

86881056

Fig. 39 Battery mounting and related components — 1995 vehicle shown

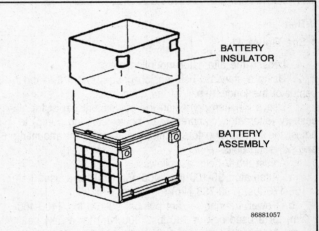

BATTERY INSULATOR

BATTERY ASSEMBLY

86881057

Fig. 40 Some vehicles may have a battery insulator. To remove the insulator, simply slide it off the top of the battery

8. If applicable, put the insulator back on the battery by sliding it on.

➡**The terminals should be coated lightly (externally) with a petroleum type jelly to prevent corrosion. Make absolutely sure that the battery is connected properly before you turn on the ignition switch. Reversed polarity can burn out your alternator and regulator within a matter of a split second.**

9. Place the battery in the battery tray making sure that the positive and negative terminals are in the same position as they were previous to removal.
10. Assemble and tighten the hold-down hardware so that the battery is secure. Do not overtighten.
11. Secure the positive, then the negative battery cable to the proper terminals. Do not overtighten.

Belts

INSPECTION

Belt tension and condition should be checked at least every 30,000 miles (48,300 km) or 24 months. Check the condition of both serpentine and V-belts for cracking, fraying and splitting on the inside of the belt.

A quick check for V-belt tension is to grasp the belt with the thumb and forefinger at the mid-point of the longest belt run and twist the belt. The belt should rotate no more than 90°. To properly check V-belt tension use a belt tension gauge and adjust to the specified tension.

Serpentine belts use a spring-loaded tensioner and do not need periodic adjustment.

ADJUSTING

V-Belt

▶ **See Figure 41**

1. Loosen the alternator mounting bolts.
2. Using a standard belt tension gauge, install it to the center of the longest span of the drive belt.
3. Use a medium prybar on the adjustment lug of the accessory (alternator, compressor or power steering pump) to adjust the belt tension to specification. Tighten the mounting and adjusting bolts.
4. Adjust the V-belts as follows:
   a. Alternator: 90-100 lbs. (400-450 Nm) for a used belt or 165-175 lbs. (750-788 Nm) for a new belt.
   b. Power steering/coolant pumps: 90-100 lbs. (400-450 Nm) for a used belt or 180 lbs. (800 Nm) for a new belt.
   c. Air conditioning compressor: 90-100 lbs. (400-450 Nm) for a used belt or 165 lbs. (750 Nm) for a new belt.

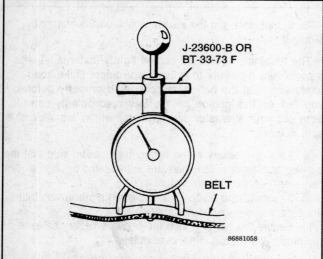

J-23600-B OR BT-33-73 F

BELT

86881058

Fig. 41 Belt tension gauge for an engine with V-belts

Serpentine Belt

▶ **See Figure 42**

A single serpentine belt may be used to drive engine-mounted accessories. Drive belt tension is maintained by a spring loaded tensioner. The drive belt tensioner can control belt tension over a broad range of belt lengths, however, there are limits to the tensioner's ability to compensate.

A belt squeak when the engine in started or stopped is normal and does not necessarily indicate a worn belt. If the squeak persists or worsens, inspect the belt for wear and replace as necessary.

1. Inspect the tensioner markings to see if the belt is within operating lengths. Replace the belt if the belt is excessively worn or is outside of the tensioner's operating range.
2. Run the engine until operating temperature is reached. Be sure all accessories are off. Turn the engine off and read the belt tension using a belt tension gauge tool placed halfway between the alternator and the air conditioning compressor. If not equipped with air conditioning, read the tension between the power steering pump and crankshaft pulley. Remove the tool.
3. Run the engine for 15 seconds, then turn it off. Using a box-end wrench, apply clockwise force to tighten to the tensioner pulley bolt. Release the force and immediately take a tension reading without disturbing belt tensioner position.
4. Using the same wrench, apply a counterclockwise force to the tensioner pulley bolt and raise the pulley to its fully raised position. Slowly lower the pulley to engage the belt. Take a tension reading without disturbing the belt tensioner position.
5. Average the 3 readings. If their average is lower than the following specifications, replace the tensioner:
   a. 2.0L and 2.3L engines: 50 lbs. (220 Nm)
   b. 3.0L engine: 79 lbs. (351 Nm)
   c. 3.3L engine: 67 lbs. (298 Nm)
   d. 3.1L engine: 50-70 lbs. (225-315 Nm)

REMOVAL & INSTALLATION

V-belt

▶ **See Figure 43**

1. Loosen the accessory-to-mounting bracket bolt(s) and adjusting bolt.
2. Rotate the accessory to relieve the belt tension.
3. Slip the drive belt from the accessory pulley and remove it from the engine.

➡**If the engine uses more than one belt, it may be necessary to remove belts that are in front of the belt being removed.**

To install:
4. Place the new belt over the crankshaft or drive pulley and stretch over the driven (accessory) pulley.
5. If removed, install the other belts in the same way.
6. Adjust the belts to the proper tension.
7. Tighten the adjusting and mounting bolts.

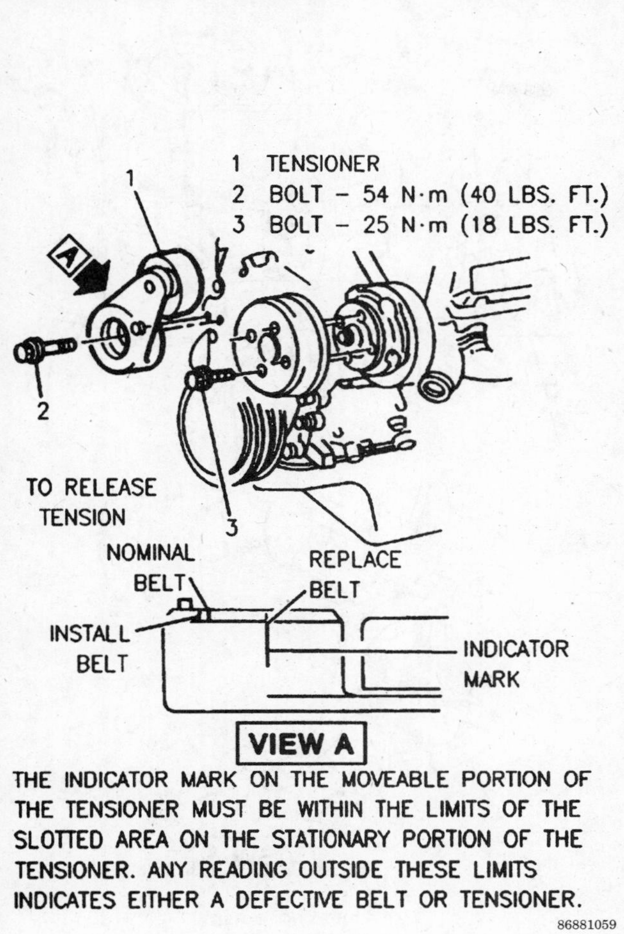

1 TENSIONER
2 BOLT – 54 N·m (40 LBS. FT.)
3 BOLT – 25 N·m (18 LBS. FT.)
A
1
2
3
TO RELEASE TENSION
NOMINAL BELT
REPLACE BELT
INSTALL BELT
INDICATOR MARK
VIEW A
THE INDICATOR MARK ON THE MOVEABLE PORTION OF THE TENSIONER MUST BE WITHIN THE LIMITS OF THE SLOTTED AREA ON THE STATIONARY PORTION OF THE TENSIONER. ANY READING OUTSIDE THESE LIMITS INDICATES EITHER A DEFECTIVE BELT OR TENSIONER.
86881059

Fig. 42 Serpentine drive belt markings

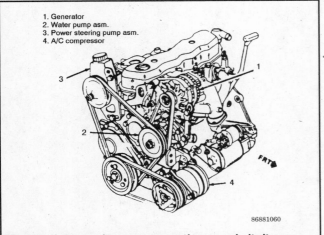

1. Generator
2. Water pump asm.
3. Power steering pump asm.
4. A/C compressor
1
2
3
4
FRT
86881060

Fig. 43 If the engine uses more than one belt, it may be necessary to remove belts that are in front of the belt being removed

Serpentine Belt

➧ See Figure 44

1. Insert a ½ in. drive breaker bar into the adjuster arm on the tensioner pulley. Later models require an 18mm box end wrench.

➡Make sure the drive end of the breaker bar is long enough to fully seat in the tensioner pulley and that both the breaker bar and box wrench are long enough to provide the proper leverage.

2. Rotate the tensioner to the left (counterclockwise) and remove the belt.
3. Slowly rotate the tensioner to the right (clockwise) to release the tension.

To install:

4. Route the belt over the pulleys following the diagram found in the engine compartment.
5. Rotate the tensioner to the left (counterclockwise) and install the belt over the remaining pulley.

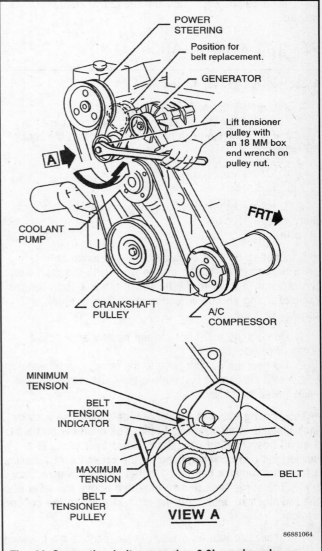

POWER STEERING
Position for belt replacement.
GENERATOR
Lift tensioner pulley with an 18 MM box end wrench on pulley nut.
A
FRT
COOLANT PUMP
CRANKSHAFT PULLEY
A/C COMPRESSOR
MINIMUM TENSION
BELT TENSION INDICATOR
MAXIMUM TENSION
BELT TENSIONER PULLEY
BELT
VIEW A
86881064

Fig. 44 Serpentine belt removal — 3.3L engine shown

6. Inspect the belt positioning over each pulley to ensure the belt is seated properly in all the grooves.

Timing Belt

INSPECTION

Vehicles equipped with the 2.0L (VIN M) engine are the only vehicles covered by this manual which utilize a timing belt. The timing belt should be inspected for cracks, wear or other damage and should be replaced every 60,000 miles (100,000 km).

For the timing belt removal and installation procedure, please refer to Section 3 of this manual.

Hoses

The hoses should be checked for deterioration, leaks and loose hose clamps every 12,000 miles (20,000 km) or 12 months.

REMOVAL & INSTALLATION

▶ **See Figures 45, 46, 47 and 48**

1. Disconnect the negative battery cable.
2. Drain the cooling system into a clean container to a level that is below the hose being removed. Save the coolant for reuse.
3. Loosen the hose clamps.
4. Disconnect the inlet hose from the radiator and thermostat housing.
5. Disconnect the outlet hose from the radiator and coolant pump or cylinder block.
   To install:

➡**If installing original equipment hoses, make sure to align the reference marks on the hose with the marks on the radiator. A twist in the hose will place a strain on the radiator fitting and could cause the fitting to crack or break.**

6. Connect the outlet hose to the radiator and coolant pump or cylinder block.
7. Connect the radiator hose to the radiator and thermostat.
8. Refill the cooling system to a level just below the filler neck. Install the radiator cap.

➡**The cooling systems on later models may use a surge tank instead of an overflow bottle. The overflow bottle has 1 small hose coming from the radiator filler neck. The surge tank can be recognized by the presence of 2 hoses, 1 from the radiator cap and 1 outlet to the lower radiator hose. The surge tank is also mounted above the level of the radiator cap, making it the highest point in the cooling system.**

9. If equipped with an overflow bottle, perform the following:
   a. Fill the overflow bottle to the "Full Hot" mark.
   b. Start the engine and allow to come to normal operating temperature.

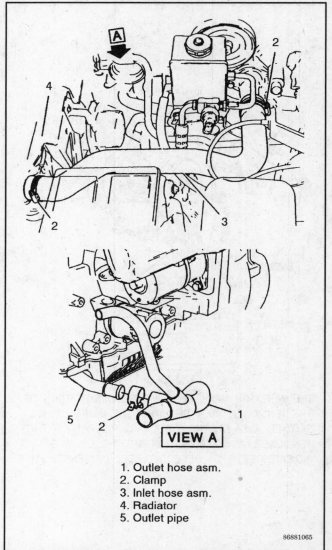

1. Outlet hose asm.
2. Clamp
3. Inlet hose asm.
4. Radiator
5. Outlet pipe

86881065

Fig. 45 Coolant hose locations — 2.3L engine shown

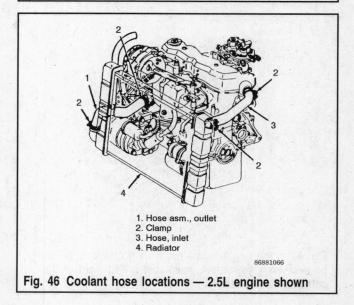

1. Hose asm., outlet
2. Clamp
3. Hose, inlet
4. Radiator

86881066

Fig. 46 Coolant hose locations — 2.5L engine shown

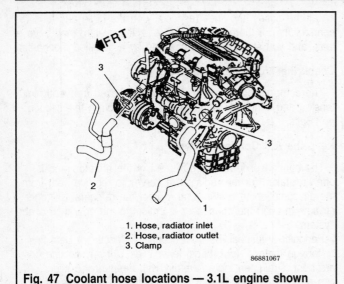

1. Hose, radiator inlet
2. Hose, radiator outlet
3. Clamp

86881067

Fig. 47 Coolant hose locations — 3.1L engine shown

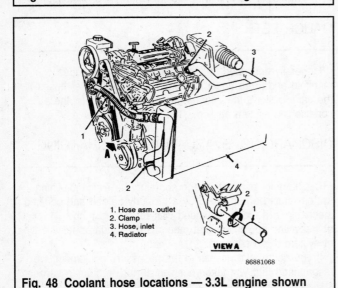

1. Hose asm. outlet
2. Clamp
3. Hose, inlet
4. Radiator

VIEW A

86881068

Fig. 48 Coolant hose locations — 3.3L engine shown

  c. Stop the engine and refill the overflow bottle to the "Full Hot" mark.

  d. Check the coolant level frequently over the next couple of days.

10. If equipped with a surge tank, perform the following:

  a. Fill the surge tank to the base of the filler neck.

  b. Install the pressure cap on the surge tank. Start the engine and allow to come to normal operating temperature or until the upper radiator hose is hot.

  c. Stop the engine and check the level of coolant in the surge tank. If the level is not above the "Full" line, allow the engine to cool enough to slowly remove the pressure cap.

  d. Add coolant to bring the level up to the "Full" line.

  e. Install the pressure cap. Make sure the arrows on the cap line up with the overflow hose.

11. Connect the negative battery cable.

CV-Boot

INSPECTION

◆ **See Figures 49 and 50**

  CV-joint boots should be periodically inspected. It would be a wise idea to examine the boot every time your vehicle is raised and supported. Check the boot for signs of cracks, tears or splits and repair/replace as necessary. For CV-boot and joint repair, as well as overhaul procedures, please refer to Section 7 of this manual.

Air Conditioning System

✳✳CAUTION

The refrigerant used in A/C systems is an extremely cold substance. When exposed to the atmosphere, it will instantly freeze any surface it comes in contact with, including your eyes. It is imperative to use eye and skin protection when working on A/C systems.

SAFETY PRECAUTIONS

➡**R-12 refrigerant is a chlorofluorocarbon which, when released into the atmosphere, contributes to the depletion of the ozone layer. Ozone filters out harmful radiation from the sun. Consult the laws in your area before servicing the air conditioning system. In most areas it is illegal to perform repairs involving refrigerant unless the work is done by a certified technician. It is also likely that you will not be able to purchase R-12 without proof that you are properly trained and certified to work on A/C systems.**

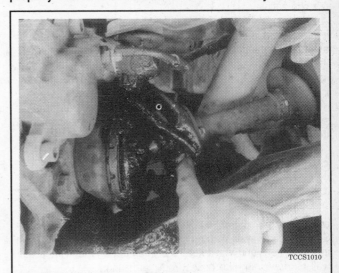

TCCS1010

Fig. 49 View of a torn CV-boot

TCCS1011

Fig. 50 View of a CV-boot in good condition

• The refrigerant used in A/C systems is an extremely cold substance. When exposed to the atmosphere, it will instantly freeze any surface it comes in contact with, including your eyes.

• Although normally non-toxic, R-12 refrigerant gas becomes highly poisonous in the presence of an open flame. One good whiff of the vapor formed by refrigerant can be fatal. Keep all forms of fire (including cigarettes) well clear of the air conditioning system.

• It has been established that the chemicals in R-12 (used on models through 1994) contribute to the damage occurring in the upper atmosphere. On some 1994 models and all 1995 models, R-134a refrigerant is used. Both of these refrigerant systems must be discharged using the proper recovery/recycling equipment.

• Do not mix refrigerants. They are NOT compatible.

• Never mix ANY parts between the systems, as they are not compatible.

• R-12 and R-134a refrigerant servicing equipment are not interchangeable. Only use recovery/recycling systems which are UL-listed and are certified to meet SAE requirements for the type of refrigerant system to be serviced. Follow the instructions provided with the equipment carefully when discharging the system.

• Servicing (recovery, evacuation and charging) of the A/C system, should be left to a professional certified mechanic with the proper equipment and related training.

SYSTEM INSPECTION

A lot of A/C problems can be avoided by running the air conditioner at least once a week, regardless of the season. Simply let the system run for at least 5 minutes a week (even in the winter), and you'll keep the internal parts lubricated as well as preventing the hoses from hardening.

Checking For A/C Oil Leaks

Refrigerant leaks show up only as oily areas on the various components because the compressor oil is transported around the entire system along with the refrigerant. Look for oily spots on all the hoses and lines (especially on the hose and tube connections). If there are oily deposits, the system may have a leak, and you should have it checked by a qualified mechanic.

Check the A/C Compressor Belt

The compressor drive belt should be checked frequently for tension and condition. Refer to the information in this section on "Belts."

Keep the A/C Condenser Clear

The condenser is mounted in front of the radiator (and is often mistaken for the radiator). It serves to remove heat from the air conditioning system and to cool the refrigerant. Proper air flow through the condenser is critical to the operation of the system.

Periodically inspect the front of the condenser for bent fins or foreign material (dirt, bugs, leaves, etc.). If any cooling fins are bent, straighten them carefully with needle-nose pliers. You can remove any debris with a stiff bristle brush or hose.

GAUGE SETS

Generally described, this tool is a set of two gauges, a manifold and three hoses. By connecting the proper hoses to the car's system, the gauges can be used to "see" the air conditioning system at work.

DISCHARGING, EVACUATING AND CHARGING

Discharging, evacuating and charging the air conditioning system must be performed by a properly trained and certified mechanic in a facility equipped with refrigerant recovery/recycling equipment that meets SAE standards for the type of system to be serviced.

If you don't have access to the necessary equipment, we recommend that you take your vehicle to a reputable service station to have the work done. If you still wish to perform repairs on the vehicle, have them discharge the system, then take your car home and perform the necessary work. When you are finished, return the vehicle to the station for evacuation and charging. Just be sure to cap ALL A/C system fittings immediately after opening them and keep them protected until the system is recharged.

Windshield Wipers

For maximum effectiveness and longest element (refill) life, the windshield and wiper blades should be kept clean. Dirt, tree sap, road tar and so on, will cause streaking, smearing and blade deterioration if left on the glass. It is advisable to wash the windshield carefully with a commercial glass cleaner at least once a month. Clean off the wiper blades with the wet rag afterwards. Do not attempt to move the wipers by hand; damage to the motor and drive mechanism could result.

To inspect and/or remove the wiper refills, place the wiper switch in the LOW speed position and the ignition switch in the ACC position. When the wiper blades are approximately vertical on the windshield, turn the ignition switch to OFF.

Examine the wiper refills. If they are cracked, broken or torn, they should be replaced immediately. Replacement intervals will vary with usage, although ozone deterioration usually limits refill life to about one year. If the wiper pattern is smeared or streaked, or if the blade chatters across the glass, the refills should be replaced. It is easiest and most sensible to replace the refills in pairs.

REMOVAL & INSTALLATION

▶ **See Figures 51 and 52**

Normally, if the wipers are not cleaning the windshield properly, only the refill has to be replaced. The blade and arm usually require replacement only in the event of damage. It is not necessary (except on new Tridon® refills) to remove the arm or the blade to replace the refill (rubber part), though you may have to position the arm higher on the glass. You can do this by turning the ignition switch **ON** and operating the wipers. When they are positioned where they are accessible, turn the ignition switch **OFF**.

If your vehicle is equipped with aftermarket blades, there are several different possible types of refills. Aftermarket wipers frequently use a different type blade or refill than the original. Here are some common aftermarket blades, though not all may be available for your car.

Most Anco® styles use a release button that is pushed down to allow the refill to slide out of the yoke jaws. The new refill slides back into the frame and locks in place.

Some Trico® refills are removed by locating where the metal backing strip or the refill is wider. Insert a small prybar between the frame and metal backing strip. Press down to release the refill from the retaining tab.

Other types of Trico® refills have two metal tabs which are unlocked by squeezing them together. The rubber filler can then be withdrawn from the frame jaws. A new refill is installed by inserting the refill into the front frame jaws and sliding it rearward to engage the remaining frame jaws. There are usually four jaws; be certain when installing, that the refill is engaged in all of them. At the end of its travel, the tabs will lock into place on the front jaws of the wiper blade frame.

Another type of refill is made from polycarbonate. The refill has a simple locking device at one end which flexes downward out of the groove into which the jaws of the holder fit, allowing easy release. By sliding the new refill through all the jaws and pushing through the slight resistance when it reaches the end of its travel, the refill will lock into position.

To replace the Tridon® refill, it is necessary to remove the wiper arm or blade. This refill has a plastic backing strip with a notch about 1 in. (25mm) from the end. Hold the blade (frame) on a hard surface so the frame is tightly bowed. Grip the tip of the backing strip and pull up while twisting counterclockwise. The backing strip will snap out of the retaining tab. Do this for the remaining tabs until the refill is free of the arm. The length of these refills is molded into the end and they should be replaced with identical types.

Regardless of the type of refill used, make sure that all of the frame jaws are engaged as the refill is pushed into place and locked. If the metal blade holder and frame are allowed to touch the glass during wiper operation, the glass will be scratched.

Tires and Wheels

▶ **See Figures 53, 54, 55 and 56**

Inspect your tires often for signs of improper inflation and uneven wear, which may indicate a need for balancing, rotation or wheel alignment. Check the tires frequently for cuts, stone bruises, abrasions, blister and for objects that may have become embedded in the tread. More frequent inspections are recommended when rapid or extreme temperature changes occur, or where road surfaces are rough and/or occasionally littered with debris. Check the condition of the wheels and replace any that are bent, cracked, severely dented or have excessive run-out.

The tires on your car have built-in wear indicators molded into the bottom of the tread grooves. The indicators will begin to appear as the tire approaches replacement tread depth. Once the indicators are visible across 2 or more adjacent grooves at 3 or more locations, the tires should be replaced.

Wear that occurs only on certain portions of the tires may indicate a particular problem, which when corrected or avoided, may significantly extend tire life. Wear that occurs only in the center of the tire indicates either overinflation or heavy acceleration on a drive wheel. Wear occurring at the outer edges of the tire and not at the center may indicate underinflation, excessively hard cornering or a lack of rotation. If wear occurs at only the outer edge of the tire, there may be a problem with the wheel alignment or the tire, when constructed, contained a non-uniformity defect.

TIRE ROTATION

▶ **See Figure 57**

Tire wear can be equalized by switching the position of the tires at 6000 miles (10,000 km) for new tires and then every 15,000 miles (24,000 km). Including a conventional spare in the rotation pattern can give up to 20% more life to a set of tires.

✳✳CAUTION

DO NOT include the temporary use spare in the rotation pattern.

There are certain exceptions to tire rotation, however. Studded snow tires should not be rotated.

➡**When studded snow tires are removed for the season, mark them so they can be reinstalled on the same side of the vehicle.**

TIRE DESIGN

For maximum service life, tires should be used in sets of five, except on vehicles equipped with a space-saver spare tire. Do not mix tires of different designs, such as steel belted radial, fiberglass belted or bias/belted, or tires of different sizes, such as P165SR-14 and P185SR-14.

Conventional bias ply tires are constructed so that the cords run bead-to-bead at an angle (bias). Alternate plies run at an

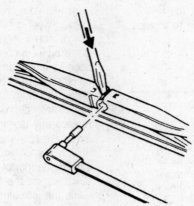

Blade replacement

1. Cycle arm and blade assembly to up position on the windshield where removal of blade assembly can be performed without difficulty. Turn ignition key off at desired position.
2. To remove blade assembly, insert screwdriver in slot, push down on spring lock and pull blade assembly from pin (View A).
3. To install, push the blade assembly on the pin so that the spring lock engages the pin (View A). Be sure the blade assembly is securely attached to pin.

VIEW A

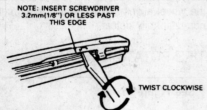

NOTE: INSERT SCREWDRIVER 3.2mm(1/8") OR LESS PAST THIS EDGE

TWIST CLOCKWISE

Element replacement

1. Insert screwdriver between the edge of the super structure and the blade backing drip (View B). Twist screwdriver slowly until element clears one side of the super structure claw.
2. Slide the element out of all the super structure claws.

VIEW B

4. Insert element into one side of the end claws (View D) and with a rocking motion push element upward until it snaps in (View E).

VIEW D

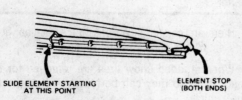

SLIDE ELEMENT STARTING AT THIS POINT

ELEMENT STOP (BOTH ENDS)

3. Slide the element into the super structure claws, starting with second set from either end (View C) and continue to slide the blade element into all the super structure claws to the element stop (View C).

VIEW C

VIEW E

86871055

Fig. 51 Wiper blade replacement — Trico®

Blade replacement

1. Cycle arm and blade assembly to a position on the windshield where removal of blade assembly can be performed without difficulty. Turn ignition key off at desired position.
2. To remove blade assembly from wiper arm, press on spring lock and pull blade assembly from pin (View A).
3. To install, push the blade assembly on the pin so that the spring lock engages the pin (View A). Be sure the blade assembly is securely attached to pin.

VIEW A

Element replacement

1. Locate the word TRIDON on the superstructure of the blade.
2. Insert a coin or similar object between the superstructure and the blade backing strip (View B). Push down and in on coin.
3. Slide the element out of all superstructures claws.
4. Locate the rectangular slot on the top/end of the element backing strip.
5. Locate the end on the blade superstructure without the word TRIDON.
6. Insert the "slot" end of the blade element into the first superstructure claw and continue to slide the blade element into all claws of the superstructure. The blade element will "snap" into place when the element is fully installed through the last superstructure claw (located at the end with the word TRIDON) (View C).

NOTE: Make sure that the element backing strip has been installed into all the superstructure claws and that the locking rib is securely engaged.

VIEW B

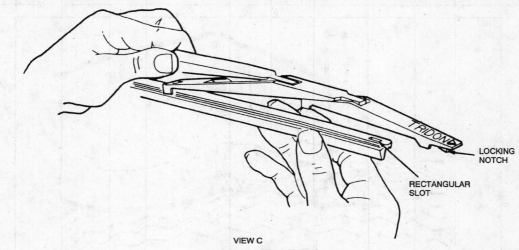

LOCKING NOTCH

RECTANGULAR SLOT

VIEW C

86871056

Fig. 52 Wiper blade replacement — Tridon®

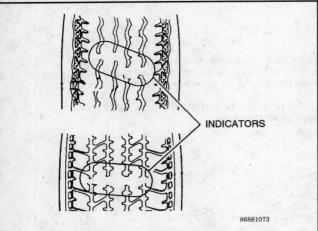

INDICATORS

86881073

Fig. 53 If the tires are used beyond the point of tread life, built-in wear indicators will begin to appear as lines across the tread

opposite angle. This type of construction gives rigidity to both tread and sidewall. Bias/belted tires are similar in construction to conventional bias ply tires. Belts run at an angel and also at a 90° angle to the bead, as in the radial tire. Tread life in improved considerably over the conventional bias tire. The radial tire differs in construction, but instead of the carcass plies running at an angle of 90° to each other, they run at an angle of 90° to the bead. This gives the tread a great deal of rigidity and the sidewall a great deal of flexibility and accounts for the characteristic bulge associated with radial tires.

All General Motors vehicles are capable of using radial tires which are the recommended type for all years. If radial tires are used, tires sizes and wheel diameters should be selected to maintain ground clearance and tire load capacity equivalent to the minimum specified tire. Radial tires should always be used in sets of 5 if the spare is a conventional tire. In an emergency, radial tires can be used with caution on the rear

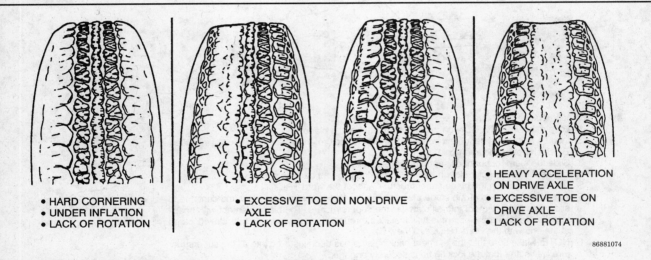

- HARD CORNERING
- UNDER INFLATION
- LACK OF ROTATION

- EXCESSIVE TOE ON NON-DRIVE AXLE
- LACK OF ROTATION

- HEAVY ACCELERATION ON DRIVE AXLE
- EXCESSIVE TOE ON DRIVE AXLE
- LACK OF ROTATION

86881074

Fig. 54 Uneven tire wear can be caused by variables from tire/vehicle condition to driving style

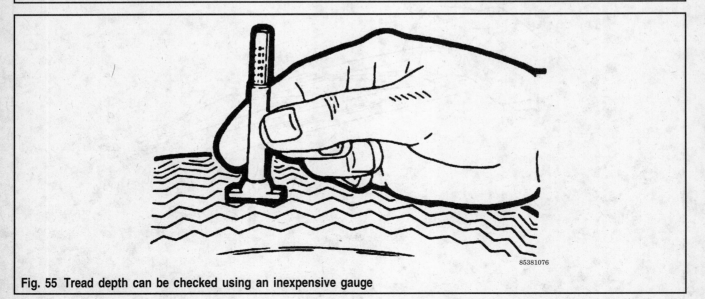

85381076

Fig. 55 Tread depth can be checked using an inexpensive gauge

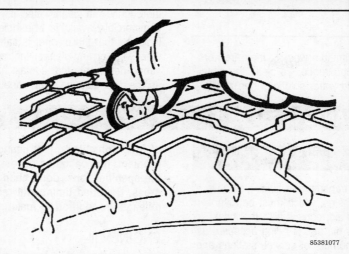

Fig. 56 If a gauge is not available, a penny may be used to check for tire tread depth; when the top of Lincoln's head is visible, it is probably time for a new tire

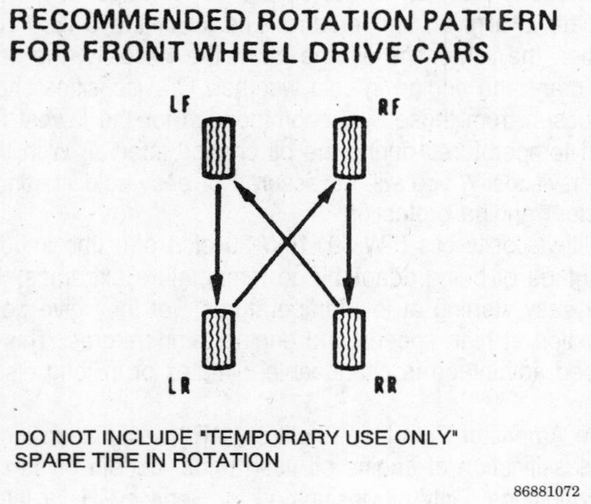

RECOMMENDED ROTATION PATTERN FOR FRONT WHEEL DRIVE CARS

LF   RF

LR   RR

DO NOT INCLUDE "TEMPORARY USE ONLY" SPARE TIRE IN ROTATION

86881072

Fig. 57 Tire rotation pattern

axle only. If this is done, both tires on the rear should be of radial design.

➡ **Radial tires should never be used on only the front axle as they can adversely effect steering if tires of different designs are mixed.**

TIRE STORAGE

Store the tires at the proper inflation pressures, if they are mounted on wheels. Keep them in a cool, dry place on their sides. If the tires are stored in a garage or basement, DO NOT, let them stand on a concrete floor; instead, set them on strips of wood.

TIRE INFLATION

Tire inflation may be the most ignored item of auto maintenance. Gasoline mileage can drop as much as 0.8% for every 1 pound/square inch (psi) of under-inflation. Tires should be checked weekly for proper air pressure. A chart should be located either in the glove compartment, on one of the vehicle's door jambs and/or in the owners manual. This chart will provide the recommended inflation pressures. Maximum fuel economy and tire life will result if the pressure maintained at/near the highest figure given on the chart.

Pressure should be checked with the tires cold (before driving 1 mile/1.6 km or more) because pressure can significantly increase, due to head build-up, as the tire is warmed. It is a good idea to have your own accurate pressure gauge, because many gauges on service station air pumps cannot be trusted. When checking pressures, do not neglect the spare tire. Note that some spare tires require pressure considerably higher than those used in the other tires.

While you are about the task of checking the air pressure, inspect the tire treads for cuts, bruises and other damage. Check the air valves to be sure that they are tight. Replace any missing valve caps. Dirt and moisture gathering in the valve stem could lead to an early demise of the stem and a subsequent flat tire.

Factory installed wheels and tires are designed to handle loads up to and including their rated load capacity when inflated to the recommended inflation pressures. Correct tire pressure and driving techniques have an important influence on tire life. Heavy cornering, excessively rapid acceleration and unnecessary braking increase tire wear. Underinflated tires can cause handling problems, poor fuel economy, shortened tire life and tire overloading.

Factory installed wheels and tires are designed to handle loads up to and including the recommended inflation pressures. Correct tire pressures and driving techniques have and important influence on tire life. Heavy cornering, excessively rapid acceleration and unnecessary braking increase tire wear. Underinflated tires can cause handling problems, poor fuel economy, shortened tire life and tire overloading.

CARE OF SPECIAL WHEELS

If your car is equipped with aluminum wheels, they are normally coated to preserve their appearance. To clean the aluminum wheels, use a mild soap and water solution, then rinse thoroughly with clean water. If you want to use on of the commercially available wheel cleaners, make sure the label indicates that the cleaner is safe for coated wheels. Never use steel wool or any cleaner that contains an abrasive, or use strong detergents that contain high alkaline or caustic agents, as they will damage your wheels.

FLUIDS AND LUBRICANTS

Fluid Disposal

Used fluids such a engine oil, transmission fluid, antifreeze and brake fluid are hazardous wastes, which must be disposed of properly. Before draining any fluid, consult with the local authorities; in many areas, waste oil, etc. is being accepted as a part of recycling programs. A number of service stations and auto parts stores are also accepting waste fluids for recycling.

Be sure of the recycling center's policies before draining any fluids, as many will not accept different fluids that have been mixed together, such as oil and antifreeze.

Fuel and Engine Oil Recommendations

FUEL

➡**Some fuel additives contain chemicals that can damage the catalytic converter and/or oxygen sensor. Read all of the labels carefully before using any additive in the engine or fuel system.**

All of the vehicles covered by this manual are designed to run on unleaded fuel. The use of a leaded fuel in a car requiring unleaded fuel will plug the catalytic converter and render it inoperative. It will also increase exhaust backpressure to the point where engine output will be severely reduced. The minimum octane rating of the the unleaded fuel being used must be at least 87, which usually means regular unleaded, but some high performance engines may require higher ratings. Fuel should be selected for the brand and octane which performs best with your engine. Judge a gasoline by its ability to prevent pinging, its engine starting capabilities (cold and hot) and general all weather performance.

As far as the octane rating is concerned, refer to the general engine specifications chart in Section 3 of this manual to find your engine and its compression ratio. If the compression ratio is 9.0:1 or lower, in most cases a regular unleaded grade of gasoline can be used. If the compression ratio is higher than 9.0:1 use a premium grade of unleaded fuel.

The use of a fuel too low in octane (a measure of anti-knock quality) will result in spark knock. Since many factors such as altitude, terrain, air temperature and humidity affect operating efficiency, knocking may result even though the recommended fuel is being used. If persistent knocking occurs, it may be necessary to switch to a higher grade of fuel. Continuous or heavy knocking may result in engine damage.

➡**Your engine's fuel requirement can change with time, mainly due to carbon build-up, which will in turn change the compression ratio. If you engine pings, knocks or diesels (runs with the ignition OFF) switch to a higher grade** of fuel. Sometimes, just changing brands will cure the problem. If it becomes necessary to retard the timing from the specifications, don't change it more than a few degrees. Retarded timing will reduce power output and fuel mileage, in addition to making the engine run hotter.

ENGINE OIL

▶ **See Figure 58**

The Society Of Automotive Engineer (SAE) grade number indicates the viscosity of the engine oil and thus its ability to lubricate at a given temperature. The lower the SAE grade number, the lighter the oil; the lower the viscosity, the easier it is to crank the engine in cold weather. Oil viscosities should be chosen from those oils recommended for the lowest anticipated temperatures during the oil change interval. With the proper viscosity, you will be assured of easy cold starting and sufficient engine protection.

Multi-viscosity oils (5W-30, 10W-30 etc.) offer the important advantage of being adaptable to temperature extremes. They allow easy starting at low temperatures, yet they give good protection at high speeds and engine temperatures. This is a decided advantage in changeable climates or in long distance driving.

The American Petroleum Institute (API) designation indicates the classification of engine oil used under certain given operating conditions. Only oil designated for Service SH, or latest superceding oil grade, should be used. Oils of the SH type perform a variety of functions inside the engine in addition to their basic function as a lubricant. Through a balanced system of metallic detergents and polymeric dispersants, the oil prevents the formation of high and low temperature deposits and also keeps sludge and particles of dirt in suspension. Acids, particularly sulfuric acid, as well as other byproducts of combustion, are neutralized. Both the SAE grade number and the API designation can be found on the side of the oil bottle.

Synthetic Oils

There are excellent synthetic and fuel-efficient oils available that, under the right circumstances, can help provide better fuel mileage and better engine protection. However, these advantages come at a price, which can be significantly more than the price per quart of conventional motor oils.

Before pouring any synthetic oils into your car's engine, you should consider the condition of the engine and the type of driving you do. It is also wise to check the vehicle manufacturer's position on synthetic oils.

Generally, it is best to avoid the use of synthetic oil in both brand new and older, high mileage engines. New engines require a proper break-in, and the synthetics are so slippery that

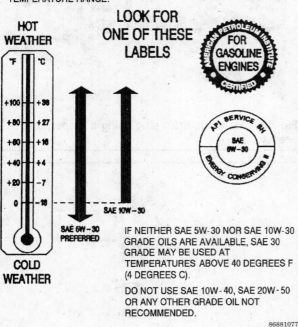

RECOMMENDED SAE VISCOSITY GRADE ENGINE OILS

FOR BEST FUEL ECONOMY AND COLD STARTING, SELECT THE LOWEST SAE VISCOSITY GRADE OIL FOR THE EXPECTED TEMPERATURE RANGE.

LOOK FOR ONE OF THESE LABELS

HOT WEATHER

COLD WEATHER

SAE 5W-30 PREFERRED

SAE 10W-30

IF NEITHER SAE 5W-30 NOR SAE 10W-30 GRADE OILS ARE AVAILABLE, SAE 30 GRADE MAY BE USED AT TEMPERATURES ABOVE 40 DEGREES F (4 DEGREES C).

DO NOT USE SAE 10W-40, SAE 20W-50 OR ANY OTHER GRADE OIL NOT RECOMMENDED.

86881077

Fig. 58 Recommended SAE engine oil viscosity grades for gasoline engines

they can impede this; most manufacturers recommend that you wait at least 5,000 miles (8,000 km) before switching to a synthetic oil. Conversely, older engines are looser and tend to lose more oil; synthetics will slip past worn parts more readily than regular oil. If your car already leaks oil, (due to worn parts or bad seals/gaskets), it may leak more with a synthetic inside.

Consider your type of driving. If most of your accumulated mileage is on the highway at higher, steadier speed, a synthetic oil will reduce friction and probably help deliver better fuel mileage. Under such ideal highway conditions, the oil change interval can be extended, as long as the oil filter can operated effectively for the extended life of the oil. If the filter can't do its job for this extended period, dirt and sludge will build up in your engine's crankcase, sump, oil pump and lines, no matter what type of oil is used. If using synthetic oil in this manner, your should continue to change the oil filter at the recommended intervals.

Cars used under harder, stop-and-go, short hop circumstances should always be serviced more frequently, and for

these cars synthetic oil may not be a wise investment. Because of the necessary shorter change interval needed for this type of driving, you cannot take advantage of the long recommended change interval of most synthetic oils.

Engine

OIL LEVEL CHECK

▶ **See Figure 59**

Every time you stop for fuel, check the engine oil making sure the engine has fully warmed and the vehicle is parked on a level surface. Because it takes some time for the oil to drain back to the oil pan, you should wait a few minutes before checking your oil. If you are doing this at a fuel stop, first fill the fuel tank, then open the hood and check the oil, but don't get so carried away as to forget to pay for the fuel. Most station attendants won't believe that you forgot.

1. Make sure the car is parked on level ground.

2. When checking the oil level, it is best for the engine to be at normal operating temperature, although checking the oil immediately after stopping will lead to a false reading. Wait a few minutes after turning off the engine to allow the oil to drain back into the crankcase.

3. Open the hood and locate the dipstick which will be in a guide tube mounted in the upper engine block. Pull the dipstick from its tube, wipe it clean (using a clean, lint free rag) and then reinsert it.

4. Pull the dipstick out again and, holding it horizontally, read the oil level. The oil should be between the FULL and ADD marks on the dipstick. The the oil is below the ADD mark, add oil of the proper viscosity through the capped opening in the top of the cylinder head cover or filler tube, as applicable. see the oil and fuel recommendations listed earlier in this section for the proper viscosity and rating of oil to use.

5. Insert the dipstick and check the oil level again after adding any oil. Approximately one quart of oil will raise the level from the ADD mark to the FULL mark. Be sure not to

86881078

Fig. 59 Open the hood and locate the dipstick

overfill the crankcase and waste the oil. Excess oil will generally be consumed at an accelerated rate.

✳✳WARNING

DO NOT overfill the crankcase. It may result in oil-fouled spark plugs, oil leaks cause by oil seal failure or engine damage due to oil foaming.

OIL AND FILTER CHANGE

▶ **See Figures 60, 61, 62, 63 and 64**

The manufacturer's recommended oil change interval is 7,500 miles (12,000 km) under normal operating conditions. We recommend an oil change interval of 3,000-3,500 miles (4,800-5,600 km) under normal conditions; more frequently under severe conditions such as when the average trip is less than 4 miles, the engine is operated for extended periods at idle or low-speed, when towing a trailer or operating is dusty areas.

In addition, we recommend that the filter be replaced EVERY time the oil is changed.

➡**Please be considerate of the environment. Dispose of waste oil properly by taking it to a service station, municipal facility or recycling center.**

1. Run the engine until it reaches normal operating temperature. The turn the engine **OFF**.
2. Raise and safely support the front of the vehicle using jackstands.
3. Slide a drain pan of at least 5 quarts capacity under the oil pan. Wipe the drain plug and surrounding area clean using an old rag.
4. Loosen the drain plug using a ratchet, short extension and socket, or a box-wrench. Turn the plug out by hand, using a rag to shield your fingers from the hot oil. By keeping an inward pressure on the plug as you unscrew it, oil won't escape past the threads and you can remove it without being burned by hot oil.
5. Quickly withdraw the plug and move your hands out of the way, but be careful not to drop the plug into the drain pan, as fishing it out can be an unpleasant mess. Allow the oil to drain completely, then reinstall the drain plug (except on 2.5L engines). Do not overtighten the plug.
6. Move the drain pan under the oil filter. Use a strap-type or cap-type wrench to loosen the oil filter. Cover your hand with a rag, and spin the filter off by hand; turn it slowly. Keep in mind that it's holding about one quart of dirty, hot oil.
7. On some vehicles such as the 2.5L engine, the oil filter is mounted inside the engine. The filter on these engines is serviced through the oil pan drain plug. To remove the oil filter on the 2.5L engines:
   a. After removing the drain plug and completely draining the oil, slowly turn the filter to begin removal, then pull it downward.
   b. Remove the filter, using pliers at the tab, then remove and discard the O-ring if it is stuck to the housing.

➡**Be careful when removing the oil filter, because the filter contains about 1 quart of hot, dirty oil.**

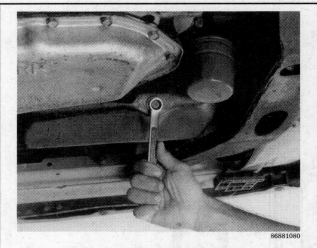

Fig. 60 Loosen the drain plug using a proper sized wrench

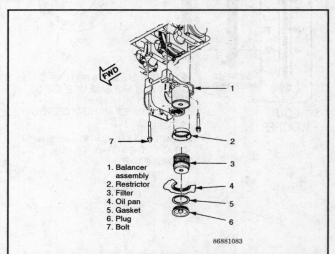

1. Balancer assembly
2. Restrictor
3. Filter
4. Oil pan
5. Gasket
6. Plug
7. Bolt

Fig. 62 Exploded view of the oil filter mounting — 2.5L engine

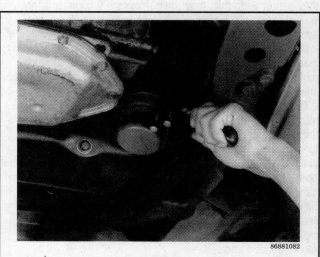

Fig. 61 Use a strap-type or cap-type wrench to loosen the oil filter

8. Empty the old oil filter into the drain pan, then properly dispose of the filter.

9. Using a clean shop towel, wipe off the filter adapter on the engine block. Be sure the towel does not leave any lint which could clog an oil passage.

10. For all vehicles except the 2.5L, coat the rubber gasket on the new filter with fresh oil. Spin the filter onto the adapter by hand until it contacts the mounting surface. Tighten the filter ¾ to 1 full turn.

11. For the 2.5L engine, coat the O-ring and grommet with clean engine oil, then press the oil filter into the housing by hand. Clean the oil pan drain plug, then coat the drain plug gasket with clean engine oil and install the plug. Tighten the plug ¼ turn after gasket contact.

12. If raised, carefully lower the vehicle.

13. Refill the crankcase with the correct amount of fresh engine oil. Please refer to the Capacities chart in this section.

14. Check the oil level on the dipstick. It is normal or the level to be a bit above the full mark until the engine is run and the new filter is filled with oil. Start the engine and allow it to idle for a few minutes.

❋❋CAUTION

Do not run the engine above idle speed until it has built up oil pressure, as indicated when the oil light goes out.

15. Shut off the engine and allow the oil to flow back to the crankcase for a minute, then recheck the oil level. Check around the filter and drain plug for any leaks, and correct as necessary.

When you have finished this job, you will notice that you now possess four or five quarts of dirty oil. The best thing to do is to pour it into plastic jugs, such as milk or old antifreeze containers. Then, locate a service station or automotive parts store where you can pour it into their used oil tank for recycling.

➡Improperly disposing of used motor oil not only pollutes the environment, it violates Federal law. Dispose of waste oil properly.

Fig. 64 Using a funnel will help prevent unnecessary mess while refilling the crankcase with fresh oil

Manual Transaxle

FLUID RECOMMENDATIONS

The recommended fluid is synchromesh transaxle fluid. The manual transaxle fluid does not require changing.

LEVEL CHECK

▶ **See Figure 65**

Check fluid level only when the engine is OFF, the vehicle is level and the transaxle is cold. To check the fluid level, remove and read the fluid level indicator/filler plug. If the indicator reads low, add the appropriate amount of synchromesh transaxle fluid to fill the transaxle to the FULL or MAX level.

➡**The fluid level indicator must be fully seated during vehicle operation or leakage will occur at the vent plug.**

Automatic Transaxle

FLUID RECOMMENDATIONS

When adding fluid or refilling the transaxle, use Dexron®IIE or Dexron® III automatic transmission fluid.

Fig. 63 Remove the oil fill cap on the valve cover to refill the crankcase with oil

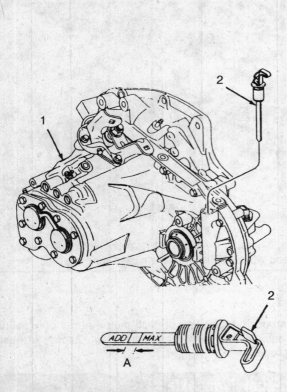

A. Level to be within "add" and "max" lines
1. Transaxle assembly
2. Indicator/fill plug

86881087

Fig. 65 View of the manual transaxle fluid level indicator/fill plug — 5TM40 5-speed manual transaxle shown

LEVEL CHECK

▶ See Figures 66 and 67

1. Start the engine and drive the vehicle for a minimum of 15 miles (24 km).

➡The automatic transmission fluid level must be checked with the vehicle at normal operating temperature; 180-200°F (82-93°C). Temperature will greatly affect transaxle fluid level.

2. Park the vehicle on a level surface.
3. Place the transaxle gear selector in P.
4. Apply the parking brake and block the drive wheels.
5. Let the vehicle idle for 3-5 minutes with the accessories OFF.
6. Pull the dipstick out and wipe with a clean, lint-free rag.
7. Push the dipstick completely into the filler tube, then wait 3 seconds and pull the dipstick out again.

8. Check both sides of the dipstick and read the lower level. The fluid level should be in the crosshatch "hot" area.

➡The fluid level is acceptable if it is anywhere within the crosshatch area. The fluid level does not have to be at the top of the crosshatch area. Do NOT add fluid unless the level is below the crosshatch area.

9. Inaccurate fluid level readings may result if the fluid is checked immediately after the vehicle has been operated under any or all of the following conditions:
   a. In high ambient temperatures above 90°F (32°C).
   b. At sustained high speeds.
   c. In heavy city traffic during hot weather.
   d. As a towing vehicle.
   e. In commercial service (taxi or police use).

10. If the vehicle has been operated under these conditions, shut the engine OFF and allow the vehicle to cool for 30 minutes. After the cooldown period, restart the vehicle and continue from Step 2.

11. If it is determined that the fluid level is low, add only enough fluid to bring the level into the crosshatch area. It generally takes less than a pint. Do NOT overfill the transaxle! If the fluid level is within specifications, simply push the dipstick back into the filler tube completely.

12. After adding fluid, if necessary, recheck the level, making sure it is within the crosshatch area. Turn the engine OFF, then unblock the drive wheels.

DRAIN AND REFILL

▶ See Figures 68, 69, 70 and 71

The car should be driven approximately 15 miles (24 km) to warm the transaxle fluid before the pan is removed.

➡The fluid should be drained while the transaxle is warm.

1. Raise and safely support the vehicle.
2. Place a drain pan under the transaxle fluid pan.
3. Remove the fluid pan bolts from the front and sides only.

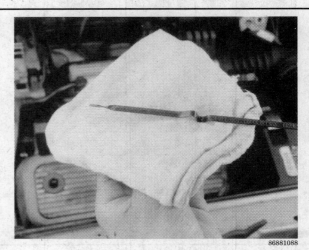

86881088

Fig. 66 The fluid level should be in the crosshatched area

Fig. 67 Use a funnel to aid in filling the transaxle

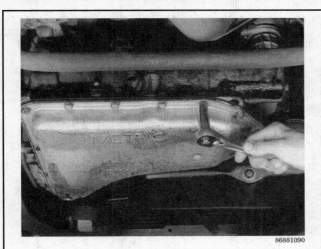

Fig. 68 Remove the fluid pan bolts from the front and sides only

Fig. 69 After removing the remaining fluid pan bolts, lower the pan from the transaxle, then . . .

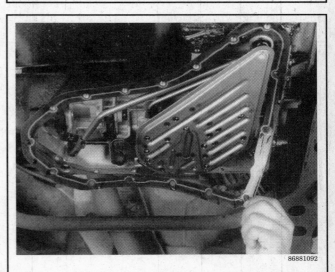

Fig. 70 . . . remove and discard the fluid pan gasket

4. Loosen, but do not remove, the bolts at the rear of the fluid pan.

5. Lightly tap the fluid pan with a rubber mallet or pry to allow the fluid to partially drain from the pan.

➡**Do not damage the transaxle case or fluid pan sealing surfaces.**

6. Remove the remaining fluid pan bolts, then lower the fluid pan from the transaxle and remove and discard the gasket.

➡**If the transaxle fluid is dark or has a burnt smell, transaxle damage is indicated. Have the transaxle checked professionally.**

7. Empty the transaxle pan of the remaining fluid, then remove the gasket material and clean with a suitable solvent.

Using a suitable scraping tool, carefully clean the gasket mounting surfaces.

To install:

8. Place a new gasket on the fluid pan.

9. Install the fluid pan to the transaxle.

➡**Apply a suitable sealant compound to the bolt shown in the illustration to prevent fluid leaks.**

10. Install the pan retaining bolts. Tighten to 133 inch lbs. (11 Nm) for vehicles through 1993. For 1994-95 vehicles, tighten the bolts to 124 inch lbs. (14 Nm).

11. Lower the vehicle.

12. Fill the transaxle to the proper level with Dexron® IIE or Dexron® III fluid. Check cold level reading for the initial fill. Do not overfill.

13. Follow the fluid check procedure earlier in this section.

14. Check the pan for leaks.

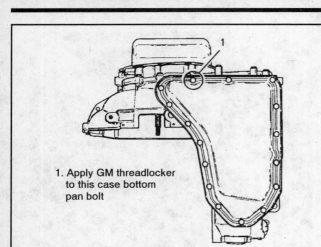

1. Apply GM threadlocker to this case bottom pan bolt

86881107

Fig. 71 Apply a suitable thread lock compound to this pan-to-case bolt

PAN AND FILTER SERVICE

▶ **See Figures 72, 73 and 74**

1. With the pan removed from the vehicle and the fluid completely drained, thoroughly clean the inside of the pan to remove all old fluid and residue.

2. Inspect the gasket sealing surface on the fluid pan and remove any remaining gasket fragments with a suitable scraper.

3. Remove the fluid filter, O-ring and/or seal from the case.

To install:

4. Apply a small amount of Transjel® to the new seal, then install the seal.

5. Install a new filter O-ring and filter.

6. Position a new gasket to the pan, then install the pan as outlined, earlier in this section.

86881093

Fig. 72 After removing the pan and gasket, remove the fluid filter

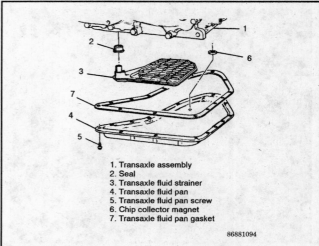

1. Transaxle assembly
2. Seal
3. Transaxle fluid strainer
4. Transaxle fluid pan
5. Transaxle fluid pan screw
6. Chip collector magnet
7. Transaxle fluid pan gasket

86881094

Fig. 73 Exploded view of the pan, filter/strainer and related components — 3T40 automatic transaxle shown

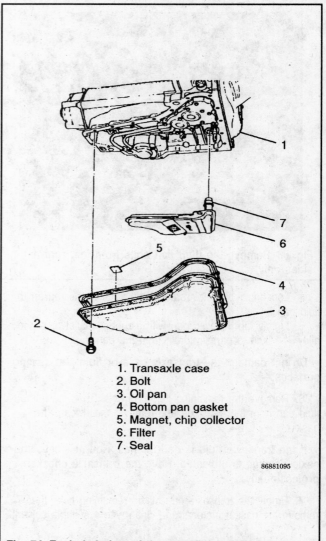

1. Transaxle case
2. Bolt
3. Oil pan
4. Bottom pan gasket
5. Magnet, chip collector
6. Filter
7. Seal

86881095

Fig. 74 Exploded view of the pan. filter and related components — 4T60E automatic transaxle shown

Cooling System

▶ **See Figures 75 and 76**

✻✻CAUTION

Never remove the radiator cap under any conditions while the engine is hot! Failure to follow these instructions could result in damage to the cooling system, engine and/or personal injury. To avoid having scalding hot coolant or steam blow out of the radiator, use extreme care whenever you are removing the radiator cap. Wait until the engine has cooled, then wrap a thick cloth around radiator cap and turn it slowly to the first stop. Step back while the pressure is released from the cooling system. When you are sure the pressure has been released, press down on the radiator cap (still have the cloth in position), turn and remove the cap.

Dealing with the cooling system can be a dangerous matter unless the proper precautions are observed. It is best to check the coolant level in the radiator when the engine is cold. All vehicles covered by this manual should be equipped with coolant recovery tank. If the coolant level is at or near the ADD/FULL COLD line (engine cold) or the FULL HOT line (engine hot), the level is satisfactory. Always be certain that the filler caps on both the radiator and the recovery tank are closed tightly.

In the event that the coolant level must be checked when the engine is hot and the vehicle is not equipped with a coolant recovery tank, place thick rag over the radiator cap and slowly turn the cap counterclockwise until it reaches the first detent. Allow all hot steam to escape. This will allow the pressure in the system to drop gradually, preventing an explosion of hot coolant. When the hissing noise stops, carefully remove the cap the rest of the way.

If the coolant level is found to be low, add a 50/50 mixture of ethylene glycol-based antifreeze and clean water. If not equipped with a recovery tank, coolant must be added through the radiator filler neck. On most models, which are equipped with a recovery bottle or surge tank, coolant may be added either through the filler neck on the radiator or directly into the recovery tank.

✻✻CAUTION

Never add coolant to a hot engine unless it is running. If it is not running, you run the risk of cracking the engine block.

It is wise to pressure check the cooling system at least once a year. If the coolant level is chronically low or rusty, the system should be thoroughly checked for leaks.

At least once every two years or 30,000 miles (50,000 km), the engine cooling system should be inspected, flushed and refilled with fresh coolant. If the coolant is left in the system too long, it loses its ability to prevent rust and corrosion. If the coolant has too much water, it won't protect against freezing.

FLUID RECOMMENDATIONS

The cooling system should be inspected, flushed and refilled with fresh coolant at least every 30,000 miles (48,000 km) or 24 months. If the coolant is left in the system too long, it loses its ability to prevent rust and corrosion.

When the coolant is being replaced, use a good quality antifreeze that is safe to be used with aluminum cooling system components. The ratio of antifreeze to water should always be a 50/50 mixture. This ratio will ensure the proper balance of cooling ability, corrosion protection and antifreeze protection. At this ratio, the antifreeze protection should be good to -34°F (-37°C). If greater antifreeze protection is needed, the ratio should not exceed 70% antifreeze to 30% water.

LEVEL CHECK

▶ **See Figures 77 and 78**

➡**When checking the coolant level, the radiator cap need not be removed. Simply check the coolant level in the recovery bottle or surge tank.**

Check the coolant level in the recovery bottle or surge tank, usually mounted on the inner fender. With the engine cold, the coolant level should be at the FULL COLD level. With the engine at normal operating temperature, the coolant level should be at the FULL HOT mark. Only add coolant to the recovery bottle or surge tank as necessary to bring the system up to a proper level.

✻✻CAUTION

Should it be necessary to remove the radiator cap, make sure the system has had time to cool, reducing the internal pressure.

On any vehicle that is not equipped with a coolant recovery bottle or surge tank, the level must be checked by removing the radiator cap. This should only be done when the cooling system has had time to sufficiently cool after the engine has been run. The coolant level should be within 2 in. (51mm) of the base of the radiator filler neck. If necessary, coolant can then be added directly to the radiator.

COOLING SYSTEM INSPECTION

Checking the Radiator Cap Seal

While you are checking the coolant level, check the radiator cap for a worn or cracked gasket. If the cap doesn't seal properly, fluid will be lost and the engine will overheat.

Worn caps should be replaced with a new one.

Checking the Radiator for Debris

Periodically clean any debris; leaves, paper, insects, etc. from the radiator fins. Pick the large pieces off by hand. The smaller pieces can be washed away with water pressure from a hose.

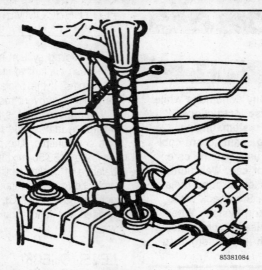

Fig. 75 Coolant protection can be easily checked using a float-type hydrometer tester

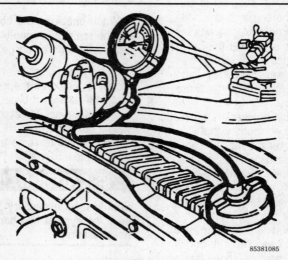

Fig. 76 If possible, a hand-held pressure tester should be used at least once a year to check system integrity

Fig. 77 Fluid level should be checked through the recovery bottle

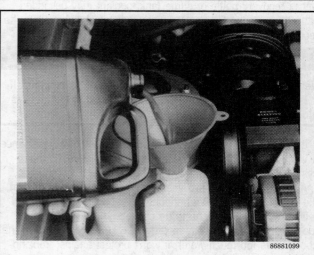

Fig. 78 The cooling system should be topped off using the recovery bottle or surge tank

Carefully straighten any bent radiator fins with a pair of needle nose pliers. Be careful, the fins are very soft. Don't wiggle the fins back and forth too much. Straighten them once and try not move them again.

DRAIN AND REFILL

▶ **See Figures 79, 80, 81 and 82**

✳✳CAUTION

When draining the coolant, keep in mind that cats and dogs are attracted by ethylene glycol antifreeze and are quite likely to drink any that is left in an uncovered container or in puddles on the ground. This will prove fatal in sufficient quantity. Always drain the coolant into a sealable container. Coolant should be reused until it is contaminated or several years old. To avoid injuries from scalding fluid and steam, DO NOT remove the radiator cap while the engine and radiator are still hot.

1. Make sure the engine is cool and the vehicle is parked on a level surface, remove the radiator cap by performing the following:
   a. Slowly rotate the cap counterclockwise to the detent.
   b. If any residual pressure is present, WAIT until the hissing stops.
   c. After the hissing noise has ceased, press down on the cap and continue rotating it counterclockwise to remove it.
2. Remove the recovery bottle or surge tank cap.
3. Place a fluid catch pan under the radiator. Place a $5/16$ in. piece of tubing through the lower tie-bar and over the drain valve, then open the valve and drain the coolant from the system.
4. Remove the engine block drain plug.
5. Install the engine block drain plug, then close the drain valve.
6. Using a 50/50 mixture of antifreeze and clean water, fill the radiator to the bottom of the filler neck and the coolant tank to the FULL mark.

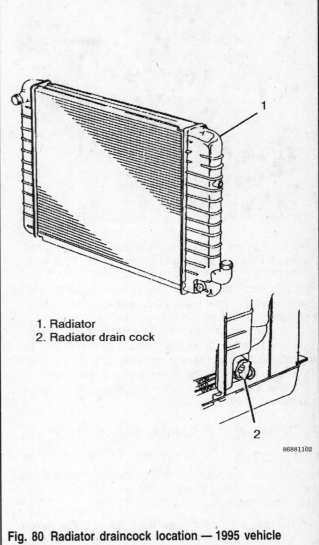

1. Radiator
2. Radiator drain cock

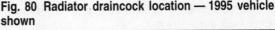

Fig. 80 Radiator draincock location — 1995 vehicle shown

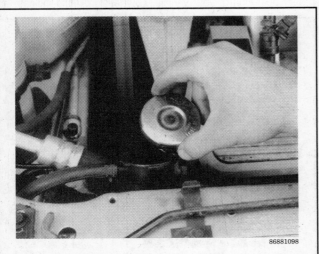

Fig. 79 When the engine is cool, carefully remove the radiator cap, then remove the recovery bottle cap

Fig. 81 Place a piece of tubing over the drain valve to help contain spillage

Fig. 82 Using a 50/50 mixture of antifreeze and clean water, fill the radiator to the bottom of the filler neck

7. Install the radiator cap, making sure the arrows line up over the overflow tube leading the reservoir or surge tank. Place the cap back on the recovery bottle or surge tank.

8. Start the engine. Select heat on the climate control panel and turn the temperature valve to full warm. Run the engine until it reaches normal operating temperature. Check to make sure there is hot air flowing from the floor ducts.

9. Check the fluid level in the reservoir or surge tank and add as necessary.

FLUSHING AND CLEANING THE SYSTEM

1. Refer to the drain and refill procedure in this section, then drain the cooling system.
2. Close the drain valve.

➡ A flushing solution may be used. Ensure it is safe for use with aluminum cooling system components. Follow the directions on the container.

3. If using a flushing solution, remove the thermostat. Reinstall the thermostat housing.
4. Add sufficient water to fill the system.
5. Start the engine and run for a few minutes. Drain the system.

➡ A flushing solution may be used. Make sure it is safe for use with aluminum cooling system components. Follow the directions given on the container.

6. If using a flushing solution, disconnect the heater hose that connects the cylinder head to the heater core (that end of the hose will clamp to a fitting on the firewall. Connect a water hose to the end of the heater hose that runs to the cylinder head and run water into the system until it begins to flow out of the top of the radiator.
7. Allow the water to flow out of the radiator until it is clear.
8. Reconnect the heater hose.
9. Drain the cooling system.
10. Reinstall the thermostat.
11. Empty the coolant reservoir or surge tank and flush it.

12. Fill the cooling system, using the correct ratio of antifreeze and water, to the bottom of the filler neck. Fill the reservoir or surge tank to the FULL mark.
13. Install the radiator cap, making sure that the arrows align with the overflow tube.

Brake Master Cylinder

▶ **See Figure 83**

The vehicles covered in this manual are equipped with a dual braking system, allowing a car to be brought to a safe stop in the event of failure in either the front or rear brakes. The dual master cylinder has two separate reservoirs, one connected to the front brakes and the other connected to the rear brakes. In the event of failure in either portion, the remaining portion is unaffected.

FLUID RECOMMENDATIONS

Use only heavy duty brake fluid meeting DOT 3 specifications. Using any other type of fluid may result in severe brake system damage.

✳✳WARNING

Brake fluid damages paint. It also absorbs moisture from the air; never leave a container or the master cylinder uncovered longer than necessary. All parts in contact with the brake fluid (master cylinder, hoses, plunger assemblies and etc.) must be kept clean, since any contamination of the brake fluid will adversely affect braking performance.

LEVEL CHECK

▶ **See Figure 84**

If should be obvious how important the brake system is to safe operation of your vehicle. The brake fluid is key to the proper operation of your vehicle. Low levels of fluid indicate a

Fig. 83 The dual brake master cylinder has two separate reservoirs

need for service (there may a leak in the system or the brake pads may just be worn and in need of replacement). In any case, the brake fluid level should be inspected at least during every oil change, but more often is desirable. Every time you open the hood is a good time to glance at the master cylinder reservoir.

To check the fluid level on most vehicles covered by this manual, you may peer through the side wall of the reservoir and observe the the level in relation to the markings. If the reservoir is opaque, simply unsnap and lift off the reservoir cover, to check the fluid level; it should be within ¼ of the tops of the reservoir walls. When making additions of brake fluid, use only fresh, uncontaminated brake fluid which meets or exceeds DOT-3 standards. Be careful not to spill any brake fluid on painted surfaces, as it will quickly eat the paint. Do not allow the brake fluid container or the master cylinder to remain open any longer than necessary; brake fluid absorbs moisture from the air, reducing the fluid's effectiveness and causing corrosion in the lines.

Clutch Master Cylinder

FLUID RECOMMENDATIONS

Use only heavy duty brake fluid meeting DOT 3 specifications. Do NOT use any other fluid because severe clutch system damage will result.

LEVEL CHECK

▶ **See Figures 85 and 86**

The clutch system fluid in the master cylinder should be checked every 6 months or 6,000 miles (10,000 km).

The clutch master cylinder reservoir is located on top of the left (driver) strut tower. Check the fluid level on the side of the reservoir. If fluid is required, remove the screw on filler cap and gasket from the master cylinder. Fill the reservoir to the

Fig. 84 When adding brake fluid to the master cylinder, use only clean, fresh fluid from a sealed container

full line in the reservoir with heavy duty brake fluid meeting DOT 3 specifications ONLY. Install the filler cap, making sure the gasket is properly seated in the cap. Make sure no dirt enters the system when adding fluid.

If fluid has to be added frequently, the system should be checked for a leak. Check for leaks at the master cylinder, slave cylinder and hose. If a leak is found, replace the component and bleed the system as outlined in Section 7.

Power Steering

FLUID RECOMMENDATIONS

When adding fluid or making a complete fluid change, always use GM P/N 1050017 power steering fluid or equivalent. Do NOT use automatic transmission fluid. Failure to use the proper fluid may cause hose and seal damage and fluid leaks.

1. Clutch master and actuator cylinder assembly
2. Bolt - 9 N.m (80 lbs. in.)
3. Remote fluid reservoir

86881108

Fig. 85 Clutch master cylinder reservoir mounting — 1992 vehicle shown

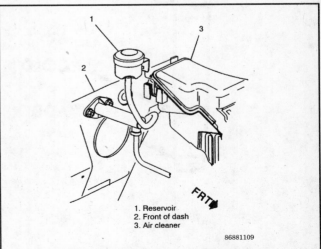

1. Reservoir
2. Front of dash
3. Air cleaner

86881109

Fig. 86 Clutch master cylinder reservoir mounting — 1995 vehicle shown

LEVEL CHECK

▶ **See Figures 87, 88 and 89**

The power steering fluid reservoir is directly above the steering pump. The pump is located on top of the engine on the right (passenger's) side.

Power steering fluid level is indicated either by marks on a see through reservoir or by marks on a fluid level indicator in the reservoir cap.

If the fluid is warmed up (about 150°F/66°C), the level should be between the HOT and COLD marks.

If the fluid is cooler than 150°F (66°C), the level should be between the ADD and COLD marks.

Chassis Greasing

Lubricate the chassis lubrication points every 7,500 miles (12,000 km) or 12 months. If your vehicle is equipped with grease fittings, lubricate the suspension and steering linkage

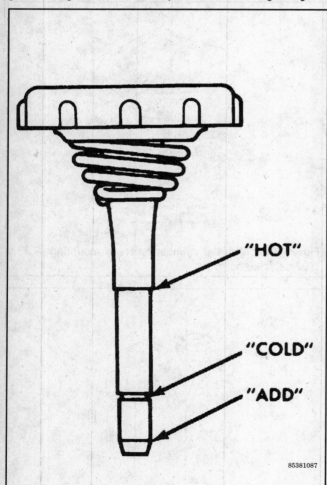

Fig. 87 The power steering reservoir cap/dipstick is marked for proper fluid levels

Fig. 88 Make sure the cap is clean before removing it; this will prevent dirt from contaminating the system

Fig. 89 Add power steering fluid through the opening while the cap is removed

with heavy duty chassis grease. Lubricate the transaxle shift linkage, parking cable guides, under body contact points and linkage with white lithium grease.

Body Lubrication and Maintenance

LOCK CYLINDERS

Apply graphite lubricant sparingly through the key slot. Insert the key and operate the lock several times to be sure that the lubricant is worked completely into the lock cylinder.

DOOR HINGES AND HINGE CHECKS

Spray a silicone lubricant on the hinge pivot points to eliminate any binding conditions. Open and close the door several times to be sure that the lubricant is evenly and thoroughly distributed.

TRUNK LID OR TAILGATE

Spray a silicone lubricant on all of the pivot and friction surfaces to eliminate any squeaks or binds. Work the tailgate to distribute the lubricant evenly.

BODY DRAIN HOLES

Be sure that the drain holes in the doors and rocker panels are cleared of obstruction. A small screwdriver can be used to carefully clear them of any debris.

Rear Wheel Bearings

The N body models are equipped with sealed hub and bearing assemblies for the rear wheels. The hub and bearing assemblies are non-serviceable. If the assembly is damaged, the complete unit must be replaced. Refer to Section 8 for the hub and bearing removal and installation procedure.

TRAILER TOWING

General Recommendations

Your vehicle is designed and intended to be used mainly to carry people. Towing a trailer will affect handling, durability and economy. Your safety and satisfaction depend upon proper use of correct equipment. Also, you should avoid overloads and other abusive use.

Factory trailer towing packages are available on most cars. However, if you are installing a trailer hitch and wiring on your car, there are a few things you should know.

Information on trailer towing, special equipment and optional equipment is available at your local dealership. You can write to Oldsmobile Customer Service Department, P.O. Box 30095, Lansing, MI 48909. In Canada, General Motors of Canada Limited, Customer Service Department, Oshawa, Ontario L1J 5Z6.

Trailer Weight

Trailer weight is the first and most important factor in determining whether or not your vehicle is suitable for towing the trailer you have in mind. The horsepower-to-weight ratio should be calculated. The basic standard is a ratio of 35:1. That is, 35 pounds (16 kg) of GVW (gross vehicle weight) for every horsepower.

To calculate this ratio, multiply you engine's rated horsepower by 35, then subtract the weight of the vehicle, including passengers and luggage. The resulting figure is the ideal maximum trailer weight that you can tow.

Hitch Weight

There are three kinds of hitches: bumper mounted, frame mounted, and load equalizing.

Bumper mounted hitches are those which attach solely to the vehicle's bumper. Many states prohibit towing with this type of hitch, when it attaches to the vehicle's stock bumper, since it subjects the bumper to stresses for which it was not de-

signed. Aftermarket rear step bumpers, designed for trailer towing, are acceptable for use with bumper mounted hitches.

➡ **Do NOT attach any hitch to the bumper bar on the vehicle. A hitch attachment may be made through the bumper mounting locations, but only if an additional attachment is also made. Frame mounted hitches can be of the type which bolts to two or more points on the frame, plus the bumper, or just to several points on the frame. Frame mounted hitches can also be of the tongue type, for Class I towing, or, of the receiver type, for classes II and III.**

Load equalizing hitches are usually used for large trailers. Most equalizing hitches are welded in place and use equalizing bars and chains to level the vehicle after the trailer is hooked up.

The bolt-on hitches are the most common, since they are relatively easy to install.

Check the gross weight rating of your trailer. Tongue weight is usually figured as 10% of gross trailer weight. Therefore, a trailer with a maximum gross weight of 2,000 lbs. (907 kg) will have a maximum tongue weight of 200 lbs. (91 kg) Class I trailers fall into this category. Class II trailers are those with a gross weight rating of 2,000-3,500 lbs. (907-1588 kg), while Class III trailers fall into the 3,500-6,000 lbs. (1588-2722 kg) category. Class IV trailers are those over 6,000 lbs. (2722 kg) and are for use with fifth wheel trucks, only.

When you have determined the hitch that you'll need, follow the manufacturer's installation instructions, exactly, especially when it comes to fastener torques. The hitch will subjected to a lot of stress and good hitches come with hardened bolts. Never substitute an inferior bolt for a hardened bolt.

Wiring

Wiring the car for towing is fairly easy. There are a number of good wiring kits available and these should be used, rather than trying to design your own. All trailers will need brake lights and turn signals as well as tail lights and side marker lights. Most states require extra marker lights for overly wide trailers. Also, most states have recently required back-up lights for trailers, and most trailer manufacturers have been building trailers with back-up lights for several years. Additionally, some

Class I, most Class II and just about all Class III trailers will have electric brakes. Add to this number an accessories wire, to operate trailer internal equipment or to charge the trailer's battery, and you can have as many as seven wires in the harness.

Determine the equipment on your trailer and buy the wiring kit necessary. The kit will contain all the wires needed, plus a plug adapter set which includes the female plug, mounted on the bumper or hitch, and the male plug, wired into, or plugged into the trailer harness.

When installing the kit, follow the manufacturer's instructions. The color coding of the wires is standard throughout the industry.

One point to note: some domestic vehicles and most imported vehicles, have separate turn signals. On most domestic vehicles, the brake lights and rear turn signals operate with the same bulb. For those vehicles with separate turn signals, you can purchase an isolation unit so that the brake lights won't blink whenever the turn signals are operated, or, you can go to your local electronics supply house and buy four diodes to wire in series with the brake and turn signal bulbs. Diodes will isolate the brake and turn signals. The choice is yours. The isolation units are simple and quick to install, but far more expensive than the diodes. The diodes, however, require more work to install properly, since they require the cutting of each bulb's wire and soldering the diode in place.

A final point, the best kits are those with a spring loaded cover on the vehicle mounted socket. This cover prevents dirt and moisture from corroding the terminals. Never let the vehicle socket hang loosely. Always mount it securely to the bumper or hitch.

TOWING THE VEHICLE

Towing the vehicle on a flat bed ("roll back") truck is the most desirable option. The car is safest and the wheels do not have to turn. It is also the most expensive way to tow and not always available.

The second best way to tow the vehicle is with the drive wheels OFF the ground.

Sometimes it is impossible to tow with the opposite wheels on ground. In that case, if the transaxle is in proper working order, the car can be towed with the front wheels on the ground (front wheel drive) for distances under 15 miles (24 km) at speeds no greater then 30 mph (48 km/h). If the transaxle is known to be damaged or if the car has to be towed over 15 miles (24 km) or over 30 mph (48km/h) the car must be dollied or towed with the rear wheels raised and the steering wheel secured so that the front wheels remain in the straight-ahead position. The steering wheel must be clamped with a special clamping device designed for towing service. If the key-controlled lock is in the locked position, damage to the lock and steering column may result.

JACKING

▶ **See Figure 90**

The jack that is furnished with the vehicle is ONLY to be used in an emergency to remove a flat tire. Never get beneath the car or, start or run the engine while the vehicle is supported by the jack. Front wheel drive cars have a center line of gravity that is far forward. Take the proper precautions to make sure the car does not fall forward while it is suspended. Personal injury may result if these procedures are not followed exactly.

When using a floor jack to lift the front of the car, lift from the center of the front crossmember. When using floor jack to lift the rear of the car, lift from the center of the rear jack pad.

After lifting the car, place jackstands under the body side pinch welds or similar strong and stable structure. Lower the car onto the jackstands slowly and carefully and check for stability before getting under the car.

Changing A Flat Tire

1. Position the vehicle on a level surface, then firmly apply the parking brake.
2. If you are in a public or in a potentially dangerous location, turn the 4-way hazard flashers ON.
3. Make sure the transaxle gear selector is in the PARK position for automatic transaxles or the NEUTRAL position for manual transaxle vehicles.
4. Remove the jacking tools and spare tire from the stowage area.

5. Connect the socket with side of ratchet marked UP/ON. Raise the jack slowly.
6. Position the jack head under the vehicle closest to the tire to be changed.
7. Raise the jack until the lift head mates with the vehicle notches as shown in the jacking previous illustration. Do NOT raise the vehicle.
8. If equipped, remove the wheel cover using the wedge end of ratchet. Connect the DOWN/OFF side of the ratchet to the socket and loosen, but do not remove the wheel nuts.
9. Connect the UP/ON side of the ratchet to the jack.
10. Raise the vehicle so the inflated spare will clear the surface when installing.
11. Remove the wheel lug nuts, then remove the wheel from the vehicle.
    To install:
12. Install the spare tire, then hand-tighten the wheel lug nuts.
13. Connect the UP/ON side of the ratchet to the socket and tighten the wheel nuts in a criss-cross sequence.
14. Carefully lower the vehicle, then remove the jack.
15. Tighten the wheel lug nuts securely to 100 ft. lbs. (140 Nm).
16. If equipped, install the wheel cover and securely store all jacking equipment.
17. Start driving the vehicle slowly to make sure everything is secure.

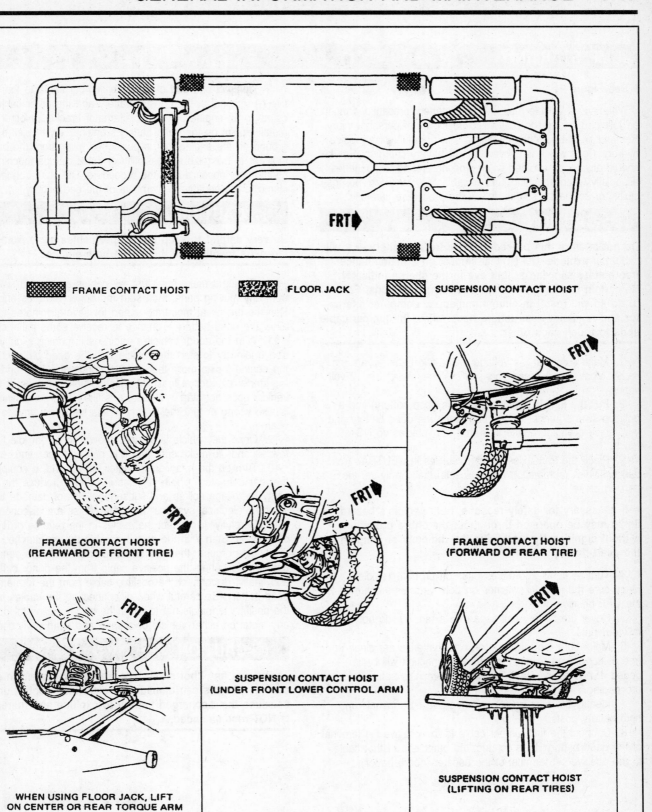

FRAME CONTACT HOIST

FLOOR JACK

SUSPENSION CONTACT HOIST

FRT

FRAME CONTACT HOIST
(REARWARD OF FRONT TIRE)

FRAME CONTACT HOIST
(FORWARD OF REAR TIRE)

SUSPENSION CONTACT HOIST
(UNDER FRONT LOWER CONTROL ARM)

WHEN USING FLOOR JACK, LIFT
ON CENTER OR REAR TORQUE ARM

SUSPENSION CONTACT HOIST
(LIFTING ON REAR TIRES)

86881113

Fig. 90 Vehicle lifting and jacking points

JUMP STARTING

♦ **See Figure 91**

Whenever a vehicle must be jump started, precautions must be followed in order to prevent to possibility of personal injury. Remember that batteries contain a small amount of explosive hydrogen gas which is a byproduct of battery charging. Sparks should always be avoided when working around the batteries, especially when attaching jumper cables. To minimize the possibility of accidental sparks, follow the procedure carefully.

❊❊CAUTION

Do not attempt this procedure on a frozen battery — it will probably explode. DO NOT attempt it on a maintenance free battery showing a light eye in the charge indicator. Be certain to observe correct polarity connections. Failure to do so will result in almost immediate computer alternator and regulator destruction. Never allow the jumper cable ends to touch each other.

1. Make sure that the voltage of the two batteries are the same. Most batteries and charging systems are of the 12 volt variety.
2. Pull the jumping vehicle (with the good battery) into a position so the jumper cables can reach the dead battery and the vehicle's engine. Make sure that the vehicles do NOT touch.
3. Place the transaxles of both vehicles in NEUTRAL (manual) or PARK (automatic), as applicable, then firmly set the parking brake.

➡**If necessary for safely reasons, both vehicle's hazard lights may be operated throughout the entire procedure without significantly increasing the difficulty of jumping the dead battery.**

4. Turn all lights and accessories off on both vehicles. Make sure the ignition switches on both vehicles are turned to the **OFF** position.
5. Cover the battery cell caps with a rag, but do not cover the terminals.
6. Make sure the terminals on both batteries are clean and free or corrosion or proper electrical connection will be impeded. If necessary, clean the battery terminals before proceeding.
7. Identify the positive (+) and negative (-) terminals on both battery posts.
8. Connect the first jumper cable to the positive (+) terminal of the dead battery, then connect the other end of that cable to the positive (+) terminal of the booster (good) battery.

9. Connect one end of the other jumper cable to the negative (-) terminal of the booster battery and the other cable clamp to an engine bolt head, alternator bracket or other solid, metallic point on the dead battery's engine. Try to pick a ground on the engine that is positioned away from the battery in order to minimize to possibility of the 2 clamps touching should one loosen during the procedure. DO NOT connect this clamp to the negative (-) terminal of the bad battery.

❊❊CAUTION

Be very careful to keep the jumper cables away from moving parts (cooling fan, belts.) on both engines.

10. Check to make sure that the cables are routed away from any moving parts, then start the donor vehicle's engine. Run the engine at moderate speed for several minutes to allow the dead battery a chance to receive some initial charge.
11. With the donor vehicle's engine still running slightly above idle, try to start the vehicle with the dead battery. Crank the engine for no more than 5-10 seconds at a time and let the starter cool for at least 20 seconds between tries. If the vehicle does not start in 3 tries, it is likely that something else is also wrong or that the battery needs additional time to charge.
12. Once the vehicle is started, allow it to run at idle for a few seconds to make sure that it is properly operating.
13. Turn on the headlights, heater blower and, if equipped, the rear defroster of both vehicles in order to reduce the severity of voltage spikes and subsequent risk of damage to vehicles' electrical systems when the cables are disconnected.
14. Carefully disconnect the cables in the reverse order of connection. Start with the negative cable that is attached to the engine ground, then the negative cable from the donor battery. Disconnect the positive cable from the donor battery and finally, disconnect the positive cable from the formerly dead battery. Be careful when disconnecting the cables from the positive terminals not to allow the alligator clips to touch any metal on either vehicle or a short and sparks will occur.

❊❊CAUTION

The use of any "hot shot" type of jumper system in excess of 12 volts can damage the electronic control units or cause the discharged battery to explode and therefore is NOT recommended.

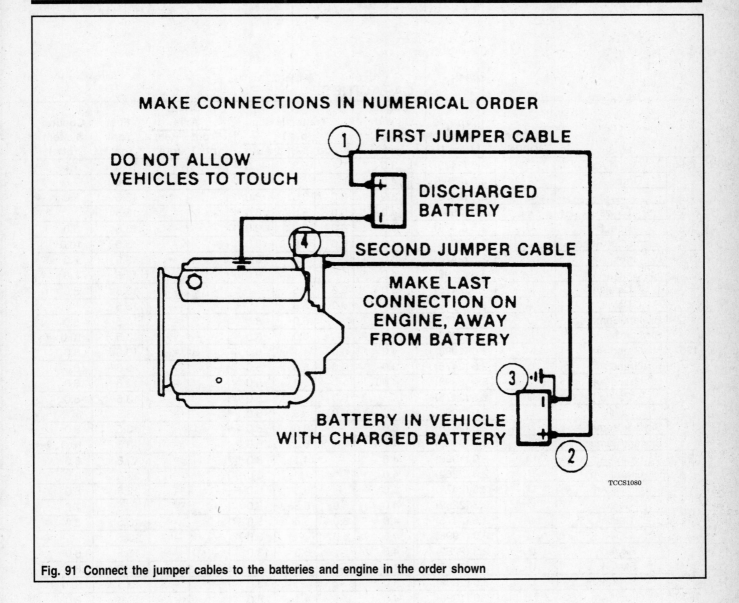

MAKE CONNECTIONS IN NUMERICAL ORDER

① FIRST JUMPER CABLE

DO NOT ALLOW
VEHICLES TO TOUCH

DISCHARGED
BATTERY

SECOND JUMPER CABLE

MAKE LAST
CONNECTION ON
ENGINE, AWAY
FROM BATTERY

③

BATTERY IN VEHICLE
WITH CHARGED BATTERY

②

TCCS1080

Fig. 91 Connect the jumper cables to the batteries and engine in the order shown

CAPACITIES

Year	Model	Engine ID/VIN	Engine Displacement Liters (cc)	Engine Oil with Filter (qts.)	Transmission (pts.)			Drive Axle		Fuel Tank (gal.)	Cooling System (qts.)
					4-Spd	5-Spd	Auto.	Front (pts.)	Rear (pts.)		
1985	Grand Am	U	2.5 (2475)	3.0 [1]	-	5.3	8.0 [12]	-	-	13.6	7.8 [12]
	Grand Am	L	3.0 (2998)	4.0 [1]	-	-	8.0 [12]	-	-	13.6	7.8 [12]
	Calais	U	2.5 (2475)	3.0 [1]	6.0	5.5	8.0 [12]	-	-	13.5	8.0
	Calais	L	3.0 (2998)	4.0 [1]	6.0	5.5	8.0 [12]	-	-	13.5	8
	Somerset Regal	U	2.5 (2475)	3.0 [1]	6.0	6.0	8.0 [12]	-	-	13.5	8.0
	Somerset Regal	L	3.0 (2998)	4.0 [1]	6.0	6.0	8.0 [12]	-	-	13.5	10.0 [9]
1986	Grand Am	U	2.5 (2475)	3.0 [1]	-	5.3	8.0 [12]	-	-	13.6	7.8 [12]
	Grand Am	L	3.0 (2998)	4.0 [1]	-	-	8.0 [12]	-	-	13.6	7.8 [12]
	Calais	U	2.5 (2475)	3.0 [1]	6.0	5.5	4	-	-	13.5	8.0
	Calais	L	3.0 (2998)	4.0 [1]	6.0	5.5	4	-	-	13.5	8
	Skylark/Somerset	U	2.5 (2475)	3.0 [1]	-	6.0	8.0 [12]	-	-	13.5	8.0
	Skylark/Somerset	L	3.0 (2998)	4.0 [1]	-	6.0	8.0 [12]	-	-	13.5	10.0 [9]
1987	Grand Am	M	2.0 (1998)	4.0 [1]	6.0	4.1	8.0 [12]	-	-	13.6	8.0
	Grand Am	U	2.5 (2475)	3.0 [1]	6.0	5.3	8.0 [12]	-	-	13.6	8.0
	Grand Am	L	3.0 (2998)	4.0 [1]	-	5.3	8.0 [12]	-	-	13.6	8.0
	Calais	U	2.5 (2475)	2	6.0	5.5	8.0 [12]	-	-	13.5	8.0
	Calais	L	3.0 (2998)	4.0 [1]	6.0	5.5	8.0 [12]	-	-	13.5	8
	Skylark/Somerset	U	2.5 (2475)	3.0 [1]	-	6.0	8.0 [5]	-	-	13.5	8.0
	Skylark/Somerset	L	3.0 (2998)	4.0 [1]	-	6.0	8.0 [5]	-	-	13.5	10.0 [9]
1988	Grand Am	M	2.0 (1998)	4.0 [1]	-	4.1	8.0 [12]	-	-	13.6	8.0
	Grand Am	D	2.3 (2262)	4.0 [1]	-	-	8.0 [12]	-	-	13.6	8.0
	Grand Am	U	2.5 (2475)	3.0 [1]	-	5.3	8.0 [12]	-	-	13.6	8.0
	Calais	D	2.3 (2262)	4.0 [1]	6.0	5.5	8.0 [12]	-	-	13.5	7.6
	Calais	U	2.5 (2475)	4.0 [1]	6.0	5.5	8.0 [12]	-	-	13.5	8.0
	Calais	L	3.0 (2998)	4.0 [1]	6.0	-	8.0 [12]	-	-	13.5	8
	Skylark	D	2.3 (2262)	4.0 [1]	-	6.0	13.0	-	-	13.5	8.0
	Skylark	U	2.5 (2475)	4.0 [1]	-	6.0	13.0	-	-	13.5	8.0
	Skylark	L	3.0 (2998)	4.0 [1]	-	-	13.0	-	-	13.5	10.0 [9]
1989	Grand Am	M	2.0 (1998)	4.0 [1]	-	4.1	8.0 [12]	-	-	13.6	8.0
	Grand Am	A	2.3 (2262)	4.0 [1]	-	5.3	8.0 [12]	-	-	13.6	8.0
	Grand Am	D	2.3 (2262)	4.0 [1]	-	5.3	8.0 [12]	-	-	13.6	8.0
	Grand Am	U	2.5 (2475)	3.0 [1]	-	5.3	8.0 [12]	-	-	13.6	8.0
	Cutlass Calais	A	2.3 (2262)	4.0 [1]	-	4.0	8.0 [12]	-	-	13.5	7.8
	Cutlass Calais	D	2.3 (2262)	4.0 [1]	-	4.0	8.0 [12]	-	-	13.5	7.8
	Cutlass Calais	U	2.5 (2475)	4.0 [1]	-	4.0	8.0 [12]	-	-	13.5	8.0
	Cutlass Calais	N	3.3 (3342)	4.0 [1]	-	4.0	8.0 [12]	-	-	13.5	8
	Skylark	D	2.3 (2262)	4.0 [1]	-	-	13.0	-	-	13.5	8.0
	Skylark	U	2.5 (2475)	4.0 [1]	-	-	13.0	-	-	13.5	8.0
	Skylark	N	3.3 (3342)	4.0 [1]	-	-	13.0	-	-	13.5	13.0
1990	Grand Am	A	2.3 (2262)	4.0 [1]	-	4.0	8.0	-	-	13.6	8.0
	Grand Am	D	2.3 (2262)	4.0 [1]	-	4.0	8.0	-	-	13.6	7.6
	Grand Am	U	2.5 (2475)	4.0 [1]	-	4.0	8.0	-	-	13.6	7.8

86881700

CAPACITIES

Year	Model	Engine ID/VIN	Engine Displacement Liters (cc)	Engine Oil with Filter (qts.)	Transmission (pts.) 4-Spd	5-Spd	Auto.	Drive Axle Front (pts.)	Rear (pts.)	Fuel Tank (gal.)	Cooling System (qts.)
1990	Cutlass Calais	A	2.3 (2262)	4.0 [1]	-	5.2	8.0 [12]	-	-	13.6	7.6
	Cutlass Calais	D	2.3 (2262)	4.0 [1]	-	5.2	8.0 [12]	-	-	13.6	8.0
	Cutlass Calais	U	2.5 (2475)	4.0 [1]	-	5.2	8.0 [12]	-	-	13.6	7.8
	Cutlass Calais	N	3.3 (3342)	4.0 [1]	-	5.2	8.0 [12]	-	-	13.6	[10]
	Skylark	D	2.3 (2262)	4.0 [1]	-	-	13.0	-	-	13.5	8.0
	Skylark	U	2.5 (2475)	4.0 [1]	-	-	13.0	-	-	13.5	8.0
	Skylark	N	3.3 (3342)	4.0 [1]	-	-	13.0	-	-	13.5	13.0
1991	Grand Am	A	2.3 (2262)	4.0 [1]	-	4.0	-	-	-	13.6	10.4
	Grand Am	D	2.3 (2262)	4.0 [1]	-	-	8.0	-	-	13.6	10.4
	Grand Am	U	2.5 (2475)	4.0 [1]	-	4.0	8.0	-	-	13.6	10.7
	Cutlass Calais	A	2.3 (2262)	4.0 [1]	-	4.0	8.0 [12]	-	-	13.6	10.8
	Cutlass Calais	D	2.3 (2262)	4.0 [1]	-	4.0	8.0 [12]	-	-	13.6	10.4
	Cutlass Calais	U	2.5 (2475)	4.0 [1]	-	4.0	8.0 [12]	-	-	13.6	10.4
	Cutlass Calais	N	3.3 (3342)	4.0 [1]	-	4.0	8.0 [12]	-	-	13.6	10.8
	Skylark	D	2.3 (2262)	4.0 [1]	-	-	8.0	-	-	13.6	8.0
	Skylark	U	2.5 (2475)	4.0 [1]	-	-	8.0	-	-	13.6	7.8
	Skylark	N	3.3 (3342)	4.0 [1]	-	-	8.0	-	-	13.6	13.0
1992	Grand Am	3	2.3 (2262)	4.0 [1]	-	4.0	8.0	-	-	13.6	9.5
	Grand Am	A	2.3 (2262)	4.0 [1]	-	4.0	8.0	-	-	13.6	9.5
	Grand Am	D	2.3 (2262)	4.0 [1]	-	4.0	8.0	-	-	13.6	9.5
	Grand Am	N	3.3 (3344)	4.0 [1]	-	-	8.0	-	-	13.6	12.7
	Achieva	A	2.3 (2262)	4.0 [1]	-	[6]	8.0 [12]	-	-	15.2	10.4
	Achieva	D	2.3 (2262)	4.0 [1]	-	[6]	8.0 [12]	-	-	15.2	10.4
	Achieva	3	2.3 (2262)	4.0 [1]	-	[6]	8.0 [12]	-	-	15.2	10.4
	Achieva	N	3.3 (3344)	4.0 [1]	-	[6]	8.0 [12]	-	-	15.2	10.8
	Skylark	D	2.3 (2262)	4.0 [1]	-	-	8.0	-	-	15.2	10.4
	Skylark	N	3.3 (3344)	4.0 [1]	-	-	8.0	-	-	15.2	13.0
1993	Grand Am	3	2.3 (2262)	4.0 [1]	-	4.0	8.0	-	-	15.2	9.5
	Grand Am	A	2.3 (2262)	4.0 [1]	-	4.0	8.0	-	-	15.2	9.5
	Grand Am	D	2.3 (2262)	4.0 [1]	-	4.0	8.0	-	-	15.2	9.5
	Grand Am	N	3.3 (3344)	4.0 [1]	-	-	8.0	-	-	15.2	12.7
	Achieva	A	2.3 (2262)	4.0 [1]	-	[7]	8.0 [12]	-	-	15.2	10.4
	Achieva	D	2.3 (2262)	4.0 [1]	-	[7]	8.0 [12]	-	-	15.2	10.4
	Achieva	3	2.3 (2262)	4.0 [1]	-	[7]	8.0 [12]	-	-	15.2	10.4
	Achieva	N	3.3 (3344)	4.0 [1]	-	[7]	8.0 [12]	-	-	15.2	10.8
	Skylark	D	2.3 (2262)	4.0 [1]	-	-	8.0	-	-	15.2	10.4
	Skylark	N	3.3 (3344)	4.0 [1]	-	-	8.0	-	-	15.2	13.0
1994	Grand Am	3	2.3 (2262)	4.5	-	4.0	8.0 [3]	-	-	15.2	10.4
	Grand Am	A	2.3 (2262)	4.5	-	4.0	8.0 [3]	-	-	15.2	10.4
	Grand Am	D	2.3 (2262)	4.5	-	4.0	8.0 [3]	-	-	15.2	10.4
	Grand Am	M	3.1 (3136)	4.5	-	4.0	8.0 [3]	-	-	15.2	13.1
	Achieva	A	2.3 (2262)	4.5	-	[7]	[11]	-	-	15.2	10.4

86881701

CAPACITIES

Year	Model	Engine ID/VIN	Engine Displacement Liters (cc)	Engine Oil with Filter (qts.)	Transmission (pts.) 4-Spd	5-Spd	Auto.	Drive Axle Front (pts.)	Rear (pts.)	Fuel Tank (gal.)	Cooling System (qts.)
1994	Achieva	D	2.3 (2262)	4.5	-	7	11	-	-	15.2	10.4
	Achieva	3	2.3 (2262)	4.5	-	7	11	-	-	15.2	10.4
	Achieva	M	3.1 (3136)	4.5	-	7	11	-	-	15.2	10.8
	Skylark	3	2.3 (2262)	4.5	-	-	8.0	-	-	15.2	10.4
	Skylark	M	3.1 (3136)	4.5	-	-	8.0	-	-	15.2	13.0
1995	Grand Am	D	2.3 (2262)	4.5	-	4.0	8.0 3	-	-	15.2	10.4
	Grand Am	M	3.1 (3136)	4.5	-	4.0	8.0 3	-	-	15.2	13.1
	Achieva	D	2.3 (2262)	4.5	-	4.0	8.0 3	-	-	15.2	10.4
	Achieva	M	3.1 (3136)	4.5	-	4.0	8.0 3	-	-	15.2	13.0
	Skylark	D	2.3 (2262)	4.5	-	-	8.0 3	-	-	15.2	10.4
	Skylark	M	3.1 (3136)	4.5	-	-	8.0 3	-	-	15.2	13.0

1 Specification is without filter replacement. Additional oil may be required.
2 Without filter replacement; With A/T: 3.0, With M/T: 4.0
3 With 3T40: pan removal 8.0 pts. - overhaul 14 pts.
  With 4T60E: pan removal 12.0 pts. - overhaul 16 pts.
4 With AT 125C: 8.0 pts.; overhaul - 18 pts.
  With AT 440-T4: 13.0 pts.: overhaul - 22 pts.
5 Overhaul: 13.0 pts.
6 With T5550: 4.2 pts.
  With Isuzu: 3.8 pts.
7 With T5550: 4.2 pts.
  With Isuzu: 4.0 pts.
8 With standard cooling: 10.3 qts.
  With A/C: 11.0 qts.
9 With A/C: 11.0 qts.
10 With standard cooling: 9.9 qts.
  With A/C: 10.4 qts.
11 Overhaul: 12.0 pts.
12 With A/C: 7.9 qts.

86881702

MAINTENANCE INTERVALS CHART I of II

Follow Schedule I if the car is mainly operated under one or more of the following conditions:
- When most trips are less than 4 miles (6 kilometers).
- When most trips are less than 10 miles (16 kilometers) and outside temperatures remain below freezing.
- Idling and/or low-speed operation in stop-and-go traffic.
- Towing a trailer
- Operating in dusty areas.

Schedule I should also be followed if the car is used for delivery service, police, taxi or other commercial applications.

ITEM NO.	TO BE SERVICED	WHEN TO PERFORM Miles (Kilometers) or Months, Whichever Occurs First	The services shown in this schedule up to 48,000 miles (80,000 km) are to be performed after 48,000 miles at the same intervals															
		MILES (000)	3	6	9	12	15	18	21	24	27	30	33	36	39	42	45	48
		KILOMETERS (000)	5	10	15	20	25	30	35	40	45	50	55	60	65	70	75	80
1	Engine Oil & Filter Change*	Every 3,000 (5,000 km) or 3 mos.	●	●	●	●	●	●	●	●	●	●	●	●	●	●	●	●
2	Chassis Lubrication	Every other oil change		●		●		●		●		●		●		●		●
3	Carb. Choke & Hose Insp.* (If Equipped)††	At 6,000 mi. (10,000 km) and then every 30,000 mi. (50,000 km)		●								●						
4	Carb. or Throttle Body Mount Bolt Torque (Some Models)*	At 6,000 mi. (10,000 km) only		●														
5	Eng. Idle Speed Adj. (Some Models)*			●														
6	Tire & Wheel Insp. and Rotation	At 6,000 mi. (10,000 km) and then every 15,000 mi. (25,000 km)		●					●					●				
7	Vac. or Air Pump Drive Belt Insp.*	Every 30,000 mi. (50,000 km) or 24 mos.										●						
8	Cooling System Service*											●						
9	Wheel Brg. Repack (Rear-Wheel-Drive Cars Only)	See explanation for service interval																
10	Transmission/Transaxle Service																	
11	Spark Plug Service*	Every 30,000 mi. (50,000 km)										●						
12	Spark Plug Wire Insp. (Some Models)*											●						
13	PCV Valve Insp. (Some Models)*††											●						
14	EGR System Insp.*††	Every 30,000 mi. (50,000 km) or 36 mos.										●						
15	Air Cleaner & PCV Filter Rep.*											●						
16	Eng. Timing Check (Some Models)*											●						
17	Fuel Tank, Cap & Lines Insp.*††	Every 30,000 (50,000 km)										●						
18	Thermostatically Controlled Air Cleaner Insp. (Some Models)*											●						

FOOTNOTES: * An Emission Control Service
†† The U.S. Environmental Protection Agency has determined that the failure to perform this maintenance item will not nullify the emission warranty or limit recall liability prior to the completion of vehicle useful life. General Motors, however, urges that all recommended maintenance services be performed at the indicated intervals and the maintenance be recorded in Section C of the owner's maintenance schedule.

86881116

MAINTENANCE INTERVALS CHART II of II

Follow Schedule II if, as a general rule, the car is driven on a daily basis for several miles (km) and none of the above conditions apply.

ITEM NO.	TO BE SERVICED	WHEN TO PERFORM Miles (Kilometers) or Months, Whichever Occurs First	The services shown in this schedule up to 45,000 miles (75,000 km) are to be performed after 45,000 miles at the same intervals					
		MILES (000)	7.5	15	22.5	30	37.5	45
		KILOMETERS (000)	12.5	25	37.5	50	62.5	75
1	Engine Oil & Filter Change*	Every 7,500 mi. (12,500 km) or 12 mos.	●	●	●	●	●	●
	Filter Change*	At first and every other oil change or 12 mos.	●		●		●	
2	Chassis Lubrication	Every 7,500 mi. (12,500 km) or 12 mos.	●	●	●	●	●	●
3	Carb. Choke & Hose Insp.* (If Equipped)††	At 7,500 mi. (12,500 km) and then at each 30,000 mi. (50,000 km) interval	●			●		
4	Carb. or Throttle Body Mount Bolt Torque (Some Models)*	At 7,500 mi. (12,500 km) only	●					
5	Eng. Idle Speed Adj. (Some Models)*		●					
6	Tire & Wheel Insp. and Rotation	At 7,500 mi. (12,500 km) and then every 15,000 mi. (25,000 km)	●		●		●	
7	Vac. or Air Pump Drive Belt Insp.*	Every 30,000 mi. (50,000 km) or 24 mos.				●		
8	Cooling System Service*					●		
9	Wheel Brg. Repack (Rear-Wheel-Drive Cars Only)	Every 30,000 mi. (50,000 km)				●		
10	Transmission/Transaxle Service	See explanation for service interval						
11	Spark Plug Service*					●		
12	Spark Plug Wire Insp. (Some Models)*	Every 30,000 mi. (50,000 km)				●		
13	PCV Valve Insp. (Some Models)*††					●		
14	EGR System Insp.*††	Every 30,000 mi. (50,000 km) or 36 mos.				●		
15	Air Cleaner & PCV Filter Rep.*					●		
16	Eng. Timing Check (Some Models)*					●		
17	Fuel Tank, Cap & Lines Insp.*††	Every 30,000 (50,000 km)				●		
18	Thermostatically Controlled Air Cleaner Insp. (Some Models)*					●		

FOOTNOTES: * An Emission Control Service
†† The U.S. Environmental Protection Agency has determined that the failure to perform this maintenance item will not nullify the emission warranty or limit recall liability prior to the completion of vehicle useful life. General Motors, however, urges that all recommended maintenance services be performed at the indicated intervals and the maintenance be recorded in Section C of the owner's maintenance schedule.

86881117

COMPUTER CONTROLLED COIL
  IGNITION (C³I)/ELECTRONIC
  IGNITION (EI) SYSTEM
  3.0L (VIN L), 3.1L (VIN M) AND 3.3L
  (VIN N) ENGINES 2-39
DIRECT IGNITION SYSTEM (DIS)
  1987-91 2.5L (VIN U) ENGINE 2-33
FIRING ORDERS 2-12
HIGH ENERGY IGNITION (HEI)
  SYSTEM
  2.0L (VIN M) AND 1985-86 2.5L (VIN
  U) ENGINES 2-13
IDLE SPEED AND MIXTURE
  ADJUSTMENTS 2-57
IGNITION TIMING
  INSPECTION AND
  ADJUSTMENT 2-56
INTEGRATED DIRECT IGNITION
  (IDI)/ELECTRONIC IGNITION SYSTEM
  2.3L (VIN A, D, AND 3)
  ENGINES 2-23
SPECIFICATIONS CHARTS
  TUNE-UP SPECIFICATIONS 2-58
TUNE-UP PROCEDURES
  SPARK PLUG WIRES 2-11
  SPARK PLUGS 2-2
VALVE LASH 2-57

2

ENGINE
PERFORMANCE
AND
TUNE-UP

COMPUTER CONTROLLED COIL
IGNITION (C³I)/ELECTRONIC
IGNITION (EI) SYSTEM 2-39
DIRECT IGNITION SYSTEM (DIS) 2-33
FIRING ORDERS 2-12
HIGH ENERGY IGNITION (HEI)
SYSTEM 2-13
IDLE SPEED AND MIXTURE
ADJUSTMENTS 2-57
IGNITION TIMING 2-56
INTEGRATED DIRECT IGNITION
(IDI)/ELECTRONIC IGNITION
SYSTEM 2-23
SPECIFICATIONS CHARTS 2-58
TUNE-UP PROCEDURES 2-2
VALVE LASH 2-57

TUNE-UP PROCEDURES

In order to extract the full measure of performance and economy from your engine, it is essential that it is properly tuned at regular intervals. A regular tune-up will keep your car's engine running smoothly and will prevent the annoying breakdowns and poor performance associated with an untuned engine.

Before the days of unleaded fuel, electronic fuel injection, and electronically controlled ignition systems (which, initially, did away with mechanical breaker points and has, on most of the newer engines, done away with the distributor altogether), the tune-up was a much more involved process, requiring a delicate ear and just the right touch in order to fine tune an engine. On today's engines, ignition timing, along with idle speed and mixture are controlled electronically, by the computer control module (ECM/PCM as applicable) and are not adjustable. The choke function has been incorporated into the fuel injection system and is no longer a separate component requiring periodic service and adjustment. In addition, with the advent of unleaded fuel and improved manufacturing techniques, spark plugs last longer. In fact, if your vehicle is equipped with the 2.3L engine, the Integrated Direct Ignition (IDI) system has even eliminated the spark plugs wires, and with them, the need for periodic inspection and replacement. Accordingly, whereas in the "old days" the engine might have received a seasonal tune-up, one for the winter months and another for summer, the tune-up now consists of replacing the spark plugs, changing the air, fuel and PCV breather filters and performing a detailed visual inspection of the spark plug wires (if equipped), vacuum, fuel and air lines and coolant hoses every 30,000 miles (48,300 km).

Under normal driving conditions, the tune-up should be performed every 30,000 miles (48,300 km). This interval should be halved if the vehicle is operated under severe conditions, such as trailer towing, prolonged idling, continual stop and start driving, or if starting or running problems are noticed. It is assumed that the routine maintenance described in Section 1 has been kept up, as this will have a decided effect on the results of a tune-up. Follow the tune-up steps in order.

If the specifications listed in the on the Tune-Up Specifications chart in this section differ from those found on the Vehicle Emission Control Information (VECI) label located in the engine compartment (usually on the radiator support), follow the specs on the VECI label. The VECI label often reflects changes made during the production run.

Spark Plugs

▶ **See Figures 1, 2, 3, 4 and 5**

A typical spark plug consists of a metal shell surrounding a ceramic insulator. A metal electrode extends downward through the center of the insulator and protrudes a small distance. Located at the end of the plug and attached to the side of the outer metal shell is the side electrode. The side electrode bends in at a 90 angle so that its tip is even with, and parallel

to, the tip of the center electrode. The distance between these two electrodes (measured in thousandths of an inch or hundredths of a millimeter) is called the spark plug gap.

The spark plug in no way produces a spark but merely provides a gap across which the current can arc. The coil produces 20,000-40,000 volts or more, which travels from the coils, through the spark plug wires to the spark plugs. The current passes along the center electrode and jumps the gap to the side electrode, and, in so doing, ignites the air/fuel mixture in the combustion chamber.

SPARK PLUG HEAT RANGE

Spark plug heat range is the ability of the plug to dissipate heat. The longer the insulator (or the farther it extends into the engine), the hotter the plug will operate; the shorter the insulator the cooler it will operate. A plug that absorbs little heat and remains too cool will quickly accumulate deposits of oil and carbon since it is not hot enough to burn them off. This leads to plug fouling and consequently to misfiring. A plug that absorbs too much heat may have deposits also, but due to the higher temperatures, the electrodes will burn away quickly. In some instances, the higher temperatures may lead to preignition. Preignition takes place when plug tips get so hot that they glow sufficiently to ignite the fuel/air mixture before the actual spark occurs. This early ignition will usually result in the "pinging" experienced during low speeds and heavy loads.

The general rule of thumb for choosing the correct heat range when picking a spark plug is, if most of your driving is long distance, high speed travel, use a colder plug; if most of your driving is stop and go, use a hotter plug. In general, however, unless you are experiencing a problem use the factory recommended spark plugs.

A set of spark plugs usually requires replacement after about 30,000 miles (48,300 km) on cars with electronic ignition, depending on your style of driving. In normal operation, plug gap increases about 0.001 in. (0.0254mm) for every 1,000-2,500 miles (1600-4000 km). As the gap increases, the plug's voltage requirement also increases. It requires a greater voltage to jump the wider gap and about two to three times as much voltage to fire a plug at high speeds than at idle.

REMOVAL & INSTALLATION

When handling spark plugs, only work on one at a time. Don't start by removing the plug wires all at once because unless you number them, they are going to get mixed up. On some models, however, it will be more convenient to remove all the wires before you start to work on the plugs. If this is necessary, take a minute before you begin and number the wires with tape before disconnecting them. The time you spend doing this will pay off later when it comes time to reconnect the wires to the plugs.

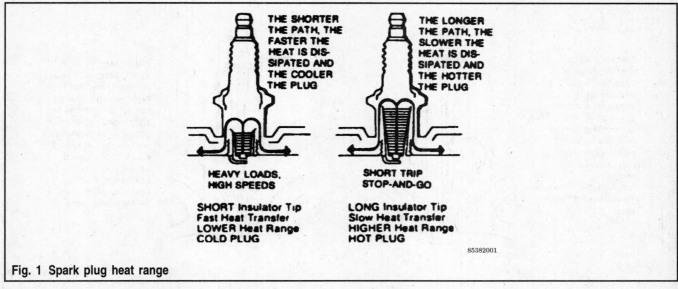

THE SHORTER THE PATH, THE FASTER THE HEAT IS DISSIPATED AND THE COOLER THE PLUG

THE LONGER THE PATH, THE SLOWER THE HEAT IS DISSIPATED AND THE HOTTER THE PLUG

HEAVY LOADS, HIGH SPEEDS

SHORT TRIP STOP-AND-GO

SHORT Insulator Tip
Fast Heat Transfer
LOWER Heat Range
COLD PLUG

LONG Insulator Tip
Slow Heat Transfer
HIGHER Heat Range
HOT PLUG

85382001

Fig. 1 Spark plug heat range

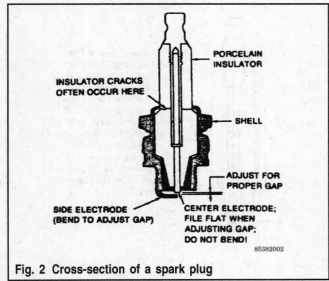

PORCELAIN INSULATOR

INSULATOR CRACKS OFTEN OCCUR HERE

SHELL

ADJUST FOR PROPER GAP

SIDE ELECTRODE (BEND TO ADJUST GAP)

CENTER ELECTRODE; FILE FLAT WHEN ADJUSTING GAP; DO NOT BEND!

85382002

Fig. 2 Cross-section of a spark plug

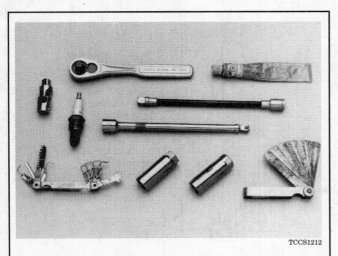

TCCS1212

Fig. 3 A variety of tools and gauges are needed for spark plug service

2.0L (VIN M) Engine

▶ See Figure 6

➡To avoid engine damage, do not remove spark plugs when the engine is warm. When removing spark plugs, only work on one at a time. Don't start by removing the plug wires all at once, because unless you number them, they may become mixed up. Take a minute before you begin and number the wires with tape. The best location for numbering is as near as possible to the spark plug boot.

1. Disconnect the negative battery cable.
2. Remove air cleaner components in order to gain access to the spark plugs.
3. Tag, then detach the first spark plug cable by pulling and twisting the boot in either direction to break loose the seal, then remove the boot from the plug. You may also use a plug wire removal tool designed especially for this purpose. Do not pull on the wire itself or you may separate the plug connector from the end of the wire. When the wire has been removed, take a wire brush and clean the area around the plug. An evaporative spray cleaner such as those designed for brake applications will also work well. Make sure that all the foreign material is removed so that none will enter the cylinder after the plug has been removed.

➡If you have access to a compressor, use the air hose the blow all material away from the spark plug bores before loosening the plug. Always protect your eyes with safety glasses when using compressed air.

4. Remove the spark plug using the proper size socket, extensions, and universals as necessary. Hold the socket or the extension close to the plug with your free hand as this will help lessen the possibility of applying a shear force which might snap the plug in half.

To install:

5. The 2.0L (VIN M) engines uses AC Type R42XLS spark plugs. Properly gap them to 0.035 in. (0.89mm) or the specification listed on the Vehicles Emission Control Information (VECI) label on the vehicle prior to installation.

Tracking Arc
High voltage arcs between a fouling deposit on the insulator tip and spark plug shell. This ignites the fuel/air mixture at some point along the insulator tip, retarding the ignition timing which causes a power and fuel loss.

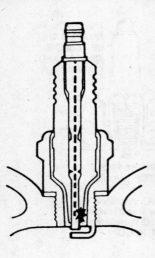

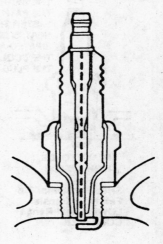

Wide Gap
Spark plug electrodes are worn so that the high voltage charge cannot arc across the electrodes. Improper gapping of electrodes on new or "cleaned" spark plugs could cause a similar condition. Fuel remains unburned and a power loss results.

Flashover
A damaged spark plug boot, along with dirt and moisture, could permit the high voltage charge to short over the insulator to the spark plug shell or the engine. AC's buttress insulator design helps prevent high voltage flashover.

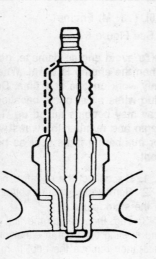

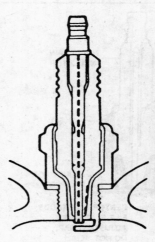

Fouled Spark Plug
Deposits that have formed on the insulator tip may become conductive and provide a "shunt" path to the shell. This prevents the high voltage from arcing between the electrodes. A power and fuel loss is the result.

Bridged Electrodes
Fouling deposits between the electrodes "ground out" the high voltage needed to fire the spark plug. The arc between the electrodes does not occur and the fuel air mixture is not ignited. This causes a power loss and exhausting of raw fuel.

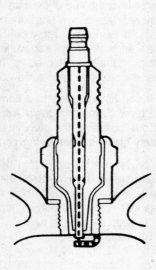

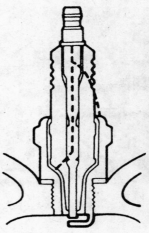

Cracked Insulator
A crack in the spark plug insulator could cause the high voltage charge to "ground out." Here, the spark does not jump the electrode gap and the fuel air mixture is not ignited. This causes a power loss and raw fuel is exhausted.

TCCS2001

Fig. 4 Used spark plugs which show damage may indicate engine problems

GAP BRIDGED

IDENTIFIED BY DEPOSIT BUILD-UP CLOSING GAP BETWEEN ELECTRODES.

CAUSED BY OIL OR CARBON FOULING. REPLACE PLUG, OR, IF DEPOSITS ARE NOT EXCESSIVE THE PLUG CAN BE CLEANED.

OIL FOULED

IDENTIFIED BY WET BLACK DEPOSITS ON THE INSULATOR SHELL BORE ELECTRODES.

CAUSED BY EXCESSIVE OIL ENTERING COMBUSTION CHAMBER THROUGH WORN RINGS AND PISTONS, EXCESSIVE CLEARANCE BETWEEN VALVE GUIDES AND STEMS, OR WORN OR LOOSE BEARINGS. CORRECT OIL PROBLEM. REPLACE THE PLUG.

CARBON FOULED

IDENTIFIED BY BLACK, DRY FLUFFY CARBON DEPOSITS ON INSULATOR TIPS, EXPOSED SHELL SURFACES AND ELECTRODES.

CAUSED BY TOO COLD A PLUG, WEAK IGNITION, DIRTY AIR CLEANER, DEFECTIVE FUEL PUMP, TOO RICH A FUEL MIXTURE, IMPROPERLY OPERATING HEAT RISER OR EXCESSIVE IDLING. CAN BE CLEANED.

NORMAL

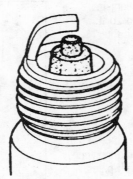

IDENTIFIED BY LIGHT TAN OR GRAY DEPOSITS ON THE FIRING TIP.

PRE-IGNITION

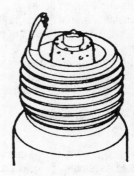

IDENTIFIED BY MELTED ELECTRODES AND POSSIBLY BLISTERED INSULATOR. METALIC DEPOSITS ON INSULATOR INDICATE ENGINE DAMAGE.

CAUSED BY WRONG TYPE OF FUEL, INCORRECT IGNITION TIMING OR ADVANCE, TOO HOT A PLUG, BURNT VALVES OR ENGINE OVERHEATING. REPLACE THE PLUG.

OVERHEATING

IDENTIFIED BY A WHITE OR LIGHT GRAY INSULATOR WITH SMALL BLACK OR GRAY BROWN SPOTS AND WITH BLUISH-BURNT APPEARANCE OF ELECTRODES.

CAUSED BY ENGINE OVER-HEATING, WRONG TYPE OF FUEL, LOOSE SPARK PLUGS, TOO HOT A PLUG, LOW FUEL PUMP PRESSURE OR INCORRECT IGNITION TIMING. REPLACE THE PLUG.

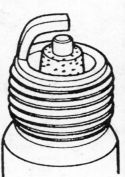

FUSED SPOT DEPOSIT

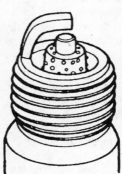

IDENTIFIED BY MELTED OR SPOTTY DEPOSITS RESEMBLING BUBBLES OR BLISTERS.

CAUSED BY SUDDEN ACCELERATION. CAN BE CLEANED IF NOT EXCESSIVE, OTHERWISE REPLACE PLUG.

TCCS2002

Fig. 5 Inspect the spark plug to determine engine running conditions

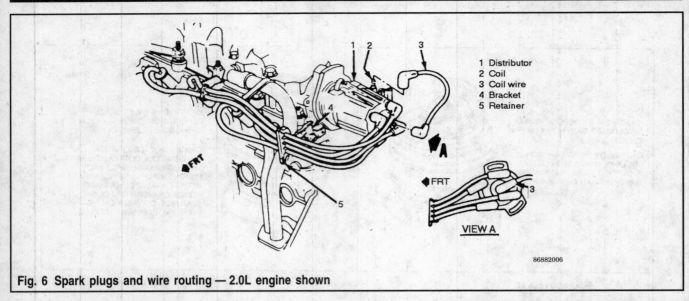

Fig. 6 Spark plugs and wire routing — 2.0L engine shown

6. Lubricate the threads lightly with an anti-seize compound, then install the spark plug. Tighten the plug to 20 ft. lbs. (27 Nm). Install the cable on the plug, making sure it snaps in place.

7. Repeat for the remaining spark plugs.

8. Install the air cleaner components.

9. Connect the negative battery cable.

2.3L Engine (VIN A, D, and 3)

▶ See Figures 7, 8 and 9

The spark plugs on this engine are located under the ignition coil and module assembly. To gain access to the spark plugs, the coil and module assembly must be removed.

➡**To avoid engine damage, do not remove the spark plugs when the engine is warm. When you're removing spark plugs, work on only one at a time. Don't start by removing the plug wires all at once, because unless you number them, they may become mixed up. Take a minute before you begin and number the wires with tape. The best location for numbering is as near as possible to the spark plug boot.**

1. Disconnect the negative battery cable.

2. Remove the 4 bolts retaining the Integrated Direct Ignition (IDI) or Electronic Ignition (EI) coil/module/cover assembly (depending upon vehicle application), then detach the electrical connector. Remove the assembly by pulling it straight up away from the engine.

3. If the connector(s) sticks to the spark plug, use spark plug connector removing tool J-36011 or equivalent, and a twisting motion to detach the connector(s) from the plugs.

4. Clean any dirt away from the spark plug recess area.

5. Remove the spark plug using the proper size socket, extensions and universal joints, as necessary. Hold the socket or the extension close to the plug with your free hand, as this will help lessen the possibility of applying a shear force which might snap the plug in half.

6. The 2.3L engine uses AC Type FR3LS plugs. Properly gap them to 0.035 in. (0.89mm), or the specification listed on the Vehicles Emission Control Information (VECI) label on the vehicle.

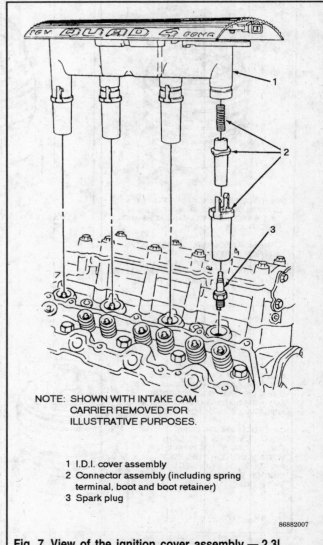

NOTE: SHOWN WITH INTAKE CAM CARRIER REMOVED FOR ILLUSTRATIVE PURPOSES.

1 I.D.I. cover assembly
2 Connector assembly (including spring terminal, boot and boot retainer)
3 Spark plug

Fig. 7 View of the ignition cover assembly — 2.3L engine (VIN's A and D) shown

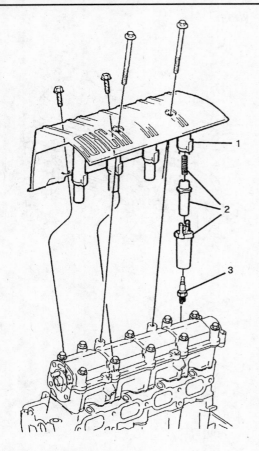

1 I.D.I. cover assembly
2 Connector assembly (including spring terminal, boot and boot retainer)
3 Spark plug

86882008

Fig. 8 To remove the cover, unfasten the four bolts, then pull the assembly straight up from the engine — 2.3L engine (VIN 3) shown

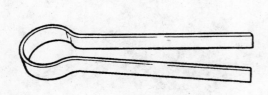

SPARK PLUG BOOT INSULATOR REMOVER
(VIN A AND D)

86882009

Fig. 9 If any of the connectors stick to the spark plug, using this tool and a twisting motion will free the connectors from the spark plugs

To install:

7. Lubricate the threads lightly with an anti-seize compound, then start the four spark plugs by hand. Tighten the plugs to 17 ft. lbs. (23 Nm).

8. If removed, install any the plug boot connectors that may have stuck to a spark plug to the IDI assembly.

➡**Check to make sure the spring terminal is inside the boot.**

9. Install the IDI or EI coil/module/cover assembly to the engine, while carefully aligning the boots with the spark plug terminals, by pushing the assembly straight down.

10. Apply Loctite® thread locking compound, or equivalent to the cover bolts. Install the bolts and tighten to 13 ft. lbs. (18 Nm).

11. If removed, engage the ignition cover electrical connectors.

12. Connect the negative battery cable.

2.5L (VIN U) Engine

▶ **See Figure 10**

1. Disconnect the negative battery cable.

2. Remove air cleaner components in order to gain access to the spark plugs.

3. Remove the first spark plug cable by pulling and twisting the boot.

4. Remove the spark plug using the proper size socket, extensions, and universals as necessary. Hold the socket or the extension close to the plug with your free hand as this will help lessen the possibility of applying a shear force which might snap the plug in half.

5. The 2.5L engine uses AC Type R43TSX or R43TS6 plugs. Properly gap them to 0.060 in. (1.5mm) or the specification listed on the Vehicles Emission Control Information (VECI) label on the vehicle prior to installation.

To install:

6. Lubricate the threads lightly with an anti-seize compound, then install the spark plug(s). Tighten the plugs to 15 ft. lbs. (21 Nm). Install the wire on the plug, making sure it snaps in place.

7. Repeat for the remaining spark plugs.

8. Install the air cleaner components.

9. Connect the negative battery cable.

3.0L (VIN L), 3.1L (VIN M), and 3.3L (VIN N) Engines

▶ **See Figures 11, 12, 13, 14 and 15**

1. Disconnect the negative battery cable.

2. Remove the first spark plug cable by twisting the boot half a turn, then pulling up.

3. Remove the spark plug using the proper size socket, extensions, and universals as necessary. Hold the socket or the extension close to the plug with your free hand as this will help lessen the possibility of applying a shear force which might snap the plug in half.

4. The 3.0L (VIN L) engine uses AC Type R44LTS plugs and they should be gapped to 0.045 in. (1.1mm) prior to installation. The 3.1L (VIN M) engine used AC type R44LTSM6 plugs and they should be gapped to 0.060 in. (1.5mm). The 3.3L (VIN N) engine uses AC Type R44LTS6 plugs for 1989-90 and R45LTS6 plugs for 1991-92. Gap both types to 0.060 in. (1.5mm).

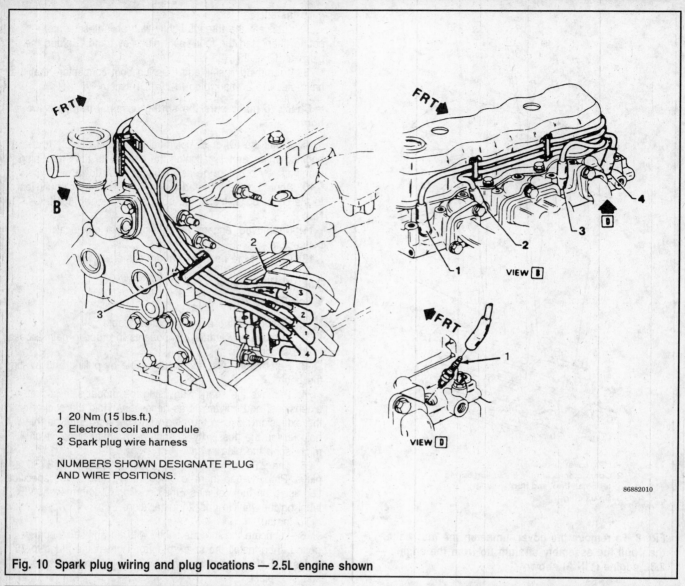

1 20 Nm (15 lbs.ft.)
2 Electronic coil and module
3 Spark plug wire harness

NUMBERS SHOWN DESIGNATE PLUG
AND WIRE POSITIONS.

86882010

Fig. 10 Spark plug wiring and plug locations — 2.5L engine shown

86882011

Fig. 11 Remove the spark plug wire by twisting the boot ½ turn, then pulling up — 1986 3.0L engine shown

86882012

Fig. 12 Using the proper size socket and ratchet combination, remove the spark plugs — 1986 3.0L engine shown

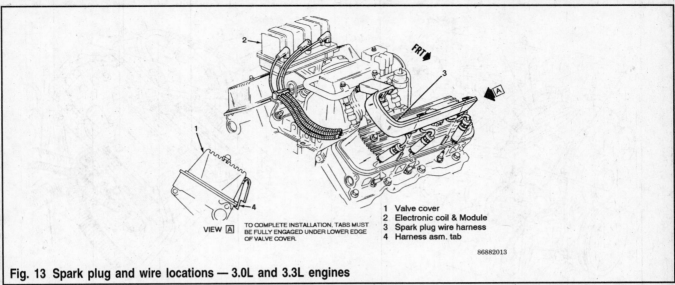

FRT
2
3
A
1
4
VIEW A
TO COMPLETE INSTALLATION, TABS MUST BE FULLY ENGAGED UNDER LOWER EDGE OF VALVE COVER.
1 Valve cover
2 Electronic coil & Module
3 Spark plug wire harness
4 Harness asm. tab
86882013

Fig. 13 Spark plug and wire locations — 3.0L and 3.3L engines

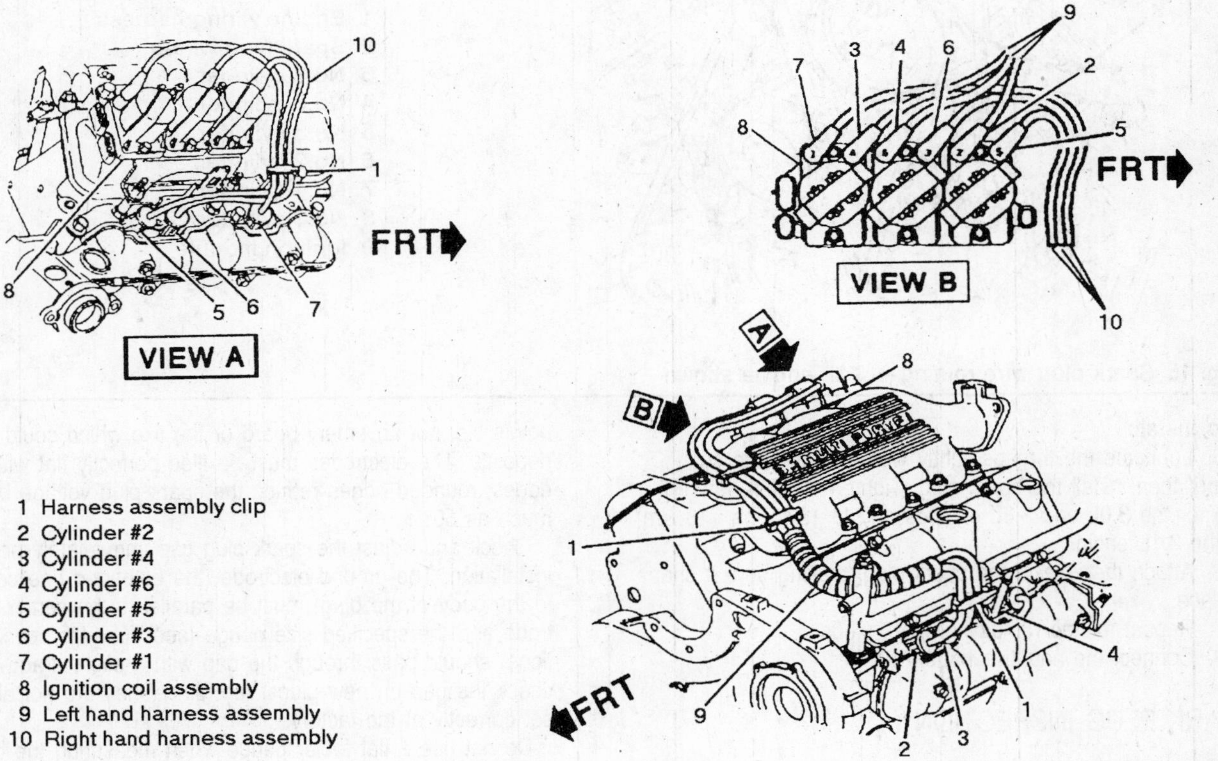

10
1
8
5
6
7
FRT
VIEW A
9
7
3
4
6
2
8
5
FRT
VIEW B
10
A
B
8
1
4
9
1
2
3
FRT
1 Harness assembly clip
2 Cylinder #2
3 Cylinder #4
4 Cylinder #6
5 Cylinder #5
6 Cylinder #3
7 Cylinder #1
8 Ignition coil assembly
9 Left hand harness assembly
10 Right hand harness assembly
86882014

Fig. 14 Spark plug locations and wire routing — 3.1L engine shown

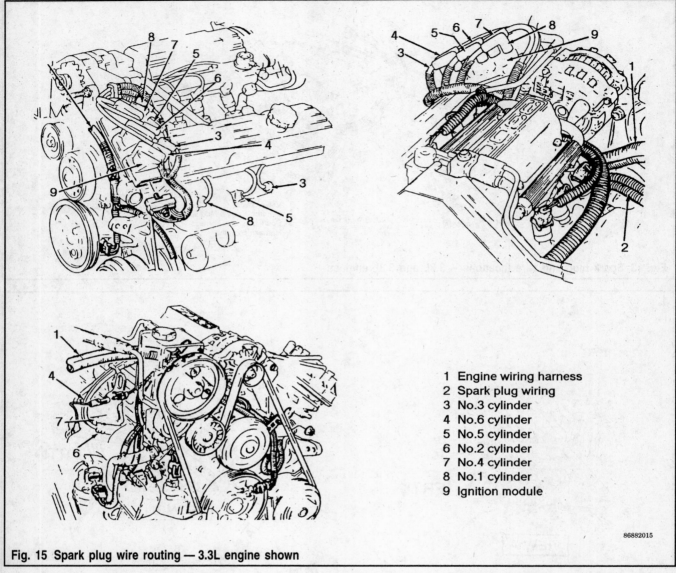

1 Engine wiring harness
2 Spark plug wiring
3 No.3 cylinder
4 No.6 cylinder
5 No.5 cylinder
6 No.2 cylinder
7 No.4 cylinder
8 No.1 cylinder
9 Ignition module

86882015

Fig. 15 Spark plug wire routing — 3.3L engine shown

To install:

5. Lubricate the threads lightly with an anti-seize compound, then install the spark plug. Tighten to 11 ft. lbs. (15 Nm) for the 3.0L and 3.3L engines and to 13 ft. lbs. (18 Nm) for the 3.1L engine.

6. Attach the wire to the spark plug, making sure it snaps in place.

7. Repeat for the remaining spark plugs.

8. Connect the negative battery cable.

SPARK PLUG INSPECTION

▶ **See Figures 16, 17 and 18**

Check the plugs for deposits and wear. If they are not going to be replaced, clean the plugs thoroughly. Remember that any kind of deposit will decrease the efficiency of the plug. Plugs can be cleaned with a spark plug cleaning machine, which can sometimes be found in some service stations, or you can do an acceptable job of cleaning with a stiff brush. If the plugs are cleaned, the electrodes must be filed flat. Use an ignition points file, not an emery board or the like which could leave deposits. The electrodes must be filed perfectly flat with sharp edges; rounded edges reduce the spark plug voltage by as much as 50%.

Check and adjust the spark plug gap immediately before installation. The ground electrode (the L-shaped one connected to the body of the plug) must be parallel to the center electrode and the specified size gauge (see Tune-Up specifications) should pass through the gap with a slight drag. Always check the gap on new plugs, too; since they are not always set correctly at the factory.

Do not use a flat feeler gauge when measuring the gap on used plugs, because the reading may be inaccurate. The ground electrode on a used plug is often rounded on the face closest to the center electrode. A flat gauge will not be able to measure the distance as accurately as a wire gauge. Most gapping tools usually have a bending tool attached. This tool may be used to adjust the side electrode until the proper distance is obtained. Never attempt to move or bend the center electrode or spark plug damage will likely occur. Also, be careful not to bend the side electrode too far or too often;

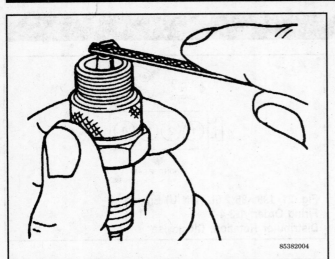

Fig. 16 Spark plugs that are in good condition can be filed and reused

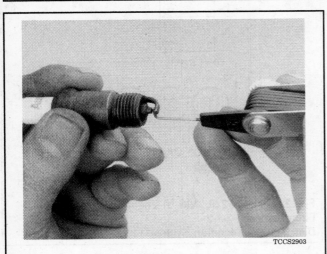

Fig. 17 Always use a wire gauge to check the electrode gap on used plugs

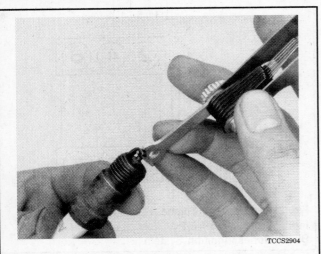

Fig. 18 Adjust the gap by bending the side electrode very slightly towards or away from the center electrode

if it is overstressed, it may weaken and break off within the engine, causing removal of the cylinder head to remove it.

Spark Plug Wires

Your vehicle is equipped with an electronic ignition system which utilizes 8mm wires to conduct the hotter spark produced (except 2.3L engine). The boots on these wires are designed to cover the spark plug cavities on the cylinder head. The 2.3L doesn't use spark plug wires. The coil assembly is connected directly to the spark plug with rubber connectors.

TESTING

Visually inspect the spark plug cables for burns, cuts, or breaks in the insulation. Check the spark plug boots and the nipples on the distributor cap and coil. Replace any damaged wiring. If no physical damage is obvious, the wires can be checked with an ohmmeter for excessive resistance or an internal break. Disconnect both ends of the wire before attaching the ohmmeter. The resistance specification is 30,000 ohms or less. Always coat the terminals of any wire that is removed or replaced with a thin layer of dielectric compound.

REMOVAL & INSTALLATION

When installing a new set of spark plug cables, replace the cables one at a time so there will be no mix-up. Start by replacing the longest cable first. Install the boot firmly over the spark plug. Route the wire exactly the same as the original; if so equipped, be sure to route the wire through the corrugated tubing. Make sure the wire is clamped in all its retainers, and that the terminals inside the boots snap into place. Repeat the process for each cable.

FIRING ORDERS

▶ See Figures 19, 20, 21, 22, 23, 24 and 25

➡To avoid confusion, label, remove and replace spark plug cables one at a time.

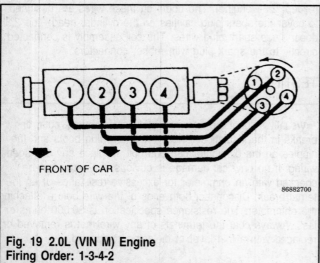

Fig. 19 2.0L (VIN M) Engine
Firing Order: 1-3-4-2
Distributor Rotation: Counterclockwise

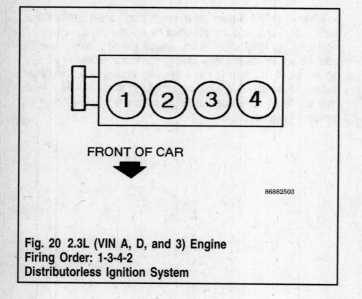

Fig. 20 2.3L (VIN A, D, and 3) Engine
Firing Order: 1-3-4-2
Distributorless Ignition System

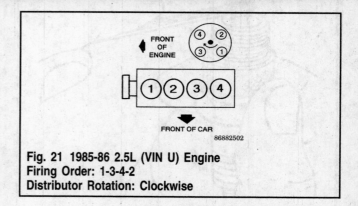

Fig. 21 1985-86 2.5L (VIN U) Engine
Firing Order: 1-3-4-2
Distributor Rotation: Clockwise

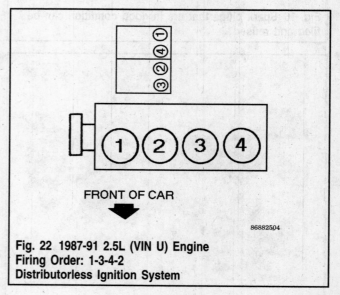

Fig. 22 1987-91 2.5L (VIN U) Engine
Firing Order: 1-3-4-2
Distributorless Ignition System

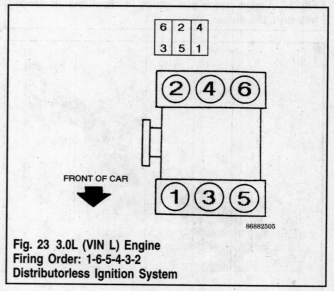

Fig. 23 3.0L (VIN L) Engine
Firing Order: 1-6-5-4-3-2
Distributorless Ignition System

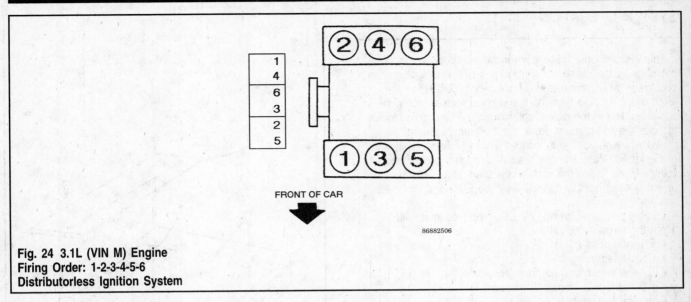

Fig. 24 3.1L (VIN M) Engine
Firing Order: 1-2-3-4-5-6
Distributorless Ignition System

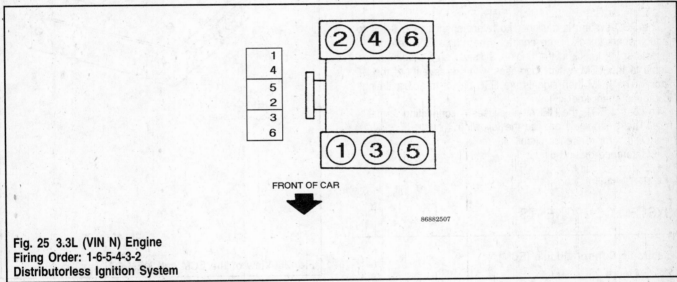

Fig. 25 3.3L (VIN N) Engine
Firing Order: 1-6-5-4-3-2
Distributorless Ignition System

HIGH ENERGY IGNITION (HEI) SYSTEM

2.0L (VIN M) and 1985-86 2.5L (VIN U) Engines

GENERAL DESCRIPTION

The High Energy Ignition (HEI) system controls fuel combustion by providing a spark to ignite the air/fuel mixture at the appropriate time. This system consists of a modified module, which is used in conjunction with the Electronic Spark Timing (EST) function of the Electronic Control Module (ECM).

The HEI system features a longer spark duration which is essential in firing lean and EGR-diluted air/fuel mixtures. The condenser (capacitor) located within the HEI distributor is provided for noise (static) suppression purposes only and is not a regularly replaced ignition system component. Dwell is controlled by the ECM and cannot be adjusted.

The HEI distributor is equipped to aid in spark timing changes necessary for optimum emissions, fuel economy and performance. All spark timing changes in the HEI (EST) distributors are performed electronically by the ECM, which monitors information from the various engine sensors, computes the desired spark timing and signals the distributor to change the timing accordingly. No vacuum or centrifugal advance is used with this distributor.

The Electronic Spark Control (ESC) system is used to control spark knock and enable maximum spark advance to improve driveability and fuel economy. This system consists of a knock sensor and an ESC module (generally part of Mem-Cal). The ECM monitors the ESC signal to determine when engine detonation occurs.

SYSTEM OPERATION

The HEI distributor uses a magnetic pickup assembly, located inside the distributor containing a permanent magnet, a pole piece with internal teeth and a pickup coil. When the teeth of the rotating timer core and pole piece align, an induced voltage in the pickup coil signals the electronic module to open the coil primary circuit. As the primary current decreases, a high voltage is induced in the secondary windings of the ignition coil, directing a spark through the rotor and high voltage leads to fire the appropriate spark plug. The dwell period is automatically controlled by the ECM and increases with engine rpm.

To control ignition timing, the ECM receives information about the following conditions:
- Engine speed (rpm)
- Crankshaft position
- Engine load (manifold pressure or vacuum)
- Atmospheric (barometric) pressure
- Engine temperature
- Exhaust Gas Recirculation (EGR)

The ESC system is designed to retard spark timing 8-10° to reduce spark knock in the engine. When the knock sensor detects spark knock in the engine, it sends an AC voltage signal to the ECM, which increases with the severity of the knock. The ECM then signals the ESC circuit to adjust timing to reduce spark knock.

To control EST, the HEI module uses 4 connecting terminals. These terminals provide the following:
- Distributor reference circuit
- Reference ground circuit
- Bypass circuit
- EST circuit

SYSTEM COMPONENTS

Electronic Control Module (ECM)

▶ See Figure 26

The Electronic Control Module (ECM) is the control center of the fuel injection system. It constantly monitors information from various sensors and controls the systems which affect vehicle performance. The ECM has 2 replaceable parts. These parts are as follows:
- The controller: ECM without the Memory and Calibration (MEM-CAL) unit
- The MEM-CAL

Memory Calibration (MEM-CAL) Unit

▶ See Figure 26

The MEM-CAL, located inside the ECM, allows the ECM to be installed in several different vehicles. It has calibration information based on the vehicle's weight, engine, transmission, axle ratio and several other factors.

Pickup Coil

The pickup coil is a device which generates an alternating current signal to determine crankshaft position.

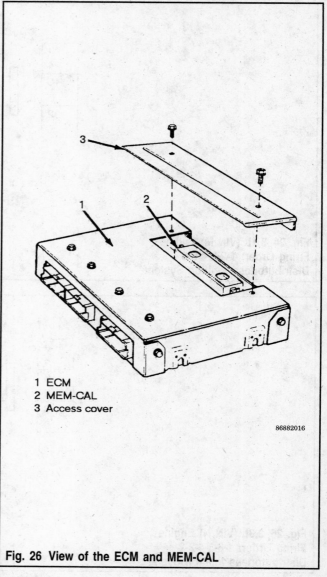

1 ECM
2 MEM-CAL
3 Access cover

86882016

Fig. 26 View of the ECM and MEM-CAL

HEI Module

The HEI module is a switching device which operates the primary circuit of the ignition coil.

Ignition Secondary

The ignition secondary consists of the ignition coil, rotor, distributor cap, plugs wires and spark plug. These components supply the high voltage to fire the spark plugs.

Electronic Spark Timing (EST)

The EST system consists of the distributor module, ECM and connecting wires. This system includes the following circuits:
- Distributor reference circuit: provides the ECM with rpm and crankshaft position information.
- Bypass signal: above 500 rpm, the ECM applies 5 volts to this circuit to switch spark timing control from the HEI module to the ECM.
- EST signal: the ECM uses this circuit to trigger the HEI module, after bypass voltage is applied to the HEI module.

• Reference ground circuit: this wire is grounded through the module and insures that the ground circuit has no voltage drop between the ignition module and the ECM which could affect performance.

DIAGNOSIS AND TESTING

Service Precautions

The HEI coil secondary voltage output capabilities can exceed 40,000 volts. Avoid body contact with the HEI high voltage secondary components when the engine is running, or personal injury may result.

➡**To avoid damage to the ECM or other ignition system components, do not use electrical test equipment such as battery or AC powered voltmeter, ohmmeter, etc. or any type of tester other than specified.**

• When making compression checks, disconnect the ignition switch feed wire at the distributor.

• Never allow the tachometer terminal to touch ground, as damage to the module and/or ignition coil can result.

• To prevent Electrostatic Discharge damage, when working with the ECM, do not touch the connector pins or soldered components on the circuit board.

• When handling a PROM, CAL-PAK or MEM-CAL, do not touch the component leads. Also, do not remove the integrated circuit from the carrier.

• Never allow welding cables to lie on, near or across any vehicle electrical wiring.

• Leave new components and modules in the shipping package until ready to install them.

• When performing electrical tests on the system, use a high impedance multimeter, digital voltmeter (DVM) J-34029-A or equivalent.

• Never pierce a high tension lead or boot for any testing purpose; otherwise, future problems are guaranteed.

Reading Codes

The Assembly Line Diagnostic Link (ALDL) connector is used for communicating with the ECM. It is usually located under the instrument panel and is sometimes covered by a plastic cover labeled DIAGNOSTIC CONNECTOR. Codes stored in the ECM's memory can be read through a hand-held diagnostic scanner plugged into the ALDL connector. Codes can also be read by connecting a jumper wires between terminals A and B of the ALDL connector and counting the number of flashes of the SERVICE ENGINE SOON light, with the ignition switch turned **ON** and the engine NOT running.

Clearing Codes

To clear codes from the ECM memory, the ECM power feed must be disconnected for at least 30 seconds. Depending on the vehicle, the ECM power feed can be disconnected at the positive battery terminal pigtail, the inline fuseholder that originates at the positive connection at the battery or the ECM fuse in the fuse block. The negative battery cable may also be disconnected; however, other on-board memory data, such as radio station presets will also be lost.

Symptom Diagnosis

An open or ground in the EST circuit, will set a Code 42 and cause the engine to run on the HEI module timing. This will cause poor performance and poor fuel economy.

Loss of the ESC signal, to the ECM, would cause the ECM to constantly retard the EST. This could result in sluggish performance and cause a Code 43 to set.

Ignition System Check
◆ **See Figures 27, 28, 29 and 30**

The accompanying wire schematics and charts can be used to diagnose and troubleshoot some HEI system component problems.

ENGINE CRANKS BUT WILL NOT RUN

1. Check that the fuel quantity is OK.
2. Turn the ignition switch **ON**. Verify that the SERVICE ENGINE SOON light is ON.
3. Install the scan tool and check the following:
   Throttle Position Sensor (TPS): if over 2.5 volts, at closed throttle, check TPS for intermittent, open or short to ground, or faulty TPS.
   Coolant: if less than 86°F (30°C), check Coolant Temperature Sensor (CTS) for intermittent, open or short to ground, or faulty CTS.
4. Connect spark checker, J 26792 or equivalent, and check for spark while cranking. Check at least 2 wires.
   a. If spark occurs, reconnect the spark plug wires and check for fuel spray at the injector(s) while cranking. If no spark is visible, go to the fuel system section in this manual.
   b. If no spark occurs, check for battery voltage to the ignition system. If OK, use the ignition diagnosis chart.

ELECTRONIC SPARK TIMING (EST) CIRCUIT

1. Clear any codes which are present.
2. Idle the engine for approximately 1 minute or until Code 42 sets. If Code 42 does not set, Code 42 is intermittent.
3. If Code 42 sets, turn the ignition **OFF** , then disengage the ECM connectors.
   a. Turn the ignition switch **ON**.
   b. Using an ohmmeter to ground, probe the ECM harness connector, at the EST circuit. Place the ohmmeter selector switch in the 1000-2000 ohms range. The meter should read less than 1000 ohms.
4. If not, check for a faulty connection, open circuit or faulty ignition module.
5. If OK, probe the bypass circuit with a test light to battery voltage.
6. If the test light is ON, disconnect the ignition 4-way connector and observe the test light.
   a. If the test light goes OFF, the problem is a faulty ignition module.
   b. If the test light stays ON, the bypass circuit is shorted to ground.
7. If the test light remains OFF, from Step 5, again probe the bypass circuit with the test light connected to battery voltage, and the ohmmeter still connected to the EST circuit and

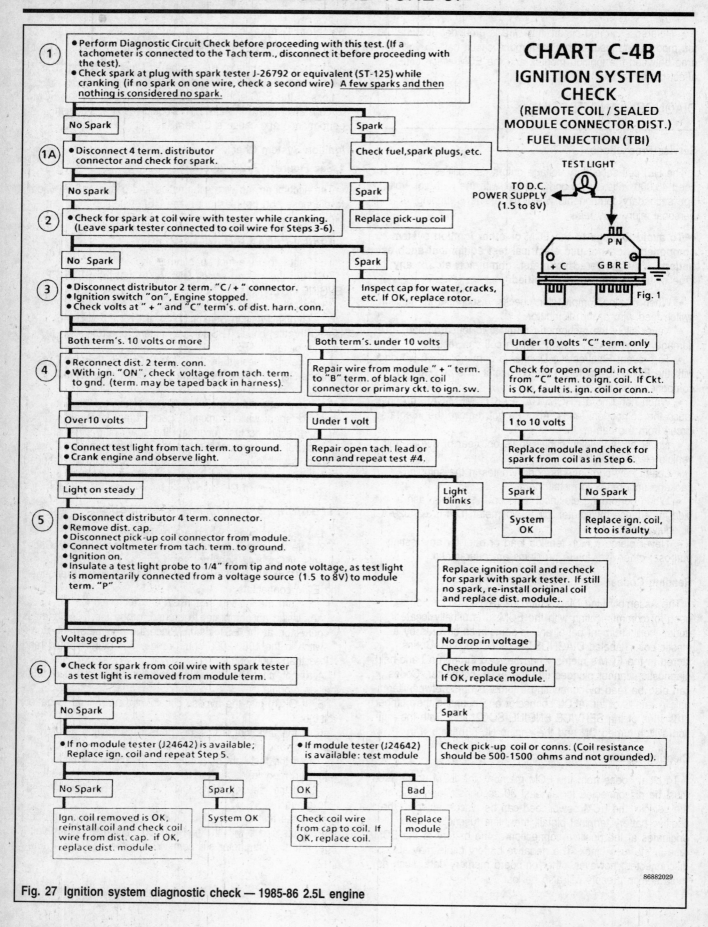

CHART C-4B

IGNITION SYSTEM CHECK
(REMOTE COIL / SEALED MODULE CONNECTOR DIST.)
FUEL INJECTION (TBI)

①
- Perform Diagnostic Circuit Check before proceeding with this test. (If a tachometer is connected to the Tach term., disconnect it before proceeding with the test).
- Check spark at plug with spark tester J-26792 or equivalent (ST-125) while cranking (if no spark on one wire, check a second wire) A few sparks and then nothing is considered no spark.

No Spark	Spark
	Check fuel, spark plugs, etc.

①A
- Disconnect 4 term. distributor connector and check for spark.

No spark	Spark
	Replace pick-up coil

②
- Check for spark at coil wire with tester while cranking. (Leave spark tester connected to coil wire for Steps 3-6).

No Spark	Spark
	Inspect cap for water, cracks, etc. If OK, replace rotor.

③
- Disconnect distributor 2 term. "C / + " connector.
- Ignition switch "on", Engine stopped.
- Check volts at " + " and "C" term's. of dist. harn. conn.

Both term's. 10 volts or more	Both term's. under 10 volts	Under 10 volts "C" term. only
	Repair wire from module " + " term. to "B" term. of black Ign. coil connector or primary ckt. to ign. sw.	Check for open or gnd. in ckt. from "C" term. to ign. coil. If Ckt. is OK, fault is. ign. coil or conn..

④
- Reconnect dist. 2 term. conn.
- With ign. "ON", check voltage from tach. term. to gnd. (term. may be taped back in harness).

Over 10 volts	Under 1 volt	1 to 10 volts
Connect test light from tach. term. to ground. • Crank engine and observe light.	Repair open tach. lead or conn and repeat test #4.	Replace module and check for spark from coil as in Step 6.

Light on steady		Light blinks	Spark	No Spark
			System OK	Replace ign. coil, it too is faulty

⑤
- Disconnect distributor 4 term. connector.
- Remove dist. cap.
- Disconnect pick-up coil connector from module.
- Connect voltmeter from tach. term. to ground.
- Ignition on.
- Insulate a test light probe to 1/4" from tip and note voltage, as test light is momentarily connected from a voltage source (1.5 to 8V) to module term. "P"

Replace ignition coil and recheck for spark with spark tester. If still no spark, re-install original coil and replace dist. module..

Voltage drops	No drop in voltage
	Check module ground. If OK, replace module.

⑥
- Check for spark from coil wire with spark tester as test light is removed from module term.

No Spark	Spark

If no module tester (J24642) is available; Replace ign. coil and repeat Step 5.	If module tester (J24642) is available: test module	Check pick-up coil or conns. (Coil resistance should be 500-1500 ohms and not grounded).

No Spark	Spark	OK	Bad
Ign. coil removed is OK, reinstall coil and check coil wire from dist. cap. if OK, replace dist. module.	System OK	Check coil wire from cap to coil. If OK, replace coil.	Replace module

TEST LIGHT

TO D.C. POWER SUPPLY (1.5 to 8V)

P N

+ C   G B R E

Fig. 1

Fig. 27 Ignition system diagnostic check — 1985-86 2.5L engine

86882029

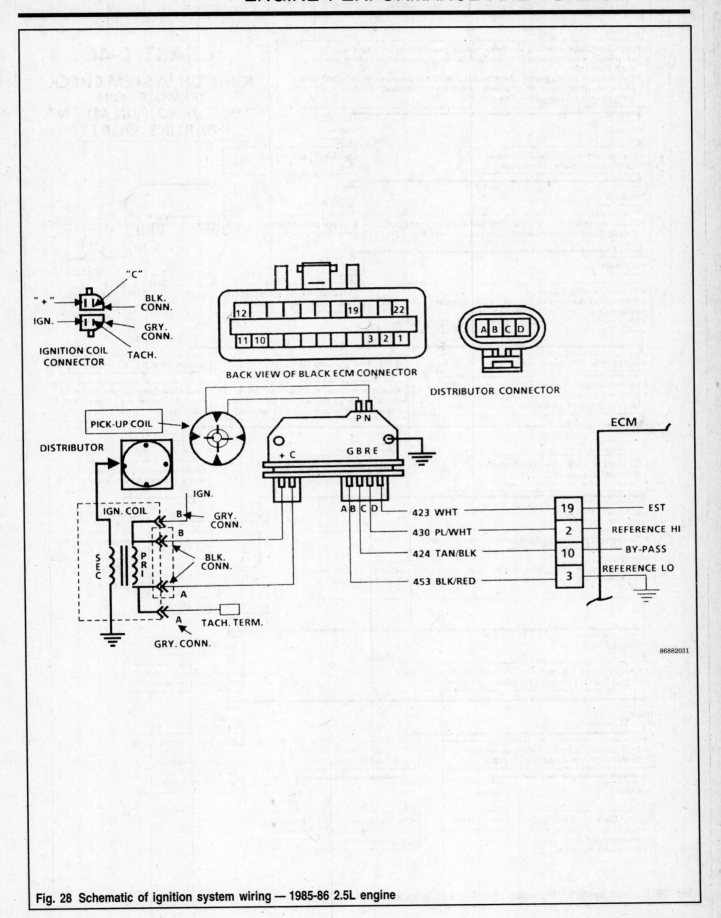

Fig. 28 Schematic of ignition system wiring — 1985-86 2.5L engine

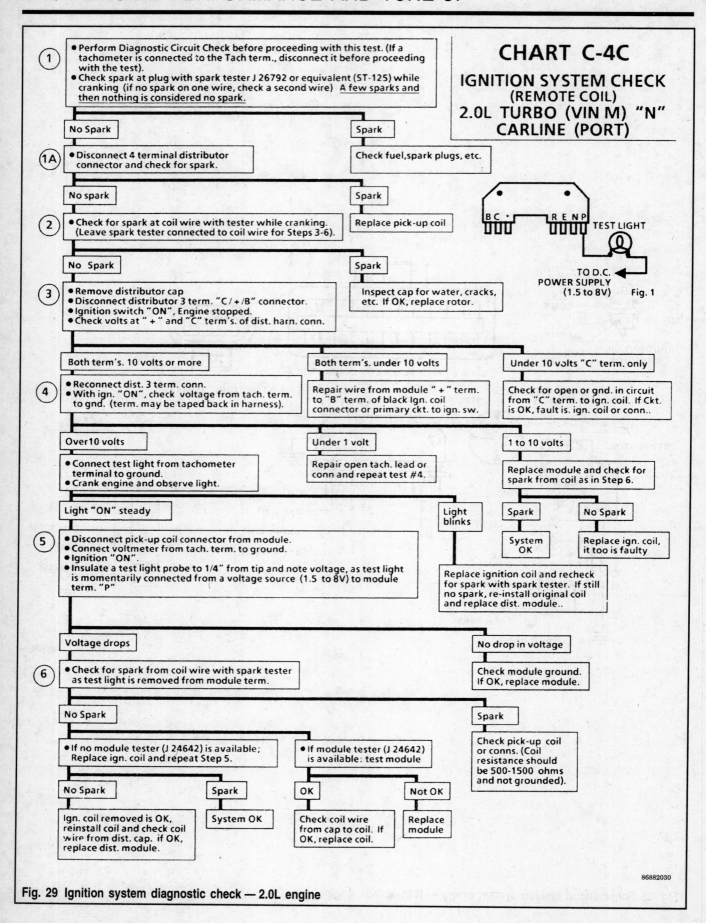

CHART C-4C
IGNITION SYSTEM CHECK
(REMOTE COIL)
2.0L TURBO (VIN M) "N"
CARLINE (PORT)

① • Perform Diagnostic Circuit Check before proceeding with this test. (If a tachometer is connected to the Tach term., disconnect it before proceeding with the test).
• Check spark at plug with spark tester J 26792 or equivalent (ST-125) while cranking (if no spark on one wire, check a second wire) A few sparks and then nothing is considered no spark.

No Spark | Spark

①A • Disconnect 4 terminal distributor connector and check for spark. | Check fuel, spark plugs, etc.

No spark | Spark

② • Check for spark at coil wire with tester while cranking. (Leave spark tester connected to coil wire for Steps 3-6). | Replace pick-up coil

No Spark | Spark

③ • Remove distributor cap
• Disconnect distributor 3 term. "C / + /B" connector.
• Ignition switch "ON", Engine stopped.
• Check volts at " + " and "C" term's of dist. harn. conn. | Inspect cap for water, cracks, etc. If OK, replace rotor.

TEST LIGHT

TO D.C. POWER SUPPLY (1.5 to 8V)   Fig. 1

Both term's. 10 volts or more | Both term's. under 10 volts | Under 10 volts "C" term. only

④ • Reconnect dist. 3 term. conn.
• With ign. "ON", check voltage from tach. term. to gnd. (term. may be taped back in harness). | Repair wire from module " + " term. to "B" term. of black Ign. coil connector or primary ckt. to ign. sw. | Check for open or gnd. in circuit from "C" term. to ign. coil. If Ckt. is OK, fault is. ign. coil or conn..

Over10 volts | Under 1 volt | 1 to 10 volts

• Connect test light from tachometer terminal to ground.
• Crank engine and observe light. | Repair open tach. lead or conn and repeat test #4. | Replace module and check for spark from coil as in Step 6.

Light "ON" steady | Light blinks | Spark | No Spark

⑤ • Disconnect pick-up coil connector from module.
• Connect voltmeter from tach. term. to ground.
• Ignition "ON".
• Insulate a test light probe to 1/4" from tip and note voltage, as test light is momentarily connected from a voltage source (1.5 to 8V) to module term. "P" | | System OK | Replace ign. coil, it too is faulty

Replace ignition coil and recheck for spark with spark tester. If still no spark, re-install original coil and replace dist. module..

Voltage drops | No drop in voltage

⑥ • Check for spark from coil wire with spark tester as test light is removed from module term. | Check module ground. If OK, replace module.

No Spark | Spark

• If no module tester (J 24642) is available; Replace ign. coil and repeat Step 5. | • If module tester (J 24642) is available: test module | Check pick-up coil or conns. (Coil resistance should be 500-1500 ohms and not grounded).

No Spark | Spark | OK | Not OK

Ign. coil removed is OK, reinstall coil and check coil wire from dist. cap. if OK, replace dist. module. | System OK | Check coil wire from cap to coil. If OK, replace coil. | Replace module

86882030

Fig. 29 Ignition system diagnostic check — 2.0L engine

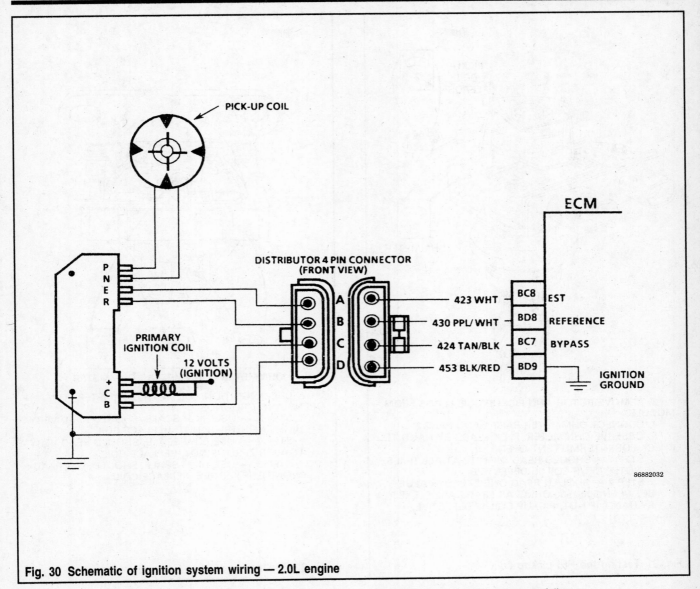

Fig. 30 Schematic of ignition system wiring — 2.0L engine

ground. As the test light contacts the bypass circuit, resistance should switch from under 1000 to over 2000 ohms.

　a. If it does, reconnect the ECM and idle the engine for approximately 1 minute or until Code 42 sets. If Code 42 sets, it is a faulty ECM.

　b. If not, Code 42 is intermittent.

8. If the results are not as indicated in Step 7, disconnect the distributor 4-way connector. With the ohmmeter still connected to the bypass circuit, resistance should have gone high (open circuit).

9. If not, the EST circuit is shorted to ground.

10. If OK, the bypass circuit is open, faulty connections or faulty ignition module.

➡When the problem has been corrected, clear codes and confirm Closed Loop operation and no SERVICE ENGINE SOON light.

PICKUP COIL

◆ See Figure 31

1. Remove the rotor and pickup coil leads from the module.

2. Using an ohmmeter, test as follow:

　a. Connect 1 lead of the ohmmeter between the distributor housing and 1 of the pickup coil lead. Meter should read infinity. Flex the leads by hand while observing the ohmmeter, to check for intermittent opens.

　b. Connect the ohmmeter between leads between both of the pickup coil leads. Meter should read a steady value between 500-1500 ohms.

3. If the readings are not as specified, the pickup coil is defective and should be replaced.

IGNITION COIL

◆ See Figure 32

1. Remove the ignition coil and check the coil with an ohmmeter for an open or ground.

2. Connect the meter as indicated in Step 1 (meter on the high scale). Should read very high or infinite. If not, replace the coil.

3. Connect the meter as indicated in Step 2 (meter on the low scale). Should read low or zero ohms. If not, replace the coil.

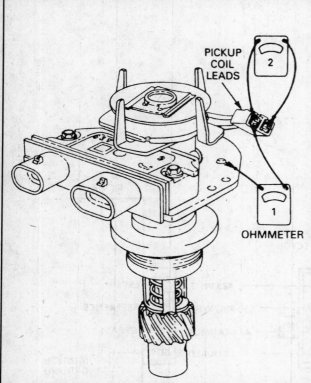

PICKUP COIL LEADS

OHMMETER

3. REMOVE ROTOR AND PICKUP COIL LEADS FROM MODULE.
4. CONNECT OHMMETER PART 1 AND PART 2.
5. OBSERVE OHMMETER. FLEX LEADS BY HAND TO CHECK FOR INTERMITTENT OPENS.
    STEP 1 — SHOULD READ INFINITE AT ALL TIMES. IF NOT, PICKUP COIL IS DEFECTIVE.
    STEP 2 — SHOULD READ ONE STEADY VALUE BETWEEN 500-1500 OHMS AS LEADS ARE FLEXED BY HAND. IF NOT, PICKUP COIL IS DEFECTIVE.

86882017

Fig. 31 Testing the HEI pickup coil

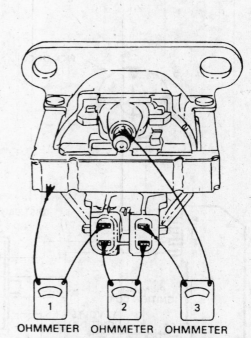

OHMMETER   OHMMETER   OHMMETER

2. CHECK IGNITION COIL WITH OHMMETER FOR OPENS AND GROUNDS:
    STEP 1. — USE HIGH SCALE. SHOULD READ VERY HIGH (INFINITE). IF NOT, REPLACE COIL.
    STEP 2. — USE LOW SCALE. SHOULD READ VERY LOW OR ZERO. IF NOT, REPLACE COIL.
    STEP 3. — USE HIGH SCALE. SHOULD NOT READ INFINITE. IF IT DOES, REPLACE COIL.

86882018

Fig. 32 Testing the HEI ignition coil

4. Connect the meter as indicated in Step 3 (meter on the high scale). Should not read infinite. If it does, replace the coil.

COMPONENT REPLACEMENT

Capacitor

The capacitor, if equipped, is part of the coil wire harness assembly. The capacitor is used only for radio noise suppression, and will seldom need replacement.

1. Disconnect the negative battery cable.
2. Remove the distributor cap by turning the four screws counterclockwise, then matchmark the location of the rotor and remove it by pulling it straight up.
3. Unfasten the capacitor attaching screw, then unplug the connector from the module and remove the capacitor from the distributor.

➡**When removing the capacitor, it may help to loosen the module.**

To install:

4. Install the capacitor in the distributor, engage the connector to the module, then install the hold-down screw making sure the ground lead is under the screw.
5. Install the rotor, then position the distributor cap and secure by tightening the four retaining screws.
6. Connect the negative battery cable.

HEI Distributor

2.0L ENGINE

➧ **See Figure 33**

1. Disconnect the negative battery cable.
2. Label and disconnect the coil and spark plug wires from the distributor cap.
3. Disconnect the coil and EST connectors.
4. Remove the distributor to cam carrier nuts.
5. Mark the tang drive and camshaft for correct positioning during installation, then remove the distributor from the engine.

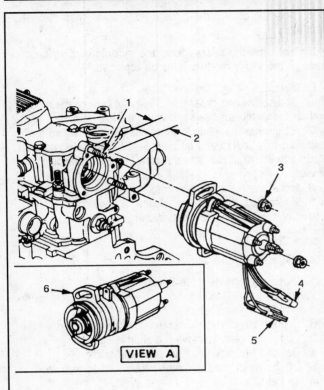

1 Stud
2 20.5±1.0 (both studs)
3 Nut asm.
4 E.S.T. connector
5 Coil connector
6 Distributor asm.

86882019

Fig. 33 View of the HEI distributor mounting — 2.0L engine shown

To install:

6. Position the distributor, aligning the tang drive to the camshaft markings made during removal.
7. Install the distributor-to-cam carrier nuts. Tighten them to 13 ft. lbs. (18 Nm).
8. Engage the coil and EST connectors.
9. Attach the coil and spark plug wires to the cap.
10. Connect the negative battery cable.
11. Check and adjust ignition timing, as required.

2.5L ENGINE — UNDISTURBED

▶ **See Figure 34**

1. Disconnect the negative battery cable.
2. Remove the air cleaner assembly.
3. If necessary, tag and disconnect the spark plug wires.
4. Detach the ignition switch battery feed wire and the tachometer lead (if equipped) from the distributor cap. Release the coil connectors from the cap, but do not use a screwdriver or tool to release the locking tabs.
5. Turn the retaining screws counterclockwise, then remove the distributor cap and place it out of the way.

6. Detach the 4-terminal ECM wiring harness from the distributor.
7. If necessary, remove the secondary wires from the cap, release the wiring harness latches, then remove the wiring harness retainer. The spark plug wire numbers are indicated on the retainer.
8. Mark the relationship of the rotor to the distributor housing and the housing relationship to the engine.
9. Remove the distributor clamp screw/bolt and the hold-down clamp.
10. Note the position of the rotor by scribing a mark on the distributor housing. Carefully pull the distributor up until the rotor just stops turning counterclockwise, then again mark the rotor position for installation purposes. The drive gear on the shaft is helical and the shaft will rotate slightly as the distributor is removed.
11. Remove the distributor from the engine. Do NOT crank the engine while the distributor is removed.

➡**To be sure of correct timing of the distributor, it must be installed with the rotor correctly positioned as noted during removal.**

To install:

12. Rotate the shaft until the rotor aligns with the second mark made during removal. As the distributor is installed, the rotor should move to the first mark made during removal. This ensures proper timing. If the marks do not align properly, remove the distributor and try again.
13. Install the distributor hold-down clamp and retaining bolt/screw.
14. If removed, install the wiring harness retainer and secondary wires.
15. Attach the 4-terminal ECM wiring harness to the distributor.
16. Install the distributor cap.
17. Fasten the coil connectors to the cap, then attach the tachometer lead (if equipped) and the ignition switch battery feed wire. Make certain the connectors are fully seated and latched.
18. Install the air cleaner assembly.
19. If necessary, connect the spark plug wires as tagged during removal.
20. Connect the negative battery cable, then start the engine, check the timing and adjust if necessary.

2.5L ENGINE — DISTURBED

➡**If the engine was accidentally cranked after the distributor was removed, the following procedure can be used to install the distributor. The engine must be set on TDC of the compression stroke to obtain proper spark timing.**

1. Remove the No. 1 spark plug.
2. Place a finger over the spark plug hole and have a helper crank the engine slowly until compression is felt.
3. Align the timing mark on the pulley to the 0 on the engine timing indicator. This will indicate that the engine is near TDC of the compression stroke.
4. Align the rotor with the marks made earlier and install the distributor as outlined in Step 12 of the undisturbed engine procedure. If no rotor alignment marks were made during removal, turn the rotor to point between the No. 1 and No. 4 spark plug towers on the distributor cap.

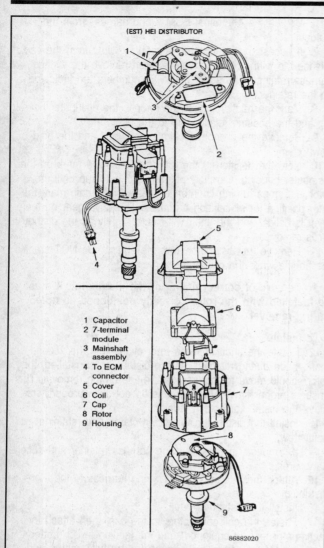

Fig. 34 Exploded view of the HEI distributor — 1985-86 2.5L engine

1 Capacitor
2 7-terminal module
3 Mainshaft assembly
4 To ECM connector
5 Cover
6 Coil
7 Cap
8 Rotor
9 Housing

86882020

5. Install the distributor assembly in the engine, then connect the ignition feed wire.

6. Install the distributor cap, then connect the spark plug wires as tagged during removal.

7. Connect the negative battery cable, then check the engine timing and adjust if necessary.

HEI Module

▶ **See Figure 35**

1. Disconnect the negative battery cable.

2. If necessary for access to the distributor, remove the air cleaner assembly.

3. Remove the distributor cap and rotor.

4. Remove the module retaining screws, then lift the stamped sheet metal shield and module upwards.

➡ **Make sure to note the color code on the leads, as these cannot be interchanged.**

5. Note the color code of the module leads, then disconnect them.

➡ **Do not wipe the grease from the module or distributor base, if the same module is to be replaced.**

To install:

6. Spread silicone grease on the metal face of the module and on the distributor base where the module seats.

7. Fit the module leads to the module. Make certain the leads are fully seated and latched. Seat the module and metal shield into the distributor, then secure using the retaining screws.

8. Install the rotor and distributor cap.

9. If removed, install the air cleaner assembly.

10. Connect the negative battery cable.

Pickup Coil

▶ **See Figures 36 and 37**

1. Disconnect the negative battery cable.

2. Remove the distributor assembly from the vehicle as described earlier in this section.

3. Support the distributor assembly in a vice and drive the roll pin from the gear. Remove the shaft assembly.

4. Remove the pickup coil retainer and shield.

5. Lift the pickup coil assembly straight up to remove it from the distributor.

To install:

6. Assemble the pickup coil, shield and retainer, then install the assembly on the distributor.

7. Install the shaft.

8. Install the gear and roll pin to the shaft. Make certain the matchmarks are aligned.

9. Spin the shaft and verify that the teeth do not touch the pole piece.

10. Install the distributor as outliner earlier in this section.

11. Connect the negative battery cable.

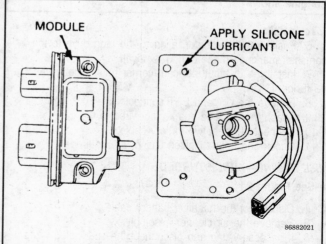

MODULE

APPLY SILICONE LUBRICANT

86882021

Fig. 35 View of an HEI module — 1986 2.5L engine shown, 2.0L similar

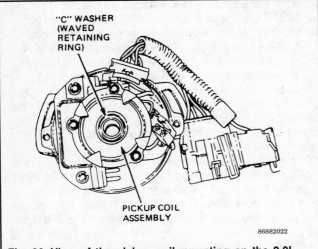

Fig. 36 View of the pickup coil mounting on the 2.0L engine

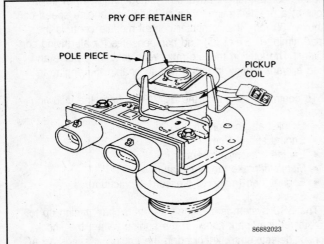

Fig. 37 View of the pickup coil mounting on the 2.5L engine

Ignition Coil

EXTERNALLY MOUNTED

▶ See Figure 38

1. Disconnect the negative battery cable.
2. Remove the air cleaner assembly, if necessary for access to the ignition coil.

3. Remove the secondary coil lead, using a twisting and pulling motion on the boot.
4. Detach the harness connectors from the coil.
5. Remove the coil mounting screws.
6. Remove the ignition coil. If necessary, drill and punch out the rivets holding the coil to the bracket.

To install:

7. Place the ignition coil into position, then install the mounting screws.
8. Attach the harness connectors to the coil. Make certain the connectors are fully seated and latched.
9. Install the secondary lead to the coil tower, making sure it is fully seated.
10. If removed, install the air cleaner assembly.
11. Connect the negative battery cable.

INTEGRAL (IN-CAP) COIL

1. Disconnect the negative battery cable.
2. Remove the distributor cap.
3. Remove the three coil cover retaining screws, then remove the cover.
4. Unfasten the coil attaching screws, then lift the ignition coil and leads from the cap.

To install:

5. Position the ignition coil and leads in the cap, then secure using the retaining screws.
6. Install the coil cover, and fasten using the three screws.
7. Install the distributor cap, then connect the negative battery cable.

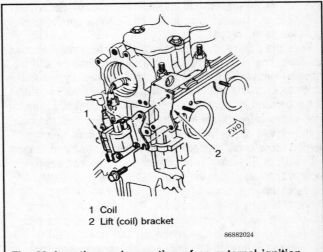

1 Coil
2 Lift (coil) bracket

Fig. 38 Location and mounting of an external ignition coil — 1989 2.0L engine shown

INTEGRATED DIRECT IGNITION (IDI)/ELECTRONIC IGNITION SYSTEM

2.3L (VIN A, D, and 3) Engines

GENERAL DESCRIPTION

Vehicles with the 2.3L engine are equipped with the Integrated Direct Ignition (IDI) or Electronic Ignition (EI) system, depending on the year of your vehicle. These systems feature distributorless ignition. The IDI or EI system consists of two separate ignition coils, an ignition module/Ignition Control Module (ICM) and a secondary conductor housing which is mounted to an aluminum cover plate. The system also consists of a Crankshaft Position (CKP) sensor, related connecting wires and the Electronic Spark Timing (EST) or Ignition Control (IC) portion of the computer control module (ECM or PCM depending upon vehicle year).

The IDI/EI system uses a magnetic crankshaft sensor (mounted remotely from the ignition module) and a reluctor to determine crankshaft position and engine speed. The reluctor is a special wheel cast into the crankshaft, with 7 slots machined into it. Six of the slots are equally spaced 60° apart and the seventh slot is spaced 10° from 1 of the other slots. This seventh slot is used to generate a sync-pulse.

The IDI/EI system uses the same Electronic Spark Timing (EST) or Ignition Control (IC) circuits as the distributor-type ignition. The computer control module (ECM/PCM) uses the EST/IC circuit to control spark advance and ignition dwell, when the ignition system is operating in the EST/IC mode.

The Electronic Spark Control (ESC) system is used to control spark knock and enable maximum spark advance to improve driveability and fuel economy. This system consists of a knock sensor and an ESC module (part of Mem-Cal). The computer control module (ECM/PCM) monitors the ESC signal to determine when engine detonation occurs.

SYSTEM OPERATION

▶ See Figure 39

The IDI or EI system uses a waste spark distribution method. Each cylinder is paired with the cylinder opposite it (1-4, 2-3). The end of each coil secondary is attached to a spark plug. These two plugs are on companion cylinders, meaning they are at top dead center at the same time. The one that is on compression is said to be the event cylinder and the one on the exhaust stroke, the waste cylinder. When the coil discharges, both plugs fire at the same time to complete the series circuit.

Since the polarity of the primary and the secondary windings are fixed, one plug always fires in a forward direction and the other in reverse. This differs from a conventional system in which all plugs fire in the same direction each time. Because of the demand for additional energy, the coil design, saturation time and primary current flow are also different. This redesign of the system allows higher energy to be available from the distributorless coils, greater than 40 kilovolts at all rpm ranges.

The IDI or EI system uses a magnetic crankshaft sensor mounted remotely from the Ignition Control Module (ICM). It protrudes into the block to within approximately 0.050 in. (1.3mm) of the crankshaft reluctor. The reluctor is a special wheel cast into the crankshaft with seven slots machined into it. Six of the slots are equally spaced (60° apart) and the seventh slot is spaced 10° from one of the other slots and serves to generate a "sync-pulse". As the crankshaft rotates, the slots of the reluctor cause a changing magnetic field at the crankshaft sensor, creating an induced voltage pulse.

The ICM or ignition module sends reference signals to the computer control module (ECM/PCM), based on the Crankshaft Position (CKP) sensor pulses, which are used to determine crankshaft position and engine speed. Reference pulses to the computer control module occur at a rate of 1 per each 180° of crankshaft rotation for vehicles through 1992, or 7 per 360° of crankshaft rotation for 1993-95 vehicles. This signal is called the 2X or 7X reference because it occurs 2 or 7 times per crankshaft revolution, depending on the year of your vehicle.

For 1993-95 vehicles, the 7X reference signal is necessary for the PCM to determine when to activate the fuel injectors.

For vehicles through 1992, a second reference signal is sent to the ECM which occurs at the same time as the sync-pulse, from the CKP sensor. This signal is called the 1X reference because it occurs 1 time per crankshaft revolution. The 1X and 2X reference signals are necessary for the ECM to determine when to activate the fuel injectors.

By comparing the time between the 1X and 2X, or 7X reference pulses, the ignition module/ICM can recognize the sync-pulse (the seventh slot) which starts the calculation of the ignition coil sequencing. The second crank pulse following the sync-pulse signals the ignition module to fire No. 2-3 ignition coil and the fifth crank pulse signals the module to fire the No. 1-4 ignition coil.

During cranking, the ignition module monitors the sync-pulse to begin the ignition firing sequence and below 700 rpm the module controls spark advance by triggering each of the 2 coils at a pre-determined interval based on engine speed only. Above 700 rpm, the computer control module controls the spark timing (EST or IC) and compensates for all driving conditions. The ignition module must receive a sync-pulse and then a crank signal, in that order, to enable the engine to start.

To control spark timing the ECM/PCM uses the following inputs:

- Crankshaft position
- Engine speed (rpm)
- Engine coolant temperature
- Manifold/Intake air temperature
- Engine load (manifold pressure or vacuum)
- Spark knock

The ESC system is designed to retard spark timing up to 15° to reduce spark knock in the engine. When the knock sensor detects spark knocking in the engine, it sends an AC voltage signal to the computer control module, which increases with the severity of the knock. The ECM or PCM then adjusts the EST/IC to reduce spark knock.

SYSTEM COMPONENTS

Crankshaft Position (CKP) Sensor

The Crankshaft Position (CKP) sensor (formerly named simply crankshaft sensor), mounted remotely from the ignition module on an aluminum cover plate, is used to determine crankshaft position and engine speed.

Ignition Coils

The two ignition coil assemblies are mounted inside the module assembly housing. Each coil distributes the spark for two plugs simultaneously.

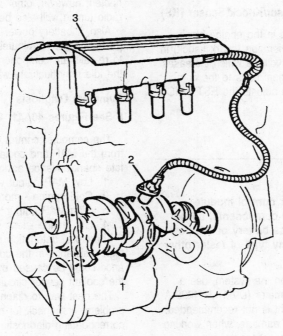

1 Crankshaft reluctor
2 Crankshaft position (CKP) sensor assembly
3 Ignition coil and electronic ignition control module (ICM)

86882043

Fig. 39 Relationship of the Crankshaft Position (CKP) sensor to the crankshaft reluctor

Electronic Spark Timing (EST)

1988-92 VEHICLES

The EST system is basically the same EST to ECM circuit used on the distributor type ignition systems with EST. This system includes the following circuits:

• Reference circuit (CKT 430) — provides the ECM with rpm and crankshaft position information from the IDI module. The IDI module receives this signal from the crank sensor.

• Bypass signal (CKT 424) — above 700 rpm, the ECM applies 5 volts to this circuit to switch spark timing control from the IDI module to the ECM.

• EST signal (CKT 42) — reference signal is sent to the ECM via the DIS module during cranking. Under 700 rpm, the IDI module controls the ignition timing. Above 700 rpm, the ECM applies 5 volts to the bypass line to switch the timing to the ECM control.

• Reference ground circuit (CKT 45) — this wire is grounded through the module and insures that the ground circuit has no voltage drop between the ignition module and the ECM which could affect performance.

Ignition Control (IC)

1993-95 VEHICLES

The IC system uses circuits between the Ignition Control Module (ICM) and the PCM similar to the type that distributor systems use. This system includes the following circuits:

• 7X Reference (CKT 430) — The CKP sensor generates a signal to the ICM, resulting in a reference pulse which is sent to the PCM. The PCM uses this signal to determine crankshaft position, engine speed and injector pulse width. The engine will not start or run if this circuit is open or grounded.

• Reference low (CKT 453) — This wire is grounded through the module and insures that the ground circuit has no voltage drop between the ICM and the PCM which may affect engine performance.

• Ignition control 1 & 2 (CKTs 423 & 406) — The PCM sends the Ignition Control (IC) pulses to the ICM on these circuits. These signals are similar to the 7X reference pulse except that the PCM uses sensor inputs to determine the pulse timing to control spark advance. When the PCM receives the 7X signal, it will determine which pair of cylinders will be fired. (1-4 or 2-3). It will tell the ICM which cylinder pair will be fired via CKTs 423 or 406.

Electronic Spark Control (ESC) Sensor/Knock Sensor (KS)

The ESC or Knock sensor, mounted in the engine block near the cylinders, detects abnormal vibration (spark knock) in the engine. It produces an AC output voltage which increases with the severity of the knock. This signal goes to the computer control module (ECM/PCM) then adjusts the EST or IC to reduce spark knocking.

DIAGNOSIS AND TESTING

Service Precautions

➡To avoid damage to the computer control module (ECM/PCM) or other ignition system components, do not use electrical test equipment such as battery or AC powered voltmeter, ohmmeter, etc. or any type of tester other than specified.

• When performing electrical tests on the system, use a high impedance multimeter, digital voltmeter (DVM) J-34029-A or equivalent. Use of a 12 volt test light is not recommended.
• To prevent electrostatic discharge damage, when working with the ECM or PCM, do not touch the connector pins or soldered components on the circuit board.
• When handling a PROM, CAL-PAK or MEM-CAL, do not touch the component leads. Also, do not remove the integrated circuit from the carrier.
• Never pierce a high tension lead or boot for any testing purpose; otherwise, future problems are almost guaranteed.
• Leave new components and modules in the shipping package until ready to install them.
• Never disconnect any electrical connection with the ignition switch ON unless instructed to do so in a test.

Reading Codes

The Assembly Line Diagnostic Link (ALDL) connector or the Data Link Connector (DLC) is used for communicating with the computer control module (ECM/PCM). It is usually located under the instrument panel and is sometimes covered by a plastic cover labeled "DIAGNOSTIC CONNECTOR." Codes stored in the computer control module's memory can be read through a hand-held diagnostic scanner plugged into the ALDL/DLC connector. If a scanner is not available, the codes can also be read by jumping from terminals A to B of the ALDL/DLC connector and counting the number of flashes of the Service Engine Soon light, with the ignition switch turned ON.

Refer to Section 4 for a more detailed explanation of diagnostic trouble codes, what they mean and how to diagnose them.

Clearing Codes

To clear codes from the computer control module (ECM/PCM) memory, the ECM power feed must be disconnected for at least 30 seconds. Depending on the vehicle, the ECM or PCM power feed can be disconnected at the positive battery terminal pigtail, the inline fuseholder that originates at the positive connection at the battery or the ECM fuse in the fuse block. The negative battery cable may also be disconnected; however, other on-board memory data, such as preset radio tuning, will also be lost.

Also, if battery power is lost, computer relearn time is approximately 5-10 minutes. This means the computer may have to re-calibrate components which set up the idle speed and the idle may fluctuate while this is occurring.

Symptom Diagnosis
▶ See Figures 40, 41, 42 and 43

The computer control module (ECM/PCM) uses information from the MAP and coolant sensors, in addition to rpm to calculate spark advance as follows:
  1. Low MAP output voltage - more spark advance.
  2. Cold engine - more spark advance.
  3. High MAP output voltage - less spark advance.
  4. Hot engine - less spark advance.
Therefore, detonation could be caused by low MAP output or high resistance in the coolant sensor circuit, and poor performance could be caused by high MAP output or low resistance in the coolant sensor circuit.

The best way to diagnose what may be an ignition-related problem, first check for codes. If codes, exist, refer to the corresponding diagnostic charts in Section 4. Otherwise, the accompanying charts may be helpful.

COMPONENT REPLACEMENT

Ignition Coil and Module Assembly
▶ See Figure 44

  1. Make sure the ignition switch is OFF.
  2. Disconnect the negative battery cable.
  3. Detach the 11-pin IDI/ICM harness connector.
  4. Remove the four ignition system assembly-to-camshaft housing bolts.
  5. Remove the ignition coil and module assembly from the engine.

➡If the boots are difficult to remove from the spark plugs, use tool J 36011 or equivalent, to remove them. First twist and then pull upward on the retainers. Reinstall the boots and retainers on the ignition coil and module housing secondary terminals. The boots and retainers must be in place on the housing secondary terminals before ignition system assembly installation or ignition system damage may result.

To install:
  6. Install the spark plug boots and retainers to the housing.
  7. Carefully aligned the boots to the spark plug terminals, while installing the ignition coil and module assembly to the engine.
  8. Coat the threads of the retaining bolts with 1052080 or equivalent, then install them. Tighten the bolts to 19 ft. lbs. (26 Nm) for vehicles through 1991. For 1992-95 vehicles, tighten the bolts to 16 ft. lbs. (22 Nm).
  9. Attach the 11-pin harness connector.

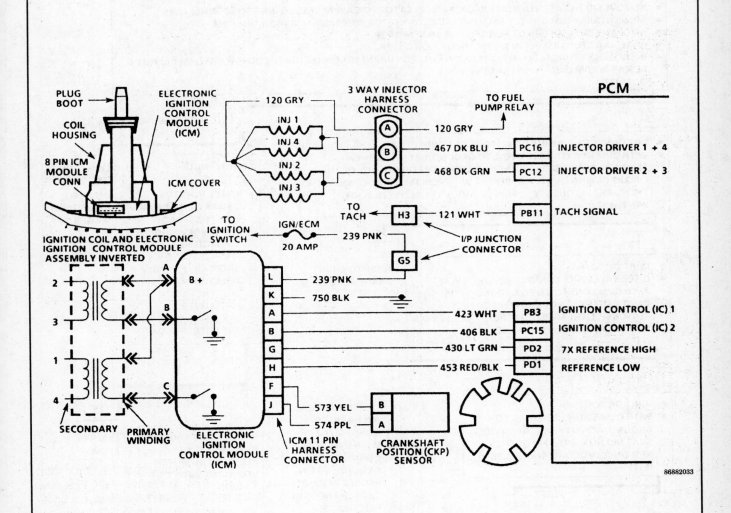

Fig. 40 Ignition system diagnosis — 2.3L engine

CHART C-4M

(Page 1 of 3)
ELECTRONIC IGNITION (EI) SYSTEM MISFIRE DIAGNOSIS
2.3L (VIN D, A & 3) "N" CARLINE

1
- IF DIAGNOSTIC TROUBLE CODES (DTCs) 19 OR 53 ARE PRESENT, REFER TO THOSE CHARTS BEFORE CONTINUING.
- ENGINE AT NORMAL OPERATING TEMPERATURE, DISCONNECT IAC VALVE.
- REMOVE CRANKCASE VENTILATION OIL/AIR SEPARATOR TO GAIN ACCESS TO INJECTOR CONNECTORS.
- MOMENTARILY DISCONNECT EACH INJECTOR CONNECTOR WHILE OBSERVING ENGINE RPM.
- NOTE ANY INJECTOR(S) NOT RESULTING IN AN RPM DROP.
- (IF ALL INJECTORS RESULT IN AN RPM DROP, GO TO STEP 2).
- INSTALL INJECTOR TEST LIGHT J 34730-2 IN INJECTOR HARNESS CONNECTOR FOR INJECTOR WHICH DID NOT RESULT IN RPM DROP. LIGHT SHOULD BLINK. DOES IT?

YES

NO

2
- DISCONNECT 3-WAY INJECTOR HARNESS CONNECTOR.
- WITH DVM NEGATIVE TERMINAL TO GROUND, BACKPROBE PCM TERMINAL CONNECTOR "PC15" AND CHECK THE FREQUENCY OF THE CIRCUIT DURING CRANKING. REPEAT WITH PCM TERMINAL CONNECTOR "PB3". THE FREQUENCY READINGS SHOULD BE BETWEEN 1-10 Hz. ARE THEY?

STEADY LIGHT

LIGHT "OFF"

4
- CHECK INJECTOR DRIVER CIRCUIT WHICH HAD THE STEADY LIGHT, FOR A SHORT TO GROUND.
- IF CIRCUIT IS NOT SHORTED, PERFORM INJECTOR COIL/BALANCE PROCEDURE.

  ARE INJECTORS OK?

REFER TO CHART C-4M (PAGE 3 OF 3).

NO

YES

REFER TO CHART C-4M (PAGE 2 OF 3).

3
- IGNITION "OFF."
- DISCONNECT PINK CONNECTORS FROM PCM. WITH DVM CONNECTED TO GROUND, PROBE THE CAVITY THAT DID NOT SHOW FREQUENCY RESPONSE, EITHER "PB3" OR "PC15". RESISTANCE SHOULD BE GREATER THAN 5K OHMS. IS IT?

YES

NO

5
- IGNITION "ON."
- WITH DVM STILL CONNECTED TO GROUND; AGAIN PROBE THE CAVITY THAT DID NOT SHOW FREQUENCY RESPONSE. VOLTAGE SHOULD BE "0". IS IT?

6
- DISCONNECT ICM 11 PIN HARNESS CONNECTOR.
- WITH DVM STILL CONNECTED TO GROUND, AGAIN PROBE THE CAVITY THAT DID NOT SHOW FREQUENCY RESPONSE. RESISTANCE SHOULD BE INFINITE. IS IT?

NO

REPLACE ANY FAULTY INJECTORS AND RECHECK FOR MISFIRE BEGINNING WITH STEP 1 AGAIN.

YES

FAULTY PCM.

YES

NO

- VISUALLY INSPECT THE PINK PCM CONNECTORS TO SEE IF THEY ARE CLEAN AND TIGHT. IF OK, REPLACE PCM.

REPAIR SHORT TO VOLTAGE IN IGNITION CONTROL CIRCUITS 1 OR 2.

NO

YES

REPAIR SHORT TO GROUND IN IGNITION CONTROL CIRCUITS 1 OR 2.

FAULTY ICM.

86882034

Fig. 41 Ignition system diagnosis (continued) — 2.3L engine

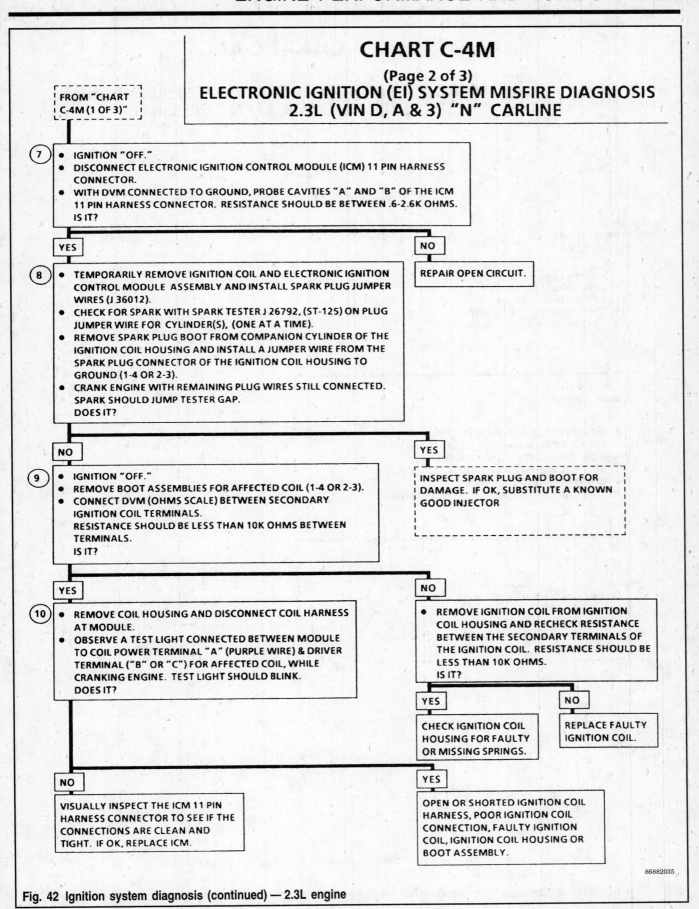

CHART C-4M

(Page 2 of 3)
ELECTRONIC IGNITION (EI) SYSTEM MISFIRE DIAGNOSIS
2.3L (VIN D, A & 3) "N" CARLINE

FROM "CHART C-4M (1 OF 3)"

7
- IGNITION "OFF."
- DISCONNECT ELECTRONIC IGNITION CONTROL MODULE (ICM) 11 PIN HARNESS CONNECTOR.
- WITH DVM CONNECTED TO GROUND, PROBE CAVITIES "A" AND "B" OF THE ICM 11 PIN HARNESS CONNECTOR. RESISTANCE SHOULD BE BETWEEN .6-2.6K OHMS. IS IT?

YES → **8**

NO → REPAIR OPEN CIRCUIT.

8
- TEMPORARILY REMOVE IGNITION COIL AND ELECTRONIC IGNITION CONTROL MODULE ASSEMBLY AND INSTALL SPARK PLUG JUMPER WIRES (J 36012).
- CHECK FOR SPARK WITH SPARK TESTER J 26792, (ST-125) ON PLUG JUMPER WIRE FOR CYLINDER(S), (ONE AT A TIME).
- REMOVE SPARK PLUG BOOT FROM COMPANION CYLINDER OF THE IGNITION COIL HOUSING AND INSTALL A JUMPER WIRE FROM THE SPARK PLUG CONNECTOR OF THE IGNITION COIL HOUSING TO GROUND (1-4 OR 2-3).
- CRANK ENGINE WITH REMAINING PLUG WIRES STILL CONNECTED. SPARK SHOULD JUMP TESTER GAP. DOES IT?

NO → **9**

YES → INSPECT SPARK PLUG AND BOOT FOR DAMAGE. IF OK, SUBSTITUTE A KNOWN GOOD INJECTOR

9
- IGNITION "OFF."
- REMOVE BOOT ASSEMBLIES FOR AFFECTED COIL (1-4 OR 2-3).
- CONNECT DVM (OHMS SCALE) BETWEEN SECONDARY IGNITION COIL TERMINALS. RESISTANCE SHOULD BE LESS THAN 10K OHMS BETWEEN TERMINALS. IS IT?

YES → **10**

NO →
- REMOVE IGNITION COIL FROM IGNITION COIL HOUSING AND RECHECK RESISTANCE BETWEEN THE SECONDARY TERMINALS OF THE IGNITION COIL. RESISTANCE SHOULD BE LESS THAN 10K OHMS. IS IT?

10
- REMOVE COIL HOUSING AND DISCONNECT COIL HARNESS AT MODULE.
- OBSERVE A TEST LIGHT CONNECTED BETWEEN MODULE TO COIL POWER TERMINAL "A" (PURPLE WIRE) & DRIVER TERMINAL ("B" OR "C") FOR AFFECTED COIL, WHILE CRANKING ENGINE. TEST LIGHT SHOULD BLINK. DOES IT?

YES → CHECK IGNITION COIL HOUSING FOR FAULTY OR MISSING SPRINGS.

NO → REPLACE FAULTY IGNITION COIL.

NO → VISUALLY INSPECT THE ICM 11 PIN HARNESS CONNECTOR TO SEE IF THE CONNECTIONS ARE CLEAN AND TIGHT. IF OK, REPLACE ICM.

YES → OPEN OR SHORTED IGNITION COIL HARNESS, POOR IGNITION COIL CONNECTION, FAULTY IGNITION COIL, IGNITION COIL HOUSING OR BOOT ASSEMBLY.

86882035

Fig. 42 Ignition system diagnosis (continued) — 2.3L engine

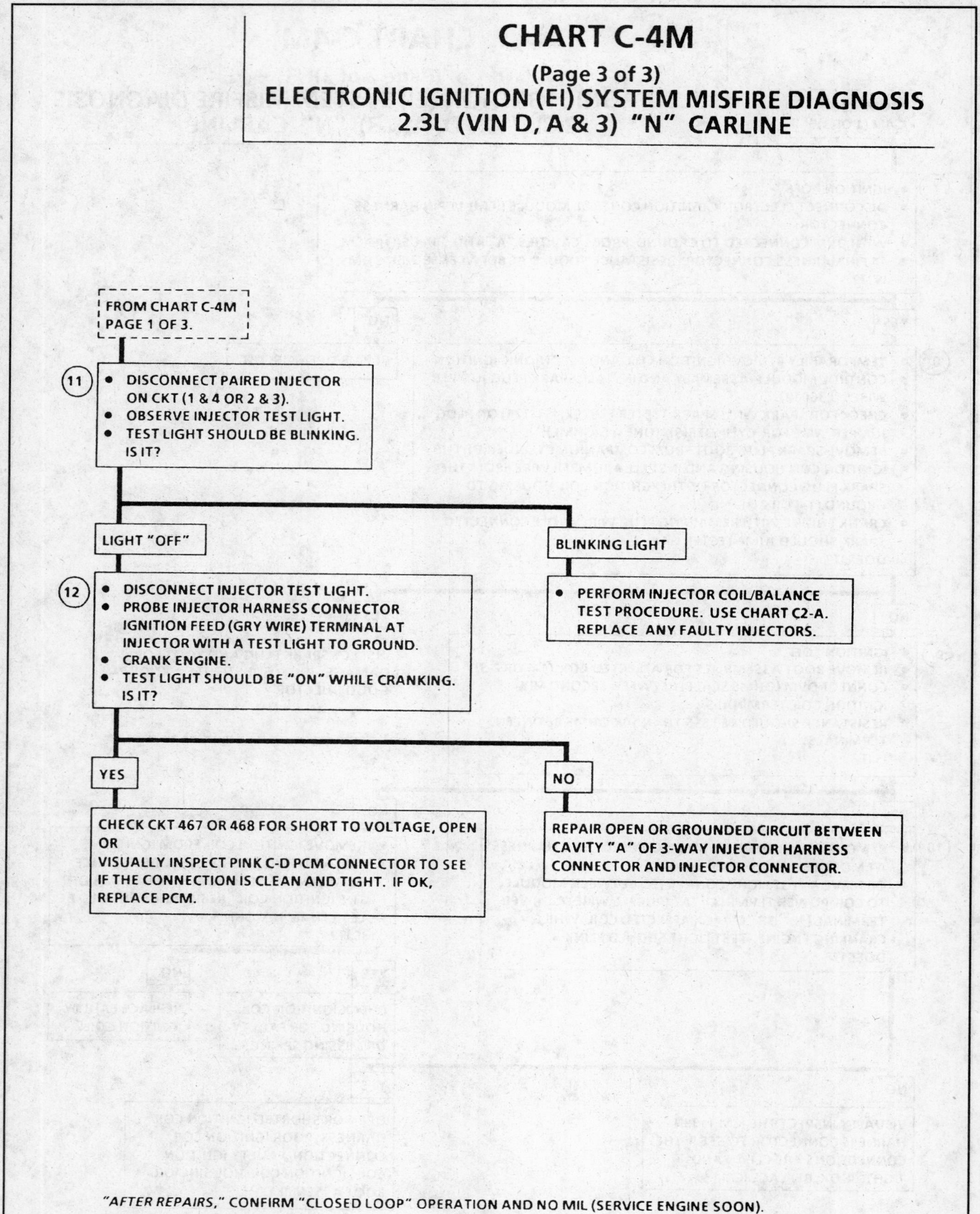

CHART C-4M

(Page 3 of 3)
ELECTRONIC IGNITION (EI) SYSTEM MISFIRE DIAGNOSIS
2.3L (VIN D, A & 3) "N" CARLINE

FROM CHART C-4M
PAGE 1 OF 3.

11
- DISCONNECT PAIRED INJECTOR ON CKT (1 & 4 OR 2 & 3).
- OBSERVE INJECTOR TEST LIGHT.
- TEST LIGHT SHOULD BE BLINKING. IS IT?

LIGHT "OFF"

BLINKING LIGHT

12
- DISCONNECT INJECTOR TEST LIGHT.
- PROBE INJECTOR HARNESS CONNECTOR IGNITION FEED (GRY WIRE) TERMINAL AT INJECTOR WITH A TEST LIGHT TO GROUND.
- CRANK ENGINE.
- TEST LIGHT SHOULD BE "ON" WHILE CRANKING. IS IT?

- PERFORM INJECTOR COIL/BALANCE TEST PROCEDURE. USE CHART C2-A. REPLACE ANY FAULTY INJECTORS.

YES

NO

CHECK CKT 467 OR 468 FOR SHORT TO VOLTAGE, OPEN OR
VISUALLY INSPECT PINK C-D PCM CONNECTOR TO SEE IF THE CONNECTION IS CLEAN AND TIGHT. IF OK, REPLACE PCM.

REPAIR OPEN OR GROUNDED CIRCUIT BETWEEN CAVITY "A" OF 3-WAY INJECTOR HARNESS CONNECTOR AND INJECTOR CONNECTOR.

"AFTER REPAIRS," CONFIRM "CLOSED LOOP" OPERATION AND NO MIL (SERVICE ENGINE SOON).

86882036

Fig. 43 Ignition system diagnosis (continued) — 2.3L engine

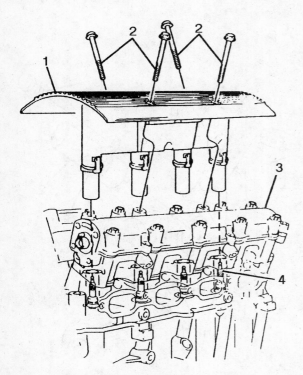

1 Ignition coil and electronic ignition
   control module (ICM)
2 Ignition coil and electronic ignition
   control module (ICM) to camshaft
   housings bolts
3 Camshaft housing (intake side) cover
4 Spark plug

86882025

Fig. 44 View of the ignition coil/module assembly and related components

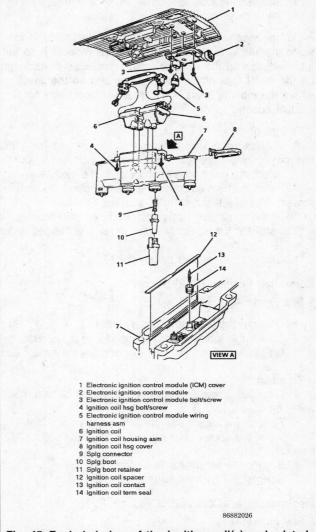

1 Electronic ignition control module (ICM) cover
2 Electronic ignition control module
3 Electronic ignition control module bolt/screw
4 Ignition coil hsg bolt/screw
5 Electronic ignition control module wiring
  harness asm
6 Ignition coil
7 Ignition coil housing asm
8 Ignition coil hsg cover
9 Splg connector
10 Splg boot
11 Splg boot retainer
12 Ignition coil spacer
13 Ignition coil contact
14 Ignition coil term seal

86882026

Fig. 45 Exploded view of the ignition coil(s) and related components — 1995 vehicle shown

10. Make sure the ignition switch is **OFF**, then connect the negative battery cable.

Ignition Coil

▶ See Figure 45

1. Disconnect the negative battery cable.
2. Detach the 11-pin IDI/ICM harness connector.
3. Remove the ignition coil and module assembly from the engine, as outlined earlier in this section.
4. Unfasten the housing to cover retaining screws, then remove the housing from the cover.
5. Disengage the coil harness connector(s).
6. Remove the coil(s), contact(s) and seal(s) from the cover.

   To install:
7. Install the coil(s) to the cover.
8. Attach the coil harness connector.
9. Install new seals to the housing.

10. Using petroleum jelly to retain the contacts, install the contacts to the housing.
11. Install the housing cover and secure using the retaining screws. Tighten the screws to 35 inch lbs. (4 Nm).
12. Fit the spark plug boots and retainers to the housing.
13. Install the IDI assembly to the engine, as outlined earlier in this section.
14. Attach the 11-pin harness connector.
15. Connect the negative battery cable.

Ignition Module/Ignition Control Module (ICM)

▶ See Figure 45

1. Disconnect the negative battery cable.
2. Remove the ignition coil and module assembly from the engine, as outlined earlier in this section.
3. Unfasten the housing-to-cover retaining screws, then remove the housing from the cover.
4. Detach the coil harness connector from the module.

5. Unfasten the module-to-cover retaining screws, then remove the module from the cover.

➡Do not wipe the grease from the module or coil, if the same module is to be replaced. If a new module is to be installed, spread the silicone grease (included in package) on the metal face of the new module and on the cover where the module seats. This grease is necessary for module cooling.

To install:

6. Position the module to the cover, then secure using the retaining screws. Tighten the screws to 35 inch lbs. (4 Nm).

7. Attach the coil harness connector to the module.

8. Install the housing cover, then secure using the retaining screws. Tighten the screws to 35 inch lbs. (4 Nm).

9. Fit the spark plug boots and retainers to the housing.

10. Install the IDI assembly to the engine, as outlined earlier in this section.

11. Connect the negative battery cable.

Crankshaft Position (CKP) Sensor

▶ **See Figure 46**

1. Disconnect the negative battery cable.

2. Detach the sensor harness connector at the sensor.

3. Unfasten the retaining bolt, then remove the sensor from the engine.

To install:

4. Lubricate a new O-ring with clean engine oil, then position it on the sensor.

5. Position the sensor into the hole in the engine block.

6. Install the sensor retaining bolt. Tighten the bolt to 88 inch lbs. (10 Nm).

7. Engage the sensor harness connector.

8. Connect the negative battery cable.

Electronic Spark Control (ESC) Knock Sensor

▶ **See Figure 47**

1. Disconnect the negative battery cable.

2. Raise and safely support the vehicle.

3. Detach the harness connector from the knock sensor.

4. Remove the sensor from the engine block.

To install:

5. Making sure the threads are clean, install the sensor. Tighten the sensor to 12-16 ft. lbs. (16-22 Nm).

6. Attach the harness connector to the knock sensor.

7. Carefully lower the vehicle.

8. Connect the negative battery cable.

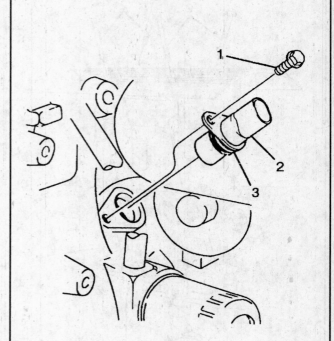

1 Crankshaft position sensor bolt
2 Crankshaft sensor asm
3 Crankshaft position sensor lubricate
  with engine oil "O" ring seal

86882027

Fig. 46 View of the Crankshaft Position (CKP) sensor location and mounting — 1995 vehicle shown

ESC KNOCK SENSOR

86882028

Fig. 47 Before installing the knock sensor, make sure the threads are clean

DIRECT IGNITION SYSTEM (DIS)

1987-91 2.5L (VIN U) Engine

GENERAL DESCRIPTION

The DIS ignition system features a distributorless ignition engine. The DIS system consists of two separate ignition coils on the 2.5L engine, a DIS ignition module, a crankshaft sensor, crankshaft reluctor ring, connecting wires and the Electronic Spark Timing (EST) portion of the Electronic Control Module (ECM).

The DIS ignition system uses a magnetic crankshaft sensor and a reluctor to determine crankshaft position and engine speed. The reluctor is a special wheel cast into the crankshaft with several machined slots. A specific slot, on the reluctor wheel, is used to generate a sync-pulse.

The DIS system uses the same Electronic Spark Timing (EST) circuits as the distributor-type ignition. The ECM uses the EST circuit to control spark advance and ignition dwell, when the ignition system is operating in the EST mode.

SYSTEM OPERATION

▶ **See Figure 48**

The DIS ignition system uses a waste spark distribution method. Each cylinder is paired with its companion cylinder (1-4, 2-3 on a 4-cylinder engine). The end of each coil secondary is attached to a spark plug. These two plugs, being companion cylinders, are at Top Dead Center (TDC) at the same time. The one that is on compression is said to be the event cylinder and the one on the exhaust stroke, the waste cylinder. When the coil discharges, both plugs fire at the same time to complete the series circuit.

Since the polarity of the primary and the secondary windings are fixed, one plug always fires in a forward direction and the other in reverse. This is differs from a conventional system in which all plugs fire in the same direction each time. Because of the demand for additional energy, the coil design, saturation time and primary current flow are also different. This redesign of the system allows higher energy to be available from the distributorless coils, greater than 40 kilovolts at all rpm ranges.

The DIS ignition system uses a magnetic crankshaft sensor which protrudes into the engine block to within approximately 0.050 in. (1.3mm) of the crankshaft reluctor. The reluctor is a special wheel cast into the crankshaft with seven slots machined into it. Six of the slots are evenly spaced (60° apart) and the seventh slot is spaced 10° from one of the other slots and serves to generate a "sync-pulse". As the crankshaft rotates, the slots of the reluctor cause a changing magnetic field at the crankshaft sensor, creating an induced voltage pulse. By counting the time between pulses, the ignition module can recognize the specified slot (sync pulse). Based on this sync pulse, the module sends reference signals to the ECM to calculate crankshaft position and engine speed.

To control EST the ECM uses the following inputs:
- Crankshaft position
- Engine Speed (rpm)
- Engine temperature
- Manifold air temperature
- Atmospheric (barometric) pressure
- Engine load (manifold pressure or vacuum)

SYSTEM COMPONENTS

Crankshaft Sensor

The crankshaft sensor is mounted to the bottom of the DIS module. It is used determine crankshaft position and engine speed.

Ignition Coils

The two ignition coil assemblies are mounted on the DIS module. Each coil distributes the spark for two plugs simultaneously (waste spark distribution). Each coil can be replaced separately.

Electronic Spark Timing (EST)

The EST system is basically the same EST to ECM circuit use on the distributor type ignition systems with EST. This system includes the following circuits:
- DIS reference circuit (CKT 430) — provides the ECM with rpm and crankshaft position information from the DIS module. The DIS module receives this signal from the crank sensor.
- Bypass signal (CKT 424) — above 400 rpm, the ECM applies 5 volts to this circuit to switch spark timing control from the DIS module to the ECM.
- EST signal (CKT 423) — reference signal is sent to the ECM via the DIS module during cranking. Under 400 rpm, the DIS module controls the ignition timing. Above 400 rpm, the ECM applies 5 volts to the bypass line to switch the timing to the ECM control.
- Reference ground circuit (CKT 453) — this wire is grounded through the module and insures that the ground circuit has no voltage drop between the ignition module and the ECM which could affect performance.

DIAGNOSIS AND TESTING

Service Precautions

➡**To avoid damage to the ECM or other ignition system components, do not use electrical test equipment such as battery or AC powered voltmeter, ohmmeter, etc. or any type of tester other than specified.**

- When performing electrical tests on the system, use a high impedance multimeter or quality digital voltmeter (DVM). Use of a 12 volt test light is not recommended.
- To prevent electrostatic discharge damage, when working with the ECM, do not touch the connector pins or soldered components on the circuit board.

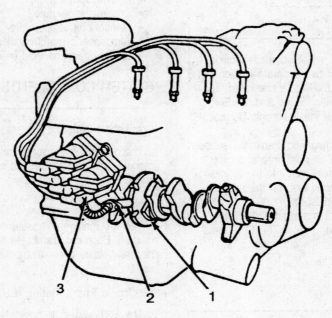

1 Crankshaft reluctor
2 Crankshaft sensor
3 Dis assembly

86882037

Fig. 48 View of the crankshaft sensor-to-crankshaft reluctor relationship

• When handling a PROM, CAL-PAK or MEM-CAL, do not touch the component leads. Also, do not remove the integrated circuit from the carrier.

• When performing electrical tests on the system, use a high impedance multimeter, digital voltmeter (DVM) J-34029-A or equivalent.

• Never pierce a high tension lead or boot for any testing purpose; otherwise, future problems are guaranteed.

• Leave new components and modules in the shipping package until ready to install them.

• Never disconnect any electrical connection with the ignition switch **ON** unless instructed to do so in a test.

Reading Codes

♦ See Figure 49

The Assembly Line Diagnostic Link (ALDL) connector is used for communicating with the ECM. It is usually located under the instrument panel and is sometimes covered by a plastic cover labeled "DIAGNOSTIC CONNECTOR." Codes stored in the ECM's memory can be read through a hand-held diagnostic scanner plugged into the ALDL connector. If a scanner is not available, the codes can also be read by jumping from terminals A to B of the ALDL connector and counting the number of flashes of the Service Engine Soon light, with the ignition switch turned **ON**.

Refer to Section 4 for a more detailed explanation of diagnostic trouble codes, what they mean and how to diagnose them.

Clearing Codes

To clear codes from the ECM memory, the ECM power feed must be disconnected for at least 30 seconds. Depending on the vehicle, the ECM power feed can be disconnected at the positive battery terminal pigtail, the inline fuseholder that originates at the positive connection at the battery or the ECM fuse in the fuse block. The negative battery cable may also be disconnected; however, other on-board memory data, such as radio station presets, will also be lost.

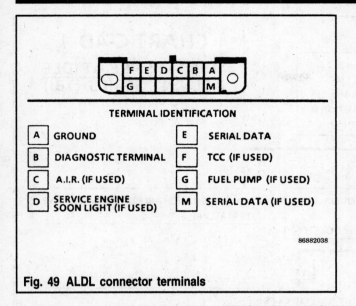

TERMINAL IDENTIFICATION

A	GROUND	E	SERIAL DATA
B	DIAGNOSTIC TERMINAL	F	TCC (IF USED)
C	A.I.R. (IF USED)	G	FUEL PUMP (IF USED)
D	SERVICE ENGINE SOON LIGHT (IF USED)	M	SERIAL DATA (IF USED)

86882038

Fig. 49 ALDL connector terminals

Symptom Diagnosis

♦ **See Figures 50, 51 and 52**

The ECM uses information from the MAP and coolant sensors, in addition to rpm to calculate spark advance as follows:
1. Low MAP output voltage — more spark advance
2. Cold engine — more spark advance
3. High MAP output voltage — less spark advance
4. Hot engine — less spark advance

Therefore, detonation could be caused by low MAP output or high resistance in the coolant sensor circuit, and poor performance could be caused by high MAP output or low resistance in the coolant sensor circuit.

The best way to diagnose what may be an ignition-related problem, first check for codes. If codes, exist, refer to the corresponding diagnostic charts in Section 4. Otherwise, the accompanying charts may be helpful.

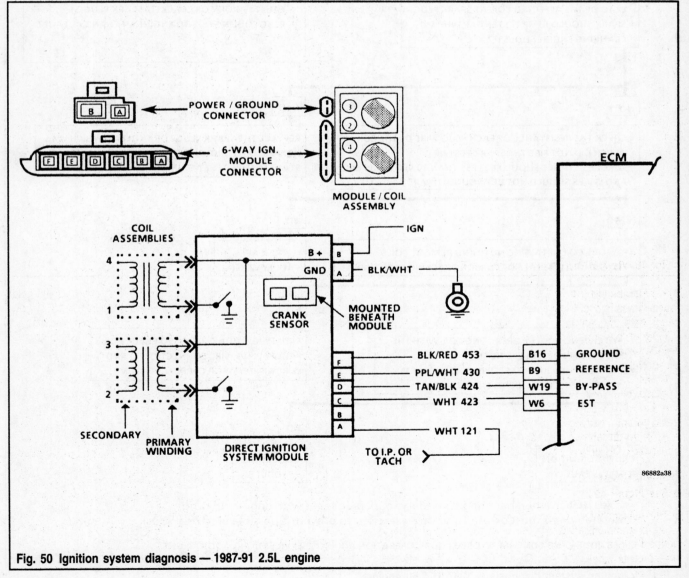

Fig. 50 Ignition system diagnosis — 1987-91 2.5L engine

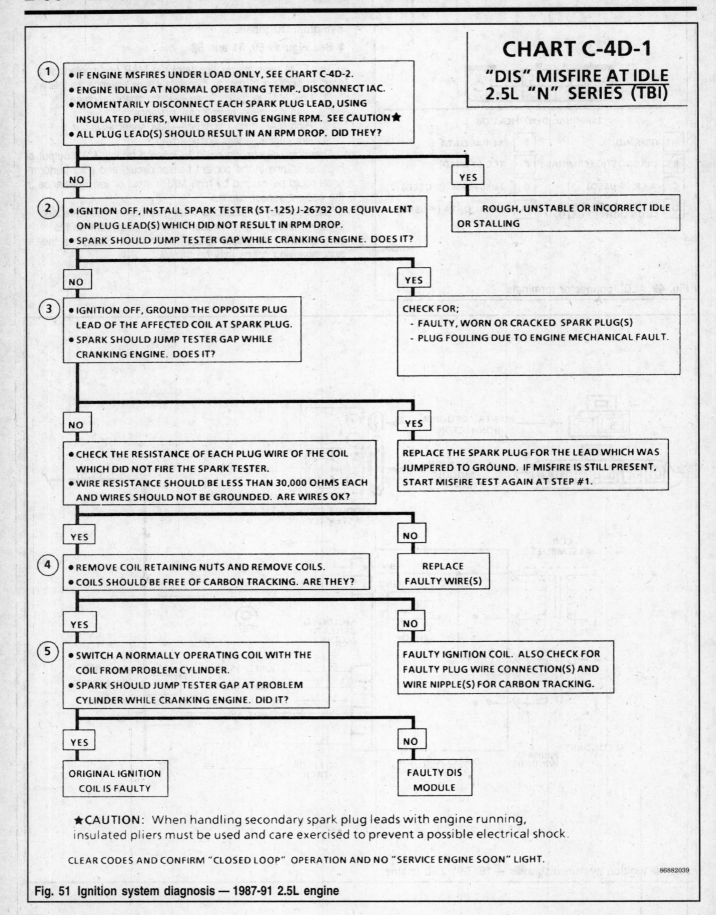

CHART C-4D-1
"DIS" MISFIRE AT IDLE
2.5L "N" SERIES (TBI)

1. • IF ENGINE MSFIRES UNDER LOAD ONLY, SEE CHART C-4D-2.
   • ENGINE IDLING AT NORMAL OPERATING TEMP., DISCONNECT IAC.
   • MOMENTARILY DISCONNECT EACH SPARK PLUG LEAD, USING INSULATED PLIERS, WHILE OBSERVING ENGINE RPM. SEE CAUTION ★
   • ALL PLUG LEAD(S) SHOULD RESULT IN AN RPM DROP. DID THEY?

   NO / YES

   YES → ROUGH, UNSTABLE OR INCORRECT IDLE OR STALLING

2. • IGNITION OFF, INSTALL SPARK TESTER (ST-125) J-26792 OR EQUIVALENT ON PLUG LEAD(S) WHICH DID NOT RESULT IN RPM DROP.
   • SPARK SHOULD JUMP TESTER GAP WHILE CRANKING ENGINE. DOES IT?

   NO / YES

   YES → CHECK FOR;
   - FAULTY, WORN OR CRACKED SPARK PLUG(S)
   - PLUG FOULING DUE TO ENGINE MECHANICAL FAULT.

3. • IGNITION OFF, GROUND THE OPPOSITE PLUG LEAD OF THE AFFECTED COIL AT SPARK PLUG.
   • SPARK SHOULD JUMP TESTER GAP WHILE CRANKING ENGINE. DOES IT?

   NO / YES

   • CHECK THE RESISTANCE OF EACH PLUG WIRE OF THE COIL WHICH DID NOT FIRE THE SPARK TESTER.
   • WIRE RESISTANCE SHOULD BE LESS THAN 30,000 OHMS EACH AND WIRES SHOULD NOT BE GROUNDED. ARE WIRES OK?

   YES → REPLACE THE SPARK PLUG FOR THE LEAD WHICH WAS JUMPERED TO GROUND. IF MISFIRE IS STILL PRESENT, START MISFIRE TEST AGAIN AT STEP #1.

   YES / NO

4. • REMOVE COIL RETAINING NUTS AND REMOVE COILS.
   • COILS SHOULD BE FREE OF CARBON TRACKING. ARE THEY?

   NO → REPLACE FAULTY WIRE(S)

   YES / NO

5. • SWITCH A NORMALLY OPERATING COIL WITH THE COIL FROM PROBLEM CYLINDER.
   • SPARK SHOULD JUMP TESTER GAP AT PROBLEM CYLINDER WHILE CRANKING ENGINE. DID IT?

   NO → FAULTY IGNITION COIL. ALSO CHECK FOR FAULTY PLUG WIRE CONNECTION(S) AND WIRE NIPPLE(S) FOR CARBON TRACKING.

   YES / NO

   YES → ORIGINAL IGNITION COIL IS FAULTY

   NO → FAULTY DIS MODULE

   ★ CAUTION: When handling secondary spark plug leads with engine running, insulated pliers must be used and care exercised to prevent a possible electrical shock.

   CLEAR CODES AND CONFIRM "CLOSED LOOP" OPERATION AND NO "SERVICE ENGINE SOON" LIGHT.

   86882039

Fig. 51 Ignition system diagnosis — 1987-91 2.5L engine

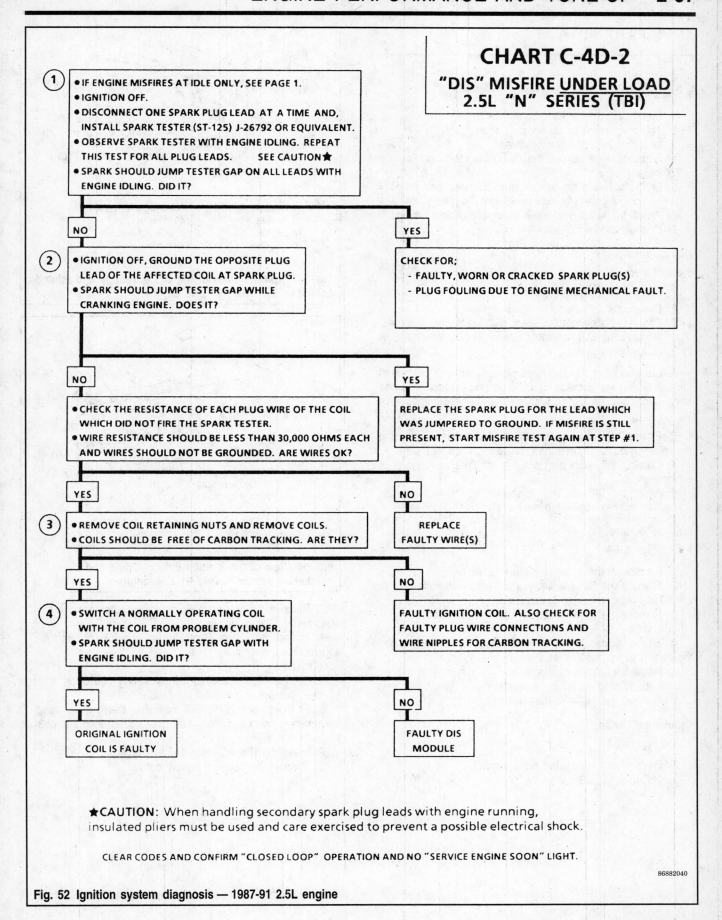

CHART C-4D-2
"DIS" MISFIRE UNDER LOAD
2.5L "N" SERIES (TBI)

1
- IF ENGINE MISFIRES AT IDLE ONLY, SEE PAGE 1.
- IGNITION OFF.
- DISCONNECT ONE SPARK PLUG LEAD AT A TIME AND, INSTALL SPARK TESTER (ST-125) J-26792 OR EQUIVALENT.
- OBSERVE SPARK TESTER WITH ENGINE IDLING. REPEAT THIS TEST FOR ALL PLUG LEADS.   SEE CAUTION ★
- SPARK SHOULD JUMP TESTER GAP ON ALL LEADS WITH ENGINE IDLING. DID IT?

NO

YES

2
- IGNITION OFF, GROUND THE OPPOSITE PLUG LEAD OF THE AFFECTED COIL AT SPARK PLUG.
- SPARK SHOULD JUMP TESTER GAP WHILE CRANKING ENGINE. DOES IT?

CHECK FOR;
- FAULTY, WORN OR CRACKED SPARK PLUG(S)
- PLUG FOULING DUE TO ENGINE MECHANICAL FAULT.

NO

YES

- CHECK THE RESISTANCE OF EACH PLUG WIRE OF THE COIL WHICH DID NOT FIRE THE SPARK TESTER.
- WIRE RESISTANCE SHOULD BE LESS THAN 30,000 OHMS EACH AND WIRES SHOULD NOT BE GROUNDED. ARE WIRES OK?

REPLACE THE SPARK PLUG FOR THE LEAD WHICH WAS JUMPERED TO GROUND. IF MISFIRE IS STILL PRESENT, START MISFIRE TEST AGAIN AT STEP #1.

YES

NO

3
- REMOVE COIL RETAINING NUTS AND REMOVE COILS.
- COILS SHOULD BE FREE OF CARBON TRACKING. ARE THEY?

REPLACE FAULTY WIRE(S)

YES

NO

4
- SWITCH A NORMALLY OPERATING COIL WITH THE COIL FROM PROBLEM CYLINDER.
- SPARK SHOULD JUMP TESTER GAP WITH ENGINE IDLING. DID IT?

FAULTY IGNITION COIL. ALSO CHECK FOR FAULTY PLUG WIRE CONNECTIONS AND WIRE NIPPLES FOR CARBON TRACKING.

YES

NO

ORIGINAL IGNITION COIL IS FAULTY

FAULTY DIS MODULE

★**CAUTION**: When handling secondary spark plug leads with engine running, insulated pliers must be used and care exercised to prevent a possible electrical shock.

CLEAR CODES AND CONFIRM "CLOSED LOOP" OPERATION AND NO "SERVICE ENGINE SOON" LIGHT.

86882040

Fig. 52 Ignition system diagnosis — 1987-91 2.5L engine

COMPONENT REPLACEMENT

Ignition Coils

▶ See Figure 53

1. Disconnect the negative battery cable.
2. Tag and detach the spark plug wires.
3. Unfasten the coil retaining nuts.
4. Separate, then remove the coil(s) from the module.

To install:

5. Fit the coil(s) to the module, then securing using the retaining nuts. Tighten the nuts to 40 inch lbs. (4.5 Nm).
6. Attach the spark plug wires as tagged during removal.
7. Connect the negative battery cable.

DIS Assembly

▶ See Figure 53

1. Disconnect the negative battery cable.
2. Detach the DIS electrical connectors.
3. Tag and disconnect the spark plug leads from the coils.
4. Remove the DIS assembly retaining bolts, then remove the unit from the engine.

➡ **Before installing the DIS assembly, check the crankshaft sensor O-ring for damage or leakage and replace if necessary. Lubricate the O-ring with engine oil before installing.**

To install:

5. Fit the DIS assembly into the engine, then secure using the retaining bolts. Tighten the bolts to 20 ft. lbs. (27 Nm).
6. Connect the spark plug wires to the coils as tagged during removal.
7. Attach the DIS electrical connectors.
8. Connect the negative battery cable.

Ignition Module

▶ See Figure 54

1. Disconnect the negative battery cable.
2. Remove the DIS assembly and the ignition coils from the engine, as outlined earlier in this section.
3. Remove the ignition module from the assembly plate.

To install:

4. Fit the module to the assembly plate. Carefully engage the sensor to the module terminals.
5. Install the ignition coils and the DIS assembly to the engine, as outlined earlier in this section.
6. Connect the negative battery cable.

Crankshaft Sensor

▶ See Figure 53

1. Disconnect the negative battery cable.
2. Remove the DIS assembly.

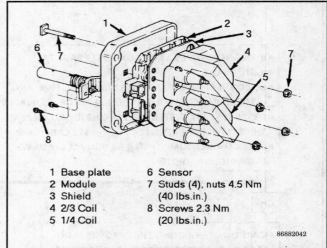

1	Base plate	6	Sensor
2	Module	7	Studs (4), nuts 4.5 Nm
3	Shield		(40 lbs.in.)
4	2/3 Coil	8	Screws 2.3 Nm
5	1/4 Coil		(20 lbs.in.)

86882042

Fig. 53 Exploded view of the DIS assembly and related components — 1987-91 2.5L engine

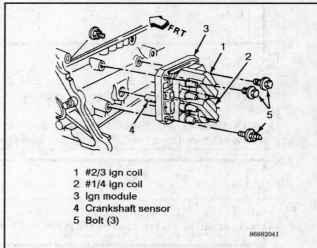

1	#2/3 ign coil
2	#1/4 ign coil
3	Ign module
4	Crankshaft sensor
5	Bolt (3)

86882041

Fig. 54 View of the ignition coils, module and crankshaft sensor — 1987-91 2.5L engine

3. Remove the sensor retaining screws, then remove the sensor from DIS assembly.
4. Inspect the sensor O-ring for wear, cracks or leakage and replace if necessary.

To install:

5. Lubricate the crankshaft sensor O-ring with clean engine oil, then install the O-ring on the sensor.
6. Fit the sensor to the DIS assembly, then secure using the retaining screws. Tighten the screws to 20 inch lbs. (2.3 Nm).
7. Install the DIS assembly to the engine.
8. Connect the negative battery cable.

COMPUTER CONTROLLED COIL IGNITION (C³I)/ELECTRONIC IGNITION (EI) SYSTEM

3.0L (VIN L), 3.1L (VIN M) and 3.3L (VIN N) Engines

GENERAL DESCRIPTION

The Computer Controlled Coil Ignition (C³I) or Electronic Ignition (EI) system features a distributorless ignition engine. The C³I/EI system consists of 3 ignition coils, a C³I ignition module/Ignition Control Module, a dual crank sensor (also referred to as the combination sensor) or two crankshaft position sensors (depending upon vehicle application), camshaft sensor, related connecting wires, and the Electronic Spark Timing (EST)/Ignition Control (IC) portion of the computer control module (ECM or PCM). The C³I/EI system uses the same Electronic Spark Timing (EST) or Ignition Control (IC) circuits as the distributor-type ignition. The computer control module (ECM/PCM) uses the EST/IC circuit to control spark advance and ignition dwell, when the ignition system is operating in the EST/IC mode. There are 2 modes of ignition system operation. These modes are as follows:

- Module mode — the ignition system operates independently of the computer control module (ECM/PCM), with module mode spark advance always at 10° BTDC. The ECM/PCM has no control of the ignition system when in this mode.
- EST/IC mode — the ignition spark timing and ignition dwell time is fully controlled by the computer control module (ECM/PCM). EST/IC spark advance and ignition dwell is calculated by the ECM/PCM.

To control spark knock, and enable maximum spark advance to improve driveability and fuel economy, an Electronic Spark Control (ESC) system is used. This system consists of a knock sensor and an ESC module (part of Mem-Cal). The computer control module monitors the ESC signal to determine when engine detonation occurs.

SYSTEM OPERATION

The C³I/EI system uses a waste spark distribution method. Each cylinder is paired with the cylinder opposite it (1-4, 2-5, 3-6). The ends of each coil secondary is attached to a spark plug. These 2 plugs, being on companion cylinders, are at top dead center at the same time. The one that is on compression is said to be the event cylinder and the one on the exhaust stroke, the waste cylinder. When the coil discharges, both plugs fire at the same time to complete the series circuit. Therefore, each pair of cylinders is fired for each crankshaft revolution.

Since the polarity of the primary and the secondary windings are fixed, one plug always fires in a forward direction and the other in reverse. This differs from a conventional system in which all plugs fire in the same direction each time. Because of the demand for additional energy; the coil design, saturation time and primary current flow are also different. This redesign of the system allows higher energy to be available from the distributorless coils, greater than 40 kilovolts at all rpm ranges.

During cranking, when the engine speed is beneath 400 rpm, the C³I module/Ignition Control Module (ICM) monitors the dual crank/CKP sensor sync signal. The sync signal is used to determine the correct pair of cylinders to be sparked first. Once the sync signal has been processed by the ignition module, it sends a fuel control reference pulse to the computer control module (ECM/PCM).

During the cranking period, the computer control module will also receive a cam pulse signal and will operate the injectors sequentially, based on true camshaft position only.

The sync signal, or pulse, is used only by the ignition module. It is used for spark synchronization at start-up only.

When the engine speed is beneath 400 rpm (during cranking), the C³I module/ICM controls the spark timing. Once the engine speed exceeds 400 rpm (engine running) spark timing is controlled by the EST/IC signal from the ECM. To control EST/IC the ECM uses the following inputs:

- Crankshaft position
- Engine speed (rpm)
- Engine Coolant Temperature Sensor (ECT)
- Intake air (Mass Air Flow — MAF)
- Throttle valve position (Throttle Position Sensor — TPS)
- Gear shift lever position (Park/Neutral Switch — P/N)
- Vehicle speed (Vehicle Speed Sensor — VSS)
- ESC signal (Knock Sensor)

The C³I ignition module/ICM provides proper ignition coil sequencing during both the module and the EST/IC modes.

The ESC system is designed to retard spark timing up to 10° to reduce spark knock in the engine. When the knock sensor detects spark knocking in the engine, it sends an AC voltage signal to the computer control module, which increases with the severity of the knock. The ECM or PCM then adjusts the EST/IC to reduce spark knock.

SYSTEM COMPONENTS

C³I Module/Ignition Control Module (ICM)

The C³I module/ICM monitors the sync-pulse and the crank signals. This information is passed on to the computer control module so that correct spark and fuel injector timing can be maintained during all driving conditions. During cranking, the module monitors the sync-pulse to begin the ignition firing sequence. Below 400 rpm, the module control spark advance by triggering each of the three coils which are fired at a predetermined interval based on engine speed only. Above 400 rpm, the C³I module/Ignition Control Module (ICM) relays the crank signal to the computer control module as a reference signal. The ECM or PCM then control t he spark timing and compensates for all driving conditions. The module must receive a sync-pulse and then a crank signal, in that order, for the engine to be able to start.

Ignition Coil

The three twin tower ignition coil assemblies are mounted on the C³I module/Ignition Control Module (ICM). Each coil distributes the spark for two plugs simultaneously (waste spark distribution).

Electronic Spark Control (ESC)

The ESC system incorporates a knock sensor and the computer control module (ECM/PCM). The knock sensor detects engine detonation. When engine detonation occurs, the computer control module (ECM/PCM) receives the ESC signal and retards EST/IC to reduce detonation.

Electronic Spark Timing (EST)/Ignition Control (IC)

The EST/IC system is basically the same EST/IC-to-computer control module (ECM/PCM) circuit used on the distributor type ignition systems with Electronic Spark Timing or Ignition Control. For vehicles equipped with either the 3.0L or 3.3L engine, this system includes the following circuits:

- Reference circuit (CKT 430) — provides the ECM with rpm and crankshaft position information from the C³I module. The C³I module receives this signal from the crank sensor's Hall effect switch.
- Bypass signal (CKT 424) — at about 400 rpm, the computer control module (ECM/PCM) applies 5 volts to this circuit to switch spark timing control from the C³I module/ICM to the ECM or PCM.
- EST/IC signal (CKT 423) — reference signal is sent to the computer control module via the C³I module/ICM during engine cranking. Under 400 rpm, the module controls the ignition timing. Above 400 rpm, the computer control module applies 5 volts to the bypass line to switch the timing to the ECM/PCM control.

For vehicles equipped with the 3.1L engine, the IC system contains the following circuits:

- 3X reference high (CKT 430) — The CKP sensor sends a signal to the electronic ignition control module which generates a reference pulse which is sent to the PCM. The PCM uses this signal to calculate crankshaft position and engine speed (and also to trigger the injector).
- 3X reference low (CKT 453) — This wire is grounded through the module and makes sure the ground circuit has no voltage drop between the ignition module and the PCM, which if open, could affect performance.
- Ignition control bypass (CKT 424) — During initial cranking, the PCM will look for synchronizing pulses from the camshaft and 3X crankshaft position sensor indicating the position of the no. 1 piston and intake valve. 5 volts are applied to the bypass circuit the instant these signals are received by the PCM.
- Ignition Control (IC) (CKT 423) — The PCM uses this circuit to trigger the ICM. The PCM uses the crankshaft reference signal to base its calculation of the amount of spark advance needed under present engine conditions.
- 24X reference signal - Additional to the electronic ignition system is the 24X crankshaft position sensor. Its function is to increase idle quality and provide good low speed driveability.

Computer Control Module (ECM/PCM)

The computer control module (ECM or PCM depending upon vehicle application) is responsible for maintaining proper spark and fuel injection timing for all driving conditions.

Dual Crank Sensor/Combination Sensor/Crankshaft Position (CKP) Sensor

Vehicles equipped with the 3.0L and 3.3L engines utilize a crankshaft position sensor. The crank sensor is mounted in a pedestal on the front of the engine near the harmonic balancer. The sensor consists of two Hall effect switches, which depend on two metal interrupter rings mounted on the harmonic balancer (crankshaft pulley) to activate them. Windows in the interrupters activate the Hall effect switches as they provide a path for the magnetic field between the switches transducers and magnets. When one of the Hall effect switches is activated, it grounds the signal line to the ignition control module, pulling that signal line's (sync-pulse or crank) applied voltage low, which is interpreted as a signal. Because of the way the signal is created, the signal circuit is always either at a high or low voltage. Three crank signal pulses and one "Sync-Pulse" are created during each crankshaft revolution. Both the CKP sensor and sync-pulse signals must be received by the ignition control module for the engine to start. A bent interrupter ring could cause rubbing of the sensor, resulting in potential driveability problems, such as rough idle, poor performance or a no-start condition.

The crankshaft position sensor is not adjustable for ignition timing, but positioning of the interrupter ring is very important. A clearance of 0.025 in. (0.64mm) is required on either side of the interrupter ring. Failure to maintain adequate clearance will damage the sensor.

24X and 3X Crankshaft Position (CKP) Sensors

Vehicles equipped with the 3.1L engine use two separately mounted crankshaft position sensors: The 24X and the 3X. The 24X crankshaft position sensor is secured in an aluminum mounting bracket and bolted to the front side of the engine timing chain cover and is located partially behind the crankshaft balancer. A three wire harness connector plugs into the 3X crankshaft position sensor, connecting it to the ignition control module.

The 24X sensor contains a Hall effect switch. The magnet and Hall effect switch are separated by an air gap. A Hall effect switch reacts like a solid-state switch, grounding a low-current signal voltage when a magnetic field is present. When the magnetic field is shielded from the switch by a piece of steel placed in the air gap between the magnet and the switch, the signal voltage is not grounded. If the piece of steel (called an interrupter) is repeatedly moved in and out of the air gap, the signal voltage will appear to go "ON-OFF-ON-OFF-ON-OFF". Compared to a conventional distributor, this "ON-OFF" signal is similar to to the signal that a set of breaker points in the distributor would generate as the distributor shaft turned and the points opened and closed.

A concentric interrupter ring mounted to the rear of the crankshaft balancer has blades and windows that, with crankshaft rotation, either block the magnetic field or allow it to reach the Hall effect switch. The Hall effect switch is called a 24X CKP sensor because the interrupter ring has 24 evenly-spaced, same-width blades and windows. The 24X sensor makes 24 "ON-OFF" pulses per crankshaft revolution. The Hall effect switch closest to the crankshaft, then 3X sensor, is called that because the interrupter ring has a special wheel cast on the crankshaft that has seven machined slots, six of which are equally spaced 60° apart. The seventh slot is spaced 10° from one of the other slots. As the interrupter ring rotates with the crankshaft, slots change the magnetic field. This will cause the 3X Hall effect switch to ground the 3X signal voltage supplied from the ignition control module. the ignition control module interprets the 3X "ON-OFF" signals as an indication of crankshaft position, and must have the 3X signal to fire the correct ignition coil.

The 24X interrupter ring and Hall effect switch react similarly. The 24X signal is used for better resolution at a calibrated rpm.

Camshaft Position (CMP) Sensor

The camshaft position sensor is located on the timing cover behind the water pump, near the camshaft sprocket.

As the camshaft sprocket turns, a magnet in it activates the Hall effect switch in the cam sensor. When the Hall effect switch is activated, it grounds the signal line to the computer control module (ECM/PCM), pulling the cam signal line's applied voltage low. This is interpreted as a cam signal.

DIAGNOSIS AND TESTING

Service Precautions

✳✳CAUTION

The ignition coil's secondary voltage output capabilities can exceed 40,000 volts. Avoid contact with the C³I/EI high voltage secondary components when the engine is running, or personal injury may result.

➡**To avoid damage to the computer control module or other ignition system components, do not use electrical test equipment such as battery or AC-powered voltmeter, ohmmeter, etc. or any type of tester other than specified.**

- To properly diagnosis the ignition systems and their problems, it will be necessary to refer to the diagnostic charts in the fuel injection section.
- When performing electrical tests on the system, use a high impedance multimeter or quality digital voltmeter (DVM). Use of a 12 volt test light is not recommended.
- To prevent electrostatic discharge damage, when working with the computer control module, do not touch the connector pins or soldered components on the circuit board.
- When handling a PROM, CAL-PAK or MEM-CAL, do not touch the component leads. Also, do not remove the integrated circuit from the carrier.
- Never pierce a high tension lead or boot for any testing purpose; otherwise, future problems are guaranteed.
- Do not allow extension cords for power tools or droplights to lie on, near or across any vehicle electrical wiring.
- Leave new components and modules in the shipping package until ready to install them.

Reading Codes

The Assembly Line Diagnostic Link (ALDL) connector is used for communicating with the ECM. It is usually located under the instrument panel and is sometimes covered by a plastic cover labeled "DIAGNOSTIC CONNECTOR." Codes stored in the ECM's memory can be read through a hand-held diagnostic scanner plugged into the ALDL connector. If a scanner is not available, the codes can also be read by jumping from terminal A to B of the ALDL connector and counting the number of flashes of the Service Engine Soon light, with the ignition switch turned **ON**.

Refer to Section 4 of this manual for a more detailed explanation of diagnostic trouble codes, what they mean and how to diagnose them.

Clearing Codes

To clear codes from the ECM memory, the ECM power feed must be disconnected for at least 30 seconds. Depending on the vehicle, the ECM power feed can be disconnected at the positive battery terminal pigtail, the inline fuseholder that originates at the positive connection at the battery or the ECM fuse in the fuse block. The negative battery cable may also be disconnected; however, other on-board memory data, such as radio station presets, will also be lost.

Also, if battery power is lost, computer relearn time is approximately 5-10 minutes. This means the computer may have to re-calibrate components which set up the idle speed and the idle may fluctuate while this is occurring.

Basic Ignition System Check
▶ **See Figures 55, 56, 57, 58, 59, 60, 61 and 62**

1. Check for diagnostic trouble codes. If any are found, refer to the appropriate chart in Section 4.
2. Turn the ignition switch **ON**. Verify that the Service Engine Soon light is ON.
3. Install the scan tool and check the following:
   a. Throttle Position Sensor (TPS) — if over 2.5 volts, at closed throttle, check the TPS and circuit.
   b. Engine Coolant Temperature (ECT) sensor — if not between 22-266°F (30-130°C), check the sensor and circuit.
4. Disconnect all injector connectors and install injector test light (J-34730-2 or equivalent) in injector harness connector. Test light should be OFF.

➡**Perform this test on one injector from each bank.**

5. Connect spark checker, (J 26792 or equivalent), and check for spark while cranking. Check at least 2 wires.
   a. If spark occurs, Connect the spark plug wires and check for fuel spray at the injector(s) while cranking.
   b. If no spark occurs, check for battery voltage to the ignition system. If OK, substitute known good parts for possible faulty ignition parts. If not, refer to the wiring diagrams to track down loss of voltage.

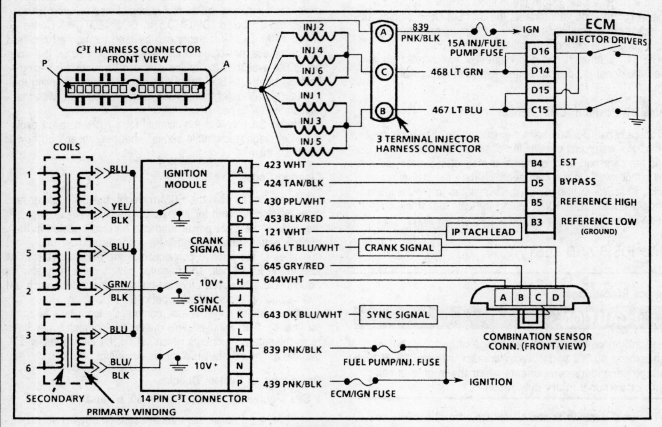

CHART C-4H-1

C³I MISFIRE AT IDLE
3.0L (VIN L) "N" SERIES (PORT)

Circuit Description:

The C³I uses a waste spark method of spark distribution. In this type of ignition system the ignition module triggers the #1/4 coil pair resulting in both #1 and #4 spark plugs firing at the same time. #1 cylinder is on the compression stroke at the same time #4 is on the exhaust stroke, resulting in a lower energy requirement to fire #4 spark plug. This leaves the remaining high voltage to fire #1 spark plug.

Test Description: Numbers below refer to circled numbers on the diagnostic chart.

1. If the "misfire" complaint exists <u>under load only</u>, the diagnostic chart C-4H-2 must be used. Engine rpm should drop approximately equally on all plug leads.

2. A spark tester such as a ST-125 must be used because it is essential to verify adequate available secondary voltage at the spark plug. (25,000 volts). Secondary voltage of at least (25,000 volts) must be present to jump the gap of a ST-125.

3. If ignition coils are carbon tracked, the coil tower spark plug wire nipples may be damaged.

4. By checking the secondary resistance, a coil with an open secondary may be located.

5. By switching a normally operating coil into the position of the malfunctioning one, a determination can be made as to fault being the coil or C³I module.

86882060

Fig. 55 Ignition system diagnosis — 3.0L engine

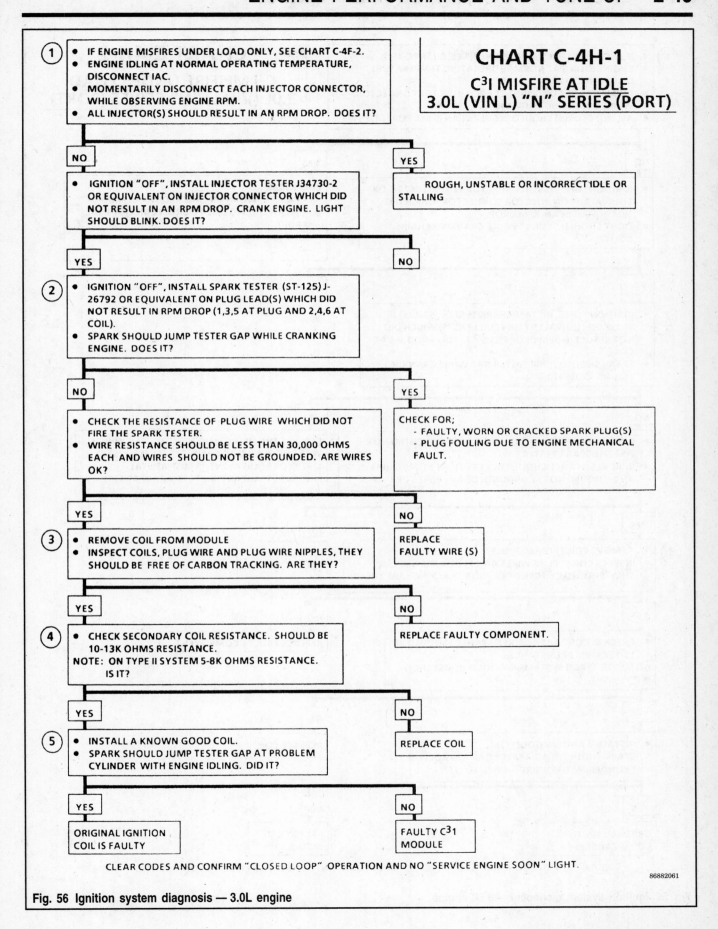

Fig. 56 Ignition system diagnosis — 3.0L engine

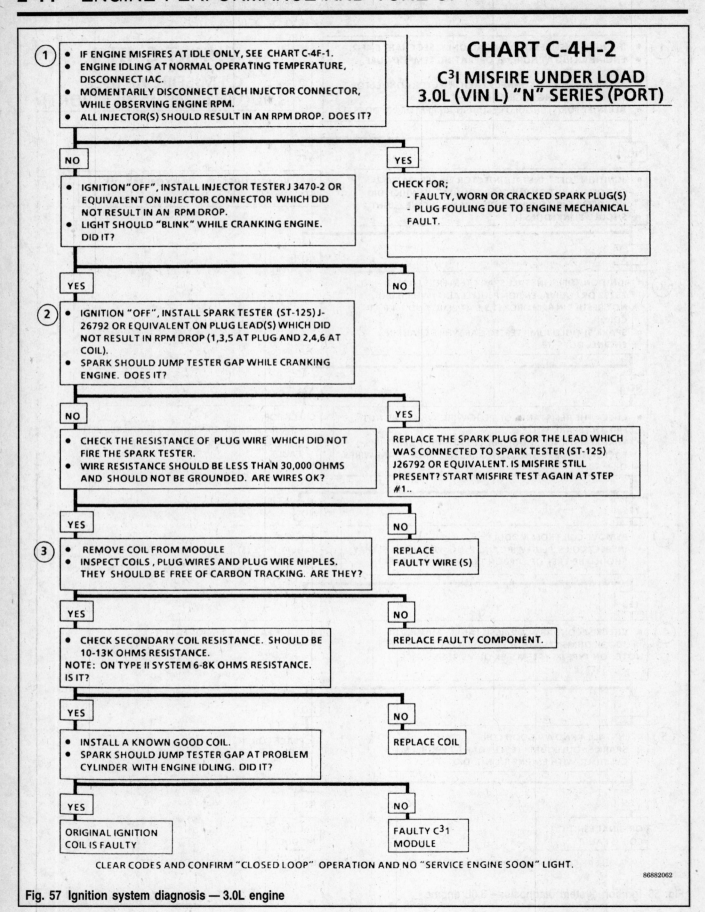

CHART C-4H-2
C³I MISFIRE UNDER LOAD
3.0L (VIN L) "N" SERIES (PORT)

1
- IF ENGINE MISFIRES AT IDLE ONLY, SEE CHART C-4F-1.
- ENGINE IDLING AT NORMAL OPERATING TEMPERATURE, DISCONNECT IAC.
- MOMENTARILY DISCONNECT EACH INJECTOR CONNECTOR, WHILE OBSERVING ENGINE RPM.
- ALL INJECTOR(S) SHOULD RESULT IN AN RPM DROP. DOES IT?

NO
- IGNITION "OFF", INSTALL INJECTOR TESTER J 3470-2 OR EQUIVALENT ON INJECTOR CONNECTOR WHICH DID NOT RESULT IN AN RPM DROP.
- LIGHT SHOULD "BLINK" WHILE CRANKING ENGINE. DID IT?

YES
CHECK FOR;
- FAULTY, WORN OR CRACKED SPARK PLUG(S)
- PLUG FOULING DUE TO ENGINE MECHANICAL FAULT.

YES — **2**
- IGNITION "OFF", INSTALL SPARK TESTER (ST-125) J-26792 OR EQUIVALENT ON PLUG LEAD(S) WHICH DID NOT RESULT IN RPM DROP (1,3,5 AT PLUG AND 2,4,6 AT COIL).
- SPARK SHOULD JUMP TESTER GAP WHILE CRANKING ENGINE. DOES IT?

NO

NO
- CHECK THE RESISTANCE OF PLUG WIRE WHICH DID NOT FIRE THE SPARK TESTER.
- WIRE RESISTANCE SHOULD BE LESS THAN 30,000 OHMS AND SHOULD NOT BE GROUNDED. ARE WIRES OK?

YES
REPLACE THE SPARK PLUG FOR THE LEAD WHICH WAS CONNECTED TO SPARK TESTER (ST-125) J26792 OR EQUIVALENT. IS MISFIRE STILL PRESENT? START MISFIRE TEST AGAIN AT STEP #1..

YES — **3**
- REMOVE COIL FROM MODULE
- INSPECT COILS, PLUG WIRES AND PLUG WIRE NIPPLES. THEY SHOULD BE FREE OF CARBON TRACKING. ARE THEY?

NO
REPLACE FAULTY WIRE (S)

YES
- CHECK SECONDARY COIL RESISTANCE. SHOULD BE 10-13K OHMS RESISTANCE.
NOTE: ON TYPE II SYSTEM 6-8K OHMS RESISTANCE.
IS IT?

NO
REPLACE FAULTY COMPONENT.

YES
- INSTALL A KNOWN GOOD COIL.
- SPARK SHOULD JUMP TESTER GAP AT PROBLEM CYLINDER WITH ENGINE IDLING. DID IT?

NO
REPLACE COIL

YES
ORIGINAL IGNITION COIL IS FAULTY

NO
FAULTY C³I MODULE

CLEAR CODES AND CONFIRM "CLOSED LOOP" OPERATION AND NO "SERVICE ENGINE SOON" LIGHT.

86882062

Fig. 57 Ignition system diagnosis — 3.0L engine

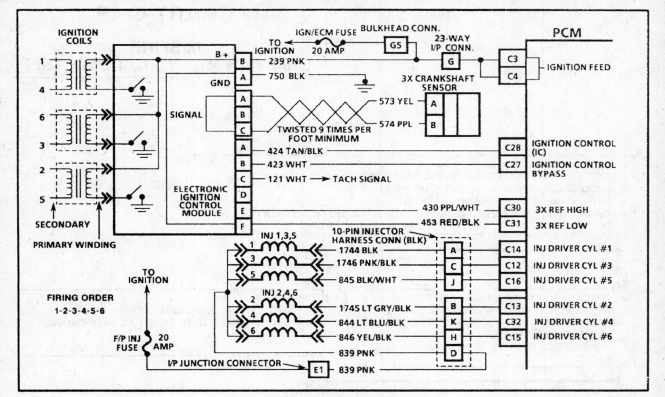

CHART C-4F

MISFIRE
3100 (VIN M) "N" CARLINE (SFI)

Circuit Description:
The Electronic Ignition (EI) system uses a waste spark method of distribution. In this type of system, the electronic ignition control module triggers the #1/4 coil pair resulting in both #1 and #4 spark plugs firing at the same time. #1 cylinder is on the compression stroke at the same time #4 is on the exhaust stroke, resulting in a lower energy requirement to fire #4 spark plug. This leaves the remainder of the high voltage to be used to fire #1 spark plug. On this application, the low resolution 3X crankshaft position sensor is mounted to the engine block and protrudes through the block to within approximately .050″ of the crankshaft reluctor. Since the reluctor is a machined portion of the crankshaft and the sensor is mounted in a fixed position on the block, timing adjustments are neither possible or necessary.

Chart Test Description: Number(s) below refer to circled number(s) on the diagnostic chart.

1. Checks for voltage output of ignition system. The companion cylinder spark plug cable in the circuit must be connected to a good ground to create a good spark and avoid over stressing the coil. Test each spark plug cable with the engine idling (the ignition must be cycled "OFF" when moving the ST-125 tester to a different spark plug cable).
   - Keep disconnected spark plug leads away from sensors and other electronic components.
   - Move quickly through this test. Don't leave any spark plug lead disconnected for longer than 15 seconds.
   - Let the engine run normally for 30 seconds between tests to avoid an excessive buildup of fuel.
2. If the spark tester fires on all wires, the ignition system, with the exception of the spark plugs, may be considered in good working order. If the spark plugs show no evidence of wear, damage or fouling, an engine mechanical fault should be suspected.

3. Plug wires should be inspected for cuts or abrasions leading to shorts to ground or other components. This would cause a weak or absent spark yet the resistance valve when measured may be correct.
4. If carbon tracking is evident replace coil and be sure plug wires relating to that coil are clean and tight. Excessive wire resistance or faulty connections could have caused the coil to be damaged.
5. If the no spark condition follows the suspected coil, that coil is faulty. Otherwise, the electronic ignition control module is the cause of no spark. This test could also be performed by substituting a known good coil for the one causing the no spark condition.

Fig. 58 Ignition system diagnosis — 3.1L engine

86882063

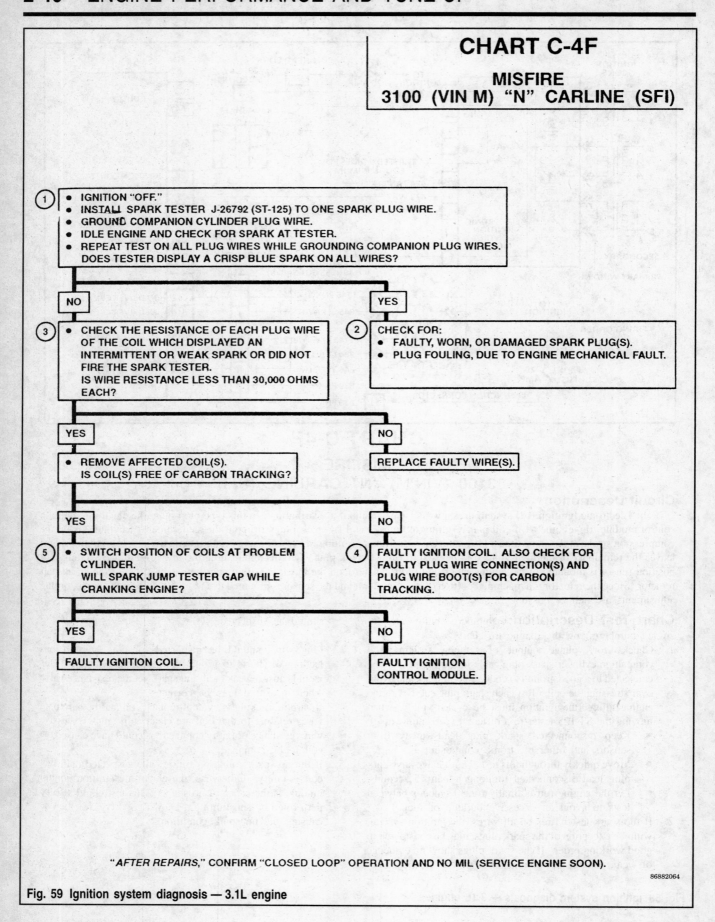

CHART C-4F

MISFIRE
3100 (VIN M) "N" CARLINE (SFI)

1
- IGNITION "OFF."
- INSTALL SPARK TESTER J-26792 (ST-125) TO ONE SPARK PLUG WIRE.
- GROUND COMPANION CYLINDER PLUG WIRE.
- IDLE ENGINE AND CHECK FOR SPARK AT TESTER.
- REPEAT TEST ON ALL PLUG WIRES WHILE GROUNDING COMPANION PLUG WIRES. DOES TESTER DISPLAY A CRISP BLUE SPARK ON ALL WIRES?

NO

3
- CHECK THE RESISTANCE OF EACH PLUG WIRE OF THE COIL WHICH DISPLAYED AN INTERMITTENT OR WEAK SPARK OR DID NOT FIRE THE SPARK TESTER. IS WIRE RESISTANCE LESS THAN 30,000 OHMS EACH?

YES

2
CHECK FOR:
- FAULTY, WORN, OR DAMAGED SPARK PLUG(S).
- PLUG FOULING, DUE TO ENGINE MECHANICAL FAULT.

YES
- REMOVE AFFECTED COIL(S). IS COIL(S) FREE OF CARBON TRACKING?

NO
REPLACE FAULTY WIRE(S).

YES

5
- SWITCH POSITION OF COILS AT PROBLEM CYLINDER. WILL SPARK JUMP TESTER GAP WHILE CRANKING ENGINE?

NO

4
FAULTY IGNITION COIL. ALSO CHECK FOR FAULTY PLUG WIRE CONNECTION(S) AND PLUG WIRE BOOT(S) FOR CARBON TRACKING.

YES
FAULTY IGNITION COIL.

NO
FAULTY IGNITION CONTROL MODULE.

"AFTER REPAIRS," CONFIRM "CLOSED LOOP" OPERATION AND NO MIL (SERVICE ENGINE SOON).

86882064

Fig. 59 Ignition system diagnosis — 3.1L engine

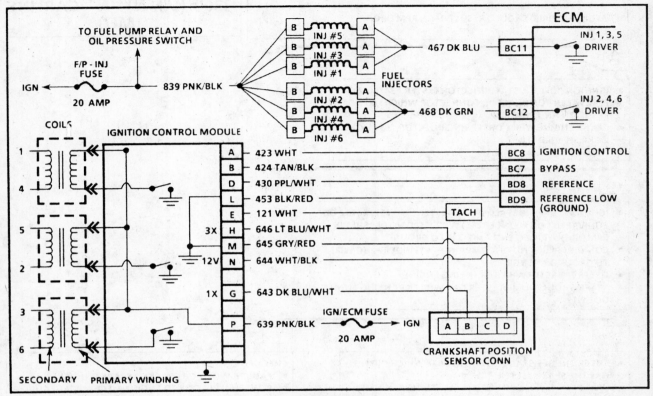

CHART C-4-1

MISFIRE AT IDLE
3300 (VIN N) "N" CARLINE (MFI)

Circuit Description:
The ignition system uses a waste spark method of spark distribution. In this type of ignition system the ignition control module triggers the #1/4 coil pair resulting in both #1 and #4 spark plugs firing at the same time. #1 cylinder is on the compression stroke at the same time #4 is on the exhaust stroke, resulting in a lower energy requirement to fire #4 spark plug. This leaves the remaining high voltage to fire #1 spark plug.

Test Description: Number(s) below refer to circled number(s) on the diagnostic chart.

1. If the "misfire" complaint exists under load only, the diagnostic CHART C-4-2 must be used. Engine RPM should drop approximately equally on all plug leads.
2. A spark tester such as a ST-125 must be used because it is essential to verify adequate available secondary voltage at the spark plug. Secondary voltage of at least 25,000 volts must be present to jump the gap of a ST-125.

3. If ignition coils are carbon tracked, the coil towers or spark plug wire boots may be damaged.
4. By checking the secondary resistance, a coil with an open secondary may be located.
5. By switching a normally operating coil into the position of the malfunctioning one, a determination can be made as to fault being the coil or ignition control module.

86882065

Fig. 60 Ignition system diagnosis — 3.3L engine

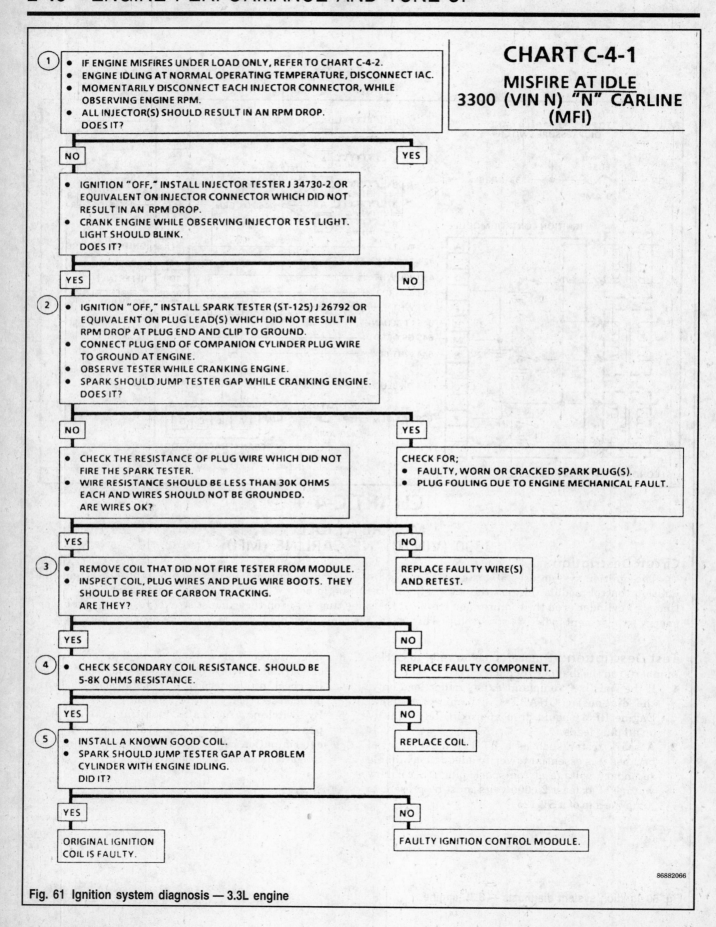

CHART C-4-1

MISFIRE AT IDLE
3300 (VIN N) "N" CARLINE (MFI)

1
- IF ENGINE MISFIRES UNDER LOAD ONLY, REFER TO CHART C-4-2.
- ENGINE IDLING AT NORMAL OPERATING TEMPERATURE, DISCONNECT IAC.
- MOMENTARILY DISCONNECT EACH INJECTOR CONNECTOR, WHILE OBSERVING ENGINE RPM.
- ALL INJECTOR(S) SHOULD RESULT IN AN RPM DROP. DOES IT?

NO → YES

- IGNITION "OFF," INSTALL INJECTOR TESTER J 34730-2 OR EQUIVALENT ON INJECTOR CONNECTOR WHICH DID NOT RESULT IN AN RPM DROP.
- CRANK ENGINE WHILE OBSERVING INJECTOR TEST LIGHT. LIGHT SHOULD BLINK. DOES IT?

YES → NO

2
- IGNITION "OFF," INSTALL SPARK TESTER (ST-125) J 26792 OR EQUIVALENT ON PLUG LEAD(S) WHICH DID NOT RESULT IN RPM DROP AT PLUG END AND CLIP TO GROUND.
- CONNECT PLUG END OF COMPANION CYLINDER PLUG WIRE TO GROUND AT ENGINE.
- OBSERVE TESTER WHILE CRANKING ENGINE.
- SPARK SHOULD JUMP TESTER GAP WHILE CRANKING ENGINE. DOES IT?

NO → YES

- CHECK THE RESISTANCE OF PLUG WIRE WHICH DID NOT FIRE THE SPARK TESTER.
- WIRE RESISTANCE SHOULD BE LESS THAN 30K OHMS EACH AND WIRES SHOULD NOT BE GROUNDED. ARE WIRES OK?

CHECK FOR;
- FAULTY, WORN OR CRACKED SPARK PLUG(S).
- PLUG FOULING DUE TO ENGINE MECHANICAL FAULT.

YES → NO

3
- REMOVE COIL THAT DID NOT FIRE TESTER FROM MODULE.
- INSPECT COIL, PLUG WIRES AND PLUG WIRE BOOTS. THEY SHOULD BE FREE OF CARBON TRACKING. ARE THEY?

REPLACE FAULTY WIRE(S) AND RETEST.

YES → NO

4
- CHECK SECONDARY COIL RESISTANCE. SHOULD BE 5-8K OHMS RESISTANCE.

REPLACE FAULTY COMPONENT.

YES → NO

5
- INSTALL A KNOWN GOOD COIL.
- SPARK SHOULD JUMP TESTER GAP AT PROBLEM CYLINDER WITH ENGINE IDLING. DID IT?

REPLACE COIL.

YES → NO

ORIGINAL IGNITION COIL IS FAULTY.

FAULTY IGNITION CONTROL MODULE.

86882066

Fig. 61 Ignition system diagnosis — 3.3L engine

CHART C-4-2

MISFIRE UNDER LOAD
3300 (VIN N) "N" CARLINE (MFI)

①
- IF ENGINE MISFIRES AT IDLE, REFER TO CHART C-4-1.
- IGNITION "OFF," INSTALL SPARK TESTER (ST-125) J 26792 OR EQUIVALENT TO #1 PLUG WIRE AT PLUG END AND CLIP TO GROUND.
- CONNECT PLUG END OF COMPANION CYLINDER (#4) PLUG WIRE TO GROUND.
- REMOVE 20 AMP FUEL PUMP/INJECTOR FUSE FROM FUSE BLOCK.
- IGNITION "ON."
- CRANK ENGINE, SPARK SHOULD JUMP TESTER GAP WHILE CRANKING.
- REPEAT ABOVE STEPS FOR EACH CYLINDER , RECORDING ANY CYLINDER(S) THAT DID NOT FIRE. RECONNECT EACH PLUG WIRE TO PLUG BEFORE MOVING ON TO NEXT CYLINDER.
- SPARK SHOULD JUMP TESTER GAP AT ALL PLUG WIRES WHILE CRANKING.

OK	CYLINDER PAIR (1-4, 2-5, OR 3-6) NOT FIRING.	SINGLE CYLINDER OR UNPAIRED CYLINDERS NOT FIRING.
• CHECK FOR FAULTY, CRACKED, FOULED OR WORN SPARK PLUG(S).	• CHECK FOR AN OPEN PLUG WIRE FOR CYLINDER PAIR THAT DID NOT FIRE (PLUG WIRES SHOULD MEASURE UNDER 30K Ω). IF OK, SWAP PROBLEM COIL WITH ONE FOR CYLINDER PAIR THAT DOES FIRE AND RETEST. IF PROBLEM FOLLOWS COIL, REPLACE COIL. IF NOT, REPLACE IGNITION CONTROL MODULE.	• CHECK FOR GROUNDED PLUG WIRE(S) FOR CYLINDER(S) THAT DID NOT FIRE AND REPLACE AS NECESSARY. IF OK, SWAP PROBLEM COIL WITH ONE THAT OPERATES PROPERLY. IF PROBLEM FOLLOWS COIL, REPLACE IT. IF NOT, REPLACE PLUG WIRE FOR CYLINDER(S) THAT DID NOT FIRE.

"*AFTER REPAIRS*," CONFIRM "CLOSED LOOP" OPERATION AND NO MIL (SERVICE ENGINE SOON).

86882067

Fig. 62 Ignition system diagnosis — 3.3L engine

COMPONENT REPLACEMENT

Ignition Coil

3.0L ENGINE

▶ See Figure 63

1. Disconnect the negative battery cable.
2. Tag and disconnect the spark plug wires from the coil.
3. Unfasten the 6 Torx® screws retaining the coil to the ignition module.

➡**Note or mark the lead colors for reassembly purposes.**

4. Tilt the coil assembly back, then detach the coil-to-module connectors and remove the coil assembly from the engine.

To install:

5. Attach the coil-to-module connectors, then install the coil assembly securing it with the retaining screws. Tighten the screws to 27 inch lbs. (3 Nm).
6. Connect the spark plug wires to the coil, as tagged during removal.
7. Connect the negative battery cable.

3.1L ENGINE

▶ See Figure 64

1. Disconnect the negative battery cable.
2. Tag and detach the spark plug wires.
3. Unfasten the two screws retaining each coil to the Ignition Control Module (ICM), then remove the coil(s) from the module.

To install:

4. Position the ignition coil(s) to the module, then install the retaining screws. Tighten the screws to 40 inch lbs. (4.5 Nm).
5. Attach the spark plug wires as tagged during removal.
6. Connect the negative battery cable.

3.3L ENGINE

▶ See Figure 65

1. Disconnect the negative battery cable.
2. Tag and disconnect the spark plug wires.

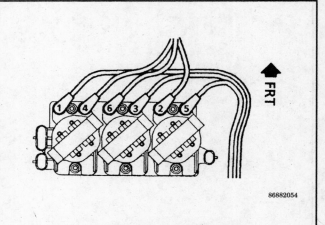

Fig. 64 View of the ignition coil assembly for the 3.1L engine; each coil is held to the module by two retaining screws

3. Remove the 2 retaining bolts securing each coil to the ignition module/Ignition Control Module (ICM).
4. Remove the coil(s) from the vehicle by lifting them off the module.

To install:

5. Fit the coil(s) to the ignition module/ICM.
6. Install the retaining bolts, then tighten them to 27 inch lbs. (3 Nm).
7. Attach the spark plug wires as tagged during removal.
8. Connect the negative battery cable.

C³I Module/Ignition Control Module (ICM)

EXCEPT 3.1L ENGINE

▶ See Figures 66 and 67

1. Disconnect the negative battery cable.
2. Disengage the 14-way connector at the ignition module.
3. Tag and disconnect the spark plug wires at the coil assembly.
4. Remove the nuts and washers retaining the module to the bracket.

Fig. 63 Tagging the spark plug wires before removing them will prevent confusion during installation

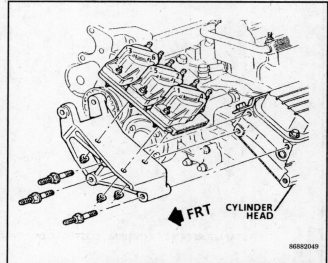

Fig. 65 View of the ignition coils — 3.3L engine shown

5. Remove the coil-to-module retaining bolts or screws.

6. Noting or marking the lead colors for reassembly, disengage the connectors between the coil and ignition module.

7. Remove the ignition module from the vehicle.

To install:

8. Fit the coils and connectors to the ignition module, then install the retaining bolts/screws. Tighten the retainers to 27 inch lbs. (3 Nm).

9. Fit the module assembly to the bracket, then install the nuts and washers.

10. Attach the spark plug wires, as tagged during removal.

11. Engage the 14-way connector to the module.

12. Connect the negative battery cable.

3.1L ENGINE

▶ See Figure 68

1. Disconnect the negative battery cable.

2. Disengage the 6, 3, and 2-way connector at the ICM.

3. Tag and detach the spark plug wires.

4. Unfasten the 6 screws securing the ignition coils to the ICM, then remove the coils from the module.

5. Remove the ignition control module.

To install:

6. Install the ICM, then position the coils to the module and fasten the 6 retaining screws. Tighten the screws to 40 inch lbs. (4.5 Nm).

7. Attach the spark plug wires as tagged during removal.

8. Engage the 2, 3, and 6-way connectors to the ICM.

9. Connect the negative battery cable.

Dual Crank Sensor/Crankshaft Position (CKP) Sensor

3.3L ENGINE

▶ See Figures 69, 70 and 71

1. Disconnect the negative battery cable.

2. Remove the serpentine belt from the crankshaft pulley (harmonic balancer).

3. Raise and safely support support the vehicle.

4. Remove the right front wheel and tire assembly, then remove the inner fender access cover.

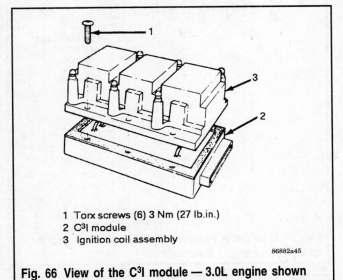

1 Torx screws (6) 3 Nm (27 lb.in.)
2 C³I module
3 Ignition coil assembly

86882a45

Fig. 66 View of the C³I module — 3.0L engine shown

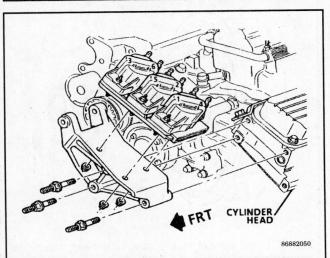

86882050

Fig. 67 View of the Ignition Control Module (ICM) — 3.3L engine shown

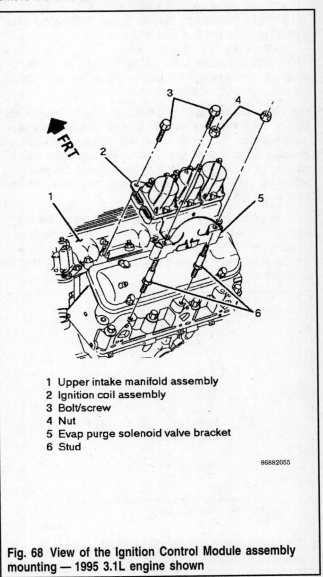

1 Upper intake manifold assembly
2 Ignition coil assembly
3 Bolt/screw
4 Nut
5 Evap purge solenoid valve bracket
6 Stud

86882055

Fig. 68 View of the Ignition Control Module assembly mounting — 1995 3.1L engine shown

5. Using a 28mm socket, disconnect the crankshaft harmonic balancer retaining bolt.

6. Using tool J-38197 or equivalent, remove the harmonic balancer.

7. Disengage the sensor electrical connector.

8. For vehicles through 1992, remove the sensor and pedestal from the engine block face, then separate the sensor from the pedestal.

9. For 1993-94 vehicles, remove the CKP sensor shield. Do NOT use a prybar. Remove the studs and sensor from the block face.

To install:

10. For vehicles through 1992:
   a. Loosely install the crankshaft sensor to the pedestal.
   b. Using tool J-37089 or equivalent, position the sensor with the pedestal attached, on the crankshaft.
   c. Install the pedestal-to-block retaining bolts. Tighten and torque to 14-28 ft. lbs. (20-40 Nm).
   d. Tighten the pedestal pinch bolt 26-44 inch lbs. (3-5 Nm), then remove tool J-37089 or equivalent.

11. For 1993-94 vehicles:
   a. Install the crankshaft position sensor.
   b. Install the studs to hold the sensor to the block face, then tighten to 6-9 ft. lbs. (8.5-12 Nm).
   c. Install the CKP sensor shield.

12. Place tool J-37089 or equivalent, on the harmonic balancer and turn. If any of the harmonic balancer vanes touch the tool, replace the balancer assembly.

➡ **A clearance of 0.025 in. (0.635mm) is required on either side of the interrupter ring. Be certain to obtain the correct clearance. Failure to do so will damage the sensor. A misadjusted sensor or bent interrupter ring could cause rubbing of the sensor, resulting in potential driveability problems, such as rough idle, poor performance, or a no start condition.**

13. Install the balancer on the crankshaft. Install the balancer retaining bolt. For vehicles through 1992, tighten the retaining bolt to 200-239 ft. lbs. (270-325 Nm). For 1993-94 vehicles, tighten the retaining bolt to 110 ft. lbs. (149 Nm) plus an additional 76° turn.

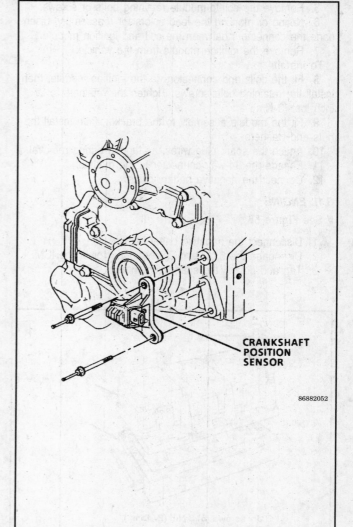

Fig. 70 Crankshaft Position (CKP) sensor/Dual crank sensor mounting — 3.3L engine

CRANKSHAFT POSITION SENSOR

86882052

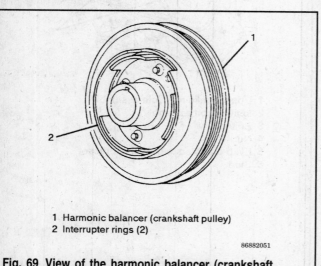

1 Harmonic balancer (crankshaft pulley)
2 Interrupter rings (2)

86882051

Fig. 69 View of the harmonic balancer (crankshaft pulley) and location of the interrupter rings

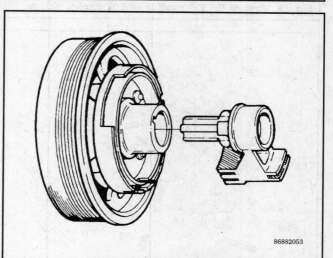

86882053

Fig. 71 Use a special tool to check the clearance of the harmonic balancer vanes

14. Install the inner fender shield.

15. Install the right front wheel and tire assembly. Tighten the wheel lug nuts to 100 ft. lbs. (140 Nm).

16. Carefully lower the vehicle.

17. Install the serpentine belt.

18. Connect the negative battery cable.

Combination Sensor

▶ See Figures 69, 72 and 73

➡The combination sensor is only found on the 3.0L engine.

1. Disconnect the negative battery cable.

2. Remove the right side lower engine compartment filler pane and the right lower wheel house-to-engine compartment bolt.

3. Detach the combination sensor harness connector.

4. Using a 28mm socket and pull handle, rotate the harmonic balancer until any window in the interrupter is aligned with the combination sensor.

5. Loosen the pinch bolt on the sensor pedestal until the sensor is free to slide in the pedestal.

6. While manipulating the sensor within the pedestal, carefully remove the sensor and pedestal as a unit.

To install:

7. If a new sensor is being installed, loosen the pinch bolt on the new sensor pedestal until the sensor is free to slide in the pedestal.

8. Make sure that the window in the interrupter is still properly positioned, then install the sensor and pedestal as a unit. Be sure that the interrupter ring is aligned with the proper slot.

9. Install the pedestal-to-engine mounting bolts, then tighten them to 22 ft. lbs. (30 Nm).

10. Fasten the lower wheel house-to-engine compartment bolt, then install the right lower filler panel.

11. Connect the negative battery cable.

INSPECTION

1. Using a 28mm socket, rotate the harmonic balancer and pull the handle until the interrupter ring(s) fill the sensor slot(s)

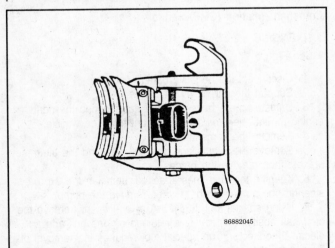

86882045

Fig. 72 View of the combination sensor which is used on the 3.0L engine

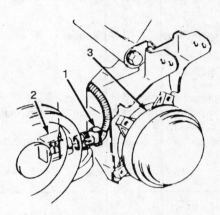

1 Crank sensor conn
2 Crank sensor
3 A/C compressor

86882047

Fig. 73 Combination (crank) sensor mounting — 1988 3.0L engine shown

and edge of the interrupter window is aligned with the edge of the deflector on the pedestal.

2. Insert adjustment tool J-36179 or equivalent into the gap between the sensor and the interrupter on each side of the interrupter ring. If the gauge will not slide past the sensor on either side of the interrupter ring, then sensor is out of adjustment or the interrupter ring is bent. This clearance should be checked at three positions around the outer interrupter ring, about 120° apart.

➡If the sensor is found to be out of adjustment, it should be removed and inspected for potential damage.

ADJUSTMENT

▶ See Figure 74

1. Loosen the pinch bolt on the sensor pedestal, then insert adjustment tool J-36179 or equivalent into the gap between the sensor and the interrupter on each side of the interrupter ring.

2. Make sure that the interrupter in sandwiched between blades of the adjustment tool and both blades are properly inserted into the sensor slot.

3. Tighten the sensor retaining pinch bolt to 30 inch lbs. (34 Nm) while keeping light pressure on the sensor against the gauge and interrupter ring. This clearance should be checked again, at three positions around the interrupter ring, about 120° apart. If the interrupter ring contacts the sensor at any point, the interrupter ring has excessive run-out and must be replaced.

24X Crankshaft Position (CKP) Sensor

3.1L ENGINE

▶ See Figure 75

1. Disconnect the negative battery cable.
2. Remove the serpentine belt from the crankshaft pulley (harmonic balancer).
3. Raise and safely support the vehicle using jackstands.

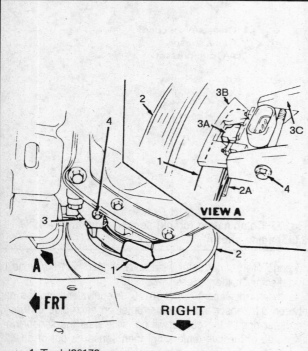

1 Tool J36179
2 Crankshaft harmonic balancer assy.
 A Interrupter ring
3 Crankshaft position sensor assy.
 A Sensor
 B Deflector
 C Pedestal
4 Pinch bolt

86882048

Fig. 74 Combination sensor adjustment — failure to maintain the correct clearance can damage the sensor

4. Unfasten the crankshaft harmonic balancer retaining bolt, then, using special tool J-24420-B or equivalent, remove the balancer.
5. Disengage the sensor electrical connector.
6. Unfasten the sensor retaining bolts, then remove the sensor from the vehicle.

To install:

7. Install the sensor, then secure using the retaining bolts. Tighten the bolts to 8 ft. lbs. (10 Nm).
8. Engage the sensor electrical connector.
9. Position the balancer on the crankshaft using special tool J-29113 or equivalent. Apply thread sealer 1052080 or equivalent to the retaining bolt threads, then install the bolt and tighten it to 110 ft. lbs. (150 Nm).
10. Carefully lower the vehicle.
11. Install the serpentine belt on the crankshaft pulley.
12. Connect the negative battery cable.

3X Crankshaft Position (CKP) Sensor

3.1L ENGINE

▶ See Figure 76

1. Disconnect the negative battery cable.
2. Remove the starter motor. For details regarding this procedure, please refer to Section 3 of this manual.
3. Detach the sensor harness connector at the module.
4. Unfasten the sensor-to-block retaining bolt, then remove the sensor from the engine.
5. Inspect the sensor O-ring for wear, cracks or leakage and replace if necessary.

To install:

6. Lubricate the sensor O-ring with clean engine oil, then position it on the sensor.
7. Place the sensor into the hole in the engine block, then install the sensor-to-block bolt. Tighten the retaining bolt to 71 inch lbs. (8 Nm).
8. Attach the sensor harness connector at the module.
9. Install the starter motor. Refer to Section 3 of this manual for details regarding this procedure.
10. Connect the negative battery cable.

Camshaft Position (CMP) Sensor

3.1L ENGINE

▶ See Figure 77

1. Disconnect the negative battery cable.
2. Support the engine by the oil pan.
3. Unfasten the 5 bolts and one nut securing the right engine mount, then remove the mount from the vehicle.
4. Remove the serpentine belt.
5. Remove the 3 nuts and one bolt retaining the alternator braces, then remove the braces.
6. Keeping the fluid lines attached, unfasten the 3 power steering pump retaining bolts, then remove the pump.
7. Using special tool J-38125-A or equivalent, remove the camshaft position sensor. It is retained by one bolt and an electrical connector. The special tool requires the removal of the plastic connector from the wires for clearance. Do NOT cut the pigtail!

To install:

8. Install the camshaft position sensor. Re-route the pigtail under the power steering pump and alternator brace. Make

sure to route the pigtail away from electronic components to avoid Electromagnetic Interference (EMI).

9. Install the power steering pump assembly, then the alternator braces.

10. Install the serpentine drive belt, then the right engine mount.

11. Connect the negative battery cable.

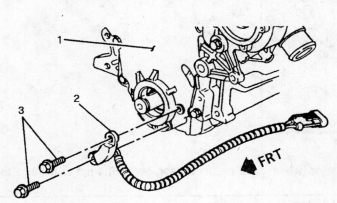

1 Front engine cover
2 24x crankshaft position sensor assembly
3 Bolt (2) torque 10 Nm (8 lb.ft.)

86882056

Fig. 75 View of the 24X CKP sensor; this sensor is used on the 3.1L engine only

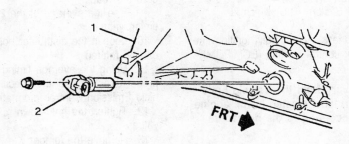

1 Engine block assembly
2 Crankshaft position (CKP) sensor

86882057

Fig. 76 View of the 3X CKP sensor location and mounting; this sensor is used on the 3.1L engine only

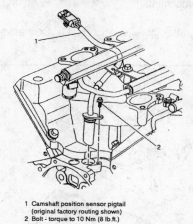

1 Camshaft position sensor pigtail
(original factory routing shown)
2 Bolt - torque to 10 Nm (8 lb.ft.)

86882058

Fig. 77 View of the factory routing of the CMP sensor. When installing the sensor, be careful not to damage the wire pigtail

IGNITION TIMING

Ignition timing can be set on the 2.0L (VIN M) engine and the 2.5L (VIN U) engine equipped with the HEI ignition system only. The 2.5L (VIN U) engine was only equipped with HEI in 1985-86. From 1987 on, the 2.5L (VIN U) engine was equipped with the Direct Ignition System (DIS) which is distributorless.

All other engines are distributorless. Accordingly, ignition timing is controlled by the computer control module (ECM/PCM) and is not adjustable.

➡If the following procedures vary from the Vehicle Emission Control Information (VECI) label located in the engine compartment, set the timing according to the procedure indicated on the VECI label.

Inspection and Adjustment

2.0L (VIN M) ENGINE

▶ **See Figure 78**

1. Start the engine, set the parking brake and run the engine until at normal operating temperature. Keep all lights and accessories off.
2. Stop the engine. Connect the red lead of a tachometer to the terminal of the coil labeled TACH and connect the black lead to a good ground.
3. If a magnetic timing unit is available, insert the probe into the receptacle near the timing scale. If a magnetic timing unit is not available, connect a conventional power timing light to the No. 1 cylinder spark plug wire.
4. Start the engine and allow it to idle.
5. With the parking brake safely set, place the automatic transaxle in D or leave the manual transaxle in Neutral.
6. Ground the ALDL connector under the dash by installing a jumper wire between the A and B terminals. The check engine light should begin flashing.

7. Aim the timing light at the timing scale or read the magnetic timing unit. Record the reading.
8. Repeat Steps 3-6 using the No. 4 spark plug wire. Record the reading.
9. Use the average of the 2 readings to derive an average timing value.
10. Loosen the distributor hold-down nuts so the distributor can be rotated.
11. Using the average timing value, turn the distributor in the proper direction until the specified timing (according to the Vehicle Emission Control Information label) is reached.
12. Tighten the hold-down nuts and recheck the timing values.
13. Remove the jumper wire from the ALDL connector. To clear the ECM memory, disconnect the ECM harness from the positive battery pigtail for 10 seconds with the key in the **OFF** position.

1985-86 2.5L (VIN U) ENGINE

1. Place the transaxle in P, set the parking brake and block the wheels.
2. Start the engine and allow it to reach normal operating temperature, then stop the engine.
3. Make sure the air conditioning is **OFF**.
4. Connect a jumper between terminals A and B of the ALDL connector.
5. Connect an inductive timing light to the coil wire. Start the engine and aim the timing light at the timing scale to check the ignition timing. Compare the reading to the specified setting on the VECI label.
6. If adjustment is necessary, loosen the distributor hold-down bolt and adjust the timing by rotating the distributor while observing the timing light.
7. When the timing is set to specification, tighten the hold-down bolt.
8. Disconnect the timing light.

9. Remove the jumper wire.

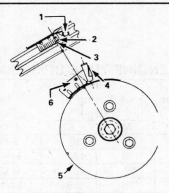

1 Magnetic timing probe hole
2 "O" stamp on pointer
3 Notch in pulley
4 Magnetic timing probe hole asm.
5 Pulley
6 Asm. mounted to front cover

86882059

Fig. 78 Common ignition timing marker with magnetic pickup

VALVE LASH

All engines in the vehicles covered by this manual are equipped with hydraulic valve lifters that do not require periodic valve lash adjustment. Adjustment to zero lash is maintained automatically by hydraulic pressure in the lifters.

IDLE SPEED AND MIXTURE ADJUSTMENTS

Idle speed and mixture for all engines covered by this manual are electronically controlled by the computerized fuel injection system. Adjustments are neither necessary nor possible. All threaded throttle stop adjusters are factory set and capped to discourage any tampering; in some areas, tampering is illegal. In most cases, proper diagnosis and parts replacement will straighten out any such problems.

GASOLINE ENGINE TUNE-UP SPECIFICATIONS

Year	Engine ID/VIN	Engine Displacement Liters (cc)	Spark Plugs Gap (in.)	Ignition Timing (deg.) MT	AT	Fuel Pump (psi)	Idle Speed (rpm) MT	AT	Valve Clearance In.	Ex.
1985	U	2.5 (2475)	0.060	8B	8B	9-13	2	2	HYD	HYD
	L	3.0 (2998)	0.040	15B	15B	34-44	2	2	HYD	HYD
1986	U	2.5 (2475)	0.060	8B	8B	9-13	2	2	HYD	HYD
	L	3.0 (2998)	0.040	15B	15B	34-44	2	2	HYD	HYD
1987	M	2.0 (1998)	0.035	8B	8B	41-47	2	2	HYD	HYD
	U	2.5 (2475)	0.060	1	1	9-13	2	2	HYD	HYD
	L	3.0 (2998)	0.040	15B	15B	41-47	2	2	HYD	HYD
1988	M	2.0 (1998)	0.035	8B	8B	25-30	2	2	HYD	HYD
	D	2.3 (2262)	0.035	1	1	34-44	2	2	HYD	HYD
	U	2.5 (2475)	0.060	1	1	9-13	2	2	HYD	HYD
	L	3.0 (2998)	0.040	15B	15B	41-47	2	2	HYD	HYD
1989	M	2.0 (1998)	0.035	8B	8B	25-30	2	2	HYD	HYD
	A	2.3 (2262)	0.035	1	1	41-47	2	2	HYD	HYD
	D	2.3 (2262)	0.035	1	1	41-47	2	2	HYD	HYD
	U	2.5 (2475)	0.060	1	1	9-13	2	2	HYD	HYD
	N	3.3 (3342)	0.045	1	1	41-47	2	2	HYD	HYD
1990	A	2.3 (2262)	0.035	1	1	41-47	2	2	HYD	HYD
	D	2.3 (2262)	0.035	1	1	41-47	2	2	HYD	HYD
	U	2.5 (2475)	0.060	1	1	9-13	2	2	HYD	HYD
	N	3.3 (3342)	0.060	1	1	41-47	2	2	HYD	HYD
1991	A	2.3 (2262)	0.035	1	1	41-47	700	700	HYD	HYD
	D	2.3 (2262)	0.035	1	1	41-47	700	700	HYD	HYD
	U	2.5 (2475)	0.060	1	1	9-13	800	700	HYD	HYD
	N	3.3 (3342)	0.060	1	1	41-47	2	2	HYD	HYD
1992	A	2.3 (2262)	0.035	1	1	34-44	2	2	HYD	HYD
	D	2.3 (2262)	0.035	1	1	34-44	2	2	HYD	HYD
	3	2.3 (2262)	0.035	1	1	34-44	2	2	HYD	HYD
	N	3.3 (3344)	0.060	-	1	41-47	-	2	HYD	HYD
1993	A	2.3 (2262)	0.035	1	1	41-47	700	700	HYD	HYD
	D	2.3 (2262)	0.035	1	1	41-47	700	700	HYD	HYD
	3	2.3 (2262)	0.035	1	1	41-47	700	700	HYD	HYD
	N	3.3 (3344)	0.060	1	1	41-47	2	2	HYD	HYD
1994	A	2.3 (2262)	0.035	1	1	41-47	700	700	HYD	HYD
	D	2.3 (2262)	0.035	1	1	41-47	700	700	HYD	HYD
	3	2.3 (2262)	0.035	1	1	41-47	700	700	HYD	HYD
	M	3.1 (3136)	0.045	-	1	41-47	2	2	HYD	HYD
1995	D	2.3 (2262)	0.035	1	1	41-47	700	700	HYD	HYD
	M	3.1 (3136)	0.045	-	1	41-47	2	2	HYD	HYD

NOTE: The Vehicle Emission Control Information label often reflects specification changes made during production. The label figures must be used if they differ from those in this chart.

B - Before top dead center

HYD - Hydraulic

1 Refer to the Vehicle Emission Control Information label

2 Idle speed is maintained by the computer control module (ECM/PCM). There is no recommended adjustment procedure.

86882500

BASIC ELECTRICITY
  BATTERY, STARTING AND
    CHARGING SYSTEMS 3-3
  UNDERSTANDING BASIC
    ELECTRICITY 3-2
BASIC MECHANICAL
TROUBLESHOOTING
  BACKFIRE — EXHAUST
    MANIFOLD 3-123
  BACKFIRE — INTAKE
    MANIFOLD 3-123
  ENGINE DETONATION
    (DIESELING) 3-123
  ENGINE SPEED OSCILLATES AT
    IDLE 3-122
  EXCESSIVE OIL LEAKAGE 3-123
  HEAVY OIL CONSUMPTION 3-123
  HIGH OIL PRESSURE 3-124
  KNOCKING CONNECTING
    RODS 3-124
  KNOCKING MAIN BEARINGS 3-124
  KNOCKING PISTONS AND
    RINGS 3-124
  KNOCKING VALVE TRAIN 3-124
  KNOCKING VALVES 3-124
  LOW OIL PRESSURE 3-124
  LOW POWER OUTPUT OF
    ENGINE 3-122
  NEGATIVE OIL PRESSURE 3-123
  POOR ACCELERATION 3-123
  POOR HIGH SPEED
    OPERATION 3-123
ENGINE ELECTRICAL
  ALTERNATOR 3-4
  REGULATOR 3-6
  SENDING UNITS AND
    SENSORS 3-10
  STARTER 3-7
ENGINE MECHANICAL
  BLOCK HEATER 3-108
  CAMSHAFT 3-93
  CRANKSHAFT AND MAIN
    BEARINGS 3-112
  CRANKSHAFT DAMPENER 3-80
  CYLINDER HEAD 3-61
  ENGINE 3-23
  ENGINE FAN 3-54
  ENGINE OVERHAUL TIPS 3-12
  EXHAUST MANIFOLD 3-47
  FLYWHEEL 3-115
  FREEZE PLUGS 3-107
  FRONT COVER OIL SEAL 3-85
  INTAKE MANIFOLD 3-40
  OIL PAN 3-72
  OIL PUMP 3-77
  PISTONS AND CONNECTING
    RODS 3-100
  RADIATOR 3-52
  REAR MAIN SEAL 3-108
  ROCKER ARM ASSEMBLY 3-36

ROCKER ARM/VALVE/CAMSHAFT
  COVER 3-30
THERMOSTAT 3-37
TIMING BELT AND TENSIONER 3-86
TIMING BELT FRONT COVER 3-80
TIMING CHAIN AND
  SPROCKETS 3-88
TIMING CHAIN FRONT COVER 3-80
TIMING GEAR FRONT COVER 3-85
TIMING GEARS 3-93
TIMING SPROCKETS 3-93
TURBOCHARGER 3-50
VALVE GUIDE SERVICE 3-70
VALVE LIFTERS 3-71
VALVE SPRINGS AND VALVE STEM
  SEALS 3-70
VALVES 3-69
WATER PUMP 3-57
EXHAUST SYSTEM
  CATALYTIC CONVERTER 3-120
  EXHAUST CROSSOVER PIPE 3-120
  FRONT EXHAUST PIPE WITH
    FLANGE/THREE WAY CATALYTIC
    CONVERTER 3-118
  FRONT EXHAUST PIPE WITHOUT
    FLANGE 3-119
  GENERAL INFORMATION 3-117
  INTERMEDIATE PIPE 3-120
  MUFFLER AND TAILPIPE 3-121
  SAFETY PRECAUTIONS 3-117
SPECIFICATIONS CHARTS
  ALTERNATOR SPECIFICATIONS 3-7
  CAMSHAFT SPECIFICATIONS 3-18
  CRANKSHAFT AND CONNECTING
    ROD SPECIFICATIONS 3-20
  ENGINE REBUILDING
    SPECIFICATIONS 3-124
  GENERAL ENGINE
    SPECIFICATIONS 3-15
  PISTON AND RING
    SPECIFICATIONS 3-22
  STARTER SPECIFICATIONS 3-10
  TORQUE SPECIFICATIONS 3-124
  VALVE SPECIFICATIONS 3-16

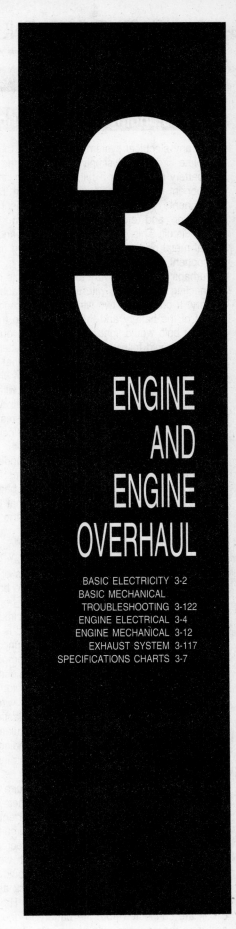

3

ENGINE AND ENGINE OVERHAUL

BASIC ELECTRICITY 3-2
BASIC MECHANICAL
TROUBLESHOOTING 3-122
ENGINE ELECTRICAL 3-4
ENGINE MECHANICAL 3-12
EXHAUST SYSTEM 3-117
SPECIFICATIONS CHARTS 3-7

BASIC ELECTRICITY

Understanding Basic Electricity

For any electrical system to operate, it must make a complete circuit. This simply means that the power flow from the battery must make a full circle. When an electrical component is operating, power flows from the battery to the components, passes through the component (load) causing it to function, and returns to the battery through the ground path of the circuit. This ground may be either another wire or the actual metal part of the vehicle depending upon how the component is designed.

Perhaps the easiest way to visualize this is to think of connecting a light bulb with two wires attached to it to the battery. If one of the two wires was attached to the negative (-) post of the battery and the other wire to the positive (+) post, the light bulb would light and the circuit would be complete. Electricity could follow a path from the battery to the bulb and back to the battery. It's not hard to see that with longer wires on our light bulb, it could be mounted anywhere on the vehicle. Further, one wire could be fitted with a switch so that the light could be turned on and off at will. Various other items could be added to our primitive circuit to make the light flash, become brighter or dimmer under certain conditions, or advise the user that it's burned out.

Some automotive components are grounded through their mounting points. The electrical current runs through the chassis of the vehicle and returns to the battery through the ground (-) cable; if you look, you'll see that the battery ground cable connects between the battery and the body of the vehicle.

Every complete circuit must include a "load" (something to use the electricity coming from the source). If you were to connect a wire between the two terminals of the battery (DON'T do this) without the light bulb, the battery would attempt to deliver its entire power supply from one pole to another almost instantly. This is a short circuit. The electricity is taking a short cut to get to ground and is not being used by any load in the circuit. This sudden and uncontrolled electrical flow can cause great damage to other components in the circuit and can develop a tremendous amount of heat. A short in an automotive wiring harness can develop sufficient heat to melt the insulation on all the surrounding wires and reduce a multiple wire cable to one sad lump of plastic and copper. Two common causes of shorts are broken insulation (thereby exposing the wire to contact with surrounding metal surfaces or other wires) or a failed switch (the pins inside the switch come out of place and touch each other).

Some electrical components which require a large amount of current to operate also have a relay in their circuit. Since these circuits carry a large amount of current (amperage or amps), the thickness of the wire in the circuit (wire gauge) is also greater. If this large wire were connected from the load to the control switch on the dash, the switch would have to carry the high amperage load and the dash would be twice as large to accommodate wiring harnesses as thick as your wrist. To prevent these problems, a relay is used. The large wires in the circuit are connected from the battery to one side of the relay and from the opposite side of the relay to the load. The relay is normally open, preventing current from passing through the circuit. An additional, smaller wire is connected from the relay to the control switch for the circuit. When the control switch is turned on, it grounds the smaller wire to the relay and completes its circuit. The main switch inside the relay closes, sending power to the component without routing the main power through the inside of the vehicle. Some common circuits which may use relays are the horn, headlights, starter and rear window defogger systems.

It is possible for larger surges of current to pass through the electrical system of your vehicle. If this surge of current were to reach the load in the circuit, it could burn it out or severely damage it. To prevent this, fuses, circuit breakers and/or fusible links are connected into the supply wires of the electrical system. These items are nothing more than a built-in weak spot in the system. It's much easier to go to a known location (the fusebox) to see why a circuit is inoperative than to dissect 15 feet of wiring under the dashboard, looking for what happened.

When an electrical current of excessive power passes through the fuse, the fuse blows and breaks the circuit, preventing the passage of current and protecting the components.

A circuit breaker is basically a self repairing fuse. It will open the circuit in the same fashion as a fuse, but when either the short is removed or the surge subsides, the circuit breaker resets itself and does not need replacement.

A fuse link (fusible link or main link) is a wire that acts as a fuse. One of these is normally connected between the starter relay and the main wiring harness under the hood. Since the starter is the highest electrical draw on the vehicle, an internal short during starting could direct about 130 amps into the wrong places. Consider the damage potential of introducing this current into a system whose wiring is rated at 15 amps and you'll understand the need for protection. Since this link is very early in the electrical path, it's the first place to look if nothing on the vehicle works, but the battery seems to be charged and is properly connected.

Electrical problems generally fall into one of three areas:

• The component that is not functioning is not receiving current.

• The component is receiving power but not using it or using it incorrectly (component failure).

• The component is improperly grounded.

The circuit can be can be checked with a test light and a jumper wire. The test light is a device that looks like a pointed screwdriver with a wire on one end and a bulb in its handle. A jumper wire is simply a piece of wire with alligator clips on each end. If a component is not working, you must follow a systematic plan to determine which of the three causes is the villain.

1. Turn on the switch that controls the item not working.

➡**Some items only work when the ignition switch is turned ON.**

2. Disconnect the power supply wire from the component.

3. Attach the ground wire on the test light to a good metal ground.

4. Touch the end probe of the test light to the power wire; if there is current in the wire, the light in the test light will come on. You have now established that current is getting to the component.

5. Turn the ignition or dash switch **OFF** and reconnect the wire to the component.

If the test light did not go on, then the problem is between the battery and the component. This includes all the switches, fuses, relays and the battery itself. The next place to look is the fusebox; check carefully either by eye or by using the test light across the fuse clips. The easiest way to check is to simply replace the fuse. If the fuse is blown, and upon replacement, immediately blows again, there is a short between the fuse and the component. This is generally (not always) a sign of an internal short in the component. Disconnect the power wire at the component again and replace the fuse; if the fuse holds, the component is the problem.

If all the fuses are good and the component is not receiving power, find the switch for the circuit. Bypass the switch with the jumper wire. This is done by connecting one end of the jumper to the power wire coming into the switch and the other end to the wire leaving the switch. If the component comes to life, the switch has failed.

✱✱✱WARNING

Never substitute the jumper for the component. The circuit needs the electrical load of the component. If you bypass it, you will cause a short circuit.

Checking the ground for any circuit can mean tracing wires to the body, cleaning connections or tightening mounting bolts for the component itself. If the jumper wire can be connected to the case of the component or the ground connector, you can ground the other end to a piece of clean, solid metal on the vehicle. Again, if the component starts working, you've found the problem.

A systematic search through the fuse, connectors, switches and the component itself will almost always yield an answer. Loose and/or corroded connectors, particularly in ground circuits, are becoming a larger problem in modern vehicles. The computers and on-board electronic (solid state) systems are highly sensitive to improper grounds and will change their function drastically if one occurs.

Remember that for any electrical circuit to work, ALL the connections must be clean and tight.

Battery, Starting and Charging Systems

BASIC OPERATING PRINCIPLES

Battery

The battery is the first link in the chain of mechanisms which work together to provide cranking of the automobile engine. In most modern vehicles, the battery is a lead/acid electrochemical device consisting of six 2v subsections (cells) connected in series so the unit is capable of producing approximately 12v of electrical pressure. Each subsection consists of a series of positive and negative plates held a short distance apart in a solution of sulfuric acid and water.

The two types of plates are of dissimilar metals. This causes a chemical reaction to be set up, and it is this reaction which produces current flow from the battery when its positive and negative terminals are connected to an electrical appliance such as a lamp or motor. The continued transfer of electrons would eventually convert the sulfuric acid to water, and make the two plates identical in chemical composition. As electrical energy is removed from the battery, its voltage output tends to drop. Thus, measuring battery voltage and battery electrolyte composition are two ways of checking the ability of the unit to supply power. During the starting of the engine, electrical energy is removed from the battery. However, if the charging circuit is in good condition and the operating conditions are normal, the power removed from the battery will be replaced by the alternator which will force electrons back through the battery, reversing the normal flow, and restoring the battery to its original chemical state.

Starting System

The battery and starting motor are linked by very heavy electrical cables designed to minimize resistance to the flow of current. Generally, the major power supply cable that leaves the battery goes directly to the starter, while other electrical system needs are supplied by a smaller cable. During starter operation, power flows from the battery to the starter and is grounded through the vehicle's frame and the battery's negative ground strap.

The starting motor is a specially designed, direct current electric motor capable of producing a great amount of power for its size. One thing that allows the motor to produce a great deal of power is its tremendous rotating speed. It drives the engine through a tiny pinion gear (attached to the starter's armature), which drives the very large flywheel ring gear at a greatly reduced speed. Another factor allowing it to produce so much power is that only intermittent operation is required of it. Thus, little allowance for air circulation is required, and the windings can be built into a very small space.

The starter solenoid is a magnetic device which employs the small current supplied by the start circuit of the ignition switch. This magnetic action moves a plunger which mechanically engages the starter and closes the heavy switch connecting it to the battery. The starting switch circuit consists of the starting switch contained within the ignition switch, a transaxle neutral safety switch or clutch pedal switch, and the wiring necessary to connect these in series with the starter solenoid or relay.

The pinion, a small gear, is mounted to a one way drive clutch. This clutch is splined to the starter armature shaft. When the ignition switch is moved to the **START** position, the solenoid plunger slides the pinion toward the flywheel ring gear via a collar and spring. If the teeth on the pinion and flywheel match properly, the pinion will engage the flywheel immediately. If the gear teeth butt one another, the spring will be compressed and will force the gears to mesh as soon as the starter turns far enough to allow them to do so. As the solenoid plunger reaches the end of its travel, it closes the contacts that connect the battery and starter and then the engine is cranked.

As soon as the engine starts, the flywheel ring gear begins turning fast enough to drive the pinion at an extremely high rate of speed. At this point, the one-way clutch begins allowing the pinion to spin faster than the starter shaft so that the starter will not operate at excessive speed. When the ignition switch is released from the starter position, the solenoid is de-energized, and a spring pulls the gear out of mesh interrupting the current flow to the starter.

Some starters employ a separate relay, mounted away from the starter, to switch the motor and solenoid current on and off. The relay replaces the solenoid electrical switch, but does not eliminate the need for a solenoid mounted on the starter used to mechanically engage the starter drive gears. The relay is used to reduce the amount of current the starting switch must carry.

Charging System

The automobile charging system provides electrical power for operation of the vehicle's ignition system, starting system and all the electrical accessories. The battery serves as an electrical surge or storage tank, storing (in chemical form) the energy originally produced by the engine driven generator. The system also provides a means of regulating output to protect the battery from being overcharged and to avoid excessive voltage to the accessories.

The storage battery is a chemical device incorporating parallel lead plates in a tank containing a sulfuric acid/water solution. Adjacent plates are slightly dissimilar, and the chemical reaction of the two dissimilar plates produces electrical energy when the battery is connected to a load such as the starter motor. The chemical reaction is reversible, so that when the generator is producing a voltage (electrical pressure) greater than that produced by the battery, electricity is forced into the battery, and the battery is returned to its fully charged state.

Newer automobiles use alternating current generators or alternators, because they are more efficient, can be rotated at higher speeds, and have fewer brush problems. In an alternator, the field rotates while all the current produced passes only through the stator winding. The brushes bear against continuous slip rings. This causes the current produced to periodically reverse the direction of its flow. Diodes (electrical one way valves) block the flow of current from traveling in the wrong direction. A series of diodes is wired together to permit the alternating flow of the stator to be rectified back to 12 volts DC for use by the vehicles's electrical system.

The voltage regulating function is performed by a regulator. The regulator is often built in to the alternator; this system is termed an integrated or internal regulator.

ENGINE ELECTRICAL

Alternator

All N-Body models use a Delco SI integral regulator alternator. Although several models of alternators are available with different idle and maximum outputs, their basic operating principles are the same.

A solid state regulator is mounted inside the alternator. All regulator components are mounted in a solid mold and this unit along with the brush holder assembly is attached to the slip ring end frame. The regulator voltage cannot be adjusted. If found to be defective, the regulator must be replaced as an assembly.

The alternator rotor bearings contain enough grease to eliminate the need for periodic lubrication. Two brushes carry current through two slip rings to the field coil mounted on the rotor. Stator windings are assembled inside a laminated core that forms part of the alternator frame. A rectifier bridge connected to the stator windings contains six diodes and electrically changes stator AC voltage to DC voltage, which is fed through the alternator output terminal. Alternator field current is supplied through a diode trio which is also connected to the stator windings. A capacitor or condenser mounted in the end frame protects the rectifier bridge and diode trio from high voltages and also suppresses radio noise. No periodic adjustment or maintenance of any kind is required on the entire alternator assembly.

ALTERNATOR PRECAUTIONS

To prevent damage to the on-board computer, alternator, and regulator, the following precautions must be taken when working with the electrical system.

• If the battery is removed for any reason, make sure it is reconnected with the correct polarity. Reversing the battery connections may result in damage to the one-way rectifiers. Always check the battery polarity visually. This is to be done before any connections are made to be sure that all of the connections correspond to the battery ground polarity.

• When utilizing a booster battery as a starting aid, always connect the positive-to-positive terminals and the negative terminals from the booster battery to a good engine ground on the vehicle being started.

• Never use a fast charger as a booster to start vehicles.

• Disconnect the battery cables when charging the battery with a fast charger; the charger has a tendency to force current through the diodes in the opposite direction for which they were designed. This burns out the diodes.

• Make sure the ignition switch if **OFF** when connecting or disconnecting any electrical component, especially on cars with any on-board computer system.

• Never attempt to polarize the alternator.

• Do not use test lights of more than 12 volts when checking diode continuity.

• Do not short across or ground any of the alternator terminals.

• The polarity of the battery, alternator and regulator must be matched and considered before making any electrical connections within the system.

• Never separate the alternator on an open circuit. Make sure all connections within the circuit are clean and tight.
• Disconnect the battery ground terminal when performing any service on electrical components.
• Disconnect the battery if arc welding is to be done on the vehicle.

REMOVAL & INSTALLATION

Except 2.3L (VIN A,D and 3)

▶ See Figures 1 and 2

1. Disconnect the negative battery cable.
2. Label and disengage the electrical connections from the alternator.
3. On the 2.5L engine, loosen the adjusting bolts and remove the alternator belt. If equipped with a serpentine belt, loosen the tensioner and turn it counterclockwise to remove the belt.
4. Unfasten the alternator mounting bolts, then detach the alternator air inlet connector (3.1L engine only) and remove the alternator from the engine.

   To install:
5. Fasten the alternator to the mounting bracket, using the retaining bolts, washers and nuts. Tighten the retainers to the specifications listed in the accompanying figures.
6. If equipped with the 3.1L engine, attach the alternator air inlet connector.
7. Install the serpentine or alternator belt, as applicable. For details, please refer to Section 1 of this manual.
8. Engage the alternator electrical connections. Tighten the "Bat" terminal nut to 65 inch lbs. (7.5 Nm).
9. Check the belt tension, then adjust if necessary.
10. Connect the negative battery cable, then check the alternator for proper operation.

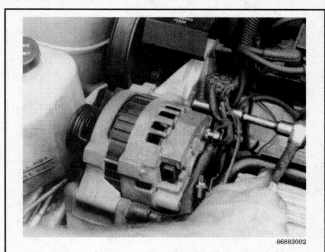

Fig. 2 Now unfasten the rear mounting bolts and remove the alternator from the vehicle

2.3L (VIN A,D and 3) Engines

1988-90 VEHICLES

▶ See Figures 3 and 4

1. Disconnect the negative battery cable.

➡ **To avoid personal injury when rotating the serpentine belt tensioner, use a tight fitting 13mm wrench that is at least 24 in. (61cm) long. Tool J 37059 can also be used to do this.**

2. Loosen the tensioner pulley bolt, turn the pulley counterclockwise and remove the serpentine belt from the alternator pulley.
3. Tag and disconnect the two vacuum lines at the front of the engine.
4. Remove the vacuum harness retaining bracket, then position the harness aside.
5. Detach the injector harness, alternator connector and the battery lead from the alternator. Position the harness out of the way.

Fig. 1 After removing the belt and detaching the electrical connections, unfasten the front retaining bolts

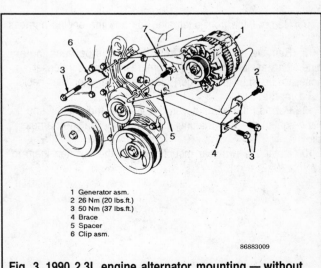

1 Generator asm.
2 26 Nm (20 lbs.ft.)
3 50 Nm (37 lbs.ft.)
4 Brace
5 Spacer
6 Clip asm.

Fig. 3 1990 2.3L engine alternator mounting — without A/C

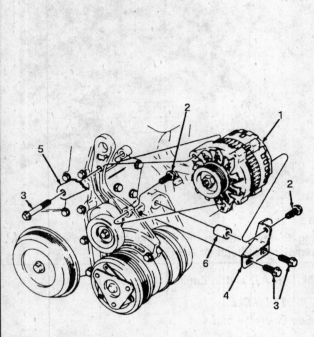

1 Generator asm.
2 26 Nm (20 lbs. in.)
3 50 Nm (37 lbs. in.)
4 Brace
5 Clip asm.
6 Spacer

86883010

Fig. 4 2.3L engine alternator mounting — with A/C

6. Unfasten and remove the two rear alternator mounting bolts.

7. Remove the front alternator bolt and the engine harness clip.

8. Remove the alternator from the vehicle between the engine lifting eyelet and the A/C compressor and condenser hose, to the right (passenger) side of the radiator filler neck.

To install:

9. Position the alternator in the vehicle, then install and hand-tighten the front mounting bolt and the engine harness clip.

10. Install the two rear mounting bolts, then tighten them to 19 ft. lbs. (26 Nm).

11. Tighten the front alternator bolt to 37 ft. lbs. (50 Nm).

12. Install the serpentine belt. For details, please refer to Section 1 of this manual.

13. Attach the injector harness wiring, alternator connector and the alternator battery lead.

14. Install the vacuum harness and the retaining clip.

15. Connect the two hoses to the vacuum harness as tagged during removal, then connect the negative battery cable.

1991-95 VEHICLES

1. Disconnect the negative battery cable at the battery.

➡To avoid personal injury when rotating the serpentine belt tensioner, use a tight fitting 13mm wrench that is at least 24 in. (61cm) long. Tool J 37059 can also be used to do this.

2. Loosen the tensioner pulley bolt, turn the pulley counterclockwise and remove the serpentine belt from the alternator pulley.

3. Label, then disconnect the oil/air separator hose and the vacuum harness at the front of the engine.

➡When removing and installing the lower alternator mounting bolts, shield the radiator core from possible tool damage to the fins and tubes.

4. Unfasten the lower alternator bolts located at the rear of the alternator. There is one 13mm head hex sized bolt and one 10mm hex head sized bolt.

5. Remove the upper alternator bolt.

6. Partially remove the alternator, then detach the alternator electrical connector and battery lead, and remove the alternator from the vehicle.

To install:

7. Position the alternator into the engine compartment, then attach the electrical connector and battery lead.

8. Install and hand-tighten the upper retaining bolt.

9. Install the two lower (rear) alternator mounting bolts. Tighten the bolts to 19 ft. lbs. (26 Nm)

10. Tighten the upper (front) alternator bolt to 37 ft. lbs. (50 Nm).

11. Install the serpentine belt. For details, please refer to Section 1 of this manual.

12. Connect the oil/air separator hose and the vacuum harness as tagged during removal.

13. Connect the negative battery cable at the battery.

Regulator

The alternator used in this vehicle has an internal regulator. The alternator is serviced as a complete unit and cannot be overhauled.

ALTERNATOR SPECIFICATIONS

Year	Engine Displacement Liters	Alternator	Model	Part No.	Output (Amps)
1985	2.5L	KG0/K99/K60	CS121/CS130/CS130	1101320/1101123/1101124	74/85/100
	3.0L	K99/K60	CS130	1101125/1101126	85/100
1986	2.5L	KG0/K99/K60	CS121/CS130/CS130	1101320/1101123/1101124	74/85/100
	3.0L	K99/K60	CS130	1101125/1101126	85/100
1987	2.0L	K99/K60	CS130	1101144/110145	85/100
	2.3L	K99/K60	CS130	1101277/1101278	85
	2.5L	KG0/K99/K60	CS121/CS130	1101320/1101123/1101124	74/85/100
	3.0L	K99/K60	CS130	1101125/1101126	85/100
1988	2.0L	K99/K60	CS130	1101144/110145	85/100
	2.3L	K99/K60	CS130	1101277/1101278	85
	2.5L	KG0/K99/K60	CS121/CS130	1101320/1101123/1101124	74/85/100
	3.0L	K99/K60	CS130	1101125/1101126	85/100
1989	2.0L	K99/K60	CS130	1101144/1101145	85/100
	2.3L	K99/K60	CS130	1101277/1101278	85/100
	2.5L	KG0/K60	CS121/CS130	1101320/1101124	74/100
	3.3L	KG0/K60	CS121/CS130	1101483/1101126	74/100
1990	2.3L	K99/K60	CS121/CS130	1101277/1101278	85/100
	2.5L	KG0	CS121	1101320	74
	3.3L	KG0	CS121	1101483	74
1991	2.3L	K99/K60	CS130CS130	1101277/1101278	85/100
	2.5L	KG0/K60	CS121/CS130	1101320/1101124	74/100
	3.3L	KG0	CS121	1101483	74
1992	2.3L	K60/K68	CS130	10479909/10479814	100/105
	3.3L	-	CS130	1101642	100
1993	2.3L	K60/K68	CS130	-	100/105
	3.3L	-	CS130	-	100
1994	2.3L	K60/K68	CS130	-	100/105
	3.1L	-	CS130	-	105
1995	2.3L	K60/K68	CS130	-	100/105
	3.1L	-	CS130	-	105

86883500

Starter

TESTING

▶ **See Figures 5 and 6**

1. Make the connections as shown in the accompanying figure.

2. Close the switch and compare the RPM, current and voltage readings with the following values, then use the test results as in the following steps:
- 2.0L engine: No load test @ 10 volts — 55-85 amps, RPM at drive pinion - 6,000-12,000 rpm
- 2.3L engine: No load test @ 10 volts — 50-75 amps, RPM at drive pinion - 6,000-12,000 rpm
- 2.5L engine: No load test @ 10 volts — 55-85 amps, RPM at drive pinion - 6,000-12,000 rpm
- 3.0L engine: No load test @ 10 volts — 52-76 amps, RPM at drive pinion - 6,000-12,000 rpm

- 3.1L engine: No load test @ 10 volts — 45-76 amps, RPM at drive pinion - 6,000-11,000 rpm
- 3.3L engine: No load test @ 10 volts — 45-74 amps, RPM at drive pinion - 8,600-12,900 rpm

3. Rated current draw and no-load speed indicates normal condition of the starter motor.

4. Low free speed and high current draw indicates:
- Too much friction. Tight, dirty, or worn bushings, bent armature shaft allowing armature to drag.
- Shorted armature. This can be further checked on a growler after disassembly.
- Grounded armature or fields. Check further after assembly.

5. Failure to operate with high current draw indicates:
- A direct ground in the terminal or fields.
- "Frozen" bearings.

6. Failure to operate with low or no current draw indicates:
- Open solenoid windings.
- Open field circuit. This can be checked after disassembly by inspecting internal connections and tracing the circuit with a test lamp.

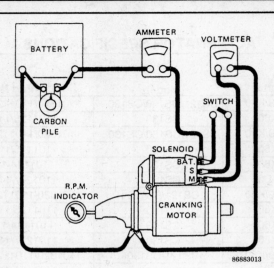

Fig. 5 Starter no load test connections

• Open armature coils. Inspect the commutator for badly burned bar after disassembly.

• Broken brush springs, worn brushes, high insulation between the commutator bars of other causes which would prevent good contact between the brushes and commutator.

7. Low no-load speed and low current draw indicates:

• High internal resistance due to poor connections, defective leads, dirty commutator and causes listed under Step 6.

8. High free speed and high current drain usually indicate shorted fields. If shorted fields are suspected, replace the field and frame assembly. Also check for shorted armature using a growler.

REMOVAL & INSTALLATION

▶ **See Figures 7, 8 and 9**

Except 2.3L Engine

1. Disconnect the negative battery cable.

2. Raise and safely support the vehicle. Disconnect the electrical wiring from the starter, if accessible.

3. If necessary for access, unfasten the three dust cover bolts, then pull the dust cover back to get to the front starter bolt. Remove the front starter bolt.

4. Remove the rear support bracket.

5. Pull the rear dust cover back to gain access to the rear starter bolt and remove the rear bolt.

6. Note the number and location of any shims.

7. Push the dust cover back into place (if removed), then lower the starter (disconnect any wiring if previously inaccessible) from the vehicle.

To install:

8. Position the starter in the vehicle, connect the wiring, then install the rear starter bolt.

9. Install the front starter bolt, then tighten both bolts to the specifications listed in the accompanying figures.

10. If removed, install the dust cover and the rear support bracket.

11. Connect the electrical wiring to the starter, if not already attached.

PROBLEM	CAUSE
1 HIGH PITCHED "WHINE" DURING CRANKING (BEFORE ENGINE FIRES) BUT ENGINE CRANKS AND FIRES OK.	DISTANCE TOO GREAT BETWEEN STARTER PINION AND FLYWHEEL.
2 HIGH PITCHED "WHINE" AFTER ENGINE FIRES, AS KEY IS BEING RELEASED. ENGINE CRANKS AND FIRES OK. THIS INTERMITTENT COMPLAINT IS OFTEN DIAGNOISED AS "STARTER HANG-IN" OR "SOLENOID WEAK".	DISTANCE TOO SMALL BETWEEN STARTER PINION AND FLYWHEEL. FLYWHEEL RUNOUT CONTRIBUTES TO THE INTERMITTENT NATURE.
3 A LOUD "WHOOP" AFTER THE ENGINE FIRES BUT WHILE THE STARTER IS STILL HELD ENGAGED. SOUNDS LIKE A SIREN IF THE ENGINE IS REVVED WHILE STARTER IS ENGAGED.	A NEW DRIVE ASSEMBLY WILL OFTEN CORRECT THIS PROBLEM.
4 A "RUMBLE", "GROWL" OR (IN SEVERE CASES) A "KNOCK" AS THE STARTER IS COASTING DOWN TO A STOP AFTER STARTING THE ENGINE.	MOST PROBABLE CAUSE IS AN UNBALANCED OR BENT STARTER ARMATURE. A NEW ARMATURE WILL OFTEN CORRECT THIS PROBLEM.

NOTE: IF THE STARTER HAS "NO SHIM" MOLDED INTO THE END FRAME HOUSING, SHIMMING THE STARTER MAY BE ATTEMPTED TO CORRECT A NOISE.

86883014

Fig. 6 Starter motor noise diagnosis

12. Carefully lower the vehicle, then connect the negative battery cable.

2.3L Engine

1988-89 (VIN D)

1. Disconnect the negative battery cable.
2. Remove the air cleaner to throttle body duct.
3. Label and detach the TPS, IAC and MAP sensor connectors.
4. Remove vacuum harness assembly and the MAP sensor vacuum hose from intake manifold, then position aside.
5. Unfasten the cooling fan shroud attaching bolts, then remove the shroud (including the MAP sensor).
6. Remove the coolant fan-to-upper radiator support bolt, then unfasten the remaining upper radiator support bolt and the upper radiator support.
7. Detach the connector from the cooling fan.

➡Because of the low clearance, be very careful not to damage the TPS lock tang with the fan bracket.

Fig. 7 Once the vehicle is raised and safely supported, you will be able to see the starter motor

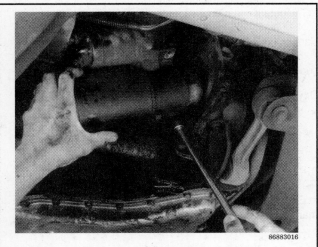

Fig. 8 After disconnecting the wiring, remove the starter mounting bolts

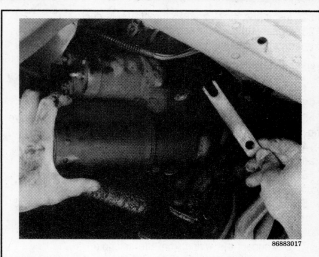

Fig. 9 When removing the starter, be sure to note the number and location of any shims

8. Lift the fan assembly out of the two lower insulators. Rotate the bracket so the two lower bracket legs point upward. Move the fan assembly toward the left (drivers) side until the fan blade overlaps the radiator tank-to-core seam about 1 in. (25mm). Lift the fan assembly from the engine compartment.
9. Remove the harness retaining clip from the engine mount bracket stud. Unfasten the starter mounting bolts.
10. Tilt the rear of starter towards the radiator, pull the starter out, then rotate solenoid towards the radiator to gain access to the electrical connections.

➡Be careful not to damage the crank sensor mounted directly to the rear of the starter. If it gets damaged, it must be replaced.

11. Detach the electrical connectors from the solenoid.
12. Move the starter toward the driver's side of the vehicle, then lift it from the vehicle.

To install:
13. Insert the starter between the throttle body and the air cleaner housing, then move it toward the right (passenger) side.
14. Attach the solenoid electrical connectors. Make sure to properly position the plastic guard over the stud and nut for the battery cable.
15. Rotate the starter into the proper position, install any shims that were removed and secure using the mounting bolt. Tighten the bolts to 74 ft. lbs. (100 Nm).
16. With the fan's bracket two lower legs facing upward, place the fan assembly between the throttle body and the radiator while overlapping the radiator tank-to-core seam with the fan blade by about 1 in. (25mm). Be careful not to damage the lock tang on the TPS.
17. Rotate the fan bracket, then place the two lower legs into the insulators.
18. Attach the electrical connector to the cooling fan.
19. Install the upper radiator support and the coolant fan should, then install the fan-to-upper radiator support mounting bolt.
20. Connect the MAP vacuum hose and the vacuum harness assembly to the intake manifold.
21. Attach the TPS, IAC and MAP sensor connectors.

22. Install the air cleaner to throttle body duct.
23. Connect the negative battery cable, then check for proper starter operation.

1990-95 (VIN D), 1989-94 (VIN A), 1992-94 (VIN 3)

1. Disconnect the negative battery cable.
2. If necessary for access, remove the air induction tube.
3. Detach the coolant fan electrical connector, then remove the fan assembly.
4. Remove the oil filter, if necessary for access to the starter.
5. For vehicles through 1990, remove the intake manifold brace.
6. Remove the mounting bolts; some engines may have 3 starter mounting bolts. Pull the starter out of the hole and move toward the front or passenger side of the vehicle.
7. Disconnect the wiring from the solenoid.
8. Remove the starter by lifting it between the intake manifold and the radiator.
   To install:
9. Lower the starter between the intake manifold and the radiator, then connect the wiring to the solenoid.
10. Rotate the starter into installation position and install the mounting bolts. For vehicles through 1994, tighten to 74 ft. lbs. (100 Nm). For 1995 vehicles, tighten the bolts to 32 ft. lbs. (43 Nm).
11. If equipped, install the intake manifold brace and oil filter, if removed.
12. Install the cooling fan assembly, then attach the electrical connector.
13. If removed, install the air induction tube.
14. Connect the negative battery cable and check the starter for proper operation.

SOLENOID REPLACEMENT

1. Disconnect the negative battery cable.
2. Detach the field strap/lead.
3. Remove the solenoid-to-drive housing retaining screws, then remove the the solenoid by using a twisting motion.
   To install:
4. Twist the solenoid into position, then secure using the retaining screws.
5. Attach the field strap/lead.
6. Connect the negative battery cable.

Sending Units and Sensors

REMOVAL & INSTALLATION

Engine Coolant Temperature (ECT) Sensor
▶ See Figure 10

➡**Be careful when handling the ECT sensor. Damage to the sensor can affect proper operation of the fuel injection system.**

1. Properly relieve cooling system pressure.
2. Make sure ignition is in the **OFF** position.

3. Disconnect the negative battery cable.
4. For the 1995 3.1L engine, remove the air intake duct.
5. Detach the ECT sensor electrical connector.
6. Carefully back out the sensor.
   To install:
7. Coat the threads of the sensor with sealer 9985253 or equivalent.

➡**For the 3.1L engine, and sure that the locking tab is in the correct position as shown in the accompanying figure.**

8. Install sensor into engine, then tighten it to 22 ft. lbs. (30 Nm) for all vehicles except the 1993 3.3L and the 3.1L engines. For the 1993 3.3L engine, tighten the sensor to 18 ft. lbs. (24 Nm). Tighten the sensor to 10 ft. lbs. (14 Nm) on the 3.1L engine. Do NOT strip the threads.
9. Attach the sensor electrical connector.
10. If removed, install the air intake duct.
11. Check coolant level and refill if necessary.
12. Connect the negative battery cable.

Intake Air Temperature (IAT) sensor
▶ See Figure 11

EXCEPT 3.1L ENGINE

1. Disconnect the negative battery cable.
2. Make sure ignition switch is in the **OFF** position.
3. Detach the electrical connector from the IAT sensor.
4. Carefully remove the sensor from the intake manifold.
   To install:
5. Coat the sensor threads with sealer 9985253 or equivalent, then install the IAT sensor in the intake manifold.
6. Tighten the sensor to 6 ft. lbs. (8 Nm)
7. Attach the electrical connector to the sensor.
8. Connect the negative battery cable.

3.1L ENGINE

➡**The IAT sensor on the 3.1L engine is located in the air cleaner.**

1. Disconnect the negative battery cable.
2. Detach the sensor electrical connector.
3. Unfasten the retaining clamp, then remove the sensors.
   To install:
4. Install the sensors, then secure using the retaining clamps.
5. Attach the sensor electrical connector, then connect the negative battery cable.

Oxygen (O2) Sensor
▶ See Figure 12

1. Disconnect the negative battery cable.
2. Make sure ignition is OFF.
3. Detach the sensor electrical connector.
4. Carefully remove sensor assembly.

➡**Excessive force may damage the threads in the intake manifold or exhaust pipe.**

   To install:
5. Coat the threads of the oxygen sensor with a suitable anti-seize compound.
6. Install the sensor and tighten to 30 ft. lbs. (41 Nm).

STARTER SPECIFICATIONS

Year	Engine Displacement (Liters)	Series	Type	No-Load Test		
				Amps	Volts	RPM
1985	2.5L	5MT	101	50-75	10	6,000-11,900
	3.0L	5MT	101	50-75	10	6,000-11,900
1986	2.5L	5MT	101	50-75	10	6,000-11,900
	3.0L	5MT	101	50-75	10	6,000-11,900
1987	2.0L	5MT	101	55-85	10	6,000-12,000
	2.3L	5MT	101	52-76	10	6,000-12,000
	2.5L	5MT	101	55-85	10	6,000-12,000
	3.0L	5MT	101	55-85	10	6,000-12,000
1988	2.0L	5MT	101	55-85	10	6,000-12,000
	2.3L	5MT	101	52-76	10	6,000-12,000
	2.5L	5MT	101	55-85	10	6,000-12,000
	3.0L	5MT	101	55-85	10	6,000-12,000
1989	2.0L	SD-200	-	55-85	10	6,000-12,000
	2.3L	SD-200	-	52-76	10	6,000-12,000
	2.5L	SD-200	-	55-85	10	6,000-12,000
	3.3L	SD-200	-	48-75	10	9,000-13,000
1990	2.3L	SD-200	-	52-76	10	6,000-12,000
	2.5L	SD-200	-	55-85	10	6,000-12,000
	3.3L	SD-250	-	45-74	10	8,600-12,900
1991	2.3L	SD-200	-	52-76	10	6,000-12,000
	2.5L	SD-200	-	55-85	10	6,000-12,000
	3.3L	SD-250	-	45-74	10	8,600-12,900
1992	2.3L	SD-200	-	52-76	10	6,000-12,000
	3.3L	SD-250	-	45-74	10	8,600-12,900
1993	2.3L	SD-200	-	50-75	10	6,000-12,000
	3.3L	SD-250	-	45-75	10	8,600-13,000
1994	2.3L	SD-200	-	50-75	10	6,000-12,000
	3.1L	SD-210	-	45-75	10	6,000-11,000
1995	2.3L	SD-200	-	50-75	10	6,000-12,000
	3.1L	SD-210	-	45-75	10	6,000-11,000

86883501

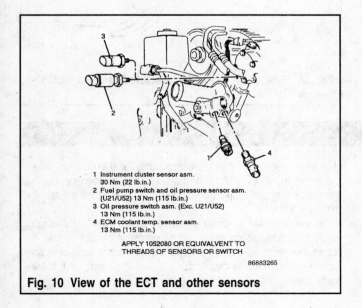

1 Instrument cluster sensor asm.
   30 Nm (22 lb.in.)
2 Fuel pump switch and oil pressure sensor asm.
   (U21/U52) 13 Nm (115 lb.in.)
3 Oil pressure switch asm. (Exc. U21/U52)
   13 Nm (115 lb.in.)
4 ECM coolant temp. sensor asm.
   13 Nm (115 lb.in.)

APPLY 1052080 OR EQUIVALVENT TO
THREADS OF SENSORS OR SWITCH

86883265

Fig. 10 View of the ECT and other sensors

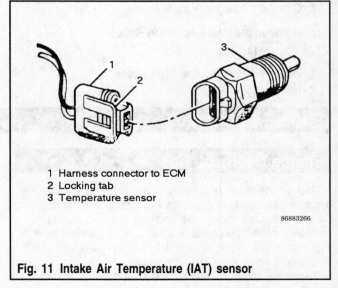

1 Harness connector to ECM
2 Locking tab
3 Temperature sensor

86883266

Fig. 11 Intake Air Temperature (IAT) sensor

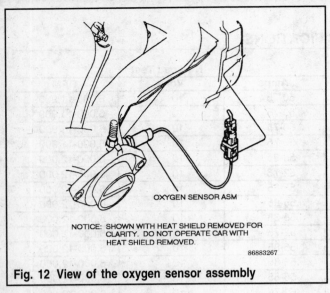

NOTICE: SHOWN WITH HEAT SHIELD REMOVED FOR CLARITY. DO NOT OPERATE CAR WITH HEAT SHIELD REMOVED.

OXYGEN SENSOR ASM

86883267

Fig. 12 View of the oxygen sensor assembly

7. Attach electrical connector.
8. Connect the negative battery cable.

Throttle Position Sensor (TPS)

▶ See Figure 13

1. Disconnect the negative battery cable.
2. Disconnect the throttle cable.
3. Remove the throttle body air duct.
4. Detach the throttle body vacuum line connector.
5. Disengage the sensor connector.
6. Remove the throttle cable bracket and the throttle body bolts.
7. Lift the throttle body until the TPS clears the fuel line.
8. Unfasten the TPS attaching screws and retainers, then remove the sensor.

To install:

9. Make sure the throttle valve is in the CLOSED position and install the sensor.
10. The remaining steps are the reversal of the removal procedure.
11. Connect the negative battery cable.

Manifold Absolute Pressure (MAP) Sensor

▶ See Figure 14

1. Disconnect the negative battery cable.
2. Unfasten the vacuum hose.

3. Detach the sensor electrical connector.
4. Unfasten the attaching screws, then remove the sensor.

To install:

5. Installation is the reverse of the removal procedure.
6. Connect the negative battery cable.

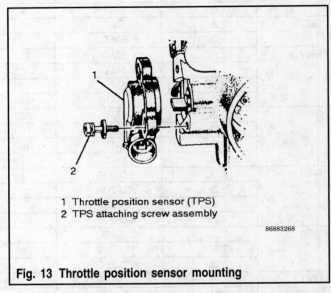

1 Throttle position sensor (TPS)
2 TPS attaching screw assembly

86883268

Fig. 13 Throttle position sensor mounting

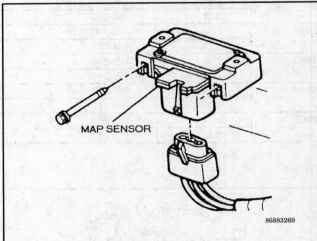

MAP SENSOR

86883269

Fig. 14 View of the Manifold Absolute Pressure (MAP) Sensor

ENGINE MECHANICAL

Engine Overhaul Tips

Most engine overhaul procedures are fairly standard. In addition to specific parts replacement procedures and specifications for your individual engine, this section is also a guide to acceptable rebuilding procedures. Examples of standard rebuilding practice are shown and should be used along with specific details concerning your particular engine.

Competent and accurate machine shop services will ensure maximum performance, reliability and engine life.

In most instances, it is more profitable for the do-it-yourself mechanic to remove, clean and inspect the component, buy the necessary parts and deliver these to a shop for actual machine work.

On the other hand, much of the rebuilding work (crankshaft, block, bearings, piston rods, and other components) is well within the scope of the do-it-yourself mechanic's tools and abilities. You will have to decide for yourself the depth of involvement you desire in an engine repair or rebuild.

TOOLS

The tools required for an engine overhaul or parts replacement will depend on the depth of your involvement. With few exceptions, they will be the tools found in a mechanic's basic tool kit (see Section 1 of this manual). More in-depth work will require some or all of the following:

• A dial indicator (reading in thousandths) mounted on a universal base
• Micrometers and telescoping gauges
• Jaw and screw-type pullers
• Scraper
• Valve spring compressor
• Ring groove cleaner
• Piston ring expander and compressor
• Ridge reamer
• Cylinder hone or glaze breaker
• Plastigage®
• Engine stand

The use of most of these tools is covered in this section. Many can be rented for a one-time use from a local parts jobber or tool supply house specializing in automotive work.

Occasionally, the use of special tools is called for. See the information on Special Tools and the Safety Notice in the front of this book before substituting another tool.

INSPECTION TECHNIQUES

Procedures and specifications are given in this section for inspecting, cleaning and assessing the wear limits of most major components. Other procedures such as Magnaflux® and Zyglo® can be used to locate material flaws and stress cracks. Magnaflux® is a magnetic process applicable only to ferrous materials. The Zyglo® process coats the material with a fluorescent dye penetrant and can be used on any material. Checking for suspected surface cracks can be more readily made using spot check dye. The dye is sprayed onto the suspected area, wiped off and the area sprayed with a developer. Cracks will show up brightly.

OVERHAUL TIPS

Aluminum has become extremely popular for use in engines, due to its low weight. Observe the following precautions when handling aluminum parts:

• Never hot tank aluminum part (the caustic hot tank solution will eat the aluminum).
• Remove all aluminum parts (identification tag, etc.) from engine parts prior to the tanking.

• Always coat threads lightly with engine oil or anti-seize compounds before installation, to prevent seizure.
• Never overtorque bolts or spark plugs, especially in aluminum threads.

When assembling the engine, any parts that will be exposed to frictional contact must be prelubed to provide lubrication at initial start-up. Any product specifically formulated for this purpose can be used, but engine oil is not recommended as a prelube in most cases.

When semi-permanent (locked, but removable) installation of bolts or nuts is desired, threads should be cleaned and coated with Loctite® or other similar, commercial non-hardening sealant.

REPAIRING DAMAGED THREADS

▶ **See Figures 15, 16, 17, 18 and 19**

Several methods of repairing damaged threads are available. Heli-Coil® (shown here), Keenserts® and Microdot® are among the most widely used. All involve basically the same principle — drilling out stripped threads, tapping the hole and installing a prewound insert — making welding, plugging and oversize fasteners unnecessary.

Two types of thread repair inserts are usually supplied: a standard type for most Inch Coarse, Inch Fine, Metric Coarse and Metric Fine thread sizes, and a spark plug type to fit most spark plug port sizes. Consult the individual manufacturer's catalog to determine exact applications. Typical thread repair kits will contain a selection of prewound threaded inserts, a tap (corresponding to the outside diameter threads of the insert) and an installation tool. Spark plug inserts usually differ because they require a tap equipped with pilot threads and a combined reamer/tap section. Most manufacturers also supply blister-packed thread repair inserts separately, in addition to a master kit containing a variety of taps and inserts plus installation tools.

Before effecting a repair to a threaded hole, remove any snapped, broken or damaged bolts or studs. Penetrating oil can be used to free frozen threads. The offending item can be removed with locking pliers or with a screw or stud extractor. After the hole is clear, the thread can be repaired, as shown in the series of accompanying illustrations and in the kit manufacturer's instructions.

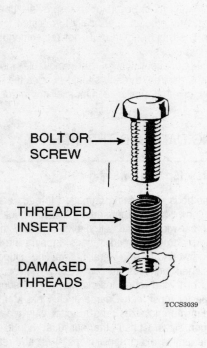

BOLT OR SCREW

THREADED INSERT

DAMAGED THREADS

TCCS3039

Fig. 15 Damaged bolt hole threads can be replaced with thread repair inserts

TANG

NOTCH

TCCS3040

Fig. 16 Standard thread repair insert (left), and spark plug thread insert

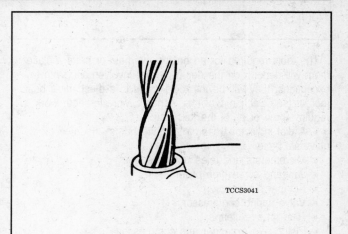

TCCS3041

Fig. 17 Drill out the damaged threads with the specified drill. Be sure to drill completely through the hole or to the bottom of a blind hole

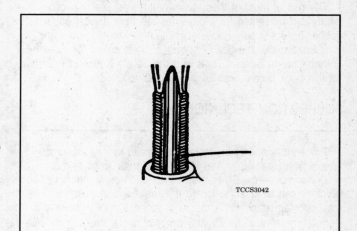

TCCS3042

Fig. 18 Using the kit, tap the hole in order to receive the thread insert. Keep the tap well oiled and back it out frequently to avoid clogging the threads

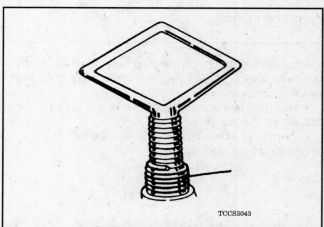

TCCS3043

Fig. 19 Screw the threaded insert onto the installer tool until the tang engages the slot. Thread the insert into the hole until it is 1/4-1/2 turn below the top surface, then remove the tool and break off the tang using a punch

GENERAL ENGINE SPECIFICATIONS

Year	Engine ID/VIN	Engine Displacement Liters (cc)	Fuel System Type	Net Horsepower @ rpm	Net Torque @ rpm (ft. lbs.)	Bore x Stroke (in.)	Compression Ratio	Oil Pressure @ rpm
1985	U	2.5 (2475)	TFI	92@4400	134@2800	4.00x3.00	9.0:1	37@2000
	L	3.0 (2998)	MFI	125@4900	150@2400	3.80x2.70	9.0:1	37@2400
1986	U	2.5 (2475)	TFI	92@4000	134@2800	4.00x3.00	9.0:1	37@2000
	L	3.0 (2998)	MFI	125@4900	150@2400	3.80x2.70	9.0:1	37@2400
1987	M	2.0 (1998)	MFI-Turbo	167@4500	175@4000	3.39x3.39	8.0:1	40@2000
	U	2.5 (2475)	TFI	92@4000	134@2800	4.00x3.00	9.0:1	37@2000
	L	3.0 (2998)	MFI	125@4900	150@2400	3.80x2.70	9.0:1	37@2400
1988	M	2.0 (1998)	MFI	167@4500	175@4000	3.40x3.40	8.0:1	45@2400
	U	2.5 (2475)	TFI	98@4400	135@2800	4.00x3.00	9.0:1	37@2000
	L	3.0 (2998)	MFI	125@4900	150@2400	3.80x2.70	9.0:1	37@2400
1989	M	2.0 (1998)	MFI-Turbo	165@5600	175@4000	3.39x3.39	8.0:1	65@2500
	A	2.3 (2262)	MFI	180@6200	180@5200	3.62x3.35	10.0:1	30@2000
	D	2.3 (2262)	MFI	150@5200	160@4000	3.62x3.35	9.5:1	30@2000
	U	2.5 (2475)	TFI	110@5200	135@3200	4.00x3.00	9.0:1	38@2000
	N	3.3 (3344)	MFI	160@5200	185@2000	3.70x3.16	9.0:1	60@1850
1990	A	2.3 (2262)	MFI	180@6200	160@5200	3.62x3.35	10.0:1	30@2000
	D	2.3 (2262)	MFI	160@6200	155@5200	3.62x3.35	9.5:1	30@2000
	U	2.5 (2475)	TFI	110@5200	135@3200	4.00x3.00	9.0:1	37@2000
	N	3.3 (3344)	MFI	160@5200	185@2000	3.70x3.16	9.0:1	60@1850
1991	A	2.3 (2262)	MFI	180@6200	160@5200	3.62x3.35	10.0:1	30@2000
	D	2.3 (2262)	MFI	160@6200	155@5200	3.62x3.35	9.5:1	30@2000
	U	2.5 (2475)	TFI	110@5200	135@3200	4.00x3.00	9.0:1	30@2000
	N	3.3 (3344)	MFI	160@5200	185@2000	3.70x3.16	9.0:1	60@1850
1992	A	2.3 (2262)	MFI	180@6200	160@5200	3.63x3.35	10.0:1	30@2000
	D	2.3 (2262)	MFI	160@6200	155@5200	3.63x3.35	9.5:1	30@2000
	3	2.3 (2262)	MFI	120@5200	140@3200	3.63x3.35	9.5:1	30@2000
	N	3.3 (3344)	MFI	160@5200	185@2000	3.70x3.16	9.0:1	60@1850
1993	3	2.3 (2262)	MFI	115@5200	140@3200	3.63x3.35	9.5:1	30@2000
	A	2.3 (2262)	MFI	175@6200	155@5200	3.63x3.35	10.0:1	30@2000
	D	2.3 (2262)	MFI	155@6000	150@4800	3.63x3.35	9.5:1	30@2000
	N	3.3 (3344)	MFI	160@5200	185@2000	3.70x3.16	9.0:1	60@1850
1994	3	2.3 (2262)	MFI	115@5200	140@3200	3.63x3.35	9.5:1	30@2000
	A	2.3 (2262)	MFI	175@6200	150@5200	3.63x3.35	10.0:1	30@2000
	D	2.3 (2262)	MFI	155@6000	150@6000	3.63x3.35	9.5:1	30@2000
	M	3.1 (3136)	MFI	155@5200	185@4000	3.51x3.31	9.5:1	15@1100
1995	D	2.3 (2262)	MFI	155@6000	150@6000	3.63x3.35	9.5:1	30@2000
	M	3.1 (3136)	MFI	155@5200	185@4000	3.51x3.31	9.5:1	15@1100

TFI - Throttle body fuel injection
MFI - Multiport fuel injection

86883502

VALVE SPECIFICATIONS

Year	Engine ID/VIN	Engine Displacement Liters (cc)	Seat Angle (deg.)	Face Angle (deg.)	Spring Test Pressure (lbs. @ in.)	Spring Installed Height (in.)	Stem-to-Guide Clearance (in.) Intake	Stem-to-Guide Clearance (in.) Exhaust	Stem Diameter (in.) Intake	Stem Diameter (in.) Exhaust
1985	U	2.5 (2475)	46	45	71-78@ 1.44	1.440	0.0010- 0.0027	0.0010- 0.0027	0.3130- 0.3140	0.3120- 0.3130
	L	3.0 (2998)	46	45	93@1.73	1.727	0.0015- 0.0035	0.0015- 0.0032	0.3401- 0.3412	0.3405- 0.3412
1986	U	2.5 (2475)	46	45	71-78@ 1.44	1.440	0.0010- 0.0027	0.0010- 0.0027	0.3130- 0.3140	0.3120- 0.3130
	L	3.0 (2998)	45	45	93@1.73	1.727	0.0015- 0.0035	0.0015- 0.0032	0.3401- 0.3412	0.3405- 0.3412
1987	M	2.0 (1998)	46	46	74-82@ 1.48	1.476	0.0006- 0.0017	0.0012- 0.0024	0.2753- 0.2747	0.2760- 0.2755
	U	2.5 (2475)	46	45	71-78@ 1.44	1.440	0.0010- 0.0027	0.0013- 0.0041	0.3130- 0.3140	0.3120- 0.3130
	L	3.0 (2998)	45	45	93@1.73	1.727	0.0015- 0.0035	0.0015- 0.0032	0.3412- 0.3401	0.3412- 0.3405
1988	M	2.0 (1998)	45	46	74-82@ 1.48	1.476	0.0006- 0.0017	0.0012- 0.0024	0.2753- 0.2747	0.2755- 0.2760
	D	2.3 (2262)	45	1	64-70@ 1.44	1.437	0.0009- 0.0027	0.0015- 0.0032	0.2751- 0.2744	0.2754- 0.2739
	U	2.5 (2475)	46	45	71-78@ 1.44	1.440	0.0010- 0.0026	0.0013- 0.0041	0.3130- 0.3140	0.3120- 0.3130
	L	3.0 (2998)	45	45	93@1.73	1.727	0.0015- 0.0035	0.0015- 0.0032	0.3412- 0.3401	0.3412- 0.3405
1989	M	2.0 (1998)	45	46	74-82@ 1.48	1.476	0.0006- 0.0017	0.0012- 0.0024	0.2753- 0.2747	0.2755- 0.2760
	A	2.3 (2262)	45	1	71-79@ 1.44	1.437	0.0010- 0.0027	0.0015- 0.0032	0.2751- 0.2745	0.2740- 0.2747
	D	2.3 (2262)	45	1	64-70@ 1.44	1.437	0.0010- 0.0027	0.0015- 0.0032	0.2751- 0.2745	0.2740- 0.2747
	U	2.5 (2475)	46	45	75@1.68	1.680	0.0010- 0.0026	0.0013- 0.0041	NA	NA
	N	3.3 (3344)	45	45	80@1.75	1.690- 1.720	0.0015- 0.0035	0.0015- 0.0035	NA	NA
1990	A	2.3 (2262)	45	1	71-79@ 1.4370	1.437	0.0010- 0.0027	0.0015- 0.0032	0.2751- 0.2745	0.2740- 0.2747
	D	2.3 (2262)	45	1	71-79@ 1.4370	1.437	0.0010- 0.0027	0.0015- 0.0032	0.2751- 0.2745	0.2740- 0.2747
	U	2.5 (2475)	46	45	75@1.68	1.680	0.0010- 0.0026	0.0013- 0.0041	NA	NA
	N	3.3 (3344)	45	45	80@1.75	1.690- 1.720	0.0015- 0.0035	0.0015- 0.0035	NA	NA
1991	A	2.3 (2262)	45	1	71-79@ 1.44	1.437	0.0010- 0.0027	0.0015- 0.0032	0.2751- 0.2745	0.2740- 0.2747
	D	2.3 (2262)	45	1	71-79@ 1.44	1.437	0.0010- 0.0027	0.0015- 0.0032	0.2751- 0.2745	0.2740- 0.2747
	U	2.5 (2475)	46	45	75@1.68	1.680	0.0010- 0.0026	0.0013- 0.0041	NA	NA
	N	3.3 (3344)	45	45	80@1.75	1.690- 1.720	0.0015- 0.0035	0.0015- 0.0035	NA	NA

86883503

VALVE SPECIFICATIONS

Year	Engine ID/VIN	Engine Displacement Liters (cc)	Seat Angle (deg.)	Face Angle (deg.)	Spring Test Pressure (lbs. @ in.)	Spring Installed Height (in.)	Stem-to-Guide Clearance (in.)		Stem Diameter (in.)	
							Intake	Exhaust	Intake	Exhaust
1992	3	2.3 (2262)	45	1	71-79@ 1.44	1.437	0.0010-0.0027	0.0015-0.0032	0.2751-0.2745	0.2740-0.2747
	A	2.3 (2262)	45	1	71-79@ 1.44	1.437	0.0010-0.0027	0.0015-0.0032	0.2751-0.2745	0.2740-0.2747
	D	2.3 (2262)	45	1	71-79@ 1.44	1.437	0.0010-0.0027	0.0015-0.0032	0.2751-0.2745	0.2740-0.2747
	N	3.3 (3344)	45	45	80@1.75	1.690-1.720	0.0015-0.0035	0.0015-0.0032	NA	NA
1993	3	2.3 (2262)	45	1	71-79@ 1.44	1.437	0.0010-0.0027	0.0015-0.0032	0.2751-0.2745	0.2740-0.2747
	A	2.3 (2262)	45	1	71-79@ 1.44	1.437	0.0010-0.0027	0.0015-0.0032	0.2751-0.2745	0.2740-0.2747
	D	2.3 (2262)	45	1	71-79@ 1.44	1.437	0.0010-0.0027	0.0015-0.0032	0.2751-0.2745	0.2740-0.2747
	N	3.3 (3344)	45	45	80@1.75	1.690-1.720	0.0015-0.0035	0.0015-0.0035	NA	NA
1994	3	2.3 (2262)	45	1	71-79@ 1.44	1.437	0.0010-0.0027	0.0015-0.0032	0.2751-0.2745	0.2740-0.2747
	A	2.3 (2262)	45	1	71-79@ 1.44	1.437	0.0010-0.0027	0.0015-0.0032	0.2751-0.2745	0.2740-0.2747
	D	2.3 (2262)	45	1	71-79@ 1.44	1.437	0.0010-0.0027	0.0015-0.0032	0.2751-0.2745	0.2740-0.2747
	M	3.1 (3136)	45	45	80@1.71	1.710	0.0010-0.0027	0.0010-0.0027	NA	NA
1995	D	2.3 (2262)	45	1	71-79@ 1.44	1.437	0.0010-0.0027	0.0015-0.0032	0.2751-0.2745	0.2740-0.2747
	M	3.1 (3136)	45	45	80@1.71	1.710	0.0010-0.0027	0.0010-0.0027	NA	NA

NA - Not Available

1 Intake: 44
Exhaust: 44.5

86883504

CAMSHAFT SPECIFICATIONS
All measurements given in inches.

Year	Engine ID/VIN	Engine Displacement Liters (cc)	Journal Diameter					Elevation		Bearing Clearance	Camshaft End Play
			1	2	3	4	5	In.	Ex.		
1985	U	2.5 (2475)	1.8690	1.8690	1.8690	1.8690	1.8690	0.3980	0.3980	0.0007-0.0027	0.0015-0.0050
	L	3.0 (2998)	1.7850-1.7860	1.7850-1.7860	1.7850-1.7860	1.7850-1.7860	NA	0.3580	0.3840	0.0005-0.0025	NA
1986	U	2.5 (2475)	1.8690	1.8690	1.8690	1.8690	1.8690	0.2320	0.2320	0.0007-0.0027	0.0015-0.0050
	L	3.0 (2998)	1.7850-1.7860	1.7850-1.7860	1.7850-1.7860	1.7850-1.7860	NA	0.3580	0.3840	0.0005-0.0025	NA
1987	M	2.0 (1998)	1.6714-1.6720	1.6810-1.6816	1.6911-1.6917	1.7009-1.7015	1.7108-1.7114	0.2409	0.2409	0.0008-0.0032	0.0016-0.0064
	U	2.5 (2475)	1.8690	1.8690	1.8690	1.8690	1.8690	0.2320	0.2320	0.0007-0.0027	0.0015-0.0050
	L	3.0 (2998)	1.7850-1.7860	1.7850-1.7860	1.7850-1.7860	1.7850-1.7860	NA	0.3580	0.3840	0.0005-0.0025	NA
1988	M	2.0 (1998)	1.6714-1.6720	1.6810-1.6816	1.6911-1.6917	1.7009-1.7015	1.7108-1.7114	0.2409	0.2409	0.0008-0.0032	0.0016-0.0064
	D	2.3 (2262)	1.3751-1.3760	1.3751-1.3760	1.3751-1.3760	1.3751-1.3760	1.3751-1.3760	0.3400	0.3500	0.0019-0.0043	0.0060-0.0140
	U	2.5 (2475)	1.8690	1.8690	1.8690	1.8690	1.8690	0.2320	0.2320	0.0007-0.0027	0.0015-0.0050
	L	3.0 (2998)	1.7850-1.7860	1.7850-1.7860	1.7850-1.7860	1.7850-1.7860	NA	0.3580	0.3840	0.0005-0.0025	NA
1989	M	2.0 (1998)	1.6714-1.6720	1.6810-1.6816	1.6911-1.6917	1.7009-1.7015	1.7108-1.7114	0.2409	0.2409	0.0008-0.0032	0.0016-0.0064
	A	2.3 (2262)	1.5728-1.5720	1.3751-1.3760	1.3751-1.3760	1.3751-1.3760	1.3751-1.3760	0.4100	0.4100	0.0019-0.0043	0.0060-0.0140
	D	2.3 (2262)	1.3751-1.3760	1.3751-1.3760	1.3751-1.3760	1.3751-1.3760	1.3751-1.3760	0.3400	0.3500	0.0019-0.0043	0.0060-0.0140
	U	2.5 (2475)	1.8690	1.8690	1.8690	1.8690	1.8690	0.2320	0.2320	0.0007-0.0027	0.0015-0.0060
	N	3.3 (3344)	1.7850-1.7860	1.7850-1.7860	1.7850-1.7860	1.7850-1.7860	NA	0.2500	0.2550	0.0005-0.0035	NA
1990	A	2.3 (2262)	1.5728-1.5720	1.3751-1.3760	1.3751-1.3760	1.3751-1.3760	1.3751-1.3760	0.4100	0.4100	0.0019-0.0043	0.0060-0.0140
	D	2.3 (2262)	1.5728-1.5720	1.3751-1.3760	1.3751-1.3760	1.3751-1.3760	1.3751-1.3760	0.3750	0.3750	0.0019-0.0043	0.0060-0.0140
	U	2.5 (2475)	1.8690	1.8690	1.8690	1.8690	1.8690	0.2480	0.2480	0.0007-0.0027	0.0015-0.0060
	N	3.3 (3344)	1.7850-1.7860	1.7850-1.7860	1.7850-1.7860	1.7850-1.7860	NA	0.2500	0.2550	0.0005-0.0035	NA
1991	A	2.3 (2262)	1.5728-1.5720	1.3751-1.3760	1.3751-1.3760	1.3751-1.3760	1.3751-1.3760	0.4100	0.4100	0.0019-0.0043	0.0060-0.0140
	D	2.3 (2262)	1.5728-1.5720	1.3751-1.3760	1.3751-1.3760	1.3751-1.3760	1.3751-1.3760	0.3750	0.3750	0.0019-0.0043	0.0060-0.0140
	U	2.5 (2475)	1.8690	1.8690	1.8690	1.8690	1.8690	0.2480	0.2480	0.0007-0.0027	0.0015-0.0060
	N	3.3 (3344)	1.7850-1.7860	1.7850-1.7860	1.7850-1.7860	1.7850-1.7860	NA	0.2500	0.2550	0.0005-0.0035	NA

86883505

CAMSHAFT SPECIFICATIONS

All measurements given in inches.

Year	Engine ID/VIN	Engine Displacement Liters (cc)	Journal Diameter					Elevation		Bearing Clearance	Camshaft End Play
			1	2	3	4	5	In.	Ex.		
1992	3	2.3 (2262)	1.5728-1.5720	1.3751-1.3760	1.3751-1.3760	1.3751-1.3760	1.3751-1.3760	0.4100	0.4100	0.0019-0.0043	0.0060-0.0140
	A	2.3 (2262)	1.5728-1.5720	1.3751-1.3760	1.3751-1.3760	1.3751-1.3760	1.3751-1.3760	0.4100	0.4100	0.0019-0.0043	0.0060-0.0140
	D	2.3 (2262)	1.5728-1.5720	1.3751-1.3760	1.3751-1.3760	1.3751-1.3760	1.3751-1.3760	0.3750	0.3750	0.0019-0.0043	0.0060-0.0140
	N	3.3 (3344)	1.7850-1.7860	1.7850-1.7860	1.7850-1.7860	1.7850-1.7860	NA	0.2500	0.2550	0.0005-0.0035	NA
1993	3	2.3 (2262)	1.5720-1.5728	1.3751-1.3760	1.3751-1.3760	1.3751-1.3760	1.3751-1.3760	0.4100	0.4100	0.0019-0.0043	0.0060-0.0140
	A	2.3 (2262)	1.5720-1.5728	1.3751-1.3760	1.3751-1.3760	1.3751-1.3760	1.3751-1.3760	0.4100	0.4100	0.0019-0.0043	0.0060-0.0140
	D	2.3 (2262)	1.5720-1.5728	1.3751-1.3760	1.3751-1.3760	1.3751-1.3760	1.3751-1.3760	0.3750	0.3750	0.0019-0.0043	0.0060-0.0140
	N	3.3 (3344)	1.7850-1.7860	1.7850-1.7860	1.7850-1.7860	1.7850-1.7860	NA	0.2500	0.2550	0.0005-0.0035	NA
1994	3	2.3 (2262)	1.5720-1.5728	1.3751-1.3760	1.3751-1.3760	1.3751-1.3760	1.3751-1.3760	0.4100	0.4100	0.0019-0.0043	0.0060-0.0140
	A	2.3 (2262)	1.5720-1.5728	1.3751-1.3760	1.3751-1.3760	1.3751-1.3760	1.3751-1.3760	0.4100	0.4100	0.0019-0.0043	0.0060-0.0140
	D	2.3 (2262)	1.5720-1.5728	1.3751-1.3760	1.3751-1.3760	1.3751-1.3760	1.3751-1.3760	0.4100	0.4100	0.0019-0.0043	0.0060-0.0140
	M	3.1 (3136)	1.8680-1.8690	1.8680-1.8690	1.8680-1.8690	1.8680-1.8690	NA	0.2727	0.2727	0.0010-0.0040	NA
1995	D	2.3 (2262)	1.5720-1.5728	1.3751-1.3760	1.3751-1.3760	1.3751-1.3760	1.3751-1.3760	0.4100	0.4100	0.0019-0.0043	0.0060-0.0140
	M	3.1 (3136)	1.8860-1.8690	1.8860-1.8690	1.8860-1.8690	1.8860-1.8690	NA	0.2727	0.2727	0.0010-0.0040	NA

NA - Not Available

86883506

CRANKSHAFT AND CONNECTING ROD SPECIFICATIONS

All measurements are given in inches.

Year	Engine ID/VIN	Engine Displacement Liters (cc)	Crankshaft Main Brg. Journal Dia.	Crankshaft Main Brg. Oil Clearance	Crankshaft Shaft End-play	Thrust on No.	Connecting Rod Journal Diameter	Connecting Rod Oil Clearance	Connecting Rod Side Clearance
1985	U	2.5 (2475)	2.2295-2.3005	0.0005-0.0022	0.0035-0.0085	5	1.9995-2.0005	0.0005-0.0026	0.0060-0.0220
	L	3.0 (2998)	2.4995	0.0003-0.0018	0.0030-0.0150	2	2.4870	0.0005-0.0026	0.0030-0.0150
1986	U	2.5 (2475)	2.2295-2.3005	0.0005-0.0022	0.0035-0.0085	5	1.9995-2.0005	0.0005-0.0026	0.0060-0.0220
	L	3.0 (2998)	2.4995	0.0003-0.0018	0.0030-0.0150	2	2.4870	0.0005-0.0026	0.0030-0.0150
1987	M	2.0 (1998)	①	0.0006-0.0016	0.0003-0.0012	3	1.9278-1.9286	0.0007-0.0024	0.0027-0.0095
	U	2.5 (2475)	2.2295-2.3005	0.0005-0.0022	0.0035-0.0085	5	1.9995-2.0005	0.0005-0.0026	0.0060-0.0220
	L	3.0 (2998)	2.4995	0.0003-0.0018	0.0030-0.0150	2	2.4870	0.0005-0.0026	0.0030-0.0150
1988	M	2.0 (1998)	①	0.0006-0.0016	0.0003-0.0012	3	1.9278-1.9286	0.0007-0.0024	0.0027-0.0095
	D	2.3 (2262)	2.0470-2.0480	0.0005-0.0023	0.0034-0.0095	3	1.8887-1.8897	0.0005-0.0020	0.0059-0.0177
	U	2.5 (2475)	2.3000	0.0005-0.0022	0.0035-0.0085	5	1.9995-2.0005	0.0005-0.0026	0.0060-0.0220
	L	3.0 (2998)	2.4995	0.0003-0.0018	0.0030-0.0150	2	2.4870	0.0005-0.0026	0.0030-0.0150
1989	M	2.0 (1998)	①	0.0006-0.0016	0.0003-0.0012	3	1.9279-1.9287	0.0007-0.0024	0.0027-0.0095
	A	2.3 (2262)	2.0470-2.4080	0.0005-0.0023	0.0034-0.0095	3	1.8887-1.8897	0.0005-0.0020	0.0059-0.0177
	D	2.3 (2262)	2.0470-2.4080	0.0005-0.0023	0.0034-0.0095	3	1.8887-1.8897	0.0005-0.0020	0.0059-0.0177
	U	2.5 (2475)	2.3000	0.0005-0.0022	0.0035-0.0085	5	1.9995-2.0005	0.0005-0.0026	0.0060-0.0220
	N	3.3 (3344)	2.4988-2.4998	0.0008-0.0022	0.0030-0.0110	3	2.2487-2.2499	0.0008-0.0022	0.0030-0.0150
1990	A	2.3 (2262)	2.0470-2.0480	0.0005-0.0023	0.0034-0.0095	3	1.8887-1.8897	0.0005-0.0020	0.0059-0.0177
	D	2.3 (2262)	2.0470-2.0480	0.0005-0.0023	0.0034-0.0095	3	1.8887-1.8897	0.0005-0.0020	0.0059-0.0177
	U	2.5 (2475)	2.3000	0.0005-0.0020	0.0051-0.0110	3	2.0000	0.0005-0.0030	0.0060-0.0240
	N	3.3 (3344)	2.4988-2.4998	0.0008-0.0022	0.0030-0.0110	3	2.2487-2.2499	0.0008-0.0022	0.0030-0.0150
1991	A	2.3 (2262)	2.0470-2.0480	0.0005-0.0023	0.0034-0.0095	3	1.8887-1.8897	0.0005-0.0020	0.0059-0.0177
	D	2..3 (2262)	2.0470-2.0480	0.0005-0.0023	0.0034-0.0095	3	1.8887-1.8897	0.0005-0.0020	0.0059-0.0177
	U	2.5 (2475)	2.3000	0.0005-0.0022	0.0059-0.0110	3	2.0000	0.0005-0.0030	0.0060-0.0240
	N	3.3 (3344)	2.4988-2.4998	0.0008-0.0022	0.0030-0.0110	3	2.2487-2.2499	0.0008-0.0022	0.0030-0.0150

86883507

CRANKSHAFT AND CONNECTING ROD SPECIFICATIONS

All measurements are given in inches.

Year	Engine ID/VIN	Engine Displacement Liters (cc)	Crankshaft				Connecting Rod		
			Main Brg. Journal Dia.	Main Brg. Oil Clearance	Shaft End-play	Thrust on No.	Journal Diameter	Oil Clearance	Side Clearance
1992	3	2.3 (2262)	2.0470-2.0480	0.0005-0.0023	0.0034-0.0095	3	1.8887-1.8897	0.0005-0.0020	0.0059-0.0177
	A	2.3 (2262)	2.0470-2.0480	0.0005-0.0023	0.0034-0.0095	3	1.8887-1.8897	0.0005-0.0020	0.0059-0.0177
	D	2.3 (2262)	2.0470-2.0480	0.0005-0.0023	0.0034-0.0095	3	1.8887-1.8897	0.0005-0.0020	0.0059-0.0177
	N	3.3 (3344)	2.4988-2.4998	0.0018-0.0030	0.0030-0.0110	3	2.2487-2.2499	0.0003-0.0026	0.0030-0.0150
1993	3	2.3 (2262)	2.0470-2.0480	0.0005-0.0023	0.0034-0.0095	3	1.8887-1.8897	0.0005-0.0020	0.0059-0.0177
	A	2.3 (2262)	2.0470-2.0480	0.0005-0.0023	0.0034-0.0095	3	1.8887-1.8897	0.0005-0.0020	0.0059-0.0177
	D	2.3 (2262)	2.0470-2.0480	0.0005-0.0023	0.0034-0.0095	3	1.8887-1.8897	0.0005-0.0020	0.0059-0.0177
	N	3.3 (3344)	2.4988-2.4998	0.0008-0.0022	0.0030-0.0110	3	2.2487-2.2499	0.0008-0.0022	0.0030-0.0150
1994	3	2.3 (2262)	2.0470-2.0480	0.0005-0.0023	0.0034-0.0095	3	1.8887-1.8897	0.0005-0.0020	0.0059-0.0177
	A	2.3 (2262)	2.0470-2.0480	0.0005-0.0023	0.0034-0.0095	3	1.8887-1.8897	0.0005-0.0020	0.0059-0.0177
	D	2.3 (2262)	2.0470-2.0480	0.0005-0.0023	0.0034-0.0095	3	1.8887-1.8897	0.0005-0.0020	0.0059-0.0177
	M	3.1 (3136)	2.6473-2.6483	0.0012-0.0030	0.0024-0.0083	3	1.9987-1.9994	0.0011-0.0037	0.0071-0.0173
1995	D	2.3 (2262)	2.0470-2.0480	0.0005-0.0023	0.0034-0.0095	3	1.8887-1.8897	0.0005-0.0020	0.0059-0.0177
	M	3.1 (3136)	2.6473-2.6483	0.0012-0.0030	0.0024-0.0083	3	1.9987-1.9994	0.0011-0.0037	0.0071-0.0173

1   Brown: 2.2830-2.2833
Green: 2.2827-2.2830

86883508

PISTON AND RING SPECIFICATIONS

All measurements are given in inches.

Year	Engine ID/VIN	Engine Displacement Liters (cc)	Piston Clearance	Ring Gap			Ring Side Clearance		
				Top Compression	Bottom Compression	Oil Control	Top Compression	Bottom Compression	Oil Control
1985	U	2.5 (2475)	0.0014-0.0022	0.0100-0.0200	0.0100-0.0200	0.0200-0.0600	0.0020-0.0030	0.0010-0.0030	0.0150-0.0550
	L	3.0 (2998)	0.0010-0.0020	0.0130-0.0230	0.0130-0.0230	0.0150-0.0350	0.0030-0.0050	0.0030-0.0050	0.0035
1986	U	2.5 (2475)	0.0014-0.0022	0.0100-0.0200	0.0100-0.0200	0.0200-0.0600	0.0020-0.0030	0.0010-0.0030	0.0150-0.0550
	L	3.0 (2998)	0.0010-0.0020	0.0130-0.0230	0.0130-0.0230	0.0150-0.0350	0.0030-0.0050	0.0030-0.0050	0.0035
1987	M	2.0 (1998)	0.0004-0.0012	0.0098-0.0177	0.0118-0.0197	NA	0.0024-0.0036	0.0019-0.0032	NA
	U	2.5 (2475)	0.0014-0.0022	0.0100-0.0200	0.0100-0.0200	0.0200-0.0600	0.0020-0.0030	0.0010-0.0030	0.0150-0.0550
	L	3.0 (2998)	0.0010-0.0020	0.0130-0.0230	0.0130-0.0230	0.0150-0.0350	0.0030-0.0050	0.0030-0.0050	0.0035
1988	M	2.0 (1998)	0.0012-0.0020	0.0098-0.0177	0.0118-0.0197	NA	0.0024-0.0036	0.0019-0.0032	NA
	D	2.3 (2262)	0.0007-0.0020	0.0160-0.0250	0.0160-0.0250	0.0160-0.0550	0.0020-0.0035	0.0016-0.0031	NA
	U	2.5 (2475)	0.0014-0.0022	0.0100-0.0200	0.0100-0.0200	0.0200-0.0600	0.0020-0.0030	0.0010-0.0030	0.0150-0.0550
	L	3.0 (2998)	0.0010-0.0020	0.0130-0.0230	0.0130-0.0230	0.0150-0.0350	0.0030-0.0050	0.0030-0.0050	0.0035
1989	M	2.0 (1998)	0.0012-0.0020	0.0098-0.0177	0.0118-0.0197	NA	0.0024-0.0036	0.0019-0.0032	NA
	A	2.3 (2262)	0.0007-0.0020	0.0138-0.0236	0.0157-0.2560	0.0157-0.0550	0.0016-0.0040	0.0016-0.0032	NA
	D	2.3 (2262)	0.0007-0.0020	0.0138-0.0236	0.0157-0.2560	0.0157-0.0550	0.0020-0.0035	0.0016-0.0032	NA
	U	2.5 (2475)	0.0014-0.0022	0.0100-0.0200	0.0100-0.0200	0.0200-0.0600	0.0020-0.0030	0.0010-0.0020	0.0150-0.0550
	N	3.3 (3344)	0.0004-0.0022	0.0100-0.0250	0.0100-0.0250	0.0150-0.0550	0.0013-0.0031	0.0013-0.0031	0.0081-0.0110
1990	A	2.3 (2262)	0.0007-0.0020	0.0138-0.0236	0.0157-0.0256	0.0157-0.0551	0.0027-0.0047	0.0016-0.0032	NA
	D	2.3 (2262)	0.0007-0.0020	0.0138-0.0236	0.0157-0.0256	0.0157-0.0551	0.0020-0.0039	0.0016-0.0032	NA
	U	2.5 (2475)	0.0014-0.0022	0.0100-0.0200	0.0100-0.0200	0.0200-0.0600	0.0020-0.0030	0.0010-0.0030	0.0150-0.0550
	N	3.3 (3344)	0.0004-0.0022	0.0100-0.0250	0.0100-0.0250	0.0150-0.0550	0.0013-0.0031	0.0013-0.0031	0.0081-0.0110
1991	A	2.3 (2262)	0.0007-0.0020	0.0138-0.0236	0.0157-0.0256	0.0157-0.0551	0.0027-0.0047	0.0016-0.0032	NA
	D	2.3 (2262)	0.0007-0.0020	0.0138-0.0236	0.0157-0.0256	0.0157-0.0551	0.0020-0.0039	0.0016-0.0032	NA
	U	2.5 (2475)	0.0014-0.0022	0.0100-0.0200	0.0100-0.0200	0.0200-0.0600	0.0020-0.0030	0.0010-0.0030	0.0150-0.0550
	N	3.3 (3344)	0.0004-0.0022	0.0100-0.0250	0.0100-0.0250	0.0150-0.0550	0.0013-0.0031	0.0013-0.0031	0.0081-0.0110

PISTON AND RING SPECIFICATIONS

All measurements are given in inches.

| Year | Engine ID/VIN | Engine Displacement Liters (cc) | Piston Clearance | Ring Gap | | | Ring Side Clearance | | |
				Top Compression	Bottom Compression	Oil Control	Top Compression	Bottom Compression	Oil Control
1992	3	2.3 (2262)	0.0007-0.0020	0.0138-0.0236	0.0157-0.0256	0.0157-0.0551	0.0020-0.0039	0.0016-0.0032	NA
	A	2.3 (2262)	0.0007-0.0020	0.0138-0.0236	0.0157-0.0256	0.0157-0.0551	0.0027-0.0047	0.0016-0.0032	NA
	D	2.3 (2262)	0.0007-0.0020	0.0138-0.0236	0.0157-0.0256	0.0157-0.0551	0.0020-0.0039	0.0016-0.0032	NA
	N	3.3 (3344)	0.0004-0.0022	0.0100-0.0250	0.0100-0.0250	0.0150-0.0550	0.0013-0.0031	0.0013-0.0031	0.0081-0.0110
1993	3	2.3 (2262)	0.0007-0.0020	0.0138-0.0236	0.0157-0.0256	0.0157-0.0551	0.0020-0.0039	0.0016-0.0032	NA
	A	2.3 (2262)	0.0007-0.0020	0.0138-0.0236	0.0157-0.0256	0.0157-0.0551	0.0027-0.0047	0.0016-0.0032	NA
	D	2.3 (2262)	0.0007-0.0020	0.0138-0.0236	0.0157-0.0256	0.0157-0.0551	0.0020-0.0039	0.0016-0.0032	NA
	N	3.3 (3344)	0.0004-0.0022	0.0100-0.0250	0.0100-0.0250	0.0150-0.0550	0.0013-0.0031	0.0013-0.0031	0.0081-0.0110
1994	3	2.3 (2262)	0.0007-0.0020	0.0138-0.0236	0.0157-0.0256	0.0157-0.0551	0.0020-0.0039	0.0016-0.0032	NA
	A	2.3 (2262)	0.0007-0.0020	0.0138-0.0236	0.0157-0.0256	0.0157-0.0551	0.0027-0.0047	0.0016-0.0032	NA
	D	2.3 (2262)	0.0007-0.0020	0.0138-0.0236	0.0157-0.0256	0.0157-0.0551	0.0020-0.0039	0.0016-0.0032	NA
	M	3.1 (3136)	0.0013-0.0027	0.0071-0.0161	0.0200-0.0280	0.0098-0.0295	0.0020-0.0035	0.0020-0.0035	0.0080
1995	D	2.3 (2262)	0.0007-0.0020	0.0138-0.0236	0.0157-0.0256	0.0157-0.0551	0.0020-0.0039	0.0016-0.0032	NA
	M	3.1 (3136)	0.0013-0.0027	0.0071-0.0161	0.0200-0.0280	0.0098-0.0295	0.0020-0.0035	0.0020-0.0035	0.0080

NA - Not Available

86883510

Engine

REMOVAL & INSTALLATION

✳✳CAUTION

When draining the coolant, keep in mind that cats and dogs are attracted by ethylene glycol antifreeze, and are quite likely to drink any that is left in an uncovered container or in puddles on the ground. This will prove fatal in sufficient quantity. Always drain the coolant into a sealable container. Coolant should be reused unless it is contaminated or several years old.

2.0L and 2.5L Engines

1. Relieve the fuel system pressure.

✳✳CAUTION

Fuel Injection systems remain under pressure, even after the engine has been turned OFF. The fuel system pressure must be relieved before disconnecting any fuel lines. Failure to do so may result in fire and/or personal injury.

2. Disconnect both battery cables and ground straps.
3. Drain the cooling system, then remove the cooling fan.
4. Remove the air cleaner assembly.
5. Detach the ECM connections and feed harness through the bulkhead. Lay the harness across the engine.
6. Label and disconnect the engine wiring harness and all engine-related connectors and lay them across the engine.
7. Tag and detach the radiator hoses and vacuum lines. Disconnect and plug the fuel lines.

8. On 2.5L engine, remove the air conditioning compressor from the engine and lay it aside, DO NOT disconnect the refrigerant lines. Remove the transaxle struts.

9. If equipped with power steering, remove the power steering pump from its mount (with the lines attached) and lay it aside.

10. If equipped with a manual transaxle, disconnect the clutch and transaxle linkage. Remove the throttle cable from the throttle body.

11. If equipped with an automatic transaxle, disconnect the transaxle cooler lines, shifter linkage, downshift cable and throttle cable from the throttle body.

12. Raise and safely support the vehicle.

13. Remove the power steering line bracket from the engine.

14. Disconnect all wiring from the transaxle.

15. On 2.0L engine, properly discharge the air conditioning system and remove the compressor. Remove the transaxle strut(s).

16. Disconnect the exhaust pipe from the exhaust manifold and hangers.

17. Disconnect and plug the heater hoses from the heater core tubes.

18. Remove the front wheels. Remove the calipers and wire them up aside. Remove the brake rotors.

19. Matchmark and remove the knuckle-to-strut bolts.

20. Remove the body-to-cradle bolts at the lower control arms. Loosen the remaining body-to-cradle bolts. Remove a bolt at each cradle side, leaving 1 bolt per corner.

21. Using the proper equipment, support the vehicle under the radiator frame support.

22. Position a jack to the rear of the body pan with a 4 in. x 4 in. x 6 ft. (10cm x 10cm x 2m) timber spanning the vehicle.

23. Raise the vehicle enough to remove the support equipment.

24. Position a dolly under the engine/transaxle assembly with 3 blocks of wood for additional support.

25. Lower the vehicle slightly, allowing the engine/transaxle assembly to rest on the dolly.

26. Remove all engine and transaxle mount bolts and brackets. Remove the remaining cradle-to-body bolts.

27. Raise the vehicle, leaving engine and transaxle assembly with the suspension on the dolly.

28. Separate the engine and transaxle.

To install:

29. Assemble the engine and transaxle assembly and position on the dolly.

30. Raise and safely support the vehicle. Roll the assembly to the installation position and lower the vehicle over the assembly.

31. Install all engine, transaxle and suspension mounting bolts. Tighten all cradle mounting bolts to 65 ft. lbs. (88 Nm). Connect the wiring to the transaxle.

32. Install the knuckle-to-strut bolts, aligning with the marks made during removal.

33. Assemble the brakes.

34. Connect the exhaust pipe to the exhaust manifold and hangers.

35. Connect the heater hoses to the heater core tubes.

36. If equipped with the 2.0L engine, install the air conditioning compressor.

37. Install the wheels and lower the vehicle.

38. If equipped with the 2.5L engine, install the air conditioning compressor.

39. Install the power steering pump and related parts.

40. If equipped with a manual transaxle, connect the clutch and transaxle linkage. Connect the throttle cable to the throttle body.

41. If equipped with an automatic transaxle, connect the transaxle cooler lines, shifter linkage, downshift cable and throttle cable to the throttle body.

42. Connect the radiator hoses, vacuum lines and fuel lines.

43. Connect the engine wiring harness and all engine-related connectors. Feed the ECM connections through the bulkhead and connect.

44. Install the air cleaner assembly.

45. Fill all fluids to their proper levels.

46. Connect the battery cables, start the engine and set the timing, if necessary. Check for leaks.

2.3L Engine

1. Relieve the fuel system pressure.

2. Disconnect the negative battery cable.

3. Drain the cooling system, making sure to recover the coolant.

4. If equipped with A/C, recover the refrigerant using an approved recycling station. See Section 1 for more information regarding the A/C system.

5. Remove the left sound insulator, then disconnect the clutch pushrod from the pedal assembly.

6. Disconnect the heater hose at the thermostat housing. Remove the radiator inlet (upper) hose.

7. Remove the air cleaner assembly.

8. Remove the coolant fan assembly.

9. If equipped with A/C, detach the compressor/condenser hose assembly at the compressor. Discard the O-rings.

10. Tag and disconnect the two vacuum hoses from the front of the engine.

11. Tag and detach the following electrical connections:
- Alternator
- A/C compressor (if equipped)
- Injector harness
- IAC and TP sensors at the throttle body
- MAP sensor
- IAT sensor
- EVAP purge canister solenoid
- Starter solenoid
- Ground connections
- Negative battery cable from the transaxle
- Ignition coil and module assembly
- ECT sensor(s)
- Oxygen sensor
- Crankshaft position sensor
- Back-up lamp switch (position the harness aside)

12. Detach the power brake vacuum hose from the throttle body. Disconnect the power brake vacuum tube-to-check valve hose from the tube.

13. Disconnect the throttle cable, then remove the bracket.

14. Remove the power steering pump rear bracket. Remove the bracket and power brake vacuum tube as an assembly.

15. Remove the power steering pivot bolt, pump and drive belt.

16. Disconnect and plug the fuel lines.

17. If equipped with a manual transaxle, disconnect the shifter cables and the clutch actuator cylinder.

18. If equipped with an automatic transaxle, disconnect the shift and TV cables.

19. Disconnect the transaxle and engine oil cooler pipes, if equipped.

20. Remove the exhaust manifold and heat shield. For details, please refer to the procedure located later in this section.

21. Remove the outlet (lower) radiator hose.

22. Install engine support fixture tool J-28467-A.

23. Remove the right engine mount.

24. Raise and safely support the vehicle.

25. Remove the front wheel and tire assemblies, right side splash shield and radiator air deflector.

26. Tag and detach the electrical connections from the following components:
- Vehicle Speed Sensor (VSS)
- Knock sensor
- Starter solenoid
- Both front ABS wheel speed sensors (if equipped).

27. Remove the engine mount strut and the transaxle mount.

28. Separate the ball joints from the steering knuckles.

29. Using the proper equipment, support the suspension supports, crossmember and stabilizer shaft. Unfasten the attaching bolts, then remove as an assembly.

30. Disconnect the heater outlet hose from the radiator outlet pipe.

31. Remove the axle shaft from the transaxle and intermediate shaft and position it aside.

32. Disconnect and plug the A/C lines from the oil pan.

33. Remove the flywheel housing cover.

34. Position a suitable support below the engine, then carefully lower the car onto the support.

35. Mark the threads on the support fixture hooks so that the setting can be duplicated when reinstalling the engine. Remove the engine support fixture J-hooks.

36. Raise the vehicle slowly off the engine and transaxle assembly. It may be necessary to move the engine/transaxle assembly rearward to clear the intake manifold.

➡**Many of the bell housing bolts are of different lengths; note their locations before removing. It is imperative that these bolts go back in their original locations when assembling the engine and transaxle or engine damage could result.**

37. Separate the engine from the transaxle.

To install:

38. Assemble the engine and transaxle. If equipped with an automatic transaxle, thoroughly clean and dry the torque converter bolts and bolt holes, apply thread locking compound to the threads and tighten the bolts to 46 ft. lbs. (63 Nm). If equipped with a manual transaxle, tighten the clutch cover bolts to 22 ft. lbs. (30 Nm).

39. Raise and safely support the vehicle. Position the engine/transaxle assembly and lower the vehicle over the assembly until the transaxle mount is indexed, then install the bolt.

40. Install the engine support fixture and adjust to previously indexed setting. Raise the vehicle off the support fixture.

41. Install the rear mount-to-body bracket and tighten the bolts to 55 ft. lbs. (75 Nm).

42. Install the rear mount nut and tighten to 55 ft. lbs. (75 Nm).

43. Install the transaxle mount through-bolt and tighten the nut to 55 ft. lbs. (75 Nm). Tighten so equal gaps are maintained.

44. Install the halfshafts.

45. Connect the heater hose to the the radiator outlet pipe.

46. Install the suspension supports, crossmember and stabilizer shaft assembly. Tighten the center bolts first, then front, then rear, to 65 ft. lbs. (90 Nm).

47. Connect the ball joints and tighten the nuts to a maximum of 50 ft. lbs. (68 Nm).

48. Install the engine strut mount.

49. If equipped, connect the A/C line to the oil pan.

50. Attach the following electrical connections as tagged during removal:
- VSS, knock sensor
- Starter solenoid
- If equipped, both ABS front wheel speed sensors.

51. For vehicles equipped with a manual transaxle, install the flywheel housing cover.

52. Install the radiator air deflector, connect the lower radiator hose, then install the splash shield.

53. Install the front wheel and tire assemblies, then carefully lower the vehicle. Remove the engine support fixture.

54. Attach the electrical connections to the following components as tagged during removal:
- Alternator
- Injector harness
- A/C compressor (if equipped)
- IAC and TPS at the throttle body
- MAP sensor
- IAT sensor
- EVAP canister purge solenoid
- Starter solenoid
- Ground connections
- Negative battery cable to the transaxle
- Engine coolant temperature sensor(s)
- Oil pressure sensor/switch
- Oxygen sensor
- Crankshaft position sensor
- Back-up light switch
- Ignition coil and module assembly

55. Connect the vacuum hoses/lines as tagged during removal.

56. If equipped with A/C, fasten the compressor/condenser hose assembly to the compressor.

57. If equipped with a manual transaxle, connect the clutch actuator line and shift cables.

58. Install the exhaust manifold and heat shield. For details, please refer to the procedure located later in this section.

59. Connect the transaxle and engine oil cooler pipes, if equipped.

60. If equipped with an automatic transaxle, connect the shift and TV cables.

61. Uncap and connect the fuel lines.

62. Connect the positive battery cable.

63. Fasten the power steering pump pivot-to-block bolt, then install the pump rear bracket and tension belt.

64. Connect the vacuum hoses to the intake manifold and to the tube from the brake booster.

65. Attach the throttle cable, then install the bracket.

66. Install the coolant fan and the air cleaner assembly.

67. Install the radiator outlet (upper) hose.

68. Install the left sound insulator, then disconnect the clutch pushrod from the pedal assembly.

69. Fasten the heater hose at the thermostat housing.

70. Fill the cooling system, transaxle and crankcase with the proper type and quantity of fluids.

71. Connect the negative battery cable.

72. If equipped with A/C, evacuate, charge and and leak test the A/C system using the proper equipment. See Section 1 for warnings concerning A/C systems.

73. Start the engine and check for leaks, then check for proper fluid levels and add as necessary.

3.0L Engine

▶ See Figures 20 and 21

1. Properly relieve the fuel system pressure. Disconnect and cap the fuel lines from the fuel rail.

2. Disconnect the negative battery cable.

3. Raise and safely support the vehicle.

4. Disengage the starter connections, then remove the starter from the vehicle.

5. Remove the flywheel dust cover, then matchmark and remove the flywheel-to-converter retaining bolts.

6. If equipped, disengage the A/C electrical connections, then remove the compressor and position aside with the lines connected.

7. Drain the cooling system, then remove the lower radiator hose.

8. Unfasten the right front engine mount bolts. Remove the right side splash guard.

9. Unfasten and remove the lower transaxle-to-engine bolts. One bolt is located between the transaxle case and engine block and is installed in the opposite direction.

10. Unfasten and remove the right rear engine mount bolts/nuts.

11. Remove the right exhaust manifold at the pipe.

12. Disconnect the heater hoses.

13. Carefully lower the vehicle.

14. Matchmark the hood hinges for installation purposes, then remove the hood.

15. Take off the serpentine belt, then remove the alternator.

16. Detach and cap the power steering pump lines, then remove the pump.

17. Disconnect and label all electrical connectors from the engine, alternator and fuel injection system, vacuum hoses, and engine ground straps.

18. Unfasten the coolant hoses from the radiator and engine. Remove the radiator and cooling fan assembly.

19. Disconnect the Mass Air Flow (MAF) sensor tubing.

20. Remove the master cylinder assembly. For details, please refer to Section 9 of this manual.

21. Disconnect the accelerator and T.V. cables from the throttle body and cable bracket.

22. Install a suitable engine lifting fixture and set up an engine hoist.

23. Remove the left side transaxle support bracket.

24. Remove the transaxle (bell house) mounting bolts.

25. Look for any vacuum or electrical connections still attached and tag and disengage as necessary.

26. Remove the engine assembly from the vehicle.

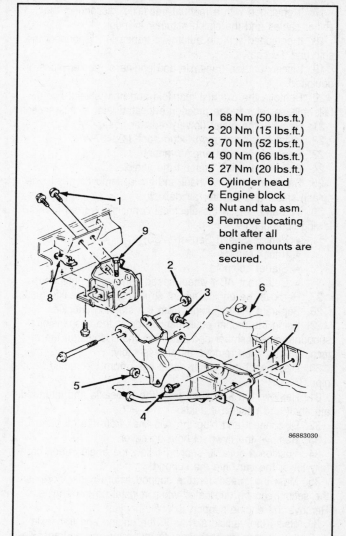

1 68 Nm (50 lbs.ft.)
2 20 Nm (15 lbs.ft.)
3 70 Nm (52 lbs.ft.)
4 90 Nm (66 lbs.ft.)
5 27 Nm (20 lbs.ft.)
6 Cylinder head
7 Engine block
8 Nut and tab asm.
9 Remove locating bolt after all engine mounts are secured.

Fig. 20 View of the right front engine mount locations — 1988 3.0L shown

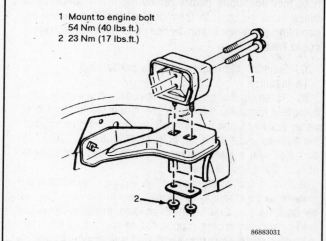

1 Mount to engine bolt
  54 Nm (40 lbs.ft.)
2 23 Nm (17 lbs.ft.)

Fig. 21 Right rear engine mount location — 1988 3.0L engine shown

To install:

27. Carefully lower the engine assembly into the vehicle.

➡**Be sure to align the flywheel-to-converter marks made during removal.**

28. Install the transaxle mounting bolts. Tighten the bolts to 55 ft. lbs. (75 Nm).
29. Install the left side transaxle support bracket.
30. Remove the engine lifting fixture.
31. Raise and safely support the vehicle.
32. Install the right front engine mount bolts and the right rear engine mount nuts.
33. Install the right exhaust manifold at the pipe.
34. Connect the heater hoses.
35. Install the right side splash guard.
36. If equipped, install the A/C compressor.
37. Install the torque converter-to-flywheel bolts, making sure to line up the marks made during removal. Tighten the bolts to 46 ft. lbs. (63 Nm). Position and secure the flywheel dust cover.
38. Connect the lower radiator hose.
39. Install the starter motor, then attach any electrical connections detached during removal.
40. Carefully lower the vehicle.
41. Uncap and connect the fuel lines to the fuel rail assembly.
42. Install the master cylinder assembly. For details, please refer to Section 9 of this manual.
43. Install the radiator, then connect the upper radiator hose.
44. Connect the Mass Air Flow (MAF) sensor tubing.
45. Install the power steering pump, then connect the lines.
46. Install the alternator, then fasten the serpentine belt.
47. Connect the negative battery cable. Align the hinge marks made during removal, then install the hood.
48. Properly fill the cooling system with the correct type and quantity of fluid.
49. Start the engine and inspect for leaks. Check the fluid levels and add as necessary.

3.1L Engine

1. Relieve the fuel system pressure.
2. Disconnect the negative battery cable.
3. Remove the top half of the air cleaner assembly and the throttle body inlet duct.
4. Drain the cooling system.
5. Remove the upper and lower radiator hoses.
6. Disconnect the coolant inlet line from the coolant surge tank.
7. Disconnect the vacuum hoses from the EVAP canister purge valve, vacuum modulator and power brake booster.
8. Disconnect the heater outlet hose from the water pump.
9. Remove the serpentine drive belt.
10. Disconnect the control cables from the throttle body lever and intake manifold bracket and position the cables out of the way.
11. Label and detach the following electrical connectors from their related components:
   - Ignition assembly
   - Oxygen sensor
   - Fuel injectors
   - Idle Air Control valve (IAC)
   - Throttle position sensor (TPS)
   - Engine Coolant Temperature (ECT) sensor
   - Park neutral switch
   - TCC solenoid
   - Shift solenoid
   - EGR valve
   - Transaxle ground
12. Remove the alternator. For details, please refer to the procedure located in this section.
13. Disconnect and cap the power steering lines from the power steering pump.
14. Disconnect and cap the fuel lines from the fuel rail.
15. Remove the cooling fan assembly.
16. Disconnect the shift control cable from the transaxle shift lever and cable bracket.
17. Disconnect the transaxle vent tube from the transaxle.
18. Disconnect the vacuum hose from the vacuum reservoir.
19. Install an engine support fixture, J-28467-A, or the equivalent.
20. Loosen, but do not remove the top 2 A/C compressor mounting bolts.
21. Raise and safely support the vehicle.
22. Remove the front tire and wheel assemblies.
23. Remove the right and left inner fender splash shields.
24. Remove the engine mount strut.
25. Disconnect the ABS sensor wires from the wheel sensors and suspension member supports, if equipped.
26. Remove the cotter pins and castle nuts from the lower ball joints. Using a suitable tool, separate the lower ball joints from the steering knuckles.
27. Remove the lower suspension support assemblies with the lower control arms attached.
28. Disconnect the halfshafts from the transaxle and support out of the way.
29. Remove the oil filter and oil filter adapter.
30. Remove the flywheel cover.
31. Remove the starter.
32. Disconnect the following electrical connectors from their related components:
   - Knock sensor
   - Front crankshaft position sensor
   - Side crankshaft position sensor
   - Oil level sensor
   - Vehicle speed sensor
   - Transaxle ground
33. Disconnect the heater hoses from the heater core.
34. Remove the A/C compressor lower mounting bolts and remove the compressor from the mounting bracket and position aside. DO NOT disconnect the refrigerant lines from the compressor or allow the lines top support the weight of the compressor.
35. Remove the vacuum reservoir tank.
36. Disconnect the exhaust pipe from the exhaust manifold and position the pipe aside.
37. Remove the engine mount strut bracket from the engine.
38. Disconnect the transaxle cooler lines from the radiator.
39. Remove the transaxle oil fill tube.
40. Lower the vehicle until the power train assembly is resting on a suitable engine table.
41. Remove the transaxle mount-to-body bolts.
42. Remove the intermediate bracket from the right engine mount.

43. Remove the engine support fixture.

44. Raise the vehicle leaving the powertrain assembly on the engine table.

45. Separate the engine and transaxle assemblies.

To install:

46. Connect the transaxle to the engine, then tighten the mounting bolts to 55 ft. lbs. (75 Nm).

47. Position the powertrain assembly under the vehicle and lower the vehicle into position.

48. Loosely install the serpentine belt.

49. Install the intermediate bracket to the right side engine mount.

50. Install the transaxle-to-body bolts.

51. Raise and safely support the vehicle.

52. Install the transaxle fill tube.

53. Connect the transaxle cooler lines to the radiator.

54. Install the engine strut bracket to the engine, then tighten the mounting bolts to 44 ft. lbs. (60 Nm).

55. Connect the exhaust pipe to the exhaust manifold, then tighten the mounting bolts to 18 ft. lbs. (25 Nm).

56. Install the vacuum reserve tank.

57. Install the A/C compressor in the mounting bracket. Install the upper bolts loosely and tighten the lower bolts.

58. Connect the heater hoses to the heater core.

59. Connect the following electrical connectors to their related components:
- Knock sensor
- Front crankshaft position sensor
- Side crankshaft position sensor
- Oil level sensor
- Vehicle speed sensor
- Transaxle ground

60. Install the starter.

61. Install the flywheel cover.

62. Install the oil filter adapter and after coating the oil filter seal with clean engine oil, install the oil filter.

63. Connect the drive axles to the transaxle.

64. Install the suspension support assemblies and lower control arms.

65. Connect the lower ball joints to the steering knuckles, then tighten the castle nuts to 41 ft. lbs. (55 Nm).

66. Attach the ABS sensor wires to the wheel sensors and suspension support wire clips.

67. Install the engine mount strut.

68. Install the left and right inner fender splash shields.

69. Install the right front tire and wheel assemblies.

70. Carefully lower the vehicle.

71. Tighten the upper A/C compressor mounting bolts.

72. Remove the engine support fixture.

73. Attach the vacuum hose to the reservoir.

74. Fasten the transaxle vent hose to the transaxle.

75. Connect the shift cable linkage to the cable bracket and shift lever on the transaxle.

76. Install the cooling fan assembly.

77. Attach the fuel lines to the fuel rail.

78. Connect the power steering lines to the power steering pump.

79. Install the alternator. For details, please refer to the procedure located in this section.

80. Connect the following electrical connectors to their related components:
- Ignition assembly
- Oxygen sensor
- Fuel injectors
- Idle Air Control valve (IAC)
- Throttle position sensor (TPS)
- Engine Coolant Temperature (ECT) sensor
- Park neutral switch
- TCC solenoid
- Shift solenoid
- EGR valve
- Transaxle ground

81. Connect the control cables to the throttle body lever and cable bracket.

82. Install the serpentine belt.

83. Connect the heater outlet hose to the water pump.

84. Connect the vacuum hoses to the power brake booster, vacuum modulator and EVAP purge solenoid.

85. Connect the coolant inlet line to the surge tank.

86. Install the upper and lower radiator hoses.

87. Install the top half of the air cleaner assembly and the throttle body air inlet duct.

88. Connect the negative battery cable.

89. Check and fill all the engine fluids as necessary.

90. Start the vehicle and bleed the power steering system.

3.3L Engine

▶ **See Figure 22**

1. Properly relieve the fuel system pressure. Detach and cap the fuel lines from the fuel rail.

2. Disconnect the negative battery cable.

3. Matchmark the position of the hood hinges, then remove the hood.

4. Drain the cooling system. Disconnect the radiator and heater hoses.

5. Remove the engine cooling fan.

6. Detach the air intake duct from the throttle body.

7. Tag and unfasten the vacuum lines from the brake power booster and the evaporative canister purge.

8. Remove the cable bracket and the cables from the throttle body.

9. Remove the accessory drive belt.

10. Remove the power steering pump and position it aside.

11. Tag and disengage all the electrical connections from the engine components.

12. Unfasten the upper transaxle-to-engine bolts.

13. Raise and safely support the vehicle.

14. If equipped, remove the A/C compressor, with the lines attached and position it aside.

15. Remove the right engine mount and torque strut.

➡ **Matchmark the relationship of the torque converter-to-flywheel for installation purposes.**

16. Remove the flywheel dust cover, then unfasten the flywheel-to-converter bolts.

17. Unfasten the lower engine-to-transaxle bolts. One bolt is located between the transaxle case and engine and is installed in the opposite direction.

18. Carefully lower the vehicle.

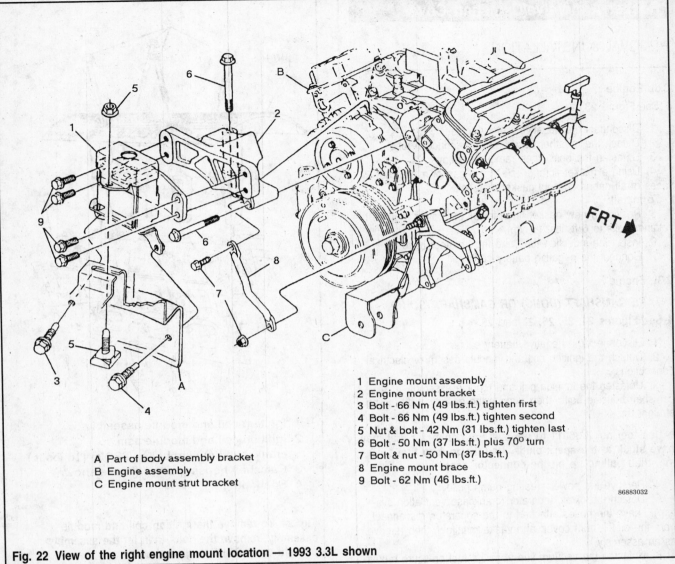

1 Engine mount assembly
2 Engine mount bracket
3 Bolt - 66 Nm (49 lbs.ft.) tighten first
4 Bolt - 66 Nm (49 lbs.ft.) tighten second
5 Nut & bolt - 42 Nm (31 lbs.ft.) tighten last
6 Bolt - 50 Nm (37 lbs.ft.) plus 70° turn
7 Bolt & nut - 50 Nm (37 lbs.ft.)
8 Engine mount brace
9 Bolt - 62 Nm (46 lbs.ft.)

A Part of body assembly bracket
B Engine assembly
C Engine mount strut bracket

86883032

Fig. 22 View of the right engine mount location — 1993 3.3L shown

19. Remove the front engine mount-to-bracket bolts or other retainers, then using a suitable lifting device, remove the engine assembly from the vehicle.

To install:

20. Carefully position the engine into the vehicle, then install the front engine mount-to-bracket bolts or other retainers.

21. Raise and safely support the vehicle.

22. Fasten the lower engine-to-transaxle bolts. One bolt is located between the transaxle case and the engine and is installed in the opposite direction.

23. Install the flywheel-to-converter bolts. Tighten the bolts twice to 46 ft. lbs. (63 Nm). Position and install the flywheel dust cover.

24. Install the right engine mount and torque strut, then tighten to the specifications shown in the accompanying figure.

25. If equipped, install the A/C compressor.

26. Carefully lower the vehicle.

27. Fasten the upper transaxle-to-engine bolts.

28. Attach all the electrical connections from the engine components, as tagged during removal.

29. Position and secure the power steering pump, then install the accessory drive belt.

30. Connect the cables to the throttle body, the install the bracket.

31. Fasten the vacuum lines to the evaporative canister purge and the brake power booster.

32. Attach the air intake duct to the throttle body.

33. Install the engine cooling fan. Connect the heater and radiator hoses

34. Refill the cooling system to the proper level.

35. Connect the negative battery cable. Install the hood, using the scribe marks made during removal.

36. Start the engine and inspect for leaks. Check the fluid levels and add if necessary.

Rocker Arm/Valve/Camshaft Cover

REMOVAL & INSTALLATION

2.0L Engine

▶ See Figure 23

1. Disconnect the negative battery cable.
2. Detach the breather hoses and the induction tube.
3. Unfasten the bolts, then remove the cover.
4. Using a gasket scraper, clean the gasket mating surfaces of all debris and old gasket material.

To install:

5. Position a new gasket, then install the cover. Tighten the retainer bolts to 6 ft. lbs. (8 Nm).
6. Install the induction tube and the breather hoses.
7. Connect the negative battery cable.

2.3L Engine

INTAKE CAMSHAFT (DOHC) OR CAMSHAFT (SOHC)

▶ See Figures 24, 25, 26, 27 and 28

1. Disconnect the negative battery cable.
2. Detach the ignition coil and module assembly electrical connections.
3. Unfasten the ignition coil and module assembly-to-camshaft housing bolts, then remove the assembly by pulling it straight up.

➡Use tool no. J 36011 to remove any connector that may have stuck to the spark plugs. Use the tool by first twisting, then pulling up on the connector assembly.

4. Remove the power steering pump pulley.
5. Detach the oil/air separator (crankcase ventilation system). Leave the hoses attached to the separator, disconnect from the oil fill, front cover, and intake manifold, then remove as an assembly.
6. Unfasten the vacuum line from the fuel pressure regulator and fuel injector harness connector.

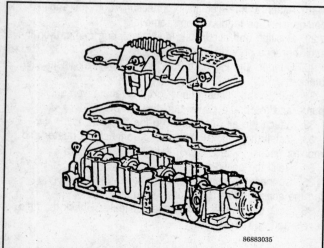

Fig. 23 When installing the camshaft cover, always use a new gasket to help prevent leakage

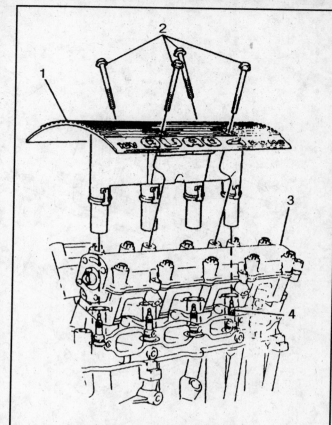

1 Ignition coil and module assembly
2 Ignition coil and module asm. to crankshaft housing bolts - 22 Nm (16 lbs.ft.)
3 Camshaft housing cover (intake shown)
4 Spark plug

86883037

Fig. 24 To remove the ignition coil and module assembly, remove the bolts then lift the assembly straight up — DOHC engine shown

7. Disconnect the fuel line retaining clamp from the bracket on top of the intake cam housing.
8. Unfasten the fuel rail-to-camshaft housing retaining bolts, then remove the fuel rail from the cylinder head. Be sure to cover the injector openings in the cylinder head, cover the injector nozzles and leave the fuel lines attached and position the fuel rail aside (on top of the master cylinder).
9. Disconnect the timing chain housing but do not remove form the vehicle.
10. Unfasten the cam housing cover-to-housing retaining bolts and the cam housing-to-cylinder head bolts.
11. Use the reverse of the tightening procedure (in the accompanying figure) when loosening the camshaft housing-to-cylinder head bolts.
12. Push the cover off the housing by threading four of the housing-to-head retaining bolts into the tapped holes in the cover. Make sure to tighten the bolts evenly remove the cover from the vehicle.
13. Remove and discard the cover-to-housing seals and clean the mating surfaces.

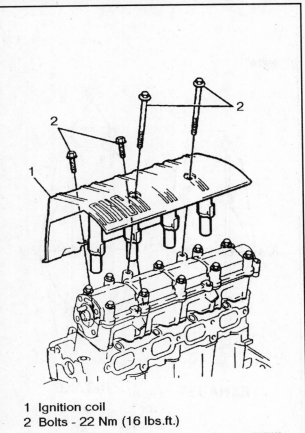

1 Ignition coil
2 Bolts - 22 Nm (16 lbs.ft.)

86883038

Fig. 25 If any of the coil assembly connectors stick to the spark plugs using tool J 36011 in a twisting and pulling motion will remove the connector — SOHC engine shown

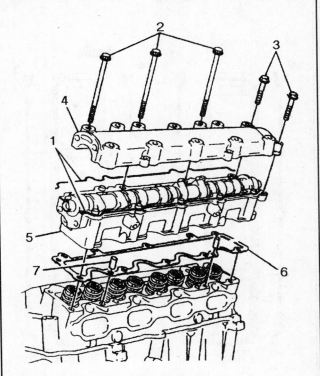

1 Camshaft housing to camshaft seals
2 Camshaft housing to cylinder head bolt
   15 Nm (11 lbs.ft.) plus turn 90o
3 Camshaft housing cover to camshaft
   housing bolt -15 Nm (11 lbs.ft.) plus turn 30 o
4 Camshaft cover
5 Camshaft housing (intake shown)
6 Camshaft housing to cylinder head gasket
7 Dowel pin (2)

86883039

Fig. 26 Exploded view of the intake cam cover and related components

To install:

14. Position new seals on the camshaft cover. Refer to the accompanying figure.

15. Apply pipe sealant 1052080 or equivalent to the camshaft housing and cover retaining bolt threads. Using J 366660, install the bolts, then tighten in sequence to the specifications in the accompanying figure.

16. Fasten the timing chain housing.

17. Uncover fuel injectors, then lubricate new injector O-ring seals with clean engine oil and install on the injectors.

18. Uncover the injector openings in the cylinder head, then install the fuel rail onto the cylinder head. Install the fuel rail-to-cylinder head retaining bolts and tighten to 19 ft. lbs. (26 Nm).

19. Install the fuel line retaining clamp and retainer to the bracket on top of the cam housing.

20. Connect the vacuum line to the fuel pressure regulator. Attach the fuel injector harness connector.

21. Install the oil/air separator assembly. You may want to lubricate the hoses to ease installation.

22. Lubricate the inner surface of the camshaft seal with clean engine oil, then install the seal into the camshaft housing using tool J 36015, or equivalent.

23. Using tool J 36015 or equivalent, install the power steering pump drive pulley onto the intake camshaft.

24. Install the power steering pump assembly and the drive belt. Adjust tension to specification.

25. Fasten any spark plug boot connector assembly that stuck to a spark plug back onto the ignition coil and module assembly.

26. Position the coil and module assembly over the spark plugs, then push the assembly straight down. Make sure it is properly seated.

27. Clean off any loose lubricant from the coil and module assembly-to-camshaft housing bolts. Apply pipe sealant 1052080 or equivalent, onto the bolts, then tighten the bolts to 16 ft. lbs. (22 Nm).

28. Attach the coil and module electrical connector.

29. Connect the negative battery cable, then start the engine and inspect for oil leaks.

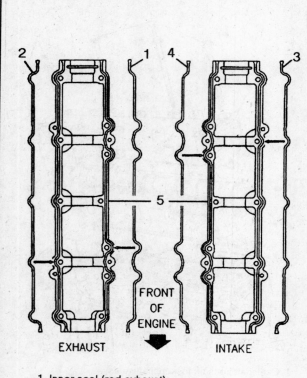

1 Inner seal (red exhaust)
2 Outer seal (red exhaust)
3 Outer seal (blue intake)
4 Inner seal (blue intake)
5 Camshaft housing cover

86883040

Fig. 27 Intake and exhaust cam housing-to-cover seal locations

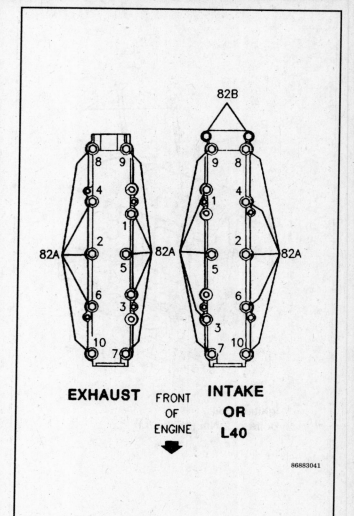

86883041

Fig. 28 Intake and exhaust camshaft bolt tightening sequence

EXHAUST CAMSHAFT (DOHC ONLY)

▶ **See Figures 27 and 28**

1. Disconnect the negative battery cable.
2. Detach the ignition coil and module electrical connection. Remove the coil and module assembly-to-camshaft housing bolts, then remove the assembly by lifting it straight up.

➡**Use tool no. J 36011 to remove any connector that may have stuck to the spark plugs. Use the tool by first twisting, then pulling up on the connector assembly.**

3. Disengage the electrical connection from the oil pressure switch.
4. For vehicles equipped with an automatic transaxle, remove the transaxle fluid level indicator tube assembly from the exhaust camshaft cover, then position it aside.
5. Disconnect, but do not remove from the vehicle, the timing chain housing at the exhaust camshaft housing.
6. Remove the exhaust camshaft cover and gasket, then discard the gasket. Clean all old gasket debris from the cover mating surfaces.

To install:

7. Position new camshaft housing-to-cover seals. No sealant is needed.
8. Apply pipe sealant 1052080 or equivalent to the threads of the camshaft housing and cover retaining bolts.
9. Position the cover onto the housing, then tighten the bolts, in sequence, to specification.
10. Tighten the timing chain housing retainers.
11. Install the transaxle fluid level indicator tube assembly to the exhaust camshaft cover.
12. Attach the oil pressure switch electrical connector.
13. Reinstall any spark plug boot connectors that may have been stuck to a spark plug, back onto the ignition coil and module assembly.
14. Position the coil and module assembly over the spark plugs then push it straight down making sure it is firmly and properly seated.
15. Clean off any lubricant on the coil and module-to-camshaft housing bolts. Apply pipe sealant 1052080 or equivalent to the bolts, then tighten them to 16 ft. lbs. (22 Nm).

16. Attach the ignition coil and module assembly electrical connector.

17. Connect the negative battery cable, then start the engine and inspect for leaks.

2.5L Engine

▶ **See Figure 29**

1. Disconnect the negative battery cable.
2. Remove the air cleaner assembly.
3. Detach the PCV valve and/or hose assembly.
4. Remove the the EGR valve.
5. Unfasten the accelerator and T.V. cables.
6. Remove the spark plug wires and the clips from the rocker arm cover.
7. Remove the rocker arm cover retaining bolts.
8. Tap the rocker arm cover gently with a rubber mallet to break the gasket loose, then remove the cover. Do not pry on the cover or damage to the sealing surfaces may result.
9. Clean the sealing surfaces of all old gasket material.

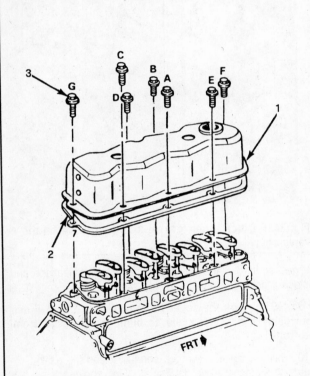

1 Rocker arm
2 Rocker arm cover gasket
3 Rocker arm cover bolt
Bolt tightening sequence:
A, B, C, D, E, F, G

86883036

Fig. 29 When removing the cover, do not pry it off as damage and distortion to the sealing surfaces may occur

To install:

10. Position a new gasket on the rocker arm cover. Be sure to remove the protective paper from the adhesive/cover side of the gasket.

11. Install the rocker arm cover, then secure using the retaining bolts. Tighten the bolts to 80 inch lbs. (9 Nm).

12. Fasten the spark plug wires and the clips to the cover.

13. Connect the PCV valve and/or hose assembly.

14. Fasten the T.V. and accelerator cables.

15. Install the air cleaner assembly.

16. Connect the negative battery cable, then start the engine and check for leaks.

3.0L Engine

FRONT (LEFT) COVER

▶ **See Figures 30, 31, 32, 33 and 34**

1. Disconnect the negative battery cable.
2. Remove the crankcase ventilation pipe.
3. Remove the spark plug wire harness cover, then tag and disconnect the wires at the spark plugs.
4. Unfasten the valve cover nuts, washers and seals, then remove the valve cover and gasket. Discard the gasket and replace any seals that are damaged.

➡ **Do NOT pry on the cover to remove it. If it sticks, use your palm or a rubber mallet to bump it rearwards, from the front.**

5. Using a suitable scraper, carefully clean the gasket mounting surfaces. Keep debris out of the engine.

To install:

6. Position a new gasket into the valve cover, then place the cover on the cylinder head. Install the seals, washers and nuts, then tighten to 88 inch lbs. (10 Nm).

7. Attach the wires to the spark plugs as tagged during removal, then install the spark plug wire harness cover.

8. Install the crankcase ventilation pipe.

9. Connect the negative battery cable, then start the engine and check for leaks.

REAR (RIGHT) COVER

1. Disconnect the negative battery cable.
2. Remove the ignition coil module using the following steps:
   a. Tag and disconnect the spark plug wires.
   b. Disengage the electrical wiring connector.
   c. Tag and detach the EGR solenoid wiring and vacuum hoses.
   d. Remove the mounting nuts.
3. Remove the serpentine belt.
4. Disengage the alternator wiring, then unfasten the rear mounting bolt and rotate the alternator toward the front of the vehicle.
5. Disconnect the power steering pump from the belt tensioner, then remove the belt tensioner assembly.
6. Remove the engine lift bracket and rear alternator brace.
7. Properly drain the coolant to a level below the heater hose.
8. Remove the throttle body heater hoses.
9. Unfasten the valve cover nuts, washers and seals, then remove the valve cover and gasket from the vehicle. Discard

Fig. 30 Remove the plastic harness cover shielding the spark plugs wires by simply pulling it off

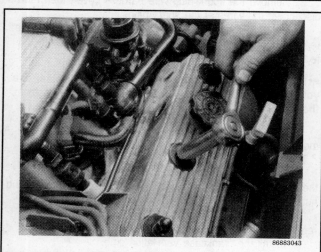

Fig. 31 Using the proper size socket, remove the valve cover retaining nuts

Fig. 32 After removing the nuts, remove the washers, then . . .

Fig. 33 . . . remove the seals. Replace any seals that are damaged or leaking

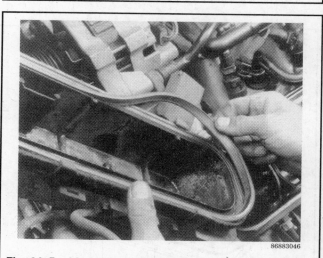

Fig. 34 Position a new gasket into the groove on the valve cover

the gasket, inspect the seals for damage and/or leakage and replace if necessary.

➡**Do NOT pry on the cover to remove it. If it sticks, use your palm or a rubber mallet to bump it rearwards, from the front.**

10. Using a suitable scraper, carefully clean the gasket mounting surfaces. Keep debris out of the engine.
   To install:
11. Position a new gasket in the groove in the valve cover.
12. Place the valve cover on the cylinder head, then install the seals, washers and retaining nuts. Tighten the nuts to 88 inch lbs. (10 Nm).
13. Connect the throttle body heater hoses.
14. Install the rear alternator brace and engine lift bracket.
15. Install the belt tensioner assembly, then secure the power steering pump to the belt tensioner.
16. Rotate the alternator into its original position, then install the rear mounting bolt and attach the wiring.
17. Install the serpentine belt.

18. Install the ignition coil module using the following steps:

a. Secure the module using the retaining bolts.

b. Attach the EGR solenoid wiring and vacuum hoses as tagged during removal.

c. Engage the electrical wiring connector.

d. Connect the spark plug wires as tagged during removal.

19. Connect the negative battery cable, then start the engine and check for leaks.

3.1L Engine

♦ See Figure 35

FRONT (LEFT) COVER

1. Disconnect the negative battery cable.

2. Drain the cooling system to a level below the coolant pipe on the front of the engine.

3. Remove the coolant bypass hose clamp at the coolant tube.

4. Unfasten the two bolts and nut securing the coolant tube to the cylinder head, then position the tube out of the way.

5. Disconnect the PCV valve from the rocker arm cover.

6. Unfasten the four rocker arm cover bolts, then remove the rocker arm cover. Discard the gasket.

To install:

7. Clean all the gasket surfaces completely.

8. Install the rocker arm cover using a new gasket, then tighten the retaining bolts to 90 inch lbs. (10 Nm).

9. Connect the PCV valve to the rocker arm cover.

10. Position the coolant tube and connect the thermostat bypass hose.

11. Install the coolant tube mounting nut and bolts. Tighten the screw at the water pump to 106 inch lbs. (12 Nm), the bolt at the corner of the cylinder head to 18 ft. lbs. (25 Nm) and the nut to 18 ft. lbs. (25 Nm).

12. Properly refill the cooling system.

13. Connect the negative battery cable, then start the vehicle. Check for leaks.

REAR (RIGHT) COVER

1. Disconnect the negative battery cable.

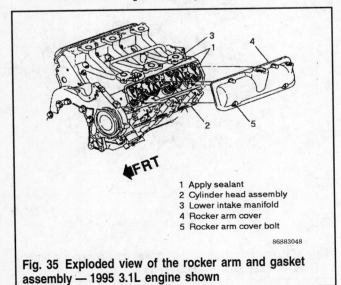

1 Apply sealant
2 Cylinder head assembly
3 Lower intake manifold
4 Rocker arm cover
5 Rocker arm cover bolt

86883048

Fig. 35 Exploded view of the rocker arm and gasket assembly — 1995 3.1L engine shown

2. Tag and disconnect the spark plug wires from the spark plugs and upper intake plenum wire retainer, then position out of the way.

3. Disconnect the power brake booster vacuum pipe from the intake plenum.

4. Remove the serpentine belt.

5. Remove the alternator.

6. Disconnect and remove the ignition assembly and EVAP canister purge solenoid as an assembly.

7. Remove the four rocker arm cover bolts, then remove the rocker arm cover. Discard the gasket.

To install:

8. Clean all the gasket surfaces completely.

9. Install the rocker arm cover using a new gasket, then tighten the rocker cover bolts to 90 inch lbs. (10 Nm).

10. Install the alternator.

11. Install the serpentine belt.

12. Connect the power brake booster vacuum pipe to the plenum.

13. Install the EVAP solenoid and ignition assembly.

14. Connect the spark plug wires to the wire retainers on the plenum and the spark plugs as tagged during removal.

15. Properly refill the cooling system.

16. Connect the negative battery cable, then start the vehicle and check for leaks.

3.3L Engine

♦ See Figure 36

FRONT (LEFT) COVER

1. Disconnect the negative battery cable.

2. Remove the accessory drive belt.

3. Unfasten the alternator-to-brace bolt, then remove the brace.

4. Remove the spark plug wire harness.

5. Unfasten the retainers, then remove the valve cover and gasket. Discard the gasket.

➡**Do NOT pry on the cover to remove it. If it sticks, use your palm or a rubber mallet to bump it rearwards, from the front.**

6. Using a suitable scraper, carefully clean the gasket mounting surfaces. Keep debris out of the engine.

To install:

7. Position a new gasket into the groove on the valve cover, then place the cover on the cylinder head. Tighten the retainers to 88 inch lbs. (10 Nm).

8. Install the spark plug wire harness.

9. Position the alternator brace, then secure using the retaining bolt.

10. Install the accessory drive belt.

11. Connect the negative battery cable, then start the engine and check for leaks.

REAR (RIGHT) COVER

1. Disconnect the negative battery cable.

2. Remove the accessory drive belt.

3. Loosen, but do not remove, the power steering pump bolts, then slide the pump forward.

4. Remove the power steering pump braces.

5. Tag and disconnect the spark plug wires.

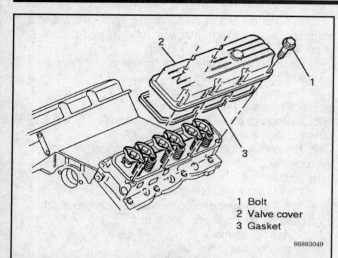

1 Bolt
2 Valve cover
3 Gasket

86883049

Fig. 36 Exploded view of the valve cover and gasket assembly — 3.3L engine shown

6. Unfasten the valve cover retainers, then remove the cover and gasket from the vehicle. Discard the gasket.

➡ Do NOT pry on the cover to remove it. If it sticks, use your palm or a rubber mallet to bump it rearwards, from the front.

7. Using a suitable scraper, carefully clean the gasket mounting surfaces. Keep debris out of the engine.

To install:

8. Position a new gasket into the groove on the valve cover, then place the cover on the cylinder head. Apply thread lock compound 12345493 or equivalent, then tighten the retainers to 88 inch lbs. (10 Nm).

9. Connect the spark plug wires as tagged during removal.

10. Install the power steering pump braces.

11. Slide the power steering pump back to its original position, then tighten the pump mounting bolts.

12. Install the accessory drive belt.

13. Connect the negative battery cable, then start the engine and inspect for leaks.

Rocker Arm Assembly

REMOVAL & INSTALLATION

2.0L Engine

1. Disconnect the negative battery cable.

2. Remove the camshaft cover. For details, please refer to the procedure located in this section.

3. Hold the valves in place with compressed air, using air adapter J 22794 or equivalent in the spark plug hole.

4. Compress the valve springs using J 33302-25 or other suitable valve spring compressor.

5. Remove rocker arms and valve lash compensators. Keep them in order if they are being reused.

6. The installation is the reverse of the removal procedure. Make sure to keep the rocker arms and valve lash compensators in their original positions if they are being reused.

7. Connect the negative battery cable and check for proper operation.

2.5L Engine

▶ See Figure 37

1. Disconnect the negative battery cable.

2. Remove the rocker arm cover. For details, please refer to the procedure located in this section.

3. Remove the rocker arm bolt and ball. If replacing the pushrod only, loosen the rocker arm bolt and swing the arm clear of the pushrod.

4. Remove the rocker arm, pushrod and guide. Store all components in order so they can be reassembled in their original location. Pushrod guides are different and must be reassembled in the previous location.

5. Installation is the reverse of removal. When new rocker arms or balls are used, coat the bearing surfaces with Molykote® or equivalent. Tighten the rocker arm bolts to 24 ft. lbs. (32 Nm).

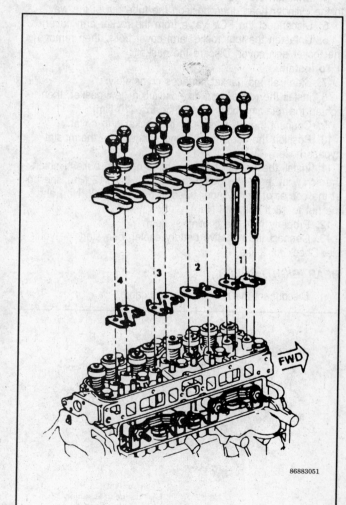

86883051

Fig. 37 Exploded view of the rocker arm assembly and related components — 2.5L engine

3.0L and 3.3L Engines
▶ **See Figures 38 and 39**

1. Disconnect the negative battery cable.
2. Remove the rocker arm cover. For details, please refer to the procedure located in this section.
3. Remove the rocker arm pedestal retaining bolts.
4. Remove the rocker arm and pedestal assembly. Note the position of the double ended bolts for reassembly. Store all components on a clean surface in order so they may be installed in their original locations.
5. Installation is the reverse of removal. Replace any components that show signs of unusual wear. For the 3.0L engine, tighten the bolts to 45 ft. lbs. (60 Nm). Tighten the bolts to 18 ft. lbs. (25 Nm) and addition 70° turn for the 3.3L engine.

3.1L Engine
▶ **See Figure 40**

1. Disconnect the negative battery cable.
2. Remove the rocker arm cover as outlined previously in this section.
3. Remove the rocker arm nuts, balls, rocker arms and pushrods.

To install:
4. Clean all the gasket surfaces completely.
5. Coat all the valve train components with engine oil prior to installation.
6. Install the pushrods and install the rocker arms on the studs. Install the rocker arm balls and mounting nuts. Make sure the pushrods are properly seated in the lifter and rocker arm. Tighten the mounting nuts to 18 ft. lbs. (24 Nm).
7. Install the rocker arm cover using a new gasket and tighten the rocker cover bolts to 90 inch lbs. (10 Nm).
8. Connect the negative battery cable.
9. Start the vehicle and verify that there are no leaks.

Fig. 38 Unfastening the rocker arm pedestal retaining bolt — 3.0L engine shown

Thermostat

REMOVAL & INSTALLATION

▶ **See Figures 41, 42, 43 and 44**

✳✳CAUTION

When draining the coolant, keep in mind that cats and dogs are attracted by the ethylene glycol antifreeze, and are quite likely to drink any that is left in an uncovered container or in puddles on the ground. This will prove fatal in sufficient quantity. Always drain the coolant into a sealable container. Coolant should be reused unless it is contaminated or several years old.

2.0L and 2.5L Engines

1. Disconnect the negative battery cable.
2. Remove the thermostat housing cap.
3. Grasp the handle of the thermostat, then gently pull it upwards to remove. Remove the gasket/O-ring and replace if damaged.
4. Clean off the thermostat housing and O-ring. After cleaning, apply a suitable lubricant to the O-ring to aid in installation.

To install:
5. Place the thermostat in the housing, pushing down to be sure it is firmly seated.
6. Install the thermostat housing cap.
7. Connect the negative battery cable.

2.3L Engines

1988-93 VEHICLES

1. Disconnect the negative battery cable.
2. Properly drain and recover the coolant to a level below the thermostat.
3. Disconnect the upper radiator hose and position it aside.
4. Remove the heater hose and position it aside.
5. Detach the ECT sensor electrical connector.
6. Remove the throttle body coolant hose.
7. Unfasten the thermostat housing retaining bolts, then remove the housing.
8. Remove the thermostat, then clean the gasket material from the mating surfaces.

To install:
9. Position the thermostat, then install the housing, using a new gasket. Tighten to 19 ft. lbs. (26 Nm).
10. Connect the throttle body and heater hoses.
11. Attach the ECT sensor electrical connector.
12. Install the upper radiator hose, then properly fill the cooling system.
13. Connect the negative battery cable.

1994-95 VEHICLES

1. Disconnect the negative battery cable.
2. Properly drain and recover the coolant to a level below the thermostat.

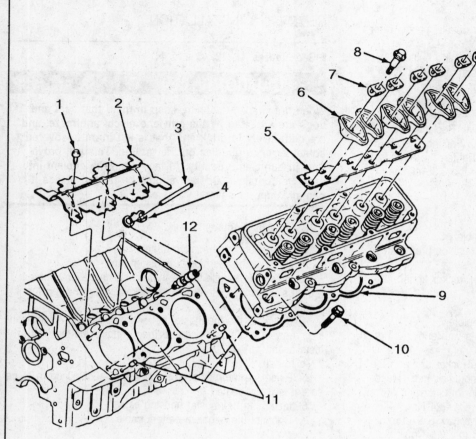

1 Bolt 37 Nm (27 lbs.ft.)
2 Lifter guide retainer
3 Pushrod
4 Lifter guide
5 Pushrod guide
6 Rocker arm
7 Rocker arm pivot
8 Bolts 51 Nm (37 lbs.ft.)
9 Head gasket
10 Head bolt
11 Dowel pin
12 Valve lifter

86883052

Fig. 39 Rocker arm and related components — 3.3L engine shown

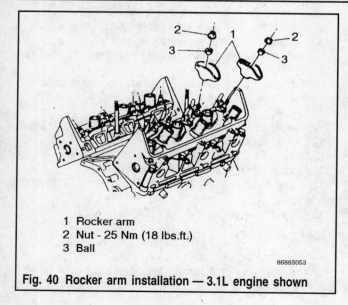

1 Rocker arm
2 Nut - 25 Nm (18 lbs.ft.)
3 Ball

86883053

Fig. 40 Rocker arm installation — 3.1L engine shown

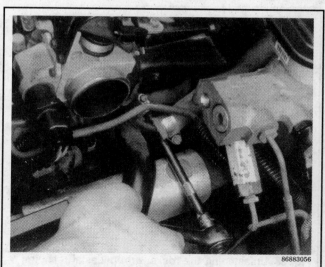

86883056

Fig. 41 Unfasten the thermostat housing retaining bolts

Fig. 42 If not done already, disconnect the throttle body outlet hose

Fig. 43 Using a pair of pliers or your hand, remove the thermostat

Fig. 44 Using a suitable scraping tool, clean the old gasket material from the housing and mating surfaces

3. Unfasten the coolant inlet housing bolt, which is accessible through the exhaust manifold.

4. Raise and safely support the vehicle.

5. Remove the radiator outlet pipe stud.

6. Remove the second coolant inlet housing bolt, then remove the coolant inlet housing.

7. Remove the thermostat, then clean the old gasket material from the mating surfaces.

To install:

8. Position the thermostat in its correct location, then install the coolant inlet housing using a new gasket. Tighten the retaining bolt to 19 ft. lbs. (26 Nm).

9. Install the radiator outlet pipe stud.

10. Carefully lower the vehicle.

11. Install the coolant inlet housing bolt through the exhaust manifold.

12. Properly fill the cooling system, then connect the negative battery cable.

3.0L Engine

1. Disconnect the negative battery cable.

2. Properly drain the coolant down to a level below the thermostat.

3. Swing aside the the air intake duct.

4. Disconnect the throttle body outlet hose.

5. Unfasten the thermostat housing attaching bolts, then remove the housing.

6. Remove the thermostat from the engine.

7. Clean the old gasket material from the housing mating surfaces.

To install:

8. Position the thermostat, be sure it is firmly seated. Use a new gasket.

9. Install the thermostat housing, then tighten the retaining bolts.

10. Connect the throttle body outlet hose.

11. Swing the air intake duct back into its original position.

12. Properly fill the cooling system.

13. Connect the negative battery cable, remove the radiator cap, then start the engine. Allow the engine to run with radiator cap removed, until the upper radiator hose becomes hot (thermostat open). With the engine idling, add coolant to the radiator until the level is up to the bottom of the filler neck.

14. Install the radiator cap, making sure the arrows line up with the overflow tube.

3.1L and 3.3L Engines

1. Disconnect the negative battery cable.

2. Drain the cooling system to a level below the thermostat housing.

3. Remove the air cleaner assembly.

4. Disconnect the surge tank line from the thermostat housing.

5. Remove thermostat housing-to-intake manifold attaching bolt and nut, then remove the housing.

6. Remove the thermostat.

To Install:

7. Clean all gasket surfaces completely.

8. Install the thermostat in the intake manifold.

9. Install the thermostat housing on the intake manifold.

10. Install the mounting bolt and nut. Tighten to 18 ft. lbs. (25 Nm) for the 3.1L engine. For the 3.3L engine, tighten to 20 ft. lbs. (27 Nm).

11. Install the air cleaner assembly.

12. Connect the surge tank line to thermostat housing.

13. Refill the cooling system.

14. Connect the negative battery cable.

Intake Manifold

REMOVAL & INSTALLATION

2.0L Engine

♦ **See Figure 45**

1. Disconnect the negative battery cable, then properly drain the cooling system and relieve the fuel system pressure.

2. Disconnect the induction tube and hoses.

3. Tag and detach the wiring to the throttle body, MAP sensor and the wastegate.

4. Disconnect the PCV hose.

5. Tag and disconnect the vacuum hoses from the throttle body.

6. Disconnect the throttle cable and, if equipped, the cruise control cable.

7. Disconnect the fuel return line from the throttle cable support bracket.

8. Tag and disconnect the wiring from the ignition coil, then remove the coil bracket.

9. Tag and detach the vacuum lines from the rear of the manifold.

10. Remove the transaxle fill tube and manifold support brackets.

11. Remove the heater tube support bracket from the lower side of the manifold.

12. Disconnect the fuel injector wiring.

13. Remove the coolant recovery tank.

14. Remove the accessory drive belt, then remove the alternator.

15. Remove the power steering adjusting bracket and the alternator front adjusting bracket.

16. Disconnect the power steering pump bracket from the cylinder head and engine block.

17. Disengage the fuel rail-to-fuel inlet fitting.

18. Detach the fuel return line from the regulator outlet.

19. Unfasten the intake manifold retaining nuts and washers, then remove the manifold from the engine.

➡**If installing a new intake manifold, transfer all necessary parts from the old manifold to the new one.**

20. Using a suitable scraping tool, clean the old gasket material from the intake manifold mating surfaces. Do NOT let any debris fall into the engine!

To install:

21. Position a new gasket on the manifold, then install the manifold. Install the retaining washers and nuts, then tighten them to 18 ft. lbs. (25 Nm) starting from the middle and working outward.

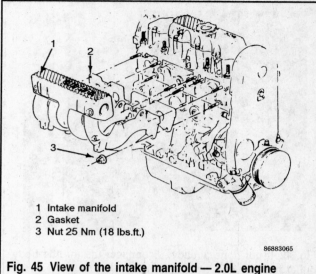

1 Intake manifold
2 Gasket
3 Nut 25 Nm (18 lbs.ft.)

86883065

Fig. 45 View of the intake manifold — 2.0L engine

22. Connect the fuel return line to the regulator outlet, then engage the fuel line to the fuel rail inlet.

23. Install the power steering pump bracket to the cylinder head and block.

24. Fasten the alternator front adjusting bracket and the power steering adjusting bracket.

25. Install the alternator, then secure the accessory drive belt.

26. Position and install the coolant recovery tank.

27. Connect the wiring to the fuel injectors.

28. Install the heater tube support bracket on the lower side of the manifold.

29. Install the manifold support and the transaxle fill tube brackets.

30. Attach the vacuum hoses to the rear of the manifold.

31. Install the ignition coil bracket, then connect the wires as tagged during removal.

32. Connect the fuel return line to the throttle cable support bracket.

33. Attach the throttle cable and the cruise control cable (if equipped).

34. Connect the vacuum hoses to the throttle body as tagged during removal.

35. Install the PCV hose.

36. Fasten the wiring to the wastegate, MAP sensor and the throttle body as tagged during removal.

37. Connect the induction tube and hoses.

38. Refill the cooling system to the proper level, then connect the negative battery cable. Start the engine and inspect for coolant leakage.

2.3L Engine

♦ **See Figures 46 and 47**

1. Disconnect the negative battery cable, then properly drain the cooling system.

2. Detach the vacuum hose and electrical connector from the MAP sensor.

3. Disengage the electrical connectors from the MAT/IAT sensor and the purge solenoid.

4. Disconnect the fuel injector harness, then position it aside.

5. Label and disconnect the vacuum hoses from the intake manifold and the hose at the fuel regulator and purge solenoid to the canister.

6. Disconnect the throttle body and vent tube-to-air cleaner ducts.

7. Remove the throttle cable bracket.

8. Disconnect the power brake vacuum line (including the retaining bracket-to-power steering bracket) and position it aside.

9. Disconnect the coolant lines from the throttle body, then remove the throttle body.

10. Remove the oil air separator (crankcase ventilation system) as an assembly. Leave the hoses attached to the separator. Disconnect the hoses from the oil fill, chain cover, intake duct and the intake manifold.

11. Detach the oil/air separator from the oil fill tube.

12. Remove the oil fill cap and oil level indicator assembly.

13. Unfasten the oil fill tube bolt/screw, then pull the tube upward to remove.

14. Detach the injector harness connector.

15. Remove the fill tube out the top, rotating as necessary to gain clearance for the oil/air separator nipple between the intake tubes and fuel rail electrical harness.

16. Remove the intake manifold support brace.

17. Unfasten the manifold retaining nuts and bolts, then remove the intake manifold from the engine.

➡If installing a new intake manifold, transfer all necessary parts from the old manifold to the new one.

18. Using a suitable scraping tool, clean the old gasket material from the intake manifold mating surfaces. Do NOT let any debris fall into the engine!

To install:

19. Install the manifold with a new gasket.

➡Make sure that the numbers stamped on the gasket are facing towards the manifold surface.

20. Follow the tightening sequence in the accompanying figure, then tighten the bolts/nuts to 19 ft. lbs. (26 Nm).

21. Install the intake manifold brace and retainers.

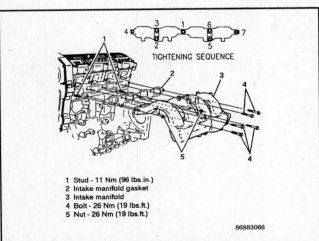

1 Stud - 11 Nm (96 lbs.in.)
2 Intake manifold gasket
3 Intake manifold
4 Bolt - 26 Nm (19 lbs.ft.)
5 Nut - 26 Nm (19 lbs.ft.)

86883066

Fig. 46 View of the mounting of the 2.3L engine intake manifold. When tightening the bolts, be sure to follow the proper tightening sequence

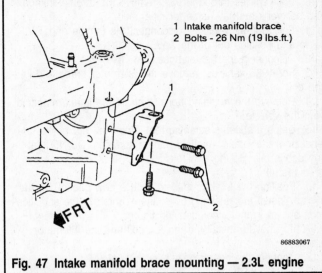

1 Intake manifold brace
2 Bolts - 26 Nm (19 lbs.ft.)

86883067

Fig. 47 Intake manifold brace mounting — 2.3L engine

22. Lubricate a new oil fill tube O-ring seal with clean engine oil, then install the tube down between intake manifold. Rotate as needed to gain clearance for the oil/air separator nipple on the fill tube.

23. Position the oil fill tube in its cylinder block opening. Align the fill tube so it is in about its proper position. Place the palm of your hand over the oil fill opening and press straight down to seat the fill tube and O-ring into the cylinder block.

24. Connect the oil/air separator hose to the oil fill tube. You can lubricate the hose as necessary to ease installation. Install the oil fill tube bolt/screw.

25. Install the throttle body to the intake manifold using a new gasket, then connect the coolant lines to the throttle body.

26. Connect the power brake vacuum hose to the throttle body, then secure the pipe to the power steering bracket.

27. Install the throttle/accelerator control cable bracket.

28. Connect the vacuum hoses to the intake manifold and connect the fuel regulator hose.

29. Attach all electrical connectors, as tagged during removal.

30. Install the air cleaner duct.

31. Install the coolant recovery tank and refill the coolant to it's proper level.

32. Connect the negative battery cable, then start the engine and inspect for leaks.

2.5L Engine

▶ See Figures 48 and 49

1. Disconnect the negative battery cable.

2. Remove the air cleaner assembly and hot air pipe (if equipped).

3. Detach the PCV valve and hose at the TBI assembly.

4. Properly drain the cooling system.

5. Properly relieve the fuel system pressure as described in Section 5, then disconnect the fuel lines.

6. Label and detach the vacuum hoses.

7. Tag and remove the wiring and throttle linkage from the TBI assembly.

8. Remove the transaxle downshift linkage.

9. If equipped, remove the cruise control linkage/servo cable.

10. For vehicles through 1987, remove the throttle linkage and bellcrank and lay aside for clearance.

11. For 1988-91 vehicles, disconnect the throttle and T.V. cable and position out of the way.

12. Disconnect the heater hose.

13. For 1986 vehicles, remove the alternator brace and ignition coil.

14. Remove the retaining bolts, then lift the intake manifold from the vehicle.

15. Using a suitable scraping tool, clean the old gasket material from the intake manifold mating surfaces. Do NOT let any debris fall into the engine!

To install:

16. Position the intake manifold, with a new gasket, on the engine. Install the retaining bolts, then tighten to the specifications shown in the accompanying figures.

17. If removed, install the ignition coil and the alternator brace.

18. Connect the heater hose.

19. For 1988-91 vehicles, connect the throttle and T.V. cable.

20. For vehicles through 1987, connect the throttle linkage and bellcrank.

21. If equipped, connect the cruise control linkage/servo cable.

22. Install the transaxle downshift linkage bracket.

23. Connect the wiring and throttle linkage to the TBI assembly.

24. Attach the vacuum hoses as tagged during removal.

25. Fasten the fuel lines.

26. Connect the PCV valve and hose at the throttle body.

27. Fill the cooling system, using the proper type and amount of coolant.

28. Install the air cleaner assembly.

29. Connect the negative battery cable, then start the engine and check for coolant and/or vacuum leaks.

3.0L Engine

▶ See Figures 50, 51, 52 and 53

➡For some vehicles, a special bolt wrench J-24394 or equivalent is required for this procedure.

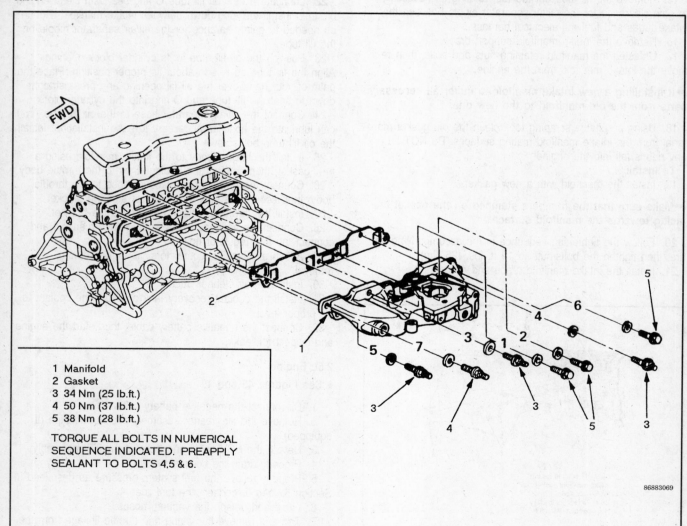

1 Manifold
2 Gasket
3 34 Nm (25 lb.ft.)
4 50 Nm (37 lb.ft.)
5 38 Nm (28 lb.ft.)

TORQUE ALL BOLTS IN NUMERICAL SEQUENCE INDICATED. PREAPPLY SEALANT TO BOLTS 4,5 & 6.

86883069

Fig. 48 Intake manifold mounting and bolt tightening specifications — 1986 2.5L engine

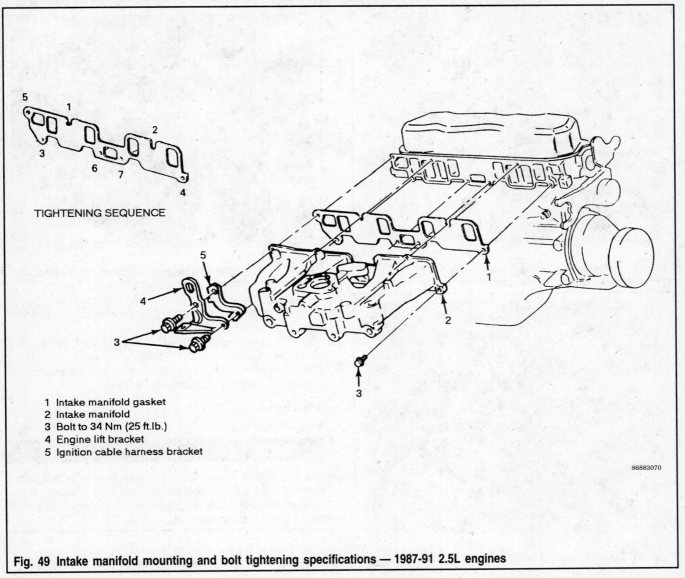

TIGHTENING SEQUENCE

1 Intake manifold gasket
2 Intake manifold
3 Bolt to 34 Nm (25 ft.lb.)
4 Engine lift bracket
5 Ignition cable harness bracket

86883070

Fig. 49 Intake manifold mounting and bolt tightening specifications — 1987-91 2.5L engines

1. Properly relieve the fuel system pressure, then disconnect the fuel lines from the fuel rail.
2. Disconnect the negative battery cable.
3. Disconnect the mass air flow sensor and air intake duct.
4. Remove the serpentine accessory drive belt, alternator and bracket.
5. Remove the the C^{3}I ignition module with the spark plug cables attached. Tag all wiring connectors before detaching from the spark plugs.
6. Label and disengage all vacuum lines and wiring connectors as necessary to gain clearance to remove the manifold.
7. Remove the throttle, cruise control (if equipped) and T.V. cables from the throttle body.
8. Properly drain the cooling system.
9. Disconnect the heater hoses from the throttle body.
10. Remove the upper radiator hose.
11. If not already done, disconnect the fuel lines, then remove the fuel rail and injectors.
12. Remove the intake manifold mounting bolts. Loosen in reverse of the torque sequence (shown in the accompany fig-

ure) to prevent manifold warping. Remove the intake manifold from the engine.
13. Using a suitable scraping tool, clean the old gasket material from the intake manifold mating surfaces. Do NOT let any debris fall into the engine!
To install:
14. Position a new manifold gasket, apply sealer No. 1050026 or equivalent if a steel gasket is used. Apply sealer 12345336 or equivalent to the ends of the manifold gasket.
15. Apply sealer 1052080 or equivalent to the manifold bolt threads, then install the bolts. Tighten the manifold bolts in the sequence in the accompanying figure to 32 ft. lbs. (44 Nm).
16. Install the injectors and fuel rail.
17. Install the upper radiator hose, then connect the heater hoses to the throttle body.
18. Connect the T.V., cruise control (if equipped), and throttle cables to the throttle body.
19. Attach all vacuum lines and wiring connectors as labeled during removal.
20. Install the ignition module, then connect the wires to the as tagged during removal.

Fig. 50 Unfasten the manifold mounting bolts, then . . .

Fig. 52 Remove and discard the old manifold gasket

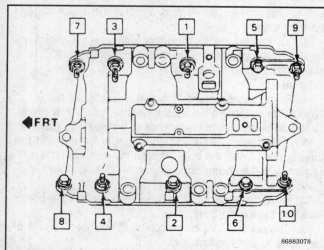

Fig. 53 Be sure to tighten the manifold bolts in the correct sequence

Fig. 51 . . . lift the intake manifold from the engine

21. Install the alternator, bracket and serpentine belt.
22. Install the air intake duct, then connect the mass airflow sensor.
23. Fill the cooling system with the proper type and quantity of coolant.
24. Connect the negative battery cable, then start the engine and check for coolant and/or vacuum leaks.

3.1L Engine

▶ See Figure 54

❋❋CAUTION

The fuel system is under pressure and must be properly relieved before disconnecting the fuel lines. Failure to properly relieve the fuel system pressure can lead to personal injury and component damage.

1. Relieve the fuel system pressure.
2. Disconnect the negative battery cable.
3. Remove top half of the air cleaner assembly and throttle body duct.
4. Properly drain and recover the cooling system.
5. Disconnect the EGR pipe from exhaust manifold.
6. Remove the serpentine belt.
7. Remove the brake vacuum pipe at the intake plenum.
8. Disconnect the control cables from the throttle body and intake plenum mounting bracket.
9. Remove the power steering lines at the alternator bracket.
10. Remove the alternator.
11. Label and disconnect the spark plug wires from the spark plugs and wire retainers on the intake plenum.
12. Remove the ignition assembly and the EVAP canister purge solenoid together.

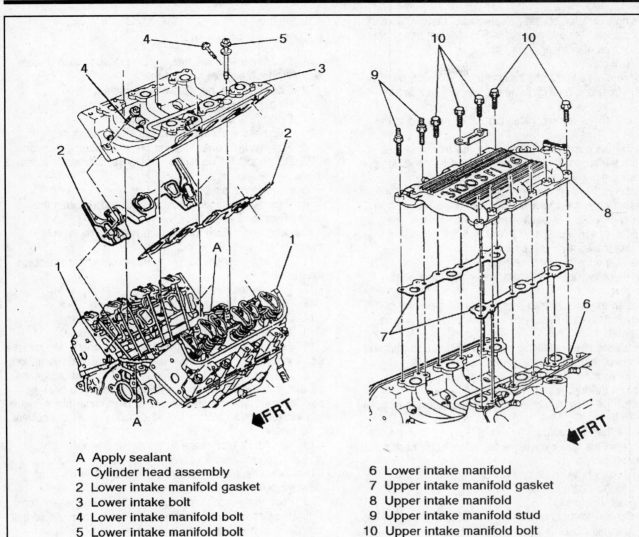

A Apply sealant
1 Cylinder head assembly
2 Lower intake manifold gasket
3 Lower intake bolt
4 Lower intake manifold bolt
5 Lower intake manifold bolt

6 Lower intake manifold
7 Upper intake manifold gasket
8 Upper intake manifold
9 Upper intake manifold stud
10 Upper intake manifold bolt

86883079

Fig. 54 View of the intake manifold installation — 3.1L engine shown

13. Disconnect the upper engine wiring harness connectors at the following components:
- Throttle Position Sensor (TPS)
- Idle Air Control (IAC)
- Fuel Injectors
- Coolant temperature sensor
- Manifold Absolute Pressure (MAP) sensor
- Camshaft Position (CMP) sensor

14. Tag and disconnect the vacuum lines from the following components:
- Vacuum modulator
- Fuel pressure regulator
- PCV valve

15. Disconnect the MAP sensor from upper intake manifold.

16. Remove the upper intake plenum mounting bolts and remove the plenum.

17. Disconnect the fuel lines from the fuel rail and fuel line bracket.

18. Install engine support fixture special tool J 28467-A or an equivalent.

19. Remove the right side engine mount.

20. Remove the power steering mounting bolts and support the pump out of the way without disconnecting the power steering lines.

21. Disconnect the coolant inlet pipe from coolant outlet housing.

22. Remove the coolant bypass hose from the water pump and the cylinder head.

23. Disconnect the upper radiator hose at thermostat housing.

24. Remove the thermostat housing.

25. Remove both rocker arm covers.

26. Remove the lower intake manifold bolts. Make sure the washers on the four center bolts are installed in their original locations.

➡ **When removing the valve train components they should be kept in order for installation the original locations.**

27. Remove the rocker arm retaining nuts and remove the rocker arms and pushrods.

28. Remove the intake manifold from the engine. Remove and discard the gasket.

29. Using a suitable scraper, clean gasket material from all mating surfaces. Remove all excess RTV sealant from front and rear ridges of cylinder block.

To install:

30. Place a 0.12 in. (3mm) bead of RTV, on each ridge, where the front and rear of the intake manifold contact the block.

31. Using a new gasket, install the intake manifold to the engine.

32. Install the pushrods, rocker arms and mounting nuts. Make sure the pushrods are properly seated in the valve lifters and rocker arms.

33. Install rocker arm nuts and tighten to 18 ft. lbs. (24 Nm).

34. Install lower the intake manifold attaching bolts. Apply sealant PN 12345739 or equivalent to the threads of bolts, and tighten bolts to 115 inch lbs. (13 Nm).

35. Install the front rocker arm cover.

36. Install the thermostat housing.

37. Connect the upper radiator hose to the thermostat housing.

38. Fasten the coolant inlet pipe to thermostat housing.

39. Connect coolant bypass pipe at the water pump and cylinder head.

40. Install the power steering pump in the mounting bracket.

41. Connect the right side engine mount.

42. Remove the special engine support tool.

43. Fasten the fuel lines to fuel rail and bracket.

44. Install the upper intake manifold and torque the mounting bolts to 18 ft. lbs. (25 Nm).

45. Install the MAP sensor.

46. Connect the upper engine wiring harness connectors to the following components:
- Throttle Position Sensor (TPS)
- Idle Air Control (IAC)
- Fuel Injectors
- Coolant temperature sensor
- Manifold Absolute Pressure (MAP) sensor
- Camshaft Position (CMP) sensor

47. Connect the vacuum lines to the following components:
- Vacuum modulator
- Fuel pressure regulator
- PCV valve

48. Install the EVAP canister purge solenoid and ignition assembly.

49. Install the alternator assembly.

50. Connect the power steering line to the alternator bracket.

51. Install the serpentine belt.

52. Connect the spark plug wires to the spark plugs and intake plenum wire retainer.

53. Install the EGR pipe to the exhaust manifold.

54. Connect the control cables to the throttle body lever and upper intake plenum mounting bracket.

55. Install air intake assembly and top half of the air cleaner assembly.

56. Install the brake vacuum pipe.

57. Fill the cooling system.

58. Connect the negative battery cable, then start the vehicle and verify that there are no leaks.

3.3L Engine

◗ See Figures 55 and 56

1. Properly relieve the fuel system pressure, then disconnect the fuel lines from the fuel rail.

2. Disconnect the negative battery cable.

3. Properly drain the coolant.

4. Disconnect the accessory drive belt.

5. Remove the alternator and the braces/supports.

6. Remove the power steering pump and braces/supports.

7. Disconnect the coolant bypass hose, the heater pipe and the upper radiator hose.

8. Remove the air inlet duct.

9. Remove the throttle cable bracket and unfasten the cables from the throttle body.

10. Label and detach the vacuum hoses from the intake manifold.

11. Tag and disengage any electrical connectors to access the manifold.

12. Remove the fuel rail.

13. Disconnect the vapor canister purge line.

14. Detach the heater hose from the throttle body.

15. Tag and disconnect the rear spark plug wires.

16. Remove the intake manifold mounting bolts, then remove the manifold from the engine. Remove and discard the gasket.

17. Using a suitable scraping tool, clean the old gasket material from the intake manifold mating surfaces. Do NOT let any debris fall into the engine! Clean the cylinder block, heads and intake manifold surfaces of all oil using a suitable solvent.

To install:

18. Apply RTV type sealer to the ends of a new manifold gasket then position the gasket.

19. Clean the intake manifold bolts and bolt holes of all adhesive compound.

20. Position the intake manifold over the new gasket. Apply a suitable thread locking compound to the intake manifold bolt threads, then install the bolts and tighten the bolts, in sequence, in two steps to 89 inch lbs. (10 Nm).

21. Attach the rear spark plugs wires at tagged during removal.

22. Connect the heater hose to the throttle body.

23. Attach the vapor canister purge line.

24. Install the fuel rail.

25. Attach any electrical connectors or vacuum lines that were removed to access the manifold.

26. Fasten the cables to the throttle body, then install the throttle cable bracket.

27. Install the air inlet duct.

28. Connect the upper radiator hose, the heater pipe and the coolant bypass hose.

29. Install the power steering braces/supports and the pump

30. Install the alternator braces/support, then install the alternator.

31. Install the accessory drive belt.

32. Fill the coolant system with the correct type and quantity of coolant.

33. Connect the negative battery cable, then start the engines and check for coolant and/or vacuum leaks.

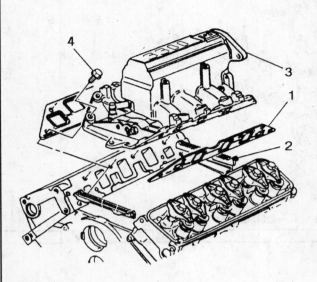

1 Intake manifold gasket
2 Intake manifold seal
3 Intake manifold
4 Bolt 10 Nm (88 lb.in.)
  TIGHTEN TWICE IN GIVEN SEQUENCE.
  APPLY P/N 1052624 TO BOLTS BEFORE
  ASSEMBLY

86883081

Fig. 55 View of the intake manifold mounting — 3.3L engine

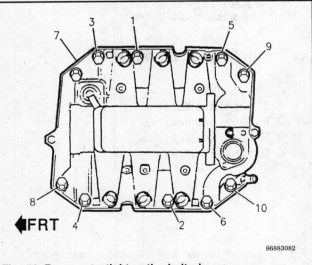

86883082

Fig. 56 Be sure to tighten the bolts in sequence

Exhaust Manifold

REMOVAL & INSTALLATION

2.0L Engine

▶ See Figures 57 and 58

1. Disconnect the negative battery cable.
2. Remove the turbo induction tube.
3. Label and detach the spark plug wires.
4. Remove the turbocharger. For details, please refer to the procedure located later in this section.
5. If applicable, detach the wiring from the oxygen sensor.
6. Unfasten the bolts and nuts retaining the exhaust manifold to the block and exhaust pipe, then remove the manifold. Remove and discard the gasket.

To Install:

7. Install the exhaust manifold with a new gasket. Install the retainers, then tighten (in the sequence shown in the accompanying figure) the studs to 20 ft. lbs. (27 Nm,) and the nuts to 16 ft. lbs. (22 Nm).
8. Connect the exhaust pipe to the exhaust manifold and tighten the nuts to 19 ft. lbs. (25 Nm).
9. Attach the wire to the oxygen sensor, if applicable.
10. Install the turbocharger. For details, please refer to the procedure located later in this section.
11. Connect the spark plug wires as tagged during removal.
12. Install the turbo induction tube.
13. Connect the negative battery cable.

2.3L Engine

▶ See Figure 59

1. Disconnect the negative battery cable
2. Detach the oxygen sensor connector.

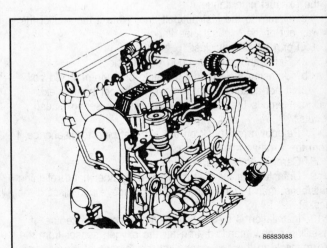

86883083

Fig. 57 Removing the turbo induction tube is simply a matter of unfastening the clamps, then removing the tube from the engine

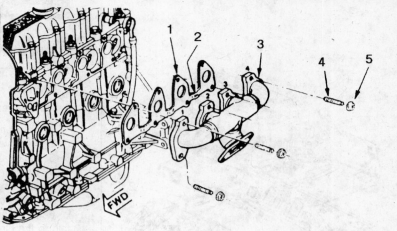

1 Gasket
2 Expansion joints face outward
3 Manifold asm.
4 Stud - 27 Nm (20 lb.ft.)
5 Nut - 22 Nm (16 lb.ft.)

TORQUE NO.2 & 3 MANIFOLD RUNNERS PRIOR TO NO.1 & 4 RUNNERS

FWD

86883084

Fig. 58 Exhaust manifold mounting and retainer tightening sequence — 2.0L engine

3. If accessible at this time, remove upper and lower exhaust manifold heat shields. Some vehicles only have one shield accessible when the vehicle is raised.

➡️**For vehicles through 1989, it is necessary to relieve the spring pressure from one nut/bolt prior to removing the second nut/bolt. If the spring pressure is not relieved it will cause the exhaust pipe to twist and bind up the bolt as it is removed.**

4. For 1988-89 vehicles:
    a. Unfasten the nut/bolt that attaches the exhaust manifold brace to the manifold.
    b. Break loose the manifold-to-exhaust pipe spring loaded nuts/bolts using a 13mm box wrench.
    c. Raise and safely support the vehicle.
5. For 1988-89 models, remove the manifold-to-exhaust pipe nuts/bolts from the exhaust pipe flange as follows:
    a. Unscrew either nut/bolt clockwise 4 turns.
    b. Move to the other nut/bolt and turn it all the way out of the exhaust pipe flange.
    c. Return to the first nut/bolt and rotate it the rest of the way out of the exhaust pipe flange.
6. For 1990-95 vehicles:
    a. Raise and safely support the vehicle.
    b. Unfasten the exhaust manifold brace-to-manifold bolt.
    c. If not already done, remove the upper heat shield.
    d. Remove the manifold-to-exhaust pipe spring loaded nuts.
7. Pull down and back on the exhaust pipe to disengage it from the exhaust manifold bolts.
8. Carefully lower the vehicle.
9. Unfasten the exhaust manifold-to-cylinder head retaining nuts/bolts, then remove the manifold. Remove and discard the gasket.
10. Installation is the reverse of the removal procedure. If installing a new manifold, transfer the oxygen sensor from the old manifold to the new one. Coat the threads of the sensor with a suitable anti-seize compound prior to installation. Make

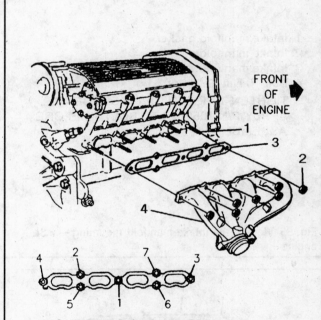

FRONT OF ENGINE

TIGHTENING SEQUENCE

1 Exhaust manifold stud
2 Exhaust manifold nut
3 Exhaust manifold gasket
4 Exhaust manifold

86883085

Fig. 59 View of the exhaust manifold mounting and tightening sequence — 1994 2.3L shown

sure to use a new gasket, then tighten the retainers, in sequence, to the following specifications:

- 1988-89 Exhaust manifold-to-cylinder head nuts: 27 ft. lbs. (37 Nm)
- 1990-95 Exhaust manifold-to-cylinder head nuts: 31 ft. lbs. (42 Nm)
- Exhaust manifold-to-cylinder head studs: 106 inch lbs. (12 Nm)

11. Install the exhaust pipe flange bolts evenly and gradually to avoid binding.

12. Connect the negative battery cable and check for leaks.

2.5L Engine

1. Disconnect the negative battery cable.
2. Remove the air cleaner assembly and the hot air tube (if equipped).
3. Remove the alternator. For details, please refer to the procedure located in this section.
4. Detach the oxygen sensor connector.
5. Remove the oil level indicator tube.
6. Raise and safely support the vehicle.
7. Disconnect the exhaust pipe from the manifold.
8. Carefully lower the vehicle.
9. Bend the locking tabs away from the mounting bolts, the unfasten the exhaust manifold retaining bolts and washers and remove the exhaust manifold. Remove and discard the gasket.
10. Clean all gasket mating surfaces on the cylinder head and manifold.
11. Installation is the reverse of removal. Make sure to use a new gasket. Tighten using a crisscross pattern to the figures shown in the torque specifications chart.

3.0L Engine

LEFT (FRONT)

▶ See Figure 60

1. Disconnect the negative battery cable.
2. Tag and disconnect the spark plug wires.
3. Remove the manifold-to-crossover retaining bolts.
4. Unfasten the air cleaner assembly mounting bolts, then remove the assembly.
5. Remove the engine cooling fan.
6. Unfasten the manifold-to-cylinder head bolts.
7. Remove the oil level indicator tube and indicator.
8. Remove the exhaust manifold from the engine, then clean the mating surfaces using a suitable solvent.
9. Installation is the reverse of the removal procedure. Tighten the manifold-to-cylinder head bolts to 37 ft. lbs. (50 Nm). Tighten the crossover-to-manifold bolts to 15 ft. lbs. (20 Nm).
10. Connect the negative battery cable.

RIGHT (REAR)

▶ See Figure 61

1. Disconnect the negative battery cable.
2. Raise and safely support the vehicle.
3. Remove the two bolts attaching the exhaust pipe to the manifold.
4. Carefully lower the vehicle.
5. Detach the oxygen sensor electrical connector.

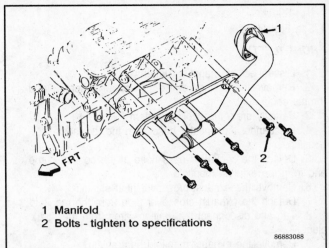

1 Manifold
2 Bolts - tighten to specifications

86883088

Fig. 60 View of the left (front) exhaust manifold mounting — 3.0L engine

6. Tag and disconnect the spark plug wires.
7. Remove the two nuts retaining the crossover pipe to the manifold.
8. Remove the serpentine drive belt.
9. Unfasten the power steering pump retaining bolts, then remove the pump.
10. Disconnect the heater hose from the tube.
11. Remove the exhaust manifold heat shield.
12. Remove the C³I bracket nuts.
13. Unfasten the six bolts attaching the exhaust manifold, then remove the manifold from the engine.
14. Using a suitable solvent, clean the exhaust manifold mating surfaces.

➡**If installing a new exhaust manifold, transfer the oxygen sensor and exhaust pipe seal (if applicable) from the old manifold to the new one.**

15. Installation is the reverse of removal. Tighten the exhaust manifold bolts to 37 ft. lbs. (50 Nm).
16. Connect the negative battery cable.

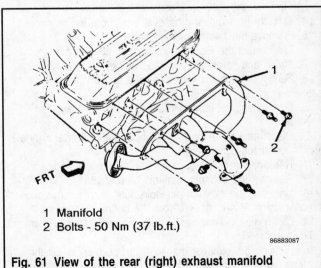

1 Manifold
2 Bolts - 50 Nm (37 lb.ft.)

86883087

Fig. 61 View of the rear (right) exhaust manifold mounting — 3.0L engine

3.1L Engine

◗ See Figure 62

FRONT (LEFT)

1. Disconnect the negative battery cable.
2. Remove the top half of the air cleaner assembly and throttle cable duct.
3. Partially drain the cooling system.
4. Disconnect the radiator hose from the thermostat housing.
5. Detach the coolant bypass hose at the coolant pump and from the exhaust manifold.
6. Remove the exhaust crossover heat shield.
7. Detach the exhaust crossover pipe from the manifold.
8. Tag and disconnect the ignition wires from the spark plugs.
9. Remove the exhaust manifold heat shield.
10. Unfasten the exhaust manifold retaining nuts, then remove the manifold and gasket from the engine.
11. Clean mating surfaces at the cylinder head and manifold.
   To install:
12. Install the exhaust manifold gasket and the exhaust manifold. Tighten the manifold mounting nuts to 12 ft. lbs (16 Nm).
13. Install the exhaust manifold heat shield.
14. Connect the exhaust crossover pipe to the manifold.
15. Install the exhaust crossover pipe heat shield.
16. Attach the secondary ignition wires to the appropriate spark plugs.
17. Connect the coolant by-pass pipe to the coolant pump and exhaust manifold.
18. Attach the radiator hose to the coolant outlet housing.
19. Install the top half of the air cleaner and the throttle body duct.
20. Connect the negative battery cable.

REAR (RIGHT)

1. Disconnect the negative battery cable.
2. Remove the top half of the air cleaner assembly and throttle cable duct.
3. Remove the exhaust crossover heat shield.
4. Detach the exhaust crossover pipe from the manifold.
5. Remove the heated oxygen sensor.
6. Disconnect the EGR pipe from the exhaust manifold.
7. Raise and safely support the vehicle.
8. Remove the transaxle oil fill tube and lever indicator assembly.
9. Disconnect the front exhaust pipe from the exhaust manifold.
10. Disconnect the exhaust pipe from the converter flange, then support the converter.
11. Remove the converter heat shield from the body.
12. Remove the exhaust manifold heat shield.
13. Unfasten the exhaust manifold nuts, then remove the exhaust manifold and gasket from the bottom of vehicle.
14. Clean mating surfaces at the cylinder head and manifold.
   To install:
15. Position the exhaust manifold gasket, then install the exhaust manifold loosely and install heat shield at this time.
16. Install the manifold nuts and tighten to 12 ft. lbs (16 Nm).

17. Install the exhaust manifold heat shield nuts.
18. Install the converter heat shield to the body.
19. Attach the exhaust pipe to the converter flange.
20. Connect the exhaust pipe to the exhaust manifold.
21. Install the transaxle oil level indicator and fill tube assembly.
22. Carefully lower the vehicle.
23. Install the heated oxygen sensor.
24. Connect the EGR pipe to exhaust manifold.
25. Install the top half of the air cleaner assembly and the throttle body duct.
26. Connect the negative battery cable.

3.3L Engine

FRONT (LEFT)

◗ See Figures 63 and 64

1. Disconnect the negative battery cable.
2. Remove the air cleaner inlet ducting
3. Tag and disconnect the spark plug wires.
4. Unfasten the exhaust crossover pipe to manifold bolts.
5. Remove the engine lift hook and manifold heat shield.
6. Remove the oil level indicator tube and the indicator.
7. Unfasten the exhaust manifold studs, then remove the manifold.
8. Installation is the reverse of the removal procedure. Tighten the nuts to 19 ft. lbs. (26 Nm) and the studs to 30 ft. lbs. (41 Nm).

REAR (RIGHT)

◗ See Figures 63 and 65

1. Disconnect the negative battery cable.
2. Tag and disconnect the spark plug wires.
3. Detach the oxygen sensor electrical connection.
4. Remove the throttle cable bracket, then unfasten the cables from the throttle body.
5. Detach the brake booster hose from the manifold.
6. Unfasten the two exhaust crossover pipe-to-manifold bolts.
7. Remove the exhaust pipe-to-manifold bolts.
8. Remove the engine lift hook.
9. Remove the transaxle oil level indicator tube.
10. Remove the manifold heat shield.
11. Unfasten the manifold studs and bolt, then remove the manifold.
12. Installation is the reverse of the removal procedure. Tighten the nuts to 19 ft. lbs. (26 Nm) and the studs to 30 ft. lbs. (41 Nm).

Turbocharger

REMOVAL & INSTALLATION

◗ See Figure 66

1. Disconnect the negative battery cable.
2. Raise and safely support the vehicle.
3. Properly drain the engine coolant.
4. Remove the lower fan attaching screw.
5. Disconnect the exhaust pipe.

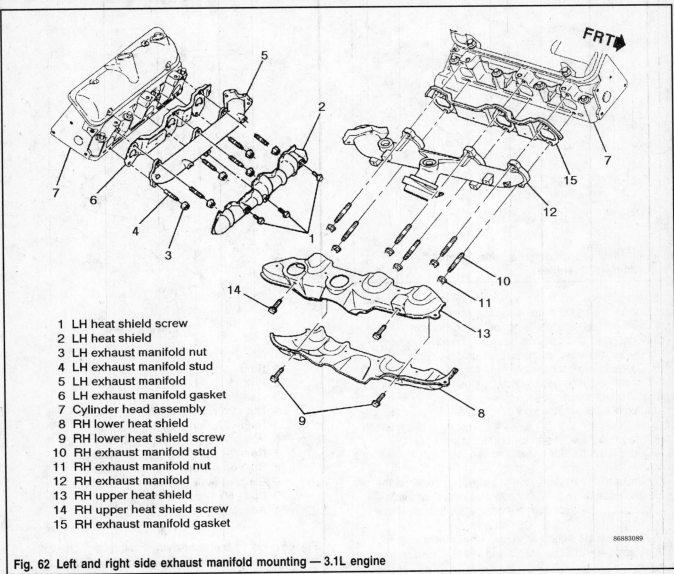

1 LH heat shield screw
2 LH heat shield
3 LH exhaust manifold nut
4 LH exhaust manifold stud
5 LH exhaust manifold
6 LH exhaust manifold gasket
7 Cylinder head assembly
8 RH lower heat shield
9 RH lower heat shield screw
10 RH exhaust manifold stud
11 RH exhaust manifold nut
12 RH exhaust manifold
13 RH upper heat shield
14 RH upper heat shield screw
15 RH exhaust manifold gasket

Fig. 62 Left and right side exhaust manifold mounting — 3.1L engine

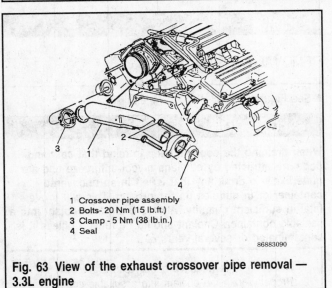

1 Crossover pipe assembly
2 Bolts- 20 Nm (15 lb.ft.)
3 Clamp - 5 Nm (38 lb.in.)
4 Seal

Fig. 63 View of the exhaust crossover pipe removal — 3.3L engine

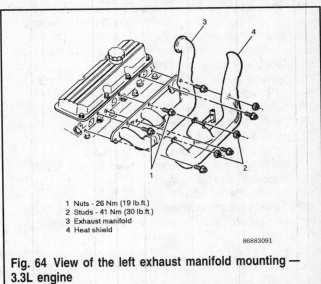

1 Nuts - 26 Nm (19 lb.ft.)
2 Studs - 41 Nm (30 lb.ft.)
3 Exhaust manifold
4 Heat shield

Fig. 64 View of the left exhaust manifold mounting — 3.3L engine

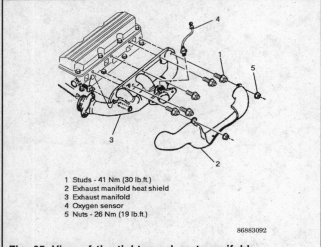

1 Studs - 41 Nm (30 lb.ft.)
2 Exhaust manifold heat shield
3 Exhaust manifold
4 Oxygen sensor
5 Nuts - 26 Nm (19 lb.ft.)

86883092

Fig. 65 View of the tighten exhaust manifold mounting — 3.3L engine

6. Remove the bolt at the rear of the A/C compressor support bracket, then loosen the remaining bolts.
7. Remove turbocharger-to-engine support bracket.
8. Disconnect and plug the oil drain pipe at turbocharger.
9. Detach the water return pipe at turbocharger.
10. Carefully lower the vehicle.
11. Disconnect the coolant recovery pipe and position it to one side, out of the way.
12. Remove the air induction tube, coolant fan, and oxygen sensor.
13. Disconnect the oil and water feed pipes.
14. Detach the air intake duct and vacuum hose at the actuator.
15. Unfasten the exhaust manifold attaching nuts and remove turbocharger and exhaust manifold as an assembly.
16. Separate the turbocharger from the exhaust manifold.
To install:
17. Assemble the turbocharger and exhaust manifold.
18. Clean the exhaust manifold and cylinder head mating surfaces.
19. Install a new gasket and install the manifold/turbocharger assembly to the engine. Tighten the Nos. 2 and 3 manifold runner nuts first, then Nos. 1 and 4, to 18 ft. lbs. (24 Nm).
20. Connect the oil and water feed and return lines.
21. Attach the oxygen sensor.
22. Connect the air intake duct and connect the vacuum hose to the actuator.
23. Install the cooling fan.
24. Install the induction tube and coolant recovery tube.
25. Raise and safely support the vehicle.
26. Install the rear turbocharger support bolt.
27. Install the compressor support bracket.
28. Install the oil drain hose.
29. Connect the exhaust pipe.
30. Connect the negative battery cable. Check the turbocharger for proper operation and the assembly for leaks.

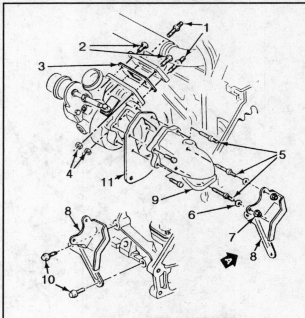

VIEW A

1 Stud
2 Bolt
3 Gasket
4 Nut - 25 Nm (18 lbs.ft.)
5 Stud - 25 Nm (18 lbs.ft.)
6 Washer
7 Nut - 25 Nm (18 lbs.ft.)
8 Support bracket
9 Exhaust outlet elbow
10 Bolt - 50 Nm (37 lbs.ft.)
11 Adapter plate

86883093

Fig. 66 View of the turbocharger mounting. The 2.0L engine is the only engine equipped with a turbocharger

Radiator

REMOVAL & INSTALLATION

▶ See Figures 67, 68, 69, 70, 71 and 72

☀☀CAUTION

When draining the coolant, keep in mind that cats and dogs are attracted by ethylene glycol antifreeze and are quite likely to drink any that is left in an uncovered container or in puddles on the ground. This will prove fatal in sufficient quantity. Always drain the coolant into a sealable container. Coolant should be reused unless it is contaminated or several years old.

1. Disconnect the negative battery cable.
2. Properly drain the coolant into a suitable container.

3. If necessary for access to the radiator, remove the air intake duct assembly or air cleaner assembly.

4. Disconnect the the engine strut brace at the radiator, loosen the engine side bolt and swing aside, if equipped.

5. Matchmark and remove the hood latch from the radiator support.

6. Detach the upper hose and coolant reserve tank hose from the radiator.

7. Disconnect the forward light harness connector and fan connector. Remove the electric cooling fan.

8. Raise and safely support the vehicle.

9. Detach the lower hose from the radiator.

10. If equipped, disconnect and plug the automatic transaxle cooler hoses.

11. Carefully lower the vehicle.

12. If equipped with air conditioning, remove the radiator to condenser bolts. Remove the refrigerant line clamp bolt.

13. Remove the mounting bolts and clamp, then remove the shroud (if equipped) and carefully lift the radiator out of the engine compartment.

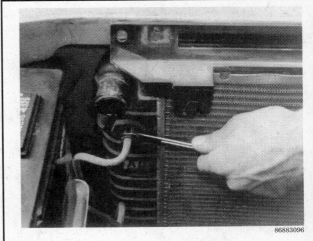

Fig. 69 Disconnect and plug the cooler lines if equipped

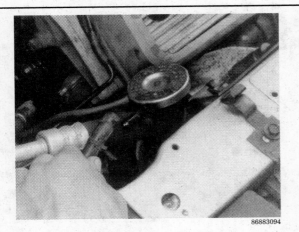

Fig. 67 Slide the tension clamp back over the overflow hose, then detach the hose from the nipple on the filler neck

Fig. 70 Unfasten the shroud mounting bolts, then . . .

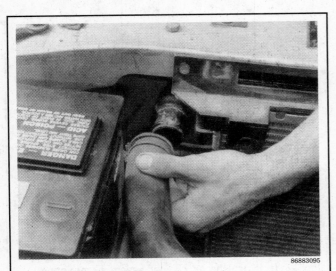

Fig. 68 Carefully pull the upper hose from the radiator

Fig. 71 . . . remove the shroud for access to the radiator

Fig. 72 Carefully lift the radiator from the front of the engine compartment

To install:

14. Lower the radiator into position.

15. Install the mounting clamps and bolts, including those associated with air conditioning parts.

16. Raise and safely support the vehicle.

17. If equipped, attach the automatic transaxle cooler lines.

18. Connect the lower hose(s).

19. Carefully lower the vehicle.

20. Install the electric cooling fan, then attach the electrical connector(s).

21. Connect the upper hose and coolant reserve tank hose.

22. Install the hood latch and strut brace.

23. Fill the system with coolant.

24. Connect the negative battery cable, then start the engine. Run the vehicle until the thermostat opens, fill the radiator and recovery tank to their correct levels, then check the automatic transaxle fluid level.

25. Turn the engine off, then once the vehicle has cooled, recheck the coolant level.

Engine Fan

REMOVAL & INSTALLATION

✳✳CAUTION

Keep hands, tools and clothing away from the engine cooling fan to help prevent personal injury. The fan is electric and can come on automatically even when the engine is off. After replacing the fan, make sure that the fan is circulating the air in the proper direction.

Except 2.3L and 3.1L Engines

▶ **See Figures 73, 74, 75, 76, 77 and 78**

1. Disconnect the negative battery cable.

2. Partially drain the cooling system, then remove the top radiator hose, if necessary for fan removal.

3. If necessary for access, remove the air cleaner assembly.

Fig. 73 Disengage the mass air flow sensor electrical connector

Fig. 74 Remove the plastic shrouding retaining the air cleaner assembly

Fig. 75 Unfasten the air cleaner assembly mounting bolts, then . . .

Fig. 76 . . . remove the air cleaner assembly for access to the fan

4. Disconnect the wiring harness from the motor and from the fan frame.

5. If necessary, remove the fan guard and hose support if necessary.

6. Unfasten the retaining bolts, then remove the fan assembly from the radiator support.

7. Installation is the reverse of the removal procedure.

2.3L Engine

1988-91 VEHICLES

▶ See Figure 79

1. Disconnect the negative battery cable.
2. Unfasten the air cleaner to the throttle body duct.
3. Detach the TPS, IAC, and MAP sensor connectors and position the harness off to the side.
4. Disconnect the vacuum harness assembly from the throttle body and place to the side.
5. Detach the MAP sensor vacuum hose from the intake manifold.

Fig. 77 Unfasten the fan retaining bolts, then . . .

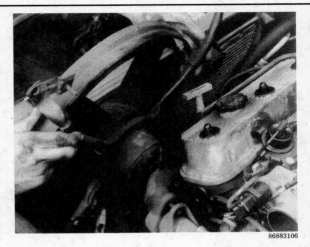

Fig. 78 . . . carefully lift the cooling fan assembly from the engine compartment

6. Unfasten the coolant fan shroud bolts and remove the fan shroud.

7. Remove the coolant fan to upper radiator support bolt and remove the upper radiator support.

8. Detach the electrical connector from the coolant fan.

9. Lift the fan out from the lower insulators. Rotate the bracket so that the two lower legs point upward.

10. Move the fan to the driver's side to ensure proper clearance and remove the fan out the top.

To install:

11. Install the fan assembly with the two lower legs pointing upward.

12. Rotate the fan, then place the two lower legs into the insulators.

13. Attach the electrical connector to the fan and install the upper radiator support.

14. Install the coolant fan shroud, then install the coolant fan-to-upper radiator support mounting bolt.

15. Fasten the MAP sensor vacuum hose to the intake manifold.

16. Attach the electrical connectors to the TPS, IAC, and MAP sensor.

17. Connect the vacuum harness to the throttle body.

18. Install the air cleaner-to-throttle body duct.

19. Connect the negative battery cable.

1992-93 VEHICLES

▶ See Figure 80

1. Disconnect the negative battery cable.
2. Remove the air intake duct assembly.
3. Unfasten the cooling fan mounting bolt.
4. Disengage the cooling fan electrical connector.
5. Remove the cooling fan assembly from the bottom of the vehicle.

To install:

6. Install the cooling fan through the bottom of the vehicle.
7. Engage the fan electrical connector.
8. Install the fan mounting bolt.
9. Connect the air intake duct assembly.
10. Connect the negative battery cable.

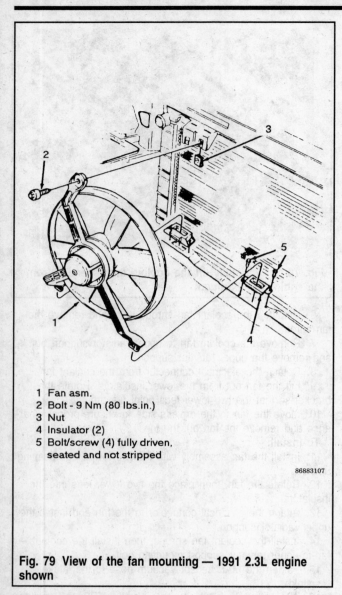

1 Fan asm.
2 Bolt - 9 Nm (80 lbs.in.)
3 Nut
4 Insulator (2)
5 Bolt/screw (4) fully driven,
  seated and not stripped

86883107

Fig. 79 View of the fan mounting — 1991 2.3L engine shown

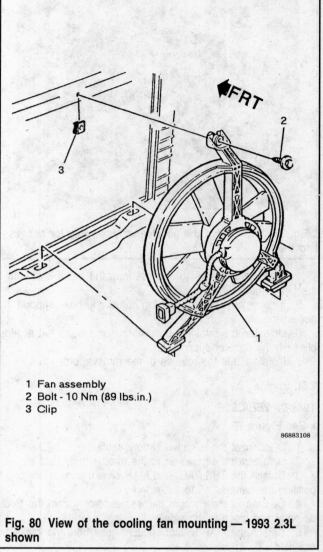

1 Fan assembly
2 Bolt - 10 Nm (89 lbs.in.)
3 Clip

86883108

Fig. 80 View of the cooling fan mounting — 1993 2.3L shown

1994-95 VEHICLES

▶ **See Figure 81**

1. Disconnect the negative battery cable.
2. Raise the vehicle enough to remove the front wheel and tire assembly.
3. Remove the bolt from the lower torque axis mount.
4. Unfasten the fan mounting bolt, then detach the electrical connector.
5. Rock the engine rearward, then remove the fan assembly.
   To install:
6. Rock the engine rearward, then install the fan assembly. Secure with the mounting bolt, then attach the electrical connector.
7. Install the bolt to the lower axis mount.
8. Install the right wheel and tire assembly, then safely lower the vehicle.
9. Connect the negative battery cable.

3.1L Engine

▶ **See Figure 81**

1. Properly drain the cooling system.
2. Disconnect the negative battery cable.
3. Remove the coolant fan mounting bolt.
4. Detach the electrical connector from the fan.
5. Disconnect the radiator inlet hose from the radiator.
6. Remove the radiator mounting bolt.
7. Pull the windshield washer fluid bottle fill tube from the bottle.
8. Remove the vacuum tank.
9. Remove the vacuum tank bracket.
10. Remove the cooling fan by sliding the fan leg into an area left from the vacuum tank.
    To install:
11. Install the coolant fan assembly.
12. Fasten the vacuum tank bracket, then install the vacuum tank.
13. Install the windshield washer fluid bottle fill tube.
14. Install the radiator mounting bolt.

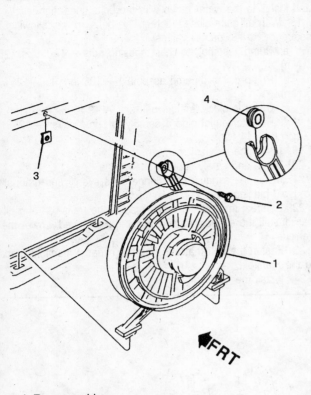

1 Fan assembly
2 Bolt - 11 Nm (97 lbs.in.)
3 Clip
4 Engine cooling fan insulator

86883109

Fig. 81 View of the coolant fan — 1995 vehicle shown

15. Connect the radiator inlet hose to the radiator.
16. Attach the electrical connector to coolant fan.
17. Install the cooling fan mounting bolt.
18. Attach the air intake duct assembly.
19. Connect the negative battery cable.

Water Pump

REMOVAL & INSTALLATION

2.0L Engine

▶ See Figure 82

1. Disconnect the negative battery cable.
2. Properly drain the engine coolant into a clean container for reuse.
3. Remove the timing belt.
4. Unfasten and remove the timing belt rear protective covers.

5. Detach the hose from the water pump.
6. Unfasten the water pump attaching bolts, then remove the water pump and seal ring.

To install:

7. Thoroughly clean and dry the mounting surfaces, bolts and bolt holes.
8. Using a new sealing ring, install the water pump to the engine and hand-tighten the retaining bolts.
9. Attach the hose to the water pump.
10. Fasten the timing belt rear protective covers, then install the timing belt and properly adjust the tension.
11. Tighten the water pump bolts to 18 ft. lbs. (24 Nm).
12. Install the timing belt cover and related parts.
13. Connect the negative battery cable.
14. Fill cooling system and check for leaks. Start the engine and allow to come to normal operating temperature. Recheck for leaks. Top-up coolant.

2.3L Engine

▶ See Figure 83

1. Disconnect the negative battery cable
2. Detach the oxygen sensor connector.
3. Properly drain the engine coolant into a suitable container. Remove the heater hose from the thermostat housing for more complete coolant drain.
4. Remove upper and lower exhaust manifold heat shields.
5. Remove the bolt that attaches the exhaust manifold brace to the manifold.
6. Break loose the manifold to exhaust pipe spring loaded bolts using a 13mm box wrench.
7. Raise and safely support the vehicle.

➡ **It is necessary to relieve the spring pressure from 1 bolt prior to removing the second bolt. If the spring pressure is not relieved, it will cause the exhaust pipe to twist and bind up the bolt as it is removed.**

8. Remove the manifold to exhaust pipe bolts from the exhaust pipe flange as follows:
   a. Unscrew either bolt clockwise 4 turns.
   b. Remove the other bolt.
   c. Remove the first bolt.

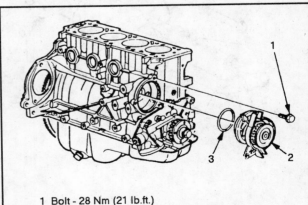

1 Bolt - 28 Nm (21 lb.ft.)
2 Coolant pump
3 Seal ring

86883110

Fig. 82 View of the water (coolant) pump mounting — 2.0L engine

9. Pull down and back on the exhaust pipe to disengage it from the exhaust manifold bolts.

10. Remove the radiator outlet pipe from the oil pan and transaxle. If equipped with a manual transaxle, remove the exhaust manifold brace. Leave the lower radiator hose attached and pull down on the outlet pipe to remove it from the water pump.

11. Carefully lower the vehicle.

12. Remove the exhaust manifold, seals and gaskets.

13. Loosen and reposition the rear engine mount and bracket for clearance, as required.

14. Remove the water pump mounting bolts and nuts. Remove the water pump and cover assembly, then separate the two pieces.

To install:

15. Thoroughly clean and dry all mounting surfaces, bolts and bolt holes. Using a new gasket, install the water pump to the cover and tighten the bolts finger-tight.

16. Lubricate the splines of the water pump with clean grease and install the assembly to the engine using new gaskets. Install the mounting bolts and nuts finger-tight.

17. Lubricate the radiator outlet pipe O-ring with antifreeze and install to the water pump with the bolts finger-tight.

18. With all gaps closed, tighten the bolts, in the following sequence, to the proper values:

a. Pump assembly-to-chain housing nuts — 19 ft. lbs. (26 Nm).

b. Pump cover-to-pump assembly — 106 inch lbs. (12 Nm).

c. Cover-to-block, bottom bolt first — 19 ft. lbs. (26 Nm).

d. Radiator outlet pipe assembly to pump cover — 125 inch lbs. (14 Nm).

19. Install the exhaust manifold.

20. Raise and safely support the vehicle.

21. Install the exhaust pipe flange bolts evenly and gradually to avoid binding.

22. Connect the radiator outlet pipe to the transaxle and oil pan. Install the exhaust manifold brace, if removed. Lower the vehicle.

23. Fasten the bolt that attaches the exhaust manifold brace to the manifold.

24. Install the heat shields.

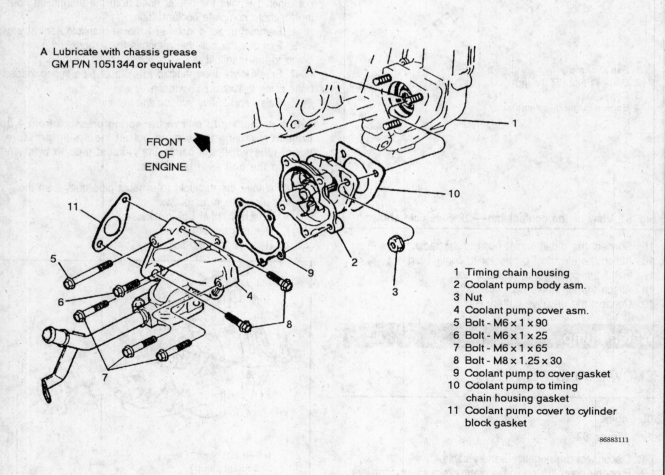

A Lubricate with chassis grease GM P/N 1051344 or equivalent

FRONT OF ENGINE

1 Timing chain housing
2 Coolant pump body asm.
3 Nut
4 Coolant pump cover asm.
5 Bolt - M6 x 1 x 90
6 Bolt - M6 x 1 x 25
7 Bolt - M6 x 1 x 65
8 Bolt - M8 x 1.25 x 30
9 Coolant pump to cover gasket
10 Coolant pump to timing chain housing gasket
11 Coolant pump cover to cylinder block gasket

86883111

Fig. 83 View of the water (coolant) pump mounting — 1994 2.3L engine shown

25. Attach the oxygen sensor connector.

26. Fill the radiator with coolant until it comes out the heater hose outlet at the thermostat housing. Then connect the heater hose. Leave the radiator cap off.

27. Connect the negative battery cable, then start the engine. Run the vehicle until the thermostat opens, fill the radiator and recovery tank to their proper levels, then turn the engine off.

28. Once the vehicle has cooled, recheck the coolant level.

2.5L Engine

▶ See Figures 84 and 85

1. Disconnect the negative battery cable.

2. Properly drain the engine coolant into a suitable container.

3. Remove the drive belts.

4. If necessary for access, remove the alternator and A/C compressor.

5. Unfasten the water pump front cover assembly mounting bolts, then remove the water pump front cover assembly.

To install:

6. If installing a new pump, transfer the water pump pulley to the new pump using tool J25034-B, J29785-A or equivalent.

7. Thoroughly clean and dry the mounting surfaces, bolts and bolt holes. Place a 1/8 in. (3mm) bead of RTV sealant on the pump's sealing surface.

8. Install the pump to the engine, coating the bolt threads with sealant as they are installed. Tighten the bolts to 25 ft. lbs. (34 Nm).

9. If removed, install the alternator and/or air conditioning compressor.

10. Install and adjust the drive belts.

11. Connect the negative battery cable.

12. Fill cooling system and check for leaks. Start the engine and allow to come to normal operating temperature. Recheck for leaks. Top off coolant level if necessary.

3.0L Engine

▶ See Figure 86

1. Disconnect the negative battery cable.

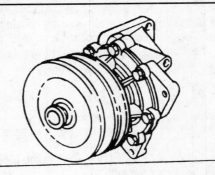

REMOVE PULLEY WITH J25034-B
OR J29785-A
INSTALL PULLEY WITH J25033-B

86883113

Fig. 85 If installing a new water pump, transfer the pulley from the old pump using the proper tool

2. Properly drain the cooling system into a suitable container.

3. Remove the drive belt.

4. Detach the coolant hoses at the water pump.

5. Unfasten the water pump pulley bolts (the long bolt can be removed through the access hole in the body side rail), then remove the pulley.

6. Unfasten the water pump mounting bolts, then remove the pulley.

7. Thoroughly clean and dry all gasket mating surfaces.

To install:

8. Using a new gasket, install the water pump on the engine. Tighten the mounting bolts to the specifications shown in the accompanying figure.

9. Install the water pump pulley, then tighten the retaining bolts to 9.6 ft. lbs. (13 Nm).

10. Attach the coolant hoses to the pump.

11. Install the drive belt.

12. Fill the cooling system to the proper level with the correct type of coolant.

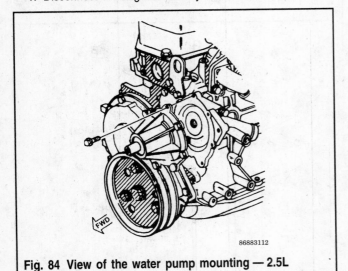

Fig. 84 View of the water pump mounting — 2.5L engine

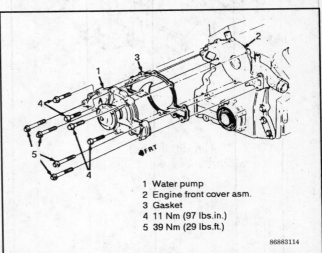

1 Water pump
2 Engine front cover asm.
3 Gasket
4 11 Nm (97 lbs.in.)
5 39 Nm (29 lbs.ft.)

86883114

Fig. 86 Water pump mounting and bolt tightening specifications — 3.0L engine shown

13. Connect the negative battery cable, then start the engine. Let the engine run until it reaches normal operating temperature, then check for leaks and coolant level. Add coolant, if necessary, then turn the engine off.

3.1L Engine

▶ See Figure 87

1. Disconnect the negative battery cable.
2. Properly drain the cooling system into a suitable container.
3. Loosen, but do not remove, the water pump pulley bolts.
4. Remove the serpentine belt.
5. Unfasten the water pump pulley bolts, then remove the pulley.
6. Remove the five water pump mounting bolts, then remove the water pump.

To install:

7. Clean all the gasket surfaces completely.
8. Apply a thin bead of sealer around the outside edge of the water pump along the gasket sealing area, then install the gasket onto the water pump.

1 Coolant pump
2 Gasket
3 Bolt - 10 Nm (89 lbs.in.)
4 Locator (must be vertical)

86883115

Fig. 87 View of the water pump mounting — 3.1L engine shown

9. Position the water pump on the engine, then tighten the water pump mounting bolts to 89 inch lbs. (10 Nm).
10. Install the water pump pulley and finger-tighten the pulley bolts.
11. Install the serpentine belt.
12. Tighten the water pump pulley bolts to 18 ft. lbs. (25 Nm).
13. Fill the cooling system.
14. Connect the negative battery cable, then start the engine. Let the engine run until it reaches normal operating temperature, then check for leaks and coolant level. Add coolant, if necessary, then turn the engine off.

3.3L Engine

▶ See Figure 88

1. Disconnect the negative battery cable.
2. Properly drain the engine coolant into a suitable container.
3. Support the engine using J 28467-A or equivalent engine support fixture.
4. Remove the right engine mount.
5. Loosen, but do not remove, the water pump pulley bolts.
6. Remove the serpentine belt.
7. Unfasten and remove the idler pulley, then remove the engine brace.
8. Unfasten the water pump pulley bolts and remove the pump with the pulley attached. Separate the pump from the pulley.
9. Thoroughly clean and dry the mounting surfaces, bolts and bolt holes.

To install:

10. Attach the water pump to the pulley, tighten the pump-to-pulley bolts to 9.6 ft. lbs. (13 Nm), then install as an assembly. Install and hand-tighten the pulley bolts.
11. Install the engine brace and idler pulley.
12. Install the serpentine belt.
13. Tighten the water pump pulley bolts to 22 ft. lbs. (30 Nm).
14. Install the right engine mount.
15. Remove the engine support fixture.
16. Fill the system with coolant.

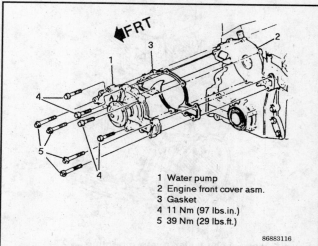

1 Water pump
2 Engine front cover asm.
3 Gasket
4 11 Nm (97 lbs.in.)
5 39 Nm (29 lbs.ft.)

86883116

Fig. 88 View of the water pump mounting and bolt tightening specifications

17. Connect the negative battery cable, run the vehicle until the thermostat opens, fill the radiator and recovery tank to the correct level.

18. Turn the engine off. Once the vehicle has cooled, recheck the coolant level and add if necessary.

Cylinder Head

REMOVAL & INSTALLATION

2.0L Engine

▶ See Figures 89, 90, 91 and 92

➡Cylinder head gasket replacement is necessary if camshaft carrier/cylinder head bolts are loosened. The head bolts should only be loosened when the engine is cold and should NEVER be reused.

1. Properly relieve the fuel system pressure. Disconnect the negative battery cable.

2. Drain the coolant into a suitable container. Remove the induction tube.

3. Remove the serpentine belt.

4. Remove the alternator and bracket.

5. Remove the ignition coil.

6. Matchmark the rotor to the distributor housing and the distributor housing to the cam carrier. Remove the distributor and tag and disconnect the spark plug wires. Refer to Section 2 of this manual for distributor removal.

7. Tag and disconnect all cables from the intake manifold, throttle body and downshift cable.

8. Label and detach all electrical connections from the throttle body and intake manifold.

9. Tag and disconnect all vacuum lines and hoses from the following components:
   - Brake booster
   - Intake manifold and water pump (coolant and heater hoses)
   - Breather from the camshaft carrier
   - Upper radiator hose

10. Disengage the exhaust manifold-to-turbo connection.

11. Unfasten the oxygen sensor electrical connector.

12. Detach and plug the fuel lines.

13. Label and disconnect the wiring at the engine harness and thermostat housing.

14. Remove the timing belt and rear cover. For details, please refer to the procedure later in this section.

15. Make sure the engine is cold, then loosen the cam carrier/cylinder head bolts gradually in the sequence shown in the accompanying figure.

16. Remove camshaft carrier, rocker arms and valve lifters/lash compensators.

17. Remove cylinder head with the intake and exhaust manifolds as an assembly. Remove the head gasket.

To install:

18. Thoroughly clean and dry the mating surfaces and bolt holes. Apply a continuous 1/8 in. (3mm) bead of RTV sealant to the sealing surface of camshaft carrier.

➡When installing the cylinder head, you MUST use a new gasket and new head bolts!

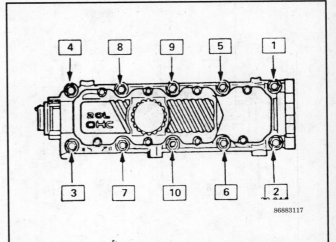

Fig. 89 When loosening the cylinder head/cam carrier bolts, make sure follow this sequence

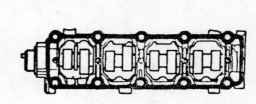

Fig. 90 After cleaning the mating surfaces, apply a continuous 1/8 in. (3mm) bead of RTV sealant to the sealing surface of camshaft carrier

19. Install a new head gasket and position the head on the engine block. Tighten the new head bolts in sequence (shown in the accompanying figure) as follows:
   - Step 1: Tighten to 18 ft. lbs. (25 Nm)
   - Step 2: Using a torque angle meter, tighten an additional 60°
   - Step 3: Tighten to 120° (another additional 60°)
   - Step 4: Tighten to 180° (a third additional 60°)

20. Install the rear cover and timing belt.

21. Connect all wiring to the engine harness and thermostat housing.

22. Attach the exhaust manifold-to-turbo connection and engage the oxygen sensor electrical connection.

23. Connect the vacuum lines and/or hoses of the following components:
   - Upper radiator hose
   - Cam carrier breather
   - Intake manifold and water pump (heater and water hoses)
   - Brake booster

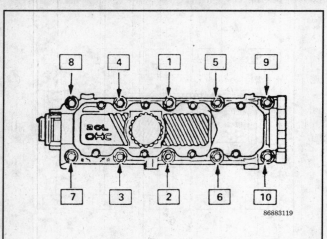

Fig. 91 To help prevent leakage, follow this sequence when tightening the new head bolts

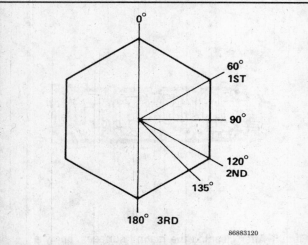

Fig. 92 Schematic of the torque degrees needed for proper bolt tightening

24. Attach all electrical connections to the throttle body and intake manifold.

25. Fasten all the fuel lines.

26. Connect all cables to the intake manifold bracket, throttle body, and downshift cable.

27. Install the distributor and spark plug wires, aligning the matchmarks.

28. Install the ignition coil.

29. Install the alternator and bracket.

30. Connect the induction tube.

31. Fill all fluids to their proper levels.

32. Connect the battery cable, start the engine and check for leaks.

33. After the engine has reached normal operation temperature (thermostat is open), tighten all head bolts, in sequence, another 30-50°. Shut the engine off.

2.3L Engine

▶ **See Figures 93, 94, 95, 96, 97 and 98**

1. Properly relieve the fuel system pressure.

2. Disconnect the negative battery cable, then drain cooling system into a suitable container.

3. Detach the heater inlet and throttle body heater hoses from water outlet. If accessible at this time, disconnect the upper radiator hose from the water outlet.

4. Remove the exhaust manifold. For details, please refer to the procedure located in this section.

5. Remove the intake (camshaft housing for SOHC) and exhaust (DOHC only) camshaft housings.

6. Unfasten the oil fill tube bolt/screw then remove the oil fill cap and level indicator assembly. Pull the oil fill tube upward to unseat from block.

7. Label and disengage the injector harness electrical connector.

8. Detach the throttle body-to-air intake duct.

9. Tag and disconnect the power brake vacuum hose from the throttle body.

10. Remove the throttle cable bracket.

11. Remove the throttle body from the intake manifold with the electrical harness and throttle cable attached and position the assembly aside.

12. Tag and disconnect the MAP sensor vacuum hose from the intake manifold, then remove the intake manifold brace.

13. Detach the electrical connectors from the MAP sensor, IAT sensor and the EVAP canister purge solenoid.

14. If not already done, detach the upper (inlet) radiator hose from the water outlet.

15. Disengage the coolant temperature sensor connector(s).

16. Unfasten the cylinder head bolts in reverse order of the installation sequence shown in the accompanying figures.

17. Lift the cylinder head from the engine block. Remove and discard the gasket. Inspect the oil flow check valve for freedom of movement.

18. Using a suitable solvent, thoroughly clean and dry all bolts, bolt holes and mating surfaces. Inspect the head bolts for any damage and replace, if necessary. If using a scraper to clean the old gasket material from the mating surfaces, use only a plastic or wood one, NOT a metal scraper. Do NOT allow any debris to fall into the engine!

To install:

19. Place a new cylinder head gasket on the cylinder block, then carefully position the cylinder head in place.

20. Sparingly coat the head bolt threads with clean engine oil, then allow the oil to drain off before installing.

21. On 1988-89 engines, install and tighten the cylinder head bolts, in sequence, as follows:

• Step 1: Tighten all head bolts in sequence to 26 ft. lbs. (35 Nm)

• Step 2: Using a torque angle meter, tighten the short bolts an additional 80° and the long bolts an additional 90° in sequence

22. On 1990-91 engines, tighten the cylinder head bolts, in sequence, as follows:

• Step 1: Tighten all head bolts in sequence to 26 ft. lbs. (35 Nm)

• Step 2: Using a torque angle meter, tighten the short bolts an additional 100° and the long bolts an additional 110° in sequence

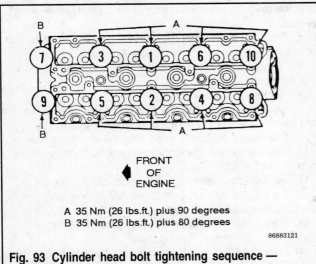

A 35 Nm (26 lbs.ft.) plus 90 degrees
B 35 Nm (26 lbs.ft.) plus 80 degrees

86883121

Fig. 93 Cylinder head bolt tightening sequence — 1988-89 2.3L ONLY

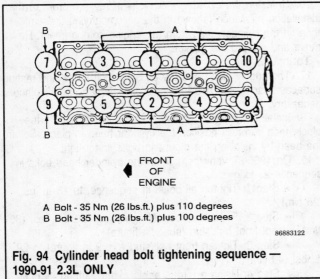

A Bolt - 35 Nm (26 lbs.ft.) plus 110 degrees
B Bolt - 35 Nm (26 lbs.ft.) plus 100 degrees

86883122

Fig. 94 Cylinder head bolt tightening sequence — 1990-91 2.3L ONLY

23. On 1992 engines, tighten the cylinder head bolts, in sequence, as follows:

• Step 1: Tighten, in sequence, head bolts 1-6 to 26 ft. lbs. (35 Nm), 7-8 to 15 ft. lbs. (20 Nm) and 9-10 to 22 ft. lbs. (30 Nm).

• Step 2: Tighten all head bolts, in sequence, an additional 90° using J 36660 or equivalent

• Step 3: In sequence, loosen each bolt one turn, then immediately re-tighten to the specified torque

• Step 4: After completing step 3 on all 10 bolts, tighten each bolt, in sequence, an additional 90°

24. On 1993-95 vehicles, tighten the cylinder head bolts to the specifications shown in the accompanying figures.

25. Engage the coolant temperature sensor electrical connector(s).

26. Connect the upper radiator hose to the water outlet.

27. Install the intake manifold bracket.

28. Attach the following electrical connections: MAP sensor, IAT sensor, and the purge solenoid.

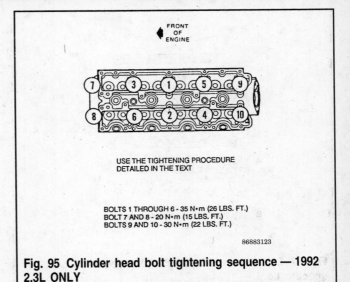

USE THE TIGHTENING PROCEDURE
DETAILED IN THE TEXT

BOLTS 1 THROUGH 6 - 35 N·m (26 LBS. FT.)
BOLT 7 AND 8 - 20 N·m (15 LBS. FT.)
BOLTS 9 AND 10 - 30 N·m (22 LBS. FT.)

86883123

Fig. 95 Cylinder head bolt tightening sequence — 1992 2.3L ONLY

USE THE TIGHTENING PROCEDURE
DETAILED IN THE TEXT

DOHC (VIN A & D)

BOLTS 1 THROUGH 6 — 25 N·m (18 LBS. FT.) PLUS 90°
BOLTS 7 AND 8 — 30 N·m (22 LBS. FT.) PLUS 60°
BOLTS 9 AND 10 — 35 N·m (26 LBS. FT.) PLUS 60°

SOHC (VIN 3)

BOLTS 1 THROUGH 6 — 25 N·m (18 LBS. FT.) PLUS 90°
BOLTS 7 AND 8 — 35 N·m (26 LBS. FT.) PLUS 60°
BOLTS 9 AND 10 — 40 N·m (30 LBS. FT.) PLUS 60°

86883124

Fig. 96 Cylinder head bolt tightening sequence and specifications — 1993 2.3L ONLY

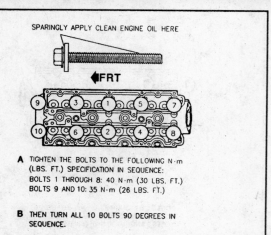

SPARINGLY APPLY CLEAN ENGINE OIL HERE

◀FRT

A TIGHTEN THE BOLTS TO THE FOLLOWING N·m
(LBS. FT.) SPECIFICATION IN SEQUENCE:
BOLTS 1 THROUGH 8: 40 N·m (30 LBS. FT.)
BOLTS 9 AND 10: 35 N·m (26 LBS. FT.)

B THEN TURN ALL 10 BOLTS 90 DEGREES IN
SEQUENCE.

86883125

Fig. 97 Cylinder head bolt tightening sequence and specifications — 1994-95 2.3L ONLY

29. Using a new gasket, install the throttle body to the intake manifold.

30. Install the accelerator control cable bracket.

31. Connect the throttle body-to-air intake duct.

32. Install the oil fill tube and level indicator.

33. Install the camshaft housing(s).

34. Install the exhaust manifold. For details, please refer to the procedure located in this section.

35. Connect the heater inlet and throttle body heater hoses to the water outlet.

36. Fill all fluids to their proper levels.

37. Connect the battery cable, start the engine and check for leaks.

2.5L Engine

▶ **See Figure 99**

1. Relieve the fuel system pressure.
2. Disconnect the negative battery cable.
3. Drain the coolant into a suitable container.
4. For 1986-88 vehicles, raise and safely support the vehicle, then disconnect the exhaust pipe from the manifold. De-

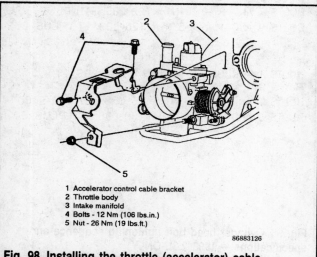

1 Accelerator control cable bracket
2 Throttle body
3 Intake manifold
4 Bolts - 12 Nm (106 lbs.in.)
5 Nut - 26 Nm (19 lbs.ft.)

86883126

Fig. 98 Installing the throttle (accelerator) cable bracket — 1994 2.3L shown

tach the oxygen sensor connector, then carefully lower the vehicle.

5. For 1989-91 vehicles, remove the exhaust manifold. For details, please refer to the procedure located in this section.

6. Remove the oil level indicator (dipstick) tube from the cylinder head.

7. Remove the air cleaner assembly.

8. Label and disconnect the electrical wiring, throttle linkage and fuel lines at the rail from the throttle body assembly.

9. Disconnect the heater hose from the intake manifold.

10. Tag and detach the wiring connections from the intake manifold and cylinder head.

11. Remove the alternator or alternator bracket for access.

12. If equipped with a top-mounted A/C compressor, remove the compressor and lay it aside.

13. If equipped with power steering, remove the upper bracket from the power steering pump.

14. Disconnect the radiator hoses from the engine.

15. Remove the rocker arm (valve) cover. Label and remove the rocker arms and pushrods.

16. Unfasten the cylinder head bolts in reverse order of the installation sequence (shown in the accompanying figures), then lift the cylinder head from the engine compartment. Remove and discard the gasket.

To install:

17. Thoroughly clean and dry all bolts, bolt holes and mating surfaces. Inspect the head bolts for any damage and replace if necessary.

18. Install a new head gasket over the dowel pins in the block, then carefully position the cylinder head in place. Secure the head by installing the mounting bolts finger-tight.

19. On 1986-87 vehicles, tighten the cylinder head bolts in sequence as follows:

- Step 1: Tighten all bolts, in sequence, to 18 ft. lbs. (25 Nm)
- Step 2: Repeat sequence, tightening to 22 ft. lbs. (30 Nm), except front bolt/stud (no. 9 in figure)
- Step 3: Tighten front bolt/stud (no. 9 in figure) to 29 ft. lbs. (40 Nm)
- Step 4: Using a torque angle meter, tighten all bolts, except no. 9, an additional 120°
- Step 5: Tighten no. 9 an additional 120°

20. On 1988-91 vehicles, tighten the cylinder head bolts in sequence as follows:

- Step 1: Tighten all bolts, in sequence, to 18 ft. lbs. (25 Nm)
- Step 2: Repeat sequence, tightening to 26 ft. lbs. (35 Nm), except front bolt/stud (no. 9 in figure)
- Step 3: Tighten front bolt/stud (no. 9 in figure) to 18 ft. lbs. (25 Nm)
- Step 4: Using a torque angle meter, tighten all bolts in sequence an additional 90°

21. Install the pushrods and rocker arms in their original positions.

22. Using a new gasket, install the rocker arm (valve) cover.

23. Connect the radiator hoses. Install the power steering pump and upper bracket.

24. If removed, install the air conditioning compressor.

25. Install the alternator and/or bracket, if removed.

26. Attach the electrical wiring connectors to the intake manifold and the cylinder head.

27. Install the heater hose to the intake manifold.

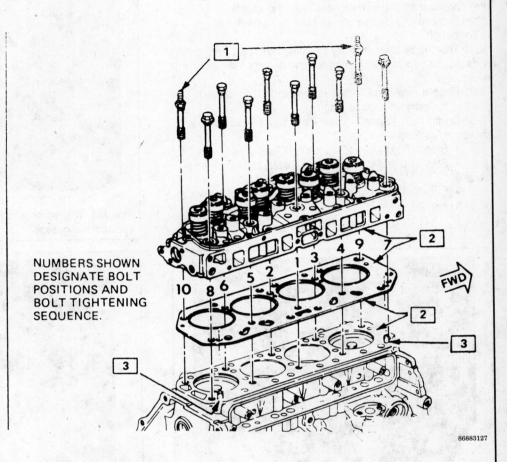

1—APPLY SEALING COM-
POUND PART NUMBER
1052080 OR EQUIVA-
LENT TO THREADS ON
BOLTS SHOWN.

2—MOUNTING SURFACES
OF BLOCK ASM., HEAD
ASM. AND BOTH SIDES
OF GASKET MUST BE
FREE OF OIL AND
FOREIGN MATERIAL.

3—LOCATING PINS

NUMBERS SHOWN
DESIGNATE BOLT
POSITIONS AND
BOLT TIGHTENING
SEQUENCE.

Fig. 99 Cylinder head bolt tightening sequence — 1986-91 2.5L

28. Connect the electrical wiring, throttle linkage and fuel lines at fuel rail to the throttle body assembly.

29. Install the oil level indicator tube to the cylinder head.

30. For 1986-88 vehicles, raise and safely support the vehicle, then connect the exhaust pipe to the manifold, then attach the oxygen sensor connector. Carefully lower the vehicle.

31. For 1989-91 vehicles, install the exhaust manifold. For details, please refer to the procedure located in this section.

32. Install the air cleaner assembly.

33. Adjust all belt tensions and fill all fluids to their proper levels.

34. Connect the battery cable, start the engine and check for leaks.

3.0L and 3.3L Engines

▶ See Figures 100, 101, 102, 103, 104 and 105

1. Properly relieve the fuel system pressure.
2. Disconnect the negative battery cable
3. Drain the coolant into a suitable container.
4. Detach the mass air flow sensor and the air intake duct.
5. Remove ignition module and wiring.

6. Remove the serpentine drive belt, the alternator and bracket.

7. Label and detach all necessary vacuum lines and electrical connections.

8. Remove the fuel lines, the fuel rail and tag and disconnect the spark plug wires.

9. Remove the heater/radiator hoses from the throttle body and intake manifold. Remove the cooling fan and the radiator.

10. Remove the intake manifold. For details, please refer to the procedure located in this section.

11. Remove the rocker arm (valve) covers. Label and remove the rocker arms, pedestals and pushrods.

12. Remove the left side exhaust manifold.

13. Remove the power steering pump.

14. Remove the oil dipstick and dipstick tube.

15. Remove the left side head bolts in reverse order of the installation sequence (shown in the accompanying figure) and lift the left cylinder head from the engine.

16. Raise and safely support the vehicle.

17. Unfasten the right exhaust manifold-to-engine bolts, then remove the right exhaust manifold.

18. Carefully lower the vehicle.

19. Remove the right cylinder head-to-engine bolts in reverse of the installation sequence (shown in the accompanying figure) and lift the right cylinder head from the engine.

20. Remove and discard the cylinder head gasket(s).

To install:

21. Thoroughly clean and dry all bolts, bolt holes and mating surfaces. Inspect the head bolts for any damage and replace if necessary.

22. Place a new head gasket to the block, then carefully position the cylinder head in place.

23. On the 3.0L engine, tighten the cylinder head bolts, in sequence, as follows:

- Step 1: Tighten to 25 ft. lbs. (34 Nm)
- Step 2: Using a torque angle meter, tighten an additional 90°
- Step 3: Tighten another additional 90°, to a maximum of 60 ft. lbs. (81 Nm)

Fig. 102 Whenever you remove the cylinder head, replace the gasket

Fig. 100 When removing cylinder head bolts, unfasten them in the reverse of installation tightening sequence

Fig. 103 Use a suitable scraper to clean the head-to-block mating surfaces. Placing clean rags in the engine block will prevent debris from falling in the block

Fig. 101 Removing the cylinder head from the engine block — 1986 3.0L engine shown

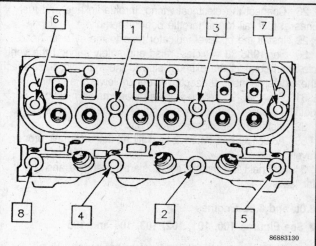

Fig. 104 View of the cylinder head bolt tightening sequence — 3.0L and 3.3L engines

24. On the 3.3L engine, tighten the cylinder head bolts, in sequence, as follows:
- Step 1: Tighten to 35 ft. lbs. (47 Nm)
- Step 2: Using a torque angle meter, tighten an additional 130°
- Step 3: Tighten the 4 center bolts an additional 30°

25. Install the intake manifold. For details, please refer to the procedure located in this section.

26. Raise and safely support the vehicle.

27. Install the exhaust manifold.

28. Carefully lower the vehicle.

29. Install the power steering pump. Install the dipstick and dipstick tube.

30. Using new gaskets, install the valve covers.

31. Install the rocker arms, pedestals and bolts. Tighten pedestal bolts to 43 ft. lbs. (58 Nm) for the 3.0L engine or 28 ft. lbs. (38 Nm) for the 3.3L engine.

32. Install the intake manifold assembly.

33. Connect the heater and radiator hoses to the throttle body and intake manifold.

34. Install the cooling fan and the radiator.

35. Attach the fuel lines, the fuel rail and the spark plug wires.

36. Engage all vacuum lines and electrical connections.

37. Install the serpentine drive belt, the alternator and bracket.

38. Install the ignition module and wiring.

39. Connect the mass air flow sensor and the air intake duct.

40. Fill all fluids to their proper levels.

41. Connect the battery cable, start the engine and check for leaks.

86883133

Fig. 105 When tightening the head bolts, always use a torque wrench

3.1L Engine
▶ See Figure 106

✳✳CAUTION

Fuel Injection systems remain under pressure, even after the engine has been turned OFF. The fuel system pressure must be relieved before disconnecting any fuel lines. Failure to do so may result in fire and/or personal injury.

LEFT CYLINDER HEAD (FRONT)

1. Properly relieve the fuel system pressure.

2. Disconnect the negative battery cable.

3. Drain the cooling system into a suitable container.

4. Disconnect the top half of the air cleaner assembly, then remove the throttle body air inlet duct.

5. Remove the exhaust crossover pipe heat shield and crossover pipe.

6. Disconnect the spark plug wires from spark plugs and wire looms and route the wires out of the way.

7. Remove the rocker arm (valve) covers. For details, please refer to the procedure located in this section.

8. Remove upper intake plenum and lower intake manifold.

9. Remove the left side exhaust manifold.

10. Remove oil level indicator tube.

➡When removing the valve train components they must be kept in order for installation in the same locations they were removed from.

11. Remove rocker arms nut, rocker arms, balls and pushrods.

12. Unfasten the cylinder head bolts evenly, then remove the cylinder head from the engine compartment. Remove and discard the gasket.

To install:

13. Clean all the gasket surfaces completely. Clean the threads on the cylinder head bolts and block threads.

14. Place the cylinder head gasket in position over the dowel pins on the cylinder block so the words **THIS SIDE UP** are showing.

15. Coat the bolt threads lightly with sealer, then install finger-tight.

16. Tighten the cylinder head bolts in sequence (shown in the accompanying figure) to 33 ft. lbs. (45 Nm). With all the bolts tightened make a second pass tightening all the bolts an additional 90°.

17. Install the pushrods, rocker arms, balls and rocker arm nuts. Tighten the rocker arm nuts to 18 ft. lbs. (25 Nm).

18. Install the lower intake manifold and upper intake plenum.

19. Install the rocker arm (valve) covers.

20. Install the oil level indicator tube.

21. Connect the spark plug wires to spark plugs and wire looms.

22. Install the left side exhaust manifold.

23. Install the exhaust crossover pipe and crossover pipe heat shield.

24. Refill the cooling system.

25. Install the top half of the air cleaner assembly and the throttle body air inlet duct.

26. Connect negative battery cable.

27. Start vehicle and verify that there are no leaks.

RIGHT CYLINDER HEAD (REAR)

❊❊CAUTION

Fuel Injection systems remain under pressure, even after the engine has been turned OFF. The fuel system pressure must be relieved before disconnecting any fuel lines. Failure to do so may result in fire and/or personal injury.

1. Relieve the fuel system pressure.
2. Disconnect the negative battery cable.
3. Drain the cooling system.
4. Remove the top half of the air cleaner assembly and remove the throttle body air inlet duct.
5. Remove the exhaust crossover pipe heat shield and crossover pipe.
6. Raise and safely support the vehicle.
7. Detach the Oxygen (O₂) sensor connector.
8. Disconnect the exhaust pipe from the exhaust manifold.

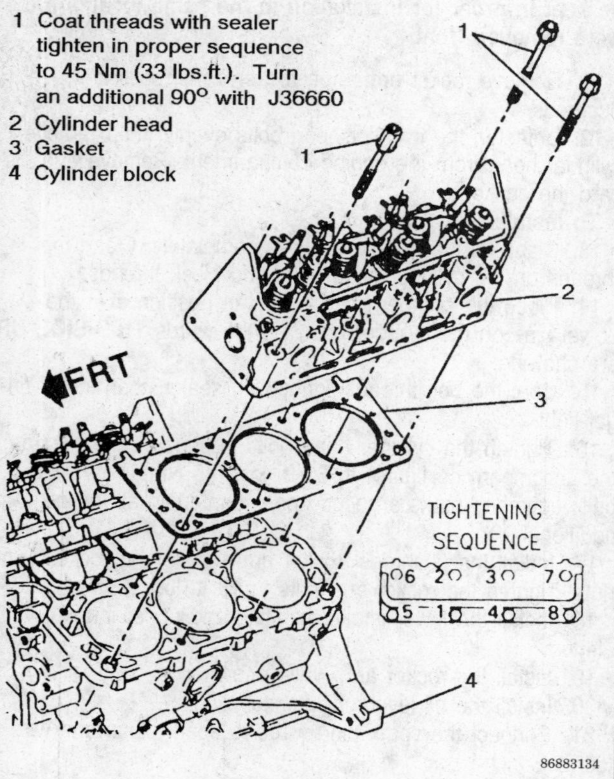

1 Coat threads with sealer tighten in proper sequence to 45 Nm (33 lbs.ft.). Turn an additional 90° with J36660
2 Cylinder head
3 Gasket
4 Cylinder block

◀FRT

TIGHTENING SEQUENCE

```
┌─────────────────┐
│ 6   2   3   7   │
│ 5   1   4   8   │
└─────────────────┘
```

86883134

Fig. 106 Cylinder head mounting and bolt tightening sequence — 3.1L engine

9. Remove the right side exhaust manifold.
10. Carefully lower the vehicle.
11. Disconnect the spark plug wires from spark plugs and wire looms and route the wires out of the way.
12. Remove the rocker arm (valve) covers.
13. Remove upper intake plenum and lower intake manifold.

➡When removing the valve train components they must be kept in order for installation in the same locations they were removed from.

14. Remove rocker arms nut, rocker arms, balls and pushrods.
15. Unfasten the cylinder head bolts evenly, then remove the cylinder head from the engine compartment. Remove and discard the gasket.
    To Install:
16. Clean all the gasket surfaces completely. Clean the threads on the cylinder head bolts and block threads.
17. Place the cylinder head gasket in position over the dowel pins on the cylinder block so the words **THIS SIDE UP** showing.
18. Coat the bolt threads lightly with sealer, then install finger-tight.
19. Tighten the cylinder head bolts in sequence to 33 ft. lbs. (45 Nm). With all the bolts tightened make a second pass tightening all the bolts an additional 90°.
20. Install the pushrods, rocker arms, balls and rocker arm nuts. Tighten the rocker arm nuts to 18 ft. lbs. (25 Nm).
21. Install the lower intake manifold and upper intake plenum.
22. Install the rocker arm covers.
23. Connect the spark plug wires to spark plugs and wire looms.
24. Raise and safely support the vehicle.
25. Install the exhaust manifold.
26. Connect the exhaust pipe to the exhaust manifold.
27. Carefully lower the vehicle.
28. Connect the Oxygen (O₂) sensor connector.
29. Install the exhaust crossover pipe and heat shield.
30. Refill the cooling system.
31. Install the top half of the air cleaner assembly and the throttle body air inlet duct.
32. Connect negative battery cable.
33. Start vehicle and verify that there are no leaks.

CLEANING & INSPECTION

▶ **See Figure 107**

1. With the valves installed to protect the valve seats, remove carbon deposits from the combustion chambers and valve heads with a drill-mounted wire brush. Be careful not to damage the cylinder head gasket surface. If the head is to be disassembled, proceed to Step 3. If the head is not to be disassembled, proceed to Step 2.
2. Remove all dirt, oil and old gasket material from the cylinder head with solvent. Clean the bolt holes and the oil passage. Be careful not to get solvent on the valve seals as the solvent may damage them. If available, dry the cylinder head with compressed air. Check the head for cracks or other damage, and check the gasket surface for burrs, nicks and

flatness. If you are in doubt about the head's serviceability, consult a reputable automotive machine shop.

3. Remove the valves, springs and retainers, then clean the valve guide bores with a valve guide cleaning tool. Remove all dirt, oil and old gasket material from the cylinder head with solvent. Clean the bolt holes and the oil passage.

4. Remove all deposits from the valves with a wire brush or buffing wheel. Inspect the valves as described later in this section.

5. Check the head for cracks using a dye penetrant in the valve seat area and ports, head surface and top. Check the gasket surface for burrs, nicks and flatness. If you are in doubt about the head's serviceability, consult a reputable automotive machine shop.

➡**If the cylinder head was removed due to an overheating condition and a crack is suspected, do not assume that the head is not cracked because a crack is not visually found. A crack can be so small that it cannot be seen by eye, but can pass coolant when the engine is at operating temperature. Consult an automotive machine shop that has testing equipment to make sure the head is not cracked.**

RESURFACING

▶ **See Figures 108 and 109**

Whenever the cylinder head is removed, check the flatness of the cylinder head gasket surface as follows:

1. Make sure all dirt and old gasket material has been cleaned from the cylinder head. Any foreign material left on the head gasket surface can cause a false measurement.

2. Place a straightedge straight across and diagonally across the gasket surface of the cylinder head (in the positions shown in the figures). Using feeler gauges, determine the clearance at the center of the straightedge.

3. If the surfaces are "out of flat" by more than 0.005 in. (0.127mm) the surface should be milled.

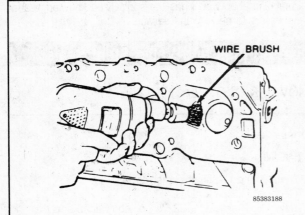

Fig. 107 Clean the combustion chamber using a drill-mounted wire brush

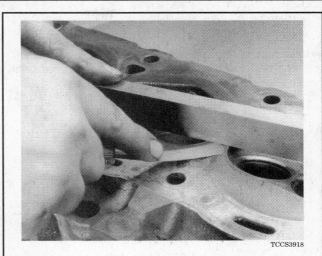

Fig. 108 Checking the cylinder head for flatness diagonally across the head surface

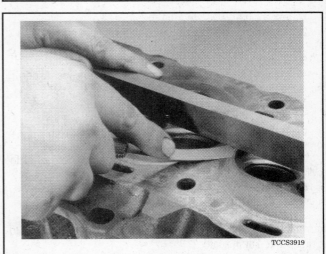

Fig. 109 Checking the cylinder head for flatness straight across the head surface

4. If warpage exceeds 0.010 in. (0.25mm) then the cylinder head should likely be replaced. Contact a reputable machine shop for machining service and recommendations.

➡**When resurfacing the cylinder head(s) on V-type engines, the intake manifold mounting position is altered and must be corrected by machining a proportionate amount from the intake manifold flange.**

Valves

REMOVAL & INSTALLATION

1. Disconnect the negative battery cable.
2. Remove the cylinder head and gasket as previously outlined.
3. Using a valve spring compressing tool, compress the valve spring and remove the valve keys.
4. Remove the retainer and spring.

5. Remove the valve seal, using tool J36017 or equivalent.

6. Remove the rotator and the valve.

➡**Make sure to keep all valve train components together and in order so that they may be reinstalled to their original positions.**

To install:

7. Install the valve and rotator.

8. Install the valve seal and properly seat it, using tool J36007 or equivalent.

9. Install the spring and the retainer.

10. Using a valve spring compressing tool, compress the valve spring and install the valve keys.

11. Install cylinder head and gasket. For details, please refer to the procedure located in this section.

12. Connect the negative battery cable.

INSPECTION

1. Inspect the valve stem tip for wear.

2. Inspect the lock/keeper grooves for chipping or wear. Replace the valve if chipped or severely worn.

3. Inspect the valve face for burn marks or cracks.

4. Inspect the valve stem for burrs and scratches. Minor scratches can be removed with an oil stone.

5. Inspect the valve stem for straightness. Bent valves must be replaced.

6. Inspect the valve face for grooves. If excessively grooved, the valve must be replaced.

7. Reinstall each valve into its respective port (guide) of the cylinder head.

8. Mount a dial indicator so that the stem is at 90° to the valve stem, as close to the valve guide as possible.

9. Move the valve off its seat, and measure the valve guide-to-stem clearance by rocking the stem back and forth to actuate the dial indicator.

10. Measure the valve stems using a micrometer, and compare to specifications, to determine whether stem or guide wear is responsible for excessive clearance.

11. If grinding the valves, measure the valve margin when done. If the margin is less that the minimum, replace the valve.

REFACING

➡**All machine work should be performed by a competent, professional machine shop. Valve face angle is not always identical to valve seat angle.**

A minimum margin of 1/32 in. (0.8mm) should remain after grinding the valve. The valve stem top should also be squared and resurfaced, by placing the stem in the V-block of the grinder, and turning it while pressing lightly against the grinding wheel. Be sure to chamfer the edge of the tip so that the squared edges don't dig into the rocker arm.

LAPPING

This procedure should be performed after the valves and seats have been machined, to insure that each valve mates to each seat precisely.

1. Invert the cylinder head, lightly lubricate the valve stems, and install the valves in the head as numbered.

2. Coat valve seats with fine grinding compound, and attach the lapping tool suction cup to a valve head. Moisten the suction cup.

3. Rotate the tool between your palms, changing position and lifting the tool often to prevent grooving.

4. Lap the valve until a smooth, polished seat is evident.

5. Remove the valve and tool, and rinse away all traces of grinding compound.

Valve Guide Service

The valve guides used in these engines are integral with the cylinder head, that is, they cannot be replaced. Refer to the previous inspection procedure under "Valves" to check the valve guides for wear.

Valve guides are most accurately repaired using the bronze wall rebuilding method. In this operation, "threads" are cut into the bore of the valve guide and bronze wire is turned into the threads. The bronze "wall" is then reamed to the proper diameter. This method is well received for a number of reasons: it is relatively inexpensive, it offers better valve lubrication (the wire forms channels which retain oil), it offers less valve friction, and it preserves the original valve guide-to-seat relationship.

Another popular method of repairing valve guides is to have the guides "knurled." Knurling entails cutting into the bore of the valve guide with a special tool The cutting action "raises" metal off of the guide bore which actually narrows the inner diameter of the bore, thereby reducing the clearance between the valve guide bore and the valve stem. This method offers the same advantages as the bronze wall method, but will generally wear faster.

Either of the above services must be performed by a professional machine shop which has the specialized knowledge and tools necessary to perform the service.

Valve Springs and Valve Stem Seals

REMOVAL & INSTALLATION

Head Installed

2.0L ENGINE

1. Remove the camshaft carrier cover.

2. Remove the spark plugs.

3. Using air line adapter J22794 or equivalent, apply air pressure to cylinder to hold valve in place.

4. Remove the rocker arms.

5. Using valve spring compressing tool J33302-25 or equivalent, compress the valve spring.

6. Remove the valve lash compensators, valve locks, and valve spring.

7. Using tool J36017 or equivalent, remove the valve seal.

To install:

8. Install the plastic sleeve to the valve stem and lubricate with engine oil.

9. Install the new oil seal over the stem and install the seat over the valve guide. Remove the plastic sleeve.

10. Using tool J33302-25, install the valve springs, caps and locks.

11. Install the rocker arms and valve lash compensators to their original positions.

12. Remove the air line adapter J22794 or equivalent and install the spark plug.

13. Install the camshaft carrier cover.

2.3L ENGINE

1. Disconnect the negative battery cable.
2. Remove the intake camshaft housing assembly.
3. Remove the exhaust camshaft housing assembly.
4. Remove the spark plugs.
5. Using the proper adapter, apply continuous air pressure to the cylinder.
6. Using a valve spring compressing tool, compress the valve spring.
7. Remove the valve keys, retainer and spring.
8. Using tool J36017 or equivalent, remove the valve seal.
9. Remove the rotator assembly.

To install:

10. Install the rotator and a new valve seal, using tool J36007 or equivalent.
11. Install the spring and retainer.
12. Using a valve spring compressing tool, compress the valve spring and install the valve keys.
13. Remove the air pressure line and install the spark plugs.
14. Install the exhaust camshaft and housing.
15. Install the intake camshaft and housing.
16. Connect the negative battery cable.
17. Start the car and inspect for any oil leakage.

3.0L AND 3.3L ENGINES

1. Remove the negative battery cable.
2. Remove the valve cover.
3. Remove the rocker arm assemblies.
4. Remove the spark plugs.
5. Using an adaptor apply air pressure to the cylinder to hold the valve closed.
6. Using a valve spring compressing tool, compress the valve spring.
7. Remove the valve keys, retainer and spring.
8. Using tool J36017 or equivalent, remove the valve seal.

To install:

9. Install the new valve seal, using tool J36007 or equivalent.
10. Install the spring and retainer.
11. Using a valve spring compressing tool, compress the valve spring and install the valve keys.
12. Remove the air pressure line and install the spark plugs.
13. Install the spark plugs.
14. Install the rocker arm assemblies and the valve cover.
15. Connect the negative battery cable.

Head Removed

1. Using a valve spring compressing tool, compress the valve spring and remove the valve keys.
2. Remove the retainer and spring.
3. Remove the valve seal, using tool J36017 or equivalent.
4. Remove the rotator.

To install:

5. Install the rotator and install the valve seal, using tool J36007 or equivalent.
6. Install the spring and the retainer.
7. Using a valve spring compressing tool, compress the valve spring and install the valve keys.

VALVE SPRING TESTING

Place the spring on a flat surface next to a square. Measure the height of the spring and rotate it against the edge of the square to measure distortion. If spring height varies (by comparison) by more than $1/16$ in. (1.6mm) or if distortion exceeds $1/16$ in. (1.6mm), replace the spring. In addition to evaluating the spring as above, test the spring pressure at the installed and compressed (installed height minus valve lift) height using a valve spring tester. Spring pressure should be within 1 lb. (0.45kg) of all other springs in either position.

Valve Lifters

REMOVAL & INSTALLATION

2.0L Engine

1. Disconnect the negative battery cable. Remove the camshaft carrier cover.
2. Hold the valves in place with compressed air, using an air adapter in the spark plug hole.
3. Compress the valve springs using a valve spring compressor.
4. Remove rocker arms; keep them in order for reassembly.
5. Remove the lifters.
6. The installation is the reverse of the removal procedure. Soak the lifters in clean engine oil prior to installation.
7. Connect the negative battery cable and check the lifters for proper operation.

2.3L Engine

1. Disconnect the negative battery cable.
2. Remove the camshafts.
3. Remove the lifters from their bores.
4. The installation is the reverse of the removal procedure. Soak the lifters in clean engine oil prior to installation.
5. Connect the negative battery cable and check the lifters for proper operation.

2.5L Engine

1. Relieve the fuel system pressure.
2. Disconnect the negative battery cable.
3. Remove the valve cover and intake manifold.

4. Remove the side pushrod cover.

5. Loosen the rocker arms in pairs and rotate them in order to clear the pushrods.

6. Remove the pushrods, retainer and guide from each cylinder.

7. Remove the valve lifters.

8. The installation is the reverse of the removal procedure. Soak the lifters in clean engine oil prior to installation.

9. Connect the negative battery cable and check the lifters for proper operation.

3.0L and 3.3L Engines

1. Relieve the fuel system pressure.

2. Disconnect the negative battery terminal.

3. Disconnect and remove the fuel rail and the throttle body from the intake manifold.

4. Drain the cooling system.

5. Remove valve covers and the intake manifold.

6. Remove the rocker arms, pedestals and pushrods. Keep these components in order for accurate installation.

7. Remove the valve lifters.

8. The installation is the reverse of the removal procedure. Soak the lifters in clean engine oil prior to installation.

9. Connect the negative battery cable and check the lifters for proper operation.

OVERHAUL

1. Remove the pushrod seat retainer by holding the plunger down and removing the retainer with a small screwdriver.

2. Remove the pushrod seat and the metering valve.

3. Remove the plunger. If plunger is stuck, tap the lifter upside down on a flat surface, if still stuck, soak in parts cleaning solvent.

4. Remove the ball check valve assembly.

5. Remove the plunger spring.

6. Clean lifter of all sludge and varnish build-up.

7. Inspect for excessive wear and scuffing. Replace if excessively worn or scuffed.

8. Inspect for flat spots on the bottom. If worn flat, replace the lifter.

9. If equipped with roller, inspect for freedom of movement, looseness, flat spots or pitting. If any detected, replace the lifter.

10. Install the check ball to the small hole in the bottom of the plunger.

11. Place ball retainer and spring over check ball and press into place using a small screwdriver.

12. Install the plunger spring over the ball retainer.

13. Install the lifter body over the spring and plunger. Make sure the oil holes in the lifter body and in the plunger line up.

14. Using a $\frac{1}{8}$ in. (3mm) drift pin, push the plunger down until the oil holes in the lifter body and plunger are aligned.

15. Insert a $\frac{1}{16}$ in. (1.6mm) pin through the oil holes to lock the plunger down.

16. Remove the $\frac{1}{8}$ in. (3mm) pin and fill the lifter with engine oil.

17. Install the metering valve, pushrod seat and pushrod seat retainer.

18. Push down on the pushrod seat to relieve the spring pressure and remove the $\frac{1}{16}$ in. (1.6mm) pin.

Oil Pan

REMOVAL & INSTALLATION

2.0L Engine

▶ **See Figure 110**

1. Disconnect the negative battery cable.

2. Raise and safely support the vehicle.

3. Remove the right front wheel assembly and the splash shield.

4. Drain the engine oil.

5. Remove the exhaust pipe from the turbocharger/wastegate.

6. Unfasten the four retaining bolts, then remove the flywheel inspection cover.

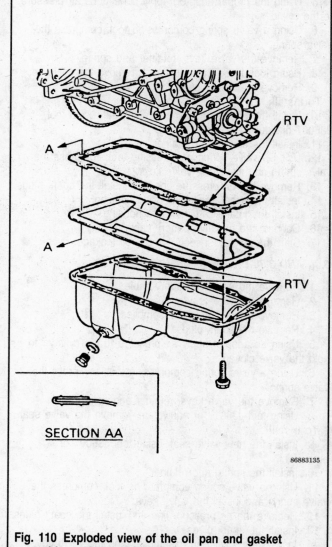

Fig. 110 Exploded view of the oil pan and gasket assembly — 1989 2.0L shown

7. Remove the oil pan attaching bolts and remove the oil pan, scraper and gasket.

8. The installation is the reverse of the removal procedure. Use a new gasket and apply sealant at the 4 engine block seams. Use thread locking compound on the bolt threads and tighten to 4 ft. lbs. (5 Nm), starting from the middle and working outward.

9. Fill the crankcase with oil to specification.

10. Connect the negative battery cable, then start the engine and check for leaks.

2.3L Engine

1988-91 VEHICLES

▶ See Figure 111

1. Disconnect the negative battery cable.
2. Raise and safely support the vehicle.
3. Remove the flywheel inspection cover.
4. Remove the splash shield-to-suspension support bolt. Remove the exhaust manifold brace, if equipped.
5. Remove the radiator outlet pipe-to-oil pan bolt.
6. Remove the transaxle-to-oil pan nut and stud using a 7mm socket.
7. Gently pry the spacer out from between oil pan and transaxle.
8. Remove the oil pan bolts. Rotate the crankshaft, if necessary, and remove the oil pan and gasket from the engine.
9. Inspect the silicone strips across the top of the aluminum carrier at the oil pan-cylinder block-seal housing 3-way joint. If damaged, these strips must be repaired with silicone sealer. Use only enough sealer to restore the strips to their original dimension; too much sealer could cause leakage.

To install:

10. Thoroughly clean and dry the mating surfaces, bolts and bolt holes. Install the oil pan with a new gasket; do not use sealer on the gasket. Loosely install the pan bolts.

11. Place the spacer in its approximate installed position but allow clearance to tighten the pan bolt above it.

12. Tighten the pan-to-block bolts to 17 ft. lbs. (24 Nm) and the remaining bolts to 106 inch lbs. (12 Nm).

13. Install the spacer and stud.

14. Fasten the oil pan transaxle nut and bolt.
15. Connect the splash shield-to-suspension support.
16. Install the radiator outlet pipe bolt.
17. Connect the exhaust manifold brace, if removed.
18. Install the flywheel inspection cover.
19. Fill the crankcase with the proper type and amount oil.
20. Connect the negative battery cable and check for leaks.

1992-95 VEHICLES

▶ See Figures 112, 113, 114 and 115

1. Disconnect the negative battery cable.
2. Raise and safely support the vehicle.
3. Drain the engine oil, then the coolant into suitable containers.
4. Unfasten the retaining bolts, then remove the flywheel housing or transaxle converter cover, as applicable.
5. Remove the right front wheel and tire assembly, then remove the splash shield.
6. Remove the serpentine drive belt.
7. Unfasten the A/C compressor from the bracket, making sure to suitably support it.
8. Remove the engine mount strut bracket.
9. Unfasten the radiator outlet pipe bolts.
10. Disconnect the A/C and radiator pipes from the oil pan.
11. Remove the exhaust manifold brace.
12. Unfasten the oil pan-to-flywheel cover bolt and nut. Remove the flywheel cover stud for clearance.
13. Detach the radiator outlet pipe from the lower radiator hose and oil pan.
14. If equipped, disengage the oil level sensor electrical connector.
15. Unfasten the oil pan bolts, then lower the oil pan from the vehicle. Remove the gasket and discard if damaged. Clean the mating surfaces.
16. Installation is the reverse of the removal procedure. Tighten the oil pan retaining bolts to the specifications shown in the accompanying figure.
17. Carefully lower the vehicle, fill the crankcase with the correct type and quantity of oil, then connect the negative battery cable. Start the engine and inspect for leaks.

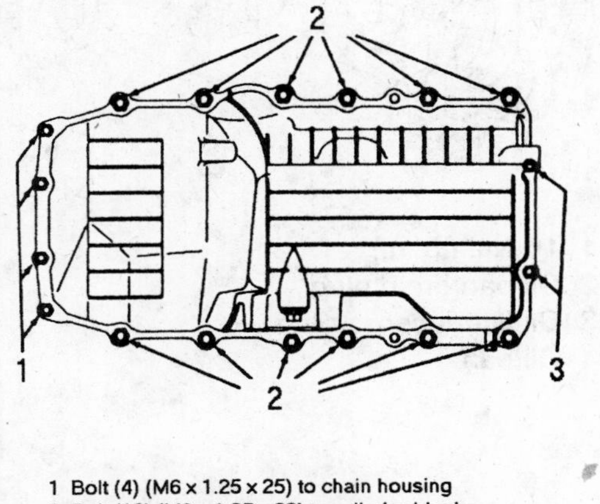

1 Bolt (4) (M6 x 1.25 x 25) to chain housing
2 Bolt (12) (M8 x 1.25 x 22) to cylinder block
3 Bolt (2) (M6 x 1.25 x 25) to rear carrier

86883138

Fig. 111 View of the oil pan fastener locations

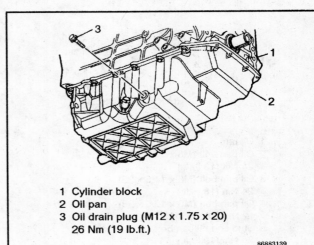

1 Cylinder block
2 Oil pan
3 Oil drain plug (M12 x 1.75 x 20)
  26 Nm (19 lb.ft.)

86883139

Fig. 112 After raising the vehicle, remove the plug and drain the engine oil

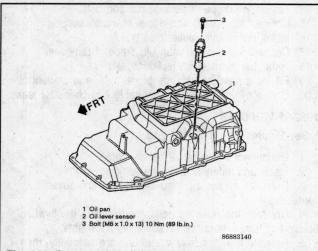

1 Oil pan
2 Oil lever sensor
3 Bolt (M6 x 1.0 x 13) 10 Nm (89 lb.in.)

86883140

Fig. 113 Remove the oil level sensor, which is mounted in the oil pan

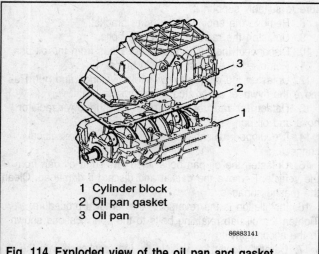

1 Cylinder block
2 Oil pan gasket
3 Oil pan

86883141

Fig. 114 Exploded view of the oil pan and gasket assembly — 1992-95 2.3L

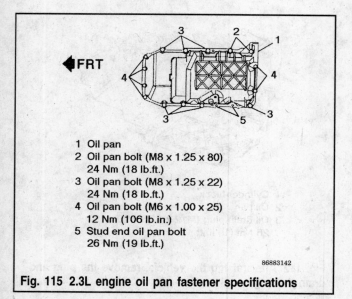

1 Oil pan
2 Oil pan bolt (M8 x 1.25 x 80)
 24 Nm (18 lb.ft.)
3 Oil pan bolt (M8 x 1.25 x 22)
 24 Nm (18 lb.ft.)
4 Oil pan bolt (M6 x 1.00 x 25)
 12 Nm (106 lb.in.)
5 Stud end oil pan bolt
 26 Nm (19 lb.ft.)

86883142

Fig. 115 2.3L engine oil pan fastener specifications

2.5L Engine

▶ **See Figure 116**

1. Disconnect the negative battery cable.

2. Raise and safely support the vehicle. Drain the engine oil.

3. Remove the exhaust pipe and hangers from the exhaust manifold and allow it to swing aside.

4. Detach the electrical connectors from the starter. Unfasten the starter-to-engine bolts, the starter and the flywheel housing inspection cover from the engine.

5. Unfasten the oil pan-to-engine bolts and the oil pan.

To install:

6. Thoroughly clean the mating surfaces, bolts and bolt holes.

7. Apply RTV sealant to the oil pan flange, surrounding all bolt holes. Also, apply sealant to the engine at the front and rear seams.

8. Install the oil pan and tighten the bolts to 20 ft. lbs. (27 Nm) for vehicles through 1988. For 1989-91 vehicles, tighten to 89 inch lbs. (10 Nm).

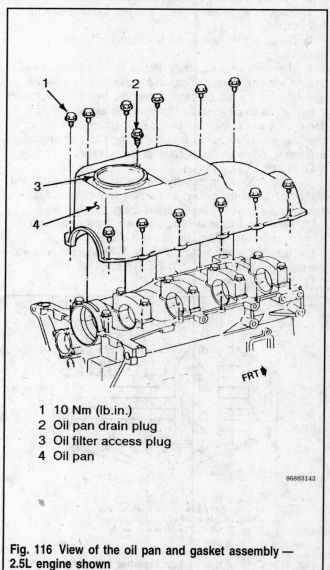

1 10 Nm (lb.in.)
2 Oil pan drain plug
3 Oil filter access plug
4 Oil pan

86883143

Fig. 116 View of the oil pan and gasket assembly — 2.5L engine shown

9. Install the flywheel housing cover and the starter. Attach the starter electrical connector.

10. Install the exhaust pipe into its original position.

11. Fill the crankcase with oil to specification.

12. Connect the negative battery cable and check for leaks.

3.0L and 1988-91 3.3L Engines

▶ See Figures 117, 118, 119 and 120

1. Disconnect the negative battery cable.

2. Raise and safely support the vehicle.

3. Drain the engine oil and remove the oil filter.

4. Remove the flywheel cover

5. For the 3.3L engine, remove the starter.

6. Unfasten the retaining bolts, then remove the oil pan, tensioner spring and formed rubber gasket.

7. The installation is the reverse of the removal procedure. Tighten the oil pan-to-engine bolts to 88 inch lbs. (10 Nm) for the 3.0L engine or 124 inch lbs. (14 Nm) for the 3.3L engine.

8. Fill the crankcase with the proper type and quantity of oil.

9. Connect the negative battery cable and check for leaks.

1992-93 3.3L Engine

▶ See Figure 121

1. Disconnect the negative battery cable.

2. Raise and safely support the vehicle.

3. Drain the engine oil.

4. Remove the lower flap and splash shield.

5. Disconnect the crankshaft pulley.

6. Remove the crankshaft position sensor cover.

7. Detach the A/C compressor electrical connector, then remove and support the compressor.

8. Disconnect the bolts at the front of the right suspension support.

9. Loosen, but do not remove, all the suspension support bolts so that the supports drop about 1.5 in. (38mm) at the front.

10. Remove the oil level sensor from the oil pan.

11. Remove the transaxle converter cover.

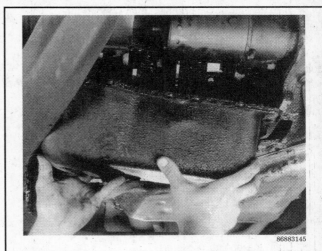

Fig. 118 You may have to maneuver the oil pan around the sub-frame

Fig. 119 After the subframe is clear, lower the oil pan, then . . .

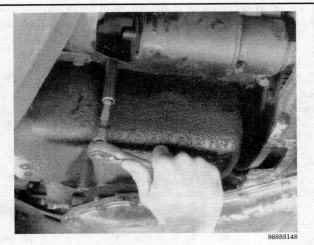

Fig. 117 Using a suitable socket extension, remove the oil pan mounting bolts

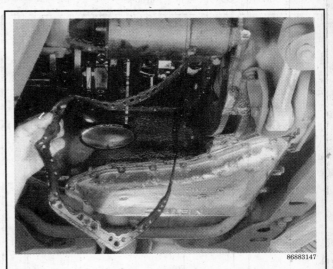

Fig. 120 . . . remove and discard the gasket

12. Unfasten the retaining bolts, then remove the oil pan. Remove and discard the gasket. Clean all mating surfaces.

13. Installation is the reverse of the removal procedure. Make sure to use a new gasket. Tighten the oil pan retaining bolts to 124 inch lbs. (14 Nm).

14. Carefully lower the car, fill the crankcase with the correct type and quantity of oil, then connect the negative battery cable. Start the engine and inspect for leaks.

3.1L Engine

▶ See Figure 122

1. Disconnect the negative battery cable.
2. Remove the serpentine belt.
3. If equipped, loosen, but do not remove, the upper A/C compressor bolts.
4. Raise and safely support the vehicle.
5. Drain the engine oil.
6. Remove the right front tire and wheel assembly.
7. Remove the right inner fender splash shield.
8. Disconnect the engine mount strut from the suspension support.
9. Unfasten the cotter pin and castle nut from the lower ball joint and separate the joint from the steering knuckle.
10. Remove the right side sway bar link.
11. Detach the ABS sensor from the right subframe.
12. Unfasten the right side subframe mounting bolts and remove the right side subframe and control arm as an assembly.
13. Remove the lower A/C compressor mounting bolts and position the compressor aside. DO NOT disconnect the refrigerant lines or allow the compressor to hang unsupported.
14. Disconnect the engine mount strut bracket from the engine.
15. Remove the engine to transaxle brace.
16. Remove the oil filter.
17. Remove the starter.
18. Remove the flywheel cover.
19. Unfasten the oil pan flange retaining bolts and the oil pan side retaining bolts, then remove the oil pan.

To install:
20. Clean the gasket mating surfaces.

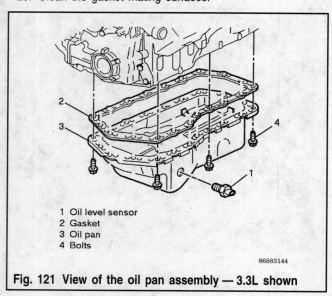

1 Oil level sensor
2 Gasket
3 Oil pan
4 Bolts

86883144

Fig. 121 View of the oil pan assembly — 3.3L shown

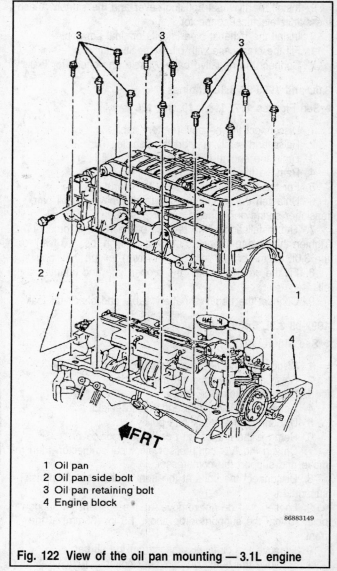

1 Oil pan
2 Oil pan side bolt
3 Oil pan retaining bolt
4 Engine block

86883149

Fig. 122 View of the oil pan mounting — 3.1L engine

21. Apply silicon sealer to the portion of the pan that contacts the rear of the block. Install a new gasket on the oil pan.
22. Position the oil pan and install the mounting bolts finger-tight.
23. With all the bolts in place, tighten the oil pan flange bolts to 18 ft. lbs. (25 Nm) and the oil pan side bolts to 37 ft. lbs. (50 Nm).
24. Install the flywheel cover. and the starter.
25. Coat the seal on the oil filter with clean engine oil, then install the filter on the engine.
26. Install the engine-to-transaxle brace and tighten the mounting bolts to 68 ft. lbs. (93 Nm).
27. Install the engine mount strut bracket. Tighten the mounting bolt at the engine bracket to 85 ft. lbs. (115 Nm).
28. Place the A/C compressor in the mounting bracket, then tighten the lower mounting bolts.
29. Install the right side subframe and control arm assembly. Tighten the subframe mounting bolts to 89 ft. lbs. (120 Nm).
30. Install the right side sway bar link and tighten to 22 ft. lbs. (30 Nm).

31. Connect the ball joint to the steering knuckle and tighten the castle nut to 48 ft. lbs. (60 Nm). Install a new cotter pin.

32. Connect the ABS sensor to the right subframe assembly.

33. Connect the engine mount strut bracket and tighten the mounting bolt at the frame to 89 ft. lbs. (120 Nm).

34. Install the right inner fender well splash shield.

35. Install the right front tire and wheel assembly and tighten to specification.

36. Carefully lower the vehicle.

37. Install the serpentine belt.

38. Fill the crankcase to the correct level.

39. Connect the negative battery cable, start the vehicle and verify that there are no leaks.

Oil Pump

REMOVAL & INSTALLATION

2.0L Engine

1. Disconnect negative battery cable.
2. Remove the timing belt and crankshaft sprocket.
3. Remove the rear timing belt cover.
4. Detach the oil pressure sending unit connector.
5. Raise and safely support the vehicle.
6. Drain the engine oil.
7. Remove the oil pan and oil filter.
8. Unfasten the oil pump mounting bolts, then remove the pump and pickup tube.

To install:

9. Prime the pump by pouring fresh oil into the pump intake and turning the driveshaft until oil comes out the pressure port. Repeat a few times until no air bubbles are present.

10. The installation is the reverse of the removal procedure. Use a new gasket and seal and tighten the oil pump bolts to 5 ft. lbs. (7 Nm). Use a new ring for the pickup tube.

11. Fill the crankcase with the proper oil.

12. Connect the negative battery cable, check the oil pressure and check for leaks.

2.3L Engine

▶ See Figure 123

1. Disconnect the negative battery cable.
2. Raise and safely support the vehicle.
3. Drain the engine oil and remove the oil pan. For details, please refer to the procedure located in this section.
4. Unfasten the oil pump attaching bolts and nut, then remove the oil pump assembly, shims if equipped, and screen.

To install:

5. With the oil pump assembly off the engine, remove 3 attaching bolts and separate the driven gear cover and screen assembly from the oil pump.

6. Install the oil pump on the block using the original shims, if equipped. Tighten the bolts to 33 ft. lbs. (45 Nm).

7. Mount a dial indicator assembly to measure backlash between oil pump to drive gear.

8. Record oil pump drive to driven gear backlash. Proper backlash is 0.010-0.018 in. (0.254-0.457mm). When measuring, do not allow the crankshaft to move.

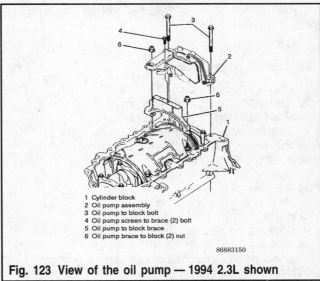

1 Cylinder block
2 Oil pump assembly
3 Oil pump to block bolt
4 Oil pump screen to brace (2) bolt
5 Oil pump to block brace
6 Oil pump brace to block (2) nut

86883150

Fig. 123 View of the oil pump — 1994 2.3L shown

9. If equipped with shims, remove shims to decrease clearance and add shims to increase clearance. If no shims were present, replace the assembly if proper backlash cannot be obtained.

10. When the proper clearance is reached, rotate crankshaft ½ turn and recheck clearance.

11. Remove oil pump from block, fill the cavity with petroleum jelly and reinstall driven gear cover and screen assembly to pump. Tighten the bolts to 106 inch lbs. (13 Nm).

12. Reinstall the pump assembly to the block. Tighten oil pump-to-block bolts 33 ft. lbs. (45 Nm).

13. Install the oil pan.

14. Fill the crankcase with the proper oil.

15. Connect the negative battery cable, check the oil pressure and check for leaks.

2.5L Engine

1. Disconnect the negative battery cable.
2. Drain the engine oil and remove the oil pan.
3. Remove the oil filter.
4. Remove the oil pump cover assembly.
5. Remove the gyrator pump gears.

✳✳CAUTION

The pressure regulator valve spring is under pressure. Exercise caution when removing the pin or personal injury may result!

6. Remove the pressure regulator pin, spring and valve.

To install:

7. Lubricate all internal parts with clean engine oil and fill all pump cavities with petroleum jelly.

8. Install the pressure regulator valve, spring and secure the pin.

9. Install the gyrator gears.

10. Install the pump cover and tighten the screws to 10 ft. lbs. (14 Nm).

11. Install the oil filter.

12. Install the oil pan.

13. Fill the crankcase with oil to specification.

14. Connect the negative battery cable, check the oil pressure and check for leaks.

3.0L and 3.3L Engines

▶ **See Figures 124 and 125**

1. Disconnect the negative battery cable.
2. Remove the timing chain front cover.
3. Raise and safely support the vehicle.
4. Drain the engine oil. Lower the vehicle.
5. Remove the oil filter adapter, the pressure regulator valve and the valve spring.
6. Remove the oil pump cover-to-oil pump screws and remove the cover.
7. Remove the oil pump gears.

To install:

8. Lubricate the oil pump gears with clean engine oil.
9. Pack the pump cavity with petroleum jelly.
10. Install the oil pump cover screws using a new gasket and tighten to 97 inch lbs. (11 Nm).

Fig. 124 Once the oil pan is removed, you can see the pump and screen assembly — 3.0L engine

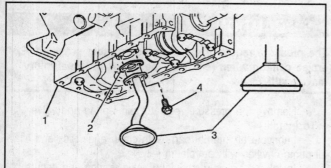

1 Cylinder block
2 Gasket
3 Oil pump pipe and screen
4 Bolt

86883151

Fig. 125 View of the oil pump mounting — 3.3L engine shown

11. Install the pressure regulator spring and valve.
12. Install the oil filter adaptor using a new gasket. Tighten the oil filter adapter-to-engine bolts to 30 ft. lbs. (41 Nm) for the 3.0L engine or 24 ft. lbs. (33 Nm) for the 3.3L engine.
13. Install the timing chain front cover to the engine.
14. Fill the crankcase with clean engine oil.
15. Connect the negative battery cable, check the oil pressure and check for leaks.

3.1L Engine

▶ **See Figures 126 and 127**

1. Disconnect the negative battery cable.
2. Raise and safely support the vehicle.
3. Drain the engine oil into a suitable container.
4. Remove the oil pan. For details, refer to the procedure located in this section.
5. Unfasten the crankshaft oil deflector bolts, then remove the crankshaft oil deflector.
6. Remove the oil pump retaining bolts, then remove the oil pump and pump driveshaft.

To install:

7. Prime the oil pump.
8. Install the oil pump and pump driveshaft. Tighten the oil pump mounting bolts to 30 ft. lbs. (41 Nm).
9. Install the crankshaft oil deflector and mounting nuts. Tighten the mounting nuts to 18 ft. lbs. (25 Nm).
10. Install the oil pan. For details, please refer to the procedure located in this section.
11. Carefully lower the vehicle.
12. Fill the crankcase to the correct level with oil.
13. Start the engine, check the oil pressure and check for leaks.

INSPECTION

▶ **See Figures 128 and 129**

2.0L Engine

1. Inspect all components carefully for physical damage of any type and replace worn parts.

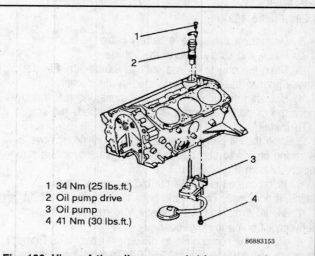

1 34 Nm (25 lbs.ft.)
2 Oil pump drive
3 Oil pump
4 41 Nm (30 lbs.ft.)

86883153

Fig. 126 View of the oil pump and drive assembly mounting — 3.1L engine

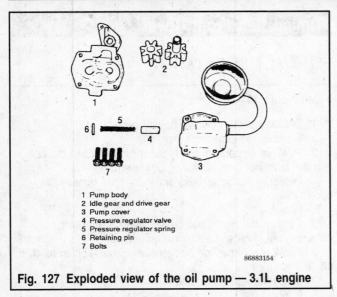

Fig. 127 Exploded view of the oil pump — 3.1L engine

1 Pump body
2 Idle gear and drive gear
3 Pump cover
4 Pressure regulator valve
5 Pressure regulator spring
6 Retaining pin
7 Bolts

86883154

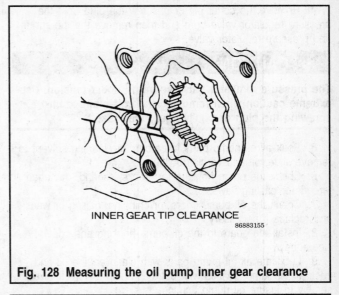

INNER GEAR TIP CLEARANCE

86883155

Fig. 128 Measuring the oil pump inner gear clearance

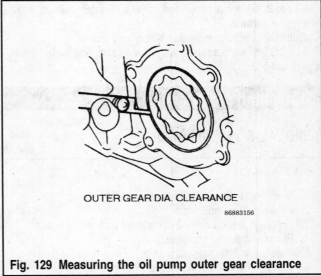

OUTER GEAR DIA. CLEARANCE

86883156

Fig. 129 Measuring the oil pump outer gear clearance

2. Check the gear pocket depth. The specification is 0.395-0.397 in. (10.03-10.08mm).

3. Check the gear pocket diameter. The specification is 3.230-3.235 in. (82.02-82.15mm).

4. Check the diameter of the gears. The specifications are 0.014-0.018 in. (0.35-0.45mm) for the drive gear and 0.004-0.007 in. (0.11-0.19mm) for the idler gear.

5. Check the side clearance. The specifications are 2.317-2.319 in. (58.85-58.90mm) for the drive gear and 3.225-3.227 in. (81.91-81.96mm) for the idler gear.

6. Check the end clearance below the pump housing. The specification is 0.001-0.004 in. (0.03-0.10mm).

2.3L Engine

1. Inspect all components carefully for physical damage of any type and replace worn parts.

2. Check the gyrator cavity depth. The specification for 1988 is 0.689-0.691 in. (17.50-17.55mm). The specification for 1989-92 is 0.67-0.676 in. (17.11-17.16mm).

3. Check the gyrator cavity diameter. The specification for 1988 is 2.010-2.012 in. (51.054-51.104mm). The specification for 1989-92 is 2.127-2.129 in. (53.95-54.00mm).

4. Check the inner gyrator tip clearance. The maximum clearance is 0.006 in. (15mm).

5. Check the outer gyrator diameter clearance. The specification is 0.010-0.014 in. (0.254-0.354mm).

2.5L Engine

1. Inspect all components carefully for physical damage of any type and replace worn parts.

2. Check the gyrator cavity depth. The specification for 1988 is 0.995-0.998 in. (25.27-25.35mm). The specification for 1989-92 is 0.514-0.516 in. (13.05-13.10mm).

3. Check the gear lash. The specification is 0.009-0.015 in. (0.23-0.38mm).

4. Check the clearance of both gears. The maximum clearance is 0.004 in. (0.10mm).

3.0L and 3.3L Engines

1. Inspect all components carefully for physical damage of any type and replace worn parts.

2. Check the gear pocket depth. The specification is 0.461-0.463 in. (11.71-11.75mm).

3. Check the gear pocket diameter. The specification is 3.508-3.512 in. (89.10-89.20mm).

4. Check the inner gear tip clearance. The maximum clearance is 0.006 in. (0.152mm).

5. Check the outer gear diameter clearance. The specification is 0.008-0.015 in. (0.025-0.089mm).

OVERHAUL

1. Remove the oil pan or front engine cover to gain access to the oil pump as previously described.

2. Remove the oil pump cover.

3. Remove the oil pump gears.

4. Remove the cotter pin or unscrew the plug from the pressure regulator valve bore and then remove the the spring and pressure regulator valve.

✳✳CAUTION

The pressure regulator valve spring is under tension. Use extreme caution when removing the cotter pin or unscrewing the plug or bodily injury may result.

5. Soak all oil pump parts in carburetor cleaning solvent to remove slide, oil and varnish build-up.
6. Check the pump housing for cracks, scoring, damaged threads or casting flaws.
7. Check the oil pump gears for chipping, galling or wear and replace if necessary.
8. Install the gears to the oil pump housing and check clearances.
9. Lubricate all oil pump parts with clean engine oil and pack all oil pump cavities with petroleum jelly before final assembly to insure oil pump priming.
10. Install oil pump cover and screws. Tighten screws to 97 inch lbs. (11 Nm).
11. Install pressure regulator spring and valve.
12. Install oil filter adapter with new gasket and install front engine cover.

Crankshaft Dampener

REMOVAL & INSTALLATION

▶ See Figure 130

1. Disconnect the negative battery cable.
2. Properly raise and support the vehicle.
3. Unfasten the crankshaft dampener bolt and washer.
4. Remove the dampener and key.
5. Installation is the reverse of the removal procedure.
6. Tighten the dampener bolt to proper torque specifications.

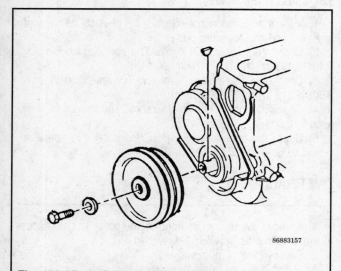

86883157

Fig. 130 View of the crankshaft dampener

Timing Belt Front Cover

REMOVAL & INSTALLATION

▶ See Figure 131

1. Disconnect the negative battery cable.
2. Remove the serpentine belt.
3. Remove serpentine belt tensioner bolt (loosen the bolt and the tensioner arm will swing downward).
4. Unfasten the cover bolts and nuts, then remove the cover.
   To install:
5. Position the timing belt cover, then secure using the bolts and nut. Tighten to 89 inch lbs. (10 Nm).
6. Install the serpentine belt tensioner, then tighten to 40 ft. lbs. (54 Nm).
7. Install the serpentine belt.
8. Connect the negative battery cable.

OIL SEAL REPLACEMENT

1. Disconnect the negative battery cable.
2. Remove the timing belt sprockets and the inner cover. Remove the crankshaft key and thrust washer.
3. Using a suitable small prybar, carefully pry out the old oil seal.

➡ **Use care to avoid damage to seal bore and crankshaft.**

4. Thoroughly clean and dry the oil seal mounting surface.
5. Use the appropriate installation tool and drive the oil seal into the front cover.
6. The installation is the reverse of the removal procedure.
7. Connect the negative battery cable and check for leaks.

Timing Chain Front Cover

REMOVAL & INSTALLATION

2.3L Engine

1. Disconnect the negative battery cable. Properly drain the engine cooling system.
2. Remove the coolant recovery reservoir.
3. Remove the serpentine drive belt using a 13mm wrench that is at least 24 in. (61cm) long.
4. Remove the alternator, then position it aside.
5. Install engine support J 28467-A or equivalent. Reinstall the alternator through-bolt, then attach the engine support fixture.
6. Remove upper cover fasteners.
7. For VIN A and D engines, detach the cover vent hose.
8. Remove the right engine mount and the engine mount bracket.
9. Raise and safely support the vehicle.
10. Remove the right front wheel and tire assembly and the splash shield.

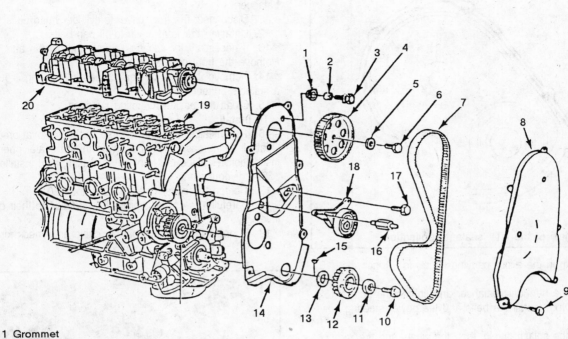

Fig. 131 View of the timing belt front cover and related components — 2.0L engine only

1 Grommet
2 Sleeve
3 Bolt 10 Nm (89 lb.in.)
4 Camshaft sprocket
5 Washer
6 Bolt 45 Nm (33 lb.ft.)
7 Timing belt
8 Front cover
9 Bolt 9 Nm (80 lb.in.)

10 Bolt 155 Nm (114 lb.ft.)
11 Washer
12 Crankshaft sprocket
13 Washer
14 Rear cover
15 Keyway

16 Stud 48 Nm (35 lb.ft.)
17 Bolt 48 Nm (35 lb.ft.)
18 Tensioner
19 Engine
20 Camshaft

86883158

11. Remove the crankshaft balancer assembly.

➡**Do not install an automatic transaxle-equipped engine balancer on a manual-transaxle equipped engine or vice-versa.**

12. Remove lower cover fasteners.
13. Carefully lower the vehicle.
14. Remove the front cover and gasket. Inspect the gasket for damage and replace if necessary.
15. The installation is the reverse of the removal procedure. Tighten the timing chain cover-to-block bolt and stud to 21 ft. lbs. (29 Nm). Tighten the balancer attaching bolt to 74 ft. lbs. (100 Nm).

2.5L Engine

1990-91 VEHICLES

▶ **See Figures 132 and 133**

1. Disconnect the negative battery cable.
2. Remove the belts. Remove the power steering pump mounting bolts and position it aside.

3. Raise and safely support the vehicle.
4. Remove the right front wheel and tire assembly, then remove the inner fender splash shield.
5. Remove the right hand cover.
6. Using a suitable tool to prevent flywheel rotation, remove the flywheel cover.
7. Unfasten the bolts and washer, then remove the crankshaft dampener.

➡**Be sure NOT to distort the cover when removing it!**

8. Unfasten the timing chain cover-to-engine bolts and the timing case cover.

To install:

9. Thoroughly clean and dry all mating surfaces. Use RTV sealant to seal all mating surfaces.
10. A centering tool fits over the crankshaft seal and is used to correctly position the timing case cover during installation. Install the cover and partially tighten the 2 opposing timing case cover screws.
11. Tighten the remaining cover screws and remove the centering tool from the timing case cover. Tighten, in the se-

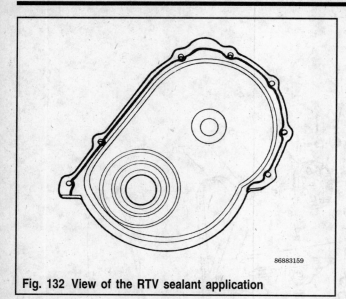

Fig. 132 View of the RTV sealant application

quence shown in the accompanying figure, to 89 inch lbs. (10 Nm).

12. Install the harmonic balancer and tighten the bolt to 162 ft. lbs. (220 Nm). Install the belts and the power steering pump.

13. Install the splash shield, then the wheel and tire assembly.

14. Connect the negative battery cable and check for leaks.

3.0L Engine

▶ **See Figures 134, 135, 136 and 137**

1. Disconnect the negative battery cable.
2. Properly drain the coolant into a suitable container.
3. Detach the upper and lower radiator hoses.
4. Disconnect the heater return hose.
5. Disengage the crankshaft sensor electrical connector.
6. Remove the serpentine belt.
7. Detach the front clamp on the coolant bypass hose.
8. Raise and safely support the vehicle. Remove the right wheel and tire assembly, then remove the splash shield.

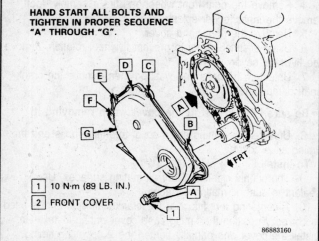

Fig. 133 Timing chain cover and tightening sequence — 1990-91 2.5L engine

9. Drain the engine oil, then remove the oil filter.
10. Unfasten the balancer bolt and washer, then remove the balancer.
11. Disconnect the front cover-to-cylinder head bolts.
12. Unfasten the front cover-to-oil pan bolts.
13. If necessary for access, remove the oil pan and gasket. Remove the front cover.
14. Remove the front oil seal by carefully prying it out using a suitable prytool.
15. Clean the gasket mounting surfaces.

To install:

16. The installation is the reverse of the removal procedure. Coat all timing case cover bolts with thread sealer prior to installation. Replace the front oil seal using seal installer tool J 35354 or equivalent.
17. Tighten the cover bolts to 22 ft. lbs. (30 Nm).
18. Carefully lower the vehicle. Fill all fluids to their proper levels.
19. Connect the negative battery cable and check for leaks.

Fig. 134 The crankshaft balancer is accessible through the right wheel well

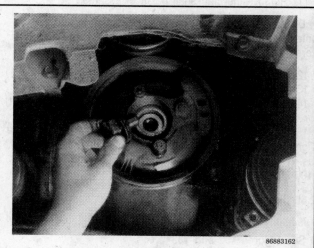

Fig. 135 Unfasten the retaining bolts and washer, then . . .

Fig. 136 . . . remove the crankshaft balancer assembly

Fig. 137 After unfastening all of the retaining bolts, remove the timing chain cover from the engine

3.1L Engine

♦ **See Figure 138**

1. Disconnect the negative battery cable.
2. Drain the cooling system into a suitable container.
3. Remove the right engine mount bracket.
4. Remove the serpentine belt.
5. Remove the crankshaft balancer as follows:
   a. Raise and safely support the vehicle.
   b. Remove the right front tire and wheel assembly.
   c. Remove the right inner fender well splash shield.
   d. Remove the flywheel cover and install a flywheel holding tool.
   e. Remove the balancer mounting bolt and washer.
   f. Using a suitable puller, J-24420-B or the equivalent remove the balancer from the crankshaft.
6. Remove the serpentine belt tensioner mounting bolt and tensioner.
7. Remove the oil pan following the procedure located in this section.

8. Detach coolant bypass pipe from the water pump and the intake manifold.
9. Disconnect the lower radiator hose to from the front cover outlet.
10. Unfasten the front cover mounting bolts and remove the front cover.

To install:

11. Clean all gasket surfaces completely.
12. Apply a thin bead of sealer around the gasket sealing area of the front cover. Install a new front cover seal on the front cover.
13. Install the front cover on the engine and tighten the mounting bolts to 15 ft. lbs (21 Nm).
14. Connect the radiator hose to the coolant outlet.
15. Install coolant bypass pipe to the water pump and the intake manifold.
16. Install the oil pan following the recommended procedure.
17. Install crankshaft balancer as follows:
   a. Coat the seal contact surface of the crankshaft balancer with clean engine oil.
   b. Line up the notch in the balancer with the crankshaft key and slide the balancer on until the key is in the balancer.
   c. Using J-29113 or an equivalent puller, seat the balancer on the crankshaft.
   d. Install the balancer mounting bolt and washer and tighten to 76 ft. lbs. (103 Nm).
   e. Install the flywheel cover.
   f. Install the right inner fender well splash shield.
   g. Install the tire and wheel assembly and tighten to specification.
18. Install the serpentine belt tensioner and tighten the mounting bolt to 40 ft. lbs. (54 Nm).
19. Install the serpentine belt.
20. Install the right engine mount bracket and tighten the bracket-to-mount bolts to 96 ft. lbs. (130 Nm).
21. Refill the cooling system.
22. Check the engine oil level and top off as necessary.
23. Connect the negative battery cable.
24. Start the vehicle and verify no oil leaks.

3.3L Engine

♦ **See Figures 139 and 140**

1. Disconnect the negative battery cable.
2. Propely drain the coolant into a suitable container.
3. Remove the accessory drive belt.
4. Disconnect the heater pipes.
5. Detach the lower radiator hose and the coolant bypass hose from the timing front cover.
6. Raise and safely support the vehicle. Remove the right front wheel and tire assembly and the right inner fender splash shield.
7. Remove the torque converter cover.
8. Holding the flywheel with tool J 37096 or equivalent, remove the the crankshaft harmonic balancer bolt and the balancer using tool J 38197 or equivalent.
9. Remove the crankshaft sensor shield.
10. Detach the electrical connections at the crankshaft sensor and the oil pressure sender.
11. Remove the crankshaft sensor.

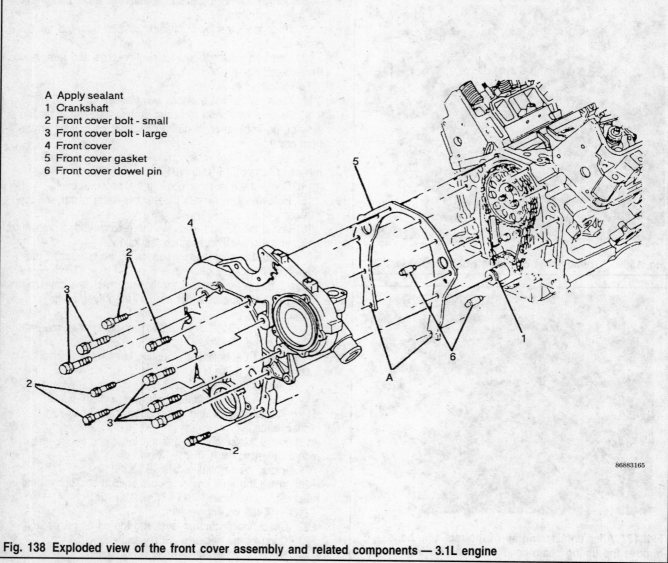

A Apply sealant
1 Crankshaft
2 Front cover bolt - small
3 Front cover bolt - large
4 Front cover
5 Front cover gasket
6 Front cover dowel pin

86883165

Fig. 138 Exploded view of the front cover assembly and related components — 3.1L engine

12. Unfasten the timing case cover-to-engine bolts, then remove timing case cover and the gasket.

13. Remove the front seal by using a suitable prytool and carefully prying the seal out of the cover. Inspect the seal and replace if necessary.

14. Clean the gasket mounting surfaces.

To install:

15. The installation is the reverse of the removal procedure. Coat all timing case cover bolts with thread sealer prior to installation. Tighten the bolts to 22 ft. lbs. (30 Nm).

16. Install the front oil seal using seal installer tool J 35354, or equivalent.

17. Fill all fluids to their proper levels.

18. Connect the negative battery cable, then start the engine and check for leaks.

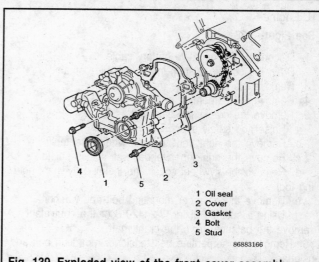

1 Oil seal
2 Cover
3 Gasket
4 Bolt
5 Stud

86883166

Fig. 139 Exploded view of the front cover assembly — 3.3L engine

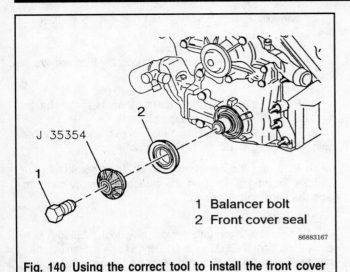

Fig. 140 Using the correct tool to install the front cover oil seal

1 Balancer bolt
2 Front cover seal

86883167

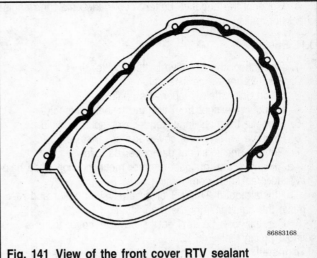

Fig. 141 View of the front cover RTV sealant application — 1986-89 2.5L engines

86883168

Timing Gear Front Cover

REMOVAL & INSTALLATION

2.5L Engine

1986-89 VEHICLES

▶ **See Figures 141 and 142**

1. Disconnect the negative battery cable.
2. Remove the drive belts.
3. Raise and safely support the vehicle. Remove the right front wheel and tire assembly and the inner fender splash shield.
4. Remove the crankshaft dampener. For details, please refer to the procedure located in this section.

➡**When removing the cover, use care not to distort it!**

5. Unfasten the front cover-to-engine retaining screw/bolts, then remove the timing gear front cover.

   To install:
6. Thoroughly clean and dry all mating surfaces. Apply a ¼ in. (6mm) wide by ⅛ in. (3mm) thick bead of RTV sealant to the front cover at the block mating surfaces.
7. A centering tool fits over the crankshaft seal and is used to correctly position the timing case cover during installation. Install the cover and partially tighten the 2 opposing timing case cover screws.
8. Tighten the remaining cover screws (in the sequence shown in the accompanying figure) to 89 inch lbs. (10 Nm), then remove the centering tool from the timing case cover.
9. Install the crankshaft dampener, then tighten the bolt to 162 ft. lbs. (220 Nm). Install the belts and the power steering pump.
10. Install the splash shield and the right wheel and tire assembly.
11. Carefully lower the vehicle.
12. Connect the negative battery cable, then start the vehicle and check for leaks.

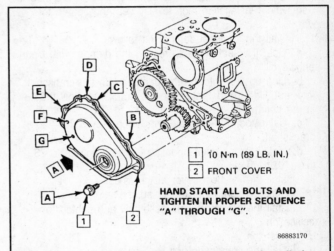

Fig. 142 View of the timing gear front cover installation and retainer tightening sequence

1 10 N·m (89 LB. IN.)
2 FRONT COVER

HAND START ALL BOLTS AND TIGHTEN IN PROPER SEQUENCE "A" THROUGH "G".

86883170

Front Cover Oil Seal

REPLACEMENT

Except 3.1L engine

1. Disconnect the negative battery cable.
2. Remove the front cover. For details, please refer to the appropriate procedure located in this section.
3. Using a small prybar, carefully pry out the old oil seal.

➡**Use care to avoid damage to seal bore or seal contact surfaces.**

4. Thoroughly clean and dry the oil seal mounting surface.
5. Use the appropriate installation tool and drive the oil seal into the front cover.
6. Lubricate balancer and seal lip with clean engine oil.
7. Install the front cover.

8. Connect the negative battery cable, then start the engine check for leaks.

3.1L Engine

1. Disconnect the negative battery cable.
2. Remove the serpentine belt.
3. Raise and safely support the vehicle.
4. Remove the right front tire and wheel assembly.
5. Remove the right inner fender well splash shield.
6. Remove the flywheel cover at the transaxle.
7. Remove the torsional dampener as follows:
   a. Remove the torsional damper mounting bolt while holding the crankshaft from turning.
   b. Install tool J 24420-B or an equivalent puller and remove the damper from the crankshaft.
8. Carefully pry the seal out of the front cover using a suitable prying tool.

To install:

9. Clean out the oil seal recess in the front cover.
10. Install the new seal in the front cover using J-34995, or an equivalent installation tool, to fully seat the seal in the cover.
11. Install the torsional damper as follows:
    a. Coat the seal contact area on the damper with clean engine oil.
    b. Line up the notch in the damper with the crankshaft key and slide the damper onto the crankshaft until the key is in the notch.
    c. Using tool J-29113, pull the damper onto the crankshaft.
    d. Install the damper mounting bolt and tighten to 76 ft. lbs. (102 Nm).
12. Install the flywheel cover at transaxle.
13. Install the right inner fender splash shield.
14. Install the tire and wheel assembly and tighten to specification.
15. Lower the vehicle.
16. Install the serpentine belt.
17. Connect the negative battery cable.
18. Start the vehicle and verify no coolant leaks or oil leaks.

Timing Belt and Tensioner

Timing belts are made of rubber and do wear out. It is recommended that the belt be replaced after approximately 60,000 miles (96,000km). Failure to do so may result in a broken belt which could cause major engine damage.

REMOVAL & INSTALLATION

2.0L Engine

1987-88 VEHICLES

▶ **See Figures 143, 144 and 145**

1. Disconnect the negative battery cable.
2. Remove the timing belt cover. For details, please refer to the procedure located in this section.
3. If not done already, raise and safely support the vehicle.
4. Remove the crankshaft pulley.

5. Carefully lower the vehicle until it is just above floor level.
6. Remove the coolant reservoir.
7. Loosen the water pump mounting bolts, then remove the timing belt.

To install:

8. Position the camshaft so the mark on its sprocket aligns with the mark on the rear timing belt cover.
9. Position the crankshaft so the mark on the pulley aligns with 10 degrees BTDC on the timing scale.

➡**Do NOT turn the camshaft. Use only the crankshaft nut to turn. Turning the nut on the camshaft directly can damage the camshaft bearings.**

10. Install the timing belt.
11. Check the timing belt tension using tool J-26486-A or equivalent. Tool J-33039 or equivalent, is used to adjust the belt tension at the water pump. With the gauge installed, adjust the tension to within the band on the gauge. Adjusting the tension with the gauge installed on the belt will ensure an initial over-tensioning with the new belt.
12. Crank the engine, but DO NOT start it, about 10 revolutions; a substantial tension loss should occur as the belt takes a set position.
13. Recheck the tension with the gauge. If a tension increase is needed, remove the gauge and adjust the water pump. Repeat until the tension is within specification.

➡**Do not increase tension with the gauge installed or the resulting tension will be inaccurate.**

14. After the proper tension has been reached, tighten the water pump bolts to 19 ft. lbs. (25 Nm).
15. Install the timing belt cover and all related parts.
16. Raise and safely support the vehicle.
17. Install the crankshaft pulley, then install the serpentine belt. If equipped, install the A/C belt.
18. Carefully lower the vehicle.
19. Install the coolant reservoir.
20. Connect the negative battery cable and road test the vehicle.

1989 VEHICLES

▶ **See Figure 146**

1. Disconnect the negative battery cable.
2. Remove the serpentine belt.
3. Remove the timing belt cover as outlined earlier in this section.
4. Loosen the water pump mounting bolts and relieve the tension using tool J-33039 or equivalent.
5. Raise and safely support the vehicle.
6. Remove the crankshaft pulley.
7. Carefully lower the vehicle.
8. Remove the timing belt.

To install:

9. Turn the crankshaft and camshaft gears clockwise to align the timing marks on the gears with the timing marks on the rear cover.
10. Install the timing belt, making sure portion of the belt between the camshaft and crankshaft gears has no slack.
11. Adjust the timing belt using tool J-33039 or equivalent, to turn the water pump eccentric clockwise until the tensioner

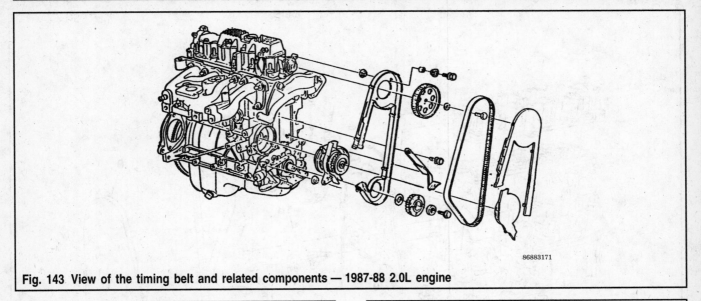

Fig. 143 View of the timing belt and related components — 1987-88 2.0L engine

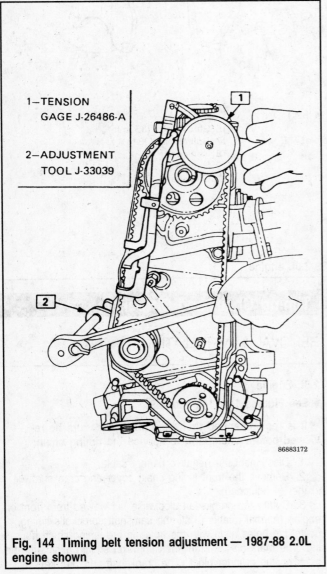

1—TENSION
GAGE J-26486-A

2—ADJUSTMENT
TOOL J-33039

Fig. 144 Timing belt tension adjustment — 1987-88 2.0L engine shown

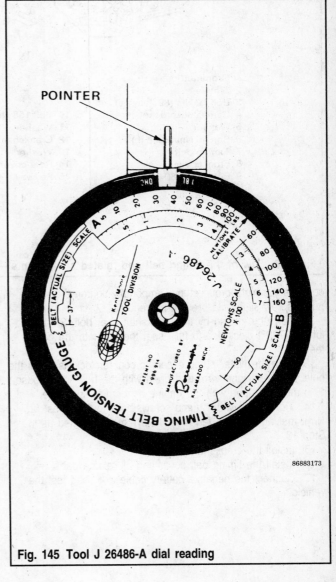

POINTER

Fig. 145 Tool J 26486-A dial reading

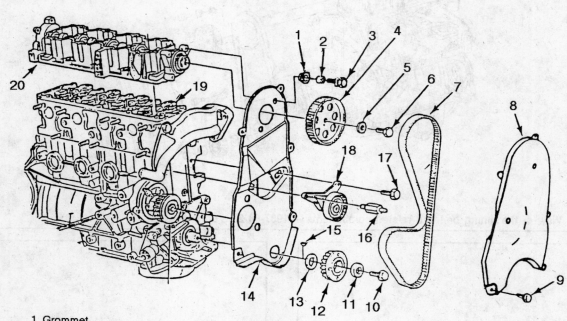

1 Grommet
2 Sleeve
3 Bolt 10 Nm (89 lb.in.)
4 Camshaft sprocket
5 Washer
6 Bolt 45 Nm (33 lb.ft.)
7 Timing belt
8 Front cover
9 Bolt 9 Nm (80 lb.in.)

10 Bolt 155 Nm (114 lb.ft.)
11 Washer
12 Crankshaft sprocket
13 Washer
14 Rear cover
15 Keyway

16 Stud 48 Nm (35 lb.ft.)
17 Bolt 48 Nm (35 lb.ft.)
18 Tensioner
19 Engine
20 Camshaft

86883174

Fig. 146 View of the timing belt and related components — 1989 2.0L engine

contacts the high torque stop. Temporarily tighten the water pump screw slightly to prevent movement.

12. Turn the engine by the crankshaft gear bolt, 2 full revolutions (720°) clockwise to fully seat the belt into the gear teeth.

13. Turn the water pump eccentric counterclockwise until the hole in the tensioner arm is aligned with the hole in the base. This must be done with the engine at room temperature.

14. Tighten the water pump screws/bolts to 19 ft. lbs. (25 Nm), making sure the tensioner hole remains aligned as in Step 13.

15. Install the crankshaft pulley.

16. Install the timing belt cover and all related parts.

17. Connect the negative battery cable and road test the vehicle.

Timing Chain and Sprockets

REMOVAL & INSTALLATION

2.3L Engine

▶ See Figures 147, 148 and 149

➡It is recommended that this entire procedure be reviewed before attempting to service the timing chain.

1. Disconnect the negative battery cable.

2. Remove the front timing chain cover and crankshaft oil slinger (if equipped).

3. Rotate the crankshaft clockwise, as viewed from front of engine (normal rotation) until the camshaft sprocket's timing dowel pin holes align with the holes in the timing chain housing. The mark on the crankshaft sprocket should align with the mark on the cylinder block. The crankshaft sprocket keyway

should point upwards and align with the centerline of the cylinder bores. This is the normal timed position.

4. Remove the timing chain guides. There are usually three.

5. Raise and safely support the vehicle.

6. Make sure all of the slack is above the tensioner. Gently pry off timing chain tensioner spring retainer, then remove the spring.

➡**Two styles of tensioner are used. Early production engines will have a spring post and late production ones will not. Both styles are identical in operation and are interchangeable.**

7. Remove the timing chain tensioner shoe retainer.

8. Make sure all the slack in the timing chain is above the tensioner assembly; remove the chain tensioner shoe. The timing chain must be disengaged from the wear grooves in the tensioner shoe in order to remove the shoe. Slide a suitable small prybar under the timing chain while pulling shoe outward.

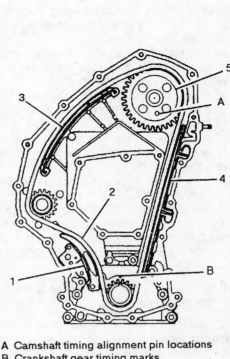

A Camshaft timing alignment pin locations
B Crankshaft gear timing marks

1 Shoe and tensioner assembly
2 Timing chain
3 R.H. timing chain guide
4 L.H. timing chain guide
5 Camshaft sprocket

86883176

Fig. 148 View of the SOHC engine "timed position"

9. If difficulty is encountered while removing chain tensioner shoe, proceed as follows:

    a. Lower the vehicle.

    b. Hold the intake camshaft sprocket with a holding tool and remove the sprocket bolt and washer.

    c. Remove the washer from the bolt and re-thread the bolt back into the camshaft by hand. The bolt provides a surface to push against.

    d. Remove intake camshaft sprocket using a 3-jaw puller in the 3 relief holes in the sprocket.

➡**Do NOT try to pry the sprocket off the camshaft or damage to the sprocket or chain housing could occur.**

10. Unfasten the tensioner assembly attaching bolts, then remove the tensioner.

✳✳CAUTION

The tensioner piston is spring loaded and could fly out causing personal injury. Use care when removing.

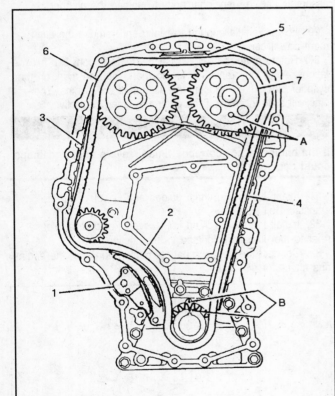

A Camshaft timing alignment pin location
B Crankshaft gear timing mark

1 Shoe assembly timing chain tensioner
2 Timing chain
3 R.H. timing chain guide
4 L.H. timing chain guide
5 Upper timing chain guide
6 Exhaust camshaft sprocket
7 Intake camshaft sprocket

86883175

Fig. 147 View of the DOHC engine "timed position"

11. Matchmark the timing chain outer surface for reassembly purposes.

12. If equipped, remove the chain housing to block stud, which is actually the timing chain tensioner shoe pivot.

13. Remove the timing chain.

14. Inspect the parts for wear, then replace if necessary. Some scoring of the timing chain shoe and guides is normal.

To install:

15. Install the intake camshaft sprocket attaching bolt and washer, tighten to 52 ft. lbs. (70 Nm), while holding the sprocket with tool J-36013, J 39579 or equivalent, if removed.

16. Install tool J 36008 or equivalent, through hole(s) in the camshaft sprocket(s) into the holes in the timing chain housing. This positions the camshafts for correct timing.

17. If the camshafts are out of position and must be rotated more than $1/8$ turn in order to install the alignment dowel pins:

   a. The crankshaft must be rotated 90° clockwise off of TDC in order to give the valves adequate clearance to open.

   b. Once the camshafts are in position and the dowels installed, rotate the crankshaft COUNTERCLOCKWISE back to TDC.

➡️**Do NOT rotate the crankshaft clockwise to TDC, or valve and piston damage could occur.**

18. For DOHC engines only, install the timing chain over the exhaust camshaft sprocket, around the idler sprocket and around the crankshaft sprocket.

19. Remove the alignment dowel pin from the intake (DOHC only) camshaft. Using dowel pin remover tool J 39579 or equivalent, rotate the intake (DOHC only) camshaft sprocket counterclockwise enough to slide the timing chain over the intake (DOHC only) camshaft sprocket. Release the camshaft sprocket wrench. The length of chain between the two camshaft sprockets will tighten. If properly timed, the intake camshaft alignment dowel pin should slide in easily. If the dowel pin does not fully index, the camshafts are not timed correctly and the procedure must be repeated.

20. Leave the alignment dowel pins installed.

21. Raise and safely support the vehicle.

22. With slack removed from chain between intake camshaft sprocket (camshaft sprocket for SOHC engines) and crankshaft sprocket, the timing marks on the crankshaft and the cylinder block should be aligned. If marks are not aligned, move the chain one tooth forward or rearward, remove the slack and recheck the marks.

23. If equipped, tighten the chain housing to block stud. The stud is installed under the timing chain. Tighten to 19 ft. lbs. (26 Nm).

24. For vehicles through 1991, reload timing chain tensioner assembly to its "zero" position as follows:

   a. Assemble restraint cylinder, spring and nylon plug into plunger. Index slot in restraint cylinder with peg in plunger. While rotating the restraint cylinder clockwise, push the restraint cylinder into the plunger until it bottoms. Keep rotating the restraint cylinder clockwise but allow the spring to push it out of the plunger. The pin in the plunger will lock the restraint in the loaded position.

   b. Install tool J-36589 or equivalent, onto plunger assembly.

   c. Install plunger assembly into tensioner body with the long end toward the crankshaft when installed.

25. For 1992-95 vehicles, reload timing chain tensioner assembly to its "zero" position as follows:

   a. Form a keeper from a piece of heavy gauge wire. See the accompanying figure.

   b. Apply slight force on the tensioner blade to compress the plunger.

   c. Insert a small prybar into the reset access hole, then pry the racket pawl away from the ratchet teeth while forcing the plunger completely in the hole.

   d. Install the keeper between the access hole and the blade.

26. Install the tensioner assembly to the chain housing. Recheck the plunger assembly installation. It is correctly installed when the long end is toward the crankshaft.

27. Install and tighten timing chain tensioner bolts. Tighten to 89 inch lbs. (10 Nm).

28. Install the tensioner shoe and tensioner shoe retainer. Remove the special tool J-36589, then squeeze the plunger assembly into the tensioner body to unload the plunger assembly.

29. Lower vehicle enough to reach and remove the alignment dowel pins.

30. Rotate crankshaft clockwise (normal rotation) two full rotations. Align the crankshaft timing mark with the mark on the cylinder block, then reinstall the alignment dowel pins. The pins will slide in easily if the engine is timed correctly.

✳✳WARNING

If the engine is not correctly timed, severe engine damage could occur.

31. Install the timing chain guides and, if equipped, the crankshaft oil slinger.

32. Install the timing chain front cover. For details, please refer to the procedure located in this section.

33. Connect the negative battery cable, then start the engine and check for oil leaks.

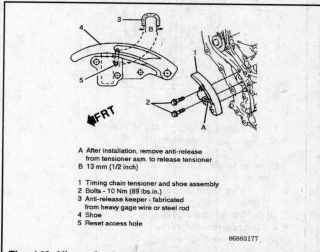

A After installation, remove anti-release from tensioner asm. to release tensioner
B 13 mm (1/2 inch)

1 Timing chain tensioner and shoe assembly
2 Bolts - 10 Nm (89 lbs.in.)
3 Anti-release keeper - fabricated from heavy gage wire or steel rod
4 Shoe
5 Reset access hole

86883177

Fig. 149 View of reloading the timing chain tensioner assembly to its "zero" position — 1992-95 vehicles

3.0L, 3.3L and 1990-91 2.5L Engines

◗ See Figures 150, 151, 152, 153, 154, 155 and 156

1. Disconnect the negative battery cable.
2. Drain the cooling system and the engine oil.
3. Remove the front cover. For details, please refer to the procedure located in this section.
4. With the engine at TDC, rotate the crankshaft to align the timing marks on the sprockets so that they are as close as possible.
5. Remove the timing chain dampener assembly.
6. Unfasten the camshaft sprocket-to-camshaft bolt(s), then remove the camshaft sprocket and chain and, if equipped, the thrust bearing.
7. Remove the crankshaft sprocket/gear by sliding it forward.
8. Clean the gasket mounting surfaces. Inspect the timing chain and the sprockets for damage and/or wear, then replace any damaged parts.

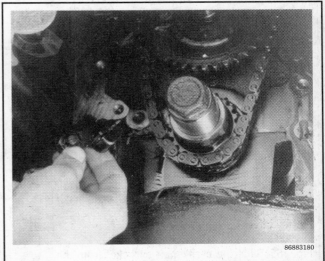

Fig. 152 . . . remove the dampener (damper) assembly

Fig. 150 View of the timing chain and sprockets, after the front cover has been removed — 1986 3.0L engine shown

Fig. 153 Use the proper size socket to unfasten the camshaft sprocket bolts, then . . .

Fig. 151 Remove the dampener retainer, then . . .

Fig. 154 . . . remove the camshaft sprocket and timing chain assembly

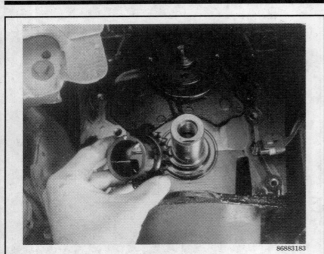

Fig. 155 Slide the crankshaft sprocket from the crankshaft by sliding it forward

To install:

9. Position the crankshaft so the No. 1 piston is at TDC of its compression stroke. On the 2.5L engine, install the thrust bearing.

10. Temporarily install the sprocket/gear on the camshaft and position the camshaft so the timing mark on the gear is pointing straight down.

11. Assemble the timing chain to the gears so the timing marks are aligned, mark-to-mark.

12. Install the camshaft sprocket attaching bolt(s).

13. Install the camshaft thrust bearing, if not already done.

14. Install the timing chain dampener.

15. Install the front cover and all related parts. For details, please refer to the procedure located in this section.

16. Connect the negative battery cable, then start the engine and check for leaks.

3.1L Engine

▶ **See Figure 157**

1. Disconnect the negative battery cable.
2. Drain the cooling system into a suitable container.

3. Remove the timing chain front cover. For details please refer to the procedure located in this section.

4. Rotate the crankshaft until the timing marks on the camshaft and crankshaft sprockets are in alignment at their closest approach.

5. Unfasten the camshaft sprocket mounting bolt, then remove the camshaft sprocket and timing chain.

6. Remove the crankshaft sprocket with gear puller J-5825-A, or equivalent.

7. Unfasten the two bolts and remove the timing chain damper.

To install:

8. Install the timing chain damper and tighten the mounting bolts to 15 ft. lbs. (21 Nm).

9. Position the crankshaft sprocket onto the crankshaft making sure the notch in the sprocket fits over the crankshaft key. Fully seat the sprocket on the crankshaft using J-38612, or an equivalent gear installer.

10. Make sure the timing mark on the crankshaft sprocket is still pointing straight up.

11. Install the camshaft sprocket inside the timing chain.

12. Pick up the chain and sprocket and hold the sprocket in such a way that the timing mark is pointing down and the timing chain is hanging down off of the sprocket.

13. Loop the timing chain under the crankshaft sprocket and install the camshaft sprocket on the camshaft. The sprocket will only fit on the camshaft if the dowel on the camshaft lines up with the hole in the sprocket.

14. Verify the timing marks are aligned. If the marks are not in alignment proceed as follows:

   a. Remove the chain and sprocket.

   b. Install the sprocket and mounting bolt loosely.

   c. Rotate the crankshaft and camshaft until the marks are in alignment.

   d. Remove the camshaft sprocket and mounting bolt.

15. Repeat steps 13 and 14.

16. Tighten the camshaft sprocket mounting bolt to 74 ft. lbs. (100 Nm).

17. Lubricate the timing chain components with engine oil.

18. Install the timing chain front cover.

19. Refill the cooling system.

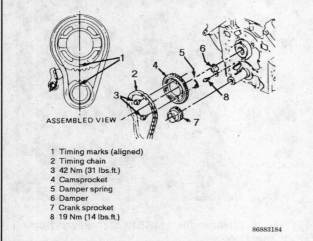

1 Timing marks (aligned)
2 Timing chain
3 42 Nm (31 lbs.ft.)
4 Camsprocket
5 Damper spring
6 Damper
7 Crank sprocket
8 19 Nm (14 lbs.ft.)

Fig. 156 Assembled view of the timing chain — 3.0L engine shown

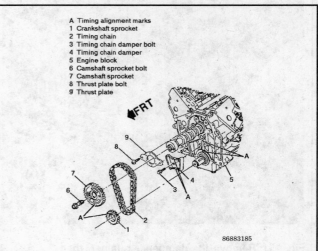

A Timing alignment marks
1 Crankshaft sprocket
2 Timing chain
3 Timing chain damper bolt
4 Timing chain damper
5 Engine block
6 Camshaft sprocket bolt
7 Camshaft sprocket
8 Thrust plate bolt
9 Thrust plate

Fig. 157 Timing chain, sprockets and related components — 1995 3.1L engine shown

20. Connect the negative battery cable, then start the engine and verify that there are no leaks.

Timing Gears

REMOVAL & INSTALLATION

1988-89 2.5L Engine

➡If the camshaft gear is to be replaced, the engine must be removed from the vehicle. The crankshaft gear may be replaced with the engine in the vehicle.

1. Disconnect the negative battery cable.
2. Raise and safely support the vehicle.
3. Remove the inner fender splash shield.
4. Remove the accessory drive belts.
5. Remove the crankshaft pulley-to-crankshaft pulley bolt and slide the pulley from the crankshaft.
6. If replacing the camshaft gear, perform the following procedures:
   a. Remove the engine from the vehicle and secure it onto a suitable holding fixture.
   b. Remove the camshaft from the engine.
   c. Using an arbor press, press the camshaft gear from the camshaft.
   d. To install the camshaft gear onto the camshaft, press the gear onto the shaft until a thrust clearance of 0.0015-0.0050 in. (0.0381-0.127mm) exists.
7. If removing the crankshaft gear, perform the following procedures:
   a. Remove the front cover-to-engine bolts.
   b. Remove the attaching bolt and slide the crankshaft gear forward off the crankshaft.
8. Clean the gasket mounting surfaces. Inspect the parts for damage and/or wear and replace damaged parts.
9. The installation is the reverse of the removal procedure. Make sure the timing marks are aligned mark-to-mark when installing.

Timing Sprockets

REMOVAL & INSTALLATION

1. Disconnect the negative battery cable.
2. If removing the camshaft sprocket, remove the camshaft carrier cover.
3. Remove the timing belt cover.
4. Position the engine so the timing marks are aligned for belt installation.
5. Remove the timing belt. For details, please refer to the procedure located in this section.
6. If removing the camshaft sprocket, hold the camshaft with an open-end wrench.
7. Remove the camshaft or crankshaft sprocket attaching bolt, washer and the sprocket.
8. The installation is the reverse of the removal procedure. Tighten the camshaft sprocket bolt to 34 ft. lbs. (45 Nm). Tighten the crankshaft sprocket bolt to 114 ft. lbs. (155 Nm).

9. Connect the negative battery cable and road test the vehicle.

Camshaft

✳✳CAUTION

Fuel Injection systems remain under pressure, even after the engine has been turned OFF. The fuel system pressure must be relieved before disconnecting any fuel lines. Failure to do so may result in fire and/or personal injury.

REMOVAL & INSTALLATION

2.0L Engine
▶ See Figure 158

1. Relieve the fuel system pressure.
2. Disconnect the negative battery cable.
3. Remove the camshaft carrier cover.
4. Hold the valves in place with compressed air, using air adapters in the spark plug holes.
5. Compress the valve springs with valve spring compressing tool J 33302-25 or equivalent.
6. Remove the rocker arms and lifters and keep them in order for reassembly. Hold the camshaft with an open-end wrench and remove the camshaft sprocket. Try to keep the valve timing by using a rubber cord, if possible. If the timing cannot be kept intact, the timing belt will have to be reset.
7. Matchmark and remove the distributor.
8. Remove the camshaft thrust plate from the rear of the carrier.
9. Remove the camshaft by sliding it toward the rear. Remove the front carrier seal.
   To install:
10. Install a new carrier seal.
11. Thoroughly lubricate the camshaft and journals with clean oil and install the camshaft. Be careful not to damage the seal.

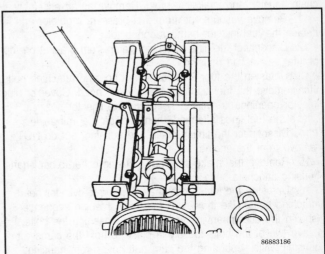

86883186

Fig. 158 Using the special tool to compress the valve springs — 1989 2.0L engine shown

12. Install the rear thrust plate, then tighten the bolts to 70 inch lbs. (8 Nm).

13. Install camshaft sprocket, timing belt and cover.

14. Install the distributor.

15. Hold the valves in place with compressed air as in Step 4, compress the valve springs and install the lifters and rocker arms.

16. Apply sealer to the camshaft carrier cover and install.

17. Connect the negative battery cable and road test the vehicle.

2.3L Engine

SOHC OR INTAKE ON DOHC

▶ See Figures 159, 160, 161, 162, 163 and 164

➡Any time the camshaft housing to cylinder head bolts are loosened or removed, the camshaft housing to cylinder head gasket must be replaced.

1. Relieve the fuel system pressure. Disconnect the negative battery cable.

2. Label and detach the ignition coil and module assembly electrical connections.

3. Unfasten the ignition coil and module assembly to camshaft housing bolts, then remove the assembly by pulling straight up. Use a special spark plug boot wire remover tool to remove connector assemblies, if they have stuck to the spark plugs.

4. If equipped, remove the idle speed power steering pressure switch connector.

5. Loosen the three power steering pump pivot bolts and remove drive belt.

6. Disconnect the two rear power steering pump bracket-to-transaxle bolts.

7. Remove the front power steering pump bracket to cylinder block bolt.

8. Disconnect the power steering pump assembly, then position it aside.

9. Using the special tool, remove the power steering pump drive pulley from the intake camshaft.

10. Remove oil/air separator bolts and hoses. Leave the hoses attached to the separator, disconnect from the oil fill, chain housing and intake manifold. Remove as an assembly.

11. Remove vacuum line from fuel pressure regulator and detach the fuel injector harness connector.

12. Disconnect fuel line attaching clamp from bracket on top of intake camshaft housing.

13. Unfasten the fuel rail-to-camshaft housing attaching bolts, then remove the fuel rail from the cylinder head. Cover or plug injector openings in cylinder head and the injector nozzles. Leave the fuel lines attached, then position fuel rail aside.

14. Disconnect the timing chain and housing, but do NOT remove from the engine.

15. Remove the intake camshaft housing cover-to-camshaft housing attaching bolts.

16. Unfasten the intake camshaft housing-to-cylinder head attaching bolts. Use the reverse of the tightening sequence (shown the accompanying figure) when loosening the bolts. Leave two of the bolts loosely in place to hold the camshaft housing while separating the camshaft cover from housing.

17. Push the cover off the housing by threading four of the housing-to-head attaching bolts into the tapped holes in the

1 Ignition coil and module assembly
2 Ignition coil and module asm. to crankshaft housing bolts - 22 Nm (16 lbs.ft.)
3 Camshaft housing cover (intake shown)
4 Spark plug

86883187

Fig. 159 View of the ignition coil and module assembly — DOHC equipped engine shown

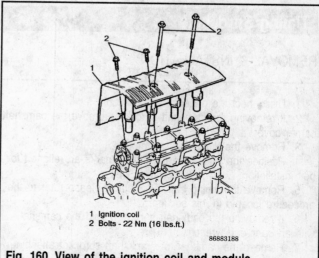

1 Ignition coil
2 Bolts - 22 Nm (16 lbs.ft.)

86883188

Fig. 160 View of the ignition coil and module assembly — SOHC equipped engine shown

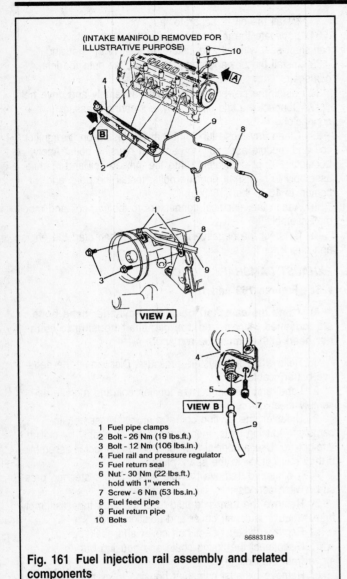

Fig. 161 Fuel injection rail assembly and related components

1 Fuel pipe clamps
2 Bolt - 26 Nm (19 lbs.ft.)
3 Bolt - 12 Nm (106 lbs.in.)
4 Fuel rail and pressure regulator
5 Fuel return seal
6 Nut - 30 Nm (22 lbs.ft.)
   hold with 1" wrench
7 Screw - 6 Nm (53 lbs.in.)
8 Fuel feed pipe
9 Fuel return pipe
10 Bolts

86883189

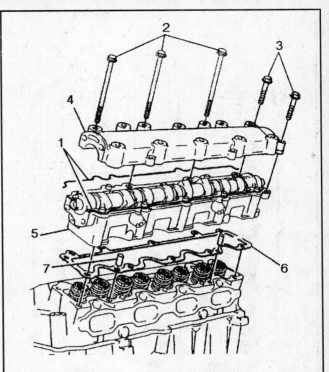

1 Camshaft housing to camshaft seals
2 Camshaft housing to cylinder head bolt
   15 Nm (11 lbs.ft.) plus turn 90 degrees
3 Camshaft housing cover to camshaft
   housing bolt - 15 Nm (11 lbs.ft.) plus
   turn 30 degrees
4 Camshaft cover
5 Camshaft housing (intake shown)
6 Camshaft housing to cylinder head gasket
7 Dowel pin (2)

86883190

Fig. 162 Exploded view of the camshaft housing, cover and gaskets — 1994 2.3L engine shown

cam housing cover. Tighten the bolts evenly so the cover does not bind on the dowel pins.

18. Remove the two loosely installed camshaft housing to head bolts and remove the cover. Discard the gaskets.

19. Note the position of the chain sprocket dowel pin for reassembly.

20. Remove intake camshaft oil seal from camshaft and discard seal. This seal must be replaced any time the housing and cover are separated.

21. Remove the camshaft carrier from the cylinder head and remove the gasket. Discard the gasket.

To install:

22. Thoroughly clean the mating surfaces of the camshaft carrier and the cylinder head, bolts and bolt holes. Install a new gasket and place the housing on the head. Install one bolt loosely to hold it in place.

23. Install the lifters into their bores. If the camshaft is being replaced, the lifters must also be replaced. Lubricate camshaft lobes, journals and lifters with camshaft and lifter prelube. The camshaft lobes and journals must be adequately lubricated or engine damage could occur upon start up.

24. Install the camshaft in the same position as when removed. The timing chain sprocket dowel pin should be straight up and align with the centerline of the lifter bores.

25. Install new camshaft housing to camshaft housing cover seals into cover; do not use sealer. Make sure the correct color seal is placed in each groove. Install the cover to the housing.

26. Apply thread locking compound to the camshaft housing and cover attaching bolt threads.

27. Install the bolts, then tighten to 11 ft. lbs. (15 Nm). Rotate the bolts (except the two rear bolts that hold the fuel pipe to the camshaft housing) an additional 75°, in sequence. Tighten the two rear bolts to 16 ft. lbs. (15 Nm), then rotate an additional 25°.

28. Install the timing chain housing and the timing chain.

29. Uncover fuel injectors, then install new fuel injector O-ring seals lubricated with oil. Install the fuel rail.

30. Fasten the fuel line attaching clamp and retainer to bracket on top of the intake camshaft housing.

31. Connect the vacuum line to the fuel pressure regulator.

32. Attach the fuel injectors harness connector.

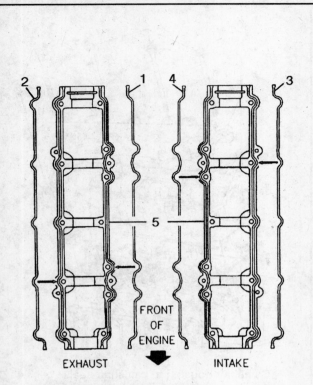

1 Inner seal (red exhaust)
2 Outer seal (red exhaust)
3 Outer seal (blue intake)
4 Inner seal (blue intake)
5 Camshaft housing cover

86883191

Fig. 163 View of the intake and exhaust camshaft-to-housing seal placement

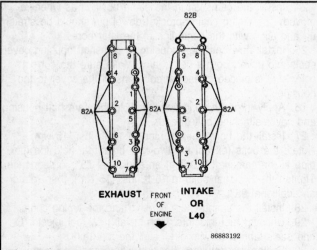

86883192

Fig. 164 Intake and exhaust camshaft housing bolt tightening sequence

33. Install the oil/air separator assembly.
34. Lubricate the inner sealing surface of the intake camshaft seal with oil and install the seal to the housing.
35. Install the power steering pump pulley onto the intake camshaft.
36. Install the power steering pump assembly and drive belt.
37. Connect the idle speed power steering pressure switch connector.
38. Clean any loose lubricant that is present on the ignition coil and module assembly to camshaft housing bolts. Apply Loctite® 592 or equivalent, onto the ignition coil and module assembly to camshaft housing bolts. Install the bolts and tighten to 13 ft. lbs. (18 Nm).
39. Attach the electrical connectors to ignition coil and module assembly.
40. Connect the negative battery cable, then start the engine and check for leaks.

EXHAUST CAMSHAFT (DOHC)

◗ See Figures 163 and 164

➡ Any time the camshaft housing-to-cylinder head bolts are loosened or removed, the camshaft housing to cylinder head gasket must be replaced.

1. Relieve the fuel system pressure. Disconnect the negative battery cable.
2. Label and disconnect the ignition coil and module assembly electrical connections.
3. Unfasten the ignition coil and module assembly-to-camshaft housing bolts, then remove the assembly by pulling straight up. Use a special tool to remove connector assemblies if they have stuck to the spark plugs.
4. If equipped, remove the idle speed power steering pressure switch connector.
5. Remove the transaxle fluid level indicator tube assembly from exhaust camshaft cover and position aside.
6. Remove exhaust camshaft cover and gasket.
7. Disconnect the timing chain and housing but do not remove from the engine.
8. Remove exhaust camshaft housing to cylinder head bolts. Use the reverse of the tightening procedure when loosening camshaft housing while separating camshaft cover from housing.
9. Push the cover off the housing by threading four of the housing to head attaching bolts into the tapped holes in the camshaft cover. When threading the bolt, tighten them evenly so the cover does not bind on the dowel pins.
10. Remove the two loosely installed camshaft housing to cylinder head bolts and remove cover, discard gaskets.
11. Loosely reinstall one camshaft housing to cylinder head bolt to retain the housing during camshaft and lifter removal.
12. Note the position of the chain sprocket dowel pin for reassembly. Remove camshaft being careful not to damage the camshaft or journals.
13. Remove the camshaft carrier from the cylinder head and remove the gasket. Discard the gasket.

To install:

14. Thoroughly clean the mating surfaces of the camshaft carrier and the cylinder head, bolts and bolt holes. Install a new gasket and place the housing on the head. Install 1 bolt loosely to hold in place.

15. Install the lifters into their bores. If the camshaft is being replaced, the lifters must also be replaced. Lubricate camshaft lobes, journals and lifters with camshaft and lifter prelube. The camshaft lobes and journals must be adequately lubricated or engine damage could occur upon start up.

16. Install camshaft in same position as when removed. The timing chain sprocket dowel pin should be straight up and align with the centerline of the lifter bores.

17. Install new camshaft housing-to-camshaft housing cover seals into the cover; do not use sealer. Make sure the correct color seal is placed in each groove. Install the cover to the housing.

18. Apply thread locking compound to the camshaft housing and cover attaching bolt threads.

19. Install bolts, then tighten, in sequence, to 11 ft. lbs. (15 Nm). Then rotate the bolts an additional 75 degrees, in sequence.

20. Install timing chain housing and timing chain.

21. Install the transaxle fluid level indicator tube assembly to the exhaust camshaft cover.

22. Attach the idle speed power steering pressure switch connector.

23. Clean any loose lubricant that is present on the ignition coil and module assembly to camshaft housing bolts. Apply Loctite® 592 or equivalent, onto the ignition coil and module assembly to camshaft housing bolts. Install the bolts and tighten to 13 ft. lbs. (18 Nm).

24. Attach the electrical connectors to ignition coil and module assembly.

25. Connect the negative battery cable, then start the engine and check for leaks.

1985-89 2.5L Engine

1. Disconnect the negative battery cable.

2. Remove the engine assembly from the vehicle. For details, please refer to the procedure located in this section.

3. Remove the rocker arm cover and pushrods, then remove the pushrod cover and valve lifters.

4. Disconnect and remove the front cover. For details, please refer to the procedure located in this section.

5. Unfasten the camshaft thrust plate screws.

➡️**Camshaft journals are the smae diameter and caution must be exercised during removal to avoid damaging the bearings.**

6. Remove the camshaft and gear from the front of the block.

7. Using a suitable arbor press and an adapter, remove the gear from the camshaft. Position the thrust plate to avoid damage by interference with the woodruff key as the gear is removed.

To install:

8. Support the camshaft at the back of the front journal in the arbor press using press plate adapters.

9. Position the spacer ring, thrust plate over the end of the shaft and the woodruff in the keyway.

10. Press the gear onto the camshaft, against the spacer ring. Measure the end clearance; it should be 0.0015 in.-0.0050 in. (0.0381-0.1270mm). If the clearance is less, replace the spacer ring. If the clearance is more, replace the thrust plate.

11. Lubricate the camshaft journals with GM E.O.S. 1052367 or equivalent.

➡️**Camshaft journals are the same diameter and care must be used when installing the camshaft to avoid damage to the bearings.**

12. Rotate the camhsaft and the crankshaft so that the timing marks on the gear teeth line up. The engine is now in the No. 4 firing position.

13. Position the camshaft thrust plate. Tighten the retaining screws to 89 inch lbs. (10 Nm).

14. Install the front cover, as outlined in this section, then install the crankshaft balancer.

15. Install the valve lifters, pushrod cover and pushrods, then secure the rocker arm cover.

16. As outlined in this section, install the engine assembly.

17. Connect the negative battery cable.

1990-91 2.5L Engine

ENGINE IN VEHICLE

▶ See Figure 165

1. Disconnect the negative battery cable. Properly relieve the fuel system pressure.

2. Remove the air cleaner assembly.

3. Drain the cooling system into a suitable container.

4. Disconnect the PCV valve and hose. Remove the EGR valve.

5. Tag and detach the spark plug wires and clips.

6. Remove the rocker arm cover. For details, please refer to the procedure located in this section.

7. Remove the fuel line bracket, then detach and plug the fuel lines.

8. Tag and disconnect the vacuum hoses, including the power brake booster hose.

9. Disconnect the wiring and throttle linkage from the TBI assembly.

10. Remove the transaxle downshift bracket.

11. Disconnect the heater hose.

12. Remove the power steering belt. Unfasten the power steering pump bolts, then position the pump aside.

13. Remove the intake manifold (including the engine lift bracket). For details, please refer to the procedure located in this section.

14. Detach the pushrod cover and the valve lifters.

15. Remove the right hand front end diagonal brace.

16. Install the engine lift bracket.

17. Unfasten the upper front engine mount-to-body bolts. Install engine support fixture tool J 28467-A or equivalent.

18. Raise and safely support the vehicle. Remove the right front wheel and tire assembly, then the inner splash shield.

19. Remove the right hand cover.

20. If equipped, unfasten and remove the A/C belt.

21. Remove the crankshaft balancer.

22. Unfasten the rear engine mount-to-bracket bolts and mount bolts. Remove the front transaxle strut bolts.

23. Remove the lower front engine mount-to-body bolts.

24. Remove the front lower air foil.

25. Unfasten the right and left front suspension bolts.

26. Drain the engine oil, then carefully lower the vehicle.

27. Unfasten the transaxle mount bolts, then lower the engine/transaxle assembly.

28. Raise and safely support the vehicle.

29. Remove the front cover as outlined in this section. Align the timing marks.

30. Unfasten the camshaft sprocket bolts, then remove the timing chain and sprockets. Remove the camshaft thrust plate.

➡**Camshaft journals are the same diameter and care must be used when removing the camshaft to avoid damage to the bearings.**

31. Remove the camshaft from the engine.

To install:

32. Lubricate the camshaft journals with GM lubricant E.O.S. 1052367 or equivalent.

33. Installation is the reverse of the removal procedure.

34. Fill the cooling system and crankcase with the proper type and amount of fluids.

35. Connect the negative battery cable, then start the engine and check for leaks.

ENGINE REMOVED

1. Disconnect the negative battery cable. Relieve the fuel system pressure before disconnecting any fuel lines.

2. As outlined in this section, remove the engine from the vehicle and secure to a suitable holding fixture.

3. Remove the valve cover, rocker arms and pushrods. Keep all parts in order for reassembly.

4. Tag and detach the spark plugs, then remove the distributor and spark plugs.

5. Detach the pushrod cover, the gasket and the lifters. Keep all parts in order for reassembly.

6. Remove the alternator, alternator lower bracket and the front engine mount bracket assembly.

7. Remove the oil pump driveshaft and gear assembly.

8. Remove the crankshaft pulley and front cover. Remove the timing chain and gears, if equipped.

9. Unfasten the two camshaft thrust plate screws by working through the holes in the gear, then remove the thrust plate.

10. Remove the camshaft, and gear assembly, if gear driven by pulling it through the front of the block. Take care not to damage the bearings while removing the camshaft.

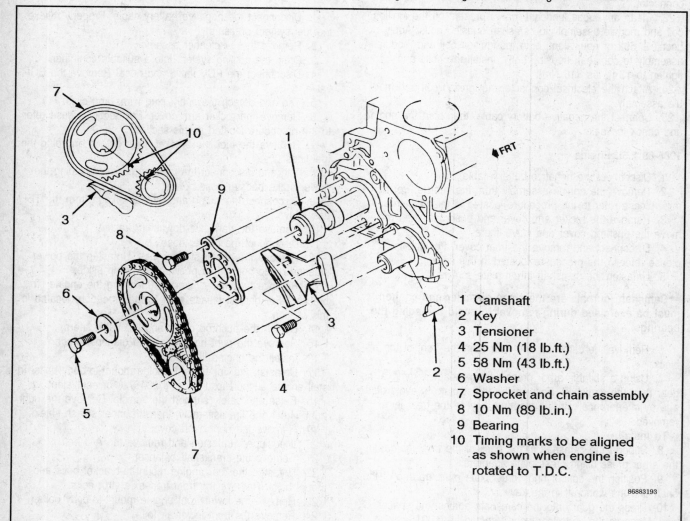

1 Camshaft
2 Key
3 Tensioner
4 25 Nm (18 lb.ft.)
5 58 Nm (43 lb.ft.)
6 Washer
7 Sprocket and chain assembly
8 10 Nm (89 lb.in.)
9 Bearing
10 Timing marks to be aligned as shown when engine is rotated to T.D.C.

86883193

Fig. 165 Exploded view of the camshaft, timing chain and related components — 1991 2.5L engine shown

To install:

11. The installation is the reverse of the removal procedure. Coat all parts with a liberal amount of clean engine oil supplement before installing.

12. Fill all fluids to their proper levels.

13. Connect the negative battery cable, then start the engine and check for leaks.

3.0L and 3.3L Engines

▶ See Figure 166

1. Disconnect the negative battery cable. Relieve the fuel system pressure before disconnecting any fuel lines.

2. Remove the engine from the vehicle and secure to a suitable holding fixture.

3. Remove the intake manifold. For details, please refer to the procedure located in this section.

4. Remove the valve covers, rocker arm assemblies, pushrods and lifters. Keep all parts in order for reassembly.

5. Remove the crankshaft balancer from the crankshaft.

6. If equipped, remove the crankshaft sensor shield, then detach the sensor electrical connector.

7. As outlined earlier in this section, remove the front cover.

8. Rotate the crankshaft to align the timing marks on the timing sprockets. Remove the camshaft sprocket and the timing chain.

9. If equipped, remove the camshaft thrust plate.

10. Remove the camshaft retainer bolts and slide the camshaft forward out of the engine. Take care not to damage the bearings while removing the camshaft.

To install:

11. The installation is the reverse of the removal procedure. Coat all parts with a liberal amount of clean engine oil supplement before installing.

12. Fill all fluids to their proper levels.

13. Connect the negative battery cable, then start the engine and check for leaks.

3.1L Engine

1. Relieve the fuel system pressure.

2. Disconnect the negative battery cable.

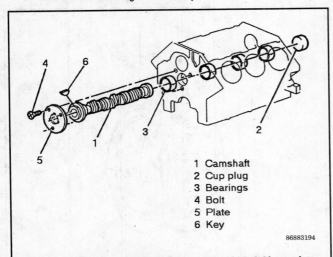

Fig. 166 View of camshaft removal — 1993 3.3L engine shown

1 Camshaft
2 Cup plug
3 Bearings
4 Bolt
5 Plate
6 Key

86883194

3. Remove the engine from the vehicle and secure to a suitable holding fixture.

➡When removing valve train components, they must be marked for installation in the same location they are removed from. When the camshaft is being replaced, the valve lifters should also be replaced.

4. Remove the intake manifold, valve cover, rocker arms, pushrods and valve lifters.

5. Remove the crankshaft balancer and front cover.

6. Remove the timing chain and sprockets.

7. Unfasten the oil pump driven gear mounting bolt, then remove the oil pump driven gear.

8. Remove the two bolts, then remove the camshaft thrust plate.

9. Carefully remove the camshaft. Avoid marring the camshaft bearing surfaces.

To install:

10. Coat the camshaft with lubricant 1052365 or equivalent, and install the camshaft.

11. Install the camshaft thrust plate, then tighten the mounting bolts to 89 inch lbs. (10 Nm).

12. Install the oil pump driven gear, then tighten the mounting bolt to 27 ft. lbs. (36 Nm).

13. Install the timing chain and sprocket.

14. Install the camshaft thrust button and front cover.

15. Install the crankshaft balancer.

16. Install the intake manifold, valve cover, rocker arms, pushrods and valve lifters.

17. Install the engine assembly into the vehicle.

18. Connect the negative battery cable.

19. Adjust the valves, as required.

20. Start the engine and verify that there are no oil leaks.

BEARING REPLACEMENT

▶ See Figure 167

1. Disconnect the negative battery cable.

2. Remove the engine assembly from the vehicle, then remove the camshaft from the engine.

3. Detach the camshaft rear plug.

4. Assemble a suitable bearing removal tool (depending upon engine application), according to the manufacturer's directions.

5. Remove the camshaft bearings.

➡Never reuse camshaft bearings once they have been removed. Always install new bearings.

To install:

6. Select and install new front, rear and intermediate camshaft bearings:

 a. Assembly a suitable bearing installation tool, following the manufacturer's instructions.

 b. Place the bearing on the tool.

 c. Index the bearing oil holes with cylinder block oil passages.

7. Apply sealer 1052914 or RTV equivalent to the camshaft plug, then install the plug.

8. Install the camshaft into the engine, then install the engine in the vehicle.

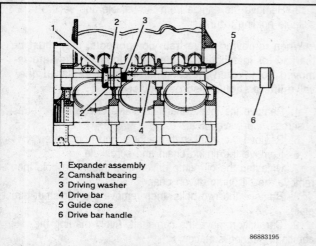

1 Expander assembly
2 Camshaft bearing
3 Driving washer
4 Drive bar
5 Guide cone
6 Drive bar handle

86883195

Fig. 167 Using the proper tool to removal and/or install camshaft bearings — 1995 3.1L engine shown

9. Connect the negative battery cable.

INSPECTION

Using a suitable solvent, degrease the camshaft and clean out all of the oil holes. Visually inspect the cam lobes and bearing journals for excessive wear, galling, gouges or overheating which may be indicated by discoloration. If a lobe is questionable, check all of the lobes. If a journal or lobe is worn, the camshaft MUST BE reground or replaced. Also, inspect the sprocket, keyway and threads.

➡️**If a journal is worn, there is a good chance that the bearings are worn and need replacement.**

If the camshaft is damaged, DO NOT attempt to repair it, it must be replaced. If a new camshaft is installed, all of the valve lifters must be replaced.
Measure cam lift using the following instructions:
1. Lubricate the camshaft bearings with a suitable camshaft and lifter prelube.
2. Carefully insert the camshaft. If the cam bearings are badly worn or damaged, set the camshaft on "V" blocks instead.
3. Install a suitable measure tool, depending upon engine application, and measure the cam lift. Compare to the specifications in the chart in this section. If any cam lift is out of specification, replace the camshaft.
Measure the run-out and diameter of the bearing journals using a micrometer. If out of specification, replace the camshaft.

Pistons and Connecting Rods

REMOVAL

▶ **See Figures 168, 169, 170, 171, 172 and 173**

1. Disconnect the negative battery cable.

2. Remove the engine assembly from the vehicle and secure on a suitable work stand.
3. Remove the intake manifold and cylinder heads.
4. Remove the oil pan and oil pump.
5. The position of each piston, connecting rod and connecting rod cap should be noted before any are removed, so they can be reinstalled in the same location.
6. Check the tops of the pistons and the sides of the connecting rods for identifying marks. In some engines, the top of the piston will be numbered to correspond with the cylinder number. The connecting rod and connecting rod cap should have numbers stamped on the machined surfaces next to the rod bolts that correspond with their cylinder number.
7. If no numbers are visible, use a number punch set and stamp the cylinder number on the connecting rod and connecting rod cap.
8. Rotate the crankshaft until the piston to be removed is at the bottom of the cylinder. Examine the cylinder bore above the ring travel. If the bore is worn so that a shoulder or ridge exists at the top of the cylinder, remove the ridge with a ridge reamer to avoid damaging the rings or cracking the ring lands in the piston during removal. Before operating the ridge reamer, place a shop towel on top of the piston to catch the metal shavings.

✳✳WARNING

Be very careful when using a ridge reamer. Only remove the cylinder bore material that is necessary to remove the ridge. If too much cylinder bore material is removed, cylinder overboring and piston replacement may be necessary.

9. Loosen the connecting rod bolt nuts until the nuts are flush with the ends of the bolts. Using a hammer and a brass drift or piece of wood, lightly tap on the nuts/bolts until the connecting rod cap is loosened from the connecting rod. Remove the nuts, rod cap and lower bearing shell.
10. Slip a piece of snug fitting rubber hose over each rod bolt, to prevent the bolt threads from damaging the crankshaft during removal. Using a hammer handle or piece of wood or plastic, push the rod and piston upward in the bore until the connecting rod is clear of the crankshaft journal.

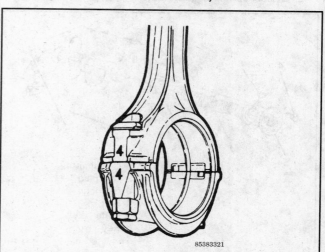

85383321

Fig. 168 Match the connecting rods to their cylinders using a number stamp

Fig. 169 Remove the ridge from the cylinder bore using a ridge cutter

Fig. 170 Place lengths of rubber hose over the connecting rod studs in order to protect the crankshaft and cylinders from damage

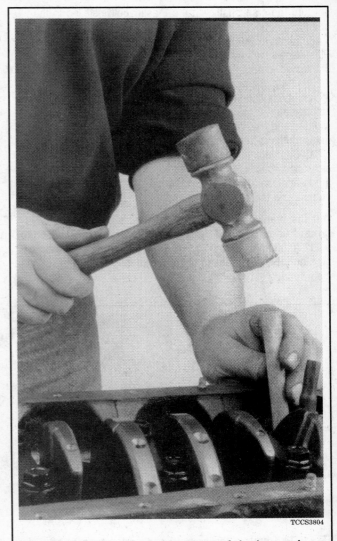

Fig. 171 Carefully tap the piston out of the bore using a wooden dowel

11. Inspect the rod bearings for scoring, chipping or other wear.

12. Inspect the crankshaft rod bearing journal for wear. Measure the journal diameter in several locations around the journal and compare to specification. If the crankshaft journal is scored or has deep ridges, or its diameter is below specification, the crankshaft must be removed from the engine and reground.

13. If the crankshaft journal appears usable, clean it and the rod bearing shells until they are completely free of oil. Blow any oil from the oil hole in the crankshaft.

➡The journal surfaces and bearing shells must be completely free of oil to get an accurate reading with Plastigage®.

14. Pull the connecting rod back onto the crankshaft rod journal and remove the rubber hoses.

15. Place a strip of Plastigage® lengthwise along the bottom center of the lower bearing shell, then install the cap with the shell and torque the connecting rod nuts to specification. Do

not turn the crankshaft with the Plastigage® installed in the bearing.

16. Remove the bearing cap with the shell. The flattened Plastigage® will either be sticking to the bearing shell or the crankshaft journal.

17. Using the printed scale on the Plastigage® package, measure the flattened Plastigage® at its widest point. The number on the scale that most closely corresponds to the width of the Plastigage® indicates the bearing clearance in thousandths of an inch or hundredths of a millimeter.

18. Compare the actual bearing clearance with the bearing clearance specification. If the bearing clearance is excessive, the bearing must be replaced or the crankshaft must be ground and the bearing replaced.

➡️**If the crankshaft is still at standard size (has not been ground undersize), bearing shell sets of 0.001, (0.0254mm) 0.002 (0.050mm) and 0.003 in. (0.0762mm) over standard size may be available to correct excessive bearing clearance.**

19. After clearance measuring is completed, be sure to remove the Plastigage® from the crankshaft and/or bearing shell.

20. Again remove the connecting rod cap and install the rubber hose on the rod bolts. Push the rod and piston upward in the bore until the piston rings clear the cylinder block. Remove the piston and connecting rod assembly from the top of the cylinder bore.

CLEANING AND INSPECTION

▶ **See Figures 174, 175, 176, 177, 178 and 179**

1. Remove the piston rings from the piston. The compression rings must be removed using a piston ring expander, to prevent breakage.

2. Clean the ring grooves with a ring groove cleaner, being careful not to cut into the piston metal. Heavy carbon deposits can be cleaned from the top of the piston with a scraper or wire brush, however, do not use a wire wheel on the ring

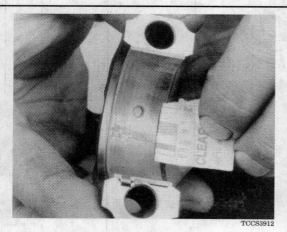

TCCS3912

Fig. 173 Remove the bearing cap and compare the gauging material to the scale provided with the package (check the journal if the material was applied there)

TCCS3211

Fig. 174 Use a ring expander tool to remove the piston rings

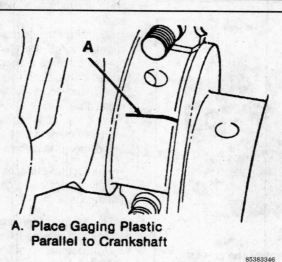

A. Place Gaging Plastic
Parallel to Crankshaft

85383346

Fig. 172 Apply a strip of gauging material to the connecting rod journal or the bearing

grooves or lands. Clean the oil drain holes in the ring grooves. Clean all remaining dirt, carbon and varnish from the piston with a suitable solvent and a brush; do not use a caustic solution.

3. After cleaning, inspect the piston for scuffing, scoring, cracks, pitting or excessive ring groove wear. Replace any piston that is obviously worn.

4. If the piston appears okay, measure the piston diameter using a micrometer. Measure the piston diameter in the thrust direction, 90° to the piston pin axis, 3/4 in. (19mm) below the center line of the piston pin bore.

5. Measure the cylinder bore diameter using a bore gauge, or with a telescope gauge and micrometer. The measurement should be made in the piston thrust direction at the top, middle and bottom of the bore.

➡**Piston diameter and cylinder bore measurements should be made with the parts at room temperature, 70°F (21°C).**

6. Subtract the piston diameter measurement made in Step 4 from the cylinder bore measurement made in Step 5. This is

Fig. 177 Measure the piston's outer diameter using a micrometer

Fig. 175 Clean the piston grooves using a ring groove cleaner

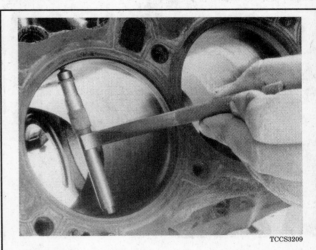

Fig. 178 A telescoping gauge may be used to measure the cylinder bore diameter

the piston-to-bore clearance. If the clearance is within specification, light finish honing is all that is necessary. If the clearance is excessive, the cylinder must be bored and the piston replaced. If the pistons are replaced, the piston rings must also be replaced.

7. If the piston-to-bore clearance is okay, check the ring groove clearance. Roll the piston ring around the ring groove in which it is to be installed and check the clearance with a feeler gauge. Compare the measurement with specification. High points in the ring groove that may cause the ring to bind may be cleaned up carefully with a points file. Replace the piston if the ring groove clearance is not within specification.

8. Check the connecting rod for damage or obvious wear. Check for signs of fractures and check the bearing bore for out-of-round and taper.

9. A shiny surface on the pin boss side of the piston usually indicates that the connecting rod is bent or the wrist pin hole is not in proper relation to the piston skirt and ring grooves.

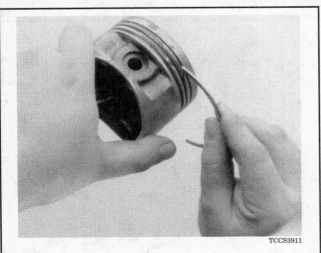

Fig. 176 You can use a piece of an old ring to clean the ring grooves, BUT be careful the ring is sharp

Fig. 179 Checking the ring-to-ring groove clearance

10. Abnormal connecting rod bearing wear can be caused by either a bent connecting rod, an improperly machined journal, or a tapered connecting rod bore.

11. Twisted connecting rods will not create an easily identifiable wear pattern, but badly twisted rods will disturb the action of the entire piston, rings, and connecting rod assembly and may be the cause of excessive oil consumption.

12. If the piston must be removed from the connecting rod, mark the side of the connecting rod that corresponds with the side of the piston that faces the front of the engine, so the new piston will be installed facing the same direction. Most pistons have an arrow or notch on the top of the piston, indicating that this side should face the front of the engine. If the original piston is to be reinstalled, use paint or a marker to indicate the cylinder number on the piston, so it can be reinstalled on the same connecting rod.

13. The piston pin is a press fit in the connecting rod. If the piston and/or connecting rod must be replaced, the pin must be pressed into the connecting rod using a fixture that will not damage or distort the piston and/or connecting rod. The piston must move freely on the pin after installation.

HONING

▶ **See Figures 180 and 181**

1. After the piston and connecting rod assembly have been removed, check the clearances as explained in the cleaning and inspection procedure, to determine whether boring and honing or just light honing are required.

2. Honing is best done with the crankshaft removed. This prevents damage to the crankshaft and makes post-honing cleaning easier, as the honing process will scatter metal particles. However, if the crankshaft is in the cylinder block, position the connecting rod journal for the cylinder being honed as far away from the bottom of the cylinder bore as possible, and wrap a shop cloth around the journal.

3. Honing can be done either with a flexible glaze breaker type hone or with a rigid hone that has honing stones and guide shoes. The flexible hone removes the least amount of metal, and is especially recommended if the piston-to-cylinder bore clearance is on the loose side. The flexible hone is useful to provide a finish on which the new piston rings will seat. A rigid hone will remove more material than the flexible hone and requires more operator skill.

4. Regardless of the type of hone used, carefully follow the manufacturers instructions for operation.

5. The hone should be moved up and down the bore at sufficient speed to obtain a uniform finish. A rigid hone will provide a more definite cross-hatch finish; operate the rigid hone at a speed to obtain a 45° included angle in the cross-hatch. The finish marks should be clean but not sharp, free from embedded particles and torn or folded metal.

6. Periodically during the honing procedure, thoroughly clean the cylinder bore and check the piston-to-bore clearance with the piston for that cylinder.

7. After honing is completed, thoroughly wash the cylinder bores and the rest of the engine with hot water and detergent. Scrub the bores well with a stiff bristle brush and rinse thoroughly with hot water. Thorough cleaning is essential, for if any abrasive material is left in the cylinder bore, it will rapidly wear the new rings and the cylinder bore. If any abrasive material is left in the rest of the engine, it will be picked up by

Fig. 180 Using a ball type cylinder hone is an easy way to hone the cylinder bore

Fig. 181 A properly cross-hatched cylinder bore

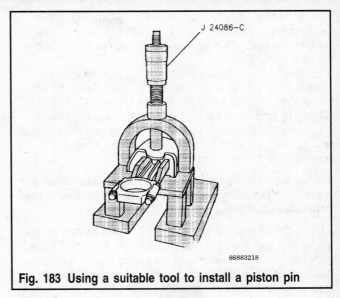

Fig. 183 Using a suitable tool to install a piston pin

the oil and carried throughout the engine, damaging bearings and other parts.

8. After the bores are cleaned, wipe them down with a clean cloth coated with light engine oil, to keep them from rusting.

PISTON PIN REPLACEMENT

▶ See Figures 182 and 183

1. Remove the piston rings using a suitable piston ring removal tool.
2. Remove the piston pin lockring, if used.
3. Install the guide bushing of the piston pin removal and installation tool.
4. Install the piston and rod assembly on a support and place the assembly in an arbor press. Press the pin out of the connecting rod using the proper piston pin tool.
5. Assembly is the reverse of the removal procedure.

PISTON RING REPLACEMENT

▶ See Figure 184

1. After the cylinder bores have been finish honed and cleaned, check the piston ring end-gap. Compress the piston rings to be used in the cylinder, one at a time, into that cylinder. Using an inverted piston, push the ring down into the cylinder bore area where normal ring wear is not encountered.
2. Measure the ring end-gap with a feeler gauge and compare to specification. A gap that is too tight is more harmful than one that is too loose (If ring end-gap is excessively loose, the cylinder bore is probably worn beyond specification).
3. If the ring end-gap is too tight, carefully remove the ring and file the ends squarely with a fine file to obtain the proper clearance.
4. Install the rings on the piston, lowest ring first. The lowest (oil) ring is installed by hand; the top 2 (compression) rings must be installed using a piston ring expander tool. There is a high risk of breaking or distorting the compression rings if they are installed by hand.

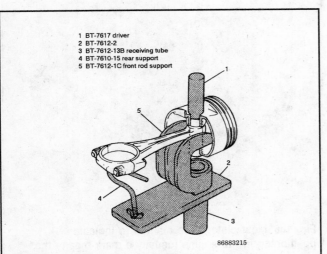

1 BT-7617 driver
2 BT-7612-2
3 BT-7612-13B receiving tube
4 BT-7610-15 rear support
5 BT-7612-1C front rod support

Fig. 182 Removing the piston pin using a suitable tool — 3.1L engine shown

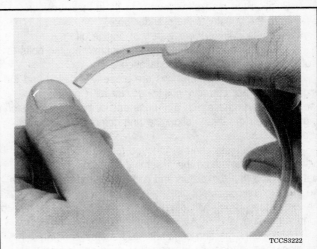

Fig. 184 Most rings are marked to show which side should face upward

5. Install the oil ring expander in the bottom ring groove. Make sure the ends butt together and do not overlap. The expander end-gap should be parallel to the piston pin, facing the right cylinder bank.

6. Start the end of an oil ring rail ring into the oil ring groove above the expander. The rail end-gap should be positioned 135° from the expander end-gap. Finish installing the rail ring by spiraling it the remainder of the way on. Repeat the rail installation with the other rail ring. Its gap position must be 135° from the other side of the expander end-gap, 90° from the other rail ring end-gap.

➡ **If the instructions on the ring packaging differ from this information regarding ring gap positioning, follow the ring manufacturers instructions.**

7. Install the lower compression ring in the piston ring expander tool with the proper side up (usually the manufacturer's mark faces UP). The piston ring packaging should contain instructions as to the directions the ring sides should face. Spread the ring with the expander tool and install it on the piston. Position the end-gap 180° from the oil ring expander end-gap.

8. Repeat Step 7 to install the top compression ring. Position the end-gap in line with the oil ring expander end-gap. The compression ring end-gaps must not be aligned.

INSTALLATION

◆ **See Figures 185, 186 and 187**

1. Make sure the connecting rod and rod cap bearing saddles are clean and free of nicks or burrs. Install the bearing shells in the connecting rod, making sure the bearing shell tangs are seated in the notches.

➡ **Be careful when handling any plain bearings. Hands and working area should be clean. Dirt is easily embedded in the bearing surface and the bearings are easily scratched or damaged.**

2. Make sure the cylinder bore and crankshaft journal are clean.

3. Position the crankshaft journal at its furthest position away from the bottom of the cylinder bore.

4. Coat the cylinder bore with light engine oil.

5. Install the rubber hoses over the connecting rod bolts to protect the crankshaft during installation.

6. Make sure the piston rings are properly installed and the ring end-gaps are correctly positioned. Install a piston ring compressor over the piston and rings and compress the piston rings into their grooves. Follow the ring compressor manufacturers instructions.

7. Place the piston and connecting rod assembly into the cylinder bore. Make sure the assembly is the correct one for that bore and that the piston and connecting rod are facing in the proper direction. Most pistons have an arrow or notch on the top of the piston, indicating that this side should face the front of the engine.

8. Make sure the ring compressor is seated squarely on the block deck surface. If the compressor is not seated squarely, a ring could pop out from beneath the compressor

and hang up on the deck surface, as the piston is tapped into the bore, possibly breaking the ring.

9. Make sure that the connecting rod is not hung up on the crankshaft counterweights and is in position to come straight on to the crankshaft.

10. Tap the piston slowly into the bore, making sure the compressor remains squarely against the block deck. When the piston is completely in the bore, remove the ring compressor.

➡ **If the connecting rod bearings were replaced, recheck the bearing clearance as described during the removal procedure, before proceeding further.**

11. Coat the crankshaft journal and the bearing shells with engine assembly lube or clean engine oil. Pull the connecting rod onto the crankshaft journal. After the rod is seated, remove the rubber hoses.

12. Install the rod bearing cap, making sure it is the correct one for the connecting rod. Lightly oil the connecting rod bolt

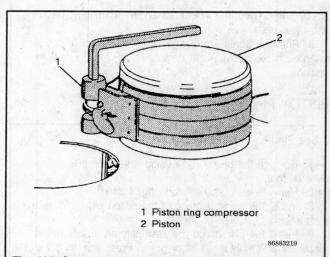

1 Piston ring compressor
2 Piston

86883219

Fig. 185 Compress the piston rings into their grooves using a suitable ring compressor

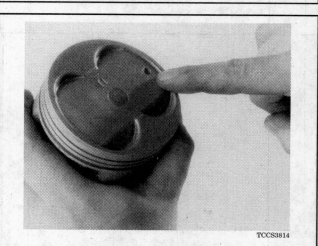

TCCS3814

Fig. 186 Most pistons are marked to indicate positioning in the engine (usually a mark means the side facing front)

Fig. 187 Using a wooden hammer handle, carefully tap the piston down through the ring compressor and into the cylinder bore

threads and install the rod nuts. Tighten the nuts to 15 ft. lbs. (20 Nm) plus 75° additional rotation.

13. After each piston and connecting rod assembly is installed, turn the crankshaft over several times and check for binding. If there is a problem and the crankshaft will not turn, or turns with great difficulty, it will be easier to find the problem (rod cap on backwards, broken ring, etc.) than if all the assemblies are installed.

14. Check the clearance between the sides of the connecting rods and the crankshaft using a feeler gauge. Spread the rods slightly with a screwdriver to insert the gauge. If the clearance is below the minimum specification, the connecting rod will have to be removed and machined to provide adequate clearance. If the clearance is excessive, substitute an unworn rod and recheck. If the clearance is still excessive, the crankshaft must be welded and reground, or replaced.

15. Install the oil pump and oil pan.

16. Install the cylinder heads and intake manifold.

17. Install the engine in the vehicle.

18. Start and run the engine, then check for leaks and proper engine operation.

Freeze Plugs

REMOVAL & INSTALLATION

▶ **See Figures 188 and 189**

1. Disconnect the negative battery cable.
2. Drain the cooling system.

✳✳CAUTION

When draining the coolant, keep in mind that cats and dogs are attracted by ethylene glycol antifreeze, and are quite likely to drink any that is left in an uncovered container or in puddles on the ground. This will prove fatal in sufficient quantity. Always drain the coolant into a sealable container. Coolant should be reused unless it is contaminated or several years old.

3. If equipped with drain plugs on the engine remove them. They would be located at the bottom of the block near the oil pan.

4. Remove any components that restrict access to the freeze plugs, like the starter or motor mounts.

5. Wearing proper eye protection, tap the bottom edge of the freeze plug with a punch and hammer. This should tilt the freeze plug, not cut it. Then use pliers to pull or pry the freeze plug from its bore. Another method is to drill the freeze plug and use a slide hammer, but more often there's not enough room to do that.

6. After the plug is removed clean the area completely. Coat the freeze plug and/or bore with gasket sealant.

To install:

7. Install the freeze plug into the hole, it must do in evenly or it will keep popping back out as you tap on it. Using a plug installer or socket that fits the edge of the plug can help keep it straight as you tap it in place.

8. Fill the engine with coolant, connect the battery cable. Start engine and check for leaks.

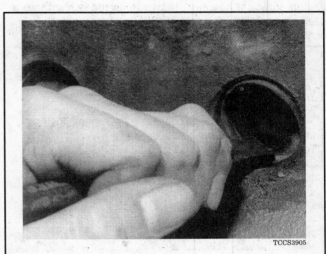

Fig. 188 Using a punch and hammer, the freeze plug can be loosened in the block

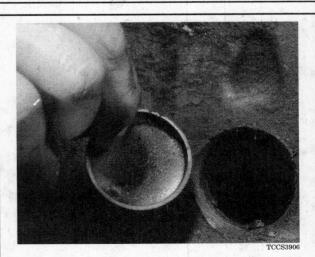

Fig. 189 Once the freeze plug has been loosened, it can be removed from the block

Block Heater

REMOVAL & INSTALLATION

Factory block heaters are not installed on these models. If an aftermarket heater has been installed the following procedure will most likely work. There are two basic types, one for the oil and one for the coolant. The oil heater usually just slips into the dipstick tube or replaces the oil drain plug. The following procedure is for the coolant type.

1. Remove the negative battery cable.
2. Drain the cooling system.

❊❊CAUTION

When draining the coolant, keep in mind that cats and dogs are attracted by ethylene glycol antifreeze, and are quite likely to drink any that is left in an uncovered container or in puddles on the ground. This will prove fatal in sufficient quantity. Always drain the coolant into a sealable container. Coolant should be reused unless it is contaminated or several years old.

3. Remove the block heater in the same way as the freeze plugs. Some heater units have a bolt that must be loosened or a V-Clamp that must be removed to remove the heating element.
4. Disconnect the heater connector and remove the heater element.

To install:
5. Coat the new heater with sealant, then install as removed.
6. Fill the engine with coolant, connect the battery cable. Start engine and check for leaks.

Rear Main Seal

REMOVAL & INSTALLATION

2.0L And 2.5L Engines

➡**The rear main seal is a one piece unit which can be replaced without removing the oil pan or crankshaft.**

1. Disconnect the negative battery cable.
2. Remove the transaxle. For details, please refer to the procedure located in Section 7 of this manual.
3. Unfasten the flywheel/flexplate-to-crankshaft bolts, then remove the flywheel.
4. If equipped with a manual transaxle, remove the pressure plate and clutch disc.
5. Using a medium prybar, pry out the old seal; be careful not to scratch the crankshaft surface.
6. Clean the block and crankshaft-to-seal mating surfaces.

To install:
7. Lubricated the outside of the seal to ease installation. Using seal installer tool J 36227 or equivalent, press the seal evenly into place.

➡**When installing the flywheel, you MUST use new bolts!**

8. If applicable, using new bolts, install the flywheel. Tighten the bolts to 48 ft. lbs. (65 Nm) plus an additional 30° turn.
9. If applicable, install the flexplate. Tighten the bolts to 48 ft. lbs. (65 Nm).
10. Install the pressure plate and clutch disc, if equipped with a manual transaxle.
11. Install the transaxle assembly as outlined in Section 7 of this manual.
12. Connect the negative battery cable, then start the engine and check for leaks.

2.3L Engine
▶ **See Figure 190**

1. Disconnect the negative battery cable.
2. Remove the transaxle assembly as outlined in Section 7 of this manual.
3. If equipped with a manual transaxle, remove the pressure plate and clutch disc.
4. Unfasten the flywheel-to-crankshaft bolts, then remove the flywheel.
5. Disconnect the oil pan-to-seal housing bolts
6. Unfasten the seal housing-to-block bolts, then remove the seal housing and gasket.
7. To support the seal housing for seal removal, place two blocks of equal thickness on a flat surface, position the seal housing and blocks so the transaxle side of the seal housing is supported across the dowel pin and center bolt holes on both sides of the seal opening.

➡**The seal housing could be damaged if not properly supported during seal removal.**

8. Drive the seal evenly out the transaxle side of the seal housing using a small prytool in the relief grooves on the crankshaft side of the seal housing. Discard the seal.

❊❊CAUTION

Be careful not to damage the seal housing sealing surface. If damaged, it may result in an oil leak.

To install:
9. Press a new seal into the housing using tool J 36005 or equivalent seal installation tool.
10. Inspect the oil pan gasket inner silicone bead for damage and repair using a silicone sealant, if necessary.
11. Position a new seal housing-to-block gasket over the alignment. The gasket is reversible.
12. Lubricate the lip of the seal with clean engine oil.
13. Install the housing assembly, then tighten the housing-to-block bolts to 106 inch lbs. (12 Nm).
14. Install the oil pan-to-seal housing bolts, then tighten to 106 inch lbs. (12 Nm).
15. Install the flywheel as outlined later in this section.

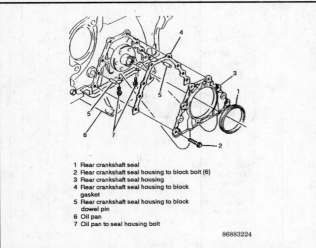

Fig. 190 Exploded view of the rear main (crankshaft) seal, housing and related components — 2.3L engine

1 Rear crankshaft seal
2 Rear crankshaft seal housing to block bolt (6)
3 Rear crankshaft seal housing
4 Rear crankshaft seal housing to block gasket
5 Rear crankshaft seal housing to block dowel pin
6 Oil pan
7 Oil pan to seal housing bolt

86883224

16. For vehicles equipped with a manual transaxle, install the clutch, pressure plate and clutch cover assembly.

17. Install the transaxle assembly as outlined in Section 7 of this manual.

18. Connect the negative battery cable, then start the engine and check for leaks.

3.0L Engine

▶ **See Figures 191, 192 and 193**

1. Disconnect the negative battery cable. Raise and safely support the vehicle.

2. Drain the engine oil, then remove the oil pan.

3. Unfasten the rear main bearing cap-to-engine bolts, then remove the bearing cap from the engine.

4. Remove the old seal from the bearing cap.

To install:

5. Using seal packing tool J 21526-2 or equivalent, insert it against one end of the seal in the cylinder block. Pack the old seal into the groove until it is packed tightly. Repeat the procedure on the other end of the seal.

6. Measure the amount the seal was driven up into the block one one side and add approximately 1/16 in. (1.6mm). Cut this length from the old seal removed from the lower bearing cap, repeat for the other side.

➡**When cutting the seal into short lengths, use a double edged blade and the lower bearing cap as a holding fixture.**

7. Install seal packing guide J 21526-1 or equivalent, onto the cylinder block.

8. Using the packing tool, work the short pieces into the guide tool and pack into the cylinder block until the tool hits the built-in stop.

➡**It may help to use a small amount of oil on the short seal pieces when packing into the block.**

9. Repeat Steps 7 and 8 for the other side.
10. Remove the guide tool.
11. Install a new rope seal into the lower bearing cap.
12. Install the lower main bearing cap and tighten the main bearing cap bolts to 100 ft. lbs. (135 Nm).

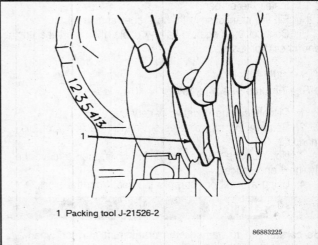

1 Packing tool J-21526-2

86883225

Fig. 191 Using the special tool to pack the seal into the block

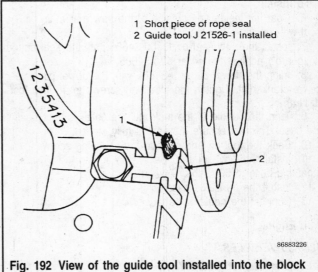

1 Short piece of rope seal
2 Guide tool J 21526-1 installed

86883226

Fig. 192 View of the guide tool installed into the block

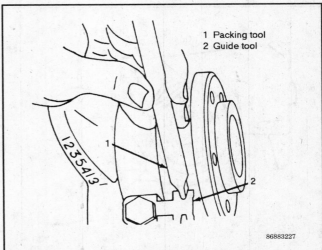

1 Packing tool
2 Guide tool

86883227

Fig. 193 Packing the short pieces of the rope seal into the guide tool and cylinder block

13. Install the oil pan.

14. Fill the crankcase with the proper engine oil.

15. Connect the negative battery cable, then start the engine and check for leaks.

3.1L Engine

▶ **See Figures 194 and 195**

1. Disconnect the negative battery cable.

2. Remove the transaxle as outlined in Section 7 of this manual.

3. Unfasten the flywheel mounting bolts, then remove the flywheel and spacer.

4. Using a small pry bar, pry the seal from the block.

✳✳CAUTION

Be careful not to damage the crankshaft surface when removing the oil seal.

5. Clean the seal mounting surface.

To install:

6. Coat the inside and outside of the new rear main oil seal with engine oil.

7. Install the new seal on tool J-34686 until the seal bottom is squarely against the collar of J-34686.

8. Align the dowel pin of J-34686 with the dowel pin hole in the crankshaft. Tighten the attaching screws to 45 inch lbs. (5 Nm).

9. Turn the handle of the tool until the collar is tight against the case. This will ensure the seal is fully seated.

10. Back the tool off and remove the attaching screws.

11. Install the flywheel and spacer and tighten the flywheel mounting bolts to 53 ft. lbs. (71 Nm).

12. Install the transaxle assembly.

13. Connect the negative battery cable.

3.3L Engine

1989-90 VEHICLES

▶ **See Figures 196 and 197**

1. Disconnect the negative battery cable.

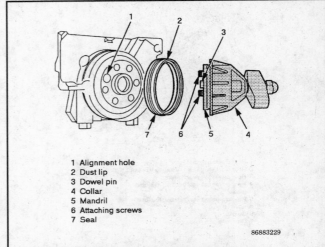

1 Alignment hole
2 Dust lip
3 Dowel pin
4 Collar
5 Mandril
6 Attaching screws
7 Seal

86883229

Fig. 195 When installing the seal, the correct installation tool must be used

2. Remove the engine from the vehicle.

3. Drain the oil and remove the oil pan.

4. Remove the crankshaft from the engine.

5. Clean the remains of the old sealer and adhesive from the upper and lower bearing groove and the mating surface of the bearing cap.

To install:

6. Install rope seal to the cap.

7. Apply GM adhesive 1052621 or equivalent to the seal groove.

8. Within one minute, install the seal into the groove. Roll it into place using a suitable tool, until the seal projects no more than $1/16$ in. (1.6mm) above the groove.

9. Seat the seal with a suitable tool.

10. Cut the excess material with a sharp knife at the bearing cap parting line using the seal installer to hold the seal in place.

11. Apply a thin film of chassis grease to the rope seal.

➡ **Use the sealer sparingly. Keep the sealer out of the bolt threads. Soak sealing strips in light oil or kerosene for 5 minutes before installing.**

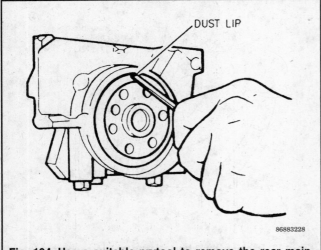

DUST LIP

86883228

Fig. 194 Use a suitable prytool to remove the rear main seal

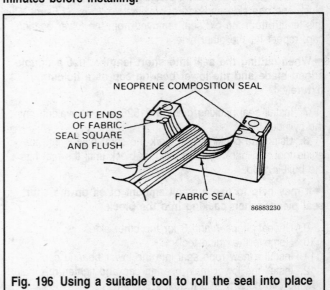

NEOPRENE COMPOSITION SEAL

CUT ENDS OF FABRIC SEAL SQUARE AND FLUSH

FABRIC SEAL

86883230

Fig. 196 Using a suitable tool to roll the seal into place

12. Apply a thin film of GM sealer 1052942 or equivalent, on the bearing cap mating surface around the seal groove.

13. Position the main bearing cap and tighten the bolts to 90 ft. lbs. (122 Nm).

14. Install the crankshaft and the oil pan.

15. Install the engine in the vehicle.

16. Fill the crankcase with the proper engine oil.

17. Connect the negative battery cable and check for leaks.

1991-93 VEHICLES

▶ **See Figures 198, 199 and 200**

1. Disconnect the negative battery cable.
2. Remove the flywheel as outlined later in this section.

➡**When prying out the seal, be very careful not to damage the crankshaft surfaces!**

3. Insert a flat bladed tool in through the dust lip at the angle shown in the accompanying figure. Pry the seal out by moving the handle of the tool towards the end of the crankshaft pilot. Repeat as necessary around the seal until it is removed.

To install:

4. Apply clean engine oil to the new seal to ease installation. Slide the seal over the mandril of the tool until the back of the seal bottom is squarely against the collar of the tool.

5. Attach tool J 38196 or equivalent to the crankshaft by hand or tighten the attaching screws to 44 inch lbs. (5 Nm).

6. Turn the "T" handle of the tool so that the collar pushes the seal into the bore, turn the handle until the collar is tight against the case. This will ensure that the seal is installed correctly.

7. Loosen the "T" handle until it comes to a stop. This will ensure that the collar will be in the correct position for installing another new seal. Remove the tool attaching screws.

8. Install the flywheel.

9. Connect the negative battery cable, then start the engine and check for leaks.

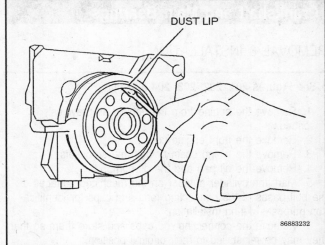

Fig. 198 Using a suitable prytool to remove the rear main seal

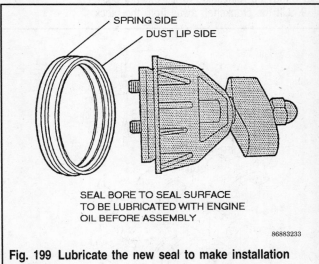

Fig. 199 Lubricate the new seal to make installation easier

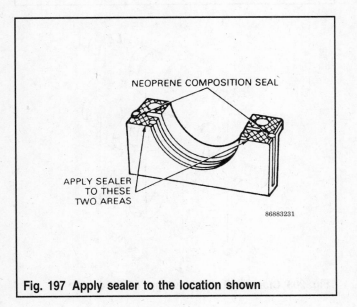

Fig. 197 Apply sealer to the location shown

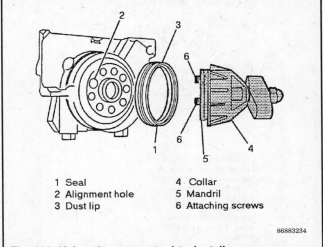

1 Seal
2 Alignment hole
3 Dust lip
4 Collar
5 Mandril
6 Attaching screws

Fig. 200 Using the proper tool to install a new rear main seal

Crankshaft and Main Bearings

REMOVAL & INSTALLATION

▶ See Figures 201, 202, 203, 204 and 205

1. Remove the engine from the vehicle as previously described.
2. Remove the front engine cover.
3. Remove the timing chain or belt and sprockets.
4. Remove the oil pan and the oil pump.
5. Mark the cylinder number on the machined surfaces of the bolt bases of the connecting rods and caps for identification purposes during installation.
6. Remove the connecting rod caps and store them so that they may be reinstalled to their original position.
7. Remove all of the main bearing caps.
8. Note the position of the keyway in the crankshaft, so that it may be reinstalled to it's original position.
9. Lift the crankshaft away from the block.

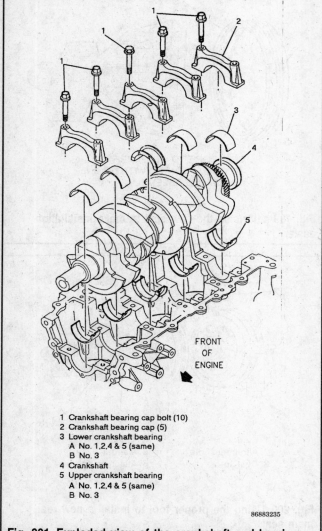

1 Crankshaft bearing cap bolt (10)
2 Crankshaft bearing cap (5)
3 Lower crankshaft bearing
  A No. 1,2,4 & 5 (same)
  B No. 3
4 Crankshaft
5 Upper crankshaft bearing
  A No. 1,2,4 & 5 (same)
  B No. 3

86883235

Fig. 201 Exploded view of the crankshaft and bearing assembly — 2.3L engine

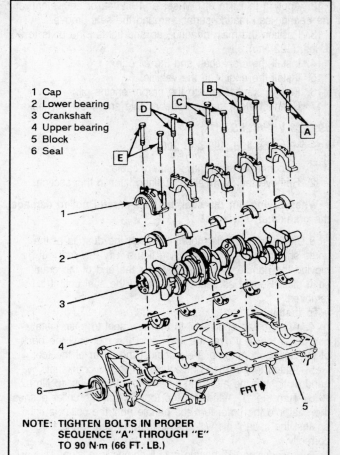

1 Cap
2 Lower bearing
3 Crankshaft
4 Upper bearing
5 Block
6 Seal

NOTE: TIGHTEN BOLTS IN PROPER SEQUENCE "A" THROUGH "E" TO 90 N·m (66 FT. LB.)

86883236

Fig. 202 Crankshaft and related components — 2.5L engine

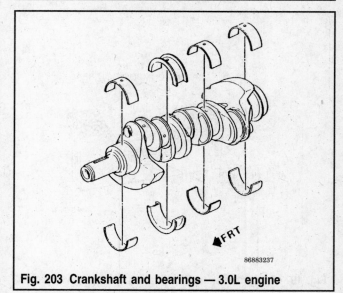

86883237

Fig. 203 Crankshaft and bearings — 3.0L engine

10. Remove the rear main oil seal.

To install:

11. Install sufficient oil pan bolts to the block to align with the connecting rod bolts. Use rubber bands between the bolts to hold the connecting rods in place.

12. Place the upper half of the main bearings in the block and lubricate them with clean engine oil.

13. Place the crankshaft keyway in the same position as removed and lower it into the block. The connecting rods should follow the crank pins into position as it is lowered.

14. Lubricate the thrust flanges with 10501609 lubricant or equivalent. Install caps with the lower half of the bearings lubricated with engine oil. Lubricate the cap bolts with engine oil and install, but do not tighten.

15. With a block of wood, tap the shaft in each direction to properly align the thrust flanges of the main bearing. Hold the shaft towards the front while torquing the thrust bearing cap bolts.

16. Tighten all of the main bearing to specifications and check crankshaft endplay.

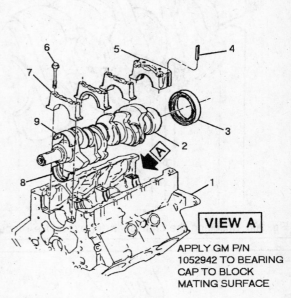

VIEW A

APPLY GM P/N 1052942 TO BEARING CAP TO BLOCK MATING SURFACE

1 Engine cylinder block
2 Crankshaft
3 Lip crankshaft rear seal
4 Crankshaft main bearing side seal
5 Crankshaft main bearing rear cap
6 Crankshaft bearing cap bolt
7 Crankshaft bearing front cap
8 Crankshaft lower bearing
9 Crankshaft upper bearing

86883239

Fig. 205 Exploded view of the crankshaft and related components — 3.3L engine

17. Lubricate the connecting rod bearings with clean oil. Install the connecting rod bearing caps to their original positions and tighten the nuts to specification.

18. Complete installation by reversing the removal steps.

CLEANING AND INSPECTION

▶ See Figures 206, 207 and 208

1. Clean the crankshaft with solvent and brush. Clean the oil passages with a suitable brush, then blow them out using compressed air.

2. Inspect the crankshaft for obvious damage or wear. Check the main and connecting rod journals for cracks, scratches, grooves or scores. Inspect the crankshaft oil seal surface for nicks, sharp edges or burrs that could damage the oil seal or cause premature wear.

3. If the crankshaft passes a visual inspection, check journal runout using a dial indicator. Support the crankshaft in V-blocks as shown in the figure and check the runout as shown. Compare to specifications.

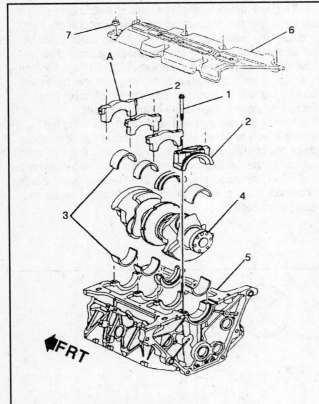

A Assemble with arrows on cap toward front of engine
1 Main bearing cap bolt
2 Main bearing cap
3 Crankshaft main bearing
4 Crankshaft
5 Engine block
6 Crankshaft oil deflector
7 Crankshaft oil deflector nut

86883238

Fig. 204 Exploded view of the crankshaft, bearings and caps — 3.1L engine

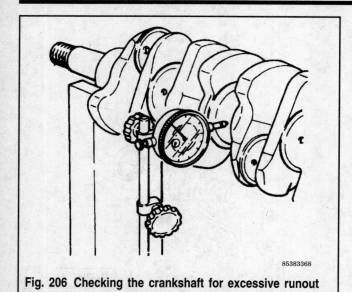

Fig. 206 Checking the crankshaft for excessive runout

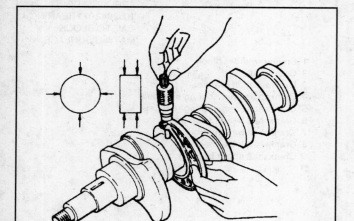

Fig. 207 Checking the main bearing journal using a micrometer

4. Measure the main and connecting rod journals for wear, out-of-roundness or taper, using a micrometer. Measure in at least four places around each journal and compare your findings with the journal diameter specifications.

5. If the crankshaft fails any inspection for wear or damage, it must be reground or replaced.

CONNECTING ROD AND MAIN BEARING REPLACEMENT

▶ See Figures 209 and 210

➡ **The following procedure requires the use of Plastigage® or a micrometer set consisting of inside and outside micrometers, and a dial indicator.**

1. Inspect the bearings for scoring, chipping or other wear.

2. Inspect the crankshaft journals as details in the Cleaning and Inspection procedure

3. If the crankshaft journals appear usable, clean them and the bearing shells until they are completely free of oil. Blow any oil from the oil hole in the crankshaft.

4. To check the crankshaft/rod bearing clearances using a micrometer, use the perform the following procedures:

  a. Set the crankshaft on V-blocks Using a dial indicator set on the center bearing journal, check the crankshaft runout. Repair or replace the crankshaft if out of specification.

  b. Using an outside micrometer, measure the crankshaft bearing journals for diameter and and out-of-round conditions; if necessary, regrind the bearing journals.

  c. Install the bearings and caps, then tightening the nuts/bolts to specifications. Using an inside micrometer, check the bearing bores in the engine block. If out of specification, regrind the bearing bores to the next largest oversize.

  d. The difference between the two readings is the bearing clearance. If out of specification, inspect for the cause and repair as necessary.

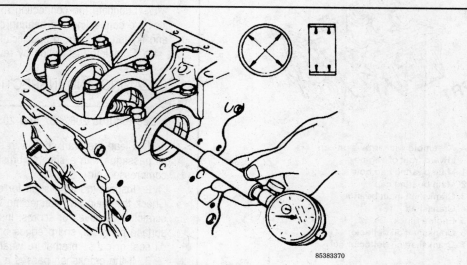

Fig. 208 Checking the main bearing bore diameter with the bearings installed

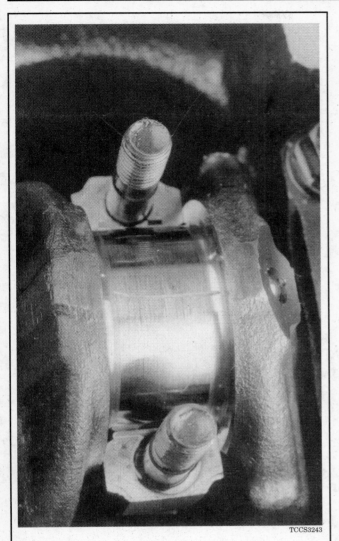

Fig. 209 Apply a strip of gauging material to the bearing, then install and torque cap

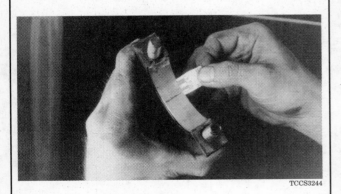

Fig. 210 As with the connecting rod bearings, remove the cap and compare the gauging material to the provided scale

5. To inspect the main bearing surfaces using the Plastigage® method, perform the following procedures:

➡**The journal surfaces and bearing shells must be completely free of oil to get an accurate reading with Plastigage®**

a. Place a strip of Plastigage® or equivalent gauging material, lengthwise along the bottom center of the lower bearing shell, then install the cap with the shell and tightening the connecting rod nuts or main cap bolt to specification.

➡**When the Plastigage® material is installed on the bearing surfaces, DO NOT rotate the crankshaft.**

b. Remove the bearing cap with the shell. The flattened Plastigage® will either be sticking to the bearing shell or the crankshaft journal.

c. Using the printed scale on the Plastigage® package, measure the flattened material at its widest point. the number on the scale that most closely corresponds to the width of the Plastigage® indicates the bearing clearance in thousandths of an inch or hundredths of a millimeter.

d. Compare your findings with the bearing clearance specification. If the bearing clearance is excessive. the bearing must be replaced or the crankshaft must be ground and the bearing replaced.

➡**The bearing shell sets over the standard size are available to correct excessive bearing clearance.**

e. After clearance measurement is completed, be sure to remove the Plastigage® from the crankshaft and/or bearing shell.

f. For final bearing shell installation, make sure the connecting rod and rod cap and/or cylinder block and main cap bearing saddles are clean and free of nicks or burrs. Install the bearing shells in the bearing saddles, making sure the shell tangs are seated in the notches.

➡**Be careful when handling any plain bearings. Your hands and the working area should be clean. Dirt is easily embedded in the bearing surface and the bearings are easily scratched or damaged.**

Flywheel

REMOVAL & INSTALLATION

▶ **See Figures 211 and 212**

1. Disconnect the negative battery cable.
2. Remove the transaxle assembly, refer to the Section 7 of this manual for details.
3. If equipped, remove the splash shield.

➡**To assure proper balance during reassembly, matchmark the relationship of the pressure plate assembly to the flywheel**

4. If equipped with a manual transaxle, remove the clutch and pressure plate.
5. Using special tool J38122 or equivalent, secure the crankshaft, then unfasten the flywheel mounting bolts. Remove the flywheel and spacer (if equipped).

To Install:

6. Remove all thread adhesive from the bolts and from the holes before installation.

7. Apply locking type adhesive to all of the flywheel-to-crankshaft mounting bolts.

8. The remaining installation steps are the reverse of the removal procedure. Tighten the flywheel bolts in stages to the following specifications:

    a. 2.0L engine: 48 ft. lbs. (65 Nm) plus an additional 30° turn.

    b. 2.3L engine: 22 ft. lbs. (30 Nm) plus an additional 45° turn.

    c. 2.5L engine: 55 ft. lbs. (75 Nm).

    d. 3.0L engine: 60 ft. lbs. (81 Nm).

    e. 3.1L engine: 61 ft. lbs. (83 Nm).

    f. 3.3L engine: 1989-92 — 61 ft. lbs. (83 Nm). 1993 — 11 ft. lbs. (15 Nm) plus an additional 50° turn.

9. Connect the negative battery cable.

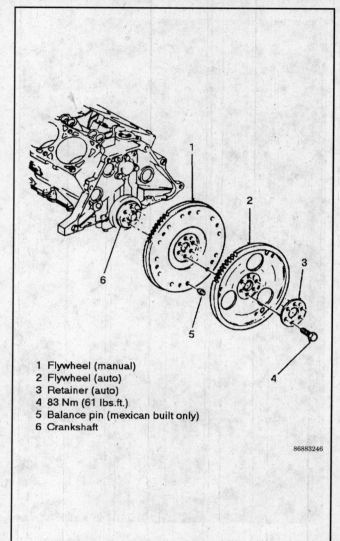

1 Flywheel (manual)
2 Flywheel (auto)
3 Retainer (auto)
4 83 Nm (61 lbs.ft.)
5 Balance pin (mexican built only)
6 Crankshaft

86883246

Fig. 212 Exploded view of the flywheel — 3.1L engine shown

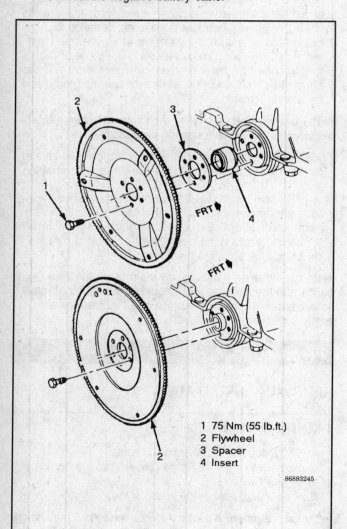

1 75 Nm (55 lb.ft.)
2 Flywheel
3 Spacer
4 Insert

86883245

Fig. 211 View of the flywheel and related components — 2.5L engine shown

EXHAUST SYSTEM

General Information

▶ **See Figures 213 and 214**

Two types of pipe connections are used on most exhaust systems; they are: the ball joint (to allow angular movement for alignment purposes) and the slip joint. Gaskets are used only with the ball joint type connections.

The system is supported by free hanging rubber mountings which permit some movement of the exhaust system but do not allow the transfer of noise and vibration into the passenger compartment. Any noise vibrations or rattles in the exhaust system are usually caused be damage or misalignment of the parts.

❊❊CAUTION

Before performing any operations on the exhaust system, be sure to allow it sufficient time to cool.

As with many areas of service on your car, the exhaust system presents its own dangers. Always follow safety precautions carefully during exhaust system service.

Safety Precautions

➡**Safety goggles should be worn at all times when working on or near the exhaust system. Older exhaust systems will almost always be covered with loose rust particles which will shower you when disturbed. These particles are more than a nuisance and could injure your eye.**

Whenever working on the exhaust system, always follow these safety precautions:

• Support the car extra securely. Not only will you often be working directly under it, but you'll frequently be using a lot of force, say, heavy hammer blows, to dislodge rusted parts. This can cause a car that's improperly supported to shift and possibly fall.

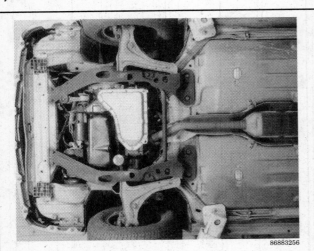

Fig. 213 View of the front exhaust system components as viewed from the under the vehicle

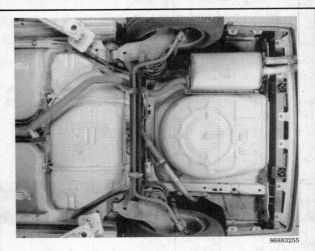

Fig. 214 Exhaust pipe routing and muffler location — 1986 3.0L vehicle shown

• Wear goggles. Exhaust system parts are always rusty. Metal chips can be dislodged, even when you're only turning rusted bolts. Attempting to pry pipes apart with a chisel makes the chips fly even more frequently.

• If you're using a cutting torch, keep it a great distance from either the fuel tank or lines. Stop what you're doing and feel the temperature of the fuel bearing pipes on the tank frequently. Even slight heat can expand and/or vaporize fuel, resulting in accumulated vapor, or even a liquid leak, near your torch.

• Watch where your hammer blows fall and make sure you hit squarely. You could easily tap a brake or fuel line when you hit an exhaust system part with a glancing blow. Inspect all lines and hoses in the area where you've been working.

❊❊CAUTION

Be very careful when working on or near the catalytic converter. External temperatures can reach 1,500°F (816°C) and more, causing severe burns. Removal or installation should be performed only on a cold exhaust system.

• Inspect inlet pipes, outlet pipes and mufflers for cracked joints, broken welds and corrosion damage that would result in a leaking exhaust system. It is normal for a certain amount of moisture and staining to be present around the muffler seams. The presence of soot, light surface rust or moisture does not indicate a faulty muffler. Inspect the clamps, brackets and insulators for cracks and stripped or badly corroded bolt threads. When flat joints are loosened and/or disconnected to replace a shield pipe or muffler, replace the bolts and flange nuts if there is reasonable doubt that its service life is limited.

• Check the complete exhaust system for open seams, holes, loose connections, or other deterioration which could permit exhaust fumes to seep into the passenger compartment.

• The exhaust system, including brush shields, must be free of leaks, binding, grounding and excessive vibrations. These conditions are usually caused by loose or broken flange bolts, shields, brackets or pipes. If any of these conditions exist, check the exhaust system components and alignment. Align or replace as necessary. Brush shields are positioned on the underside of the catalytic converter and should be free from bends which would bring any part of the shield in contact with the catalytic converter or muffler. The shield should also be clear of any combustible material such as dried grass or leaves.

• Before removing any component of the exhaust system, ALWAYS squirt a liquid rust dissolving agent onto the fasteners for ease of removal. A lot of knuckle skin will be saved by following this rule.

• Coat all of the exhaust connections and bolt threads with anti-seize compound to prevent corrosion from making the next disassembly difficult.

Front Exhaust Pipe with Flange/Three Way Catalytic Converter

REMOVAL & INSTALLATION

▶ See Figures 215, 216, 217, 218, 219, 220, 221 and 222

1. Raise and safely support the vehicle.
2. Remove the bolts from between the exhaust pipe and the manifold.
3. Support the catalytic converter and remove the attaching bolts from between the converter and the intermediate pipe.
4. Remove the manifold and converter seals, then remove the pipe.

To install:

5. Properly clean the flange surfaces and install the manifold and catalytic converter seals.
6. Install the exhaust pipe to the manifold with bolts, then tighten the bolts to the specifications shown the accompanying figures.
7. Connect the exhaust pipe to the converter and install the bolts. Tighten the bolts to specifications.
8. Carefully lower the vehicle.

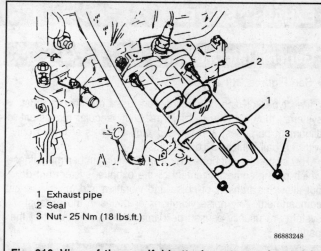

1 Exhaust pipe
2 Seal
3 Nut - 25 Nm (18 lbs.ft.)

86883248

Fig. 216 View of the manifold attachment — early model 2.3L shown

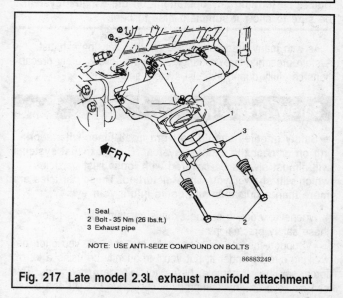

1 Seal
2 Bolt - 35 Nm (26 lbs.ft.)
3 Exhaust pipe

NOTE: USE ANTI-SEIZE COMPOUND ON BOLTS

86883249

Fig. 217 Late model 2.3L exhaust manifold attachment

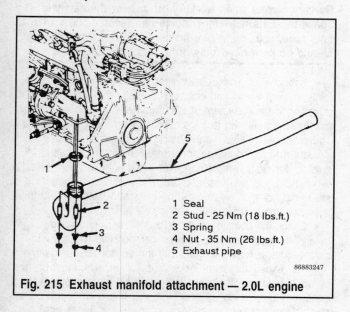

1 Seal
2 Stud - 25 Nm (18 lbs.ft.)
3 Spring
4 Nut - 35 Nm (26 lbs.ft.)
5 Exhaust pipe

86883247

Fig. 215 Exhaust manifold attachment — 2.0L engine

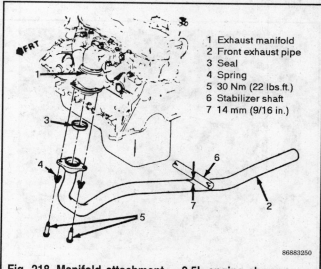

1 Exhaust manifold
2 Front exhaust pipe
3 Seal
4 Spring
5 30 Nm (22 lbs.ft.)
6 Stabilizer shaft
7 14 mm (9/16 in.)

86883250

Fig. 218 Manifold attachment — 2.5L engine shown

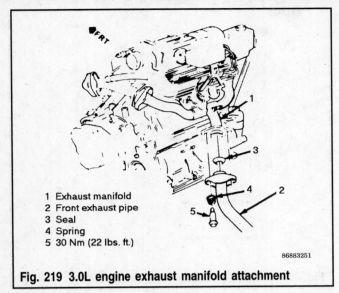

1 Exhaust manifold
2 Front exhaust pipe
3 Seal
4 Spring
5 30 Nm (22 lbs. ft.)

86883251

Fig. 219 3.0L engine exhaust manifold attachment

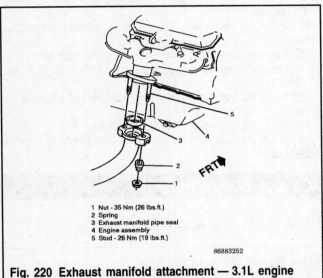

1 Nut - 35 Nm (26 lbs.ft.)
2 Spring
3 Exhaust manifold pipe seal
4 Engine assembly
5 Stud - 26 Nm (19 lbs.ft.)

86883252

Fig. 220 Exhaust manifold attachment — 3.1L engine

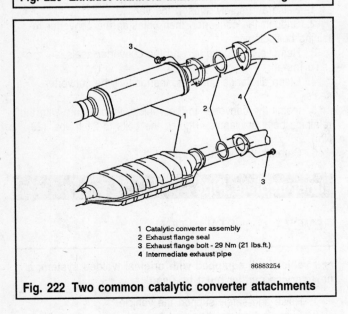

1 Catalytic converter assembly
2 Exhaust flange seal
3 Exhaust flange bolt - 29 Nm (21 lbs.ft.)
4 Intermediate exhaust pipe

86883254

Fig. 222 Two common catalytic converter attachments

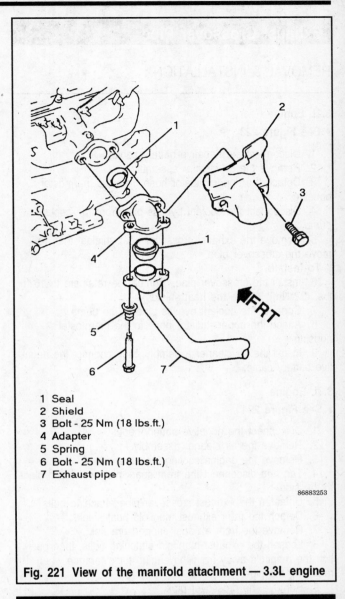

1 Seal
2 Shield
3 Bolt - 25 Nm (18 lbs.ft.)
4 Adapter
5 Spring
6 Bolt - 25 Nm (18 lbs.ft.)
7 Exhaust pipe

86883253

Fig. 221 View of the manifold attachment — 3.3L engine

Front Exhaust Pipe without Flange

REMOVAL & INSTALLATION

1. Raise and safely support the vehicle.
2. Support the catalytic converter.
3. Unfasten the clamps, then disconnect the exhaust pipe from the catalytic converter.
4. Detach the exhaust pipe from the manifold, then remove the pipe.
5. Remove the manifold seal.
   To install:
6. Connect the exhaust pipe to the catalytic converter and install the clamp.
7. Install the manifold seal and connect the exhaust pipe to the manifold.
8. Carefully lower the vehicle.

Exhaust Crossover Pipe

REMOVAL & INSTALLATION

3.1L Engine

♦ See Figure 223

1. Disconnect the negative battery cable.
2. Remove the air cleaner assembly.
3. Detach the upper radiator hose from the thermostat housing.
4. Disconnect the coolant bypass pipe from the coolant pump.
5. Remove the exhaust crossover heat shields, then remove the crossover pipe.

To install:

6. Install the crossover pipe. Tighten the retainers to 16 ft. lbs. (22 Nm). Attach the heat shields.
7. Connect the coolant bypass pipe to the pump.
8. Attach the upper radiator hose to the thermostat housing.
9. Install the air cleaner assembly, then connect the negative battery cable.

3.3L Engine

♦ See Figure 224

1. Disconnect the negative battery cable.
2. Remove the air cleaner assembly.
3. Remove the engine cooling fan assembly.
4. Tag and disconnect the front spark plug wires and place to the side.
5. Unfasten the exhaust crossover pipe attaching bolts.
6. Detach the front exhaust manifold heat shield.
7. Remove the front exhaust support bracket.
8. Loosen the exhaust manifold attaching bolts, then position the manifold away from the engine for clearance when removing the pipe.
9. Remove the crossover pipe.

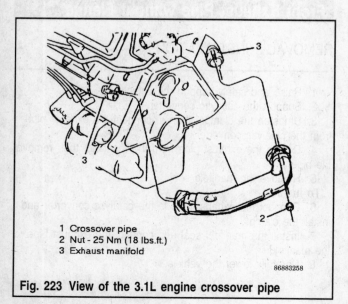

1 Crossover pipe
2 Nut - 25 Nm (18 lbs.ft.)
3 Exhaust manifold

86883258

Fig. 223 View of the 3.1L engine crossover pipe

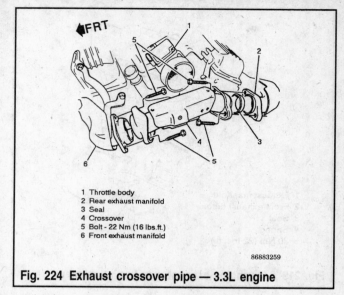

1 Throttle body
2 Rear exhaust manifold
3 Seal
4 Crossover
5 Bolt - 22 Nm (16 lbs.ft.)
6 Front exhaust manifold

86883259

Fig. 224 Exhaust crossover pipe — 3.3L engine

To install:

10. Install the crossover pipe, but do not install bolts at this time.
11. Connect the exhaust manifold and tighten the bolts.
12. Install the crossover pipe bolts, then tighten to 16 ft. lbs. (22 Nm).
13. Install the exhaust manifold support bracket and heat shield.
14. Install the engine cooling fan assembly.
15. Install the air cleaner assembly and connect the negative battery cable.

Catalytic Converter

REMOVAL & INSTALLATION

♦ See Figures 225 and 226

1. Raise and safely support the vehicle.
2. Support the converter, then unfasten the converter retaining bolts/clamps.
3. Remove the converter and the converter seals.

To install:

4. Clean all flange surfaces, then install the converter seals.
5. Install the converter to the vehicle, then secure with the retaining bolts or clamps. Tighten the bolts to 21 ft. lbs. (29 Nm).
6. Carefully lower the vehicle.

Intermediate Pipe

REMOVAL & INSTALLATION

➡If vehicle still equipped with original welded system, a new service muffler must be used.

1. Raise and safely support the vehicle.
2. Support the catalytic converter and muffler assembly.

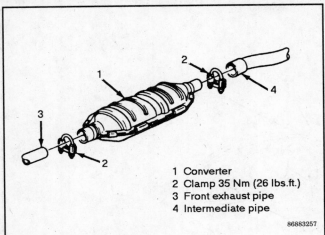

Fig. 225 Catalytic converter assembly without flange

1 Converter
2 Clamp 35 Nm (26 lbs.ft.)
3 Front exhaust pipe
4 Intermediate pipe

86883257

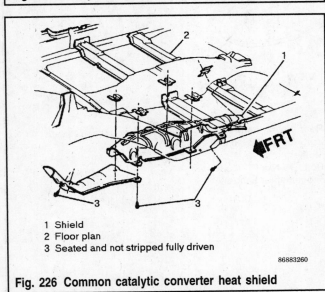

1 Shield
2 Floor plan
3 Seated and not stripped fully driven

86883260

Fig. 226 Common catalytic converter heat shield

3. Disconnect the intermediate pipe hanger.

4. Unbolt the pipe from the converter, then disconnect the intermediate pipe.

5. Remove the muffler hangers and the muffler and remove the converter seal.

To Install:

6. Install the converter seal and install the muffler to the intermediate pipe and to the hanger.

7. Install the intermediate pipe to the converter and connect to the hanger.

8. Lower the vehicle.

Muffler and Tailpipe

REMOVAL & INSTALLATION

◆ **See Figures 227, 228 and 229**

1. Raise and safely support the vehicle.

2. Support the intermediate pipe and muffler.

3. Using exhaust pipe cutting tool J 29800 or equivalent, cut the intermediate pipe as close to the weld as possible.

4. Remove the muffler hangers, then the muffler.

To Install:

5. Connect the muffler to the intermediate pipe and install the hangers.

6. Install a U-Bolt type clamp and tighten.

7. Carefully lower the vehicle.

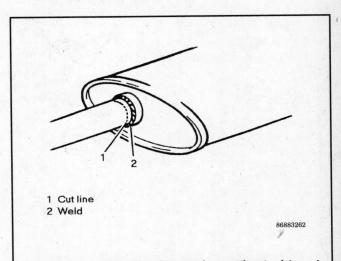

1 Cut line
2 Weld

86883262

Fig. 227 Use a suitable exhaust pipe cutting tool to cut the intermediate pipe as close to the weld as you can

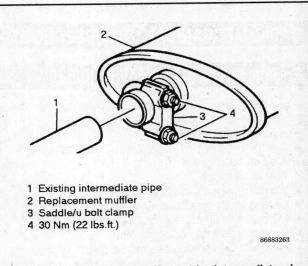

1 Existing intermediate pipe
2 Replacement muffler
3 Saddle/u bolt clamp
4 30 Nm (22 lbs.ft.)

86883263

Fig. 228 Connecting the muffler to the intermediate pipe

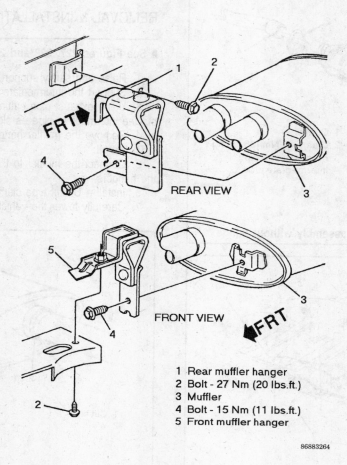

1 Rear muffler hanger
2 Bolt - 27 Nm (20 lbs.ft.)
3 Muffler
4 Bolt - 15 Nm (11 lbs.ft.)
5 Front muffler hanger

86883264

Fig. 229 A view of the muffler attachment

BASIC MECHANICAL TROUBLESHOOTING

Engine Speed Oscillates at Idle

When the engine idle speed will not remain constant, check for the following, as necessary:
- A faulty fuel pump
- A leaky Exhaust Gas Recirculation (EGR) valve
- A blown head gasket
- A worn camshaft
- Worn timing gears, chain or sprockets
- Leaking intake manifold-to-engine gasket
- A blocked Positive Crankcase Ventilation (PCV) valve
- Overheating of the cooling system
- Fault with the computerized engine control system

Low Power Output of Engine

When the engine power output is below normal, check for the following, as necessary:
- Overheating of the cooling system
- Leaks in the vacuum system
- Leaking of the fuel pump or hoses
- Unadjusted valve timing
- A blown head gasket
- A slipping clutch disc or unadjusted pedal
- Excessive piston-to-bore clearance
- Worn piston rings
- A worn camshaft
- Sticking valve(s) or weak valve spring(s)

- A poorly operating diverter valve
- A faulty pressure regulator valve (Automatic Transaxle)
- Low fluid level (Automatic Transaxle)
- Fault with the computerized engine control system

Poor High Speed Operation

When the engine cannot maintain high speed operations, check for the following, as necessary:
- A faulty fuel pump producing low fuel volume
- A restriction in the intake manifold
- A worn distributor shaft
- Leaking valves or worn valve springs
- Fault with the computerized engine control system

Poor Acceleration

When the engine experiences poor acceleration characteristics, check for the following, as necessary:
- Incorrect ignition timing
- Poorly seated valves
- Fault with the computerized engine control system

Backfire — Intake Manifold

When the engine backfires through the intake manifold, check for the following, as necessary:
- Incorrect ignition timing
- Defective Exhaust Gas Recirculation (EGR) valve
- Fault with the computerized engine control system

Backfire — Exhaust Manifold

When the engine backfires through the exhaust manifold, check for the following, as necessary:
- Leaks in the vacuum hose system
- Leaks in the exhaust system
- Faulty vacuum diverter valve
- Fault with the computerized engine control system

Engine Detonation (Dieseling)

When the engine operates beyond the controlled limits, check for the following, as necessary:
- Faulty ignition electrical system components
- Ignition timing that is too far advanced
- Inoperative Exhaust Gas Recirculation (EGR) valve
- Inoperative Positive Crankcase Ventilation (PCV) valve
- Faulty or loose spark plugs
- Clogged fuel delivery system
- Sticking, leaking or broken valves
- Excessive deposits in the combustion chambers
- Leaks in the vacuum system
- Fault with the computerized engine control system

Excessive Oil Leakage

When large amounts of oil are noticed under the engine after each operation, check for the following, as necessary:
- Damaged or broken oil filter gasket
- Leaking oil pressure sending switch
- Worn rear main oil seal gasket
- Worn front main oil seal gasket
- Damaged or broken fuel pump gasket (mechanical pump)
- Damaged or loose valve cover gasket
- Damaged oil pan gasket or bent oil pan
- Improperly seated oil pan drain plug
- Broken timing chain cover gasket
- Blocked camshaft bearing drain hole

Heavy Oil Consumption

When the engine is burning large amounts of oil, check for the following, as necessary:
- Engine oil level that is too high
- Engine oil that is too thin
- Wrong size of piston rings.
- Clogged piston ring grooves or oil return slots
- Insufficient tension of the piston rings
- Piston rings that are sticking in the grooves
- Excessively worn piston ring grooves
- Reversed (up-side-down) compression rings
- Non-staggered piston ring gaps
- Improper Positive Crankcase Ventilation (PCV) valve operation
- Damaged valve O-ring seals
- Restricted oil drain back holes
- Worn valve stem or guides
- Damaged valve stem oil deflectors
- Too long intake gasket dowels
- Mismatched rail and expander of the oil ring
- Excessive clearance of the main and connecting rods
- Scored or worn cylinder walls

Negative Oil Pressure

When the engine presents no oil pressure, check for the following, as necessary:
- Low oil level in the crankcase
- Broken oil pressure gauge or sender
- Blocked oil pump passages
- Blocked oil pickup screen or tube
- Malfunctioning oil pump
- Sticking oil pressure relief valve
- Leakage of the internal oil passages
- Worn (loose) camshaft bearings

Low Oil Pressure

When the engine presents low oil pressure, check for the following, as necessary:
- Low oil level in the crankcase
- Blocked oil pickup screen or tube
- Malfunctioning or excessive clearance of the oil pump
- Sticking oil pressure relief valve
- Very thin engine oil
- Worn (loose) main, rod or camshaft bearings

High Oil Pressure

When the engine presents high oil pressure, check for the following, as necessary:
- Sticking (closed) oil pressure relief valve
- Wrong grade of oil
- Faulty oil pressure gauge or sender

Knocking Main Bearings

When the main bearings are constantly making noise, check for the following, as necessary:
- Oval shaped crankshaft journals
- Loose torque converter or flywheel mounting bolts
- Loose damper pulley hub
- Excessive clearance of the main bearings
- Excessive belt tension
- Low oil supply to the main bearings
- Extreme crankshaft end-play

Knocking Connecting Rods

When the connecting rod bearings are constantly making noise, check for the following, as necessary:
- Misaligned connecting rod or cap
- Missing bearing shell or excessive bearing clearance
- Incorrectly torqued connecting rod bolts
- Connecting rod journal of the crankshaft is out-of-round

Knocking Pistons and Rings

When the pistons and/rings are constantly making noise, check for the following, as necessary:
- Misaligned connecting rods
- Out-of-round or tapered cylinder bore
- Loose or tight ring side clearance
- Build-up of carbon on the piston(s)
- Piston-to-cylinder bore clearance is excessive
- Broken piston rings
- Loose or seized piston pin(s)

Knocking Valve Train

When the valve train is constantly making noise, check for the following, as necessary:
- Loose rocker arms
- Dirt or chips in the valve lifters
- Excessive valve stem-to-guide clearance
- Restrictions in valve lifter oil holes
- Incorrect valve lifter(s)
- Missing valve lock(s)
- Faulty valve lifter check ball
- Excessive valve lifter leak down
- Reversed rocker arm nut (installed up-side-down)
- Excessively worn camshaft lobes
- Bent or worn pushrods
- Excessively worn bridged pivots or rocker arms
- Cocked or broken valve springs
- Bent valve(s)
- Worn valve lifter face(s)
- Damaged lifter plunger or pushrod seat

Knocking Valves

When the valves are constantly noisy, check for the following, as necessary:
- Unadjusted valve lash
- Broken valve springs
- Bent pushrods
- Excessively worn camshaft lobes
- Dirty or worn valve lifters
- Worn valve guides
- Excessive valve seat or face run-out
- Loose rocker arm studs

TORQUE SPECIFICATIONS

Component			US	Metric
Cylinder Head				
	2.0L	1st step:	18 ft. lbs.	25 Nm
		2nd step:	Plus 60 degree turn	
		3rd step:	Plus 60 degree turn (to 120 degrees)	
		4th step:	Plus 60 degree turn (to 180 degrees)	
		5th step:	After engine is warmed up, tighten an additional 30-50 degrees	
	2.3L			
		1988-89	26 ft. lbs.	35 Nm
			Tighten short bolts an additional 80 degrees and long bolts 90 degrees	
		1990-91	26 ft. lbs.	35 Nm
			Tighten short bolts an additional 100 degrees and long bolts 110 degrees	
		1992		
		1st step:	bolts #1-6 26 ft. lbs.	35 Nm
			bolts #7-8 15 ft. lbs.	20 Nm
			bolts #9-10 22 ft. lbs.	30 Nm
		2nd step:	Tighten an additional 90 degrees	
		3rd step:	Loosen 1 turn, retighten to specifications	
		4th step:	Tighten an additional 90 degrees	
		1993-95		
		1st step:	bolts # 1-8 30 ft. lbs.	40 Nm
			bolts # 9-10 26 ft. lbs.	35 Nm
		2nd step:	Tighten all bolts and additional 90 degrees	
	2.5L	1986-87		
		1st step:		
		2nd step:	22 ft. lbs. except bolt #9	30 Nm
		3rd step:	Tighten #9 to 29 ft. lbs.	40 Nm
		4th step:	Plus 120 degree turn, except #9	
		5th step:	Tighten #9 an additional 120 degree turn	
		1989-91		
		1st step:	18 ft. lbs.	25 Nm
		2nd step:	26 ft. lbs. except bolt #9	35 Nm
		3rd step:	Retighten bolt #9 to 18 ft. lbs.	25 Nm
		4th step:	Tighten an additional 90 degrees	
	3.0L			
		1st step:	25 ft. lbs.	34 Nm
		2nd step:	Tighten an additional 90 degrees	
		3rd step:	An additional 90 degrees to a maximum torque of 60 ft. lbs.	81 Nm
	3.1L			
		1st step:	33 ft. lbs.	45 Nm
		2nd step:	Tighten an additional 90 degrees	
	3.3L			
		1st step:	35 ft. lbs.	47 Nm
		2nd step:	Tighten an additional 130 degrees	
		3rd step:	Tighten the 4 center bolts an additional 30 degrees	
Engine Coolant Temperature (ECT) Sensor				
	All engines except 3.1L and 1993 3.3L		22 ft. lbs.	30 Nm
	3.1L		10 ft. lbs.	14 Nm
	1993 3.3L		18 ft. lbs.	24 Nm
Exhaust Manifold				
	2.0L	studs	20 ft. lbs.	27 Nm

86883700

TORQUE SPECIFICATIONS

Component			US	Metric
Exhaust Manifold	2.0L	nuts	16 ft. lbs.	22 Nm
	2.3L			
		1988–89	27 ft. lbs.	37 Nm
		1990–95		
		studs	106 inch lbs.	12 Nm
		nuts	31 ft. lbs.	42 Nm
	2.5L			
		outside	26 ft. lbs.	35 Nm
		inside	37 ft. lbs.	50 Nm
	3.0L		37 ft. lbs.	50 Nm
	3.1L		12 ft. lbs.	16 Nm
	3.3L			
		studs	30 ft. lbs.	41 Nm
		nuts	19 ft. lbs.	26 Nm
Intake Manifold				
	2.0L		18 ft. lbs.	25 Nm
	2.3L		19 ft. lbs.	26 Nm
	2.5L		25 ft. lbs.	34 Nm
	3.0L		32 ft. lbs.	44 Nm
	3.1L			
		lower manifold bolts	115 inch lbs.	13 ft. lbs
		upper manifold bolts	18 ft. lbs.	25 Nm
	3.3L			
		(tighten two times)	89 inch lbs.	10 Nm
Oil Pan				
	2.0L		4 ft. lbs.	5 Nm
	2.3L	1988–91	17 ft. lbs.	24 Nm
		1992–95		
		baffle bolts and studs	30 ft. lbs.	44 Nm
	2.5L			
		1985–88	20 ft. lbs.	27 Nm
		1989–91	89 inch lbs.	10 Nm
	3.0L		89 inch lbs.	10 Nm
	3.1L			
		flange bolts	18 ft. lbs.	25 Nm
		side bolts	37 ft. lbs.	50 Nm
	3.3L		124 inch lbs.	14 Nm
Oil Pump				
	2.0L		5 ft. lbs.	7 Nm
	2.3L		33 ft. lbs.	45 Nm
	2.5L		10 ft. lbs.	14 Nm
	3.0L and 3.3L		97 inch lbs.	11 Nm
	3.1L		30 ft. lbs.	41 Nm
Rocker Arm/Valve Cover				
	2.0L		6 ft. lbs.	8 Nm
	2.3L			
		1st step:	11 ft. lbs.	15 Nm
		2nd step:	Plus 90 degrees for 82A bolts and or 30 degrees for 82B bolts	
	2.5L		80 inch lbs.	9 Nm
	3.0L and 3.3L		88 inch lbs.	10 Nm
	3.1L		90 inch lbs.	10 Nm

86883701

TORQUE SPECIFICATIONS

Component	US	Metric
Rocker Arms		
2.5L	24 ft. lbs.	32 Nm
3.0L	45 ft. lbs.	60 Nm
3.1L	18 ft. lbs.	24 Nm
3.3	18 ft. lbs.	24 Nm
	plus an additional 70 degree turn	
Thermostat Housing		
2.3L	19 ft. lbs.	26 Nm
2.5L	20 ft. lbs.	27 Nm
3.0L	22 ft. lbs.	30 Nm
3.1L	18 ft. lbs.	25 Nm
3.3L	20 ft. lbs.	27 Nm
Timing Belt Front Cover		
2.0L	89 inch lbs.	10 Nm
Timing Chain Front Cover		
2.3L	21 ft. lbs.	29 ft. lbs.
2.5L		
1990-91	89 inch lbs.	10 Nm
3.0L and 3.3L	22 ft. lbs.	30 Nm
3.1L	15 ft. lbs.	21 Nm
Timing Gear Front Cover		
2.5L		
1986-89	89 inch lbs.	10 Nm
Turbocharger		
2.0L	18 ft. lbs.	24 Nm
Water Pump		
2.0L	18 ft. lbs.	24 Nm
2.3L		
pump-to-chain housing nuts	19 ft. lbs.	26 Nm
pump cover-to-pump	106 inch lbs.	12 Nm
cover-to-block (bottom bolt first)	19 ft. lbs.	26 Nm
outlet pipe-to-cover	125 inch lbs.	14 Nm
2.5L	25 ft. lbs.	34 Nm
3.0L and 3.3L	9.6 ft. lbs.	13 Nm
3.1L	89 inch lbs.	10 Nm

86883702

ENGINE REBUILDING SPECIFICATIONS

Component		US	Metric
Bore x Stroke			
2.0L		3.39 x 3.39 in.	86.1 x 86.1 mm
2.3L		3.63 x 3.35 in.	92.2 x 85.1 mm
2.5L		4.00 x 3.00 in.	101.6 x 76.2 mm
3.0L		3.80 x 2.70 in.	96.5 x 68.6 mm
3.1L		3.51 x 3.31 in.	89.2 x 84.1 mm
3.3L		3.70 x 3.16 in.	93.9 x 80.3 mm
Camshaft End Play			
2.0L		0.0016-0.0064 in.	0.0406-0.1626 mm
2.3L		0.0060-0.0140 in.	0.1524-0.3556 mm
2.5L		0.0015-0.0060 in.	0.0381-0.1524 mm
Camshaft Journal-to-Bearing Clearance			
2.0L		0.0008-0.0032 in.	0.0203-0.0813 mm
2.3L		0.0019-0.0043 in.	0.0483-0.1092 mm
2.5L		0.0007-0.0027 in.	0.0178-0.0686 mm
3.0L		0.0005-0.0025 in.	0.0127-0.0686 mm
3.1L		0.0010-0.0040 in.	0.0254-0.1016 mm
3.8L		0.0005-0.0035 in.	0.0127-0.0889 mm
Camshaft Lobe Lift			
2.0L			
	Intake	0.241 in.	6.121 mm
	Exhaust	0.241 in.	6.121 mm
2.3L			
	1988-89 VIN D		
	Intake	0.340 in.	8.636 mm
	Exhaust	0.350 in.	8.890 mm
	1990-93 VIN D		
	Intake	0.375 in.	9.525 mm
	Exhaust	0.375 in.	9.525 mm
	VIN A, 3 and 1994-95 D		
	Intake	0.410 in.	10.414 mm
	Exhaust	0.410 in.	10.414 mm
2.5L			
	1985		
	Intake	0.398 in.	10.109 mm
	Exhaust	0.398 in.	10.109 mm
	1986-89		
	Intake	0.232 in.	5.893 mm
	Exhaust	0.232 in.	5.893 mm
	1990-91		
	Intake	0.248 in.	6.299 mm
	Exhaust	0.248 in.	6.299 mm
3.0L			
	Intake	0.358 in.	9.093 mm
	Exhaust	0.384 in.	9.753 mm
3.1L			
	Intake	0.2727 in.	6.926 mm
	Exhaust	0.2727 in.	6.926 mm
3.3L			
	Intake	0.250 in.	6.350 mm
	Exhaust	0.255 in.	6.477 mm

86883703

ENGINE REBUILDING SPECIFICATIONS

Component	US	Metric
Connecting Rod OIl Clearance		
2.5L	0.0008-0.0014 in.	0.0203-0.0355 mm
3.0L	0.0010-0.0014 in.	0.0254-0.0355 mm
3.0L/3.2L SHO	0.0009-0.0022 in.	0.0229-0.0559 mm
3.8L	0.0010-0.0014 in.	0.0254-0.0355 mm
Connecting Rod-to-Crankshaft Side Clearance		
2.0L	0.0007-0.0024 in.	0.0178-0.0609 mm
2.3L	0.0005-0.0025 in.	0.0127-0.0635 mm
2.5L		
1985-89	0.0005-0.0026 in.	0.0127-0.0660 mm
1990-91	0.0005-0.0030 in.	0.0127-0.0762 mm
1993-95	0.0063-0.0138 in.	0.1600-0.3505 mm
3.0L	0.0005-0.0026 in.	0.0127-0.0609 mm
3.1L	0.0011-0.0037 in.	0.0279-0.0939 mm
3.3L	0.0008-0.0022 in.	0.0203-0.0559 mm
Connecting Rod Journal Diameter		
2.0L	1.9279-1.9287 in.	48.969-48.989 mm
2.3L	1.8887-1.8897 in.	47.973-47.998 mm
2.5L		
1985-89	1.9995-2.0005 in.	50.673-50.813 mm
1990-91	2.0000 in.	50.800 mm
3.0L	2.4870 in.	63.169 mm
3.1L	1.9987-1.9994 in	50.767-50.785 mm
3.3L	2.2487-2.2499 in.	57.117-57.147 mm
Crankshaft Endplay		
2.0L	0.0003-0.0012 in	
2.3L	0.0034-0.0095 in.	51.994-52.019 mm
2.5L		58.420 mm
1985-89	0.0035-0.0085 in.	
1990-91	0.0059-0.0110 in.	
3.0L	2.4870 in.	63.487 mm
3.1L	0.0024-0.0083 in.	67.241-67.267 mm
3.3L	0.0030-0.0110 in.	63.469-63.495 mm
Cylinder Bore Diameter		
2.0L	3.3852-3.3868 in.	85.985-86.025 mm
2.3L	3.6217-3.6223 in.	91.992-92.008 mm
2.5L	4.0 in.	101.6 mm
3.0L	3.80 in.	96.50 mm
3.1L	3.6220-3.6232 in.	91.998-92.029 mm
3.3L	3.70 in.	93.90 mm
Cylinder Bore Max Taper		
2.0L	0.0005 in.	0.0130 mm
2.3L	0.0003 in.	0.0080 mm
2.5L	0.0050 in.	0.1270 mm
3.0L	0.0050 in.	0.1270 mm
3.1L	0.0008 in.	0.0203 mm
3.3L	0.0005 in.	0.0130 mm
Cylinder Bore Out-Of-Round (Max.)		
2.0L	0.0005 in.	0.0130 mm
2.3L	0.0004 in	0.0100 mm
2.5L	0.0010 in.	0.0254 mm

ENGINE REBUILDING SPECIFICATIONS

Component		US	Metric
Cylinder Bore Out-Of-Round (Max.)			
3.0L		0.00039 in.	0.0100 mm
3.1L		0.0005 in.	0.0140 mm
3.3L		0.0004 in.	0.0100 mm
Main Bearing Journal Diameter			
2.0L			
	Brown	2.2830-2.2833 in	57.988-57.996 mm
	Green	2.2827-2.2830 in.	57.980-57.988 mm
2.3L		2.0470-2.0480 in.	51.994-52.019 mm
2.5L		2.3000 in.	58.420 mm
3.0L		2.4995 in.	63.487 mm
3.1L		2.6473-2.6483 in.	67.241-67.267 mm
3.3L		2.4988-2.4998 in.	63.469-63.495 mm
Main Bearing Clearance			
2.0L		0.0006-0.0016 in.	0.0152-0.0406 mm
2.3L		0.0005-0.0023 in.	0.0127-0.0584 mm
2.5L		0.0005-0.0022 in.	0.0127-0.0558 mm
3.0L		0.0003-0.0018 in.	0.0076-0.0457 mm
3.1L		0.0012-0.0030 in.	0.0305-0.0762 mm
3.3L		0.0008-0.0022 in.	0.0203-0.0558 mm
Piston-to-Bore or Liner Clearance			
2.0L		0.0012-0.0020 in.	0.0304-0.0508 mm
2.3L		0.0007-0.0020 in.	0.0178-0.0508 mm
2.5L		0.0014-0.0022 in.	0.0355-0.0559 mm
3.0L		0.0010-0.0020 in.	0.0254-0.0508 mm
3.1L		0.0013-0.0027 in.	0.0330-0.0686 mm
3.3L		0.0004-0.0022 in.	0.0102-0.0559 mm
Piston Ring End Gap			
2.0L			
	Top	0.0098-0.0177 in.	0.2489-0.4496 mm
	Bottom	0.0118-0.0197 in.	0.2997-0.5004 mm
	Oil	NA	NA
2.3L			
	Top	0.0138-0.0236 in.	0.3505-0.5994 mm
	Bottom	0.0157-0.0551 in.	0.3988-1.3994 mm
	Oil	0.0020-0.0035 in.	0.0508-0.0889 mm
2.5L			
	Top	0.0100-0.0200 in.	0.2540-0.0508 mm
	Bottom	0.0100-0.0200 in.	0.2540-0.0508 mm
	Oil	0.0200-0.0600 in.	0.0508-1.5240 mm
3.0L			
	Top	0.0130-0.0230 in.	0.3302-0.5842 mm
	Bottom	0.0130-0.0230 in.	0.3302-0.5842 mm
	Oil	0.0150-0.0350 in.	0.3810-0.8890 mm
3.1L			
	Top	0.0071-0.0161 in.	0.1803-0.4089 mm
	Bottom	0.0200-0.0280 in.	0.0508-0.7112 mm
	Oil	0.0098-0.0295 in.	0.2489-0.7493 mm
3.3L			
	Top	0.0100-0.0250 in.	0.2540-0.6350 mm

86883705

ENGINE REBUILDING SPECIFICATIONS

Component		US	Metric
Piston Ring End Gap (cont.)			
3.3L			
	Bottom	0.0100-0.0250 in.	0.2540-0.6350 mm
	Oil	0.0150-0.0550 in.	0.3810-1.3970 mm
Piston Ring Side Clearance			
2.0L			
	Top	0.0024-0.0036 in.	0.0508-0.0914 mm
	Bottom	0.0019-0.0032 in.	0.0482-0.0813 mm
	Oil	NA	NA
2.3L			
	Top	0.0020-0.0039 in.	0.0508-0.0991 mm
	Bottom	0.0016-0.0032 in.	0.0406-0.0813 mm
	Oil	NA	NA
2.5L			
	Top	0.0020-0.0030 in.	0.0508-0.0762 mm
	Bottom	0.0010-0.0030 in.	0.0254-0.0762 mm
	Oil	0.0150-0.0550 in.	0.3810-1.3970 mm
3.0L			
	Top	0.0030-0.0050 in.	0.0762-0.1270 mm
	Bottom	0.0030-0.0050 in.	0.0762-0.1270 mm
	Oil	0.0035 in.	0.0889 mm
3.1L			
	Top	0.0020-0.0035 in.	0.0508-0.0889 mm
	Bottom	0.0020-0.0035 in.	0.0508-0.0889 mm
	Oil	0.0080 in.	0.2032 mm
3.3L			
	Top	0.0013-0.0031 in.	0.0330-0.0787 mm
	Bottom	0.0013-0.0031 in.	0.0330-0.0787 mm
	Oil	0.0081-0.0110 in.	0.02057-0.2794 mm
Valve Face Angle			
2.0L			46 degrees
2.3L			
	Intake		44 degrees
	Exhaust		44.5 degrees
2.5L			45 degrees
3.0L			45 degrees
3.1L			45 degrees
3.3L			45 degrees
Valve Seat Angle			
2.0L			45 degrees
2.3L			45 degrees
2.5L			46 degrees
3.0L			45 degrees
3.1L			45 degrees
3.3L			45 degrees
Valve Spring Pressure (closed)			
2.0L		74-82 lbs. @ 1.48 in.	34-37 kg @ 38 mm
2.3L		71-79 lbs. @ 1.44 in.	32-36 kg @ 51 mm
2.5L			
	1985-88	71-78 lbs. @ 1.44 in.	32-35 kg @ 37 mm
	1989-91	75 lbs. @ 1.68 in.	34 kg @ 42.7 mm

86883706

ENGINE REBUILDING SPECIFICATIONS

Component		US	Metric
Valve Spring Pressure (closed) cont.			
3.0L		93 lbs. @ 1.73 in.	42 kg @ 43.9 mm
3.1L		80 lbs. @ 1.71 in.	36 kg @ 43.4 mm
3.3L		80 lbs. @ 1.75 in.	36 kg @ 44.5 mm
Valve Spring Installed Height			
2.0L		1.476 in.	37.49 mm
2.3L		1.437 in.	36.50 mm
2.5L			
	1985-88	1.440 in	36.58 mm
	1989-91	1.680 in.	42.67 mm
3.0L		1.727 in.	43.87 mm
3.1L		1.710 in.	43.43 mm
3.3L		1.690-1.720 in.	42.93-43.69 mm
Valve Stem-to-Guide Clearance			
2.0L			
	Intake	0.0006-0.0017 in.	0.0152-0.0432 mm
	Exhaust	0.0012-0.0024 in.	0.0305-0.0610 mm
2.3L			
	Intake	0.0010-0.0027 in.	0.0254-0.0686 mm
	Exhaust	0.0015-0.0032 in.	0.0381-0.0813 mm
2.5L			
	Intake	0.0010-0.0026 in.	0.0254-0.0660 mm
	Exhaust	0.0013-0.0041 in.	0.0330-0.1041 mm
3.0L			
	Intake	0.0015-0.0035 in.	0.0381-0.0889 mm
	Exhaust	0.0015-0.0032 in.	0.0381-0.0813 mm
3.1L			
	Intake	0.0010-0.0027 in.	0.0254-0.0432 mm
	Exhaust	0.0010-0.0027 in.	0.0254-0.0432 mm
3.3L			
	Intake	0.0015-0.0035 in.	0.0381-0.0889 mm
	Exhaust	0.0015-0.0035 in.	0.0381-0.0889 mm

86883707

AIR POLLUTION
  AUTOMOTIVE POLLUTANTS 4-2
  INDUSTRIAL POLLUTANTS 4-2
  INTERNAL COMBUSTION ENGINE
    POLLUTANTS 4-3
  NATURAL POLLUTANTS 4-2
  TEMPERATURE INVERSION 4-2
AUTOMOTIVE EMISSIONS
  CRANKCASE EMISSIONS 4-5
  EVAPORATIVE EMISSIONS 4-5
  EXHAUST GASES 4-3
DIAGNOSTIC TROUBLE CODES AND
  CHARTS 4-27
ELECTRONIC ENGINE CONTROLS
  ENGINE COOLANT TEMPERATURE
    (ECT) SENSOR 4-17
  ENGINE/POWERTRAIN CONTROL
    MODULE (ECM/PCM) 4-16
  ESC KNOCK SENSOR (KS) 4-23
  IDLE AIR CONTROL (IAC)
    VALVE 4-18
  MANIFOLD ABSOLUTE PRESSURE
    (MAP) SENSOR 4-20
  MANIFOLD AIR TEMPERATURE
    (MAT)/INTAKE AIR TEMPERATURE
    (IAT) SENSOR 4-20
  MASS AIR FLOW (MAF)
    SENSOR 4-20
  OPERATION 4-16
  OXYGEN (O_2) SENSOR 4-20
  THROTTLE POSITION SENSOR
    (TPS) 4-22
  VEHICLE SPEED SENSOR
    (VSS) 4-23
EMISSION CONTROLS
  CATALYTIC CONVERTER 4-14
  CRANKCASE VENTILATION
    SYSTEM 4-6
  EVAPORATIVE EMISSION CONTROL
    SYSTEM 4-7
  EXHAUST GAS RECIRCULATION
    SYSTEM 4-8
SELF-DIAGNOSTIC SYSTEMS
  DASHBOARD WARNING LAMP 4-24
  DIAGNOSIS AND TESTING 4-25
  GENERAL INFORMATION 4-24
  INTERMITTENTS 4-24
  LEARNING ABILITY 4-24
  TOOLS AND EQUIPMENT 4-25
VACUUM DIAGRAMS 4-117

4

EMISSION CONTROLS

AIR POLLUTION 4-2
AUTOMOTIVE EMISSIONS 4-3
DIAGNOSTIC TROUBLE CODES
AND CHARTS 4-27
ELECTRONIC ENGINE CONTROLS 4-16
EMISSION CONTROLS 4-6
SELF-DIAGNOSTIC SYSTEMS 4-24
VACUUM DIAGRAMS 4-117

AIR POLLUTION

The earth's atmosphere, at or near sea level, consists of 78% nitrogen, 21% oxygen and 1% other gases, approximately. If it were possible to remain in this state, 100% clean air would result. However, many varied causes allow other gases and particulates to mix with the clean air, causing the air to become unclean or polluted.

Certain of these pollutants are visible while others are invisible, with each having the capability of causing distress to the eyes, ears, throat, skin and respiratory system. Should these pollutants be concentrated in a specific area and under the right conditions, death could result due to the displacement or chemical change of the oxygen content in the air. These pollutants can cause much damage to the environment and to the many man made objects that are exposed to the elements.

To better understand the causes of air pollution, the pollutants can be categorized into 3 separate types: natural, industrial and automotive.

Natural Pollutants

Natural pollution has been present on earth before man appeared and is still a factor to be considered when discussing air pollution, although it causes only a small percentage of the present overall pollution problem existing in our country. It is the direct result of decaying organic matter, wind born smoke and particulates from such natural events as plains and forest fires (ignited by heat or lightning), volcanic ash, sand and dust which can spread over a large area of the countryside.

Such a phenomenon of natural pollution has been recent volcanic eruptions, with the resulting plume of smoke, steam and volcanic ash blotting out the sun's rays as it spreads and rises higher into the atmosphere, where the upper air currents catch and carry the smoke and ash, while condensing the steam back into water vapor. As the water vapor, smoke and ash traveled on their journey, the smoke dissipates into the atmosphere while the ash and moisture settle back to earth in a trail hundred of miles long. In many cases, lives are lost and millions of dollars of property damage result, and ironically, man can only stand by and watch it happen.

Industrial Pollutants

Industrial pollution is caused primarily by industrial processes, the burning of coal, oil and natural gas, which in turn produces smoke and fumes. Because the burning fuels contain much sulfur, the principal ingredients of smoke and fumes are sulfur dioxide (SO_2) and particulate matter. This type of pollutant occurs most severely during still, damp and cool weather, such as at night. Even in its less severe form, this pollutant is not confined to just cities. Because of air movements, the pollutants move for miles over the surrounding countryside, leaving in its path a barren and unhealthy environment for all living things.

Working with Federal, State and Local mandated rules, regulations and by carefully monitoring the emissions, industries have greatly reduced the amount of pollutant emitted from their industrial sources, striving to obtain an acceptable level. Because of the mandated industrial emission clean up, many land areas and streams in and around the cities that were formerly barren of vegetation and life, have now begun to move back in the direction of nature's intended balance.

Automotive Pollutants

The third major source of air pollution is the automotive emissions. The emissions from the internal combustion engine were not an appreciable problem years ago because of the small number of registered vehicles and the nation's small highway system. However, during the early 1950's, the trend of the American people was to move from the cities to the surrounding suburbs. This caused an immediate problem in the transportation areas because the majority of the suburbs were not afforded mass transit conveniences. This lack of transportation created an attractive market for the automobile manufacturers, which resulted in a dramatic increase in the number of vehicles produced and sold, along with a marked increase in highway construction between cities and the suburbs. Multi-vehicle families emerged with much emphasis placed on the individual vehicle per family member. As the increase in vehicle ownership and usage occurred, so did the pollutant levels in and around the cities, as the suburbanites drove daily to their businesses and employment in the city and its fringe area, returning at the end of the day to their homes in the suburbs.

It was noted that a fog and smoke type haze was being formed and at times, remained in suspension over the cities and did not quickly dissipate. At first this "smog," derived from the words "smoke" and "fog," was thought to result from industrial pollution but it was determined that the automobile emissions were largely to blame. It was discovered that as normal automobile emissions were exposed to sunlight for a period of time, complex chemical reactions would take place.

It was found the smog was a photo chemical layer and was developed when certain oxides of nitrogen (NOx) and unburned hydrocarbons (HC) from the automobile emissions were exposed to sunlight and was more severe when the smog would remain stagnant over an area in which a warm layer of air would settle over the top of a cooler air mass at ground level, trapping and holding the automobile emissions, instead of the emissions being dispersed and diluted through normal air flows. This type of air stagnation was given the name "Temperature Inversion."

Temperature Inversion

In normal weather situations, the surface air is warmed by the heat radiating from the earth's surface and the sun's rays and will rise upward, into the atmosphere, to be cooled through a convection type heat expands with the cooler upper air. As the warm air rises, the surface pollutants are carried upward and dissipated into the atmosphere.

When a temperature inversion occurs, we find the higher air is no longer cooler but warmer than the surface air, causing the cooler surface air to become trapped and unable to move. This warm air blanket can extend from above ground level to a few hundred or even a few thousand feet into the air. As the surface air is trapped, so are the pollutants, causing a severe smog condition. Should this stagnant air mass extend to a few thousand feet high, enough air movement with the inversion takes place to allow the smog layer to rise above ground level but the pollutants still cannot dissipate. This inversion can remain for days over an area, with only the smog level rising or lowering from ground level to a few hundred feet high. Meanwhile, the pollutant levels increases, causing eye irritation, respirator problems, reduced visibility, plant damage and in some cases, cancer type diseases.

This inversion phenomenon was first noted in the Los Angeles, California area. The city lies in a basin type of terrain and during certain weather conditions, a cold air mass is held in the basin while a warmer air mass covers it like a lid.

Because this type of condition was first documented as prevalent in the Los Angeles area, this type of smog was named Los Angeles Smog, although it occurs in other areas where a large concentration of automobiles are used and the air remains stagnant for any length of time.

Internal Combustion Engine Pollutants

Consider the internal combustion engine as a machine in which raw materials must be placed so a finished product comes out. As in any machine operation, a certain amount of wasted material is formed. When we relate this to the internal combustion engine, we find that by putting in air and fuel, we obtain power from this mixture during the combustion process to drive the vehicle. The by-product or waste of this power is, in part, heat and exhaust gases with which we must concern ourselves.

AUTOMOTIVE EMISSIONS

Before emission controls were mandated on the internal combustion engines, other sources of engine pollutants were discovered, along with the exhaust emission. It was determined the engine combustion exhaust produced 60% of the total emission pollutants, fuel evaporation from the fuel tank and carburetor vents produced 20%, with the another 20% being produced through the crankcase as a by-product of the combustion process.

Exhaust Gases

The exhaust gases emitted into the atmosphere are a combination of burned and unburned fuel. To understand the exhaust emission and its composition review some basic chemistry.

When the air/fuel mixture is introduced into the engine, we are mixing air, composed of nitrogen (78%), oxygen (21%) and other gases (1%) with the fuel, which is 100% hydrocarbons (HC), in a semi-controlled ratio. As the combustion process is accomplished, power is produced to move the vehicle while the heat of combustion is transferred to the cooling system. The exhaust gases are then composed of nitrogen, a diatomic gas (N_2), the same as was introduced in the engine, carbon dioxide (CO_2), the same gas that is used in beverage carbonation and water vapor (H_2O). The nitrogen (N_2), for the

HEAT TRANSFER

The heat from the combustion process can rise to over 4000°F (2204°C). The dissipation of this heat is controlled by a ram air effect, the use of cooling fans to cause air flow and having a liquid coolant solution surrounding the combustion area and transferring the heat of combustion through the cylinder walls and into the coolant. The coolant is then directed to a thin-finned, multi-tubed radiator, from which the excess heat is transferred to the outside air by one or all of the 3 heat transfer methods: conduction, convection or radiation.

The cooling of the combustion area is an important part in the control of exhaust emissions. To understand the behavior of the combustion and transfer of its heat, consider the air/fuel charge. It is ignited and the flame front burns progressively across the combustion chamber until the burning charge reaches the cylinder walls. Some of the fuel in contact with the walls is not hot enough to burn, thereby snuffing out or quenching the combustion process. This leaves unburned fuel in the combustion chamber. This unburned fuel is then forced out of the cylinder along with the exhaust gases and into the exhaust system.

Many attempts have been made to minimize the amount of unburned fuel in the combustion chambers due to the snuffing out or quenching, by increasing the coolant temperature and lessening the contact area of the coolant around the combustion area. Design limitations within the combustion chambers prevent the complete burning of the air/fuel charge, so a certain amount of the unburned fuel is still expelled into the exhaust system, regardless of modifications to the engine.

most part passes through the engine unchanged, while the oxygen (O_2) reacts (burns) with the hydrocarbons (HC) and produces the carbon dioxide (CO_2) and the water vapors (H_2O). If this chemical process would be the only process to take place, the exhaust emissions would be harmless. However, during the combustion process, other pollutants are formed and are considered dangerous. These pollutants are carbon monoxide (CO), hydrocarbons (HC), oxides of nitrogen (NOx) oxides of sulfur (SOx) and engine particulates.

Lead (Pb), is considered 1 of the particulates and is present in the exhaust gases whenever leaded fuels are used. Lead (Pb) does not dissipate easily. Levels can be high along roadways when it is emitted from vehicles and can pose a health threat. Since the increased usage of unleaded gasoline and the phasing out of leaded gasoline for fuel, this pollutant is gradually diminishing. While not considered a major threat lead is still considered a dangerous pollutant.

HYDROCARBONS

Hydrocarbons (HC) are essentially unburned fuel that have not been successfully burned during the combustion process or have escaped into the atmosphere through fuel evaporation. The main sources of incomplete combustion are rich air/fuel mixtures, low engine temperatures and improper spark timing.

The main sources of hydrocarbon emission through fuel evaporation come from the vehicle's fuel tank and carburetor bowl.

To reduce combustion hydrocarbon emission, engine modifications were made to minimize dead space and surface area in the combustion chamber. In addition the air/fuel mixture was made more lean through improved carburetion, fuel injection and by the addition of external controls to aid in further combustion of the hydrocarbons outside the engine. Two such methods were the addition of an air injection system, to inject fresh air into the exhaust manifolds and the installation of a catalytic converter, a unit that is able to burn traces of hydrocarbons without affecting the internal combustion process or fuel economy.

To control hydrocarbon emissions through fuel evaporation, modifications were made to the fuel tank and carburetor bowl to allow storage of the fuel vapors during periods of engine shut-down, and at specific times during engine operation, to purge and burn these same vapors by blending them with the air/fuel mixture.

CARBON MONOXIDE

Carbon monoxide is formed when not enough oxygen is present during the combustion process to convert carbon (C) to carbon dioxide (CO_2). An increase in the carbon monoxide (CO) emission is normally accompanied by an increase in the hydrocarbon (HC) emission because of the lack of oxygen to completely burn all of the fuel mixture.

Carbon monoxide (CO) also increases the rate at which the photochemical smog is formed by speeding up the conversion of nitric oxide (NO) to nitrogen dioxide (NO_2). To accomplish this, carbon monoxide (CO) combines with oxygen (O_2) and nitric oxide (NO) to produce carbon dioxide (CO_2) and nitrogen dioxide (NO_2). ($CO + O_2S + NO = CO_2 + NO_2$).

The dangers of carbon monoxide, which is an odorless, colorless toxic gas are many. When carbon monoxide is inhaled into the lungs and passed into the blood stream, oxygen is replaced by the carbon monoxide in the red blood cells, causing a reduction in the amount of oxygen being supplied to the many parts of the body. This lack of oxygen causes headaches, lack of coordination, reduced mental alertness and should the carbon monoxide concentration be high enough, death could result.

NITROGEN

Normally, nitrogen is an inert gas. When heated to approximately 2500°F (1371°C) through the combustion process, this gas becomes active and causes an increase in the nitric oxide (NOx) emission.

Oxides of nitrogen (NOx) are composed of approximately 97-98% nitric oxide (NO_2). Nitric oxide is a colorless gas but when it is passed into the atmosphere, it combines with oxygen and forms nitrogen dioxide (NO_2). The nitrogen dioxide then combines with chemically active hydrocarbons (HC) and when in the presence of sunlight, causes the formation of photo chemical smog.

OZONE

To further complicate matters, some of the nitrogen dioxide (NO_2) is broken apart by the sunlight to form nitric oxide and oxygen. (NO_2 + sunlight = NO + O). This single atom of oxygen then combines with diatomic (meaning 2 atoms) oxygen (O_2S) to form ozone (O_3). Ozone is 1 of the smells associated with smog. It has a pungent and offensive odor, irritates the eyes and lung tissues, affects the growth of plant life and causes rapid deterioration of rubber products. Ozone can be formed by sunlight as well as electrical discharge into the air.

The most common discharge area on the automobile engine is the secondary ignition electrical system, especially when inferior quality spark plug cables are used. As the surge of high voltage is routed through the secondary cable, the circuit builds up an electrical field around the wire, acting upon the oxygen in the surrounding air to form the ozone. The faint glow along the cable with the engine running that may be visible on a dark night, is called the "corona discharge." It is the result of the electrical field passing from a high along the cable, to a low in the surrounding air, which forms the ozone gas. The combination of corona and ozone has been a major cause of cable deterioration. Recently, different types and better quality insulating materials have lengthened the life of the electrical cables.

Although ozone at ground level can be harmful, ozone is beneficial to the earth's inhabitants. By having a concentrated ozone layer called the "ozonosphere," between 10 and 20 miles (16-32 km) up in the atmosphere much of the ultra violet radiation from the sun's rays are absorbed and screened. If this ozone layer were not present, much of the earth's surface would be burned, dried and unfit for human life.

There is much discussion concerning the ozone layer and its density. A feeling exists that this protective layer of ozone is slowly diminishing and corrective action must be directed to this problem. Much experimenting is presently being conducted to determine if a problem exists and if so, the short and long term effects of the problem and how it can be remedied.

OXIDES OF SULFUR

Oxides of sulfur (SOx) were initially ignored in the exhaust system emissions, since the sulfur content of gasoline as a fuel is less than $1/10$ of 1%. Because of this small amount, it was felt that it contributed very little to the overall pollution problem. However, because of the difficulty in solving the sulfur emissions in industrial pollutions and the introduction of catalytic converter to the automobile exhaust systems, a change was mandated. The automobile exhaust system, when equipped with a catalytic converter, changes the sulfur dioxide (SO_2) into the sulfur trioxide (SO_3).

When this combines with water vapors (H_2O), a sulfuric acid mist (H_2SO_4) is formed and is a very difficult pollutant to handle and is extremely corrosive. This sulfuric acid mist that is formed, is the same mist that rises from the vents of an automobile storage battery when an active chemical reaction takes place within the battery cells.

When a large concentration of vehicles equipped with catalytic converters are operating in an area, this acid mist will rise and be distributed over a large ground area causing land, plant, crop, paints and building damage.

PARTICULATE MATTER

A certain amount of particulate matter is present in the burning of any fuel, with carbon constituting the largest percentage of the particulates. In gasoline, the remaining percentage of particulates is the burned remains of the various other compounds used in its manufacture. When a gasoline engine is in good internal condition, the particulate emissions are low but as the engine wears internally, the particulate emissions increase. By visually inspecting the tail pipe emissions, a determination can be made as to where an engine defect may exist. An engine with light gray smoke emitting from the tail pipe normally indicates an increase in the oil consumption through burning due to internal engine wear. Black smoke would indicate a defective fuel delivery system, causing the engine to operate in a rich mode. Regardless of the color of the smoke, the internal part of the engine or the fuel delivery system should be repaired to a "like new" condition to prevent excess particulate emissions.

Diesel and turbine engines emit a darkened plume of smoke from the exhaust system because of the type of fuel used. Emission control regulations are mandated for this type of emission and more stringent measures are being used to prevent excess emission of the particulate matter. Electronic components are being introduced to control the injection of the fuel at precisely the proper time of piston travel, to achieve the optimum in fuel ignition and fuel usage. Other particulate after-burning components are being tested to achieve a cleaner particular emission.

Good grades of engine lubricating oils should be used, meeting the manufacturers specification. "Cut-rate" oils can contribute to the particulate emission problem because of their low "flash" or ignition temperature point. Such oils burn prematurely during the combustion process causing emissions of particulate matter.

The cooling system is an important factor in the reduction of particulate matter. With the cooling system operating at a temperature specified by the manufacturer, the optimum of combustion will occur. The cooling system must be maintained in the same manner as the engine oiling system, as each system is required to perform properly in order for the engine to operate efficiently for a long time.

Crankcase Emissions

Crankcase emissions are made up of water, acids, unburned fuel, oil fumes and particulates. The emissions are classified as hydrocarbons (HC) and are formed by the small amount of unburned, compressed air/fuel mixture entering the crankcase from the combustion area during the compression and power strokes, between the cylinder walls and piston rings. The head of the compression and combustion help to form the remaining crankcase emissions.

Since the first engines, crankcase emissions were allowed to go into the air through a road draft tube, mounted on the lower side of the engine block. Fresh air came in through an open oil filler cap or breather. The air passed through the crankcase mixing with blow-by gases. The motion of the vehicle and the air blowing past the open end of the road draft tube caused a low pressure area at the end of the tube. Crankcase emissions were simply drawn out of the road draft tube into the air.

To control the crankcase emission, the road draft tube was deleted. A hose and/or tubing was routed from the crankcase to the intake manifold so the blow-by emission could be burned with the air/fuel mixture. However, it was found that intake manifold vacuum, used to draw the crankcase emissions into the manifold, would vary in strength at the wrong time and not allow the proper emission flow. A regulating type valve was needed to control the flow of air through the crankcase.

Testing, showed the removal of the blow-by gases from the crankcase as quickly as possible, was most important to the longevity of the engine. Should large accumulations of blow-by gases remain and condense, dilution of the engine oil would occur to form water, soots, resins, acids and lead salts, resulting in the formation of sludge and varnishes. This condensation of the blow-by gases occur more frequently on vehicles used in numerous starting and stopping conditions, excessive idling and when the engine is not allowed to attain normal operating temperature through short runs. The crankcase purge control or PCV system will be described in detail later in this section.

Evaporative Emissions

Gasoline fuel is a major source of pollution, before and after it is burned in the automobile engine. From the time the fuel is refined, stored, pumped and transported, again stored until it is pumped into the fuel tank of the vehicle, the gasoline gives off unburned hydrocarbons (HC) into the atmosphere. Through redesigning of the storage areas and venting systems, the pollution factor has been diminished but not eliminated, from the refinery standpoint. However, the automobile still remained the primary source of vaporized, unburned hydrocarbon (HC) emissions.

Fuel pumped form an underground storage tank is cool but when exposed to a warmer ambient temperature, will expand. Before controls were mandated, an owner would fill the fuel tank with fuel from an underground storage tank and park the vehicle for some time in warm area, such as a parking lot. As the fuel would warm, it would expand and should no provisions or area be provided for the expansion, the fuel would spill out the filler neck and onto the ground, causing hydrocarbon (HC) pollution and creating a severe fire hazard. To correct this condition, the vehicle manufacturers added overflow plumbing and/or gasoline tanks with built in expansion areas or domes.

However, this did not control the fuel vapor emission from the fuel tank and the carburetor bowl. It was determined that most of the fuel evaporation occurred when the vehicle was stationary and the engine not operating. Most vehicles carry 5-25 gallons (19-95 liters) of gasoline. Should a large concentration of vehicles be parked in one area, such as a large parking lot, excessive fuel vapor emissions would take place, increasing as the temperature increases.

To prevent the vapor emission from escaping into the atmosphere, the fuel system is designed to trap the fuel vapors while the vehicle is stationary, by sealing the fuel system from the atmosphere. A storage system is used to collect and hold the fuel vapors from the carburetor and the fuel tank when the engine is not operating. When the engine is started, the storage system is then purged of the fuel vapors, which are drawn into the engine and burned with the air/fuel mixture.

The components of the fuel evaporative system will be described in detail later in this section.

EMISSION CONTROLS

Crankcase Ventilation System

OPERATION

▶ **See Figures 1, 2 and 3**

The Crankcase Ventilation system is used on all vehicles to evacuate the crankcase vapors. There are 2 types of ventilation systems: Crankcase Ventilation (CV) and Positive Crankcase Ventilation (PCV). Both systems purge crankcase vapors and differ only in the use of fresh air.

The CV system, used on the 2.3L and some 2.5L engines, allows crankcase vapors to escape but does not introduce fresh air into the crankcase. However, the CV system on the 3.1L engine, does introduce fresh air into the crankcase.

The PCV system and the CV system on the 3.1L engine, circulates fresh air from the air cleaner or intake duct through the crankcase, where it mixes with blow-by gases and then passes through the Positive Crankcase Ventilation (PCV) valve or constant bleed orifice into the intake manifold.

When manifold vacuum is high, such as at idle, the orifice or valve restricts the flow of blow-by gases into the intake manifold. If abnormal operating conditions occur, the system will allow excessive blow-by gases to back flow through the hose into the air cleaner. These blow-by gases will then be mixed with the intake air in the air cleaner instead of the manifold. The air cleaner has a small filter attached to the inside wall that connects to the breather hose to trap impurities flowing in either direction.

A plugged PCV valve, orifice or hose may cause rough idle, stalling or slow idle speed, oil leaks, oil in the air cleaner or sludge in the engine. A leak could cause rough idle, stalling or high idle speed. The condition of the grommets in the valve cover will also affect system and engine performance.

TESTING

PCV Valve/Constant Bleed Orifice

1. Run the engine at idle at normal operating temperature.
2. Remove the PCV valve or orifice from the grommet in the valve cover and place your thumb over the end to check if vacuum is present. If vacuum is not present, check for plugged hoses or manifold port. Repair or replace as necessary.
3. If the engine is equipped with a PCV valve, stop the engine and remove the valve. Shake and listen for the rattle of the check valve needle. If no rattle is heard, replace the valve.

PCV System/CV System On 3.1L Engines

1. Check to make sure the engine has the correct PCV valve or bleed orifice.

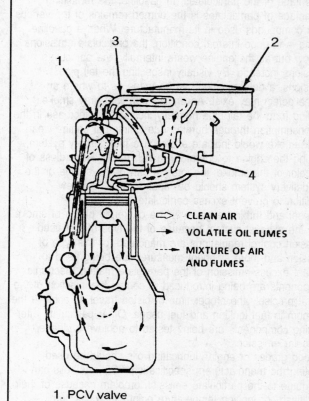

| CLEAN AIR |
| VOLATILE OIL FUMES |
| MIXTURE OF AIR AND FUMES |

1. PCV valve
2. Air cleaner
3. Crankcase vent hose
4. PCV valve hose

86884001

Fig. 1 The PCV system circulates crankcase vapors into the intake manifold for burning — 2.0L and 2.5L engines shown

2. Start the engine and bring to normal operating temperature.
3. Block off PCV system fresh air intake passage.
4. Remove the engine oil dipstick and install a vacuum gauge on the dipstick tube.
5. Run the engine at 1500 rpm for 30 seconds then read the vacuum gauge with the engine at 1500 rpm.
   • If vacuum is present, the PCV system is functioning properly.
   • If there is no vacuum, the engine may not be sealed and/or is drawing in outside air. Check the grommets and valve cover or oil pan gasket for leaks.

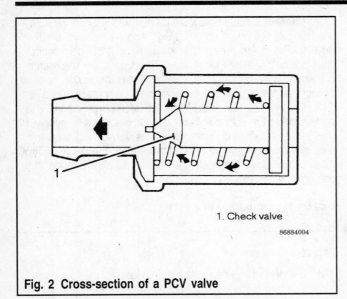

1. Check valve

86884004

Fig. 2 Cross-section of a PCV valve

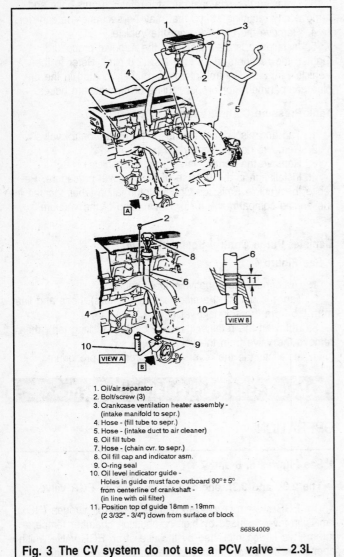

1. Oil/air separator
2. Bolt/screw (3)
3. Crankcase ventilation heater assembly -
   (intake manifold to sepr.)
4. Hose - (fill tube to sepr.)
5. Hose - (intake duct to air cleaner)
6. Oil fill tube
7. Hose - (chain cvr. to sepr.)
8. Oil fill cap and indicator asm.
9. O-ring seal
10. Oil level indicator guide -
    Holes in guide must face outboard 90° ± 5°
    from centerline of crankshaft -
    (in line with oil filter)
11. Position top of guide 18mm - 19mm
    (2 3/32" - 3/4") down from surface of block

86884009

Fig. 3 The CV system do not use a PCV valve — 2.3L engine shown

• If the vacuum gauge registers a pressure or the vacuum gauge is pushed out of the dipstick tube, check for the correct PCV valve or bleed orifice, a plugged hose or excessive engine blow-by.

CV System

1. Check the CV system for proper flow by looking for oil sludging or leaks.
2. If noted, check the smaller nipple of the oil/air separator by blowing through it or inserting a 0.06 in. (1.52mm) plug gauge into the orifice inside the nipple.
3. If the orifice is plugged, replace the CV oil/air separator assembly.

Evaporative Emission Control System

OPERATION

The Evaporative Emission Control System is designed to prevent fuel tank vapors from being emitted into the atmosphere. When the engine is not running, gasoline vapors from the tank are stored in a charcoal canister, mounted under the hood. The charcoal canister absorbs the gasoline vapors and stores them until certain engine conditions are met and the vapors can be purged and burned by the engine. In some vehicles with fuel injection, any liquid fuel entering the canister goes into a reservoir in the bottom of the canister to protect the integrity of the carbon element in the canister above. Three different methods (depending upon application) are used to control the purge cycle of the charcoal canister.

In the first method, the charcoal canister purge cycle is controlled by throttle position without the use of a valve on the canister. A vacuum line connects the canister to a ported vacuum source on the throttle body. When the throttle is at any position above idle, a vacuum is created in the throttle body venturi. That vacuum acts on the canister causing fresh air to be drawn into the bottom of the canister and the fuel vapors to be carried into the throttle body at that vacuum port. The air/vapor flow volume is only what can be drawn through the vacuum port and is fairly constant.

For the second method, the flow volume is modulated with throttle position through a vacuum valve. The ported vacuum from the throttle body is used to open a diaphragm valve on top of the canister. When the valve is open, air and vapors are drawn into the intake manifold, usually through the same manifold port as the PCV system. With this method, the purge valve cycle is slaved to the throttle opening; more throttle opening, more purge air flow.

And third, the charcoal canister purge valve cycle is controlled by the computer control module through a solenoid valve mounted on or remotely from the canister. When the solenoid is activated, full manifold vacuum is applied to the top of the purge valve diaphragm to open the valve all the way. A high volume of fresh air is drawn into the canister and the

gasoline vapors are purged quickly. The ECM activates the solenoid valve when the following conditions are met:
- The engine is at normal operating temperature.
- After the engine has been running a specified period of time.
- Vehicle speed is above a predetermined speed.
- Throttle opening is above a predetermined value.

➡**Remember that the fuel tank filler cap is an integral part of the system in that it was designed to seal in fuel vapors. If it is lost or damaged, make sure the replacement is of the correct size and fit so a proper seal can be obtained.**

A vent pipe allows fuel vapors to flow to the charcoal canister. On some vehicles, the tank is isolated from the charcoal canister by a tank pressure control valve, located either in the tank or in the vapor line near the canister. It is a combination roll-over, integral pressure and vacuum relief valve. When the vapor pressure in the tank exceeds 0.73 psi (5 kPa), the valve opens to allow vapors to vent to the canister. The valve also provides vacuum relief to protect against vacuum build-up in the fuel tank and roll-over spill protection.

Poor engine idle, stalling and poor driveability can be caused by an inoperative canister purge solenoid, a damaged canister or split, damaged or improperly connected hoses.

The most common symptom of problems in this system is fuel odors coming from under the hood. If there is no liquid fuel leak, check for a cracked or damaged vapor canister, inoperative or always open canister control valve, disconnected, mis-routed, kinked or damaged vapor pipe or canister hoses; or a damaged air cleaner or improperly seated air cleaner gasket.

TESTING

Charcoal Canister

1. Visually check the canister for cracks or damage.
2. If fuel is leaking from the bottom of the canister, replace canister and check for proper hose routing.
3. Check the filter at the bottom of the canister. If dirty, replace the filter.

Tank Pressure Control Valve

1. Using a hand-held vacuum pump, apply a vacuum of 15 in. Hg (51 kPa) through the control vacuum signal tube to the purge valve diaphragm. If the diaphragm does not hold vacuum for at least 20 seconds, the diaphragm is leaking. Replace the control valve.
2. With the vacuum still applied to the control vacuum tube, attach a short piece of hose to the valve's tank tube side and blow into the hose. Air should pass through the valve. If it does not, replace the control valve.

Canister Purge Control Valve

1. Connect a clean length of hose to the fuel tank vapor line connection on the canister and attempt to blow through the purge control valve. It should be difficult or impossible to blow through the valve. If air passes easily, the valve is stuck open and should be replaced.

2. Connect a hand-held vacuum pump to the top vacuum line fitting of the purge control valve. Apply a vacuum of 15 in. Hg (51 kPa) to the purge valve diaphragm. If the diaphragm does not hold vacuum for at least 20 seconds the diaphragm is leaking. Replace the control valve. If it is impossible to blow through the valve, it is stuck closed and must be replaced.

3. On vehicles with a solenoid activated purge control valve, unplug the connector and use jumper wires to supply 12 volts to the solenoid connections on the valve. With the vacuum still applied to the control vacuum tube, the purge control valve should open and it should be easy to blow through. If not, replace the valve.

REMOVAL & INSTALLATION

Charcoal Canister

1. Disconnect the negative battery cable.
2. Tag and disconnect the hoses from the canister.
3. Unfasten the charcoal canister retaining nuts/bolts and remove any retaining straps that may be securing the canister.
4. Remove the canister from the vehicle.
5. Installation is the reverse of the removal procedure. Tighten the retainers to 25 inch lbs. (2.8 Nm). Refer to the Vehicle Emission Control Information label, located in the engine compartment, for proper routing of the vacuum hoses.

Tank Pressure Control Valve

1. Tag and disconnect the hoses from the control valve.
2. Remove the mounting hardware.
3. Remove the control valve from the vehicle.
4. Installation is the reverse of the removal procedure. Refer to the Vehicle Emission Control Information label, located in the engine compartment, for proper routing of the vacuum hoses.

Canister Purge Control Solenoid Valve
▶ See Figure 4

1. Disconnect the negative battery cable.
2. Tag and detach the electrical connector(s), hose and line from the from the solenoid valve.
3. Unfasten the retainer (screws, bolts or locking tab), then remove the valve from the vehicle.
4. Installation is the reverse of the removal procedure.

Exhaust Gas Recirculation System

OPERATION

▶ See Figures 5, 6 and 7

➡**The 2.3L and 3.3L engines do not use an EGR valve.**

The EGR system is used to reduce oxides of nitrogen (NOx) emission levels caused by high combustion chamber temperatures. This is accomplished by the use of an EGR valve which opens, under specific engine operating conditions, to admit a small amount of exhaust gas into the intake manifold, below the throttle plate. The exhaust gas mixes with the incoming air charge and displaces a portion of the oxygen in the air/fuel

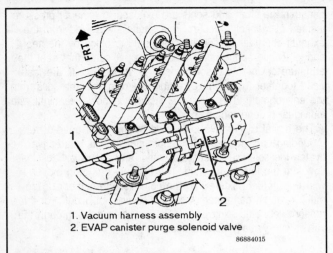

1. Vacuum harness assembly
2. EVAP canister purge solenoid valve

86884015

Fig. 4 View of the solenoid valve assembly mounting — 3.1L engine shown

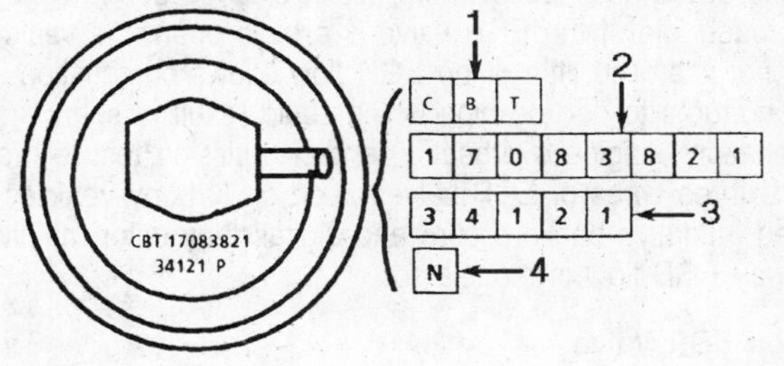

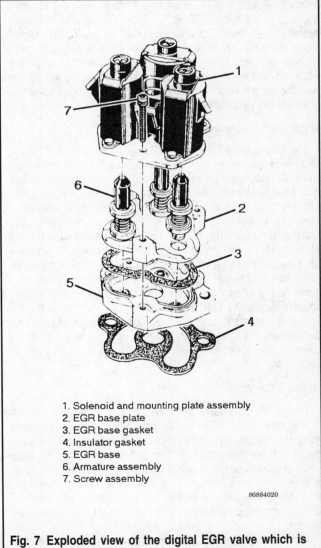

1. Assembly plant code
2. Part number
3. Date built
4. Look here for letter:
   P = Positive back pressure
   N = Negative back pressure
   BLANK = Ported valve

86884017

Fig. 6 Ported and negative back pressure EGR valve identification

mixture entering the combustion chamber. The exhaust gas does not support combustion of the air/fuel mixture but it takes up volume, the net effect of which is to lower the temperature of the combustion process. This lower temperature also helps control detonation.

The EGR valve is a mounted on the intake manifold and has an opening into the exhaust manifold. The EGR valve is opened by ported vacuum and allows exhaust gases to flow into the intake manifold. If too much exhaust gas enters, combustion will not occur. Because of this, very little exhaust gas is allowed to pass through the valve. The EGR system will be activated once the engine reaches normal operating temperature and the EGR valve will open when engine operating conditions are above idle speed and below Wide Open Throttle (WOT). On California vehicles equipped with a Vehicle Speed Sensor (VSS), the EGR valve opens when the VSS signal is greater than 2 mph. The EGR system is deactivated on vehicles equipped with a Transmission Converter Clutch (TCC) when the TCC is engaged.

Too much EGR flow at idle, cruise, or during cold operation may result in the engine stalling after cold start, the engine

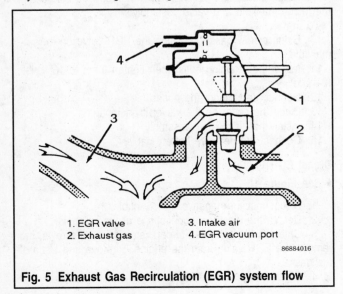

1. EGR valve
2. Exhaust gas
3. Intake air
4. EGR vacuum port

86884016

Fig. 5 Exhaust Gas Recirculation (EGR) system flow

1. Solenoid and mounting plate assembly
2. EGR base plate
3. EGR base gasket
4. Insulator gasket
5. EGR base
6. Armature assembly
7. Screw assembly

86884020

Fig. 7 Exploded view of the digital EGR valve which is used on the 3.1L engine

stalling at idle after deceleration, vehicle surge during cruise and rough idle. If the EGR valve is always open, the vehicle may not idle. Too little or no EGR flow allows combustion temperatures to get too high which could result in spark knock (detonation), engine overheating and/or emission test failure.

The three types of EGR valves used on N body vehicles are ported, negative backpressure and digital; they differ mainly in the way EGR flow is modulated.

Ported EGR Valve

The ported EGR valve, used on the 2.0L and 3.0L engines, takes its name from the fact that it uses a ported vacuum source to open the EGR valve and modulate the EGR flow. The ported vacuum source is a small opening just above the throttle blade in the throttle body. When the throttle begins to open the air passing through the venturi, creates a low pressure which draws on the EGR valve diaphragm causing it to open. As the throttle blade opens further, the ported vacuum increases and opens the valve further.

The ECM controls EGR operation through an EGR control solenoid. Ported vacuum must flow through the EGR control solenoid to open the EGR valve. The ECM uses information received from the Coolant Temperature Sensor (CTS), Throttle Position Sensor (TPS) and the Mass Air Flow (MAF) sensor to determine when to allow EGR operation. When certain parameters are met, such as engine at normal operating temperature and the engine speed is above idle, the ECM signals the solenoid to open, allowing EGR operation.

Negative Backpressure EGR Valve

The negative backpressure EGR valve, used on the 2.5L engine, varies the amount of exhaust gas flow into the intake manifold depending on manifold vacuum and variations in exhaust backpressure. Like the ported EGR valve, the negative backpressure EGR valve uses a ported vacuum source. An air bleed valve, located inside the EGR valve assembly acts as a vacuum regulator. The bleed valve controls the amount of vacuum in the vacuum chamber by bleeding vacuum to outside air during the open phase of the cycle. The diaphragm on the valve has an internal air bleed hole which is held closed by a small spring when there is no exhaust backpressure. Engine vacuum opens the EGR valve against the pressure of a spring. When manifold vacuum combines with negative exhaust backpressure, the vacuum bleed hole opens and the EGR valve closes. This valve will open if vacuum is applied with the engine not running.

Digital EGR Valve

The digital EGR valve, used on the 3.1L engine, is designed to accurately supply EGR to an engine, independent of intake manifold vacuum. The valve controls EGR flow from the exhaust to the intake manifold through three orifices which increment in size to produce seven combinations. When a solenoid is energized, the armature, with attached shaft and swivel pintle is lifted, opening the orifice. The flow accuracy is dependent on metering orifice size only, which results in improved control.

The swivel pintle feature insures good sealing of exhaust gas, reducing the need of critical assembly alignment. In addition, the effects of EGR leakage on idle quality are reduced

because the shaft and seals are exposed to exhaust pressure instead of manifold vacuum. The shafts are sealed from the exhaust chamber by floating seals held in place by the seal spring. These springs also hold the upper seals that seal the armature cavity in the solenoids. The solenoid coils are fastened together to maximize reliability and to seal the coils from the environment. The coils use a common power terminal with individual ground terminals.

The digital EGR valve is opened by the PCM quad-driver, grounding each respective solenoid circuit. This quad-driver activates the solenoid, raises the pintle, and allows exhaust gas flow into the intake manifold. The exhaust gas then moves with the air/fuel mixture into the combustion chamber. If too much exhaust gas enters, combustion will not occur. For this reason, very little exhaust gas is allowed to pass through the valve, with virtually none at idle.

TESTING

▶ See Figures 8, 9 and 10

Refer to the appropriate chart to test the EGR system.

REMOVAL & INSTALLATION

Ported and Negative Backpressure EGR Valves
▶ See Figures 11, 12, 13 and 14

1. Disconnect the negative battery cable.
2. If necessary for valve access, remove the air cleaner assembly.
3. If equipped, remove the EGR valve cover.
4. Tag and disconnect the necessary EGR valve hoses and wiring.
5. Unfasten the EGR valve retaining bolts.
6. Remove the EGR valve. Discard the gasket.
7. Buff the exhaust deposits from the mounting surface and around the valve using a wire wheel.
8. Remove deposits from the valve outlet.
9. Clean the gasket material from the mounting surfaces of the intake manifold and valve assembly.

To install:
10. Using a new gasket, position the EGR valve on the manifold.
11. Install the retaining bolts, then tighten them to 16 ft. lbs. (22 Nm).
12. Connect the wiring and hoses.
13. Place the cover on the valve, if equipped.
14. Install the air cleaner assembly.
15. Connect the negative battery cable.

Digital EGR Valve
▶ See Figure 15

1. Disconnect the negative battery cable.
2. Detach the electrical connections at the solenoid.
3. Unfasten the two base-to-pad retaining bolts/screws, then remove the EGR valve from the engine. Remove and discard the gasket.
4. Clean the gasket mating surfaces.

EXHAUST GAS RECIRCULATION (EGR) CHECK

ASSUMES NO CODE 32 IS STORED FOR EGR VALVE. MAKE PHYSICAL INSPECTION OF EGR VACUUM HOSE FOR RESTRICTIONS.

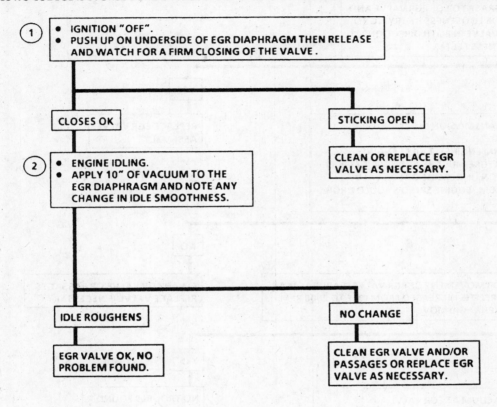

1
- IGNITION "OFF".
- PUSH UP ON UNDERSIDE OF EGR DIAPHRAGM THEN RELEASE AND WATCH FOR A FIRM CLOSING OF THE VALVE.

CLOSES OK

STICKING OPEN

CLEAN OR REPLACE EGR VALVE AS NECESSARY.

2
- ENGINE IDLING.
- APPLY 10" OF VACUUM TO THE EGR DIAPHRAGM AND NOTE ANY CHANGE IN IDLE SMOOTHNESS.

IDLE ROUGHENS

NO CHANGE

EGR VALVE OK, NO PROBLEM FOUND.

CLEAN EGR VALVE AND/OR PASSAGES OR REPLACE EGR VALVE AS NECESSARY.

CLEAR CODES AND CONFIRM "CLOSED LOOP" OPERATION AND NO "SERVICE ENGINE SOON" LIGHT.

86884022

Fig. 8 Ported EGR system check

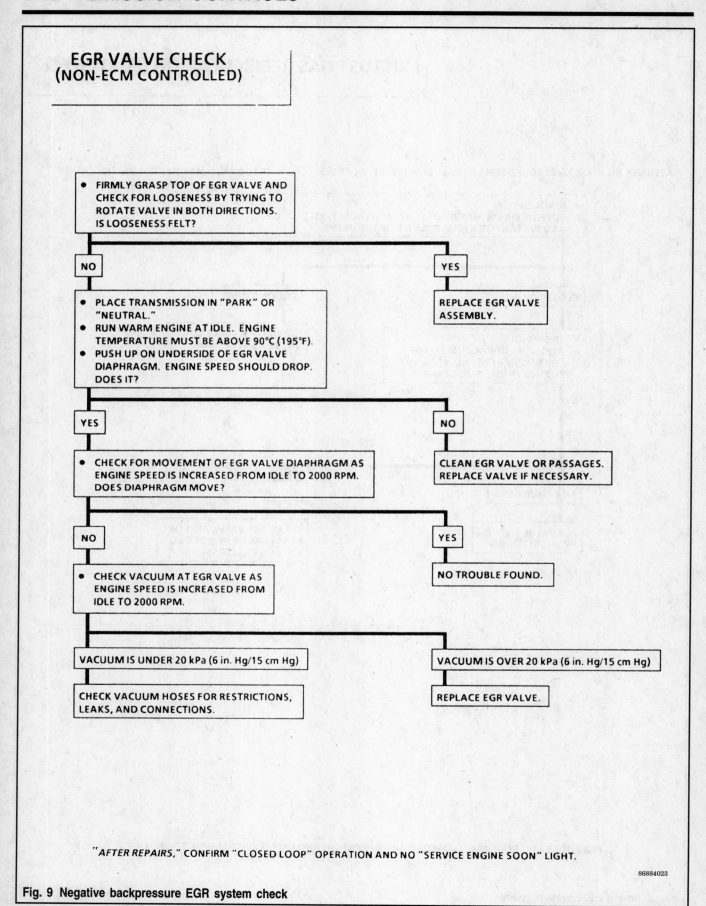

EGR VALVE CHECK
(NON-ECM CONTROLLED)

- FIRMLY GRASP TOP OF EGR VALVE AND CHECK FOR LOOSENESS BY TRYING TO ROTATE VALVE IN BOTH DIRECTIONS. IS LOOSENESS FELT?

NO

YES

- PLACE TRANSMISSION IN "PARK" OR "NEUTRAL."
- RUN WARM ENGINE AT IDLE. ENGINE TEMPERATURE MUST BE ABOVE 90°C (195°F).
- PUSH UP ON UNDERSIDE OF EGR VALVE DIAPHRAGM. ENGINE SPEED SHOULD DROP. DOES IT?

REPLACE EGR VALVE ASSEMBLY.

YES

NO

- CHECK FOR MOVEMENT OF EGR VALVE DIAPHRAGM AS ENGINE SPEED IS INCREASED FROM IDLE TO 2000 RPM. DOES DIAPHRAGM MOVE?

CLEAN EGR VALVE OR PASSAGES. REPLACE VALVE IF NECESSARY.

NO

YES

- CHECK VACUUM AT EGR VALVE AS ENGINE SPEED IS INCREASED FROM IDLE TO 2000 RPM.

NO TROUBLE FOUND.

VACUUM IS UNDER 20 kPa (6 in. Hg/15 cm Hg)

VACUUM IS OVER 20 kPa (6 in. Hg/15 cm Hg)

CHECK VACUUM HOSES FOR RESTRICTIONS, LEAKS, AND CONNECTIONS.

REPLACE EGR VALVE.

"AFTER REPAIRS," CONFIRM "CLOSED LOOP" OPERATION AND NO "SERVICE ENGINE SOON" LIGHT.

86884023

Fig. 9 Negative backpressure EGR system check

EXHAUST GAS RECIRCULATION (EGR) FLOW CHECK

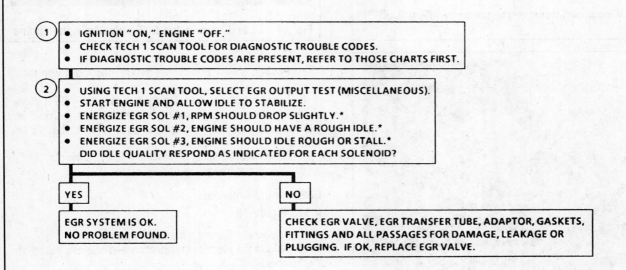

① • IGNITION "ON," ENGINE "OFF."
   • CHECK TECH 1 SCAN TOOL FOR DIAGNOSTIC TROUBLE CODES.
   • IF DIAGNOSTIC TROUBLE CODES ARE PRESENT, REFER TO THOSE CHARTS FIRST.

② • USING TECH 1 SCAN TOOL, SELECT EGR OUTPUT TEST (MISCELLANEOUS).
   • START ENGINE AND ALLOW IDLE TO STABILIZE.
   • ENERGIZE EGR SOL #1, RPM SHOULD DROP SLIGHTLY.*
   • ENERGIZE EGR SOL #2, ENGINE SHOULD HAVE A ROUGH IDLE.*
   • ENERGIZE EGR SOL #3, ENGINE SHOULD IDLE ROUGH OR STALL.*
     DID IDLE QUALITY RESPOND AS INDICATED FOR EACH SOLENOID?

YES

EGR SYSTEM IS OK.
NO PROBLEM FOUND.

NO

CHECK EGR VALVE, EGR TRANSFER TUBE, ADAPTOR, GASKETS,
FITTINGS AND ALL PASSAGES FOR DAMAGE, LEAKAGE OR
PLUGGING. IF OK, REPLACE EGR VALVE.

* THESE STEPS MUST BE DONE VERY QUICKLY, AS THE PCM WILL
   ADJUST THE IDLE AIR CONTROL VALVE TO CORRECT IDLE SPEED.

"AFTER REPAIRS," CONFIRM "CLOSED LOOP" OPERATION AND NO MIL (SERVICE ENGINE SOON).

86884021

Fig. 10 Digital EGR system check

Fig. 11 If equipped, remove the cover by lifting it off the valve

Fig. 12 Disconnect the vacuum hose

Fig. 13 Unfasten the EGR retaining bolts or nuts . . .

Fig. 14 . . . and remove the EGR valve from the engine

To install:

5. Position a new EGR valve gasket, aligning it with the holes.

6. Install then bolts, aligning them through the EGR valve assembly and cast EGR pad of the upper intake manifold and into the pipe assembly. Tighten the bolts to 18 ft. lbs. (25 Nm).

7. Attach the electrical connections to the solenoid.

8. Connect the negative battery cable.

EGR Control Solenoid

▶ See Figure 16

1. Disconnect the negative battery cable.

2. Detach the electrical connection and vacuum hoses at the solenoid.

3. Unfasten the retaining nut, then remove the solenoid.

To install:

4. Install the solenoid and bracket. Tighten the retaining nut to 17 ft. lbs. (24 Nm).

5. Attach the vacuum hoses and electrical connector.

6. Connect the negative battery cable.

Filter Replacement

1. Grasp the filter and pull it off with a rocking motion.

2. Install a new filter by pushing it on. Make sure the cutouts for the wires are properly aligned.

Catalytic Converter

OPERATION

All engines covered by this manual are equipped with a catalytic converter in order to reduce tail pipe emissions. The catalytic converter is mounted in the engine exhaust stream ahead of the muffler. Its function is to combine carbon monoxide (CO) and hydrocarbons (HC) with oxygen and break down nitrogen oxide (NOx) compounds. These gasses are converted to mostly CO_2 and water. It heats to operating temperature within about 1-2 minutes, depending on ambient temperature

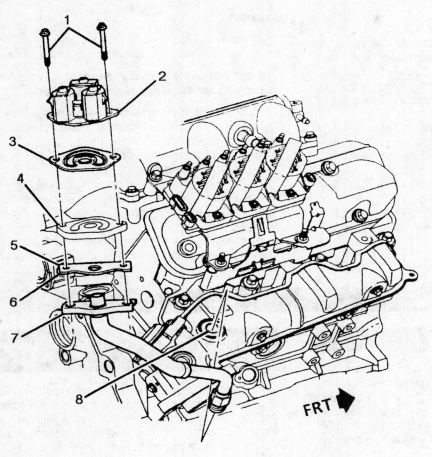

1. Bolt/screw
2. Digital EGR valve
3. Gasket
4. EGR pad - (Part of the upper intake manifold)
5. Gasket
6. Folded tabs
7. Bracket - (Part of the EGR pipe assembly)
8. Exhaust manifold

86884029

Fig. 15 View of the digital EGR valve mounting — 3.1L engine

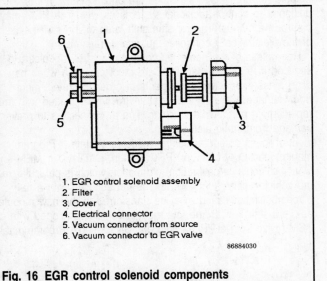

1. EGR control solenoid assembly
2. Filter
3. Cover
4. Electrical connector
5. Vacuum connector from source
6. Vacuum connector to EGR valve

86884030

Fig. 16 EGR control solenoid components

and driving conditions and will operate at temperatures up to about 1500°F. Inside the converter housing is a single or dual bed ceramic monolith, coated with various combinations of platinum, palladium and rhodium.

The catalytic converter is not serviceable. If tests and visual inspection show the converter to be damaged, it must be replaced. There are 2 types of failures: melting or fracturing. The most common failure is melting, resulting from unburned gasoline contacting the monolith, such as when a cylinder does not fire. Usually when the monolith melts, high backpressure results. When it cracks, it begins to break up into small particles that get blown out the tail pipe.

Poor fuel mileage and/or a lack of power can often be traced to a melted or plugged catalytic converter. The damage may be the result of engine malfunction or the use of leaded gasoline in the vehicle. Proper diagnosis for a restricted exhaust system is essential before any components are replaced. The following procedure that can be used to determine if the exhaust system is restricted.

TESTING

Backpressure Diagnosis Test

1. Carefully remove the oxygen sensor.
2. Install an adapter that has the same size threads as the sensor and that will hook up to a pressure gauge. Install in place of the sensor.
3. With engine idling at normal operating temperature, observe the backpressure reading on the gauge. The reading should not exceed 1.25 psi (8.6 kPa).
4. Increase engine speed to 2000 rpm and observe gauge. The reading should not exceed 3 psi (20.7 kPa).
5. If the backpressure at either speed exceeds specification, a restricted exhaust is indicated.
6. Inspect the entire exhaust system for a collapsed pipe, heat distress or possible internal muffler failure.
7. If there are no obvious reasons for the excessive backpressure, the catalytic converter is suspected and should be removed for inspection or replacement.

8. When test is complete, remove the pressure gauge and adapter. Lightly coat the threads of the oxygen sensor with an anti-seize compound. Reinstall the oxygen sensor.

Inspection

1. Raise and safely support the vehicle.
2. Inspect the catalytic converter protector for any damage.

➡**If any part of the protector is dented to the extent that is contacts the converter, replace the protector.**

3. Check the heat insulator for adequate clearance between the converter and the heat insulator. Repair or replace any damaged components.
4. Unfasten the retaining bolts at the front and the rear, then remove the converter.
5. On units with a ceramic monolith, it should be possible to look into the end of the housing and see light through the other end. If it is melted enough to cause high exhaust backpressure, it will be obvious.
6. Installation is the reverse of the removal procedure. Lower the vehicle, start the engine and check for exhaust leaks.

ELECTRONIC ENGINE CONTROLS

Operation

The fuel injection system, described in detail in Section 5 of this manual, is operated along with the ignition system to obtain optimum performance and fuel economy while producing a minimum of exhaust emissions. The various sensors described in this section are used by the computer control module (ECM or PCM depending upon application) for feedback to determine proper engine operating conditions.

➡**Although most diagnosis may be conducted using a Digital Volt/Ohm Meter (DVOM), certain steps or procedures may require use of the TECH 1® diagnostic scan tool (a specialized tester) or an equivalent scan/testing tool. If the proper tester is not available, the vehicle should be taken to a reputable service station which has the appropriate equipment.**

When dealing with the electronic engine control system, keep in mind that the system is sensitive to improperly connected electrical and vacuum circuits. The condition and connection of all hoses and wires should always be the first step when attempting to diagnose a driveability problem. Worn or deteriorated hoses and damaged or corroded wires may well make a good component appear faulty.

➡**When troubleshooting the system, always check the electrical and vacuum connectors which may cause the problem before testing or replacing a component.**

For more information on troubleshooting the electronic engine control system, please refer to the information on self-diagnostics later in this section.

Engine/Powertrain Control Module (ECM/PCM)

The heart of the electronic control system which is found on all vehicles covered by this manual is a computer control module. The module gathers information from various sensors, then controls fuel supply and engine emission systems. Most vehicles are equipped with an Engine Control Module (ECM) which, as its name implies, controls the engine and related emissions systems. Some ECMs may also control the Torque Converter Clutch (TCC) on automatic transmission vehicles or the manual upshift light on manual transmission vehicles. Later model vehicles may be equipped with a Powertrain Control Module (PCM). This is similar to the original ECM, but is designed to control additional systems as well. The PCM may control the manual transmission shift lamp or the shift functions of the electronically controlled automatic transmission.

Regardless of the name, all computer control modules are serviced in a similar manner. Care must be taken when handling these expensive components in order to protect them from damage. Carefully follow all instructions included with the replacement part. Avoid touching pins or connectors to prevent damage from static electricity.

All of these computer control modules contain a Programmable Read Only Memory (PROM) chip, CALPAK or MEM-CAL that contains calibration information which is particular to the vehicle application. This chip is not supplied with a replacement module and must be transferred to the new module before installation. Some late models vehicles equipped with a PCM utilize both a PROM chip and an Erasable Programmable

Read Only Memory (EPROM). which must be programmed with a scan tool after installation.

❊❊WARNING

To prevent the possibility of permanent control module damage, the ignition switch MUST always be OFF when disconnecting power from or reconnecting power to the module. This includes unplugging the module connector, disconnecting the negative battery cable, removing the module fuse or even attempting to jump your dead battery using jumper cables.

REMOVAL & INSTALLATION

▶ **See Figures 17, 18, 19, 20 and 21**

1. Turn the ignition switch **OFF**.
2. Disconnect the negative battery cable.
3. Remove the right side hush panel, as required.
4. Detach the electrical harness connectors from the computer control module.
5. Unfasten the module-to-bracket retaining screws, then remove the ECM or PCM as applicable.
6. If replacement of the calibration unit is required, unfasten the access cover retaining screws, then remove the cover from the computer control module. Carefully remove the calibration unit from the ECM/PCM, as follows:
    a. If the ECM contains a PROM carrier, use the rocker type PROM removal tool.
    b. If the ECM contains a CAL-PAK, grasp the CAL-PAK carrier (at the narrow end only), using the removal tool. Remove the Cal-Pak carrier.
    c. If the ECM/PCM contains a MEM-CAL or EPROM, push both retaining clips back away from the MEM-CAL/EPROM. At the same time, grasp it at both ends and lift it up out of the socket. Do not remove the cover of the MEM-CAL/EPROM.

➡**Before replacement of a defective computer control module, first check the resistance of each ECM/PCM controlled solenoid. This can be done at the module connector, using an ohmmeter and the ECM or PCM connector wiring diagram. Any computer control module controlled device with low resistance will damage the replacement ECM/PCM due to high current flow through the internal circuits.**

To install:
7. Fit the replacement calibration unit into the socket.

➡**The small notch of the carrier should be aligned with the small notch in the socket. Press on the ends of the carrier until it is firmly seated in the socket. Do not press on the calibration unit, only the carrier.**

8. Install the access cover, then secure using the retaining screws.
9. Position the computer control module in the vehicle, then install the module-to-bracket retaining screws.

10. Attach the module electrical harness connectors.
11. Install the right side hush panel, as required.
12. Check that the ignition switch is **OFF**, then connect the negative battery cable.
13. If your vehicle has the 3.1L engine which is equipped with a PCM with EPROM, the EPROM must be reprogrammed using a scan tool and the latest available software. In all likelihood, the vehicle must be towed to a dealer or repair shop containing the suitable equipment for this service.
14. Enter the self-diagnostic system and check for trouble codes to be sure the module and calibration unit are properly installed. For details, refer to the procedure for checking trouble codes, later in this section.

FUNCTIONAL CHECK

1. Turn the ignition switch **ON**.
2. Enter diagnostics, by grounding the appropriate ALDL terminals. Refer to diagnostics procedures in this section.
3. Allow Code 12 to flash 4 times to verify that no other codes are present. This indicates the PROM or MEM-CAL is installed properly.
4. If trouble Codes 42, 43 or 51 are present or if the SERVICE ENGINE SOON light is ON constantly with no codes, the PROM/MEM-CAL is not fully seated, installed backward, has bent pins or is defective.

➡**Anytime the calibration unit is installed backward and the ignition switch is turned ON, the unit is destroyed.**

5. If it is not fully seated, press firmly on the ends of the MEM-CAL.

Engine Coolant Temperature (ECT) Sensor

OPERATION

▶ **See Figure 22**

The Engine Coolant Temperature (ECT) sensor, sometimes referred to as the Coolant Temperature Sensor (CTS), is a thermistor (resistor which changes value based on temperature) mounted in the engine coolant stream. Low coolant temperatures produce a high resistance — 100,000 ohms at -40°F (-40°C), while high temperatures cause low resistance — 70 ohms at 266°F (130°C).

The control module provides a 5 volt reference signal to the sensor through a resistor in the module and measures the voltage. The voltage will be high when the engine is cold and low when the engine is hot. By measuring the voltage, the control module knows the engine coolant temperature. The engine coolant temperature affects most other systems controlled by the module.

➡**Removal and installation of the coolant temperature sensor is covered in Section 3 of this manual. Please refer there for further information.**

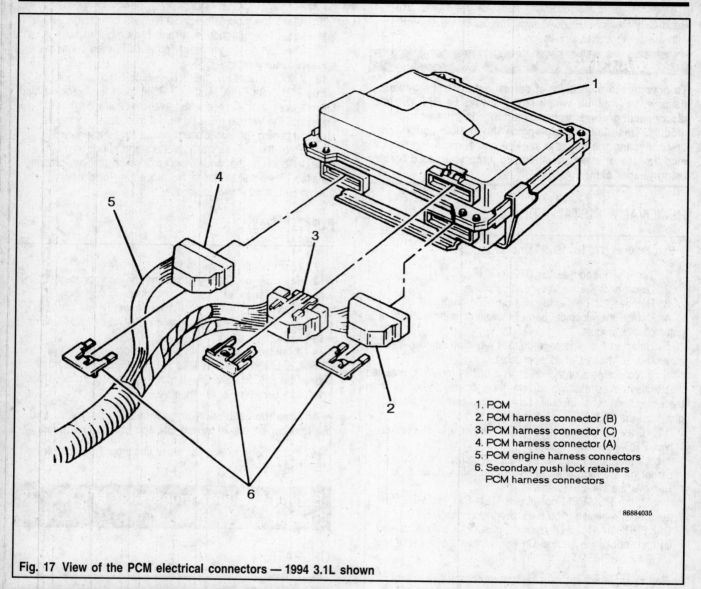

1. PCM
2. PCM harness connector (B)
3. PCM harness connector (C)
4. PCM harness connector (A)
5. PCM engine harness connectors
6. Secondary push lock retainers
   PCM harness connectors

86884035

Fig. 17 View of the PCM electrical connectors — 1994 3.1L shown

Idle Air Control (IAC) Valve

OPERATION

Engine idle speeds are controlled by the computer control module (ECM/PCM) through the IAC valve mounted on the throttle body. The ECM or PCM sends voltage pulses to the IAC motor windings causing the IAC motor shaft and pintle to move in or out a given distance (number of steps) for each pulse (called counts). The movement of the pintle controls the airflow around the throttle plate, which in turn, controls engine idle speed. Idle air control valve pintle position counts can be observed using a scan tool. Zero (0) counts corresponds to a fully closed passage, while 140 counts or more correspond to full flow.

Idle speed can be categorized in 2 ways: actual (controlled) idle speed and minimum idle speed. Controlled idle speed is obtained by the ECM positioning the IAC valve pintle. Resulting idle speed is determined by total air flow (IAC passage + PCV + throttle valve + calibrated vacuum leaks). Controlled idle speed is specified at normal operating conditions, which consists of engine coolant at normal operating temperature, air conditioning compressor OFF, manual transmission in neutral or automatic transmission in D.

Minimum idle air speed is set at the factory with a stop screw. This setting allows enough air flow by the throttle valves to cause the IAC valve pintle to be positioned a calibrated number of steps (counts) from the seat during normal controlled idle operation.

The idle speed is controlled by the computer control module through the IAC valve. No adjustment is required during routine maintenance. Tampering with the minimum idle speed adjustment is highly discouraged and may result in premature failure of the IAC valve.

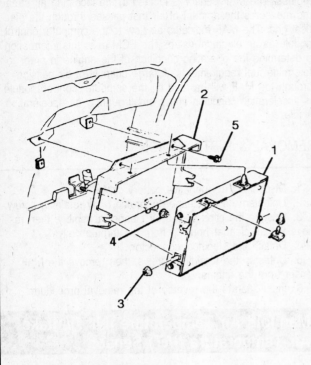

1. ECM Module assembly
2. Bracket
3. Nut (2)
   1.2 - 1.6 Nm (10 - 14 lb. in.)
4. Nut
   4.5 -7.0 Nm (39 - 61 lb. in.)
5. Bolt/screw (2)
   Fully driven seated and not stripped

86884032

Fig. 18 View of the computer control module mounting — 1992 3.3L shown

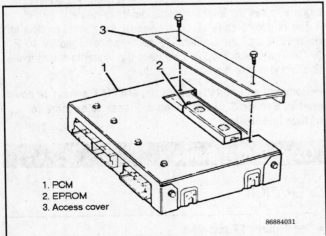

1. PCM
2. EPROM
3. Access cover

86884031

Fig. 19 In order to remove the calibration unit, you must first remove the access cover from the control module

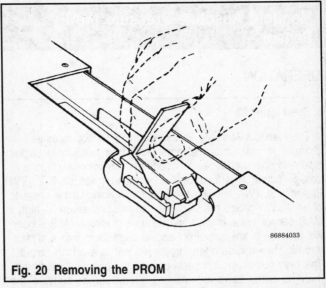

86884033

Fig. 20 Removing the PROM

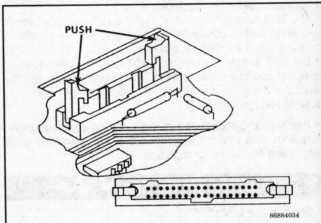

PUSH

86884034

Fig. 21 To remove the EPROM from the PCM, push the retaining clips back away from the unit, grasping both ends, then lift it up out of the socket

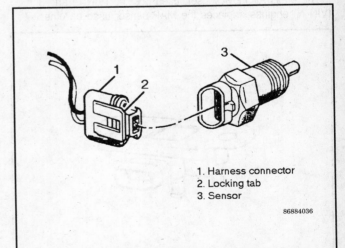

1. Harness connector
2. Locking tab
3. Sensor

86884036

Fig. 22 Engine Coolant Temperature (ECT) sensor and connector

Manifold Absolute Pressure (MAP) Sensor

OPERATION

▶ **See Figure 23**

The Manifold Absolute Pressure (MAP) sensor measures the changes in intake manifold pressure, which result from engine load and speed changes and converts this information to a voltage output. It is found on all engines except the 3.0L (VIN L) and 3.3L (VIN N). The MAP sensor reading is the opposite of a vacuum gauge reading: when manifold pressure is high, MAP sensor value is high and vacuum is low. A MAP sensor will produce a low output on engine coastdown with a closed throttle while a wide open throttle will produce a high output. The high output is produced because the pressure inside the manifold is the same as outside the manifold, so 100% of the outside air pressure is measured.

The MAP sensor is also used to measure barometric pressure under certain conditions, which allows the ECM to automatically adjust for different altitudes.

The MAP sensor changes the 5 volt signal supplied by the computer control module (ECM or PCM as applicable), which reads the change and uses the information to control fuel delivery and ignition timing.

➡**Removal and installation of the manifold absolute pressure sensor is covered in Section 3 of this manual. Please refer there for further information.**

Mass Air Flow (MAF) Sensor

▶ **See Figures 24 and 25**

OPERATION

The Mass Air Flow sensor, used on 3.0L (VIN L) and 3.3L (VIN N) engines, replaces the MAP sensor used on other

86884037

Fig. 23 MAP sensor — 1995 2.3L shown

engines. The MAF sensor is located in the incoming air stream and measures the amount of air that passes through the electrical grid. The MAF indicates air flow to the computer control module as an electrical value. The ECM uses this information to determine the operating condition of the engine in order to determine fuel requirements. A large quantity of air passing through the MAF will be read by the computer control module as acceleration condition and a small quantity as deceleration or idle.

REMOVAL & INSTALLATION

1. Disconnect the negative battery cable.
2. Unfasten the air cleaner-to-throttle body retaining screw.
3. Unsnap the clips on the air cleaner assembly, then remove the air cleaner housing from the throttle body.
4. Detach the electrical connector.
5. Unfasten the retaining screws, then remove the MAF sensor from the engine.
6. Installation is the reverse of the removal procedure.

Manifold Air Temperature (MAT)/Intake Air Temperature (IAT) Sensor

OPERATION

▶ **See Figure 26**

The MAT or IAT sensor (as equipped), is a thermistor (resistor which changes value based on temperature) mounted either in the air intake snorkel or the manifold (depending on the application). Low intake air temperatures produce a high resistance — 100,000 ohms at -40°F (-40°C), while high temperatures cause low resistance — 70 ohms at 266°F (130°C).

The control module provides a 5 volt reference signal to the sensor through a resistor in the module and measures the voltage. The voltage will be high when the air is cold and low when the air is hot. By measuring the voltage, the control module knows the intake/manifold air temperature.

The air temperature signal is used by the control module to delay EGR until the temperature reaches approximately 40°F (5°C). The control module also uses the signal to retard ignition timing during high air temperatures.

➡**Removal and installation of the MAT/IAT sensor is covered in Section 3 of this manual. Please refer there for further information.**

Oxygen (O₂) Sensor

OPERATION

▶ **See Figures 27 and 28**

The oxygen sensor is essentially a small variable battery; it has the ability to produce a low voltage signal that feeds information on engine exhaust oxygen content to the control module.

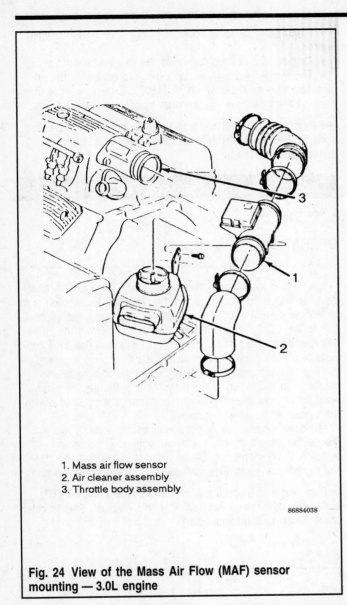

1. Mass air flow sensor
2. Air cleaner assembly
3. Throttle body assembly

86884038

Fig. 24 View of the Mass Air Flow (MAF) sensor mounting — 3.0L engine

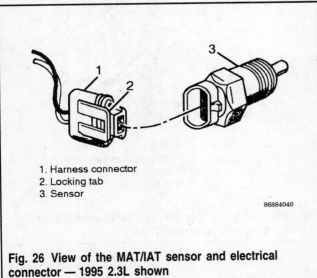

1. Harness connector
2. Locking tab
3. Sensor

86884040

Fig. 26 View of the MAT/IAT sensor and electrical connector — 1995 2.3L shown

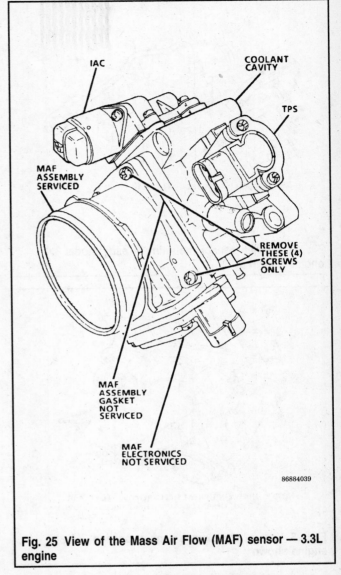

IAC

COOLANT CAVITY

TPS

MAF ASSEMBLY SERVICED

REMOVE THESE (4) SCREWS ONLY

MAF ASSEMBLY GASKET NOT SERVICED

MAF ELECTRONICS NOT SERVICED

86884039

Fig. 25 View of the Mass Air Flow (MAF) sensor — 3.3L engine

The sensor is constructed from a zirconia/platinum electrolytic element. Zirconia is an electrolyte that conducts electricity under certain chemical conditions. The element is made up of a ceramic material which acts as an insulator when cold. At operating temperatures of approximately 600°F (315°C), the element becomes a semiconductor. A platinum coating on the outer surface of the element stimulates further combustion of the exhaust gases right at the surface and this helps to keep the element up to the desired temperature.

The oxygen sensor has an inner cavity which is filled with reference (atmospheric) air. The atmosphere has approximately 21 percent oxygen in it. In the circuit, this inner cavity is the positive terminal, while the outer surface (exposed to the exhaust stream) is the negative or ground terminal.

Due to the element's electrolytic properties, oxygen concentration differences between the reference air and exhaust gases produce small voltages. A rich exhaust (excess fuel) has almost no oxygen. So when there is a large difference in the amount of oxygen touching the inside and outside surfaces, more conduction occurs and the sensor puts out a voltage

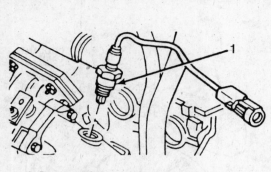

1. Oxygen (O_2) sensor - 41 Nm (30 ft. lb.)

86884041

Fig. 27 Oxygen sensor mounting — early model 3.0L engine shown

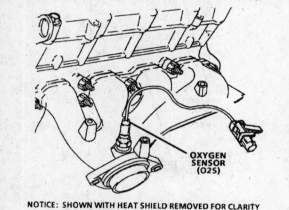

OXYGEN SENSOR (O2S)

NOTICE: SHOWN WITH HEAT SHIELD REMOVED FOR CLARITY
DO NOT OPERATE CAR WITH HEAT SHIELD REMOVED

86884042

Fig. 28 View of the oxygen sensor location — 2.3L engine shown

signal above 0.6 V (600 mV). The signal may vary as high as 0.9 V (999 mV).

With a lean exhaust (excessive oxygen), there is about 2 percent oxygen in the gases. The smaller difference in oxygen content causes less conduction and the sensor produces a smaller voltage somewhere below 0.3 V (300 mV). The signal could drop as low as 0.1 V (100 mV). Commonly, values outside this range will cause a trouble code to set for most control systems.

Precautions:

• Careful handling of the oxygen sensor is essential.
• The electrical pigtail and connector are permanently attached and should not be removed from the oxygen sensor.
• The in-line electrical connector and louvered end of the oxygen sensor must be kept free of grease, dirt and other contaminants.

• Avoid using cleaning solvents of any type on the oxygen sensor.
• Do not drop or roughly handle the oxygen sensor.
• The oxygen sensor may be difficult to remove if the engine temperature is below 120°F (48°C). Excessive force may damage the threads in the exhaust manifold or exhaust pipe.

➡Removal and installation of the oxygen sensor is covered in Section 3 of this manual. Please refer there for further information.

Throttle Position Sensor (TPS)

◆ **See Figure 29**

OPERATION

The TPS is mounted to the throttle body, opposite the throttle lever and is connected to the throttle shaft. Its function is to sense the current throttle valve position and relay that information to the ECM. Throttle position information allows the ECM to generate the required injector control signals. The TPS consists of a potentiometer which alters the flow of voltage according to the position of a wiper on the variable resistor windings, in proportion to the movement of the throttle shaft. As throttle angle is changed (the accelerator is pressed down), the output of the sensor changes.

At closed throttle, the output of the sensor is fairly low (0.5 V). As the throttle opens, the output voltage should rise towards 5 V. By monitoring the sensor output voltage, the control module can determine fuel delivery based on throttle angle.

➡Removal and installation of the Throttle Position (TP) sensor is covered in Section 3 of this manual. Please refer there for further information.

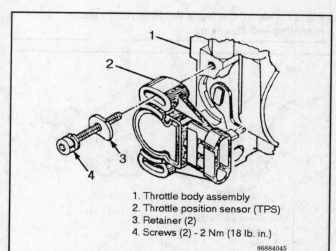

1. Throttle body assembly
2. Throttle position sensor (TPS)
3. Retainer (2)
4. Screws (2) - 2 Nm (18 lb. in.)

86884045

Fig. 29 The throttle position sensor is mounted on the throttle body — 3.3L engine shown

Vehicle Speed Sensor (VSS)

OPERATION

The VSS is located on the transmission and sends a pulsing voltage signal to the ECM which is converted to miles per hour. This sensor mainly controls the operation of the TCC system, shift light, cruise control and activation of the EGR system.

REMOVAL & INSTALLATION

1. Disconnect the negative battery cable.
2. Raise and safely support the vehicle.
3. Detach the VSS lead from the transaxle.
4. If necessary, unfasten the governor housing bolts, then remove the housing.
5. Unfasten the bolt or screw and retainer, then remove the VSS assembly from the vehicle. Remove and discard the O-ring.

To install:

6. Lubricate a new O-ring with sychromesh transaxle fluid part no. 12345349 or equivalent, then install on the sensor.
7. Install the VSS assembly, then secure with the retainer and bolt/screw.
8. If removed, install the governor housing and secure with the retaining bolts.
9. Attach the VSS lead to the transaxle.
10. Carefully lower the vehicle.
11. Connect the negative battery cable.

ESC Knock Sensor (KS)

▶ **See Figures 30 and 31**

OPERATION

The Knock Sensor (KS) detects abnormal vibration (spark knocking) in the engine. The sensor is mounted in the engine block near the cylinders. The sensor produces an AC output voltage which increases with the severity of the knock. This signal voltage inputs to the ECM/PCM. The computer control module then adjusts the timing to reduce the knock. This allows the engine to use maximum spark advance to improve driveability and fuel economy.

REMOVAL & INSTALLATION

1. Disconnect the negative battery cable.
2. Raise and safely support the vehicle.
3. Detach the wiring harness connector from the Knock Sensor (KS).
4. Remove the knock sensor from the engine block.

To install:

5. Install the knock sensor into the engine block. Tighten to 14 ft. lbs. (19 Nm).
6. Attach the wiring harness connector to the sensor.
7. Carefully lower the vehicle.
8. Connect the negative battery cable.

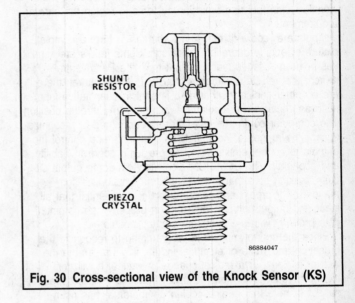

Fig. 30 Cross-sectional view of the Knock Sensor (KS)

ESC KNOCK SENSOR

86884046

Fig. 31 The Knock Sensor (KS) is mounted in the engine block near the cylinders

SELF-DIAGNOSTIC SYSTEMS

General Information

The computer control module (ECM/PCM) is required to maintain the exhaust emissions at acceptable levels. The module is a small, solid state computer which receives signals from many sources and sensors; it uses these data to make judgments about operating conditions and then control output signals to the fuel and emission systems to match the current requirements.

Inputs are received from many sources to form a complete picture of engine operating conditions. Some inputs are simply yes or no messages, such as that from the Park/Neutral switch; the vehicle is either in gear or in Park/Neutral; there are no other choices. Other data is sent in quantitative input, such as engine RPM, coolant temperature and throttle position. The computer control module is pre-programmed to recognize acceptable ranges or combinations of signals and control the outputs to control emissions while providing good driveability and economy. The ECM/PCM also monitors some output circuits, making sure that the components function as commanded. For proper engine operation, it is essential that all input and output components function properly and communicate properly with the computer control module.

Since the control module is programmed to recognize the presence and value of electrical inputs, it will also note the lack of a signal or a radical change in values. It will, for example, react to the loss of signal from the vehicle speed sensor or note that engine coolant temperature has risen beyond acceptable (programmed) limits. Once a fault is recognized, a numeric code is assigned and held in memory. The dashboard warning lamp: CHECK ENGINE or SERVICE ENGINE SOON will illuminate to advise the operator that the system has detected a fault.

More than one code may be stored. Although not every engine uses every code, possible codes range from 12 to 100. Additionally, the same code may carry different meanings relative to each engine or engine family.

In the event of an computer control module failure, the system will default to a pre-programmed set of values. These are compromise values which allow the engine to operate, although possibly at reduced efficiency. This is variously known as the default, limp-in or back-up mode. Driveability is almost always affected when the ECM/PCM enters this mode.

Learning Ability

The computer control module can compensate for minor variations within the fuel system through the block learn and fuel integrator systems. The fuel integrator monitors the oxygen sensor output voltage, adding or subtracting fuel to drive the mixture rich or lean as needed to reach the ideal air fuel ratio of 14.7:1. The integrator values may be read with a scan tool; the display will range from 0-255 and should center on 128 if the oxygen sensor is seeing a 14.7:1 mixture.

The temporary nature of the integrator's control is expanded by the block learn function. The name is derived from the fact that the entire engine operating range (load vs. rpm) is divided into 16 sections or blocks. Within each memory block is stored the correct fuel delivery value for that combination of load and engine speed. Once the operating range enters a certain block, that stored value controls the fuel delivery unless the integrator steps in to change it. If changes are made by the integrator, the new value is memorized and stored within the block. As the block learn makes the correction, the integrator correction will be reduced until the integrator returns to 128; the block learn then controls the fuel delivery with the new value.

The next time the engine operates within the block's range, the new value will be used. The block learn data can also be read by a scan tool; the range is the same as the integrator and should also center on 128. In this way, the systems can compensate for engine wear, small air or vacuum leaks or reduced combustion.

Any time the battery is disconnected, the block learn values are lost and must be relearned by the ECM. This loss of corrected values may be noticed as a significant change in driveability. To reteach the system, make certain the engine is fully warmed up. Drive the vehicle at part throttle using moderate acceleration and idle until normal performance is felt.

Dashboard Warning Lamp

The primary function of the dash warning lamp is to advise the operator and that a fault has been detected, and, in most cases, a code stored. Under normal conditions, the dash warning lamp will illuminate when the ignition is turned **ON**. Once the engine is started and running, the computer control module will perform a system check and extinguish the warning lamp if no fault is found.

Additionally, the dash warning lamp can be used to retrieve stored codes after the system is placed in the Diagnostic Mode. Codes are transmitted as a series of flashes with short or long pauses. When the system is placed in the Field Service Mode, the dash lamp will indicate open loop or closed loop function to the technician.

Intermittents

If a fault occurs intermittently, such as a loose connector pin breaking contact as the vehicle hits a bump, the computer control module (ECM or PCM depending upon application) will note the fault as it occurs and energize the dash warning lamp. If the problem self-corrects, as with the terminal pin again making contact, the dash lamp will extinguish after 10 seconds but a code will remain stored in the computer control module's memory.

When an unexpected code appears during diagnostics, it may have been set during an intermittent failure that self-corrected; the codes are still useful in diagnosis and should not be discounted.

Tools and Equipment

SCAN TOOLS

Although stored Diagnostic Trouble Codes (DTC's) may be read with only the use of a small jumper wire, the use of a hand-held scan tool such as GM's TECH-1® or equivalent is recommended. There are many manufacturers of these tools; a purchaser must be certain that the tool is proper for the intended use. If you own a scan type tool, it probably came with comprehensive instructions on proper use. Be sure to follow the instructions that came with your unit if they differ from what is given here; this is a general guide with useful information included.

The scan tool allows any stored codes to be read from the ECM or PCM memory. The tool also allows the operator to view the data being sent to the computer control module while the engine is running. This ability has obvious diagnostic advantages; the use of the scan tool is frequently required by the diagnostic charts. Use of the scan tool provides additional data but does not eliminate the need for use of the charts. The scan tool makes collecting information easier; the data must be correctly interpreted by an operator familiar with the system.

An example of the usefulness of the scan tool may be seen in the case of a temperature sensor which has changed its electrical characteristics. The ECM is reacting to an apparently warmer engine (causing a driveability problem), but the sensor's voltage has not changed enough to set a fault code. Connecting the scan tool, the voltage signal being sent to the ECM may be viewed; comparison to either a chart of normal values or a known good vehicle reveals the problem quickly.

The ECM is capable of communicating with a scan tool in 3 modes:

1. Normal or Open Mode. This mode is not applicable to all engines. When engaged, certain engine data can be observed on the scanner without affecting engine operating characteristics. The number of items readable in this mode varies with engine family. Most scan tools are designed to change automatically to the ALDL mode if this mode is not available.

2. ALDL Mode. Also referred to as the 10K or SPECIAL mode, the scanner will present all readable data as available. Certain operating characteristics of the engine are changed or controlled when this mode is engaged. The closed loop timers are bypassed, the spark (EST) is advanced and the PARK/NEUTRAL restriction is bypassed. If applicable, the IAC controls the engine speed to 950-1050 rpm, and, on some engines, the canister purge solenoid is energized.

3. Factory Test. Sometimes referred to as BACK-UP mode, this level of communication is primarily used during vehicle assembly and testing. This mode will confirm that the default or limp-in system is working properly within the computer control module. Other data obtainable in this mode has little use in diagnosis.

➡**A scan tool that is known to display faulty data should not be used for diagnosis. Although the fault may be believed to be in only one area, it can possibly affect many other areas during diagnosis, leading to errors and incorrect repair.**

To properly read system values with a scan tool, the following conditions must be met. All normal values given in the charts will be based on these conditions:
- Engine running at idle, throttle closed
- Engine warm, upper radiator hose hot
- Vehicle in park or neutral
- System operating in closed loop
- All accessories OFF

ELECTRICAL TOOLS

The most commonly required electrical diagnostic tool is the Digital Multimeter, allowing voltage, ohmage (resistance) and amperage to be read by one instrument. The multimeter must be a high-impedance unit, with 10 megohms of impedance in the voltmeter. This type of meter will not place an additional load on the circuit it is testing; this is extremely important in low voltage circuits. The multimeter must be of high quality in all respects. It should be handled carefully and protected from impact or damage. Replace batteries frequently in the unit.

Other necessary tools include an unpowered test light, a quality tachometer with an inductive (clip-on) pick up, and the proper tools for releasing GM's Metri-Pack, Weather Pack and Micro-Pack terminals as necessary. The Micro-Pack connectors are used at the computer control module electrical connector. A vacuum pump/gauge may also be required for checking sensors, solenoids and valves.

Diagnosis and Testing

TROUBLESHOOTING

Diagnosis of a driveablility and/or emissions problems requires attention to detail and following the diagnostic procedures in the correct order. Resist the temptation to perform any repairs before performing the preliminary diagnostic steps. In many cases this will shorten diagnostic time and often cure the problem without electronic testing.

The proper troubleshooting procedure for these vehicles is as follows:

Visual/Physical Underhood Inspection

This is possibly the most critical step of diagnosis. A detailed examination of connectors, wiring and vacuum hoses can often lead to a repair without further diagnosis. Performance of this step relies on the skill of the technician performing it; a careful inspector will check the undersides of hoses as well as the integrity of hard-to-reach hoses blocked by the air cleaner or other component. Wiring should be checked carefully for any sign of strain, burning, crimping, or terminal pull-out from a connector. Checking connectors at components or in harnesses is required; usually, pushing them together will reveal a loose fit.

Diagnostic Circuit Check

This step is used to check that the on-board diagnostic system is working correctly. A system which is faulty or shorted may not yield correct codes when placed in the Diagnostic

Mode. Performing this test confirms that the diagnostic system is not failed and is able to communicate through the dash warning lamp.

If the diagnostic system is not operating correctly, or if a problem exists without the dash warning lamp being lit, refer to the specific engine's A-Charts. These charts cover such conditions as "Engine Cranks But Will Not Run" or "No Service Engine Soon Light".

Reading Codes and Use of Scan Tool

Once the integrity of the system is confirmed, enter the Diagnostic Mode and read any stored codes. To enter the diagnostic mode:

1. Turn the ignition switch OFF.
2. Locate the Assembly Line Diagnostic Link (ALDL), usually under the instrument panel. It may be within a plastic cover or housing labeled DIAGNOSTIC CONNECTOR. This link is used to communicate with the ECM.
3. The code(s) stored in memory may be read either through counting the flashes of the dashboard warning lamp or through the use of a hand-held scan tool. If using the scan tool, connect it correctly to the ALDL.
4. If reading codes via the dash warning lamp, use a small jumper wire to connect Terminal B to Terminal A of the ALDL. As the ALDL connector is viewed from the front, Terminal A is on the extreme right of the upper row; Terminal B is second from the right on the upper row.
5. After the terminals are connected, turn the ignition switch to the ON position, but DO NOT start the engine. The dash warning lamp should begin to flash Code 12. The code will display as one flash, a pause and two flashes. Code 12 is not a fault code. It is used as a system acknowledgment or handshake code; its presence indicates that the ECM can communicate as requested. Code 12 is used to begin every diagnostic sequence. Some vehicles also use Code 12 after all diagnostic codes have been sent.
6. After Code 12 has been transmitted 3 times, the fault codes, if any, will each be transmitted 3 times. The codes are stored and transmitted in numeric order from lowest to highest.

➡ **The order of codes in the memory does not indicate the order of occurrence.**

7. If there are no codes stored, but a driveability or emissions problem is evident, refer to the Symptoms and Intermittents Chart for the specific fuel system.
8. If one or more codes are stored, record them. At the end of the procedure, refer to the applicable Diagnostic Code chart.
9. If no fault codes are transmitted, connect the scan tool (if not already connected). Use the scan functions to view the values being sent to the ECM. Compare the actual values to the typical or normal values for the engine.
10. Switch the ignition OFF when finished with code retrieval or scan tool readings.

Circuit/Component Diagnosis and Repair

Using the appropriate chart(s) based on the Diagnostic Circuit Check, the fault codes and the scan tool data will lead to diagnosis and checking of a particular circuit or component. It is important to note that the fault code indicates a fault or loss of signal in an ECM-controlled system, not necessarily in the specific component. Detailed procedures to isolate the problem are included in each code chart; these procedures must be followed accurately to insure timely and correct repair. Following the procedure will also insure that only truly faulty components are replaced.

DIAGNOSTIC MODE

The ECM may be placed into the diagnostic mode by turning the ignition switch from OFF to ON, then grounding ALDL Terminal B to Terminal A. When in the Diagnostic Mode, the ECM will:

• Display Code 12, indicating the system is operating correctly.
• Display any stored fault codes 3 times in succession.
• Energize all the relays controlled by the ECM except the fuel pump relay. This will allow the relays and circuits to be checked in the shop without recreating certain driving conditions.
• Move the IAC valve to its fully extended position, closing the idle air passage.

➡ **Due to increased battery draw, do not allow the vehicle to remain in the Diagnostic Mode for more than 30 minutes. If longer periods are necessary, connect a battery charger.**

FIELD SERVICE MODE

If ALDL terminal B is grounded to terminal A with the engine running, the system enters the Field Service Mode. In this mode, the dash warning lamp will indicate whether the system is operating in open loop or closed loop.

If working in open loop, the dash warning lamp will flash rapidly 2½ times per second. In closed loop, the flash rate slows to once per second. Additionally, if the system is running lean in closed loop, the lamp will be off most of the cycle. A rich condition in closed loop will cause the lamp to remain lit for most of the 1 second cycle.

When operating in the Field Service Mode, additional codes cannot be stored by the ECM. The closed loop timer is bypassed in this mode.

CLEARING THE TROUBLE CODES

Stored fault codes may be erased from memory at any time by removing power from the ECM for at least 30 seconds. It may be necessary to clear stored codes during diagnosis to check for any recurrence during a test drive, but the stored codes must be written down when retrieved. The codes may still be required for subsequent troubleshooting. Whenever a repair is complete, the stored codes must be erased and the vehicle test driven to confirm correct operation and repair.

✳✳WARNING

The ignition switch must be OFF any time power is disconnected or restored to the ECM. Severe damage may result if this precaution is not observed.

Depending on the electrical distribution of the particular vehicle, power to the ECM may be disconnected by removing the ECM fuse in the fusebox, disconnecting the in-line fuse holder near the positive battery terminal or disconnecting the ECM power lead at the battery terminal. Disconnecting the negative battery cable to clear codes is not recommended as this will also clear other memory data in the vehicle such as radio presets or seat memory.

DIAGNOSTIC TROUBLE CODES AND CHARTS

Listings of the Diagnostic Trouble Codes (DTCs) for the various engine control systems covered in this manual are located in this section. When using these charts along with the computer module's self-diagnostic system, remember that a code only points to the faulty circuit NOT necessarily to a faulty component. Loose, damaged or corroded connections may contribute to a fault code on a circuit when the sensor or component is operating properly. Be sure that components are faulty before replacing them, especially the expensive ones.

Following the DTC listings are code charts which have been are provided to help track down what part of the circuit is at fault for the irregular readings and has caused the computer control module to set a trouble code. The charts should be used along with the information in this section, the engine performance symptom charts and the information in Sections 2, 3, 5 and 6 of this manual, as necessary. Keep in mind that most charts are only valid when the trouble is present. If the trouble is intermittent (often caused by loose or corroded terminals on circuit connections), the chart may lead to a dead end or "Intermittent code" ending in which the exact cause of the fault is still left undetermined. In these cases, check all related vacuum hoses and/or wiring for poor, worn or damaged connections. If bad connections are found, wiggle the connection in attempt to duplicate the fault condition so that troubleshooting may continue. Also, before replacing a computer control module, be ABSOLUTELY certain that the module is at fault. The price of a module is usually quite significant and they are usually NON-RETURNABLE components.

➡**After making repairs, clear the trouble codes and operate the vehicle to see if it will reset, indicating further problems.**

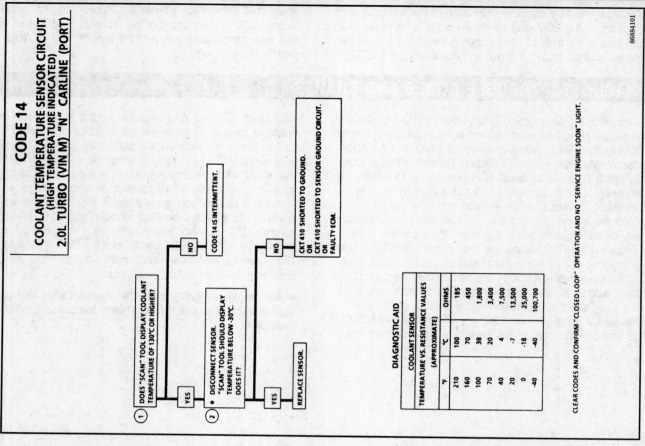

DTC CHART — 2.0L MFI-TURBO

CODE 14

COOLANT TEMPERATURE SENSOR CIRCUIT
(HIGH TEMPERATURE INDICATED)
2.0L TURBO (VIN M) "N" CARLINE (PORT)

86684101

1. DOES "SCAN" TOOL DISPLAY COOLANT TEMPERATURE OF 130°C OR HIGHER?
   - NO → CODE 14 IS INTERMITTENT.
   - YES
2. • DISCONNECT SENSOR.
   • "SCAN" TOOL SHOULD DISPLAY TEMPERATURE BELOW -30°C.
   DOES IT?
   - YES → REPLACE SENSOR.
   - NO → CKT 410 SHORTED TO GROUND.
     OR
     CKT 410 SHORTED TO SENSOR GROUND CIRCUIT.
     OR
     FAULTY ECM.

DIAGNOSTIC AID

COOLANT SENSOR		
TEMPERATURE VS. RESISTANCE VALUES (APPROXIMATE)		
°F	°C	OHMS
210	100	185
160	70	450
100	38	1,800
70	20	3,400
40	4	7,500
20	-7	13,500
0	-18	25,000
-40	-40	100,700

CLEAR CODES AND CONFIRM "CLOSED LOOP" OPERATION AND NO "SERVICE ENGINE SOON" LIGHT.

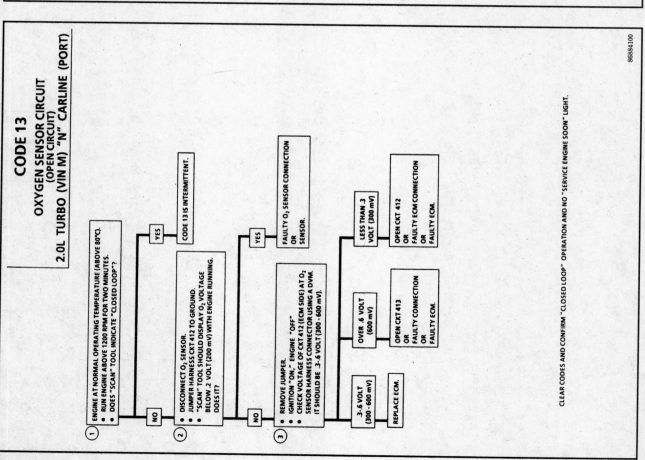

DTC CHART — 2.0L MFI-TURBO

CODE 13

OXYGEN SENSOR CIRCUIT
(OPEN CIRCUIT)
2.0L TURBO (VIN M) "N" CARLINE (PORT)

86684100

1. • ENGINE AT NORMAL OPERATING TEMPERATURE (ABOVE 80°C).
   • RUN ENGINE ABOVE 1200 RPM FOR TWO MINUTES.
   • DOES "SCAN" TOOL INDICATE "CLOSED LOOP"?
   - YES → CODE 13 IS INTERMITTENT.
   - NO
2. • DISCONNECT O₂ SENSOR.
   • JUMPER HARNESS CKT 412 TO GROUND.
   • "SCAN" TOOL SHOULD DISPLAY O₂ VOLTAGE BELOW .2 VOLT (200 mV) WITH ENGINE RUNNING.
   DOES IT?
   - YES → FAULTY O₂ SENSOR CONNECTION OR SENSOR.
   - NO
3. • REMOVE JUMPER.
   • IGNITION "ON," ENGINE "OFF"
   • CHECK VOLTAGE OF CKT 412 (ECM SIDE) AT O₂ SENSOR HARNESS CONNECTOR USING A DVM. IT SHOULD BE .3-.6 VOLT (300 - 600 mV).

   - .3-.6 VOLT (300 - 600 mV) → REPLACE ECM.
   - OVER .6 VOLT (600 mV) → OPEN CKT 413 OR FAULTY CONNECTION OR FAULTY ECM.
   - LESS THAN .3 VOLT (300 mV) → OPEN CKT 412 OR FAULTY ECM CONNECTION OR FAULTY ECM.

CLEAR CODES AND CONFIRM "CLOSED LOOP" OPERATION AND NO "SERVICE ENGINE SOON" LIGHT.

DTC CHART — 2.0L MFI-TURBO

CODE 22

THROTTLE POSITION SENSOR (TPS) CIRCUIT
(SIGNAL VOLTAGE LOW)
2.0L TURBO (VIN M) "N" CARLINE (PORT)

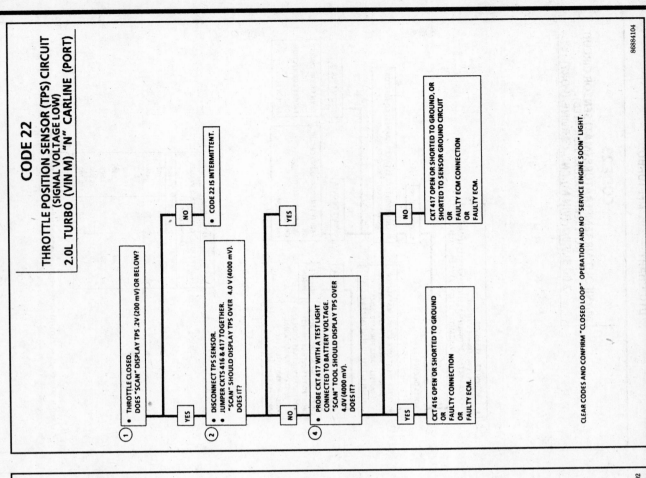

86884104

CLEAR CODES AND CONFIRM "CLOSED LOOP" OPERATION AND NO "SERVICE ENGINE SOON" LIGHT.

DTC CHART — 2.0L MFI-TURBO

CODE 15

COOLANT TEMPERATURE SENSOR CIRCUIT
(LOW TEMPERATURE INDICATED)
2.0L TURBO (VIN M) "N" CARLINE (PORT)

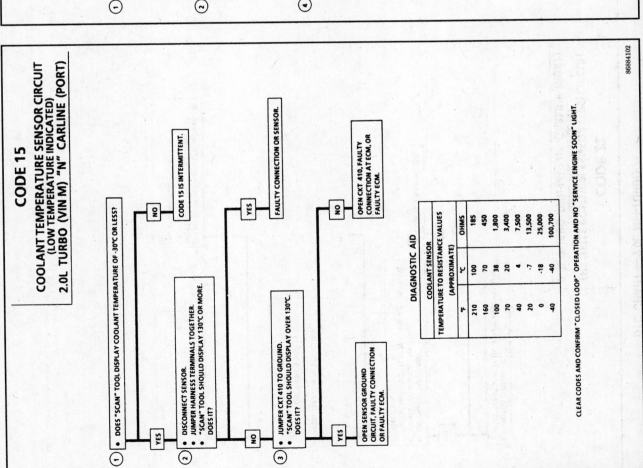

86884102

CLEAR CODES AND CONFIRM "CLOSED LOOP" OPERATION AND NO "SERVICE ENGINE SOON" LIGHT.

DTC CHART — 2.0L MFI-TURBO

CODE 23

MANIFOLD AIR TEMPERATURE (MAT) SENSOR CIRCUIT
(LOW TEMPERATURE INDICATED)
2.0L TURBO (VIN M) "N" CARLINE (PORT)

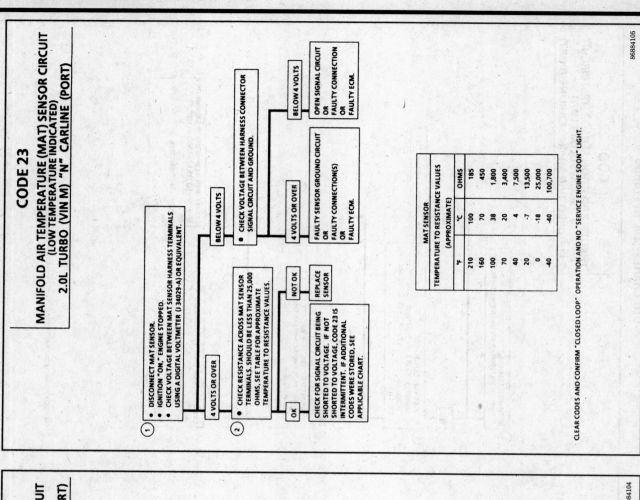

MAT SENSOR		
TEMPERATURE TO RESISTANCE VALUES		
(APPROXIMATE)		
°F	°C	OHMS
210	100	185
160	70	450
100	38	1,800
70	20	3,400
40	4	7,500
20	-7	13,500
0	-18	25,000
-40	-40	100,700

CLEAR CODES AND CONFIRM "CLOSED LOOP" OPERATION AND NO "SERVICE ENGINE SOON" LIGHT.

DTC CHART — 2.0L MFI-TURBO

CODE 22

THROTTLE POSITION SENSOR (TPS) CIRCUIT
(SIGNAL VOLTAGE LOW)
2.0L TURBO (VIN M) "N" CARLINE (PORT)

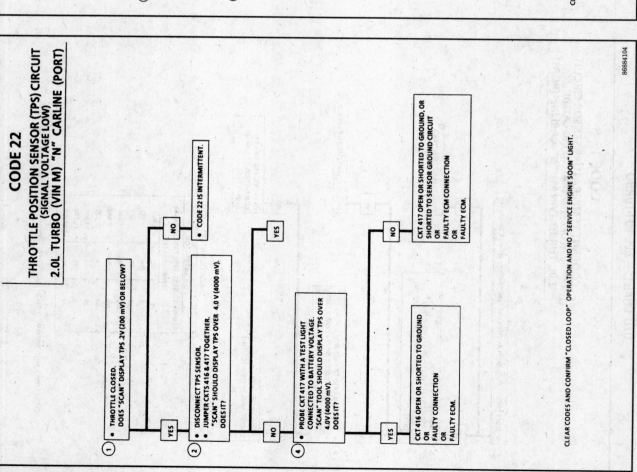

CLEAR CODES AND CONFIRM "CLOSED LOOP" OPERATION AND NO "SERVICE ENGINE SOON" LIGHT.

DTC CHART — 2.0L MFI-TURBO

CODE 25

MANIFOLD AIR TEMPERATURE (MAT) SENSOR CIRCUIT
(HIGH TEMPERATURE INDICATED)
2.0L TURBO (VIN M) "N" CARLINE (PORT)

NOTE: A "SCAN" TOOL MAY NOT BE USED TO DIAGNOSE THIS FAULT, DUE TO THE ECM TRANSMITTING "DEFAULT" (SUBSTITUTE) VALUES WHEN THE FAULT IS PRESENT.

1
- DISCONNECT MAT SENSOR.
- IGNITION "ON," ENGINE STOPPED.
- CHECK VOLTAGE BETWEEN HARNESS CONNECTOR TERMINALS.

4 VOLTS OR OVER

BELOW 4 VOLTS

CKT 472 SHORTED TO GROUND.
OR
CKT 472 SHORTED TO SENSOR GROUND CIRCUIT.
OR
FAULTY ECM.

2
- CHECK RESISTANCE ACROSS MAT SENSOR TERMINALS. SHOULD BE MORE THAN 185 OHMS. SEE TABLE FOR APPROXIMATE TEMPERATURE TO RESISTANCE VALUES.

OK

NOT OK

REPLACE SENSOR

INTERMITTENT FAULT IN SENSOR CIRCUIT OR CONNECTOR. IF ADDITIONAL CODES WERE STORED, SEE APPLICABLE CHART.

MAT SENSOR TEMPERATURE TO RESISTANCE VALUES (APPROXIMATE)		
°F	°C	OHMS
210	100	185
160	70	450
100	38	1,600
70	20	3,400
40	4	7,500
20	-7	13,500
0	-18	25,000
-40	-40	100,700

CLEAR CODES AND CONFIRM "CLOSED LOOP" OPERATION AND NO "SERVICE ENGINE SOON" LIGHT.

86884107

DTC CHART — 2.0L MFI-TURBO

CODE 24

VEHICLE SPEED SENSOR (VSS) CIRCUIT
2.0L TURBO (VIN M) "N" CARLINE (PORT)

DISREGARD CODE 24 IF SET WHILE DRIVE WHEELS ARE NOT TURNING.

1
- RAISE DRIVE WHEELS
- "NOTICE": DO NOT PERFORM THIS TEST WITHOUT SUPPORTING THE LOWER CONTROL ARMS SO THAT THE DRIVE AXLES ARE IN A NORMAL HORIZONTAL POSITION. RUNNING THE VEHICLE IN GEAR WITH THE WHEELS HANGING DOWN AT FULL TRAVEL MAY DAMAGE THE DRIVE AXLES.
- WITH ENGINE IDLING IN GEAR, "SCAN" TOOL SHOULD DISPLAY VEHICLE SPEED ABOVE 0. DOES IT?

NO

DOES SPEEDOMETER WORK?

YES

CODE 24 IS INTERMITTENT.

NO

- IGNITION "OFF"
- DISCONNECT VSS AT TRANSAXLE.
- CONNECT SIGNAL GENERATOR TESTER J 33431-8 OR EQUIVALENT TO VSS HARNESS CONNECTOR.
- IGNITION "ON," TOOL "ON" AND SET TO GENERATE A VSS SIGNAL. "SCAN" TOOL SHOULD DISPLAY VEHICLE SPEED ABOVE 0. DOES IT?

YES

2
REPLACE ECM.

NO

CKT 400 OR 401 OPEN, SHORTED TO GROUND, SHORTED TOGETHER, FAULTY CONNECTIONS, OR FAULTY ECM.

YES

REPLACE VEHICLE SPEED SENSOR.

CLEAR CODES AND CONFIRM "CLOSED LOOP" OPERATION AND NO "SERVICE ENGINE SOON" LIGHT.

86884106

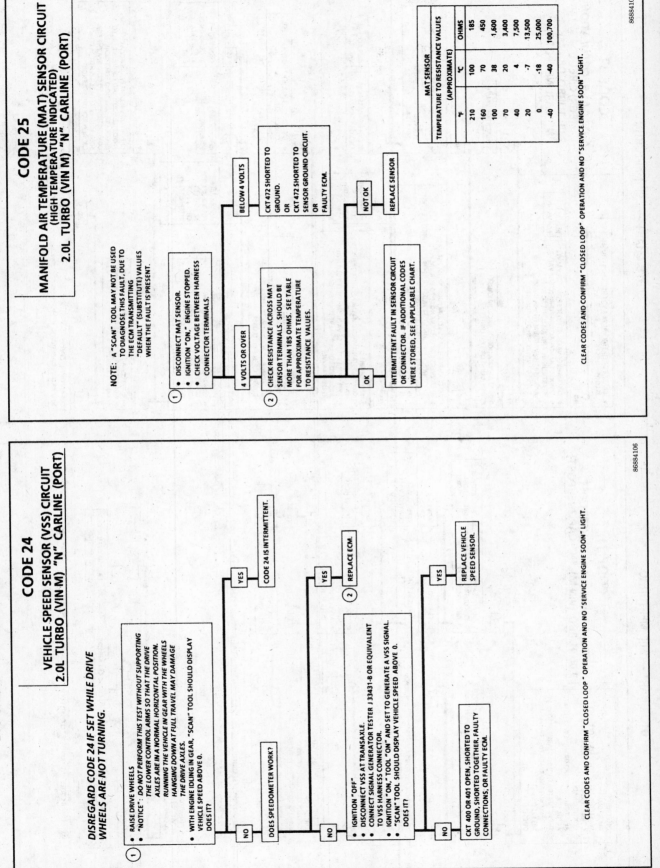

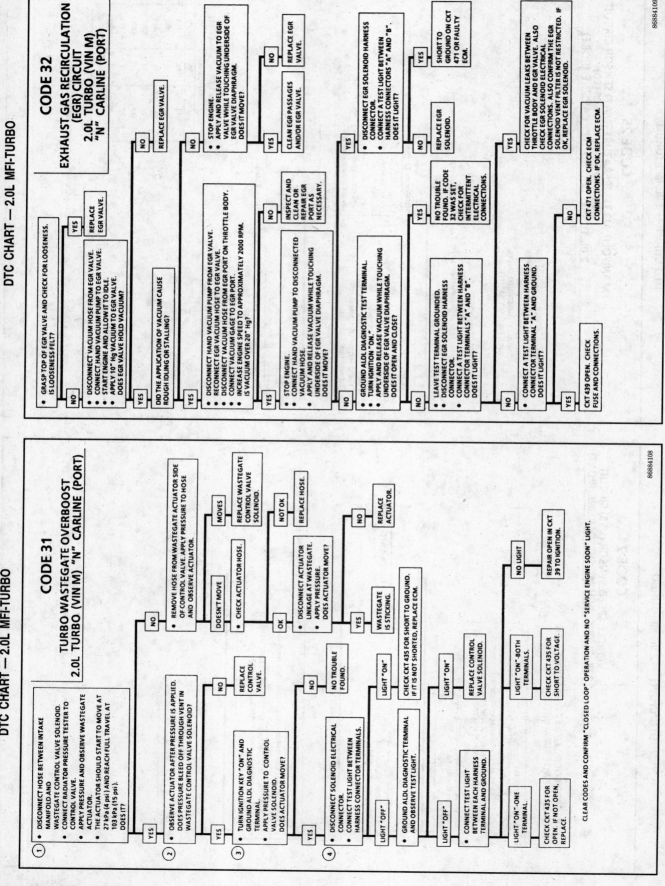

DTC CHART — 2.0L MFI-TURBO

CODE 32
EXHAUST GAS RECIRCULATION (EGR) CIRCUIT
2.0L TURBO (VIN M) "N" CARLINE (PORT)

CODE 31
TURBO WASTEGATE OVERBOOST
2.0L TURBO (VIN M) "N" CARLINE (PORT)

CLEAR CODES AND CONFIRM "CLOSED LOOP" OPERATION AND NO "SERVICE ENGINE SOON" LIGHT.

DTC CHART — 2.0L MFI-TURBO

CODE 34

MANIFOLD ABSOLUTE PRESSURE (MAP) SENSOR CIRCUIT
(SIGNAL VOLTAGE LOW - HIGH VACUUM)
2.0L TURBO (VIN M) "N" CARLINE (PORT)

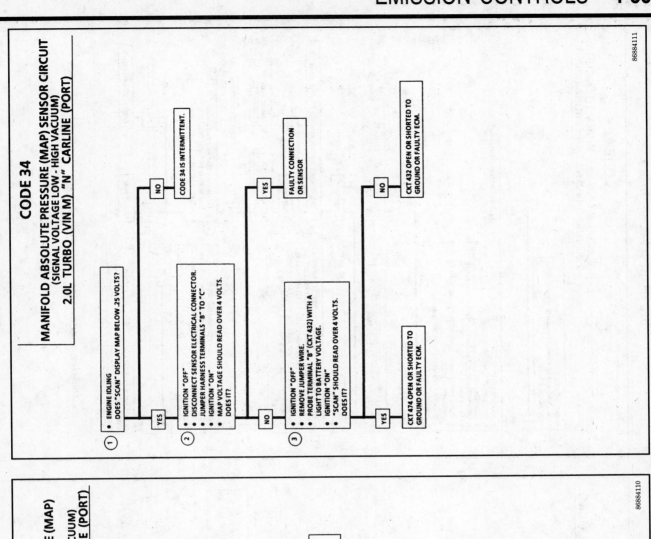

DTC CHART — 2.0L MFI-TURBO

"SCAN" DIAGNOSTICS

CODE 33

MANIFOLD ABSOLUTE PRESSURE (MAP)
SENSOR CIRCUIT
(SIGNAL VOLTAGE HIGH - LOW VACUUM)
2.0L TURBO (VIN M) "N" CARLINE (PORT)

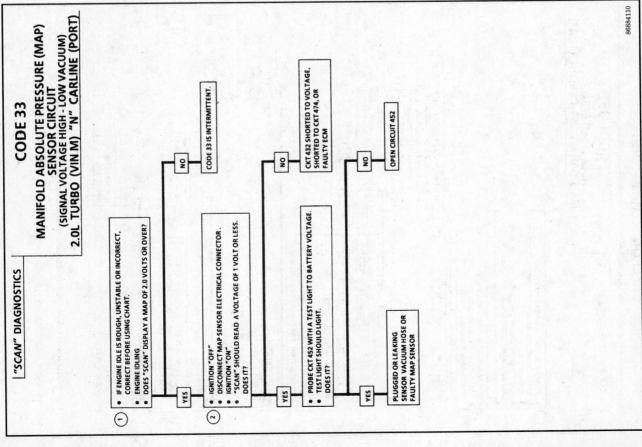

DTC CHART — 2.0L MFI-TURBO

CODE 42
ELECTRONIC SPARK TIMING (EST) CIRCUIT
2.0L TURBO (VIN M) "N" CARLINE (PORT)

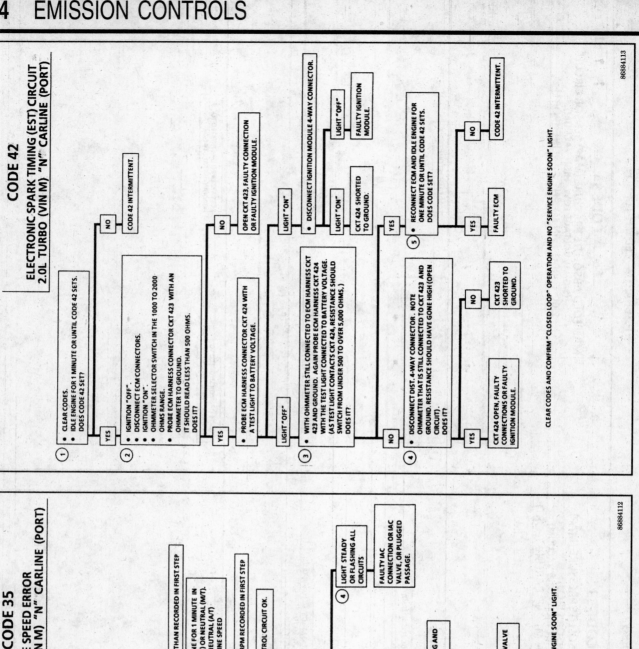

① • CLEAR CODES.
• IDLE ENGINE FOR 1 MINUTE OR UNTIL CODE 42 SETS.
  DOES CODE 42 SET?

NO → CODE 42 INTERMITTENT.

YES

② • IGNITION "OFF".
• DISCONNECT ECM CONNECTORS.
• IGNITION "ON".
• OHMMETER SELECTOR SWITCH IN THE 1000 TO 2000-OHMS RANGE.
• PROBE ECM HARNESS CONNECTOR CKT 423 WITH AN OHMMETER TO GROUND.
  IT SHOULD READ LESS THAN 500 OHMS.
  DOES IT?

NO → OPEN CKT 423, FAULTY CONNECTION OR FAULTY IGNITION MODULE.

YES

• PROBE ECM HARNESS CONNECTOR CKT 424 WITH A TEST LIGHT TO BATTERY VOLTAGE.

LIGHT "OFF"

LIGHT "ON"

③ • WITH OHMMETER STILL CONNECTED TO ECM HARNESS CKT 423 AND GROUND. AGAIN PROBE ECM HARNESS CKT 424 WITH THE TEST LIGHT CONNECTED TO BATTERY VOLTAGE. (AS TEST LIGHT CONTACTS CKT 424, RESISTANCE SHOULD SWITCH FROM UNDER 500 TO OVER 5,000 OHMS.)
  DOES IT?

• DISCONNECT IGNITION MODULE 4-WAY CONNECTOR.

LIGHT "OFF" → CKT 424 SHORTED TO GROUND.

LIGHT "ON" → FAULTY IGNITION MODULE.

YES

⑤ • RECONNECT ECM AND IDLE ENGINE FOR ONE MINUTE OR UNTIL CODE 42 SETS.
  DOES CODE SET?

NO → CODE 42 INTERMITTENT.

YES → FAULTY ECM

NO

④ • DISCONNECT DIST. 4-WAY CONNECTOR. NOTE OHMMETER THAT IS STILL CONNECTED TO CKT 423 AND GROUND. RESISTANCE SHOULD HAVE GONE HIGH (OPEN CIRCUIT).
  DOES IT?

NO → CKT 423 SHORTED TO GROUND.

YES → CKT 424 OPEN, FAULTY CONNECTIONS OR FAULTY IGNITION MODULE.

CLEAR CODES AND CONFIRM "CLOSED LOOP" OPERATION AND NO "SERVICE ENGINE SOON" LIGHT.

DTC CHART — 2.0L MFI-TURBO

CODE 35
IDLE SPEED ERROR
2.0L TURBO (VIN M) "N" CARLINE (PORT)

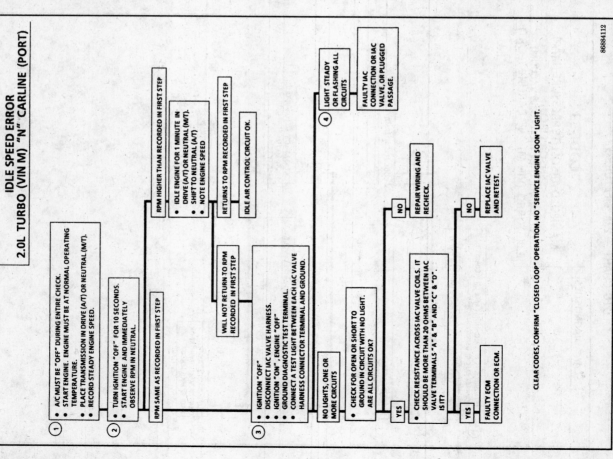

① • A/C MUST BE "OFF" DURING ENTIRE CHECK.
• START ENGINE. ENGINE MUST BE AT NORMAL OPERATING TEMPERATURE.
• PLACE TRANSMISSION IN DRIVE (A/T) OR NEUTRAL (M/T).
• RECORD STEADY ENGINE SPEED.

② • TURN IGNITION "OFF" FOR 10 SECONDS.
• START ENGINE AND IMMEDIATELY OBSERVE RPM IN NEUTRAL.

RPM SAME AS RECORDED IN FIRST STEP

RPM HIGHER THAN RECORDED IN FIRST STEP
• IDLE ENGINE FOR 1 MINUTE IN DRIVE (A/T) OR NEUTRAL (M/T).
• SHIFT TO NEUTRAL (A/T)
• NOTE ENGINE SPEED

WILL NOT RETURN TO RPM RECORDED IN FIRST STEP

RETURNS TO RPM RECORDED IN FIRST STEP → IDLE AIR CONTROL CIRCUIT OK.

③ • IGNITION "OFF".
• DISCONNECT IAC VALVE HARNESS.
• IGNITION "ON", ENGINE "OFF"
• GROUND DIAGNOSTIC TEST TERMINAL.
• CONNECT A TEST LIGHT BETWEEN EACH IAC VALVE HARNESS CONNECTOR TERMINAL AND GROUND.

NO LIGHTS, ONE OR MORE CIRCUITS

• CHECK FOR OPEN OR SHORT TO GROUND IN CIRCUIT WITH NO LIGHT. ARE ALL CIRCUITS OK?

LIGHT STEADY OR FLASHING ALL CIRCUITS

④ → FAULTY IAC CONNECTION OR IAC VALVE, OR PLUGGED PASSAGE.

NO → REPAIR WIRING AND RECHECK.

YES

• CHECK RESISTANCE ACROSS IAC VALVE COILS. IT SHOULD BE MORE THAN 20 OHMS BETWEEN IAC VALVE TERMINALS "A" & "B" AND "C" & "D".
  IS IT?

NO → REPLACE IAC VALVE AND RETEST.

YES → FAULTY ECM CONNECTION OR ECM.

CLEAR CODES, CONFIRM "CLOSED LOOP" OPERATION, NO "SERVICE ENGINE SOON" LIGHT.

86884113

86884112

DTC CHART — 2.0L MFI-TURBO

CODE 44

OXYGEN SENSOR CIRCUIT
(LEAN EXHAUST INDICATED)
2.0L TURBO (VIN M) "N" CARLINE (PORT)

1
- RUN WARM ENGINE (75 TO 95)°C AT 1200 RPM.
- DOES "SCAN" TOOL INDICATE O_2 SENSOR VOLTAGE FIXED BELOW .35 VOLT (350 mV)?

NO → CODE 44 IS INTERMITTENT.

YES →
- DISCONNECT O_2 SENSOR.
- WITH ENGINE IDLING, "SCAN" TOOL SHOULD DISPLAY O_2 SENSOR VOLTAGE BETWEEN .35 VOLT AND .55 VOLT (350 mV AND 550 mV). DOES IT?

NO → CKT 412 SHORTED TO GROUND OR FAULTY ECM.

YES →

CLEAR CODES AND CONFIRM "CLOSED LOOP" OPERATION AND NO "SERVICE ENGINE SOON" LIGHT.

86884115

DTC CHART — 2.0L MFI-TURBO

CODE 43

ELECTRONIC SPARK CONTROL (ESC) CIRCUIT
2.0L TURBO (VIN M) "N" CARLINE (PORT)

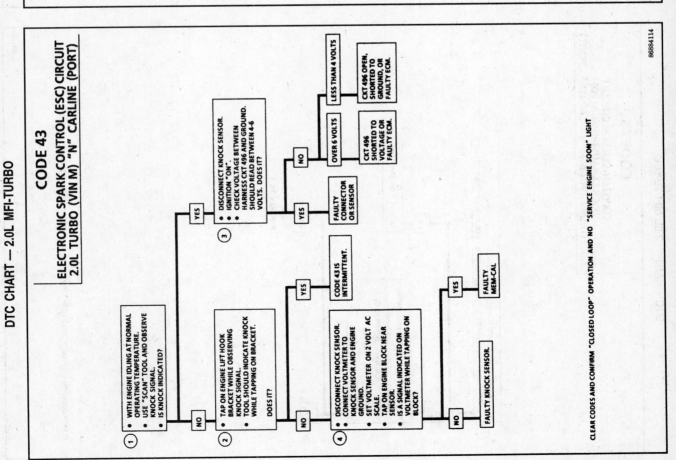

1
- WITH ENGINE IDLING AT NORMAL OPERATING TEMPERATURE.
- USE "SCAN" TOOL AND OBSERVE KNOCK SIGNAL.
- IS KNOCK INDICATED?

NO →

2
- TAP ON ENGINE LIFT HOOK BRACKET WHILE OBSERVING KNOCK SIGNAL.
- TOOL SHOULD INDICATE KNOCK WHILE TAPPING ON BRACKET.
  DOES IT?

NO →

4
- DISCONNECT KNOCK SENSOR. CONNECT VOLTMETER TO KNOCK SENSOR AND ENGINE GROUND.
- SET VOLTMETER ON 2 VOLT AC SCALE.
- TAP ON ENGINE BLOCK NEAR SENSOR.
- IS A SIGNAL INDICATED ON VOLTMETER WHILE TAPPING ON BLOCK?

YES → CODE 43 IS INTERMITTENT.

YES →

3
- DISCONNECT KNOCK SENSOR. IGNITION "ON".
- CHECK VOLTAGE BETWEEN HARNESS CKT 496 AND GROUND. SHOULD READ BETWEEN 4-6 VOLTS. DOES IT?

YES → FAULTY CONNECTOR OR SENSOR

NO →

OVER 6 VOLTS → CKT 496 SHORTED TO VOLTAGE OR FAULTY ECM.

LESS THAN 4 VOLTS → CKT 496 OPEN, SHORTED TO GROUND, OR FAULTY ECM.

YES → FAULTY MEM-CAL

NO → FAULTY KNOCK SENSOR.

CLEAR CODES AND CONFIRM "CLOSED LOOP" OPERATION AND NO "SERVICE ENGINE SOON" LIGHT

86884114

DTC CHART — 2.0L MFI-TURBO

CODE 45
OXYGEN SENSOR CIRCUIT
(RICH EXHAUST INDICATED)
2.0L TURBO (VIN M) "N" CARLINE (PORT)

(1)
- RUN WARM ENGINE (75°C TO 95°C) AT 1200 RPM.
- DOES "SCAN" TOOL DISPLAY O_2 SENSOR VOLTAGE FIXED ABOVE .75 VOLT (750 mV)?

YES		NO

NO → CODE 45 IS INTERMITTENT.

YES →
- DISCONNECT O_2 SENSOR AND JUMPER HARNESS CKT 412 TO GROUND.
- "SCAN" TOOL SHOULD DISPLAY O_2 BELOW .35 VOLT (350 mV).
- DOES IT?

YES →

NO → REPLACE ECM.

CLEAR CODES AND CONFIRM "CLOSED LOOP" OPERATION AND NO "SERVICE ENGINE SOON" LIGHT.

86884116

DTC CHART — 2.0L MFI-TURBO

CODE 51
PROM ERROR
(FAULTY OR INCORRECT PROM)
2.0L TURBO (VIN M) "N" CARLINE (PORT)

CHECK THAT ALL PINS ARE FULLY INSERTED IN THE SOCKET AND THAT PROM IS PROPERLY SEATED. IF OK, REPLACE PROM, CLEAR MEMORY, AND RECHECK. IF CODE 51 REAPPEARS, REPLACE ECM.

CLEAR CODES AND CONFIRM "CLOSED LOOP" OPERATION AND NO "SERVICE ENGINE SOON" LIGHT.

86884117

DTC CHART — 2.3L MFI

DTC 14

ENGINE COOLANT TEMPERATURE (ECT) SENSOR CIRCUIT
(HIGH TEMPERATURE INDICATED)
2.3L (VIN D, A & 3) "N" CARLINE

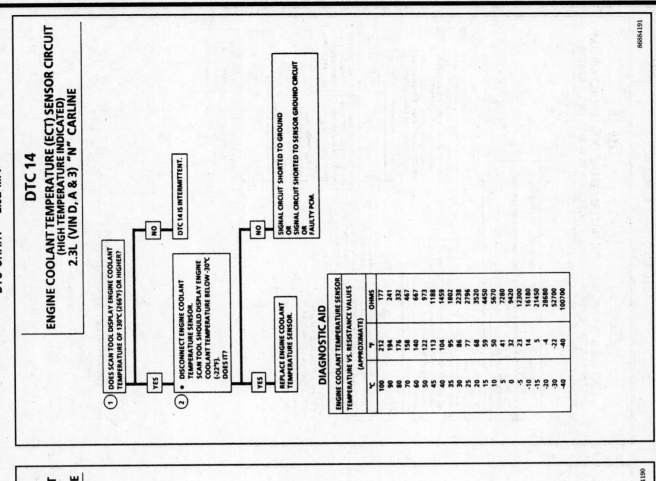

DIAGNOSTIC AID

ENGINE COOLANT TEMPERATURE SENSOR
TEMPERATURE VS. RESISTANCE VALUES
(APPROXIMATE)

°C	°F	OHMS
100	212	177
90	194	241
80	176	332
70	158	467
60	140	667
50	122	973
45	113	1188
40	104	1459
35	95	1802
30	86	2238
25	77	2796
20	68	3520
15	59	4450
10	50	5670
5	41	7280
0	32	9420
-5	23	12300
-10	14	16180
-15	5	21450
-20	-4	28680
-30	-22	52700
-40	-40	100700

86684191

DTC CHART — 2.3L MFI

DTC 13

OXYGEN SENSOR (O2S) CIRCUIT
(OPEN CIRCUIT)
2.3L (VIN D, A & 3) "N" CARLINE

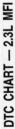
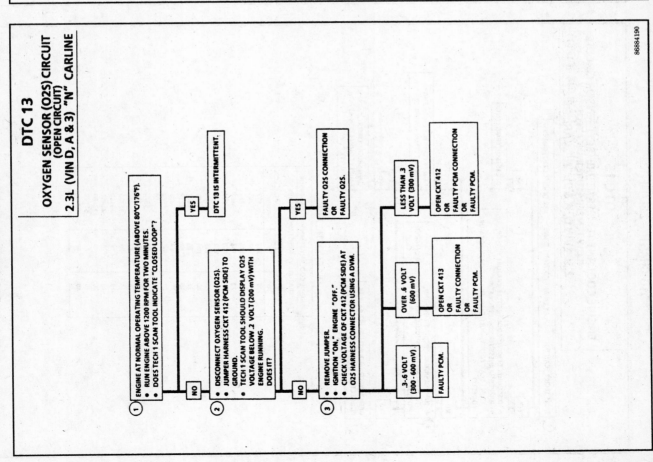

86684190

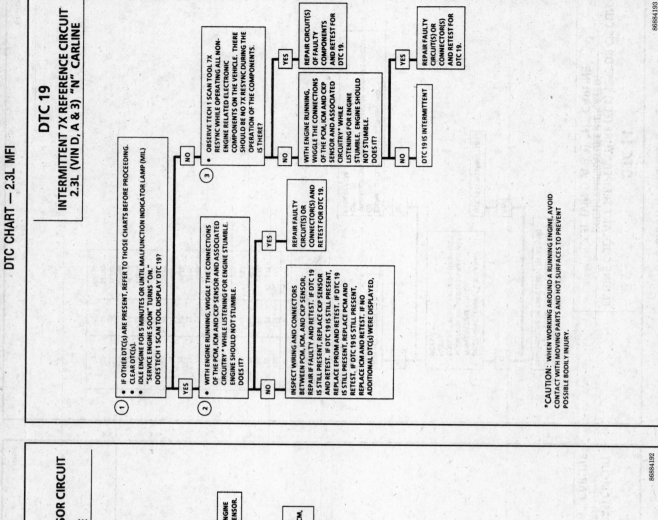

DTC CHART — 2.3L MFI

DTC 19
INTERMITTENT 7X REFERENCE CIRCUIT
2.3L (VIN D, A & 3) "N" CARLINE

① IF OTHER DTC(s) ARE PRESENT, REFER TO THOSE CHARTS BEFORE PROCEEDING.
- CLEAR DTC(s).
- IDLE ENGINE FOR 5 MINUTES OR UNTIL MALFUNCTION INDICATOR LAMP (MIL) "SERVICE ENGINE SOON" TURNS "ON."
DOES TECH 1 SCAN TOOL DISPLAY DTC 19?

② WITH ENGINE RUNNING, WIGGLE THE CONNECTIONS OF THE PCM, ICM AND CKP SENSOR AND ASSOCIATED CIRCUITRY* WHILE LISTENING FOR ENGINE STUMBLE. ENGINE SHOULD NOT STUMBLE. DOES IT?

REPAIR FAULTY CIRCUIT(S) OR CONNECTOR(S) AND RETEST FOR DTC 19.

INSPECT WIRING AND CONNECTORS BETWEEN PCM, ICM, AND CKP SENSOR. REPAIR IF FAULTY AND RETEST. IF DTC 19 IS STILL PRESENT, REPLACE CKP SENSOR AND RETEST. IF DTC 19 IS STILL PRESENT, REPLACE EPROM AND RETEST. IF DTC 19 IS STILL PRESENT, REPLACE PCM AND RETEST. IF DTC 19 IS STILL PRESENT, REPLACE ICM AND RETEST. IF NO ADDITIONAL DTC(s) WERE DISPLAYED,

③ OBSERVE TECH 1 SCAN TOOL 7X RESYNC WHILE OPERATING ALL NON-ENGINE RELATED ELECTRONIC COMPONENTS ON THE VEHICLE. THERE SHOULD BE NO 7X RESYNC DURING THE OPERATION OF THE COMPONENTS. IS THERE?

REPAIR CIRCUIT(S) OF FAULTY COMPONENTS AND RETEST FOR DTC 19.

WITH ENGINE RUNNING, WIGGLE THE CONNECTIONS OF THE PCM, ICM AND CKP SENSOR AND ASSOCIATED CIRCUITRY* WHILE LISTENING FOR ENGINE STUMBLE. ENGINE SHOULD NOT STUMBLE. DOES IT?

REPAIR FAULTY CIRCUIT(S) OR CONNECTOR(S) AND RETEST FOR DTC 19.

DTC 19 IS INTERMITTENT

*CAUTION: WHEN WORKING AROUND A RUNNING ENGINE, AVOID CONTACT WITH MOVING PARTS AND HOT SURFACES TO PREVENT POSSIBLE BODILY INJURY.

86884193

DTC CHART — 2.3L MFI

DTC 15
ENGINE COOLANT TEMPERATURE (ECT) SENSOR CIRCUIT
(LOW TEMPERATURE INDICATED)
2.3L (VIN D, A & 3) "N" CARLINE

① DOES TECH 1 SCAN TOOL DISPLAY ENGINE COOLANT TEMPERATURE OF -30°C (-22°F) OR LESS?

DTC 15 IS INTERMITTENT.

② - DISCONNECT ENGINE COOLANT TEMPERATURE SENSOR.
- JUMPER HARNESS TERMINALS TOGETHER.
TECH 1 SCAN TOOL SHOULD DISPLAY 130°C (266°F) OR MORE. DOES IT?

FAULTY CONNECTION OR ENGINE COOLANT TEMPERATURE SENSOR.

③ JUMPER SIGNAL CIRCUIT TO GROUND. TECH 1 SCAN TOOL SHOULD DISPLAY OVER 130°C (266°F). DOES IT?

OPEN SIGNAL CIRCUIT, FAULTY CONNECTION AT PCM, OR FAULTY PCM.

OPEN SENSOR GROUND CIRCUIT, FAULTY CONNECTION OR FAULTY PCM.

DIAGNOSTIC AID

ENGINE COOLANT TEMPERATURE SENSOR
TEMPERATURE VS. RESISTANCE VALUES (APPROXIMATE)

°C	°F	OHM
100	212	177
90	194	241
80	176	332
70	158	467
60	140	667
50	122	973
45	113	1188
40	104	1459
35	95	1802
30	86	2238
25	77	2796
20	68	3520
15	59	4450
10	50	5670
5	41	7280
0	32	9420
-5	23	12300
-10	14	16180
-15	5	21450
-20	-4	28680
-30	-22	52700
-40	-40	100700S-

86884192

DTC CHART — 2.3L MFI

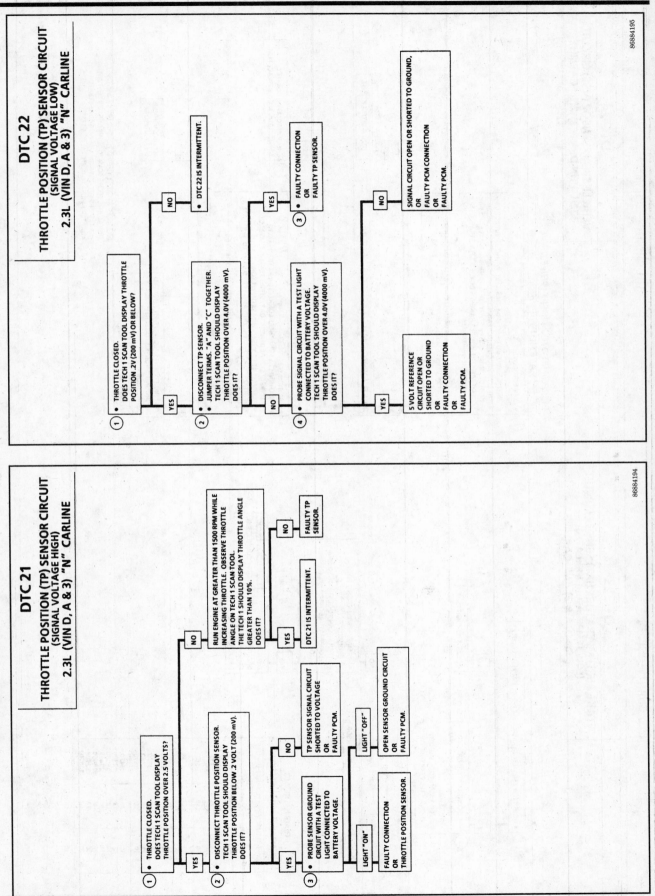

DTC 22

THROTTLE POSITION (TP) SENSOR CIRCUIT
(SIGNAL VOLTAGE LOW)
2.3L (VIN D, A & 3) "N" CARLINE

86884195

1. THROTTLE CLOSED.
   DOES TECH 1 SCAN TOOL DISPLAY THROTTLE POSITION .2V (200 mV) OR BELOW?

   NO → DTC 22 IS INTERMITTENT.

   YES →

2. DISCONNECT TP SENSOR.
   JUMPER TERMS. "A" AND "C" TOGETHER.
   TECH 1 SCAN TOOL SHOULD DISPLAY THROTTLE POSITION OVER 4.0V (4000 mV).
   DOES IT?

   YES → 3 FAULTY CONNECTION OR FAULTY TP SENSOR.

   NO →

4. PROBE SIGNAL CIRCUIT WITH A TEST LIGHT CONNECTED TO BATTERY VOLTAGE.
   TECH 1 SCAN TOOL SHOULD DISPLAY THROTTLE POSITION OVER 4.0V (4000 mV).
   DOES IT?

   NO → SIGNAL CIRCUIT OPEN OR SHORTED TO GROUND, OR FAULTY PCM CONNECTION OR FAULTY PCM.

   YES → 5 VOLT REFERENCE CIRCUIT OPEN OR SHORTED TO GROUND OR FAULTY CONNECTION OR FAULTY PCM.

DTC CHART — 2.3L MFI

DTC 21

THROTTLE POSITION (TP) SENSOR CIRCUIT
(SIGNAL VOLTAGE HIGH)
2.3L (VIN D, A & 3) "N" CARLINE

86884194

1. THROTTLE CLOSED.
   DOES TECH 1 SCAN TOOL DISPLAY THROTTLE POSITION OVER 2.5 VOLTS?

   NO → RUN ENGINE AT GREATER THAN 1500 RPM WHILE INCREASING THROTTLE. OBSERVE THROTTLE ANGLE ON TECH 1 SCAN TOOL.
   THE TECH 1 SHOULD DISPLAY THROTTLE ANGLE GREATER THAN 10%.
   DOES IT?

   NO → FAULTY TP SENSOR.

   YES → DTC 21 IS INTERMITTENT.

   YES →

2. DISCONNECT THROTTLE POSITION SENSOR.
   TECH 1 SCAN TOOL SHOULD DISPLAY THROTTLE POSITION BELOW .2 VOLT (200 mV).
   DOES IT?

   NO → TP SENSOR SIGNAL CIRCUIT SHORTED TO VOLTAGE OR FAULTY PCM.

   YES →

3. PROBE SENSOR GROUND CIRCUIT WITH A TEST LIGHT CONNECTED TO BATTERY VOLTAGE.

   LIGHT "OFF" → OPEN SENSOR GROUND CIRCUIT OR FAULTY PCM.

   LIGHT "ON" → FAULTY CONNECTION OR THROTTLE POSITION SENSOR.

DTC CHART — 2.3L MFI

DTC 24
VEHICLE SPEED SENSOR (VSS) CIRCUIT
2.3L (VIN D, A & 3) "N" CARLINE

DISREGARD DTC 24 IF SET WHILE DRIVE WHEELS ARE NOT TURNING.

(1)
- RAISE DRIVE WHEELS.
- NOTICE: DO NOT PERFORM THIS TEST WITHOUT SUPPORTING THE LOWER CONTROL ARMS SO THAT THE DRIVE AXLES ARE IN A NORMAL HORIZONTAL POSITION. RUNNING THE VEHICLE IN GEAR WITH THE WHEELS HANGING DOWN AT FULL TRAVEL MAY DAMAGE THE DRIVE AXLES.
- WITH ENGINE IDLING IN GEAR, TECH 1 SCAN TOOL SHOULD DISPLAY VEHICLE SPEED ABOVE 0. DOES IT?

YES → DTC 24 IS INTERMITTENT.

NO → DOES SPEEDOMETER WORK?

YES → CHECK EPROM FOR CORRECT APPLICATION. IF OK, REPLACE PCM. (2)

NO →
(2)
- IGNITION "OFF."
- DISCONNECT VSS HARNESS CONNECTOR AT TRANSAXLE.
- CONNECT SIGNAL GENERATOR TESTER J 33431-B, J 38522 OR EQUIVALENT TO VSS HARNESS CONNECTOR.
- IGNITION "ON," TESTER "ON" AND SET TO 60 Hz TO GENERATE A VSS SIGNAL.
- SCAN TOOL SHOULD DISPLAY VEHICLE SPEED ABOVE 0. DOES IT?

YES → REPLACE VEHICLE SPEED SENSOR.

NO → VSS "HIGH" OR VSS "LOW" OPEN, SHORTED TO GROUND, SHORTED TOGETHER, FAULTY CONNECTIONS, OR FAULTY PCM.

NOTICE: BECAUSE THE VSS OUTPUT USES A 4000 PPM SIGNAL, THE TECH 1 SCAN TOOL WILL READ 9 MPH WITH THE TESTERS SET ON 60 Hz. USE SIGNAL GENERATOR ADAPTER J 41059 TO PERFORM THIS TEST.

86884197

DTC CHART — 2.3L MFI

DTC 23
INTAKE AIR TEMPERATURE (IAT) SENSOR CIRCUIT
(LOW TEMPERATURE INDICATED)
2.3L (VIN D, A & 3) "N" CARLINE

(1)
- DOES TECH 1 SCAN TOOL DISPLAY IAT -30°C (-22°F) OR COLDER?

NO → DTC 23 IS INTERMITTENT.

YES →
(2)
- DISCONNECT SENSOR.
- JUMPER HARNESS TERMINALS TOGETHER.
- TECH 1 SCAN TOOL SHOULD DISPLAY TEMPERATURE OVER 130°C (266°F). DOES IT?

YES → FAULTY CONNECTION OR SENSOR.

NO →
(3)
- JUMPER SIGNAL CIRCUIT TO GROUND.
- TECH 1 SCAN TOOL SHOULD DISPLAY TEMPERATURE OVER 130°C (266°F). DOES IT?

YES → OPEN SENSOR GROUND CIRCUIT, FAULTY CONNECTION OR FAULTY PCM.

NO → OPEN SIGNAL CIRCUIT, FAULTY CONNECTION OR FAULTY PCM.

DIAGNOSTIC AID

INTAKE AIR TEMPERATURE SENSOR
TEMPERATURE VS. RESISTANCE VALUES (APPROXIMATE)

°C	°F	OHMS
100	212	177
90	194	241
80	176	332
70	158	467
60	140	667
50	122	973
45	113	1188
40	104	1459
35	95	1802
30	86	2238
25	77	2796
20	68	3520
15	59	4450
10	50	5670
5	41	7280
0	32	9420
-5	23	12300
-10	14	16180
-15	5	21450
-20	-4	28680
-30	-22	52700
-40	-40	100700

86884196

DTC CHART — 2.3L MFI

DTC 26
QUAD-DRIVER MODULE (QDSM) CIRCUIT
2.3L (VIN D, A & 3) "N" CARLINE

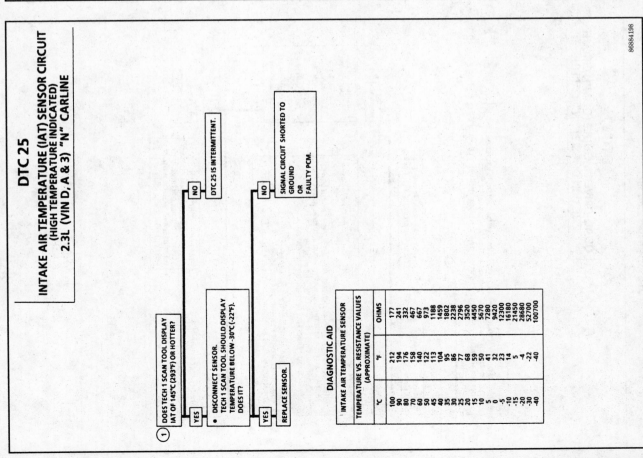

1. • INSTALL TECH 1 SCAN TOOL.
   • IGNITION "ON," ENGINE "OFF."
   • SCAN DTC(s).
   IS DTC 26 SET?

   NO → DTC 26 FAULT IS INTERMITTENT. CHECK FOR POOR TERMINAL CONTACT AT PCM AND QDSM CIRCUITRY.

2. • ENGINE RUNNING
   • USING TECH 1 SCAN TOOL, COMMAND MIL "ON" THEN "OFF." DOES MIL TURN "ON" AND "OFF" WHEN COMMANDED?

   NO → REFER TO "CHART A-1".

3. • USING TECH 1 SCAN TOOL OUTPUT CONTROL FUNCTION, COMMAND, TEMPERATURE/CHECK GAUGES LIGHT "ON" AND THEN "OFF." DOES TEMPERATURE/CHECK GAUGES LIGHT TURN "ON" AND "OFF" WHEN COMMANDED?

   YES → DTC 26 FAULT IS INTERMITTENT. CHECK FOR POOR TERMINAL CONTACT AT PCM AND QDSM CIRCUITRY. IF OK, CLEAR DTC(s) AND RE-CHECK. IF DTC 26 RESETS, REPLACE PCM.

DTC CHART — 2.3L MFI

DTC 25
INTAKE AIR TEMPERATURE (IAT) SENSOR CIRCUIT
(HIGH TEMPERATURE INDICATED)
2.3L (VIN D, A & 3) "N" CARLINE

1. DOES TECH 1 SCAN TOOL DISPLAY IAT OF 145°C (293°F) OR HOTTER?

   NO → DTC 25 IS INTERMITTENT.

   • DISCONNECT SENSOR. TECH 1 SCAN TOOL SHOULD DISPLAY TEMPERATURE BELOW -30°C (-22°F). DOES IT?

   NO → SIGNAL CIRCUIT SHORTED TO GROUND OR FAULTY PCM.

   YES → REPLACE SENSOR.

DIAGNOSTIC AID

INTAKE AIR TEMPERATURE SENSOR

TEMPERATURE VS. RESISTANCE VALUES (APPROXIMATE)		
°C	°F	OHMS
100	212	177
90	194	241
80	176	332
70	158	467
60	140	667
50	122	973
45	113	1188
40	104	1459
35	95	1802
30	86	2238
25	77	2796
20	68	3520
15	59	4450
10	50	5670
5	41	7280
0	32	9420
-5	23	12300
-10	14	16180
-15	5	21450
-20	-4	28680
-30	-22	52700
-40	-40	100700

86684199

86684198

DTC CHART — 2.3L MFI

DTC 28
QUAD-DRIVER MODULE (QDM 2) CIRCUIT
2.3L (VIN D, A & 3) "N" CARLINE

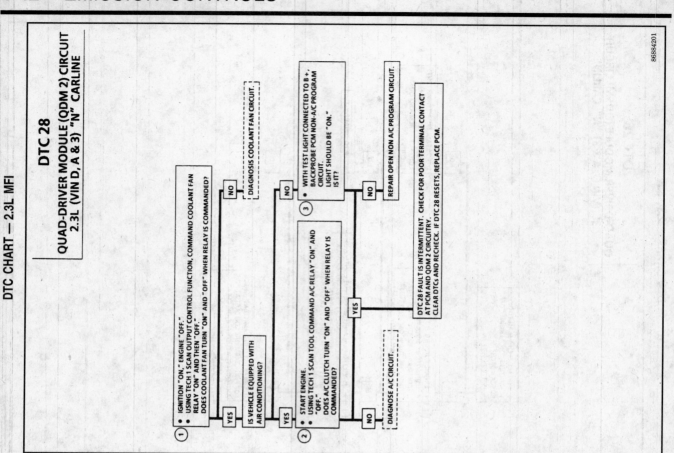

① • IGNITION "ON," ENGINE "OFF."
• USING TECH 1 SCAN OUTPUT CONTROL FUNCTION, COMMAND COOLANT FAN RELAY "ON" AND THEN "OFF."
• DOES COOLANT FAN TURN "ON" AND "OFF" WHEN RELAY IS COMMANDED?

YES → IS VEHICLE EQUIPPED WITH AIR CONDITIONING?

NO → DIAGNOSIS COOLANT FAN CIRCUIT.

② • START ENGINE.
• USING TECH 1 SCAN TOOL COMMAND A/C RELAY "ON" AND "OFF."
• DOES A/C CLUTCH TURN "ON" AND "OFF" WHEN RELAY IS COMMANDED?

YES

NO → DIAGNOSE A/C CIRCUIT.

③ WITH TEST LIGHT CONNECTED TO B +, BACKPROBE PCM NON-A/C PROGRAM CIRCUIT.
LIGHT SHOULD BE "ON."
IS IT?

NO → REPAIR OPEN NON A/C PROGRAM CIRCUIT.

DTC 28 FAULT IS INTERMITTENT. CHECK FOR POOR TERMINAL CONTACT AT PCM AND QDM 2 CIRCUITRY. CLEAR DTCs AND RECHECK. IF DTC 28 RESETS, REPLACE PCM.

86884201

DTC CHART — 2.3L MFI

DTC 27
QUAD-DRIVER MODULE (QDM 1) CIRCUIT
2.3L (VIN D, A & 3) "N" CARLINE

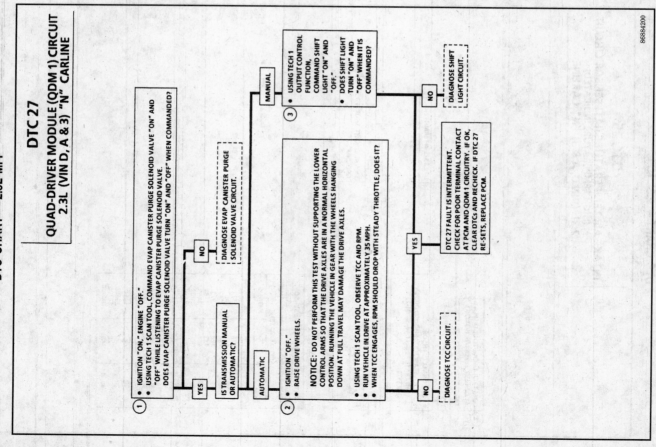

① • IGNITION "ON," ENGINE "OFF."
• USING TECH 1 SCAN TOOL, COMMAND EVAP CANISTER PURGE SOLENOID VALVE "ON" AND "OFF" WHILE LISTENING TO EVAP CANISTER PURGE SOLENOID VALVE.
• DOES EVAP CANISTER PURGE SOLENOID VALVE TURN "ON" AND "OFF" WHEN COMMANDED?

YES → IS TRANSMISSION MANUAL OR AUTOMATIC?

NO → DIAGNOSE EVAP CANISTER PURGE SOLENOID VALVE CIRCUIT.

AUTOMATIC

② • IGNITION "OFF."
• RAISE DRIVE WHEELS.
NOTICE: DO NOT PERFORM THIS TEST WITHOUT SUPPORTING THE LOWER CONTROL ARMS SO THAT THE DRIVE AXLES ARE IN A NORMAL HORIZONTAL POSITION. RUNNING THE VEHICLE IN GEAR WITH THE WHEELS HANGING DOWN AT FULL TRAVEL MAY DAMAGE THE DRIVE AXLES.
• USING TECH 1 SCAN TOOL, OBSERVE TCC AND RPM.
• RUN VEHICLE IN DRIVE AT APPROXIMATELY 35 MPH.
• WHEN TCC ENGAGES, RPM SHOULD DROP WITH STEADY THROTTLE, DOES IT?

NO → DIAGNOSE TCC CIRCUIT.

YES → DTC 27 FAULT IS INTERMITTENT. CHECK FOR POOR TERMINAL CONTACT AT PCM AND QDM 1 CIRCUITRY. IF OK, CLEAR DTCs AND RECHECK. IF DTC 27 RE-SETS, REPLACE PCM.

MANUAL

③ • USING TECH 1 OUTPUT CONTROL FUNCTION, COMMAND SHIFT LIGHT "ON" AND "OFF."
• DOES SHIFT LIGHT TURN "ON" AND "OFF" WHEN IT IS COMMANDED?

NO → DIAGNOSE SHIFT LIGHT CIRCUIT.

86884200

DTC CHART — 2.3L MFI

DTC 33

MANIFOLD ABSOLUTE PRESSURE (MAP) SENSOR CIRCUIT
(SIGNAL VOLTAGE HIGH - LOW VACUUM)
2.3L (VIN D, A & 3) "N" CARLINE

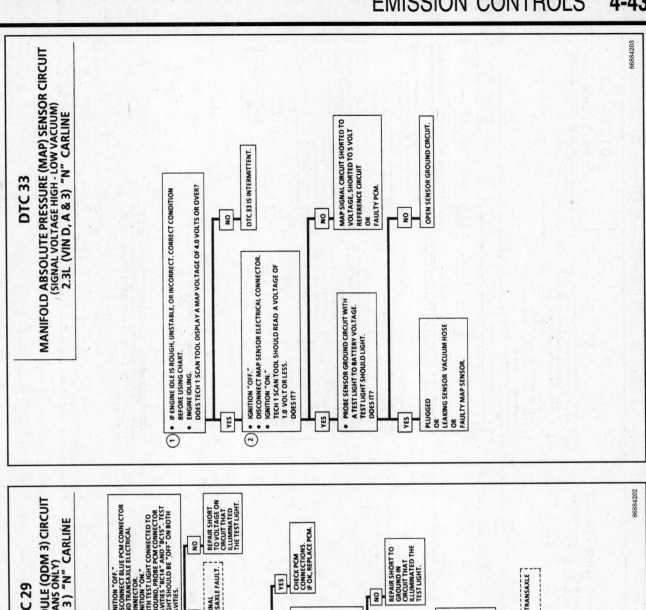

DTC CHART — 2.3L MFI

DTC 29

QUAD-DRIVER MODULE (QDM 3) CIRCUIT
(4T60E TRANS ONLY)
2.3L (VIN D, A & 3) "N" CARLINE

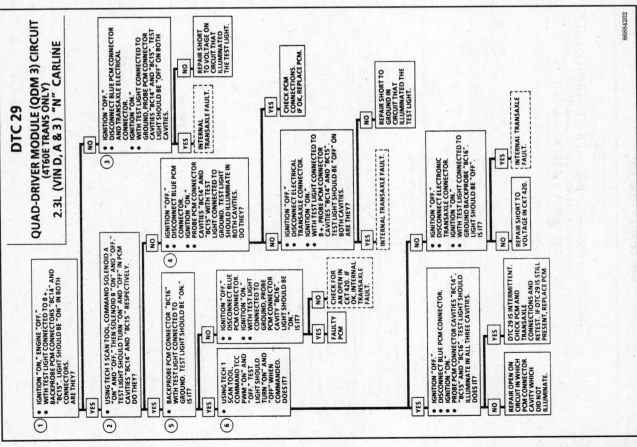

DTC CHART — 2.3L MFI

DTC 35

IDLE SPEED ERROR
2.3L (VIN D, A & 3) "N" CARLINE

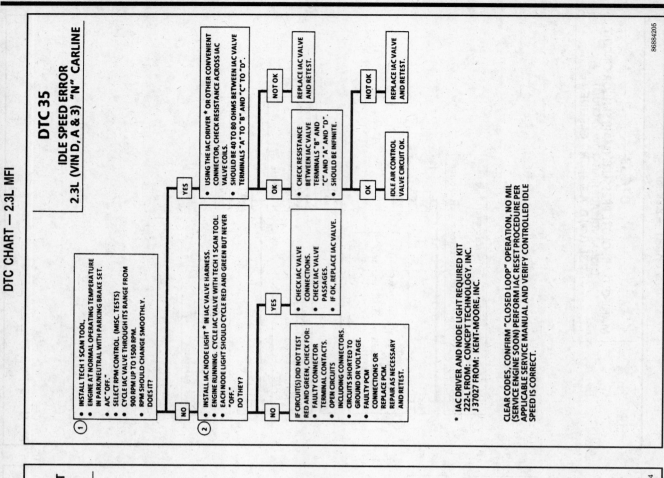

(1)
- INSTALL TECH 1 SCAN TOOL.
- ENGINE AT NORMAL OPERATING TEMPERATURE IN PARK/NEUTRAL WITH PARKING BRAKE SET.
- A/C "OFF."
- SELECT RPM CONTROL. (MISC. TESTS)
- CYCLE IAC VALVE THROUGH ITS RANGE FROM 900 RPM UP TO 1500 RPM.
- RPM SHOULD CHANGE SMOOTHLY.
  DOES IT?

NO

(2)
- INSTALL IAC NODE LIGHT * IN IAC VALVE HARNESS.
- ENGINE RUNNING. CYCLE IAC VALVE WITH TECH 1 SCAN TOOL.
- EACH NODE LIGHT SHOULD CYCLE RED AND GREEN BUT NEVER "OFF."
  DO THEY?

YES

- USING THE IAC DRIVER * OR OTHER CONVENIENT CONNECTOR, CHECK RESISTANCE ACROSS IAC VALVE COILS.
- SHOULD BE 40 TO 80 OHMS BETWEEN IAC VALVE TERMINALS "A" TO "B" AND "C" TO "D".

OK / NOT OK → REPLACE IAC VALVE AND RETEST.

CHECK RESISTANCE BETWEEN IAC VALVE TERMINALS "B" AND "C" AND "A" AND "D". SHOULD BE INFINITE.

OK → IDLE AIR CONTROL VALVE CIRCUIT OK.

NOT OK → REPLACE IAC VALVE AND RETEST.

NO

IF CIRCUIT(S) DID NOT TEST RED AND GREEN, CHECK FOR:
- FAULTY CONNECTOR TERMINAL CONTACTS.
- OPEN CIRCUITS
- CIRCUITS SHORTED TO GROUND OR VOLTAGE.
- FAULTY PCM CONNECTIONS OR REPLACE PCM.
  REPAIR AS NECESSARY AND RETEST.

YES

- CHECK IAC VALVE CONNECTIONS.
- CHECK IAC VALVE PASSAGES.
- IF OK, REPLACE IAC VALVE.

* IAC DRIVER AND NODE LIGHT REQUIRED KIT 222-L FROM: CONCEPT TECHNOLOGY, INC. J 37027 FROM: KENT-MOORE, INC.

CLEAR CODES, CONFIRM "CLOSED LOOP" OPERATION, NO MIL (SERVICE ENGINE SOON) PERFORM IAC RESET PROCEDURE PER APPLICABLE SERVICE MANUAL AND VERIFY CONTROLLED IDLE SPEED IS CORRECT.

86884205

DTC CHART — 2.3L MFI

DTC 34

MANIFOLD ABSOLUTE PRESSURE (MAP) SENSOR CIRCUIT
(SIGNAL VOLTAGE LOW - HIGH VACUUM)
2.3L (VIN D, A & 3) "N" CARLINE

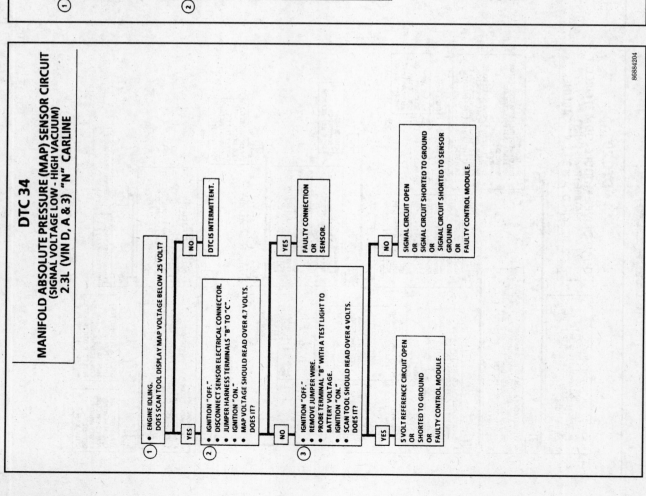

(1)
- ENGINE IDLING.
  DOES SCAN TOOL DISPLAY MAP VOLTAGE BELOW .25 VOLT?

YES

NO → DTC IS INTERMITTENT.

(2)
- IGNITION "OFF."
- DISCONNECT SENSOR ELECTRICAL CONNECTOR. JUMPER HARNESS TERMINALS "B" TO "C".
- IGNITION "ON."
- MAP VOLTAGE SHOULD READ OVER 4.7 VOLTS. DOES IT?

NO

YES → FAULTY CONNECTION OR SENSOR.

(3)
- IGNITION "OFF."
- REMOVE JUMPER WIRE.
- PROBE TERMINAL "B" WITH A TEST LIGHT TO BATTERY VOLTAGE.
- IGNITION "ON."
- SCAN TOOL SHOULD READ OVER 4 VOLTS. DOES IT?

YES → 5 VOLT REFERENCE CIRCUIT OPEN
OR
SHORTED TO GROUND
OR
FAULTY CONTROL MODULE.

NO → SIGNAL CIRCUIT OPEN
OR
SIGNAL CIRCUIT SHORTED TO GROUND
OR
SIGNAL CIRCUIT SHORTED TO SENSOR GROUND
OR
FAULTY CONTROL MODULE.

86884204

DTC CHART — 2.3L MFI

CODE 42
ELECTRONIC SPARK TIMING (EST) CIRCUIT
2.3L (VIN D & A) "N" CARLINE (PORT)

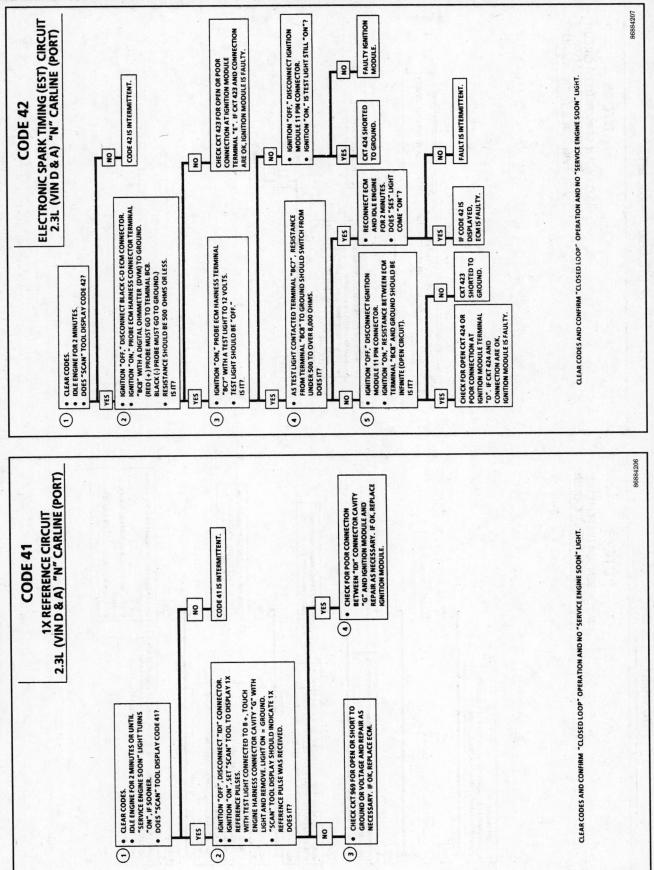

1. • CLEAR CODES.
   • IDLE ENGINE FOR 2 MINUTES.
   • DOES "SCAN" TOOL DISPLAY CODE 42?

NO → CODE 42 IS INTERMITTENT.

YES

2. • IGNITION "OFF." DISCONNECT BLACK C-D ECM CONNECTOR.
   • IGNITION "ON." PROBE ECM HARNESS CONNECTOR TERMINAL "BC8" WITH A DIGITAL OHMMETER (DVM) TO GROUND. (RED (+) PROBE MUST GO TO TERMINAL BC8. BLACK (-) PROBE MUST GO TO GROUND.) RESISTANCE SHOULD BE 500 OHMS OR LESS. IS IT?

NO → CHECK CKT 423 FOR OPEN OR POOR CONNECTION AT IGNITION MODULE TERMINAL "E". IF CKT 423 AND CONNECTION ARE OK, IGNITION MODULE IS FAULTY.

YES

3. • IGNITION "ON." PROBE ECM HARNESS TERMINAL "BC7" WITH A TEST LIGHT TO 12 VOLTS.
   • TEST LIGHT SHOULD BE "OFF."
   • IS IT?

NO → • IGNITION "OFF." DISCONNECT IGNITION MODULE 11 PIN CONNECTOR.
   • IGNITION "ON," IS TEST LIGHT STILL "ON"?

   NO → FAULTY IGNITION MODULE.

   YES → CKT 424 SHORTED TO GROUND.

YES

4. • AS TEST LIGHT CONTACTED TERMINAL "BC7", RESISTANCE FROM TERMINAL "BC8" TO GROUND SHOULD SWITCH FROM UNDER 500 TO OVER 8,000 OHMS. DOES IT?

NO → • IGNITION "OFF." DISCONNECT IGNITION MODULE 11 PIN CONNECTOR.
   • IGNITION "ON," RESISTANCE BETWEEN ECM TERMINAL "BC8" AND GROUND SHOULD BE INFINITE (OPEN CIRCUIT). IS IT?

   YES → CHECK FOR OPEN CKT 424 OR POOR CONNECTION AT IGNITION MODULE TERMINAL "D". IF CKT 424 AND CONNECTION ARE OK, IGNITION MODULE IS FAULTY.

   NO → CKT 423 SHORTED TO GROUND.

YES

5. • RECONNECT ECM AND IDLE ENGINE FOR 2 MINUTES.
   • DOES "SES" LIGHT COME "ON"?

YES → IF CODE 42 IS DISPLAYED, ECM IS FAULTY.

NO → FAULT IS INTERMITTENT.

CLEAR CODES AND CONFIRM "CLOSED LOOP" OPERATION AND NO "SERVICE ENGINE SOON" LIGHT.

86884207

DTC CHART — 2.3L MFI

CODE 41
1X REFERENCE CIRCUIT
2.3L (VIN D & A) "N" CARLINE (PORT)

1. • CLEAR CODES.
   • IDLE ENGINE FOR 2 MINUTES OR UNTIL "SERVICE ENGINE SOON" LIGHT TURNS "ON", IF SOONER.
   • DOES "SCAN" TOOL DISPLAY CODE 41?

NO → CODE 41 IS INTERMITTENT.

YES

2. • IGNITION "OFF". DISCONNECT "IDI" CONNECTOR.
   • IGNITION "ON", SET "SCAN" TOOL TO DISPLAY 1X REFERENCE PULSES.
   • WITH TEST LIGHT CONNECTED TO B+, TOUCH ENGINE HARNESS CONNECTOR CAVITY "G" WITH LIGHT AND REMOVE. LIGHT ON = GROUND.
   • "SCAN" TOOL DISPLAY SHOULD INDICATE 1X REFERENCE PULSE WAS RECEIVED.
   • DOES IT?

YES → CHECK FOR POOR CONNECTION BETWEEN "IDI" CONNECTOR CAVITY "G" AND IGNITION MODULE AND REPAIR AS NECESSARY. IF OK, REPLACE IGNITION MODULE.

NO

3. • CHECK CKT 969 FOR OPEN OR SHORT TO GROUND OR VOLTAGE AND REPAIR AS NECESSARY. IF OK, REPLACE ECM.

CLEAR CODES AND CONFIRM "CLOSED LOOP" OPERATION AND NO "SERVICE ENGINE SOON" LIGHT.

86884206

DTC CHART — 2.3L MFI

DTC 45
OXYGEN SENSOR (O2S) CIRCUIT
(RICH EXHAUST INDICATED)
2.3L (VIN D, A & 3) "N" CARLINE

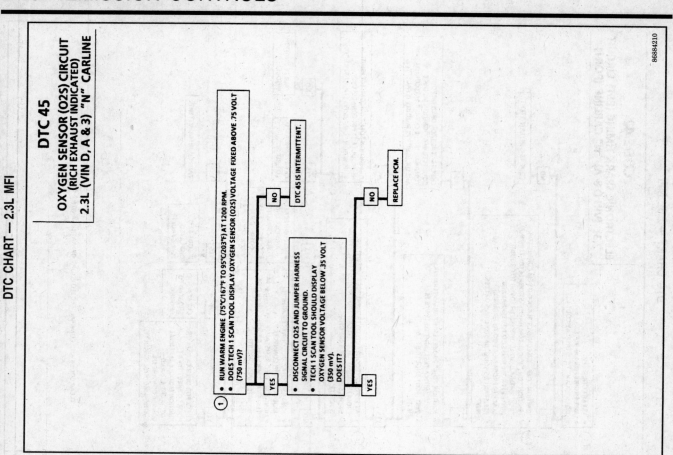

1.
- RUN WARM ENGINE (75°C/167°F TO 95°C/203°F) AT 1200 RPM.
- DOES TECH 1 SCAN TOOL DISPLAY OXYGEN SENSOR (O2S) VOLTAGE FIXED ABOVE .75 VOLT (750 mV)?

YES →
- DISCONNECT O2S AND JUMPER HARNESS SIGNAL CIRCUIT TO GROUND.
- TECH 1 SCAN TOOL SHOULD DISPLAY OXYGEN SENSOR VOLTAGE BELOW .35 VOLT (350 mV).
  DOES IT?

YES → REPLACE PCM.

NO → DTC 45 IS INTERMITTENT.

NO → REPLACE PCM.

86884210

DTC CHART — 2.3L MFI

DTC 43
KNOCK SENSOR (KS) CIRCUIT
2.3L (VIN D, A & 3) "N" CARLINE

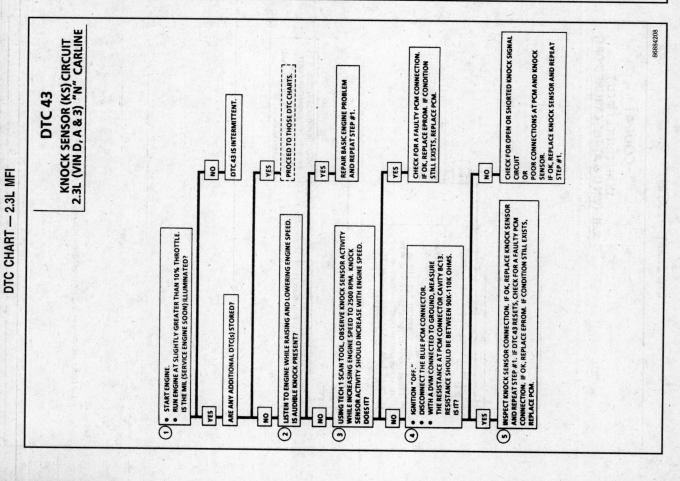

1.
- START ENGINE.
- RUN ENGINE AT SLIGHTLY GREATER THAN 10% THROTTLE.
  IS THE MIL (SERVICE ENGINE SOON) ILLUMINATED?

YES → ARE ANY ADDITIONAL DTC(s) STORED?

NO → DTC 43 IS INTERMITTENT.

YES → PROCEED TO THOSE DTC CHARTS.

2.
- LISTEN TO ENGINE WHILE RAISING AND LOWERING ENGINE SPEED.
  IS AUDIBLE KNOCK PRESENT?

YES → REPAIR BASIC ENGINE PROBLEM AND REPEAT STEP #1.

3.
- USING TECH 1 SCAN TOOL, OBSERVE KNOCK SENSOR ACTIVITY WHILE INCREASING ENGINE SPEED TO 2500 RPM. KNOCK SENSOR ACTIVITY SHOULD INCREASE WITH ENGINE SPEED.
  DOES IT?

YES → CHECK FOR A FAULTY PCM CONNECTION. IF OK, REPLACE EPROM. IF CONDITION STILL EXISTS, REPLACE PCM.

4.
- IGNITION "OFF."
- DISCONNECT THE BLUE PCM CONNECTOR.
- WITH A DVM CONNECTED TO GROUND, MEASURE THE RESISTANCE AT PCM CONNECTOR CAVITY BC13. RESISTANCE SHOULD BE BETWEEN 90K-110K OHMS.
  IS IT?

NO → CHECK FOR OPEN OR SHORTED KNOCK SIGNAL CIRCUIT
OR
POOR CONNECTIONS AT PCM AND KNOCK SENSOR.
IF OK, REPLACE KNOCK SENSOR AND REPEAT STEP #1.

5.
- INSPECT KNOCK SENSOR CONNECTION. IF OK, REPLACE KNOCK SENSOR AND REPEAT STEP #1. IF DTC 43 RESETS, CHECK FOR A FAULTY PCM CONNECTION. IF OK, REPLACE EPROM. IF CONDITION STILL EXISTS, REPLACE PCM.

86884208

DTC CHART — 2.3L MFI

DTC 45
OXYGEN SENSOR (O2S) CIRCUIT
(RICH EXHAUST INDICATED)
2.3L (VIN D, A & 3) "N" CARLINE

① • RUN WARM ENGINE (75°C/167°F TO 95°C/203°F) AT 1200 RPM.
  • DOES TECH 1 SCAN TOOL DISPLAY OXYGEN SENSOR (O2S) VOLTAGE FIXED ABOVE .75 VOLT (750 mV)?

YES	NO

NO → DTC 45 IS INTERMITTENT.

• DISCONNECT O2S AND JUMPER HARNESS SIGNAL CIRCUIT TO GROUND.
• TECH 1 SCAN TOOL SHOULD DISPLAY OXYGEN SENSOR VOLTAGE BELOW .35 VOLT (350 mV).
  DOES IT?

YES	NO

NO → REPLACE PCM.

86884210

DTC CHART — 2.3L MFI

DTC 51
EPROM ERROR
(FAULTY OR INCORRECT EPROM)
2.3L (VIN D, A & 3) "N" CARLINE

CHECK THAT ALL PINS ARE FULLY INSERTED IN THE SOCKET AND THAT EPROM IS PROPERLY LATCHED. IF OK, REPLACE EPROM, CLEAR MEMORY, AND RECHECK. IF DTC 51 REAPPEARS, REPLACE PCM.

NOTICE: TO PREVENT POSSIBLE ELECTROSTATIC DISCHARGE DAMAGE TO THE PCM OR EPROM, DO NOT TOUCH THE COMPONENT LEADS, AND DO NOT REMOVE THE EPROM COVER OR THE INTEGRATED CIRCUIT FROM CARRIER.

86884211

DTC CHART — 2.3L MFI

DTC 53
BATTERY VOLTAGE ERROR
2.3L (VIN D, A & 3) "N" CARLINE

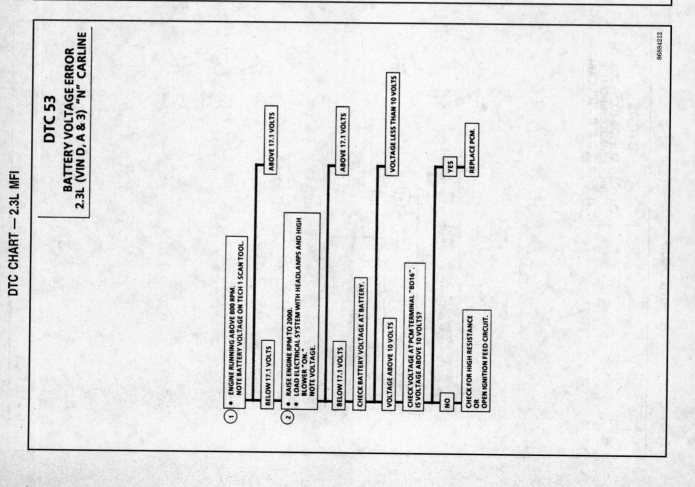

1. ● ENGINE RUNNING ABOVE 800 RPM.
   ● NOTE BATTERY VOLTAGE ON TECH 1 SCAN TOOL.

   BELOW 17.1 VOLTS

   ABOVE 17.1 VOLTS

2. ● RAISE ENGINE RPM TO 2000.
   ● LOAD ELECTRICAL SYSTEM WITH HEADLAMPS AND HIGH BLOWER "ON."
   ● NOTE VOLTAGE.

   BELOW 17.1 VOLTS

   ABOVE 17.1 VOLTS

   CHECK BATTERY VOLTAGE AT BATTERY.

   VOLTAGE ABOVE 10 VOLTS

   VOLTAGE LESS THAN 10 VOLTS

   CHECK VOLTAGE AT PCM TERMINAL "BD16". IS VOLTAGE ABOVE 10 VOLTS?

   YES

   REPLACE PCM.

   NO

   CHECK FOR HIGH RESISTANCE OR OPEN IGNITION FEED CIRCUIT.

86884212

DTC CHART — 2.3L MFI

DTC 55
FUEL LEAN MONITOR
2.3L (VIN D, A, & 3) "N" CARLINE

Important
- DTC 55 MAY SET AS A RESULT OF THE VEHICLE RUNNING OUT OF FUEL.

1. ● CHECK TO SEE IF THERE IS ADEQUATE FUEL IN THE VEHICLE'S TANK BEFORE PROCEEDING.
   ● IF OTHER DTC(s) ARE SET, REFER TO THOSE DTC CHARTS BEFORE PROCEEDING WITH THIS CHART.
   ● IF ENGINE IS IDLING ROUGH, REFER TO CHART C-4M (ELECTRONIC IGNITION (E1) SYSTEM MISFIRE) FOR FURTHER DIAGNOSIS.
   ● USING TECH 1 SCAN TOOL, OBSERVE O2S VOLTAGE WHILE RUNNING WARM ENGINE (75°C/167°F TO 95°C/203°F) AT 1200 RPM. O2S VOLTAGE SHOULD VARY FROM 100 TO 900 mV AND SHOULD OCCASIONALLY TOGGLE ABOVE 447 MV. DOES IT?

   YES

   NO

   O2S VOLTAGE READING LOW. REFER TO DTC 44 FOR FURTHER DIAGNOSIS.

86884213

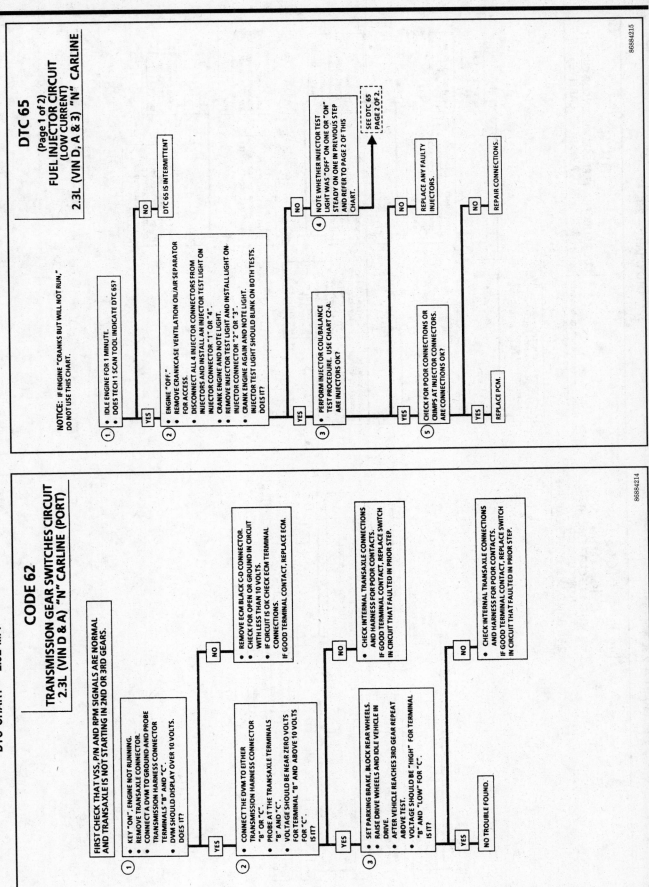

DTC CHART — 2.3L MFI

DTC 65
(Page 1 of 2)
FUEL INJECTOR CIRCUIT
(LOW CURRENT)
2.3L (VIN D, A & 3) "N" CARLINE

NOTICE: IF ENGINE "CRANKS BUT WILL NOT RUN,"
DO NOT USE THIS CHART.

1. • IDLE ENGINE FOR 1 MINUTE.
   • DOES TECH 1 SCAN TOOL INDICATE DTC 65?

NO → DTC 65 IS INTERMITTENT

YES

2. • ENGINE "OFF."
   • REMOVE CRANKCASE VENTILATION OIL/AIR SEPARATOR FOR ACCESS.
   • DISCONNECT ALL 4 INJECTOR CONNECTORS FROM INJECTORS AND INSTALL AN INJECTOR TEST LIGHT ON INJECTOR CONNECTOR "1" OR "4".
   • CRANK ENGINE AND NOTE LIGHT.
   • REMOVE INJECTOR TEST LIGHT AND INSTALL LIGHT ON INJECTOR CONNECTOR "2" OR "3".
   • CRANK ENGINE AGAIN AND NOTE LIGHT. INJECTOR TEST LIGHT SHOULD BLINK ON BOTH TESTS. DOES IT?

NO

4. NOTE WHETHER INJECTOR TEST LIGHT WAS "OFF" ON ONE OR "ON" STEADY ON ONE IN PREVIOUS STEP AND REFER TO PAGE 2 OF THIS CHART.

→ SEE DTC 65 PAGE 2 OF 2.

YES

3. • PERFORM INJECTOR COIL/BALANCE TEST PROCEDURE. USE CHART C2-A.
   • ARE INJECTORS OK?

NO → REPLACE ANY FAULTY INJECTORS.

YES

5. • CHECK FOR POOR CONNECTIONS OR CRIMPS AT INJECTOR CONNECTORS.
   • ARE CONNECTIONS OK?

NO → REPAIR CONNECTIONS.

YES → REPLACE PCM.

86684215

DTC CHART — 2.3L MFI

CODE 62
TRANSMISSION GEAR SWITCHES CIRCUIT
2.3L (VIN D & A) "N" CARLINE (PORT)

FIRST CHECK THAT VSS, P/N AND RPM SIGNALS ARE NORMAL AND TRANSAXLE IS NOT STARTING IN 2ND OR 3RD GEARS.

1. • KEY "ON", ENGINE NOT RUNNING.
   • REMOVE TRANSAXLE CONNECTOR.
   • CONNECT A DVM TO GROUND AND PROBE TRANSMISSION HARNESS CONNECTOR TERMINALS "B" AND "C".
   • DVM SHOULD DISPLAY OVER 10 VOLTS. DOES IT?

NO → • REMOVE ECM BLACK C-D CONNECTOR.
   • CHECK FOR OPEN OR GROUND IN CIRCUIT WITH LESS THAN 10 VOLTS.
   • IF CIRCUIT IS OK CHECK ECM TERMINAL CONNECTIONS.
   • IF GOOD TERMINAL CONTACT, REPLACE ECM.

YES

2. • CONNECT THE DVM TO EITHER TRANSMISSION HARNESS CONNECTOR "B" OR "C".
   • PROBE AT THE TRANSAXLE TERMINALS "B" AND "C".
   • VOLTAGE SHOULD BE NEAR ZERO VOLTS FOR TERMINAL "B" AND ABOVE 10 VOLTS FOR "C". IS IT?

NO → • CHECK INTERNAL TRANSAXLE CONNECTIONS AND HARNESS FOR POOR CONTACTS.
   • IF GOOD TERMINAL CONTACT, REPLACE SWITCH IN CIRCUIT THAT FAULTED IN PRIOR STEP.

YES

3. • SET PARKING BRAKE, BLOCK REAR WHEELS.
   • RAISE DRIVE WHEELS AND IDLE VEHICLE IN DRIVE.
   • AFTER VEHICLE REACHES 3RD GEAR REPEAT ABOVE TEST.
   • VOLTAGE SHOULD BE "HIGH" FOR TERMINAL "B" AND "LOW" FOR "C". IS IT?

NO → • CHECK INTERNAL TRANSAXLE CONNECTIONS AND HARNESS FOR POOR CONTACTS.
   • IF GOOD TERMINAL CONTACT, REPLACE SWITCH IN CIRCUIT THAT FAULTED IN PRIOR STEP.

YES → NO TROUBLE FOUND.

86684214

DTC CHART — 2.3L MFI

DTC 66

A/C REFRIGERANT PRESSURE SENSOR CIRCUIT
2.3L (VIN D, A & 3) "N" CARLINE

NOTICE: IF VEHICLE IS NOT EQUIPPED WITH AIR CONDITIONING, DO NOT USE THIS CHART.

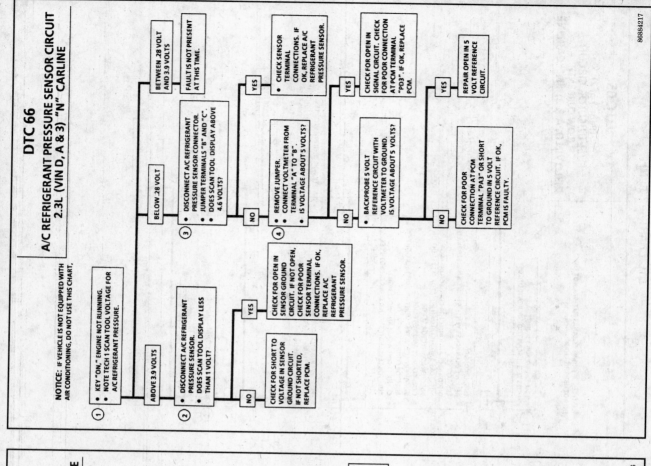

DTC CHART — 2.3L MFI

DTC 65

(Page 2 of 2)
FUEL INJECTOR CIRCUIT
(LOW CURRENT)
2.3L (VIN D, A & 3) "N" CARLINE

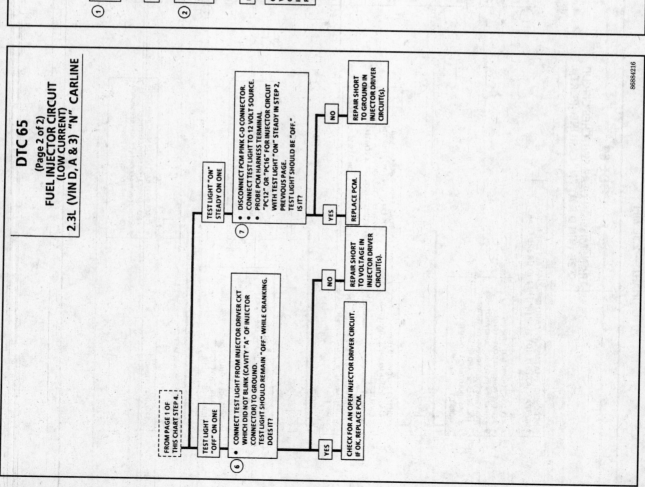

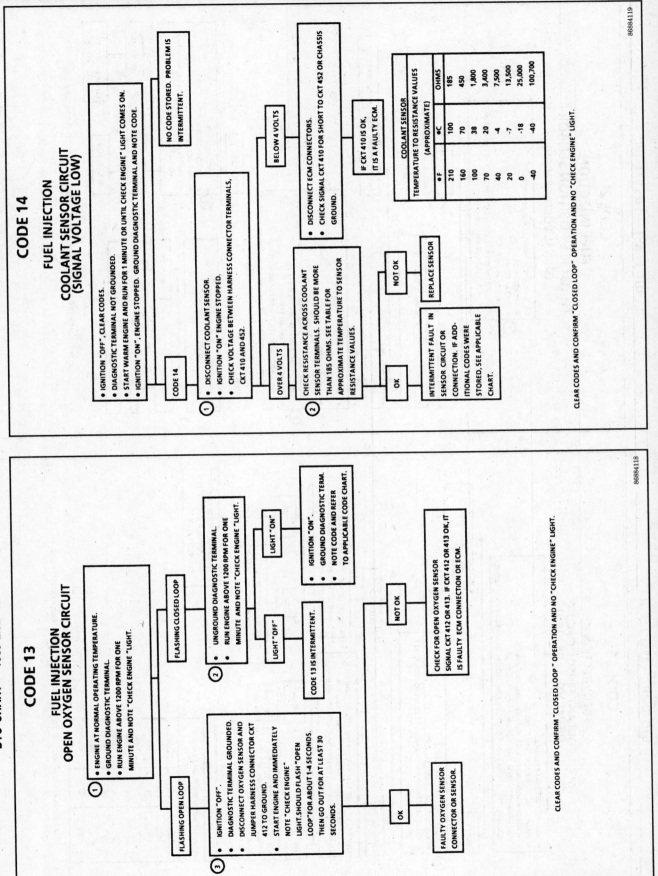

DTC CHART — 1985 2.5L TBI

CODE 14

FUEL INJECTION
COOLANT SENSOR CIRCUIT
(SIGNAL VOLTAGE LOW)

1.
- IGNITION "OFF", CLEAR CODES.
- DIAGNOSTIC TERMINAL NOT GROUNDED.
- START WARM ENGINE AND RUN FOR 1 MINUTE OR UNTIL CHECK ENGINE" LIGHT COMES ON.
- IGNITION "ON", ENGINE STOPPED. GROUND DIAGNOSTIC TERMINAL AND NOTE CODE.

→ NO CODE STORED. PROBLEM IS INTERMITTENT.

→ CODE 14

1.
- DISCONNECT COOLANT SENSOR.
- IGNITION "ON" ENGINE STOPPED.
- CHECK VOLTAGE BETWEEN HARNESS CONNECTOR TERMINALS, CKT 410 AND 452.

→ OVER 4 VOLTS

2.
CHECK RESISTANCE ACROSS COOLANT SENSOR TERMINALS. SHOULD BE MORE THAN 185 OHMS. SEE TABLE FOR APPROXIMATE TEMPERATURE TO SENSOR RESISTANCE VALUES.

→ OK → INTERMITTENT FAULT IN SENSOR CIRCUIT OR CONNECTION. IF ADDITIONAL CODES WERE STORED, SEE APPLICABLE CHART.

→ NOT OK → REPLACE SENSOR

→ BELOW 4 VOLTS

- DISCONNECT ECM CONNECTORS.
- CHECK SIGNAL CKT 410 FOR SHORT TO CKT 452 OR CHASSIS GROUND.

→ IF CKT 410 IS OK, IT IS A FAULTY ECM.

COOLANT SENSOR TEMPERATURE TO RESISTANCE VALUES (APPROXIMATE)		
°F	°C	OHMS
210	100	185
160	70	450
100	38	1,800
70	20	3,400
40	4	7,500
20	-7	13,500
0	-18	25,000
-40	-40	100,700

CLEAR CODES AND CONFIRM "CLOSED LOOP" OPERATION AND NO "CHECK ENGINE" LIGHT.

86884119

DTC CHART — 1985 2.5L TBI

CODE 13

FUEL INJECTION
OPEN OXYGEN SENSOR CIRCUIT

1.
- ENGINE AT NORMAL OPERATING TEMPERATURE.
- GROUND DIAGNOSTIC TERMINAL.
- RUN ENGINE ABOVE 1200 RPM FOR ONE MINUTE AND NOTE "CHECK ENGINE "LIGHT.

→ FLASHING OPEN LOOP

3.
- IGNITION "OFF".
- DIAGNOSTIC TERMINAL GROUNDED.
- DISCONNECT OXYGEN SENSOR AND JUMPER HARNESS CONNECTOR CKT 412 TO GROUND.
- START ENGINE AND IMMEDIATELY NOTE "CHECK ENGINE" LIGHT. SHOULD FLASH "OPEN LOOP" FOR ABOUT 1-4 SECONDS. THEN GO OUT FOR AT LEAST 30 SECONDS.

→ OK → FAULTY OXYGEN SENSOR CONNECTOR OR SENSOR.

→ NOT OK → CHECK FOR OPEN OXYGEN SENSOR SIGNAL CKT 412 OR 413. IF CKT 412 OR 413 OK, IT IS FAULTY ECM CONNECTION OR ECM.

→ FLASHING CLOSED LOOP

2.
- UNGROUND DIAGNOSTIC TERMINAL.
- RUN ENGINE ABOVE 1200 RPM FOR ONE MINUTE AND NOTE "CHECK ENGINE "LIGHT.

→ LIGHT "OFF" → CODE 13 IS INTERMITTENT.

→ LIGHT "ON"
- IGNITION "ON".
- GROUND DIAGNOSTIC TERM.
- NOTE CODE AND REFER TO APPLICABLE CODE CHART.

CLEAR CODES AND CONFIRM "CLOSED LOOP" OPERATION AND NO "CHECK ENGINE" LIGHT.

86884118

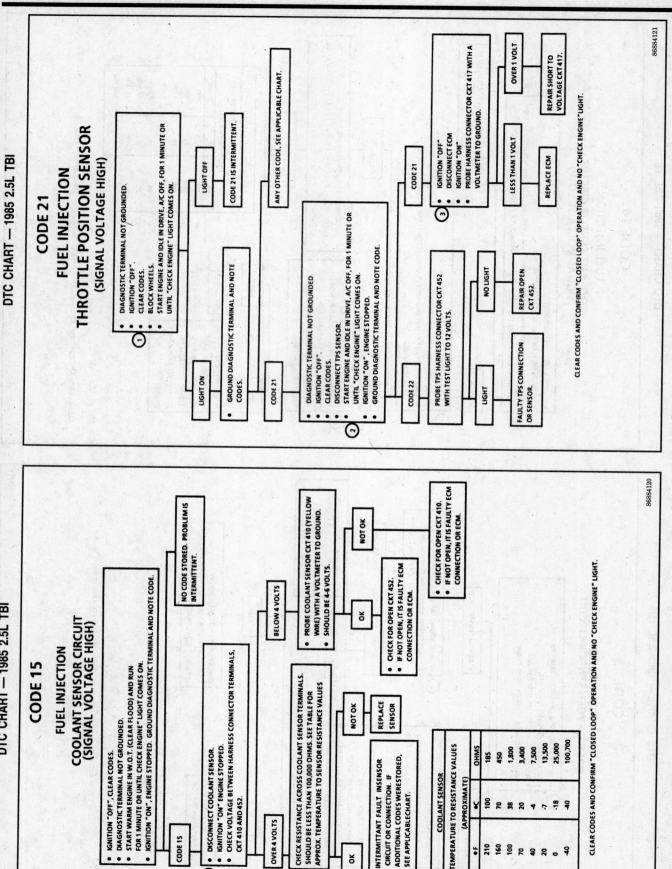

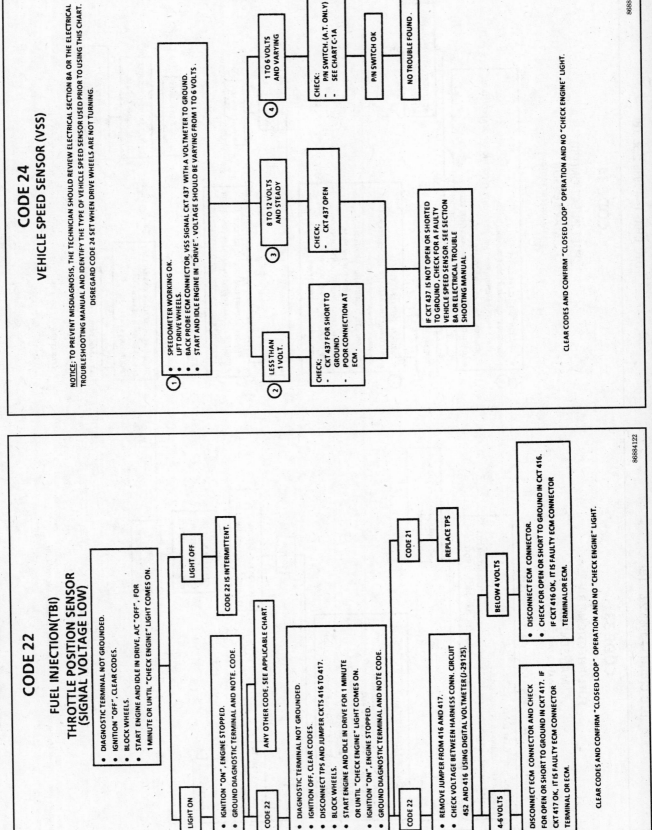

DTC CHART — 1985 2.5L TBI

CODE 24
VEHICLE SPEED SENSOR (VSS)

NOTICE: TO PREVENT MISDIAGNOSIS, THE TECHNICIAN SHOULD REVIEW ELECTRICAL SECTION 8A OR THE ELECTRICAL TROUBLESHOOTING MANUAL AND IDENTIFY THE TYPE OF VEHICLE SPEED SENSOR USED PRIOR TO USING THIS CHART. DISREGARD CODE 24 SET WHEN DRIVE WHEELS ARE NOT TURNING.

①
- SPEEDOMETER WORKING OK.
- LIFT DRIVE WHEELS.
- BACK PROBE ECM CONNECTOR, VSS SIGNAL CKT 437 WITH A VOLTMETER TO GROUND.
- START AND IDLE ENGINE IN "DRIVE". VOLTAGE SHOULD BE VARYING FROM 1 TO 6 VOLTS.

② LESS THAN 1 VOLT.

CHECK:
- CKT 437 FOR SHORT TO GROUND.
- POOR CONNECTION AT ECM.

IF CKT 437 IS NOT OPEN OR SHORTED TO GROUND, CHECK FOR A FAULTY VEHICLE SPEED SENSOR. SEE SECTION 8A OR ELECTRICAL TROUBLE SHOOTING MANUAL.

③ 8 TO 12 VOLTS AND STEADY

CHECK:
- CKT 437 OPEN

④ 1 TO 6 VOLTS AND VARYING

CHECK:
- P/N SWITCH. (A.T. ONLY) SEE CHART C-1A

P/N SWITCH OK

NO TROUBLE FOUND.

CLEAR CODES AND CONFIRM "CLOSED LOOP" OPERATION AND NO "CHECK ENGINE" LIGHT.

86884123

DTC CHART — 1985 2.5L TBI

CODE 22
FUEL INJECTION(TBI)
THROTTLE POSITION SENSOR (SIGNAL VOLTAGE LOW)

①
- DIAGNOSTIC TERMINAL NOT GROUNDED.
- IGNITION "OFF", CLEAR CODES.
- BLOCK WHEELS.
- START ENGINE AND IDLE IN DRIVE, A/C "OFF", FOR 1 MINUTE OR UNTIL "CHECK ENGINE" LIGHT COMES ON.

LIGHT ON
- IGNITION "ON", ENGINE STOPPED.
- GROUND DIAGNOSTIC TERMINAL AND NOTE CODE.

LIGHT OFF

CODE 22 IS INTERMITTENT.

CODE 22

ANY OTHER CODE, SEE APPLICABLE CHART.

②
- DIAGNOSTIC TERMINAL NOT GROUNDED.
- IGNITION OFF, CLEAR CODES.
- DISCONNECT TPS AND JUMPER CKTS 416 TO 417.
- BLOCK WHEELS.
- START ENGINE AND IDLE IN DRIVE FOR 1 MINUTE OR UNTIL "CHECK ENGINE" LIGHT COMES ON.
- IGNITION "ON", ENGINE STOPPED.
- GROUND DIAGNOSTIC TERMINAL AND NOTE CODE.

CODE 22
- REMOVE JUMPER FROM 416 AND 417.
- CHECK VOLTAGE BETWEEN HARNESS CONN. CIRCUIT 452 AND 416 USING DIGITAL VOLTMETER (J-29125).

CODE 21

REPLACE TPS

BELOW 4 VOLTS
- DISCONNECT ECM CONNECTOR.
- CHECK FOR OPEN OR SHORT TO GROUND IN CKT 416. IF CKT 416 OK, IT IS FAULTY ECM CONNECTOR TERMINAL OR ECM.

③
- DISCONNECT ECM CONNECTOR AND CHECK FOR OPEN OR SHORT TO GROUND IN CKT 417. IF CKT 417 OK, IT IS FAULTY ECM CONNECTOR TERMINAL OR ECM.

4-6 VOLTS

CLEAR CODES AND CONFIRM "CLOSED LOOP" OPERATION AND NO "CHECK ENGINE" LIGHT.

86884122

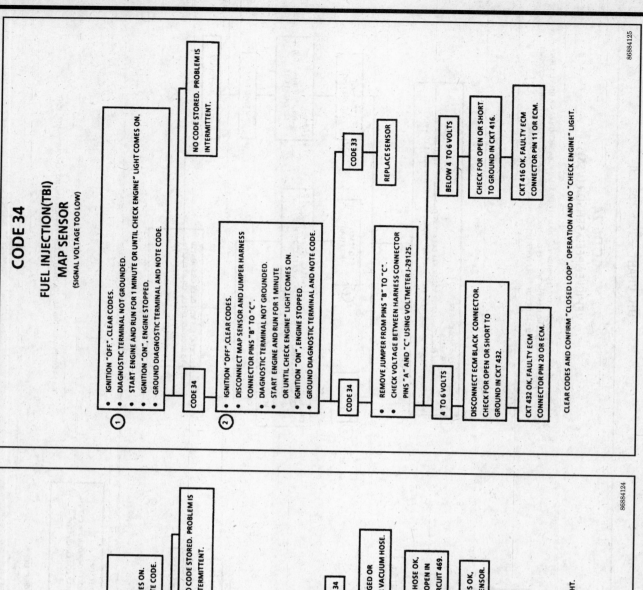

DTC CHART — 1985 2.5L TBI

CODE 34

FUEL INJECTION(TBI)
MAP SENSOR

(SIGNAL VOLTAGE TOO LOW)

①
- IGNITION "OFF", CLEAR CODES.
- DIAGNOSTIC TERMINAL NOT GROUNDED.
- START ENGINE AND RUN FOR 1 MINUTE OR UNTIL CHECK ENGINE" LIGHT COMES ON.
- IGNITION "ON", ENGINE STOPPED.
- GROUND DIAGNOSTIC TERMINAL AND NOTE CODE.

CODE 34

NO CODE STORED. PROBLEM IS INTERMITTENT.

②
- IGNITION "OFF",CLEAR CODES.
- DISCONNECT MAP SENSOR AND JUMPER HARNESS CONNECTOR PINS "B" TO "C".
- DIAGNOSTIC TERMINAL NOT GROUNDED.
- START ENGINE AND RUN FOR 1 MINUTE OR UNTIL CHECK ENGINE" LIGHT COMES ON.
- IGNITION "ON", ENGINE STOPPED.
- GROUND DIAGNOSTIC TERMINAL AND NOTE CODE.

CODE 34
- REMOVE JUMPER FROM PINS "B" TO "C".
- CHECK VOLTAGE BETWEEN HARNESS CONNECTOR PINS "A" AND "C" USING VOLTMETER J-29125.

CODE 33

REPLACE SENSOR.

BELOW 4 TO 6 VOLTS

CHECK FOR OPEN OR SHORT TO GROUND IN CKT 416.

CKT 416 OK, FAULTY ECM CONNECTOR PIN 11 OR ECM.

4 TO 6 VOLTS

DISCONNECT ECM BLACK CONNECTOR. CHECK FOR OPEN OR SHORT TO GROUND IN CKT 432.

CKT 432 OK, FAULTY ECM CONNECTOR PIN 20 OR ECM.

CLEAR CODES AND CONFIRM "CLOSED LOOP" OPERATION AND NO "CHECK ENGINE" LIGHT.

86884125

DTC CHART — 1985 2.5L TBI

CODE 33

FUEL INJECTION(TBI)
MAP SENSOR

(SIGNAL VOLTAGE TOO HIGH)

IF ENGINE IDLE IS LOW AND UNSTABLE, CORRECT BEFORE USING CHART.

①
- IGNITION "OFF", CLEAR CODES.
- DIAGNOSTIC TERMINAL NOT GROUNDED.
- START ENGINE AND RUN FOR 1 MINUTE OR UNTIL CHECK ENGINE" LIGHT COMES ON.
- IGNITION "ON", ENGINE STOPPED. GROUND DIAGNOSTIC TERMINAL AND NOTE CODE.

CODE 33

NO CODE STORED. PROBLEM IS INTERMITTENT.

②
- IGNITION "OFF",CLEAR CODES.
- DISCONNECT MAP SENSOR CONNECTOR.
- DIAGNOSTIC TERMINAL NOT GROUNDED.
- START ENGINE AND RUN FOR 1 MINUTE OR UNTIL CHECK ENGINE" LIGHT COMES ON.
- IGNITION "ON" ENGINE STOPPED.
- GROUND DIAGNOSTIC TERMINAL AND NOTE CODE.

CODE 33

CHECK FOR SHORT TO VOLTAGE IN CKT 432.

IF CKT 432 IS OK, REPLACE ECM.

CODE 34

CHECK FOR PLUGGED OR LEAKING SENSOR VACUUM HOSE.

IF VACUUM HOSE OK, CHECK FOR OPEN IN GROUND CIRCUIT 469.

IF CKT 469 IS OK, REPLACE SENSOR.

CLEAR CODES AND CONFIRM "CLOSED LOOP" OPERATION AND NO "CHECK ENGINE" LIGHT.

86884124

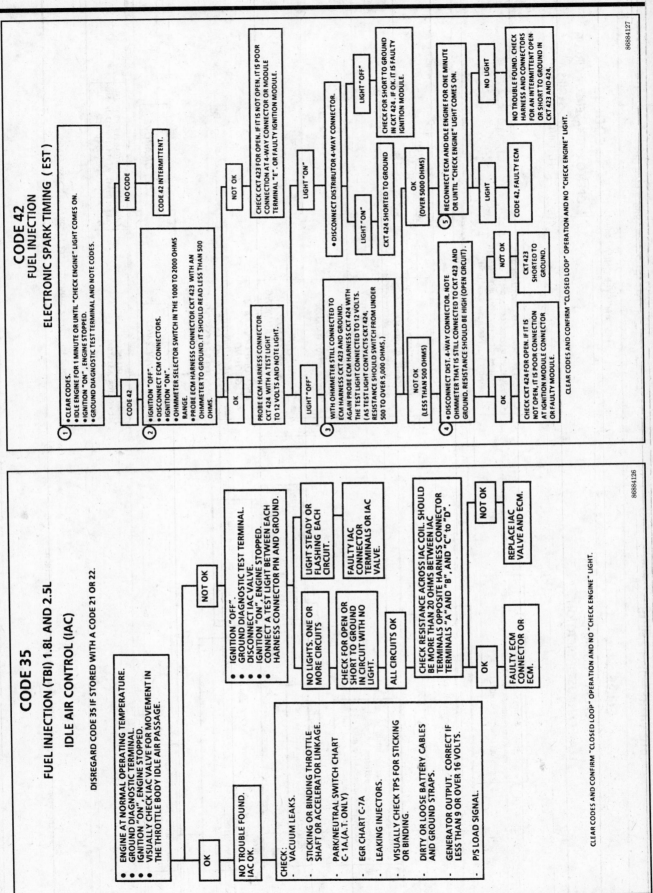

DTC CHART — 1985 2.5L TBI

CODE 42
FUEL INJECTION
ELECTRONIC SPARK TIMING (EST)

1
- CLEAR CODES.
- IDLE ENGINE FOR 1 MINUTE OR UNTIL "CHECK ENGINE" LIGHT COMES ON.
- IGNITION "ON", ENGINE STOPPED.
- GROUND DIAGNOSTIC TEST TERMINAL AND NOTE CODES.

NO CODE → CODE 42 INTERMITTENT.

CODE 42

2
- IGNITION "OFF".
- DISCONNECT ECM CONNECTORS.
- IGNITION "ON".
- OHMMETER SELECTOR SWITCH IN THE 1000 TO 2000 OHMS RANGE.
- PROBE ECM HARNESS CONNECTOR CKT 423 WITH AN OHMMETER TO GROUND. IT SHOULD READ LESS THAN 500 OHMS.

OK

PROBE ECM HARNESS CONNECTOR CKT 424 WITH A TEST LIGHT TO 12 VOLTS AND NOTE LIGHT.

NOT OK → CHECK CKT 423 FOR OPEN. IF IT IS NOT OPEN, IT IS POOR CONNECTION AT 4-WAY CONNECTOR OR MODULE TERMINAL "E". OR FAULTY IGNITION MODULE.

LIGHT "OFF"

3
WITH OHMMETER STILL CONNECTED TO ECM HARNESS CKT 423 AND GROUND. AGAIN PROBE ECM HARNESS CKT 424 WITH THE TEST LIGHT CONNECTED TO 12 VOLTS. (AS TEST LIGHT CONTACTS CKT 424, RESISTANCE SHOULD SWITCH FROM UNDER 500 TO OVER 5,000 OHMS.)

LIGHT "ON" → • DISCONNECT DISTRIBUTOR 4-WAY CONNECTOR.

LIGHT "ON"

CKT 424 SHORTED TO GROUND

LIGHT "OFF"

CHECK FOR SHORT TO GROUND IN CKT 424. IF OK, IT IS FAULTY IGNITION MODULE.

OK (OVER 5000 OHMS)

NOT OK (LESS THAN 500 OHMS)

4
• DISCONNECT DIST. 4-WAY CONNECTOR. NOTE OHMMETER THAT IS STILL CONNECTED TO CKT 423 AND GROUND. RESISTANCE SHOULD BE HIGH (OPEN CIRCUIT).

NOT OK → CKT 423 SHORTED TO GROUND.

OK

CHECK CKT 424 FOR OPEN. IF IT IS NOT OPEN, IT IS POOR CONNECTION AT IGNITION MODULE CONNECTOR OR FAULTY MODULE.

5
RECONNECT ECM AND IDLE ENGINE FOR ONE MINUTE OR UNTIL "CHECK ENGINE" LIGHT COMES ON.

NO LIGHT → NO TROUBLE FOUND. CHECK HARNESS AND CONNECTORS FOR AN INTERMITTENT OPEN OR SHORT TO GROUND IN CKT 423 AND 424.

LIGHT

CODE 42, FAULTY ECM

CLEAR CODES AND CONFIRM "CLOSED LOOP" OPERATION AND NO "CHECK ENGINE" LIGHT.

DTC CHART — 1985 2.5L TBI

CODE 35
FUEL INJECTION (TBI) 1.8L AND 2.5L
IDLE AIR CONTROL (IAC)

DISREGARD CODE 35 IF STORED WITH A CODE 21 OR 22.

ENGINE AT NORMAL OPERATING TEMPERATURE.
GROUND DIAGNOSTIC TERMINAL.
IGNITION "ON". ENGINE STOPPED.
VISUALLY CHECK IAC VALVE FOR MOVEMENT IN THE THROTTLE BODY IDLE AIR PASSAGE.

OK

NO TROUBLE FOUND. IAC OK.

CHECK:
- VACUUM LEAKS.
- STICKING OR BINDING THROTTLE SHAFT OR ACCELERATOR LINKAGE.
- PARK/NEUTRAL SWITCH CHART C-1A.(A.T. ONLY)
- EGR CHART C-7A
- LEAKING INJECTORS.
- VISUALLY CHECK TPS FOR STICKING OR BINDING.
- DIRTY OR LOOSE BATTERY CABLES AND GROUND STRAPS.
- GENERATOR OUTPUT. CORRECT IF LESS THAN 9 OR OVER 16 VOLTS.
- P/S LOAD SIGNAL.

NOT OK

- IGNITION "OFF".
- GROUND DIAGNOSTIC TEST TERMINAL.
- DISCONNECT IAC VALVE.
- IGNITION "ON", ENGINE STOPPED.
- CONNECT A TEST LIGHT BETWEEN EACH HARNESS CONNECTOR PIN AND GROUND.

LIGHT STEADY OR FLASHING EACH CIRCUIT. → FAULTY IAC CONNECTOR TERMINALS OR IAC VALVE.

NO LIGHTS, ONE OR MORE CIRCUITS

CHECK FOR OPEN OR SHORT TO GROUND IN CIRCUIT WITH NO LIGHT.

ALL CIRCUITS OK

CHECK RESISTANCE ACROSS IAC COIL. SHOULD BE MORE THAN 20 OHMS BETWEEN IAC TERMINALS OPPOSITE HARNESS CONNECTOR TERMINALS "A" AND "B", AND "C" to "D".

NOT OK → REPLACE IAC VALVE AND ECM.

OK

FAULTY ECM CONNECTOR OR ECM.

CLEAR CODES AND CONFIRM "CLOSED LOOP" OPERATION AND NO "CHECK ENGINE" LIGHT.

DTC CHART — 1986 2.5L TBI

CODE 13
OPEN OXYGEN SENSOR CIRCUIT
2.5L "N" SERIES
FUEL INJECTION (TBI)

■ "SCAN" STEP ONLY

START NON-SCAN

①
- ENGINE AT NORMAL OPERATING TEMPERATURE.
- GROUND DIAGNOSTIC TERMINAL.
- RUN ENGINE ABOVE 1200 RPM FOR ONE MINUTE AND NOTE "SERVICE ENGINE SOON" LIGHT.

FLASHING "OPEN LOOP" ── FLASHING "CLOSED LOOP"

CODE 13 IS INTERMITTENT.

②
- IGNITION "OFF".
- DIAGNOSTIC TERMINAL GROUNDED.
- DISCONNECT OXYGEN SENSOR AND JUMPER HARNESS CONNECTOR CKT 412 TO GROUND.
- START ENGINE AND IMMEDIATELY NOTE "SERVICE ENGINE SOON" LIGHT. IT SHOULD FLASH "OPEN LOOP" FOR ABOUT 1-4 SECONDS, THEN GO OFF FOR AT LEAST 30 SECONDS.

START SCAN

■ "SCAN" IS FIXED BETWEEN .35 TO .55 V. WITH ENGINE RUNNING.
■ DISCONNECT SENSOR AND JUMPER CKT 412 TO GROUND.
■ ENGINE RUNNING.
SENSOR VOLTAGE SHOULD BE LESS THAN .2 VOLT (200MV)

OK ── ■ LESS THAN .2 VOLT.

FAULTY OXYGEN SENSOR CONNECTOR OR SENSOR.

NOT OK ── ■ .2 VOLT OR ABOVE

CHECK FOR OPEN OXYGEN SENSOR SIGNAL CKT 412 OR 413. IF CKT 412 OR 413 OK, IT IS FAULTY ECM CONNECTION OR ECM.

CLEAR CODES AND CONFIRM "CLOSED LOOP" OPERATION AND NO "SERVICE ENGINE SOON" LIGHT.

86884129

DTC CHART — 1985 2.5L TBI

CODE 44
FUEL INJECTION
LEAN EXHAUST INDICATION

①
- GROUND DIAGNOSTIC TERMINAL.
- RUN WARM ENGINE AT APPROX. 1200 TO 1800 RPM FOR 1 MINUTE AND NOTE LIGHT.

LIGHT STAYING "OFF" MORE THAN "ON" OR FLASHING "OPEN LOOP". ── FLASHING "CLOSED LOOP"

CODE IS INTERMITTENT.

②
- IGNITION "OFF".
- DIAGNOSTIC TERMINAL GROUNDED.
- DISCONNECT OXYGEN SENSOR.
- START ENGINE AND IMMEDIATELY NOTE "CHECK ENGINE" LIGHT.

"CHECK ENGINE" LIGHT FLASHING OPEN LOOP.

"CHECK ENGINE" LIGHT WENT OFF FOR AT LEAST 30 SECONDS

CHECK SIGNAL CKT 412 FOR SHORT TO GROUND. IF OK, IT IS A FAULTY ECM.

③
- CHECK :
  - FUEL PRESSURE, SHOULD BE 62-90 KPA (9-13 PSI).
  - WATER IN FUEL SYSTEM.
  - MAP SENSOR
  - OPEN CKT 413

IF ALL CHECKS OK, IT IS A FAULTY OXYGEN SENSOR.

CLEAR CODES AND CONFIRM "CLOSED LOOP" OPERATION AND NO "CHECK ENGINE" LIGHT.

86884128

DTC CHART — 1986 2.5L TBI

CODE 15

**COOLANT SENSOR CIRCUIT
(SIGNAL VOLTAGE HIGH)
2.5L "N" SERIES
FUEL INJECTION (TBI)**

■ "SCAN" STEP ONLY

START NON-SCAN

- IGNITION "OFF", CLEAR CODES.
- DIAGNOSTIC TERMINAL NOT GROUNDED.
- START WARM ENGINE IN W.O.T. (CLEAR FLOOD) AND RUN FOR 1 MINUTE OR UNTIL "SERVICE ENGINE SOON" LIGHT COMES ON.
- IGNITION "ON", ENGINE STOPPED.
- GROUND DIAGNOSTIC TERMINAL AND NOTE CODE.

NO CODE 15. PROBLEM IS INTERMITTENT.

CODE 15

① **START SCAN**

- DISCONNECT COOLANT SENSOR CONNECTOR
- IGNITION "ON" ENGINE STOPPED.
- CHECK VOLTAGE BETWEEN HARNESS CONNECTOR TERMINALS, CKT 410 AND 452.

■ **IF COOLANT TEMP. IS FIXED BELOW -30°C, DISCONNECT SENSOR AND JUMPER HARNESS TERMINALS TOGETHER**

■ **BELOW -30°C** / BELOW 4 VOLTS

■ **ABOVE 135°C** / 4 VOLTS OR OVER

OK

FAULTY COOLANT SENSOR CONNECTION OR FAULTY SENSOR.

- PROBE COOLANT SENSOR CKT 410 (YELLOW WIRE) WITH A VOLTMETER TO GROUND. SHOULD BE 4-6 VOLTS.
- **JUMPER CKT 410 TO CHASSIS GROUND**

■ **BELOW -30°C** / VOLTAGE NOT OK

■ **ABOVE 135°C** / VOLTAGE OK

- CHECK FOR OPEN CKT 410.
- IF NOT OPEN, IT IS FAULTY ECM CONNECTION OR ECM.

- CHECK FOR OPEN CKT 452.
- IF NOT OPEN, IT IS FAULTY ECM CONNECTION OR ECM.

COOLANT SENSOR TEMPERATURE TO RESISTANCE VALUES (APPROXIMATE)		
°F	°C	OHMS
275	135	68
210	100	185
160	70	450
100	38	1,800
70	20	3,400
40	4	7,500
20	-7	13,500
0	-18	25,000
-22	-30	53,000
-40	-40	100,700

CLEAR CODES AND CONFIRM "CLOSED LOOP" OPERATION AND NO "SERVICE ENGINE SOON" LIGHT.

86884131

DTC CHART — 1986 2.5L TBI

CODE 14

**COOLANT SENSOR CIRCUIT
(SIGNAL VOLTAGE LOW)
2.5L "N" SERIES
FUEL INJECTION (TBI)**

■ "SCAN" STEP ONLY

START NON-SCAN

- IGNITION "OFF", CLEAR CODES.
- DIAGNOSTIC TERMINAL NOT GROUNDED.
- START WARM ENGINE AND RUN FOR 1 MINUTE OR UNTIL "SERVICE ENGINE SOON" LIGHT COMES ON.
- IGNITION "ON", ENGINE STOPPED. GROUND DIAGNOSTIC TERMINAL AND NOTE CODE.

NO CODE 14 STORED. PROBLEM IS INTERMITTENT.

CODE 14

① **START SCAN**

- DISCONNECT COOLANT SENSOR.
- IGNITION "ON" ENGINE STOPPED.
- CHECK VOLTAGE BETWEEN HARNESS CONNECTOR TERMINALS, CKT 410 AND 452.

■ **IF COOLANT IS FIXED ABOVE 135°C, DISCONNECT SENSOR**

■ **ABOVE 135°C** / BELOW 4 VOLTS

■ **BELOW -30°C** / OVER 4 VOLTS

REPLACE SENSOR

- IGNITION "OFF"
- DISCONNECT ECM CONNECTORS.
- CHECK SIGNAL CKT 410 FOR SHORT TO CKT 452 OR CHASSIS GROUND.

IF CKT 410 IS OK, IT IS A FAULTY ECM.

COOLANT SENSOR TEMPERATURE TO RESISTANCE VALUES (APPROXIMATE)		
°F	°C	OHMS
210	100	185
160	70	450
100	38	1,800
70	20	3,400
40	4	7,500
20	-7	13,500
0	-18	25,000
-40	-40	100,700

CLEAR CODES AND CONFIRM "CLOSED LOOP" OPERATION AND NO "SERVICE ENGINE SOON" LIGHT.

86884130

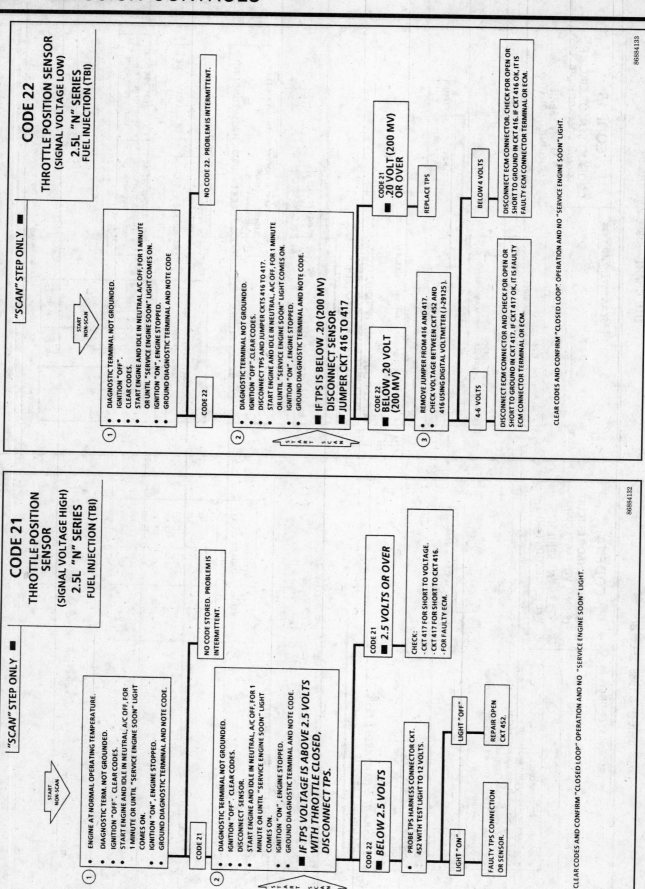

DTC CHART — 1986 2.5L TBI

CODE 22
THROTTLE POSITION SENSOR
(SIGNAL VOLTAGE LOW)
2.5L "N" SERIES
FUEL INJECTION (TBI)

"SCAN" STEP ONLY ■

START NON-SCAN

① • DIAGNOSTIC TERMINAL NOT GROUNDED.
• IGNITION "OFF".
• CLEAR CODES.
• START ENGINE AND IDLE IN NEUTRAL, A/C OFF, FOR 1 MINUTE OR UNTIL "SERVICE ENGINE SOON" LIGHT COMES ON.
• IGNITION "ON", ENGINE STOPPED.
• GROUND DIAGNOSTIC TERMINAL AND NOTE CODE

CODE 22 ⟶ NO CODE 22. PROBLEM IS INTERMITTENT.

② • DIAGNOSTIC TERMINAL NOT GROUNDED.
• IGNITION "OFF". CLEAR CODES.
• DISCONNECT TPS AND JUMPER CKTS 416 TO 417.
• START ENGINE AND IDLE IN NEUTRAL, A/C OFF, FOR 1 MINUTE OR UNTIL "SERVICE ENGINE SOON" LIGHT COMES ON.
• IGNITION "ON", ENGINE STOPPED.
• GROUND DIAGNOSTIC TERMINAL AND NOTE CODE.

START SCAN

■ IF TPS IS BELOW .20 (200 MV)
■ DISCONNECT SENSOR
■ JUMPER CKT 416 TO 417

CODE 22
■ BELOW .20 VOLT (200 MV)

CODE 21
■ .20 VOLT (200 MV) OR OVER ⟶ REPLACE TPS

③ • REMOVE JUMPER FROM 416 AND 417.
• CHECK VOLTAGE BETWEEN CKT 452 AND 416 USING DIGITAL VOLTMETER (J-29125).

4-6 VOLTS ⟶ DISCONNECT ECM CONNECTOR AND CHECK FOR OPEN OR SHORT TO GROUND IN CKT 417. IF CKT 417 OK, IT IS FAULTY ECM CONNECTOR TERMINAL OR ECM.

BELOW 4 VOLTS ⟶ DISCONNECT ECM CONNECTOR. CHECK FOR OPEN OR SHORT TO GROUND IN CKT 416. IF CKT 416 OK, IT IS FAULTY ECM CONNECTOR TERMINAL OR ECM.

CLEAR CODES AND CONFIRM "CLOSED LOOP" OPERATION AND NO "SERVICE ENGINE SOON" LIGHT.

86884133

DTC CHART — 1986 2.5L TBI

CODE 21
THROTTLE POSITION SENSOR
(SIGNAL VOLTAGE HIGH)
2.5L "N" SERIES
FUEL INJECTION (TBI)

"SCAN" STEP ONLY ■

START NON-SCAN

① • ENGINE AT NORMAL OPERATING TEMPERATURE.
• DIAGNOSTIC TERM. NOT GROUNDED.
• IGNITION "OFF". CLEAR CODES.
• START ENGINE AND IDLE IN NEUTRAL, A/C OFF, FOR 1 MINUTE OR UNTIL "SERVICE ENGINE SOON" LIGHT COMES ON.
• IGNITION "ON", ENGINE STOPPED.
• GROUND DIAGNOSTIC TERMINAL AND NOTE CODE.

CODE 21 ⟶ NO CODE STORED. PROBLEM IS INTERMITTENT.

② • DIAGNOSTIC TERMINAL NOT GROUNDED.
• IGNITION "OFF". CLEAR CODES.
• DISCONNECT SENSOR.
• START ENGINE AND IDLE IN NEUTRAL, A/C OFF, FOR 1 MINUTE OR UNTIL "SERVICE ENGINE SOON" LIGHT COMES ON.
• IGNITION "ON", ENGINE STOPPED.
• GROUND DIAGNOSTIC TERMINAL AND NOTE CODE.

START SCAN

■ IF TPS VOLTAGE IS ABOVE 2.5 VOLTS WITH THROTTLE CLOSED, DISCONNECT TPS.

CODE 22
■ BELOW 2.5 VOLTS

CODE 21
■ 2.5 VOLTS OR OVER ⟶ CHECK:
- CKT 417 FOR SHORT TO VOLTAGE.
- CKT 417 FOR SHORT TO CKT 416.
- FOR FAULTY ECM.

• PROBE TPS HARNESS CONNECTOR CKT. 452 WITH TEST LIGHT TO 12 VOLTS.

LIGHT "OFF" ⟶ REPAIR OPEN CKT 452.

LIGHT "ON" ⟶ FAULTY TPS CONNECTION OR SENSOR.

CLEAR CODES AND CONFIRM "CLOSED LOOP" OPERATION AND NO "SERVICE ENGINE SOON" LIGHT.

86884132

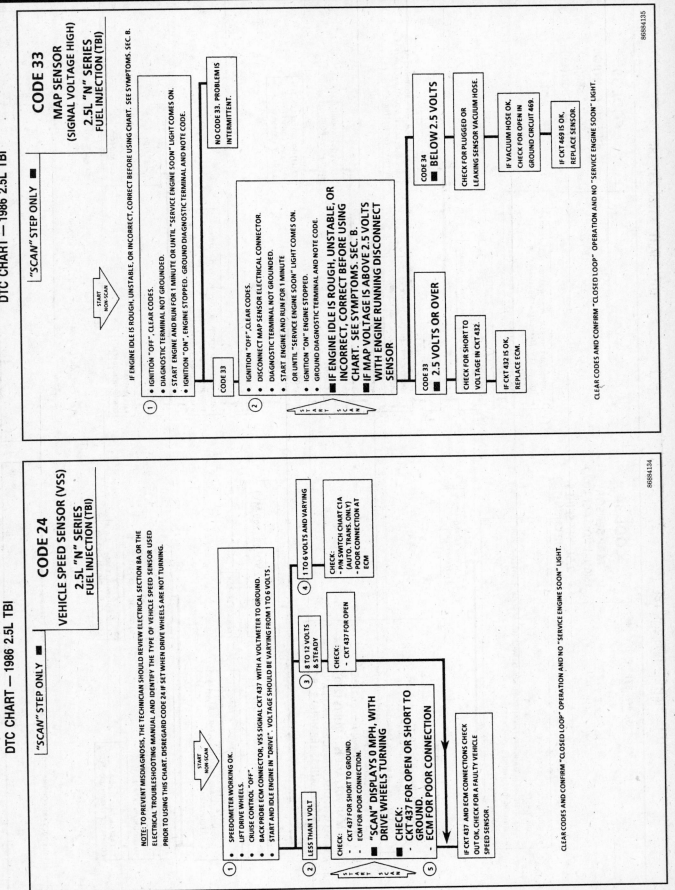

DTC CHART — 1986 2.5L TBI

"SCAN" STEP ONLY ■ CODE 33

MAP SENSOR
(SIGNAL VOLTAGE HIGH)

2.5L "N" SERIES
FUEL INJECTION (TBI)

IF ENGINE IDLE IS ROUGH, UNSTABLE, OR INCORRECT, CORRECT BEFORE USING CHART. SEE SYMPTOMS. SEC. B.

START NON-SCAN

① ● IGNITION "OFF", CLEAR CODES.
● DIAGNOSTIC TERMINAL NOT GROUNDED.
● START ENGINE AND RUN FOR 1 MINUTE OR UNTIL "SERVICE ENGINE SOON" LIGHT COMES ON.
● IGNITION "ON", ENGINE STOPPED. GROUND DIAGNOSTIC TERMINAL AND NOTE CODE.

CODE 33

NO CODE 33. PROBLEM IS INTERMITTENT.

② ● IGNITION "OFF", CLEAR CODES.
● DISCONNECT MAP SENSOR ELECTRICAL CONNECTOR.
● DIAGNOSTIC TERMINAL NOT GROUNDED.
● START ENGINE AND RUN FOR 1 MINUTE OR UNTIL "SERVICE ENGINE SOON" LIGHT COMES ON.
● IGNITION "ON" ENGINE STOPPED.
● GROUND DIAGNOSTIC TERMINAL AND NOTE CODE.
■ IF ENGINE IDLE IS ROUGH, UNSTABLE, OR INCORRECT, CORRECT BEFORE USING CHART. SEE SYMPTOMS. SEC. B.
■ IF MAP VOLTAGE IS ABOVE 2.5 VOLTS WITH ENGINE RUNNING DISCONNECT SENSOR

START SCAN

CODE 33
■ 2.5 VOLTS OR OVER

CHECK FOR SHORT TO VOLTAGE IN CKT 432.

IF CKT 432 IS OK, REPLACE ECM.

CODE 34
■ BELOW 2.5 VOLTS

CHECK FOR PLUGGED OR LEAKING SENSOR VACUUM HOSE.

IF VACUUM HOSE OK, CHECK FOR OPEN IN GROUND CIRCUIT 469.

IF CKT 469 IS OK, REPLACE SENSOR.

CLEAR CODES AND CONFIRM "CLOSED LOOP" OPERATION AND NO "SERVICE ENGINE SOON" LIGHT.

86884135

DTC CHART — 1986 2.5L TBI

"SCAN" STEP ONLY ■ CODE 24

VEHICLE SPEED SENSOR (VSS)

2.5L "N" SERIES
FUEL INJECTION (TBI)

NOTE: TO PREVENT MISDIAGNOSIS, THE TECHNICIAN SHOULD REVIEW ELECTRICAL SECTION 8A OR THE ELECTRICAL TROUBLESHOOTING MANUAL AND IDENTIFY THE TYPE OF VEHICLE SPEED SENSOR USED PRIOR TO USING THIS CHART. DISREGARD CODE 24 IF SET WHEN DRIVE WHEELS ARE NOT TURNING.

START NON-SCAN

① ● SPEEDOMETER WORKING OK.
● LIFT DRIVE WHEELS.
● CRUISE CONTROL "OFF".
● BACK PROBE ECM CONNECTOR, VSS SIGNAL CKT 437 WITH A VOLTMETER TO GROUND.
● START AND IDLE ENGINE IN "DRIVE". VOLTAGE SHOULD BE VARYING FROM 1 TO 6 VOLTS.

② LESS THAN 1 VOLT
CHECK:
- CKT 437 FOR SHORT TO GROUND.
- ECM FOR POOR CONNECTION.
■ "SCAN" DISPLAYS 0 MPH, WITH DRIVE WHEELS TURNING
■ CHECK:
- CKT 437 FOR OPEN OR SHORT TO GROUND.
- ECM FOR POOR CONNECTION

START SCAN

③ 8 TO 12 VOLTS & STEADY
CHECK:
- CKT 437 FOR OPEN

④ 1 TO 6 VOLTS AND VARYING
CHECK:
- P/N SWITCH CHART C1A (AUTO. TRANS. ONLY)
- POOR CONNECTION AT ECM

⑤ IF CKT 437 AND ECM CONNECTIONS CHECK OUT OK, CHECK FOR A FAULTY VEHICLE SPEED SENSOR.

CLEAR CODES AND CONFIRM "CLOSED LOOP" OPERATION AND NO "SERVICE ENGINE SOON" LIGHT.

86884134

DTC CHART — 1986 2.5L TBI

CODE 35
IDLE AIR CONTROL
2.5L "N" SERIES
FUEL INJECTION (TBI)

①
- DISREGARD CODE 35 IF SET WITH A CODE 21, 22, 44, OR 45.
- ENGINE AT NORMAL OPERATING TEMPERATURE.
- A/C OFF.
- RECORD CLOSED THROTTLE IDLE RPM IN "PARK OR NEUTRAL."

②
- IGNITION "OFF".
- DISCONNECT IAC VALVE.
- START ENGINE. NOTE RPM IN PARK/NEUTRAL.

③ IDLE RPM, NO INCREASE
- IGNITION "ON". ENGINE STOPPED.
- GROUND DIAGNOSTIC TEST TERMINAL.
- CONNECT A TEST LIGHT BETWEEN EACH HARNESS CONNECTOR PIN AND GROUND.

IDLE RPM INCREASE → IAC OK. IGNITION "OFF". RECONNECT IAC, PROBABLE CAUSE IS A SMALL VACUUM LEAK OR INTERMITTENT ELECTRICAL PROBLEM.

LIGHT OFF, ONE OR MORE CIRCUITS.
- CHECK FOR OPEN OR SHORT TO GROUND IN CIRCUIT(S) WITH LIGHT OFF

STEADY OR FLASHING LIGHT EACH CIRCUIT.
- IF ALL ITEMS CHECKED OK, IT IS FAULTY IAC CONNECTOR OR IAC VALVE ASSEMBLY.

ALL CIRCUITS OK
- CHECK RESISTANCE ACROSS IAC COILS. (SHOULD BE MORE THAN 20 OHMS BETWEEN IAC TERMINALS OPPOSITE HARNESS CONNECTOR TERMS. "A" TO "B", AND "C" TO "D".)

OK → FAULTY ECM CONNECTION OR ECM

NOT OK → REPLACE IAC VALVE AND ECM.

CLEAR CODES AND CONFIRM "CLOSED LOOP" OPERATION AND NO "SERVICE ENGINE SOON" LIGHT.

DTC CHART — 1986 2.5L TBI

"SCAN" STEP ONLY ■

CODE 34
MAP SENSOR
(SIGNAL VOLTAGE LOW)
2.5L "N" SERIES
FUEL INJECTION (TBI)

START NON-SCAN →

①
- IGNITION "OFF", CLEAR CODES.
- DIAGNOSTIC TERMINAL NOT GROUNDED.
- START ENGINE AND RUN FOR 1 MINUTE OR UNTIL "SERVICE ENGINE SOON" LIGHT COMES ON.
- IGNITION "ON", ENGINE STOPPED.
- GROUND DIAGNOSTIC TERMINAL AND NOTE CODE.

NO CODE 34. PROBLEM IS INTERMITTENT.

CODE 34

②
- IGNITION "OFF", CLEAR CODES.
- DISCONNECT MAP SENSOR AND JUMPER HARNESS CONNECTOR TERMINAL "B" TO "C".
- DIAGNOSTIC TERMINAL NOT GROUNDED.
- START ENGINE AND RUN FOR 1 MINUTE OR UNTIL "SERVICE ENGINE SOON" LIGHT COMES ON.
- IGNITION "ON", ENGINE STOPPED.
- GROUND DIAGNOSTIC TERMINAL AND NOTE CODE.

START SCAN

■ IF MAP VOLTAGE IS .2 VOLTS (200 MV) OR BELOW, DISCONNECT SENSOR AND JUMPER HARNESS TERMINALS "B" TO "C"

CODE 33 ■ ABOVE .2 VOLTS (200 MV) → REPLACE SENSOR

CODE 34 ■ .2 VOLTS (200 MV) OR BELOW
- REMOVE JUMPER FROM TERMINAL "B" TO "C".
- CHECK VOLTAGE BETWEEN HARNESS CONNECTOR TERMINAL "A" AND "C" USING VOLTMETER J-29125 OR EQUIVALENT.

4 TO 6 VOLTS
- CHECK FOR OPEN OR SHORT TO GROUND IN CKT 432.
- CKT 432 OK, FAULTY ECM CONNECTOR TERMINAL OR ECM.

BELOW 4 TO 6 VOLTS
- CHECK FOR OPEN OR SHORT TO GROUND IN CKT 416.
- CKT 416 OK, FAULTY ECM CONNECTOR TERMINAL OR ECM.

CLEAR CODES AND CONFIRM "CLOSED LOOP" OPERATION AND NO "SERVICE ENGINE SOON" LIGHT.

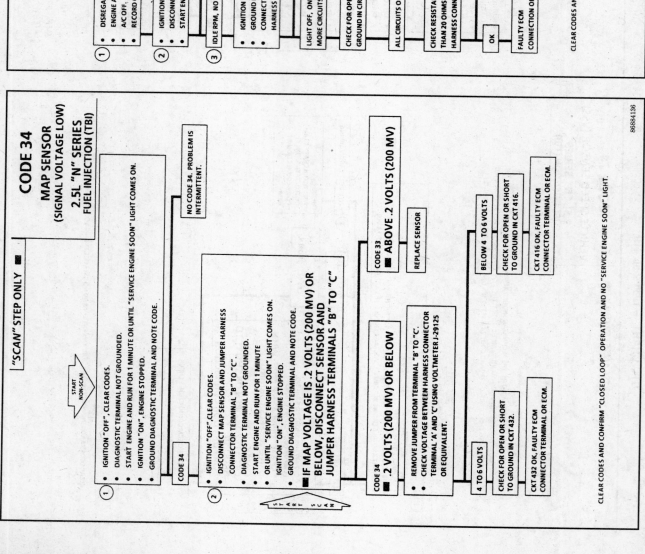

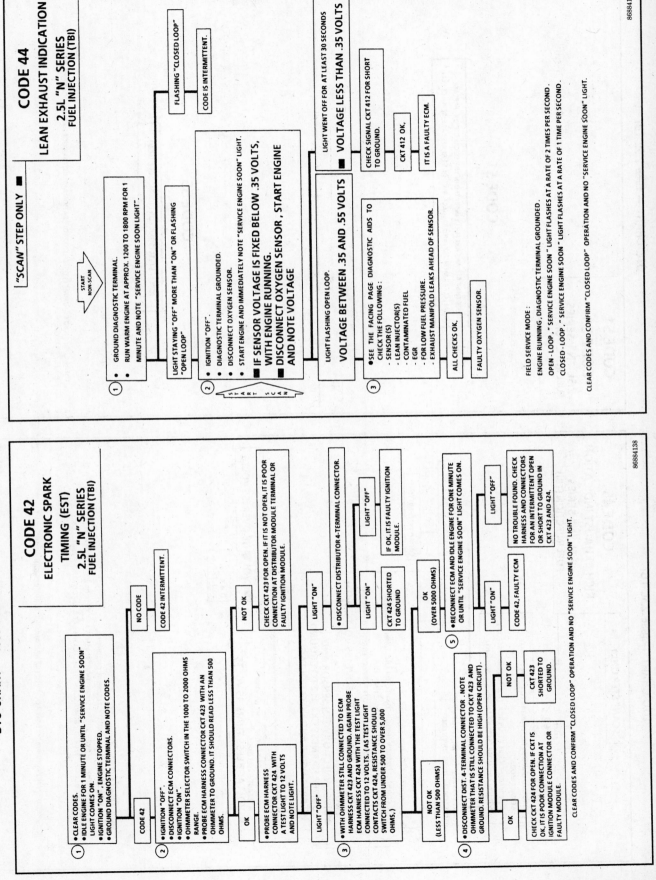

DTC CHART — 1986 2.5L TBI

CODE 44
LEAN EXHAUST INDICATION
2.5L "N" SERIES FUEL INJECTION (TBI)

"SCAN" STEP ONLY ■

START NON-SCAN

1.
- GROUND DIAGNOSTIC TERMINAL.
- RUN WARM ENGINE AT APPROX. 1200 TO 1800 RPM FOR 1 MINUTE AND NOTE "SERVICE ENGINE SOON LIGHT".

LIGHT STAYING "OFF" MORE THAN "ON" OR FLASHING "OPEN LOOP"

FLASHING "CLOSED LOOP"

CODE IS INTERMITTENT.

2.
- IGNITION "OFF".
- DIAGNOSTIC TERMINAL GROUNDED.
- DISCONNECT OXYGEN SENSOR.
- START ENGINE AND IMMEDIATELY NOTE "SERVICE ENGINE SOON" LIGHT.

■ IF SENSOR VOLTAGE IS FIXED BELOW .35 VOLTS, WITH ENGINE RUNNING. DISCONNECT OXYGEN SENSOR, START ENGINE AND NOTE VOLTAGE

START SCAN

LIGHT FLASHING OPEN LOOP.

VOLTAGE BETWEEN .35 AND .55 VOLTS

LIGHT WENT OFF FOR AT LEAST 30 SECONDS

■ VOLTAGE LESS THAN .35 VOLTS

CHECK SIGNAL CKT 412 FOR SHORT TO GROUND.

CKT 412 OK,

IT IS A FAULTY ECM.

3.
- SEE THE FACING PAGE DIAGNOSTIC AIDS TO CHECK THE FOLLOWING :
  - SENSOR (S)
  - LEAN INJECTOR(S)
  - CONTAMINATED FUEL
  - EGR
  - FOR LOW FUEL PRESSURE.
  - EXHAUST MANIFOLD LEAKS AHEAD OF SENSOR.

ALL CHECKS OK,

FAULTY OXYGEN SENSOR.

FIELD SERVICE MODE :
ENGINE RUNNING , DIAGNOSTIC TERMINAL GROUNDED.
OPEN - LOOP , " SERVICE ENGINE SOON " LIGHT FLASHES AT A RATE OF 2 TIMES PER SECOND .
CLOSED - LOOP , " SERVICE ENGINE SOON " LIGHT FLASHES AT A RATE OF 1 TIME PER SECOND .

CLEAR CODES AND CONFIRM "CLOSED LOOP" OPERATION AND NO "SERVICE ENGINE SOON" LIGHT.

86884139

DTC CHART — 1986 2.5L TBI

CODE 42
ELECTRONIC SPARK TIMING (EST)
2.5L "N" SERIES FUEL INJECTION (TBI)

1.
- CLEAR CODES.
- IDLE ENGINE FOR 1 MINUTE OR UNTIL "SERVICE ENGINE SOON" LIGHT COMES ON.
- IGNITION "ON" , ENGINE STOPPED.
- GROUND DIAGNOSTIC TERMINAL AND NOTE CODES.

CODE 42

NO CODE

CODE 42 INTERMITTENT.

2.
- IGNITION "OFF".
- DISCONNECT ECM CONNECTORS.
- IGNITION "ON".
- OHMMETER SELECTOR SWITCH IN THE 1000 TO 2000 OHMS RANGE.
- PROBE ECM HARNESS CONNECTOR CKT 423 WITH AN OHMMETER TO GROUND. IT SHOULD READ LESS THAN 500 OHMS.

OK

NOT OK

CHECK CKT 423 FOR OPEN. IF IT IS NOT OPEN, IT IS POOR CONNECTION AT DISTRIBUTOR MODULE TERMINAL OR FAULTY IGNITION MODULE.

- PROBE ECM HARNESS CONNECTOR CKT 424 WITH A TEST LIGHT TO 12 VOLTS AND NOTE LIGHT.

LIGHT "ON"

LIGHT "OFF"

3.
- WITH OHMMETER STILL CONNECTED TO ECM HARNESS CKT 423 AND GROUND. AGAIN PROBE ECM HARNESS CKT 424 WITH THE TEST LIGHT CONNECTED TO 12 VOLTS. (AS TEST LIGHT CONTACTS CKT 424, RESISTANCE SHOULD SWITCH FROM UNDER 500 TO OVER 5,000 OHMS.)

NOT OK (LESS THAN 500 OHMS)

OK (OVER 5000 OHMS)

- DISCONNECT DISTRIBUTOR 4-TERMINAL CONNECTOR.

LIGHT "ON"

LIGHT "OFF"

CKT 424 SHORTED TO GROUND

IF OK, IT IS FAULTY IGNITION MODULE.

- DISCONNECT DIST. 4-TERMINAL CONNECTOR . NOTE OHMMETER THAT IS STILL CONNECTED TO CKT 423 AND GROUND. RESISTANCE SHOULD BE HIGH (OPEN CIRCUIT).

OK

NOT OK

CKT 423 SHORTED TO GROUND.

CHECK CKT 424 FOR OPEN. IF CKT IS OK, IT IS POOR CONNECTION AT IGNITION MODULE CONNECTOR OR FAULTY MODULE.

5.
- RECONNECT ECM AND IDLE ENGINE FOR ONE MINUTE OR UNTIL "SERVICE ENGINE SOON" LIGHT COMES ON.

LIGHT "ON"

LIGHT "OFF"

CODE 42, FAULTY ECM

NO TROUBLE FOUND. CHECK HARNESS AND CONNECTORS FOR AN INTERMITTENT OPEN OR SHORT TO GROUND IN CKT 423 AND 424.

CLEAR CODES AND CONFIRM "CLOSED LOOP" OPERATION AND NO "SERVICE ENGINE SOON" LIGHT.

86884138

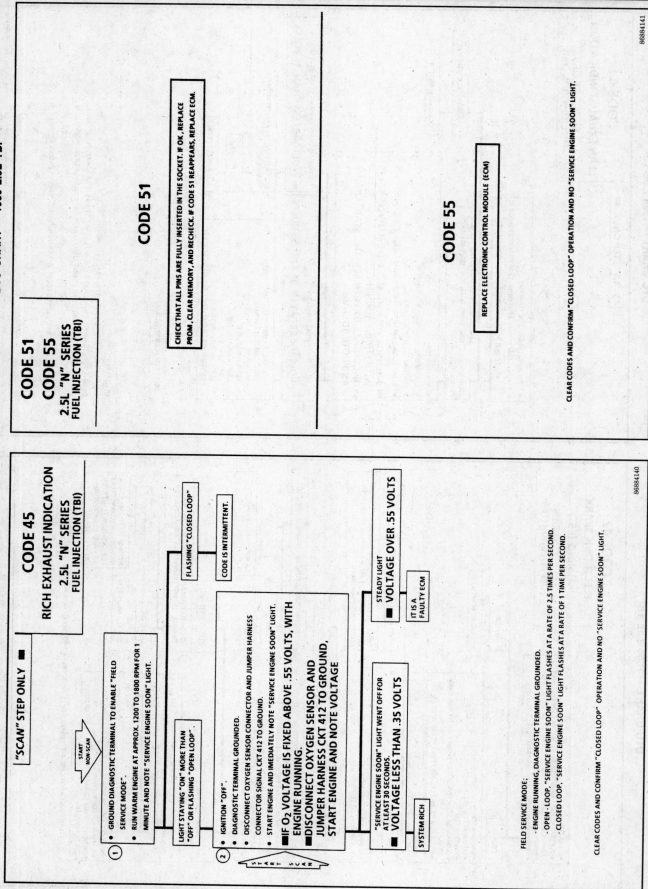

DTC CHART — 1986 2.5L TBI

CODE 51
CODE 55
2.5L "N" SERIES
FUEL INJECTION (TBI)

CODE 51

CHECK THAT ALL PINS ARE FULLY INSERTED IN THE SOCKET. IF OK, REPLACE PROM, CLEAR MEMORY, AND RECHECK. IF CODE 51 REAPPEARS, REPLACE ECM.

CODE 55

REPLACE ELECTRONIC CONTROL MODULE (ECM)

CLEAR CODES AND CONFIRM "CLOSED LOOP" OPERATION AND NO "SERVICE ENGINE SOON" LIGHT.

DTC CHART — 1986 2.5L TBI

CODE 45
RICH EXHAUST INDICATION
2.5L "N" SERIES
FUEL INJECTION (TBI)

■ "SCAN" STEP ONLY

START NON-SCAN

1.
- GROUND DIAGNOSTIC TERMINAL TO ENABLE "FIELD SERVICE MODE".
- RUN WARM ENGINE AT APPROX. 1200 TO 1800 RPM FOR 1 MINUTE AND NOTE "SERVICE ENGINE SOON" LIGHT.

LIGHT STAYING "ON" MORE THAN "OFF" OR FLASHING "OPEN LOOP".

FLASHING "CLOSED LOOP"

CODE IS INTERMITTENT.

2.
- IGNITION "OFF".
- DIAGNOSTIC TERMINAL GROUNDED.
- DISCONNECT OXYGEN SENSOR CONNECTOR AND JUMPER HARNESS CONNECTOR SIGNAL CKT 412 TO GROUND.
- START ENGINE AND IMMEDIATELY NOTE "SERVICE ENGINE SOON" LIGHT.

■ IF O$_2$ VOLTAGE IS FIXED ABOVE .55 VOLTS, WITH ENGINE RUNNING.
■ DISCONNECT OXYGEN SENSOR AND JUMPER HARNESS CKT 412 TO GROUND, START ENGINE AND NOTE VOLTAGE

START SCAN

STEADY LIGHT
■ VOLTAGE OVER .55 VOLTS

IT IS A FAULTY ECM

"SERVICE ENGINE SOON" LIGHT WENT OFF FOR AT LEAST 30 SECONDS.
■ VOLTAGE LESS THAN .35 VOLTS

SYSTEM RICH

FIELD SERVICE MODE;
- ENGINE RUNNING, DIAGNOSTIC TERMINAL GROUNDED.
- OPEN - LOOP, "SERVICE ENGINE SOON" LIGHT FLASHES AT A RATE OF 2.5 TIMES PER SECOND.
- CLOSED LOOP, "SERVICE ENGINE SOON" LIGHT FLASHES AT A RATE OF 1 TIME PER SECOND.

CLEAR CODES AND CONFIRM "CLOSED LOOP" OPERATION AND NO "SERVICE ENGINE SOON" LIGHT.

86884140
86884141

DTC CHART — 1987-91 2.5L TBI

CODE 14
COOLANT TEMPERATURE SENSOR (CTS) CIRCUIT
(HIGH TEMPERATURE INDICATED)
2.5L (VIN U) "N" CARLINE (TBI)

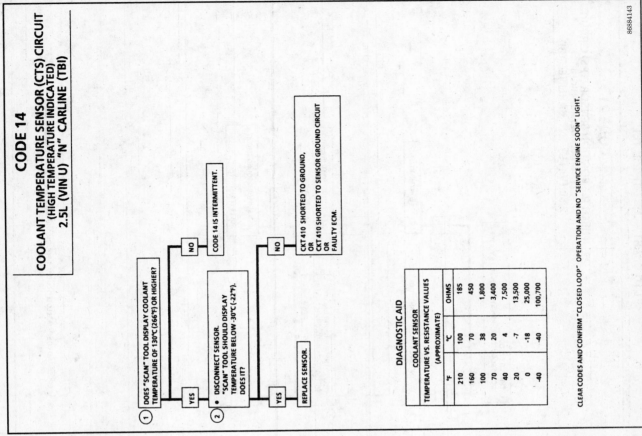

DTC CHART — 1987-91 2.5L TBI

CODE 13
OXYGEN (O₂) SENSOR CIRCUIT
(OPEN CIRCUIT)
2.5L (VIN U) "N" CARLINE (TBI)

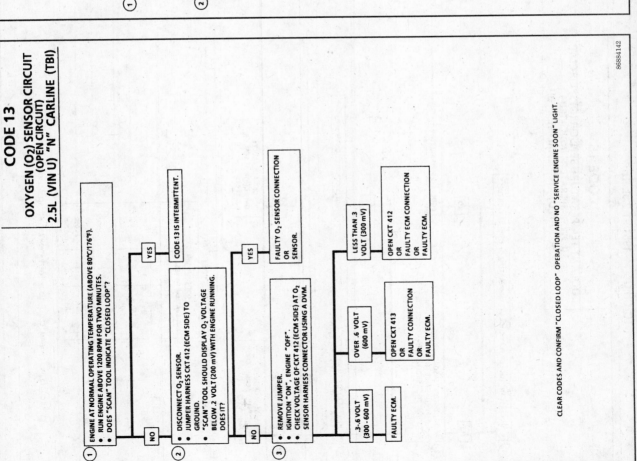

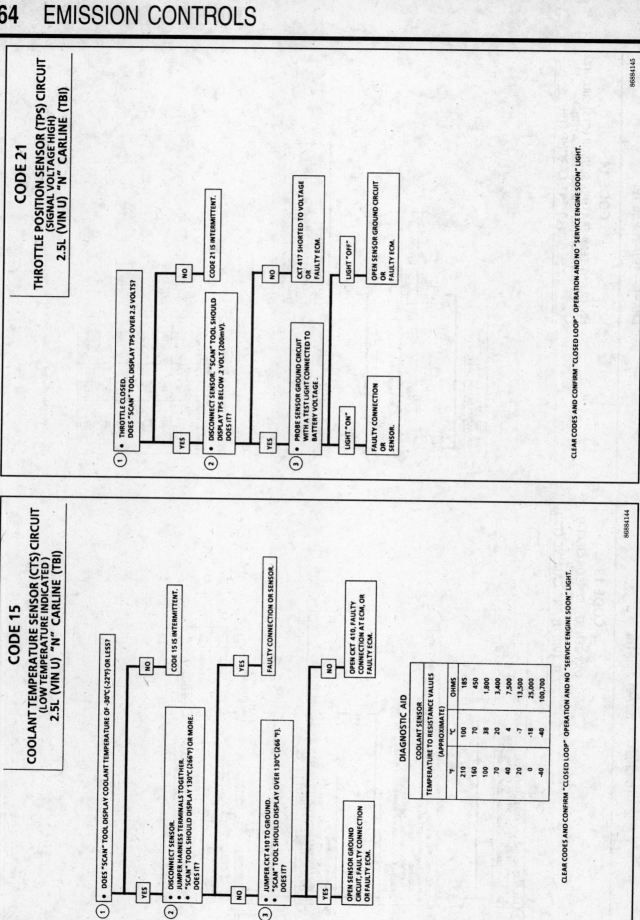

DTC CHART — 1987-91 2.5L TBI

86884145

CODE 21

THROTTLE POSITION SENSOR (TPS) CIRCUIT
(SIGNAL VOLTAGE HIGH)
2.5L (VIN U) "N" CARLINE (TBI)

① • THROTTLE CLOSED.
   DOES "SCAN" TOOL DISPLAY TPS OVER 2.5 VOLTS?

YES

NO → CODE 21 IS INTERMITTENT.

② • DISCONNECT SENSOR. "SCAN" TOOL SHOULD DISPLAY TPS BELOW .2 VOLT (200mV).
   DOES IT?

YES

NO → CKT 417 SHORTED TO VOLTAGE OR FAULTY ECM.

③ • PROBE SENSOR GROUND CIRCUIT WITH A TEST LIGHT CONNECTED TO BATTERY VOLTAGE.

LIGHT "ON" → FAULTY CONNECTION OR SENSOR.

LIGHT "OFF" → OPEN SENSOR GROUND CIRCUIT OR FAULTY ECM.

CLEAR CODES AND CONFIRM "CLOSED LOOP" OPERATION AND NO "SERVICE ENGINE SOON" LIGHT.

DTC CHART — 1987-91 2.5L TBI

86884144

CODE 15

COOLANT TEMPERATURE SENSOR (CTS) CIRCUIT
(LOW TEMPERATURE INDICATED)
2.5L (VIN U) "N" CARLINE (TBI)

① • DOES "SCAN" TOOL DISPLAY COOLANT TEMPERATURE OF -30°C (-22°F) OR LESS?

YES

NO → CODE 15 IS INTERMITTENT.

② • DISCONNECT SENSOR.
   • JUMPER HARNESS TERMINALS TOGETHER.
   • "SCAN" TOOL SHOULD DISPLAY 130°C (266°F) OR MORE.
   DOES IT?

YES → FAULTY CONNECTION OR SENSOR.

NO

③ • JUMPER CKT 410 TO GROUND.
   • "SCAN" TOOL SHOULD DISPLAY OVER 130°C (266°F).
   DOES IT?

NO → OPEN CKT 410, FAULTY CONNECTION AT ECM, OR FAULTY ECM.

YES → OPEN SENSOR GROUND CIRCUIT, FAULTY CONNECTION OR FAULTY ECM.

DIAGNOSTIC AID

COOLANT SENSOR TEMPERATURE TO RESISTANCE VALUES (APPROXIMATE)		
°F	°C	OHMS
210	100	185
160	70	450
100	38	1,800
70	20	3,400
40	4	7,500
20	-7	13,500
0	-18	25,000
-40	-40	100,700

CLEAR CODES AND CONFIRM "CLOSED LOOP" OPERATION AND NO "SERVICE ENGINE SOON" LIGHT.

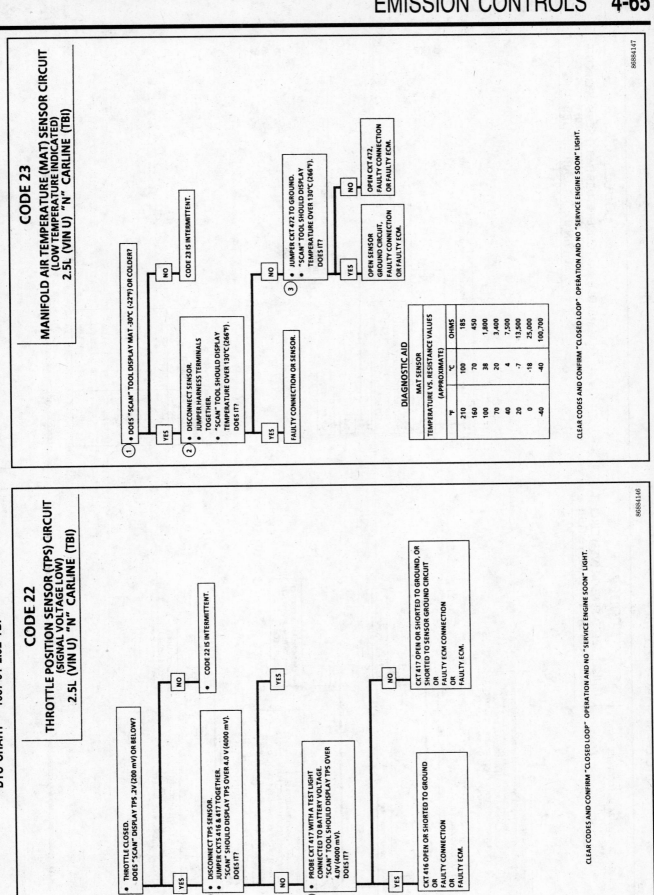

DTC CHART — 1987-91 2.5L TBI

CODE 23

MANIFOLD AIR TEMPERATURE (MAT) SENSOR CIRCUIT
(LOW TEMPERATURE INDICATED)
2.5L (VIN U) "N" CARLINE (TBI)

1. • DOES "SCAN" TOOL DISPLAY MAT -30°C (-22°F) OR COLDER?
   - **NO** → CODE 23 IS INTERMITTENT.
   - **YES** ↓

2. • DISCONNECT SENSOR.
   • JUMPER HARNESS TERMINALS TOGETHER.
   • "SCAN" TOOL SHOULD DISPLAY TEMPERATURE OVER 130°C (266°F). DOES IT?
   - **YES** → FAULTY CONNECTION OR SENSOR.
   - **NO** ↓

3. • JUMPER CKT 472 TO GROUND.
   • "SCAN" TOOL SHOULD DISPLAY TEMPERATURE OVER 130°C (266°F). DOES IT?
   - **YES** → OPEN SENSOR GROUND CIRCUIT, FAULTY CONNECTION OR FAULTY ECM.
   - **NO** → OPEN CKT 472, FAULTY CONNECTION OR FAULTY ECM.

DIAGNOSTIC AID

MAT SENSOR
TEMPERATURE VS. RESISTANCE VALUES
(APPROXIMATE)

°F	°C	OHMS
210	100	185
160	70	450
100	38	1,800
70	20	3,400
40	4	7,500
20	-7	13,500
0	-18	25,000
-40	-40	100,700

CLEAR CODES AND CONFIRM "CLOSED LOOP" OPERATION AND NO "SERVICE ENGINE SOON" LIGHT.

86884147

DTC CHART — 1987-91 2.5L TBI

CODE 22

THROTTLE POSITION SENSOR (TPS) CIRCUIT
(SIGNAL VOLTAGE LOW)
2.5L (VIN U) "N" CARLINE (TBI)

1. • THROTTLE CLOSED.
   • DOES "SCAN" DISPLAY TPS .2V (200 mV) OR BELOW?
   - **NO** → CODE 22 IS INTERMITTENT.
   - **YES** ↓

2. • DISCONNECT TPS SENSOR.
   • JUMPER CKTS 416 & 417 TOGETHER.
   • "SCAN" SHOULD DISPLAY TPS OVER 4.0 V (4000 mV). DOES IT?
   - **YES** ↓
   - **NO** ↓

4. • PROBE CKT 417 WITH A TEST LIGHT CONNECTED TO BATTERY VOLTAGE.
   • "SCAN" TOOL SHOULD DISPLAY TPS OVER 4.0V (4000 mV). DOES IT?
   - **YES** → CKT 416 OPEN OR SHORTED TO GROUND OR FAULTY CONNECTION OR FAULTY ECM.
   - **NO** → CKT 417 OPEN OR SHORTED TO GROUND, OR SHORTED TO SENSOR GROUND CIRCUIT OR FAULTY ECM CONNECTION OR FAULTY ECM.

CLEAR CODES AND CONFIRM "CLOSED LOOP" OPERATION AND NO "SERVICE ENGINE SOON" LIGHT.

86884146

DTC CHART — 1987-91 2.5L TBI

CODE 25

MANIFOLD AIR TEMPERATURE (MAT) SENSOR CIRCUIT
(HIGH TEMPERATURE INDICATED)
2.5L (VIN U) "N" CARLINE (TBI)

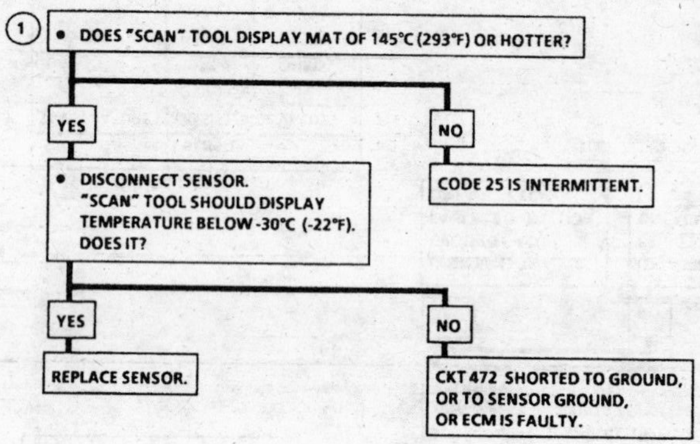

① • DOES "SCAN" TOOL DISPLAY MAT OF 145°C (293°F) OR HOTTER?

YES → • DISCONNECT SENSOR.
"SCAN" TOOL SHOULD DISPLAY TEMPERATURE BELOW -30°C (-22°F). DOES IT?

NO → CODE 25 IS INTERMITTENT.

YES → REPLACE SENSOR.

NO → CKT 472 SHORTED TO GROUND, OR TO SENSOR GROUND, OR ECM IS FAULTY.

DIAGNOSTIC AID

MAT SENSOR
TEMPERATURE VS. RESISTANCE VALUES
(APPROXIMATE)

°F	°C	OHMS
210	100	185
160	70	450
100	38	1,800
70	20	3,400
40	4	7,500
20	-7	13,500
0	-18	25,000
-40	-40	100,700

CLEAR CODES AND CONFIRM "CLOSED LOOP" OPERATION AND NO "SERVICE ENGINE SOON" LIGHT.

86884149

DTC CHART — 1987-91 2.5L TBI

CODE 24

VEHICLE SPEED SENSOR (VSS) CIRCUIT
2.5L (VIN U) "N" CARLINE (TBI)

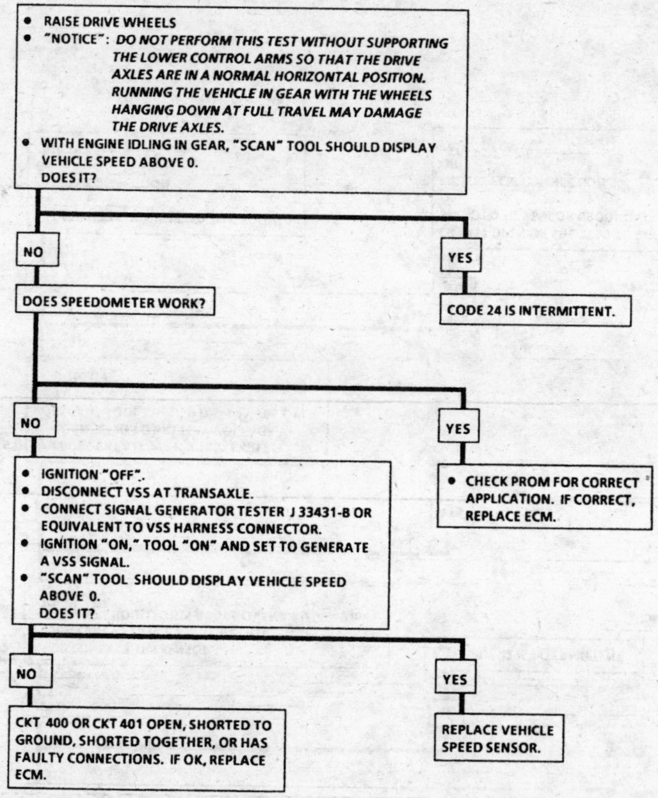

DISREGARD CODE 24 IF SET WHILE DRIVE WHEELS ARE NOT TURNING.

• RAISE DRIVE WHEELS
• "NOTICE": DO NOT PERFORM THIS TEST WITHOUT SUPPORTING THE LOWER CONTROL ARMS SO THAT THE DRIVE AXLES ARE IN A NORMAL HORIZONTAL POSITION. RUNNING THE VEHICLE IN GEAR WITH THE WHEELS HANGING DOWN AT FULL TRAVEL MAY DAMAGE THE DRIVE AXLES.
• WITH ENGINE IDLING IN GEAR, "SCAN" TOOL SHOULD DISPLAY VEHICLE SPEED ABOVE 0. DOES IT?

YES → CODE 24 IS INTERMITTENT.

NO → DOES SPEEDOMETER WORK?

YES → • CHECK PROM FOR CORRECT APPLICATION. IF CORRECT, REPLACE ECM.

NO → • IGNITION "OFF".
• DISCONNECT VSS AT TRANSAXLE.
• CONNECT SIGNAL GENERATOR TESTER J 33431-B OR EQUIVALENT TO VSS HARNESS CONNECTOR.
• IGNITION "ON," TOOL "ON" AND SET TO GENERATE A VSS SIGNAL.
• "SCAN" TOOL SHOULD DISPLAY VEHICLE SPEED ABOVE 0. DOES IT?

YES → REPLACE VEHICLE SPEED SENSOR.

NO → CKT 400 OR CKT 401 OPEN, SHORTED TO GROUND, SHORTED TOGETHER, OR HAS FAULTY CONNECTIONS. IF OK, REPLACE ECM.

CLEAR CODES AND CONFIRM "CLOSED LOOP" OPERATION AND NO "SERVICE ENGINE SOON" LIGHT.

86884148

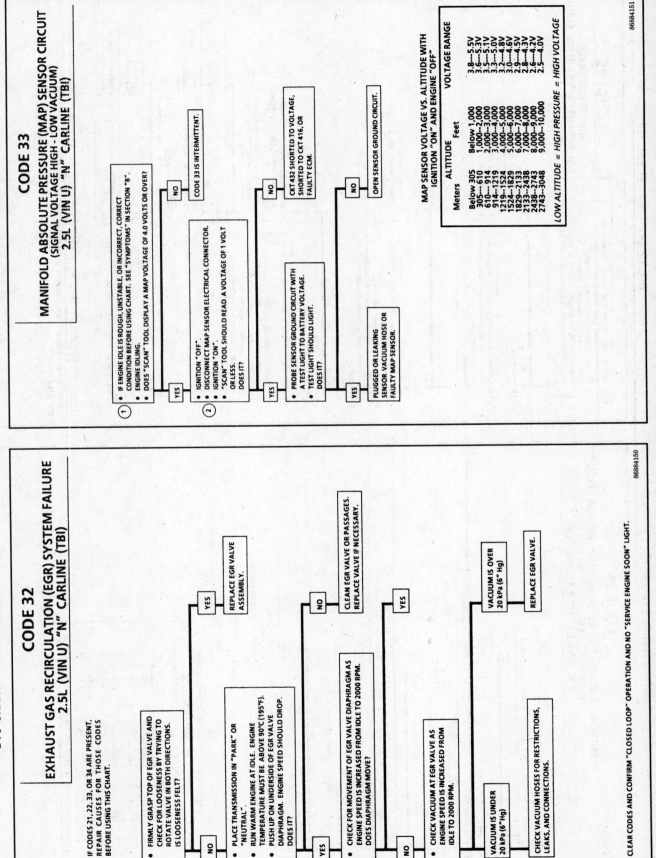

DTC CHART — 1987-91 2.5L TBI

CODE 33

MANIFOLD ABSOLUTE PRESSURE (MAP) SENSOR CIRCUIT
(SIGNAL VOLTAGE HIGH - LOW VACUUM)
2.5L (VIN U) "N" CARLINE (TBI)

(1)
- IF ENGINE IDLE IS ROUGH, UNSTABLE, OR INCORRECT, CORRECT CONDITION BEFORE USING CHART. SEE "SYMPTOMS" IN SECTION "B".
- ENGINE IDLING.
- DOES "SCAN" TOOL DISPLAY A MAP VOLTAGE OF 4.0 VOLTS OR OVER?

NO → CODE 33 IS INTERMITTENT.

YES

(2)
- IGNITION "OFF".
- DISCONNECT MAP SENSOR ELECTRICAL CONNECTOR.
- IGNITION "ON".
- "SCAN" TOOL SHOULD READ A VOLTAGE OF 1 VOLT OR LESS.
- DOES IT?

NO → CKT 432 SHORTED TO VOLTAGE, SHORTED TO CKT 416, OR FAULTY ECM.

YES

- PROBE SENSOR GROUND CIRCUIT WITH A TEST LIGHT TO BATTERY VOLTAGE.
- TEST LIGHT SHOULD LIGHT.
- DOES IT?

NO → OPEN SENSOR GROUND CIRCUIT.

YES

PLUGGED OR LEAKING SENSOR VACUUM HOSE OR FAULTY MAP SENSOR.

MAP SENSOR VOLTAGE VS. ALTITUDE WITH IGNITION "ON" AND ENGINE "OFF"

ALTITUDE		VOLTAGE RANGE
Meters	Feet	
Below 305	Below 1,000	3.8—5.5V
305— 610	1,000—2,000	3.6—5.3V
610— 914	2,000—3,000	3.5—5.1V
914—1219	3,000—4,000	3.3—5.0V
1219—1524	4,000—5,000	3.2—4.8V
1524—1829	5,000—6,000	3.0—4.6V
1829—2133	6,000—7,000	2.9—4.5V
2133—2438	7,000—8,000	2.8—4.3V
2438—2743	8,000—9,000	2.6—4.2V
2743—3048	9,000—10,000	2.5—4.0V

LOW ALTITUDE = HIGH PRESSURE = HIGH VOLTAGE

86884151

DTC CHART — 1987-91 2.5L TBI

CODE 32

EXHAUST GAS RECIRCULATION (EGR) SYSTEM FAILURE
2.5L (VIN U) "N" CARLINE (TBI)

IF CODES 21, 22, 33, OR 34 ARE PRESENT, REPAIR CAUSES FOR THOSE CODES BEFORE USING THIS CHART.

- FIRMLY GRASP TOP OF EGR VALVE AND CHECK FOR LOOSENESS BY TRYING TO ROTATE VALVE IN BOTH DIRECTIONS. IS LOOSENESS FELT?

YES → REPLACE EGR VALVE ASSEMBLY.

NO

- PLACE TRANSMISSION IN "PARK" OR "NEUTRAL".
- RUN WARM ENGINE AT IDLE. ENGINE TEMPERATURE MUST BE ABOVE 90°C(195°F).
- PUSH UP ON UNDERSIDE OF EGR VALVE DIAPHRAGM. ENGINE SPEED SHOULD DROP. DOES IT?

NO → CLEAN EGR VALVE OR PASSAGES. REPLACE VALVE IF NECESSARY.

YES

- CHECK FOR MOVEMENT OF EGR VALVE DIAPHRAGM AS ENGINE SPEED IS INCREASED FROM IDLE TO 2000 RPM. DOES DIAPHRAGM MOVE?

YES → CLEAN EGR VALVE OR PASSAGES. REPLACE VALVE IF NECESSARY.

NO

- CHECK VACUUM AT EGR VALVE AS ENGINE SPEED IS INCREASED FROM IDLE TO 2000 RPM.

VACUUM IS UNDER 20 kPa (6"Hg) → CHECK VACUUM HOSES FOR RESTRICTIONS, LEAKS, AND CONNECTIONS.

VACUUM IS OVER 20 kPa (6" Hg) → REPLACE EGR VALVE.

CLEAR CODES AND CONFIRM "CLOSED LOOP" OPERATION AND NO "SERVICE ENGINE SOON" LIGHT.

86884150

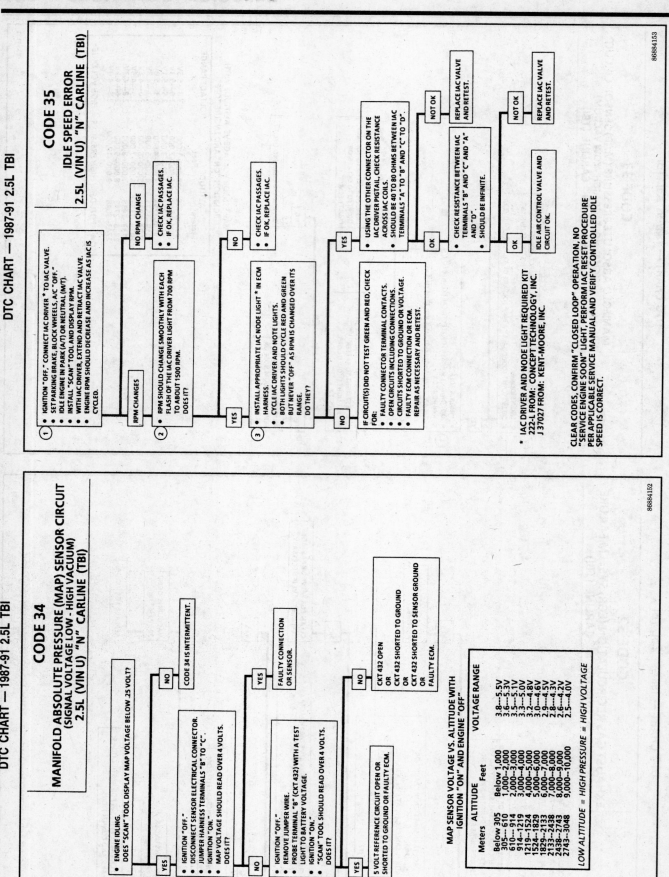

DTC CHART — 1987-91 2.5L TBI

CODE 35
IDLE SPEED ERROR
2.5L (VIN U) "N" CARLINE (TBI)

86884153

1.
- IGNITION "OFF." CONNECT IAC DRIVER * TO IAC VALVE.
- SET PARKING BRAKE, BLOCK WHEELS, A/C "OFF."
- IDLE ENGINE IN PARK (A/T) OR NEUTRAL (M/T).
- INSTALL "SCAN" TOOL AND DISPLAY RPM.
- WITH IAC DRIVER, EXTEND AND RETRACT IAC VALVE.
- ENGINE RPM SHOULD DECREASE AND INCREASE AS IAC IS CYCLED.

RPM CHANGES

NO RPM CHANGE

→ • CHECK IAC PASSAGES.
  • IF OK, REPLACE IAC.

2. RPM SHOULD CHANGE SMOOTHLY WITH EACH FLASH OF THE IAC DRIVER LIGHT FROM 700 RPM TO ABOUT 1500 RPM. DOES IT?

YES

NO

→ • CHECK IAC PASSAGES.
  • IF OK, REPLACE IAC.

3. INSTALL APPROPRIATE IAC NODE LIGHT * IN ECM HARNESS.
- CYCLE IAC DRIVER AND NOTE LIGHTS.
- BOTH LIGHTS SHOULD CYCLE RED AND GREEN BUT NEVER "OFF" AS RPM IS CHANGED OVER IT'S RANGE.
DO THEY?

YES

NO

IF CIRCUIT(S) DID NOT TEST GREEN AND RED, CHECK FOR:
- FAULTY CONNECTOR TERMINAL CONTACTS.
- OPEN CIRCUITS INCLUDING CONNECTIONS.
- CIRCUITS SHORTED TO GROUND OR VOLTAGE.
- FAULTY ECM CONNECTION OR ECM.
- REPAIR AS NECESSARY AND RETEST.

USING THE OTHER CONNECTOR ON THE IAC DRIVER PIGTAIL, CHECK RESISTANCE ACROSS IAC COILS.
SHOULD BE 40 TO 80 OHMS BETWEEN IAC TERMINALS "A" TO "B" AND "C" TO "D".

OK

NOT OK → REPLACE IAC VALVE AND RETEST.

CHECK RESISTANCE BETWEEN IAC TERMINALS "B" AND "C" AND "A" AND "D".
SHOULD BE INFINITE.

OK

NOT OK → REPLACE IAC VALVE AND RETEST.

IDLE AIR CONTROL VALVE AND CIRCUIT OK.

* IAC DRIVER AND NODE LIGHT REQUIRED KIT 222-L FROM: CONCEPT TECHNOLOGY, INC. J 37027 FROM: KENT-MOORE, INC.

CLEAR CODES, CONFIRM "CLOSED LOOP" OPERATION. NO "SERVICE ENGINE SOON" LIGHT, PERFORM IAC RESET PROCEDURE PER APPLICABLE SERVICE MANUAL AND VERIFY CONTROLLED IDLE SPEED IS CORRECT.

DTC CHART — 1987-91 2.5L TBI

CODE 34
MANIFOLD ABSOLUTE PRESSURE (MAP) SENSOR CIRCUIT
(SIGNAL VOLTAGE LOW - HIGH VACUUM)
2.5L (VIN U) "N" CARLINE (TBI)

86884152

1.
- ENGINE IDLING.
- DOES "SCAN" TOOL DISPLAY MAP VOLTAGE BELOW .25 VOLT?

YES

NO → CODE 34 IS INTERMITTENT.

2.
- IGNITION "OFF."
- DISCONNECT SENSOR ELECTRICAL CONNECTOR.
- JUMPER HARNESS TERMINALS "B" TO "C".
- IGNITION "ON."
- MAP VOLTAGE SHOULD READ OVER 4 VOLTS. DOES IT?

NO

YES → FAULTY CONNECTION OR SENSOR.

3.
- IGNITION "OFF."
- REMOVE JUMPER WIRE.
- PROBE TERMINAL "B" (CKT 432) WITH A TEST LIGHT TO BATTERY VOLTAGE.
- IGNITION "ON."
- "SCAN" TOOL SHOULD READ OVER 4 VOLTS. DOES IT?

YES → 5 VOLT REFERENCE CIRCUIT OPEN OR SHORTED TO GROUND OR FAULTY ECM.

NO →
CKT 432 OPEN
OR
CKT 432 SHORTED TO GROUND
OR
CKT 432 SHORTED TO SENSOR GROUND
OR
FAULTY ECM.

MAP SENSOR VOLTAGE VS. ALTITUDE WITH IGNITION "ON" AND ENGINE "OFF"

ALTITUDE		VOLTAGE RANGE
Meters	Feet	
Below 305	Below 1,000	3.8—5.5V
305— 610	1,000—2,000	3.6—5.3V
610— 914	2,000—3,000	3.5—5.1V
914—1219	3,000—4,000	3.3—5.0V
1219—1524	4,000—5,000	3.2—4.8V
1524—1829	5,000—6,000	3.0—4.6V
1829—2133	6,000—7,000	2.9—4.5V
2133—2438	7,000—8,000	2.8—4.3V
2438—2743	8,000—9,000	2.6—4.2V
2743—3048	9,000—10,000	2.5—4.0V

LOW ALTITUDE = HIGH PRESSURE = HIGH VOLTAGE

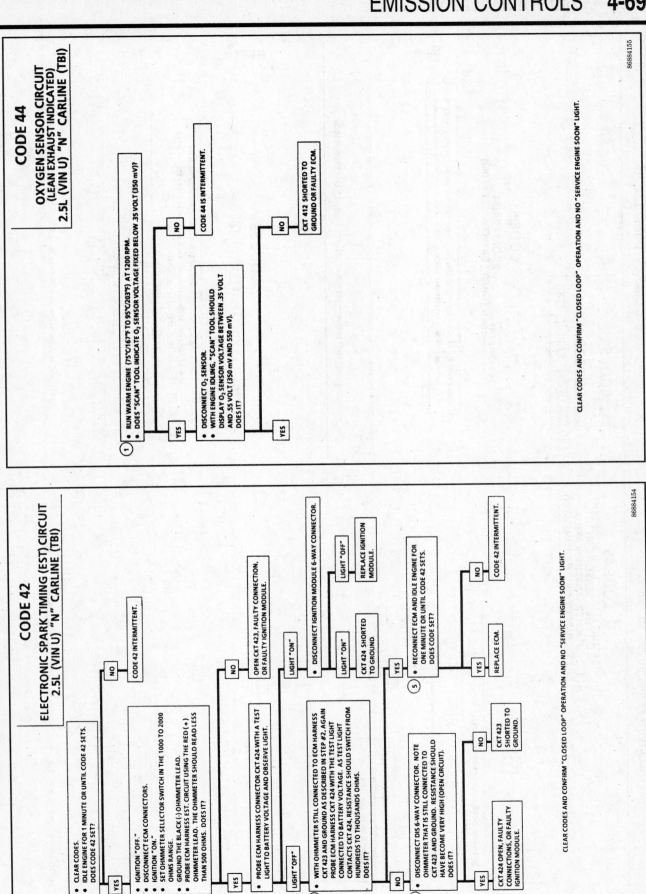

DTC CHART — 1987-91 2.5L TBI

CODE 44

OXYGEN SENSOR CIRCUIT
(LEAN EXHAUST INDICATED)
2.5L (VIN U) "N" CARLINE (TBI)

86884155

1.
- RUN WARM ENGINE (75°C/167°F TO 95°C/203°F) AT 1200 RPM.
- DOES "SCAN" TOOL INDICATE O₂ SENSOR VOLTAGE FIXED BELOW .35 VOLT (350 mV)?

NO → CODE 44 IS INTERMITTENT.

YES →
- DISCONNECT O₂ SENSOR.
- WITH ENGINE IDLING, "SCAN" TOOL SHOULD DISPLAY O₂ SENSOR VOLTAGE BETWEEN .35 VOLT AND .55 VOLT (350 mV AND 550 mV).
  DOES IT?

NO → CKT 412 SHORTED TO GROUND OR FAULTY ECM.

YES →

CLEAR CODES AND CONFIRM "CLOSED LOOP" OPERATION AND NO "SERVICE ENGINE SOON" LIGHT.

DTC CHART — 1987-91 2.5L TBI

CODE 42

ELECTRONIC SPARK TIMING (EST) CIRCUIT
2.5L (VIN U) "N" CARLINE (TBI)

86884154

1.
- CLEAR CODES.
- IDLE ENGINE FOR 1 MINUTE OR UNTIL CODE 42 SETS.
  DOES CODE 42 SET?

NO → CODE 42 INTERMITTENT.

YES →

2.
- IGNITION "OFF."
- DISCONNECT ECM CONNECTORS.
- IGNITION "ON."
- SET OHMMETER SELECTOR SWITCH IN THE 1000 TO 2000 OHMS RANGE.
- GROUND THE BLACK (-) OHMMETER LEAD.
- PROBE ECM HARNESS EST. CIRCUIT USING THE RED (+) OHMMETER LEAD. THE OHMMETER SHOULD READ LESS THAN 500 OHMS. DOES IT?

NO → OPEN CKT 423, FAULTY CONNECTION, OR FAULTY IGNITION MODULE.

YES →

- PROBE ECM HARNESS CONNECTOR CKT 424 WITH A TEST LIGHT TO BATTERY VOLTAGE AND OBSERVE LIGHT.

LIGHT "OFF" →

3.
- WITH OHMMETER STILL CONNECTED TO ECM HARNESS CKT 423 AND GROUND AS DESCRIBED IN STEP #2, AGAIN PROBE ECM HARNESS CKT 424 WITH THE TEST LIGHT CONNECTED TO BATTERY VOLTAGE. AS TEST LIGHT CONTACTS CKT 424, RESISTANCE SHOULD SWITCH FROM HUNDREDS TO THOUSANDS OHMS.
  DOES IT?

LIGHT "ON" → DISCONNECT IGNITION MODULE 6-WAY CONNECTOR.

LIGHT "OFF" → REPLACE IGNITION MODULE.

LIGHT "ON" → CKT 424 SHORTED TO GROUND

4.
- DISCONNECT DIS 6-WAY CONNECTOR. NOTE OHMMETER THAT IS STILL CONNECTED TO CKT 423 AND GROUND. RESISTANCE SHOULD HAVE BECOME VERY HIGH (OPEN CIRCUIT).
  DOES IT?

NO → CKT 423 SHORTED TO GROUND.

YES → CKT 424 OPEN, FAULTY CONNECTIONS, OR FAULTY IGNITION MODULE.

5.
- RECONNECT ECM AND IDLE ENGINE FOR ONE MINUTE OR UNTIL CODE 42 SETS. DOES CODE SET?

NO → CODE 42 INTERMITTENT.

YES → REPLACE ECM.

CLEAR CODES AND CONFIRM "CLOSED LOOP" OPERATION AND NO "SERVICE ENGINE SOON" LIGHT.

DTC CHART — 1987-91 2.5L TBI

CODE 51
CODE 53
2.5L (VIN U) "N" CARLINE (TBI)

CODE 51
PROM ERROR
(FAULTY OR INCORRECT PROM)

CHECK THAT ALL PINS ARE FULLY INSERTED IN THE SOCKET AND THAT PROM IS PROPERLY SEATED. IF OK, REPLACE PROM, CLEAR MEMORY, AND RECHECK. IF CODE 51 REAPPEARS, REPLACE ECM.

CLEAR CODES AND CONFIRM "CLOSED LOOP" OPERATION AND NO "SERVICE ENGINE SOON" LIGHT.

CODE 53
SYSTEM OVERVOLTAGE

THIS CODE INDICATES THAT THERE IS A BASIC GENERATOR PROBLEM.
- CODE 53 WILL SET IF BATTERY VOLTAGE AT THE ECM IS GREATER THAN 16.9 VOLTS FOR AT LEAST 50 SECONDS.
- CHECK AND REPAIR CHARGING SYSTEM.

CLEAR CODES AND CONFIRM "CLOSED LOOP" OPERATION AND NO "SERVICE ENGINE SOON" LIGHT.

86884157

DTC CHART — 1987-91 2.5L TBI

CODE 45
OXYGEN SENSOR CIRCUIT
(RICH EXHAUST INDICATED)
2.5L (VIN U) "N" CARLINE (TBI)

1
- RUN WARM ENGINE (75°C/167°F TO 95°C/203°F) AT 1200 RPM.
- DOES "SCAN" TOOL DISPLAY O_2 SENSOR VOLTAGE FIXED ABOVE .75 VOLT (750 mV)?

YES

- DISCONNECT O_2 SENSOR AND JUMPER HARNESS CKT 412 TO GROUND.
- "SCAN" TOOL SHOULD DISPLAY O_2 BELOW .35 VOLT (350 mV).
- DOES IT?

NO

CODE 45 IS INTERMITTENT.

YES

NO

REPLACE ECM.

CLEAR CODES AND CONFIRM "CLOSED LOOP" OPERATION AND NO "SERVICE ENGINE SOON" LIGHT.

86884156

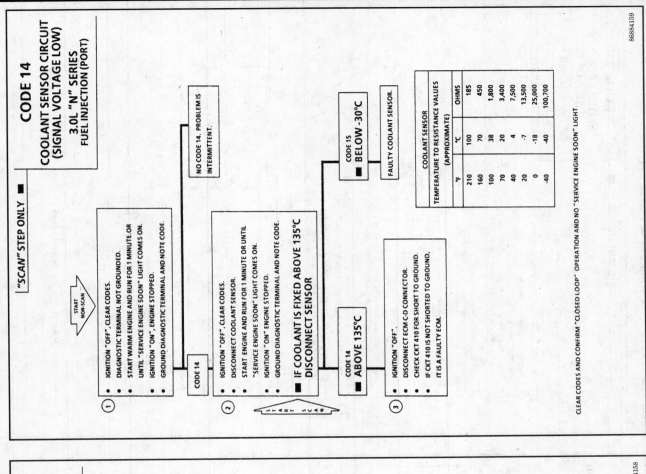

DTC CHART — 1985-86 3.0L MFI

"SCAN" STEP ONLY ■   CODE 14
COOLANT SENSOR CIRCUIT
(SIGNAL VOLTAGE LOW)
3.0L "N" SERIES
FUEL INJECTION (PORT)

START NON-SCAN

1
- IGNITION "OFF", CLEAR CODES.
- DIAGNOSTIC TERMINAL NOT GROUNDED.
- START WARM ENGINE AND RUN FOR 1 MINUTE, OR UNTIL "SERVICE ENGINE SOON" LIGHT COMES ON.
- IGNITION "ON", ENGINE STOPPED.
- GROUND DIAGNOSTIC TERMINAL AND NOTE CODE.

CODE 14

NO CODE 14. PROBLEM IS INTERMITTENT.

2
- IGNITION "OFF", CLEAR CODES.
- DISCONNECT COOLANT SENSOR.
- START ENGINE AND RUN FOR 1 MINUTE OR UNTIL "SERVICE ENGINE SOON" LIGHT COMES ON.
- IGNITION "ON", ENGINE STOPPED.
- GROUND DIAGNOSTIC TERMINAL AND NOTE CODE.

■ IF COOLANT IS FIXED ABOVE 135°C DISCONNECT SENSOR

START SCAN

CODE 14
■ ABOVE 135°C

CODE 15
■ BELOW -30°C

FAULTY COOLANT SENSOR.

3
- IGNITION "OFF".
- DISCONNECT ECM C-D CONNECTOR.
- CHECK CKT 410 FOR SHORT TO GROUND.
- IF CKT 410 IS NOT SHORTED TO GROUND, IT IS A FAULTY ECM.

COOLANT SENSOR TEMPERATURE TO RESISTANCE VALUES (APPROXIMATE)		
°F	°C	OHMS
210	100	185
160	70	450
100	38	1,800
70	20	3,400
40	4	7,500
20	-7	13,500
0	-18	25,000
-40	-40	100,700

CLEAR CODES AND CONFIRM "CLOSED LOOP" OPERATION AND NO "SERVICE ENGINE SOON" LIGHT.

86884159

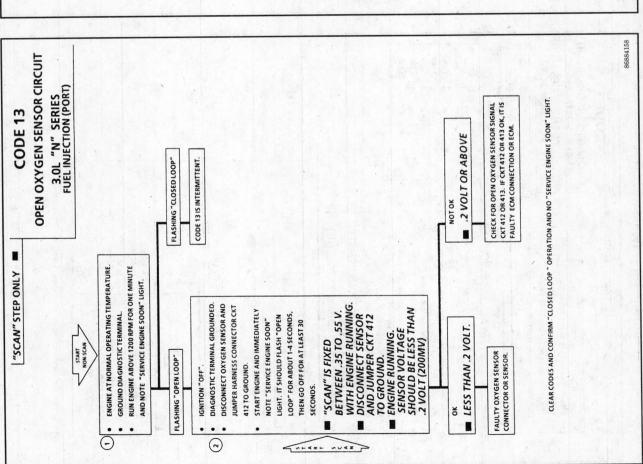

DTC CHART — 1985-86 3.0L MFI

"SCAN" STEP ONLY ■   CODE 13
OPEN OXYGEN SENSOR CIRCUIT
3.0L "N" SERIES
FUEL INJECTION (PORT)

START NON-SCAN

1
- ENGINE AT NORMAL OPERATING TEMPERATURE.
- GROUND DIAGNOSTIC TERMINAL.
- RUN ENGINE ABOVE 1200 RPM FOR ONE MINUTE AND NOTE "SERVICE ENGINE SOON" LIGHT.

FLASHING "OPEN LOOP"

FLASHING "CLOSED LOOP"

CODE 13 IS INTERMITTENT.

2
- IGNITION "OFF".
- DIAGNOSTIC TERMINAL GROUNDED.
- DISCONNECT OXYGEN SENSOR AND JUMPER HARNESS CONNECTOR CKT 412 TO GROUND.
- START ENGINE AND IMMEDIATELY NOTE "SERVICE ENGINE SOON" LIGHT. IT SHOULD FLASH "OPEN LOOP" FOR ABOUT 1-4 SECONDS, THEN GO OFF FOR AT LEAST 30 SECONDS.
- "SCAN" IS FIXED BETWEEN .35 TO .55 V. WITH ENGINE RUNNING.
- DISCONNECT SENSOR AND JUMPER CKT 412 TO GROUND.
- ENGINE RUNNING. SENSOR VOLTAGE SHOULD BE LESS THAN .2 VOLT (200MV)

START SCAN

OK
■ LESS THAN .2 VOLT.

FAULTY OXYGEN SENSOR CONNECTOR OR SENSOR.

NOT OK
■ .2 VOLT OR ABOVE

CHECK FOR OPEN OXYGEN SENSOR SIGNAL CKT 412 OR 413. IF CKT 412 OR 413 OK, IT IS FAULTY ECM CONNECTION OR ECM.

CLEAR CODES AND CONFIRM "CLOSED LOOP" OPERATION AND NO "SERVICE ENGINE SOON" LIGHT.

86884158

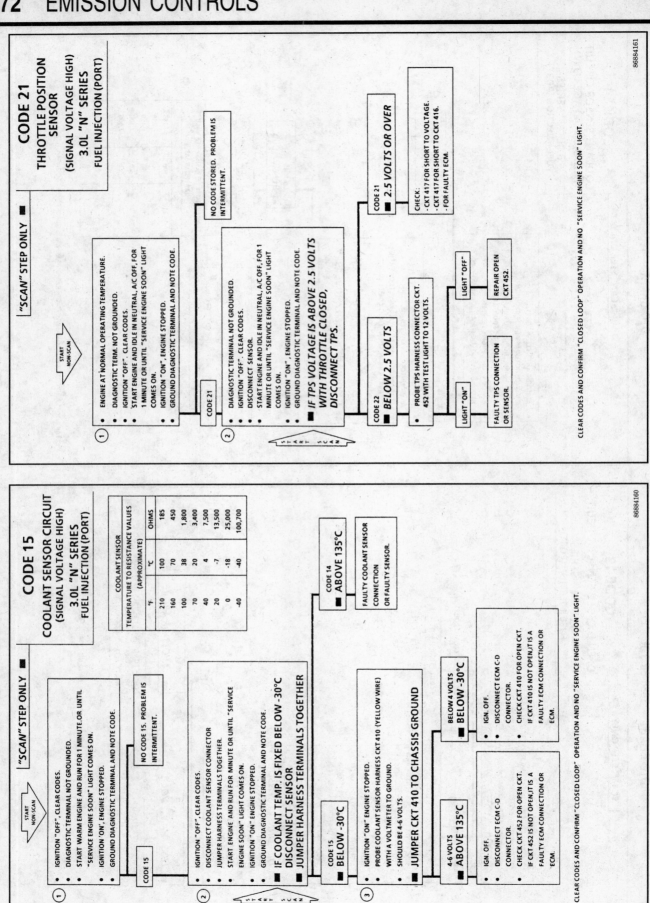

DTC CHART — 1985-86 3.0L MFI

"SCAN" STEP ONLY ■

CODE 21
THROTTLE POSITION SENSOR
(SIGNAL VOLTAGE HIGH)
3.0L "N" SERIES
FUEL INJECTION (PORT)

86884161

START NON-SCAN

(1)
- ENGINE AT NORMAL OPERATING TEMPERATURE.
- DIAGNOSTIC TERM. NOT GROUNDED.
- IGNITION "OFF". CLEAR CODES.
- START ENGINE AND IDLE IN NEUTRAL, A/C OFF, FOR 1 MINUTE OR UNTIL "SERVICE ENGINE SOON" LIGHT COMES ON.
- IGNITION "ON", ENGINE STOPPED.
- GROUND DIAGNOSTIC TERMINAL AND NOTE CODE.

CODE 21
- NO CODE STORED. PROBLEM IS INTERMITTENT.

(2)
- DIAGNOSTIC TERMINAL NOT GROUNDED.
- IGNITION "OFF". CLEAR CODES.
- DISCONNECT SENSOR.
- START ENGINE AND IDLE IN NEUTRAL, A/C OFF, FOR 1 MINUTE OR UNTIL "SERVICE ENGINE SOON" LIGHT COMES ON.
- IGNITION "ON", ENGINE STOPPED.
- GROUND DIAGNOSTIC TERMINAL AND NOTE CODE.
- ■ IF TPS VOLTAGE IS ABOVE 2.5 VOLTS WITH THROTTLE CLOSED, DISCONNECT TPS.

START NON-SCAN

CODE 21 ■ **2.5 VOLTS OR OVER**

CHECK:
- CKT 417 FOR SHORT TO VOLTAGE.
- CKT 417 FOR SHORT TO CKT 416.
- FOR FAULTY ECM.

CODE 22 ■ **BELOW 2.5 VOLTS**
- PROBE TPS HARNESS CONNECTOR CKT. 452 WITH TEST LIGHT TO 12 VOLTS.

LIGHT "ON"
- FAULTY TPS CONNECTION OR SENSOR.

LIGHT "OFF"
- REPAIR OPEN CKT. 452.

CLEAR CODES AND CONFIRM "CLOSED LOOP" OPERATION AND NO "SERVICE ENGINE SOON" LIGHT.

DTC CHART — 1985-86 3.0L MFI

"SCAN" STEP ONLY ■

CODE 15
COOLANT SENSOR CIRCUIT
(SIGNAL VOLTAGE HIGH)
3.0L "N" SERIES
FUEL INJECTION (PORT)

86884160

COOLANT SENSOR
TEMPERATURE TO RESISTANCE VALUES
(APPROXIMATE)

°F	°C	OHMS
210	100	185
160	70	450
100	38	1,800
70	20	3,400
40	4	7,500
20	-7	13,500
0	-18	25,000
-40	-40	100,700

START NON-SCAN

(1)
- IGNITION "OFF", CLEAR CODES.
- DIAGNOSTIC TERMINAL NOT GROUNDED.
- START WARM ENGINE AND RUN FOR 1 MINUTE, OR UNTIL "SERVICE ENGINE SOON" LIGHT COMES ON.
- IGNITION "ON", ENGINE STOPPED.
- GROUND DIAGNOSTIC TERMINAL AND NOTE CODE.

CODE 15
- NO CODE 15. PROBLEM IS INTERMITTENT.

(2)
- IGNITION "OFF", CLEAR CODES.
- DISCONNECT COOLANT SENSOR CONNECTOR
- JUMPER HARNESS TERMINALS TOGETHER.
- START ENGINE AND RUN FOR MINUTE OR UNTIL "SERVICE ENGINE SOON" LIGHT COMES ON.
- IGNITION "ON" ENGINE STOPPED.
- GROUND DIAGNOSTIC TERMINAL AND NOTE CODE.
- ■ IF COOLANT TEMP. IS FIXED BELOW -30°C DISCONNECT SENSOR
- ■ JUMPER HARNESS TERMINALS TOGETHER

CODE 14 ■ **ABOVE 135°C**
- FAULTY COOLANT SENSOR CONNECTION OR FAULTY SENSOR.

CODE 15 ■ **BELOW -30°C**
- IGNITION "ON" ENGINE STOPPED.
- PROBE COOLANT SENSOR HARNESS CKT 410 (YELLOW WIRE) WITH A VOLTMETER TO GROUND.
  SHOULD BE 4-6 VOLTS.

(3) ■ JUMPER CKT 410 TO CHASSIS GROUND

4-6 VOLTS ■ **ABOVE 135°C**
- IGN. OFF.
- DISCONNECT ECM C-D CONNECTOR.
- CHECK CKT 452 FOR OPEN CKT.
- IF CKT 452 IS NOT OPEN, IT IS A FAULTY ECM CONNECTION OR ECM.

BELOW 4 VOLTS ■ **BELOW -30°C**
- IGN. OFF.
- DISCONNECT ECM C-D CONNECTOR.
- CHECK CKT 410 FOR OPEN CKT.
- IF CKT 410 IS NOT OPEN, IT IS A FAULTY ECM CONNECTION OR ECM.

CLEAR CODES AND CONFIRM "CLOSED LOOP" OPERATION AND NO "SERVICE ENGINE SOON" LIGHT.

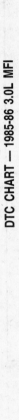

DTC CHART — 1985-86 3.0L MFI

CODE 23
MANIFOLD AIR TEMPERATURE SENSOR (MAT) CIRCUIT (SIGNAL VOLTAGE HIGH)
3.0L "N" SERIES FUEL INJECTION (PORT)

"SCAN" STEP ONLY

START NON-SCAN

1.
- DISCONNECT MAT SENSOR.
- IGNITION "ON", ENGINE STOPPED.
- CHECK VOLTAGE BETWEEN HARNESS CONNECTOR TERMINALS, CKT 472 AND 452.

IF MAT TEMP. IS FIXED BELOW -30°C DISCONNECT SENSOR
JUMPER HARNESS TERMINALS TOGETHER

- 4 VOLTS OR OVER ABOVE 135°C
- BELOW 4 VOLTS BELOW -30°C
  - CHECK VOLTAGE BETWEEN HARNESS CONNECTOR CKT 472 AND GROUND.
  - JUMPER CKT 472 TO CHASSIS GROUND
    - 4 VOLTS OR OVER ABOVE 135°C
    - BELOW 4 VOLTS BELOW -30°C
      - CHECK FOR OPEN IN CKT 452 AND CHECK TERMINAL CONNECTIONS.
      - CHECK FOR OPEN IN CKT 472 AND CHECK TERMINAL CONNECTIONS.
      - IF WIRE AND CONNECTIONS ARE OK, IT IS A FAULTY ECM.
      - IF WIRE AND CONNECTIONS ARE OK, IT IS FAULTY ECM.

2.
- CHECK RESISTANCE ACROSS MAT SENSOR TERMINALS. SHOULD BE LESS THAN 25,000 OHMS. SEE TABLE FOR APPROXIMATE TEMPERATURE TO RESISTANCE VALUES.

- NOT OK — REPLACE SENSOR
- OK — INTERMITTENT FAULT IN SENSOR CIRCUIT OR CONNECTOR. IF ADDITIONAL CODES WERE STORED, SEE APPLICABLE CHART.

CLEAR CODES AND CONFIRM "CLOSED LOOP" OPERATION AND NO "SERVICE ENGINE SOON" LIGHT.

MAT SENSOR
TEMPERATURE TO RESISTANCE VALUES (APPROXIMATE)

°F	°C	OHMS
210	100	185
160	70	450
100	38	1,800
70	20	3,400
40	4	7,500
20	-7	13,500
0	-18	25,000
-40	-40	100,700

86884173

DTC CHART — 1985-86 3.0L MFI

CODE 22
THROTTLE POSITION SENSOR (SIGNAL VOLTAGE LOW)
3.0L "N" SERIES FUEL INJECTION (PORT)

"SCAN" STEP ONLY

START NON-SCAN

1.
- DIAGNOSTIC TERMINAL NOT GROUNDED.
- IGNITION "OFF".
- CLEAR CODES.
- START ENGINE AND IDLE IN NEUTRAL A/C OFF, FOR 1 MINUTE OR UNTIL "SERVICE ENGINE SOON" LIGHT COMES ON.
- IGNITION "ON", ENGINE STOPPED.
- GROUND DIAGNOSTIC TERMINAL AND NOTE CODE

- CODE 22
- NO CODE 22. PROBLEM IS INTERMITTENT.

2.
- DIAGNOSTIC TERMINAL NOT GROUNDED.
- IGNITION "OFF". CLEAR CODES.
- DISCONNECT TPS AND JUMPER CKTS 416 TO 417.
- START ENGINE AND IDLE IN NEUTRAL, A/C OFF, FOR 1 MINUTE OR UNTIL "SERVICE ENGINE SOON" LIGHT COMES ON.
- IGNITION "ON", ENGINE STOPPED.
- GROUND DIAGNOSTIC TERMINAL AND NOTE CODE.

IF TPS IS BELOW .20 (200 MV) DISCONNECT SENSOR
JUMPER CKT 416 TO 417

- CODE 22 BELOW .20 VOLT (200 MV)
- CODE 21 .20 VOLT (200 MV) OR OVER

3.
- REMOVE JUMPER FROM 416 AND 417.
- CHECK VOLTAGE BETWEEN CKT 452 AND 416 USING DIGITAL VOLTMETER (J-29125).

- 4-6 VOLTS
- BELOW 4 VOLTS
  - CHECK TPS ADJUSTMENT. IF ADJUSTMENT OK, REPLACE TPS.
  - DISCONNECT ECM CONNECTOR AND CHECK FOR OPEN OR SHORT TO GROUND IN CKT 417. IF CKT 417 OK, IT IS FAULTY ECM CONNECTOR TERMINAL OR ECM.
  - DISCONNECT ECM CONNECTOR. CHECK FOR OPEN OR SHORT TO GROUND IN CKT 416. IF CKT 416 OK, IT IS FAULTY ECM CONNECTOR TERMINAL OR ECM.

CLEAR CODES AND CONFIRM "CLOSED LOOP" OPERATION AND NO "SERVICE ENGINE SOON" LIGHT.

86884162

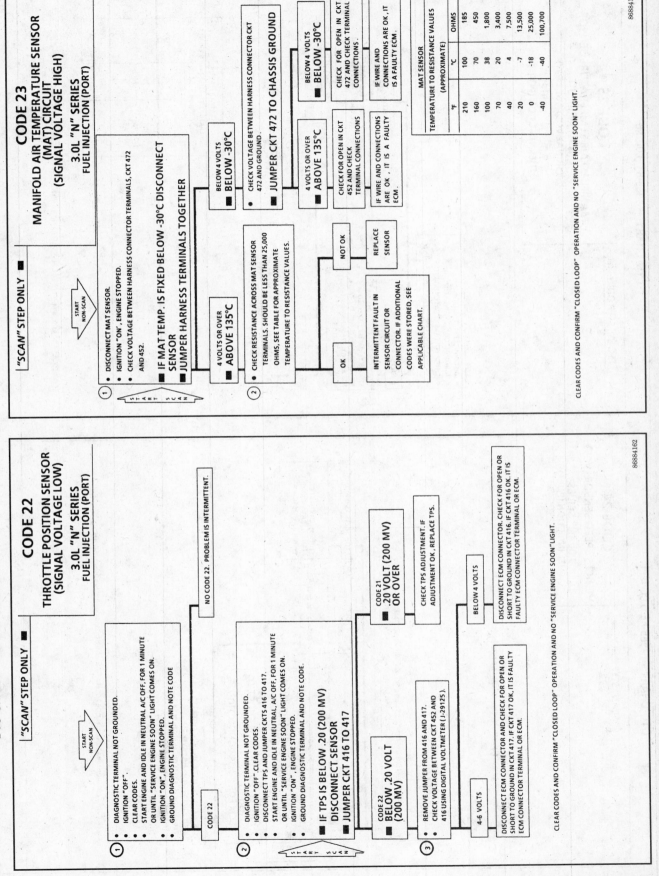

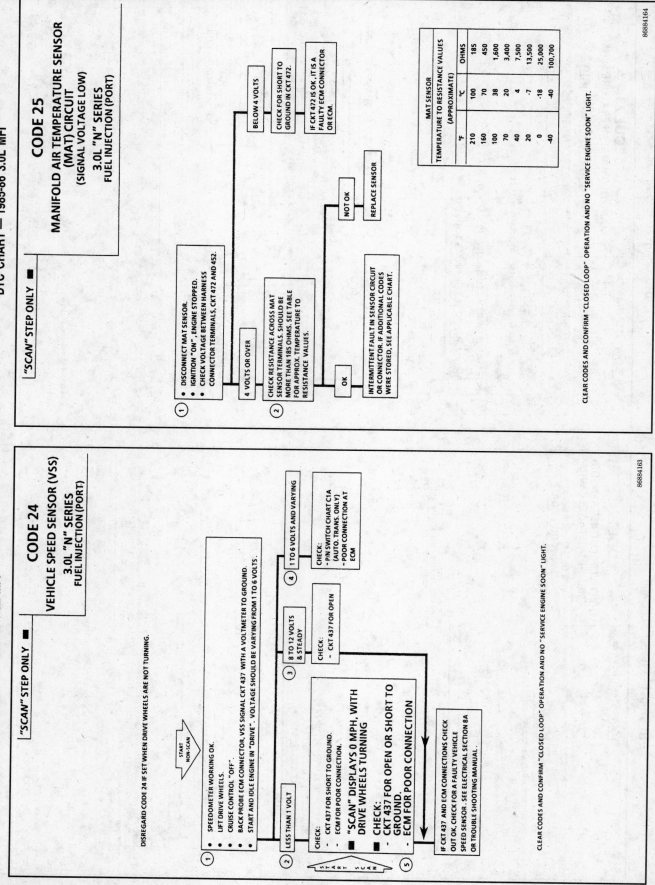

DTC CHART — 1985-86 3.0L MFI

"SCAN" STEP ONLY ■

CODE 25

MANIFOLD AIR TEMPERATURE SENSOR (MAT) CIRCUIT
(SIGNAL VOLTAGE LOW)
3.0L "N" SERIES
FUEL INJECTION (PORT)

1
- DISCONNECT MAT SENSOR.
- IGNITION "ON", ENGINE STOPPED.
- CHECK VOLTAGE BETWEEN HARNESS CONNECTOR TERMINALS, CKT 472 AND 452.

4 VOLTS OR OVER

BELOW 4 VOLTS

CHECK FOR SHORT TO GROUND IN CKT 472.

IF CKT 472 IS OK, IT IS A FAULTY ECM CONNECTOR OR ECM.

2
CHECK RESISTANCE ACROSS MAT SENSOR TERMINALS. SHOULD BE MORE THAN 185 OHMS. SEE TABLE FOR APPROX. TEMPERATURE TO RESISTANCE VALUES.

OK

NOT OK

REPLACE SENSOR

INTERMITTENT FAULT IN SENSOR CIRCUIT OR CONNECTOR. IF ADDITIONAL CODES WERE STORED, SEE APPLICABLE CHART.

MAT SENSOR TEMPERATURE TO RESISTANCE VALUES (APPROXIMATE)		
°F	°C	OHMS
210	100	185
160	70	450
100	38	1,600
70	20	3,400
40	4	7,500
20	-7	13,500
0	-18	25,000
-40	-40	100,700

CLEAR CODES AND CONFIRM "CLOSED LOOP" OPERATION AND NO "SERVICE ENGINE SOON" LIGHT.

86884164

DTC CHART — 1985-86 3.0L MFI

"SCAN" STEP ONLY ■

CODE 24

VEHICLE SPEED SENSOR (VSS)
3.0L "N" SERIES
FUEL INJECTION (PORT)

DISREGARD CODE 24 IF SET WHEN DRIVE WHEELS ARE NOT TURNING.

START NON-SCAN

1
- SPEEDOMETER WORKING OK.
- LIFT DRIVE WHEELS.
- CRUISE CONTROL "OFF".
- BACK PROBE ECM CONNECTOR, VSS SIGNAL CKT 437 WITH A VOLTMETER TO GROUND.
- START AND IDLE ENGINE IN "DRIVE". VOLTAGE SHOULD BE VARYING FROM 1 TO 6 VOLTS.

LESS THAN 1 VOLT

8 TO 12 VOLTS & STEADY

1 TO 6 VOLTS AND VARYING

2
CHECK:
- CKT 437 FOR SHORT TO GROUND.
- ECM FOR POOR CONNECTION.

3
CHECK:
- CKT 437 FOR OPEN

4
CHECK:
- P/N SWITCH CHART C1A (AUTO. TRANS. ONLY)
- POOR CONNECTION AT ECM

START SCAN

"SCAN" DISPLAYS 0 MPH, WITH DRIVE WHEELS TURNING

CHECK:
■ CKT 437 FOR OPEN OR SHORT TO GROUND.
■ ECM FOR POOR CONNECTION

5
IF CKT 437 AND ECM CONNECTIONS CHECK OUT OK, CHECK FOR A FAULTY VEHICLE SPEED SENSOR. SEE ELECTRICAL SECTION 8A OR TROUBLE SHOOTING MANUAL.

CLEAR CODES AND CONFIRM "CLOSED LOOP" OPERATION AND NO "SERVICE ENGINE SOON" LIGHT.

86884163

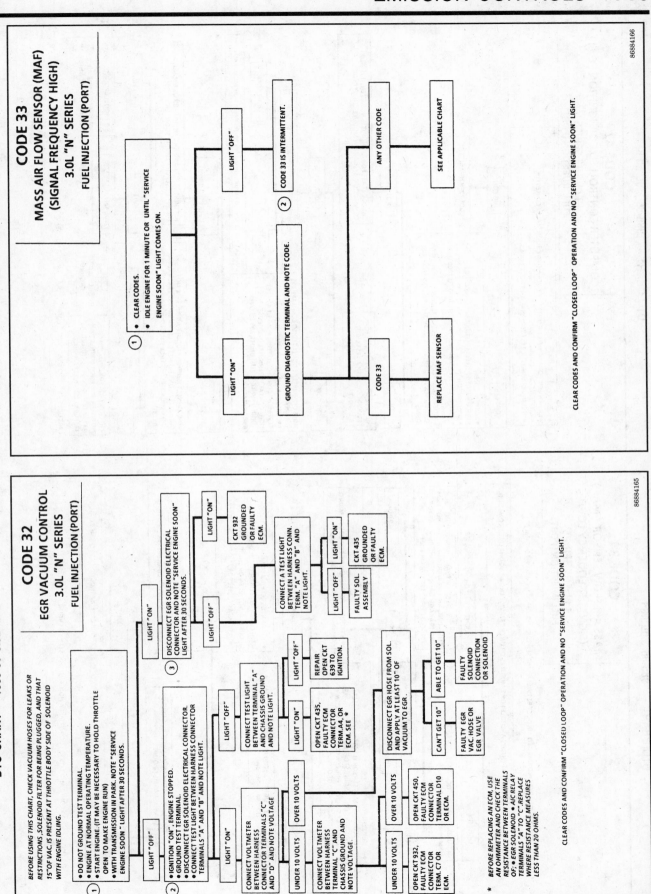

DTC CHART — 1985-86 3.0L MFI

CODE 33
MASS AIR FLOW SENSOR (MAF) (SIGNAL FREQUENCY HIGH)
3.0L "N" SERIES
FUEL INJECTION (PORT)

86884166

(1)
- CLEAR CODES.
- IDLE ENGINE FOR 1 MINUTE OR UNTIL "SERVICE ENGINE SOON" LIGHT COMES ON.

LIGHT "ON"

LIGHT "OFF"

GROUND DIAGNOSTIC TERMINAL AND NOTE CODE.

CODE 33 IS INTERMITTENT.

(2)

CODE 33

ANY OTHER CODE

REPLACE MAF SENSOR

SEE APPLICABLE CHART

CLEAR CODES AND CONFIRM "CLOSED LOOP" OPERATION AND NO "SERVICE ENGINE SOON" LIGHT.

DTC CHART — 1985-86 3.0L MFI

CODE 32
EGR VACUUM CONTROL
3.0L "N" SERIES
FUEL INJECTION (PORT)

86884165

BEFORE USING THIS CHART, CHECK VACUUM HOSES FOR LEAKS OR RESTRICTIONS, SOLENOID FILTER FOR BEING PLUGGED, AND THAT 15" OF VAC. IS PRESENT AT THROTTLE BODY SIDE OF SOLENOID WITH ENGINE IDLING.

(1)
- DO NOT GROUND TEST TERMINAL.
- ENGINE AT NORMAL OPERATING TEMPERATURE.
- START ENGINE. (IT MAY BE NECESSARY TO HOLD THROTTLE OPEN TO MAKE ENGINE RUN)
- WITH TRANSMISSION IN PARK, NOTE "SERVICE ENGINE SOON" LIGHT AFTER 30 SECONDS.

LIGHT "OFF"

LIGHT "ON"

(2)
- IGNITION "ON", ENGINE STOPPED.
- GROUND TEST TERMINAL.
- DISCONNECT EGR SOLENOID ELECTRICAL CONNECTOR.
- CONNECT TEST LIGHT BETWEEN HARNESS CONNECTOR TERMINALS "A" AND "B" AND NOTE LIGHT.

(3)
- DISCONNECT EGR SOLENOID ELECTRICAL CONNECTOR AND NOTE "SERVICE ENGINE SOON" LIGHT AFTER 30 SECONDS.

LIGHT "OFF"

LIGHT "ON"

CKT 932 GROUNDED OR FAULTY ECM.

CONNECT A TEST LIGHT BETWEEN HARNESS CONN. TERM. "A" AND "B" AND NOTE LIGHT.

LIGHT "ON"

LIGHT "OFF"

FAULTY SOL. ASSEMBLY

CKT 435 GROUNDED OR FAULTY ECM.

LIGHT "ON"

LIGHT "OFF"

CONNECT VOLTMETER BETWEEN HARNESS CONNECTOR TERMINALS "C" AND "D" AND NOTE VOLTAGE.

CONNECT TEST LIGHT BETWEEN TERMINAL "A" AND CHASSIS GROUND AND NOTE LIGHT.

UNDER 10 VOLTS

OVER 10 VOLTS

LIGHT "ON"

LIGHT "OFF"

CONNECT VOLTMETER BETWEEN HARNESS TERMINAL "C" AND CHASSIS GROUND AND NOTE VOLTAGE.

OPEN CKT 435, FAULTY ECM CONNECTOR TERM.A4, OR ECM. SEE *

REPAIR OPEN CKT 639 TO IGNITION.

UNDER 10 VOLTS

OVER 10 VOLTS

OPEN CKT 932, FAULTY ECM CONNECTOR TERM. C7 OR ECM.

OPEN CKT 450, FAULTY ECM CONNECTOR TERMINAL D10 OR ECM.

DISCONNECT EGR HOSE FROM SOL. AND APPLY AT LEAST 10" OF VACUUM TO EGR.

CAN'T GET 10"

ABLE TO GET 10"

FAULTY EGR VAC. HOSE OR EGR VALVE

FAULTY SOLENOID CONNECTION OR SOLENOID

* BEFORE REPLACING AN ECM, USE AN OHMMETER AND CHECK THE RESISTANCE BETWEEN TERMINALS OF: • EGR SOLENOID • AIC RELAY TERMINALS "A" TO "C". REPLACE WHERE RESISTANCE MEASURES LESS THAN 20 OHMS.

CLEAR CODES AND CONFIRM "CLOSED LOOP" OPERATION AND NO "SERVICE ENGINE SOON" LIGHT.

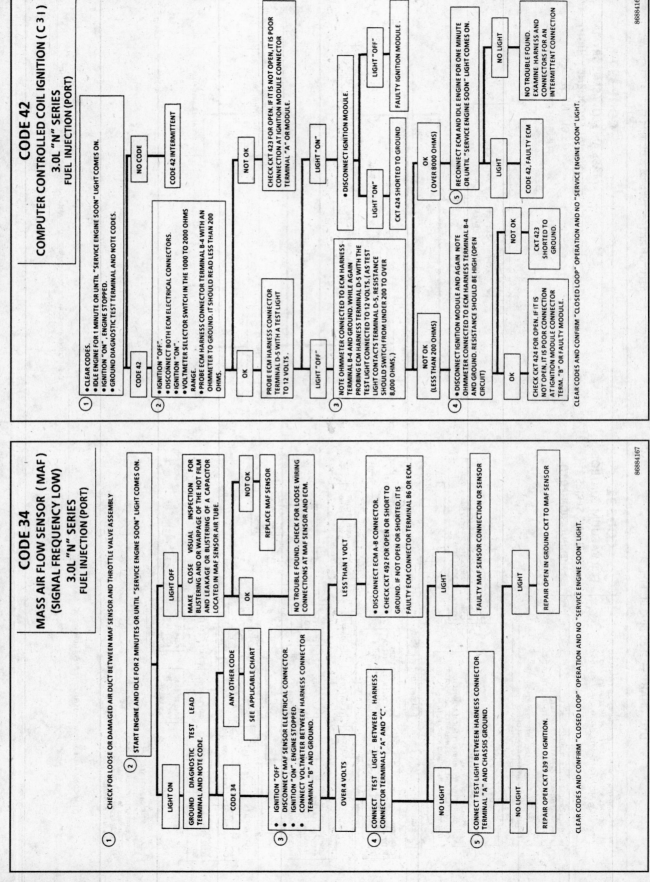

86884170

86884169

DTC CHART — 1985-86 3.0L MFI

CODE 44
LEAN EXHAUST INDICATION
3.0L "N" SERIES
FUEL INJECTION (PORT)

"SCAN" STEP ONLY ■

START NON-SCAN

①
- GROUND DIAGNOSTIC TERMINAL.
- RUN WARM ENGINE AT APPROX. 1200 TO 1800 RPM FOR 1 MINUTE AND NOTE "SERVICE ENGINE SOON LIGHT".

- LIGHT STAYING "OFF" MORE THAN "ON" OR FLASHING "OPEN LOOP"
  - FLASHING "CLOSED LOOP"
    - CODE IS INTERMITTENT.

②
- IGNITION "OFF".
- DIAGNOSTIC TERMINAL GROUNDED.
- DISCONNECT OXYGEN SENSOR.
- START ENGINE AND IMMEDIATELY NOTE "SERVICE ENGINE SOON" LIGHT.

■ IF SENSOR VOLTAGE IS FIXED BELOW .35 VOLTS, WITH ENGINE RUNNING.
■ DISCONNECT OXYGEN SENSOR, START ENGINE AND NOTE VOLTAGE

START SCAN

- LIGHT FLASHING OPEN LOOP.
- **VOLTAGE BETWEEN .35 AND .55 VOLTS**
  - LIGHT WENT OFF FOR AT LEAST 30 SECONDS
  - ■ **VOLTAGE LESS THAN .35 VOLTS**
    - CHECK SIGNAL CKT 412 FOR SHORT TO GROUND.
      - CKT 412 OK.
        - IT IS A FAULTY ECM.

③
- CHECK THE FOLLOWING :
  - SENSOR (S)
  - LEAN INJECTOR(S)
  - CONTAMINATED FUEL
  - EGR
  - FOR LOW FUEL PRESSURE.
  - EXHAUST MANIFOLD LEAKS AHEAD OF SENSOR.

- ALL CHECKS OK,
  - FAULTY OXYGEN SENSOR.

FIELD SERVICE MODE :
ENGINE RUNNING , DIAGNOSTIC TERMINAL GROUNDED.
OPEN - LOOP , " SERVICE ENGINE SOON " LIGHT FLASHES AT A RATE OF 2 TIMES PER SECOND .
CLOSED - LOOP , " SERVICE ENGINE SOON " LIGHT FLASHES AT A RATE OF 1 TIME PER SECOND

CLEAR CODES AND CONFIRM "CLOSED LOOP" OPERATION AND NO "SERVICE ENGINE SOON" LIGHT.

DTC CHART — 1985-86 3.0L MFI

CODE 43
ELECTRONIC SPARK CONTROL (ESC)
3.0L "N" SERIES
FUEL INJECTION (PORT)

①
- IGNITION "OFF" , CLEAR CODES.
- IDLE ENGINE FOR 1 MINUTE OR UNTIL " SERVICE ENGINE SOON" LIGHT COMES ON.
- GROUND DIAGNOSTIC TERMINAL AND NOTE CODE.

- CODE 43
- NO CODE

②
- DIAGNOSTIC TERMINAL UNGROUNDED.
- CONNECT TACHOMETER.
- ENGINE RUNNING AT ABOUT 1500 RPM.
- TRANS . IN P/N AND AT NORM. OPERATING TEMP.
- TAP ENGINE BLOCK IN AREA OF KNOCK SENSOR AND CHECK FOR RPM DROP.

  - RPM DROPS
    - PROBLEM IS INTERMITTENT.
  - NO RPM DROP

③
- ENGINE IDLING.
- BACK PROBE ECM A-B CONNECTOR TERMINAL B 7 WITH A VOLTMETER TO GROUND AND NOTE VOLTAGE.

  - UNDER 6 VOLTS
  - OVER 6 VOLTS
    - IT IS FAULTY CONNECTION AT ECM A-B CONNECTOR TERMINAL B7 OR ECM.

④
- IGNITION "ON" , ENGINE STOPPED.
- RECHECK VOLTAGE AT ECM TERM. B7.

  - UNDER 6 VOLTS
  - OVER 6 VOLTS
    - REPLACE ESC MODULE.

⑤
- IGNITION "OFF"
- DISCONNECT ECM A-B CONNECTOR.
- IGNITION "ON"
- RECHECK VOLTAGE ON CKT 457

  - UNDER 6 VOLTS
  - OVER 6 VOLTS
    - REPLACE ECM

⑥
- DISCONNECT ESC MODULE . CHECK VOLTAGE FROM ESC CONNECTOR TERM. B TO GROUND.
- SHOULD READ BATTERY VOLTAGE

  - OK
  - NOT OK
    - REPAIR OPEN IN. CKT 439.

CHECK FOR OPEN OR SHORT TO GROUND IN CKT 457. IF NOT OPEN OR SHORTED TO GROUND, IT IS FAULTY ESC CONNECTION OR ESC MODULE.

CLEAR CODES AND CONFIRM "CLOSED LOOP" OPERATION AND NO "SERVICE ENGINE SOON" LIGHT.

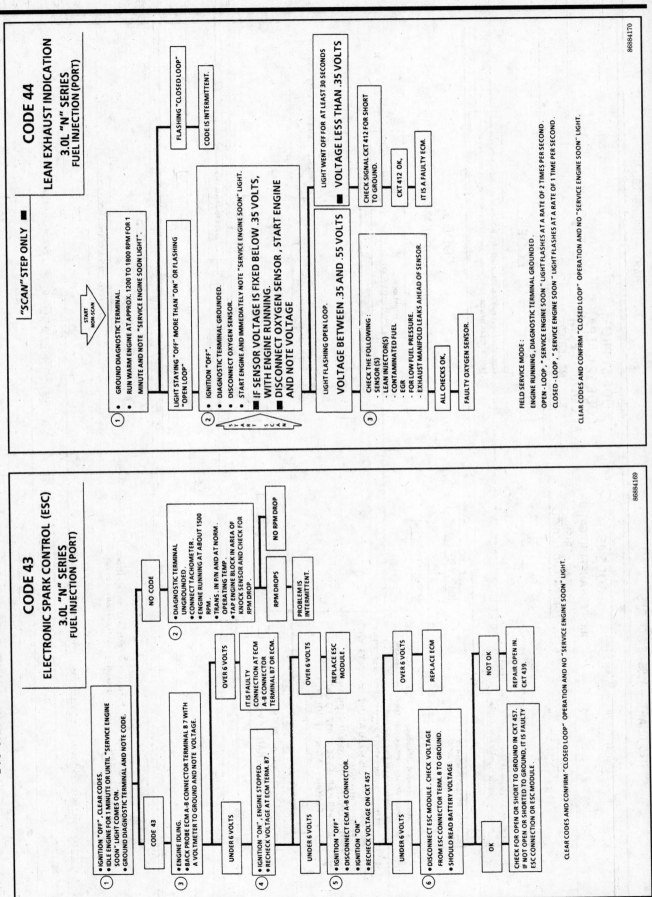

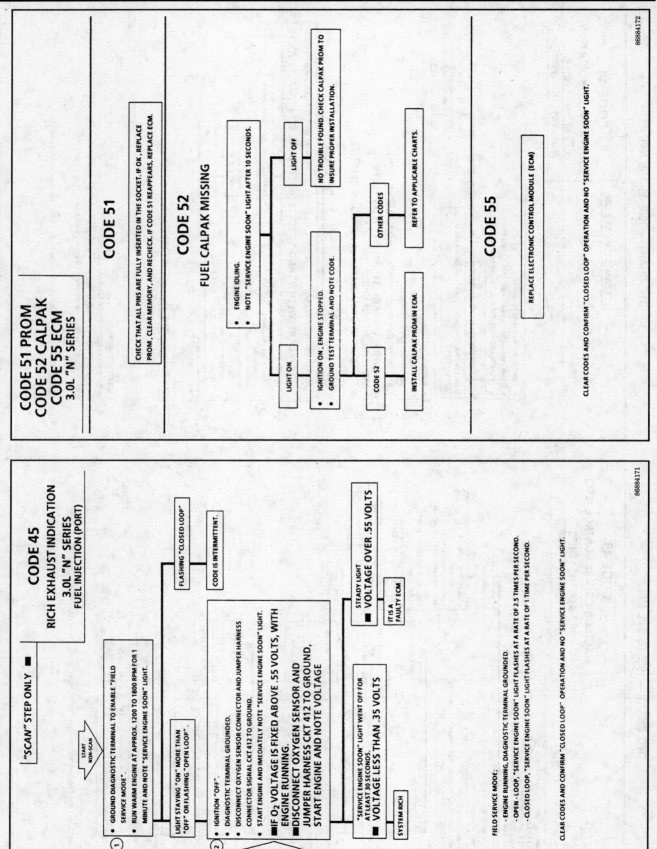

DTC CHART — 1985-86 3.0L MFI

86884172

CODE 51 PROM
CODE 52 CALPAK
CODE 55 ECM
3.0L "N" SERIES

CODE 51

CHECK THAT ALL PINS ARE FULLY INSERTED IN THE SOCKET. IF OK, REPLACE PROM, CLEAR MEMORY, AND RECHECK. IF CODE 51 REAPPEARS, REPLACE ECM.

CODE 52
FUEL CALPAK MISSING

- ENGINE IDLING.
- NOTE "SERVICE ENGINE SOON" LIGHT AFTER 10 SECONDS.

LIGHT ON
- IGNITION ON , ENGINE STOPPED.
- GROUND TEST TERMINAL AND NOTE CODE.

LIGHT OFF
NO TROUBLE FOUND. CHECK CALPAK PROM TO INSURE PROPER INSTALLATION.

CODE 52
INSTALL CALPAK PROM IN ECM.

OTHER CODES
REFER TO APPLICABLE CHARTS.

CODE 55

REPLACE ELECTRONIC CONTROL MODULE (ECM)

CLEAR CODES AND CONFIRM "CLOSED LOOP" OPERATION AND NO "SERVICE ENGINE SOON" LIGHT.

DTC CHART — 1985-86 3.0L MFI

86884171

■ "SCAN" STEP ONLY

CODE 45
RICH EXHAUST INDICATION
3.0L "N" SERIES
FUEL INJECTION (PORT)

START NON-SCAN

①
- GROUND DIAGNOSTIC TERMINAL TO ENABLE "FIELD SERVICE MODE".
- RUN WARM ENGINE AT APPROX. 1200 TO 1800 RPM FOR 1 MINUTE AND NOTE "SERVICE ENGINE SOON" LIGHT.

LIGHT STAYING "ON" MORE THAN "OFF" OR FLASHING "OPEN LOOP".

FLASHING "CLOSED LOOP"
CODE IS INTERMITTENT.

②
- IGNITION "OFF".
- DIAGNOSTIC TERMINAL GROUNDED.
- DISCONNECT OXYGEN SENSOR CONNECTOR AND JUMPER HARNESS CONNECTOR SIGNAL CKT 412 TO GROUND.
- START ENGINE AND IMMEDIATELY NOTE "SERVICE ENGINE SOON" LIGHT.

■ IF O₂ VOLTAGE IS FIXED ABOVE .55 VOLTS, WITH ENGINE RUNNING.
■ DISCONNECT OXYGEN SENSOR AND JUMPER HARNESS CKT 412 TO GROUND, START ENGINE AND NOTE VOLTAGE

START SCAN

STEADY LIGHT
■ VOLTAGE OVER .55 VOLTS

IT IS A FAULTY ECM

"SERVICE ENGINE SOON" LIGHT WENT OFF FOR AT LEAST 30 SECONDS.
■ VOLTAGE LESS THAN .35 VOLTS

SYSTEM RICH

FIELD SERVICE MODE:
- ENGINE RUNNING, DIAGNOSTIC TERMINAL GROUNDED.
- OPEN - LOOP, "SERVICE ENGINE SOON" LIGHT FLASHES AT A RATE OF 2.5 TIMES PER SECOND.
- CLOSED LOOP, "SERVICE ENGINE SOON" LIGHT FLASHES AT A RATE OF 1 TIME PER SECOND.

CLEAR CODES AND CONFIRM "CLOSED LOOP" OPERATION AND NO "SERVICE ENGINE SOON" LIGHT.

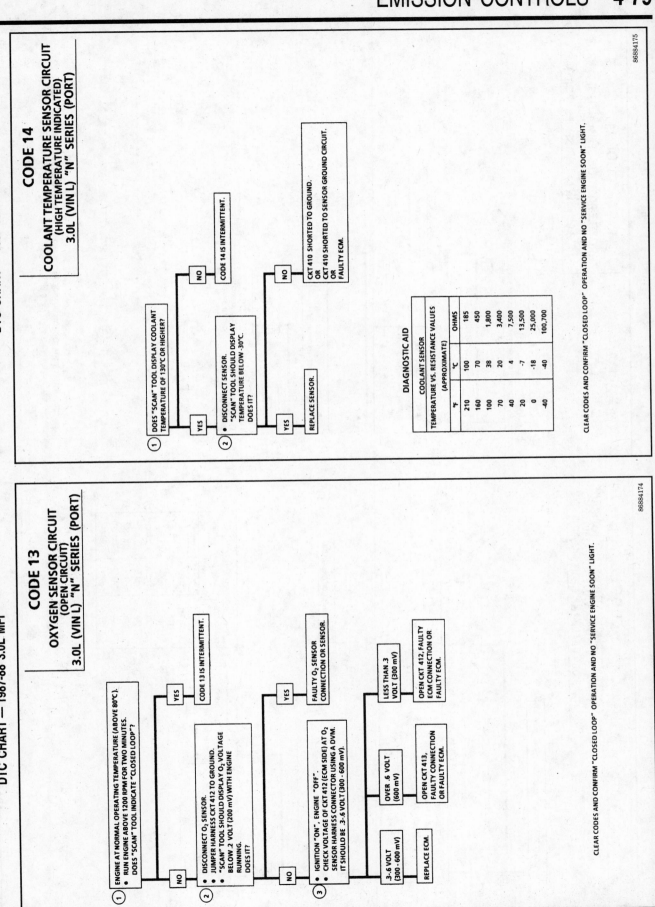

DTC CHART — 1987-88 3.0L MFI

CODE 14

COOLANT TEMPERATURE SENSOR CIRCUIT
(HIGH TEMPERATURE INDICATED)
3.0L (VIN L) "N" SERIES (PORT)

86884175

1. DOES "SCAN" TOOL DISPLAY COOLANT TEMPERATURE OF 130°C OR HIGHER?

- NO → CODE 14 IS INTERMITTENT.

- YES →

2. DISCONNECT SENSOR.
   "SCAN" TOOL SHOULD DISPLAY TEMPERATURE BELOW -30°C.
   DOES IT?

- NO → CKT 410 SHORTED TO GROUND.
  OR
  CKT 410 SHORTED TO SENSOR GROUND CIRCUIT.
  OR
  FAULTY ECM.

- YES → REPLACE SENSOR.

DIAGNOSTIC AID

COOLANT SENSOR
TEMPERATURE VS. RESISTANCE VALUES
(APPROXIMATE)

°F	°C	OHMS
210	100	185
160	70	450
100	38	1,800
70	20	3,400
40	4	7,500
20	-7	13,500
0	-18	25,000
-40	-40	100,700

CLEAR CODES AND CONFIRM "CLOSED LOOP" OPERATION AND NO "SERVICE ENGINE SOON" LIGHT.

DTC CHART — 1987-88 3.0L MFI

CODE 13

OXYGEN SENSOR CIRCUIT
(OPEN CIRCUIT)
3.0L (VIN L) "N" SERIES (PORT)

86884174

1. ENGINE AT NORMAL OPERATING TEMPERATURE (ABOVE 80°C).
   - RUN ENGINE ABOVE 1200 RPM FOR TWO MINUTES.
   - DOES "SCAN" TOOL INDICATE "CLOSED LOOP"?

- YES → CODE 13 IS INTERMITTENT.

- NO →

2. DISCONNECT O₂ SENSOR.
   - JUMPER HARNESS CKT 412 TO GROUND.
   - "SCAN" TOOL SHOULD DISPLAY O₂ VOLTAGE BELOW .2 VOLT (200 mV) WITH ENGINE RUNNING.
   DOES IT?

- YES → FAULTY O₂ SENSOR CONNECTION OR SENSOR.

- NO →

3. IGNITION "ON", ENGINE "OFF".
   - CHECK VOLTAGE OF CKT 412 (ECM SIDE) AT O₂ SENSOR HARNESS CONNECTOR USING A DVM. IT SHOULD BE .3 -.6 VOLT (300 - 600 mV).

- 3 -.6 VOLT (300 - 600 mV) → REPLACE ECM.

- OVER .6 VOLT (600 mV) → OPEN CKT 413, FAULTY CONNECTION OR FAULTY ECM.

- LESS THAN .3 VOLT (300 mV) → OPEN CKT 412, FAULTY ECM CONNECTION OR FAULTY ECM.

CLEAR CODES AND CONFIRM "CLOSED LOOP" OPERATION AND NO "SERVICE ENGINE SOON" LIGHT.

DTC CHART — 1987-88 3.0L MFI

CODE 21
THROTTLE POSITION SENSOR (TPS) CIRCUIT
(SIGNAL VOLTAGE HIGH)
3.0L (VIN L) "N" SERIES (PORT)

1. • THROTTLE CLOSED.
   • DOES "SCAN" TOOL DISPLAY TPS OVER 2.5 VOLTS?

   NO → CODE 21 IS INTERMITTENT.

   YES →

2. • DISCONNECT SENSOR.
   • "SCAN" TOOL SHOULD DISPLAY TPS BELOW .2 VOLT (200mV).
   • DOES IT?

   NO → CKT 417 SHORTED TO VOLTAGE OR FAULTY ECM.

   YES →

3. • PROBE SENSOR GROUND CIRCUIT WITH A TEST LIGHT CONNECTED TO 12 VOLTS.

   LIGHT "OFF" → OPEN SENSOR GROUND CIRCUIT OR FAULTY ECM.

   LIGHT "ON" → FAULTY CONNECTION OR SENSOR.

CLEAR CODES AND CONFIRM "CLOSED LOOP" OPERATION AND NO "SERVICE ENGINE SOON" LIGHT.

86884177

DTC CHART — 1987-88 3.0L MFI

CODE 15
COOLANT TEMPERATURE SENSOR CIRCUIT
(LOW TEMPERATURE INDICATED)
3.0L (VIN L) "N" SERIES (PORT)

1. • DOES "SCAN" DISPLAY COOLANT -30°C OR COLDER?

   NO → CODE 15 IS INTERMITTENT.

   YES →

2. • DISCONNECT SENSOR
   • JUMPER HARNESS TERMINALS TOGETHER
   • "SCAN" SHOULD DISPLAY 130°C OR MORE.
   • DOES IT?

   YES → FAULTY CONNECTION OR SENSOR.

   NO →

3. • JUMPER CKT 410 TO GROUND.
   • "SCAN" SHOULD DISPLAY OVER 130°C.
   • DOES IT?

   NO → OPEN CKT 410, FAULTY CONNECTION AT ECM, OR FAULTY ECM.

   YES → OPEN SENSOR GROUND CIRCUIT, FAULTY CONNECTION OR FAULTY ECM.

DIAGNOSTIC AID

COOLANT SENSOR TEMPERATURE TO RESISTANCE VALUES (APPROXIMATE)		
°F	°C	OHMS
210	100	185
160	70	450
100	38	1,800
70	20	3,400
40	4	7,500
20	-7	13,500
0	-18	25,000
-40	-40	100,700

CLEAR CODES AND CONFIRM "CLOSED LOOP" OPERATION AND NO "SERVICE ENGINE SOON" LIGHT.

86884176

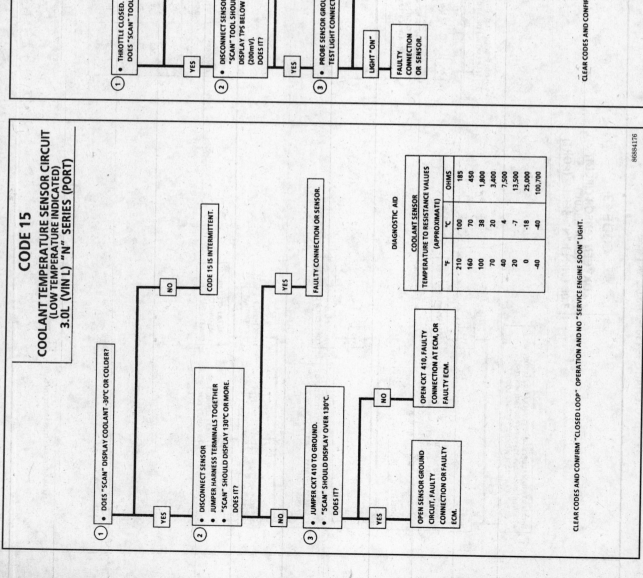

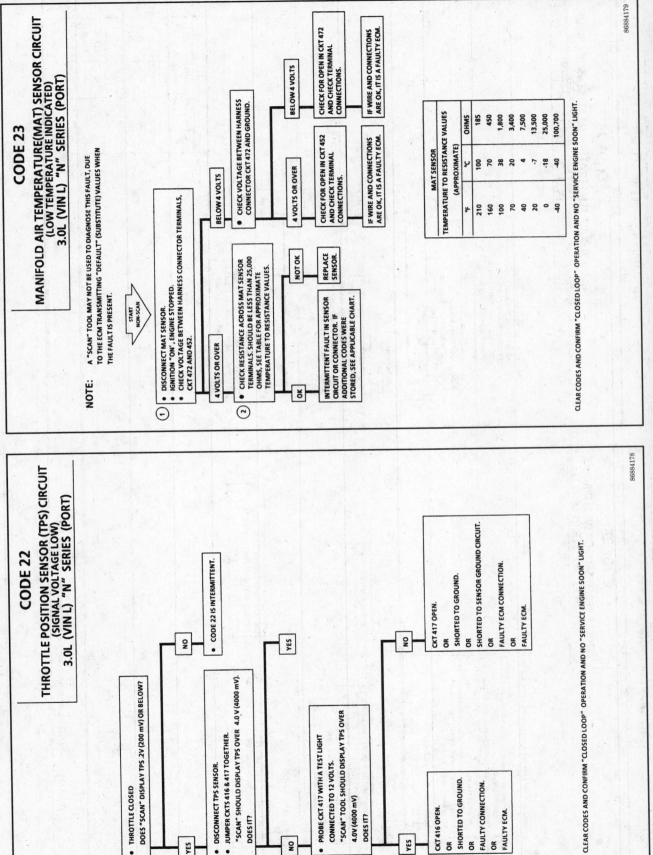

DTC CHART — 1987-88 3.0L MFI

CODE 23

MANIFOLD AIR TEMPERATURE (MAT) SENSOR CIRCUIT
(LOW TEMPERATURE INDICATED)
3.0L (VIN L) "N" SERIES (PORT)

NOTE: A "SCAN" TOOL MAY NOT BE USED TO DIAGNOSE THIS FAULT, DUE TO THE ECM TRANSMITTING "DEFAULT" (SUBSTITUTE) VALUES WHEN THE FAULT IS PRESENT.

START NON-SCAN

(1)
- DISCONNECT MAT SENSOR.
- IGNITION "ON", ENGINE STOPPED.
- CHECK VOLTAGE BETWEEN HARNESS CONNECTOR TERMINALS, CKT 472 AND 452.

4 VOLTS OR OVER

(2)
- CHECK RESISTANCE ACROSS MAT SENSOR TERMINALS. SHOULD BE LESS THAN 25,000 OHMS. SEE TABLE FOR APPROXIMATE TEMPERATURE TO RESISTANCE VALUES.

OK — INTERMITTENT FAULT IN SENSOR CIRCUIT OR CONNECTOR. IF ADDITIONAL CODES WERE STORED, SEE APPLICABLE CHART.

NOT OK — REPLACE SENSOR.

BELOW 4 VOLTS — CHECK VOLTAGE BETWEEN HARNESS CONNECTOR CKT 472 AND GROUND.

4 VOLTS OR OVER — CHECK FOR OPEN IN CKT 452 AND CHECK TERMINAL CONNECTIONS. IF WIRE AND CONNECTIONS ARE OK, IT IS A FAULTY ECM.

BELOW 4 VOLTS — CHECK FOR OPEN IN CKT 472 AND CHECK TERMINAL CONNECTIONS. IF WIRE AND CONNECTIONS ARE OK, IT IS A FAULTY ECM.

MAT SENSOR
TEMPERATURE TO RESISTANCE VALUES
(APPROXIMATE)

°F	°C	OHMS
210	100	185
160	70	450
100	38	1,800
70	20	3,400
40	4	7,500
20	-7	13,500
0	-18	25,000
-40	-40	100,700

CLEAR CODES AND CONFIRM "CLOSED LOOP" OPERATION AND NO "SERVICE ENGINE SOON" LIGHT.

86884179

DTC CHART — 1987-88 3.0L MFI

CODE 22

THROTTLE POSITION SENSOR (TPS) CIRCUIT
(SIGNAL VOLTAGE LOW)
3.0L (VIN L) "N" SERIES (PORT)

(1)
- THROTTLE CLOSED
  DOES "SCAN" DISPLAY TPS .2V (200 mV) OR BELOW?

YES

(2)
- DISCONNECT TPS SENSOR.
- JUMPER CKTS 416 & 417 TOGETHER.
  "SCAN" SHOULD DISPLAY TPS OVER 4.0 V (4000 mV). DOES IT?

NO — CODE 22 IS INTERMITTENT.

YES

(4)
- PROBE CKT 417 WITH A TEST LIGHT CONNECTED TO 12 VOLTS.
  "SCAN" TOOL SHOULD DISPLAY TPS OVER 4.0V (4000 mV)
  DOES IT?

YES — CKT 416 OPEN.
OR
SHORTED TO GROUND.
OR
FAULTY CONNECTION.
OR
FAULTY ECM.

NO — CKT 417 OPEN.
OR
SHORTED TO GROUND.
OR
SHORTED TO SENSOR GROUND CIRCUIT.
OR
FAULTY ECM CONNECTION.
OR
FAULTY ECM.

CLEAR CODES AND CONFIRM "CLOSED LOOP" OPERATION AND NO "SERVICE ENGINE SOON" LIGHT.

86884178

DTC CHART — 1987-88 3.0L MFI

CODE 25
MANIFOLD AIR TEMPERATURE (MAT) SENSOR CIRCUIT
(HIGH TEMPERATURE INDICATED)
3.0L (VIN L) "N" SERIES (PORT)

NOTE: A "SCAN" TOOL MAY NOT BE USED TO DIAGNOSE THIS FAULT, DUE TO THE ECM TRANSMITTING "DEFAULT" (SUBSTITUTE) VALUES WHEN THE FAULT IS PRESENT.

1.
- DISCONNECT MAT SENSOR.
- IGNITION "ON", ENGINE STOPPED.
- CHECK VOLTAGE BETWEEN HARNESS CONNECTOR TERMINALS.

4 VOLTS OR OVER | **BELOW 4 VOLTS**

BELOW 4 VOLTS:
CKT 472 SHORTED TO GROUND.
OR
CKT 472 SHORTED TO SENSOR GROUND CIRCUIT.
OR
FAULTY ECM.

2. CHECK RESISTANCE ACROSS MAT SENSOR TERMINALS. SHOULD BE MORE THAN 185 OHMS. SEE TABLE FOR APPROXIMATE TEMPERATURE TO RESISTANCE VALUES.

OK | **NOT OK**

NOT OK: REPLACE SENSOR

OK: INTERMITTENT FAULT IN SENSOR CIRCUIT OR CONNECTOR. IF ADDITIONAL CODES WERE STORED, SEE APPLICABLE CHART.

MAT SENSOR
TEMPERATURE TO RESISTANCE VALUES (APPROXIMATE)

°F	°C	OHMS
210	100	185
160	70	450
100	38	1,600
70	20	3,400
40	4	7,500
20	-7	13,500
0	-18	25,000
-40	-40	100,700

CLEAR CODES AND CONFIRM "CLOSED LOOP" OPERATION AND NO "SERVICE ENGINE SOON" LIGHT.

86884181

DTC CHART — 1987-88 3.0L MFI

CODE 24
VEHICLE SPEED SENSOR (VSS) CIRCUIT
3.0L (VIN L) "N" SERIES (PORT)

DISREGARD CODE 24, IF SET WHILE DRIVE WHEELS ARE NOT TURNING.

1.
- RAISE DRIVE WHEELS
- "NOTICE": DO NOT PERFORM THIS TEST WITHOUT SUPPORTING THE LOWER CONTROL ARMS SO THAT THE DRIVE AXLES ARE IN A NORMAL HORIZONTAL POSITION. RUNNING THE VEHICLE IN GEAR WITH THE WHEELS HANGING DOWN AT FULL TRAVEL MAY DAMAGE THE DRIVE AXLES.
- WITH ENGINE IDLING IN GEAR, "SCAN" SHOULD DISPLAY MPH ABOVE 0.
DOES IT?

NO | **YES**

YES: CODE 24 IS INTERMITTENT.

2.
- IGNITION "OFF", DISCONNECT VSS BUFFER, IGNITION "ON".
- PROBE 8 WAY CONNECTOR TERMINAL "F" WITH A VOLTMETER TO GROUND.
- SHOULD BE 10 VOLTS OR MORE.
IS IT?

NO | **YES**

NO: CHECK CKT 437 FOR OPENS OR SHORT TO GROUND, INCLUDING ECM TERMINAL "A-10". IF CIRCUIT IS OK, REPLACE ECM.

YES: SEE SECTION "8A", PAGE 33-0, FOR VSS BUFFER AND PM GENERATOR DIAGNOSTICS.

CLEAR CODES AND CONFIRM "CLOSED LOOP" OPERATION AND NO "SERVICE ENGINE SOON" LIGHT.

86884180

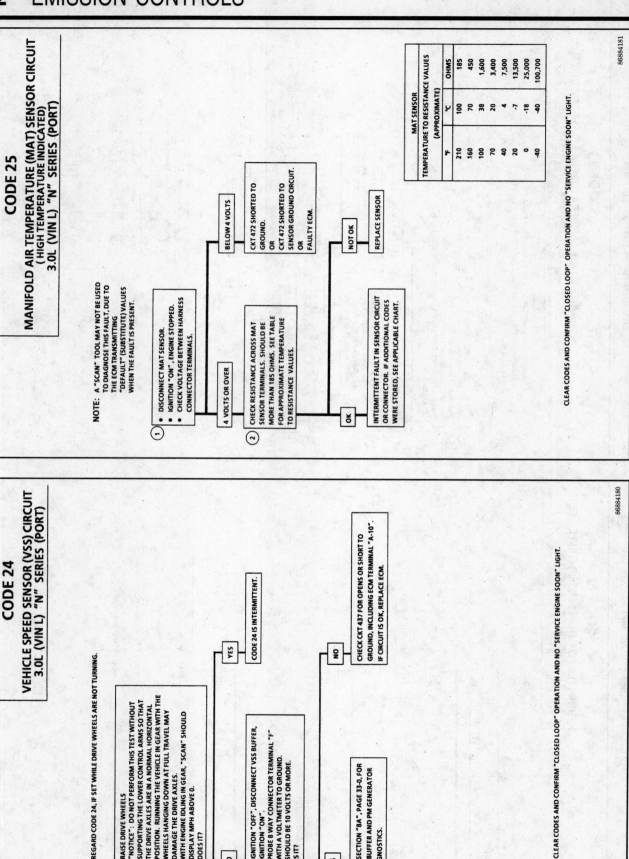

DTC CHART — 1987-88 3.0L MFI

CODE 33
MASS AIR FLOW (MAF) SENSOR CIRCUIT
(GM/SEC HIGH)
3.0L (VIN L) "N" SERIES (PORT)

DTC CHART — 1987-88 3.0L MFI

CODE 32
EXHAUST GAS RECIRCULATION (EGR) CIRCUIT
3.0L (VIN L) "N" SERIES (PORT)

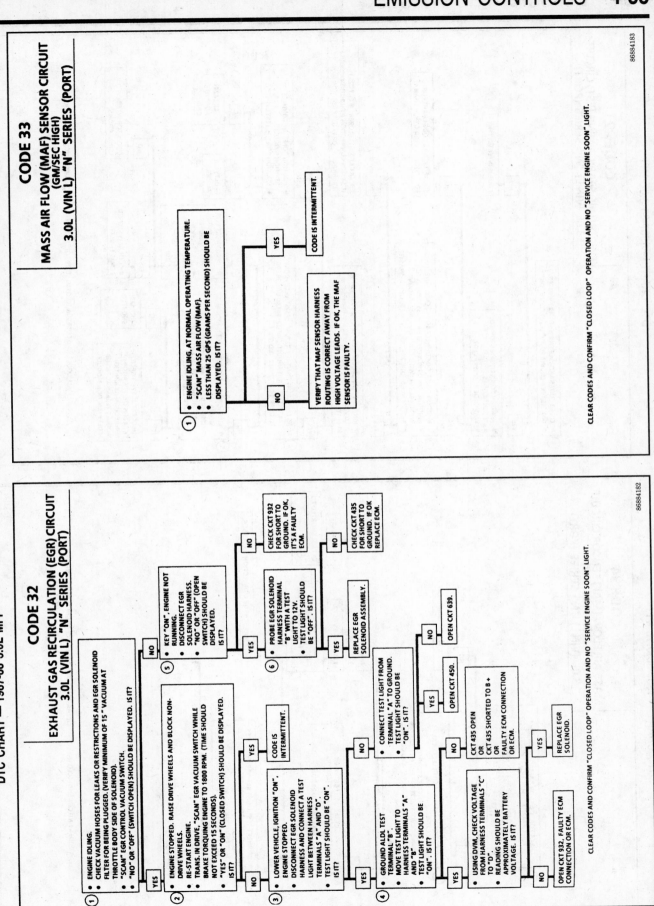

86884183

86884182

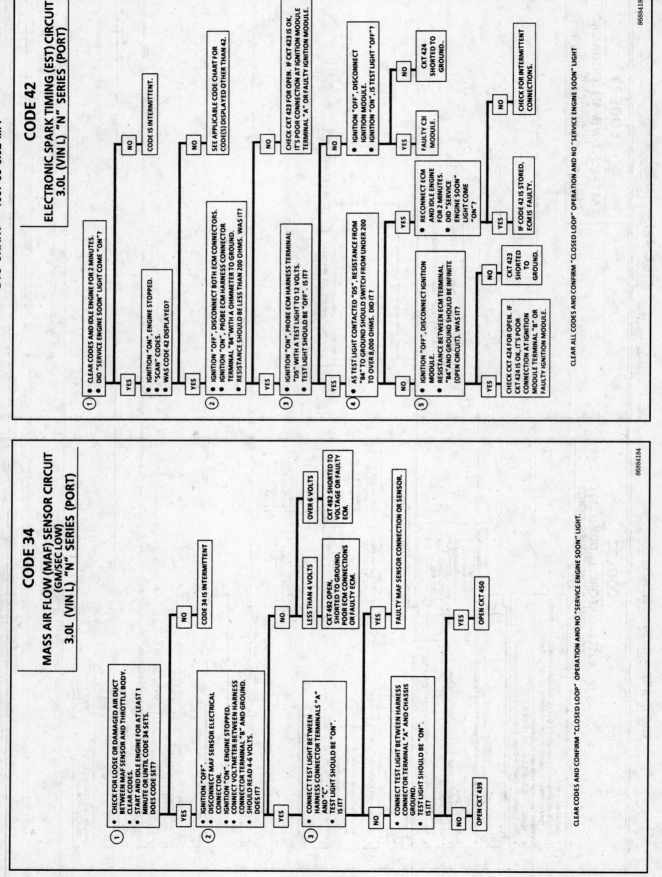

DTC CHART — 1987-88 3.0L MFI

CODE 42
ELECTRONIC SPARK TIMING (EST) CIRCUIT
3.0L (VIN L) "N" SERIES (PORT)

86884185

DTC CHART — 1987-88 3.0L MFI

CODE 34
MASS AIR FLOW (MAF) SENSOR CIRCUIT
(GM/SEC LOW)
3.0L (VIN L) "N" SERIES (PORT)

86884184

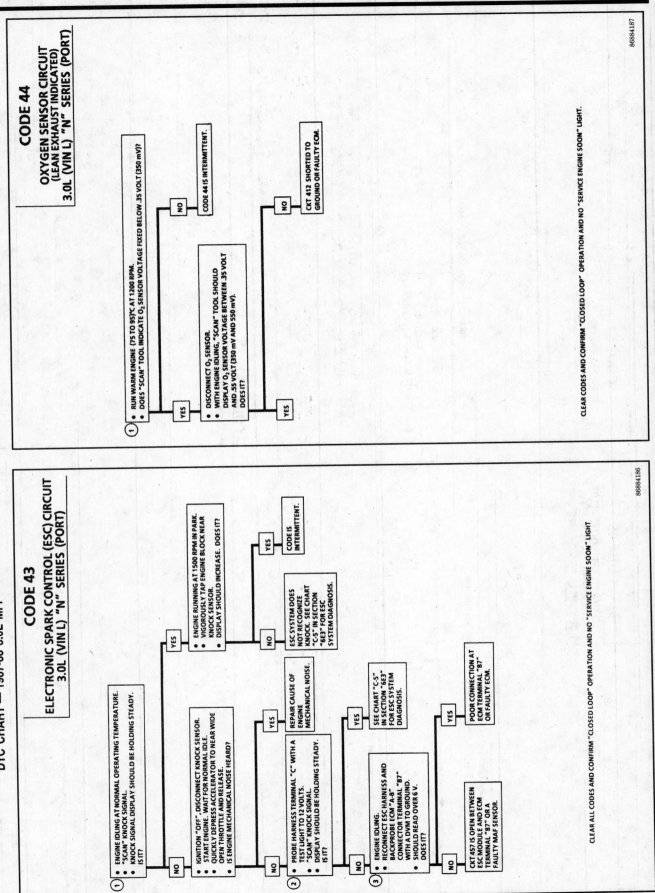

DTC CHART — 1987-88 3.0L MFI

CODE 44

OXYGEN SENSOR CIRCUIT
(LEAN EXHAUST INDICATED)
3.0L (VIN L) "N" SERIES (PORT)

1.
- RUN WARM ENGINE (75 TO 95)°C AT 1200 RPM.
- DOES "SCAN" TOOL INDICATE O₂ SENSOR VOLTAGE FIXED BELOW .35 VOLT (350 mV)?

YES → DISCONNECT O₂ SENSOR.
- WITH ENGINE IDLING, "SCAN" TOOL SHOULD DISPLAY O₂ SENSOR VOLTAGE BETWEEN .35 VOLT AND .55 VOLT (350 mV AND 550 mV).
DOES IT?

YES → CKT 412 SHORTED TO GROUND OR FAULTY ECM.

NO → CODE 44 IS INTERMITTENT.

NO →

CLEAR CODES AND CONFIRM "CLOSED LOOP" OPERATION AND NO "SERVICE ENGINE SOON" LIGHT.

86884187

DTC CHART — 1987-88 3.0L MFI

CODE 43

ELECTRONIC SPARK CONTROL (ESC) CIRCUIT
3.0L (VIN L) "N" SERIES (PORT)

1.
- ENGINE IDLING AT NORMAL OPERATING TEMPERATURE.
- "SCAN" KNOCK SIGNAL.
- KNOCK SIGNAL DISPLAY SHOULD BE HOLDING STEADY.
IS IT?

YES → ENGINE RUNNING AT 1500 RPM IN PARK.
- VIGOROUSLY TAP ENGINE BLOCK NEAR KNOCK SENSOR.
- DISPLAY SHOULD INCREASE. DOES IT?

YES → CODE IS INTERMITTENT.

NO → ESC SYSTEM DOES NOT RECOGNIZE KNOCK. SEE CHART "C-5" IN SECTION "6E3" FOR ESC SYSTEM DIAGNOSIS.

NO →
2.
- IGNITION "OFF", DISCONNECT KNOCK SENSOR.
- START ENGINE, WAIT FOR NORMAL IDLE.
- QUICKLY DEPRESS ACCELERATOR TO NEAR WIDE OPEN THROTTLE AND RELEASE.
- IS ENGINE MECHANICAL NOISE HEARD?

YES → REPAIR CAUSE OF ENGINE MECHANICAL NOISE.

NO → PROBE HARNESS TERMINAL "C" WITH A TEST LIGHT TO 12 VOLTS.
- "SCAN" KNOCK SIGNAL.
- DISPLAY SHOULD BE HOLDING STEADY.
IS IT?

YES → SEE CHART "C-5" IN SECTION "6E3" FOR ESC SYSTEM DIAGNOSIS.

NO →
3.
- ENGINE IDLING.
- RECONNECT ESC HARNESS AND BACKPROBE ECM "A-8" CONNECTOR TERMINAL "B7" WITH A DVM TO GROUND.
- SHOULD READ OVER 6 V.
DOES IT?

YES → POOR CONNECTION AT ECM TERMINAL "B7" OR FAULTY ECM.

NO → CKT 457 IS OPEN BETWEEN ESC MODULE AND ECM TERMINAL "B7" OR A FAULTY MAF SENSOR.

CLEAR ALL CODES AND CONFIRM "CLOSED LOOP" OPERATION AND NO "SERVICE ENGINE SOON" LIGHT

86884186

DTC CHART — 1987-88 3.0L MFI

CODE 51
PROM ERROR
(FAULTY OR INCORRECT CALPAK)

CHECK THAT ALL PINS ARE FULLY INSERTED IN THE SOCKET. IF OK, REPLACE PROM, CLEAR MEMORY AND RECHECK. IF CODE 51 REAPPEARS, REPLACE ECM.

CLEAR ALL CODES AND CONFIRM "CLOSED LOOP" OPERATION AND NO "SERVICE ENGINE SOON" LIGHT

CODE 52
CALPAK ERROR
(FAULTY OR INCORRECT CALPAK)

CHECK THAT ALL PINS ARE FULLY INSERTED IN THE SOCKET. IF OK, REPLACE CALPAK, CLEAR MEMORY AND RECHECK. IF CODE 52 REAPPEARS, REPLACE ECM.

CLEAR ALL CODES AND CONFIRM "CLOSED LOOP" OPERATION AND NO "SERVICE ENGINE SOON" LIGHT

CODE 55
ECM ERROR

REPLACE ELECTRONIC CONTROL MODULE (ECM).

CLEAR ALL CODES AND CONFIRM "CLOSED LOOP" OPERATION AND NO "SERVICE ENGINE SOON" LIGHT

86884189

DTC CHART — 1987-88 3.0L MFI

CODE 45
OXYGEN SENSOR CIRCUIT
(RICH EXHAUST INDICATED)
3.0L (VIN L) "N" SERIES (PORT)

(1)
- RUN WARM ENGINE (75°C TO 95°C) AT 1200 RPM.
- DOES "SCAN" TOOL DISPLAY O_2 SENSOR VOLTAGE FIXED ABOVE .75 VOLT (750 mV)?

YES

NO → CODE 45 IS INTERMITTENT.

- DISCONNECT O_2 SENSOR AND JUMPER HARNESS CKT 412 TO GROUND.
- "SCAN" TOOL SHOULD DISPLAY O_2 BELOW .35 VOLT (350 mV).
  DOES IT?

YES

NO → REPLACE ECM.

CLEAR CODES AND CONFIRM "CLOSED LOOP" OPERATION AND NO "SERVICE ENGINE SOON" LIGHT.

86884188

DTC CHART — 3.1L SFI

DTC 14

ENGINE COOLANT TEMPERATURE (ECT) SENSOR CIRCUIT
(HIGH TEMPERATURE INDICATED)
3100 (VIN M) "N" CARLINE (SFI)

1. DOES SCAN TOOL DISPLAY ENGINE COOLANT TEMPERATURE OF 134°C (273°F) OR HIGHER?

YES / NO

NO → DTC 14 IS INTERMITTENT.

2. DISCONNECT ENGINE COOLANT TEMPERATURE SENSOR. SCAN TOOL SHOULD DISPLAY ENGINE COOLANT TEMPERATURE BELOW -30°C (-22°F). DOES IT?

YES / NO

YES → REPLACE ENGINE COOLANT TEMPERATURE SENSOR.

NO → CKT 410 SHORTED TO GROUND OR CKT 410 SHORTED TO SENSOR GROUND CIRCUIT OR FAULTY PCM.

DIAGNOSTIC AID

ENGINE COOLANT TEMPERATURE SENSOR
TEMPERATURE VS. RESISTANCE VALUES
(APPROXIMATE)

°C	°F	OHMS
100	212	177
90	194	241
80	176	332
70	158	467
60	140	667
50	122	973
45	113	1188
40	104	1459
35	95	1802
30	86	2238
25	77	2796
20	68	3520
15	59	4450
10	50	5670
5	41	7280
0	32	9420
-5	23	12300
-10	14	16180
-15	5	21450
-20	-4	28680
-30	-22	52700
-40	-40	100700

86884219

DTC CHART — 3.1L SFI

DTC 13

HEATED OXYGEN SENSOR (HO2S) OPEN CIRCUIT
3100 (VIN M) "N" CARLINE (SFI)

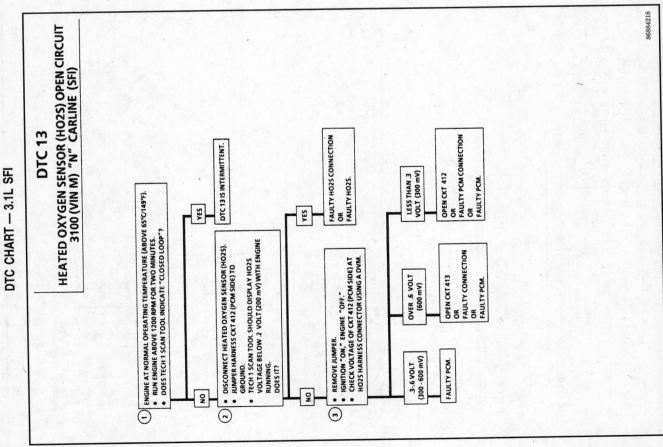

1. • ENGINE AT NORMAL OPERATING TEMPERATURE (ABOVE 65°C/149°F).
   • RUN ENGINE ABOVE 1200 RPM FOR TWO MINUTES.
   • DOES TECH 1 SCAN TOOL INDICATE "CLOSED LOOP"?

YES / NO

YES → DTC 13 IS INTERMITTENT.

2. • DISCONNECT HEATED OXYGEN SENSOR (HO2S).
   • JUMPER HARNESS CKT 412 (PCM SIDE) TO GROUND.
   • TECH 1 SCAN TOOL SHOULD DISPLAY HO2S VOLTAGE BELOW .2 VOLT (200 mV) WITH ENGINE RUNNING. DOES IT?

YES / NO

YES → FAULTY HO2S CONNECTION OR FAULTY HO2S.

3. • REMOVE JUMPER.
   • IGNITION "ON," ENGINE "OFF."
   • CHECK VOLTAGE OF CKT 412 (PCM SIDE) AT HO2S HARNESS CONNECTOR USING A DVM.

.3-.6 VOLT (300 - 600 mV) → FAULTY PCM.

OVER .6 VOLT (600 mV) → OPEN CKT 413 OR FAULTY CONNECTION OR FAULTY PCM.

LESS THAN .3 VOLT (300 mV) → OPEN CKT 412 OR FAULTY PCM CONNECTION OR FAULTY PCM.

86884218

DTC CHART — 3.1L SFI

DTC 16
SYSTEM VOLTAGE LOW
3100 (VIN M) "N" CARLINE (SFI)

DTC CHART — 3.1L SFI

DTC 15
ENGINE COOLANT TEMPERATURE (ECT) SENSOR CIRCUIT
(LOW TEMPERATURE INDICATED)
3100 (VIN M) "N" CARLINE (SFI)

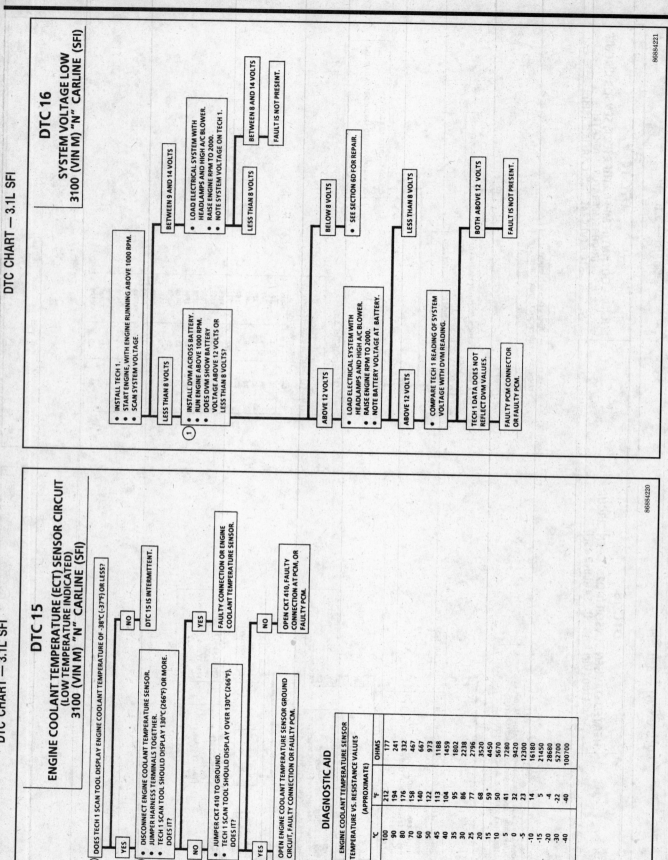

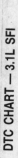

DIAGNOSTIC AID

ENGINE COOLANT TEMPERATURE SENSOR
TEMPERATURE VS. RESISTANCE VALUES
(APPROXIMATE)

°C	°F	OHMS
100	212	177
90	194	241
80	176	332
70	158	467
60	140	667
50	122	973
45	113	1188
40	104	1459
35	95	1802
30	86	2238
25	77	2796
20	68	3520
15	59	4450
10	50	5670
5	41	7280
0	32	9420
-5	23	12300
-10	14	16180
-15	5	21450
-20	-4	28680
-30	-22	52700
-40	-40	100700

86884221

86884220

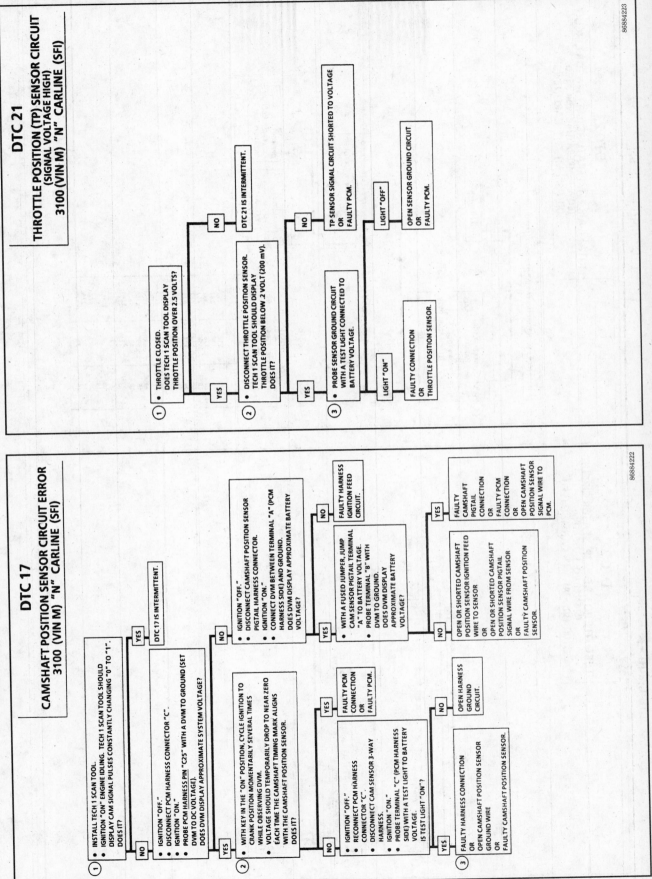

DTC CHART — 3.1L SFI

DTC 21

THROTTLE POSITION (TP) SENSOR CIRCUIT (SIGNAL VOLTAGE HIGH) 3100 (VIN M) "N" CARLINE (SFI)

1. THROTTLE CLOSED. DOES TECH 1 SCAN TOOL DISPLAY THROTTLE POSITION OVER 2.5 VOLTS?
   - NO → DTC 21 IS INTERMITTENT.
   - YES →

2. DISCONNECT THROTTLE POSITION SENSOR. TECH 1 SCAN TOOL SHOULD DISPLAY THROTTLE POSITION BELOW .2 VOLT (200 mV). DOES IT?
   - NO → TP SENSOR SIGNAL CIRCUIT SHORTED TO VOLTAGE OR FAULTY PCM.
   - YES →

3. PROBE SENSOR GROUND CIRCUIT WITH A TEST LIGHT CONNECTED TO BATTERY VOLTAGE.
   - LIGHT "ON" → FAULTY CONNECTION OR THROTTLE POSITION SENSOR.
   - LIGHT "OFF" → OPEN SENSOR GROUND CIRCUIT OR FAULTY PCM.

DTC CHART — 3.1L SFI

DTC 17

CAMSHAFT POSITION SENSOR CIRCUIT ERROR 3100 (VIN M) "N" CARLINE (SFI)

1. INSTALL TECH 1 SCAN TOOL. IGNITION "ON" ENGINE IDLING. TECH 1 SCAN TOOL SHOULD DISPLAY CAM SIGNAL PULSES CONSTANTLY CHANGING "0" TO "1". DOES IT?
   - YES → DTC 17 IS INTERMITTENT.
   - NO →
     - IGNITION "OFF."
     - DISCONNECT PCM HARNESS CONNECTOR "C".
     - IGNITION "ON."
     - PROBE PCM HARNESS PIN "C25" WITH A DVM TO GROUND (SET DVM TO DC VOLTAGE). DOES DVM DISPLAY APPROXIMATE SYSTEM VOLTAGE?
   - NO →

2. WITH KEY IN THE "ON" POSITION, CYCLE IGNITION TO CRANK POSITION MOMENTARILY SEVERAL TIMES WHILE OBSERVING DVM. VOLTAGE SHOULD TEMPORARILY DROP TO NEAR ZERO EACH TIME THE CAMSHAFT TIMING MARK ALIGNS WITH THE CAMSHAFT POSITION SENSOR. DOES IT?
   - NO →
     - IGNITION "OFF."
     - DISCONNECT CAMSHAFT POSITION SENSOR PIGTAIL HARNESS CONNECTOR.
     - IGNITION "ON."
     - CONNECT DVM BETWEEN TERMINAL "A" (PCM HARNESS SIDE) AND GROUND. DOES DVM DISPLAY APPROXIMATE BATTERY VOLTAGE?
       - NO → FAULTY HARNESS IGNITION FEED CIRCUIT.
       - YES →
         - WITH A FUSED JUMPER, JUMP CAM SENSOR PIGTAIL TERMINAL "A" TO BATTERY VOLTAGE.
         - PROBE TERMINAL "B" WITH DVM TO GROUND. DOES DVM DISPLAY APPROXIMATE BATTERY VOLTAGE?
           - NO → OPEN OR SHORTED CAMSHAFT POSITION SENSOR IGNITION FEED WIRE TO SENSOR OR OPEN OR SHORTED CAMSHAFT POSITION SENSOR PIGTAIL SIGNAL WIRE FROM SENSOR OR FAULTY CAMSHAFT POSITION SENSOR.
           - YES → FAULTY CAMSHAFT PIGTAIL CONNECTION OR FAULTY PCM CONNECTION OR OPEN CAMSHAFT POSITION SENSOR SIGNAL WIRE TO PCM.
   - YES →

3.
   - IGNITION "OFF."
   - RECONNECT PCM HARNESS CONNECTOR "C".
   - DISCONNECT CAM SENSOR 3-WAY HARNESS.
   - IGNITION "ON."
   - PROBE TERMINAL "C" (PCM HARNESS SIDE) WITH A TEST LIGHT TO BATTERY VOLTAGE. IS TEST LIGHT "ON"?
     - YES → FAULTY PCM CONNECTION OR FAULTY PCM.
     - NO → OPEN HARNESS GROUND CIRCUIT.

FAULTY HARNESS CONNECTION OR OPEN CAMSHAFT POSITION SENSOR GROUND WIRE OR FAULTY CAMSHAFT POSITION SENSOR.

86884223

86884222

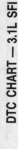

DTC CHART — 3.1L SFI

DTC 23

INTAKE AIR TEMPERATURE (IAT) SENSOR CIRCUIT
(LOW TEMPERATURE INDICATED)
3100 (VIN M) "N" CARLINE (SFI)

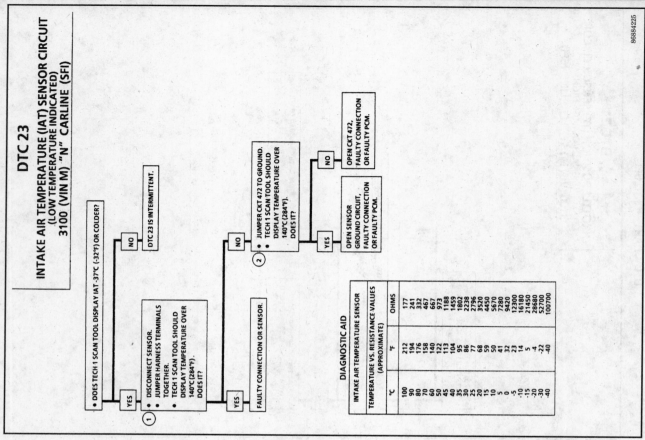

86884225

- DOES TECH 1 SCAN TOOL DISPLAY IAT -37°C (-32°F) OR COLDER?

NO → DTC 23 IS INTERMITTENT.

YES →

①
- DISCONNECT SENSOR.
- JUMPER HARNESS TERMINALS TOGETHER.
- TECH 1 SCAN TOOL SHOULD DISPLAY TEMPERATURE OVER 140°C (284°F).
DOES IT?

NO →

②
- JUMPER CKT 472 TO GROUND.
- TECH 1 SCAN TOOL SHOULD DISPLAY TEMPERATURE OVER 140°C (284°F).
DOES IT?

NO → OPEN CKT 472, FAULTY CONNECTION OR FAULTY PCM.

YES → OPEN SENSOR GROUND CIRCUIT, FAULTY CONNECTION OR FAULTY PCM.

YES → FAULTY CONNECTION OR SENSOR.

DIAGNOSTIC AID

INTAKE AIR TEMPERATURE SENSOR
TEMPERATURE VS. RESISTANCE VALUES
(APPROXIMATE)

°C	°F	OHMS
100	212	177
90	194	241
80	176	332
70	158	467
60	140	667
50	122	973
45	113	1188
40	104	1459
35	95	1802
30	86	2238
25	77	2796
20	68	3520
15	59	4450
10	50	5670
5	41	7280
0	32	9420
-5	23	12300
-10	14	16180
-15	5	21450
-20	-4	28680
-30	-22	52700
-40	-40	100700

DTC CHART — 3.1L SFI

DTC 22

THROTTLE POSITION (TP) SENSOR CIRCUIT
(SIGNAL VOLTAGE LOW)
3100 (VIN M) "N" CARLINE (SFI)

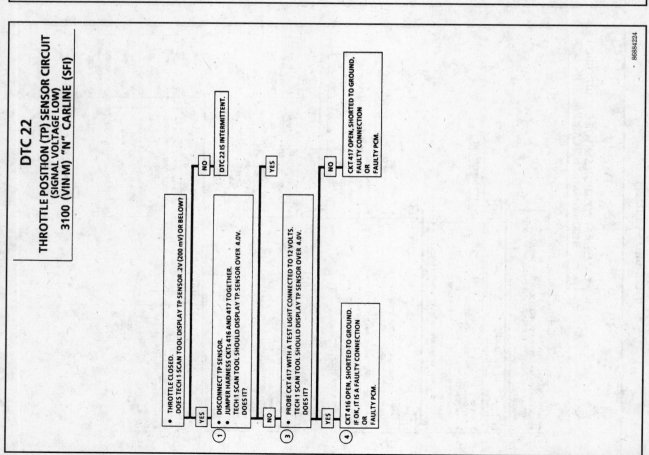

86884224

- THROTTLE CLOSED.
- DOES TECH 1 SCAN TOOL DISPLAY TP SENSOR .2V (200 mV) OR BELOW?

NO → DTC 22 IS INTERMITTENT.

YES →

①
- DISCONNECT TP SENSOR.
- JUMPER HARNESS CKTS 416 AND 417 TOGETHER.
- TECH 1 SCAN TOOL SHOULD DISPLAY TP SENSOR OVER 4.0V.
DOES IT?

YES →

③
- PROBE CKT 417 WITH A TEST LIGHT CONNECTED TO 12 VOLTS.
- TECH 1 SCAN TOOL SHOULD DISPLAY TP SENSOR OVER 4.0V.
DOES IT?

NO → CKT 417 OPEN, SHORTED TO GROUND, FAULTY CONNECTION OR FAULTY PCM.

YES →

④
CKT 416 OPEN, SHORTED TO GROUND. IF OK, IT IS A FAULTY CONNECTION OR FAULTY PCM.

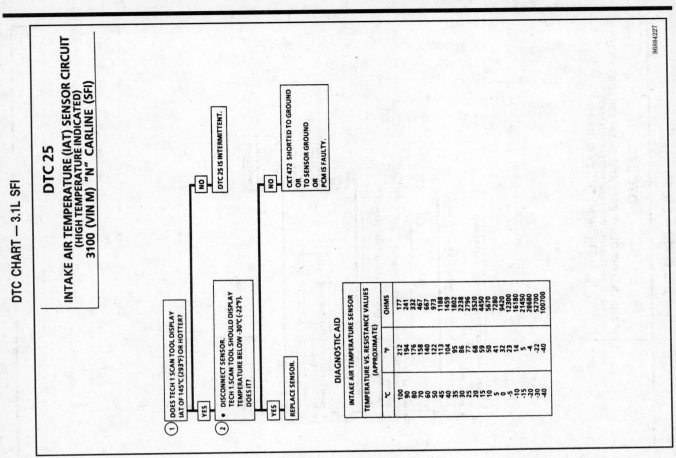

DTC CHART — 3.1L SFI

DTC 25
INTAKE AIR TEMPERATURE (IAT) SENSOR CIRCUIT
(HIGH TEMPERATURE INDICATED)
3100 (VIN M) "N" CARLINE (SFI)

① DOES TECH 1 SCAN TOOL DISPLAY IAT OF 145°C (293°F) OR HOTTER?

NO → DTC 25 IS INTERMITTENT.

YES ↓

② DISCONNECT SENSOR.
• TECH 1 SCAN TOOL SHOULD DISPLAY TEMPERATURE BELOW -30°C (-22°F). DOES IT?

NO → CKT 472 SHORTED TO GROUND
OR
TO SENSOR GROUND
OR
PCM IS FAULTY.

YES ↓

REPLACE SENSOR.

DIAGNOSTIC AID

INTAKE AIR TEMPERATURE SENSOR

TEMPERATURE VS. RESISTANCE VALUES (APPROXIMATE)		
°C	°F	OHMS
100	212	177
90	194	241
80	176	332
70	158	467
60	140	667
50	122	973
45	113	1188
40	104	1459
35	95	1802
30	86	2238
25	77	2796
20	68	3520
15	59	4450
10	50	5670
5	41	7280
0	32	9420
-5	23	12300
-10	14	16180
-15	5	21450
-20	-4	28680
-30	-22	52700
-40	-40	100700

86884227

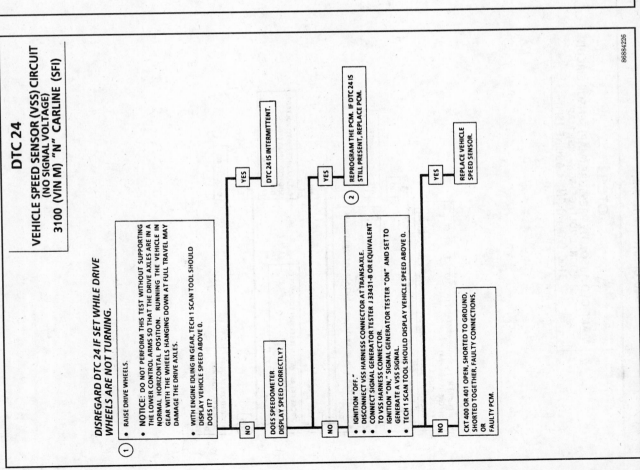

DTC CHART — 3.1L SFI

DTC 24
VEHICLE SPEED SENSOR (VSS) CIRCUIT
(NO SIGNAL VOLTAGE)
3100 (VIN M) "N" CARLINE (SFI)

DISREGARD DTC 24 IF SET WHILE DRIVE WHEELS ARE NOT TURNING.

① • RAISE DRIVE WHEELS.
• **NOTICE:** DO NOT PERFORM THIS TEST WITHOUT SUPPORTING THE LOWER CONTROL ARMS SO THAT THE DRIVE AXLES ARE IN A NORMAL HORIZONTAL POSITION. RUNNING THE VEHICLE IN GEAR WITH THE WHEELS HANGING DOWN AT FULL TRAVEL MAY DAMAGE THE DRIVE AXLES.
• WITH ENGINE IDLING IN GEAR, TECH 1 SCAN TOOL SHOULD DISPLAY VEHICLE SPEED ABOVE 0. DOES IT?

NO ↓

DOES SPEEDOMETER DISPLAY SPEED CORRECTLY?

YES → DTC 24 IS INTERMITTENT.

NO ↓

• IGNITION "OFF."
• DISCONNECT VSS HARNESS CONNECTOR AT TRANSAXLE.
• CONNECT SIGNAL GENERATOR TESTER J 33431-B OR EQUIVALENT TO VSS HARNESS CONNECTOR.
• IGNITION "ON," SIGNAL GENERATOR TESTER "ON" AND SET TO GENERATE A VSS SIGNAL.
• TECH 1 SCAN TOOL SHOULD DISPLAY VEHICLE SPEED ABOVE 0.

YES → ② REPROGRAM THE PCM. IF DTC 24 IS STILL PRESENT, REPLACE PCM.

NO ↓

CKT 400 OR 401 OPEN, SHORTED TO GROUND, SHORTED TOGETHER, FAULTY CONNECTIONS, OR FAULTY PCM.

YES → REPLACE VEHICLE SPEED SENSOR.

86884226

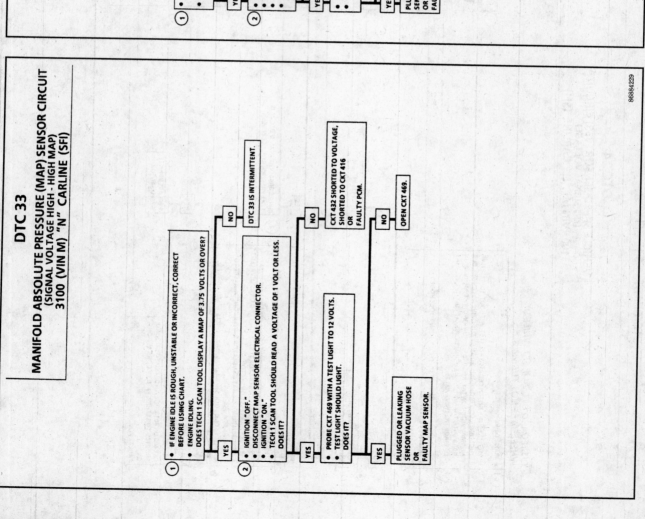

DTC CHART — 3.1L SFI

DTC 33

MANIFOLD ABSOLUTE PRESSURE (MAP) SENSOR CIRCUIT
(SIGNAL VOLTAGE HIGH - HIGH MAP)
3100 (VIN M) "N" CARLINE (SFI)

① • IF ENGINE IDLE IS ROUGH, UNSTABLE OR INCORRECT, CORRECT BEFORE USING CHART.
• ENGINE IDLING.
DOES TECH 1 SCAN TOOL DISPLAY A MAP OF 3.75 VOLTS OR OVER?

NO → DTC 33 IS INTERMITTENT.

YES

② • IGNITION "OFF."
• DISCONNECT MAP SENSOR ELECTRICAL CONNECTOR.
• IGNITION "ON."
• TECH 1 SCAN TOOL SHOULD READ A VOLTAGE OF 1 VOLT OR LESS.
DOES IT?

NO → CKT 432 SHORTED TO VOLTAGE, SHORTED TO CKT 416 OR FAULTY PCM.

YES

• PROBE CKT 469 WITH A TEST LIGHT TO 12 VOLTS.
• TEST LIGHT SHOULD LIGHT.
DOES IT?

NO → OPEN CKT 469.

YES

PLUGGED OR LEAKING SENSOR VACUUM HOSE OR FAULTY MAP SENSOR.

86884229

DTC CHART — 3.1L SFI

DTC 35
IDLE SPEED ERROR
3100 (VIN M) "N" CARLINE (SFI)

1
- INSTALL TECH 1 SCAN TOOL.
- ENGINE AT NORMAL OPERATING TEMPERATURE IN PARK/NEUTRAL WITH PARKING BRAKE SET.
- A/C "OFF."
- SELECT RPM CONTROL. (MISC. TESTS)
- CYCLE IAC THROUGH ITS RANGE FROM 700 RPM UP TO 1500 RPM.
- RPM SHOULD CHANGE SMOOTHLY. DOES IT?

NO →

2
- INSTALL IAC NODE LIGHT * IN IAC HARNESS.
- ENGINE RUNNING. CYCLE IAC WITH TECH 1 SCAN TOOL.
- EACH NODE LIGHT SHOULD CYCLE RED AND GREEN BUT NEVER "OFF."
- DO THEY?

NO →
- IF CIRCUIT(S) DID NOT TEST RED AND GREEN, CHECK FOR:
- FAULTY CONNECTOR TERMINAL CONTACTS.
- OPEN CIRCUITS INCLUDING CONNECTORS.
- CIRCUITS SHORTED TO GROUND OR VOLTAGE.
- FAULTY PCM CONNECTIONS OR REPLACE PCM.
- REPAIR AS NECESSARY AND RETEST.

YES →
- CHECK IAC CONNECTIONS.
- CHECK IAC PASSAGES.
- IF OK, REPLACE IAC.

YES →
- USING THE IAC DRIVER * OR OTHER CONVENIENT CONNECTOR, CHECK RESISTANCE ACROSS IAC COILS.
- SHOULD BE 40 TO 80 OHMS BETWEEN IAC TERMINALS "A" TO "B" AND "C" TO "D".

NOT OK →
REPLACE IAC VALVE AND RETEST.

OK →
- CHECK RESISTANCE BETWEEN IAC TERMINALS "B" AND "C" AND "A" AND "D".
- SHOULD BE INFINITE.

NOT OK →
REPLACE IAC VALVE AND RETEST.

OK →
IDLE AIR CONTROL CIRCUIT OK.

* IAC DRIVER AND NODE LIGHT REQUIRED KIT 222-L FROM: CONCEPT TECHNOLOGY, INC. J 37027 FROM: KENT-MOORE, INC.

CLEAR DIAGNOSTIC TROUBLE CODES, CONFIRM "CLOSED LOOP" OPERATION, NO MALFUNCTION INDICATOR LAMP (MIL). PERFORM IAC RESET PROCEDURE PER APPLICABLE SERVICE MANUAL AND VERIFY CONTROLLED IDLE SPEED IS CORRECT.

86884231

DTC CHART — 3.1L SFI

DTC 34
MANIFOLD ABSOLUTE PRESSURE (MAP) SENSOR CIRCUIT
(SIGNAL VOLTAGE LOW - LOW MAP)
3100 (VIN M) "N" CARLINE (SFI)

1
- IGNITION "OFF" FOR 10 SECONDS.
- START ENGINE AND IMMEDIATELY NOTE MAP VALUE ON TECH 1 SCAN TOOL.
- DOES SCAN DISPLAY MAP BELOW .25 VOLT?

YES →
- IGNITION "OFF."
- DISCONNECT SENSOR ELECTRICAL CONNECTOR.
- JUMPER HARNESS TERMINALS "B" TO "C".
- IGNITION "ON."
- DOES MAP VOLTAGE READ OVER 4 VOLTS?

NO →

2
- IGNITION "OFF."
- REMOVE JUMPER WIRE.
- PROBE TERMINAL "B" (CKT 432) WITH A LIGHT TO 12 VOLTS.
- IGNITION "ON."
- DOES TECH 1 SCAN TOOL READ OVER 4 VOLTS?

YES →
CKT 416 OPEN OR SHORTED TO GROUND OR FAULTY PCM.

NO →
DTC 34 IS INTERMITTENT.

YES →
FAULTY CONNECTION OR SENSOR.

NO →
CKT 432 OPEN OR SHORTED TO GROUND OR FAULTY PCM.

86884230

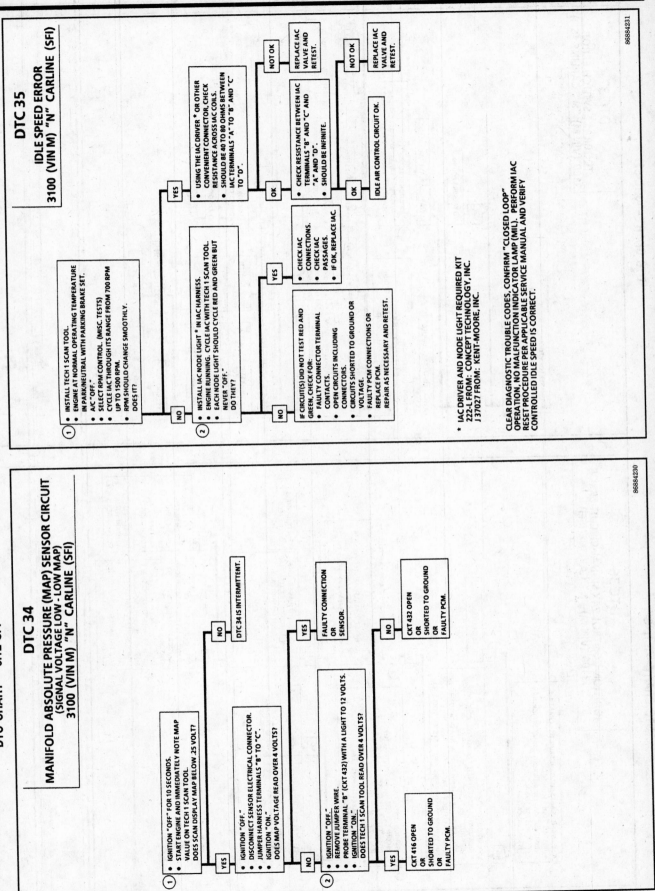

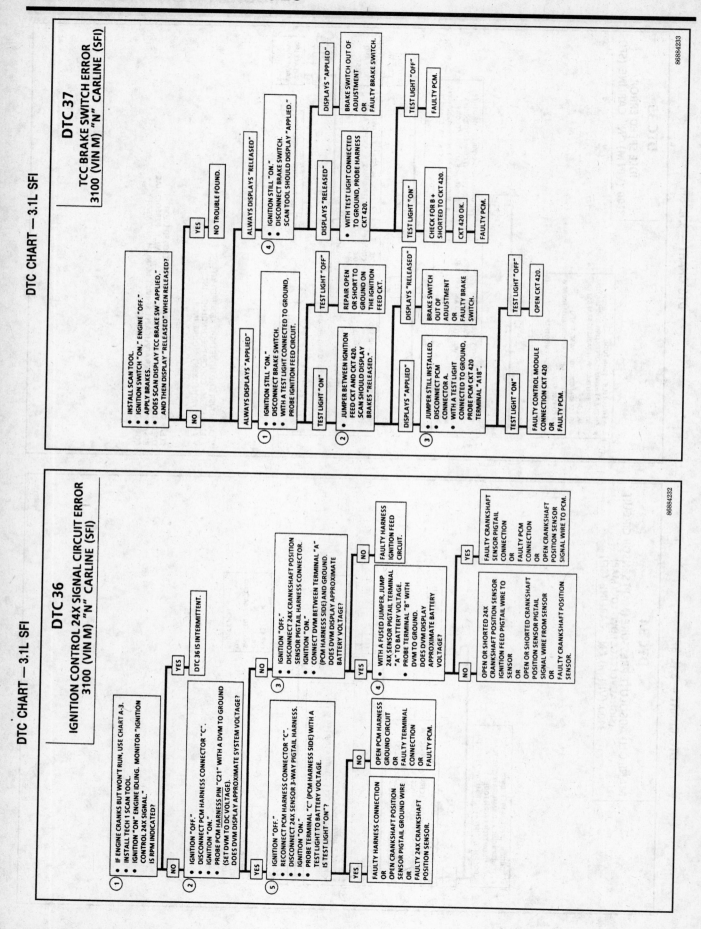

DTC CHART — 3.1L SFI

DTC 37
TCC BRAKE SWITCH ERROR
3100 (VIN M) "N" CARLINE (SFI)

- INSTALL SCAN TOOL.
- IGNITION SWITCH "ON," ENGINE "OFF."
- APPLY BRAKES.
- DOES SCAN DISPLAY TCC BRAKE SW "APPLIED," AND THEN DISPLAY "RELEASED" WHEN RELEASED?

YES → NO TROUBLE FOUND.

NO

ALWAYS DISPLAYS "APPLIED" | **ALWAYS DISPLAYS "RELEASED"**

①
- IGNITION STILL "ON."
- DISCONNECT BRAKE SWITCH.
- WITH A TEST LIGHT CONNECTED TO GROUND, PROBE IGNITION FEED CIRCUIT.

TEST LIGHT "ON" | TEST LIGHT "OFF"

REPAIR OPEN OR SHORT TO GROUND ON THE IGNITION FEED CKT.

②
- JUMPER BETWEEN IGNITION FEED CKT AND CKT 420. SCAN SHOULD DISPLAY BRAKES "RELEASED."

DISPLAYS "APPLIED" | DISPLAYS "RELEASED"

BRAKE SWITCH OUT OF ADJUSTMENT OR FAULTY BRAKE SWITCH.

③
- JUMPER STILL INSTALLED.
- DISCONNECT PCM CONNECTOR A.
- WITH A TEST LIGHT CONNECTED TO GROUND, PROBE PCM CKT 420 TERMINAL "A18".

TEST LIGHT "ON" | TEST LIGHT "OFF"

FAULTY CONTROL MODULE CONNECTION CKT 420 OR FAULTY PCM. | OPEN CKT 420.

④
- IGNITION STILL "ON."
- DISCONNECT BRAKE SWITCH. SCAN TOOL SHOULD DISPLAY "APPLIED."

DISPLAYS "RELEASED" | DISPLAYS "APPLIED"

BRAKE SWITCH OUT OF ADJUSTMENT OR FAULTY BRAKE SWITCH.

- WITH TEST LIGHT CONNECTED TO GROUND, PROBE HARNESS CKT 420.

TEST LIGHT "ON" | TEST LIGHT "OFF"

CHECK FOR B + SHORTED TO CKT 420. | FAULTY PCM.

CKT 420 OK.

FAULTY PCM.

86884233

DTC CHART — 3.1L SFI

DTC 36
IGNITION CONTROL 24X SIGNAL CIRCUIT ERROR
3100 (VIN M) "N" CARLINE (SFI)

①
- IF ENGINE CRANKS BUT WON'T RUN, USE CHART A-3.
- INSTALL TECH 1 SCAN TOOL.
- IGNITION "ON" ENGINE IDLING. MONITOR "IGNITION CONTROL 24X SIGNAL."
- IS RPM INDICATED?

YES → DTC 36 IS INTERMITTENT.

NO

②
- IGNITION "OFF."
- DISCONNECT PCM HARNESS CONNECTOR "C".
- IGNITION "ON."
- PROBE PCM HARNESS PIN "C21" WITH A DVM TO GROUND (SET DVM TO DC VOLTAGE).
- DOES DVM DISPLAY APPROXIMATE SYSTEM VOLTAGE?

YES | **NO**

③
- IGNITION "OFF."
- DISCONNECT 24X CRANKSHAFT POSITION SENSOR PIGTAIL HARNESS CONNECTOR.
- IGNITION "ON."
- CONNECT DVM BETWEEN TERMINAL "A" (PCM HARNESS SIDE) AND GROUND. DOES DVM DISPLAY APPROXIMATE BATTERY VOLTAGE?

NO → FAULTY HARNESS IGNITION FEED CIRCUIT.

YES

④
- WITH A FUSED JUMPER, JUMP 24X SENSOR PIGTAIL TERMINAL "A" TO BATTERY VOLTAGE.
- PROBE TERMINAL "B" WITH DVM TO GROUND.
- DOES DVM DISPLAY APPROXIMATE BATTERY VOLTAGE?

YES → FAULTY CRANKSHAFT SENSOR PIGTAIL CONNECTION OR FAULTY PCM CONNECTION OR OPEN CRANKSHAFT POSITION SENSOR SIGNAL WIRE TO PCM.

NO → OPEN OR SHORTED 24X CRANKSHAFT POSITION SENSOR IGNITION FEED PIGTAIL WIRE TO SENSOR OR OPEN OR SHORTED CRANKSHAFT POSITION SENSOR PIGTAIL SIGNAL WIRE FROM SENSOR OR FAULTY CRANKSHAFT POSITION SENSOR.

⑤
- IGNITION "OFF."
- RECONNECT PCM HARNESS CONNECTOR "C".
- DISCONNECT 24X SENSOR 3-WAY PIGTAIL HARNESS.
- IGNITION "ON."
- PROBE TERMINAL "C" (PCM HARNESS SIDE) WITH A TEST LIGHT TO BATTERY VOLTAGE. IS TEST LIGHT "ON"?

YES | **NO**

FAULTY HARNESS CONNECTION OR OPEN CRANKSHAFT POSITION SENSOR PIGTAIL GROUND WIRE OR FAULTY 24X CRANKSHAFT POSITION SENSOR.

OPEN PCM HARNESS GROUND CIRCUIT OR FAULTY TERMINAL CONNECTION OR FAULTY PCM.

86884232

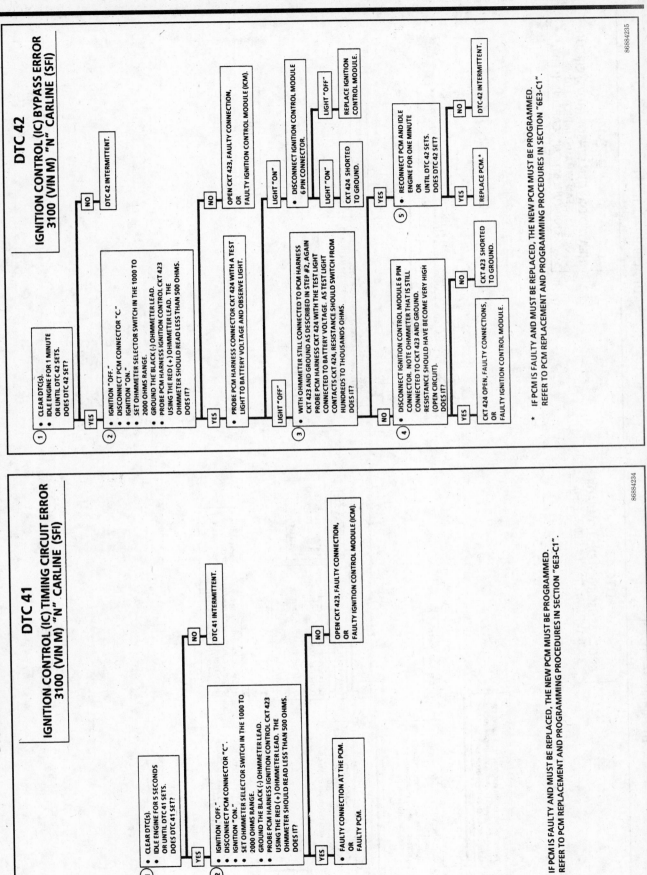

DTC CHART — 3.1L SFI

DTC 42
IGNITION CONTROL (IC) BYPASS ERROR
3100 (VIN M) "N" CARLINE (SFI)

86884235

1. • CLEAR DTC(s).
   • IDLE ENGINE FOR 1 MINUTE OR UNTIL DTC 42 SETS.
   DOES DTC 42 SET?

   NO → DTC 42 INTERMITTENT.

   YES ↓

2. • IGNITION "OFF."
   • DISCONNECT PCM CONNECTOR "C."
   • IGNITION "ON."
   • SET OHMMETER SELECTOR SWITCH IN THE 1000 TO 2000 OHMS RANGE.
   • GROUND THE BLACK (-) OHMMETER LEAD.
   • PROBE PCM HARNESS IGNITION CONTROL CKT 423 USING THE RED (+) OHMMETER LEAD. THE OHMMETER SHOULD READ LESS THAN 500 OHMS.
   DOES IT?

   NO → OPEN CKT 423, FAULTY CONNECTION, OR FAULTY IGNITION CONTROL MODULE (ICM).

   YES ↓

   • PROBE PCM HARNESS CONNECTOR CKT 424 WITH A TEST LIGHT TO BATTERY VOLTAGE AND OBSERVE LIGHT.

   LIGHT "ON" → • DISCONNECT IGNITION CONTROL MODULE 6 PIN CONNECTOR.
   LIGHT "ON" → CKT 424 SHORTED TO GROUND.
   LIGHT "OFF" → REPLACE IGNITION CONTROL MODULE.

   LIGHT "OFF" ↓

3. • WITH OHMMETER STILL CONNECTED TO PCM HARNESS CKT 423 AND GROUND AS DESCRIBED IN STEP #2, AGAIN PROBE PCM HARNESS CKT 424 WITH THE TEST LIGHT CONNECTED TO BATTERY VOLTAGE. AS TEST LIGHT CONTACTS CKT 424, RESISTANCE SHOULD SWITCH FROM HUNDREDS TO THOUSANDS OHMS.
   DOES IT?

   NO ↓

4. • DISCONNECT IGNITION CONTROL MODULE 6 PIN CONNECTOR. NOTE OHMMETER THAT IS STILL CONNECTED TO CKT 423 AND GROUND. RESISTANCE SHOULD HAVE BECOME VERY HIGH (OPEN CIRCUIT).
   DOES IT?

   NO → CKT 423 SHORTED TO GROUND.

   YES → CKT 424 OPEN, FAULTY CONNECTIONS, OR FAULTY IGNITION CONTROL MODULE.

   YES (step 3) ↓

5. • RECONNECT PCM AND IDLE ENGINE FOR ONE MINUTE OR UNTIL DTC 42 SETS.
   DOES DTC 42 SET?

   YES → REPLACE PCM.*

   NO → DTC 42 INTERMITTENT.

* IF PCM IS FAULTY AND MUST BE REPLACED, THE NEW PCM MUST BE PROGRAMMED. REFER TO PCM REPLACEMENT AND PROGRAMMING PROCEDURES IN SECTION "6E3-C1".

DTC CHART — 3.1L SFI

DTC 41
IGNITION CONTROL (IC) TIMING CIRCUIT ERROR
3100 (VIN M) "N" CARLINE (SFI)

86884234

1. • CLEAR DTC(s).
   • IDLE ENGINE FOR 5 SECONDS OR UNTIL DTC 41 SETS.
   DOES DTC 41 SET?

   NO → DTC 41 INTERMITTENT.

   YES ↓

2. • IGNITION "OFF."
   • DISCONNECT PCM CONNECTOR "C."
   • IGNITION "ON."
   • SET OHMMETER SELECTOR SWITCH IN THE 1000 TO 2000 OHMS RANGE.
   • GROUND THE BLACK (-) OHMMETER LEAD.
   • PROBE PCM HARNESS IGNITION CONTROL CKT 423 USING THE RED (+) OHMMETER LEAD. THE OHMMETER SHOULD READ LESS THAN 500 OHMS.
   DOES IT?

   NO → OPEN CKT 423, FAULTY CONNECTION, OR FAULTY IGNITION CONTROL MODULE (ICM).

   YES → FAULTY CONNECTION AT THE PCM. OR FAULTY PCM.

* IF PCM IS FAULTY AND MUST BE REPLACED, THE NEW PCM MUST BE PROGRAMMED. REFER TO PCM REPLACEMENT AND PROGRAMMING PROCEDURES IN SECTION "6E3-C1".

DTC CHART — 3.1L SFI

DTC 44

HEATED OXYGEN SENSOR (HO2S) CIRCUIT
(LEAN EXHAUST INDICATED)
3100 (VIN M) "N" CARLINE (SFI)

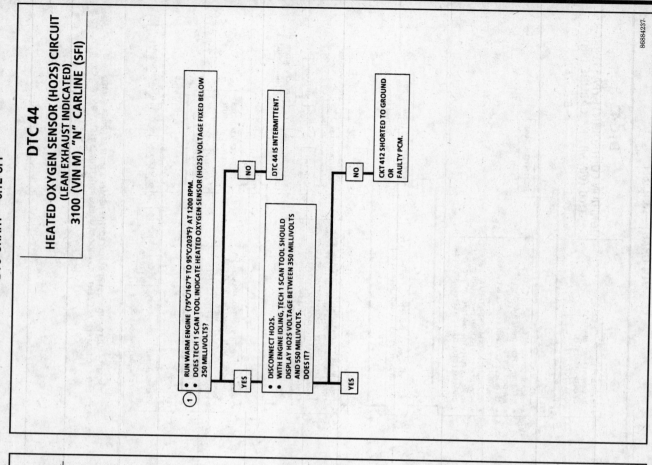

(1)
- RUN WARM ENGINE (75°C/167°F TO 95°C/203°F) AT 1200 RPM.
- DOES TECH 1 SCAN TOOL INDICATE HEATED OXYGEN SENSOR (HO2S) VOLTAGE FIXED BELOW 250 MILLIVOLTS?

YES

- DISCONNECT HO2S.
- WITH ENGINE IDLING, TECH 1 SCAN TOOL SHOULD DISPLAY HO2S VOLTAGE BETWEEN 350 MILLIVOLTS AND 550 MILLIVOLTS. DOES IT?

YES

NO — DTC 44 IS INTERMITTENT.

NO — CKT 412 SHORTED TO GROUND OR FAULTY PCM.

86884237.

DTC CHART — 3.1L SFI

DTC 43

KNOCK SENSOR (KS) CIRCUIT CIRCUIT ERROR
3100 (VIN M) "N" CARLINE (SFI)

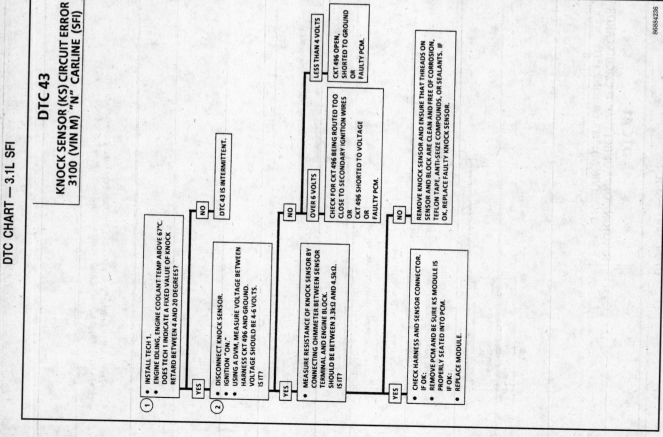

(1)
- INSTALL TECH 1.
- ENGINE IDLING, ENGINE COOLANT TEMP ABOVE 67°C. DOES TECH 1 INDICATE A FIXED VALUE OF KNOCK RETARD BETWEEN 4 AND 20 DEGREES?

YES

NO — DTC 43 IS INTERMITTENT.

(2)
- DISCONNECT KNOCK SENSOR.
- IGNITION "ON."
- USING A DVM, MEASURE VOLTAGE BETWEEN HARNESS CKT 496 AND GROUND. VOLTAGE SHOULD BE 4-6 VOLTS. IS IT?

YES

- MEASURE RESISTANCE OF KNOCK SENSOR BY CONNECTING OHMMETER BETWEEN SENSOR TERMINAL AND ENGINE BLOCK. SHOULD BE BETWEEN 3.3kΩ AND 4.5kΩ. IS IT?

YES

NO — OVER 6 VOLTS — CHECK FOR CKT 496 BEING ROUTED TOO CLOSE TO SECONDARY IGNITION WIRES OR CKT 496 SHORTED TO VOLTAGE OR FAULTY PCM.

LESS THAN 4 VOLTS — CKT 496 OPEN, SHORTED TO GROUND OR FAULTY PCM.

NO —
- CHECK HARNESS AND SENSOR CONNECTOR. IF OK:
- REMOVE PCM AND BE SURE KS MODULE IS PROPERLY SEATED INTO PCM. IF OK:
- REPLACE MODULE.

REMOVE KNOCK SENSOR AND ENSURE THAT THREADS ON SENSOR AND BLOCK ARE CLEAN AND FREE OF CORROSION, TEFLON TAPE, ANTI-SEIZE COMPOUNDS, OR SEALANTS. IF OK, REPLACE FAULTY KNOCK SENSOR.

86884236

DTC CHART — 3.1L SFI

DTC 51
PROM ERROR
(FAULTY OR INCORRECT CALIBRATION)
3100 (VIN M) "N" CARLINE (SFI)

DTC 51 WILL BE STORED WHEN AN INVALID PROGRAM IS DETECTED BY THE PCM. CHECK THAT ALL CONNECTIONS ARE FULLY INSERTED IN THE SOCKET. IF OK, REPROGRAM THE PCM. REFER TO SECTION "6E3-C1" (PCM AND SENSORS). IF PCM WILL NOT REPROGRAM, REPLACE PCM.

NOTICE: REPLACEMENT PCMs MUST BE REPROGRAMMED. IT IS ALSO NECESSARY TO TRANSFER THE KNOCK SENSOR (KS) MODULE WHEN REPLACING THE PCM. TO PREVENT POSSIBLE ELECTROSTATIC DISCHARGE DAMAGE TO THE PCM, DO NOT TOUCH THE COMPONENT LEADS.

86884239

DTC CHART — 3.1L SFI

DTC 45
HEATED OXYGEN SENSOR (HO2S) CIRCUIT
(RICH EXHAUST INDICATED)
3100 (VIN M) "N" CARLINE (SFI)

- RUN WARM ENGINE (75°C/167°F TO 95°C/203°F) AT 1200 RPM.
- DOES TECH 1 SCAN TOOL DISPLAY HO2S VOLTAGE FIXED ABOVE 750 MILLIVOLTS?

NO → DTC 45 IS INTERMITTENT.

YES ↓

- DISCONNECT O2S AND JUMPER HARNESS CKT 413 TO GROUND.
- JUMPER HARNESS CKT 412 TO GROUND.
- TECH 1 SCAN TOOL SHOULD DISPLAY HO2S VOLTAGE BELOW 350 MILLIVOLTS. DOES IT?

NO → FAULTY PCM. REFER TO SECTION "6E3-C1" FOR PCM REPLACEMENT.

YES

86884238

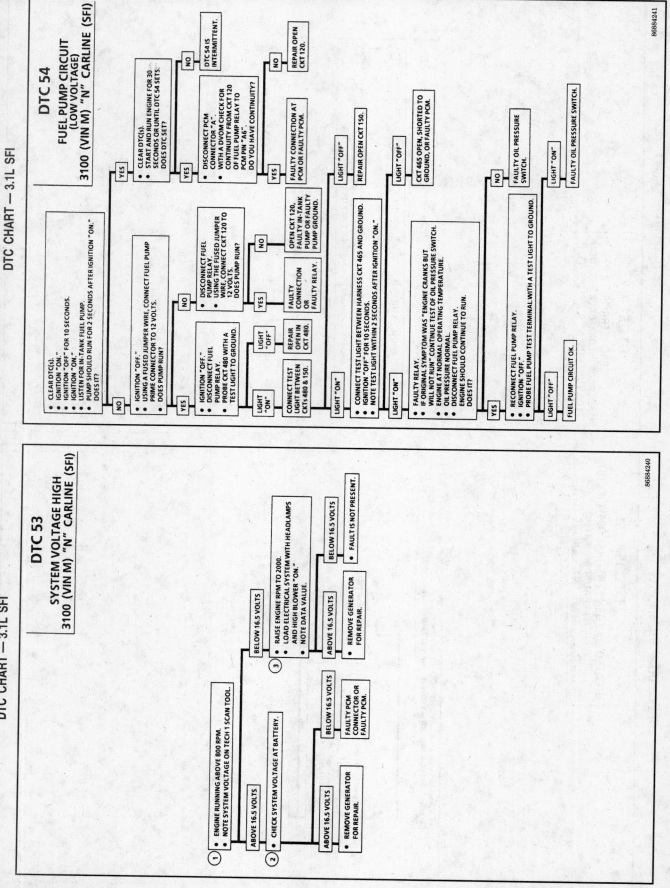

DTC CHART — 3.1L SFI

DTC 54
FUEL PUMP CIRCUIT
(LOW VOLTAGE)
3100 (VIN M) "N" CARLINE (SFI)

86884241

- CLEAR DTC(s).
- IGNITION "ON."
- IGNITION "OFF" FOR 10 SECONDS.
- IGNITION "ON."
- LISTEN FOR IN-TANK FUEL PUMP.
- PUMP SHOULD RUN FOR 2 SECONDS AFTER IGNITION "ON." DOES IT?

NO →

- IGNITION "OFF."
- USING A FUSED JUMPER WIRE, CONNECT FUEL PUMP PRIME CONNECTOR TO 12 VOLTS.
- DOES PUMP RUN?

YES →

- CLEAR DTC(s).
- START AND RUN ENGINE FOR 30 SECONDS OR UNTIL DTC 54 SETS. DOES DTC SET?

NO → DTC 54 IS INTERMITTENT.

YES →

- DISCONNECT PCM CONNECTOR "A".
- WITH A DVOM CHECK FOR CONTINUITY FROM CKT 120 OF FUEL PUMP RELAY TO PCM PIN "A6". DO YOU HAVE CONTINUITY?

NO → REPAIR OPEN CKT 120.

YES → FAULTY CONNECTION AT PCM OR FAULTY PCM.

YES →

- IGNITION "OFF."
- DISCONNECT FUEL PUMP RELAY.
- USING THE FUSED JUMPER WIRE, CONNECT CKT 120 TO 12 VOLTS. DOES PUMP RUN?

NO → OPEN CKT 120, FAULTY IN-TANK PUMP OR FAULTY PUMP GROUND.

YES → FAULTY CONNECTION OR FAULTY RELAY.

NO →

- IGNITION "OFF."
- DISCONNECT FUEL PUMP RELAY.
- PROBE CKT 480 WITH A TEST LIGHT TO GROUND.

LIGHT "OFF" → REPAIR OPEN IN CKT 480.

LIGHT "ON" → CONNECT TEST LIGHT BETWEEN CKTS 480 & 150.

LIGHT "OFF" → CONNECT TEST LIGHT BETWEEN HARNESS CKT 465 AND GROUND.
- IGNITION "OFF" FOR 10 SECONDS.
- NOTE TEST LIGHT WITHIN 2 SECONDS AFTER IGNITION "ON."

LIGHT "ON" → REPAIR OPEN CKT 150.

LIGHT "ON" → FAULTY RELAY.

LIGHT "OFF" → CKT 465 OPEN, SHORTED TO GROUND, OR FAULTY PCM.

- IF ORIGINAL SYMPTOM WAS "ENGINE CRANKS BUT WILL NOT RUN" CONTINUE TEST OF OIL PRESSURE SWITCH. ENGINE AT NORMAL OPERATING TEMPERATURE. OIL PRESSURE NORMAL.
- DISCONNECT FUEL PUMP RELAY. ENGINE SHOULD CONTINUE TO RUN. DOES IT?

NO → FAULTY OIL PRESSURE SWITCH.

YES →
- RECONNECT FUEL PUMP RELAY.
- IGNITION "OFF."
- PROBE FUEL PUMP TEST TERMINAL WITH A TEST LIGHT TO GROUND.

LIGHT "OFF" → FUEL PUMP CIRCUIT OK.

LIGHT "ON" → FAULTY OIL PRESSURE SWITCH.

DTC CHART — 3.1L SFI

DTC 53
SYSTEM VOLTAGE HIGH
3100 (VIN M) "N" CARLINE (SFI)

86884240

(1)
- ENGINE RUNNING ABOVE 800 RPM.
- NOTE SYSTEM VOLTAGE ON TECH 1 SCAN TOOL.

ABOVE 16.5 VOLTS →

(2) CHECK SYSTEM VOLTAGE AT BATTERY.

ABOVE 16.5 VOLTS →
- REMOVE GENERATOR FOR REPAIR.

BELOW 16.5 VOLTS → FAULTY PCM CONNECTOR OR FAULTY PCM.

BELOW 16.5 VOLTS →

(3)
- RAISE ENGINE RPM TO 2000.
- LOAD ELECTRICAL SYSTEM WITH HEADLAMPS AND HIGH BLOWER "ON."
- NOTE DATA VALUE.

ABOVE 16.5 VOLTS → REMOVE GENERATOR FOR REPAIR.

BELOW 16.5 VOLTS → FAULT IS NOT PRESENT.

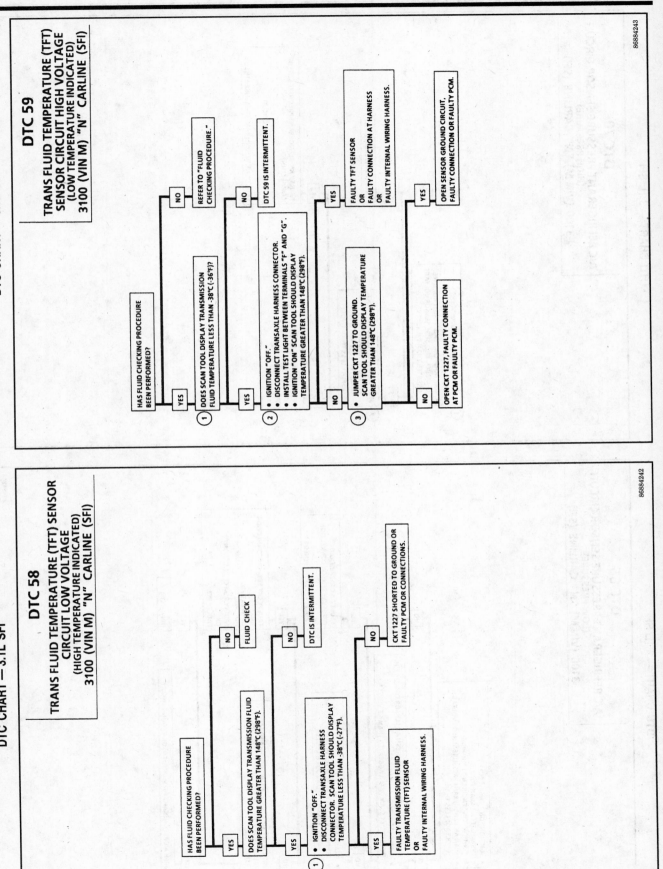

DTC CHART — 3.1L SFI

DTC 59

TRANS FLUID TEMPERATURE (TFT)
SENSOR CIRCUIT HIGH VOLTAGE
(LOW TEMPERATURE INDICATED)
3100 (VIN M) "N" CARLINE (SFI)

HAS FLUID CHECKING PROCEDURE BEEN PERFORMED?

NO → REFER TO "FLUID CHECKING PROCEDURE."

YES

(1) DOES SCAN TOOL DISPLAY TRANSMISSION FLUID TEMPERATURE LESS THAN -38°C (-36°F)?

NO → DTC 59 IS INTERMITTENT.

YES

(2)
- IGNITION "OFF."
- DISCONNECT TRANSAXLE HARNESS CONNECTOR.
- INSTALL TEST LIGHT BETWEEN TERMINALS "F" AND "G".
- IGNITION "ON" SCAN TOOL SHOULD DISPLAY TEMPERATURE GREATER THAN 148°C (298°F).

YES → FAULTY TFT SENSOR
OR
FAULTY CONNECTION AT HARNESS
OR
FAULTY INTERNAL WIRING HARNESS.

NO

(3) JUMPER CKT 1227 TO GROUND.
SCAN TOOL SHOULD DISPLAY TEMPERATURE GREATER THAN 148°C (298°F).

YES → OPEN SENSOR GROUND CIRCUIT,
FAULTY CONNECTION OR FAULTY PCM.

NO → OPEN CKT 1227, FAULTY CONNECTION AT PCM OR FAULTY PCM.

86884243

DTC CHART — 3.1L SFI

DTC 58

TRANS FLUID TEMPERATURE (TFT) SENSOR
CIRCUIT LOW VOLTAGE
(HIGH TEMPERATURE INDICATED)
3100 (VIN M) "N" CARLINE (SFI)

HAS FLUID CHECKING PROCEDURE BEEN PERFORMED?

NO → FLUID CHECK

YES

DOES SCAN TOOL DISPLAY TRANSMISSION FLUID TEMPERATURE GREATER THAN 148°C (298°F).

NO → DTC IS INTERMITTENT.

YES

(1)
- IGNITION "OFF."
- DISCONNECT TRANSAXLE HARNESS CONNECTOR. SCAN TOOL SHOULD DISPLAY TEMPERATURE LESS THAN -38°C (-27°F).

YES → FAULTY TRANSMISSION FLUID TEMPERATURE (TFT) SENSOR
OR
FAULTY INTERNAL WIRING HARNESS.

NO → CKT 1227 SHORTED TO GROUND OR FAULTY PCM OR CONNECTIONS.

86884242

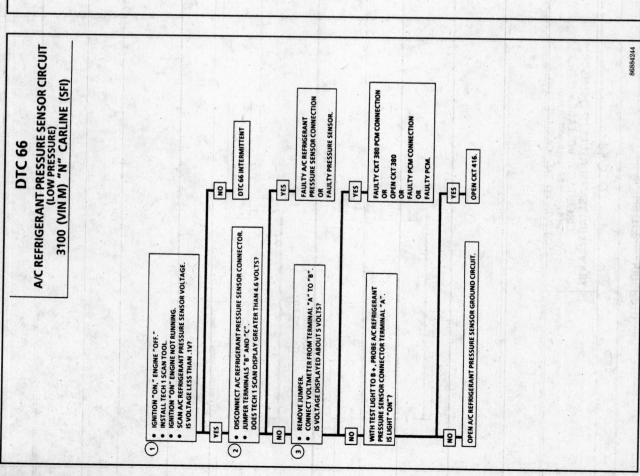

DTC CHART — 3.1L SFI

DTC 70

A/C REFRIGERANT PRESSURE SENSOR CIRCUIT
(HIGH PRESSURE)
3100 (VIN M) "N" CARLINE (SFI)

1.
- IGNITION "OFF," ENGINE "OFF."
- INSTALL TECH 1 SCAN TOOL.
- IGNITION "ON" ENGINE NOT RUNNING.
  IS A/C REF. PRESSURE SENSOR VOLTAGE
  GREATER THAN 1.8 VOLTS?

YES
NO — DTC 70 IS INTERMITTENT.

2.
- DISCONNECT A/C REFRIGERANT
  PRESSURE SENSOR.
  DOES TECH 1 SCAN TOOL
  DISPLAY LESS THAN 1 VOLT?

YES — FAULTY A/C REFRIGERANT PRESSURE SENSOR
CONNECTION
OR
OPEN SENSOR GROUND CIRCUIT
OR
FAULTY A/C REFRIGERANT PRESSURE SENSOR.

NO — A/C REFRIGERANT PRESSURE SENSOR
SIGNAL CIRCUIT SHORTED TO VOLTAGE
OR
FAULTY PCM.

DTC CHART — 3.1L SFI

DTC 66

A/C REFRIGERANT PRESSURE SENSOR CIRCUIT
(LOW PRESSURE)
3100 (VIN M) "N" CARLINE (SFI)

1.
- IGNITION "ON," ENGINE "OFF."
- INSTALL TECH 1 SCAN TOOL.
- IGNITION "ON" ENGINE NOT RUNNING.
- SCAN A/C REFRIGERANT PRESSURE SENSOR VOLTAGE.
  IS VOLTAGE LESS THAN .1V?

YES
NO — DTC 66 INTERMITTENT

2.
- DISCONNECT A/C REFRIGERANT PRESSURE SENSOR CONNECTOR.
- JUMPER TERMINALS "B" AND "C".
  DOES TECH 1 SCAN DISPLAY GREATER THAN 4.6 VOLTS?

YES — FAULTY A/C REFRIGERANT
PRESSURE SENSOR CONNECTION
OR
FAULTY PRESSURE SENSOR.

NO

3.
- REMOVE JUMPER.
- CONNECT VOLTMETER FROM TERMINAL "A" TO "B".
  IS VOLTAGE DISPLAYED ABOUT 5 VOLTS?

YES — FAULTY CKT 380 PCM CONNECTION
OR
OPEN CKT 380
OR
FAULTY PCM CONNECTION
OR
FAULTY PCM.

NO

WITH TEST LIGHT TO B +, PROBE A/C REFRIGERANT
PRESSURE SENSOR CONNECTOR TERMINAL "A".
IS LIGHT "ON"?

YES — OPEN CKT 416.

NO — OPEN A/C REFRIGERANT PRESSURE SENSOR GROUND CIRCUIT.

86884245

86884244

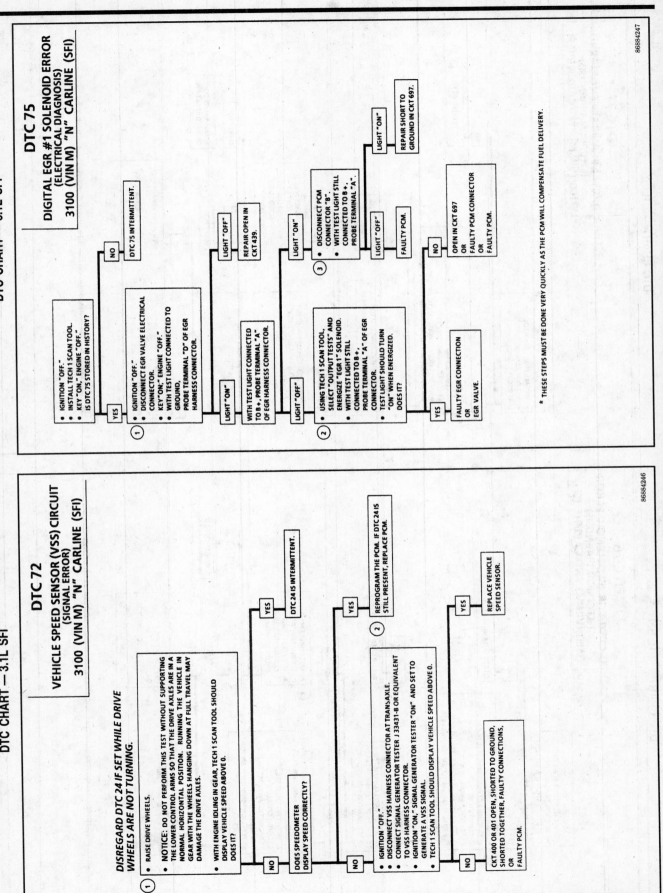

DTC CHART — 3.1L SFI

DTC 75
DIGITAL EGR #1 SOLENOID ERROR
(ELECTRICAL DIAGNOSIS)
3100 (VIN M) "N" CARLINE (SFI)

- IGNITION "OFF."
- INSTALL TECH 1 SCAN TOOL.
- KEY "ON," ENGINE "OFF."
- IS DTC 75 STORED IN HISTORY?

NO → DTC 75 INTERMITTENT.

YES

① • IGNITION "OFF."
- DISCONNECT EGR VALVE ELECTRICAL CONNECTOR.
- KEY "ON," ENGINE "OFF."
- WITH TEST LIGHT CONNECTED TO B +, PROBE TERMINAL "D" OF EGR HARNESS CONNECTOR.

LIGHT "ON"

LIGHT "OFF" → REPAIR OPEN IN CKT 439.

WITH TEST LIGHT CONNECTED TO B +, PROBE TERMINAL "A" OF EGR HARNESS CONNECTOR.

LIGHT "OFF"

LIGHT "ON"

② • USING TECH 1 SCAN TOOL, SELECT "OUTPUT TESTS" AND ENERGIZE "EGR 1" SOLENOID.
- WITH TEST LIGHT STILL CONNECTED TO B +, PROBE TERMINAL "A" OF EGR CONNECTOR.
- TEST LIGHT SHOULD TURN "ON" WHEN ENERGIZED. DOES IT?

③ • DISCONNECT PCM CONNECTOR "B".
- WITH TEST LIGHT STILL CONNECTED TO B +, PROBE TERMINAL "A".

LIGHT "ON" → REPAIR SHORT TO GROUND IN CKT 697.

LIGHT "OFF" → FAULTY PCM.

YES → FAULTY EGR CONNECTION OR EGR VALVE.

NO → OPEN IN CKT 697 OR FAULTY PCM CONNECTOR OR FAULTY PCM.

* THESE STEPS MUST BE DONE VERY QUICKLY AS THE PCM WILL COMPENSATE FUEL DELIVERY.

86884247

DTC CHART — 3.1L SFI

DTC 72
VEHICLE SPEED SENSOR (VSS) CIRCUIT
(SIGNAL ERROR)
3100 (VIN M) "N" CARLINE (SFI)

DISREGARD DTC 24 IF SET WHILE DRIVE WHEELS ARE NOT TURNING.

① • RAISE DRIVE WHEELS.
- NOTICE: DO NOT PERFORM THIS TEST WITHOUT SUPPORTING THE LOWER CONTROL ARMS SO THAT THE DRIVE AXLES ARE IN A NORMAL HORIZONTAL POSITION. RUNNING THE VEHICLE IN GEAR WITH THE WHEELS HANGING DOWN AT FULL TRAVEL MAY DAMAGE THE DRIVE AXLES.
- WITH ENGINE IDLING IN GEAR, TECH 1 SCAN TOOL SHOULD DISPLAY VEHICLE SPEED ABOVE 0. DOES IT?

YES → DTC 24 IS INTERMITTENT.

NO

DOES SPEEDOMETER DISPLAY SPEED CORRECTLY?

YES

② REPROGRAM THE PCM. IF DTC 24 IS STILL PRESENT, REPLACE PCM.

NO

• IGNITION "OFF."
- DISCONNECT VSS HARNESS CONNECTOR AT TRANS/AXLE.
- CONNECT SIGNAL GENERATOR TESTER J 33431-B OR EQUIVALENT TO VSS HARNESS CONNECTOR.
- IGNITION "ON," SIGNAL GENERATOR TESTER "ON" AND SET TO GENERATE A VSS SIGNAL.
- TECH 1 SCAN TOOL SHOULD DISPLAY VEHICLE SPEED ABOVE 0.

YES → REPLACE VEHICLE SPEED SENSOR.

NO

CKT 400 OR 401 OPEN, SHORTED TO GROUND, SHORTED TOGETHER, FAULTY CONNECTIONS, OR FAULTY PCM.

86884246

DTC CHART — 3.1L SFI

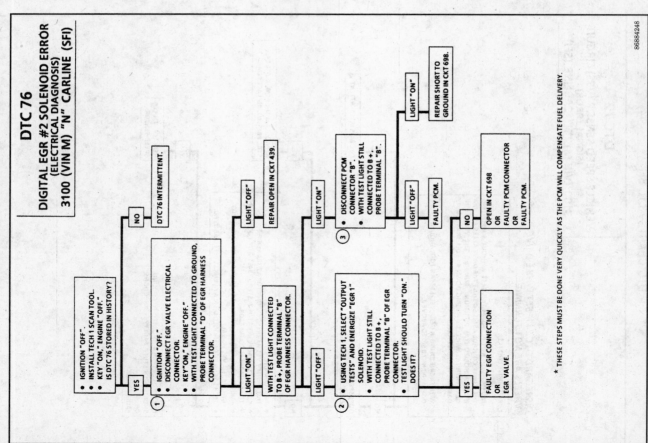

DTC CHART — 3.1L SFI

DTC CHART — 3.1L SFI

DTC 80
TRANSMISSION COMPONENT ERROR 3100 (VIN M) "N" CARLINE (SFI)

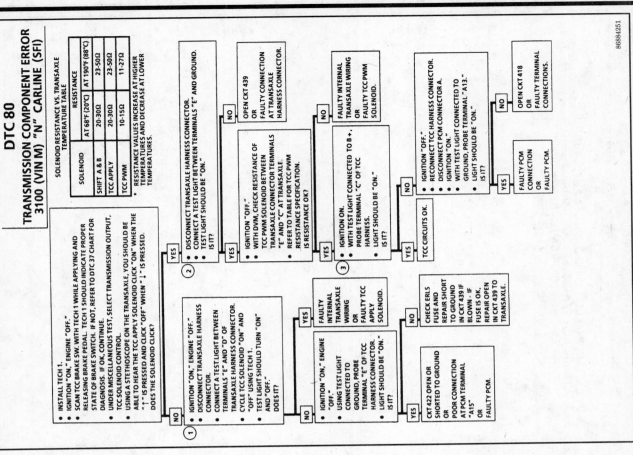

SOLENOID RESISTANCE VS. TRANSAXLE TEMPERATURE TABLE

SOLENOID	RESISTANCE	
	AT 68°F (20°C)	AT 190°F (88°C)
SHIFT A & B	20-30Ω	23-50Ω
TCC APPLY	20-30Ω	23-50Ω
TCC PWM	10-15Ω	11-27Ω

* RESISTANCE VALUES INCREASE AT HIGHER TEMPERATURES AND DECREASE AT LOWER TEMPERATURES.

- INSTALL TECH 1.
- IGNITION "ON," ENGINE "OFF."
- SCAN TCC BRAKE SW. WITH TECH 1 WHILE APPLYING AND RELEASING BRAKE PEDAL. TECH 1 SHOULD INDICATE PROPER STATE OF BRAKE SWITCH. IF NOT, REFER TO DTC 37 CHART FOR DIAGNOSIS. IF OK, CONTINUE.
- UNDER MISCELLANEOUS TEST, SELECT TRANSMISSION OUTPUT, TCC SOLENOID CONTROL.
- USING A STETHOSCOPE ON THE TRANSAXLE, YOU SHOULD BE ABLE TO HEAR THE TCC APPLY SOLENOID CLICK "ON" WHEN THE "↑" IS PRESSED AND CLICK "OFF" WHEN "↓" IS PRESSED.
DOES THE SOLENOID CLICK?

NO →

①
- IGNITION "ON," ENGINE "OFF."
- DISCONNECT TRANSAXLE HARNESS CONNECTOR.
- CONNECT A TEST LIGHT BETWEEN TERMINALS "E" AND "D" OF TRANSAXLE HARNESS CONNECTOR.
- CYCLE TCC SOLENOID "ON" AND "OFF" USING TECH 1.
- TEST LIGHT SHOULD TURN "ON" AND "OFF."
DOES IT?

YES →
FAULTY INTERNAL TRANSAXLE WIRING OR FAULTY TCC APPLY SOLENOID.

NO →
- IGNITION "ON," ENGINE "OFF."
- USING TEST LIGHT CONNECTED TO GROUND, PROBE TERMINAL "E" OF TCC HARNESS CONNECTOR.
- LIGHT SHOULD BE "ON."
IS IT?

YES →
CKT 422 OPEN OR SHORTED TO GROUND OR POOR CONNECTION AT PCM TERMINAL "A15" OR FAULTY PCM.

NO →
CHECK ERLS FUSE AND REPAIR SHORT TO GROUND IN CKT 439 IF BLOWN - IF FUSE IS OK, REPAIR OPEN IN CKT 439 TO TRANSAXLE.

YES →

②
- DISCONNECT TRANSAXLE HARNESS CONNECTOR.
- CONNECT A TEST LIGHT BETWEEN TERMINALS "E" AND GROUND.
TEST LIGHT SHOULD BE "ON."
IS IT?

YES →
- IGNITION "OFF."
- WITH DVM, CHECK RESISTANCE OF TCC PWM SOLENOID BETWEEN TRANSAXLE CONNECTOR TERMINALS "E" AND "C" AT TRANSAXLE.
- REFER TO TABLE FOR TCC PWM RESISTANCE SPECIFICATION.
IS RESISTANCE OK?

YES →

③
- IGNITION ON.
- WITH TEST LIGHT CONNECTED TO B +, PROBE TERMINAL "C" OF TCC HARNESS.
- LIGHT SHOULD BE "ON."
IS IT?

YES →
TCC CIRCUITS OK.

NO →
- IGNITION "OFF."
- RECONNECT TCC HARNESS CONNECTOR.
- DISCONNECT PCM CONNECTOR A.
- IGNITION "ON."
- WITH TEST LIGHT CONNECTED TO GROUND, PROBE TERMINAL "A13."
- LIGHT SHOULD BE "ON."
IS IT?

YES →
FAULTY PCM CONNECTION OR FAULTY PCM.

NO →
OPEN CKT 418 OR FAULTY TERMINAL CONNECTIONS.

NO →
FAULTY INTERNAL TRANSAXLE WIRING OR FAULTY TCC PWM SOLENOID.

NO →
OPEN CKT 439 OR FAULTY CONNECTION AT TRANSAXLE HARNESS CONNECTOR.

86884251

DTC CHART — 3.1L SFI

DTC 79
TRANSMISSION FLUID OVERTEMP 3100 (VIN M) "N" CARLINE (SFI)

DTC 79 INDICATES A TRANSMISSION FLUID OVER TEMPERATURE CONDITION HAS OCCURRED. THE PCM DETERMINES IF THE TFT TEMPERATURE IS ACCURATE BY CHECKING FOR GROSS FAILURES OF THE TFT SENSOR FIRST (DTC 58, 59). WHEN VALID DATA IS ESTABLISHED, A DTC 79 WILL BE SET IF THE TFT SENSOR INDICATES ABOVE 130°C AND WILL CLEAR FROM CURRENT DTC WHEN THE TEMPERATURE FALLS BELOW 120°C. SECTION 7A SHOULD BE CONSULTED FOR POSSIBLE CONDITIONS THAT WOULD CAUSE A TRANSMISSION OVER TEMPERATURE CONDITION. DRIVING CONDITIONS i.e. TRAILER TOWING, STEEP GRADES ect., SHOULD NOT BE DISCOUNTED. REFER TO SECTION / FOR TRANSMISSION FLUID CHECKING PROCEDURES.

86884250

DTC CHART — 3.1L SFI

DTC 85, 87

85 EPROM ERROR (FAULTY OR INCORRECT CALIBRATION)
87 ELECTRONICALLY ERASABLE PROGRAMMABLE READ
ONLY MEMORY (EEPROM) ERROR
3100 (VIN M) "N" CARLINE (SFI)

DTC(s) 51, 85, 87 WILL BE STORED WHEN AN INVALID PROGRAM IS DETECTED BY THE PCM. CHECK THAT ALL CONNECTORS ARE FULLY INSERTED IN THE SOCKET. IF OK, REPROGRAM THE PCM. REFER TO SECTION "6E3-C1" (PCM AND SENSORS). IF PCM WILL NOT REPROGRAM, REPLACE PCM.

NOTICE: REPLACEMENT PCM's MUST BE REPROGRAMMED. IT IS ALSO NECESSARY TO TRANSFER THE KNOCK SENSOR (KS) MODULE WHEN REPLACING THE PCM. TO PREVENT POSSIBLE ELECTROSTATIC DISCHARGE DAMAGE TO THE PCM, DO NOT TOUCH THE COMPONENT LEADS.

86884253

DTC CHART — 3.1L SFI

DTC 82

IGNITION CONTROL 3X SIGNAL ERROR
3100 (VIN M) "N" CARLINE (SFI)

86884252

(1)
NO IGNITION CONTROL 3X SIGNAL RPM AND NO SPARK.

- DISCONNECT ELECTRONIC ICM 2 PIN CONNECTOR.
- IGNITION "ON."
- CONNECT TEST LIGHT BETWEEN HARNESS TERMINALS.
- TEST LIGHT SHOULD TURN "ON."
- DOES IT?

YES →

- IGNITION "OFF."
- DISCONNECT IGNITION 6-WAY CONNECTOR.
- IGNITION "ON."
- MOMENTARILY TOUCH CKT 430 WITH A TEST LIGHT TO 12 VOLTS WHILE OBSERVING ENGINE SPEED WITH TECH 1.
- IS RPM INDICATED?

YES →

(2)
- DISCONNECT 3X CRANKSHAFT POSITION SENSOR 3-WAY CONNECTOR FROM IGNITION CONTROL MODULE (ICM) WITH OHMMETER IN 2K OHMS POSITION, PROBE HARNESS TERMINALS "A" & "C" (SHOULD DISPLAY BETWEEN 900-1200 OHMS).
- DOES IT?

NO →
CKT 430 OPEN OR SHORTED TO GROUND OR FAULTY PCM.

NO (from first box) →
- CONNECT TEST LIGHT FROM HARNESS TERMINAL "B" TO GROUND.
- IGNITION "ON."
- TEST LIGHT SHOULD TURN "ON."
- DOES IT?

NO →
REPAIR OPEN IGNITION FEED CKT 239.

YES →
REPAIR OPEN GROUND CKT 750.

YES (from box 2) →

GREATER THAN 1200 OHMS
OPEN CRANK SENSOR CIRCUIT, FAULTY CONNECTION OR FAULTY CRANKSHAFT POSITION SENSOR.

NO →
LESS THAN 900 OHMS
CRANK SENSOR LEADS SHORTED TOGETHER OR FAULTY CRANKSHAFT POSITION SENSOR.

(3)
- SET VOLTMETER ON 2 VOLT AC POSITION.
- CRANK ENGINE AND OBSERVE VOLTAGE READING. READING SHOULD BE GREATER THAN .1 VOLT (100 mV).
- IS IT?

YES →
REPLACE ELECTRONIC IGNITION CONTROL MODULE (ICM).

NO →
FAULTY CONNECTION OR FAULTY CRANKSHAFT POSITION SENSOR.

DTC CHART — 3.1L SFI

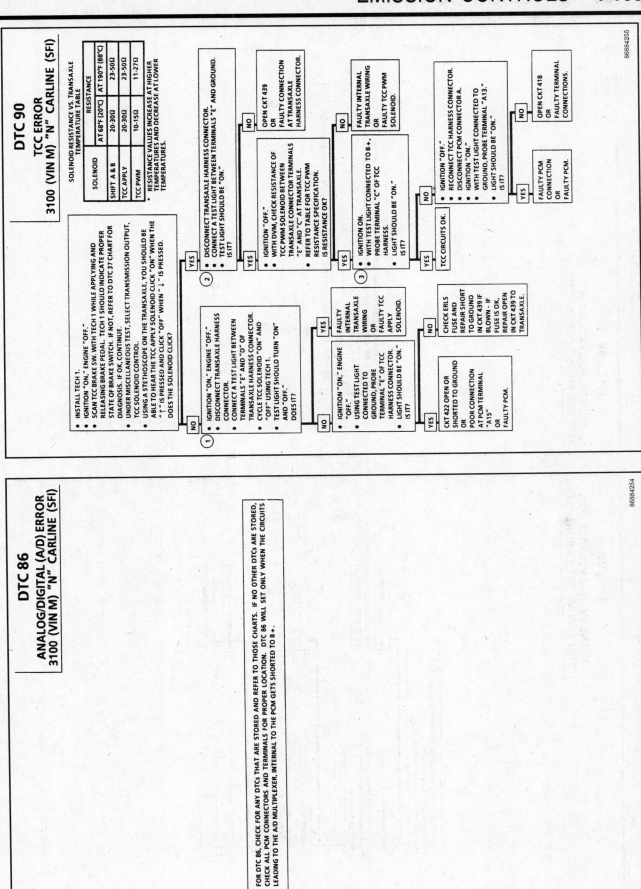

DTC 90
TCC ERROR
3100 (VIN M) "N" CARLINE (SFI)

SOLENOID RESISTANCE VS. TRANSAXLE TEMPERATURE TABLE

SOLENOID	RESISTANCE AT 68°F (20°C)	RESISTANCE AT 190°F (88°C)
SHIFT A & B	20-30Ω	23-50Ω
TCC APPLY	20-30Ω	23-50Ω
TCC PWM	10-15Ω	11-27Ω

* RESISTANCE VALUES INCREASE AT HIGHER TEMPERATURES AND DECREASE AT LOWER TEMPERATURES.

- INSTALL TECH 1.
- IGNITION "ON," ENGINE "OFF."
- SCAN TCC BRAKE SW, WITH TECH 1 WHILE APPLYING AND RELEASING BRAKE PEDAL. TECH 1 SHOULD INDICATE PROPER STATE OF BRAKE SWITCH. IF NOT, REFER TO DTC 37 CHART FOR DIAGNOSIS. IF OK, CONTINUE.
- UNDER MISCELLANEOUS TEST, SELECT TRANSMISSION OUTPUT, TCC SOLENOID CONTROL.
- USING A STETHOSCOPE ON THE TRANSAXLE, YOU SHOULD BE ABLE TO HEAR THE TCC APPLY SOLENOID CLICK "ON" WHEN THE "↑" IS PRESSED AND CLICK "OFF" WHEN "↓" IS PRESSED.
DOES THE SOLENOID CLICK?

NO → (1) YES → (2)

(1)
- IGNITION "ON," ENGINE "OFF."
- DISCONNECT TRANSAXLE HARNESS CONNECTOR.
- CONNECT A TEST LIGHT BETWEEN TERMINALS "E" AND "D" OF TRANSAXLE HARNESS CONNECTOR.
- CYCLE TCC SOLENOID "ON" AND "OFF" USING TECH 1.
- TEST LIGHT SHOULD TURN "ON" AND "OFF."
DOES IT?

YES → FAULTY INTERNAL TRANSAXLE WIRING OR FAULTY TCC APPLY SOLENOID.

NO →
- IGNITION "ON," ENGINE "OFF."
- USING TEST LIGHT CONNECTED TO GROUND, PROBE TERMINAL "E" OF TCC HARNESS CONNECTOR.
- LIGHT SHOULD BE "ON."
IS IT?

YES → CKT 422 OPEN OR SHORTED TO GROUND OR POOR CONNECTION AT PCM TERMINAL "A15" OR FAULTY PCM.

NO → CHECK ERLS FUSE AND REPAIR SHORT TO GROUND IN CKT 439 IF BLOWN - IF FUSE IS OK, REPAIR OPEN IN CKT 439 TO TRANSAXLE.

(2)
- DISCONNECT TRANSAXLE HARNESS CONNECTOR.
- CONNECT A TEST LIGHT BETWEEN TERMINALS "E" AND GROUND.
- TEST LIGHT SHOULD BE "ON."
IS IT?

NO → OPEN CKT 439 OR FAULTY CONNECTION AT TRANSAXLE HARNESS CONNECTOR.

YES →
- IGNITION "OFF."
- WITH DVM, CHECK RESISTANCE OF TCC PWM SOLENOID BETWEEN TRANSAXLE CONNECTOR TERMINALS "E" AND "C" AT TRANSAXLE.
- REFER TO TABLE FOR TCC PWM RESISTANCE SPECIFICATION.
IS RESISTANCE OK?

NO → FAULTY INTERNAL TRANSAXLE WIRING OR FAULTY TCC PWM SOLENOID.

YES →
- IGNITION ON.
- WITH TEST LIGHT CONNECTED TO B+, PROBE TERMINAL "C" OF TCC HARNESS.
- LIGHT SHOULD BE "ON."
IS IT? → (3)

(3)
NO → TCC CIRCUITS OK.

YES →
- IGNITION "OFF."
- RECONNECT TCC HARNESS CONNECTOR.
- DISCONNECT PCM CONNECTOR A.
- IGNITION "ON."
- WITH TEST LIGHT CONNECTED TO GROUND, PROBE TERMINAL "A13."
- LIGHT SHOULD BE "ON."
IS IT?

YES → FAULTY PCM CONNECTION OR FAULTY PCM.

NO → OPEN CKT 418 OR FAULTY TERMINAL CONNECTIONS.

86884255

DTC CHART — 3.1L SFI

DTC 86
ANALOG/DIGITAL (A/D) ERROR
3100 (VIN M) "N" CARLINE (SFI)

FOR DTC 86, CHECK FOR ANY DTCs THAT ARE STORED AND REFER TO THOSE CHARTS. IF NO OTHER DTCs ARE STORED, CHECK ALL PCM CONNECTORS AND TERMINALS FOR PROPER LOCATION. DTC 86 WILL SET ONLY WHEN THE CIRCUITS LEADING TO THE A/D MULTIPLEXER, INTERNAL TO THE PCM GETS SHORTED TO B+.

86884254

DTC CHART — 3.1L SFI

DTC 96

TRANS SYSTEM VOLTAGE LOW
3100 (VIN M) "N" CARLINE (SFI)

1. ENGINE OPERATING AT NORMAL TEMPERATURE AND ENGINE SPEED GREATER THAN 1000 RPM.
   NOTE BATTERY VOLTAGE ON SCAN TOOL.

LESS THAN 9 VOLTS

GREATER THAN 9 VOLTS

FAULT IS NOT PRESENT.

2. CHECK BATTERY VOLTAGE AT BATTERY WITH DVM.

GREATER THAN 9 VOLTS

LESS THAN 9 VOLTS

- IGNITION "OFF."
- DISCONNECT PCM CONNECTOR "C".
- WITH DVM, PROBE CKT 639.

LESS THAN 9 VOLTS

GREATER THAN 9 VOLTS

OPEN OR FAULTY CKT 639.

FAULTY PCM CONNECTOR OR FAULTY PCM.

86884256

DTC CHART — 3.1L SFI

DTCs 98, 99

INVALID PCM PROGRAM
3100 (VIN M) "N" CARLINE (SFI)

DTC 98 OR 99 WILL BE STORED WHEN AN INVALID PROGRAM IS DETECTED BY THE PCM.
REFER TO REPROGRAMMING PROCEDURES. IF DTC 98 OR 99 CONTINUES TO BE DISPLAYED
USING A TECH 1, REPLACE PCM.

Important
- THE KNOCK SENSOR (KS) MODULE MUST BE TRANSFERRED TO THE REPLACEMENT PCM.

86884257

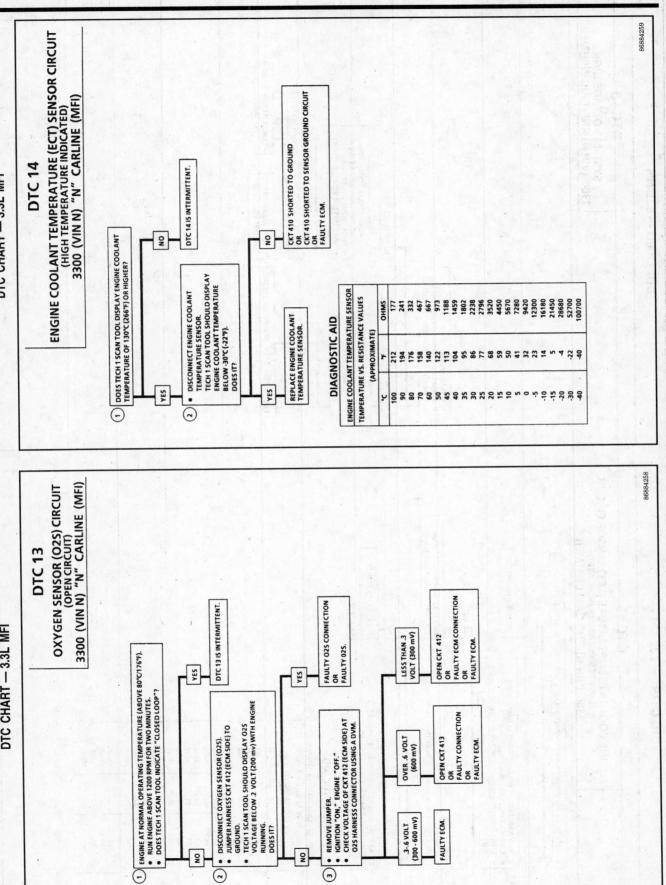

DTC CHART — 3.3L MFI

DTC 14

ENGINE COOLANT TEMPERATURE (ECT) SENSOR CIRCUIT
(HIGH TEMPERATURE INDICATED)
3300 (VIN N) "N" CARLINE (MFI)

1. DOES TECH 1 SCAN TOOL DISPLAY ENGINE COOLANT TEMPERATURE OF 130°C (266°F) OR HIGHER?

   NO → DTC 14 IS INTERMITTENT.

   YES →

2. • DISCONNECT ENGINE COOLANT TEMPERATURE SENSOR.
   TECH 1 SCAN TOOL SHOULD DISPLAY ENGINE COOLANT TEMPERATURE BELOW -30°C (-22°F).
   DOES IT?

   NO → CKT 410 SHORTED TO GROUND
   OR
   CKT 410 SHORTED TO SENSOR GROUND CIRCUIT
   OR
   FAULTY ECM.

   YES → REPLACE ENGINE COOLANT TEMPERATURE SENSOR.

DIAGNOSTIC AID

ENGINE COOLANT TEMPERATURE SENSOR
TEMPERATURE VS. RESISTANCE VALUES
(APPROXIMATE)

°C	°F	OHMS
100	212	177
90	194	241
80	176	332
70	158	467
60	140	667
50	122	973
45	113	1188
40	104	1459
35	95	1802
30	86	2238
25	77	2796
20	68	3520
15	59	4450
10	50	5670
5	41	7280
0	32	9420
-5	23	12300
-10	14	16180
-15	5	21450
-20	-4	28680
-30	-22	52700
-40	-40	100700

86884259

DTC CHART — 3.3L MFI

DTC 13

OXYGEN SENSOR (O2S) CIRCUIT
(OPEN CIRCUIT)
3300 (VIN N) "N" CARLINE (MFI)

1. • ENGINE AT NORMAL OPERATING TEMPERATURE (ABOVE 80°C/176°F).
   • RUN ENGINE ABOVE 1200 RPM FOR TWO MINUTES.
   • DOES TECH 1 SCAN TOOL INDICATE "CLOSED LOOP"?

   YES → DTC 13 IS INTERMITTENT.

   NO →

2. • DISCONNECT OXYGEN SENSOR (O2S).
   • JUMPER HARNESS CKT 412 (ECM SIDE) TO GROUND.
   • TECH 1 SCAN TOOL SHOULD DISPLAY O2S VOLTAGE BELOW .2 VOLT (200 mv) WITH ENGINE RUNNING.
   DOES IT?

   YES → FAULTY O2S CONNECTION
   OR
   FAULTY O2S.

   NO →

3. • REMOVE JUMPER.
   • IGNITION "ON," ENGINE "OFF."
   • CHECK VOLTAGE OF CKT 412 (ECM SIDE) AT O2S HARNESS CONNECTOR USING A DVM.

   LESS THAN .3 VOLT (300 mV) → OPEN CKT 412
   OR
   FAULTY ECM CONNECTION
   OR
   FAULTY ECM.

   OVER .6 VOLT (600 mV) → OPEN CKT 413
   OR
   FAULTY CONNECTION
   OR
   FAULTY ECM.

   .3 - .6 VOLT (300 - 600 mV) → FAULTY ECM.

86884258

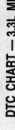

DTC CHART — 3.3L MFI

DTC 16
SYSTEM VOLTAGE HIGH
3300 (VIN N) "N" CARLINE (MFI)

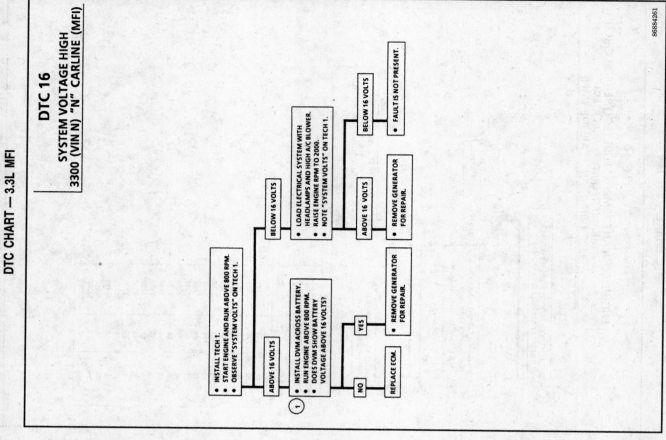

- INSTALL TECH 1.
- START ENGINE AND RUN ABOVE 800 RPM.
- OBSERVE "SYSTEM VOLTS" ON TECH 1.

ABOVE 16 VOLTS

- INSTALL DVM ACROSS BATTERY.
- RUN ENGINE ABOVE 800 RPM.
- DOES DVM SHOW BATTERY VOLTAGE ABOVE 16 VOLTS?

YES → REMOVE GENERATOR FOR REPAIR.

NO → REPLACE ECM.

BELOW 16 VOLTS

- LOAD ELECTRICAL SYSTEM WITH HEADLAMPS AND HIGH A/C BLOWER.
- RAISE ENGINE RPM TO 2000.
- NOTE "SYSTEM VOLTS" ON TECH 1.

ABOVE 16 VOLTS → REMOVE GENERATOR FOR REPAIR.

BELOW 16 VOLTS → FAULT IS NOT PRESENT.

DTC CHART — 3.3L MFI

DTC 15
ENGINE COOLANT TEMPERATURE (ECT) SENSOR CIRCUIT
(LOW TEMPERATURE INDICATED)
3300 (VIN N) "N" CARLINE (MFI)

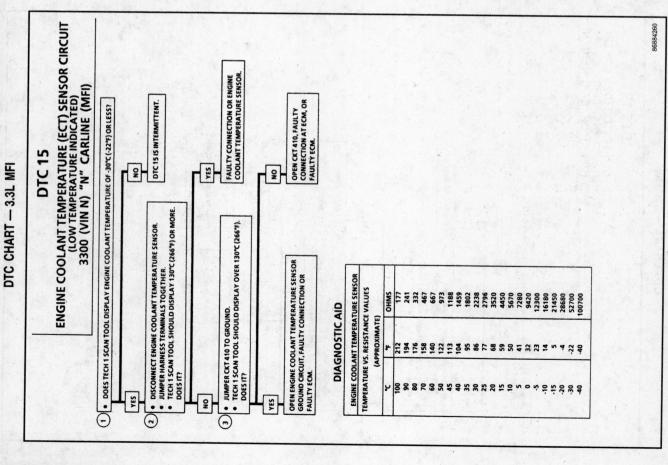

1. DOES TECH 1 SCAN TOOL DISPLAY ENGINE COOLANT TEMPERATURE OF -30°C (-22°F) OR LESS?

NO → DTC 15 IS INTERMITTENT.

YES

2.
- DISCONNECT ENGINE COOLANT TEMPERATURE SENSOR.
- JUMPER HARNESS TERMINALS TOGETHER.
- TECH 1 SCAN TOOL SHOULD DISPLAY 130°C (266°F) OR MORE.

DOES IT?

YES → FAULTY CONNECTION OR ENGINE COOLANT TEMPERATURE SENSOR.

NO

3.
- JUMPER CKT 410 TO GROUND.
- TECH 1 SCAN TOOL SHOULD DISPLAY OVER 130°C (266°F).

DOES IT?

YES → OPEN ENGINE COOLANT TEMPERATURE SENSOR GROUND CIRCUIT, FAULTY CONNECTION OR FAULTY ECM.

NO → OPEN CKT 410, FAULTY CONNECTION AT ECM, OR FAULTY ECM.

DIAGNOSTIC AID

ENGINE COOLANT TEMPERATURE SENSOR
TEMPERATURE VS. RESISTANCE VALUES
(APPROXIMATE)

°C	°F	OHMS
100	212	177
90	194	241
80	176	332
70	158	467
60	140	667
50	122	973
45	113	1188
40	104	1459
35	95	1802
30	86	2238
25	77	2796
20	68	3520
15	59	4450
10	50	5670
5	41	7280
0	32	9420
-5	23	12300
-10	14	16180
-15	5	21450
-20	-4	28680
-30	-22	52700
-40	-40	100700

86884261

86884260

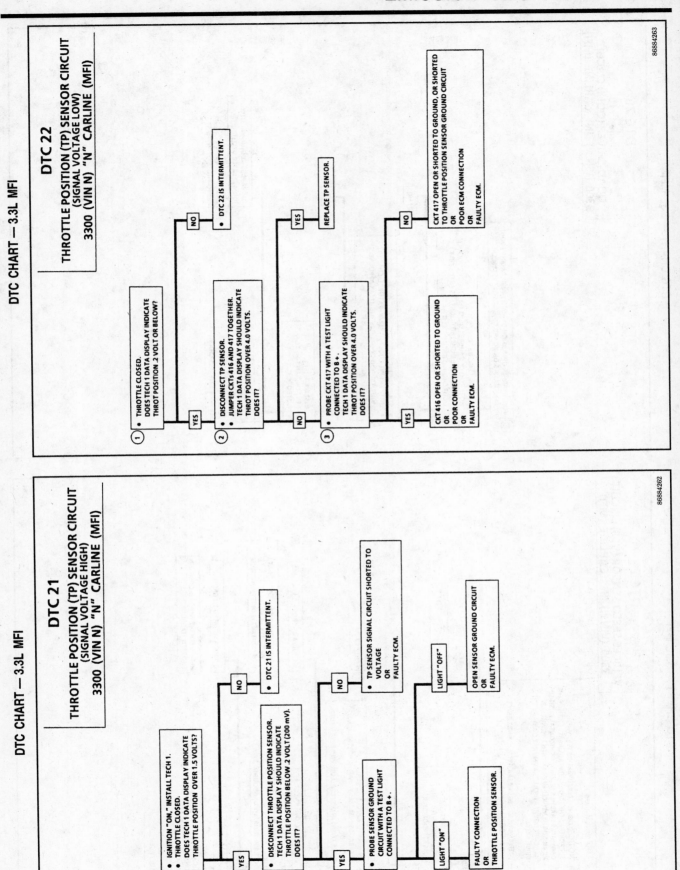

DTC CHART — 3.3L MFI

DTC 22

THROTTLE POSITION (TP) SENSOR CIRCUIT
(SIGNAL VOLTAGE LOW)
3300 (VIN N) "N" CARLINE (MFI)

1. • THROTTLE CLOSED.
   DOES TECH 1 DATA DISPLAY INDICATE
   THROT POSITION .2 VOLT OR BELOW?

   NO → • DTC 22 IS INTERMITTENT.

   YES →

2. • DISCONNECT TP SENSOR.
   JUMPER CKTs 416 AND 417 TOGETHER.
   TECH 1 DATA DISPLAY SHOULD INDICATE
   THROT POSITION OVER 4.0 VOLTS.
   DOES IT?

   YES → REPLACE TP SENSOR.

   NO →

3. • PROBE CKT 417 WITH A TEST LIGHT
   CONNECTED TO B+.
   TECH 1 DATA DISPLAY SHOULD INDICATE
   THROT POSITION OVER 4.0 VOLTS.
   DOES IT?

   NO → CKT 417 OPEN OR SHORTED TO GROUND, OR SHORTED
   TO THROTTLE POSITION SENSOR GROUND CIRCUIT
   OR
   POOR ECM CONNECTION
   OR
   FAULTY ECM.

   YES → CKT 416 OPEN OR SHORTED TO GROUND
   OR
   POOR CONNECTION
   OR
   FAULTY ECM.

86884263

DTC CHART — 3.3L MFI

DTC 21

THROTTLE POSITION (TP) SENSOR CIRCUIT
(SIGNAL VOLTAGE HIGH)
3300 (VIN N) "N" CARLINE (MFI)

1. • IGNITION "ON," INSTALL TECH 1.
   • THROTTLE CLOSED.
   DOES TECH 1 DATA DISPLAY INDICATE
   THROTTLE POSITION OVER 1.5 VOLTS?

   NO → • DTC 21 IS INTERMITTENT.

   YES →

2. • DISCONNECT THROTTLE POSITION SENSOR.
   TECH 1 DATA DISPLAY SHOULD INDICATE
   THROTTLE POSITION BELOW .2 VOLT (200 mV).
   DOES IT?

   NO → TP SENSOR SIGNAL CIRCUIT SHORTED TO
   VOLTAGE
   OR
   FAULTY ECM.

   YES →

3. • PROBE SENSOR GROUND
   CIRCUIT WITH A TEST LIGHT
   CONNECTED TO B+.

   LIGHT "OFF" → OPEN SENSOR GROUND CIRCUIT
   OR
   FAULTY ECM.

   LIGHT "ON" → FAULTY CONNECTION
   OR
   THROTTLE POSITION SENSOR.

86884262

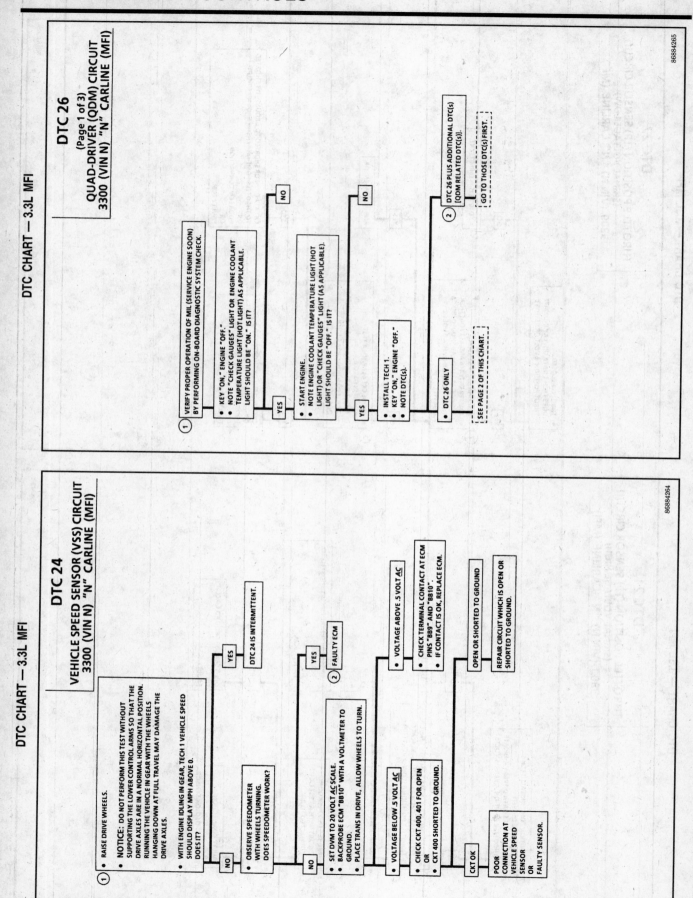

DTC CHART — 3.3L MFI

DTC 26
(Page 1 of 3)
QUAD-DRIVER (QDM) CIRCUIT
3300 (VIN N) "N" CARLINE (MFI)

1. • VERIFY PROPER OPERATION OF MIL (SERVICE ENGINE SOON) BY PERFORMING ON-BOARD DIAGNOSTIC SYSTEM CHECK.

• KEY "ON," ENGINE "OFF."
• NOTE "CHECK GAUGES" LIGHT OR ENGINE COOLANT TEMPERATURE LIGHT (HOT LIGHT) AS APPLICABLE. LIGHT SHOULD BE "ON." IS IT?

YES | NO

• START ENGINE.
• NOTE ENGINE COOLANT TEMPERATURE LIGHT (HOT LIGHT) OR "CHECK GAUGES" LIGHT (AS APPLICABLE). LIGHT SHOULD BE "OFF." IS IT?

YES | NO

• INSTALL TECH 1.
• KEY "ON," ENGINE "OFF."
• NOTE DTC(s).

• DTC 26 ONLY

SEE PAGE 2 OF THIS CHART.

• DTC 26 PLUS ADDITIONAL DTC(s) (QDM RELATED DTC(s)).

2. GO TO THOSE DTC(s) FIRST.

86884265

DTC CHART — 3.3L MFI

DTC 24
VEHICLE SPEED SENSOR (VSS) CIRCUIT
3300 (VIN N) "N" CARLINE (MFI)

1. • RAISE DRIVE WHEELS.
• NOTICE: DO NOT PERFORM THIS TEST WITHOUT SUPPORTING THE LOWER CONTROL ARMS SO THAT THE DRIVE AXLES ARE IN A NORMAL HORIZONTAL POSITION. RUNNING THE VEHICLE IN GEAR WITH THE WHEELS HANGING DOWN AT FULL TRAVEL MAY DAMAGE THE DRIVE AXLES.
• WITH ENGINE IDLING IN GEAR, TECH 1 VEHICLE SPEED SHOULD DISPLAY MPH ABOVE 0. DOES IT?

NO | YES

• OBSERVE SPEEDOMETER WITH WHEELS TURNING. DOES SPEEDOMETER WORK?

DTC 24 IS INTERMITTENT.

NO | YES

FAULTY ECM

• SET DVM TO 20 VOLT AC SCALE.
• BACKPROBE ECM "BB10" WITH A VOLTMETER TO GROUND.
• PLACE TRANS IN DRIVE, ALLOW WHEELS TO TURN.

2.

• VOLTAGE BELOW .5 VOLT AC

• VOLTAGE ABOVE .5 VOLT AC

• CHECK CKT 400, 401 FOR OPEN OR CKT 400 SHORTED TO GROUND.

• CHECK TERMINAL CONTACT AT ECM PINS "BB9" AND "BB10". IF CONTACT IS OK, REPLACE ECM.

CKT OK

OPEN OR SHORTED TO GROUND

POOR CONNECTION AT VEHICLE SPEED SENSOR OR FAULTY SENSOR.

REPAIR CIRCUIT WHICH IS OPEN OR SHORTED TO GROUND.

86884264

DTC CHART — 3.3L MFI

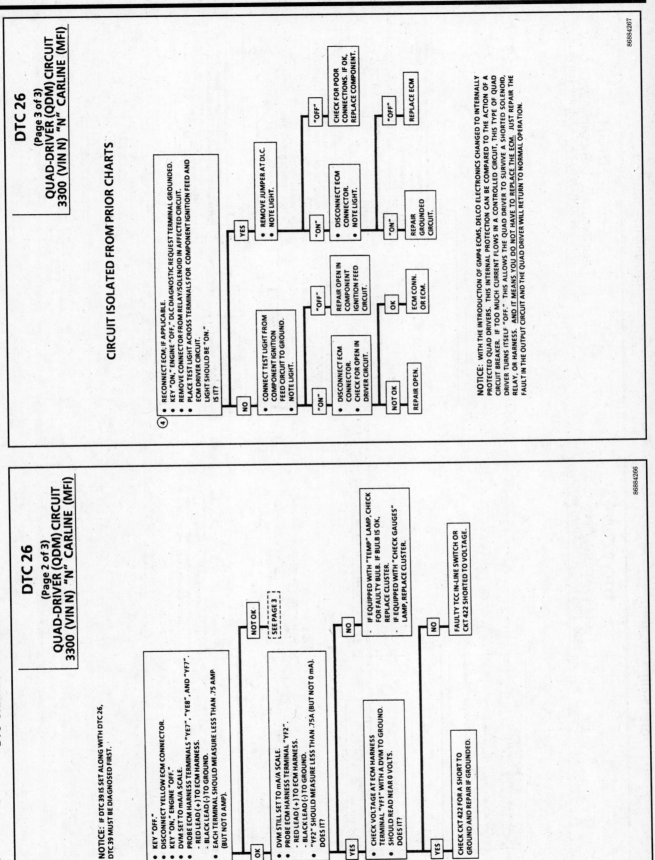

DTC 26
(Page 3 of 3)
QUAD-DRIVER (QDM) CIRCUIT
3300 (VIN N) "N" CARLINE (MFI)

CIRCUIT ISOLATED FROM PRIOR CHARTS

④
- RECONNECT ECM, IF APPLICABLE.
- KEY "ON," ENGINE "OFF," DLC DIAGNOSTIC REQUEST TERMINAL GROUNDED.
- REMOVE CONNECTOR FROM RELAY/SOLENOID IN AFFECTED CIRCUIT.
- PLACE TEST LIGHT ACROSS TERMINALS FOR COMPONENT IGNITION FEED AND ECM DRIVER CIRCUIT.
LIGHT SHOULD BE "ON."
IS IT?

YES

NO

- REMOVE JUMPER AT DLC.
- NOTE LIGHT.

- CONNECT TEST LIGHT FROM COMPONENT IGNITION FEED CIRCUIT TO GROUND.
- NOTE LIGHT.

"ON"

"OFF"

"ON"

"OFF"

- DISCONNECT ECM CONNECTOR.
- NOTE LIGHT.

- DISCONNECT ECM CONNECTOR.
- CHECK FOR OPEN IN DRIVER CIRCUIT.

REPAIR OPEN IN COMPONENT IGNITION FEED CIRCUIT.

CHECK FOR POOR CONNECTIONS. IF OK, REPLACE COMPONENT.

"ON"

"OFF"

NOT OK

OK

REPAIR GROUNDED CIRCUIT.

REPLACE ECM

REPAIR OPEN.

ECM CONN. OR ECM.

NOTICE: WITH THE INTRODUCTION OF GMP4 ECMS, DELCO ELECTRONICS CHANGED TO INTERNALLY PROTECTED QUAD DRIVERS. THIS INTERNAL PROTECTION CAN BE COMPARED TO THE ACTION OF A CIRCUIT BREAKER. IF TOO MUCH CURRENT FLOWS IN A CONTROLLED CIRCUIT, THIS TYPE OF QUAD DRIVER TURNS ITSELF "OFF." THIS ALLOWS THE QUAD DRIVER TO SURVIVE A SHORTED SOLENOID, RELAY, OR HARNESS. AND IT MEANS YOU DO NOT HAVE TO REPLACE THE ECM. JUST REPAIR THE FAULT IN THE OUTPUT CIRCUIT AND THE QUAD DRIVER WILL RETURN TO NORMAL OPERATION.

86884267

DTC CHART — 3.3L MFI

DTC 26
(Page 2 of 3)
QUAD-DRIVER (QDM) CIRCUIT
3300 (VIN N) "N" CARLINE (MFI)

NOTICE: IF DTC 39 IS SET ALONG WITH DTC 26, DTC 39 MUST BE DIAGNOSED FIRST.

③
- KEY "OFF."
- DISCONNECT YELLOW ECM CONNECTOR.
- KEY "ON," ENGINE "OFF."
- DVM SET TO mA/A SCALE.
- PROBE ECM HARNESS TERMINALS "YF7", "YE8", AND "YF7".
  = RED LEAD (+) TO ECM HARNESS.
  = BLACK LEAD (-) TO GROUND.
- EACH TERMINAL SHOULD MEASURE LESS THAN .75 AMP. (BUT NOT 0 AMP).

OK

NOT OK

- DVM STILL SET TO mA/A SCALE.
- PROBE ECM HARNESS TERMINAL "YF2".
  = RED LEAD (+) TO ECM HARNESS.
  = BLACK LEAD (-) TO GROUND.
- "YF2" SHOULD MEASURE LESS THAN .75A (BUT NOT 0 mA).
DOES IT?

SEE PAGE 3

YES

- CHECK VOLTAGE AT ECM HARNESS TERMINAL "YF1" WITH A DVM TO GROUND.
- SHOULD READ NEAR 0 VOLTS.
DOES IT?

NO

- IF EQUIPPED WITH "TEMP" LAMP, CHECK FOR FAULTY BULB. IF BULB IS OK, REPLACE CLUSTER.
- IF EQUIPPED WITH "CHECK GAUGES" LAMP, REPLACE CLUSTER.

YES

NO

CHECK CKT 422 FOR A SHORT TO GROUND AND REPAIR IF GROUNDED.

FAULTY TCC IN-LINE SWITCH OR CKT 422 SHORTED TO VOLTAGE.

86884266

DTC CHART — 3.3L MFI

DTC 31

PARK/NEUTRAL POSITION (PNP) INPUT CIRCUIT
3300 (VIN N) "N" CARLINE (MFI)

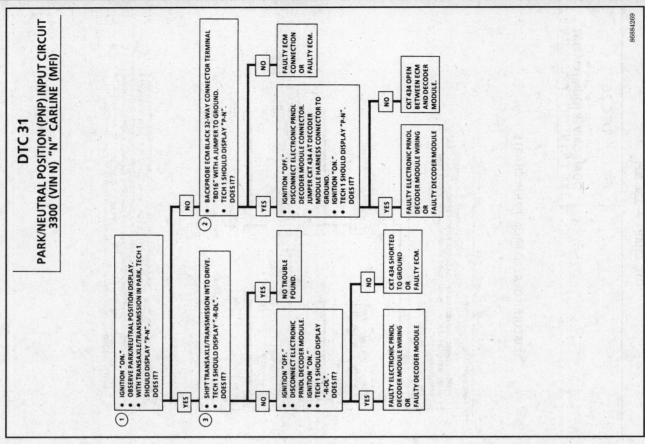

DTC CHART — 3.3L MFI

DTCs 27, 28

GEAR SWITCHES CIRCUITS
3300 (VIN N) "N" CARLINE (MFI)

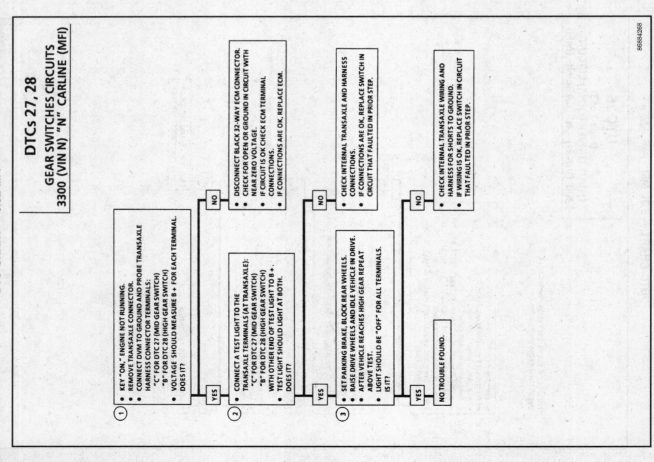

DTC CHART — 3.3L MFI

DTC 38
BRAKE SWITCH CIRCUIT
3300 (VIN N) "N" CARLINE (MFI)

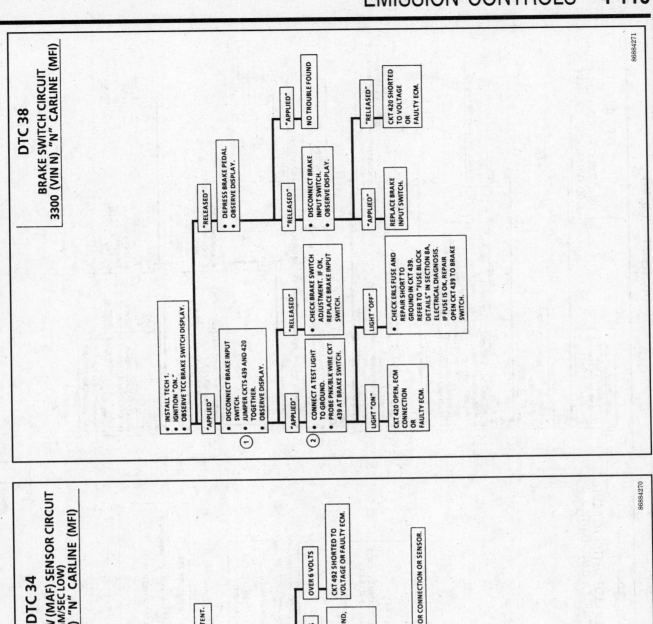

DTC CHART — 3.3L MFI

DTC 34
MASS AIR FLOW (MAF) SENSOR CIRCUIT
(GM/SEC LOW)
3300 (VIN N) "N" CARLINE (MFI)

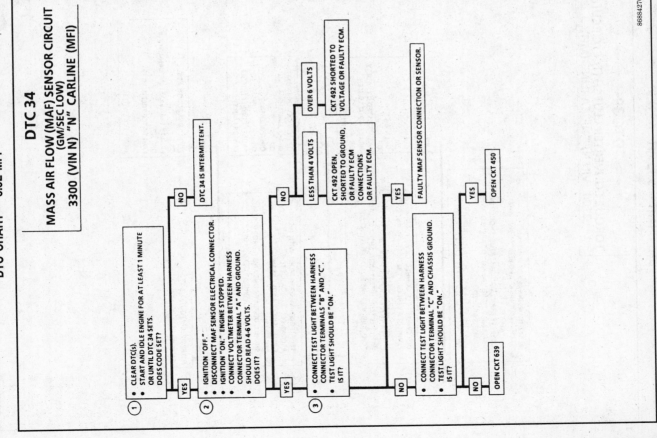

DTC CHART — 3.3L MFI

DTC 42

IGNITION CONTROL (IC) CIRCUIT 3300 (VIN N) "N" CARLINE (MFI)

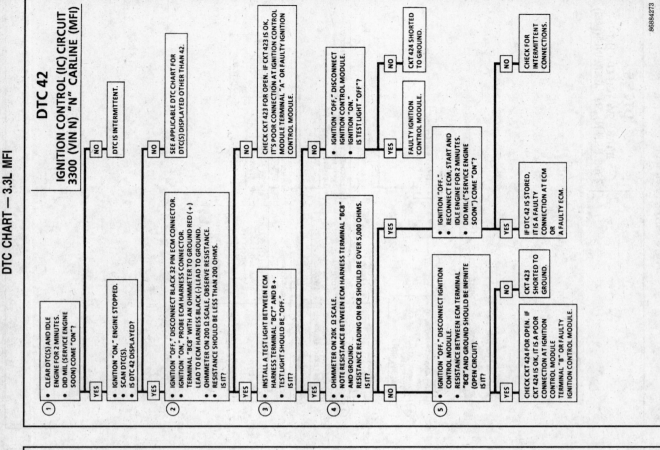

DTC CHART — 3.3L MFI

DTC 39

TORQUE CONVERTER CLUTCH (TCC) CIRCUIT 3300 (VIN N) "N" CARLINE (MFI)

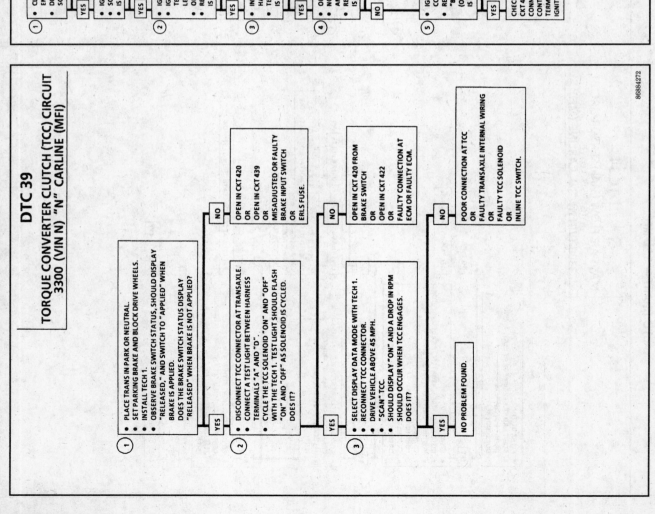

DTC CHART — 3.3L MFI

DTC 44
OXYGEN SENSOR (O2S) CIRCUIT
(LEAN EXHAUST INDICATED)
3300 (VIN N) "N" CARLINE (MFI)

(1)
- RUN WARM ENGINE (75°C/167°F TO 95°C/203°F) AT 1200 RPM.
- DOES TECH 1 DATA DISPLAY INDICATE OXYGEN SENSOR (O2S) VOLTAGE FIXED BELOW .3 VOLT (300 mV)?

NO → DTC 44 IS INTERMITTENT.

YES →
- DISCONNECT OXYGEN SENSOR.
- WITH ENGINE IDLING, TECH 1 DATA DISPLAY SHOULD INDICATE OXYGEN SENSOR VOLTAGE BETWEEN .35 VOLT AND .55 VOLT (350 mV AND 550 mV). DOES IT?

NO → CKT 412 SHORTED TO GROUND OR FAULTY ECM.

YES → (1)

86884275

DTC CHART — 3.3L MFI

DTC 43
KNOCK SENSOR (KS) CIRCUIT
3300 (VIN N) "N" CARLINE (MFI)

(1)
- INSTALL TECH 1.
- ENGINE IDLING, ENGINE COOLANT TEMP ABOVE 67°C.
- DOES TECH 1 INDICATE A FIXED VALUE OF KNOCK RETARD BETWEEN 4 AND 20 DEGREES?

NO → DTC 43 IS INTERMITTENT.

YES →

(2)
- DISCONNECT KNOCK SENSOR.
- IGNITION "ON."
- USING A DVM, MEASURE VOLTAGE BETWEEN HARNESS CKT 496 AND GROUND. VOLTAGE SHOULD BE 4-6 VOLTS. IS IT?

LESS THAN 4 VOLTS → CKT 496 OPEN, SHORTED TO GROUND OR FAULTY ECM.

OVER 6 VOLTS → CHECK FOR CKT 496 BEING ROUTED TOO CLOSE TO SECONDARY IGNITION WIRES OR CKT 496 SHORTED TO VOLTAGE OR FAULTY ECM.

YES →

(3)
- MEASURE RESISTANCE OF KNOCK SENSOR BY CONNECTING OHMMETER BETWEEN SENSOR TERMINAL AND ENGINE BLOCK. SHOULD BE BETWEEN 3.3KΩ & 4.5KΩ. IS IT?

NO → REMOVE KNOCK SENSOR AND ENSURE THAT THREADS ON SENSOR AND BLOCK ARE CLEAN AND FREE OF CORROSION, TEFLON TAPE, ANTI-SEIZE COMPOUNDS, OR SEALANTS. IF OK, REPLACE FAULTY KNOCK SENSOR.

YES →
- CHECK HARNESS AND SENSOR CONNECTOR. IF OK:
- REMOVE ECM AND BE SURE PROM IS PROPERLY SEATED INTO ECM. IF OK:
- REPLACE PROM.

86884274

DTC CHART — 3.3L MFI

DTC 45

OXYGEN SENSOR (O2S) CIRCUIT
(RICH EXHAUST INDICATED)
3300 (VIN N) "N" CARLINE (MFI)

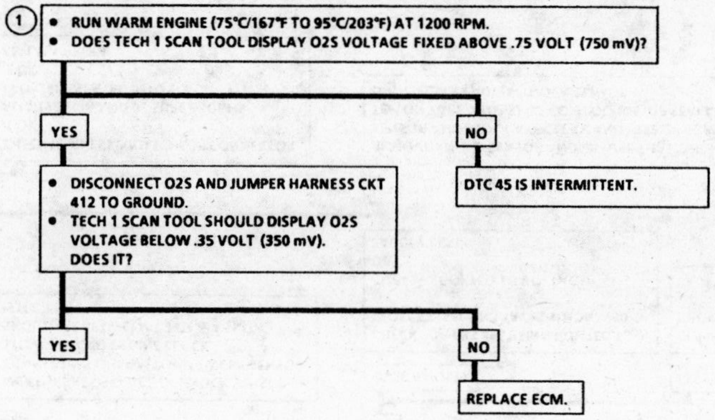

① • RUN WARM ENGINE (75°C/167°F TO 95°C/203°F) AT 1200 RPM.
  • DOES TECH 1 SCAN TOOL DISPLAY O2S VOLTAGE FIXED ABOVE .75 VOLT (750 mV)?

YES

NO — DTC 45 IS INTERMITTENT.

• DISCONNECT O2S AND JUMPER HARNESS CKT 412 TO GROUND.
• TECH 1 SCAN TOOL SHOULD DISPLAY O2S VOLTAGE BELOW .35 VOLT (350 mV).
  DOES IT?

YES

NO — REPLACE ECM.

86884276

DTC CHART — 3.3L MFI

DTC 51

PROM ERROR
(FAULTY OR INCORRECT PROM)
3300 (VIN N) "N" CARLINE (MFI)

CHECK THAT ALL PINS ARE FULLY INSERTED IN THE SOCKET. IF OK, REPLACE PROM, CLEAR MEMORY AND RECHECK. IF DTC 51 REAPPEARS, REPLACE ECM.

NOTICE: To prevent possible Electrostatic Discharge damage to the ECM or PROM, Do Not touch the component leads. Do Not remove integrated circuit from carrier.

86884277

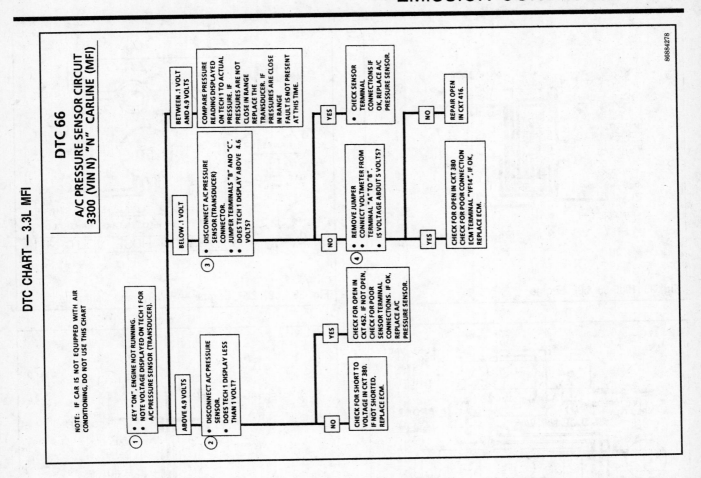

DTC CHART — 3.3L MFI

DTC 66
A/C PRESSURE SENSOR CIRCUIT
3300 (VIN N) "N" CARLINE (MFI)

NOTE: IF CAR IS NOT EQUIPPED WITH AIR CONDITIONING, DO NOT USE THIS CHART

1
- KEY "ON", ENGINE NOT RUNNING.
- NOTE VOLTAGE DISPLAYED ON TECH 1 FOR A/C PRESSURE SENSOR (TRANSDUCER).

ABOVE 4.9 VOLTS

BELOW .1 VOLT

BETWEEN .1 VOLT AND 4.9 VOLTS

2
- DISCONNECT A/C PRESSURE SENSOR.
- DOES TECH 1 DISPLAY LESS THAN 1 VOLT?

3
- DISCONNECT A/C PRESSURE SENSOR (TRANSDUCER) CONNECTOR.
- JUMPER TERMINALS "B" AND "C".
- DOES TECH 1 DISPLAY ABOVE 4.6 VOLTS?

COMPARE PRESSURE READING DISPLAYED ON TECH 1 TO ACTUAL PRESSURE. IF PRESSURES ARE NOT CLOSE IN RANGE REPLACE THE TRANSDUCER. IF PRESSURES ARE CLOSE IN RANGE FAULT IS NOT PRESENT AT THIS TIME.

NO

YES

NO

YES

CHECK FOR SHORT TO VOLTAGE IN CKT 380. IF NOT SHORTED, REPLACE ECM.

CHECK FOR OPEN IN CKT 452. IF NOT OPEN, CHECK FOR POOR SENSOR TERMINAL CONNECTIONS. IF OK, REPLACE A/C PRESSURE SENSOR.

4
- REMOVE JUMPER
- CONNECT VOLTMETER FROM TERMINAL "A" TO "B".
- IS VOLTAGE ABOUT 5 VOLTS?

CHECK SENSOR TERMINAL CONNECTIONS IF OK, REPLACE A/C PRESSURE SENSOR.

YES

NO

CHECK FOR OPEN IN CKT 380 CHECK FOR POOR CONNECTION AT ECM TERMINAL "YF14", IF OK, REPLACE ECM.

REPAIR OPEN IN CKT 416.

VACUUM DIAGRAMS

Following is a listing of vacuum diagrams for most of the engine and emissions package combinations covered by this manual. Because vacuum circuits will vary based on various engine and vehicle options, always refer first to the vehicle emission control information label. Should the label be missing, or should the vehicle be equipped with a different engine from the original equipment, refer to the diagrams below for the same or similar configuration.

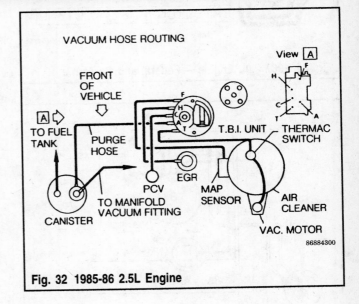

Fig. 32 1985-86 2.5L Engine

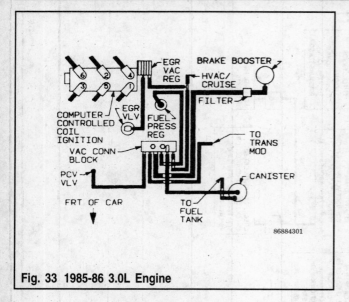

Fig. 33 1985-86 3.0L Engine

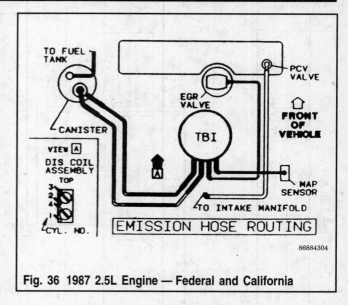

Fig. 36 1987 2.5L Engine — Federal and California

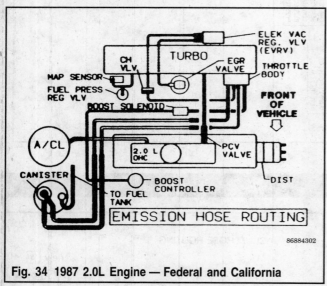

Fig. 34 1987 2.0L Engine — Federal and California

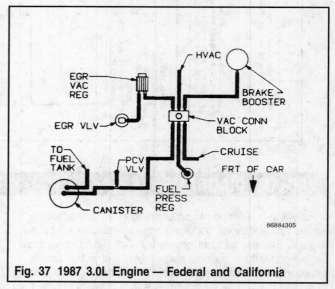

Fig. 37 1987 3.0L Engine — Federal and California

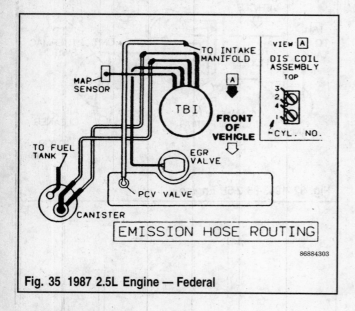

Fig. 35 1987 2.5L Engine — Federal

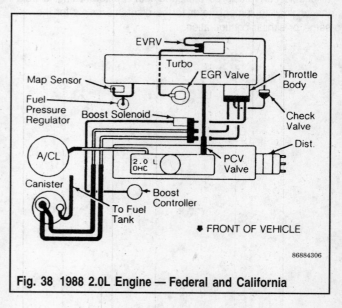

Fig. 38 1988 2.0L Engine — Federal and California

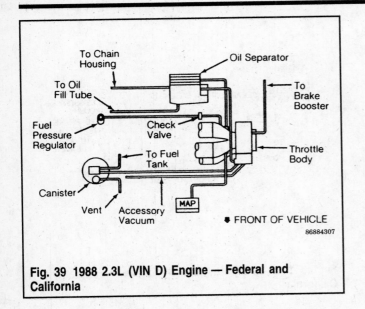

Fig. 39 1988 2.3L (VIN D) Engine — Federal and California

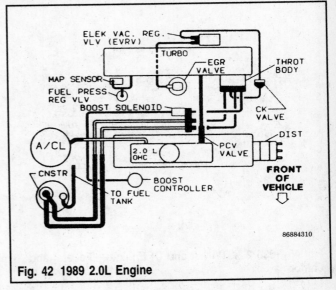

Fig. 42 1989 2.0L Engine

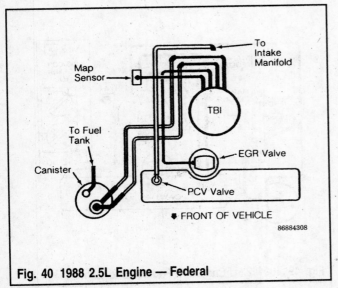

Fig. 40 1988 2.5L Engine — Federal

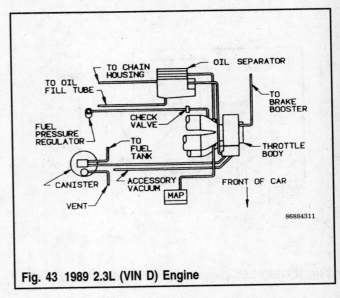

Fig. 43 1989 2.3L (VIN D) Engine

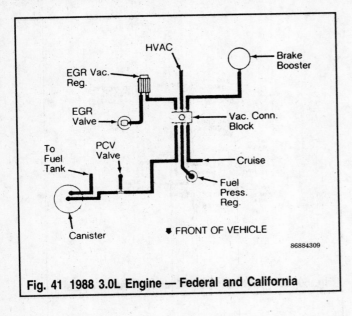

Fig. 41 1988 3.0L Engine — Federal and California

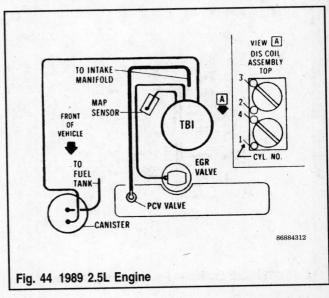

Fig. 44 1989 2.5L Engine

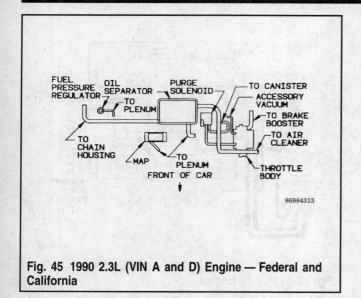

Fig. 45 1990 2.3L (VIN A and D) Engine — Federal and California

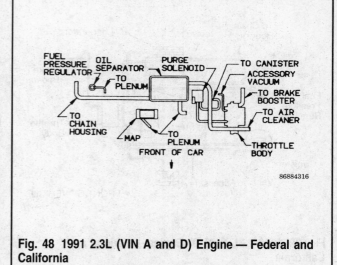

Fig. 48 1991 2.3L (VIN A and D) Engine — Federal and California

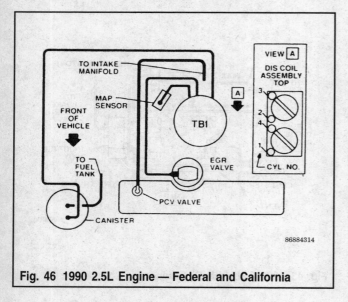

Fig. 46 1990 2.5L Engine — Federal and California

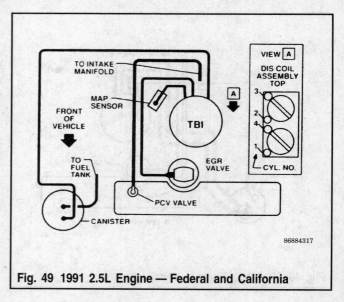

Fig. 49 1991 2.5L Engine — Federal and California

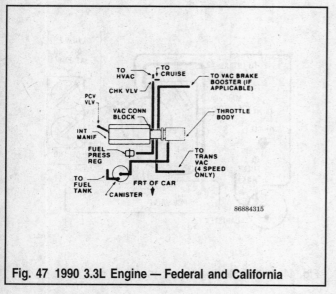

Fig. 47 1990 3.3L Engine — Federal and California

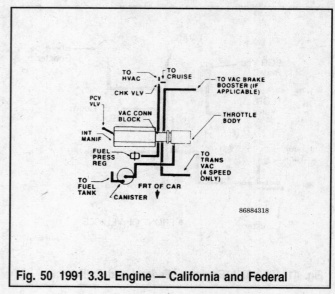

Fig. 50 1991 3.3L Engine — California and Federal

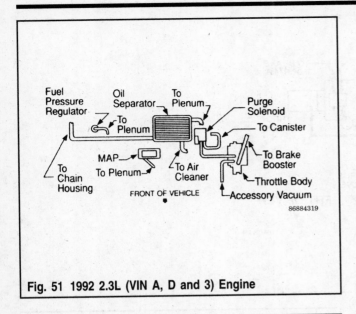

Fig. 51 1992 2.3L (VIN A, D and 3) Engine

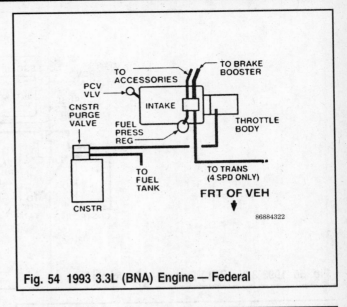

Fig. 54 1993 3.3L (BNA) Engine — Federal

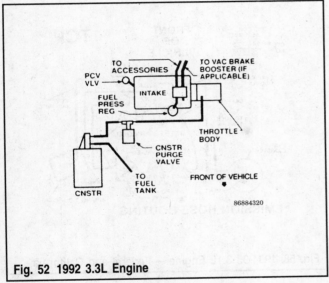

Fig. 52 1992 3.3L Engine

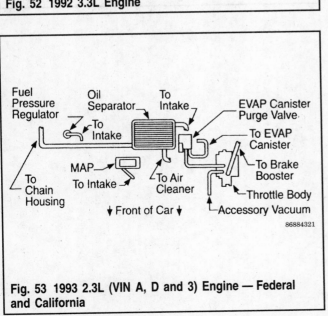

Fig. 53 1993 2.3L (VIN A, D and 3) Engine — Federal and California

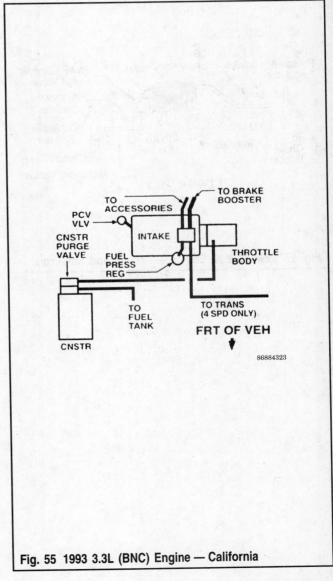

Fig. 55 1993 3.3L (BNC) Engine — California

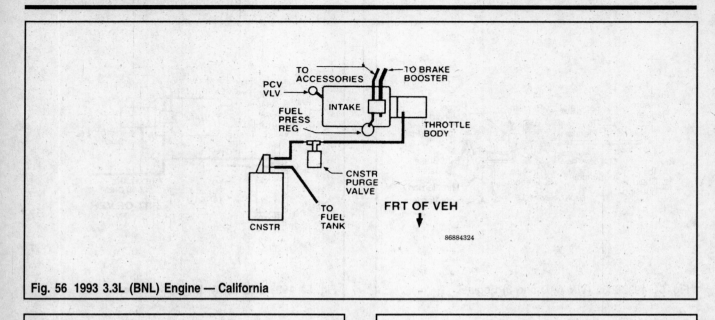

Fig. 56 1993 3.3L (BNL) Engine — California

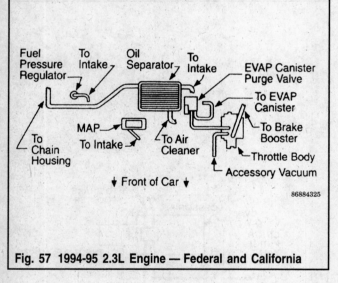

Fig. 57 1994-95 2.3L Engine — Federal and California

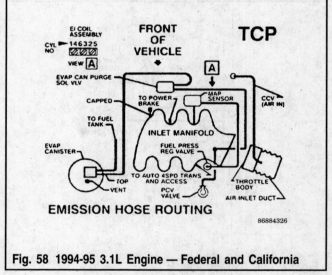

Fig. 58 1994-95 3.1L Engine — Federal and California

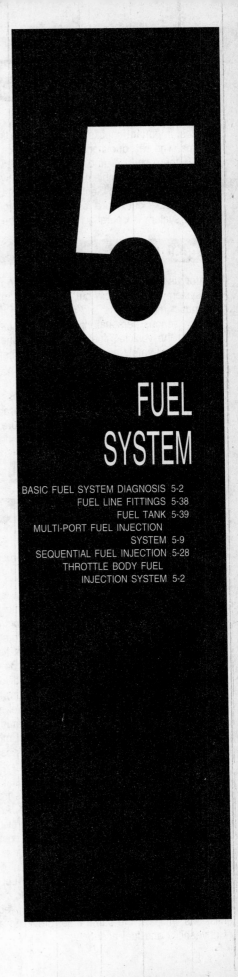

BASIC FUEL SYSTEM DIAGNOSIS
PRECAUTIONS 5-2
FUEL LINE FITTINGS
QUICK-CONNECT FITTINGS 5-38
FUEL TANK
TANK ASSEMBLY 5-39
**MULTI-PORT FUEL INJECTION
SYSTEM**
ELECTRIC FUEL PUMP 5-13
FUEL INJECTORS 5-22
FUEL PRESSURE REGULATOR 5-23
FUEL PUMP RELAY 5-26
FUEL RAIL ASSEMBLY 5-18
IDLE AIR CONTROL (IAC)
VALVE 5-25
RELIEVING FUEL SYSTEM
PRESSURE 5-12
SYSTEM DESCRIPTION 5-9
THROTTLE BODY 5-15
THROTTLE POSITION (TP)
SENSOR 5-24
SEQUENTIAL FUEL INJECTION
ELECTRIC FUEL PUMP 5-31
FUEL INJECTORS 5-33
FUEL PRESSURE REGULATOR 5-36
FUEL PUMP RELAY 5-38
FUEL RAIL ASSEMBLY 5-35
IDLE AIR CONTROL (IAC)
VALVE 5-37
INTAKE MANIFOLD PLENUM 5-33
RELIEVING FUEL SYSTEM
PRESSURE 5-31
SYSTEM DESCRIPTION 5-28
THROTTLE BODY 5-33
THROTTLE POSITION (TP)
SENSOR 5-37
**THROTTLE BODY FUEL INJECTION
SYSTEM**
ELECTRIC FUEL PUMP 5-4
FUEL METER BODY 5-6
FUEL PRESSURE REGULATOR 5-7
FUEL PUMP RELAY 5-8
IDLE AIR CONTROL (IAC) VALVE 5-8
RELIEVING FUEL SYSTEM
PRESSURE 5-4
SYSTEM DESCRIPTION 5-2
THROTTLE BODY 5-5
THROTTLE POSITION (TP)
SENSOR 5-7
TUBE MODULE 5-8

5

FUEL
SYSTEM

BASIC FUEL SYSTEM DIAGNOSIS 5-2
FUEL LINE FITTINGS 5-38
FUEL TANK 5-39
MULTI-PORT FUEL INJECTION
SYSTEM 5-9
SEQUENTIAL FUEL INJECTION 5-28
THROTTLE BODY FUEL
INJECTION SYSTEM 5-2

BASIC FUEL SYSTEM DIAGNOSIS

When there is a problem starting or driving a vehicle, two of the most important checks involve the ignition and the fuel systems. The two questions that mechanics attempt to answer first, "is there spark?" and "is there fuel?" will often lead to solving most basic problems. For ignition system diagnosis and testing, please refer to Section 2 of this manual. If the ignition system checks out (there is spark), then you must determine if the fuel system is operating properly (is there fuel?).

Precautions

Safety is the most important factor when performing not only fuel system maintenance, but any type of maintenance. Failure to conduct maintenance and repairs in a safe manner may result in serious personal injury or death. Maintenance and testing of the vehicle's fuel system components can be accomplished safely and effectively by adhering to the following rules and guidelines:

• To avoid the possibility of fire and personal injury, always disconnect the negative battery cable unless the repair or test procedure requires that battery voltage be applied.

• Always relieve the fuel system pressure prior to disconnecting any fuel system component (injector, fuel rail, pressure regulator, etc.), fitting or fuel line connection. Exercise extreme caution whenever relieving fuel system pressure to avoid exposing skin, face and eyes to fuel spray. Please be advised that fuel under pressure may penetrate the skin or any part of the body that it contacts.

• Always place a shop towel or cloth around the fitting or connection prior to loosening to absorb any excess fuel due to spillage. Ensure that all fuel spillage (should it occur) is quickly removed from engine surfaces. Ensure that all fuel soaked cloths or towels are deposited into a suitable waste container.

• Always keep a dry chemical (Class B) fire extinguisher near the work area.

• Do not allow fuel spray or fuel vapors to come into contact with a spark or open flame.

• Always use a backup wrench when loosening and tightening fuel line connection fittings. This will prevent unnecessary stress and torsion to fuel line piping. Always follow the proper torque specifications.

• Always replace worn fuel fitting O-rings with new ones. Do not substitute fuel hose or equivalent where fuel pipe is installed.

• Due to the possibility of a fire or explosion, never drain or store gasoline in an open container.

THROTTLE BODY FUEL INJECTION SYSTEM

System Description

▶ See Figure 1

➡Throttle body fuel injection is found on vehicles equipped with a 2.5L engine.

The Throttle Body Injection (TBI) system is an electronic fuel metering system in which the amount of fuel delivered by the injector is determined by the Electronic Control Module (ECM). This small, on-board microcomputer monitors various engine and vehicle conditions to calculate the fuel delivery time (pulse width) of the injector. The fuel pulse may be modified by the ECM to account for special operating conditions, such as cranking, cold starting, altitude, acceleration, and deceleration.

The TBI system provides a means of fuel distribution for controlling exhaust emissions within legislated limits. The TBI system, by precisely controlling the air/fuel mixture under all operating conditions, provides as near as possible complete combustion.

In order to regulate the fuel delivery in such an efficient manner, the ECM receives electrical inputs from various sensors about engine operating conditions. An oxygen sensor in the main exhaust stream functions to provide feedback information to the ECM regarding oxygen content in the exhaust. The ECM uses this information from the oxygen sensor, and other sensors, in modifying fuel delivery to achieve, as near as possible, an ideal air/fuel ratio of 14.7:1. This air/fuel ratio allows the 3-way catalytic converter to be more efficient in the conversion process of reducing exhaust emissions while, at the same time, providing acceptable levels of driveability and fuel economy.

The basic TBI model 700 is made up of 2 major casting assemblies: (1) a throttle body with a valve to control airflow and (2) a fuel body assembly with an integral pressure regulator and fuel injector to supply the required fuel. A device to control idle speed (IAC) and a device to provide information about throttle valve position (TPS) are included as part of the TBI unit.

OPERATING MODES

The computer control module uses voltage input from various sensors to determine how much fuel to give the engine. The fuel is delivered under one of several conditions, called modes. All modes are controlled by the computer control module.

Starting Mode

When the key is first turned **ON**, before the starter is engaged, the ECM turns the fuel pump relay on for two seconds, and the fuel pump builds up fuel pressure at the TBI unit. The ECM then monitors the coolant temperature, throttle position, manifold pressure, and ignition signal to determine the proper air/fuel ratio for starting. This ranges from 1.5:1 at -33°F (-36°C) to 14.7:1 at 201°F (94°C).

Clear Flood Mode

If the engine floods, it can be cleared by pressing the accelerator pedal all the way to the floor. The ECM then pulses the injector for an air/fuel ratio of approximately 20:1. The ECM maintains this injector rate as long as the throttle stays wide

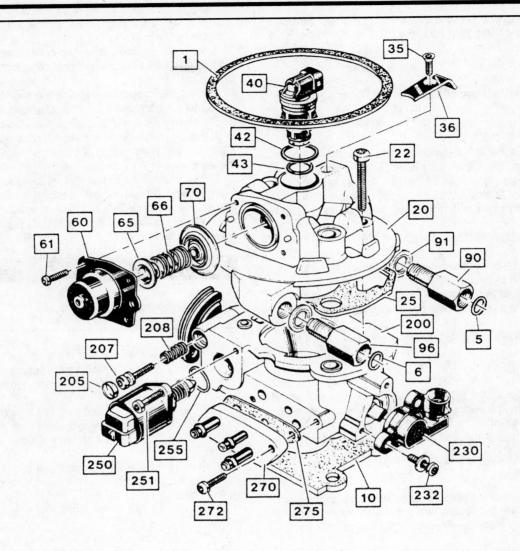

Part Names

1	Gasket - Air Cleaner
5	O-ring - Fuel Line Inlet Nut
6	O-ring - Fuel Line Outlet Nut
10	Gasket - Flange
20	Fuel Meter Body Assembly
22	Screw - Fuel Meter Body - Throttle Body Attaching
25	Gasket - Fuel Meter Body to Throttle Body
35	Screw - Injector Retainer Attaching
36	Retainer - Injector
40	TBI Injector Assembly
42	O-ring - Fuel Injector - Upper
43	O-ring - Fuel Injector - Lower
60	Pressure Regulator Cover Assembly
61	Screw - Pressure Regulator Attaching
65	Seat - Pressure Regulator Spring
66	Spring - Pressure Regulator

70	Pressure Regulator Diaphragm Assembly
90	Fitting - Fuel Inlet
91	Seal - Fuel Fitting
96	Fitting - Fuel Outlet
200	Throttle Body Assembly
205	Plug - Idle Stop Screw
207	Idle Stop Screw Assembly
208	Spring - Idle Stop Screw
230	Sensor - Throttle Position (TPS)
232	Screw Assembly - TPS Attaching
250	Idle Air Control (IAC) Valve Assembly
251	Screw - IAC Valve Attaching
255	O-ring - IAC Valve
270	Tube Module Assembly
272	Screw - Tube Module Assembly Attaching
275	Gasket - Tube Module Assembly

86885002

Fig. 1 Exploded view of the throttle body assembly and related components of the 2.5L engine

open and the engine speed is below 600 rpm. If the throttle position becomes less than 80%, the ECM returns to the Starting Mode.

Run Mode

The run mode has two conditions called "Open Loop" and "Closed Loop".

OPEN LOOP

When the engine is first started and the engine speed is above 400 rpm, the system is in "Open Loop" operation. The ECM ignores the signal from the oxygen sensor, because it is not warmed up, and calculates the air/fuel ratio based on inputs from coolant temperature and manifold absolute pressure sensors.

The system stays in "Open Loop" until the following conditions are met:

1. The O_2 sensor has varying voltage output, showing that it is hot enough to operate properly.
2. The coolant temperature is above a specified value.
3. A specific amount of time has elapsed after starting the engine.

When the values are met, the engine enters "Closed Loop" operation.

CLOSED LOOP

In "Closed Loop", the ECM continues to calculate the air/fuel ratio required by the engine, but trims the actual amount of fuel delivered according to the signal from the O_2 sensor. A 14.7:1 air/fuel ratio is required for efficient catalytic converter operation.

Acceleration Mode

When the ECM senses rapid changes in throttle position and manifold pressure, the system enters the acceleration model and provides the extra fuel needed for smooth acceleration.

Fuel Cutoff Mode

To prevent possible engine damage from overspeed, the ECM "cuts off" fuel from the injector at approximately 5700 rpm. Fuel "cutoff" remains in effect until engine speed drops below 5600 rpm. A false high rpm indication could activate this mode and cause the vehicle to surge or hesitate at road speeds. Also refer to "Deceleration Mode" for very fast deceleration.

Deceleration Mode

When deceleration occurs, the fuel remaining in the intake manifold can cause excessive emissions and backfiring. When the ECM observes a fast reduction in throttle opening and a sharp decrease in manifold pressure, it causes the system to enter the deceleration mode, reducing the amount of fuel delivered to the engine. When deceleration is very fast, the ECM cuts off fuel completely for short periods.

Relieving Fuel System Pressure

1. Loosen the fuel filler cap to relieve fuel tank vapor pressure.

2. For vehicles through 1990, remove the fuel pump fuse from the fuse panel.

3. For 1991 vehicles, raise and safely support the vehicle, then detach the fuel pump electrical connector. Carefully lower the vehicle.

4. Start the engine and run until the engine stalls. Engage the starter an additional 3 seconds to assure complete relief.

5. For vehicles through 1990, reinstall the fuel pump fuse.

6. For 1991 vehicles, raise and safely support the vehicle, attach the fuel pump electrical connector, then carefully lower the vehicle.

7. Disconnect the negative battery cable to avoid possible fuel discharge if an accidental attempt is made to start the engine, then continue with fuel system work.

8. When your finished the fuel system work, don't forget to tighten the fuel filler cap.

Electric Fuel Pump

REMOVAL & INSTALLATION

▶ **See Figure 2**

1. Properly relieve the fuel system pressure.

2. If not done already, disconnect the negative battery cable.

3. Raise and safely support the vehicle with jackstands.

4. Safely drain, then remove the fuel tank assembly as outlined in the "Fuel Tank" removal procedure located in this section.

5. Remove the fuel tank sending unit and pump assembly by turning the fuel pump cam lock ring counterclockwise, then lift the assembly out of the tank.

6. Remove the fuel pump from the level sensor unit as follows:

   a. Pull the pump up into the attaching hose or pulsator while pulling outward away from the bottom support.

   b. Take care to prevent damage to the rubber insulator and strainer during removal.

   c. When the pump assembly is clear of the bottom support, pull the pump out of the rubber connector for removal.

To install:

7. Replace any attaching hoses or rubber sound insulator that show signs of deterioration.

8. Push the fuel pump into the attaching hoses and install the pump/sensor assembly into the tank. Always use a new O-ring seal.

9. Be careful not to fold over or twist the strainer when installing the sensor unit. Also, make sure the strainer does not block full travel of the float arm.

10. Position the cam lock and turn clockwise to lock.

11. Install the fuel tank as outlined in this Section.

12. Fill the tank with gas and check for fuel leaks.

13. Connect the negative battery cable.

FUEL PRESSURE TESTING

1. Relieve the fuel pressure from the fuel system.

2. Turn the ignition **OFF**.

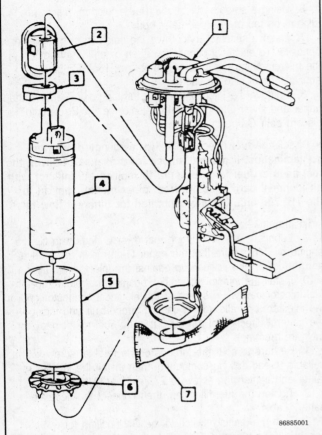

1. FUEL TANK METER ASSY.
2. PULSATOR
3. BUMPER
4. FUEL PUMP
5. SOUND ISOLATOR SLEEVE
6. SOUND INSULATOR
7. FILTER

86885001

Fig. 2 Exploded view of the TBI system fuel pump and related components

3. Uncouple the fuel supply flexible hose in the engine compartment and install fuel pressure gauge J29658/BT8205 or equivalent in the pressure line.

4. Be sure to tighten the fuel line to the gauge to ensure that there are no leaks during testing.

5. Start the engine and observe the fuel pressure reading. The fuel pressure should be 9-13 psi (62-90 kPa).

6. Relieve the fuel pressure. Remove the fuel pressure gauge and reinstall the fuel line. Be sure to install a new O-ring on the fuel feed line.

7. Start the engine, then check for fuel leaks.

Throttle Body

REMOVAL & INSTALLATION

▶ See Figure 3

➡This procedure covers removal and installation of the entire throttle body assembly, including the fuel meter body. If you only need to remove the fuel meter body, refer to the following procedure.

1. Relieve the fuel system pressure.
2. Disconnect the negative battery cable.
3. Raise the hood, install fender covers and remove the air cleaner assembly.
4. Tag and detach the electrical connectors for the idle speed control motor/idle air control valve, the throttle position sensor, fuel injectors and any other component necessary in order to remove the throttle body.
5. Unfasten the grommet with the wires from the throttle body.
6. Remove the throttle return spring, cruise control, throttle linkage and downshift cable.
7. Tag and disconnect all necessary vacuum lines, the fuel inlet line, fuel return line, brake booster line, MAP sensor hose and the AIR hose. Be sure to use a back-up wrench on all metal lines. Remove and discard the fuel line O-rings.
8. Remove the PCV, EVAP and/or EGR hoses from the front of the throttle body.
9. Unfasten the throttle body mounting screws/bolts, then remove the throttle body and flange gasket. Discard the gasket.

To install:

10. The installation is the reverse order of the removal procedure.
11. Tighten the throttle body retaining screws to 18 ft. lbs. (24 Nm) and fuel lines to 20 ft. lbs. (27 Nm). Always use new gaskets and O-rings.
12. Make certain cruise and shift cables do not hold the throttle above the idle stop. Reset the IAC by depressing the

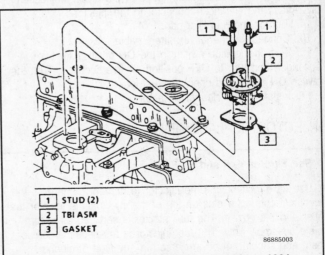

1. STUD (2)
2. TBI ASM
3. GASKET

86885003

Fig. 3 Removing the throttle body assembly — 1991 2.5L engine shown

accelerator slightly, run engine for 3-4 seconds and turn ignition **OFF** for 10 seconds.

Fuel Meter Body

REMOVAL & INSTALLATION

▶ See Figure 1

1. Relieve the fuel system pressure.
2. Raise the hood, install fender covers and remove the air cleaner assembly.
3. If not done already, disconnect the negative battery cable.
4. Detach the electrical connector from the injector. Remove the grommet with wires from the fuel meter assembly.
5. Remove the fuel inlet and outlet lines and O-rings. Be sure to use a back-up wrench to keep the TBI nuts from turning. Be sure to discard the old O-rings.
6. Unfasten the TBI mounting hardware and the 2 fuel meter body attaching screws.
7. Remove the fuel meter assembly from the throttle body, then remove the fuel meter-to-throttle body gasket, and discard the gasket.
   To install:
8. Install the new throttle body to fuel meter body gasket. Match the cut portions in the gasket with the opening in the throttle body.
9. Install the fuel meter body assembly onto the throttle body assembly.
10. Install the fuel meter body to the throttle body attaching screw assemblies, pre-coated with a suitable thread sealer.
11. Tighten the screw assemblies to 53 inch lbs. (6 Nm). Install the fuel inlet and outlet nuts with new gaskets to the fuel meter body assembly. Tighten the inlet and outlet nut to 20 ft. lbs. (27 Nm).
12. Install the fuel inlet and return lines and new O-rings. Be sure to use a back-up wrench to keep the TBI nuts from turning.
13. Install the grommet with wires to the fuel meter assembly. Attach the electrical connector to the injector.
14. Tighten the fuel filler cap.
15. Connect the negative battery cable.
16. Turn the ignition switch to the **ON** position for two seconds, then turn to **OFF** position for five seconds. Turn the switch **ON** again and check for fuel leaks.
17. Install the air cleaner assembly.

INJECTOR REPLACEMENT

▶ See Figures 4, 5 and 6

Use care in removing the injector to prevent damage to the electrical connector pins on top of the injector, the injector fuel filter and the nozzle. The fuel injector is serviced as a complete assembly only. The fuel injector is an electrical component and should not be immersed in any type of cleaner.

1. Relieve the fuel system pressure.

2. Raise the hood, install fender covers, then remove the air cleaner assembly.
3. If not done already, disconnect the negative battery cable.
4. Detach the electrical connector to the injector by squeezing on tow tabs, then pulling straight up.
5. Remove the injector retainer screw and retainer.
6. Using a smooth object, such as a fulcrum, place the fulcrum on top of the fuel meter body.
7. Insert a suitable prytool into the small lip of the injector opposite the electrical connection, then carefully pry against the fulcrum lifting the injector straight up. Tool J-26868 or equivalent can also be used.
8. Remove the injector from the throttle body. Remove the upper and lower O-ring from the injector cavity. Be sure to discard both O-rings.

➡ **Check the fuel injector filter for evidence of dirt and contamination. If present, check for presence of dirt in the fuel lines or fuel tank. Be sure to replace the injector with an identical part. Injectors from other models may fit in the TBI 700 unit, but are calibrated for different flow rates.**

To install:
9. Lubricate the new upper and lower O-rings with clean engine oil. Make sure that the upper O-ring is in the groove and the lower one is flush up against the injector fuel filter.
10. Install the injector assembly, pushing it straight into the fuel injector cavity. Be sure that the electrical connector end of the injector is parallel to the casting support rib and facing in the general direction of the cut-out in the fuel meter body for the wire grommet.
11. Be sure to coat the threads of the retainer screw with a suitable thread locking compound, then install the injector retainer and tighten the screw to 27 inch lbs. (3 Nm).
12. Tighten the fuel filler cap, then connect the negative battery cable.
13. Turn the ignition switch to the **ON** position for two seconds, then turn to **OFF** position for five seconds. Turn the switch **ON** again, then check for fuel leaks.
14. Install the air cleaner assembly.

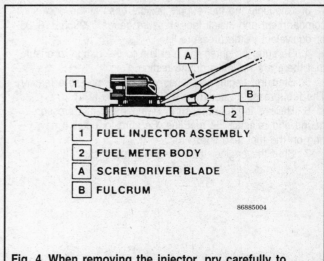

1	FUEL INJECTOR ASSEMBLY
2	FUEL METER BODY
A	SCREWDRIVER BLADE
B	FULCRUM

86885004

Fig. 4 When removing the injector, pry carefully to avoid damage

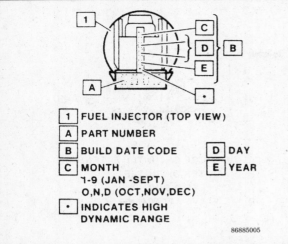

1	FUEL INJECTOR (TOP VIEW)
A	PART NUMBER
B	BUILD DATE CODE	D	DAY
C	MONTH	E	YEAR
	1-9 (JAN.-SEPT)		
	O,N,D (OCT,NOV,DEC)		
·	INDICATES HIGH DYNAMIC RANGE

86885005

Fig. 5 Check the part number on the injector to make sure you are replacing it with an identical part

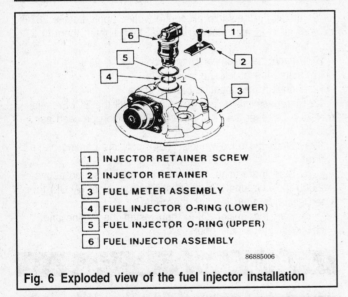

1	INJECTOR RETAINER SCREW
2	INJECTOR RETAINER
3	FUEL METER ASSEMBLY
4	FUEL INJECTOR O-RING (LOWER)
5	FUEL INJECTOR O-RING (UPPER)
6	FUEL INJECTOR ASSEMBLY

86885006

Fig. 6 Exploded view of the fuel injector installation

Fuel Pressure Regulator

REMOVAL & INSTALLATION

♦ See Figure 7

➡To prevent leaks, the pressure regulator diaphragm assembly must be replaced whenever the cover is removed.

1. Properly relieve the fuel system pressure as outlined earlier in this section.
2. Raise the hood, install fender covers and remove the air cleaner assembly. Disconnect the negative battery cable.

➡The pressure regulator contains a large spring under heavy compression. Use care when removing the screws to prevent personal injury.

3. While keeping the pressure regulator cover compressed, unfasten the 4 pressure regulator retaining screws.

4. Remove the pressure regulator cover assembly, then remove the spring, spring seat and diaphragm assembly. Discard the diaphragm assembly.

5. Check the pressure regulator seat in the fuel meter body cavity for pitting, nicks or irregularities. Use a magnifying glass if necessary. If any of the above is present, the whole fuel body casting must be replaced.

To install:

6. Install the new pressure regulator diaphragm assembly, making sure it is seated in the groove in the fuel meter body.

7. Install the regulator spring seat and spring into the cover assembly.

8. Install the cover assembly over the diaphragm, while aligning the mounting holes. Be sure to use care while installing the pressure regulator to prevent misalignment of the diaphragm and possible leaks.

9. Coat the regulator retaining screws with Loctite 262® or equivalent suitable thread sealer, then install the screws and tighten 22 inch lbs. (2.5 Nm).

10. Tighten the fuel filler cap, then connect the negative battery cable.

11. Turn the ignition switch to the **ON** position for two seconds, then turn to **OFF** position for five seconds. Turn the switch **ON** again and check for fuel leaks.

12. Install the air cleaner assembly.

Throttle Position (TP) Sensor

REMOVAL & INSTALLATION

The TP sensor is not adjustable and is not supplied with attaching screw retainers. Since these TPS configurations can be mounted interchangeably, be sure to order the correct one for your engine with the identical part number of the one being replaced.

1. Disconnect the negative battery cable.
2. Remove the air cleaner assembly along with the necessary duct work.
3. Detach the TP electrical connector.

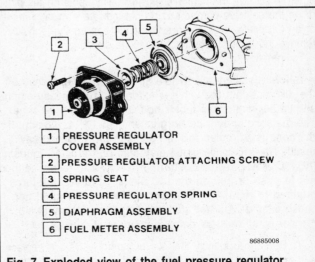

1	PRESSURE REGULATOR COVER ASSEMBLY
2	PRESSURE REGULATOR ATTACHING SCREW
3	SPRING SEAT
4	PRESSURE REGULATOR SPRING
5	DIAPHRAGM ASSEMBLY
6	FUEL METER ASSEMBLY

86885008

Fig. 7 Exploded view of the fuel pressure regulator components

4. Unfasten the TP sensor attaching screws. If the sensor is riveted to the throttle body, it will be necessary to drill out the rivets.

5. Remove the TP sensor from the throttle body assembly.

➡**The throttle position sensor is an electrical component and should not be immersed in any type of liquid solvent or cleaner, as damage may result.**

To install:

6. With the throttle valve closed, install the TP sensor onto the throttle shaft. Rotate the TPS counterclockwise to align the mounting holes.

7. Apply Loctite 262® or equivalent to the retaining screws. Install the retaining screws or rivets, then tighten the screws to 18 inch lbs. (2.0 Nm).

8. Attach the sensor electrical connector.

9. Install the air cleaner assembly, then connect the negative battery cable.

Idle Air Control (IAC) Valve

REMOVAL & INSTALLATION

◆ **See Figure 8**

1. Disconnect the negative battery cable.
2. Remove the air cleaner assembly.
3. Detach the electrical connection from the idle air control assembly.
4. Unfasten the retaining screws, then remove the idle air control valve from the throttle body assembly. Discard the O-ring.
5. Clean the IAC valve O-ring sealing surface, pintle valve seat and air passage.

➡**Be sure that the cleaner is safe to use on systems equipped with an oxygen sensor. Do not use a cleaner containing methyl ethyl ketone.**

6. Use a suitable carburetor cleaner and a parts cleaning brush to remove the carbon deposits. Shiny spots on the pintle or on the seat are normal and do not indicate a misalignment or a bent pintle shaft. If the air passage has heavy deposits, remove the throttle body for a complete cleaning.

To install:

➡**Before installing a new idle air control valve, measure the distance that the valve is extended. This measurement should be made from motor housing to end of the cone. The distance should be no greater than 1⅛ in. (28mm). If the cone is extended too far, damage to the valve may result. The IAC valve pintle may also be retracted by using IAC/ISC Motor Tester J-37027/BT-8256K. It is recommended not to push or pull on the IAC pintle. However, the force required to retract the pintle of a NEW valve should not cause damage. Do not soak the IAC valve in any liquid cleaner or solvent, as damage may result.**

7. Be sure to identify the idle air control valve and replace with an identical part. The IAC valve pintle shape and diameter are designed for specific applications.

8. Lubricate a new IAC valve O-ring with clean engine oil.

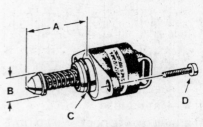

A DISTANCE OF PINTLE EXTENSION
B DIAMETER OF PINTLE
C IAC VALVE O-RING
D IAC VALVE ATTACHING SCREW

86885007

Fig. 8 View of a flange mount IAC valve

9. Install the new idle air control valve, apply Loctite 262® or equivalent to the retaining screws, then tighten them to 27 inch lbs. (3 Nm).

10. Attach the electrical connection.

11. Install the air cleaner assembly.

12. Connect the negative battery cable.

13. The base idle will not be correct until the ECM resets the IAC. To reset the IAC valve pintle position proceed as follows:

a. Block the drive wheels, then apply the parking brake firmly.

b. Start the engine, then hold the engine speed above 2,000 rpm. Ground the diagnostic test terminal (ALDL) for ten seconds, then remove the ground.

c. Turn the ignition **OFF**, then restart the engine and check for proper idle operation.

Fuel Pump Relay

REMOVAL & INSTALLATION

◆ **See Figure 9**

➡**The fuel pump relay is located in the engine compartment, mounted on the firewall.**

1. Disconnect the negative battery cable.
2. Detach the fuel pump relay electrical connector, then remove the relay.

To install:

3. Install the relay, then attach the electrical connector.
4. Connect the negative battery cable.

Tube Module

REMOVAL & INSTALLATION

◆ **See Figure 10**

1. Disconnect the negative battery cable.

2. Remove the air cleaner assembly.

3. Tag and disconnect the vacuum hoses.

4. Unfasten the tube module assembly attaching screws, then remove the tube module and gasket. Discard the gasket. Clean the gasket mating surfaces.

To install:

5. Using a new gasket, install the tube module assembly. Apply Loctite 26® or equivalent to the retaining screws, then install them and tighten to 27 inch lbs. (3.0 Nm).

6. Attach the vacuum hoses as tagged during removal.

7. Install the air cleaner assembly.

8. Connect the negative battery cable.

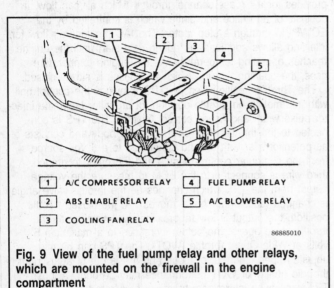

1	A/C COMPRESSOR RELAY	4	FUEL PUMP RELAY
2	ABS ENABLE RELAY	5	A/C BLOWER RELAY
3	COOLING FAN RELAY		

86885010

Fig. 9 View of the fuel pump relay and other relays, which are mounted on the firewall in the engine compartment

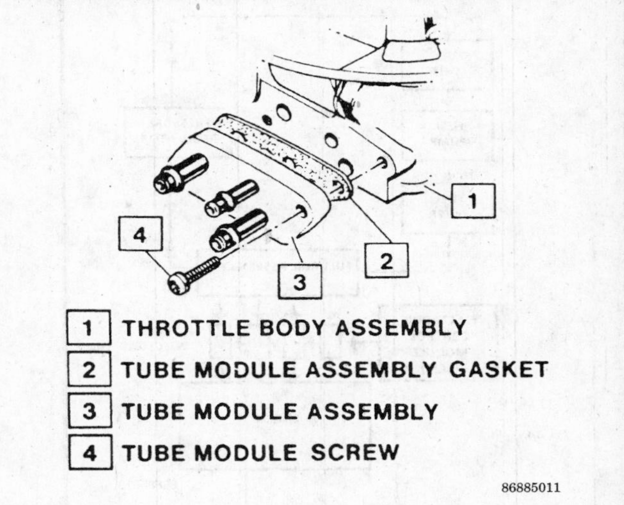

1	THROTTLE BODY ASSEMBLY
2	TUBE MODULE ASSEMBLY GASKET
3	TUBE MODULE ASSEMBLY
4	TUBE MODULE SCREW

86885011

Fig. 10 Tube module assembly mounting

MULTI-PORT FUEL INJECTION SYSTEM

System Description

▶ See Figures 11, 12, 13, 14 and 15

➡ **Multi-port fuel injection is found on vehicles equipped with 2.0L, 2.3L, 3.0L and 3.3L engines.**

The Multi-Port Fuel Injection (MPI) system is controlled by an computer control module (ECM or PCM depending upon vehicle application) which monitors engine operations and generates output signals to provide the correct air/fuel mixture, ignition timing and engine idle speed control. Input to the control unit is provided by an oxygen sensor, coolant temperature sensor, detonation (knock) sensor on some engines, hot film Mass Air Flow (MAF) sensor or Manifold Absolute Pressure (MAP) sensor and Throttle Position Sensor (TPS). The ECM/PCM also receives information concerning engine rpm, vehicle speed, transaxle selector position, power steering and air conditioning.

The injectors are located, one at each intake port, rather than the single injector found on the throttle body system. The injectors are mounted on a fuel rail and are activated by a signal from the computer control module. The injector is a solenoid-operated valve which remains open depending on the width of the electronic pulses (length of the signal) from the ECM/PCM; the longer the open time, the more fuel is injected.

In this manner, the air/fuel mixture can be precisely controlled for maximum performance with minimum emissions. On all multi-port fuel injection systems, except the 2.3L engine, the computer control module fires all of the injectors at once.

The system on 2.3L engines is slightly different in that the injectors are paired by companion cylinders and are fired in pairs. This system is called Alternating Synchronous Double Fire (ASDF) fuel injection. It is similar in operation to the other injection systems except that each pair of cylinders fires once per crankshaft revolution. This means that cylinders 1 and 4, as well as 2 and 3, fire once per crankshaft revolution. In this way, a cylinder's injector fires on the intake stroke and exhaust stroke. Firing the injector on the exhaust stroke (when the intake valve is closed) helps provide better fuel vaporization.

Fuel is pumped from the tank by a high pressure fuel pump, located inside the fuel tank. It is a positive displacement roller vane pump. The impeller serves as a vapor separator and precharges the high pressure assembly. A pressure regulator maintains 28-36 psi (193-248 kPa), 28-50 psi (193-345 kPa) on turbocharged engines, in the fuel line to the injectors and the excess fuel is fed back to the tank. A fuel accumulator is used to dampen the hydraulic line hammer in the system created when all injectors open simultaneously.

The MAP sensor, used on all except the 3.0L and 3.3L engines, measures the changes in intake manifold pressure,

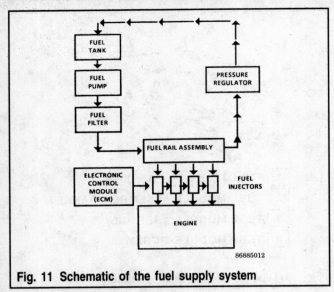

86885012

Fig. 11 Schematic of the fuel supply system

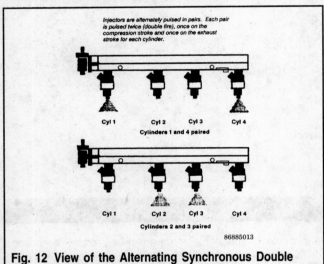

Injectors are alternately pulsed in pairs. Each pair is pulsed twice (double fire), once on the compression stroke and once on the exhaust stroke for each cylinder.

Cyl 1   Cyl 2   Cyl 3   Cyl 4

Cylinders 1 and 4 paired

Cyl 1   Cyl 2   Cyl 3   Cyl 4

Cylinders 2 and 3 paired

86885013

Fig. 12 View of the Alternating Synchronous Double Fire (ASDF), found on the 2.3L engine only

which result from engine load and speed changes and converts this information to a voltage output. The MAP sensor reading is the opposite of a vacuum gauge reading: when manifold pressure is high, MAP sensor value is high and vacuum is low. A MAP sensor will produce a low output on engine coastdown with a closed throttle while a wide open throttle will produce a high output. The high output is produced because the pressure inside the manifold is the same as outside the manifold, so 100 percent of the outside air pressure is measured.

The MAP sensor is also used to measure barometric pressure under certain conditions, which allows the computer control module to automatically adjust for different altitudes. The MAP sensor changes the 5 volt signal supplied by the ECM/PCM, which reads the change and uses the information to control fuel delivery and ignition timing.

The Mass Air Flow (MAF) Sensor used on 3.0L and 3.3L engines, measures the mass of air that is drawn into the engine. It is located just ahead of the throttle in the intake system and consists of a heated grid which measures the

mass of air, rather than just the volume. A resistor is used to measure the temperature of the film at 75°F (24°C) above ambient temperature. As the ambient (outside) air temperature rises and the rate of air flowing through the grid increases (indicating the throttle opening), more energy is required to maintain the heated grid at the higher temperature. The computer control module calculates the difference in energy required to maintain the grid temperature in order to determine the mass of the incoming air. The control unit uses this information to determine the duration of fuel injection pulse, timing and EGR.

The throttle body incorporates an Idle Air Control (IAC) that provides for a bypass channel through which air can flow. It consists of an orifice and pintle which is controlled by the ECM/PCM through a step motor. The IAC provides air flow for idle and allows additional air during cold start until the engine reaches operating temperature. As the engine temperature rises, the opening through which air passes is slowly closed.

The Throttle Position Sensor (TPS) provides the control unit with information on throttle position, in order to determine injector pulse width and hence correct mixture. The TPS is connected to the throttle shaft on the throttle body and consists of as potentiometer with on end connected to a 5 volt source from the computer control module and the other to ground. A third wire is connected to the ECM to measure the voltage output from the TPS which changes as the throttle valve angle is changed (accelerator pedal moves). At the closed throttle position, the output is low (approximately 0.4 volts); as the throttle valve opens, the output increases to a maximum 5 volts at Wide Open Throttle (WOT). The TPS can be misadjusted open, shorted, or loose and if it is out of adjustment, the idle quality or WOT performance may be poor. A loose TPS can cause intermittent bursts of fuel from the injectors and an unstable idle because the computer thinks the throttle is moving. This should cause a trouble code to be set. Once a trouble code is set, the computer control module will use a preset value for TPS and some vehicle performance may return. A small amount of engine coolant is routed through the throttle assembly to prevent freezing inside the throttle bore during cold operation.

OPERATING MODES

The computer control module uses voltage input from various sensors to determine how much fuel to give the engine. The fuel is delivered under one of several conditions, called modes. All modes are controlled by the computer control module.

Starting Mode

When the ignition is first turned **ON** (before engaging the starter), the computer control module (ECM/PCM) energizes the fuel pump relay for a calibrated time (approximately 2 seconds) to allow the fuel pump to build up pressure. The ECM/PCM also checks the ECT and the TP sensors to determine the proper air/fuel ratio for starting. This ranges from 1.5:1 at -33°F (-36°C) to 14.7:1 at 201°F (94°C), for early model vehicles, or 0.8:1 at -40°F (-40°C) to 16.8:1 at 220°F (104°C), for later model vehicles, engine coolant temperature. The computer controls the amount of fuel delivered by chang-

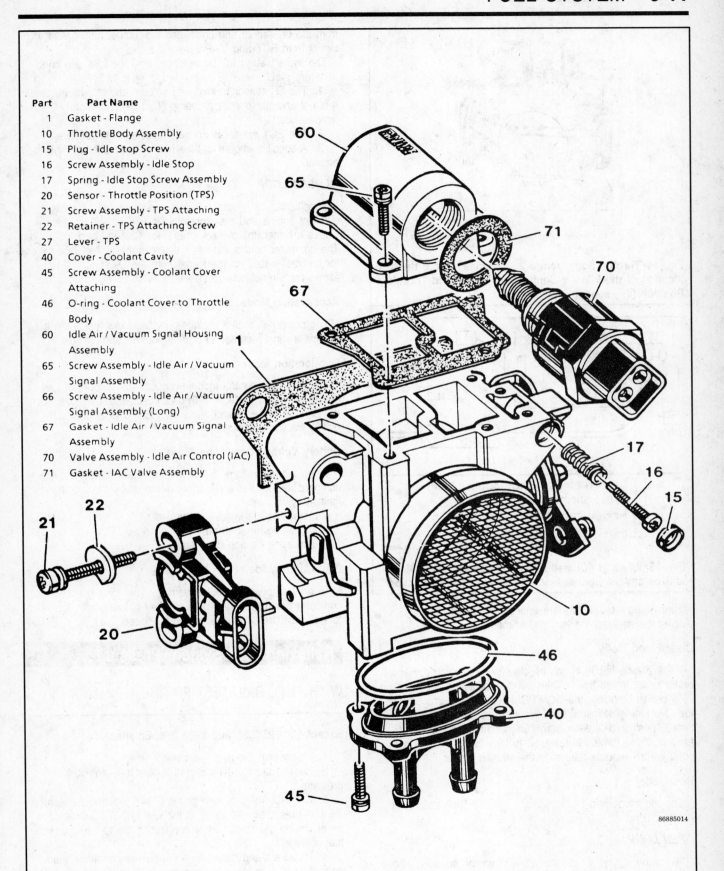

Part	Part Name
1	Gasket - Flange
10	Throttle Body Assembly
15	Plug - Idle Stop Screw
16	Screw Assembly - Idle Stop
17	Spring - Idle Stop Screw Assembly
20	Sensor - Throttle Position (TPS)
21	Screw Assembly - TPS Attaching
22	Retainer - TPS Attaching Screw
27	Lever - TPS
40	Cover - Coolant Cavity
45	Screw Assembly - Coolant Cover Attaching
46	O-ring - Coolant Cover to Throttle Body
60	Idle Air / Vacuum Signal Housing Assembly
65	Screw Assembly - Idle Air / Vacuum Signal Assembly
66	Screw Assembly - Idle Air / Vacuum Signal Assembly (Long)
67	Gasket - Idle Air / Vacuum Signal Assembly
70	Valve Assembly - Idle Air Control (IAC)
71	Gasket - IAC Valve Assembly

86885014

Fig. 13 Exploded view of an MFI throttle body assembly from a 3.0L engine

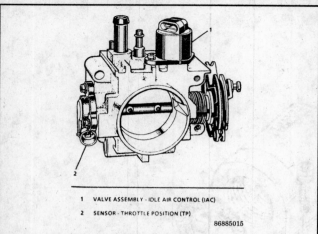

1 VALVE ASSEMBLY - IDLE AIR CONTROL (IAC)
2 SENSOR - THROTTLE POSITION (TP)

86885015

Fig. 14 Throttle body from a 2.3L engine — note the location of the Idle Air Control (IAC) valve and Throttle Position (TP) sensor

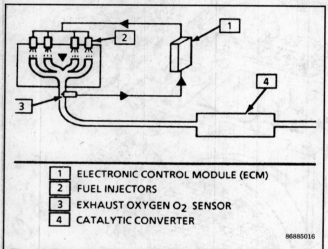

1	ELECTRONIC CONTROL MODULE (ECM)
2	FUEL INJECTORS
3	EXHAUST OXYGEN O$_2$ SENSOR
4	CATALYTIC CONVERTER

86885016

Fig. 15 When in "Closed Loop" operations, the ECM utilizes oxygen sensor feedback to adjust fuel injection

ing how long the injectors are energized. This is done by pulsing the injectors for very short times.

Clear Flood Mode

If the engine floods, it can be cleared by pushing the accelerator pedal to the floor. When throttle position is greater than 75% during cranking, the ECM/PCM completely turns off the fuel. No fuel is delivered from the injectors as long as the throttle position is greater than 75%, and the engine is not running. If the throttle is released to less than 75%, the computer control module returns to the starting mode.

Run Mode

The run mode had two conditions called "Open Loop" and "Closed Loop".

OPEN LOOP

When the engine is first started, and engine speed is above approximately 637 rpm, the system goes into "Open Loop" operation. The computer control module ignores the signal from the O$_2$ sensor and calculates the air/fuel ratio based on inputs from ECT and MAP sensors.

The system stays in "Open Loop" until the following conditions are met:

1. The O$_2$ sensor has varying voltage output, showing that it is hot enough to work properly. (This depends upon temperature.)

2. The ECT sensor is above a specified temperature.

3. A specific amount of time has elapsed after starting the engine.

CLOSED LOOP

Specific values for the previous conditions exist for each different engine and are stores in the PROM. When these values are met, the system goes into "Closed Loop" operation. The computer control module calculates the air/fuel ratio (injector on-time) based on the signal from the O$_2$ sensor. This allows the air/fuel ratio to stay very close to 14.7:1.

Acceleration Mode

The computer control module provides extra fuel when it detects a rapid increase in throttle position and air flow.

Deceleration Mode

The computer control module reduces the amount of fuel delivered when it detects in throttle position and air flow. If deceleration is very rapid, the ECM/PCM cuts off fuel completely for short periods.

Battery Voltage Correction Mode

When battery voltage is low, the computer control module compensates for the weak spark delivered by the electronic ignition system by:

• Increasing the injector pulse width.
• Increasing the idle rpm.
• Increasing ignition dwell time.

Fuel Cutoff Mode

To prevent possible engine damage from overspeed, the computer control module "cuts off" fuel delivery from the injectors at a calibrated engine or vehicle speed.

Relieving Fuel System Pressure

WITH FUEL RAIL TEST FITTING

Except 1991-95 2.3L and 1988 3.0L Engines

1. Disconnect the negative battery cable.

2. Loosen the fuel filler cap to relieve fuel tank vapor pressure.

3. Connect fuel pressure gauge J 34730-1 or equivalent, to the fuel pressure relief valve at the fuel rail. Wrap a shop towel around the fittings while connecting the tool to prevent fuel spillage.

4. Install a bleed hose into an approved container, then open the valve to bleed the system pressure. Drain any fuel still in the gauge into an approved container.

5. Install the fuel filler cap.

WITHOUT FUEL RAIL TEST FITTING

1991-95 2.3L and 1988 3.0L Engines

1. Remove the fuel filler cap to relieve fuel tank vapor pressure.
2. Raise and safely support the vehicle with jackstands.
3. From under the vehicle, detach the fuel pump electrical connector. It should be the only connector coming from the fuel tank.
4. Carefully lower the vehicle.
5. Start the engine and run until the engine stalls. Engage the starter an additional 3 seconds to assure complete relief.
6. Raise and safely support the vehicle.
7. Attach the fuel pump electrical connector, then carefully lower the vehicle.
8. Install the fuel filler cap.
9. Disconnect the negative battery cable, to avoid possible fuel discharge if an accidental attempt is made to start the engine, then continue with fuel system work.

Electric Fuel Pump

REMOVAL & INSTALLATION

1985-91 Vehicles
▶ See Figure 16

1. Properly relieve the fuel system pressure.
2. If not done already, disconnect the negative battery cable.
3. Raise and safely support the vehicle with jackstands.
4. Safely drain, then remove the fuel tank assembly, as outlined in the fuel tank removal procedure later in this section.
5. Remove the fuel tank sending unit and pump assembly by turning the fuel pump cam lock ring counterclockwise, then lift the assembly out of the tank.
6. Remove the fuel pump from the level sensor unit as follows:
   a. Pull the pump up into the attaching hose or pulsator while pulling outward away from the bottom support.
   b. Take care to prevent damage to the rubber insulator and strainer during removal.
   c. When the pump assembly is clear of the bottom support, pull the pump out of the rubber connector for removal.
To install:
7. Replace any attaching hoses or rubber sound insulator that show signs of deterioration.
8. Push the fuel pump into the attaching hoses and install the pump/sensor assembly into the tank. Always use a new O-ring seal.
9. Be careful not to fold over or twist the strainer when installing the sensor unit. Also, make sure the strainer does not block full travel of the float arm.
10. Position the cam lock and turn clockwise to lock.
11. Install the fuel tank as outlined in this Section.
12. Fill the tank with gas and check for fuel leaks.
13. Connect the negative battery cable.

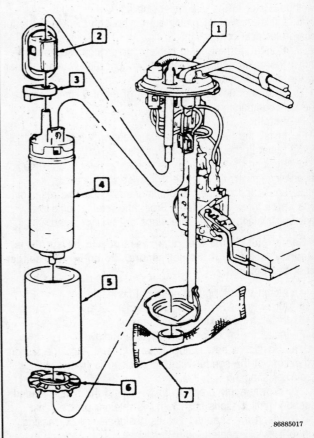

1. FUEL TANK METER ASSY.
2. PULSATOR
3. BUMPER
4. FUEL PUMP
5. SOUND ISOLATOR SLEEVE
6. SOUND INSULATOR
7. FILTER

86885017

Fig. 16 Exploded view of the MFI system fuel pump and related components — 1985-91 vehicles

1992-95 Vehicles
▶ See Figures 17, 18, 19, 20 and 21

1. Properly relieve the fuel system pressure.
2. If not already done, disconnect the negative battery cable.
3. Drain, then remove the fuel tank. For details, please refer to the procedure later in this section.

➡Be careful when removing the modular fuel sender because it may spring up from its position.

4. Remove the modular fuel sender as follows:
   a. While holding the modular fuel sender assembly down, remove the snapring from the designated slots located on the retainer.
   b. Keep in mind that the reservoir bucket is full of fuel. It must be tipped slightly during removal to avoid damage to the float. Place the reservoir fuel into an approved container.
   c. Remove and discard the fuel sender O-ring.
5. Remove the external fuel strainer.

6. Remove the Connector Position Assurance (CPA) from the electrical connector, then detach the fuel pump electrical connector.

7. Gently release the tabs on the sides of the fuel sender-to-cover assembly. Begin by starting at the sides of the reservoir and releasing the tab opposite the fuel level sensor. Move clockwise to release the second and third tab using the same method. Refer to the accompanying figure.

8. Lift the cover assembly out far enough to detach the fuel pump electrical connection.

9. Rotate the fuel pump baffle counterclockwise, then remove the baffle and pump assembly from their retainer. Refer to the accompanying figure.

10. Slide the fuel pump outlet out of the slot, then remove the seal/dampener.

To install:

11. Install the fuel pump seal/dampener, then slide the fuel pump outlet in the slots of the reservoir cover.

12. Position the fuel pump and baffle assembly onto the reservoir retainer, then rotate clockwise until seated.

13. Lower the retainer assembly partially into the reservoir. Line up all three sleeve tabs. Press the retainer onto the reservoir making sure all three tabs are firmly seated.

➡**Gently pull on the fuel pump reservoir to be sure it is securely fastened. If it's not secure, the entire fuel sender must be replaced.**

14. Attach the fuel pump electrical connector.
15. Attach the CPA to the fuel sender cover.
16. Install a new external fuel strainer.
17. Install the modular fuel sender as follows:

   a. Position a new sender-to-tank O-ring. Align the tab on the front of the sender with the slot on the front of the retainer snapring.

   b. Slowly apply pressure to the top of the spring loaded sender until it aligns flush with the retainer on the tank.

   c. Insert the snapring into its designated slots, making sure it is fully seated.

18. Install the fuel tank as outlined later in this section.
19. Carefully lower the vehicle, then fill the fuel tank.

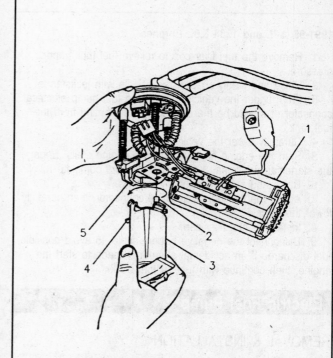

1 RESERVOIR ASSEMBLY
2 TUBE, OUTLET
3 PUMP, FUEL ASSEMBLY
4 MEMBER, FLEX
5 RESERVOIR, RETAINER–FUEL PUMP

86885019

Fig. 18 To remove the fuel pump and baffle assembly, you must rotate it counterclockwise

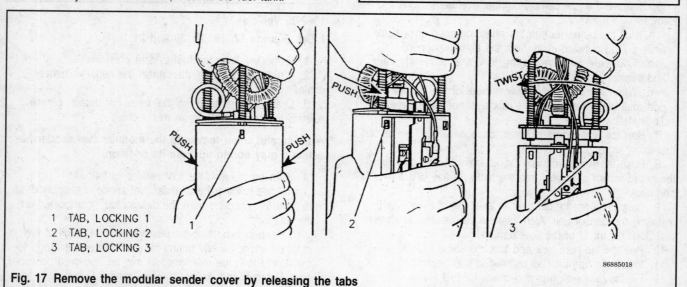

1 TAB, LOCKING 1
2 TAB, LOCKING 2
3 TAB, LOCKING 3

Fig. 17 Remove the modular sender cover by releasing the tabs

86885018

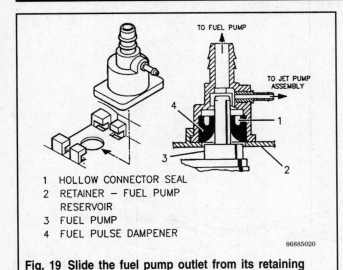

1 HOLLOW CONNECTOR SEAL
2 RETAINER – FUEL PUMP
   RESERVOIR
3 FUEL PUMP
4 FUEL PULSE DAMPENER

86885020

Fig. 19 Slide the fuel pump outlet from its retaining slot, then . . .

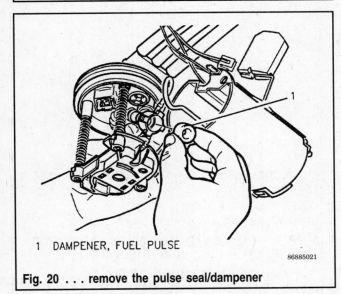

1 DAMPENER, FUEL PULSE

86885021

Fig. 20 . . . remove the pulse seal/dampener

20. Connect the negative battery cable. Turn the ignition to the **ON** position for two seconds, then turn it to the **OFF** position for ten seconds. Turn again to the **ON** position and check for fuel leaks.

FUEL PRESSURE TESTING

1. Connect pressure gauge J-34730-1, or equivalent, to fuel pressure test point on the fuel rail. Wrap a rag around the pressure tap to absorb any leakage that may occur when installing the gauge.
2. Turn the ignition **ON**. The fuel pump pressure should read as follows:
   - 2.0L engine: 35-38 psi (245-256 kPa)
   - 2.3L engine: 41-47 psi (280-325 kPa)
   - 1985-86 3.0L engine: 37-43 psi (255-298 kPa)
   - 1987-88 3.0L engine: 41-47 psi (280-325 kPa)
   - 3.3L engine: 41-47 psi (280-325 kPa)

3. Start the engine and allow it to idle. The fuel pressure should drop no more than 3-10 psi (21-69 kPa).

➡**The idle pressure will vary somewhat depending on barometric pressure. Check for a drop in pressure indicating regulator control, rather than specific values.**

4. On turbocharged vehicles, use a low pressure air pump to apply air pressure to the regulator to simulate turbocharger boost pressure. Boost pressure should increase fuel pressure 1 psi (7 kPa) for every lb. of boost. Again, look for changes rather than specific pressures. The maximum fuel pressure should not exceed 46 psi (317 kPa).
5. If the fuel pressure drops, check the operation of the check valve, the pump coupling connection, fuel pressure regulator valve and the injectors. A restricted fuel line or filter may also cause a pressure drip. To check the fuel pump output, restrict the fuel return line and run 12 volts to the pump. The fuel pressure should rise to approximately 75 psi (517 kPa) with the return line restricted.
6. Before attempting to remove or service any fuel system component, it is necessary to relieve the fuel system pressure.

Throttle Body

REMOVAL & INSTALLATION

2.0L Engine
◆ **See Figure 22**

1. Properly relieve the fuel system pressure.
2. If not done already, disconnect the negative battery cable.
3. Remove the air inlet duct.
4. Detach the IAC valve and TPS electrical connectors.
5. Tag and disconnect the vacuum lines from the throttle body.
6. Disconnect the throttle, Throttle Valve (TV) and, if equipped, cruise control cables.
7. Unfasten the retaining bolts, then remove the throttle body assembly and flange gasket. Discard the gasket.
8. Clean the gasket mating surfaces.
To install:

➡**Use care when cleaning the old gasket material from machined aluminum surfaces. Sharp tools may cause damage to sealing surfaces.**

9. Install the throttle body assembly with a new flange gasket, then secure using the retaining bolts. Tighten to 10-15 ft. lbs. (14-20 Nm).
10. Connect the throttle, TV and cruise control cables.

➡**Ensure that the throttle and cruise control linkage does not hold the throttle open.**

11. Connect the vacuum lines as tagged during removal.
12. Attach the TPS and IAC valve electrical connectors.
13. Install the air inlet duct.
14. Connect the negative battery cable.
15. With the ignition switch in the **OFF** position, ensure that the movement of the accelerator is free.

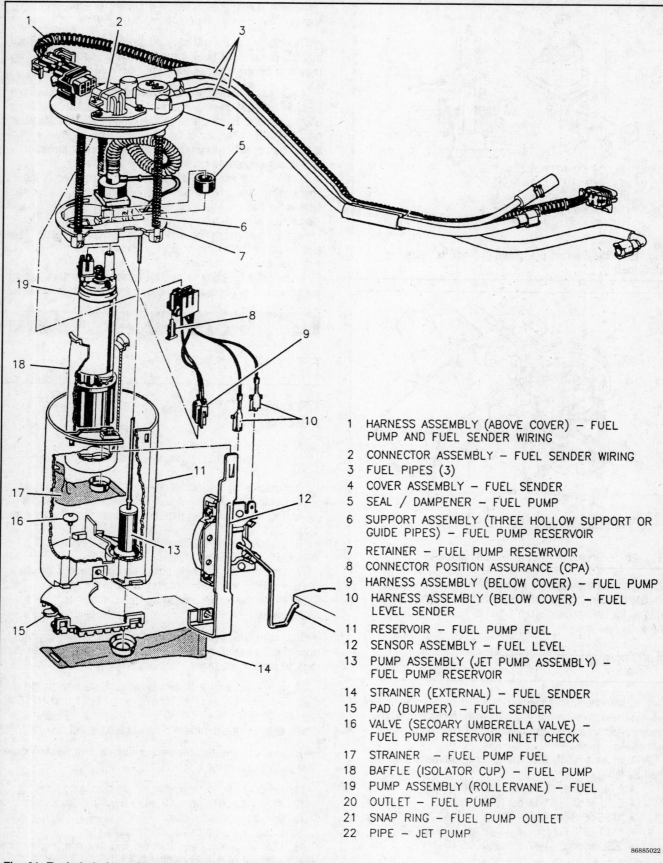

1 HARNESS ASSEMBLY (ABOVE COVER) – FUEL PUMP AND FUEL SENDER WIRING
2 CONNECTOR ASSEMBLY – FUEL SENDER WIRING
3 FUEL PIPES (3)
4 COVER ASSEMBLY – FUEL SENDER
5 SEAL / DAMPENER – FUEL PUMP
6 SUPPORT ASSEMBLY (THREE HOLLOW SUPPORT OR GUIDE PIPES) – FUEL PUMP RESERVOIR
7 RETAINER – FUEL PUMP RESEWRVOIR
8 CONNECTOR POSITION ASSURANCE (CPA)
9 HARNESS ASSEMBLY (BELOW COVER) – FUEL PUMP
10 HARNESS ASSEMBLY (BELOW COVER) – FUEL LEVEL SENDER
11 RESERVOIR – FUEL PUMP FUEL
12 SENSOR ASSEMBLY – FUEL LEVEL
13 PUMP ASSEMBLY (JET PUMP ASSEMBLY) – FUEL PUMP RESERVOIR
14 STRAINER (EXTERNAL) – FUEL SENDER
15 PAD (BUMPER) – FUEL SENDER
16 VALVE (SECOARY UMBERELLA VALVE) – FUEL PUMP RESERVOIR INLET CHECK
17 STRAINER – FUEL PUMP FUEL
18 BAFFLE (ISOLATOR CUP) – FUEL PUMP
19 PUMP ASSEMBLY (ROLLERVANE) – FUEL
20 OUTLET – FUEL PUMP
21 SNAP RING – FUEL PUMP OUTLET
22 PIPE – JET PUMP

86885022

Fig. 21 Exploded view of the modular fuel sender and related components

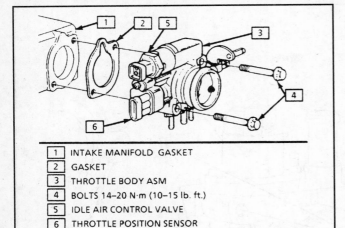

1	INTAKE MANIFOLD GASKET
2	GASKET
3	THROTTLE BODY ASM
4	BOLTS 14–20 N·m (10–15 lb. ft.)
5	IDLE AIR CONTROL VALVE
6	THROTTLE POSITION SENSOR

86885023

Fig. 22 View of the throttle body mounting — 2.0L engine

2.3L Engine

▶ See Figures 23 and 24

1. Properly relieve the fuel system pressure.
2. If not done already, disconnect the negative battery cable.
3. Partially drain the coolant into a suitable drain pan, to allow the coolant hoses at the throttle body to be removed.
4. Remove the air inlet duct.
5. Detach the IAC valve and TP sensor connectors.
6. Tag and detach all necessary vacuum lines.
7. Disconnect and plug the 2 coolant hoses.
8. Unfasten the accelerator cable bracket retaining nut and bolts, then remove the bracket.
9. Remove the throttle, Throttle Valve (TV) and cruise control cables.
10. Remove the power steering pump brace.
11. Disconnect the power brake vacuum hose at the throttle body.
12. Unfasten the throttle body retaining bolts, then remove the throttle body assembly. Remove and discard the gasket.
13. Clean the gasket mating surfaces.

➡**Use care when cleaning the old gasket material from machined aluminum surfaces. Sharp tools may cause damage to sealing surfaces.**

14. Installation is the reverse order of the removal procedure. Tighten the retaining bolts to 19 ft. lbs. (26 Nm).
15. Connect the negative battery cable. Refill the cooling system.
16. For 1990-95 2.3L vehicles you must reset the IAC valve pintle position:
    a. Turn the ignition switch to the **ON** position (engine off).
    b. Ground the diagnostic test terminal (ALDL) for five seconds, then remove the ground.
    c. Turn the ignition **OFF** for ten seconds.
    d. Start the engine and check for proper idle operation.

3.0L Engine

1. Disconnect the negative battery cable.

2. Partially drain the cooling system to allow the coolant hoses at the throttle body to be removed.
3. Remove the air inlet duct at the throttle body.
4. Detach the TPS and IAC valve electrical connectors.
5. Tag and disconnect the vacuum lines from the throttle body.
6. Detach and plug the coolant hoses from the throttle body.
7. Disconnect the throttle, Throttle Valve (TV) and cruise control cables.
8. Unfasten the throttle body attaching bolts, then remove the throttle body assembly and flange gasket. Discard the gasket.

To install:

➡**Use care in the cleaning of old gasket material from machined aluminum surfaces. Sharp tools may cause damage to sealing surfaces.**

9. Install the throttle body assembly with a new flange gasket, then secure using the attaching bolts. Tighten the bolts to 11 ft. lbs. (15 Nm).
10. Connect the throttle, TV and cruise cables.

➡**Ensure that the throttle and cruise control linkage does not hold the throttle open.**

11. Attach the coolant hoses to the throttle body.
12. Connect the vacuum lines as tagged during removal.
13. Attach the TPS and IAC valve electrical connectors.
14. Connect the air inlet duct to the throttle body.
15. Refill the radiator.
16. Connect the negative battery cable.
17. With the ignition switch in the **OFF** position, ensure that the movement of the accelerator is free.

3.3L Engine

▶ See Figure 25

1. Properly relieve the fuel system pressure.
2. If not done already, disconnect the negative battery cable.
3. Partially drain the cooling system to allow for removal of the the coolant hose at the throttle body.
4. Remove the air cleaner and related duct work for clearance.
5. Unfasten the vacuum harness attaching screw from the throttle cable bracket.
6. Disconnect the throttle, Throttle Valve (TV) and cruise control cables.
7. Tag and disconnect the necessary vacuum lines from the throttle body.
8. Disconnect the IAC valve, TP sensor and MAF sensor electrical connectors.
9. Remove the coolant hose from the throttle body.
10. Unfasten the nuts/bolts securing the throttle body to the intake manifold, then remove the throttle body assembly and flange gasket. Discard the gasket.

➡**Use care in the cleaning of old gasket material from machined aluminum surfaces. Sharp tools may cause damage to sealing surfaces.**

11. Clean the gasket mating surfaces.

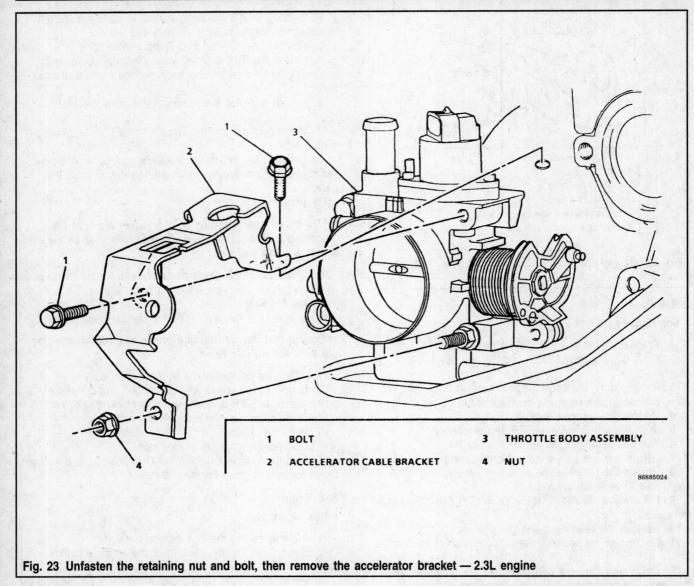

| 1 | BOLT | 3 | THROTTLE BODY ASSEMBLY |
| 2 | ACCELERATOR CABLE BRACKET | 4 | NUT |

86885024

Fig. 23 Unfasten the retaining nut and bolt, then remove the accelerator bracket — 2.3L engine

To install:

12. Using a new gasket, install the throttle body assembly and secure using the retaining nuts/bolts. Tighten to 21 ft. lbs. (28 Nm).

13. Connect the coolant hose to the throttle body.

14. Connect the throttle, TV and cruise cables.

➡**Ensure that the throttle and cruise control linkage does not hold the throttle open.**

15. Connect the vacuum lines as tagged during removal.

16. Attach the TPS and IAC valve electrical connectors.

17. Install the vacuum harness attaching screw. Tighten to 66 inch lbs. (7.5 Nm).

18. Connect the air inlet duct to the throttle body. Install the air cleaner and duct work.

19. Refill the radiator, then connect the negative battery cable.

20. With the ignition switch in the **OFF** position, ensure that the movement of the accelerator is free.

21. Reset the IAC valve pintle position by turning the ignition **ON**, then **OFF**. Start the engine and check for proper idle operation.

Fuel Rail Assembly

When servicing the fuel rail assembly, be careful to prevent dirt and other contaminants from entering the fuel passages. Fittings should be capped and holes plugged during servicing. At any time the fuel system is opened for service, the O-ring seals and retainers used with related components should be replaced.

Before removing the fuel rail, the fuel rail assembly may be cleaned with a spray type cleaner, GM-30A or equivalent, following package instructions. Do not immerse fuel rails in liquid cleaning solvent. Be sure to always use new O-rings and seals when reinstalling the fuel rail assemblies.

There is an 8-digit number stamped on the under side of the fuel rail assembly on 4 cylinder engines and on the left hand fuel rail on dual rail assemblies (fueling even cylinders No. 2,

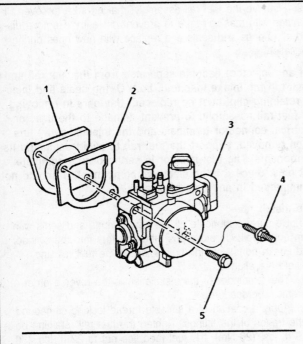

1   INTAKE MANIFOLD

2   GASKET

3   THROTTLE BODY ASSEMBLY

4   BOLT - STUD END

5   BOLT

86885025

Fig. 24 MFI throttle body assembly removal — 2.3L engine

4, 6). Refer to this number if servicing or part replacement is required.

REMOVAL & INSTALLATION

2.0L Engine
▶ **See Figure 26**

1. Properly relieve fuel system pressure.
2. If not done already, disconnect the negative battery cable.
3. Remove the air intake ducts and/or passages in order to gain access to the fuel rail.
4. Disconnect and plug the fuel line from the fuel rail.
5. Carefully detach the fuel injector electrical connectors, then lay the harness aside.
6. Remove the pressure regulator assembly, as required to ease removal of the fuel rail.
7. Unfasten the fuel rail mounting hardware.
8. Carefully remove the fuel injectors from the intake manifold.
9. Remove the fuel rail from the vehicle.
10. Remove and discard the fuel injector O-rings.
To install:
11. Lubricate new O-rings with a light coating of clean engine oil. Install the O-rings.
12. Carefully install the fuel injectors to the intake manifold.
13. Install the fuel rail attaching hardware.
14. If removed, install the pressure regulator.
15. Attach the fuel injector electrical connectors.
16. Connect the fuel line to the fuel rail.
17. Install the air intake ducts and/or passages.
18. Connect the negative battery cable.
19. Turn the ignition key to the **ON** position. Check for fuel leaks.
20. Start the engine and allow to idle. Recheck for leaks.

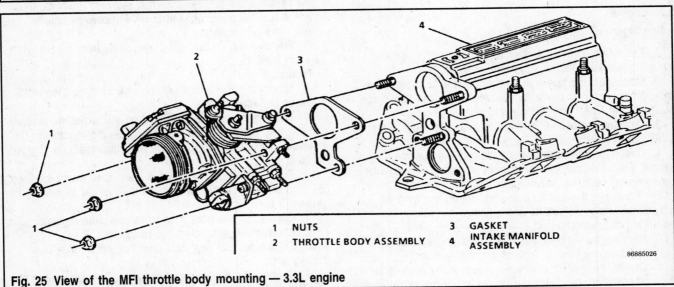

| 1 | NUTS | 3 | GASKET |
| 2 | THROTTLE BODY ASSEMBLY | 4 | INTAKE MANIFOLD ASSEMBLY |

86885026

Fig. 25 View of the MFI throttle body mounting — 3.3L engine

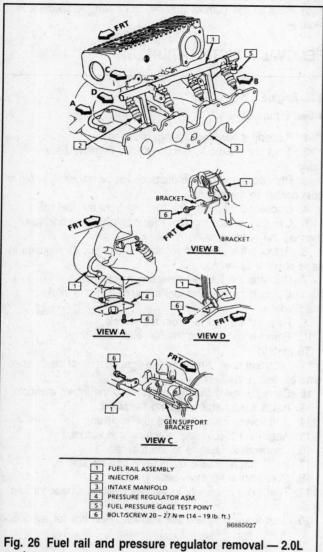

1	FUEL RAIL ASSEMBLY
2	INJECTOR
3	INTAKE MANIFOLD
4	PRESSURE REGULATOR ASM.
5	FUEL PRESSURE GAGE TEST POINT
6	BOLT/SCREW 20 – 27 N·m (14 – 19 lb. ft.)

86885027

Fig. 26 Fuel rail and pressure regulator removal — 2.0L engine

2.3L Engine
▶ See Figure 27

1. Properly relieve the fuel system pressure. If not done already, disconnect the negative battery cable.
2. Disconnect the hoses at the front and side of the crankcase ventilation oil/air separator. Leave the vacuum hoses connected to the EVAP canister purge control solenoid.
3. Unfasten the bolts attaching the oil/air separator and the EVAP solenoid valve.
4. Disconnect the hose to the bottom of the separator, then remove the crankcase ventilation oil/air separator. Position the canister purge solenoid valve out of the way.
5. Disconnect the fuel feed line and return line from the fuel rail assembly, be sure to use a backup wrench on the inlet fitting to prevent turning.
6. Remove the vacuum line at the pressure regulator.
7. Unfasten the fuel rail assembly retaining bolts.
8. Detach the injector electrical connectors by pushing in the wire connector clip, while pulling the connector away from the injector.

9. Remove the fuel rail assembly, making sure to cover all openings with masking tape to prevent dirt entry. Remove discard all O-rings and seals and replace with new ones during installation.

➡️ If any injectors become separated from the fuel rail and remain in the intake manifold, both O-ring seals and injector retaining clip must be replaced. Use care in removing the fuel rail assembly, to prevent damage to the injector electrical connector terminals and the injector spray tips. When removed, support the fuel rail to avoid damaging its components. The fuel injector is serviced as a complete unit only. Since it is an electrical component, it should not be immersed in any type of cleaner.

To install:

10. Be sure to lubricate all the new O-rings and seals with clean engine oil. Carefully push the injectors into the cylinder head intake ports until the bolt holes on the fuel rail and manifold are aligned.
11. The remainder of the installation is the reverse order of the removal procedure.
12. Apply a coating of a suitable thread locking compound on the treads of the fittings. Tighten the fuel rail retaining bolts to 19 ft. lbs. (26 Nm), the fuel feed line nut to 22 ft. lbs. (30 Nm) and the fuel pipe fittings to 20 ft. lbs. (26 Nm).
13. Connect the negative battery cable. Turn the ignition to the **ON** position for two seconds, then turn it to the **OFF** position for ten seconds. Turn again to the **ON** position and check for fuel leaks.

3.0L and 3.3L Engines
▶ See Figures 28 and 29

1. Properly relieve the fuel system pressure.
2. Disconnect the negative battery cable.
3. Detach the fuel injector electrical connectors.
4. Remove the vacuum hose from the pressure regulator.
5. Disconnect the fuel feed land return lines from the fuel rail assembly, be sure to use a backup wrench on the inlet fitting to prevent turning. Remove and discard the O-ring(s).
6. Unfasten the fuel rail assembly retaining nut/bolts, then rove the fuel rail assembly and cover all openings tape to prevent dirt from entering.
7. Remove and discard the O-ring seals from the spray tip of each injector.

To install:

8. Lubricate new O-rings with clean engine oil, then install them on the injectors.
9. Position the fuel rail assembly on the intake manifold, the carefully push down on the rail to seal the injectors in the manifold. Secure the rail using the retaining nuts/bolts. Tighten to 20 ft. lbs. (27 Nm).
10. Put new O-ring(s) on the fuel lines, then install the lines. Be sure to use a backup wrench on the fuel rail inlet fitting to prevent it from turning.
11. Connect the vacuum hose to the pressure regulator.
12. Attach the injector electrical connectors.
13. Tighten the fuel filler cap, then connect the negative battery cable.
14. Connect the negative battery cable. Turn the ignition to the **ON** position for two seconds, then turn it to the **OFF**

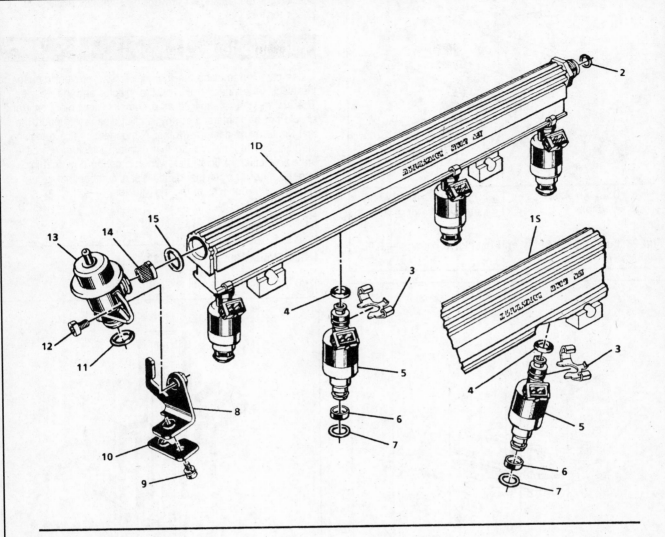

1 RAIL ASSEMBLY - MFI FUEL (S = SOHC; D = DOHC)

2 O-RING - FUEL INLET LINE

3 CLIP - INJECTOR RETAINER

4 O-RING - UPPER INJECTOR (BLACK)

5 INJECTOR ASSEMBLY - MFI FUEL

6 BACKUP - O-RING

7 O-RING - LOWER INJECTOR (BROWN)

8 RETAINER AND SPACER ASSEMBLY

9 SCREW - BRACKET ATTACHING

10 BRACKET - RETURN LINE ATTACHING

11 O-RING - FUEL RETURN LINE

12 SCREW - FUEL PRESSURE REGULATOR ATTACHING

13 REGULATOR ASSEMBLY - FUEL PRESSURE

14 SCREEN - FILTER (IF SO EQUIPPED)

15 O-RING - FUEL INLET FITTING

86885028

Fig. 27 Exploded view of the fuel rail and related components — 2.3L engine

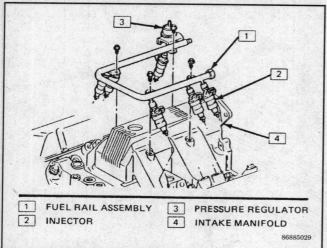

1	FUEL RAIL ASSEMBLY	3	PRESSURE REGULATOR
2	INJECTOR	4	INTAKE MANIFOLD

86885029

Fig. 28 Fuel rail assembly and injector locations — 3.0L engine

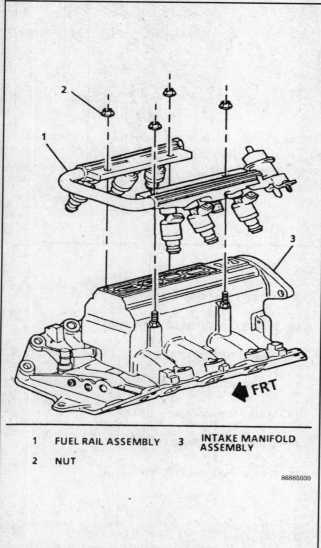

1	FUEL RAIL ASSEMBLY	3	INTAKE MANIFOLD ASSEMBLY
2	NUT		

86885030

Fig. 29 View of the fuel rail mounting — 3.3L engine

position for ten seconds. Turn again to the **ON** position and check for fuel leaks.

Fuel Injectors

Use care in removing the fuel injectors to prevent damage to the electrical connector pins on the injector and the nozzle. The fuel injector is serviced as a complete assembly only and should not be immersed in any kind of cleaner. Support the fuel rail to avoid damaging other components while removing the injector. Be sure to note that different injectors are calibrated for different flow rates. When ordering new fuel injectors, be sure to order the identical part number that is inscribed on the bottom of the old injector.

REMOVAL & INSTALLATION

▶ See Figures 30, 31, 32 and 33

1. Properly relieve fuel system pressure.

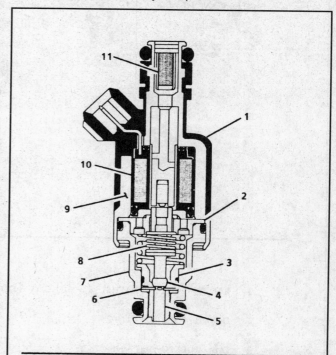

1	SOLENOID ASSEMBLY	7	HOUSING - SPRAY
2	SPACER AND GUIDE ASSEMBLY	8	SPRING - CORE
3	CORE SEAT	9	HOUSING - SOLENOID
4	VALVE - BALL	10	SOLENOID
5	SPRAY TIP	11	FILTER - FUEL INLET
6	PLATE - DIRECTOR		

86885031

Fig. 30 Cross-sectional view of an MFI fuel injector

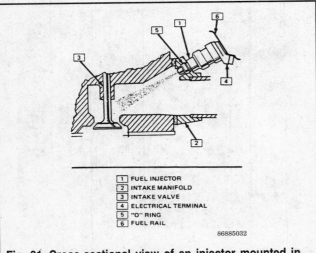

1 FUEL INJECTOR
2 INTAKE MANIFOLD
3 INTAKE VALVE
4 ELECTRICAL TERMINAL
5 "O" RING
6 FUEL RAIL

86885032

Fig. 31 Cross-sectional view of an injector mounted in the intake manifold

2. If not done already, disconnect the negative battery cable.

3. Detach the injector electrical connections.

4. Remove the fuel rail assembly, as outlined earlier in this section.

5. Unfasten the injector retaining clip. Separate the injector from the fuel rail.

6. Remove the O-ring seals from the injector and discard.

To install:

7. Prior to installing the injectors, coat the new injector O-ring seals with clean engine oil. Install the seals on the injector assembly.

8. Use new injector retainer clips on the injector assembly. Position the open end of the clip facing the injector electrical connector.

9. Install the injector into the fuel rail injector socket with the electrical connectors facing outward. Push the injector in firmly until it engages with the retainer clip locking it in place.

10. Install the fuel rail and injector assembly.

11. Attach the injector electrical connectors.

12. Connect the negative battery cable. Turn the ignition to the **ON** position for two seconds, then turn it to the **OFF** position for ten seconds. Turn again to the **ON** position and check for fuel leaks.

Fuel Pressure Regulator

➡On some applications, the pressure regulator and fuel rail are only available as an assembly. Check with your local parts retailer for parts availability and compatibility.

REMOVAL & INSTALLATION

◆ **See Figures 34, 35 and 36**

1. Properly relieve the fuel system pressure.

2. If not done already, disconnect the negative battery cable.

3. Detach the vacuum line from the regulator.

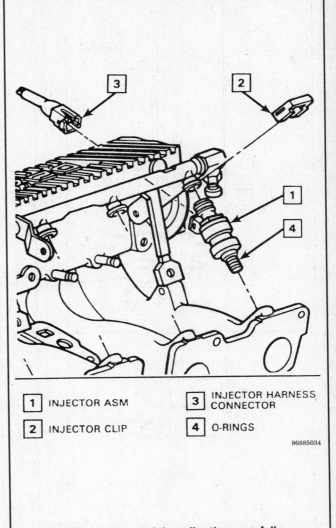

| 1 | INJECTOR ASM | 3 | INJECTOR HARNESS CONNECTOR |
| 2 | INJECTOR CLIP | 4 | O-RINGS |

86885034

Fig. 32 Unfasten the retaining clip, then carefully remove the fuel injector from the fuel rail

86885033

Fig. 33 After removing the injector from the fuel rail, remove and discard the O-ring seals

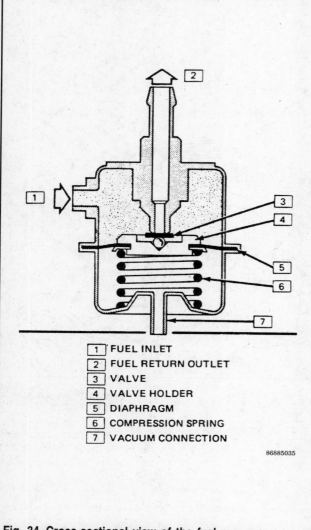

1 FUEL INLET
2 FUEL RETURN OUTLET
3 VALVE
4 VALVE HOLDER
5 DIAPHRAGM
6 COMPRESSION SPRING
7 VACUUM CONNECTION

86885035

Fig. 34 Cross-sectional view of the fuel pressure regulator which is located on the fuel rail assembly

86885036

Fig. 35 When disconnecting the fuel lines, be sure to use a backup wrench

86885037

Fig. 36 Before removing the regulator assembly, place a clean shop towel under the regulator to catch any fuel drips

4. Disconnect the fuel inlet and return lines from the fuel regulator assembly, be sure to use a backup wrench on the fittings to prevent turning.

5. For the 2.3L engine, remove the fuel rail assembly from the engine.

6. Unfasten the pressure regulator mounting screw or retainer. Place a clean shop rag under the regulator to catch any fuel that may spill out of the regulator.

7. Remove the pressure regulator from the rail assembly by twisting back and forth while pulling apart. Remove and discard the O-ring seal.

To install:

8. Prior to assembling the pressure regulator to the fuel rail, lubricate the new rail-to-regulator O-ring seal with clean engine oil.

9. Place the O-ring on the pressure regulator and install the pressure regulator to the fuel rail.

10. Install the retainer or coat the regulator mounting screws with an approved tread locking compound and secure the pressure regulator in place. Tighten the mounting screws to 102 inch lbs. (11.5 Nm).

11. If removed, install the fuel rail assembly to the engine.

12. Connect the fuel feed line and return line to the fuel rail assembly, use a backup wrench on the fittings to prevent turning.

13. Attach the vacuum line to the regulator.

14. Connect the negative battery cable. Turn the ignition to the **ON** position for two seconds, then turn it to the **OFF** position for ten seconds. Turn again to the **ON** position and check for fuel leaks.

Throttle Position (TP) Sensor

REMOVAL & INSTALLATION

♦ See Figure 37

1. Disconnect the negative battery cable.

2. If necessary for access to the sensor, remove the air cleaner tube resonator assembly.

3. Detach the electrical connector from the TP sensor.

4. Unfasten the attaching screws, lock washers and retainers, as applicable.

5. Remove the throttle position sensor. If necessary, remove the screw holding the actuator to the end of the throttle shaft.

To install:

6. With the throttle valve in the normal closed idle position, install the TP sensor on the throttle body assembly, making sure the sensor pickup lever is located above the tang on the throttle actuator lever.

7. Install the retainers, screws and lock washers using a thread locking compound. Tighten to 18 inch lbs. (2 Nm).

8. Attach the sensor electrical connector.

9. If removed, install the air cleaner tube resonator assembly.

10. Connect the negative battery cable.

ADJUSTMENT

3.0L and 3.3L Engines

1. Install three jumper wires between the TP sensor and the harness connector or use a "SCAN" tool and view throttle position

2. With the ignition in the **ON** position and the throttle closed, use a digital voltmeter connected between "A" and "B'", adjust the position of the throttle sensor to obtain a reading of 0.50-0.59 volts for a 3.0L engine and 0.38-0.42 volts for a 3.3L engine.

3. Tighten the screws to 18 inch lbs. (2.0 Nm), recheck the reading to make sure the adjustment has not changed.

4. With the ignition **OFF**, remove the jumper wires, then connect the harness to the TP sensor.

TPS Output Check Test

WITH SCAN TOOL

1. Use a suitable scan tool to read the TPS voltage.

2. With the ignition switch **ON** and the engine **OFF**, the TPS voltage should be less, than 1.25 volts.

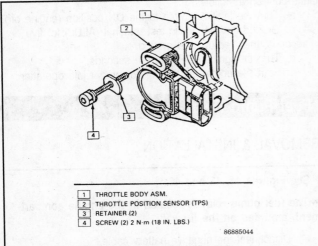

1	THROTTLE BODY ASM.
2	THROTTLE POSITION SENSOR (TPS)
3	RETAINER (2)
4	SCREW (2) 2 N·m (18 IN. LBS.)

86885044

Fig. 37 View of the Throttle Position (TP) sensor mounting — 3.0L engine shown

3. If the voltage reading is higher than specified, replace the throttle position sensor.

WITHOUT SCAN TOOL

1. Disconnect the TPS harness from the TPS.

2. Using suitable jumper wires, connect a digital voltmeter to terminals A and B on the TPS.

3. With the ignition **ON** and the engine running, the TPS voltage should be 0.450-1.25 volts at base idle to approximately 4.5 volts at wide open throttle.

4. If the reading on the TPS is out of specification, replace it.

5. Turn ignition **OFF**, remove jumper wires, then reconnect harness to throttle position switch.

Idle Air Control (IAC) Valve

REMOVAL & INSTALLATION

▶ **See Figures 38, 39, 40, 41, 42 and 43**

1. Disconnect the negative battery cable.

2. Detach electrical connector from idle air control valve.

3. Unfasten the retaining screws, then remove the idle air control valve from its mounting position.

To install:

✳✳WARNING

If re-installing the used IAC valve, DO NOT push or pull on the valve pintle! The force required to move the pintle may damage the threads on the worm drive. Also, do not soak the valve in any liquid cleaner; this will damage the valve

4. If installing a new idle air control valve, measure the distance the valve plunger is extended. Measurement should be made from the edge of the valves mounting flange to the end of the cone. The distance should not exceed $1\frac{1}{8}$ in. (28mm), or damage to the valve may occur when installed. If measuring distance is greater than specified above, use finger pressure to slowly retract the pintle, by using a slight side to side motion to help it retract easier (valve with collar at electric terminal end) or compress the retaining spring from the valve while turning the valve "in" with a clockwise motion. Return the spring to its original position with the straight part of the spring end aligned with the flat surface of the valve (valve without collar at electric terminal end).

5. Use a new gasket, then position the idle air control valve in its mounting position.

6. Install the retaining screws, then tighten them to 27 inch lbs. (3 Nm).

7. Attach the IAC valve electrical connector.

8. Connect the negative battery cable.

9. For most vehicles, the idle may be unstable for up to 7 minutes upon restarting, while the ECM resets the IAC valve pintle to the correct position.

10. For vehicles equipped with a 3.0L engine, reset the IAC valve by turning the ignition switch **ON**, and then **OFF**.

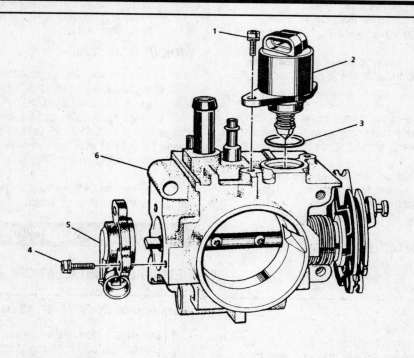

1   SCREW - IAC VALVE ATTACHING

2   VALVE ASSEMBLY - IDLE AIR CONTROL (IAC)

3   O-RING - IAC VALVE

4   SCREW - TP SENSOR ATTACHING

5   SENSOR - THROTTLE POSITION (TP)

6   BODY ASSEMBLY - THROTTLE

86885038

Fig. 38 View of the Idle Air Control (IAC) valve mounting in the throttle body assembly

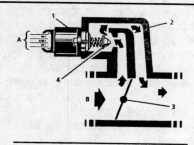

1   VALVE ASSEMBLY - IDLE AIR CONTROL (IAC)

2   BODY ASSEMBLY - THROTTLE

3   VALVE - THROTTLE

4   PINTLE - IAC VALVE

A   ELECTRICAL INPUT SIGNAL

B   AIR INLET

86885039

Fig. 39 IAC valve air flow diagram

11. For 1990-95 2.3L vehicles you must reset the IAC valve pintle position as follows:

    a. Turn the ignition switch to the **ON** position (engine off).

    b. Ground the diagnostic test terminal (ALDL) for five seconds, then remove the ground.

    c. Turn the ignition **OFF** for ten seconds.

    d. Start the engine and check for proper idle operation.

Fuel Pump Relay

REMOVAL & INSTALLATION

▶ See Figures 44, 45 and 46

➡The fuel pump relay is located in the engine compartment, mounted on the firewall.

1. Disconnect the negative battery cable.

2. On some vehicles, there is cover over the relays that must be removed for access.

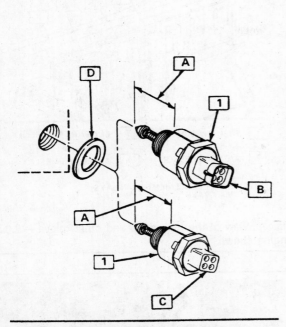

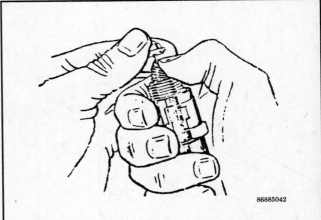

Fig. 42 For new IAC valves without a collar, compress the retaining spring from the valve while turning the valve "in" with a clockwise motion, then . . .

1	IDLE AIR CONTROL VALVE
A	LESS THAN 28mm (1-1/8 IN.)
B	TYPE I (WITH COLLAR)
C	TYPE II (WITHOUT COLLAR)
D	GASKET (PART OF IAC VALVE SERVICE KIT)

86885040

Fig. 40 There are two types of IAC valves; one has a collar at the electric terminal end and one doesn't

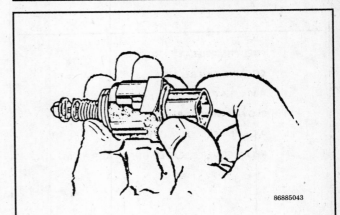

86885043

Fig. 43 . . . return the spring to its original position with the straight part of the spring end aligned with the flat surface of the valve

3. Detach the fuel pump relay electrical connector, then remove the relay.

To install:
4. Install the relay, then attach the electrical connector.
5. If equipped, install the relay cover.
6. Connect the negative battery cable.

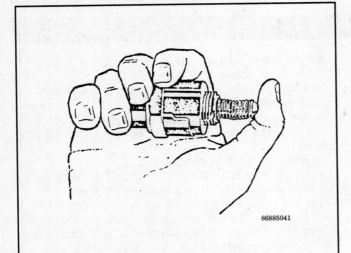

86885041

Fig. 41 Adjusting a new IAC valve — with collar

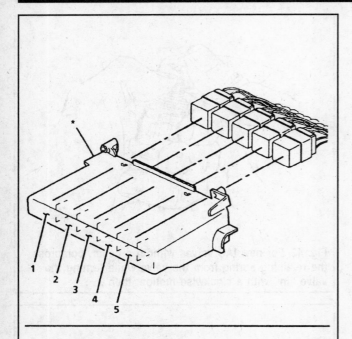

1   FUEL PUMP RELAY

2   COOLING FAN RELAY

3   ABS RELAY

4   BLOWER MOTOR RELAY

5   A/C COMPRESSOR RELAY

*   RELAY COVER LOCATED UNDER ABS EBCM

86885045

Fig. 44 On some vehicles, such as this 2.3L engine, there is a cover over the relays which must be removed in order to access the relays

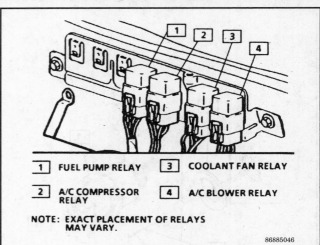

| 1 | FUEL PUMP RELAY | 3 | COOLANT FAN RELAY |
| 2 | A/C COMPRESSOR RELAY | 4 | A/C BLOWER RELAY |

NOTE: EXACT PLACEMENT OF RELAYS MAY VARY.

86885046

Fig. 45 View of the fuel pump and other relays — 2.0L engine shown

86885047

Fig. 46 View of the relays mounted on the engine compartment firewall — 1986 3.0L engine shown

SEQUENTIAL FUEL INJECTION

System Description

▶ See Figures 47, 48, 49, 50 and 51

The Sequential Fuel Injection (SFI) system, found on 3.1L engines, is a multi-port system in which the Powertrain Control Module (PCM) monitors engine operations and generates output signals to provide the correct air/fuel mixture, ignition timing and engine idle speed control. Fuel is delivered to the engine by individual injectors mounted in the intake manifold near each cylinder.

The main control sensor is the Heated Oxygen Sensor (HO$_2$S) which is located in the exhaust manifold. This sensor tells the PCM how much oxygen is in the exhaust gas, and the PCM changes the air/fuel ratio to the engine by controlling the fuel injectors. The best mixture to minimize exhaust emissions is 14.7:1 which allows the catalytic converter to operate most efficiently. Because of the constant measuring and adjust-

ing of the air/fuel ratio, the fuel injection system is called a "Closed Loop" system.

The fuel metering system components in the SFI system include the following:

• Fuel supply components: fuel tank, pump and pipes
• Fuel rail assembly, including the SFI fuel injectors and the pressure regulator
• Fuel pump electrical circuit
• Throttle body assembly, which includes the Idle Air Control (IAC) valve and the Throttle Position (TP) sensor

The fuel supply is stored in the fuel tank. An electric fuel pump, located in the fuel tank with the gauge sending unit, pumps fuel through an in-pipe fuel filter to the fuel rail assembly. The pump provides fuel at a pressure greater than is needed by the injectors. A fuel pressure regulator, part of the fuel rail assembly, keeps fuel available to the injectors at a controlled pressure. Unused fuel is returned to the fuel tank by a separate pipe. When the ignition switch is turned to the **ON** position, without the engine running, the PCM energizes the fuel pump relay for two seconds, causing the fuel pump to pressurize the fuel system. If the PCM does not receive ignition reference pulses (engine cranking or running) within two seconds, it shuts off the fuel pump or relay, causing the fuel pump to stop.

The fuel rail assembly is made up of the left-hand rail, which delivers fuel to the even number cylinders (2, 4, 6); the right-hand rail, which delivers fuel to the odd number cylinders (1, 3, 5); the fuel injectors and the fuel pressure regulator. The rail assembly is mounted to the lower section of the intake manifold and distributes fuel to the cylinder through the individual injectors. Fuel is delivered from the pump through the fuel feed pipe to the inlet fitting on the fuel rail. From there it is directed, by the crossover tube, to the other fuel rail. Fuel in each rail flows through the main supply conduit, and excess fuel flows back through the pressure regulator assembly, which maintains correct system pressure. Fuel then flows from the regulator through the fuel return pipe back to the tank.

The fuel pressure regulator is a diaphragm-operated relief valve with fuel pump pressure on one side, and regulator spring pressure intake manifold vacuum on the other. the function of the regulator is the maintain a constant pressure across the injectors at all times. The pressure regulator compensates for engine load by increasing fuel pressure as engine vacuum drops. With the ignition **ON** and the engine **OFF** (zero vacuum), fuel pressure at the pressure connection should be 41-47 psi (284-325 kPa). If the pressure is too low, poor performance could result. If the pressure is too high, excessive odor and DTC 45 may result.

The accelerator control system is cable type. There are no linkage adjustments. Therefore, the specific cable for each application must be used. Only the specific replacement part will work. When work has been performed on accelerator controls, always make sure that all components are installed correctly and that linkage and cables are not rubbing or binding in any manner. The throttle should operate freely without bind between full closed and wide open throttle (WOT).

The throttle body assembly is mounted on the intake manifold plenum, and is used to control air flow into the engine,

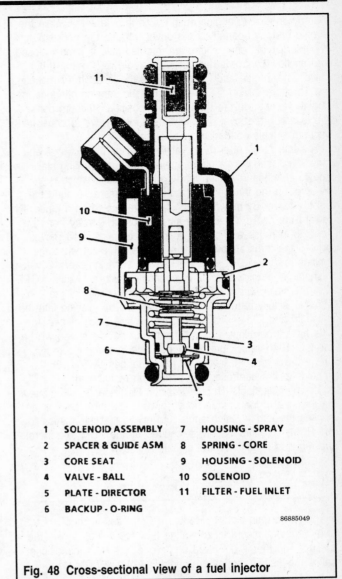

1	SOLENOID ASSEMBLY	**7**	HOUSING - SPRAY
2	SPACER & GUIDE ASM	**8**	SPRING - CORE
3	CORE SEAT	**9**	HOUSING - SOLENOID
4	VALVE - BALL	**10**	SOLENOID
5	PLATE - DIRECTOR	**11**	FILTER - FUEL INLET
6	BACKUP - O-RING		

86885049

Fig. 48 Cross-sectional view of a fuel injector

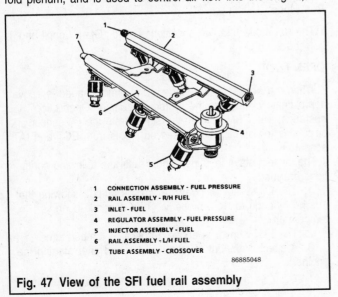

1 CONNECTION ASSEMBLY - FUEL PRESSURE
2 RAIL ASSEMBLY - R/H FUEL
3 INLET - FUEL
4 REGULATOR ASSEMBLY - FUEL PRESSURE
5 INJECTOR ASSEMBLY - FUEL
6 RAIL ASSEMBLY - L/H FUEL
7 TUBE ASSEMBLY - CROSSOVER

86885048

Fig. 47 View of the SFI fuel rail assembly

1 COVER
2 VACUUM CHAMBER
(VACUUM SOURCE TUBE NOT SHOWN)
3 SEAL - O-RING
4 VALVE - FUEL PRESSURE REGULATOR
5 BASE ASSEMBLY
6 FILTER - SCREEN (IF EQUIPPED)
7 DIAPHRAGM
8 SPRING

86885050

Fig. 49 The fuel pressure regulator is mounted on the fuel rail

thereby controlling engine output. The throttle valve within the throttle body is opened by the driver through the accelerator controls. During engine idle, the throttle valve is almost closed, and air flow control is handled by the Idle Air Control (IAC) valve. The throttle body also provides the location for mounting the Throttle Position (TP) sensor and the sensing changes in engine vacuum due to throttle valve position. Vacuum ports are located at, above, or below the throttle valve to generate vacuum signals needed by various components.

The Idle Air Control (IAC) valve's function is to control engine idle speed, as its name implies, while preventing stalls due to changes in engine load. The IAC valve, which is mounted in the throttle body, controls bypass air around the throttle valve. By moving a conical valve known as a pintle, IN toward the seat (to decrease air flow) or OUT away from the seat (to increase air flow), a controlled amount of air moves around the throttle plate. The IAC valve will reset when the ignition is turned **ON**, then **OFF**. When servicing the IAC valve, it should only disconnected or connected with the ignition **OFF**. The IAC valve affects only the idle characteristics of the vehicle. If it is fully retracted, too much air will be allowed into the manifold and idle speed will be high. If it is stuck closed, too little air will be allowed in the manifold, and idle speed will be too low. If it is stuck part way open, the idle may be rough, and will not respond to engine load changes. A DTC 35 should set if a controlled idle cannot be maintained.

The nonadjustable Throttle Position (TP) sensor is mounted on the side of the throttle body opposite the throttle lever. It senses the throttle valve angle and relays that information to the PCM. This information is required by the PCM to generate the required injector control signals (pulses).

OPERATING MODES

The Powertrain Control Module (PCM) uses voltage input from various sensors to determine how much fuel to give the engine. The fuel is delivered under one of several conditions, called modes. All modes are controlled by the PCM.

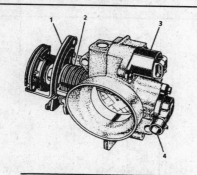

1	LEVER ASSSEMBLY - THROTTLE SHAFT AND CAM
2	SPRING - THROTTLE RETURN
3	VALVE ASSEMBLY - IDLE AIR CONTROL (IAC)
4	SENSOR ASSEMBLY - THROTTLE POSITION (TP)

86885051

Fig. 50 View of the throttle body used on the SFI system

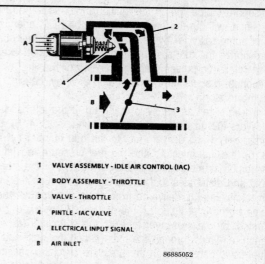

1	VALVE ASSEMBLY - IDLE AIR CONTROL (IAC)
2	BODY ASSEMBLY - THROTTLE
3	VALVE - THROTTLE
4	PINTLE - IAC VALVE
A	ELECTRICAL INPUT SIGNAL
B	AIR INLET

86885052

Fig. 51 Idle Air Control (IAC) valve air flow diagram

Starting Mode

When the ignition is first turned **ON** (before engaging the starter), the PCM energizes the fuel pump relay for a calibrated time (approximately 2 seconds) to allow the fuel pump to build up pressure. The PCM also checks the ECT, MAP and TP sensors to determine the proper air/fuel ratio for starting. This ranges from 1.5:1 at -33°F (-36°C) to 14.7:1 at 201°F (94°C), operating temperature. The PCM controls the amount of fuel delivered by changing how long the injectors are energized. This is done by pulsing the injectors for very short times.

Clear Flood Mode

If the engine floods, it can be cleared by pushing the accelerator all the way down. The PCM then completely turns off the fuel. No fuel is delivered from the injectors as long as the throttle stays wide open and the engine speed is below 600 rpm. If the throttle position becomes less than 80% the PCM returns to the starting mode.

Run Mode

The run mode had two conditions called "Open Loop" and "Closed Loop".

OPEN LOOP

When the engine is first started, and engine speed is above approximately 400 rpm, the system goes into "Open Loop" operation. The PCM ignores the signal from the O_2 sensor and calculates the air/fuel ratio based on inputs from ECT and IAT sensors.

The system stays in "Open Loop" until the following conditions are met:

1. The O_2 sensor has varying voltage output, showing that it is hot enough to work properly. (This depends upon temperature.)

2. The ECT sensor is above a specified temperature.

3. A specific amount of time has elapsed after starting the engine.

CLOSED LOOP

Specific values for the previous conditions exist for each different engine and are stores in the PROM. When these values are met, the system goes into "Closed Loop" operation. The PCM calculates the air/fuel ratio (injector on-time) based on the signal from the O_2 sensor. This allows the air/fuel ratio to stay very close to 14.7:1.

Acceleration Mode

When the driver pushes on the accelerator pedal, air flow into the cylinders increased rapidly, while fuel flow tends to lag behind. To prevent possible hesitation, the PCM increases the pulse width to the injectors to provide extra fuel during acceleration. The amount of fuel required is based on throttle position, manifold air pressure, and engine speed.

Fuel Cutoff Mode

To prevent possible engine damage from over-speed, the PCM will cut off fuel from the injectors when engine speed is about 6,200 rpm with the vehicle in any forward gear or reverse, and approximately 4,000 rpm in park or neutral. To prevent tire damage, the PCM also has a fuel cut off in excess of 100 mph (161 km/h) based on the speed rating of the tires.

Deceleration Mode

When the driver released the accelerator pedal, air flow in the engine is reduced. The corresponding changes in throttle position and manifold air pressure are relayed to the PCM, which reduces the injector pulse width to reduce fuel flow. If the deceleration is very rapid, or for long periods (such as long closed throttle coast-down), the PCM shuts off fuel completely for short periods in order to protect the catalytic converter.

Converter Protection Mode

The PCM constantly monitors engine operation and estimates conditions that could result in high converter temperatures. If the PCM determines the converter may overheat, it causes the system to return to "Open Loop" operation and enriches the fuel mixture.

Battery Voltage Correction Mode

When battery voltage is low, the PCM can compensate for the weak spark delivered by the electronic ignition system by:
- Increasing the injector pulse width.
- Increasing the idle rpm.
- Increasing ignition dwell time.

Relieving Fuel System Pressure

1. Disconnect the negative battery cable to avoid possible fuel discharge if an accidental attempt is made to start the engine.
2. Loosen the fuel filler cap to relieve fuel tank vapor pressure.
3. Connect fuel pressure gauge J 34730-1 or equivalent, to the fuel pressure connection at the fuel rail. Wrap a shop towel around the fittings while connecting the tool to avoid fuel spillage.
4. Install a bleed hose into an approved container, then open the valve to bleed the system pressure. Drain any fuel still in the gauge into an approved container.
5. After service is completed, don't forget to tighten the fuel filler cap.

Electric Fuel Pump

REMOVAL & INSTALLATION

▶ **See Figures 52, 53, 54, 55 and 56**

1. Disconnect the negative battery cable.
2. Properly relieve the fuel system pressure.
3. Drain then remove the fuel tank from the vehicle. For details, please refer to the procedure located in this section.

✳✳CAUTION

Observe all applicable safety precautions when working around fuel. Do not allow fuel spray or fuel vapors to come in contact with a spark or open flame. Keep a dry chemical (Class B) fire extinguisher near the work area. Never drain or store fuel in an open container due to the possibility of fire or explosion.

4. While holding the modulator fuel sender assembly down, remove the snapring from the designated slots located on the retainer.

➡**The modular fuel sender assembly may spring up from its position. When removing the modular fuel sender from the tank, be aware that the reservoir bucket is full of fuel. It must be tipped slightly during removal to avoid damage to the float.**

5. Remove the external fuel strainer.
6. Separate the Connector Position Assurance (CPA) from the electrical connector and detach the fuel pump electrical connector.
7. Gently release the tabs on the sides of the fuel sender at the cover assembly. Begin by squeezing the sides of the reservoir and releasing the tab opposite the fuel level sensor. Move clockwise to release the second and third tab in the same manner.
8. Lift the cover assembly out far enough to disconnect the fuel pump electrical connection.
9. Rotate the fuel pump baffle counterclockwise and remove the baffle and pump assembly from the retainer.
10. Slide the fuel pump outlet from its slot, then remove the fuel pump outlet seal.
   To install:
11. Install the fuel pump outlet seal.
12. Slide the fuel pump outlet into the slots of the reservoir cover.
13. Install the fuel pump and baffle assembly onto the reservoir retainer and rotate clockwise until seated.

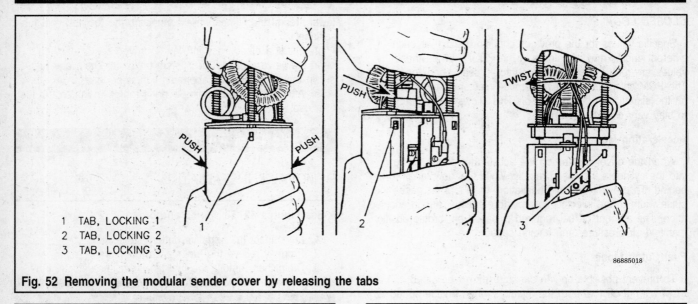

1 TAB, LOCKING 1
2 TAB, LOCKING 2
3 TAB, LOCKING 3

86885018

Fig. 52 Removing the modular sender cover by releasing the tabs

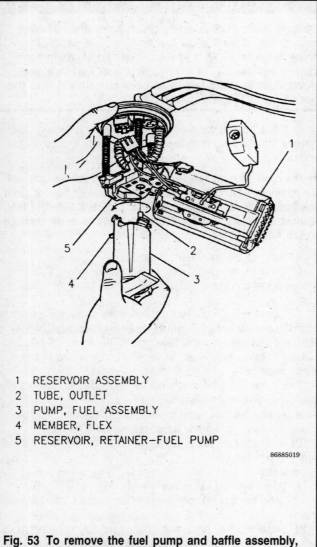

1 RESERVOIR ASSEMBLY
2 TUBE, OUTLET
3 PUMP, FUEL ASSEMBLY
4 MEMBER, FLEX
5 RESERVOIR, RETAINER—FUEL PUMP

86885019

Fig. 53 To remove the fuel pump and baffle assembly, you must rotate it counterclockwise

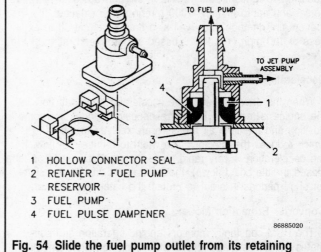
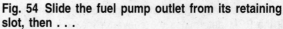

1 HOLLOW CONNECTOR SEAL
2 RETAINER – FUEL PUMP
   RESERVOIR
3 FUEL PUMP
4 FUEL PULSE DAMPENER

86885020

Fig. 54 Slide the fuel pump outlet from its retaining slot, then . . .

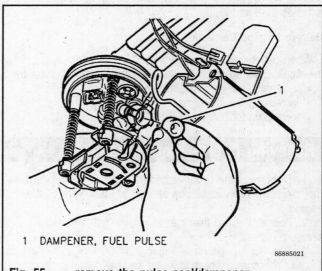

1 DAMPENER, FUEL PULSE

86885021

Fig. 55 . . . remove the pulse seal/dampener

14. Install the lower retainer assembly partially into the reservoir. Line up all 3 sleeve tabs. Press the retainer onto the reservoir making sure all 3 tabs are firmly seated.

➡**Gently pull on the fuel pump reservoir to assure a secure fastening. If not secure, replace the entire fuel sender.**

15. Attach the fuel pump connector.
16. Connect the CPA to the fuel sender cover.
17. Install a new external fuel strainer.
18. Install the modular fuel sender as follows:
   a. Position a new sender-to-tank O-ring. Align the tab on the front of the sender with the slot on the front of the retainer snapring.
   b. Slowly apply pressure to the top of the spring loaded sender until it aligns flush with the retainer on the tank.
   c. Insert the snapring into its designated slots, making sure it is fully seated.
19. Install the fuel tank as outlined later in this section.
20. Carefully lower the vehicle, then fill the fuel tank.
21. Connect the negative battery cable. Turn the ignition to the **ON** position for two seconds, then turn it to the **OFF** position for ten seconds. Turn again to the **ON** position and check for fuel leaks.

Throttle Body

REMOVAL & INSTALLATION

▶ **See Figure 57**

1. Disconnect the negative battery cable.
2. Properly relieve the fuel system pressure.
3. Remove the air inlet duct.
4. Detach the IAC valve and the TP sensor electrical connectors.
5. Disconnect the throttle and cruise control cables.
6. Unfasten the accelerator cable bracket bolts, then remove the bracket.
7. Remove the engine coolant pipe nut to gain access to the throttle body attaching stud.
8. Unfasten the throttle body retaining nut/stud, then remove the throttle body assembly. Remove and discard the flange gasket.
9. Clean the gasket mating surfaces.

✳✳CAUTION

Be careful when cleaning the mating surfaces because sharp tools may scratch and/or damage the sealing surfaces.

To install:
10. Position a new flange gasket, then install the throttle body assembly and secure with the retaining bolt/stud. Tighten to 18 ft. lbs. (25 Nm).
11. Fasten the coolant pipe nut, then install the accelerator cable bracket.

12. Connect the throttle and cruise control cables.

➡**Make sure the throttle and cruise control linkage does not hold the throttle open.**

13. Attach the TP sensor and IAC valve electrical connectors.
14. Install the air inlet duct, then connect the negative battery cable.
15. With the engine off, check to make sure the accelerator pedal if free by depressing it to the floor, then releasing it.

Fuel Injectors

REMOVAL & INSTALLATION

▶ **See Figure 58**

1. Disconnect the negative battery cable.
2. Properly relieve the fuel system pressure.
3. Remove the intake manifold plenum and the fuel rail assembly. Refer to the procedures later in this section for details.
4. Unfasten and discard the injector retaining clip, then remove the fuel injector. Remove and discard the O-rings from both ends of the injector. Save the O-ring backups for use during installation.

To install:
5. Make sure the O-ring backups are on the injectors prior to installing new O-rings. Lubricate new injector O-rings with clean engine oil, then install them on the injector assembly.
6. Place new injector retaining clips on the injector assembly. Position the open end of the clip facing the injector electrical connector.
7. Install the fuel injector assembly into the fuel rail injector socket with the electrical connectors facing outward. Push in far enough to engage the retainer clip with the machined slots on the rail socket.
8. Install the fuel rail assembly and intake manifold plenum. Refer to the procedures later in this section for details.
9. Connect the negative battery cable.

Intake Manifold Plenum

Removing the fuel rail and/or injectors requires removal of the top portion of the intake manifold, which is called the plenum.

REMOVAL & INSTALLATION

▶ **See Figure 59**

1. Disconnect the negative battery cable.
2. Tag and disconnect the vacuum hoses.
3. Unfasten the EGR-to-plenum nuts.
4. Remove the throttle body assembly. Refer to the procedure located earlier in this section for details.
5. Remove the ignition coil assembly front retaining bolts.
6. Remove the alternator braces.
7. Detach the MAP sensor connector, then remove the sensor and bracket.

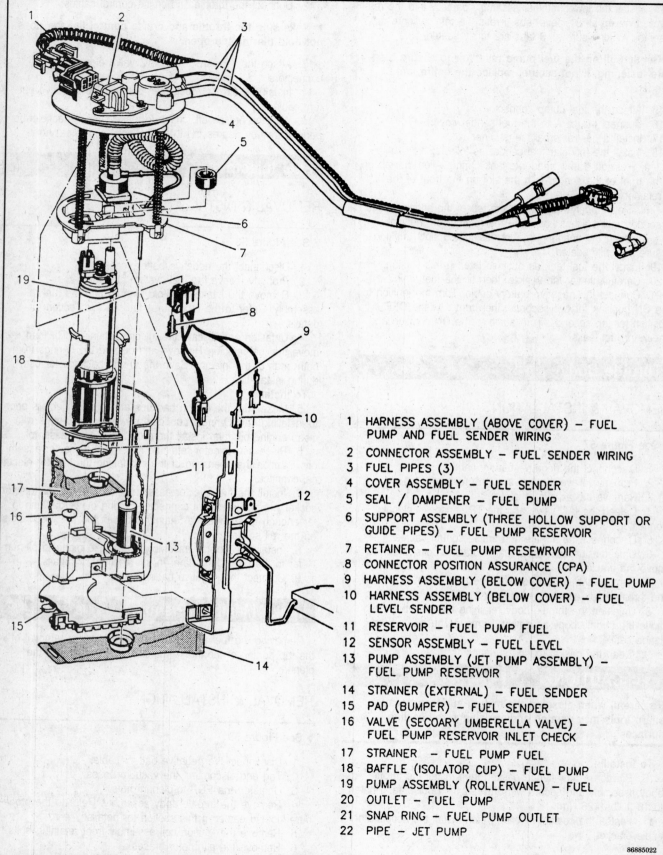

1 HARNESS ASSEMBLY (ABOVE COVER) – FUEL PUMP AND FUEL SENDER WIRING
2 CONNECTOR ASSEMBLY – FUEL SENDER WIRING
3 FUEL PIPES (3)
4 COVER ASSEMBLY – FUEL SENDER
5 SEAL / DAMPENER – FUEL PUMP
6 SUPPORT ASSEMBLY (THREE HOLLOW SUPPORT OR GUIDE PIPES) – FUEL PUMP RESERVOIR
7 RETAINER – FUEL PUMP RESEWRVOIR
8 CONNECTOR POSITION ASSURANCE (CPA)
9 HARNESS ASSEMBLY (BELOW COVER) – FUEL PUMP
10 HARNESS ASSEMBLY (BELOW COVER) – FUEL LEVEL SENDER
11 RESERVOIR – FUEL PUMP FUEL
12 SENSOR ASSEMBLY – FUEL LEVEL
13 PUMP ASSEMBLY (JET PUMP ASSEMBLY) – FUEL PUMP RESERVOIR
14 STRAINER (EXTERNAL) – FUEL SENDER
15 PAD (BUMPER) – FUEL SENDER
16 VALVE (SECOARY UMBERELLA VALVE) – FUEL PUMP RESERVOIR INLET CHECK
17 STRAINER – FUEL PUMP FUEL
18 BAFFLE (ISOLATOR CUP) – FUEL PUMP
19 PUMP ASSEMBLY (ROLLERVANE) – FUEL
20 OUTLET – FUEL PUMP
21 SNAP RING – FUEL PUMP OUTLET
22 PIPE – JET PUMP

86885022

Fig. 56 Exploded view of the modular fuel sender and related components

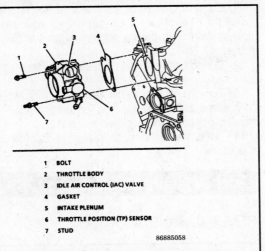

1 BOLT
2 THROTTLE BODY
3 IDLE AIR CONTROL (IAC) VALVE
4 GASKET
5 INTAKE PLENUM
6 THROTTLE POSITION (TP) SENSOR
7 STUD

86885058

Fig. 57 Removing the throttle body assembly — 3.1L SFI engine

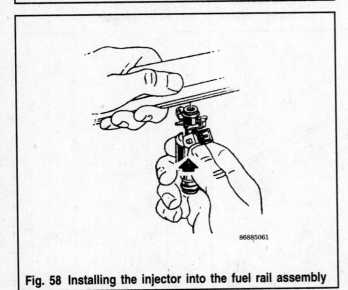

86885061

Fig. 58 Installing the injector into the fuel rail assembly

8. Unfasten the plenum retaining bolts, then remove the plenum. Remove and discard the gaskets.

➡ **Be careful when cleaning the mating surfaces because sharp tools may damage the sealing surfaces and possibly cause leaks.**

9. Carefully clean the gasket mating surfaces.
To install:

➡ **Make sure you route the MAP sensor electrical connector to the outside of the plenum gasket.**

10. Position new plenum gaskets. Install the plenum, then securing using the retaining bolts. Tighten the bolts to 18 ft. lbs. (25 Nm).
11. Install the MAP sensor and bracket. Attach the electrical connector.
12. Install the alternator braces, then fasten the coil front retaining bolts.
13. Fasten the EGR-to-plenum bolts.
14. Connect the vacuum lines as tagged during removal.

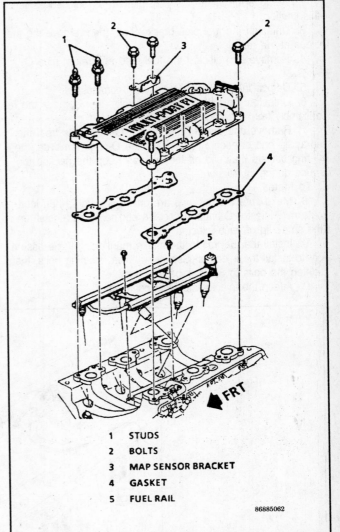

1 STUDS
2 BOLTS
3 MAP SENSOR BRACKET
4 GASKET
5 FUEL RAIL

86885062

Fig. 59 The intake plenum must be removed in order to remove the fuel rail and injectors

15. Install the throttle body assembly as outlined earlier in this section.
16. Connect the negative battery cable. With the engine off, make sure the accelerator cable is free by depressing the pedal to the floor then release it.

Fuel Rail Assembly

REMOVAL & INSTALLATION

▶ See Figure 60

➡ **Be careful when removing the fuel rail assembly to avoid damage to the injector electrical connector terminals and spray tips. Prevent dirt and other debris from entering open lines and passages. Fittings should be capped and holes should be plugged during servicing.**

1. Disconnect the negative battery cable, then properly relieve the fuel system pressure.

2. Remove the intake manifold plenum as outlined earlier in this section.

3. Unfasten the fuel pipe bracket bolt, then remove the fuel pipes at the rail.

4. Remove and discard the fuel feed and return pipe O-rings.

5. Detach the fuel injector electrical connectors.

6. Unfasten the fuel rail retaining bolts, then remove the rail assembly from the engine.

7. Remove and discard the injector O-ring seals from the spray tip end of each injector. With the O-rings removed, the O-ring backup may slip off the injector. Keep the backup for reuse during installation.

To install:

8. Make sure the backups are on the injectors, then lubricate new injector O-rings with clean engine oil and install on the spray tip of each injector.

9. Install the fuel rail in the intake manifold. Tilt the assembly to install the injectors. Secure with the retaining bolts, then tighten the bolts to 89 inch lbs. (10 Nm).

10. Attach the injector electrical connectors.

11. Put new O-rings on the fuel feed and return pipes, then install the pipes. Using a backup wrench on the fittings to prevent them from turning, tightening the fuel pipe nuts to 13 ft. lbs. (17 Nm).

12. Connect the negative battery cable, then tighten the fuel filler cap.

13. Turn the ignition to the **ON** position for two seconds, then turn it to the **OFF** position for ten seconds. Turn again to the **ON** position and check for fuel leaks.

14. Install the intake manifold plenum as outlined earlier in this section.

Fuel Pressure Regulator

REMOVAL & INSTALLATION

▶ See Figure 60

1. Disconnect the negative battery cable.
2. Properly relieve the fuel system pressure.

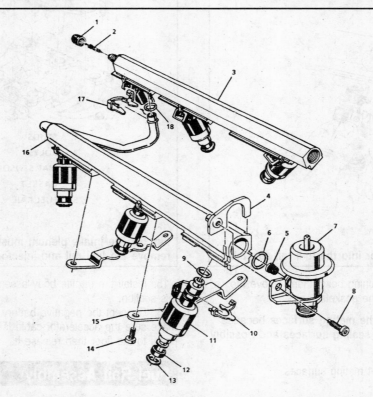

1	CAP - FUEL PRESSURE CONNECTION
2	VALVE ASSEMBLY - FUEL PRESSURE CONNECTION
3	RAIL ASSEMBLY - RH FUEL
4	BRACKET - RETAINER AND SPACER
5	SCREEN - FILTER
6	O-RING - PRESSURE REGULATOR INLET
7	REGULATOR ASSEMBLY - FUEL PRESSURE
8	SCREW - PRESSURE REGULATOR ATTACHING
9	O-RING - UPPER INJECTOR (BLACK)
10	CLIP - INJECTOR RETAINER
11	INJECTOR ASSEMBLY - FUEL
12	BACKUP - O-RING
13	O-RING - LOWER INJECTOR (BROWN)
14	SCREW - RAIL MOUNTING BRACKET ATTACHING
15	BRACKET - RAIL MOUNTING (2 EA.)
16	RAIL ASSEMBLY - LH FUEL (WITH CROSSOVER TUBE)
17	CLIP - CROSSOVER TUBE RETAINER
18	O-RING - CROSSOVER TUBE

86885063

Fig. 60 View of the fuel rail assembly, injectors and fuel pressure regulator — 3.1L SFI engine

3. Remove the intake manifold plenum as described earlier in this section.

4. Disconnect the vacuum line from the regulator.

5. Place a shop towel under the regulator to catch any fuel that may drip out. Unfasten the fuel pressure regulator retaining screw, then remove the regulator by twisting and pulling it from the fuel rail.

6. Remove and discard the retainer and spacer bracket from the fuel rail.

7. Disconnect the regulator from the fuel return pipe.

8. Remove and discard the regulator inlet O-ring. Inspect the filter screen for contamination and replace if necessary.

To install:

9. Lubricate a new pressure regulator inlet O-ring with clean engine oil, then install on the regulator inlet.

➡**The fuel return pipe must be connected before tightening the regulator retaining screw to prevent the regulator from rotating. Rotation of the regulator could damage the retainer and spacer bracket and lead to a fuel leak at the regulator inlet.**

10. Connect the fuel return pipe to the regulator.

11. Install a new retainer and spacer bracket into the slot on the fuel rail.

12. Connect the regulator to the fuel rail. Tighten the fuel return pipe nut to 13 ft. lbs. (17 Nm). Secure the regulator with the retaining screw. Tighten the screw to 6 ft. lbs. (8.5 Nm).

13. Attach the vacuum line to the regulator.

14. Make sure that the retainer and spacer bracket is engages in the slots in the fuel rail.

15. Turn the ignition to the **ON** position for two seconds, then turn it to the **OFF** position for ten seconds. Turn again to the **ON** position and check for fuel leaks.

16. Install the intake manifold plenum as outlined earlier in this section.

Throttle Position (TP) Sensor

REMOVAL & INSTALLATION

▶ **See Figure 62**

1. Disconnect the negative battery cable.
2. Remove the air inlet duct.
3. Detach the TP sensor electrical connector.
4. Unfasten the attaching screws and retainers, then remove the TP sensor. Remove and discard the O-ring.

To install:

5. With the throttle valve in the normal closed idle position, install the TP sensor, with a new O-ring, on the throttle body. Secure using the two retaining screw, then tighten the screws to 18 inch lbs. (2 Nm).

6. Attach the TP sensor electrical connector.
7. Install the air inlet duct.
8. Connect the negative battery cable.

Idle Air Control (IAC) Valve

REMOVAL & INSTALLATION

▶ **See Figures 61 and 62**

➡**If installing a new IAC valve, be sure to replace with an identical part. IAC valve pintle shape and diameter are designed for the specific application.**

1. Disconnect the negative battery cable.
2. Detach the IAC valve electrical connector.
3. Unfasten the IAC valve retaining screws, then remove the valve.
4. Use a suitable carburetor cleaner and parts cleaning brush to clean carbon deposits from the valve. Shiny spots on the pintle seat are normal and do not indicate a need for replacement.
5. Inspect the IAC valve O-ring for damage, and replace if necessary.

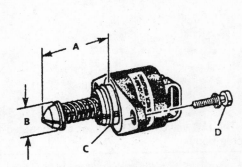

A	DISTANCE OF PINTLE EXTENSION
B	DIAMETER OF PINTLE
C	IACV O-RING
D	IACV ATTACHING SCREW ASSEMBLY

86885060

Fig. 61 If installing a new valve, measure the distance between the tip of the IAC valve pintle and mounting flange

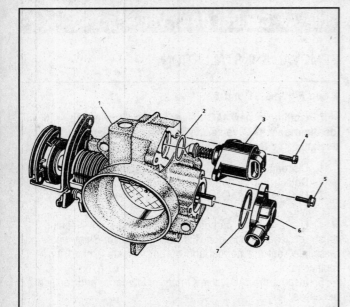

```
1   BODY ASSEMBLY - THROTTLE
2   O-RING - IAC VALVE
3   VALVE ASSEMBLY - IDLE AIR CONTROL (IAC)
4   SCREW - IAC VALVE ATTACHING
5   SCREW - TP SENSOR ATTACHING
6   SENSOR - THROTTLE POSITION (TP)
7   O-RING - TP SENSOR
```

86885059

Fig. 62 The IAC valve and TP sensor are mounted to the throttle body

FUEL LINE FITTINGS

Quick-Connect Fittings

REMOVAL & INSTALLATION

▶ **See Figure 64**

➡ **This procedure requires Tool Set J37088-A fuel line quick-connect separator.**

1. Grasp both sides of the fitting. Twist the female connector $\frac{1}{4}$ turn in each direction to loosen any dirt within the fit-

To install:

> ✳✳**CAUTION**
>
> **If re-installing the old IAC valve, DO NOT push or pull on the valve pintle. The force required to move the pintle may damage the threads on the worm drive. Also, DO NOT soak the valve in any type of liquid cleaner or solvent, as this may damage the valve.**

6. If installing a new valve, measure the distance between the tip of the IAC valve pintle and mounting flange. If the distance is greater than 1 $\frac{1}{8}$ in. (28mm), use finger pressure to slowly retract the pintle. The force required to retract the pintle of a new valve will not cause damage to the valve.

7. Lubricate the IAC valve O-ring with clean engine oil, then position on the valve.

8. Install the IAC valve assembly and secure with the retaining screws. Tighten the screws to 27 inch lbs. (3 Nm).

9. Attach the valve electrical connector.

10. Connect the negative battery cable, then reset the IAC valve pintle position as follows:

   a. Turn the ignition **ON** for five seconds.

   b. Turn the ignition **OFF** for ten seconds.

   c. Start the engine and check for proper idle operation.

Fuel Pump Relay

REMOVAL & INSTALLATION

▶ **See Figure 63**

1. Disconnect the negative battery cable.

2. Detach the fuel pump relay electrical connector, then remove the relay.

To install:

3. Install the fuel pump relay, then attach the relay electrical connector.

4. Connect the negative battery cable.

tings. Using compressed air, blow out the dirt from the quick-connect fittings at the end of the fittings.

> ✳✳**CAUTION**
>
> **Safety glasses MUST be worn when using compressed air to avoid eye injury due to flying dirt particles!**

2. For plastic (hand releasable) fittings, squeeze the plastic retainer release tabs, then pull the connection apart.

3. For metal fittings, choose the correct tool from kit J37088-A for the size of the fitting to be disconnected. Insert the proper tool into the female connector, then push inward to release the locking tabs. Pull the connection apart.

4. If it is necessary to remove rust or burrs from the male tube end of a quick-connect fitting, use emery cloth in a radial motion with the tube end to prevent damage to the O-ring sealing surfaces. Using a clean shop towel, wipe off the male

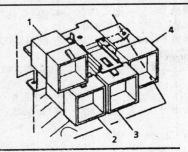

1   FUEL PUMP RELAY
2   COOLING FAN RELAY
3   BLOWER MOTOR RELAY
4   A/C COMPRESSOR RELAY

NOTICE: POSITION OF RELAYS MAY VARY

86885064

Fig. 63 View of the fuel pump and other relays — 3.1L SFI engine shown

tube ends. Inspect all connectors for dirt and burrs. Clean and/or replace if required.

To install:

❈❈CAUTION

Before installing a new filter, always apply a few drops of clean engine oil to the male tube end of the filter and to the fuel level meter assembly. This will ensure proper reconnection and prevent a possible fuel leak. During normal operation, the O-rings located in the female connector will swell and may prevent proper reconnection if not lubricated.

5. Apply a few drops of clean engine oil to the male tube end of the fitting.
6. Push the connectors together to cause the retaining tabs/fingers to snap into place.
7. Once installed, pull on both ends of each connection to make sure they are secure.

FUEL TANK

Tank Assembly

DRAINING

1. Disconnect the negative battery cable.

❈❈CAUTION

To reduce the risk of fire and personal injury, always keep a dry chemical (Class B) fire extinguisher near the work area.

2. Remove the fuel cap.
3. Raise the vehicle and safely support with jackstands.
4. Disconnect the filler vent hose from the tank.

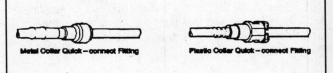

Metal Collar Quick—connect Fitting   Plastic Collar Quick—connect Fitting

Installation

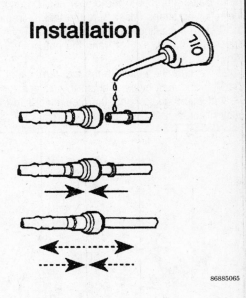

86885065

Fig. 64 Make sure you lubricate the male fitting before fastening the quick-connect fittings

5. Use a hand operated pump approved for gasoline to drain as much fuel as possible through the filler vent hose.
6. Reconnect the filler vent hose and tighten the clamp.
7. Install any removed lines, hoses and cap. Connect the negative battery cable.

REMOVAL & INSTALLATION

1985-91 Vehicles
▶ See Figure 65

1. Disconnect the negative battery cable.
2. Drain the fuel tank as outlined earlier in this section.
3. Remove the fuel filler door assembly and disconnect the screw retaining the filler pipe-to-body bracket.
4. Raise and safely support the vehicle with jackstands.
5. Detach the tank level sender lead connector.

6. If equipped, remove the ground wire retaining screw from the underbody of the vehicle.

7. Disconnect the hoses from the tank meter assembly and the hoses at the tank from the filler and vent pipes.

8. Support the tank with a transmission jack or equivalent.

9. Unfasten the two tank retaining straps, then remove the tank from the vehicle slowly to ensure all connections and hoses have been detached.

To install:

10. Position the tank sound insulators in their original positions and raise the tank far enough to connect the electrical and hose connectors.

11. Raise the tank to the proper position and loosely install the retaining straps. Make sure the tank is in the proper position before tightening the retaining straps. Tighten the strap bolts to 25 ft. lbs. (33 Nm) and the nuts to 106 inch lbs. (12 Nm).

12. Connect the hoses to the fuel tank meter assembly and the filler and vent pipes. Tighten the clamps.

13. If equipped, connect the grounding lead to the underbody of the car.

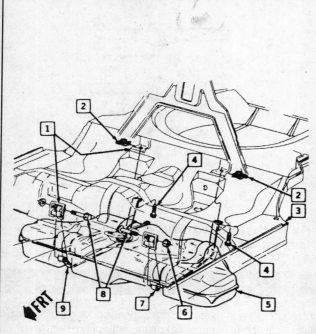

Fig. 65 View of the fuel tank mounting — 1991 vehicle shown

1. SUPPORTS, UNDERBODY
2. NUT
3. BODY ASM.
4. BOLT — 33 N·m (25 LBS. FT.)
5. TANK ASM., FUEL
6. NUT — 12 N·m (106 LBS. IN.)
7. STRAP ASM., LEFT
8. BOLT
9. STRAP ASM., RIGHT

86885066

14. Attach the fuel tank meter assembly harness connector to the body harness connector.

15. Lower the car, install the filler pipe-to-body bracket and the fuel filler door.

16. Connect the negative battery cable, then fill the gas tank with fuel.

17. With the engine OFF, turn the ignition key to the ON position and check for fuel leaks at the tank.

1992-95 Vehicles

▶ See Figure 66

➡Two people are required to perform this procedure.

1. Disconnect the negative battery cable.
2. Properly drain the fuel tank as outlined earlier.
3. Raise and safely support the vehicle.
4. Detach the fuel sender connector.
5. Unfasten the muffler hanger bolts.
6. Remove the exhaust rubber hangers and allow the exhaust system to rest on the rear axle.
7. Disconnect the hoses from the fuel tank sender. For details, please refer to quick-connect fitting removal, located in this section.
8. Detach the hoses, at the tank, from the filler, vent and vapor pipes.
9. With an assistant's help, support the tank, then unfasten the two fuel tank retaining straps. Remove the tank from the vehicle slowly to ensure all connections and hoses have been detached.
10. Remove the sound insulators.
11. Inspect the fuel line O-rings for damage, and replace if necessary.

To install:

12. Install the sound insulators.
13. With an assistant's help, position the fuel tank to the body of the car. Secure using the retaining straps, then tighten the bolts to 24 ft. lbs. (33 Nm).
14. Connect the hoses to the filler, vent and vapor pipes.
15. Attach the fuel feed and return connecting line quick-connect fittings to the fuel sender.
16. Install the exhaust rubber hangers, then secure the muffler hanger bolts. Tighten the bolts to 11 ft. lbs. (15 Nm).
17. Attach the fuel tank sender electrical connector.
18. Carefully lower the vehicle, then refill the fuel tank.
19. Connect the negative battery cable, then turn the ignition to the ON position for two seconds, then turn it to the OFF position for ten seconds. Turn again to the ON position and check for fuel leaks.

SENDING UNIT REPLACEMENT

1985-91 Vehicles

▶ See Figure 67

1. Disconnect the negative battery cable.
2. Remove the fuel tank from the vehicle as outlined earlier.
3. Using locking cam tool J 24187 or equivalent, remove the cam, sender assembly and gasket. Discard the gasket.

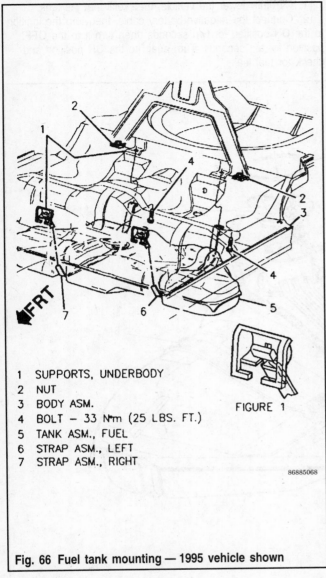

1 SUPPORTS, UNDERBODY
2 NUT
3 BODY ASM.
4 BOLT — 33 N·m (25 LBS. FT.)
5 TANK ASM., FUEL
6 STRAP ASM., LEFT
7 STRAP ASM., RIGHT

FIGURE 1

86885068

Fig. 66 Fuel tank mounting — 1995 vehicle shown

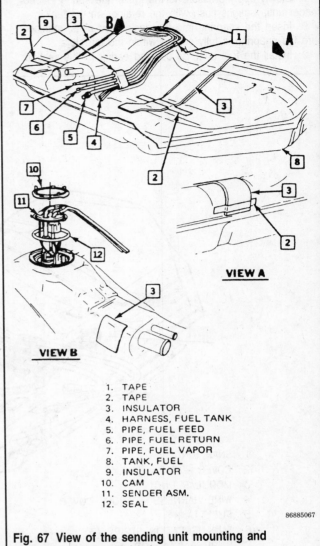

1. TAPE
2. TAPE
3. INSULATOR
4. HARNESS, FUEL TANK
5. PIPE, FUEL FEED
6. PIPE, FUEL RETURN
7. PIPE, FUEL VAPOR
8. TANK, FUEL
9. INSULATOR
10. CAM
11. SENDER ASM.
12. SEAL

86885067

Fig. 67 View of the sending unit mounting and location — 1991 vehicle shown

To install:

✳✳WARNING

Do not twist the strainer when installing the pump/sender assembly. Make sure the strainer does not block the full travel of the float arm.

4. Using a new gasket, install the sender assembly and lock the cam in position with tool J 24187 or equivalent.
5. Install the fuel tank as outlined earlier.
6. Connect the negative battery cable.

1992-95 Vehicles

▶ **See Figure 68**

1. Disconnect the negative battery cable.
2. Properly relieve the fuel system pressure.

3. Drain, then remove the fuel tank, as outlined earlier in this section.

✳✳CAUTION

The modular fuel sender assembly may spring up from its position!

4. While holding the modular fuel sender assembly down, remove the snapring from the designated slots located on the retainer. When removing the sender assembly from the fuel tank, keep in mind that the reservoir bucket is full of fuel. It must be tipped slightly during removal to avoid damage to the float. Make sure to discard the reservoir fuel into an approved container.
5. Remove and discard the fuel sender O-ring.
   To install:
6. Position a new O-ring on the modular fuel sender.
7. Align the tab on the front of the sender with the slot on the front of the retainer snapring.

8. Slowly apply pressure to the top of the spring loaded sender until it aligns flush with the retainer on the tank.

9. Insert the snapring into the designated slots, making sure the snapring is fully seated within the tab slots.

10. Install the fuel tank, as outlined earlier in this section.

11. Carefully lower the vehicle, then refill the gas tank.

12. Connect the negative battery cable, then turn the ignition to the **ON** position for two seconds, then turn it to the **OFF** position for ten seconds. Turn again to the **ON** position and check for fuel leaks.

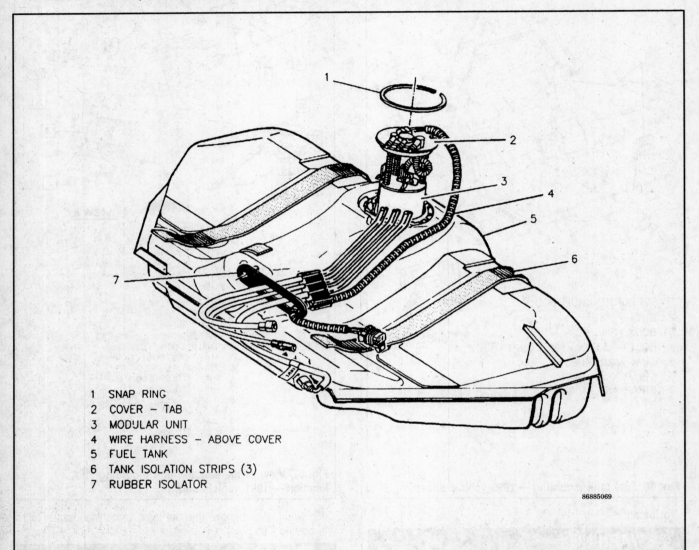

1   SNAP RING
2   COVER – TAB
3   MODULAR UNIT
4   WIRE HARNESS – ABOVE COVER
5   FUEL TANK
6   TANK ISOLATION STRIPS (3)
7   RUBBER ISOLATOR

86885069

Fig. 68 Modular fuel sender mounting on the fuel tank — 1995 vehicle shown

AIR CONDITIONER
ACCUMULATOR 6-27
COMPRESSOR 6-20
CONDENSER 6-24
CONTROL CABLES 6-31
EVAPORATOR CORE 6-25
GENERAL INFORMATION 6-20
HEATER/AIR CONDITIONER
  CONTROL PANEL 6-31
ORIFICE (EXPANSION) TUBE 6-31
RECEIVER DEHYDRATOR 6-30
REFRIGERANT LINES 6-30
THERMAL EXPANSION VALVE
  (TXV) 6-32
VACUUM MOTORS 6-31
CIRCUIT PROTECTION
CIRCUIT BREAKERS 6-68
FLASHERS 6-68
FUSE BLOCK AND FUSES 6-66
FUSIBLE LINKS 6-67
CRUISE CONTROL
ACTUATOR SWITCH 6-33
BRAKE/CLUTCH RELEASE
  SWITCHES 6-35
SPEED SENSOR 6-35
VACUUM RESERVOIR/TANK 6-38
VACUUM SERVO UNIT 6-37
ENTERTAINMENT SYSTEMS
RADIO RECEIVER/AMPLIFIER/TAPE
  PLAYER/COMPACT DISC
  PLAYER 6-38
SPEAKERS 6-39
HEATER
BLOWER MOTOR AND FAN 6-14
BLOWER SWITCH 6-18
CONTROL PANEL/HEAD 6-16
GENERAL INFORMATION 6-14
HEATER CORE 6-15
TEMPERATURE CONTROL
  CABLE 6-16
INSTRUMENTS AND SWITCHES
HEADLIGHT SWITCH 6-55
INSTRUMENT CLUSTER 6-49
PRINTED CIRCUIT BOARD 6-53
SPEEDOMETER 6-53
SPEEDOMETER CABLE 6-53
WINDSHIELD WIPER SWITCH 6-54
LIGHTING
FOG LIGHTS 6-64
HEADLIGHTS 6-56
SIGNAL AND MARKER LIGHTS 6-59
**SUPPLEMENTAL INFLATABLE
RESTRAINT (SIR) SYSTEM**
GENERAL INFORMATION 6-10
TRAILER WIRING 6-65
**UNDERSTANDING AND
TROUBLESHOOTING ELECTRICAL
SYSTEMS**
MECHANICAL TEST EQUIPMENT 6-9
SAFETY PRECAUTIONS 6-2
WIRING HARNESSES 6-7

WINDSHIELD WIPERS AND WASHERS
WINDSHIELD WASHER FLUID
  RESERVOIR 6-48
WINDSHIELD WASHER MOTOR 6-48
WINDSHIELD WIPER BLADE AND
  ARM 6-43
WINDSHIELD WIPER MOTOR 6-43
WIPER LINKAGE 6-43
WIRING DIAGRAMS 6-69

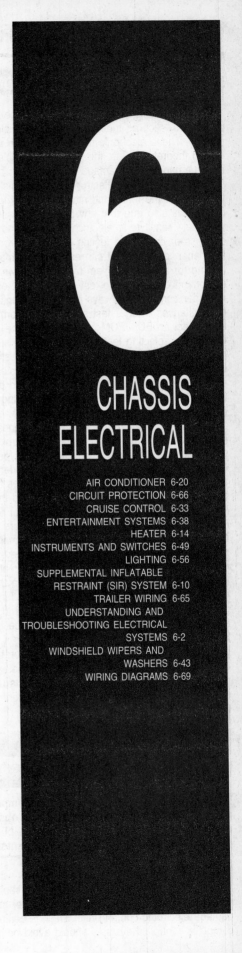

6

CHASSIS ELECTRICAL

AIR CONDITIONER 6-20
CIRCUIT PROTECTION 6-66
CRUISE CONTROL 6-33
ENTERTAINMENT SYSTEMS 6-38
HEATER 6-14
INSTRUMENTS AND SWITCHES 6-49
LIGHTING 6-56
SUPPLEMENTAL INFLATABLE
RESTRAINT (SIR) SYSTEM 6-10
TRAILER WIRING 6-65
UNDERSTANDING AND
TROUBLESHOOTING ELECTRICAL
SYSTEMS 6-2
WINDSHIELD WIPERS AND
WASHERS 6-43
WIRING DIAGRAMS 6-69

UNDERSTANDING AND TROUBLESHOOTING ELECTRICAL SYSTEMS

Most new vehicles are equipped with one or more on-board computers, such as those installed on vehicles covered by this manual. These electronic components (with no moving parts) should theoretically last the life of the vehicle, provided nothing external happens to damage the circuits or memory chips.

While it is true that electronic components should never wear out, in the real world malfunctions can, and often do, occur. It is also true that any computer-based system is extremely sensitive to electrical voltages and cannot tolerate careless or haphazard testing or service procedures. An inexperienced individual can easily cause major damage looking for a minor problem by using the wrong kind of test equipment or connecting test leads or connectors under improper conditions. Always pay close attention to the circumstances when a test should be performed. NEVER disconnect an ECM/PCM connector with the ignition switch **ON**. When selecting test equipment, make sure the manufacturer's instructions state that the tester is compatible with whatever type of electronic control system is being serviced. Read all instructions carefully and double check all test points before installing probes or making any test connections.

The following section outlines basic diagnosis techniques for dealing with computerized automotive control systems. Along with a general explanation of the various types of test equipment available to aid in servicing modern electronic automotive systems, basic repair techniques for wiring harnesses and connectors are given. Read the basic information before attempting any repairs or testing any computerized system, to provide the background of information necessary in order to avoid the most common and obvious mistakes that can cost both time and money. Although the replacement and testing procedures are simple in themselves, the systems are not, and unless one has a thorough understanding of all components and their function within a particular computerized control system, the logical test sequence these systems demand cannot be followed. Minor malfunctions can make a big difference, so it is important to know how each component affects the operation of the overall electronic system in order to find the ultimate cause of a problem without replacing good components unnecessarily. It is not enough to use the correct test equipment; the test equipment must be used correctly.

Safety Precautions

✳✳WARNING

Whenever working on or around any computer based microprocessor control system, always observe these general precautions to prevent the possibility of personal injury or damage to electronic components.

• Never install or remove battery cables with the ignition switch **ON** or the engine running. Jumper cables should be connected with the key **OFF** to avoid power surges that can damage electronic control units. Engines equipped with computer controlled systems should avoid both giving and getting jump starts due to the possibility of serious damage to components from arcing in the engine compartment when connections are made with the ignition **ON**.

• Always remove the battery cables before charging the battery. Never use a high output charger on an installed battery or attempt to use any type of "hot shot" (24 volt) starting aid.

• Exercise care when inserting test probes into connectors to insure good connections without damaging the connector or spreading the pins. Always probe connectors from the rear (wire) side, NOT the pin side, in order to avoid accidental shorting of terminals during test procedures.

• Never remove or attach wiring harness connectors with the ignition switch **ON** unless the instructions specifically direct you to do so. NEVER disengage/engage the computer control module wiring connectors with the ignition **ON**.

• Do not drop any components during service procedures and never apply 12 volts directly to any component (like a solenoid or relay) unless instructed specifically to do so. Some component electrical windings are designed to safely handle only 4 or 5 volts and can be destroyed in seconds if 12 volts are applied directly to the connector.

• Remove the electronic control unit if the vehicle is to be placed in an environment where temperatures exceed approximately 176°F (80°C), such as a paint spray booth or when arc or gas welding near the control unit location in the car.

ORGANIZED TROUBLESHOOTING

When diagnosing a specific problem, organized troubleshooting is a must. The complexity of a modern vehicle demands that you approach any problem in a logical, organized manner. There are certain troubleshooting techniques that are standard:

1. Establish when the problem occurs. Does the problem appear only under certain conditions? Were there any noises, odors, or other unusual symptoms?

2. Isolate the problem area. To do this, make some simple tests and observations; then, eliminate the systems that are working properly. Check for obvious problems such as broken wires, dirty connections, and split or disconnected vacuum hoses. ALWAYS check the obvious before assuming something complicated is the cause.

3. Test for problems systematically to determine the cause once the problem area is isolated. Are all the components functioning properly? Is there power going to electrical switches and motors? Is there vacuum at vacuum switches and/or actuators? Is there a mechanical problem such as bent linkage or loose mounting screws? Performing careful, systematic checks will often turn up most causes on the first inspection without wasting time checking components that have little or no relationship to the problem.

4. Test all repairs after the work is done to make sure that the problem is fixed. Some causes can be traced to more than one component, so a careful verification of repair work is important to pick up additional malfunctions that may cause a problem to reappear or a different problem to arise. A blown

fuse, for example, is a simple problem that may require more than another fuse to repair. If you don't look for a problem that caused a fuse to blow, for example, a shorted wire may go undetected.

Experience has shown that most problems tend to be the result of a fairly simple and obvious cause, such as loose or corroded connectors or air leaks in the intake system; a careful inspection of components during testing is essential for quick and accurate troubleshooting. Special, hand held computerized testers designed specifically for diagnosing the system are available from a variety of aftermarket sources, as well as from the vehicle manufacturer, but care should be taken to assure that any test equipment being used is designed to diagnose that particular computer controlled system accurately without damaging the computer control module or other components being tested.

➡**Pinpointing the exact cause of trouble in an electrical system can sometimes only be accomplished by the use of special test equipment. The following describes commonly used test equipment and explains how to put it to best use in diagnosis. In addition to the information covered here, the manufacturer's instruction booklet provided with the tester should be read and clearly understood before attempting any test procedures.**

TEST EQUIPMENT

Jumper Wires

Jumper wires are simple, yet extremely valuable, pieces of test equipment. Jumper wires are simply wires that are used to bypass sections of a circuit. The simplest type of jumper wire is merely a length of multi-strand wire with an alligator clip at each end. Jumper wires are usually fabricated from lengths of standard automotive wire and whatever type of connector (alligator clip, spade connector or pin connector) that is required for the particular vehicle being tested. The well equipped tool box will have several different styles of jumper wires in several different lengths. Some jumper wires are made with three or more terminals coming from a common splice for special purpose testing. In cramped, hard-to-reach areas it is advisable to have insulated boots over the jumper wire terminals in order to prevent accidental grounding, sparks, and possible fire, especially when testing fuel system components.

Jumper wires are used primarily to locate open electrical circuits, on either the ground (-) side of the circuit or on the hot (+) side. If an electrical component fails to operate, connect the jumper wire between the component and a good ground. If the component operates only with the jumper installed, the ground circuit is open. If the ground circuit is good, but the component does not operate, the circuit between the power feed and component is open. You can sometimes connect the jumper wire directly from the battery to the hot terminal of the component, but first make sure the component uses 12 volts in operation. Some electrical components, such as fuel injectors, are designed to operate on about 4 volts and running 12 volts directly to the injector terminals can burn out

the wiring. By inserting an inline fuseholder between a set of test leads, a fused jumper wire can be used for bypassing open circuits. Use a 5 amp fuse to provide protection against voltage spikes. When in doubt, use a voltmeter to check the voltage input to the component and measure how much voltage is being applied normally. By moving the jumper wire successively back from the lamp toward the power source, you can isolate the area of the circuit where the open is located. When the component stops functioning, or the power is cut off, the open is in the segment of wire between the jumper and the point previously tested.

✳✳CAUTION

Never use jumpers made from wire that is of lighter gauge than used in the circuit under test. If the jumper wire is of too small a gauge, it may overheat and possibly melt. Never use jumpers to bypass high resistance loads (such as motors) in a circuit. Bypassing resistances, in effect, creates a short circuit which may, in turn, cause damage and fire. Never use a jumper for anything other than temporary bypassing of components in a circuit.

12 Volt Test Light

The 12 volt test light is used to check circuits and components while electrical current is flowing through them. It is used for voltage and ground tests. Twelve volt test lights come in different styles but all have three main parts; a ground clip, a probe, and a light. The most commonly used 12 volt test lights have pick-type probes. To use a 12 volt test light, connect the ground clip to a good ground and probe wherever necessary with the pick. The pick should be sharp so that it can penetrate wire insulation to make contact with the wire, without making a large hole in the insulation. The wrap-around light is handy in hard to reach areas or where it is difficult to support a wire to push a probe pick into it. To use the wrap around light, hook the wire to be probed with the hook and pull the trigger. A small pick will be forced through the wire insulation into the wire core.

✳✳WARNING

Do not use a test light to probe electronic ignition spark plug or coil wires. Never use a pick-type test light to probe wiring on computer controlled systems unless specifically instructed to do so. Any wire insulation that is pierced by the test light probe should be taped and sealed with silicone after testing.

Like the jumper wire, the 12 volt test light is used to isolate opens in circuits. But, whereas the jumper wire is used to bypass the open to operate the load, the 12 volt test light is used to locate the presence of voltage in a circuit. If the test light glows, you know that there is power up to that point; if the 12 volt test light does not glow when its probe is inserted into the wire or connector, you know that there is an open circuit (no power). Move the test light in successive steps back toward the power source until the light in the handle does glow. When it does glow, the open is between the probe and point previously probed.

➡The test light does not detect that 12 volts (or any particular amount of voltage) is present; it only detects that some voltage is present. It is advisable before using the test light to touch its terminals across the battery posts to make sure the light is operating properly.

Self-Powered Test Light

The self-powered test light usually contains a 1.5 volt penlight battery. One type of self-powered test light is similar in design to the 12 volt test light. This type has both the battery and the light in the handle and pick-type probe tip. The second type has the light toward the open tip, so that the light illuminates the contact point. The self-powered test light is a dual purpose piece of test equipment. It can be used to test for either open or short circuits when power is isolated from the circuit (continuity test). A powered test light should NOT be used on any computer controlled system or component unless specifically instructed to do so. Many engine sensors can be destroyed by even this small amount of voltage applied directly to the terminals.

Open Circuit Testing

To use the self-powered test light to check for open circuits, first isolate the circuit from the vehicle's 12 volt power source by disconnecting the battery or wiring harness connector. Connect the test light ground clip to a good ground and probe sections of the circuit sequentially with the test light. Start testing from either end of the circuit. If the light is out, the open is between the probe and the circuit ground. If the light is on, the open is between the probe and end of the circuit toward the power source.

Short Circuit Testing

By isolating the circuit both from power and from ground, and using a self-powered test light, you can check for shorts to ground in the circuit. Isolate the circuit from power and ground. Connect the test light ground clip to a good ground and probe any easy-to-reach test point in the circuit. If the light comes on, there is a short somewhere in the circuit. To isolate the short, probe a test point at either end of the isolated circuit (the light should be on). Leave the test light probe connected and open connectors, switches, remove parts, etc., sequentially, until the light goes out. When the light goes out, the short is between the last circuit component opened and the previous circuit opened.

➡The 1.5 volt battery in the test light does not provide much current. A weak battery may not provide enough power to illuminate the test light even when a complete circuit is made (especially if there are high resistances in the circuit). Always make sure that the test battery is strong. To check the battery, briefly touch the ground clip to the probe; if the light glows brightly the battery is strong enough for testing. Never use a self-powered test light to perform checks for opens or shorts when power is applied to the electrical system under test. The 12 volt vehicle power will quickly burn out the 1.5 volt light bulb in the test light.

Voltmeter

A voltmeter is used to measure voltage at any point in a circuit, or to measure the voltage drop across any part of a circuit. It can also be used to check continuity in a wire or circuit by indicating current flow from one end to the other. Voltmeters usually have various scales on the meter dial and a selector switch to allow the detection of different voltages. The voltmeter has a positive and a negative lead. To avoid damage to the meter, always connect the negative lead to the negative (-) side of circuit (to ground or nearest the ground side of the circuit) and connect the positive lead to the positive (+) side of the circuit (to the power source or nearest the power source). Note that the negative voltmeter lead will always be black and that the positive voltmeter will always be some color other than black (usually red). Depending on how the voltmeter is connected into the circuit, it has several uses.

A voltmeter can be connected either in parallel or in series with a circuit, and has a very high resistance to current flow. When connected in parallel, only a small amount of current will flow through the voltmeter current path; the rest will flow through the normal circuit current path and the circuit will work normally. When the voltmeter is connected in series with a circuit, only a small amount of current can flow through the circuit. The circuit will not work properly, but the voltmeter reading will show if the circuit is complete or not.

✳✳WARNING

Do not use a multimeter to probe electronic ignition spark plug or coil wires. Small pin holes in secondary ignition wires will allow high voltage to arc from the wire to a metal part, external to the secondary ignition circuit. This arcing may cause misfiring, leading to a driveability complaint.

Available Voltage Measurement

Set the voltmeter selector switch to the 20V position and connect the meter negative lead to the negative post of the battery. Connect the positive meter lead to the positive post of the battery and turn the ignition switch **ON** to provide a load. Read the voltage on the meter or digital display. A well charged battery should register over 12 volts. If the meter reads below 11.5 volts, the battery power may be insufficient to operate the electrical system properly. This test determines voltage available from the battery and should be the first step in any electrical trouble diagnosis procedure. Many electrical problems, especially on computer controlled systems, can be caused by a low state of charge in the battery. Excessive corrosion at the battery cable terminals can cause a poor contact that will prevent proper charging and full battery current flow.

Normal battery voltage is 12 volts when fully charged. When the battery is supplying current to one or more circuits it is said to be "under load". When everything is off the electrical system is under a "no-load" condition. A fully charged battery may show about 12.5 volts at no load, will drop to 12 volts under medium load, and will drop even lower under heavy load. If the battery is partially discharged, the voltage decrease under heavy load may be excessive, even though the battery shows 12 volts or more at no load. When allowed to discharge further, the battery's available voltage under load will decrease more severely. For this reason, it is important that the battery be fully charged during all testing procedures to avoid errors in diagnosis and incorrect test results.

Voltage Drop

When current flows through a resistance, the voltage beyond the resistance is reduced (the larger the current, the greater the reduction in voltage). When no current is flowing, there is no voltage drop because there is no current flow. All points in the circuit which are connected to the power source are at the same voltage as the power source. The total voltage drop always equals the total source voltage. In a long circuit with many connectors, a series of small, unwanted voltage drops due to corrosion at the connectors can add up to a total loss of voltage which impairs the operation of the normal loads in the circuit.

INDIRECT COMPUTATION OF VOLTAGE DROPS

1. Set the voltmeter selector switch to the 20 volt position.
2. Connect the meter negative lead to a good ground.
3. Probe all resistances in the circuit with the positive meter lead.
4. Operate the circuit in all modes and observe the voltage readings.

DIRECT MEASUREMENT OF VOLTAGE DROPS

1. Set the voltmeter switch to the 20 volt position.
2. Connect the voltmeter negative lead to the ground side of the resistance load to be measured.
3. Connect the positive lead to the positive side of the resistance or load to be measured.
4. Read the voltage drop directly on the 20 volt scale.

Too high a voltage indicates too high a resistance. If, for example, a blower motor runs too slowly, you can determine if there is too high a resistance in the resistor pack. By taking voltage drop readings in all parts of the circuit, you can isolate the problem. Too low a voltage drop indicates too low a resistance. If, for example, a blower motor runs too fast in the MED and/or LOW position, the problem can be isolated in the resistor pack by taking voltage drop readings in all parts of the circuit to locate a possibly shorted resistor. The maximum allowable voltage drop under load is critical, especially if there is more than one high resistance problem in a circuit because all voltage drops are cumulative. A small drop is normal due to the resistance of the conductors.

HIGH RESISTANCE TESTING

1. Set the voltmeter selector switch to the 4 volt position.
2. Connect the voltmeter positive lead to the positive post of the battery.
3. Turn on the headlights and heater blower to provide a load.
4. Probe various points in the circuit with the negative voltmeter lead.
5. Read the voltage drop on the 4 volt scale. Some average maximum allowable voltage drops are:

FUSE PANEL — 0.7 volts
IGNITION SWITCH — 0.5 volts
HEADLIGHT SWITCH — 0.7 volts
IGNITION COIL (+) — 0.5 volts
ANY OTHER LOAD — 1.3 volts

➡ **Voltage drops are all measured while a load is operating; without current flow, there will be no voltage drop.**

Ohmmeter

The ohmmeter is designed to read resistance (ohms) in a circuit or component. Although there are several different styles of ohmmeters, all will usually have a selector switch which permits the measurement of different ranges of resistance (usually the selector switch allows the multiplication of the meter reading by 10, 100, 1000, and 10,000). A calibration knob allows the meter to be set at zero for accurate measurement. Since all ohmmeters are powered by an internal battery (usually 9 volts), the ohmmeter can be used as a self-powered test light. When the ohmmeter is connected, current from the ohmmeter flows through the circuit or component being tested. Since the ohmmeter's internal resistance and voltage are known values, the amount of current flow through the meter depends on the resistance of the circuit or component being tested.

The ohmmeter can be used to perform continuity tests for opens or shorts (either by observation of the meter needle or as a self-powered test light), and to read actual resistance in a circuit. It should be noted that the ohmmeter is used to check the resistance of a component or wire while there is no voltage applied to the circuit. Current flow from an outside voltage source (such as the vehicle battery) can damage the ohmmeter, so the circuit or component should be isolated from the vehicle electrical system before any testing is done. Since the ohmmeter uses its own voltage source, either lead can be connected to any test point.

➡ **When checking diodes or other solid state components, the ohmmeter leads can only be connected one way in order to measure current flow in a single direction. Make sure the positive (+) and negative (-) terminal connections are as described in the test procedures to verify the one-way diode operation.**

In using the meter for making continuity checks, do not be concerned with the actual resistance readings. Zero resistance, or any resistance readings, indicate continuity in the circuit. Infinite resistance indicates an open in the circuit. A high resistance reading where there should be none indicates a problem in the circuit. Checks for short circuits are made in the same manner as checks for open circuits except that the circuit must be isolated from both power and normal ground. Infinite resistance indicates no continuity to ground, while zero resistance indicates a dead short to ground.

RESISTANCE MEASUREMENT

The batteries in an ohmmeter will weaken with age and temperature, so the ohmmeter must be calibrated or "zeroed" before taking measurements. Many modern digital meters are self-zeroing and will require no adjustment. If your meter must be zeroed, be sure to check this each time it is used. To zero the meter, place the selector switch in its lowest range and touch the two ohmmeter leads together. Turn the calibration knob until the meter needle is exactly on zero.

➡All analog (needle) type ohmmeters must be zeroed before use, but most digital ohmmeter models are automatically calibrated when the switch is turned on. Self-calibrating digital ohmmeters do not have an adjusting knob, but it's a good idea to check for a zero readout before use by touching the leads together. All computer controlled systems require the use of a digital ohmmeter with at least 10 megohms impedance for testing. Before any test procedures are attempted, make sure the ohmmeter used is compatible with the electrical system, or damage to the on-board computer could result.

To measure resistance, first isolate the circuit from the vehicle power source by disconnecting the battery cables or the harness connector. Make sure the ignition key is **OFF** when disconnecting any components or the battery. Where necessary, also isolate at least one side of the circuit to be checked to avoid reading parallel resistances. Parallel circuit resistances will always give a lower reading than the actual resistance of either of the branches. When measuring the resistance of parallel circuits, the total resistance will always be lower than the smallest resistance in the circuit. Connect the meter leads to both sides of the circuit (wire or component) and read the actual measured ohms on the meter scale. Make sure the selector switch is set to the proper ohm scale for the circuit being tested to avoid misreading the ohmmeter test value.

✳✳WARNING

Never use an ohmmeter with power applied to the circuit. Like the self-powered test light, the ohmmeter is designed to operate on its own power supply. The normal 12 volt automotive electrical system current could damage the meter.

Ammeters

An ammeter measures the amount of current flowing through a circuit in units called amperes or amps. Amperes are units of electron flow which indicate the speed at which electrons are flowing through the circuit. Since Ohm's Law dictates that current flow in a circuit is equal to the circuit voltage divided by the total circuit resistance, increasing voltage also increases the current level (amps). Likewise, any decrease in resistance will increase the amount of amps in a circuit. At normal operating voltage, most circuits have a characteristic amount of amperes, called "current draw" which can be measured using an ammeter. By referring to a specified current draw rating, measuring the amperes, and comparing the two values, one can determine what is happening within the circuit to aid in diagnosis. An open circuit, for example, will not allow any current to flow so the ammeter reading will be zero. More current flows through a heavily loaded circuit or when the charging system is operating.

An ammeter is always connected in series with the circuit being tested. All of the current that normally flows through the circuit must also flow through the ammeter; if there is any other path for the current to follow, the ammeter reading will not be accurate. The ammeter itself has very little resistance

to current flow and therefore will not affect the circuit, but it will measure current draw only when the circuit is closed and electricity is flowing. Excessive current draw can blow fuses and drain the battery, while a reduced current draw can cause motors to run slowly, lights to dim and other components to not operate properly. The ammeter can help diagnose these conditions by locating the cause of the high or low reading.

Multimeters

Different combinations of test meters can be built into a single unit designed for specific tests. Some of the more common combination test devices are known as Volt/Amp testers, Tach/Dwell meters, or Digital Multimeters. The Volt/Amp tester is used for charging system, starting system or battery tests and consists of a voltmeter, an ammeter and a variable resistance carbon pile. The voltmeter will usually have at least two ranges for use with 6, 12 and 24 volt systems. The ammeter also has more than one range for testing various levels of battery loads and starter current draw and the carbon pile can be adjusted to offer different amounts of resistance. The Volt/Amp tester has heavy leads to carry large amounts of current and many later models have an inductive ammeter pickup that clamps around the wire to simplify test connections. On some models, the ammeter also has a zero-center scale to allow testing of charging and starting systems without switching leads or polarity. A digital multimeter is a voltmeter, ammeter and ohmmeter combined in an instrument which gives a digital readout. These are often used when testing solid state circuits because of their high input impedance (usually 10 megohms or more).

The tach/dwell meter combines a tachometer and a dwell (cam angle) meter and is a specialized kind of voltmeter. The tachometer scale is marked to show engine speed in rpm and the dwell scale is marked to show degrees of distributor shaft rotation. In most electronic ignition systems, dwell is determined by the control unit, but the dwell meter can also be used to check the duty cycle (operation) of some electronic engine control systems. Some tach/dwell meters are powered by an internal battery, while others take their power from the vehicle battery in use. The internal battery powered testers usually require calibration much like an ohmmeter before testing.

Special Test Equipment

A variety of diagnostic tools are available to help troubleshoot and repair computerized engine control systems. The most sophisticated of these devices are the console type engine analyzers that usually occupy a garage service bay, but there are several types of aftermarket electronic testers available that will allow quick circuit tests of the engine control system by plugging directly into a special connector located in the engine compartment or under the dashboard. Several tool and equipment manufacturers offer simple, hand held testers that measure various circuit voltage levels on command to check all system components for proper operation. Although these testers often cost about $300-$500, consider that the average computer control unit can cost just as much and the money saved by not replacing perfectly good sensors or components in an attempt to correct a problem could justify the purchase price of a special diagnostic tester the first time it's used.

These computerized testers can allow quick and easy test measurements while the engine is operating or while the vehicle is being driven. In addition, the on-board computer memory can be read to access any stored trouble codes, in effect allowing the computer to tell you "where it hurts" and aid trouble diagnosis by pinpointing exactly which circuit is malfunctioning. In the same manner, repairs can be tested to make sure the problem has been corrected. The biggest advantage these special testers have is their relatively easy hookups that minimize or eliminate the chances of making the wrong connections and getting false voltage readings or damaging the computer accidentally.

➡It should be remembered that these testers check voltage levels in circuits; they don't detect mechanical problems or failed components. Testers simply can inform you if the circuit voltage falls within the pre-programmed limits stored in the tester PROM unit. Also, most of the hand held testers are designed to work only on one or two systems made by a specific manufacturer.

A variety of aftermarket testers are available to help diagnose different computerized control systems. Owatonna Tool Company (OTC), for example, markets a device called the OTC Monitor which plugs directly into the Assembly Line Diagnostic Link (ALDL). The OTC tester makes diagnosis a simple matter of pressing the correct buttons and, by changing the internal PROM or inserting a different diagnosis cartridge, it will work on any model from full size to subcompact, over a wide range of years. An adapter is supplied with the tester to allow connection to all types of ALDL links, regardless of the number of pin terminals used. By inserting an updated PROM into the OTC tester, it can be easily updated to diagnose any new modifications of computerized control systems.

Wiring Harnesses

The average vehicle contains about 1/2 mile (0.805 km) of wiring, with hundreds of individual connections. To protect the many wires from damage and to keep them from becoming a confusing tangle, they are organized into bundles, enclosed in plastic or taped together and called wiring harnesses. Different wiring harnesses serve different parts of the vehicle. Individual wires are color coded to help trace them through a harness where sections are hidden from view.

A loose or corroded connection or a replacement wire that is too small for the circuit will add extra resistance and an additional voltage drop to the circuit. A ten percent voltage drop can result in slow or erratic motor operation, for example, even though the circuit is complete. Automotive wiring or circuit conductors can be in any one of three forms:
1. Single-strand wire
2. Multi-strand wire
3. Printed circuitry

Single-strand wire has a solid metal core and is usually used inside such components as alternators, motors, relays and other devices. Multi-strand wire has a core made of many small strands of wire twisted together into a single conductor. Most of the wiring in an automotive electrical system is made up of multi-strand wire, either as a single conductor or grouped together in a harness. All wiring is color coded on the insulator, either as a solid color or as a colored wire with an identification stripe. A printed circuit is a thin film of copper or other conductor that is printed on an insulator backing. Occasionally, a printed circuit is sandwiched between two sheets of plastic for more protection and flexibility. A complete printed circuit, consisting of conductors, insulating material and connectors for lamps or other components is called a printed circuit board. Printed circuitry is used in place of individual wires or harnesses in places where space is limited, such as behind instrument panels.

WIRE GAUGE

Since computer controlled automotive electrical systems are very sensitive to changes in resistance, the selection of properly sized wires is critical when systems are repaired. The wire gauge number is an expression of the cross-section area of the conductor. The most common system for expressing wire size is the American Wire Gauge (AWG) system.

Wire cross-section area is measured in circular mils. A mil is $1/1000$ in. (0.001 in. or 0.0254mm); a circular mil is the area of a circle one mil in diameter. For example, a conductor with 1/4 in. (6.35mm) diameter is 0.250 in. or 250 mils. The circular mil cross-section area of the wire is 250 squared (250^2) or 62,500 circular mils. Imported vehicles usually use metric wire gauge designations, which is simply the cross-section area of the conductor in square millimeters (mm^2).

Gauge numbers are assigned to conductors of various cross-section areas. As gauge number increases, area decreases and the conductor becomes smaller. A 5 gauge conductor is smaller than a 1 gauge conductor and a 10 gauge is smaller than a 5 gauge. As the cross-section area of a conductor decreases, resistance increases and so does the gauge number. A conductor with a higher gauge number will carry less current than a conductor with a lower gauge number.

➡Gauge wire size refers to the size of the conductor, not the size of the complete wire. It is possible to have two wires of the same gauge with different diameters because one may have thicker insulation than the other.

12 volt automotive electrical systems generally use 10, 12, 14, 16 and 18 gauge wire. Main power distribution circuits and larger accessories usually use 10 and 12 gauge wire. Battery cables are usually 4 or 6 gauge, although 1 and 2 gauge wires are occasionally used. Wire length must also be considered when making repairs to a circuit. As conductor length increases, so does resistance. An 18 gauge wire, for example, can carry a 10 amp load for 10 feet without excessive voltage drop; however if a 15 foot wire is required for the same 10 amp load, it must be a 16 gauge wire.

WIRING DIAGRAMS

An electrical schematic shows the electrical current paths when a circuit is operating properly. It is essential to understand how a circuit works before trying to figure out why it doesn't. Schematics break the entire electrical system down into individual circuits and show only one particular circuit. In a schematic, no attempt is made to represent wiring and components as they physically appear on the vehicle; switches and other components are shown as simply as possible. Face views of harness connectors show the cavity or terminal locations in all multi-pin connectors to help locate test points.

If you need to backprobe a connector while it is on the component, the order of the terminals must be mentally reversed. The wire color code can help in this situation, as well as a keyway, lock tab or other reference mark.

WIRING REPAIR

Soldering is a quick, efficient method of joining metals permanently. Everyone who has the occasion to make wiring repairs should know how to solder. Electrical connections that are soldered are far less likely to come apart and will conduct electricity much better than connections that are only "pigtailed" together. The most popular (and preferred) method of soldering is with an electric soldering gun or iron. Soldering irons are available in many sizes and wattage ratings. Irons with higher wattage ratings deliver higher temperatures and recover lost heat faster. A small soldering iron rated for no more than 50 watts is recommended, especially on electrical systems where excess heat can damage the components being soldered.

There are three ingredients necessary for successful soldering; proper flux, good solder and sufficient heat. A soldering flux is necessary to clean the metal of tarnish, prepare it for soldering and to enable the solder to spread into tiny crevices. When soldering, always use a rosin flux or rosin core solder which is non-corrosive and will not attract moisture once the job is finished. Other types of flux (acid core) will leave a residue that will attract moisture and cause the wires to corrode. Tin is a unique metal with a low melting point. In a molten state, it dissolves and alloys easily with many metals. Solder is often made by mixing tin with lead. The most common proportions are 40/60, 50/50 and 60/40, with the percentage of tin listed first. Low priced solders usually contain less tin, making them very difficult for a beginner to use because more heat is required to melt the solder. A common solder is 40/60 which is well suited for all-around general use, but 60/40 melts easier, has more tin for a better joint and is preferred for electrical work.

Soldering Techniques

Successful soldering requires that the metals to be joined are heated to a temperature that will melt the solder — usually 360-460°F (182-238°C). Contrary to popular belief, the purpose of the soldering iron is not to melt the solder itself, but to heat the parts being soldered to a temperature high enough to melt the solder when it is touched to the work. Melting flux-cored solder on the soldering iron will usually destroy the effectiveness of the flux.

➡**Soldering tips are made of copper for good heat conductivity, but must be "tinned" regularly for quick transference of heat to the project and to prevent the solder from sticking to the iron. To "tin" the iron, simply heat it and touch the flux-cored solder to the tip; the solder will flow over the hot tip. Wipe the excess off with a clean rag, but be careful as the iron will be hot.**

After some use, the tip may become pitted. If so, simply dress the tip with a smooth file and "tin" the tip again. An old saying holds that "metals well cleaned are half soldered." Flux-cored solder will remove oxides but rust, bits of insulation and oil or grease must be removed with a wire brush or emery cloth. For maximum strength in soldered parts, the joint must start off clean and tight. Weak joints will result in gaps too wide for the solder to bridge.

If a separate soldering flux is used, it should be brushed or swabbed on only those areas that are to be soldered. Most solders contain a core of flux and separate fluxing is unnecessary. Hold the work to be soldered firmly. It is best to solder on a wooden board, because a metal vise will only rob the piece to be soldered of heat and make it difficult to melt the solder. Hold the soldering tip with the broadest face against the work to be soldered. Apply solder under the tip close to the work, using enough solder to give a heavy film between the iron and the piece being soldered, while moving slowly and making sure the solder melts properly. Keep the work level or the solder will run to the lowest part and favor the thicker parts, because these require more heat to melt the solder. If the soldering tip overheats (the solder coating on the face of the tip burns up), it should be retinned. Once the soldering is completed, let the soldered joint stand until cool. Tape and seal all soldered wire splices after the repair has cooled.

Wire Harness and Connectors

The on-board computer wire harness electrically connects the control unit to the various solenoids, switches and sensors used by the control system. Most connectors located in the engine compartment or which are otherwise exposed to the elements are protected against moisture and dirt which could create oxidation and deposits on the terminals. This protection is important because of the very low voltage and current levels used by the computer and sensors. All connectors have a lock which secures the male and female terminals together, with a secondary lock holding the seal and terminal into the connector. Both terminal locks must be released when disconnecting module connectors.

These special connectors are weather-proof and all repairs require the use of a special terminal and the tool required to service it. This tool is used to remove the pin and sleeve terminals. If removal is attempted with an ordinary pick, there is a good chance that the terminal will be bent or deformed. Unlike standard blade type terminals, these terminals cannot be straightened once they are bent. Make certain that the connectors are properly seated and all of the sealing rings in place when connecting leads. On some models, a hinge-type flap provides a backup or secondary locking feature for the terminals. Most secondary locks are used to improve the connector reliability by retaining the terminals if the small terminal lock tangs are not positioned properly.

Molded-on connectors require complete replacement of the connection. This means splicing a new connector assembly into the harness. All splices in on-board computer systems should be soldered to insure proper contact. Use care when probing the connections or replacing terminals in them as it is possible to short between opposite terminals. If this happens to the wrong terminal pair, it is possible to damage certain components. Always use jumper wires between connectors for circuit checking and never probe through weatherproof seals.

Open circuits are often difficult to locate by sight because corrosion or terminal misalignment can be hidden by the connectors. Merely wiggling a connector on a sensor or in the wiring harness may correct the open circuit condition. This should always be considered when an open circuit or a failed sensor is indicated. Intermittent problems may also be caused by oxidized or loose connections. When using a circuit tester for diagnosis, always probe connections from the wire side. Be careful not to damage sealed connectors with test probes.

All wiring harnesses should be replaced with identical parts, using the same gauge wire and connectors. When signal wires are spliced into a harness, use wire with high temperature insulation only. With the low voltage and current levels found in the system, it is important that the best possible connection at all wire splices be made by soldering the splices together. It is seldom necessary to replace a complete harness. If replacement is necessary, pay close attention to insure proper harness routing. Secure the harness with suitable plastic wire clamps to prevent vibrations from causing the harness to wear in spots or contact any hot components.

➡Weatherproof connectors cannot be replaced with standard connectors. Instructions are provided with replacement connector and terminal packages. Some wire harnesses have mounting indicators (usually pieces of colored tape) to mark where the harness is to be secured.

In making wiring repairs, it's important that you always replace damaged wires with wires that are the same gauge as the wire being replaced. The heavier the wire, the smaller the gauge number. Wires are color-coded to aid in identification and whenever possible the same color coded wire should be used for replacement. A wire stripping and crimping tool is necessary to install solderless terminal connectors. Test all crimps by pulling on the wires; it should not be possible to pull the wires out of a good crimp.

Wires which are open, exposed or otherwise damaged are repaired by simple splicing. Where possible, if the wiring harness is accessible and the damaged place in the wire can be located, it is best to open the harness and check for all possible damage. In an inaccessible harness, the wire must be bypassed with a new insert, usually taped to the outside of the old harness.

When replacing fusible links, be sure to use fusible link wire, NOT ordinary automotive wire. Make sure the fusible segment is of the same gauge and construction as the one being replaced and double the stripped end when crimping the terminal connector for a good contact. The melted (open) fusible link segment of the wiring harness should be cut off as close to the harness as possible, then a new segment spliced in as described. In the case of a damaged fusible link that feeds two harness wires, the harness connections should be replaced with two fusible link wires so that each circuit will have its own separate protection.

➡Most of the problems caused in the wiring harness are due to bad ground connections. Always check all vehicle ground connections for corrosion or looseness before performing any power feed checks to eliminate the chance of a bad ground affecting the circuit.

Repairing Hard Shell Connectors

Unlike molded connectors, the terminal contacts in hard shell connectors can be replaced. Replacement usually involves the use of a special terminal removal tool to depress the locking tangs (barbs) on the connector terminal and allow the connector to be removed from the rear of the shell. The connector shell should be replaced if it shows any evidence of burning, melting, cracks, or breaks. Replace individual terminals that are burnt, corroded, distorted or loose.

➡The insulation crimp must be tight to prevent the insulation from sliding back on the wire when the wire is pulled. The insulation must be visibly compressed under the crimp tabs, and the ends of the crimp should be turned in for a firm grip on the insulation.

The wire crimp must be made with all wire strands inside the crimp. The terminal must be fully compressed on the wire strands with the ends of the crimp tabs turned in to make a firm grip on the wire. Check all connections with an ohmmeter to insure a good contact. There should be no measurable resistance between the wire and the terminal when connected.

Mechanical Test Equipment

VACUUM GAUGE

Most gauges are graduated in inches of mercury (in. Hg), although a device called a manometer reads vacuum in inches of water (in. H_2O). The normal vacuum reading usually varies between 18 and 22 in. Hg (60.78-74.29 kPa) at sea level. To test engine vacuum, the gauge must be connected to a source of manifold vacuum. Many engines have a plug in the intake manifold which can be removed and replaced with an adapter fitting. Connect the vacuum gauge to the fitting with a suitable rubber hose or, if no manifold plug is available, connect the vacuum gauge to any device using manifold vacuum, such as EGR valves, etc. The vacuum gauge can be used to determine if enough vacuum is reaching a component to allow its actuation.

HAND VACUUM PUMP

Small, hand-held vacuum pumps come in a variety of designs. Most have a built-in vacuum gauge and allow the component to be tested without removing it from the vehicle. Operate the pump lever or plunger to apply the correct amount of vacuum required for the test specified in the diagnosis routines. The level of vacuum in inches of Mercury (in. Hg) is indicated on the pump gauge. For some testing, an additional vacuum gauge may be necessary.

Intake manifold vacuum is used to operate various systems and devices on late model vehicles. To correctly diagnose and solve problems in vacuum control systems, a vacuum source is necessary for testing. In some cases, vacuum can be taken from the intake manifold when the engine is running, but vacuum is normally provided by a hand vacuum pump. These hand vacuum pumps have a built-in vacuum gauge that allows testing while the device is still attached to the component. For some tests, an additional vacuum gauge may be necessary.

SUPPLEMENTAL INFLATABLE RESTRAINT (SIR) SYSTEM

General Information

▶ See Figure 1

Beginning in 1994, a driver's side air bag became standard equipment for the Grand Am, Skylark and Achieva. The Supplemental Inflatable Restraint (SIR) system offers protection in addition to that provided by the driver's seat belt by deploying an air bag from the center of the steering wheel. The air bag deploys when the vehicle is involved in a frontal crash of sufficient force up to 30° off the centerline of the vehicle. To further absorb the crash energy, there is also a knee bolster located beneath the instrument panel in the driver's area and the steering wheel is collapsible.

The system has an energy reserve, which can store a large enough electrical charge to deploy the air bag(s) for up to ten minutes after the battery has been disconnected or damaged. The system **MUST** be disabled before any service is performed on or around SIR components or SIR wiring.

SYSTEM OPERATION

The SIR system contains a deployment loop for each air bag and a Diagnostic Energy Reserve Module (DERM). The deployment loop supplies current through the inflator module which will cause air bag deployment in the event of a frontal collision of sufficient force. The DERM supplies the necessary power, even if the battery has been damaged.

The deployment loop is made up of the arming sensors, coil assembly, inflator module and the discriminating sensors. The inflator module is only supplied sufficient current when the arming sensor and at least one of the two discriminating sensors close simultaneously. The function of the DERM is to supply the deployment loop a 36 Volt Loop Reserve (36VLR)

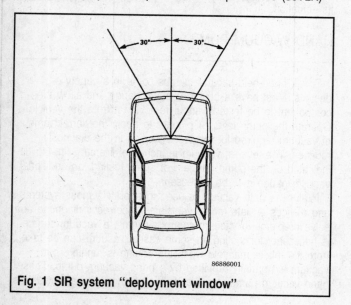

86886001

Fig. 1 SIR system "deployment window"

to assure sufficient voltage to deploy the air bag if ignition voltage is lost in a frontal crash.

The DERM, in conjunction with the sensor resistors, makes it possible to detect circuit and component malfunctions within the deployment loop. If the voltages monitored by the DERM fall outside expected limits, the DERM will indicate a malfunction by storing a diagnostic trouble code and illuminating the 7AIR BAG lamp.

SYSTEM COMPONENTS

▶ See Figures 2, 3, 4, 5, 6, 7 and 8

Diagnostic Energy Reserve Module (DERM)

The DERM is designed to perform five main functions: energy reserve, malfunction detection, malfunction recording, driver notification and frontal crash recording.

The DERM maintains a reserve voltage supply to provide deployment energy for a few seconds when the vehicle voltage is low or lost in a frontal crash. The DERM performs diagnostic monitoring of the SIR system and records malfunctions in the form of diagnostic trouble codes, which can be obtained from a hand scan tool and/or on-board diagnostics. The DERM warns the driver of SIR system malfunctions by controlling the AIR BAG warning lamp and records SIR system status during a frontal crash.

AIR BAG Warning Lamp

The AIR BAG warning/indicator lamp is used to verify lamp and DERM operation by flashing 7 times when the ignition is first turned **ON**. It is also used to warn the driver of an SIR system malfunction.

Discriminating Sensors

Vehicles equipped with driver's side air bag only, have two discriminating sensors. The forward discriminating sensor is located in front of the radiator. The passenger compartment discriminating sensor is located behind the right side of the instrument panel.

The discriminating sensor consists of a sensing element, diagnostic resistor and normally open switch contacts. The sensing element closes the switch contact when vehicle velocity changes are severe enough to warrant air bag deployment.

Arming Sensor

The arming sensor is contained in the same housing as the passenger compartment discriminating sensor and is referred to as the dual sensor.

The arming sensor is a switch located in the power side of the deployment loop. It is calibrated to close at low level velocity changes (lower than the discriminating sensors), assuring that the inflator module is connected directly to the 36VLR output of the DERM or Ignition 1 voltage when any discriminating sensor closes.

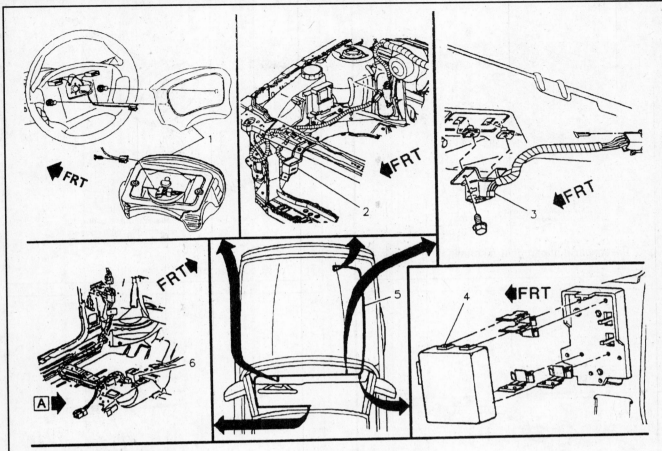

1 Inflator module
2 Forward discriminating sensor
3 Arming sensor
4 Derm
5 Sir wiring harness
6 Passenger compartment discriminating sensor

86886002

Fig. 2 Exploded view of a DERM

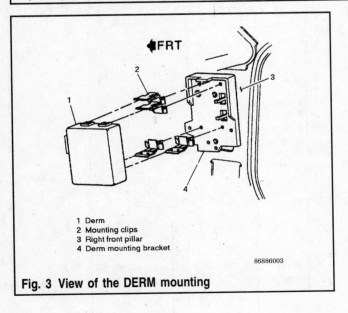

1 Derm
2 Mounting clips
3 Right front pillar
4 Derm mounting bracket

86886003

Fig. 3 View of the DERM mounting

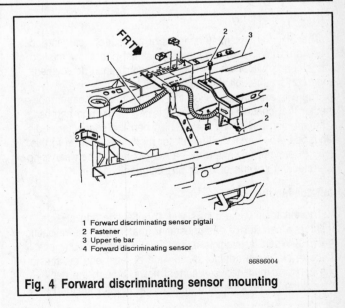

1 Forward discriminating sensor pigtail
2 Fastener
3 Upper tie bar
4 Forward discriminating sensor

86886004

Fig. 4 Forward discriminating sensor mounting

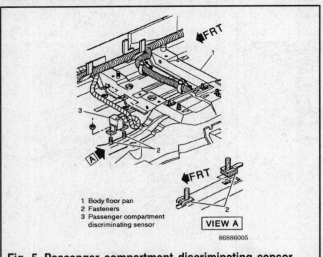

1 Body floor pan
2 Fasteners
3 Passenger compartment discriminating sensor

VIEW A

86886005

Fig. 5 Passenger compartment discriminating sensor mounting

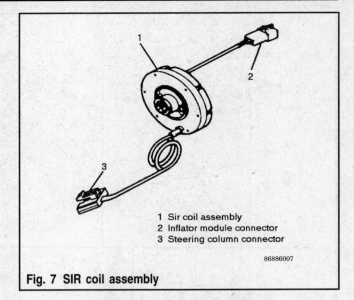

1 Sir coil assembly
2 Inflator module connector
3 Steering column connector

86886007

Fig. 7 SIR coil assembly

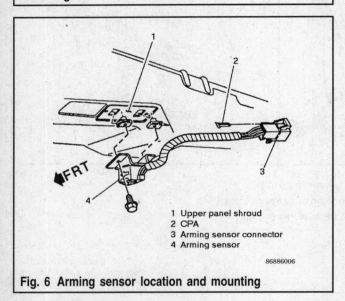

1 Upper panel shroud
2 CPA
3 Arming sensor connector
4 Arming sensor

86886006

Fig. 6 Arming sensor location and mounting

SIR Coil Assembly

The SIR coil assembly consists of two current carrying coils. They are attached to the steering column and allow rotation of the steering wheel while maintaining continuous deployment loop contact through the inflator module.

There is a shorting bar on the lower steering column connector that connects the SIR coil to the SIR wiring harness. The shorting bar shorts the circuit when the connector is disengaged. The circuit to the inflator module is shorted in this way to prevent unwanted air bag deployment when servicing the steering column or other SIR components.

Inflator Module

The inflator module consists of an inflatable bag and an inflator (a canister of gas-generating material and an initiating device). When the vehicle is in a frontal crash of sufficient force to close the arming sensor and at least one discriminating sensor simultaneously, current flows through the deployment loop. Current passing through the initiator ignites the

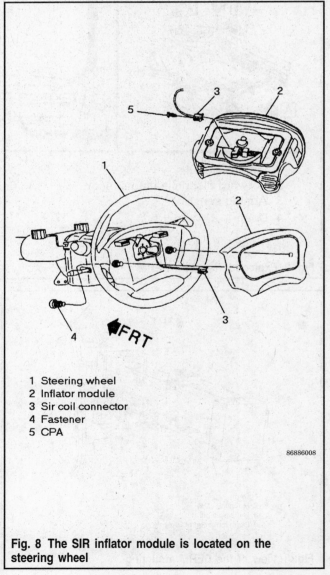

1 Steering wheel
2 Inflator module
3 Sir coil connector
4 Fastener
5 CPA

86886008

Fig. 8 The SIR inflator module is located on the steering wheel

material in the inflator module, causing a reaction which produces a gas that rapidly inflates the air bag.

All vehicles are equipped with an inflator module located in the steering wheel.

SERVICE PRECAUTIONS

▶ **See Figure 9**

• When performing service around the SIR system components or wiring, the SIR system **MUST** be disabled. Failure to do so could result in possible air bag deployment, personal injury or unneeded SIR system repairs.

• When carrying a live inflator module, make sure that the bag and trim cover are pointed away from you. Never carry the inflator module by the wires or connector on the underside of the module. In case of accidental deployment, the bag will then deploy with minimal chance of injury.

• When placing a live inflator module on a bench or other surface, always face the bag and trim cover up, away from the surface.

DISABLING THE SYSTEM

▶ **See Figure 10**

1. Turn the steering wheel so that the vehicle's wheels are pointing straight ahead.
2. Turn the ignition switch to **LOCK**, remove the key, then disconnect the negative battery cable.
3. Remove the "AIR BAG" fuse from the fuse block.
4. Remove the steering column filler panel.
5. Disengage the Connector Position Assurance (CPA) and yellow two way connector at the base of the steering column.
6. Connect the negative battery cable.

ENABLING THE SYSTEM

1. Disconnect the negative battery cable.
2. Turn the ignition switch to **LOCK**, then remove the key.
3. Engage the two way connector at the base of the steering column and the Connector Position Assurance (CPA).
4. Install the steering column filler panel.
5. Install the "AIR BAG" fuse to the fuse block.
6. Connect the negative battery cable.
7. Turn the ignition switch to **RUN** and make sure that the "AIR BAG" warning lamp flashes seven times and then shuts off. If the warning lamp does not shut off, make sure that the wiring is properly connected. If the light remains on, take the vehicle to a reputable repair facility for service.

ALWAYS CARRY INFLATOR MODULE WITH TRIM COVER AWAY FROM BODY.

ALWAYS PLACE INFLATOR MODULE ON WORKBENCH WITH TRIM COVER UP, AWAY FROM LOOSE OBJECTS.

86886009

Fig. 9 When carrying a live inflator module, make sure that the bag and trim cover are pointed away from you. Never carry the inflator module by the wires or connector on the underside of the module

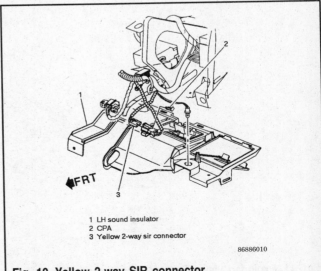

1 LH sound insulator
2 CPA
3 Yellow 2-way sir connector

86886010

Fig. 10 Yellow 2-way SIR connector

HEATER

General Information

The heater and air conditioning systems are controlled manually. The manual system controls air temperature through a cable-actuated lever and air flow through a vacuum switching valve and vacuum actuators.

The heating system provides heating, ventilation and defrosting for the windshield and side windows. The heater core is a heat exchanger supplied with coolant from the engine cooling system. Temperature is controlled by the temperature valve which moves an air door that directs air flow through the heater core for more heat or bypasses the heater core for less heat.

Vacuum actuators control the mode doors which direct air flow to the outlet ducts. The mode selector on the control panel directs engine vacuum to the actuators. The position of the mode doors determines whether air flows from the floor, panel, defrost or panel and defrost ducts (bi-level mode).

Blower Motor and Fan

REMOVAL & INSTALLATION

▶ **See Figures 11, 12, 13 and 14**

1. Disconnect negative battery cable.
2. For the 3.1L engine, remove the alternator belt, then remove the alternator and position aside.
3. For the 2.5L and 3.3L engines, remove the power steering pressure hose from the power steering pump.
4. For the 3.0L engine, remove the serpentine belt.
5. For the 3.0L and 3.3L engines, remove the retaining bolts from the power steering pump bracket, then set the pump aside.

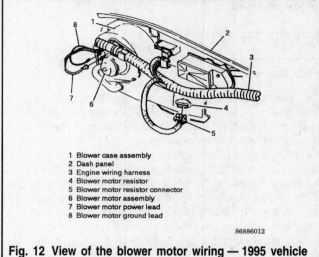

1 Blower case assembly
2 Dash panel
3 Engine wiring harness
4 Blower motor resistor
5 Blower motor resistor connector
6 Blower motor assembly
7 Blower motor power lead
8 Blower motor ground lead

86886012

Fig. 12 View of the blower motor wiring — 1995 vehicle shown

6. Detach the blower electrical connector, then, if accessible, remove the cooling tube.

➡**When cutting the blower motor cover, make the cut just the thickness of the cover, which is ⅛ in. (2mm) thick. Cutting deeper than that may damage the cooling tube.**

7. For 1992-95 vehicles, partially cut the blower motor case cover, as shown on the cover. Cutting completely around the cover is NOT required. Swing the cut potion of the cover down.
8. If previously accessible, disconnect the cooling tube.
9. Unfasten the attaching screws/bolts and remove the blower motor from the case.
10. If necessary, remove the fan from the blower motor.
11. The installation is the reverse of the removal procedure.
12. If the case was cut during removal, secure the cover using the three retaining clips.

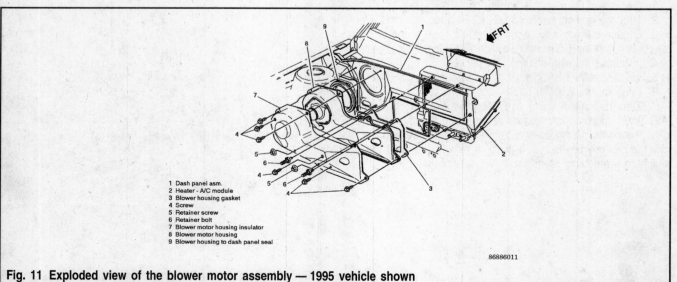

1 Dash panel asm.
2 Heater - A/C module
3 Blower housing gasket
4 Screw
5 Retainer screw
6 Retainer bolt
7 Blower motor housing insulator
8 Blower motor housing
9 Blower housing to dash panel seal

86886011

Fig. 11 Exploded view of the blower motor assembly — 1995 vehicle shown

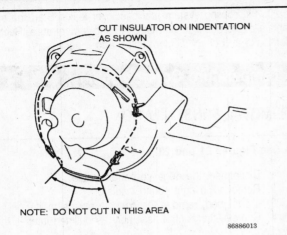

Fig. 13 Some later model vehicles require you to cut the case, on the indicated lines, in order to access the blower motor

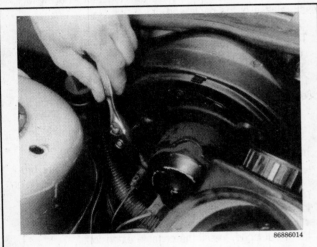

Fig. 14 On 3.0L engines, you must remove the power steering pump for access to the blower motor

13. Connect the negative battery cable, then start the engine and check the blower motor for proper operation.

Heater Core

REMOVAL & INSTALLATION

▶ See Figures 15, 16, 17, 18, 19 and 20

1. Disconnect the negative battery cable.
2. Drain the engine cooling system into a suitable container for reuse.
3. Raise and safely support the vehicle.
4. If necessary, remove the rear lateral transaxle strut mount.
5. Detach the drain tube, then disconnect the heater hoses from the core tubes.
6. Carefully lower the vehicle.

7. Unfasten and remove the sound insulators, console extensions and/or steering column filler, as required.
8. Remove the floor or console outlet ductwork and hoses.
9. Remove the heater core access cover.
10. Unfasten the heater core mounting clamps/bolts, then remove the heater core from the vehicle.

To install:

11. Install the heater core, then secure using the clamps/bolts.
12. Fasten the heater core cover.
13. Connect the outlet hoses and ducts.
14. Install the sound insulators, console extensions and/or steering column filler.
15. Raise and safely support the vehicle.
16. Install the drain tube and connect the heater hoses to the core tubes.
17. If removed, install the rear lateral transaxle strut mount, if removed.
18. Carefully lower the vehicle.
19. Connect the negative battery cable.

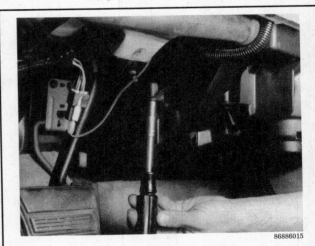

Fig. 15 Unfasten the sound insulator retaining bolts, then . . .

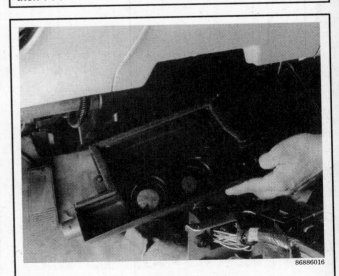

Fig. 16 . . . remove the sound insulator

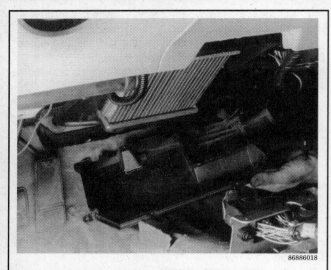

Fig. 17 Remove the heater core access cover

Fig. 18 Unfasten the heater core retaining bolts; most later models are secured with clamps

Fig. 19 Remove the heater core from the vehicle

20. Fill cooling system and check for leaks. Start the engine and allow to come to normal operating temperature. Recheck for leaks and check coolant level. Add if necessary.

Temperature Control Cable

REMOVAL & INSTALLATION

◆ **See Figures 21 and 22**

1. Disconnect the negative battery cable.
2. Remove the right sound insulator.
3. If equipped, remove the console extension.
4. Remove the control assembly as outlined later in this section.
5. Disconnect the cable from the control assembly.
6. Detach the control cable from the heater module. On some vehicles it will help to use a 7mm socket to push the retaining "fingers" on the module arm together to allow for easy release of the cable end.
7. Remove the control cable from the vehicle.
   To install:
8. Install the control cable.
9. Connect the cable to the heater module.
10. Attach the cable to the control assembly. If the cable does not snap in to the control assembly, do the following:
    a. Remove the cable end from the heater control.
    b. Rotate the cable "snap in" 90°.
    c. Secure the cable to the heater control with a hex headed, self-tapping screw.
    d. Reinstall the cable. If the retaining "fingers" are broken, break off the remaining "fingers" and install a push-on clip.
11. Install the control assembly as outlined later in this section.
12. If equipped, install the console extension.
13. Install the right sound insulator.
14. Connect the negative battery cable.

ADJUSTMENT

◆ **See Figure 23**

After cable installation, move the temperature knob quickly from full cold to full hot position. At about two-thirds control travel, additional effort may be required to complete the adjustment. During adjustment, a "click" may be heard as the cable end is brought into proper position. The cable is now set and should provide uniform effort from full cold to full hot and back with audible temperature valve stop contact upon reaching these positions. If not, remove the cable end from the actuator and turn the eyelet until the cable end is flush with the end of the eyelet. Reinstall, then adjust the cable.

Control Panel/Head

The following procedure covers removal and installation of the control head for vehicles equipped with heat only, and also for vehicles equipped with heat and air conditioning.

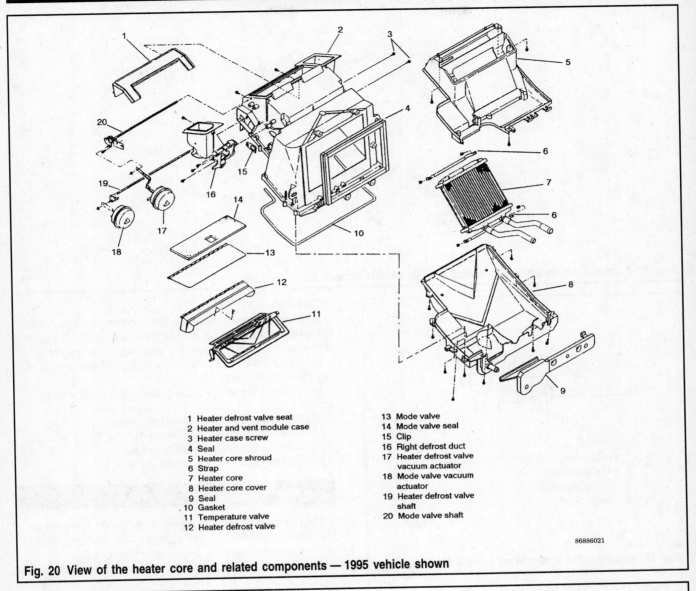

1 Heater defrost valve seat
2 Heater and vent module case
3 Heater case screw
4 Seal
5 Heater core shroud
6 Strap
7 Heater core
8 Heater core cover
9 Seal
10 Gasket
11 Temperature valve
12 Heater defrost valve

13 Mode valve
14 Mode valve seal
15 Clip
16 Right defrost duct
17 Heater defrost valve vacuum actuator
18 Mode valve vacuum actuator
19 Heater defrost valve shaft
20 Mode valve shaft

86886021

Fig. 20 View of the heater core and related components — 1995 vehicle shown

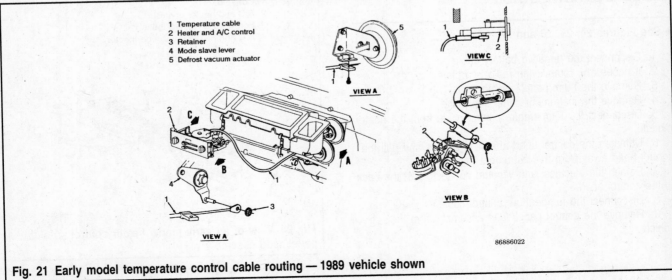

1 Temperature cable
2 Heater and A/C control
3 Retainer
4 Mode slave lever
5 Defrost vacuum actuator

VIEW A

VIEW C

VIEW B

VIEW A

86886022

Fig. 21 Early model temperature control cable routing — 1989 vehicle shown

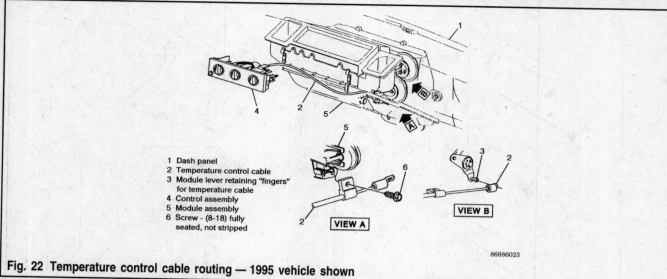

1 Dash panel
2 Temperature control cable
3 Module lever retaining "fingers" for temperature cable
4 Control assembly
5 Module assembly
6 Screw - (8-18) fully seated, not stripped

Fig. 22 Temperature control cable routing — 1995 vehicle shown

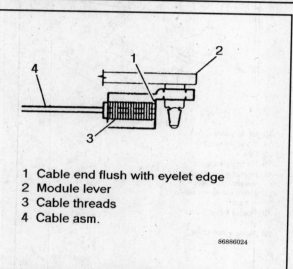

1 Cable end flush with eyelet edge
2 Module lever
3 Cable threads
4 Cable asm.

Fig. 23 Adjusting the temperature control cable

REMOVAL & INSTALLATION

▶ **See Figures 24, 25, 26 and 27**

1. Disconnect the negative battery cable.
2. If necessary, remove the radio trim plate.
3. Remove the hush panel, as required.
4. Remove the instrument panel trim plate.
5. Disconnect the temperature control cable from the heater module.
6. Unfasten the control head attaching screws and pull the control head away from the instrument panel.
7. Detach the electrical and vacuum connectors at the back of the control head.
8. Disconnect the temperature control cable.
9. Remove the control panel/head assembly from the vehicle.

To install:

10. Position control head near the mounting location. Attach the electrical and vacuum connectors and cables to the back of the control head. Connect the temperature control cable.
11. Install the control panel/head assembly, then secure using the attaching screws.
12. Connect the temperature control cable to the heater module.
13. Install the instrument panel trim plate.
14. Install the hush panel, if removed.
15. If removed, install the radio trim panel.
16. Connect the negative battery cable.

Blower Switch

The following procedure covers removal and installation of the blower switch for vehicles equipped with heat only, and also for vehicles equipped with heat and air conditioning.

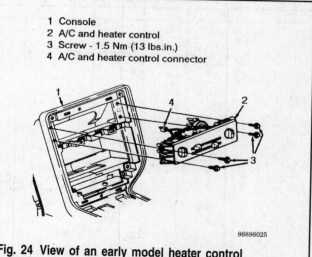

1 Console
2 A/C and heater control
3 Screw - 1.5 Nm (13 lbs.in.)
4 A/C and heater control connector

Fig. 24 View of an early model heater control panel/head assembly

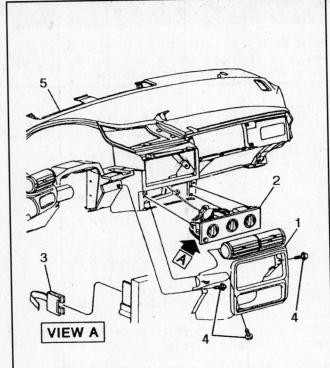

1 I/P trim plate
2 Heater/AC control assembly
3 Heater/AC control push-in retainer (3)
4 I/P trim plate screws (3)-
   2.3 Nm (20 lbs.in.)
5 I/P pad assembly

86886026

Fig. 25 Heater and A/C control assembly — 1995 Grand Am shown

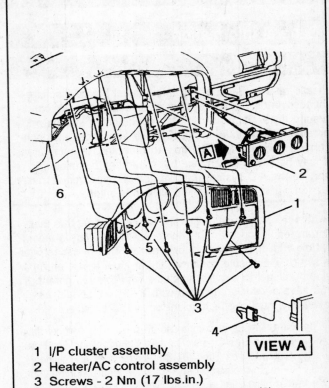

1 I/P cluster assembly
2 Heater/AC control assembly
3 Screws - 2 Nm (17 lbs.in.)
4 Heater/AC control push-in retainer (3)
5 I/P cluster trim push-in retainer (2)
6 I/P pad assembly

86886027

Fig. 26 View of the heater control assembly and related components — 1995 Achieva shown

REMOVAL & INSTALLATION

1. Disconnect the negative battery cable.
2. Remove the heater/air conditioner control assembly as outlined earlier in this section.
3. Remove the blower switch knob.
4. Detach the switch electrical connector.
5. Unfasten the blower switch attaching screws, then remove the blower switch.

To install:

6. Install the blower switch, then secure using the attaching screws.
7. Attach the blower switch electrical connector.
8. Install the control assembly as outlined earlier in this section.
9. Connect the negative battery cable.

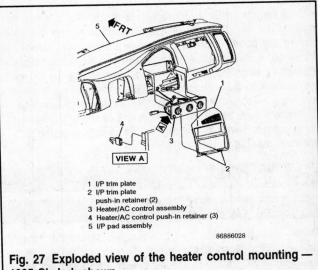

1 I/P trim plate
2 I/P trim plate
   push-in retainer (2)
3 Heater/AC control assembly
4 Heater/AC control push-in retainer (3)
5 I/P pad assembly

86886028

Fig. 27 Exploded view of the heater control mounting — 1995 Skylark shown

AIR CONDITIONER

General Information

✳✳CAUTION

Please refer to Section 1 of this manual before discharging/recovering the A/C system or disconnecting air conditioning lines. Damage to the air conditioning system or personal injury could result. Consult your local laws concerning refrigerant discharge and recycling. In many areas it may be illegal for anyone but a certified technician to service the A/C system. Always use an approved recovery station when discharging the air conditioning.

➡All 1995 and some 1994 vehicles covered by this manual are equipped with a refrigerant (R-134a) that is incompatible with the older R-12 or Freon®. This newer refrigerant is NOT available commercially in most areas, and it may be illegal to service a vehicle with this refrigerant. If you have a vehicle equipped with R-134a, it should be taken to a qualified technician for all A/C service.

There are 2 types of compressors used on front-wheel drive car air conditioning systems. The HR-6 compressor, used on Cycling Clutch Orifice Tube (CCOT) systems, is a 6 cylinder axial compressor consisting of 3 double-ended pistons actuated by a swash plate shaft assembly. The compressor cycles on and off according to system demands. The compressor driveshaft is driven by the serpentine belt when the electromagnetic clutch is engaged.

The V-5 compressor, used on Variable Displacement Orifice Tube (VDOT) systems, is designed to meet the demands of the air conditioning system without cycling. The compressor employs a variable angle wobble plate controlling the displacement of 5 axially oriented cylinders. Displacement is controlled by a bellows actuated control valve located in the rear head of the compressor. The electromagnetic compressor clutch connects the compressor shaft to the serpentine drive belt when the coil is energized.

➡R-12 refrigerant is a chlorofluorocarbon which, when released into the atmosphere, can contribute to the depletion of the ozone layer in the upper atmosphere. Ozone filters out harmful radiation from the sun. It is essential that every effort be made to avoid discharging the refrigerant system to the atmosphere. When discharging the system, use an approved R-12 Recovery/Recycling machine that meets SAE standards. Follow the operating instructions provided with the approved equipment exactly to properly discharge the system.

Compressor

✳✳CAUTION

Please refer to Section 1 of this manual before discharging/recovering the A/C system or disconnecting air conditioning lines. Damage to the air conditioning system or personal injury could result. Consult your local laws concerning refrigerant discharge and recycling. In many areas

it may be illegal for anyone but a certified technician to service the A/C system. Always use an approved recovery station when discharging the air conditioning.

REMOVAL & INSTALLATION

➡Please refer to Section 1 for important instructions pertaining to discharging, evacuating and recharging the system.

2.0L Engine

▶ See Figure 28

1. Disconnect the negative battery cable.
2. Properly discharge the air conditioning system.
3. Remove the serpentine belt.
4. Raise and safely support the vehicle.
5. Unfasten the retaining bolts, then remove the right side splash shield.
6. Disconnect the compressor/condenser hose assembly. Remove and discard the O-rings.

➡Cap the refrigerant lines when opening the system to prevent the entry of dirt and moisture and the loss of refrigerant lubricant.

7. Unfasten the two compressor bolts at the rear mounting bracket.
8. Detach the pressure switch and the clutch connectors from the compressor.
9. Unfasten the compressor attaching bolts and nut, then remove the compressor assembly.
10. Drain and measure the refrigerant oil from the compressor. Discard the old oil.

To install:

11. If the compressor is to be replaced, drain the oil from the new compressor and discard. Add new refrigerant oil equivalent to the amount drained from the old compressor. If less than 1 oz. (30ml) was drained from the old compressor, add 2 oz. (60ml).

➡Any repair to the A/C compressor or belt system will require loosening some A/C bracket bolts. To prevent future torque loss after retightening these bolts, the bolt or stud should be replaced with an appropriate new on or apply Loctite 242®, or equivalent, before installing the old bolt or stud.

12. Install the compressor and secure using the four front mounting bolts. Install the two rear mounting bolts and nut.
13. Install new O-rings to the compressor refrigerant lines. Lubricate with refrigerant oil.
14. Attach the pressure switch and clutch connectors to the compressor.
15. Using new O-rings, connect the compressor/condenser hose assembly.
16. Install the right side splash shield.
17. Carefully lower the vehicle.
18. Install the serpentine belt.
19. Connect the negative battery cable.

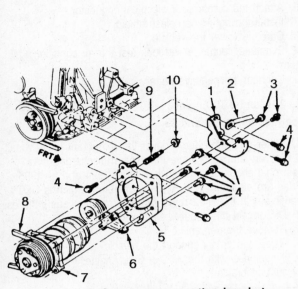

Fig. 28 A/C compressor mounting — 2.0L engine

1 Comp. rear mounting bracket
2 Brace
3 Bolt - 26 Nm (19 lbs.ft.)
4 Bolt - 50 Nm (36 lbs.ft.)
5 Compressor front mounting bracket
6 Idler pulley asm.
7 Compressor asm.
8 Belt
9 Stud
10 Nut - 50 Nm (36 lbs.ft.)

86886029

20. Evacuate, recharge and leak test the air conditioning system.

2.3L Engine
▶ See Figure 29

1. Either discharge and recover the refrigerant using a suitable recovery station or have the system discharged by a professional shop. Remember that some 1994 and all 1995 vehicles are equipped with R-134a refrigerant which is NOT compatible with the R-12 refrigerant used in previous vehicles.
2. Disconnect the negative battery cable.
3. Raise and safely support the vehicle.
4. Remove the right front wheel and tire assembly. Unfasten the retaining bolts, then remove the engine splash shield.
5. Remove the serpentine belt.
6. Disconnect the compressor hose assembly, then discard the sealing O-rings/washers.

➡**Cap the refrigerant lines when opening the system to prevent the entry of dirt and moisture and the loss of refrigerant lubricant.**

7. If necessary for access, remove the oil filter.
8. With a 7mm wrench, remove and discard the stud in the back of the compressor. The stud was only needed for assembly line purposes.
9. Detach the clutch electrical connector from the compressor.
10. Unfasten the compressor attaching bolts, then remove the compressor.
11. Drain and measure the refrigerant oil from the compressor. Discard the old oil.

To install:

12. If the compressor is to be replaced, drain the oil from the new compressor and discard. Add new refrigerant oil equivalent to the amount drained from the old compressor. If less than 1 oz. (30ml) was drained from the old compressor, add 2 oz. (60ml).
13. Position the compressor, then secure using the attaching bolts.
14. Install the serpentine drive belt.
15. Attach the compressor electrical connector.
16. Connect the compressor hose assembly, using new sealing washers/O-rings.
17. Install the engine splash shield, and the right front wheel and tire assembly.
18. Carefully lower the vehicle.
19. Evacuate, recharge and leak test the air conditioning system.
20. Connect the negative battery cable, then check the system operation.

2.5L Engine
▶ See Figure 30

1. Properly discharge the air conditioning system.
2. Disconnect the negative battery cable.
3. Raise and safely support the vehicle.
4. Unfasten the retaining bolts, then remove the right side splash shield.
5. Remove the serpentine belt.
6. Unfasten the compressor front bracket bolts.

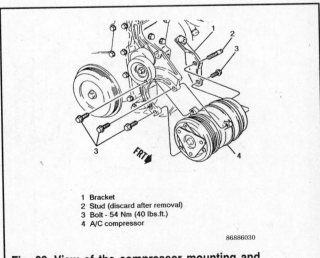

1 Bracket
2 Stud (discard after removal)
3 Bolt - 54 Nm (40 lbs.ft.)
4 A/C compressor

86886030

Fig. 29 View of the compressor mounting and location — 2.3L engine

7. Disconnect the compressor/condenser hose from the compressor. Remove and discard the O-rings.

➡Cap the refrigerant lines when opening the system to prevent the entry of dirt and moisture and the loss of refrigerant lubricant.

8. Detach the compressor electrical connector.
9. Unfasten the attaching bolts, then remove the compressor from the vehicle.
10. Drain and measure the refrigerant oil from the compressor. Discard the old oil.

To install:

11. If the compressor is to be replaced, drain the oil from the new compressor and discard. Add new refrigerant oil equivalent to the amount drained from the old compressor. If less than 1 oz. (30ml) was drained from the old compressor, add 2 oz. (60ml).
12. Position the compressor, then secure using the attaching bolts.
13. Install the front bracket.
14. Install the serpentine belt.

15. Using new O-rings, connect the compressor/condenser hose to the compressor.
16. Attach the compressor electrical connector.
17. Install the right side splash shield.
18. Carefully lower the vehicle.
19. Evacuate, recharge and leak test the air conditioning system.
20. Connect the negative battery cable.

3.0L, 3.1L and 3.3L Engines
▶ **See Figures 31, 32 and 33**

1. Either discharge and recover the refrigerant using a suitable recovery station or have the system discharged by a professional shop. Remember that some 1994 and all 1995 vehicles are equipped with R-134a refrigerant which is NOT compatible with the R-12 refrigerant used in previous vehicles.
2. Disconnect the negative battery cable.
3. Remove the serpentine belt.
4. Raise and safely support the vehicle.
5. If equipped with the 3.0L or 3.3L engine, remove the lower support bracket.

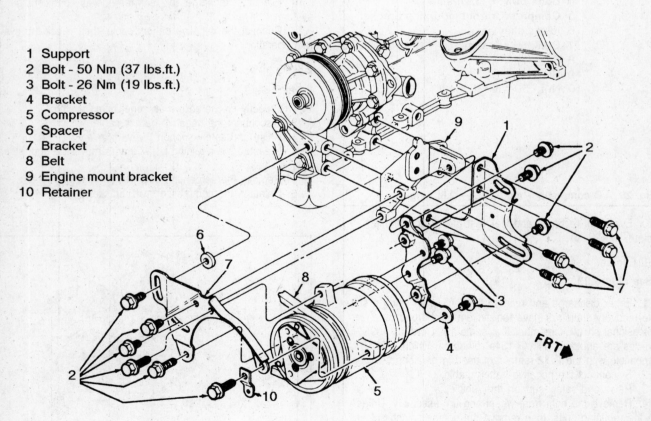

1 Support
2 Bolt - 50 Nm (37 lbs.ft.)
3 Bolt - 26 Nm (19 lbs.ft.)
4 Bracket
5 Compressor
6 Spacer
7 Bracket
8 Belt
9 Engine mount bracket
10 Retainer

86886031

Fig. 30 Exploded view of the compressor assembly mounting — 2.5L engine

6. Disconnect the compressor/condenser hose from the compressor. Remove and discard the O-ring seals.

➡ **Cap the refrigerant lines when opening the system to prevent the entry of dirt and moisture and the loss of refrigerant lubricant.**

7. Detach the clutch electrical connector.
8. Remove the splash shield.
9. Unfasten the attaching bolts, then remove the compressor.
10. Drain and measure the refrigerant oil from the compressor. Discard the old oil.

To install:

11. If the compressor is to be replaced, drain the oil from the new compressor and discard. Add new refrigerant oil equivalent to the amount drained from the old compressor. If

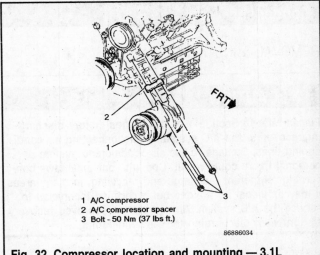

1 A/C compressor
2 A/C compressor spacer
3 Bolt - 50 Nm (37 lbs. ft.)

86886034

Fig. 32 Compressor location and mounting — 3.1L engine

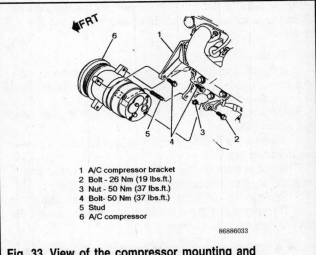

1 A/C compressor bracket
2 Bolt - 26 Nm (19 lbs.ft.)
3 Nut - 50 Nm (37 lbs.ft.)
4 Bolt- 50 Nm (37 lbs.ft.)
5 Stud
6 A/C compressor

86886033

Fig. 33 View of the compressor mounting and location — 3.3L engine

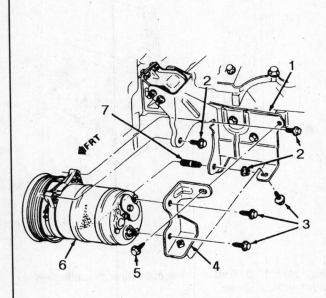

1 Engine mounting bracket
2 50 Nm (37 lbs.ft.)
3 13 Nm (115 lbs.in.)
4 A/C compressor rear support bracket
5 90 Nm (66 lbs.ft.)
6 Compressor asm. (V5)
7 Stud - 13 Nm (115 lbs.in.)

86886032

Fig. 31 A/C compressor mounting — 3.0L engine

less than 1 oz. (30ml) was drained from the old compressor, add 2 oz. (60ml).

12. Install the compressor and secure using the attaching bolts.
13. Install the splash shield.
14. Attach the electrical connector.
15. Using new O-rings, connect the compressor/condenser hose.
16. If removed, install the lower support bracket.
17. Carefully lower the vehicle.
18. Install the serpentine belt.
19. Evacuate, recharge and leak test the air conditioning system.
20. Connect the negative battery cable, then check for proper system operation.

Condenser

REMOVAL & INSTALLATION

✳✳CAUTION

Please refer to Section 1 of this manual before discharging/recovering the A/C system or disconnecting air conditioning lines. Damage to the air conditioning system or personal injury could result. Consult your local laws concerning refrigerant discharge and recycling. In many areas it may be illegal for anyone but a certified technician to service the A/C system. Always use an approved recovery station when discharging the air conditioning.

1985-91 Vehicles
▶ **See Figure 34**

➡**Please refer to Section 1 for important instructions pertaining to discharging, evacuating and recharging the system.**

1. Disconnect the negative battery cable.
2. Properly discharge the air conditioning system.
3. If equipped, unclip the plastic covers over the condenser.
4. Remove the grille and molding.
5. If necessary for access, remove the right and left headlight assemblies.
6. Remove the headlight mounting panel/front end panel and mounting brackets.
7. Scribe a mark on the radiator support for use during reinstallation, then remove the hood latch assembly.
8. Remove the condenser retainers and splash shields.
9. Disconnect and plugs the lines from the condenser. Remove and discard the O-rings.

➡**Use a backup wrench on the condenser fittings when removing the high-pressure and liquid lines. Cap the refrigerant lines when opening the system to prevent the entry of dirt and moisture and the loss of refrigerant lubricant.**

10. Carefully remove the condenser from the vehicle.
11. Transfer the splash shields, as required.
To install:

➡**If replacing the condenser or if the original condenser was flushed during service, add 1 fluid oz. (30ml) of refrigerant lubricant to the system.**

12. Install the condenser in the vehicle.
13. Install the condenser retainers and splash shield.
14. Lubricate new O-rings with clean refrigerant oil, then install on the condenser refrigerant line fittings.
15. Connect the refrigerant lines at the condenser.

➡**Use a backup wrench on the condenser fittings when tightening lines.**

16. Install the headlight mounting panel/front end panel and mounting brackets.
17. Using the marks made during removal, install the hood latch assembly.

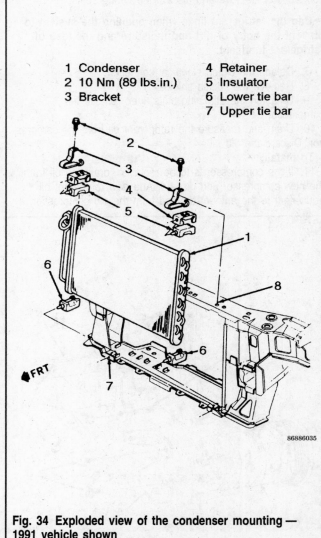

1	Condenser	4	Retainer
2	10 Nm (89 lbs.in.)	5	Insulator
3	Bracket	6	Lower tie bar
		7	Upper tie bar

Fig. 34 Exploded view of the condenser mounting — 1991 vehicle shown

18. Install the headlight assemblies.
19. Fasten the grille and molding to the headlight mounting panel/front end panel.
20. If removed, clip the cover over the condenser.
21. Evacuate, recharge and leak test the air conditioning system.
22. Connect the negative battery cable, then check the system for proper operation.

1992-95 Vehicles
▶ **See Figure 35**

1. Either discharge and recover the refrigerant using a suitable recovery station or have the system discharged by a professional shop. Remember that some 1994 and all 1995 vehicles are equipped with R-134a refrigerant which is NOT compatible with the R-12 refrigerant used in previous vehicles.
2. Disconnect the negative battery cable.
3. Scribe the location of the hood latch attaching nuts for installation purposes, then remove the latch.
4. Remove the hood latch support assembly.

5. Disconnect and plug the condenser outlet line. Remove and discard the O-rings.

6. Remove the condenser inlet line and retaining clamp on the radiator side tank. Remove and discard the O-rings.

7. Unfasten the retaining bolts from the radiator, then remove the condenser by lifting upward and turning slightly in a counter-clockwise direction.

To install:

8. Position the condenser, then install it by turning it slightly in a clockwise direction.

9. Using new O-rings, connect the condenser inlet line and secure using the retaining clamp.

10. Using new O-rings, fasten the condenser outlet line.

11. Install the hood latch support, then, using the marks made during removal, install the hood latch assembly.

12. Evacuate, recharge and leak test the air conditioning system.

13. Connect the negative battery cable, then check the system for proper operation.

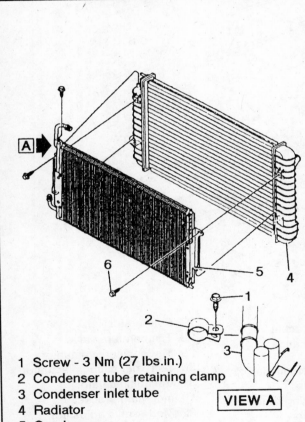

1 Screw - 3 Nm (27 lbs.in.)
2 Condenser tube retaining clamp
3 Condenser inlet tube
4 Radiator
5 Condenser
6 Screw - 6 Nm (54 lbs.in.)

VIEW A

86886036

Fig. 35 View of the condenser mounting — 1995 vehicle shown

Evaporator Core

REMOVAL & INSTALLATION

✳✳CAUTION

Please refer to Section 1 of this manual before discharging/recovering the A/C system or disconnecting air conditioning lines. Damage to the air conditioning system or personal injury could result. Consult your local laws concerning refrigerant discharge and recycling. In many areas it may be illegal for anyone but a certified technician to service the A/C system. Always use an approved recovery station when discharging the air conditioning.

1985-87 Vehicles

▶ **See Figure 36**

1. Either discharge and recover the refrigerant using a suitable recovery station or have the system discharged by a professional shop.

2. Drain the cooling system into a suitable container, then disconnect the negative battery cable.

3. Disconnect the console extensions.

4. Remove the right hush panel.

5. For access, lower the right-hand air duct, the plenum and the housing.

6. Raise and safely support the vehicle.

7. For vehicles equipped with an automatic transaxle, remove the transaxle support bolt.

8. Disconnect and plug the evaporator core and heater hoses.

9. Carefully lower the vehicle.

10. Remove the heater cover and baffle plate.

11. Remove the evaporator core from the vehicle.

To install:

12. Install the evaporator core.

13. Fasten the baffle plate and the heater cover.

14. Raise and safely support the vehicle.

15. Connect the heater and evaporator hoses.

16. For vehicles equipped with an automatic transaxle, install the support bolt.

17. Carefully lower the vehicle.

18. Raise and install the housing, plenum and the right-hand air duct.

19. Install the right hush panel, then connect the console extensions.

20. Evacuate, recharge and leak test the air conditioning system.

21. Connect the negative battery cable, then check the system for proper operation.

1988-91 Vehicles

▶ **See Figure 36**

1. Either discharge and recover the refrigerant using a suitable recovery station or have the system discharged by a professional shop.

2. Disconnect the negative battery cable.

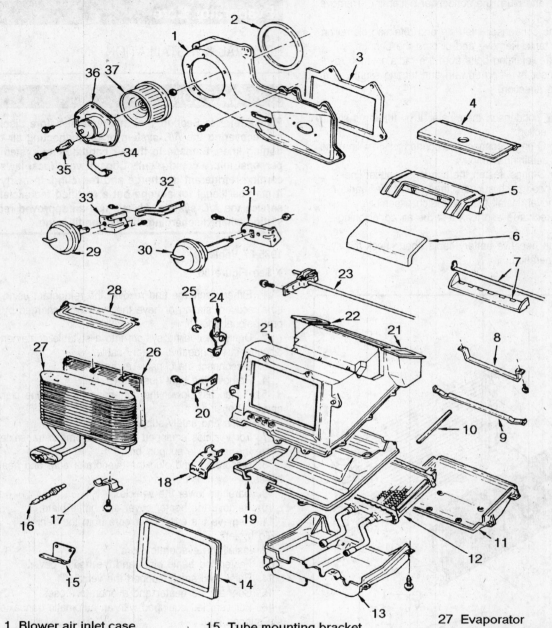

1 Blower air inlet case
2 Blower gasket
3 Blower air inlet flange mount
4 Mode valve
5 Defroster valve seat
6 Evaporator case seal
7 Defroster valve
8 Core mounting strap
9 Evaporator case seal
10 Evaporator to case seal
11 Rear core cover
12 Heater core
13 Front core cover
14 Evaporator core seal

15 Tube mounting bracket
16 Orifice (remote location in evaporator tube next to the accumulator)
17 Special tube clamp
18 Evaporator mounting bracket
19 Heater core shroud
20 Vacuum reservoir retaining clip
21 Evaporator case
22 Defroster duct
23 Mode valve shaft
24 Mode slave lever
25 Retainer (push on)
26 Water core filter

27 Evaporator
28 Temperature valve
29 Mode vacuum actuator
30 Defroster vacuum actuator
31 Vacuum actuator mounting bracket
32 Mode valve adjusting slave link
33 Mode valve actuator bracket
34 Lower motor cooling tube
35 Blower motor ground terminal
36 Blower motor
37 Blower fan

86886037

Fig. 36 Exploded view of the evaporator core, as well as related heater and A/C components

3. Properly drain the cooling system into a suitable container.

4. Raise and safely support the vehicle.

5. Disconnect the heater hoses at the heater core.

6. Remove the drain tube.

7. Disconnect the block fitting at the evaporator and discard the O-rings.

➡**Cap the refrigerant lines when opening the system to prevent the entry of dirt and moisture and the loss of refrigerant lubricant.**

8. Carefully lower the vehicle.

9. Remove the right and left sound insulators.

10. Disconnect the floor air outlet duct and hoses from the duct.

11. Unfasten the heater core cover, then remove the heater core.

12. Remove the evaporator core cover, then remove the evaporator core.

To install:

➡**If replacing the evaporator or if the original evaporator was flushed during service, add 3 fluid oz. (90ml) of refrigerant lubricant to the system.**

13. Install the evaporator core, then install the cover.

14. Install the heater core and the core cover.

15. Connect the floor air outlet duct and hoses.

16. Install the right and left sound insulators.

17. Raise and safely support the vehicle.

18. Lubricate new O-rings with clean refrigerant oil, then install them on the evaporator refrigerant lines.

19. Connect the block fitting to the evaporator.

20. Install the drain tube.

21. Connect the heater hoses to the heater core.

22. Carefully lower the vehicle.

23. Evacuate, recharge and leak test the air conditioning system.

24. Connect the negative battery cable.

25. Fill cooling system and check for leaks. Start the engine and allow to come to normal operating temperature. Recheck for coolant leaks. Allow the engine to warm up sufficiently to confirm operation of cooling fan.

1992-95 Vehicles
▶ **See Figure 37**

1. Either discharge and recover the refrigerant using a suitable recovery station or have the system discharged by a professional shop. Remember that some 1994 and all 1995 vehicles are equipped with R-134a refrigerant which is NOT compatible with the R-12 refrigerant used in previous vehicles.

2. Disconnect the negative battery cable.

3. Raise and safely support the vehicle.

4. Remove the front exhaust shield.

5. Unfasten three of the cradle cross brace, then swing the brace aside.

6. Disconnect the lines from the evaporator, then remove and discard the O-rings.

7. Carefully lower the vehicle.

8. Remove the right side under dash insulator panel.

9. Disconnect the electrical junction box at the heater core cover.

10. Remove the left side insulator panel, then remove the steering column filler.

11. If equipped, partially remove the shift console to get access to the floor duct and heater core cover.

12. Disconnect the floor duct.

13. Remove the heater core cover.

➡**The heater core will be suspended by the core pipes. Do not apply any downward pressure on the core, or damage may occur to the pipes.**

14. Remove the heater core shroud and straps, then remove the evaporator assembly.

To install:

15. Install the evaporator assembly.

16. Fasten the heater core shroud and straps, then install the core cover.

17. Connect the floor duct.

18. Install the steering column filler.

19. Fasten the left side insulator panel.

20. Connect the electrical junction box to the heater core cover, then install the right hand insulation panel.

21. If necessary, fasten the shift console.

22. Raise and safely support the vehicle.

23. Uncap and attach the evaporator lines.

24. Swing the cross brace into position then install the retaining bolts.

25. Install the exhaust heat shield, then carefully lower the vehicle.

26. Evacuate, recharge and leak test the air conditioning system.

27. Connect the negative battery cable.

28. Fill cooling system and check for leaks. Start the engine and allow to come to normal operating temperature. Recheck for coolant leaks. Allow the engine to warm up sufficiently to confirm operation of cooling fan.

Accumulator

REMOVAL & INSTALLATION

1985-91 Vehicles
▶ **See Figures 38, 39 and 40**

❊❊CAUTION

Please refer to Section 1 of this manual before discharging/recovering the A/C system or disconnecting air conditioning lines. Damage to the air conditioning system or personal injury could result. Consult your local laws concerning refrigerant discharge and recycling. In many areas it may be illegal for anyone but a certified technician to service the A/C system. Always use an approved recovery station when discharging the air conditioning.

1. Either discharge and recover the refrigerant using a suitable recovery station or have the system discharged by a professional shop. Remember that some 1994 and all 1995 vehicles are equipped with R-134a refrigerant which is NOT compatible with the R-12 refrigerant used in previous vehicles.

2. Disconnect the negative battery cable.

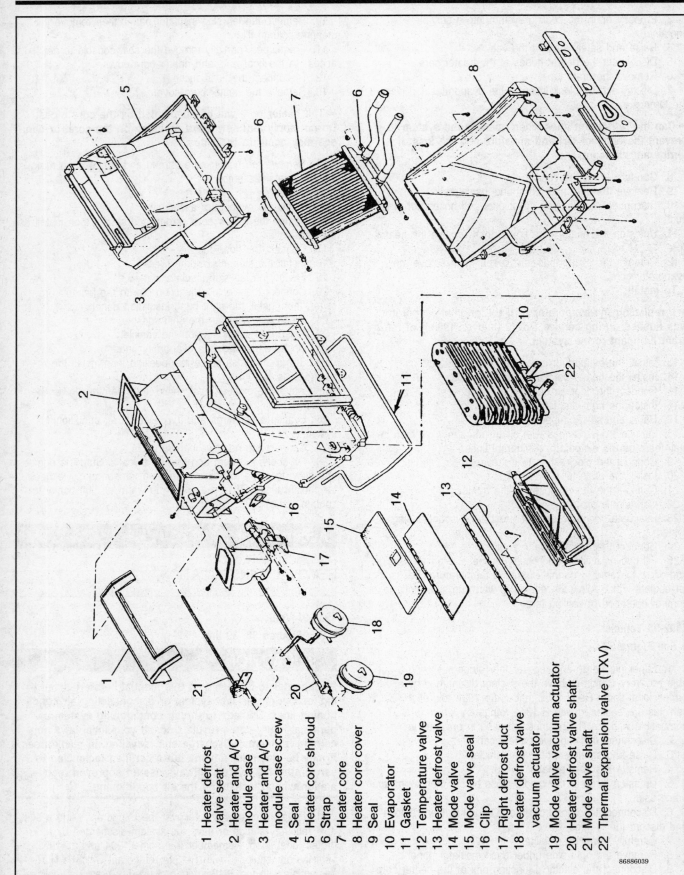

1. Heater defrost valve seat
2. Heater and A/C module case
3. Heater and A/C module case screw
4. Seal
5. Heater core shroud
6. Strap
7. Heater core
8. Heater core cover
9. Seal
10. Evaporator
11. Gasket
12. Temperature valve
13. Heater defrost valve
14. Mode valve
15. Mode valve seal
16. Clip
17. Right defrost duct
18. Heater defrost valve vacuum actuator
19. Mode valve vacuum actuator
20. Heater defrost valve shaft
21. Mode valve shaft
22. Thermal expansion valve (TXV)

86886039

Fig. 37 Exploded view of the evaporator assembly and related components — 1995 vehicle shown

3. Disconnect the low-pressure lines at the inlet and outlet fittings on the accumulator.

➡**Cap the refrigerant lines when opening the system to prevent the entry of dirt and moisture and the loss of refrigerant lubricant.**

4. Disconnect the pressure cycling switch connection and remove the switch, as required.

5. Loosen the lower strap bolt and spread the strap. Turn the accumulator and remove.

6. Drain and measure the oil in the accumulator. Discard the old oil.

To install:

7. Add new oil equivalent to the amount drained from the old accumulator. Add an additional 2-3 oz. (60-90ml) of oil to compensate for the oil retained by the accumulator desiccant.

8. Position the accumulator in the securing bracket and tighten the clamp bolt.

9. Lubricate new O-rings with clean refrigerant oil, then install on the inlet and outlet connections of the accumulator.

1 Bolt/screw
2 Parallel to center line of car
3 Accumulator asm.
4 Bracket asm.
5 Bolt/screw - 1 Nm (8 lbs.in.)
6 Canister asm.
7 Retainer

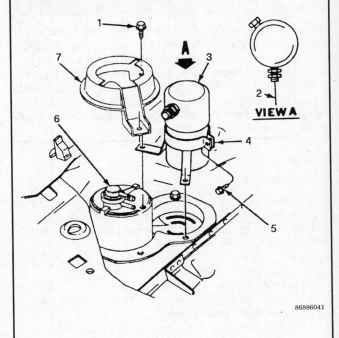

Fig. 39 Exploded view of the accumulator mounting and location — 2.5L engine

1 Bolt/screw
2 Parallel to center line of car
3 Accumulator asm.
4 Bracket asm.
5 Bolt/screw - 1 Nm (8 lbs.in.)
6 Canister asm.
7 Retainer

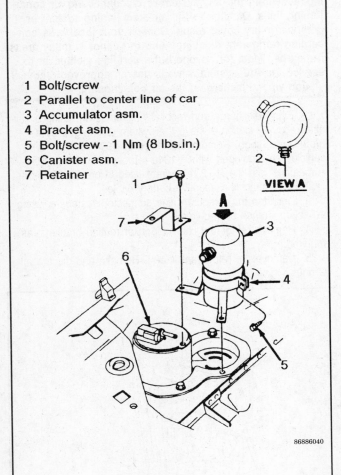

Fig. 38 Exploded view of the accumulator mounting — 2.3L engine

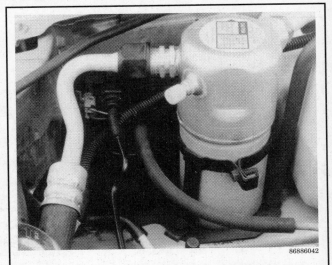

Fig. 40 Accumulator location — 1986 3.0L engine shown

10. Connect the low-pressure inlet and outlet lines to the accumulator.

11. Connect the negative battery cable.

12. Evacuate, charge and leak test the system.

Receiver Dehydrator

REMOVAL & INSTALLATION

> **❋❋CAUTION**
>
> **Please refer to Section 1 of this manual before discharging/recovering the A/C system or disconnecting air conditioning lines. Damage to the air conditioning system or personal injury could result. Consult your local laws concerning refrigerant discharge and recycling. In many areas it may be illegal for anyone but a certified technician to service the A/C system. Always use an approved recovery station when discharging the air conditioning.**

1992-95 Vehicles

▶ **See Figure 41**

1. Either discharge and recover the refrigerant using a suitable recovery station or have the system discharged by a professional shop. Remember that some 1994 and all 1995 vehicles are equipped with R-134a refrigerant which is NOT compatible with the R-12 refrigerant used in previous vehicles.

2. Disconnect the negative battery cable.

3. Raise and safely support the vehicle.

4. Remove the right front wheel and tire assembly, then partially remove the splash shield.

5. Detach both lines at the receiver dehydrator, then remove and discard the O-rings.

6. Unfasten the bracket bolt(s), then remove the receiver dehydrator assembly from the vehicle and remove the assembly from the bracket.

To install:

7. Position the receiver dehydrator into the bracket, then install the assembly into the vehicle. Secure using the bracket bolt(s).

8. Using a new O-ring seals, connect both lines to the receiver dehydrator.

9. Install the right splash shield, then the right wheel and tire assembly.

10. Carefully lower the vehicle.

11. Connect the negative battery cable.

12. Evacuate, charge and leak test the system.

Refrigerant Lines

REMOVAL & INSTALLATION

> **❋❋CAUTION**
>
> **Please refer to Section 1 of this manual before discharging/recovering the A/C system or disconnecting air conditioning lines. Damage to the air conditioning system or personal injury could result. Consult your local laws concerning refrigerant discharge and recycling. In many areas it may be illegal for anyone but a certified technician to service the A/C system. Always use an approved recovery station when discharging the air conditioning.**

1. Either discharge and recover the refrigerant using a suitable recovery station or have the system discharged by a professional shop. Remember that some 1994 and all 1995 vehicles are equipped with R-134a refrigerant which is NOT compatible with the R-12 refrigerant used in previous vehicles.

2. Disconnect the negative battery cable.

3. Unfasten the refrigerant line connectors/fasteners, using a backup wrench as required.

4. Remove refrigerant line support or routing brackets, as required.

5. Remove the refrigerant line(s). Remove and discard all O-rings.

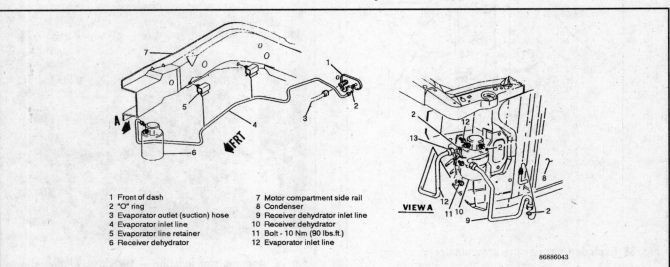

1	Front of dash	7	Motor compartment side rail
2	"O" ring	8	Condenser
3	Evaporator outlet (suction) hose	9	Receiver dehydrator inlet line
4	Evaporator inlet line	10	Receiver dehydrator
5	Evaporator line retainer	11	Bolt - 10 Nm (90 lbs.ft.)
6	Receiver dehydrator	12	Evaporator inlet line

86886043

Fig. 41 1992-95 vehicles are equipped with a receiver dehydrator in place of an accumulator

To install:

6. Position new refrigerant line in place, leaving protective caps installed until ready to connect.

7. Lubricate new O-rings with clean refrigerant oil, then install then on the refrigerant line connector fittings.

8. Connect and secure the refrigerant line(s), using a backup wrench, as required.

9. Install refrigerant line support or routing brackets, as required.

10. Evacuate, recharge and leak test the system.

11. Connect the negative battery cable.

Vacuum Motors

REMOVAL & INSTALLATION

1. Remove the vacuum lines from the actuator.
2. Disconnect the linkage from the actuator.
3. Remove the hardware attaching the actuator.
4. Remove the actuator.

To install:

5. Install the actuator and attaching hardware.
6. Connect the linkage to the actuator.
7. Connect the vacuum lines to the actuator.
8. Test system to confirm proper functioning of the actuator.

Control Cables

REMOVAL & INSTALLATION

1. Disconnect the negative battery cable.
2. Remove the screws securing the cluster trim plate to the instrument panel.
3. Tilt the top of the cluster trim plate downward releasing the clips that mount the bottom of the trim plate to the dash. Remove the trim plate.
4. Remove the screws attaching the accessory trim center plate to the dash.
5. Tilt the top of accessory trim plate downward releasing the clips that mount the bottom of the plate to the instrument panel. Remove the plate.
6. Remove the screws attaching the control assembly to the dash.
7. Remove the control assembly from the dash.
8. Disconnect the control assembly electrical connectors.
9. Remove the control assembly.

To install:

10. Install the control assembly.
11. Connect the control assembly electrical connectors.
12. Install the control assembly attaching screws.
13. Push the mounting clips into place and roll the top of the accessory trim plate upward into position.
14. Install the screws attaching the accessory trim plate to the dash.

15. Push the mounting clips into place and roll the top of the cluster trim plate upward into position.

16. Install the screws attaching the cluster trim plate to the instrument panel.

17. Connect the negative battery cable.

Heater/Air Conditioner Control Panel

REMOVAL & INSTALLATION

1. Disconnect the negative battery cable.
2. Remove the lower center trim plate by removing the screws or by gently prying the tabs out of the retainers.
3. Remove the control panel attaching screws and pull the control assembly away from the instrument panel.
4. Disconnect the electrical connectors.
5. Label and disconnect the control cables.

To install:

6. Connect the control cables to the new control panel assembly.
7. Connect the electrical connectors.
8. Reposition the control panel assembly and install the attaching screws.
9. Install the lower center trim plate by removing the screws or gently pressing on the plate until the tabs snap into the retainers.
10. Connect the negative battery cable.

Orifice (Expansion) Tube

REMOVAL & INSTALLATION

1985-91 Vehicles
◗ **See Figure 42**

❈❈CAUTION

Please refer to Section 1 of this manual before discharging/recovering the A/C system or disconnecting air conditioning lines. Damage to the air conditioning system or personal injury could result. Consult your local laws concerning refrigerant discharge and recycling. In many areas it may be illegal for anyone but a certified technician to service the A/C system. Always use an approved recovery station when discharging the air conditioning.

1. Either discharge and recover the refrigerant using a suitable recovery station or have the system discharged by a professional shop.
2. Disconnect the negative battery cable.
3. Loosen the fitting at the liquid line outlet on the condenser or evaporator inlet pipe, then separate the liquid line from the condenser outlet pipe. Remove and discard the O-ring.

➠**Use a backup wrench on the condenser outlet fitting when loosening the lines.**

4. Using needle-nosed pliers, tools AC-1002, and J 26549 or equivalent, carefully, remove the fixed orifice tube from the tube fitting in the evaporator inlet line.

➡**If the system has a pressure switch near the orifice tube, it should be removed prior to heating the pipe to avoid damage to the switch.**

5. In the event that the restricted or plugged orifice tube is difficult to remove, perform the following:

a. Remove as much of the impacted residue as possible.

b. Using a hair dryer, epoxy drier or equivalent, carefully apply heat approximately ¼ in. (6mm) from the dimples on the inlet pipe. Do not overheat the pipe.

c. While applying heat, use special tool J 26549-C or equivalent to grip the orifice tube. Use a turning motion along with a push-pull motion to loosen the impacted orifice tube and remove it.

6. Swab the inside of the evaporator inlet pipe with R-11 to remove any remaining residue.

7. Add 1 oz. of 525 viscosity refrigerant oil to the system.

8. Lubricate the new O-ring and orifice tube with refrigerant oil and insert into the inlet pipe.

➡**Ensure that the new orifice tube is inserted in the inlet tube with the smaller screen end first.**

9. Connect the evaporator inlet pipe with the condenser outlet fitting.

➡**Use a backup wrench on the condenser outlet fitting when tightening the lines.**

10. Evacuate, recharge and leak test the system.
11. Connect the negative battery cable.

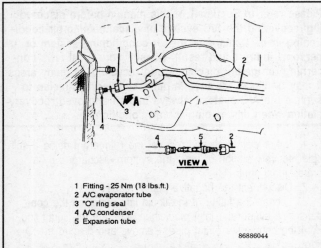

1 Fitting - 25 Nm (18 lbs.ft.)
2 A/C evaporator tube
3 "O" ring seal
4 A/C condenser
5 Expansion tube

86886044

Fig. 42 View of the expansion tube which is used on 1985-91 vehicles

Thermal Expansion Valve (TXV)

REMOVAL & INSTALLATION

1992-95 Vehicles
▶ See Figure 43

⁂CAUTION

Please refer to Section 1 of this manual before discharging/recovering the A/C system or disconnecting air conditioning lines. Damage to the air conditioning system or personal injury could result. Consult your local laws concerning refrigerant discharge and recycling. In many areas it may be illegal for anyone but a certified technician to service the A/C system. Always use an approved recovery station when discharging the air conditioning.

1. Either discharge and recover the refrigerant using a suitable recovery station or have the system discharged by a professional shop. Remember that some 1994 and all 1995 vehicles are equipped with R-134a refrigerant which is NOT compatible with the R-12 refrigerant used in previous vehicles.

2. Disconnect the negative battery cable.
3. Remove the right side under-dash insulator panel.
4. Remove the electrical junction box at the heater core cover.
5. Remove the left side insulator panel, then detach the steering column filler.
6. If equipped, partially move the shift console to gain access to the floor duct and heater core cover.
7. Unfasten the floor duct, then remove the heater core cover.

➡**The heater core will be suspended by the heater core pipes. Do not apply any downward pressure on the core, or damage may occur to the heater core pipes.**

8. Unfasten the heater core shroud and straps, then unfasten the insulation tape from the valve fittings.
9. Remove the thermal expansion valve. Clean all of the insulation tape from the evaporator fittings to be sure the correct seating of the O-rings.

To install:
10. Using new insulation wrap, install the thermal expansion valve.
11. Fasten the heater core shroud and straps, then install the core cover.
12. The fittings on the TXV should be leak checked before finishing installation. This can be done without running the vehicle:

a. Evacuate and partially recharge the A/C system with 1 lb. (48kg) of the proper refrigerant. Again, REMEMBER that some 1994 and all 1995 vehicles are equipped with R-134a refrigerant which is NOT compatible with the R-12 refrigerant used in previous vehicles.

b. Properly leak test the system.
13. Install the floor duct and the steering column filler.
14. Attach the left side insulation panel.

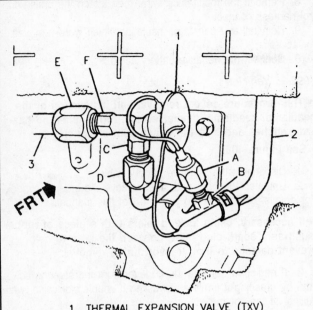

1 THERMAL EXPANSION VALVE (TXV)
2 EVAP. OUTLET LINE
3 EVAP. INLET LINE

WRENCH SIZES:

A	15 mm	D	19 mm
B	9/16 "	E	23 mm
C	13 mm	F	16 mm

NOTE: INSULATION REMOVED FOR ILLUSTRATION
PURPOSE ONLY — INSULATION MUST BE
INSTALLED ON VALVE

86886045

**Fig. 43 View of the Thermal Expansion Valve (TXV),
which is used on 1992-95 vehicles**

15. Fasten the electrical junction box to the heater core cover.

16. Install the right side insulation panel. If equipped, fasten the console.

17. Evacuate, recharge and leak test the system.

18. Connect the negative battery cable.

CRUISE CONTROL

Actuator Switch

The cruise control actuator switch on most vehicles is part of the multi-function lever located on the steering column. On some vehicles, separate set/coast and resume/accel switches are mounted on the steering wheel.

REMOVAL & INSTALLATION

Multi-Function Lever

1985-91 Vehicles

▶ **See Figures 44 and 45**

1. Disconnect the negative battery terminal.

2. Detach cruise control switch connector at the base of steering column, it may be necessary to remove an under dash panel or trim piece for access.

3. Make sure lever is in the CENTER or OFF position.

4. Pull lever straight out of retaining clip within the steering column.

5. Attach mechanic's wire or similar to the connector; gently pull the harness through the column, leaving the pull wire in place.

To install:

6. Place the transaxle selector in LOW or 1. Attach the mechanic's wire to the connector. Gently pull the harness into place, checking that the harness is completely clear of any moving or movable components such as tilt-column, telescoping column, brake pedal linkage, etc.

7. Position the lever and push it squarely into the retainer until it snaps in place.

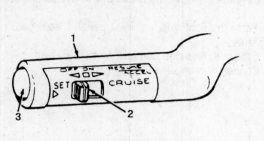

1 Turn signal lever
2 Off/on, resume/accel switch
3 Set/coast switch

86886046

Fig. 44 The cruise control engagement switch is part of the multi-function lever assembly; the cruise control switch and the lever must be replaced as an assembly

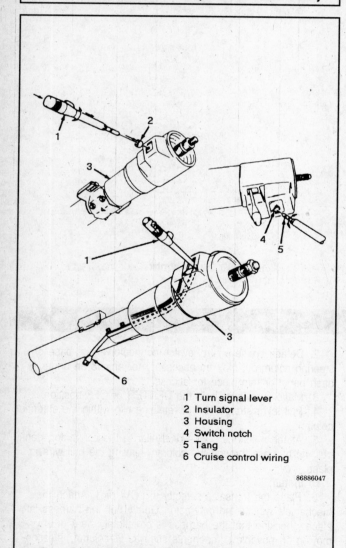

1 Turn signal lever
2 Insulator
3 Housing
4 Switch notch
5 Tang
6 Cruise control wiring

86886047

Fig. 45 Removing the multi-function turn signal lever in order to replace the cruise control switch

8. Remove the mechanics' wire, then attach the cruise control harness connector.
9. Reinstall any panels or insulation which were removed for access.
10. Connect the negative battery cable.

1992-95 Vehicles

➡This procedure covers removal and installation of the headlamp, headlamp dimmer switch, turn signal and hazard switches and also the cruise control switch.

◆ See Figure 46

1. Disconnect the negative battery cable.
2. Unfasten the horn pad, then remove the steering wheel. For details, please refer to Section 8 of this manual.

➡If necessary, using locking pliers with a piece of rubber (such as a spark plug boot) between the jaws to help prevent damage to the tilt lever during removal.

3. If equipped, remove the tilt lever from the steering column by grasping it firmly and twisting it counterclockwise, while pulling off the column.
4. Remove the upper and lower steering column covers.
5. Remove the dampener assembly, then unfasten and remove the switch assembly from the vehicle.

To install:

6. Position and secure the switch assembly.
7. Install the dampener and the upper and lower steering column covers.
8. If equipped, attach the tilt lever to the column.
9. Install the steering wheel, then fasten the horn pad.
10. Connect the negative battery cable.

Steering Wheel Mounted Switches

1. Disconnect the negative battery cable.
2. Remove the horn pad.
3. Unfasten the retainer and nut.
4. Remove the steering wheel.
5. Detach the electrical connectors.
6. Remove the horn switch, if necessary.

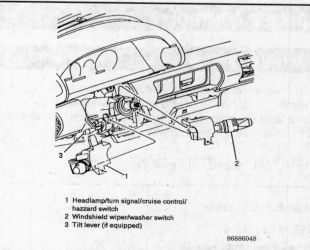

1 Headlamp/turn signal/cruise control/ hazzard switch
2 Windshield wiper/washer switch
3 Tilt lever (if equipped)

86886048

Fig. 46 View of the steering column showing the cruise control switch location — 1992-95 vehicles

To install:

7. If removed, install the horn switch. Attach the electrical connectors.

8. Install the steering wheel; tighten the nut to 30 ft. lbs. (41 Nm).

9. Install the retainer and clip.

10. Fasten the horn pad.

11. Connect the negative battery cable.

Brake/Clutch Release Switches

All factory or dealer installed cruise control systems for these vehicles are equipped with either a brake or clutch release switch. The purpose of the switch is to deactivate the system when the driver begins to depress the pedal. most of the switches found on earlier models are vacuum break switches (vacuum release valves) which will therefore have a vacuum line attached to the rear or side of the switch. A vacuum brake switch is used to quickly vent vacuum to the atmosphere so a vacuum controlled servo may return the throttle to the idle position. Later models may use a vacuum switch, and electric switch or a combined vacuum and electric switch.

REMOVAL & INSTALLATION

▶ **See Figures 47, 48, 49 and 50**

1. Disconnect the negative battery cable.

2. If necessary for access, remove the left sound insulator.

3. At the brake switch, detach either the two electrical connectors or the electrical connector and the vacuum hose.

4. Pull the switch rearward to remove the switch from the retainer.

To install:

5. Position the retainer into the bracket.

6. With the brake or clutch pedal depressed, insert the switch into the retainer until the switch seats on the retainer. You will head "clicks" as the ribbed part of the switch is pushed forward through the retainer.

7. Connect the wiring and/or vacuum lines. Adjust the switch as follows:

    a. Pull the brake or clutch pedal fully rearward against the pedal stop until audible "clicks" can not be heard. The switch will be moved in the retainer providing adjustment.

    b. Release the brake or clutch pedal and repeat Step A to be sure that the switch is properly adjusted.

8. If removed, install the left sound insulator.

9. Connect the negative battery cable.

ADJUSTMENT

1. Press the brake pedal assembly and insert the switch assembly and the stoplamp switch assembly into the retainers until fully seated.

2. Slowly release the brake pedal assembly back to its fully retracted position. The release switch assembly will move within the retainers to their "adjusted" position.

3. Measure pedal travel and check switch engagement. The release switch assembly contact should be open at $1/8$ to $1/2$ in.

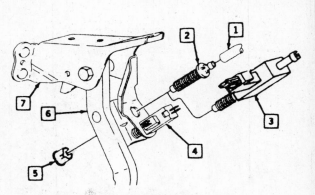

1. SERVO VACUUM RELEASE HOSE
2. CRUISE CONTROL RELEASE VALVE (MAN. ONLY)
3. CRUISE CONTROL VACUUM RELEASE & T.C.C. RELEASE SWITCH
4. BRAKE LAMP AND CRUISE RELEASE SWITCH
5. RETAINER
6. BRAKE PEDAL
7. BRACKET

CRUISE CONTROL VACUUM RELEASE VALVE ADJUSTMENT PROCEDURE:

1. INSTALL RETAINER.
2. WITH BRAKE PEDAL DEPRESSED, INSERT VALVE INTO TUBULAR RETAINER UNTIL VALVE SEATS ON RETAINER. NOTE THAT AUDIBLE "CLICKS" CAN BE HEARD AS THREADED PORTION OF VALVE IS PUSHED THROUGH THE RETAINER TOWARD THE BRAKE PEDAL.
3. PULL BRAKE PEDAL FULLY REARWARD AGAINST PEDAL STOP UNTIL AUDIBLE "CLICK" SOUNDS CAN NO LONGER BE HEARD. VALVE WILL BE MOVED IN TUBULAR RETAINER PROVIDING ADJUSTMENT.
4. RELEASE BRAKE PEDAL AND REPEAT STEP (3) TO ASSURE THAT NO AUDIBLE "CLICK" SOUNDS REMAIN.

86886049

Fig. 47 Early model cruise control electrical and vacuum brake switch mounting

(3.5 to 12.5mm). brake pedal assembly travel, measured at the centerline of the brake pedal assembly pad. Nominal actuation of the stoplamp switch assembly contacts is about $3/16$ in. (4.5mm) after the cruise control switch assembly contacts close.

Speed Sensor

REMOVAL & INSTALLATION

Optical Type With Buffer

1. Disconnect the negative battery cable.

2. To gain access to the sensor and buffer behind the speedometer, the instrument cluster must be partially removed. When doing so, disconnect the harness connector at the rear of the cluster; if the cluster is pulled too far outward with the harness attached, both may be damaged.

3. Disconnect the amplifier connector.

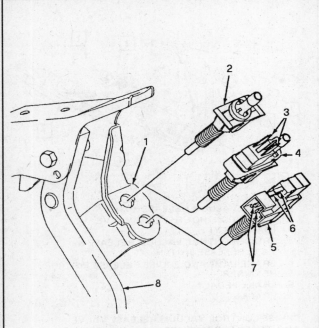

1 Brake pedal mounting bracket
2 Cruise control release valve (vacuum)
   (manual transaxle only)
3 Torque converter clutch terminals
4 TCC and cruise control release switch/
   valve (automatic transaxle only)
5 Stoplamp switch
6 Cruise control release switch terminals
7 Stop lamp switch terminals
8 Brake pedal asm

86886050

Fig. 48 View of the cruise control release switch and related components — 1992 vehicle shown

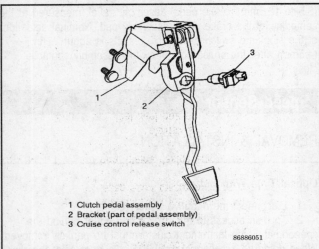

1 Clutch pedal assembly
2 Bracket (part of pedal assembly)
3 Cruise control release switch

86886051

Fig. 49 View of the cruise control clutch pedal release switch — 1995 vehicle shown

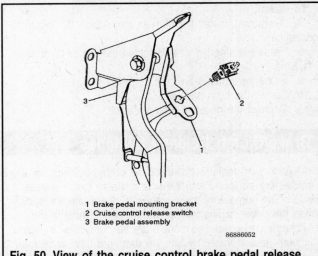

1 Brake pedal mounting bracket
2 Cruise control release switch
3 Brake pedal assembly

86886052

Fig. 50 View of the cruise control brake pedal release switch — 1995 vehicle shown

4. Remove the speed sensor attaching screw and remove the sensor through the opening in the base of the instrument panel.

To install:

5. Route the sensor wire connector and harness through the opening in the base of the instrument panel.

6. Install the sensor on its bracket and install the retaining screw.

7. Connect the amplifier connector.

8. Reinstall the instrument cluster and connect the electrical harness.

9. Connect the negative battery cable.

Permanent Magnet Type

▶ **See Figures 51 and 52**

1. Disconnect the negative battery cable.

2. If necessary for access, raise and safely support the vehicle.

3. Detach the wiring harness from the speed sensor. If the sensor also contains the speedometer cable, remove the cable.

4. Unfasten the retainer clip/bolt.

5. Carefully lift the sensor out of the transaxle or transaxle case extension.

6. Remove and discard the O-ring from the sensor.

To install:

7. Lubricate a new O-ring with Dexron® II or equivalent transmission fluid, then install the ring on the sensor.

8. Install the sensor into the transaxle/case extension, then secure the retaining clip/bolt.

9. Connect the speedometer cable if it was removed; connect the wiring harness. Make certain the harness is routed clear of moving or hot components.

10. If raised, carefully lower the vehicle.

11. Connect the negative battery cable.

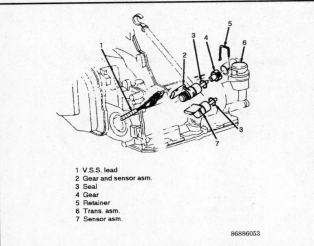

Fig. 51 Exploded view of an early model Vehicle Speed Sensor (VSS) mounting — 1989 vehicle shown

1 V.S.S. lead
2 Gear and sensor asm.
3 Seal
4 Gear
5 Retainer
6 Trans. asm.
7 Sensor asm.

86886053

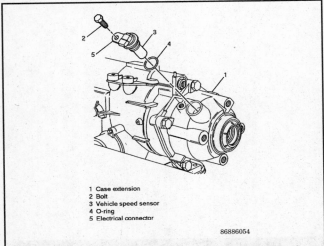

Fig. 52 Exploded view of a late model Vehicle Speed Sensor (VSS) mounting — 1995 vehicle shown

1 Case extension
2 Bolt
3 Vehicle speed sensor
4 O-ring
5 Electrical connector

86886054

Vacuum Servo Unit

REMOVAL & INSTALLATION

♦ See Figures 53 and 54

1. Disconnect the negative battery cable.
2. Detach the electrical connector and vacuum hoses at the servo.
3. Disconnect the actuating chain, cable or rod from the servo.
4. Unfasten the screws holding the vacuum servo and solenoid unit to the bracket, then remove the unit from the vehicle.

To install:

5. Connect the larger diameter brake release vacuum line to the servo unit. Connect the vacuum hose from the vacuum control valve to the servo unit.
6. Attach the actuating chain, rod or cable to the servo.

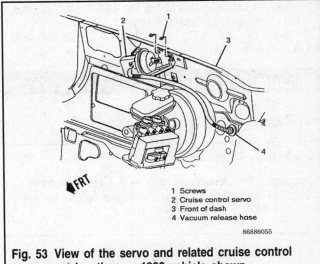

Fig. 53 View of the servo and related cruise control component locations — 1992 vehicle shown

1 Screws
2 Cruise control servo
3 Front of dash
4 Vacuum release hose

86886055

7. Install the servo unit to the bracket; tighten the screws to 12 inch lbs. (1.4 Nm).
8. Attach the electrical connector to the servo.
9. Adjust the cable, rod or chain.
10. Connect the negative battery cable.

VACUUM SYSTEM LINKAGE ADJUSTMENT

✳✳WARNING

Do not stretch cables to make pins fit or holes align. This will prevent the engine from returning to idle.

Cable Type

1. Check that the cable is properly installed and that the throttle is closed to the idle position.
2. Pull the servo end of the cable toward the linkage bracket of the servo. Place the servo connector in one of the

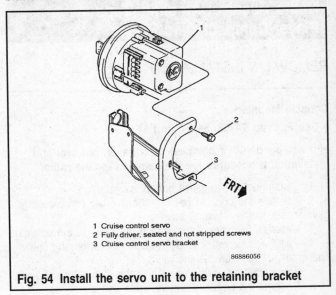

1 Cruise control servo
2 Fully driver, seated and not stripped screws
3 Cruise control servo bracket

86886056

Fig. 54 Install the servo unit to the retaining bracket

6 holes in the bracket which allows the least amount of slack and does not move the throttle linkage.

3. Install the retainer clip. Check that the throttle linkage is still in the idle position.

Vacuum Reservoir/Tank

REMOVAL & INSTALLATION

▶ See Figures 55 and 56

Disconnect the vacuum line, remove the retaining screws and remove the reservoir. When reinstalling, tighten the retaining screws to 35-97 inch lbs. (4-11 Nm).

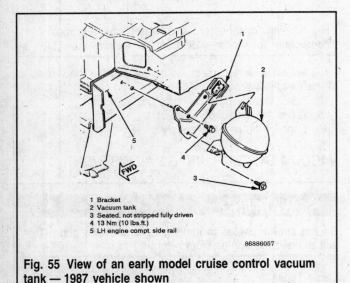

1 Bracket
2 Vacuum tank
3 Seated, not stripped fully driven
4 13 Nm (10 lbs.ft.)
5 LH engine compt. side rail

86886057

Fig. 55 View of an early model cruise control vacuum tank — 1987 vehicle shown

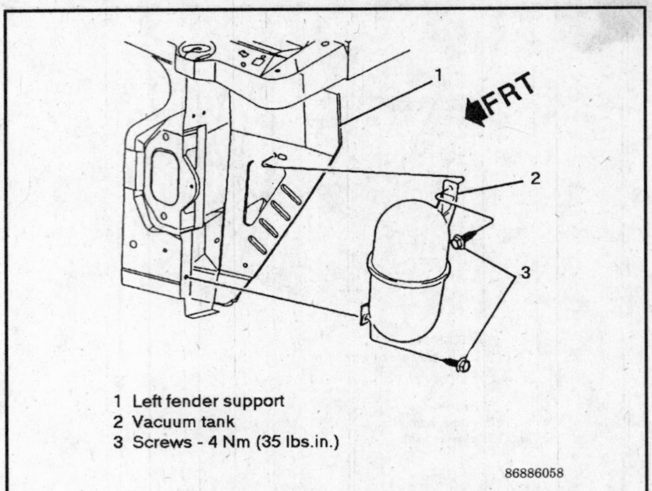

1 Left fender support
2 Vacuum tank
3 Screws - 4 Nm (35 lbs.in.)

86886058

Fig. 56 Cruise control vacuum tank mounting — 1993 vehicle shown

ENTERTAINMENT SYSTEMS

Radio Receiver/Amplifier/Tape Player/Compact Disc Player

REMOVAL & INSTALLATION

Console Mounted

▶ See Figures 57, 58, 59, 60 and 61

➡ If equipped with a compact disc player, removal and installation procedures are the same as for the radio.

1. Disconnect the negative battery cable.

2. Remove the console bezel and any other trim pieces to gain access to the retaining screws.

3. Unfasten the screws that attach the radio to the console.

4. Pull the radio out, detach the connectors, ground cable and antenna, then remove the radio.

5. The installation is the reverse of the removal procedure.

6. Connect the negative battery cable and check the radio for proper operation.

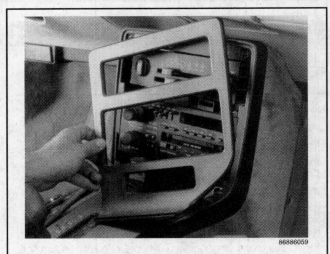

86886059

Fig. 57 Remove the console bezel for access to the radio retaining screws

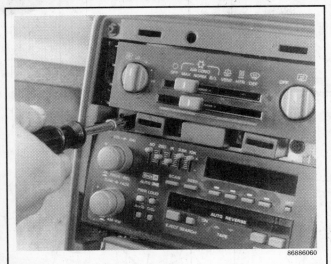

Fig. 58 Unfasten the retaining screws, then . . .

Fig. 59 . . . carefully pull out the radio

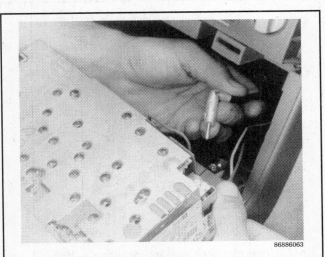

Fig. 60 Disconnect the antenna from the rear of the radio

Fig. 61 Detach the electrical connector from the radio

Dash Mounted

1. Disconnect the negative battery cable.
2. Remove the instrument panel extension bezel and any other trim pieces required for access.
3. Remove the radio bracket.
4. Unfasten the screws that attach the radio to the instrument panel.
5. Pull the radio out, detach the connectors, ground cable and antenna, then remove the radio.
6. The installation is the reverse of the removal procedure.
7. Connect the negative battery cable and check the radio for proper operation.

Speakers

REMOVAL & INSTALLATION

Front Speakers

DASH MOUNTED

▶ **See Figure 62**

1. Disconnect the negative battery cable.
2. For 1985-87 vehicles, remove the light and wiper switches, then unfasten the air deflectors and trim.
3. Remove the speaker/defroster grille or dash pad from the instrument panel.
4. Unfasten the speaker attaching screws.
5. Lift the speaker partially out, then detach the electrical connector(s).
6. Remove the speaker.
   To install:
7. Attach the speaker electrical connector(s).
8. Place the speaker into position, then secure using the attaching screws.
9. Install the speaker/defroster grille or dash pad to the instrument panel.
10. For 1985-87 vehicles, connect the light and wiper switches, then install the air deflectors and trim.

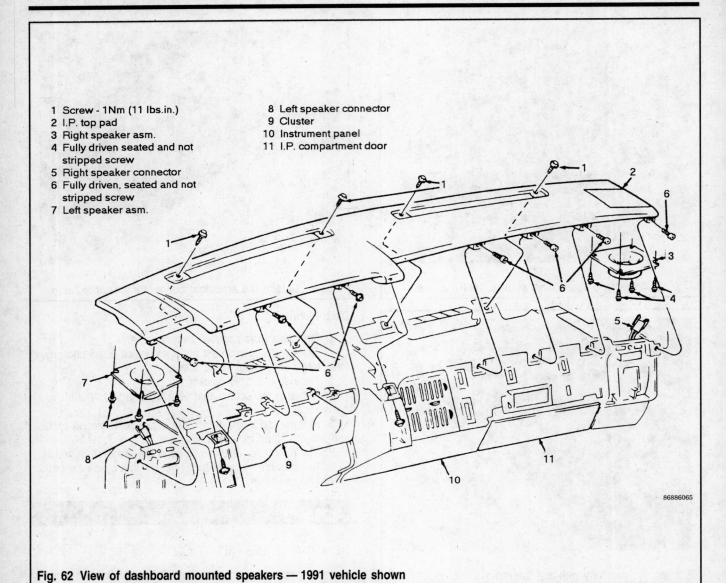

1 Screw - 1Nm (11 lbs.in.)
2 I.P. top pad
3 Right speaker asm.
4 Fully driven seated and not stripped screw
5 Right speaker connector
6 Fully driven, seated and not stripped screw
7 Left speaker asm.
8 Left speaker connector
9 Cluster
10 Instrument panel
11 I.P. compartment door

Fig. 62 View of dashboard mounted speakers — 1991 vehicle shown

11. Connect the negative battery cable.

DOOR MOUNTED

▶ **See Figure 63**

1. Disconnect the negative battery cable.
2. Remove the door trim panel.
3. Unfasten the door speaker retaining screws, then pull the speakers out to detach the electrical connector.

To install:

4. Attach the speaker electrical connector, then position it into the recess in the door.
5. Secure the speaker using the retaining screws. Be sure not to overtighten and strip the screws.
6. Install the door trim panel.
7. Connect the negative battery cable.

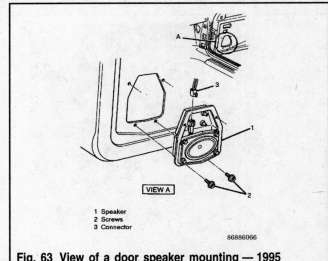

1 Speaker
2 Screws
3 Connector

Fig. 63 View of a door speaker mounting — 1995 vehicle shown

Rear Speakers

1985-90 VEHICLES

◗ **See Figures 64, 65, 66 and 67**

The rear speakers for 1985-90 vehicles are serviced from inside the trunk area.

1. Disconnect the negative battery cable.

2. From inside the trunk, unfasten the retainer, then remove the speaker cover.

3. Remove the speaker by sliding the lever on the speaker bracket out of the clip, then carefully lower the speaker.

4. Detach the speaker electrical wires, then remove the speaker assembly from the vehicle.

To install:

5. Attach the electrical wires to the speaker.

6. Position the speaker into the bracket, then hold the speaker against the shelf in its proper position and slide the lever on the speaker retainer into the clip.

7. Install the speaker cover, then close the trunk lid.

8. Connect the negative battery cable.

Fig. 66 Unclip the retaining lever, then carefully lower the speaker and detach the wiring

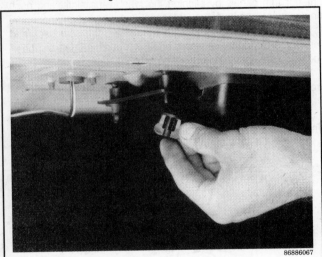
Fig. 64 Unfasten the speaker cover retainer, then . . .

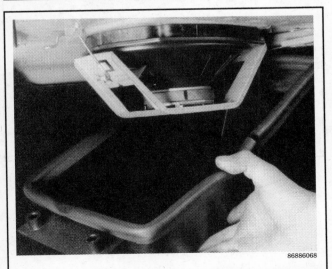
Fig. 65 . . . remove the cover for access to the speaker

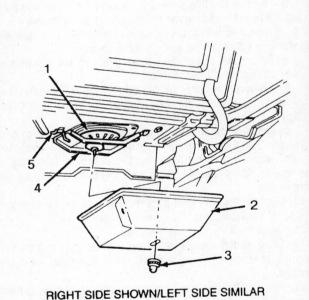

RIGHT SIDE SHOWN/LEFT SIDE SIMILAR

1 Speaker
2 Cover
3 Nut
4 Bracket
5 Lever

Fig. 67 View of the rear speaker mounting — 1985-90 vehicles

1991-95 VEHICLES

♦ **See Figure 68**

1. Disconnect the negative battery cable.
2. Remove the rear seat cushion by unfasten the bolts from the bracket at the front of the seat.
3. Grasp the seat cushion and lift up and outward, then remove the cushion from the vehicle.
4. Remove the anchor bolts from the bottom of the seatback securing the rear seat retainers and center seat safety belts.
5. Grasp the bottom of the seatback and swing upward to disengage the offsets on the back upper frame bar from the hangers; lift the seatback upward to remove.
6. If equipped with 4 doors, remove the upper rear quarter interior trim panels by performing the following:
   a. Disconnect the tabs on the trim pale from the slots in the body by grasping the trim panel and pulling toward the front of the car.
   b. Remove the trim panel by rotating it inboard.
7. If equipped with 4 doors, remove the lower rear quarter interior trim panels by performing the following:
   a. Unfasten the 2 attaching screws.
   b. Remove the trim panel by grasping the panel and pulling it inboard to disengage the tabs from the retainers.
8. If equipped with 2 doors, remove the lower rear quarter interior trim panels by performing the following:
   a. Detach the carpet retainer by removing the screws and lifting up on the carpet retainer.
   b. Remove the upper windshield molding by grasping the molding and pulling down to disengage the molding from the clips.
   c. Unfasten the trim panel attaching screws, then remove the trim panel by grasping the panel and pulling it inboard.
9. Remove the center high-mount stop light by removing the screws, lifting the light, then detaching the electrical connector.
10. Remove the rear seat back-to-window panel by sliding the panel out from under the remaining quarter trim.
11. Disconnect the speaker harness.
12. Unfasten the speaker attaching screws, then remove the speaker assembly by lifting and sliding the assembly out of the slots.
13. Remove the speaker from the retainer by removing the screws.

To install:

14. Install the speaker to the retainer and secure using the attaching screws.
15. Attach the speaker assembly by inserting the tabs into the slots.
16. Install the speaker retainer assembly attaching screws.
17. Attach the speaker electrical connectors.

18. Fasten the rear seat-to-back window trim panel by sliding the panel under the quarter trim.
19. Install the center high-mount stop light by connecting the electrical connector, positioning the assembly and installing the attaching screws.
20. If equipped with 2 doors, install the lower rear quarter interior trim panels by performing the following:
   a. Align the fasteners to the retainers in the body and pushing outboard on the panel.
   b. Install the two attaching screws.
   c. Install the upper windshield molding by starting at the top rear of the body lock pillar and engaging the tabs on the molding clips in the body.
   d. Install the carpet retainer.
21. If equipped with 4 doors, install the lower upper rear quarter interior trim panels by performing the following:
   a. Align the tabs to the retainers and press the trim panel until the tabs are fully engaged to the retainers.
   b. Install the attaching screws.
22. If equipped with 4 doors, install the upper rear quarter interior trim panels by aligning the tabs in the slots, and pushing rearward and rotating outboard.
23. Install the rear seat back by aligning the seat back and engaging the upper retaining hook. An audible snap will be heard to indicate proper engagement.
24. Install the safety belt anchors on the top of the seat retainer brackets. Install the attaching bolts and tighten to 28 ft. lbs. (38 Nm).
25. Install the rear seat by aligning to the proper position. Install the attaching bolts and tighten to 13 ft. lbs. (18 Nm).
26. Connect the negative battery cable.

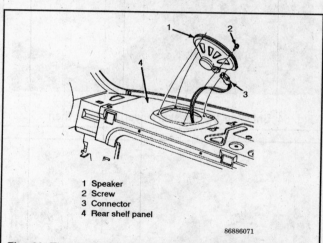

1 Speaker
2 Screw
3 Connector
4 Rear shelf panel

86886071

Fig. 68 The rear speakers are accessible after you remove the rear seat-to-back window trim panel — 1995 vehicle shown

WINDSHIELD WIPERS AND WASHERS

Windshield Wiper Blade and Arm

REMOVAL & INSTALLATION

1985-91 Vehicles
▶ See Figure 69

1. Turn the ignition switch to the **ON** position. Turn the windshield wiper switch to the ON position.
2. When the wiper arms have reached the center of the windshield, turn the ignition switch to the **OFF** position.
3. Place a piece of masking tape on the windshield under each wiper arm and mark the position of the wiper arm.
4. Lift the wiper arm from the windshield and pull the retaining latch.
5. Remove the wiper arm from the transaxle shaft.

To install:
6. Align the wiper arm with the marks made before removal and slide the wiper arm onto the transmission shaft.
7. Push the retaining latch in and allow the wiper arm to return to the windshield. Make sure the marks are still in alignment.
8. Remove the masking tape.

1992-95 Vehicles
▶ See Figures 70, 71, 72, 73 and 74

1. Turn the ignition switch to the **ON** position. Turn the windshield wiper switch to the ON position.
2. When the wiper arms have reached the center of the windshield, turn the ignition switch to the **OFF** position.
3. Detach the washer hose from the plastic connector.
4. Remove the protective cap.
5. Lift the wiper arm and insert a suitable pin or pop rivet completely through the two holes located next to the pivot of the arm.
6. Unfasten the arm retaining nut.
7. Using a battery terminal puller or equivalent tool, pull the arm off its drive shaft. If necessary replace the wiper blade.
8. Clean the knurls of the drive shaft with a suitable wire brush.

To install:
9. Install the wiper arm 1 in. (25mm) below the park ramp. Refer to the accompanying figure.
10. Connect the pivot prevention arm from the wiper arm.
11. Secure the arm with a new nut. Tighten the nut to 22.5 ft. lbs. (30.5 Nm).
12. Run the wiper system and check for correct wipe pattern. The left hand side blade tip should wipe to a limit of 1-1.5 in. (25-38mm) from the outside edge of the glass. The right hand side blade should overlap into the left hand wipe pattern as shown in the accompanying figure.

13. Connect the washer hose, then install the protective cap.

Windshield Wiper Motor

REMOVAL & INSTALLATION

▶ See Figures 75, 76, 77, 78, 79, 80 and 81

1. Remove the wiper arm and blade assemblies as described earlier in this section.
2. Remove the cowl cover, if necessary for access.
3. Disconnect the negative battery cable.
4. Remove the wiper arm drive link from the crank arm.
5. Detach the connectors from the motor.
6. Unfasten the wiper motor attaching bolts/screws.
7. Remove the wiper motor and crank arm by guiding the assembly through the access hole in the upper shroud panel. Remove the seal from the motor assembly

To install:
8. Install the seal to the motor assembly.
9. Guide the wiper motor and crank arm assembly through the access hole and into position.
10. Secure using the the wiper motor attaching bolts/screws.
11. Attach the wiper motor electrical connector.
12. Install the wiper arm drive link to the crank arm.
13. If removed, install the wiper arm and blade assemblies and cowl cover.
14. Connect the negative battery cable. Start the vehicle and check for proper wiper operation.

Wiper Linkage

REMOVAL & INSTALLATION

▶ See Figure 82

1. Remove the wiper arms and the wiper motor as outlined earlier in this section.
2. Disconnect the negative battery cable.
3. Unfasten the bolts attaching the left and right side linkage/transmission assemblies.
4. Remove the wiper linkage/transmission assembly.

To install:
5. Install the wiper linkage.
6. Install the bolts attaching the left and right side linkage/transmission assemblies.
7. Install the wiper motor and wiper arms as outlined earlier in this section.
8. Connect the negative battery cable, then start the engine and check for proper wiper operation.

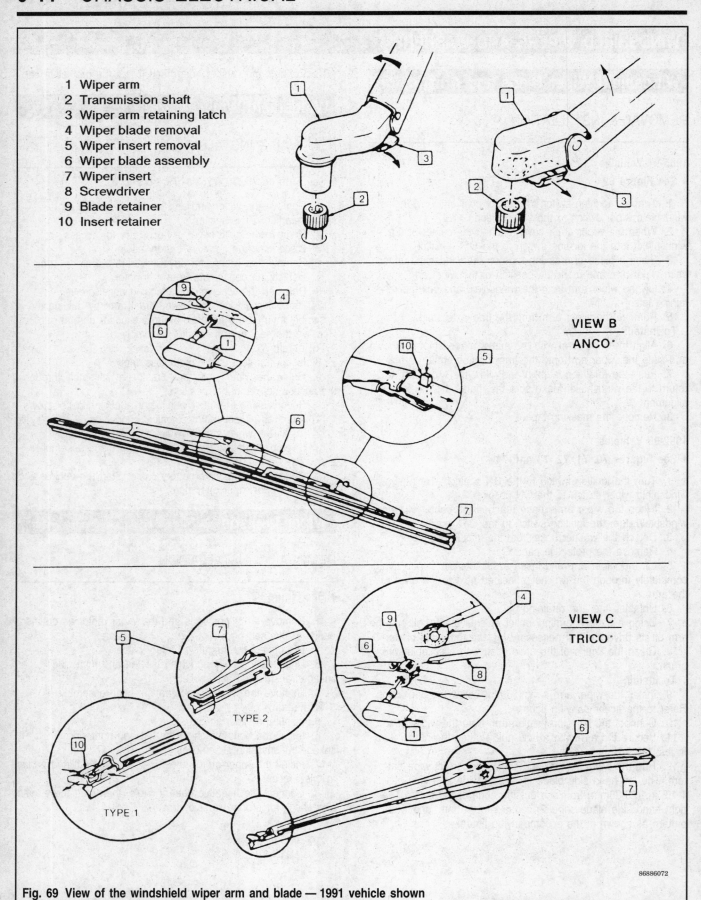

1 Wiper arm
2 Transmission shaft
3 Wiper arm retaining latch
4 Wiper blade removal
5 Wiper insert removal
6 Wiper blade assembly
7 Wiper insert
8 Screwdriver
9 Blade retainer
10 Insert retainer

VIEW B
ANCO*

VIEW C
TRICO*

TYPE 2

TYPE 1

86886072

Fig. 69 View of the windshield wiper arm and blade — 1991 vehicle shown

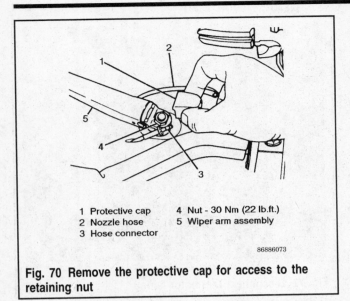

1 Protective cap
2 Nozzle hose
3 Hose connector
4 Nut - 30 Nm (22 lb.ft.)
5 Wiper arm assembly

86886073

Fig. 70 Remove the protective cap for access to the retaining nut

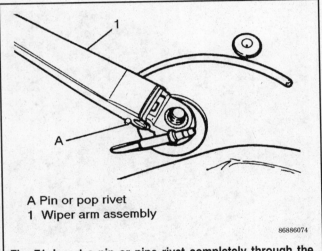

A Pin or pop rivet
1 Wiper arm assembly

86886074

Fig. 71 Insert a pin or pipe rivet completely through the holes next to the pivot of the arm

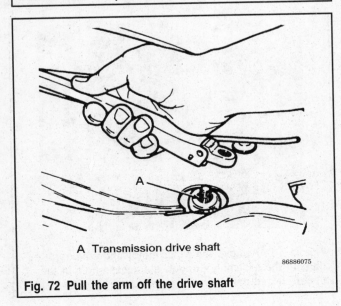

A Transmission drive shaft

86886075

Fig. 72 Pull the arm off the drive shaft

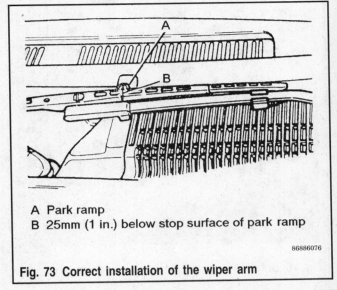

A Park ramp
B 25mm (1 in.) below stop surface of park ramp

86886076

Fig. 73 Correct installation of the wiper arm

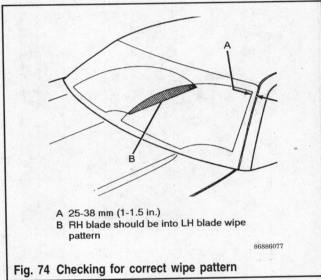

A 25-38 mm (1-1.5 in.)
B RH blade should be into LH blade wipe pattern

86886077

Fig. 74 Checking for correct wipe pattern

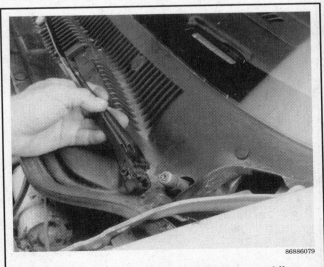

86886079

Fig. 75 Remove the wiper arm and blade assemblies

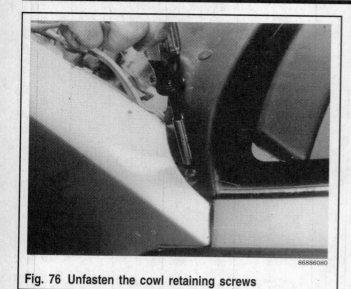

Fig. 76 Unfasten the cowl retaining screws

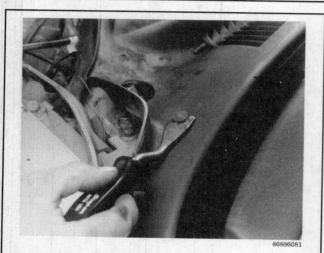

Fig. 77 Using a suitable tool, detach the cowl fasteners, then . . .

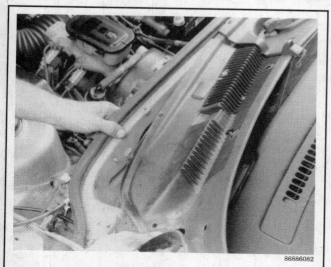

Fig. 78 . . . remove the cowl cover from the vehicle

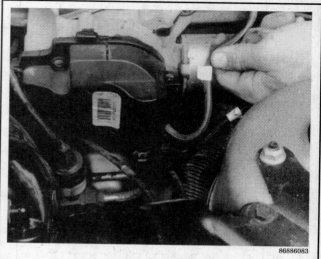

Fig. 79 Disconnect the motor wiring

Fig. 80 Unfasten the motor retaining bolts, then . . .

Fig. 81 . . . Remove the wiper motor and crank arm by guiding the assembly through the access hole in the upper shroud panel

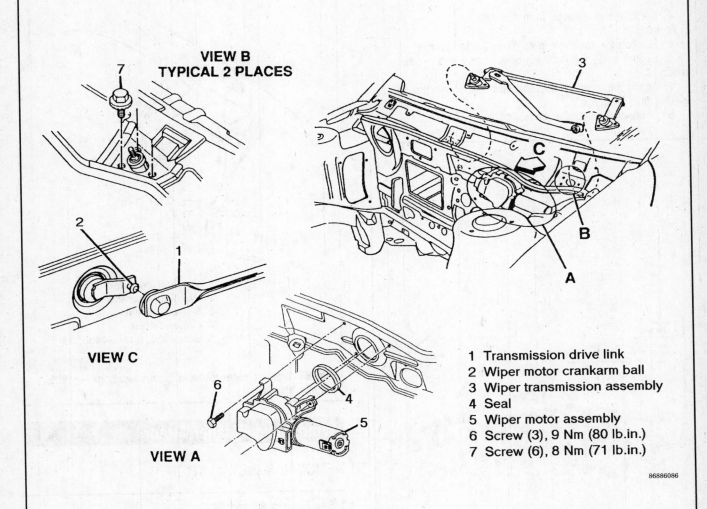

VIEW B
TYPICAL 2 PLACES

7

3

C

B

A

2

1

VIEW C

6

4

5

VIEW A

1 Transmission drive link
2 Wiper motor crankarm ball
3 Wiper transmission assembly
4 Seal
5 Wiper motor assembly
6 Screw (3), 9 Nm (80 lb.in.)
7 Screw (6), 8 Nm (71 lb.in.)

86886086

Fig. 82 View of the wiper motor and transmission (linkage) assembly — 1995 vehicle shown

Windshield Washer Fluid Reservoir

REMOVAL & INSTALLATION

▶ **See Figures 83 and 84**

1. Disconnect the negative battery cable.
2. Detach the electrical connectors and washer hose from the reservoir.
3. Unfasten the reservoir attaching bolts/screws and retainers.
4. Remove the reservoir from the vehicle.

To install:

5. Position the reservoir in its mounting location.
6. Secure using the retaining bolts/screws and/or other retainers.
7. Attach the washer hose and electrical connectors to the washer fluid reservoir.
8. Connect the negative battery cable.

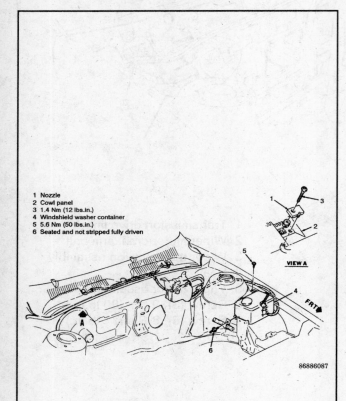

1 Nozzle
2 Cowl panel
3 1.4 Nm (12 lbs.in.)
4 Windshield washer container
5 5.6 Nm (50 lbs.in.)
6 Seated and not stripped fully driven

Fig. 83 View of the washer reservoir and related components — 1989 vehicle shown

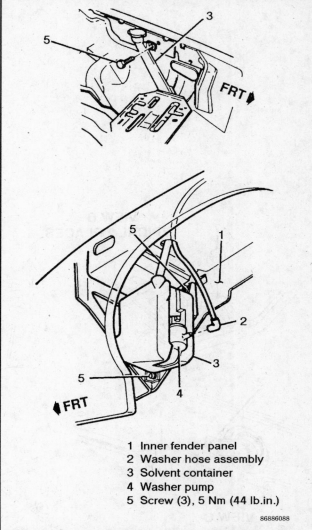

1 Inner fender panel
2 Washer hose assembly
3 Solvent container
4 Washer pump
5 Screw (3), 5 Nm (44 lb.in.)

86886088

Fig. 84 Washer reservoir and pump locations — 1995 vehicle shown

Windshield Washer Motor

REMOVAL & INSTALLATION

▶ **See Figures 83 and 84**

1. Disconnect the negative battery cable.
2. Siphon the washer solvent from the reservoir.
3. If equipped, remove the brace or other retainers.
4. Unfasten the reservoir bolts.
5. Detach the electrical connectors and washer hose from the reservoir.
6. Remove the washer pump (motor) from the reservoir.

To install:

7. Install the washer pump to the reservoir.

➡**Make sure the new washer pump is pushed all the way into the reservoir gasket.**

8. Attach the electrical connectors and washer hose.

9. Secure using the reservoir attaching screws.
10. If equipped, install the brace.

11. Refill the reservoir with washer solvent.
12. Connect the negative battery cable.

INSTRUMENTS AND SWITCHES

Instrument Cluster

REMOVAL & INSTALLATION

➡ For Instrument panel and console removal and installation procedures, please refer to Section 10.

Skylark

1985-89 VEHICLES

▶ See Figures 85 and 86

1. Disconnect the negative battery cable.
2. Remove the cluster trim plate, headlight and wiper switch trim plates and the switches.
3. Remove the screws fastening the cluster to the instrument panel pad, pull the cluster out to unplug all connectors and, then remove the cluster.
4. Remove the lens and gauge trim plate to gain access to the speedometer assembly attaching screws and remove the speedometer or gauges. If equipped with digital gauges, replace them as an assembly.
5. The installation is the reverse of the removal procedure.
6. Connect the negative battery cable and check all cluster-related components for proper operation.

1990-92 VEHICLES

▶ See Figures 87 and 88

1. Disconnect the negative battery cable.
2. Remove the steering column opening filler.
3. Remove the cluster trim plate.
4. If equipped with a column-mounted shifter, disconnect the PRNDL cable clip from the shift collar on the steering column.

5. Unfasten the screws retaining the cluster to the instrument panel pad, pull the cluster out to unplug all connectors, then remove the cluster.
6. Remove the lens and gauge trim plate to gain access to the speedometer assembly attaching screws and remove the speedometer or gauges. If equipped with digital dash, replace it as an assembly.
7. The installation is the reverse of the removal procedure.
8. Connect the negative battery cable and check all cluster-related components for proper operation.

1993-95 VEHICLES

▶ See Figures 89 and 90

1. If applicable, properly disable the SIR system. For details, please refer to the procedure located in this section.
2. Disconnect the negative battery cable.
3. Remove the cluster trim plate by unfastening the two retaining screws and pulling the plate rearward the disengage the clips.
4. Unfasten the four cluster retaining screws, then rock the top of the cluster rearward to remove it from the vehicle.
   To install:
5. Position the cluster to the instrument panel, then secure using the four retaining screws. Tighten the screws to 17 inch lbs. (2 Nm).
6. Install the trim plate by aligning the clips to the holes and pressing in, then securing with the retaining screws. Tighten the screws to 17 inch lbs. (2 Nm).

Calais

1985-91 VEHICLES

▶ See Figure 91

1. Disconnect the negative battery cable.
2. Remove the steering column collar.

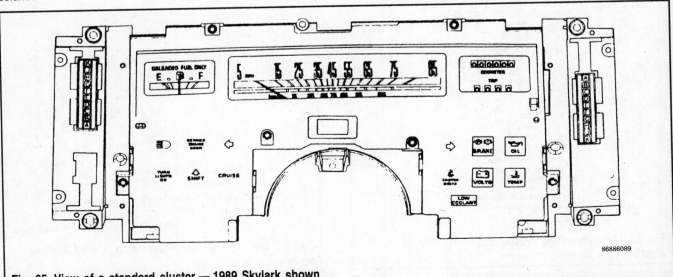

Fig. 85 View of a standard cluster — 1989 Skylark shown

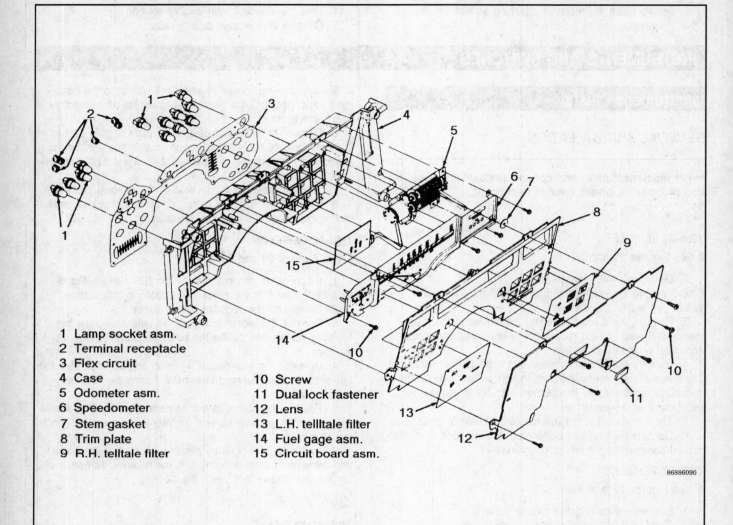

1 Lamp socket asm.
2 Terminal receptacle
3 Flex circuit
4 Case
5 Odometer asm.
6 Speedometer
7 Stem gasket
8 Trim plate
9 R.H. telltale filter

10 Screw
11 Dual lock fastener
12 Lens
13 L.H. telltale filter
14 Fuel gage asm.
15 Circuit board asm.

86886090

Fig. 86 Exploded view of a disassembled cluster — 1989 Skylark shown

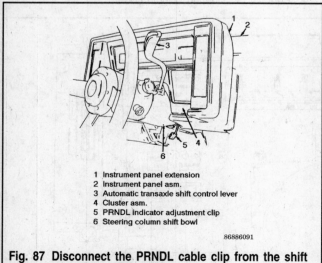

1 Instrument panel extension
2 Instrument panel asm.
3 Automatic transaxle shift control lever
4 Cluster asm.
5 PRNDL indicator adjustment clip
6 Steering column shift bowl

86886091

Fig. 87 Disconnect the PRNDL cable clip from the shift collar on the steering column

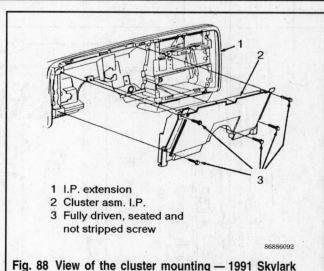

1 I.P. extension
2 Cluster asm. I.P.
3 Fully driven, seated and not stripped screw

86886092

Fig. 88 View of the cluster mounting — 1991 Skylark shown

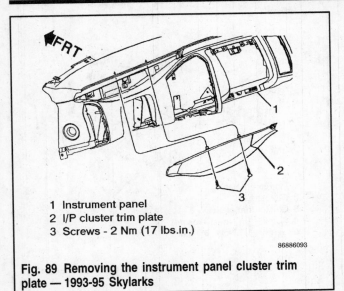

1 Instrument panel
2 I/P cluster trim plate
3 Screws - 2 Nm (17 lbs.in.)

86886093

Fig. 89 Removing the instrument panel cluster trim plate — 1993-95 Skylarks

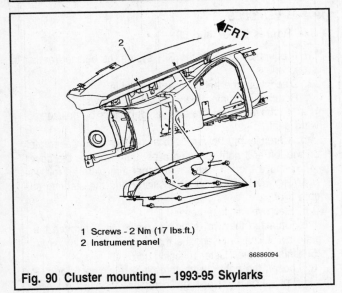

1 Screws - 2 Nm (17 lbs.ft.)
2 Instrument panel

86886094

Fig. 90 Cluster mounting — 1993-95 Skylarks

3. Remove the steering column opening filler and cluster trim plates.

4. Lower the steering column.

5. Remove the screws fastening the cluster to the instrument panel pad, pull the cluster out to unplug all connectors and remove the cluster.

6. Remove the lens and applique, if necessary, to gain access to the speedometer or gauges attaching screws and remove the speedometer or gauges.

7. The installation is the reverse of the removal procedure.

8. Connect the negative battery cable and check all cluster-related components for proper operation.

Achieva

1992-95 VEHICLES

◆ See Figures 92 and 93

1. If applicable, properly disable the SIR system as outlined earlier in this section.

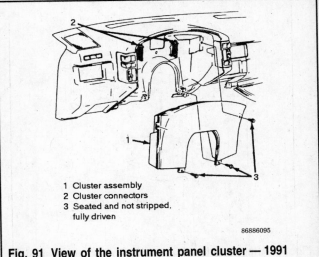

1 Cluster assembly
2 Cluster connectors
3 Seated and not stripped, fully driven

86886095

Fig. 91 View of the instrument panel cluster — 1991 Calais shown

2. Disconnect the negative battery cable.

3. Remove the instrument cluster trim plate as follows:

   a. Remove the steering wheel and column cover.

   b. Unfasten the retaining screws, then pull the trim plate back enough to detach the electrical connectors.

   c. Remove the trim plate.

4. Unfasten the four cluster retaining screws, then remove the cluster from the vehicle.

To install:

5. Position the cluster to the instrument panel, then install the retaining screws. Tighten the screws to 17 inch lbs. (2 Nm).

6. Install the instrument panel cluster trim plate as follows:

   a. Attach the cluster electrical connectors, then position the panel, and secure with the retaining screws. Tighten the screws to 17 inch lbs. (2 Nm).

   b. Install the steering wheel and column cover.

7. Enable the SIR system as outlined earlier in this section, if applicable.

8. If not done already, connect the negative battery cable.

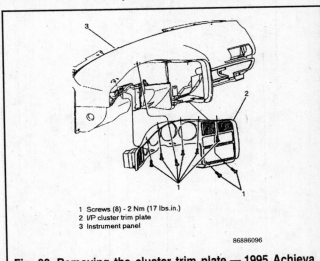

1 Screws (8) - 2 Nm (17 lbs.in.)
2 I/P cluster trim plate
3 Instrument panel

86886096

Fig. 92 Removing the cluster trim plate — 1995 Achieva shown

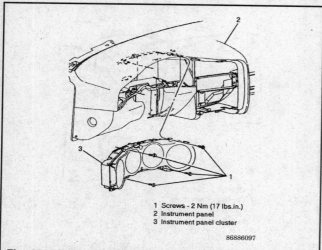

Fig. 93 After unfastening the retaining screws, remove the cluster assembly — Achieva shown

1 Screws - 2 Nm (17 lbs.in.)
2 Instrument panel
3 Instrument panel cluster

86886097

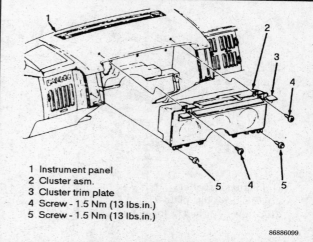

Fig. 95 Removing the cluster assembly — 1991 Grand Am

1 Instrument panel
2 Cluster asm.
3 Cluster trim plate
4 Screw - 1.5 Nm (13 lbs.in.)
5 Screw - 1.5 Nm (13 lbs.in.)

86886099

Grand Am

1985-91 VEHICLES

▶ See Figures 94 and 95

1. Disconnect the negative battery cable.
2. Unfasten the three screws at the lower edge of the cluster, then remove the trim plate.
3. Remove the steering column cover and lower the column, as required.
4. Remove the screws fastening the cluster to the instrument panel pad, pull the cluster out to unplug all connectors and remove the cluster.
5. Remove the lens and gauge trim plate to gain access to the speedometer assembly or gauges attaching screws and remove the speedometer or gauges. If equipped with digital dash, replace it as an assembly.
6. The installation is the reverse of the removal procedure.
7. Connect the negative battery cable and check all cluster-related components for proper operation.

1992-95 VEHICLES

▶ See Figures 96, 97 and 98

1. If equipped, disable the SIR system as outlined earlier in this section.
2. Disconnect the negative battery cable.
3. Remove instrument panel cover as follows:
    a. Remove the drivers side air deflectors by pulling rearward gently.
    b. Carefully pry upward with a rocking motion alternately on the left and right retaining clips, then remove the cover.
4. Remove the left instrument panel trim plate as follows:
    a. Remove the left sound insulator and the steering column filler.
    b. Remove the fuse cover.
    c. Unfasten the two retaining screws, then remove the plate by pulling to disengage the clips.
5. Unfasten the cluster retaining screws.
6. Loosen the right cluster trim plate retaining screws. Pull the trim panel back far enough to remove the cluster.

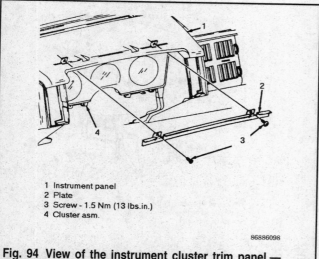

1 Instrument panel
2 Plate
3 Screw - 1.5 Nm (13 lbs.in.)
4 Cluster asm.

86886098

Fig. 94 View of the instrument cluster trim panel — 1991 Grand Am shown

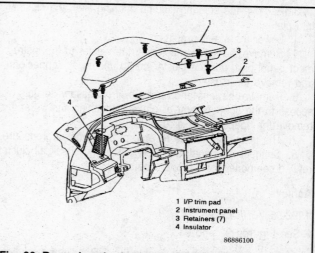

1 I/P trim pad
2 Instrument panel
3 Retainers (7)
4 Insulator

86886100

Fig. 96 Removing the instrument panel cover — 1994 Grand Am shown

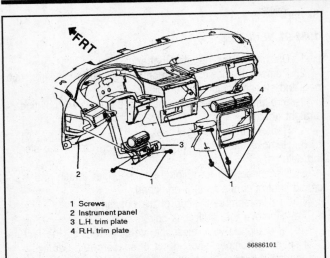

Fig. 97 Location of the left and right instrument panel trim plates

1 Screws
2 Instrument panel
3 L.H. trim plate
4 R.H. trim plate

86886101

7. If applicable, detach the electrical connector(s), then remove the cluster completely from the vehicle.
8. The installation is the reverse of the removal procedure.
9. Connect the negative battery cable and check all cluster-related components for proper operation.

Speedometer

REMOVAL & INSTALLATION

➡**If equipped with electronic instrumentation, the speedometer cannot be replaced separately; the entire instrument cluster must be replaced.**

Standard Cluster

1. Disconnect the negative battery cable.
2. Remove the instrument cluster as outlined earlier in this section.
3. Unfasten the screws from the cluster lens.

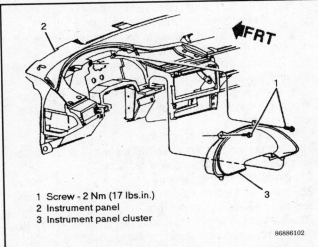

1 Screw - 2 Nm (17 lbs.in.)
2 Instrument panel
3 Instrument panel cluster

86886102

Fig. 98 Removing the instrument cluster — 1994 Grand Am

4. Remove the cluster lens. Be careful not to scratch the lens.
5. Carefully, lift the speedometer facing.
6. Unplug the odometer motor leads.
To install:
7. Plug the odometer motor leads.
8. Install the speedometer facing.
9. Carefully, install the cluster lens.
10. Secure using the the cluster lens attaching screws.
11. Install the instrument cluster as outlined earlier in this section.
12. Connect the negative battery cable.

Speedometer Cable

REMOVAL & INSTALLATION

➡**Only vehicles equipped with standard gauge clusters have mechanically driven speedometers. Electronic gauges use a vehicle speed sensor to drive the speedometer.**

1. Disconnect the negative battery cable.
2. Remove the instrument cluster far enough to reach behind and disconnect the speedometer cable from the back of the cluster.
3. Remove the left side sound insulator panel.
4. Push the speedometer cable grommet through the fire wall.
5. Observe the routing of the speedometer cable from the firewall up to the instrument cluster. If possible, tape a length of wire or string to the cable to aid installation of the new cable. Feed the cable down and through the hole in firewall.
6. Disconnect the speedometer cable from the transaxle by removing the bolt attaching the cable to the drive assembly on the transaxle.
7. Remove the speedometer cable.
To install:
8. Attach the length of wire or string to the new speedometer cable and pull through the firewall and up behind the instrument panel.
9. Connect the speedometer cable to the speedometer drive assembly on the transaxle. Install the attaching bolt.
10. Connect the speedometer cable to the speedometer.
11. Install the instrument cluster.
12. Make sure the speedometer cable is routed freely and has no kinks or sharp bends.
13. Install the grommet in the firewall.
14. Install the left side sound insulator panel.
15. Connect the negative battery cable.

Printed Circuit Board

REMOVAL & INSTALLATION

1. Disconnect the negative battery cable.
2. Remove the instrument cluster.
3. Unfasten the screws from the cluster lens.
4. Carefully, lift up on the lens and trim plate.

5. Remove the foam gasket from the trip odometer reset.

6. Remove the screws from the fuel gauge, speedometer and odometer.

7. Disconnect the fuel gauge.

8. Remove the speedometer and odometer.

9. Detach the odometer connector from the circuit board.

10. Remove the circuit board from inside the case.

To install:

11. Install the circuit board inside the case.

12. Attach the odometer connector to the circuit board.

13. Install the speedometer and odometer.

14. Connect the fuel gauge electrical connector.

15. Install the screws to the fuel gauge, speedometer and odometer.

16. Secure the foam gasket on the trip odometer reset.

17. Install the trim plate and lens.

18. Secure the screws through the lens and trim plate into the case.

19. Install the instrument cluster as outlined earlier in this section.

20. Connect the negative battery cable.

Windshield Wiper Switch

REMOVAL & INSTALLATION

Grand Am

1985-91 VEHICLES

▶ **See Figure 99**

1. Disconnect the negative battery cable.

2. Remove the cluster trim, instrument panel trim or wiper switch trim screws, as required.

3. Unfasten the wiper switch attaching screws.

4. Pull the switch out, unplug the connectors, then remove the switch assembly.

5. The installation is the reverse of the removal procedure.

6. Connect the negative battery cable and check the wipers and washers for proper operation.

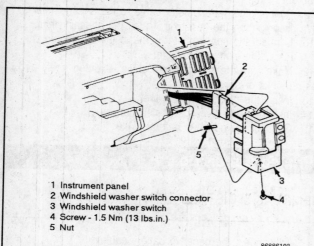

1 Instrument panel
2 Windshield washer switch connector
3 Windshield washer switch
4 Screw - 1.5 Nm (13 lbs.in.)
5 Nut

86886103

Fig. 99 Windshield wiper washer switch location — 1985-91 Grand Am

Skylark

1988-91 VEHICLES

1. Disconnect the negative battery cable.

2. Remove the lower instrument panel sound insulator, trim pad and steering column trim collar.

3. Straighten the steering wheel so the tires are pointing straight ahead.

4. Remove the steering wheel.

5. Remove the plastic wire protector from under the steering column.

6. Disconnect the turn signal switch, wiper switch and cruise control connectors, if equipped.

7. To disassemble the top of the column:

   a. Remove the shaft lock cover.

   b. If equipped with telescope steering, remove the first set of spacers, bumper, second set of spacers and carrier snapring retainer.

   c. Depress the lockplate with the proper depressing tool and remove the retaining ring from its groove.

   d. Remove the tool, retaining ring, lockplate, canceling cam and spring.

8. Pull the turn signal lever straight out of the wiper switch.

9. Remove the 3 screws and remove the turn signal switch and actuator lever.

10. Remove the ignition key light.

11. Place the key in the **RUN** position and use a thin suitable tool to remove the buzzer switch.

12. Remove the key lock cylinder attaching screw and remove the lock cylinder.

13. Remove the 3 housing cover screws and remove the housing cover assembly.

14. Remove the wiper switch pivot pin and remove the switch.

To install:

15. Run the wiring through the opening and down the steering column, position the switch and install the wiper switch pivot pin.

16. Install the housing cover assembly, making sure the dimmer switch actuator is properly aligned.

17. Install the key lock cylinder and place in the RUN position. Install the buzzer switch and key light.

18. Install the turn signal switch and lever.

19. To assemble the top end of the column:

   a. Install the spring, canceling cam, lockplate and retaining ring on the steering shaft.

   b. Depress the plate with the depressing tool and install the ring securely in the groove. Remove the tool slowly.

   c. If equipped with telescopic steering, install the carrier snapring retainer, lower set of spacers, bumper and upper set of spacers.

   d. Install the shaft lock cover.

20. Connect the turn signal switch, wiper switch and cruise control connectors. Install the wire protector.

21. Install and steering wheel.

22. Install the steering column trim collar, lower instrument panel trim pad and sound insulator.

23. Connect the negative battery cable and check the key lock cylinder, wiper and washer, cruise control, turn signal switch and dimmer switch for proper operation.

Calais

1985-91 VEHICLES

▶ **See Figure 100**

1. Disconnect the negative battery cable.
2. Remove the steering column cover.
3. Unfasten the four retaining screws from the steering column opening filler and the four screws from the cluster trim plate.
4. Remove the screw mounting the wiper and rear window defogger switch.
5. Pull the switch rearward to detach both connectors, then remove the switch.
6. The installation is the reverse of the removal procedure.
7. Connect the negative battery cable, then check the wipers for proper operation.

Grand Am, Skylark and Achieva

1992-95 VEHICLES

▶ **See Figure 101**

1. If equipped, disable the SIR system as outlined earlier in this section.
2. Disconnect the negative battery cable.
3. Remove the horn pad and the steering wheel. For details, please refer to Section 8 of this manual.
4. If applicable, remove the tilt lever from the column. If necessary, use locking pliers with a piece of rubber (such as a spark plug boot) between the jaws to help prevent damage to the tilt lever during removal.

5. Remove the upper and lower steering column covers, then remove the dampener assembly.
6. Detach and remove the headlight switch assembly, then remove the windshield wiper switch assembly.
7. The installation is the reverse of the removal procedure.
8. Connect the negative battery cable, the check the wipers for proper operation.

Headlight Switch

REMOVAL & INSTALLATION

➡**For 1992-95 vehicles, please refer to the cruise control actuator switch (multi-function lever) procedure earlier in this section for removal and installation of the integral headlight switch.**

1985-91 Vehicles

▶ **See Figures 102 and 103**

1. Disconnect the negative battery cable.
2. Remove the cluster trim, instrument panel trim or headlight switch trim screws, as required.
3. Unfasten the headlight switch attaching screws.
4. Pull the switch out, unplug the connectors, then remove the switch assembly.
5. The installation is the reverse of the removal procedure.
6. Connect the negative battery cable and check the headlight switch for proper operation.

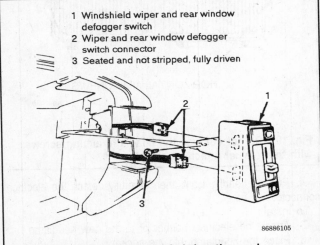

1 Windshield wiper and rear window defogger switch
2 Wiper and rear window defogger switch connector
3 Seated and not stripped, fully driven

86886105

Fig. 100 Windshield wiper switch location and mounting — 1991 Calais shown

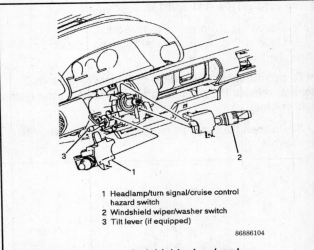

1 Headlamp/turn signal/cruise control hazard switch
2 Windshield wiper/washer switch
3 Tilt lever (if equipped)

86886104

Fig. 101 View of the windshield wiper/washer mounting — 1995 Grand Am shown

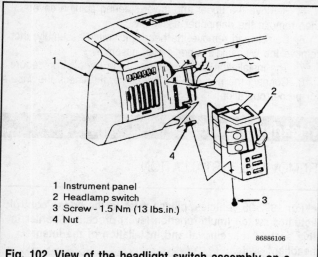

Fig. 102 View of the headlight switch assembly on a 1991 Grand Am

1 Instrument panel
2 Headlamp switch
3 Screw - 1.5 Nm (13 lbs.in.)
4 Nut

86886106

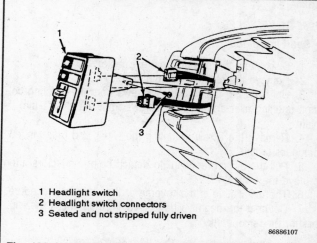

Fig. 103 Headlight switch mounting and location — 1991 Calais shown

1 Headlight switch
2 Headlight switch connectors
3 Seated and not stripped fully driven

86886107

LIGHTING

Headlights

REMOVAL & INSTALLATION

Sealed Beam

▶ **See Figures 104, 105 and 106**

1. Disconnect the negative battery cable.
2. Unfasten the headlight bezel attaching screws, then remove the bezel.

➡**To avoid turning the vertical or horizontal aiming screws, refer to the illustration before removing the headlight retainer.**

3. Unfasten the headlight retainer attaching screws, then remove the retainer.

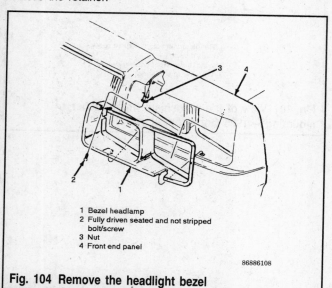

Fig. 104 Remove the headlight bezel

1 Bezel headlamp
2 Fully driven seated and not stripped bolt/screw
3 Nut
4 Front end panel

86886108

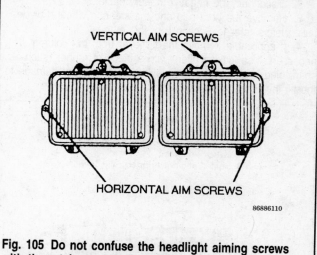

VERTICAL AIM SCREWS

HORIZONTAL AIM SCREWS

86886110

Fig. 105 Do not confuse the headlight aiming screws with the retainer attaching screws

4. Pull the headlight out, then carefully detach the electrical connector.

To install:

5. Attach the electrical connector to the new headlamp.
6. Place the headlamp into the socket.
7. Install the retainer, then tighten the attaching screws.
8. Connect the negative battery cable, then turn the headlight switch on, to be sure the headlights are operating.
9. Install the headlight bezel and secure using the attaching screws.

Composite

▶ **See Figures 107, 108, 109, 110, 111 and 112**

Most of the vehicles covered by this manual are equipped with composite headlight assemblies. Due to space constraints, no access may be provided to withdraw the bulbs, so the

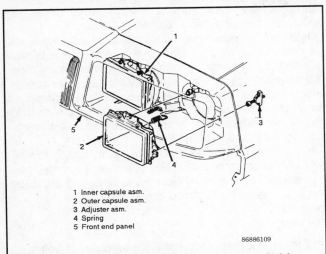

1 Inner capsule asm.
2 Outer capsule asm.
3 Adjuster asm.
4 Spring
5 Front end panel

86886109

Fig. 106 View of the headlight mounting — sealed beam shown

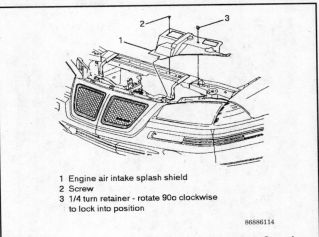

1 Engine air intake splash shield
2 Screw
3 1/4 turn retainer - rotate 90o clockwise
  to lock into position

86886114

Fig. 107 For some vehicles, such as this 1995 Grand Am, you must remove the splash shield to access the bulb

replacement usually requires removal of the composite assembly.

➡The composite headlight assemblies use Halogen bulbs which contain a gas under pressure. Improper handling of the bulb could cause it to shatter into flying glass fragments. To help avoid personal injury, follow the precautions closely.

Whenever handling a Halogen bulb, ALWAYS follow these precautions:
• Turn the headlight switch OFF and allow the bulb to cool before changing it. Leave the switch OFF until the change is complete.
• ALWAYS wear eye protection when changing a halogen bulb.
• Handle the bulb only by its base. Avoid touching the glass.
• DO NOT drop or scratch the bulb.
• Keep dirt and moisture off the bulb.
• Place the used bulb in the new bulb's carton and dispose of it properly.

1. Raise the hood and locate the bulb mounting location at the rear of the composite headlamp body.
2. Disconnect the negative battery cable.
3. If necessary for access, remove the splash shield or side marker lamp(s).
4. If there is enough room to access the plastic base, press in and turn the base 1/4 turn counterclockwise and remove from the metal retaining ring by gently pulling back and away from the headlight. Remove the electrical connector from the bulb by raising the lock tab and pulling the connector down and away from the bulb's plastic base.
5. If you can't access the bulb from the engine compartment, unfasten the thumb screws, and/or other retainers, then pull the composite headlight assembly forward slightly and disengage the wiring connector. Press in and turn the base 1/4 turn counterclockwise and remove the bulb from the metal retaining ring by gently pulling back and away from the headlight.

86886111

Fig. 108 Unfasten the thumb screws, then . . .

86886112

Fig. 109 . . . pull the headlight assembly away from the vehicle for access to the bulb and connector

Fig. 110 Remove the retaining ring from the base of the bulb, then . . .

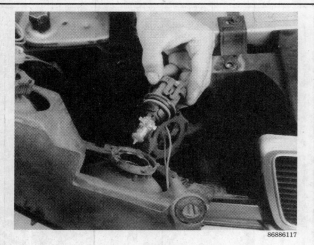

Fig. 111 . . . turn the bulb and remove it from the headlight assembly

To install:

6. Attach the electrical connector on the new bulb's plastic base making sure that the lock tab is in place.

7. Install the bulb by inserting the smallest tab located on top of the plastic base into the corresponding notch in the metal retaining ring. Turn clockwise ¼ turn until it stops. The small plastic tab should be at the top of the metal ring.

8. Install the composite headlight assembly, then secure with the retainers.

9. Connect the negative battery cable, then check for proper headlight operation.

AIMING

▶ See Figure 113

The headlights must be properly aimed to provide the best, safest road illumination. The lights should be checked for proper aim and adjusted as necessary. Certain state and local authorities have requirements for headlight aiming; these should be checked before adjustment is made.

Headlight adjustment may be temporarily made using a wall, as described below, or on the rear of another vehicle. When adjusted, the lights should not glare in oncoming car or truck windshields, nor should they illuminate the passenger compartment of vehicles driving in front of you. These adjustments are rough and should always be fine-tuned by a repair shop which is equipped with headlight aiming tools. Improper adjustments may be both dangerous and illegal.

For most of the vehicles covered by this manual, horizontal and vertical aiming of each sealed beam unit is provided by two adjusting screws which move the retaining ring and adjusting plate against the tension of a coil spring. There is no adjustment for focus; this is done during headlight manufacturing.

➡Because the composite headlight assembly is bolted into position, no adjustment should be necessary or possible. Some applications, however, may be bolted to an adjuster plate or may be retained used adjusting screws. If so, follow this procedure when adjusting the lights, BUT always have the adjustment checked by a reputable shop.

Before removing the headlight bulb or disturbing the headlamp in any way, note the current settings in order to ease headlight adjustment upon reassembly. If the high or low beam setting of the old lamp still works, this can be done using the wall of a garage or a building:

1. Park the car on a level surface, with the fuel tank about ½ full and with the vehicle empty of all extra cargo (unless normally carried). The vehicle should be facing a wall which is no less than 6 feet high and 12 feet wide. The front of the vehicle should be about 25 feet from the wall.

➡The car's fuel tank should be about half full when adjusting the headlights. Tires should be properly inflated, and if a heavy load is normally carried in the vehicle, it should remain there.

2. If aiming is to be performed outdoors, it is advisable to wait until dusk in order to properly see the headlight beams on the wall. If done in a garage, darken the area around the wall as much as possible by closing shades or hanging cloth over the windows.

3. Turn the headlights **ON** and mark the wall at the center of each light's low beam, then switch on the brights and mark the center of each light's high beam. A short length of masking tape which is visible from the front of the truck may be used. Although marking all four positions is advisable, marking one position from each light should be sufficient.

4. If neither beam on one side of the vehicle is working, and if another like-sized car is available, park the second car in the exact spot where the vehicle was and mark the beams using the same-side light on that truck. Then switch the cars so the one to be aimed is back in the original spot. The car must be parked no closer to or farther away from the wall than the second vehicle.

5. Perform any necessary repairs, but make sure the car is not moved, or is returned to the exact spot from which the lights were marked. Turn the headlights **ON** and adjust the beams to match the marks on the wall.

6. Have the headlight adjustment checked as soon as possible by a reputable repair shop.

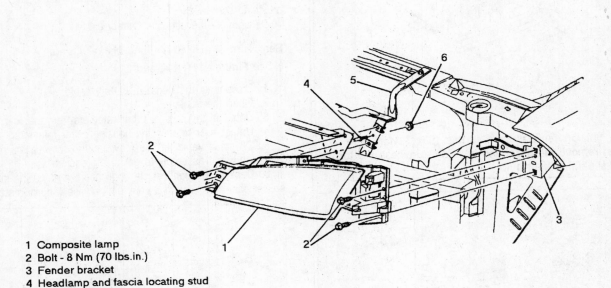

1 Composite lamp
2 Bolt - 8 Nm (70 lbs.in.)
3 Fender bracket
4 Headlamp and fascia locating stud
5 Center support

86886115

Fig. 112 Exploded view of the composite headlight mounting — 1995 vehicle shown

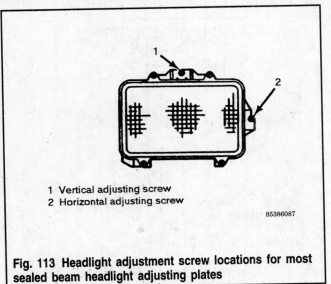

1 Vertical adjusting screw
2 Horizontal adjusting screw

85386087

Fig. 113 Headlight adjustment screw locations for most sealed beam headlight adjusting plates

Signal and Marker Lights

REMOVAL & INSTALLATION

Front Turn Signal and Parking Lights
▶ See Figures 114 and 115

1. Disconnect the negative battery cable.

2. On early model vehicles, unfasten the retaining screws, then remove the bezel and light housing from the front fascia of the vehicle. Remove the bulb.

3. On later model vehicles, remove the lamp assembly, unfasten the socket from the lamp housing by turning it counterclockwise, then remove the lamp from the socket by pressing in and turning counterclockwise.

To install:

4. Install the replacement lamp into the socket, matching the directional alignment pins on the base of the bulb with the complementary slots in the socket. This will assure that the

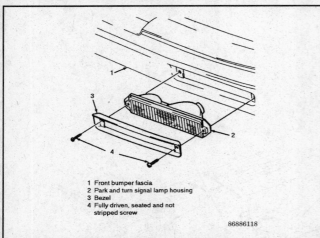

1 Front bumper fascia
2 Park and turn signal lamp housing
3 Bezel
4 Fully driven, seated and not
   stripped screw

86886118

Fig. 114 On vehicles such as this 1991 Skylark, you must remove the bezel and housing to access the turn signal/parking light bulb

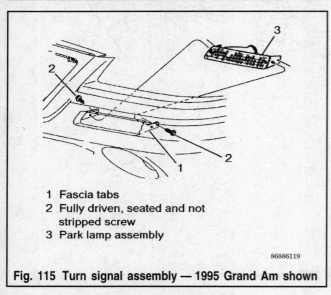

1 Fascia tabs
2 Fully driven, seated and not
   stripped screw
3 Park lamp assembly

86886119

Fig. 115 Turn signal assembly — 1995 Grand Am shown

proper filament is energized at the right time; i.e.: the turn signal filament and not the parking lamp filament is energized when the turn signal is turned on.

5. If you can get to the bulb from the engine compartment, push the lamp into the socket and turn clockwise. Install the socket to the lamp housing by turning clockwise.

6. If the bulb can't be accessed from the engine compartment, after the bulb is installed, fasten the housing and bezel to the front fascia of the vehicle.

7. Connect the negative battery cable.

8. Check operation of the parking lamp and turn signal.

Front Side Marker Lights

▶ **See Figure 116**

1. Disconnect the negative battery cable.
2. Unfasten the side marker housing attaching screws.
3. Lower the housing far enough to remove the socket from the housing by turning 45° counterclockwise.
4. Remove the bulb and socket assembly from the housing, then detach the bulb from the socket.

To install:

5. Position the bulb into the socket making sure it is secure.

6. Install the socket to the lamp housing.

7. Secure the socket to the lamp housing by turning 45° clockwise.

8. Install the side marker housing, then fasten using the attaching screws.

9. Connect the negative battery cable.

Rear Turn Signal, Brake, and Marker Lights

▶ **See Figures 117, 118 and 119**

1. Disconnect the negative battery cable.
2. Open the trunk.
3. Unfasten the nuts or other retainers from the rear trim.
4. Unfasten or release the housing cover retainers.
5. On some vehicles, you may have to remove the rear fascia and light assembly to get to the sockets.
6. Depending upon vehicle application, remove the lamp socket either by rotating it counterclockwise (approximately ¼

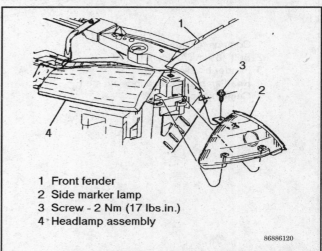

1 Front fender
2 Side marker lamp
3 Screw - 2 Nm (17 lbs.in.)
4 Headlamp assembly

86886120

Fig. 116 Side marker lamp mounting — 1995 vehicle shown

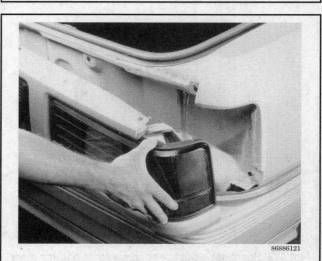

86886121

Fig. 117 On some vehicles, such as this 1986 Grand Am, you must remove the rear fascia

turn) until the plastic tabs disengage, or by squeezing the metal tangs while pulling the socket from the light assembly.

➥**Generally, side marker lamps use small bulbs with flat, blade-type bases, and tail lights/turn signals use larger, round-based ("bayonet") bulbs.**

7. Remove the bulb from the socket using the appropriate method. Bulbs with blade-type bases pull straight out, while those with round bases and protuding pins (bayonet-type bulbs) must be depressed, then rotated counterclockwise (approximately ⅛ turn) before pulling out.

To install:

8. Secure the bulb in the socket using the appropriate method. Bulbs with blade-type bases push straight in, while those with round bases and protuding pins (bayonet-type bulbs) must be inserted, then depressed and rotated clockwise (approximately ⅛ turn).

9. Install the lamp socket using the appropriate method. Depending on the type of socket, either engage the plastic

tabs, and rotate the socket clockwise (approximately ¼ turn), or push on the socket until the metal tangs engage.

10. Install the housing cover nuts.
11. If removed, install the rear fascia and light assembly.
12. Install the rear trim.
13. Connect the negative battery cable, then check the operation of the rear lights.

High-Mount Brake Light

1985-91 VEHICLES WITHOUT LUGGAGE RACK

▶ **See Figure 120**

1. Disconnect the negative battery cable.
2. Unfasten the two lamp housing mounting screws, then remove the housing.
3. Detach the electrical connector.
4. Unfasten the two cover screws remove the cover, then disconnect the bulb from the socket.

To install:

5. Position the bulb in the socket.

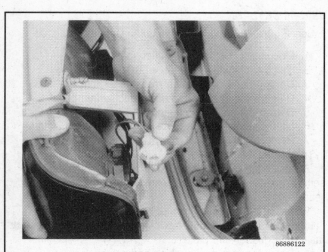

Fig. 118 Remove the lamp socket assembly by turning it counterclockwise, then pulling it out

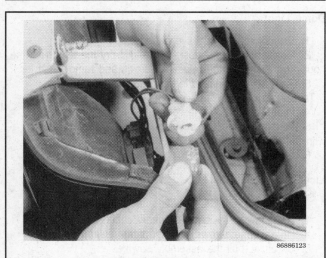

Fig. 119 Remove the side marker bulb from its socket by pulling straight out

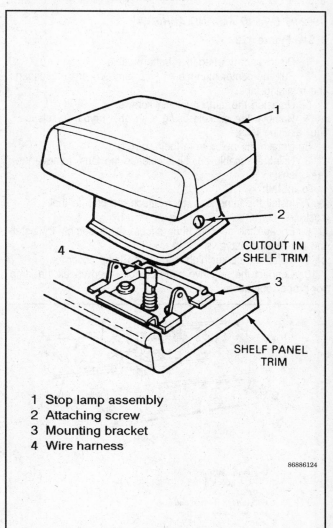

1 Stop lamp assembly
2 Attaching screw
3 Mounting bracket
4 Wire harness

Fig. 120 View of the center high-mount stop lamp — 1985-91 vehicles without luggage racks

6. Install the cover and secure with the two retaining screws.

7. Attach the electrical connector.

8. Position the housing, then secure with the retaining screws.

9. Connect the negative battery cable, then check operation of the light.

1985-91 VEHICLES WITH LUGGAGE RACK

▶ See Figure 121

1. Disconnect the negative battery cable.

2. Unfasten the two lens retaining screws, then remove the lens.

3. Remove the bulb from the socket.

To install:

4. Install the bulb into the socket.

5. Install the lens, then secure with the two retaining screws.

6. Connect the negative battery cable, then check the operation of the light.

1992-95 GRAND AM AND ACHIEVA

▶ See Figure 122

1. Disconnect the negative battery cable.

2. Pull the center high-mount stop lamp cover to disengage the retaining tabs.

3. Unfasten the lamp retaining screws.

4. Remove the sockets using a suitable prybar to release the retaining tabs.

5. Detach the bulbs from their sockets.

6. Using a suitable prybar to release the tabs, remove the lamp lens.

To install:

7. Install the lamp lens, then attach the bulb in their sockets.

8. Engage the sockets, then secure the assembly by installing the retaining screws.

9. Install the center high-mount stop lamp cover.

10. Connect the negative battery cable, then check the lamp for proper operation.

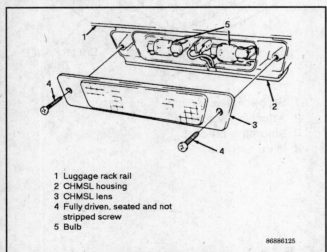

1 Luggage rack rail
2 CHMSL housing
3 CHMSL lens
4 Fully driven, seated and not
   stripped screw
5 Bulb

86886125

Fig. 121 After unfastening the lens, you can remove the bulb — 1985-91 vehicles with a luggage rack

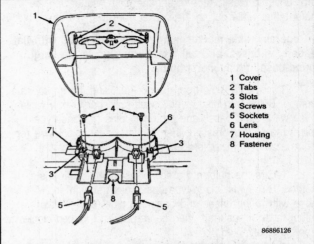

1 Cover
2 Tabs
3 Slots
4 Screws
5 Sockets
6 Lens
7 Housing
8 Fastener

86886126

Fig. 122 View of the center high-mount stop lamp assembly — 1995 Grand Am and Achieva shown

1992-95 SKYLARK

▶ See Figure 123

1. Disconnect the negative battery cable.

2. Remove the rear seat cushion and seatback.

3. Unfasten and remove the rear quarter trim panels.

4. Remove the rear seat-to-back window trim panel.

5. Detach the electrical connector.

6. Lift the retainers, then slide the tabs from the slots.

7. Remove the lamp assembly, then detach the bulb(s).

To install:

8. Install the bulb(s), then insert the tabs of the lamp assembly into the slots, pushing rearward until secure against rear window.

9. Attach the electrical connector.

10. Install the rear seat-to-back window trim panel, then fasten the quarter trim panels.

11. Install the rear seat cushion and seatback.

12. Connect the negative battery cable, then check the light for proper operation.

Dome Light

1. Disconnect the negative battery cable.

2. Depending on the design, carefully pry the lens from the housing or unfasten the retaining screws and remove the lens.

3. Remove the bulb from its socket.

To install:

4. Install the bulb in the socket.

5. Fasten the lens by pushing it into position or securing with the retaining screws.

6. Connect the negative battery cable.

License Plate Lights

▶ See Figure 124

1. Disconnect the negative battery cable.

2. Remove the screws from the lamp assembly.

3. Carefully, pull the assembly down.

4. Remove the bulb from the socket by turning counterclockwise.

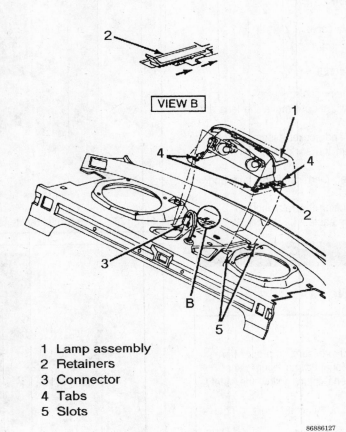

1 Lamp assembly
2 Retainers
3 Connector
4 Tabs
5 Slots

86886127

Fig. 123 View of the center high-mount brake light — 1995 Skylark shown

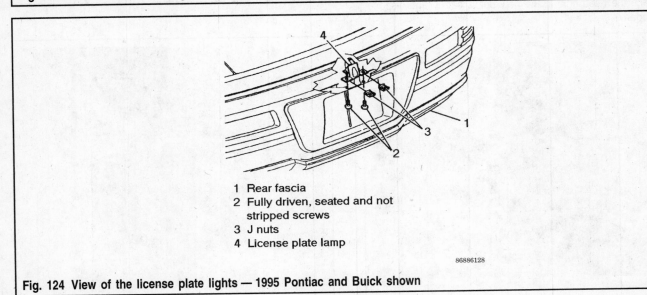

1 Rear fascia
2 Fully driven, seated and not
   stripped screws
3 J nuts
4 License plate lamp

86886128

Fig. 124 View of the license plate lights — 1995 Pontiac and Buick shown

To install:

5. Install the bulb to the socket by pressing in and turning clockwise.
6. Reposition the lamp assembly.
7. Install the mounting screws.
8. Connect the negative battery cable.

Back-up Lamp

▶ **See Figures 125, 126, 127 and 128**

1. Disconnect the negative battery cable.
2. Unfasten the retaining screws, then remove the lens and molding, if equipped.
3. Twist and remove the bulb and socket assembly from the lens, then detach the bulb from the socket.

To install:

4. Attach the bulb to the socket, then install the bulb and socket assembly into the lens.
5. Install the lens and secure using the retainers.
6. Connect the negative battery cable.

Fog Lights

REMOVAL & INSTALLATION

▶ **See Figures 129 and 130**

Halogen bulbs contain gas under pressure. Improper handling of the bulb could cause it to shatter into flying glass fragments. To avoid possible personal injury, follow the safety precautions listed below.

• Turn off the headlight switch and allow the bulb to cool before attempting to change.
• Always wear eye protection when changing a halogen bulb.
• Handle the bulb only by its base. Avoid touching the glass.
• Do not drop or scratch the bulb.
• Keep dirt and moisture off the bulb.
• Place the used bulb in the new bulb's carton and dispose of it properly.

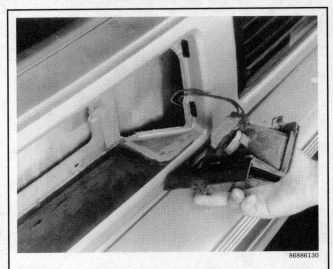

Fig. 126 . . . remove the lens assembly from the vehicle

Fig. 127 Twist and remove the bulb and socket assembly from the lens, then . . .

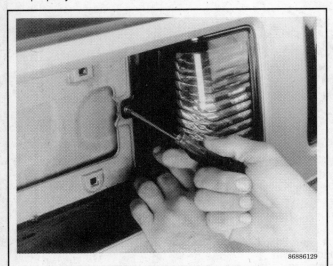

Fig. 125 Unfasten the retaining screws, then . . .

Fig. 128 . . . carefully remove the bulb from the socket

1. Disconnect the negative battery cable.
2. Remove the screw and nut behind the assembly
3. Remove the upper screw and spring.
4. Detach the electrical connector.

To install:

5. Attach the electrical connector.
6. Install the upper screw and spring.
7. Install the screw and spring behind the assembly
8. Connect the negative battery cable, then check the operation and aim of the fog lamps.

AIMING

1. Park the car on level ground so that it is facing (perpendicular to) a flat wall at a distance of 25 ft. (7.62m).
2. Remove any stone shields and switch on the fog lights.
3. Loosen the mounting hardware and aim as follows:
  a. The horizontal distance between the light beams on the wall should be the same as between the lights themselves.
  b. The vertical height of the light beams above the ground should be 4 in. (102mm) less than the distance between the ground and the center of the lamp lenses.
4. Tighten the mounting hardware.

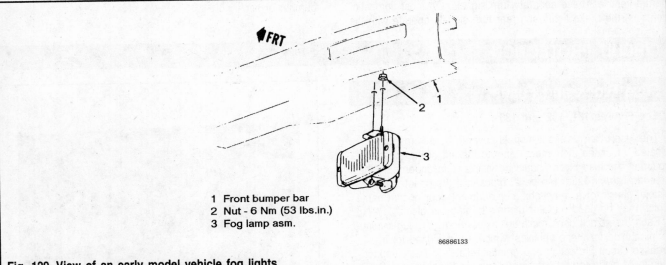

1 Front bumper bar
2 Nut - 6 Nm (53 lbs.in.)
3 Fog lamp asm.

86886133

Fig. 129 View of an early model vehicle fog lights

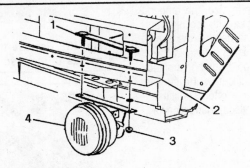

1 Retainer/stud
2 Impact bar
3 Fully driven, seated and not stripped nuts
4 Fog lamp assembly

86886134

Fig. 130 Late model fog light assembly — 1993 Grand Am shown

TRAILER WIRING

Wiring the car for towing is fairly easy. There are a number of good wiring kits available and these should be used, rather than trying to design your own. All trailers will need brake lights and turn signals as well as tail lights and side marker lights. Most states require extra marker lights for overly wide trailers. Also, most states have recently required back-up lights for trailers, and most trailer manufacturers have been building trailers with back-up lights for several years.

Additionally, some Class I, most Class II and just about all Class III trailers will have electric brakes.

Add to this number an accessories wire, to operate trailer internal equipment or to charge the trailer's battery, and you can have as many as seven wires in the harness.

Determine the equipment on your trailer and buy the wiring kit necessary. The kit will contain all the wires needed, plus a plug adapter set which included the female plug, mounted on the bumper or hitch, and the male plug, wired into, or plugged into the trailer harness.

When installing the kit, follow the manufacturer's instructions. The color coding of the wires is standard throughout the industry.

One point to note: some domestic vehicles, and most imported vehicles, have separate turn signals. On most domestic vehicles, the brake lights and rear turn signals operate with the same bulb. For those vehicles without separate turn signals, you can purchase an isolation unit so that the brake lights won't blink whenever the turn signals are operated, or, you can go to your local electronics supply house and buy four diodes to wire in series with the brake and turn signal bulbs. Diodes will isolate the brake and turn signals. The choice is yours. The isolation units are simple and quick to install, but far more expensive than the diodes. The diodes, however, require more work to install properly, since they require the cutting of each bulb's wire and soldering in place of the diode.

One final point, the best kits are those with a spring loaded cover on the vehicle mounted socket. This cover prevents dirt and moisture from corroding the terminals. Never let the vehicle socket hang loosely; always mount it securely to the bumper or hitch.

CIRCUIT PROTECTION

Fuse Block and Fuses

▶ **See Figures 131, 132 and 133**

The fuse block on most models covered by this manual is located under the instrument panel to the left of the steering column. The fuse block should be visible from underneath the steering column, near the pedal bracket. If the panel is not visible, check for a removable compartment door or trim panel which may be used on later models to hide the block.

Each fuse block uses miniature fuses (normally plug-in blade terminal-type for these vehicles) which are designed for increased circuit protection and greater reliability. The compact plug-in or blade terminal design allows for fingertip removal and replacement.

Although most fuses are interchangeable in size, the amperage values are not. Should you install a fuse with too high a value, damaging current could be allowed to destroy the component you were attempting to protect by using a fuse in the first place. The plug-in type fuses have a bold number molded on them and are color coded for easy identification. Be sure to only replace a fuse with the proper amperage rated substitute.

A blown fuse can easily be checked by visual inspection or by continuity checking.

REPLACEMENT

1. Locate the fuse for the circuit in question.

➡**When replacing the fuse, DO NOT use one with a higher amperage rating.**

2. Check the fuse by pulling it from the fuse block and observing the element. If it is broken, install a replacement fuse the same amperage rating. If the fuse blows again, check the circuit for a short to ground or faulty device in the circuit protected by the fuse.

3. Continuity can also be checked with the fuse installed in the fuse block with the use of a test light connected across the 2 test points on the end of the fuse. If the test light lights, replace the fuse. Check the circuit for a short to ground or faulty device in the circuit protected by the fuse.

Fig. 131 Remove the compartment door/trim panel for access to the fuse block

Fig. 132 Common fuse block location — 1986 vehicle shown

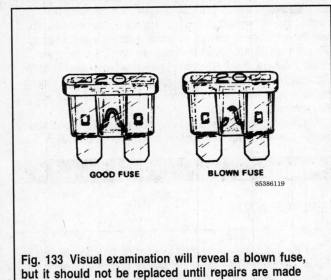

Fig. 133 Visual examination will reveal a blown fuse, but it should not be replaced until repairs are made

Fusible Links

A fusible link is a protective device used in an electrical circuit that acts very much like a standard fuse. The major difference is that fusible links are larger and capable of conducting a higher amperage than most fuses. When the current increases beyond the rated amperage for a given link, the fusible metal of the wire link will melt, thus breaking the electrical circuit and preventing further damage to any other components or wiring. Whenever a fusible link is melted because of a short circuit, correct the cause before installing a new one. There are four different gauge sizes commonly used and they are usually color coded so that they may be easily installed in their original positions.

REPLACEMENT

▶ **See Figure 134**

1. Disconnect the negative battery cable, followed by the positive cable.
2. Locate the burned out link.
3. If both ends of the link are ring terminal connectors which are easily accessed:
   a. Measure the installed length necessary for the new link.
   b. Unbolt and remove the link and connector pieces.
   c. Obtain a suitable length of link, then strip the insulation off the harness wire back 1/2 in. (12.7mm) to allow soldering of the new connectors.
   d. Position the new connector around the new link and crimp it securely. Then, solder the connection, using rosin core solder and sufficient heat to guarantee a good connection. Repeat for the remaining connection.

➡**Whenever splicing a new wire, always bond the splice with rosin core solder, then cover with electrical tape. Using acid core solder may cause corrosion.**

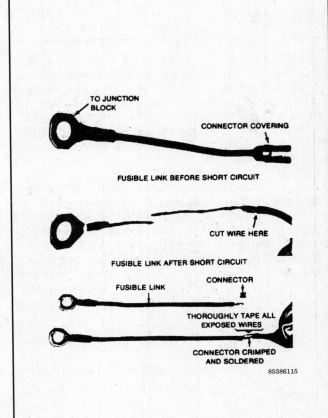

Fig. 134 Fusible links may be repaired by soldering a new link into the wire

4. If the ends of the connector are not easily accessed, repair the length in the vehicle.
   a. Strip away the melted insulation and cut the burned link ends from the wire.
   b. Strip the wire back 1/2 in. (12.7mm) to allow soldering of the new link.
   c. Using a new fusible link of appropriate gauge and length, solder it into the circuit.
5. Tape all exposed wiring with electrical tape and seal with silicone or use a heat shrink tube, if available, to weatherproof the repair.
6. If removed from the vehicle, install the link and secure the connectors.
7. Reconnect the positive, followed by the negative battery cables.

Circuit Breakers

REPLACEMENT

Circuit breakers differ from fuses in that they are reusable. Circuit breakers open when the flow of current exceeds specified value and will close after a few seconds when current flow returns to normal. Some of the circuits protected by circuit breakers include electric windows and power accessories. Circuits breakers are used in these applications due to the fact that they must operated at times under prolonged high current flow due to demand even though there is not malfunction in the circuit.

There are 2 types of circuit breakers. The first type opens when high current flow is detected. A few seconds after the excessive current flow has been removed, the circuit breaker will close. If the high current flow is experienced again, the circuit will open again.

The second type is referred to as the Positive Temperature Coefficient (PTC) circuit breaker. When excessive current flow passes through the PTC circuit breaker, the circuit is not opened but its resistance increases. As the device heats ups with the increase in current flow, the resistance increases to the point where the circuit is effectively open. Unlike other circuit breakers, the PTC circuit breaker will not reset until the circuit is opened, removing voltage from the terminals. Once the voltage is removed, the circuit breaker will re-close within a few seconds.

Replace the circuit breaker by unplugging the old one and plugging in the new one. Confirm proper circuit operation.

Flashers

REPLACEMENT

The hazard flasher is located forward of the console on all N-Body vehicles. The turn signal flasher is located behind the instrument panel, on the left side of the steering column bracket. Replace the flasher by unplugging the old one and plugging in the new one. Confirm proper flasher operation.

WIRING DIAGRAMS

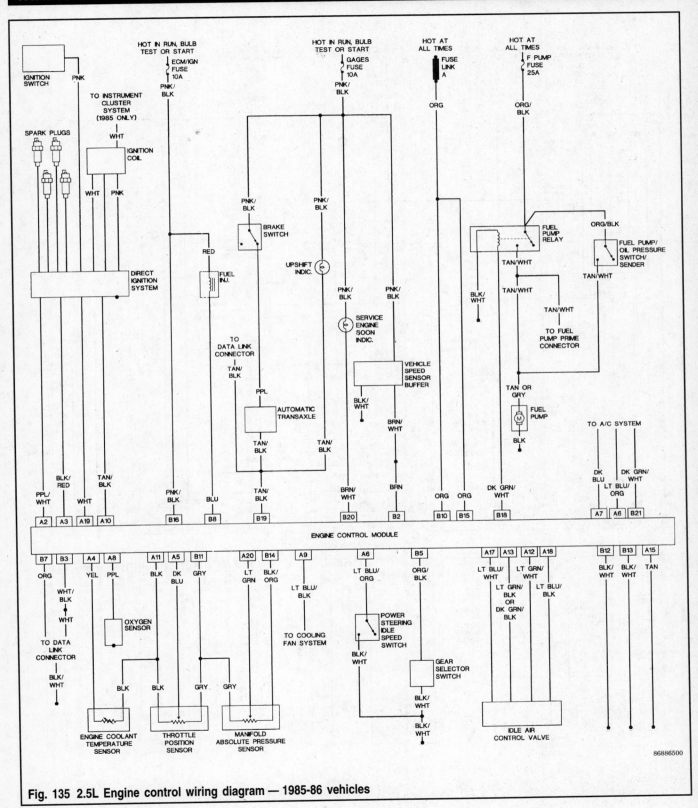

Fig. 135 2.5L Engine control wiring diagram — 1985-86 vehicles

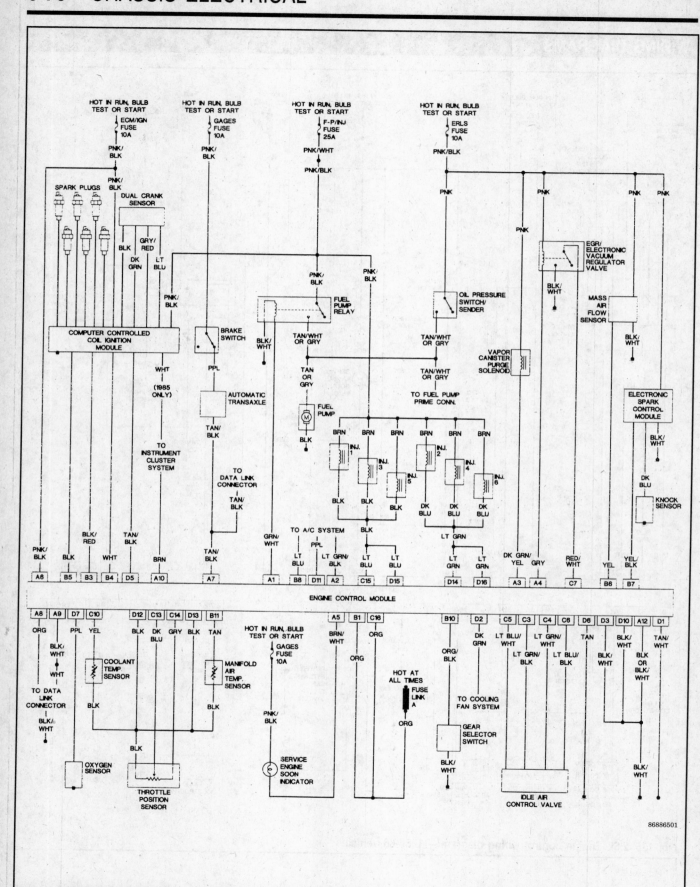

Fig. 136 3.0L Engine control wiring diagram — 1985-86 vehicles

86886501

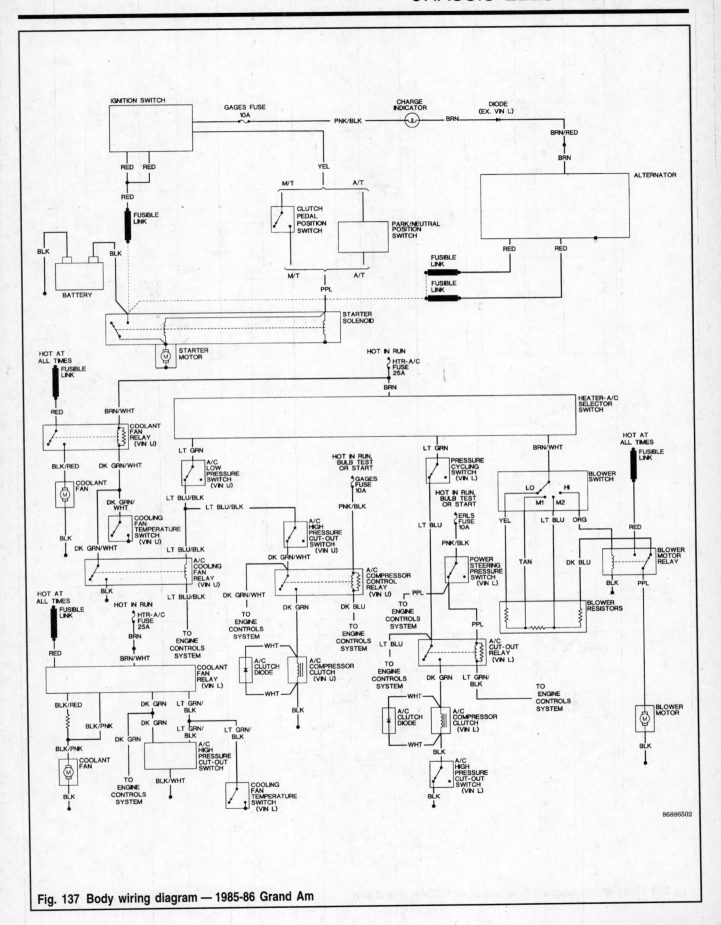

Fig. 137 Body wiring diagram — 1985-86 Grand Am

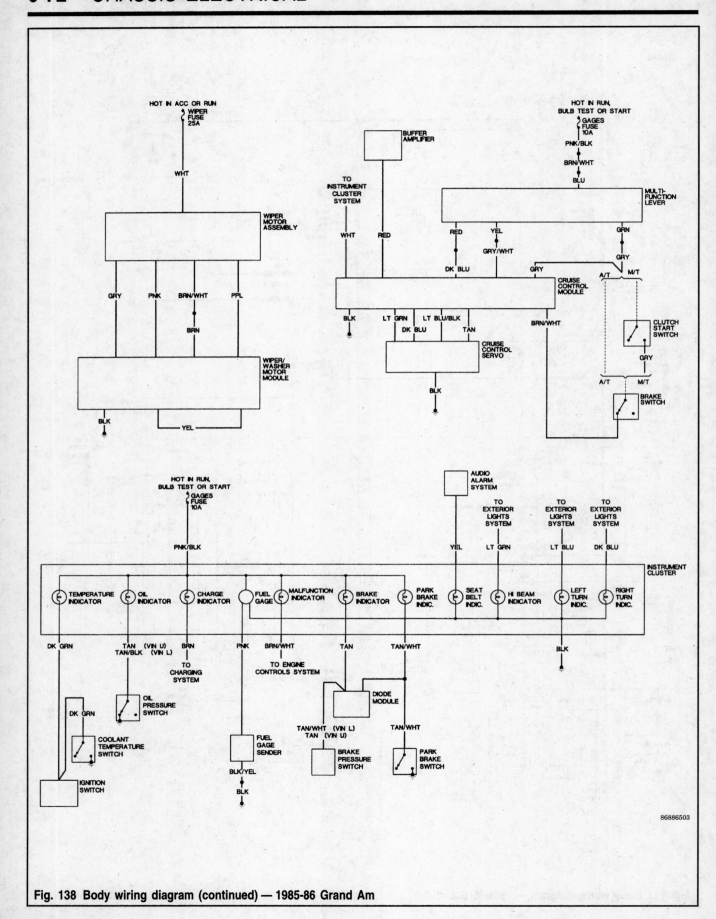

Fig. 138 Body wiring diagram (continued) — 1985-86 Grand Am

86886503

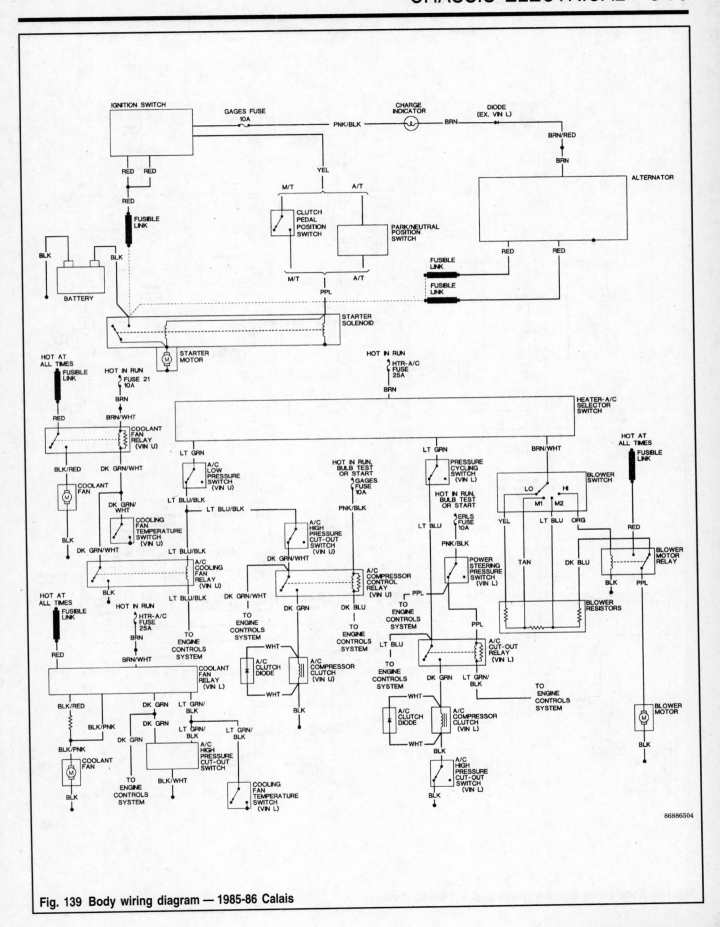

Fig. 139 Body wiring diagram — 1985-86 Calais

86886504

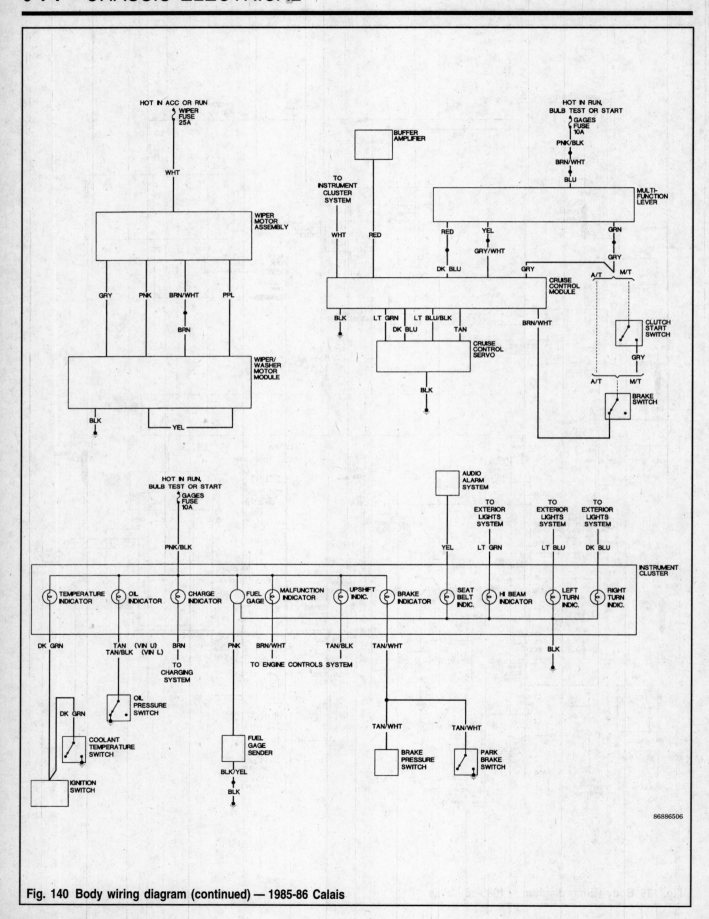

Fig. 140 Body wiring diagram (continued) — 1985-86 Calais

86886506

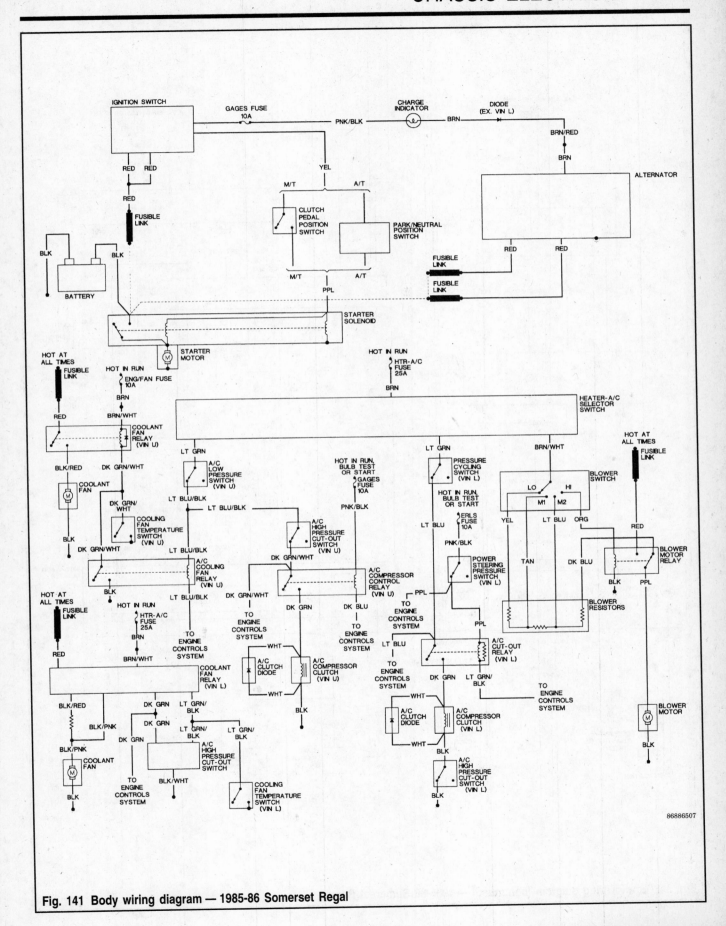

Fig. 141 Body wiring diagram — 1985-86 Somerset Regal

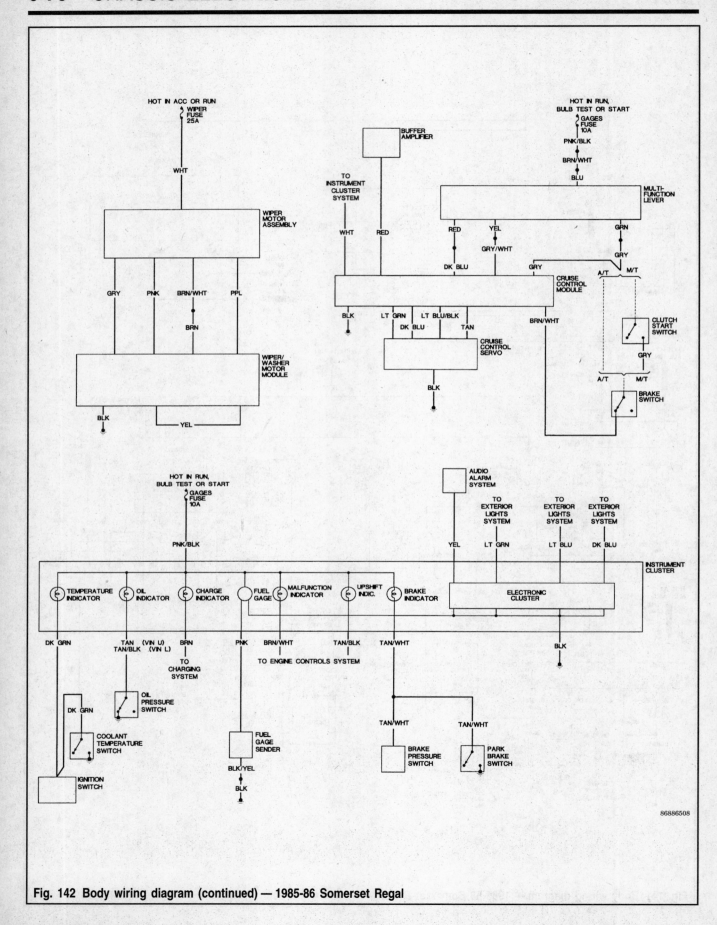

Fig. 142 Body wiring diagram (continued) — 1985-86 Somerset Regal

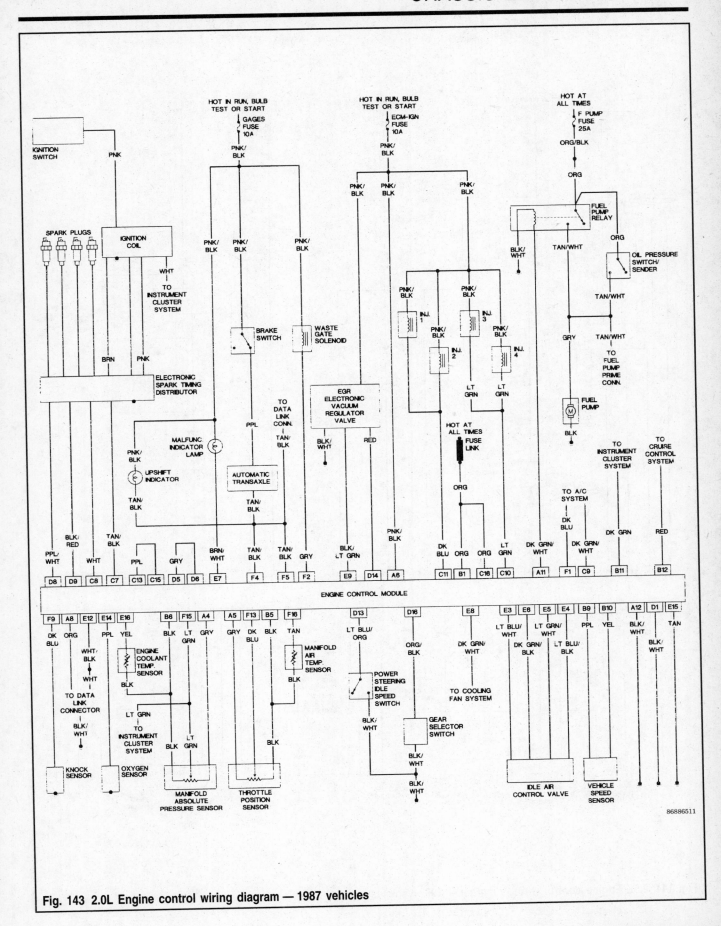

Fig. 143 2.0L Engine control wiring diagram — 1987 vehicles

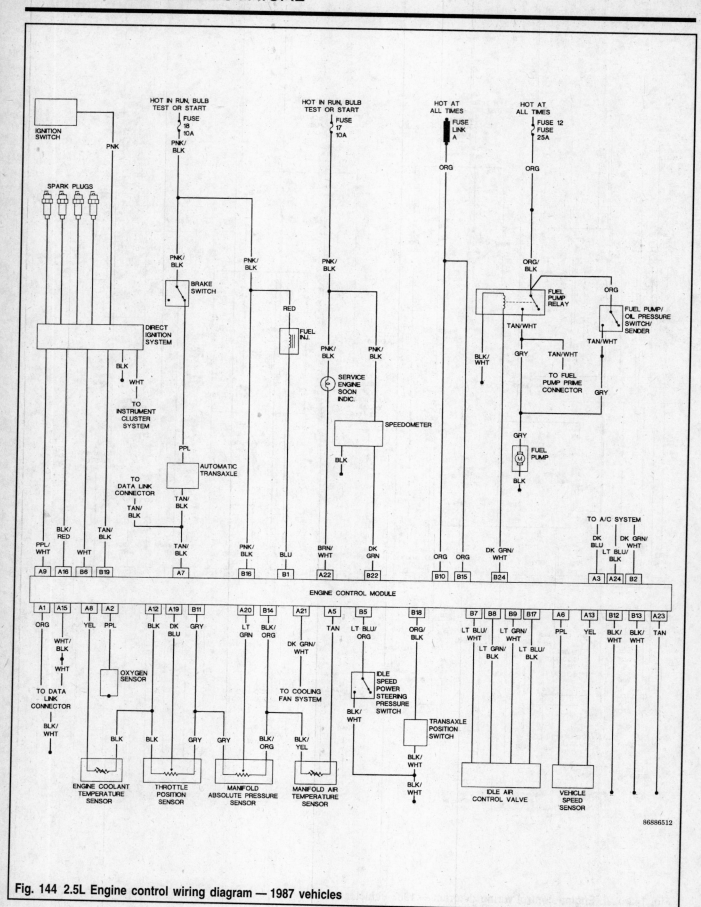

Fig. 144 2.5L Engine control wiring diagram — 1987 vehicles

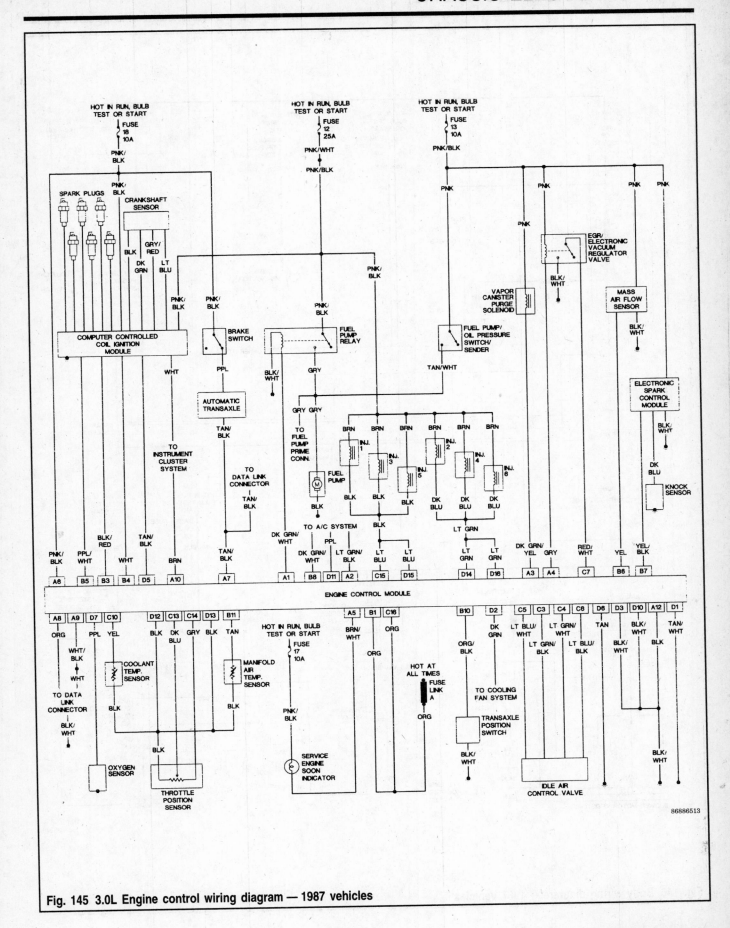

Fig. 145 3.0L Engine control wiring diagram — 1987 vehicles

86886513

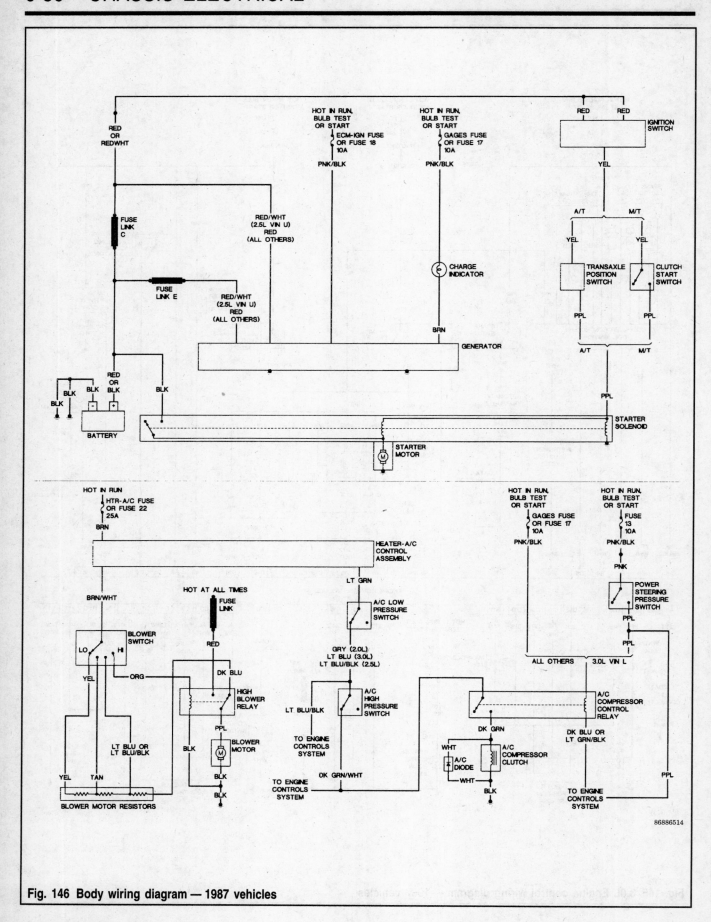

Fig. 146 Body wiring diagram — 1987 vehicles

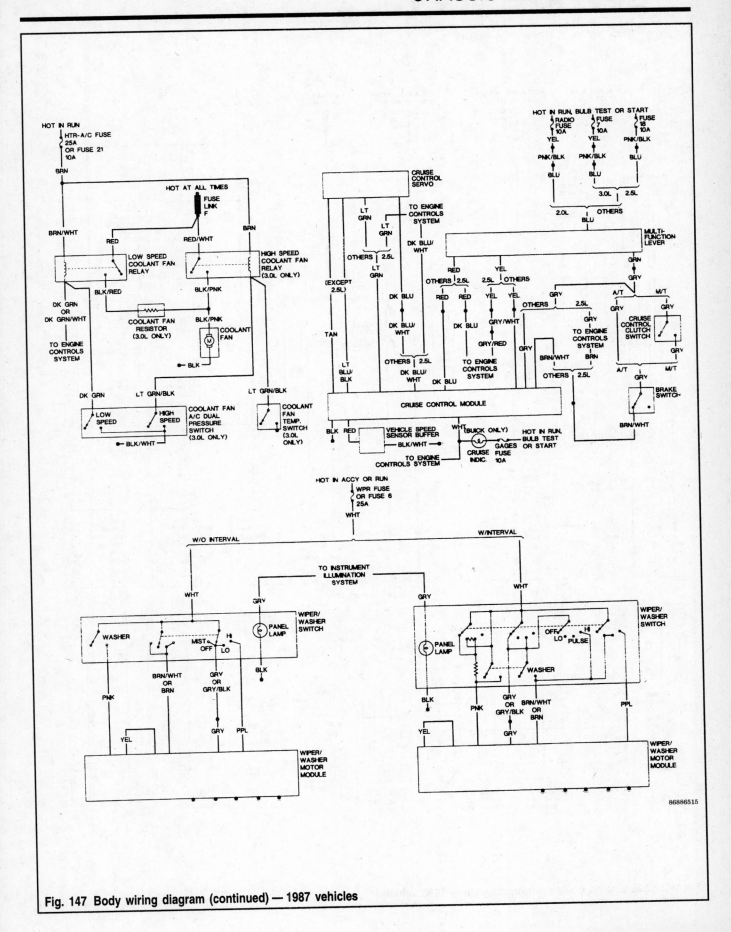

Fig. 147 Body wiring diagram (continued) — 1987 vehicles

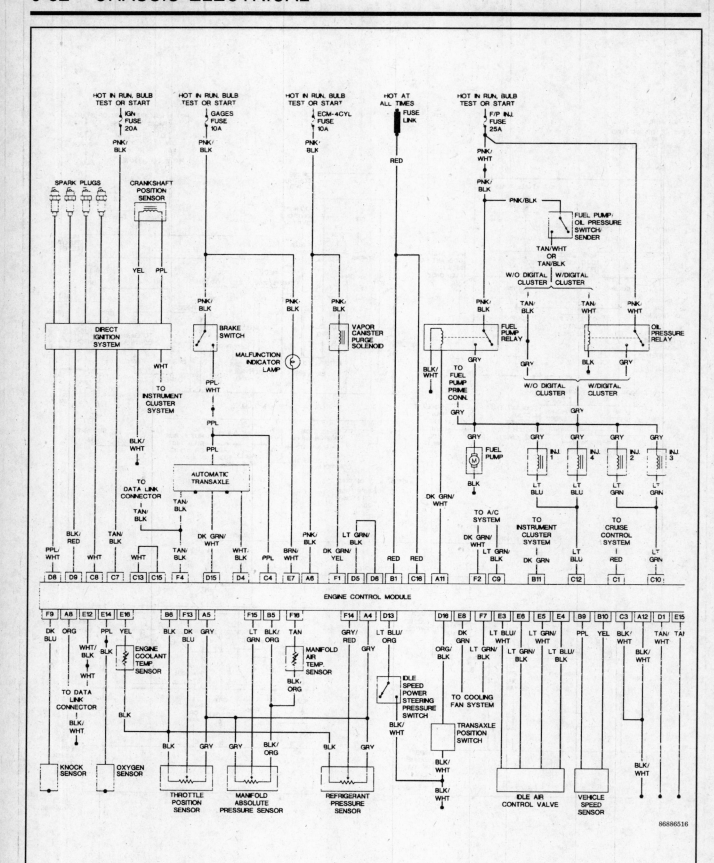

Fig. 148 2.3L Engine control wiring diagram — 1988 vehicles

86886516

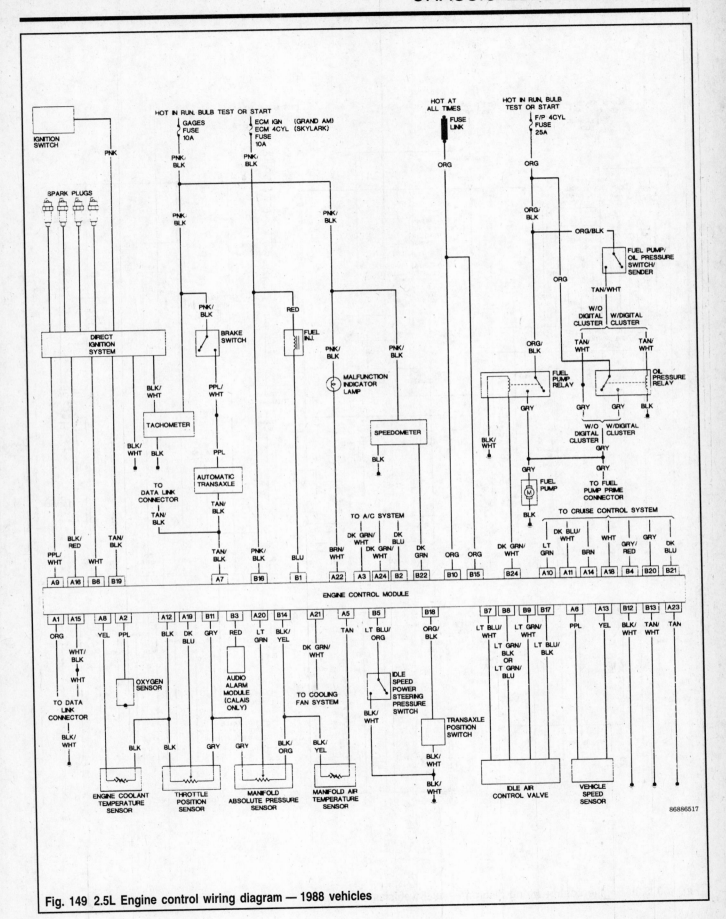

Fig. 149 2.5L Engine control wiring diagram — 1988 vehicles

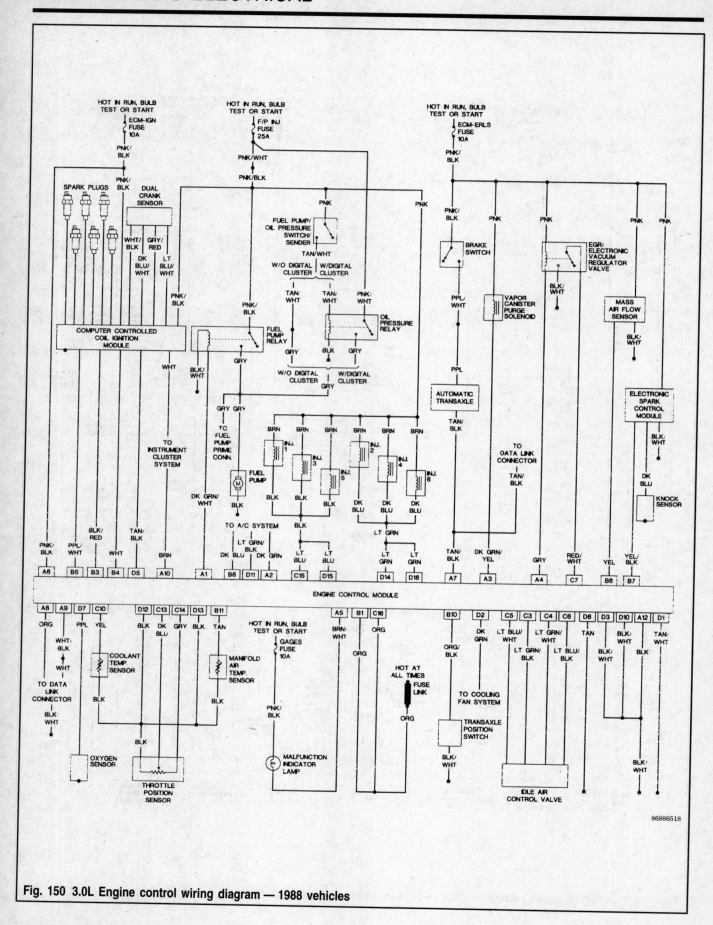

Fig. 150 3.0L Engine control wiring diagram — 1988 vehicles

86886518

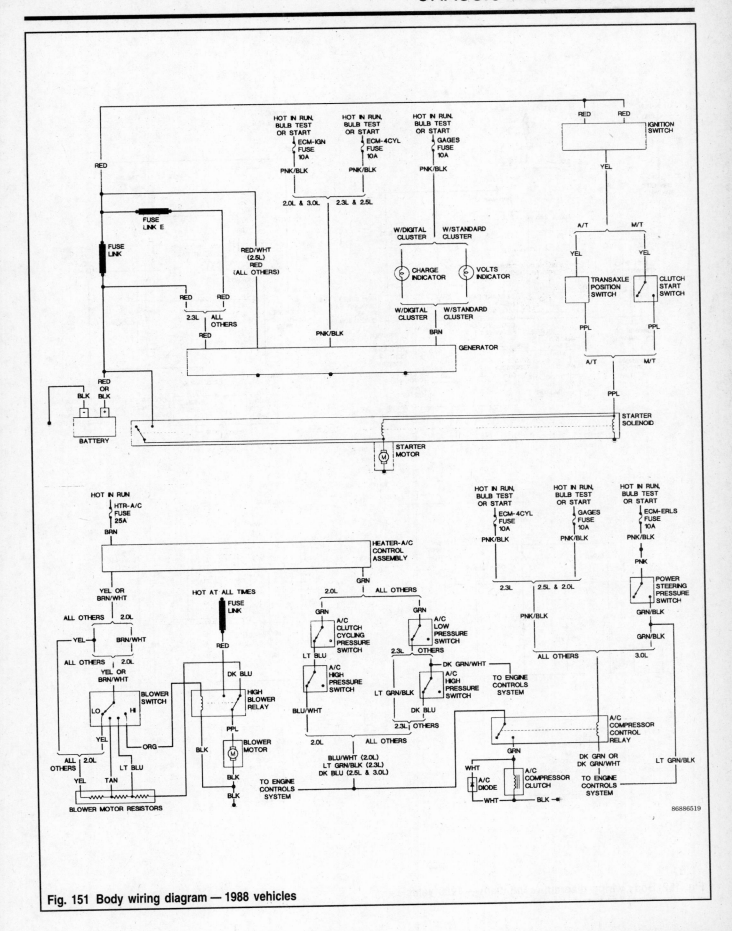

Fig. 151 Body wiring diagram — 1988 vehicles

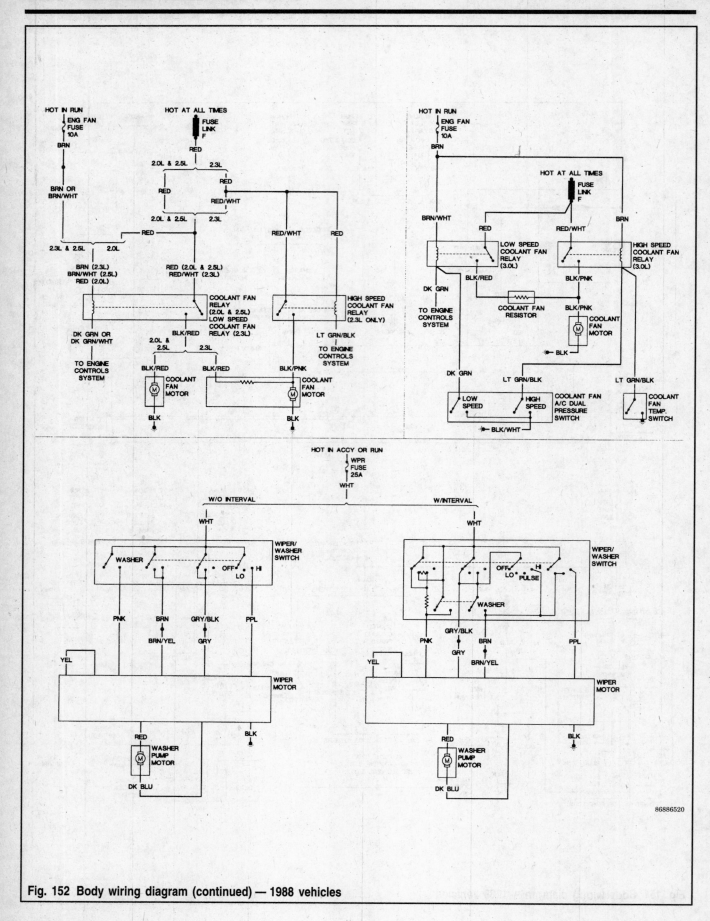

Fig. 152 Body wiring diagram (continued) — 1988 vehicles

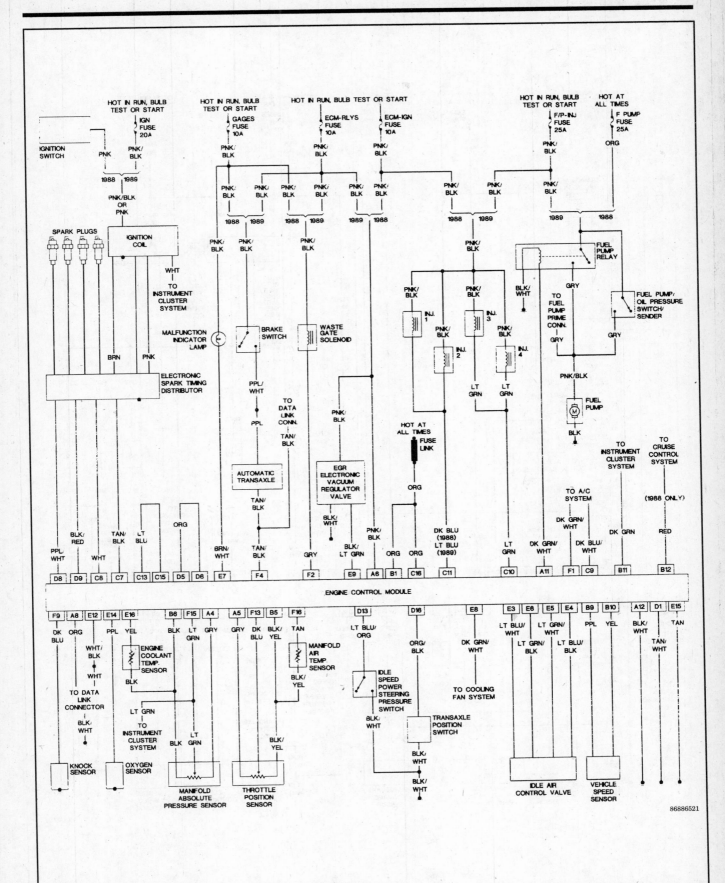

Fig. 153 2.0L Engine control wiring diagram — 1988-89 vehicles

86886521

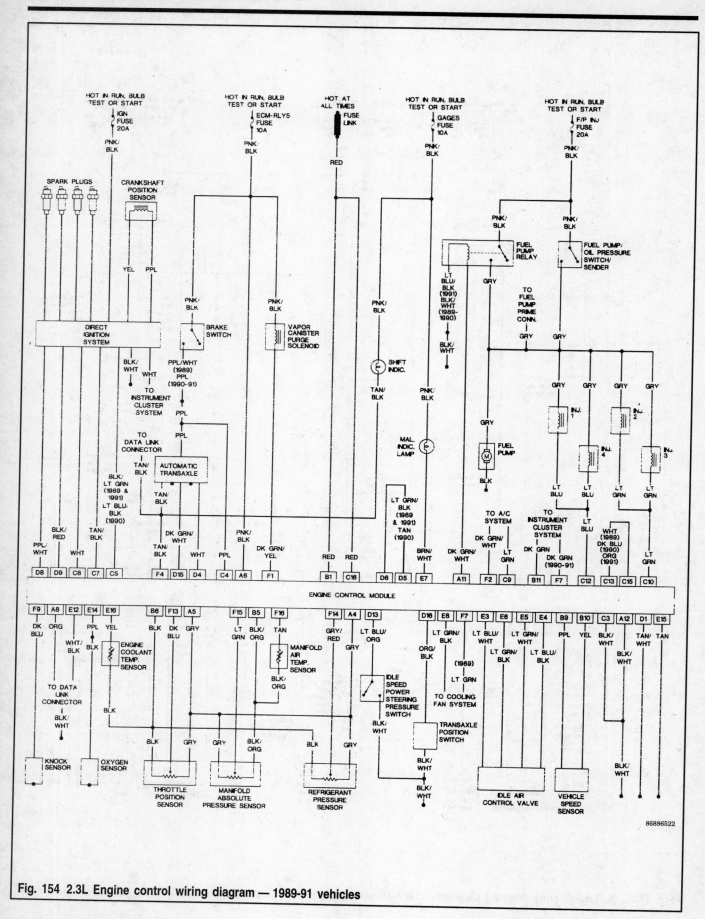

Fig. 154 2.3L Engine control wiring diagram — 1989-91 vehicles

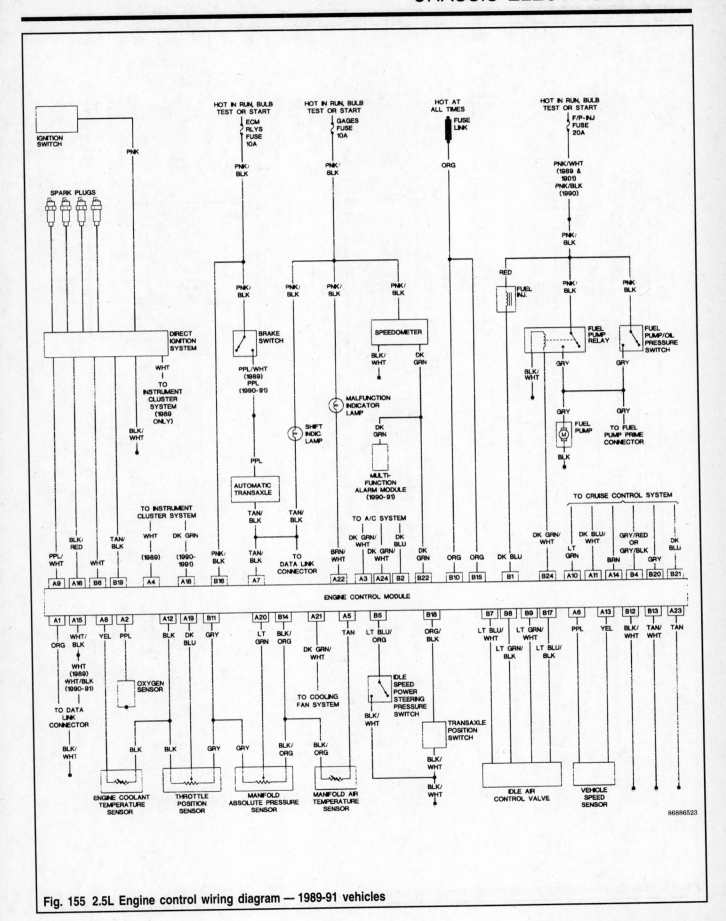

Fig. 155 2.5L Engine control wiring diagram — 1989-91 vehicles

86886523

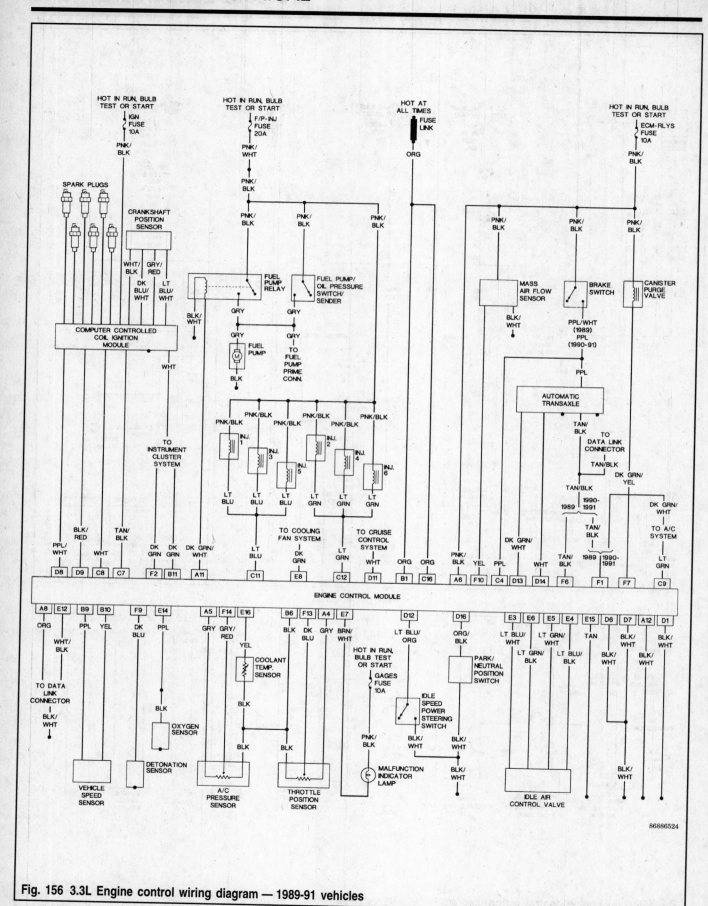

Fig. 156 3.3L Engine control wiring diagram — 1989-91 vehicles

86886524

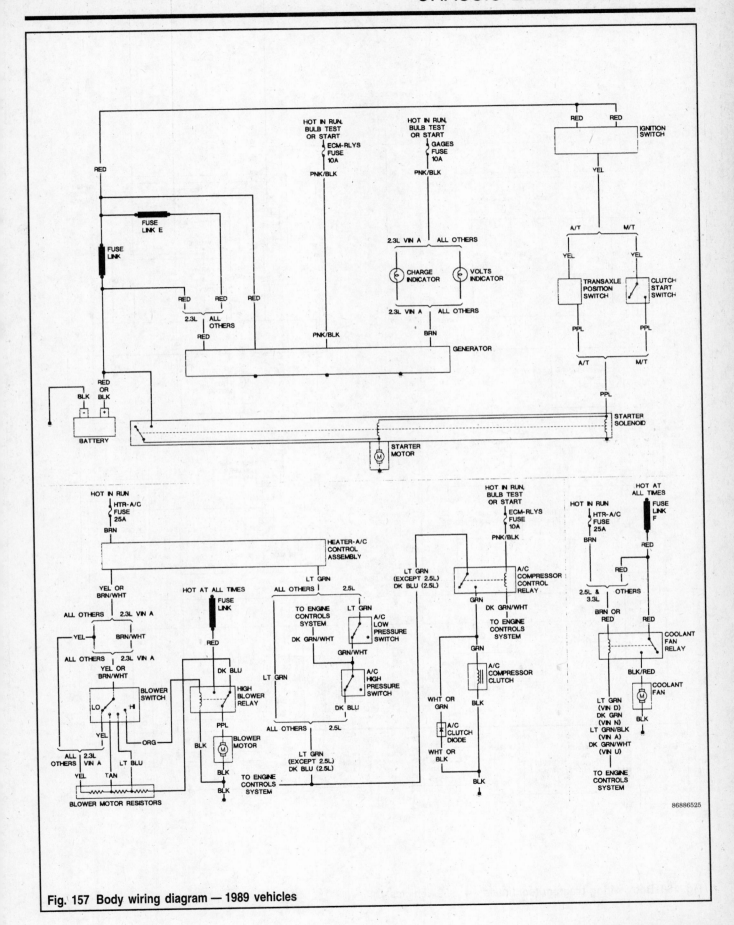

Fig. 157 Body wiring diagram — 1989 vehicles

86886525

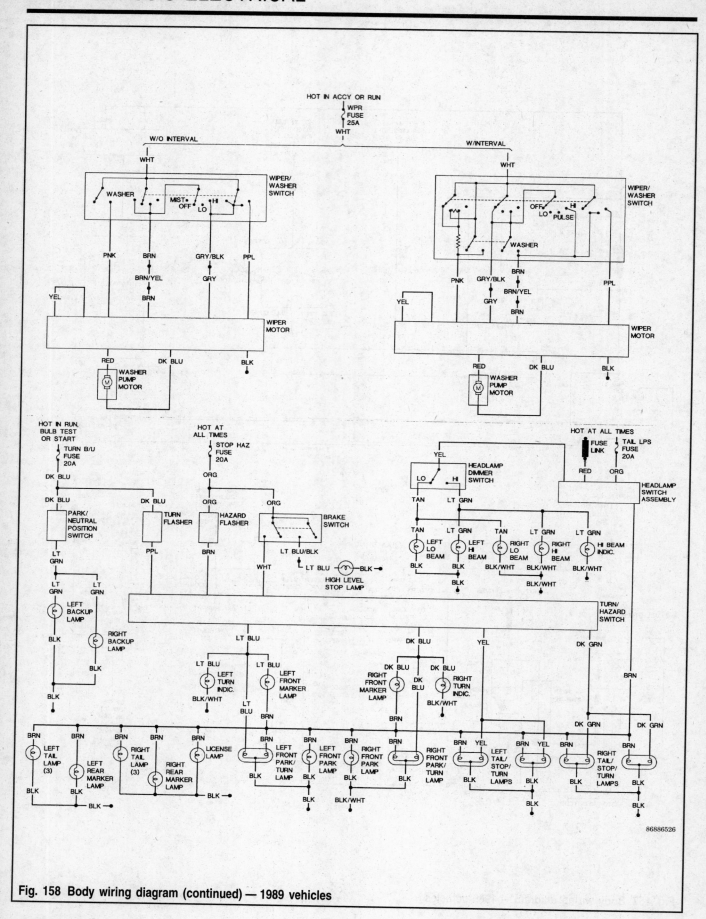

Fig. 158 Body wiring diagram (continued) — 1989 vehicles

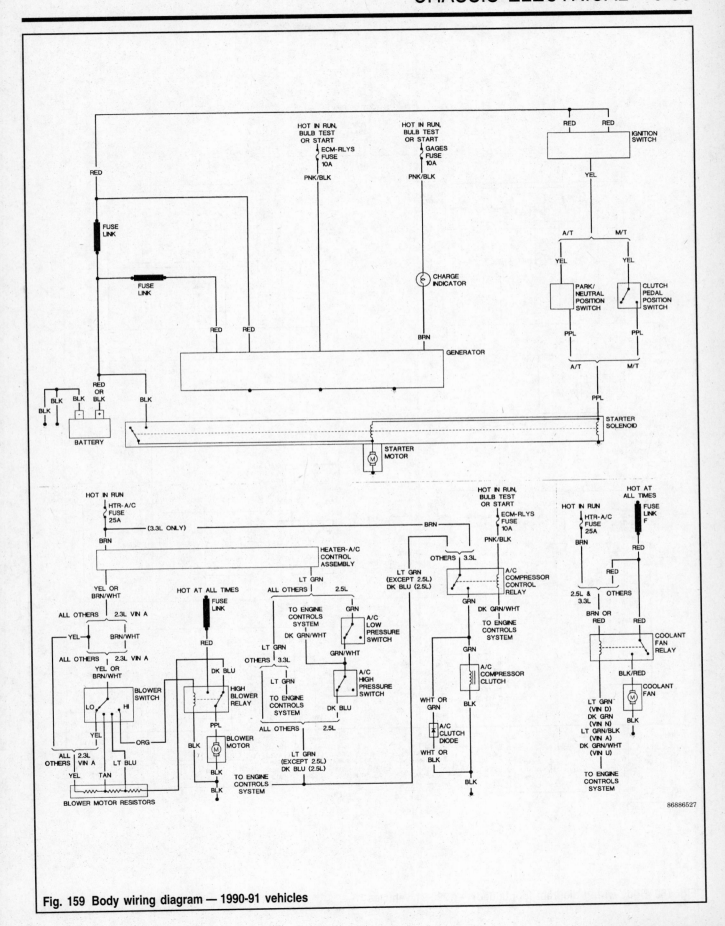

Fig. 159 Body wiring diagram — 1990-91 vehicles

86886527

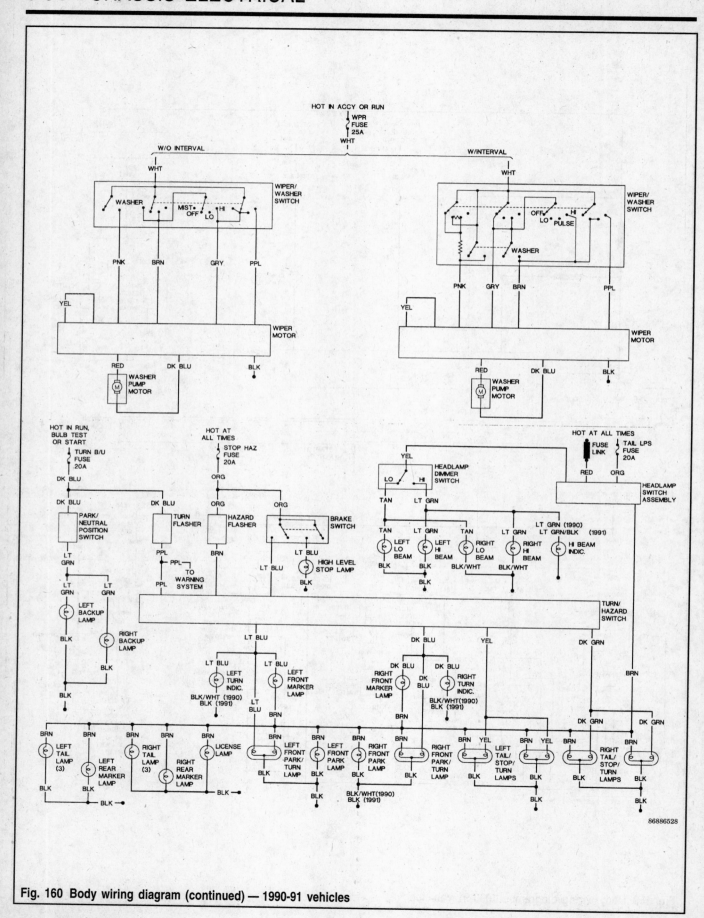

Fig. 160 Body wiring diagram (continued) — 1990-91 vehicles

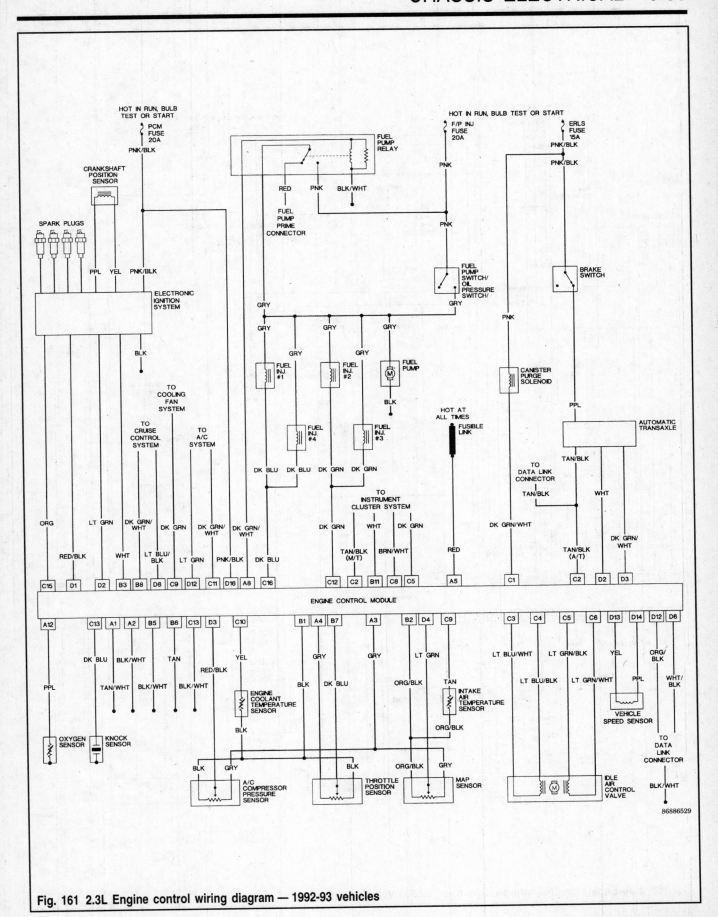

Fig. 161 2.3L Engine control wiring diagram — 1992-93 vehicles

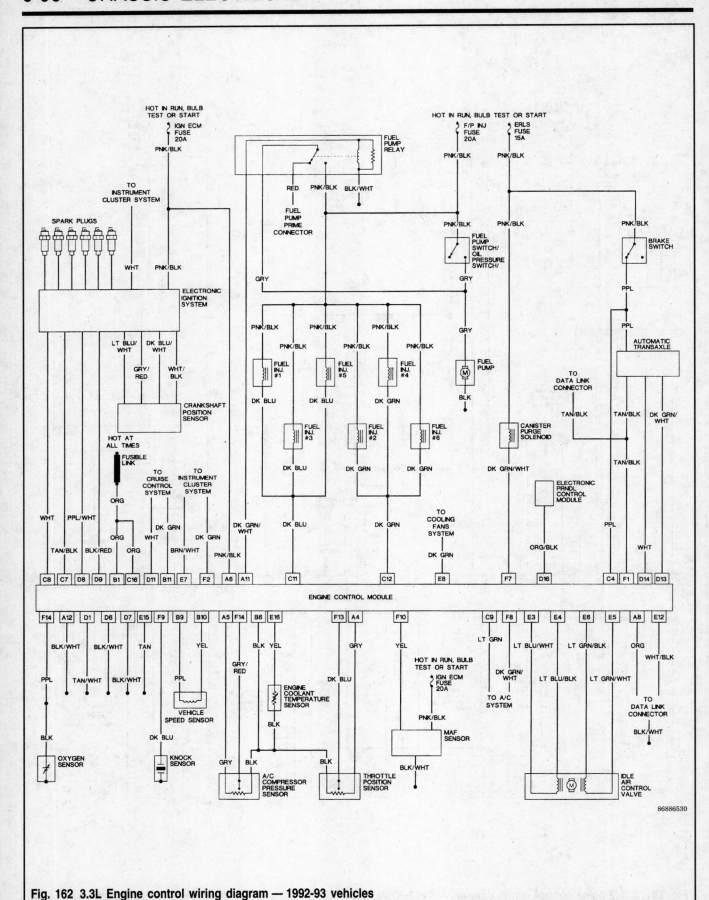

Fig. 162 3.3L Engine control wiring diagram — 1992-93 vehicles

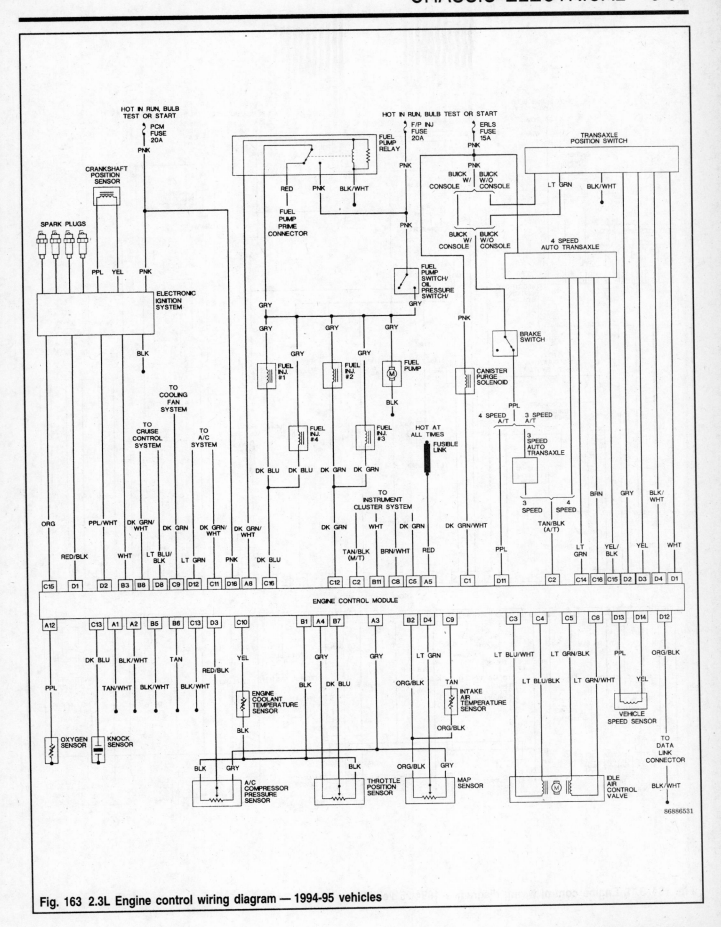

Fig. 163 2.3L Engine control wiring diagram — 1994-95 vehicles

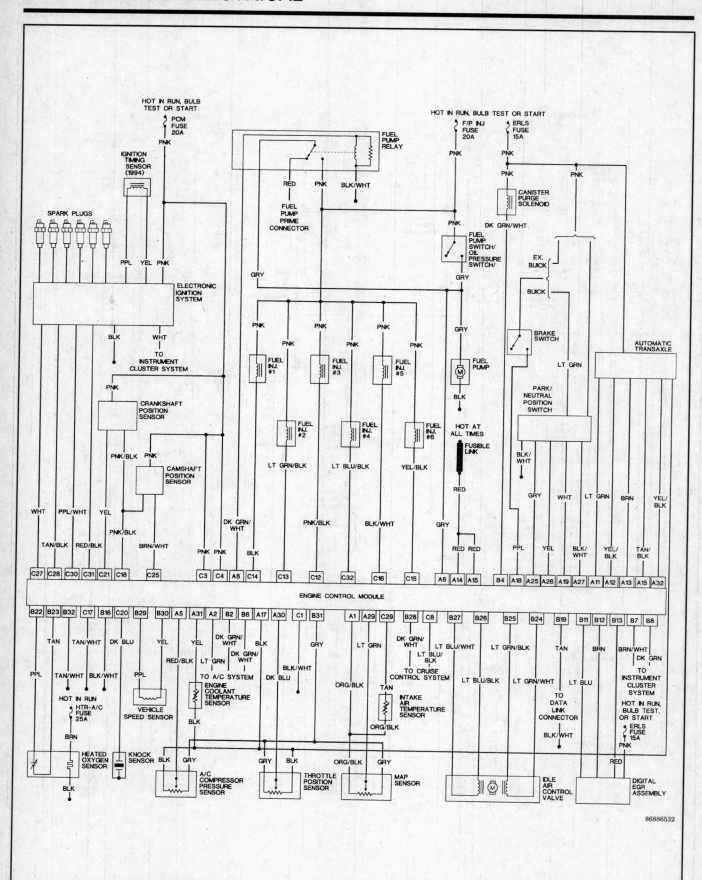

Fig. 164 3.1L Engine control wiring diagram — 1994-95 vehicles

86886532

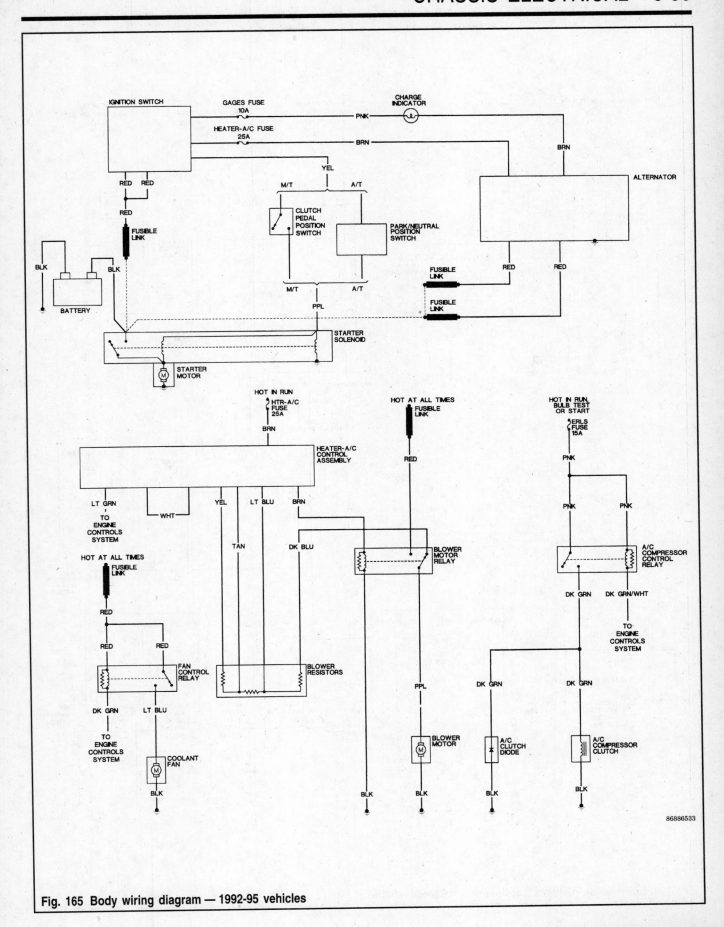

Fig. 165 Body wiring diagram — 1992-95 vehicles

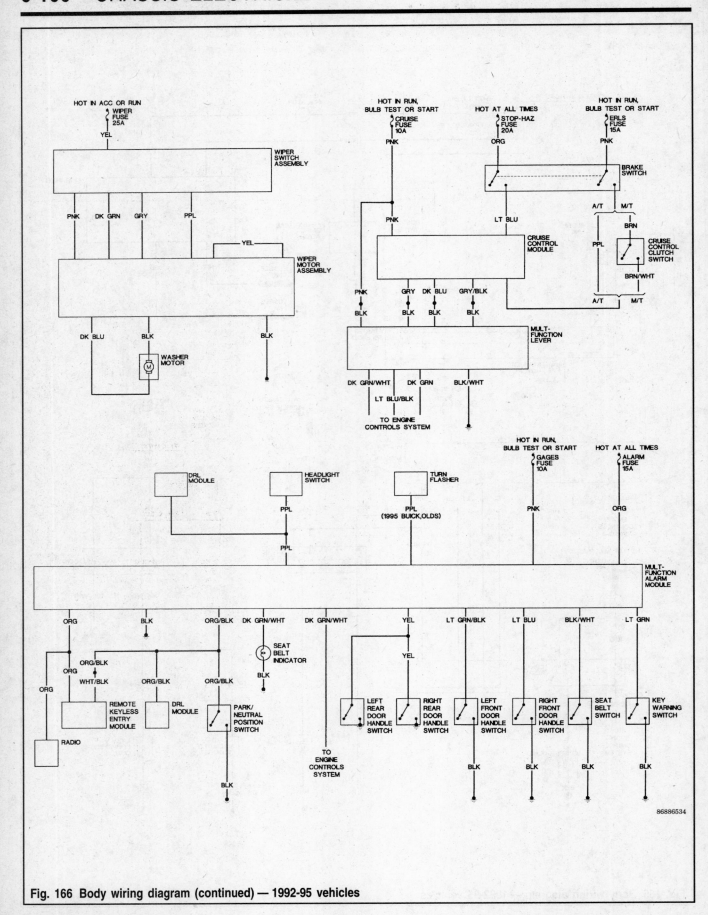

Fig. 166 Body wiring diagram (continued) — 1992-95 vehicles

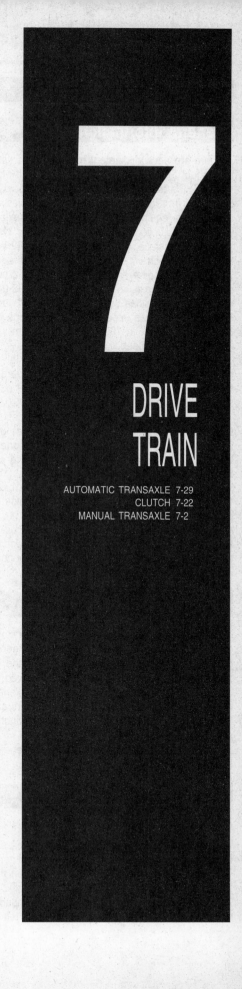

AUTOMATIC TRANSAXLE
ADJUSTMENTS 7-32
FLUID PAN 7-30
GENERAL INFORMATION 7-29
HALFSHAFTS 7-37
IDENTIFICATION 7-30
NEUTRAL SAFETY AND BACK-UP
 SWITCH 7-33
TRANSAXLE 7-34
CLUTCH
ADJUSTMENTS 7-22
CLUTCH CABLE 7-22
CLUTCH MASTER AND SLAVE
 CYLINDER ASSEMBLY 7-25
CLUTCH PEDAL 7-22
DRIVEN DISC AND PRESSURE
 PLATE 7-24
HYDRAULIC CLUTCH SYSTEM
 BLEEDING 7-29
MANUAL TRANSAXLE
ADJUSTMENTS 7-2
BACK-UP LIGHT SWITCH 7-2
GENERAL INFORMATION 7-2
HALFSHAFTS/DRIVE AXLES 7-14
IDENTIFICATION 7-2
METRIC FASTENERS 7-2
TRANSAXLE 7-2

7

DRIVE
TRAIN

AUTOMATIC TRANSAXLE 7-29
CLUTCH 7-22
MANUAL TRANSAXLE 7-2

MANUAL TRANSAXLE

General Information

There are several different manual transaxles used throughout the years on vehicles covered by this manual. In 1985-87, the Isuzu and Muncie 76mm transaxles were used. Beginning in 1988, manual transaxle vehicles with the 2.5L engine were equipped with the Isuzu transaxle and vehicles with the 2.0L or 2.3L used the Hydra-matic Muncie 282 (HM-282) transaxle. In 1990-91, the HM-282 was replaced with the 5TM40 which was installed on vehicles equipped with the 2.3L (VIN A) engine and 2.3L (VIN D); 2.5L engines were still equipped with the Isuzu transaxle. For 1992-94, the NV-T550 was used on vehicles with the 2.3L (VIN A) engine and the Isuzu transaxle was used on all other engine applications with manual transaxles. In 1995 the Isuzu 76mm was the only manual transaxle used.

These transaxles are constant mesh design units with gearing that provides for synchronized forward speeds, a reverse speed, a final drive with differential output and speedometer drive.

The input and output gear clusters are nested very close together, requiring extremely tight tolerances of shafts, gears and synchronizers. The input shaft is supported by a roller bearing in the clutch and differential housing and a ball bearing in the transaxle case.

The output shaft is supported by a roller bearing in the clutch and differential housing and a combination ball-and-roller bearing in the transaxle case.

The differential case is supported by opposed tapered roller bearings which are under preload. The speed gears are supported by roller bearings. A bushing supports the reverse idler gear.

Metric Fasteners

The metric fastener dimensions are very close to the dimensions of the familiar inch system fasteners and, for this reason, replacement fasteners must have the same measurement and strength as those removed.

Do not attempt to interchange metric fasteners with standard fasteners. Mismatched or incorrect fasteners can result in damage to the transaxle unit through malfunctions, breakage or possible personal injury.

Care should be taken to re-use the fasteners in the same locations as removed.

Identification

▶ **See Figures 1 and 2**

On HM-282, 5TM40 and NVT550 transaxles, the identification stamp is located at the center top of the case. The transaxle identification tag is located on the left side near the left side cover.

On Isuzu transaxles, the number is stamped into a tag mounted on the shift quadrant box on the left side.

Adjustments

SHIFT LINKAGE

▶ **See Figure 3**

The shift linkage procedure shown in the illustration is for 1985-87 vehicles equipped with an Isuzu 5-speed manual transaxle. No adjustment procedure is available for 1988-95 models.

Back-up Light Switch

REMOVAL & INSTALLATION

▶ **See Figures 4 and 5**

1. Disconnect the negative battery cable.
2. Detach the back-up light connector.
3. Remove the back-up light switch assembly from the transaxle.

   To install:
4. Using a suitable pipe sealant compound, install the back-up light switch assembly. Tighten to 24 ft. lbs. (33 Nm).
5. Attach the back-up light switch connector.
6. Connect the negative battery cable.

Transaxle

REMOVAL & INSTALLATION

2.0L Engines

▶ **See Figures 6 and 7**

1. Disconnect the negative battery cable.
2. Properly drain the cooling system into a suitable container.
3. Unfasten the heater hose at the core using tool J 37097 or equivalent.
4. Install the engine support fixture tool J-28467 or equivalent. Raise the engine enough to take pressure off the motor mounts.
5. Remove the left sound panel/insulator.
6. Remove the clutch master cylinder pushrod from the clutch pedal.
7. Remove the air cleaner and air intake duct assembly.
8. Remove the clutch slave (actuator) cylinder from the transaxle support bracket, then lay it aside.
9. Remove the transaxle mount through-bolt.
10. Raise and safely support the vehicle.
11. Unfasten and remove the exhaust crossover bolts at the right manifold.
12. Carefully lower the vehicle.

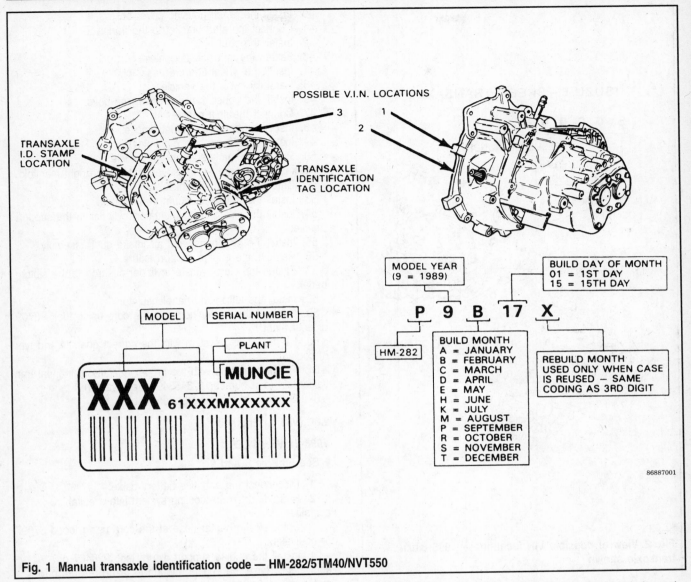

POSSIBLE V.I.N. LOCATIONS

TRANSAXLE I.D. STAMP LOCATION

TRANSAXLE IDENTIFICATION TAG LOCATION

MODEL	SERIAL NUMBER

PLANT

MUNCIE

XXX 61XXXMXXXXXX

MODEL YEAR (9 = 1989)

BUILD DAY OF MONTH
01 = 1ST DAY
15 = 15TH DAY

P 9 B 17 X

HM-282

BUILD MONTH
A = JANUARY
B = FEBRUARY
C = MARCH
D = APRIL
E = MAY
H = JUNE
K = JULY
M = AUGUST
P = SEPTEMBER
R = OCTOBER
S = NOVEMBER
T = DECEMBER

REBUILD MONTH
USED ONLY WHEN CASE
IS REUSED — SAME
CODING AS 3RD DIGIT

86887001

Fig. 1 Manual transaxle identification code — HM-282/5TM40/NVT550

13. Remove the left exhaust manifold. For details, please refer to Section 3 of this manual.
14. Detach the transaxle mount bracket.
15. Disconnect the shift cables.
16. Unfasten the upper transaxle-to-engine bolts.
17. Raise and safely support the vehicle.
18. Remove the left front wheel and tire assembly.
19. Take off the left front inner splash shield.
20. Remove the transaxle strut and bracket.
21. Drain the transaxle.
22. Remove the clutch housing cover bolts.
23. Disconnect the speedometer cable.
24. Detach the stabilizer bar at the left suspension support and control arm.
25. Remove the left suspension support attaching bolts and remove the support and control arm as an assembly.

✳✳CAUTION

Drive axle boot protector J 34754 or equivalent should be modified and installed on any drive axle before service procedures on or near the drive axle. Failure to do this may result in boot damage and possible joint failure.

26. Unfasten the left hand suspension support attaching bolts, then swing it aside.
27. Remove the left hand drive axle from the transaxle.
28. Unfasten the intermediate shaft housing-to-transaxle bolts, then slide the housing away from the transaxle. Using a suitable prytool, disengage the intermediate shaft from the transaxle.
29. Attach the transaxle case to a jack.
30. Unfasten the remaining transaxle-to-engine bolts.

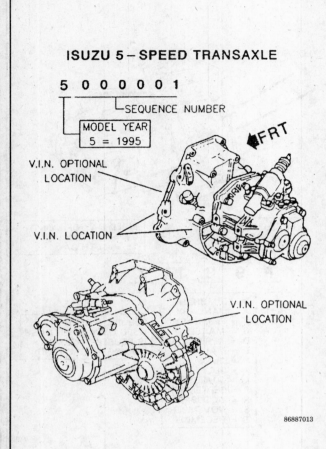

ISUZU 5 – SPEED TRANSAXLE

5 0 0 0 0 0 1

SEQUENCE NUMBER

MODEL YEAR
5 = 1995

V.I.N. OPTIONAL LOCATION

FRT

V.I.N. LOCATION

V.I.N. OPTIONAL LOCATION

86887013

Fig. 2 View of possible VIN locations — 1995 Isuzu transaxle shown

31. Remove the transaxle by sliding toward the driver's side, away from the engine. Carefully lower the jack, guiding the intermediate shaft out of the transaxle.

To install:

32. When installing the transaxle, guide the right driveshaft/intermediate shaft into its bore as the transaxle is being raised. The right driveshaft/intermediate shaft CAN NOT be readily installed after the transaxle is connected to the engine.

33. Install the transaxle-to-engine mounting bolts and tighten to specifications.

34. Seat the intermediate shaft in the transaxle, then install the intermediate shaft housing bolts.

35. Install the left drive axle into its bore at the transaxle, then seat the drive axle into the transaxle. Remove the drive axle boot protectors.

36. Install the suspension support-to-body bolts.

37. Fasten the ball joint to the steering knuckle.

38. Connect the stabilizer bar to the suspension support and control arm.

39. Attach the speedometer cable.

40. Install the clutch housing cover bolts.

41. Connect the strut bracket to the transaxle.

42. Install the strut.

43. Fasten the inner splash shield.

44. Install the wheel and tire assembly.

45. Carefully lower the vehicle.

46. Install the upper transaxle-to-engine bolts.

47. Connect the shift cables.

48. Install the transaxle mount bracket.

49. Install the left exhaust manifold.

50. Raise and safely support the vehicle.

51. Install the exhaust crossover bolts at the right manifold.

52. Carefully lower the vehicle.

53. Install the transaxle mount through-bolt.

54. Install the clutch slave (actuator) cylinder to the support bracket.

55. Install the air cleaner and air intake duct assembly.

56. Remove the engine support fixture.

57. Fasten the clutch master cylinder pushrod to the clutch pedal.

58. Install the left sound panel/insulator.

59. Connect the heater hoses at the core using tool J 37097 or equivalent.

60. Fill the cooling system with the correct quantity and type of coolant.

61. Fill the transaxle with the proper quantity of manual transaxle fluid (part number 12345349 or equivalent).

62. Connect the negative battery cable.

2.3L (VIN A) Engines

1988-91 VEHICLES

▶ **See Figures 8 and 9**

1. Disconnect the negative battery cable.

2. Properly drain the cooling system into a suitable container.

3. Unfasten the heater hose at the core using tool J 37097 or equivalent.

4. Install the engine support fixture tool J-28467 or equivalent. Raise the engine enough to take pressure off the motor mounts.

5. Remove the left sound panel/insulator.

6. Remove the clutch master cylinder pushrod from the clutch pedal.

7. Detach the air cleaner-to-throttle body duct and hose.

8. Remove the clutch slave (actuator) cylinder from the transaxle support bracket, then lay it aside.

9. Unfasten the retaining bolts, then remove the power steering pump and set it aside.

10. Disconnect the shift cables.

11. Unfasten the two transaxle mount bracket upper bolts from the transaxle. Unfasten the upper transaxle-to-engine bolts.

12. For 1990-91 vehicles, remove the transaxle vent tube.

13. Raise and safely support the vehicle.

14. Remove the left front wheel and tire assemblies. Detach the left inner splash shield.

15. Properly drain the transaxle.

16. Detach the speedometer connection.

17. Disconnect the radiator outlet pipe (water pump inlet) from the transaxle.

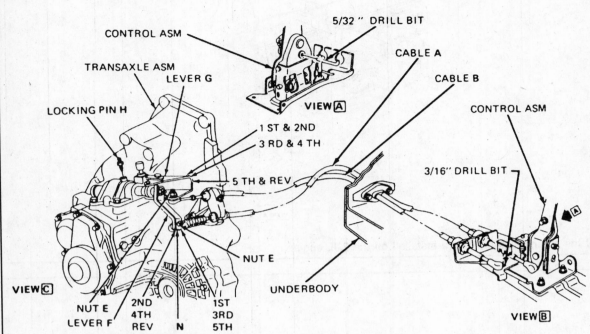

1. Disconnect negative cable at battery.
2. Shift transaxle into third gear. Remove lock pin (H) and reinstall with tapered end down. This will lock transaxle in third gear.
3. Loosen shift cable attaching nuts (E) at transaxle levers (G) and (F).
4. Remove console trim plate and slide shifter boot up shifter handle. Remove console.
5. Install a 5/32" or No. 22 drill bit into alignment hole at side of shifter assembly, as shown in View A.
6. Align the hole in the select lever (View B) with the slot in the shifter plate and install a 3/16" drill bit.
7. Tighten nuts E at levers G and F. Remove drill bits from alignments holes at the shifter. Remove lockpin (H) and reinstall with tapered end up.
8. Install console, shifter boot and trim plate.
9. Connect negative cable at battery.
10. Road test vehicle to check for a good neutral gate feel during shifting. It may be necessary to fine tune the adjustment after testing.

86887014

Fig. 3 Manual shift linkage adjustment — 1985-87 vehicles equipped with the Isuzu transaxle

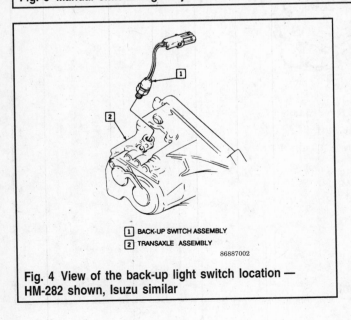

1 BACK-UP SWITCH ASSEMBLY
2 TRANSAXLE ASSEMBLY

86887002

Fig. 4 View of the back-up light switch location — HM-282 shown, Isuzu similar

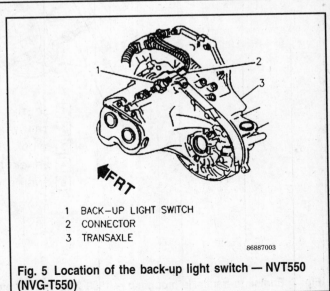

1 BACK-UP LIGHT SWITCH
2 CONNECTOR
3 TRANSAXLE

86887003

Fig. 5 Location of the back-up light switch — NVT550 (NVG-T550)

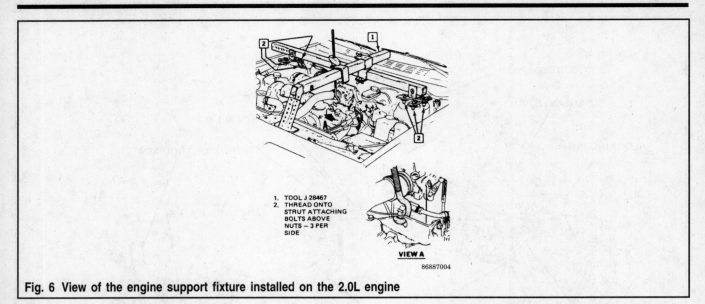

1. TOOL J 28467
2. THREAD ONTO STRUT ATTACHING BOLTS ABOVE NUTS — 3 PER SIDE

VIEW A

86887004

Fig. 6 View of the engine support fixture installed on the 2.0L engine

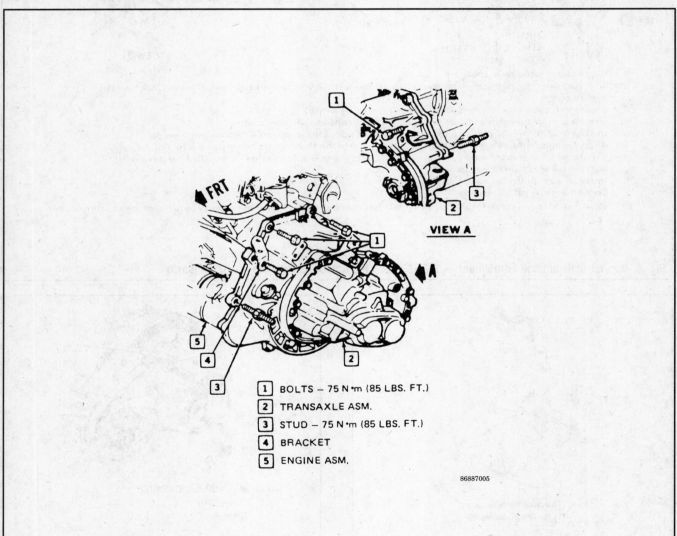

VIEW A

FRT

1. BOLTS — 75 N•m (85 LBS. FT.)
2. TRANSAXLE ASM.
3. STUD — 75 N•m (85 LBS. FT.)
4. BRACKET
5. ENGINE ASM.

86887005

Fig. 7 Engine-to-transaxle mounting — 1989 2.0L engine shown

18. Unfasten the engine mount crossmember retaining nuts from the left suspension support.

19. Remove the stabilizer shaft from the left suspension support and left control arm.

20. Unfasten the left suspension support retaining bolts, then swing it aside and support it with wire.

✳✳CAUTION

Drive axle boot protector J 34754 or equivalent should be modified and installed on any drive axle before service procedures on or near the drive axle. Failure to do this may result in boot damage and possible joint failure.

21. Remove the left drive axle from the transaxle and position it aside.

22. Unfasten the lower transaxle mount bracket bolt and the transaxle mount through-bolt.

23. Remove the rear engine mount bracket from the engine block.

24. Detach the stabilizer shaft from the right control arm.

25. Separate the ball joint from the strut assembly.

26. Disengage the right drive axle from the intermediate shaft and position it aside.

27. Unfasten the remaining intermediate shaft-to-block retainer, then remove the shaft.

28. Remove the two flywheel housing covers.

29. Install a suitable transaxle support jack.

30. Disconnect the negative battery cable from the transaxle.

31. Unfasten the remaining transaxle-to-engine bolts, and the spacer and stud, then carefully lower the transaxle from the vehicle.

To install:

32. Using a suitable jack, raise the the transaxle into position. Install the lower engine-to-transaxle bolts, spacer stud and nut. Tighten to the specifications shown in the accompanying figure.

33. Connect the negative battery cable to the transaxle.

34. Install the lower transaxle mount bracket bolt.

35. Fasten the two flywheel housing covers.

36. Install the intermediate shaft and lower retaining bolt (the shorter bolt).

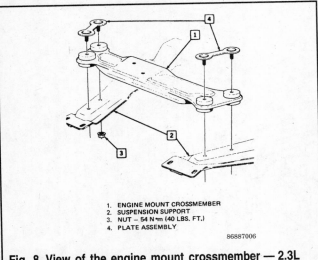

1. ENGINE MOUNT CROSSMEMBER
2. SUSPENSION SUPPORT
3. NUT — 54 N•m (40 LBS. FT.)
4. PLATE ASSEMBLY

86887006

Fig. 8 View of the engine mount crossmember — 2.3L (VIN A) engine through 1991

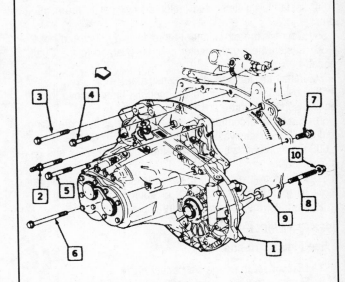

1. TRANSAXLE
2. STUD — 96 N•m (71 LBS. FT.) POSITION 2
3. BOLT — 96 N•m (71 LBS. FT.) POSITION 3
4. BOLT — 96 N•m (71 LBS. FT.) POSITION 4
5. BOLT — 96 N•m (71 LBS. FT.) POSITION 5
6. BOLT — 56 N•m (41 LBS. FT.)
7. BOLT — 96 N•m (71 LBS. FT.)
8. STUD — 12 N•m (106 LBS. IN.)
9. SPACER
10. NUT — 56 N•m (41 LBS. FT.)

86887008

Fig. 9 Transaxle retainer locations and torque specifications — 2.3L (VIN A) engines through 1991

37. Install the rear engine mount bracket to the block, then install the rear engine mount and body bracket.

38. Engage the right drive axle into the intermediate shaft and index ball joint. Install the ball joint nut.

39. Connect the stabilizer shaft to the right control arm, then connect the left drive axle to the transaxle.

40. Install the left suspension support indexing the engine mount crossmember.

41. Install the engine mount crossmember retaining nuts.

42. Connect the stabilizer shaft to the suspension support and control arm.

43. Attach the radiator outlet pipe to the transaxle.

44. Fasten the speedometer connection.

45. Fasten the inner splash shield.

46. Remove drive axle boot protectors J 34754.

47. Install the wheel and tire assembly.

48. Carefully lower the vehicle.

49. Making sure they're in the correct positions, install the upper transaxle-to-engine bolts.

50. If equipped, install the transaxle vent tube.

51. Install the transaxle mount bracket-to-upper bolts.

52. Connect the shift cables.

53. Install the power steering pump and bracket, then tighten the belt to specifications.

54. Install the clutch slave (actuator) cylinder to the support bracket.

55. Connect the air cleaner-to-throttle body duct and hose.

56. Fasten the clutch master cylinder pushrod to the clutch pedal.

57. Install the left sound panel/insulator.

58. Lower the engine onto the mounts, then remove the engine support fixture.

59. If removed, connect the heater hoses at the core using tool J 37097 or equivalent.

60. Fill the cooling system with the correct quantity and type of coolant.

61. Fill the transaxle with the proper quantity of manual transaxle oil (part number 12345349 or equivalent).

62. Connect the negative battery cable.

1992-93 VEHICLES

▶ See Figures 10 and 11

1. Disconnect the negative battery cable.

2. Remove the left sound insulator, then disconnect the clutch pushrod from the pedal.

3. Remove the air cleaner assembly and the bracket.

4. Remove the clutch slave cylinder and position it aside.

5. Remove the power steering pump bracket.

6. Disconnect the shift cables and levers from the transaxle.

7. Detach the electrical connector from the vehicle speed sensor.

8. Tag and disconnect the vacuum lines.

9. Remove the shift cable bracket.

10. Unfasten the upper transaxle-to-engine bolts.

11. Install a suitable engine support fixture as shown in the accompanying figure.

12. Remove the the upper transaxle mount and through-bolt.

13. Raise and safely support the vehicle.

14. Remove the left front wheel and tire assembly.

15. Unfasten the left drive axle nut and left ball joint nut. Discard the cotter pin.

✳✳CAUTION

Drive axle boot protector J 34754 or equivalent should be modified and installed on any drive axle before service procedures on or near the drive axle. Failure to do this may result in boot damage and possible joint failure.

16. Remove the left drive axle. Unfasten the left stabilizer link nut.

17. Properly drain the transaxle.

18. Remove the left inner splash shield.

19. Unfasten the attaching bolts and remove the left suspension support.

20. Disconnect the heater hose bolt.

21. Remove the flywheel inspection cover.

22. Remove the lower transaxle mount and through-bolt.

23. Carefully lower the vehicle, then lower the engine and transaxle assembly.

24. Detach the back-up light switch connector.

25. Raise and safely support the vehicle.

26. Support the transaxle with a suitable jackstand.

27. Unfasten the remaining transaxle-to-engine bolts. Detach the ground connections.

28. Remove the transaxle by sliding it away from the engine and carefully lowering the jack while guiding the intermediate shaft out of the transaxle.

To install:

29. Position the transaxle to the engine and intermediate shaft. Install the lower transaxle-to-engine bolts, tighten the bolts to the specifications shown in the accompanying figure.

30. Remove the transaxle jack.

31. Attach the back-up light switch connector.

32. Install the heater hose bolt, then tighten to 40 ft. lbs. (54 Nm).

33. Fasten the transaxle shift levers.

34. Carefully lower the vehicle.

35. Raise the engine and transaxle assembly.

36. Install the upper transaxle mount and through-bolt. Tighten the mount bolts to 55 ft. lbs. (75 Nm) and the through-

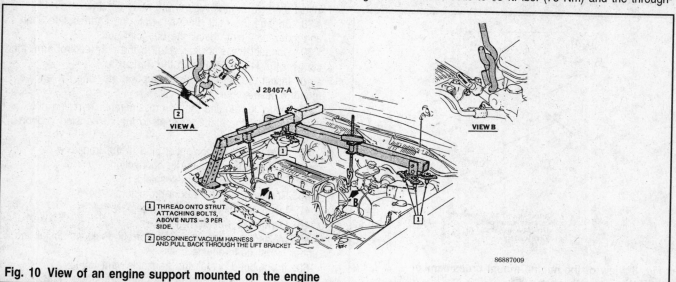

Fig. 10 View of an engine support mounted on the engine

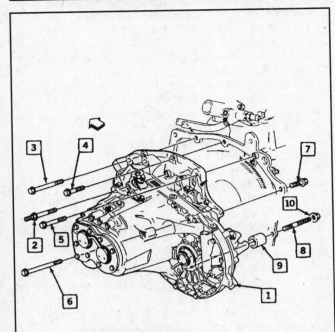

1. TRANSAXLE
2. STUD — 96 N·m (71 LBS. FT.) POSITION 2
3. BOLT — 96 N·m (71 LBS. FT.) POSITION 3
4. BOLT — 96 N·m (71 LBS. FT.) POSITION 4
5. BOLT — 96 N·m (71 LBS. FT.) POSITION 5
6. BOLT — 56 N·m (41 LBS. FT.)
7. BOLT — 96 N·m (71 LBS. FT.)
8. STUD — 12 N·m (106 LBS. IN.)
9. SPACER
10. NUT — 56 N·m (41 LBS. FT.)

86887010

Fig. 11 Transaxle-to-engine bolt locations and torque specifications — 1992-93 vehicles

bolt to 33 ft. lbs. (45 Nm), then turn an addition 120° using tool J 36660 or equivalent.

37. Attach the vehicle speed sensor connector.
38. Raise and safely support the vehicle.
39. Install the left drive axle, then fasten the left drive axle nut.
40. Install the left suspension support, then secure with the attaching bolts and nuts.
41. Fasten the left ball joint with a new cotter pin.
42. Install the left stabilizer link nut. Tighten the link nut to 10 ft. lbs. (17 Nm) except for the direct acting stabilizer. For the direct acting stabilizer, tighten the link nut to 70 ft. lbs. (95 Nm).
43. Remove the seal protector(s) used when removing and installing the drive axle.
44. Install the left inner splash shield, then the tire and wheel assembly. Tighten the lug nuts to 100 ft. lbs. (140 Nm).
45. Install the lower transaxle mount and through-bolt. Tighten the mount bolts to 55 ft. lbs. (75 Nm) and the through-bolt to 33 ft. lbs. (45 Nm), then turn an addition 120° using tool J 36660 or equivalent.

46. Carefully lower the vehicle.
47. Remove the engine support fixture.
48. Install the upper engine-to-transaxle bolts. Tighten the bolts to 71 ft. lbs. (96 Nm).
49. Fasten the shift cable bracket, tighten the retaining nut to 89 inch lbs. (10 Nm).
50. Connect the shift cables.
51. Install the clutch slave cylinder. For details, please refer to the procedure located later in this section.
52. Fasten the power steering pump bracket.
53. Connect the vacuum lines as tagged during removal.
54. Install the air cleaner assembly and bracket.
55. Connect the negative battery cable.
56. Fasten the clutch pushrod to the clutch pedal, then install the left sound insulator.
57. Fill the transaxle with the proper quantity of manual transaxle fluid, part number 12345349 or equivalent.

2.3L (VIN A and 3)

1994 VEHICLES ONLY

See Figures 10 and 12

1. Disconnect the negative battery cable.
2. Remove the left sound insulator, then disconnect the clutch pushrod from the pedal.
3. Remove the air cleaner assembly and the bracket.
4. Disconnect the brake booster line from the throttle body, then position it aside.
5. Detach the hydraulic line from the slave cylinder.
6. Remove the power steering pump bracket.
7. Disconnect the shift cables from the transaxle.
8. Detach the electrical connector from the back-up light switch.
9. Tag and disconnect the vacuum lines.
10. Remove the shift cable bracket.
11. Unfasten the upper transaxle-to-engine bolts.
12. Install a suitable engine support fixture as shown in the accompanying figure.
13. Remove the the upper transaxle mount and through-bolt.
14. Raise and safely support the vehicle.
15. Drain the transaxle.
16. Detach both from ABS wheel speed sensor connectors and the left side harness from the suspension support.
17. Remove both front wheel and tire assemblies.
18. Remove both drive axles.
19. Unfasten the both stabilizer link nuts.
20. Remove the left front inner splash shield.
21. Unfasten the attaching bolts and remove the left suspension support.
22. Detach the vehicle speed sensor electrical connector from the transaxle.
23. Disconnect the heater hose bolt.
24. Remove the flywheel housing cover.
25. Remove the lower transaxle mount and through-bolt.
26. Carefully lower the vehicle, then lower the engine and transaxle assembly enough to remove the transaxle from the vehicle. Note the number of turns for ease of installation.
27. Raise and safely support the vehicle.
28. Support the transaxle with a suitable jackstand.
29. Unfasten the remaining transaxle-to-engine bolts. Detach any ground connections.

30. Remove the transaxle by sliding it away from the engine and carefully lowering the jack while guiding the intermediate shaft out of the transaxle.

To install:

31. Position the transaxle to the engine and intermediate shaft. Install the lower transaxle-to-engine bolts, tighten the bolts to the specifications shown in the accompanying figure.

32. Raise the engine and transaxle assembly.

33. Install the lower transaxle mount and through-bolt. Tighten the bolt to 44 ft. lbs. (60 Nm).

34. Remove the transaxle jack.

35. Attach the back-up light switch connector.

36. Install the heater hose bolt, then tighten to 40 ft. lbs. (54 Nm).

37. Fasten the transaxle shift levers.

38. Carefully lower the vehicle.

39. Install the upper transaxle mount and through-bolt. Tighten the mount bolts to 96 ft. lbs. (130 Nm) and the through-bolt to 44 ft. lbs. (60 Nm).

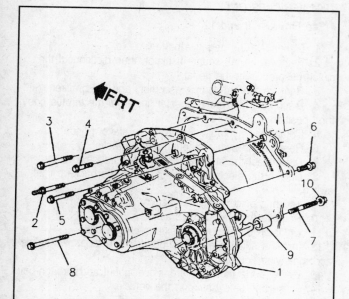

1 TRANSAXLE
2 STUD – 75 N·m (55 LBS. FT.) POSITION 2
3 BOLT – 75 N·m (55 LBS. FT.) POSITION 3
4 BOLT – 75 N·m (55 LBS. FT.) POSITION 4
5 BOLT – 75 N·m (55 LBS. FT.) POSITION 5
6 BOLT – 75 N·m (55 LBS. FT.) POSITION 6
7 STUD – 13 N·m (115 LBS. IN.) POSITION 7
8 BOLT – 75 N·m (55 LBS. FT.) POSITION 8
9 SPACER
10 NUT – 75 N·m (55 LBS. FT.)

86887012

Fig. 12 Transaxle-to-engine bolt locations and torque specifications — 1994 vehicles

40. Attach the vehicle speed sensor connector.

41. Raise and safely support the vehicle.

42. Install the drive axles.

43. Install the left suspension support, then secure with the attaching bolts and nuts.

44. Fasten the ball joints with new cotter pins.

45. Install the stabilizer link nuts.

46. Attach both front ABS wheel speed sensors.

47. Install the left inner splash shield.

48. Fasten the flywheel housing cover.

49. Install the wheel and tire assemblies.

50. Carefully lower the vehicle.

51. Remove the engine support fixture.

52. Install the upper engine-to-transaxle bolts. Tighten the bolts to 71 ft. lbs. (96 Nm).

53. Fasten the shift cable bracket, tighten the retaining nut to 89 inch lbs. (10 Nm).

54. Connect the shift cables.

55. Attach the hydraulic line to the slave cylinder.

56. Fasten the power steering pump bracket, then adjust the belt tension.

57. Connect the vacuum lines as tagged during removal.

58. Install the air cleaner assembly and bracket.

59. Connect the negative battery cable.

60. Attach the brake booster line to the throttle body.

61. Fasten the clutch pushrod to the clutch pedal, then install the left sound insulator.

62. Fill the transaxle with the proper quantity of manual transaxle fluid (part number 12345349 or equivalent).

2.3L (VIN 3) Engine

1992-93 VEHICLES

▶ See Figures 10, 13 and 14

1. Disconnect the negative battery cable.

2. Install the engine support fixture tool J-28467 or equivalent. Raise the engine enough to take pressure off the motor mounts.

3. Remove the left sound insulator.

4. Detach the clutch master cylinder pushrod from the clutch pedal.

5. Remove the clutch slave (actuator) cylinder from the transaxle support bracket, then lay it aside.

6. Disconnect the wire harness at the mount bracket.

7. Unfasten the transaxle mount through-bolt, then remove the mount.

8. Detach the shift cables and the retaining clamp at the transaxle.

9. Remove the ground cables at the transaxle mounting studs.

10. Detach the back-up switch connector.

11. Raise and safely support the vehicle. Properly drain the transaxle.

12. Remove the front wheel and tire assemblies. Detach the left front inner splash shield.

13. Unfasten the flywheel housing cover bolts, then remove the cover.

14. Detach the vehicle speed sensor at the transaxle.

15. Unfasten the left and right drive axle nuts, and the left and right ball joint nuts.

16. Remove the left and right stabilizer links.

✸✸CAUTION

Drive axle boot protector J 34754 or equivalent should be modified and installed on any drive axle before service procedures on or near the drive axle. Failure to do this may result in boot damage and possible joint failure.

17. Remove the drive axles.

18. Unfasten the left side U-bolt from the stabilizer bar. Unfasten the left suspension support attaching bolts.

19. Disconnect the through-bolt then remove the lower transaxle mount.

20. Attach the transaxle case to a suitable support jack.

21. Disconnect the negative battery cable from the transaxle.

22. Unfasten the transaxle-to-engine bolts, then carefully slide the transaxle away from the engine and lower the jack.

To install:

23. Position the transaxle. Secure with the transaxle-to-engine mounting bolts and tighten to 55 ft. lbs. (75 Nm).

24. Install the flywheel housing cover, then secure with the bolts. Tighten the bolts to 89 inch lbs. (10 Nm).

25. Position the lower transaxle mount, secure with the through-bolt, then tighten the retaining bolts to 55 ft. lbs. (75 Nm) and the through-bolt to 39 ft. lbs. (54 Nm).

26. Install the left suspension support and retaining bolts.

27. Fasten the left U-bolt to the stabilizer bar.

28. Secure axle seal protector J 37292-B.

29. Install the left and right drive axles, then secure using the retaining nuts. Install the left and right ball joint nuts.

30. Install the left and right stabilizer link nuts. Tighten the link nuts to 10 ft. lbs. (17 Nm).

31. Remove the axle seal protector and boot protector.

32. Connect the vehicle speed sensor at the transaxle.

33. Fasten the inner splash shield.

34. Install the wheel and tire assembly.

35. Carefully lower the vehicle, then final tighten the wheel lug nuts to 100 ft. lbs. (140 Nm).

36. Connect the ground cables at the transaxle mounting studs.

37. Attach the back-up light switch connector.

38. Install the clutch slave (actuator) cylinder to the transaxle bracket aligning the pushrod into the pocket of the clutch release lever, then install the retaining nuts and tighten evenly to prevent damage to the cylinder.

39. Install the upper transaxle mount and through-bolt. Tighten the mount bolts to 55 ft. lbs. (75 Nm) and the through-bolt to 39 ft. lbs. (54 Nm).

40. Attach the wire harness at the mount bracket.

41. Remove the engine support fixture.

42. Install the shift cables and clamp.

43. Fasten the clutch master cylinder pushrod to the clutch pedal.

44. Install the left sound panel/insulator.

45. Fill the transaxle with the proper quantity of manual transaxle fluid (part number 12345349 or equivalent).

46. Connect the negative battery cable.

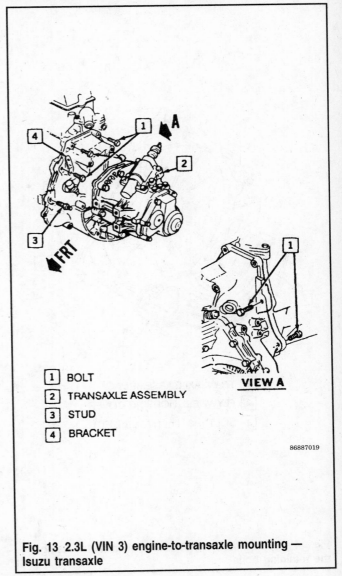

1	BOLT
2	TRANSAXLE ASSEMBLY
3	STUD
4	BRACKET

86887019

Fig. 13 2.3L (VIN 3) engine-to-transaxle mounting — Isuzu transaxle

2.3L (VIN D) Engine

1995 VEHICLES ONLY

1. Disconnect the negative battery cable.

2. Install the engine support fixture tool J-28467 or equivalent. Raise the engine enough to take pressure off the motor mounts.

3. Remove the left sound insulator. Detach the clutch master cylinder pushrod from the clutch pedal.

4. Remove the air cleaner and duct assembly from the throttle body.

5. Disconnect the wire harness at the mount bracket.

6. Unfasten the upper transaxle mount-to-transaxle bolts.

7. Remove the ground cables at the transaxle mounting studs.

8. Disengage the clutch master cylinder from the clutch actuator cylinder.

9. Disconnect the ground cables at the transaxle mounting studs.

10. Detach the back-up switch connector.

11. Remove the transaxle vent tube.

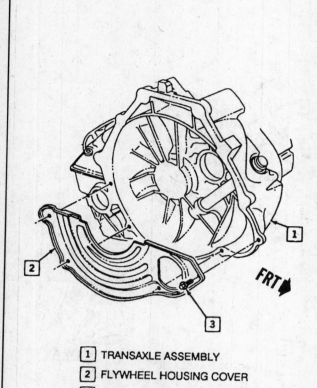

1 TRANSAXLE ASSEMBLY
2 FLYWHEEL HOUSING COVER
3 BOLT - 13 N.m (115 LBS. FT.)

86887020

Fig. 14 Position the flywheel cover, then fasten using the retaining bolts

12. Unfasten the rear transaxle-to-engine bolts.

13. Lower the engine with the engine support fixture at least 30 revolutions (keep count) to ease removal and installation of the transaxle.

14. Raise and safely support the vehicle. Properly drain the transaxle.

15. Remove the front wheel and tire assemblies. Detach the left front inner splash shield.

16. Detach both from ABS wheel speed sensor harness connectors, then unroute the left side harness.

17. Unfasten the flywheel housing cover bolts, then remove the cover.

18. Disconnect the vehicle speed sensor at the transaxle.

19. Unfasten the left and right ball joint nuts, then separate the ball joints.

20. Remove the stabilizer link pin. Unfasten the left side U-bolt from the stabilizer bar.

21. Unfasten the left suspension support attaching bolts.

❊❊CAUTION

Drive axle boot protector J 34754 or equivalent should be modified and installed on any drive axle before service procedures on or near the drive axle. Failure to do this may result in boot damage and possible joint failure.

22. Remove the drive axles from the transaxle.

23. Remove the front lower transaxle mount.

24. Attach the transaxle case to a suitable support jack.

25. Disconnect the negative battery cable from the transaxle.

26. Unfasten the transaxle-to-engine bolts, then carefully slide the transaxle away from the engine and lower the jack.

To install:

27. Position the transaxle. Secure with the transaxle-to-engine mounting bolts and tighten to 55 ft. lbs. (75 Nm).

28. Install the front transaxle mount.

29. Install the flywheel housing cover, then secure with the bolts. Tighten the bolts to 89 inch lbs. (10 Nm).

30. Connect the drive axles to the transaxle.

31. Install the left suspension support and retaining bolts.

32. Fasten the left U-bolt to the stabilizer bar.

33. Connect the left and right ball joint nuts.

34. Install the left side stabilizer link nuts.

35. Route the left side ABS wheel speed sensor wiring harness and attach both front harnesses to the sensor.

36. Fasten the inner splash shield.

37. Install the wheel and tire assembly. Connect the vehicle speed sensor at the transaxle.

38. Carefully lower the vehicle, then final tighten the wheel lug nuts to 100 ft. lbs. (140 Nm).

39. Connect the ground cables at the transaxle mounting studs.

40. Fasten the transaxle vent tube.

41. Attach the back-up light switch connector.

42. Secure the upper transaxle-to-engine bolts. Tighten to 55 ft. lbs. (75 Nm).

43. Connect the clutch master cylinder to the clutch actuator (slave) cylinder.

44. Install the rear transaxle mount.

45. Attach the wire harness at the mount bracket.

46. Remove the engine support fixture.

47. Install the shift cables, clamp and nut. Tighten the clamp nut to 89 inch lbs. (10 Nm).

48. Fasten the clutch master cylinder pushrod to the clutch pedal.

49. Install the left sound panel/insulator.

50. Fill the transaxle with the proper quantity of manual transaxle fluid (part number 12345349 or equivalent).

51. Connect the negative battery cable.

2.5L Engines

▶ See Figures 15, 16 and 17

1. Disconnect the negative battery cable.

2. Install the engine support fixture tool J-28467 or equivalent. Raise the engine enough to take pressure off the motor mounts.

3. Remove the left sound panel/insulator.

4. Remove the clutch master cylinder pushrod from the clutch pedal.

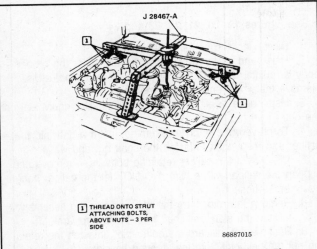

Fig. 15 Engine support fixture installed on the 2.5L engine

5. Remove the clutch slave (actuator) cylinder from the transaxle support bracket, then lay it aside.

6. Disconnect the wire harness at the mount bracket.

7. Unfasten the transaxle mount attaching bolts, then remove the mount bracket bolts and nuts and remove the bracket.

8. Detach the shift cables and the retaining clamp at the transaxle.

9. Remove the ground cables at the transaxle mounting studs.

10. Detach the back-up switch connector.

11. Raise and safely support the vehicle. Properly drain the transaxle.

12. Remove the left front wheel and tire assemblies. Detach the left inner splash shield.

13. Remove the transaxle front strut and strut bracket.

14. Unfasten the clutch (flywheel) cover housing bolts, then remove the cover.

15. Disconnect the vehicle speed sensor at the transaxle.

16. Remove the stabilizer shaft from the left suspension support and left control arm.

17. Unfasten the left suspension support retaining bolts, then swing it aside.

❊❊WARNING

Drive axle boot protector J 34754 or equivalent should be modified and installed on any drive axle before service procedures on or near the drive axle. Failure to do this may result in boot damage and possible joint failure.

18. Detach the drive axles from the transaxle, then remove the left shaft from the transaxle.

19. Attach the transaxle case to a suitable support jack.

20. Disconnect the negative battery cable from the transaxle.

21. Unfasten the transaxle-to-engine bolts, then carefully slide it away from the engine and lower the jack while guiding the right drive axle out of the transaxle.

To install:

22. Position the transaxle. Guide the right drive axle into its bore at the transaxle is being raised. The right drive axle CAN

NOT be readily installed after the transaxle is connected to the engine. Secure with the transaxle-to-engine mounting bolts and tighten to 55 ft. lbs. (75 Nm).

23. Install the left drive axle into its bore at the transaxle, then seat both drive axles at the transaxle.

24. Remove boot protector J 34754.

25. Fasten the suspension support-to-body bolts. Connect the stabilizer shaft to the suspension support and control arm.

26. Connect the vehicle speed sensor at the transaxle.

27. Install the clutch (flywheel) cover, then secure using the retaining bolts. Tighten the bolts to 115 inch lbs. (13 Nm).

28. Fasten the front strut bracket to the transaxle, then install the front strut.

29. Fasten the inner splash shield.

30. Install the wheel and tire assembly.

31. Carefully lower the vehicle, then final tighten the wheel lug nuts to 100 ft. lbs. (140 Nm).

32. Attach the back-up light switch connector.

33. Connect the shift cables.

34. Install the clutch slave (actuator) cylinder to the transaxle bracket aligning the pushrod into the pocket of the clutch re-

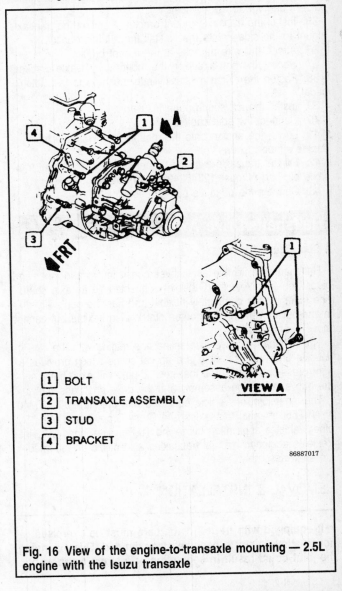

1. BOLT
2. TRANSAXLE ASSEMBLY
3. STUD
4. BRACKET

Fig. 16 View of the engine-to-transaxle mounting — 2.5L engine with the Isuzu transaxle

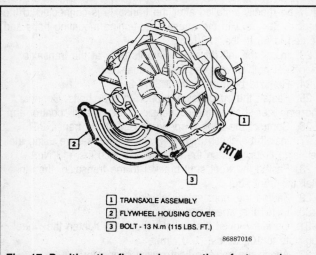

[1] TRANSAXLE ASSEMBLY
[2] FLYWHEEL HOUSING COVER
[3] BOLT - 13 N.m (115 LBS. FT.)

86887016

Fig. 17 Position the flywheel cover, then fasten using the retaining bolts

lease lever, then install the retaining nuts and tighten evenly to prevent damage to the cylinder.

35. Install the transaxle mount bracket. Position the transaxle mount to the side frame, then install the retaining bolts.

36. Attach the wire harness at the mount bracket.

37. Secure the bolt attaching the mount-to-transaxle bracket.

38. Fasten the clutch master cylinder pushrod to the clutch pedal.

39. Install the left sound panel/insulator.

40. Connect the shift cables.

41. Lower the engine onto the mounts, then remove the engine support fixture.

42. Fill the transaxle with the proper quantity of manual transaxle oil, part number 12345349 or equivalent.

43. Connect the negative battery cable.

Halfshafts/Drive Axles

▶ **See Figure 18**

Halfshafts are flexible assemblies consisting of and inner and outer Constant Velocity (CV) joint connected by an axle shaft. The inner joint is completely flexible and has the capability of in-and-out movement. The outer joint is also flexible but cannot move in-and-out.

The halfshaft or drive axle spline end mating with the knuckle and hub assembly is a helical spline which provides a tight press-fit and assures that no end-play will exist between the hub and bearing assembly and the drive shaft assembly.

The inner joint on vehicle equipped with the HM-282, 5TM40 or NVT550 manual transaxles is a Cross-Groove type. All other vehicles application utilize the Tri-Pot type inner CV joint. Vehicles equipped manual transaxles also utilize an intermediate shaft assembly.

REMOVAL & INSTALLATION

➡**If equipped with tri-pot joints, care must be exercised not to allow joints to become overextended. Overextending the joint could result in separation of internal components.**

1985-88 Vehicles

▶ **See Figures 19, 20, 21, 22, 23 and 24**

1. Disconnect the negative battery cable.

2. Raise and safely support the vehicle under the proper body lift points. Do NOT support under lower control arms. Remove the wheel and tire assemblies.

3. Install drive axle boot protector J 34754 or equivalent on the outer joint.

4. To prevent the rotor from turning, insert a drift into the caliper and rotor, then unfasten the shaft nut and washer.

5. Disconnect the caliper retaining bolts, then remove and support the caliper with a wire; DO NOT let the caliper hang by its brake hose.

6. Remove the rotor from the hub and bearing assembly.

7. Detach the stabilizer shaft from the control arm.

8. Remove and discard the cotter pin, unfasten the retaining nut the ball joint from the steering knuckle.

9. Pry the halfshaft from the transaxle or intermediate shaft.

10. Using tool J 28733 or suitable halfshaft pressing tool, remove the halfshaft/drive axle from the hub and bearing assembly, by pressing the halfshaft in and away from hub. The halfshaft should only be pressed in until the press fit between the halfshaft and hub is loose.

11. To remove the intermediate shaft on manual transaxles:

   a. Remove the detonation sensor.

   b. Remove the power steering pump brace.

   c. Remove the intermediate shaft bracket bolts and remove the assembly.

To install:

12. Install the intermediate shaft, if removed. Tighten the bracket bolts to 35 ft. lbs. (47 Nm).

13. Install halfshaft seal boot protectors on all tri-pot inner joints with silicone boots.

14. Start splines of halfshaft into transaxle and push halfshaft until it snaps into place.

15. Start the splines by inserting halfshaft into the hub assembly.

16. Secure lower ball joint into the steering knuckle and install the attaching nut. Install a new cotter pin.

17. Install the rotor and caliper.

18. Secure the washer and hub nut, tighten to 191 ft. lbs. (260 Nm).

19. Install stabilizer bar bushing assembly to lower control arm and tighten to 13 ft. lbs. (18 Nm).

20. Remove halfshaft seal boot protector.

21. Install the wheel and tire assemblies.

22. Carefully lower the vehicle.

23. Connect the negative battery cable and check for proper operation.

1989-95 Vehicles

▶ **See Figure 25**

1. Disconnect the negative battery cable.

2. Raise and safely support the vehicle.

3. Remove the wheel and tire assemblies.

4. Install a suitable halfshaft seal protector on the outer joint or place shop towels under the outer joint to protect the joint from any sharp edges.

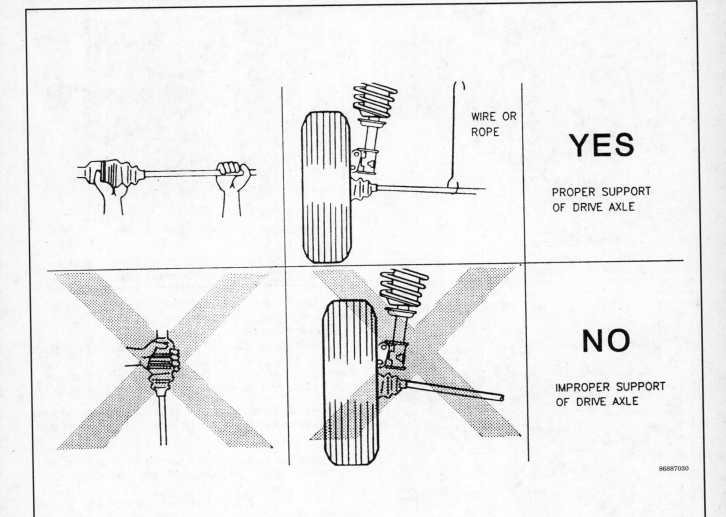

WIRE OR ROPE

YES

PROPER SUPPORT OF DRIVE AXLE

NO

IMPROPER SUPPORT OF DRIVE AXLE

86887030

Fig. 18 Always handle the drive axle/halfshaft assembly properly to avoid damage

86887021

Fig. 19 Insert a brass drift to prevent the rotor from turning and remove the shaft nut

86887023

Fig. 20 Using needle-nose pliers, remove and discard the ball joint cotter pin

Fig. 21 Unfasten the retaining nut

Fig. 22 Use a suitable tool to carefully pry the halfshaft from the transaxle

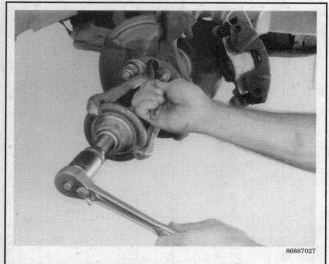

Fig. 23 Press the halfshaft out of the hub

Fig. 24 Once the halfshaft is loose, pull the knuckle away and remove the joint from the hub

5. Insert a drift into the caliper and rotor to prevent the rotor from turning, then unfasten the shaft nut and washer. Discard the shaft nut.

6. Remove the lower ball joint cotter pin and attaching nut, then using toll J 38892 or equivalent, loosen the joint. If removing the right axle, turn the wheel to the left. If removing the left axle, turn the wheel to the right. Discard the cotter pin.

➡**To avoid damage to the ball joint and seal, use only the recommended tools for separating the ball joint from the knuckle.**

7. Separate the joint using a suitable prybar between the suspension support and lower control arm. Remove the stabilizer shaft, if necessary.

8. For vehicles through 1990, pull out on the lower steering knuckle area. Using a plastic or rubber mallet, strike the end of the halfshaft to disengage it from the hub and bearing assembly. The shaft nut can be partially installed to protect the threads.

9. For 1991-95 vehicles, use tool J 28733-A or equivalent, to disengage the halfshaft/axle from the hub and bearing assembly.

10. Separate the halfshaft/drive axle from the hub and bearing assembly and move the strut assembly rearward.

11. Remove the inner joint from the transaxle using tools J 28468 or J 33008, or equivalent, attached to tools J 29794 and J 2619-01, or equivalent, for intermediate shaft (if equipped).

12. To remove the intermediate shaft, remove the rear engine mount through-bolt. Then remove the intermediate shaft bracket bolts and remove the assembly.

To install:

13. Install the seal protector to the transaxle. Install the intermediate shaft, if removed. Tighten the bracket bolts to 35 ft. lbs. (47 Nm).

14. Drive the halfshaft into the transaxle or intermediate shaft by placing a non-iron drift or other suitable tool into the groove on the joint housing and tapping until seated. Be careful not to damage the axle seal or spring. Verify that the axle is seated by grasping the inner joint housing and pulling outboard.

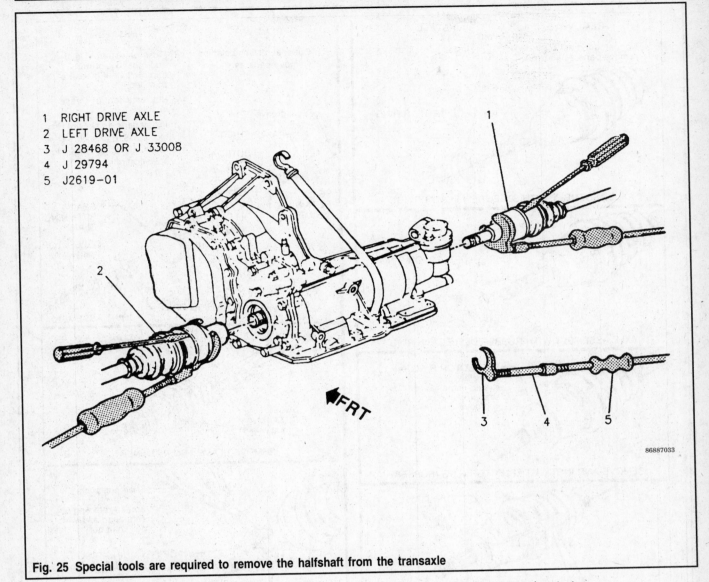

1 RIGHT DRIVE AXLE
2 LEFT DRIVE AXLE
3 J 28468 OR J 33008
4 J 29794
5 J2619—01

FRT

86887033

Fig. 25 Special tools are required to remove the halfshaft from the transaxle

15. Install the halfshaft/drive axle to the hub and bearing assembly.

➡**Do NOT loosen the steering knuckle nut at any time during installation.**

16. Connect the ball joint to the steering knuckle, then tighten the steering knuckle nut to 48-63 ft. lbs. (65-85 Nm) to install the cotter pin. Fasten a new cotter pin on the assembly. Install the stabilizer shaft, if removed.

17. Install the washer and a new drive shaft nut. Insert a drift to keep the rotor from turning, then tighten the nut to 185 ft. lbs. (260 Nm).

18. Remove the CV-joint seal protectors.
19. Install the wheels and tire assemblies.
20. Carefully lower the vehicle, then connect the negative battery cable.

CV-JOINT OVERHAUL

▶ **See Figures 26, 27, 28 and 29**

Please refer to the appropriate illustration for overhaul procedures.

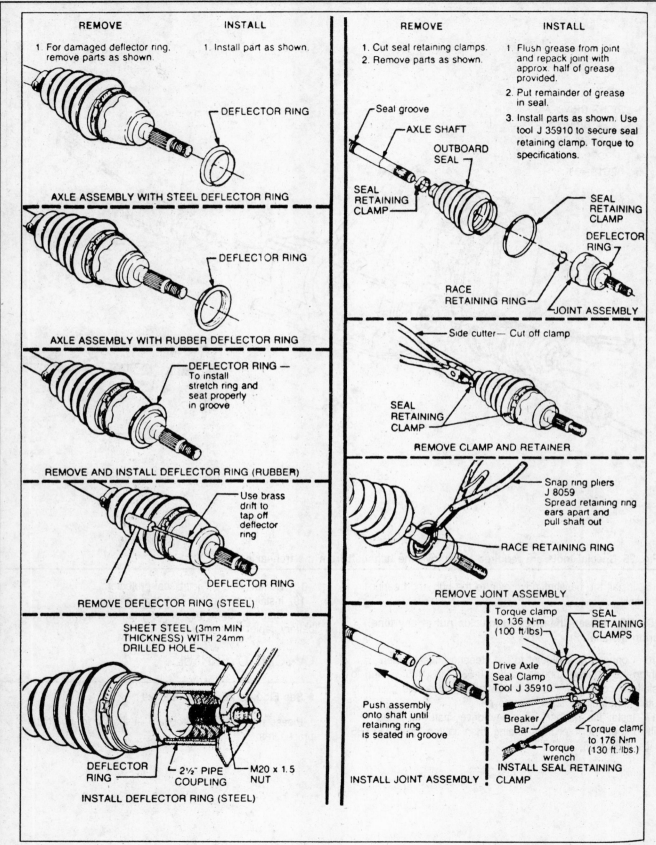

REMOVE

1. For damaged deflector ring, remove parts as shown.

INSTALL

1. Install part as shown.

DEFLECTOR RING

AXLE ASSEMBLY WITH STEEL DEFLECTOR RING

DEFLECTOR RING

AXLE ASSEMBLY WITH RUBBER DEFLECTOR RING

DEFLECTOR RING —
To install stretch ring and seat properly in groove

REMOVE AND INSTALL DEFLECTOR RING (RUBBER)

Use brass drift to tap off deflector ring

DEFLECTOR RING

REMOVE DEFLECTOR RING (STEEL)

SHEET STEEL (3mm MIN THICKNESS) WITH 24mm DRILLED HOLE

DEFLECTOR RING

2½" PIPE COUPLING

M20 x 1.5 NUT

INSTALL DEFLECTOR RING (STEEL)

REMOVE

1. Cut seal retaining clamps.
2. Remove parts as shown.

INSTALL

1. Flush grease from joint and repack joint with approx. half of grease provided.
2. Put remainder of grease in seal.
3. Install parts as shown. Use tool J 35910 to secure seal retaining clamp. Torque to specifications.

Seal groove

AXLE SHAFT

OUTBOARD SEAL

SEAL RETAINING CLAMP

SEAL RETAINING CLAMP

DEFLECTOR RING

RACE RETAINING RING

JOINT ASSEMBLY

Side cutter — Cut off clamp

SEAL RETAINING CLAMP

REMOVE CLAMP AND RETAINER

Snap ring pliers J 8059
Spread retaining ring ears apart and pull shaft out

RACE RETAINING RING

REMOVE JOINT ASSEMBLY

Push assembly onto shaft until retaining ring is seated in groove

INSTALL JOINT ASSEMBLY

Torque clamp to 136 N·m (100 ft./lbs)

SEAL RETAINING CLAMPS

Drive Axle Seal Clamp Tool J 35910

Breaker Bar

Torque wrench

Torque clamp to 176 N·m (130 ft./lbs.)

INSTALL SEAL RETAINING CLAMP

Fig. 26 Tri-pot halfshaft/drive axle unit repair

86887034

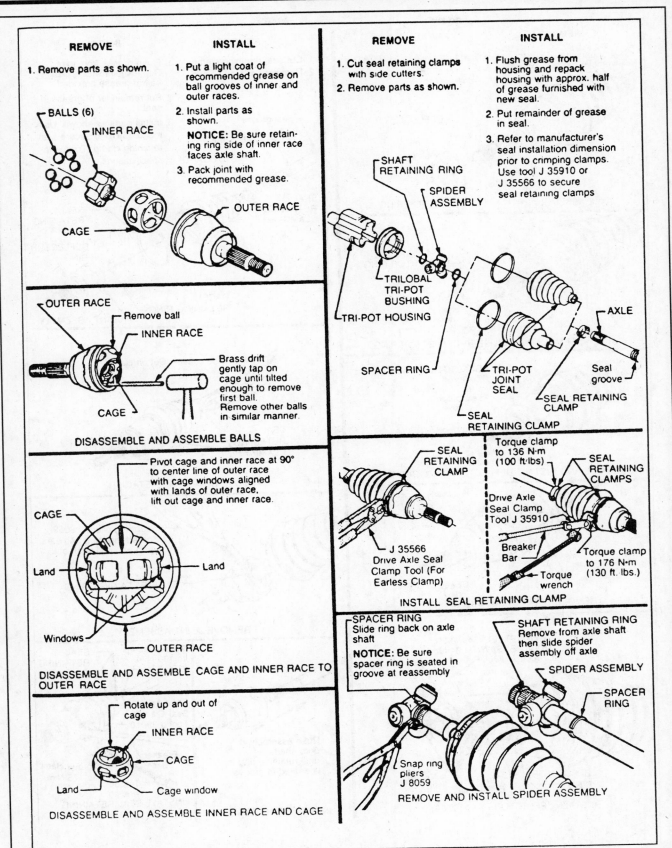

REMOVE

1. Remove parts as shown.

BALLS (6)

INNER RACE

CAGE

OUTER RACE

INSTALL

1. Put a light coat of recommended grease on ball grooves of inner and outer races.

2. Install parts as shown.

NOTICE: Be sure retaining ring side of inner race faces axle shaft.

3. Pack joint with recommended grease.

REMOVE

1. Cut seal retaining clamps with side cutters.

2. Remove parts as shown.

INSTALL

1. Flush grease from housing and repack housing with approx. half of grease furnished with new seal.

2. Put remainder of grease in seal.

3. Refer to manufacturer's seal installation dimension prior to crimping clamps. Use tool J 35910 or J 35566 to secure seal retaining clamps

SHAFT RETAINING RING

SPIDER ASSEMBLY

TRILOBAL TRI-POT BUSHING

TRI-POT HOUSING

SPACER RING

TRI-POT JOINT SEAL

SEAL RETAINING CLAMP

AXLE

Seal groove

SEAL RETAINING CLAMP

OUTER RACE

Remove ball

INNER RACE

CAGE

Brass drift gently tap on cage until tilted enough to remove first ball. Remove other balls in similar manner.

DISASSEMBLE AND ASSEMBLE BALLS

Pivot cage and inner race at 90° to center line of outer race with cage windows aligned with lands of outer race, lift out cage and inner race.

CAGE

Land

Land

Windows

OUTER RACE

DISASSEMBLE AND ASSEMBLE CAGE AND INNER RACE TO OUTER RACE

Rotate up and out of cage

INNER RACE

CAGE

Land

Cage window

DISASSEMBLE AND ASSEMBLE INNER RACE AND CAGE

SEAL RETAINING CLAMP

J 35566 Drive Axle Seal Clamp Tool (For Earless Clamp)

Torque clamp to 136 N·m (100 ft/lbs)

SEAL RETAINING CLAMPS

Drive Axle Seal Clamp Tool J 35910

Breaker Bar

Torque wrench

Torque clamp to 176 N·m (130 ft. lbs.)

INSTALL SEAL RETAINING CLAMP

SPACER RING Slide ring back on axle shaft

NOTICE: Be sure spacer ring is seated in groove at reassembly

SHAFT RETAINING RING Remove from axle shaft then slide spider assembly off axle

SPIDER ASSEMBLY

SPACER RING

Snap ring pliers J 8059

REMOVE AND INSTALL SPIDER ASSEMBLY

86887035

Fig. 27 Tri-pot halfshaft/drive axle unit repair

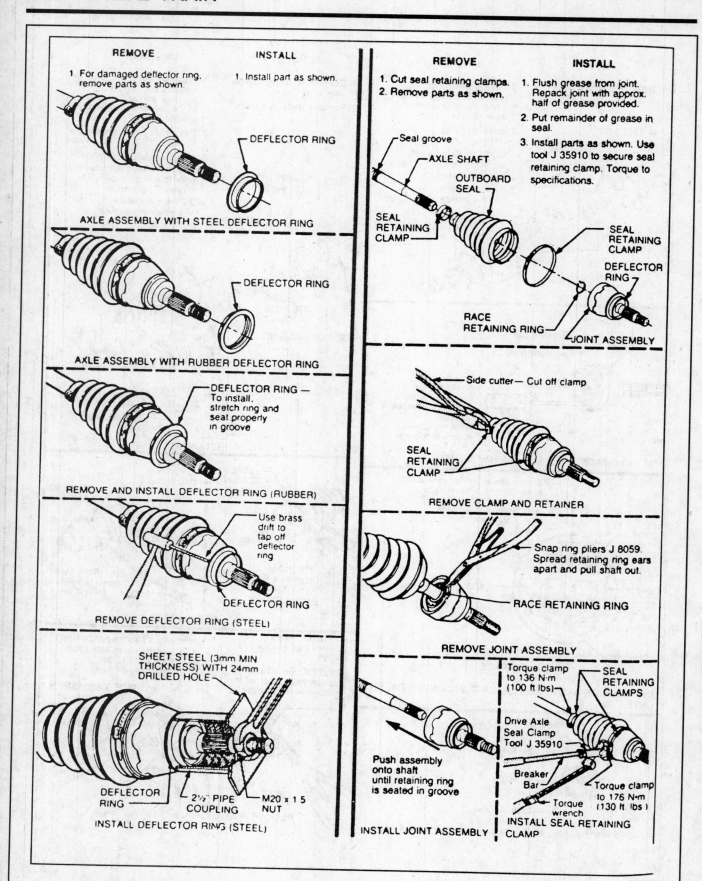

REMOVE

1. For damaged deflector ring, remove parts as shown.

INSTALL

1. Install part as shown.

DEFLECTOR RING

AXLE ASSEMBLY WITH STEEL DEFLECTOR RING

DEFLECTOR RING

AXLE ASSEMBLY WITH RUBBER DEFLECTOR RING

DEFLECTOR RING — To install, stretch ring and seat properly in groove

REMOVE AND INSTALL DEFLECTOR RING (RUBBER)

Use brass drift to tap off deflector ring

DEFLECTOR RING

REMOVE DEFLECTOR RING (STEEL)

SHEET STEEL (3mm MIN THICKNESS) WITH 24mm DRILLED HOLE

DEFLECTOR RING

2½" PIPE COUPLING

M20 x 1.5 NUT

INSTALL DEFLECTOR RING (STEEL)

REMOVE

1. Cut seal retaining clamps.
2. Remove parts as shown.

INSTALL

1. Flush grease from joint. Repack joint with approx. half of grease provided.
2. Put remainder of grease in seal.
3. Install parts as shown. Use tool J 35910 to secure seal retaining clamp. Torque to specifications.

Seal groove

AXLE SHAFT

OUTBOARD SEAL

SEAL RETAINING CLAMP

SEAL RETAINING CLAMP

DEFLECTOR RING

RACE RETAINING RING

JOINT ASSEMBLY

Side cutter — Cut off clamp

SEAL RETAINING CLAMP

REMOVE CLAMP AND RETAINER

Snap ring pliers J 8059. Spread retaining ring ears apart and pull shaft out.

RACE RETAINING RING

REMOVE JOINT ASSEMBLY

Torque clamp to 136 N·m (100 ft lbs)

SEAL RETAINING CLAMPS

Drive Axle Seal Clamp Tool J 35910

Push assembly onto shaft until retaining ring is seated in groove

Breaker Bar

Torque wrench

Torque clamp to 176 N·m (130 ft lbs)

INSTALL JOINT ASSEMBLY

INSTALL SEAL RETAINING CLAMP

Fig. 28 Cross-groove halfshaft/drive axle unit repair

86887036

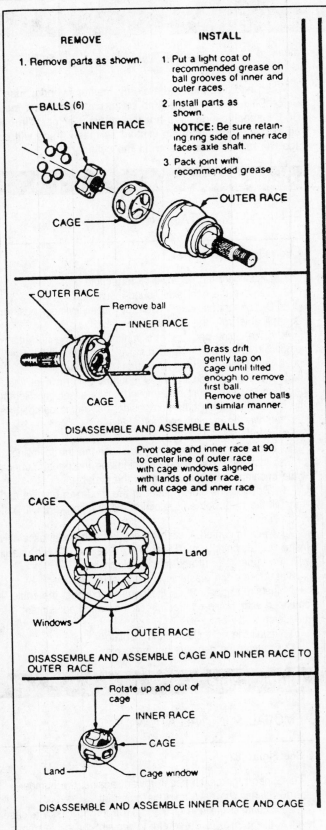

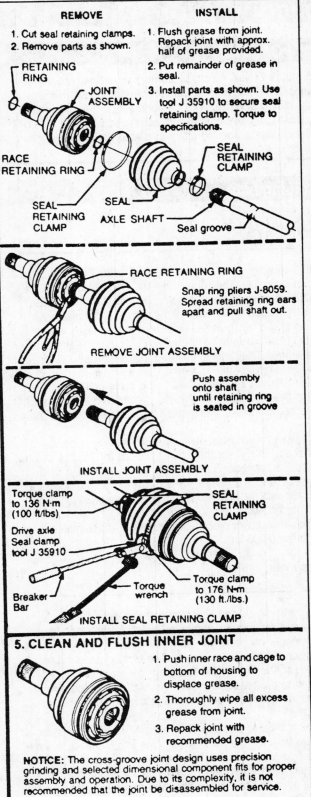

REMOVE

1. Remove parts as shown.

- BALLS (6)
- INNER RACE
- CAGE
- OUTER RACE

INSTALL

1. Put a light coat of recommended grease on ball grooves of inner and outer races.
2. Install parts as shown.

NOTICE: Be sure retaining ring side of inner race faces axle shaft.

3. Pack joint with recommended grease.

- OUTER RACE
- Remove ball
- INNER RACE
- Brass drift gently tap on cage until tilted enough to remove first ball. Remove other balls in similar manner.
- CAGE

DISASSEMBLE AND ASSEMBLE BALLS

- Pivot cage and inner race at 90 to center line of outer race with cage windows aligned with lands of outer race. lift out cage and inner race
- CAGE
- Land
- Land
- Windows
- OUTER RACE

DISASSEMBLE AND ASSEMBLE CAGE AND INNER RACE TO OUTER RACE

- Rotate up and out of cage
- INNER RACE
- CAGE
- Land
- Cage window

DISASSEMBLE AND ASSEMBLE INNER RACE AND CAGE

REMOVE

1. Cut seal retaining clamps.
2. Remove parts as shown.

- RETAINING RING
- JOINT ASSEMBLY
- RACE RETAINING RING
- SEAL RETAINING CLAMP
- SEAL
- AXLE SHAFT
- SEAL RETAINING CLAMP
- Seal groove

INSTALL

1. Flush grease from joint. Repack joint with approx. half of grease provided.
2. Put remainder of grease in seal.
3. Install parts as shown. Use tool J 35910 to secure seal retaining clamp. Torque to specifications.

RACE RETAINING RING

Snap ring pliers J-8059. Spread retaining ring ears apart and pull shaft out.

REMOVE JOINT ASSEMBLY

Push assembly onto shaft until retaining ring is seated in groove

INSTALL JOINT ASSEMBLY

- Torque clamp to 136 N·m (100 ft/lbs)
- Drive axle Seal clamp tool J 35910
- Breaker Bar
- Torque wrench
- SEAL RETAINING CLAMP
- Torque clamp to 176 N·m (130 ft./lbs.)

INSTALL SEAL RETAINING CLAMP

5. CLEAN AND FLUSH INNER JOINT

1. Push inner race and cage to bottom of housing to displace grease.
2. Thoroughly wipe all excess grease from joint.
3. Repack joint with recommended grease.

NOTICE: The cross-groove joint design uses precision grinding and selected dimensional component fits for proper assembly and operation. Due to its complexity, it is not recommended that the joint be disassembled for service.

86887037

Fig. 29 Cross-groove halfshaft/drive axle unit repair

CLUTCH

✳✳CAUTION

The clutch driven disc may contain asbestos, which has been determined to be a cancer causing agent. Never clean clutch surfaces with compressed air! Avoid inhaling any dust from any clutch surface! When cleaning clutch surfaces, use a commercially available brake cleaning fluid.

Adjustments

CLUTCH CABLE

The adjusting mechanism is mounted to the clutch pedal and bracket assembly. The cable is a fixed length and cannot be lengthened or shortened; however, the position of the cable can be changed by adjusting the position of the quadrant in relation to the clutch pedal. This mechanism makes adjustments in the quadrant position which changes the effective cable length. This is done by lifting the clutch pedal to disengage the pawl from the quadrant. The spring in the hub of the quadrant applies a tension load to the cable and keeps the release bearing in contact with the clutch levers. This results in a balanced condition, with the correct tension applied to the cable.

As the clutch friction material wears, the cable must be lengthened. This is accomplished by simply pulling the clutch pedal up to its rubber bumper. This action forces the pawl against its stop and rotates it out of mesh with the quadrant teeth, allowing the cable to play out until the quadrant spring load is balanced against the load applied by the release bearing. This adjustment procedure is required approximately every 5000 miles (8000 km).

HYDRAULIC CLUTCH

The hydraulic clutch release system consists of a clutch master cylinder with an integral or remote reservoir and a slave cylinder connected to the master cylinder by a hydraulic line, much like the brake system. The clutch master cylinder is mounted to the front of the dash and the slave cylinder is mounted to the transaxle support bracket. The clutch master cylinder is operated directly off the clutch pedal by the pushrod.

When the clutch pedal is depressed, hydraulic fluid under pressure from the master cylinder flows into the slave cylinder. As the hydraulic force reaches the slave cylinder, the pushrod movement rotates the clutch fork which forces the release bearing into the clutch diaphragm and disengages the clutch. The hydraulic clutch system provides automatic clutch adjust-

ment, so no periodic adjustment of the clutch linkage or pedal is required.

➡When adding fluid to the clutch master cylinder, use Delco Supreme 11 brake fluid or an equivalent that meets DOT 3 specifications. Do not use mineral or paraffin based oil in the clutch hydraulic system as these fluids will damage the rubber components in the cylinders.

Clutch Pedal

REMOVAL & INSTALLATION

▶ See Figures 30 and 31

1. Disconnect the negative battery cable.
2. Remove the right side sound insulator.
3. Disconnect the clutch cable or master cylinder pushrod, as applicable from the clutch pedal.
4. If the clutch pedal pivot is mounted using a nut and bolt, remove from the bracket and remove the clutch pedal. Remove the spacers and bushings from the pedal.
5. If the clutch pedal pivot is mounted using a rivet, the pedal and bracket must be removed as an assembly. Remove the bracket attaching nuts from inside the engine compartment and remove the bracket and pedal assembly.

   To install:
6. If mounted with a nut and bolt, perform the following;
   a. Install the spacer and bushings on the pedal. Lubricate the bushings before installing on the pedal.
   b. Position the clutch pedal to the mounting bracket and install the pivot bolt and retaining nut. Tighten to 23 ft. lbs. (31 Nm).
7. If rivet mounted, install the bracket and pedal assembly. Install the attaching nuts. Tighten to 16 ft. lbs. (22 Nm) starting with the upper left nut and moving clockwise.
8. Lubricate the master cylinder pushrod bushing
9. Install the pushrod on the pedal or connect the cable. If equipped with cruise control, check the switch adjustment at the clutch pedal bracket.
10. Install the right side sound insulator.
11. Connect the negative battery cable.

Clutch Cable

REMOVAL & INSTALLATION

▶ See Figure 32

1. Support the clutch pedal upward against the bumper stop to release the pawl from the quadrant.
2. Disconnect the end of the cable from the clutch release lever at the transaxle. Be careful to prevent the cable from snapping toward the rear of the car. The quadrant in the adjusting mechanism can be damaged by allowing the cable to snap back.

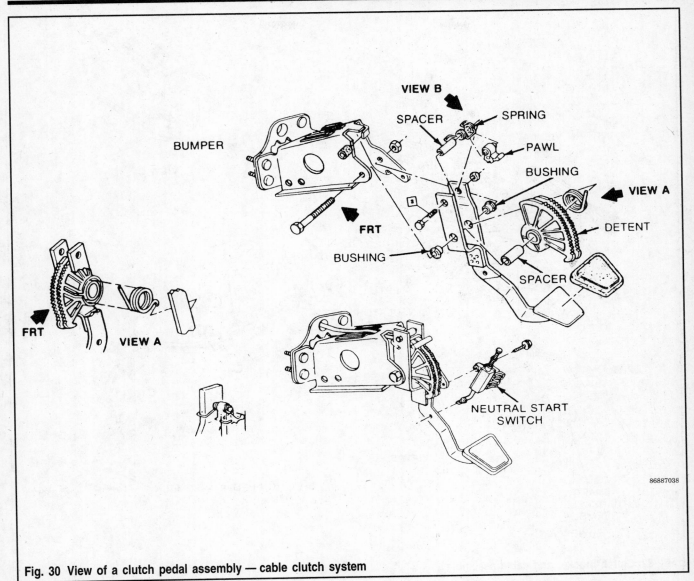

Fig. 30 View of a clutch pedal assembly — cable clutch system

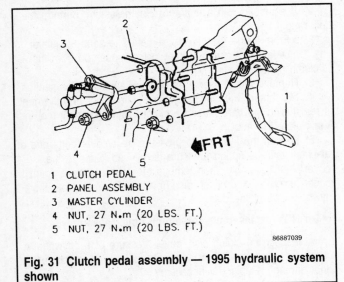

1 CLUTCH PEDAL
2 PANEL ASSEMBLY
3 MASTER CYLINDER
4 NUT, 27 N•m (20 LBS. FT.)
5 NUT, 27 N•m (20 LBS. FT.)

86887039

Fig. 31 Clutch pedal assembly — 1995 hydraulic system shown

3. From inside the car, remove the hush panel.

4. Disconnect the clutch cable from the quadrant. Lift the locking pawl away from the quadrant, then slide the cable out on the right side of the quadrant.

5. If necessary for access in the engine compartment, remove the windshield washer bottle.

6. From the engine side of the cowl, disconnect the two upper nuts holding the cable retainer to the upper studs. Disconnect the cable from the bracket mounted to the transaxle and remove the cable.

7. Inspect the clutch cable from signs of fraying, kinks, worn ends or excessive cable friction. Replace the cable if any of these problems are noted.

To install:

8. Place the gasket into position on the two upper studs, then position the cable with the retaining flange against the bracket.

9. Attach the end of the cable to the quadrant, being sure to route the cable underneath the pawl. Attach the 2 upper nuts to the retainer mounting studs and tighten.

10. Attach the cable to the bracket mounted to the transaxle.

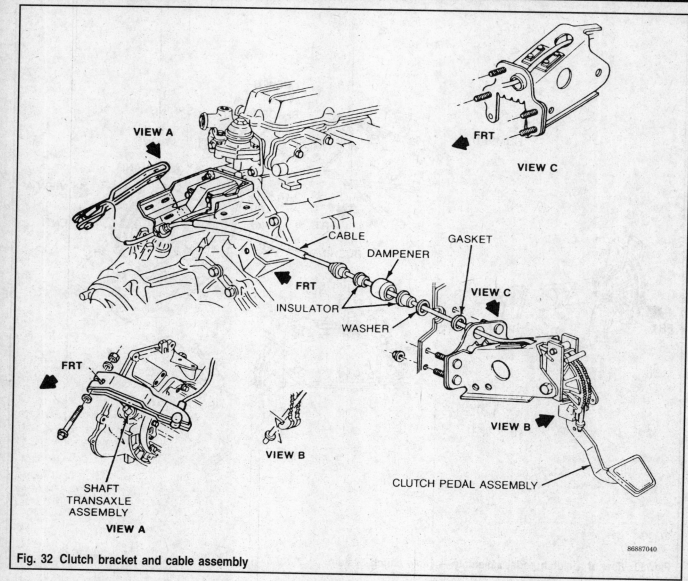

VIEW A

FRT

VIEW C

CABLE

DAMPENER

GASKET

VIEW C

INSULATOR

WASHER

FRT

VIEW B

FRT

VIEW B

CLUTCH PEDAL ASSEMBLY

SHAFT
TRANSAXLE
ASSEMBLY

VIEW A

86887040

Fig. 32 Clutch bracket and cable assembly

11. Install the windshield washer bottle.

12. Support the clutch pedal upward against the bumper to release the pawl from the quadrant. Attach the outer end of the cable to the clutch release lever.

➡ **Be sure NOT to yank on the cable, since overloading the cable could damage the quadrant.**

13. Check clutch operation and adjust by lifting the clutch pedal up to allow the mechanism to adjust the cable length. Depress the pedal slowly several times to set the pawl into mesh with the quadrant teeth.

Driven Disc and Pressure Plate

REMOVAL & INSTALLATION

▶ **See Figures 33 and 34**

1. Disconnect the negative battery cable.

2. If equipped with a hydraulic clutch system, perform the following:

   a. From inside the vehicle, remove the sound insulator.

   b. Detach the clutch master cylinder pushrod from the clutch pedal.

3. Remove the transaxle as outlined earlier in this section.

4. Matchmark the clutch/pressure plate cover and flywheel, if reinstalling old parts. Insert a clutch plate alignment tool into the clutch disc hub.

5. Loosen the flywheel to pressure plate/cover bolts one at at time, until the spring pressure is relieved. Support the cover/plate assembly, then remove the pressure plate/clutch cover assembly and clutch disc from the flywheel. Note the flywheel side of the disc.

➡ **Do NOT disassemble the clutch cover assembly.**

6. Inspect the clutch disc, cover/pressure plate, flywheel, clutch fork, and pivot shaft assembly for scoring, cracks or heat damage. Replace if necessary.

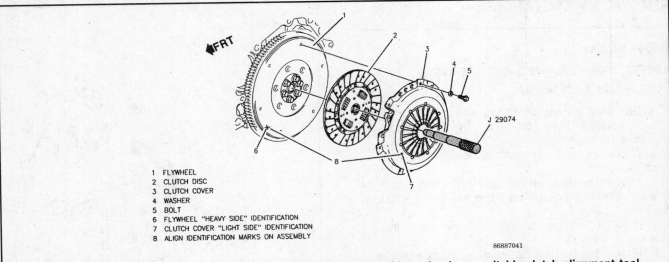

1 FLYWHEEL
2 CLUTCH DISC
3 CLUTCH COVER
4 WASHER
5 BOLT
6 FLYWHEEL "HEAVY SIDE" IDENTIFICATION
7 CLUTCH COVER "LIGHT SIDE" IDENTIFICATION
8 ALIGN IDENTIFICATION MARKS ON ASSEMBLY

86887041

Fig. 33 Exploded view of the clutch disc, cover (pressure plate) assembly and using a suitable clutch alignment tool

To install:

7. Sparingly apply anti-seize compound to the input shaft and clutch disc splines. Install a new release bearing.

8. Align the "heavy side" of the flywheel assembly, stamped with an "X", with the clutch cover "light side" marked with paint. Support with clutch alignment arbor tool J 29074 or equivalent. The clutch disc is installed with the damper springs offset towards the transaxle. There should be stamped letters on the clutch disc to identify the flywheel side.

9. Tighten the pressure plate/clutch-to-flywheel mounting bolts, in the sequence shown in the accompanying figure, gradually and evenly to 12-18 ft. lbs. (16-24 Nm).

10. Remove the clutch alignment tool.

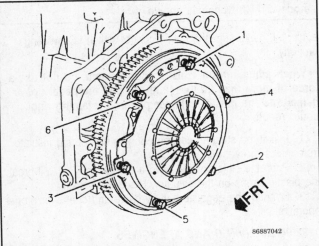

Fig. 34 Proper clutch cover bolt/pressure plate tightening sequence

86887042

11. Lightly lubricate the clutch fork ends which contact the bearing with chassis grease 1051344 or equivalent.

a. On vehicles equipped with Isuzu transaxles, pack the inside diameter recess of the release bearing completely full with chassis grease part no. 1051344 or equivalent.

b. On all other manual transaxle applications, lubricate the inside diameter of the bearing with clutch bearing lubricant part no. 12345777 or equivalent.

➡**On the Isuzu transaxle, make sure the bearing pads are located on the fork ends (pads must be indexed) and both spring ends are in the fork holes with the spring completely seated in the bearing groove.**

12. To avoid transaxle damage, the clutch lever must not be moved toward the flywheel until the transaxle is bolted to the engine.

13. Install the transaxle as outlined earlier in this section.

14. Attach the clutch master cylinder pushrod to the clutch pedal, then secure with the retaining clip. If equipped with cruise control, check the switch adjustment at the clutch pedal bracket.

➡**When adjusting the cruise control switch, do not exert an upward force on the clutch pedal pad of more than 20 lbs. (9 kg) or damage to the master cylinder pushrod retaining ring can result.**

15. Install the sound insulator.

16. Connect the negative battery cable and check the clutch and reverse lights for proper operation.

Clutch Master and Slave Cylinder Assembly

For some early model vehicles, the master cylinder and slave cylinders are removed from the vehicle as an assembly. For later model vehicles, there is a separate removal and installation procedure for each component.

REMOVAL & INSTALLATION

1985-94 Vehicles

EXCEPT 1992-94 2.3L (VIN D AND A) ENGINES

▶ **See Figures 35, 36 and 37**

1. Disconnect the negative battery cable.
2. Remove the steering column opening filler/sound insulator from inside the vehicle.
3. Disconnect the clutch master cylinder pushrod from the clutch pedal.
4. Remove the clutch master cylinder attaching nuts at the front of the dash and disconnect the remote fluid reservoir, if equipped.
5. Unfasten the actuator cylinder attaching nuts at the transaxle.
6. Remove the hydraulic system assembly as a unit from the vehicle.

To install:

7. Bleed the system, if necessary.
8. Install the actuator cylinder to the transaxle, aligning the pushrod into the pocket on the lever. Tighten the attaching nuts evenly to 16 ft. lbs. (22 Nm) to prevent damage.

➡**New actuators are packaged with plastic straps to retain the pushrod. Do not break the strap off; it will break upon the first clutch application.**

9. Install the master cylinder to the front of the dash. Tighten the attaching nuts to 15 ft. lbs. (21 Nm) evenly to prevent damage. Connect the remote fluid reservoir, if equipped. If equipped with a bleed screw, bleed the system.
10. Remove the pushrod restrictor from the master cylinder pushrod. Lubricate the bushing on the clutch pedal. Connect the pushrod to the pedal and install the retaining clip. If

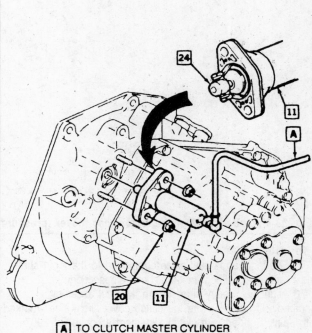

A TO CLUTCH MASTER CYLINDER

11 CLUTCH MASTER AND ACTUATOR CYLINDER ASSEMBLY

20 NUT

24 PUSHROD RETAINER (DO NOT REMOVE)

86887044

Fig. 36 View of the clutch actuator (slave cylinder) — model 5TM40 transaxle shown

equipped, make sure the cruise control switch is operating properly.

➡**When adjusting the cruise control switch, do not use a force of more than 20 lbs. (9 kg) to pull the pedal up, or damage to the master cylinder pushrod retaining ring could result.**

11. Install the steering column opening filler/sound insulator from inside the vehicle.
12. Push the clutch pedal down a few times. This will break the plastic straps on the actuator. Bleed the system.
13. Connect the negative battery cable and check for proper operation.

1992-94 2.3L (VIN D AND A) ENGINES

▶ **See Figures 38 and 39**

1. Remove the air intake duct from the air cleaner.
2. Disconnect the negative, then the positive battery cables.
3. Remove the left fender brace.
4. Unfasten the battery hold-down clamp bolt, then remove the battery.

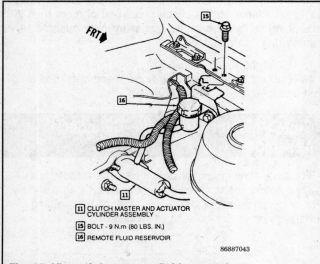

11 CLUTCH MASTER AND ACTUATOR CYLINDER ASSEMBLY

15 BOLT - 9 N.m (80 LBS. IN.)

16 REMOTE FLUID RESERVOIR

86887043

Fig. 35 View of the remote fluid reservoir

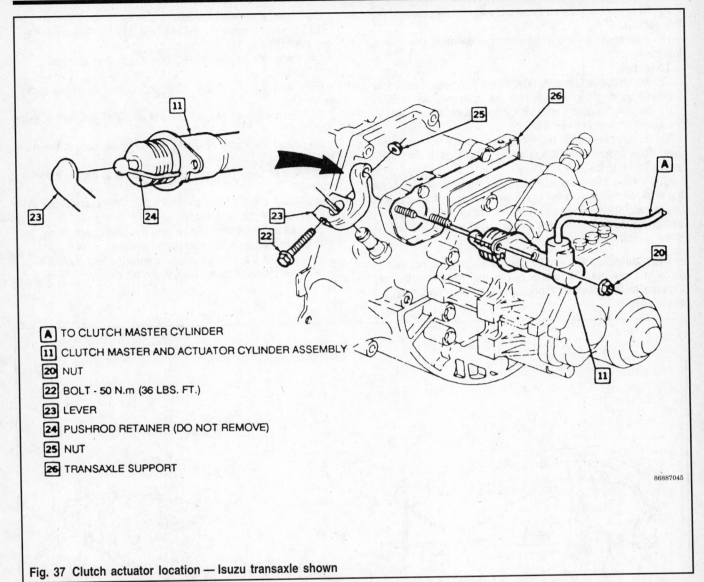

A TO CLUTCH MASTER CYLINDER

11 CLUTCH MASTER AND ACTUATOR CYLINDER ASSEMBLY

20 NUT

22 BOLT - 50 N.m (36 LBS. FT.)

23 LEVER

24 PUSHROD RETAINER (DO NOT REMOVE)

25 NUT

26 TRANSAXLE SUPPORT

86887045

Fig. 37 Clutch actuator location — Isuzu transaxle shown

5. Detach the Intake Air Temperature (IAT) sensor lead at the air cleaner.

6. Disconnect the Mass Air Flow (MAF) sensor lead.

7. Detach the PCV pipe retaining clamp from the air intake duct.

8. Unfasten the air cleaner bracket mounting bolts at the battery tray.

9. Remove the air cleaner, MAF sensor and air intake duct as an assembly.

10. Disconnect the electrical lead at the washer bottle, then unfasten the attaching bolts and remove the washer bottle.

11. If equipped, remove the cruise control mounting bracket retaining nuts from the strut tower.

12. From inside the vehicle, detach the sound insulator.

13. Disconnect the clutch master cylinder pushrod from the clutch pedal.

14. Unfasten the master cylinder retaining nuts at the front of the dash.

15. Detach the clutch actuator cylinder quick disconnect fitting from the clutch master cylinder line.

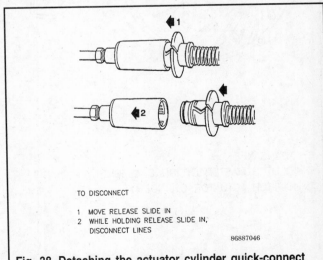

TO DISCONNECT

1 MOVE RELEASE SLIDE IN
2 WHILE HOLDING RELEASE SLIDE IN, DISCONNECT LINES

86887046

Fig. 38 Detaching the actuator cylinder quick-connect fitting from the clutch master cylinder line

16. Remove the transaxle assembly as outlined earlier in this section.

17. Disconnect the clutch actuator cylinder from the transaxle.

To install:

18. Attach the actuator cylinder to the transaxle. Install the transaxle assembly into the vehicle as outlined in this section.

19. Fasten the clutch actuator cylinder quick disconnect to the clutch master cylinder line.

20. Position the clutch master cylinder to the front of the dash, then secure using the retaining nuts. Tighten the nuts evenly to 15 ft. lbs. (21 Nm).

21. Remove the pedal restrictor from the pushrod. Lubricate the pushrod bearing on the clutch pedal. Connect the pushrod to the clutch pedal, then install the retaining clip. If equipped with cruise control, check the switch adjustment at the clutch pedal bracket.

➡**When adjusting the cruise control switch, do not use a force of more than 20 lbs. (9 kg) to pull the pedal up, or damage to the master cylinder pushrod retaining ring could result.**

22. Install the sound insulator.

23. Bleed the hydraulic system. For details, please refer to the procedure in this section.

24. Install the washer bottle, then attach the electrical connector.

25. Install the air cleaner, MAF sensor and air intake duct assembly.

26. Fasten the air cleaner bracket and MAF sensor mounting bolts.

27. Install the clamp retaining the air intake duct to the throttle body.

28. Fasten the PCV pipe retaining clamp to the air intake duct.

29. Attach the MAF sensor connector, then connect the IAT sensor lead at the air cleaner.

30. Install the battery, secure with the hold-down clamp. Install the left fender brace. Bleed the system.

31. Connect the positive, then negative battery cables.

32. Attach the air intake duct to the air cleaner.

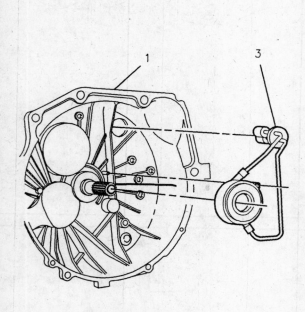
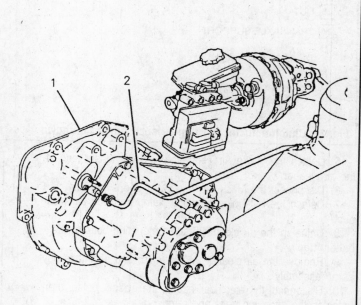

1 TRANSAXLE
2 CLUTCH MASTER CYLINDER ASSEMBLY
3 CLUTCH ACTUATOR CYLINDER

86887047

Fig. 39 After removing the transaxle, disconnect and remove the clutch actuator cylinder

1995 Vehicles

MASTER CYLINDER

▶ **See Figure 40**

1. Disconnect the negative battery cable.
2. From inside the vehicle, remove the sound insulator.
3. Disconnect the clutch master cylinder pushrod from the clutch pedal.
4. Unfasten the clutch master cylinder retaining nuts at the front of the dash.
5. Remove the remote fluid reservoir.
6. Detach the clutch master cylinder assembly from the actuator assembly, then remove from the vehicle.

To install:

7. Connect the master cylinder to the actuator cylinder assembly.
8. Install the remote fluid reservoir.
9. Fasten the master cylinder retaining nuts at the front of the dash. Tighten the nuts evenly to 18 ft. lbs. (25 Nm).
10. Connect the pushrod to the clutch pedal. If equipped, adjust the cruise control switch as outlined in Section 6.
11. Install the sound insulator.
12. Bleed the hydraulic system as outlined later in this section.
13. Connect the negative battery cable.

CLUTCH ACTUATOR (SLAVE) CYLINDER

1. Disconnect the negative battery cable.
2. Detach the master cylinder from the clutch actuator cylinder.
3. Remove the transaxle. For details, refer to the procedure located in this section.

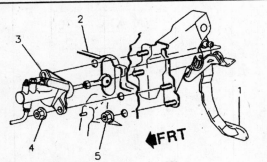

1 CLUTCH PEDAL
2 PANEL ASSEMBLY
3 MASTER CYLINDER
4 NUT, 27 N•m (20 LBS. FT.)
5 NUT, 27 N•m (20 LBS. FT.)

86887048

Fig. 40 Relation of the clutch master cylinder to the clutch pedal

4. Detach the actuator cylinder from the transaxle.

To install:

5. Lubricate the inside of the bearing with clutch bearing lubricant part. no. 12345777 or equivalent.
6. Install the actuator cylinder to the transaxle.
7. Install the transaxle as outlined earlier in this section.
8. Connect the master cylinder to the actuator cylinder.
9. Bleed the hydraulic system.
10. Connect the negative battery cable.

Hydraulic Clutch System Bleeding

WITH BLEED SCREW

1. Make sure the reservoir is full of DOT 3 fluid and is kept topped off throughout this procedure.
2. Loosen the bleed screw, located on the actuator cylinder body next to the inlet connection.
3. When a steady stream of fluid comes out the bleeder, tighten it to 17 inch lbs. (2 Nm).
4. Refill the fluid reservoir.
5. To check the system, start the engine and wait 10 seconds.
6. Depress the clutch pedal and shift into Reverse. If there is any gear clash, air may still be present.

WITHOUT BLEED SCREW

1. Remove the actuator cylinder from the transaxle.
2. Loosen the master cylinder attaching nuts to the ends of the studs.
3. Remove the reservoir cap and diaphragm.
4. Depress the actuator cylinder pushrod about ¾ in. (19mm) into its bore and hold the position.
5. Install the reservoir diaphragm and cap while holding the actuator pushrod.
6. Release the pushrod when the diaphragm and cap are properly installed.
7. With the actuator lower than the master cylinder, hold the actuator vertically with the pushrod end facing the ground.
8. Press the actuator pushrod into its bore with ½ in. (13mm) strokes. Check the reservoir for bubbles. Continue until no bubbles enter the reservoir.
9. Install the master cylinder and actuator.
10. Refill the fluid reservoir.
11. To check the system, start the engine and wait 10 seconds.
12. Depress the clutch pedal and shift into Reverse. If there is any gear clash, air may still be present.

AUTOMATIC TRANSAXLE

General Information

Vehicles through 1989 used the THM 125/125 C automatic transaxle. In 1990, the Hydra-matic 3T40 automatic transaxle was introduced. The 1993-95 vehicles either came equipped with the 3T40 or the optional 4T60-E Hydra-matic automatic transaxles. All transaxles should use Dexron® IIE or III transmission fluid.

Identification

▶ **See Figures 41, 42, 43 and 44**

All of the automatic transaxles covered by this manual should have a metal identification nameplate attached to the transaxle case exterior. Additional transaxle information is usually provided on the Service Parts Identification label. This label is affixed to the inside of each vehicle at the assembly plant.

Fluid Pan

▶ **See Figure 45**

REMOVAL & INSTALLATION

1. Raise and safely support the vehicle.
2. Place the drain pan under the transaxle fluid pan.

3. Remove the fluid pan bolts from the front and sides only.
4. Loosen, but do not remove the 4 bolts at the rear of the fluid pan.
5. Lightly tap the fluid pan with a rubber mallet or pry to allow the fluid to partially drain from the pan.

➡ **Do not damage the transaxle case or fluid pan sealing surfaces.**

6. Remove the remaining fluid pan bolts, fluid pan and gasket.
   To install:
7. Install a new gasket to the fluid pan.
8. Install the fluid pan to the transaxle.

➡ **Apply a suitable sealant compound to the bolt shown in the illustration to prevent fluid leaks.**

9. Install the pan bolts. Tighten to 133 inch lbs. (11 Nm).
10. Lower the vehicle.
11. Fill the transaxle to the proper level with Dexron® IIE or III fluid. Check cold level reading. Do not overfill.

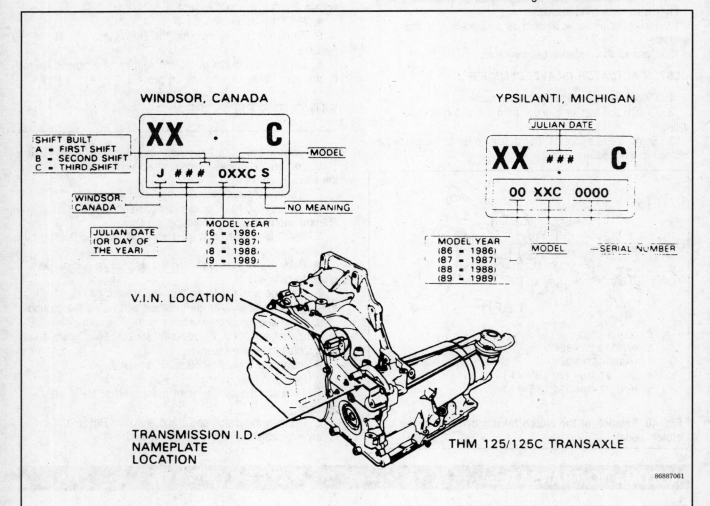

Fig. 41 Transaxle identification label location — 1985-89 vehicles equipped with the 125-C automatic transaxle

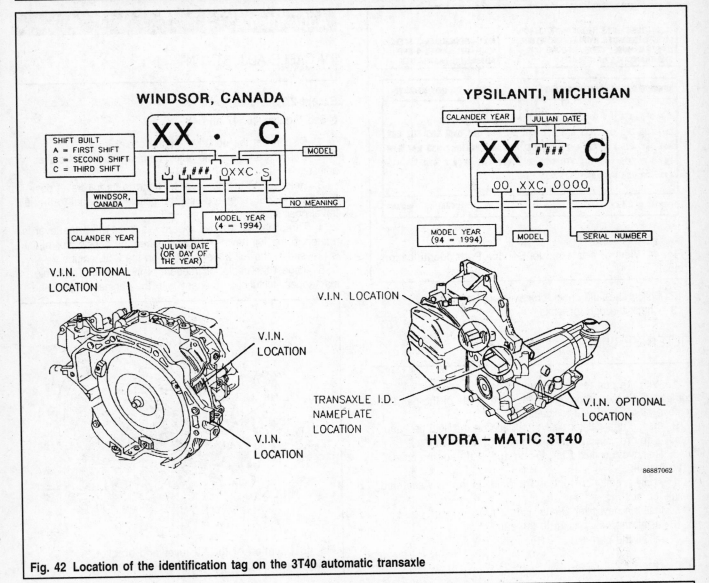

Fig. 42 Location of the identification tag on the 3T40 automatic transaxle

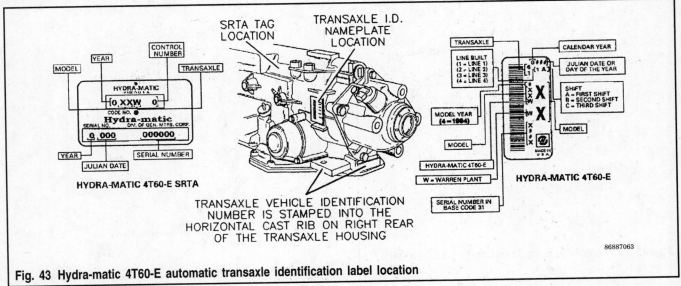

Fig. 43 Hydra-matic 4T60-E automatic transaxle identification label location

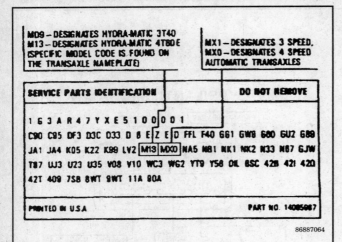

86887064

Fig. 44 View of a late model Service Parts Identification label

12. Follow the fluid check procedure in Section 1.
13. Check the pan for leaks.

FILTER SERVICE

1. With the pan removed from the vehicle and the fluid completely drained, thoroughly clean the inside of the pan to remove all old fluid and residue.
2. Inspect the gasket sealing surface on the fluid pan and remove any remaining gasket fragments with a scraper.
3. Remove the fluid filter, O-ring and seal from the case.
To install:
4. Apply a small amount of Transjel® to the new seal and install the seal.
5. Install a new filter O-ring and filter.
6. Install the new gasket to the pan.
7. Install the pan.

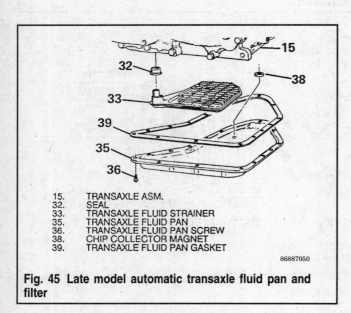

15.	TRANSAXLE ASM.
32.	SEAL
33.	TRANSAXLE FLUID STRAINER
35.	TRANSAXLE FLUID PAN
36.	TRANSAXLE FLUID PAN SCREW
38.	CHIP COLLECTOR MAGNET
39.	TRANSAXLE FLUID PAN GASKET

86887050

Fig. 45 Late model automatic transaxle fluid pan and filter

Adjustments

TV CABLE ADJUSTMENT

Except 2.3L Engine
♦ See Figures 46, 47 and 48

1. Disconnect the negative battery cable.
2. Depress and hold the adjustment tap at the TV cable adjuster.
3. Release the throttle lever by hand to its full travel position. On the 2.5L engine press, the accelerator pedal to the full travel position.
4. The slider must move toward the lever when the lever is rotated to the full travel position or when the accelerator pedal is pressed to the full travel position on the 2.5L engine.
5. Inspect the cable for freedom of movement. The cable may appear to function properly with the engine stopped and

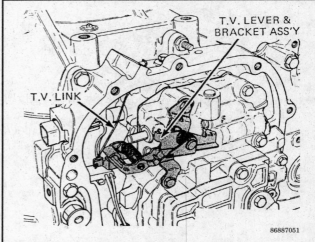

86887051

Fig. 46 Location of the TV lever and bracket assembly — 3.3L engine shown

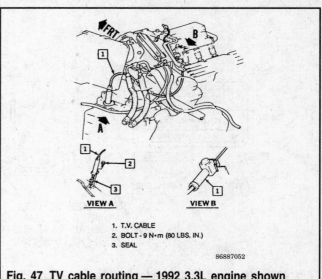

1. T.V. CABLE
2. BOLT - 9 N·m (80 LBS. IN.)
3. SEAL

86887052

Fig. 47 TV cable routing — 1992 3.3L engine shown

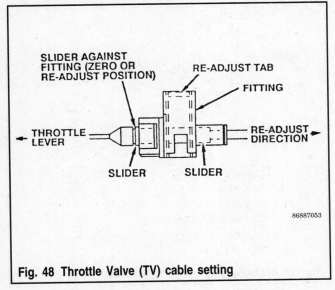

Fig. 48 Throttle Valve (TV) cable setting

cold, so recheck the cable after the engine is warm. Don't forget to connect the negative battery cable first.

6. Road test the vehicle and check for proper shifting.

2.3L Engine

▶ **See Figures 49 and 50**

1. Disconnect the negative battery cable.
2. Rotate the TV cable adjuster body at the transaxle 90° and pull the cable conduit out until the slider mechanism contacts the stop.
3. Rotate the adjuster body back to the original position.
4. Using a torque wrench, rotate the TV cable adjuster until 75-120 inch lbs. (9-14 Nm) is reached.
5. Connect the negative battery cable, then road test the vehicle and check for proper shifting.

SHIFT CABLE ADJUSTMENT

1. Place the selector in the N detent.
2. Raise the locking tab on the cable adjuster.
3. Place the shift control assembly on the transaxle in the neutral position.
4. Push the locking tab back into position.

Neutral Safety and Back-Up Switch

REMOVAL & INSTALLATION

▶ **See Figures 51 and 52**

1. Disconnect the negative battery cable.
2. Remove the shifter linkage.
3. Detach the switch electrical connector.
4. Unfasten the mounting bolts and remove the switch from the transaxle.

To install:

5. Place the shifter shaft in the N detent.
6. Align the flats of the shift shaft with those of the switch.

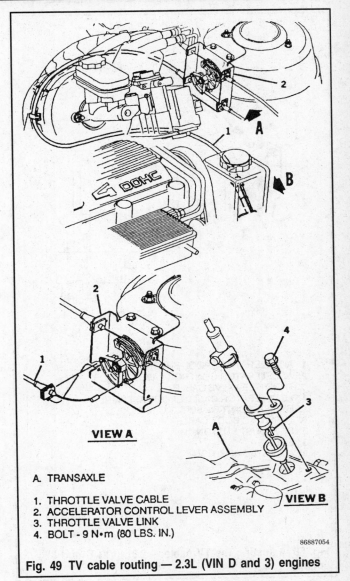

VIEW A

A. TRANSAXLE

1. THROTTLE VALVE CABLE
2. ACCELERATOR CONTROL LEVER ASSEMBLY
3. THROTTLE VALVE LINK
4. BOLT - 9 N·m (80 LBS. IN.)

VIEW B

Fig. 49 TV cable routing — 2.3L (VIN D and 3) engines

7. If replacing the switch, tighten the mounting bolts to 18 ft. lbs. (24 Nm) and remove the pre-installed alignment pin.

8. If reinstalling the old switch, install the mounting bolts loosely and adjust the switch as follows:

a. Insert a 3/32 in. (2.34mm) max diameter gauge pin in the service adjustment hole and rotate the switch until the pin drops in to a depth of 5/8 in. (9mm).

b. Tighten the mounting bolts to 18 ft. lbs. (24 Nm). Remove the gauge pin.

9. Connect the negative battery cable and check the switch for proper operation. The reverse lights should come on when the transaxle is shifted into R. If the engine can be started in any gear except P or N, readjust the switch.

ADJUSTMENT

1. Place the shifter in the N detent.
2. The switch is located on the shift shaft on the top of the automatic transaxle. Loosen the switch attaching bolts.

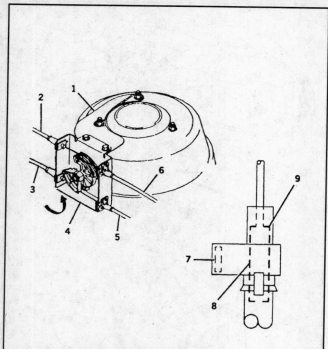

1. ACCELERATOR SPOOL BRACKET
2. ACCELERATOR CONTROL CABLE
3. THROTTLE VALVE CABLE
4. ACCELERATOR CABLE SPOOL ASSEMBLY
5. CRUISE CONTROL SERVO CABLE
6. THROTTLE BODY CABLE
7. RE-ADJUST BUTTON
8. SLIDER
9. ADJUSTED POSITION

86887055

Fig. 50 Adjusting the TV cable — 2.3L (VIN D and 3) engines

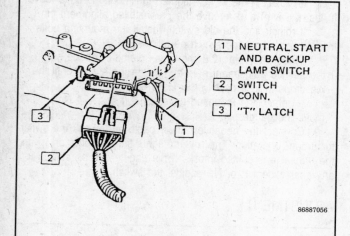

1	NEUTRAL START AND BACK-UP LAMP SWITCH
2	SWITCH CONN.
3	"T" LATCH

86887056

Fig. 51 Detach the "T" latch electrical connector from the switch

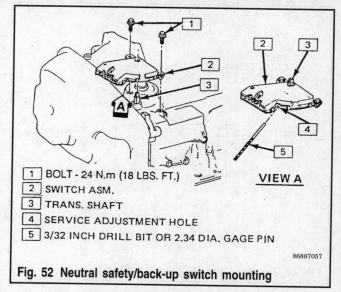

1	BOLT - 24 N.m (18 LBS. FT.)
2	SWITCH ASM.
3	TRANS. SHAFT
4	SERVICE ADJUSTMENT HOLE
5	3/32 INCH DRILL BIT OR 2.34 DIA. GAGE PIN

86887057

Fig. 52 Neutral safety/back-up switch mounting

3. Rotate the switch on the shifter assembly to align the service adjustment hole with the carrier tang hole.

4. Insert a $3/32$ in. (2.34mm) maximum diameter gauge pin into the hole to a depth of $5/8$ in. (9mm)

5. Tighten the mounting bolts and remove the pin.

Transaxle

REMOVAL & INSTALLATION

▶ **See Figures 53, 54 and 55**

1985-93 Vehicles

1. Disconnect the negative battery cable. If necessary, drain the coolant and disconnect the heater core hoses.

2. Remove the air cleaner assembly. If equipped with a 3.0L or 3.3L engine, remove the mass air flow sensor and air intake duct.

3. Disconnect the Throttle Valve (TV) cable from the throttle lever and the transaxle.

4. If equipped with a 2.3L engine, remove the power steering pump and bracket and position it aside.

5. Remove the transaxle dipstick and tube.

6. Install J 28468 or equivalent suitable engine support fixture. Insert a $1/4$ x 2 in. long bolt in the hole at the front right motor mount to maintain driveline alignment.

7. Remove the wiring harness-to-transaxle nut. Detach the wiring connectors from the speed sensor, TCC connector, neutral safety switch and reverse light switch.

8. Disconnect the shift linkage from the transaxle.

9. Remove the upper two transaxle-to-engine bolts and the upper left transaxle mount along with the bracket assembly.

10. Remove the rubber hose from the transaxle vent pipe. Remove the remaining upper engine-to-transaxle bolts.

11. Raise and safely support the vehicle. Remove both front wheel and tire assemblies.

12. If equipped with a 2.3L engine, remove both lower ball joints and stabilizer shafts links.

13. Drain the transaxle fluid.

14. Remove the shift linkage bracket from the transaxle.

✱✱CAUTION

On some vehicles, the sub-frame must be lowered for clearance. This means the intermediate shaft must be disconnected from the rack and pinion stub shaft. Failure to disconnect the intermediate shaft from the rack and pinion steering gear stub can result in damage to the steering gear and/or intermediate shaft. This damage can cause loss of steering control, which could result in an accident and possibly personal injury.

15. Install a halfshaft boot seal protector on the inner seals.

➡Some vehicles may use a gray silicone boot on the inboard axle joint. Use boot protector tool on these boots. All other boots are made from a black thermo-plastic material and do not require the use of a boot seal protector.

16. Remove both ball joint-to-control arm nuts, then separate the ball joints from the control arms.
17. Remove both halfshafts and support them with a cord or wire.
18. Unfasten and remove the transaxle mounting strut.
19. Remove the left stabilizer bar link pin bolt, left frame bushing clamp nuts and left frame support assembly.
20. Remove the torque converter cover. Matchmark the flexplate and torque converter for installation purposes. Remove the torque converter-to-flexplate bolts.
21. Disconnect and plug the transaxle oil cooler lines.
22. Remove the transaxle-to-engine support bracket, then install a suitable transaxle removal jack.
23. Unfasten the remaining transaxle-to-engine attaching bolts, then carefully remove the transaxle from the vehicle.

To install:
24. Securely mount the transaxle on the jack.
25. Apply a small amount of grease on the torque converter hub and seat in the oil pump.
26. Position the transaxle in the vehicle, then install the lower engine to transaxle bolts.
27. Install the transaxle to engine support bracket. Once the transaxle is securely held in place, remove the jack. Connect the cooler lines.
28. Install the torque converter bolts and tighten to specification.
29. Fasten the torque converter cover.
30. Install the left frame support assembly.
31. Fasten the left stabilizer shaft frame busing nuts and link pin bolt.
32. Install the transaxle mounting strut.
33. Install the halfshafts and the ball joints.

34. Position and secure the shift linkage bracket to the transaxle.
35. If equipped attach the ABS connectors. Install the inner splash shields.
36. Install the wheel and tire assemblies, then carefully lower the vehicle.
37. Fasten the upper transaxle to engine bolts.
38. Install the left side transaxle mount.
39. Connect the shift linkage to the transaxle.
40. Attach the wiring connectors to their switches on the transaxle.
41. Remove the 1/4 x 2 in. bolt that was placed in the hole at the front right motor mount to maintain driveline alignment. Remove an engine support tool.
42. Replace the O-ring, lubricate it and install the dipstick tube and dipstick.
43. Install the TV cable and rubber vent tube.
44. Install the air cleaner assembly and air tubes.
45. If detached, connect the heater hoses.
46. Fill all fluids to their proper levels. Adjust cables as required.
47. Connect the negative battery cable, then check the transaxle for proper operation and leaks.

1994-95 Vehicles

1. Disconnect the negative battery cable.
2. Remove the air intake duct.
3. Disconnect the Throttle Valve (TV) cable. Remove the shift cable and bracket.
4. Tag and disconnect the vacuum lines. Detach the transaxle electrical connectors.
5. Remove the power steering pump from it bracket and set it aside.
6. Remove the transaxle filler tube.
7. Install engine support fixture J 28467-A or equivalent.
8. Unfasten the top engine-to-transaxle bolts.
9. Raise and safely support the vehicle. Remove both wheel and tire assemblies, then remove the left splash shield.
10. Remove both ABS wheel speed sensors and harness from the left suspension support.
11. Remove both lower ball joints and the stabilizer shaft links.
12. Detach the front air deflector.
13. Remove the left suspension supports.
14. As outlined earlier, remove both halfshafts (drive axles).
15. Unfasten and remove the transaxle-to-engine brace.
16. Remove the starter. For details, please refer to the procedure in Section 3 of this manual.
17. Unfasten the flywheel-to-torque converter bolts.
18. Remove the transaxle fluid cooler pipes.
19. Disconnect the ground wires from the engine to the transaxle bolt.

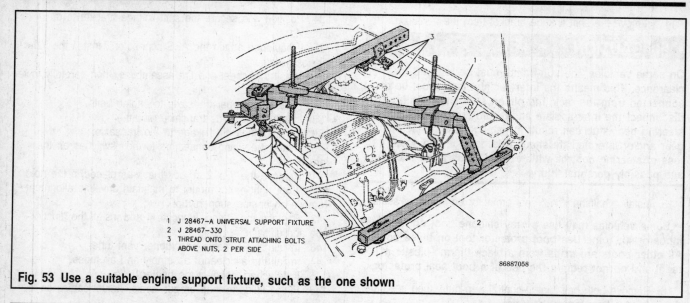

1 J 28467–A UNIVERSAL SUPPORT FIXTURE
2 J 28467–330
3 THREAD ONTO STRUT ATTACHING BOLTS
  ABOVE NUTS, 2 PER SIDE

86887058

Fig. 53 Use a suitable engine support fixture, such as the one shown

1 BOLT – 66 N·m (49 LBS. FT.)
2 BOLT – TRANSAXLE SUPPORT PIPE
  EXPANSION – 55 N·m (41 LBS. FT.)
3 BOLTS – 130 N·m (96 LBS. FT.)
4 TRANSAXLE
5 BODY

86887059

Fig. 54 View of the transaxle mount

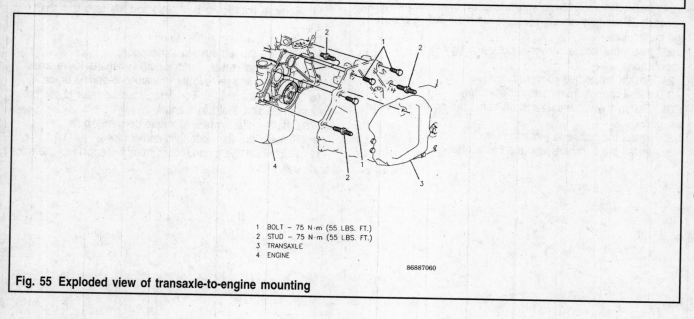

1 BOLT – 75 N·m (55 LBS. FT.)
2 STUD – 75 N·m (55 LBS. FT.)
3 TRANSAXLE
4 ENGINE

86887060

Fig. 55 Exploded view of transaxle-to-engine mounting

20. Remove the fluid cooler pipe brace and the exhaust brace.

21. Support the transaxle with a suitable jack.

22. Remove the transaxle mount-to-body bolts.

23. Unfasten the heater core hose pipe brace-to-transaxle nut and bolt.

24. Unfasten the remaining engine-to-transaxle bolts, then carefully remove the transaxle assembly from the vehicle.

To install:

25. Place a thin film of grease on the torque converter pilot knob. Make sure to properly seat the torque converter in the oil pump.

26. Move the transaxle assembly into position with the jack, while installing the right drive axle (halfshaft).

27. Fasten the lower engine-to-transaxle bolts into their proper locations.

28. Install the transaxle mount-to-body bolts.

29. Fasten the engine and transaxle attaching bolts.

30. Install the exhaust brace and the fluid cooler pipe brace.

31. Connect the ground wire at the engine to the transaxle bolt.

32. Attach the transaxle fluid cooler pipes.

33. Apply a suitable sealant compound on the flywheel-to-torque converter bolts, then install the bolts.

34. Fasten the transaxle converter cover.

35. Install the starter, as outlined in Section 3 of this manual.

36. Connect the engine-to-transaxle brace.

37. Install the halfshafts (drive axles).

38. Install the left suspension support.

39. Fasten the air deflector.

40. Install the stabilizer shaft links and the lower ball joints.

41. Connect both ABS wheel speed sensors.

42. Install the left splash shield.

43. Fasten the heater core pipe brace nut and bolt.

44. Install both wheel and tire assemblies, then carefully lower the vehicle.

45. Fasten the top engine-to-transaxle bolts.

46. Remove the engine support fixture.

47. Install the transaxle filler tube.

48. Install the power steering pump assembly, then adjust the belt.

49. Attach the electrical connections and vacuum lines as tagged during removal.

50. Install the shift cable and bracket.

51. Install the TV cable, then connect the air intake duct.

52. Properly fill the transaxle, then connect the negative battery cable.

Halfshafts

For halfshaft removal and installation and CV-joint overhaul, please refer to the procedures located under manual transaxle, earlier in this section.

Troubleshooting the Manual Transmission

Problem	Cause	Solution
Transmission shifts hard	• Clutch adjustment incorrect • Clutch linkage or cable binding • Shift rail binding	• Adjust clutch • Lubricate or repair as necessary • Check for mispositioned selector arm roll pin, loose cover bolts, worn shift rail bores, worn shift rail, distorted oil seal, or extension housing not aligned with case. Repair as necessary.
	• Internal bind in transmission caused by shift forks, selector plates, or synchronizer assemblies • Clutch housing misalignment • Incorrect lubricant • Block rings and/or cone seats worn	• Remove, dissemble and inspect transmission. Replace worn or damaged components as necessary. • Check runout at rear face of clutch housing • Drain and refill transmission • Blocking ring to gear clutch tooth face clearance must be 0.030 inch or greater. If clearance is correct it may still be necessary to inspect blocking rings and cone seats for excessive wear. Repair as necessary.
Gear clash when shifting from one gear to another	• Clutch adjustment incorrect • Clutch linkage or cable binding • Clutch housing misalignment • Lubricant level low or incorrect lubricant • Gearshift components, or synchronizer assemblies worn or damaged	• Adjust clutch • Lubricate or repair as necessary • Check runout at rear of clutch housing • Drain and refill transmission and check for lubricant leaks if level was low. Repair as necessary. • Remove, disassemble and inspect transmission. Replace worn or damaged components as necessary.
Transmission noisy	• Lubricant level low or incorrect lubricant • Clutch housing-to-engine, or transmission-to-clutch housing bolts loose • Dirt, chips, foreign material in transmission • Gearshift mechanism, transmission gears, or bearing components worn or damaged • Clutch housing misalignment	• Drain and refill transmission. If lubricant level was low, check for leaks and repair as necessary. • Check and correct bolt torque as necessary • Drain, flush, and refill transmission • Remove, disassemble and inspect transmission. Replace worn or damaged components as necessary. • Check runout at rear face of clutch housing

Troubleshooting Basic Clutch Problems

Problem	Cause
Excessive clutch noise	Throwout bearing noises are more audible at the lower end of pedal travel. The usual causes are: · Riding the clutch · Too little pedal free-play · Lack of bearing lubrication A bad clutch shaft pilot bearing will make a high pitched squeal, when the clutch is disengaged and the transmission is in gear or within the first 2″ of pedal travel. The bearing must be replaced. Noise from the clutch linkage is a clicking or snapping that can be heard or felt as the pedal is moved completely up or down. This usually requires lubrication. Transmitted engine noises are amplified by the clutch housing and heard in the passenger compartment. They are usually the result of insufficient pedal free-play and can be changed by manipulating the clutch pedal.
Clutch slips (the car does not move as it should when the clutch is engaged)	This is usually most noticeable when pulling away from a standing start. A severe test is to start the engine, apply the brakes, shift into high gear and SLOWLY release the clutch pedal. A healthy clutch will stall the engine. If it slips it may be due to: · A worn pressure plate or clutch plate · Oil soaked clutch plate · Insufficient pedal free-play
Clutch drags or fails to release	The clutch disc and some transmission gears spin briefly after clutch disengagement. Under normal conditions in average temperatures, 3 seconds is maximum spin-time. Failure to release properly can be caused by: · Too light transmission lubricant or low lubricant level · Improperly adjusted clutch linkage
Low clutch life	Low clutch life is usually a result of poor driving habits or heavy duty use. Riding the clutch, pulling heavy loads, holding the car on a grade with the clutch instead of the brakes and rapid clutch engagement all contribute to low clutch life.

Troubleshooting Basic Automatic Transmission Problems

Problem	Cause	Solution
Fluid leakage	· Defective pan gasket · Loose filler tube · Loose extension housing to transmission case · Converter housing area leakage	· Replace gasket or tighten pan bolts · Tighten tube nut · Tighten bolts · Have transmission checked professionally
Fluid flows out the oil filler tube	· High fluid level · Breather vent clogged · Clogged oil filter or screen · Internal fluid leakage	· Check and correct fluid level · Open breather vent · Replace filter or clean screen (change fluid also) · Have transmission checked professionally

Troubleshooting Basic Automatic Transmission Problems

Problem	Cause	Solution
Transmission overheats (this is usually accompanied by a strong burned odor to the fluid)	• Low fluid level • Fluid cooler lines clogged • Heavy pulling or hauling with insufficient cooling • Faulty oil pump, internal slippage	• Check and correct fluid level • Drain and refill transmission. If this doesn't cure the problem, have cooler lines cleared or replaced. • Install a transmission oil cooler • Have transmission checked professionally
Buzzing or whining noise	• Low fluid level • Defective torque converter, scored gears	• Check and correct fluid level • Have transmission checked professionally
No forward or reverse gears or slippage in one or more gears	• Low fluid level • Defective vacuum or linkage controls, internal clutch or band failure	• Check and correct fluid level • Have unit checked professionally
Delayed or erratic shift	• Low fluid level • Broken vacuum lines • Internal malfunction	• Check and correct fluid level • Repair or replace lines • Have transmission checked professionally

Lockup Torque Converter Service Diagnosis

Problem	Cause	Solution

No lockup	• Faulty oil pump
	• Sticking governor valve
	• Valve body malfunction
	  (a) Stuck switch valve
	  (b) Stuck lockup valve
	  (c) Stuck fail-safe valve
	• Failed locking clutch
	• Leaking turbine hub seal
	• Faulty input shaft or seal ring
		• Replace oil pump
		• Repair or replace as necessary
		• Repair or replace valve body or its internal components as necessary
		
		• Replace torque converter
		• Replace torque converter
		• Repair or replace as necessary

Will not unlock	• Sticking governor valve
	• Valve body malfunction
	  (a) Stuck switch valve
	  (b) Stuck lockup valve
	  (c) Stuck fail-safe valve
		• Repair or replace as necessary
		• Repair or replace valve body or its internal components as necessary

Stays locked up at too low a speed in direct	• Sticking governor valve
	• Valve body malfunction
	  (a) Stuck switch valve
	  (b) Stuck lockup valve
	  (c) Stuck fail-safe valve
		• Repair or replace as necessary
		• Repair or replace valve body or its internal components as necessary

Locks up or drags in low or second	• Faulty oil pump
	• Valve body malfunction
	  (a) Stuck switch valve
	  (b) Stuck fail-safe valve
		• Replace oil pump
		• Repair or replace valve body or its internal components as necessary

86887068

FRONT SUSPENSION
  FRONT END ALIGNMENT 8-13
  FRONT HUB AND BEARING 8-12
  LOWER BALL JOINT 8-6
  LOWER CONTROL
    ARM/SUSPENSION SUPPORT 8-8
  MACPHERSON STRUTS 8-3
  STABILIZER SHAFT AND
    BUSHINGS 8-7
  STEERING KNUCKLE 8-9
REAR SUSPENSION
  COIL SPRINGS AND
    INSULATORS 8-16
  CONTROL ARM BUSHING 8-16
  REAR END ALIGNMENT 8-20
  REAR HUB AND BEARING 8-19
  SHOCK ABSORBERS 8-16
  STABILIZER BAR 8-19
SPECIFICATIONS CHARTS
  WHEEL ALIGNMENT
    SPECIFICATIONS 8-14
STEERING
  IGNITION LOCK CYLINDER 8-28
  IGNITION SWITCH 8-26
  POWER STEERING PUMP 8-33
  POWER STEERING RACK AND
    PINION 8-31
  STEERING COLUMN 8-28
  STEERING LINKAGE 8-30
  STEERING WHEEL 8-21
  TURN SIGNAL SWITCH 8-22
WHEELS
  FRONT AND REAR WHEELS 8-2
  WHEEL LUG STUDS 8-2

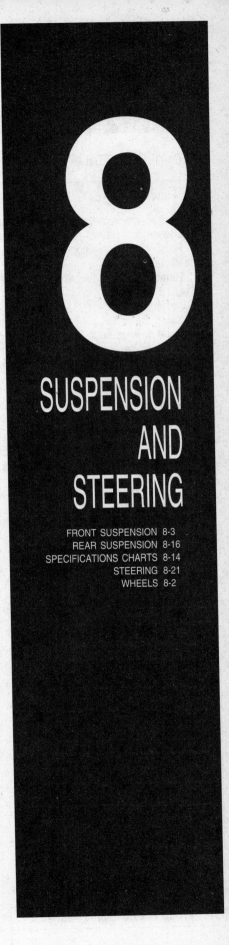

8

SUSPENSION AND STEERING

FRONT SUSPENSION 8-3
REAR SUSPENSION 8-16
SPECIFICATIONS CHARTS 8-14
STEERING 8-21
WHEELS 8-2

WHEELS

Front and Rear Wheels

REMOVAL & INSTALLATION

▶ **See Figure 1**

1. If equipped, remove the wheel cover.
2. Loosen, but do not remove the lug nuts.
3. Raise and safely support the vehicle so the tire is clear of the ground.
4. Remove the lug nuts, then remove the wheel from the vehicle.

To install:

5. Install the wheel.
6. Install the lug nuts, then hand-tighten in a star pattern.
7. Carefully lower the vehicle.
8. Final tighten the lug nuts in a star pattern to 103 ft. lbs. (140 Nm).
9. If equipped, install the wheel cover.

INSPECTION

1. Inspect the wheels for dents, excess corrosion and build-up of dried mud, especially on the inside surface of the wheel.
2. Inspect the tires for uneven wear, tread separation and cracks in the sidewalls due to dry rotting or curb damage.
3. Inspect the tire valve for leaking and proper sealing in the wheel assembly.
4. Take corrective action or replace as necessary.

Wheel Lug Studs

REPLACEMENT

Front Wheels

▶ **See Figures 2 and 3**

1. Remove the tire and wheel assembly.
2. As described later in this section, remove the hub and bearing assembly.
3. Using tool J 6627-A or equivalent wheel stud remover tool, remove and discard the wheel stud(s).

To install:

4. Insert the new stud from the rear of the hub.
5. Install flat washers and nut (flat side down), onto the wheel stud, then tighten until the wheel stud is fully seated.
6. Remove the nut and washers.
7. Install the hub and bearing assembly as outlined later in this section.
8. Install the tire and wheel assembly.

Rear Wheels

▶ **See Figures 2 and 3**

1. Remove the tire and wheel assembly.
2. Remove the brake drum, then remove the hub and bearing assembly. For details, please refer to the procedure located later in this section.
3. Unfasten and remove the wheel stud(s) using tool J 6627-A or an equivalent wheel stud removal tool. Discard the removed stud(s).

To install:

4. Insert the new stud from the rear of the hub.
5. Install 4 flat washers onto the stud.
6. Install the wheel nut with the flat side toward the washers.

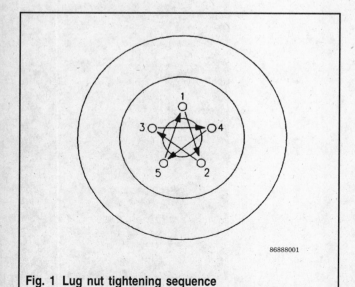

86888001

Fig. 1 Lug nut tightening sequence

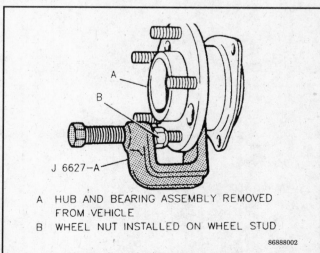

A HUB AND BEARING ASSEMBLY REMOVED
   FROM VEHICLE
B WHEEL NUT INSTALLED ON WHEEL STUD

86888002

Fig. 2 Once the hub and bearing is removed from the vehicle, use the proper tool to remove the wheel stud(s)

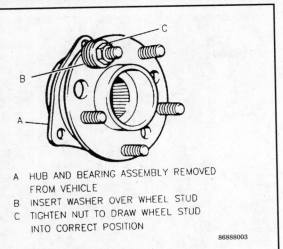

A HUB AND BEARING ASSEMBLY REMOVED
  FROM VEHICLE
B INSERT WASHER OVER WHEEL STUD
C TIGHTEN NUT TO DRAW WHEEL STUD
  INTO CORRECT POSITION

86888003

Fig. 3 Install washers and a nut on the wheel stud, then tighten until the stud is properly seated

7. Tighten the nut until the stud head is properly seated in the hub flange.

8. Remove the nut and washers.

9. Install the hub and bearing assembly and the brake drum.

10. Install the tire and wheel assembly.

FRONT SUSPENSION

The front suspension on all N-Body models utilizes MacPherson struts, which are specially suited to front wheel drive. The lower control arm pivots from the engine cradle, which has isolation mounts to the body and conventional rubber bushings for the lower control arm pivots. The upper end of the strut is isolated by a rubber mount which contains a nonserviceable bearing for wheel turning.

The lower end of the wheel steering knuckle pivots on a ball stud for wheel turning. The ball stud is retained in the lower control arm and the steering knuckle clamps to the stud portion.

All front suspension fasteners are an important attaching part in that it could affect the performance of vital parts and systems and/or could result in major repair expense. They must be replaced with one of the same part number or with an equivalent part if replacement becomes necessary. Do not use a replacement part of lesser quality or substitute design. Never attempt to heat, quench or straighten any front suspension part. Doing so may lessen the integrity of the part. If bent or damaged, the part should be replaced.

MacPherson Struts

REMOVAL & INSTALLATION

▶ See Figures 4, 5, 6, 7, 8, 9, 10, 11, 12, 13 and 14

➡Before removing front suspension components, their positions should be marked so they may assembled correctly. Scribe the knuckle along the lower outboard strut radius (A), the strut flange on the inboard side along the curve of the knuckle (B) and make a chisel mark across the strut/knuckle interface (C). When reassembling, carefully match the marks to the components.

1. From inside the engine compartment, remove the three nuts attaching the top of the strut assembly to the body.

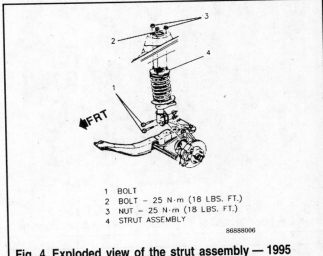

1 BOLT
2 BOLT – 25 N·m (18 LBS. FT.)
3 NUT – 25 N·m (18 LBS. FT.)
4 STRUT ASSEMBLY

86888006

Fig. 4 Exploded view of the strut assembly — 1995 vehicle shown

2. Raise and safely support the vehicle.

3. Place jackstands under the frame.

4. Lower the car slightly so that the weight rests on the jackstands and not on the control arms.

5. Remove the front tire and wheel assemblies.

✳✳CAUTION

Whenever working near the drive axles, take care to prevent the inner Tri-pot joints from being overextended. Overextension of the joint could result in separation of internal components which could go undetected and result in failure of the joint.

6. Some vehicles may use a silicone (gray) boot on the inboard axle joint. Use boot protector J-33162 or equivalent on these boots. All other boots are made from a thermoplastic

(black) material and do not require the use of a boot seal protector.

7. Remove the cotter pin and nut, then separate the tie rod end from the strut assembly, using tool J 24319-01 or equivalent. Discard the cotter pin.

8. Disconnect the brake line bracket from the strut assembly.

9. Scribe a mark on the strut flange as shown in the accompanying figure.

10. Unfasten and remove the strut-to-steering knuckle bolts.

➡ **The steering knuckle MUST be supported to prevent axle joint overextension.**

11. Remove the strut assembly from the vehicle. Be careful to avoid chipping or cracking the spring coating when handling the front suspension coil spring assembly.

To install:

12. Move the strut into position, then install the three nuts connecting the strut assembly to the body.

Fig. 7 Unfasten the tie rod-to-strut retaining nut

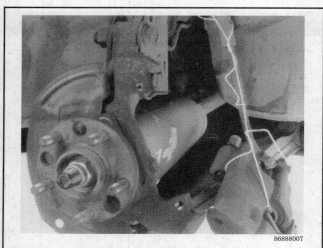

Fig. 5 If your vehicle has a gray CV-boot, install a suitable boot protector to protect the boot from damage

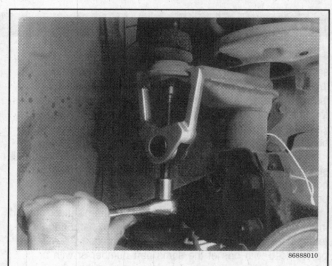

Fig. 8 Using a suitable tie rod end threaded puller . . .

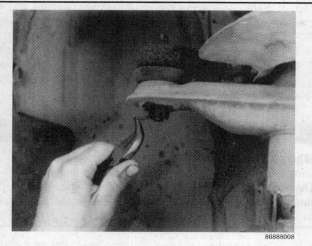

Fig. 6 Use suitable pliers to remove, then discard the tie rod end cotter pin

Fig. 9 . . . separate the tie rod end from the strut assembly

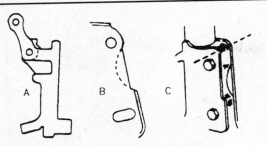

A SCRIBE KNUCKLE ALONG LOWER
  OUTBOARD STRUT RADIUS
B SCRIBE STRUT FLANGE ON INBOARD
  SIDE ALONG CURVE OF KNUCKLE
C SCRIBE ACROSS STRUT/KNUCKLE
  INTERFACE

Fig. 10 Scribe a matchmark as illustrated, for alignment purposes during installation

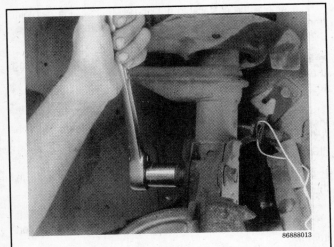

Fig. 11 Unfasten the strut-to-steering knuckle retaining bolts

Fig. 12 Remove the retaining bolts, then . . .

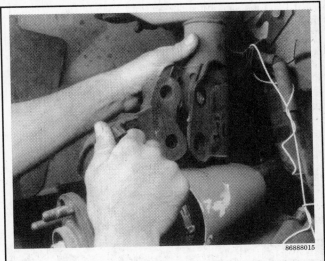

Fig. 13 . . . detach the strut from the steering knuckle

Fig. 14 When removing the strut assembly from the vehicle, be careful not to chip or crack the coil spring coating

13. Align the steering knuckle with the strut flange scribe mark made during removal, then install the bolts and nuts. Tighten the nuts to 133 ft. lbs. (180 Nm).

14. Position the tie rod end into the strut assembly, then secure with the tie rod end bolt and new cotter pin. Tighten the tie rod end bolt to 44 ft. lbs. (60 Nm).

15. Tighten the nuts and bolts attaching the top of the strut assembly to the body to the following specifications:

    a. Stabilizer-to-strut nut: 70 ft. lbs. (95 Nm).
    b. Nuts and bolt to 18 ft. lbs. (25 Nm).

16. Install the brake line bracket.

17. Slightly raise the vehicle, then remove the jackstands from under the suspension supports.

18. Install the tire and wheel assembly.

19. Carefully lower the vehicle, then final tighten the lug nuts to 103 ft. lbs. (140 Nm).

Lower Ball Joint

INSPECTION

1. Raise and safely support the vehicle on jackstands. Allow the suspension to hang freely.

2. Grasp the tire at the top and bottom and move the top of the tire in and out.

3. Observe for any horizontal movement of the steering knuckle relative to the front lower control arm. If any movement is detected, replace the ball joint.

4. If the ball stud is disconnected from the steering knuckle and any looseness is detected, or if the ball stud can be twisted in its socket using finger pressure, replace the ball joint.

REMOVAL & INSTALLATION

▶ **See Figures 15 and 16**

1. Raise and safely support the vehicle.
2. Place jackstands under the frame.
3. Lower the car slightly so the weight rests on the jackstands and not the control arm.
4. Remove the front tire and wheel assembly.

➡ **Be careful to avoid over-extending the axle shaft joints. When either end of the shaft is disconnected, over-extension of the joint could result in separation of internal components and possible joint failure. Failure to observe this can result in interior joint or boot damage and possible joint failure.**

5. If a silicone (gray) boot is used on the inboard axle joint, install boot seal protector J-33162 or equivalent. If a thermoplastic (black) boot is used, no protector is necessary.

6. Remove the cotter pin from the ball joint castellated nut. Discard the pin.

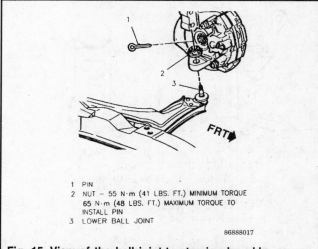

1 PIN
2 NUT – 55 N·m (41 LBS. FT.) MINIMUM TORQUE
   65 N·m (48 LBS. FT.) MAXIMUM TORQUE TO
   INSTALL PIN
3 LOWER BALL JOINT

86888017

Fig. 15 View of the ball joint-to-steering knuckle attachment

7. Remove the castellated nut and disconnect the ball joint from the steering knuckle using ball joint separator J-34505, J-29330, or equivalent.

➡ **Be sure to use on the recommended tool for separating the ball joint from the knuckle. Failure to use the proper tool may cause damage to the ball joint and seal.**

8. Drill out the three rivets retaining the ball joint to the lower control arm. Use a 1/8 in. (3mm) drill bit to make a pilot hole through the rivets. Finish drilling the rivets with a 1/2 in. (13mm) drill bit.

➡ **Be careful not to damage the drive axle boot when drilling out the ball joint rivets.**

9. Unfasten the nut attaching the link to the stabilizer shaft.

10. Remove the ball joint from the steering knuckle and control arm.

To install:

11. Piston the ball joint in the control arm.

12. Install the three ball joint bolts and nuts as shown on the instructions sheet in the ball joint kit, then tighten the bolts to specifications.

13. Position the ball joint stud through the steering knuckle.

14. Install the ball joint nut. Tighten the stabilizer shaft bushing clamp nuts to 15-22 ft. lbs. (20-30 Nm).

15. Fasten the ball joint-to-steering knuckle nut to 55 ft. lbs. (75 Nm), plus a 60° rotation. Do NOT loosen the nut at any time during installation.

16. Install a new cotter pin to the ball joint castellated nut.

17. If installed, remove the boot protector.

18. Fasten the nut attaching the stabilizer link to the stabilizer shaft. Tighten to 22 ft. lbs. (30 Nm), then slightly raise the vehicle and remove the jackstands from under the suspension.

19. Install the front tire and wheel assembly and hand-tighten the lug nuts.

20. Carefully lower the vehicle, then tighten the wheel lug nuts to 103 ft. lbs. (140 Nm).

➡ **The front end alignment should be checked and adjusted whenever the strut assemblies are removed.**

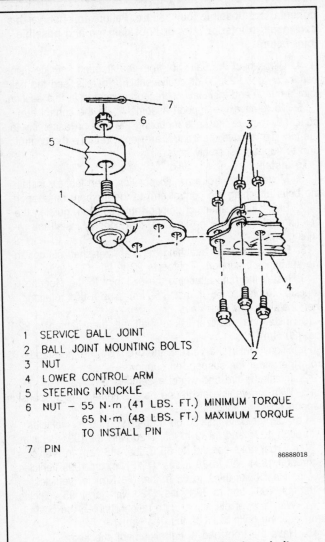

1 SERVICE BALL JOINT
2 BALL JOINT MOUNTING BOLTS
3 NUT
4 LOWER CONTROL ARM
5 STEERING KNUCKLE
6 NUT — 55 N·m (41 LBS. FT.) MINIMUM TORQUE
   65 N·m (48 LBS. FT.) MAXIMUM TORQUE
   TO INSTALL PIN
7 PIN

86888018

Fig. 16 Attach a new ball joint using the three bolts and nuts

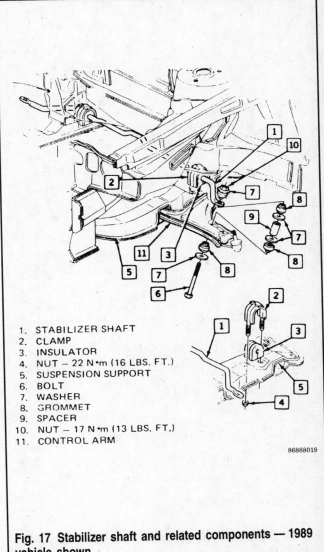

1. STABILIZER SHAFT
2. CLAMP
3. INSULATOR
4. NUT — 22 N·m (16 LBS. FT.)
5. SUSPENSION SUPPORT
6. BOLT
7. WASHER
8. GROMMET
9. SPACER
10. NUT — 17 N·m (13 LBS. FT.)
11. CONTROL ARM

86888019

Fig. 17 Stabilizer shaft and related components — 1989 vehicle shown

Stabilizer Shaft and Bushings

REMOVAL & INSTALLATION

▶ See Figures 17 and 18

1. Raise and safely support the vehicle with jackstands, allowing the front suspension to hang freely.
2. Remove the front tire and wheel assemblies.
3. Unfasten the nuts attaching the stabilizer shafts to the links.
4. Disconnect the clamps securing the stabilizer shaft to the suspension support assemblies.
5. Loosen the front bolts and remove the rear and center bolts from the support assemblies to lower them enough to remove the stabilizer shaft.
6. Remove the stabilizer shaft and bushings/insulators.
To install:
7. Install the stabilizer shaft with bushings and insulators.

8. Secure the clamps attaching the stabilizer shaft to the suspension support assemblies and hand-tighten.
9. Move the suspension support assemblies into position, then install and hand-tighten the retaining bolts.
10. Install the nuts attaching the stabilizer shaft to the links. Tighten to 22 ft. lbs. (30 Nm).
11. Tighten the suspension support bolts, center first, front second, and rear third, to the following specifications:
   • Center bolts first, to 66 ft. lbs. (90 Nm) for vehicles through 1994 and to 89 ft. lbs. (120 Nm) for 1995 vehicles
   • Front bolts second, to 65 ft. lbs. (88 Nm) for vehicles through 1994 and to 89 ft. lbs. (120 Nm) for 1995 vehicles
   • Rear bolts third, to 65 ft. lbs. (88 Nm) for vehicles through 1994 and to 89 ft. lbs. (120 Nm) for 1995 vehicles
12. Tighten the stabilizer shaft-to-support assembly nuts to 16-22 ft. lbs. (22-30 Nm) and the stabilizer shaft to control arm nuts to 13-22 ft. lbs. (17-30 Nm).
13. Tighten the clamp nuts to 22 ft. lbs. (30 Nm).
14. Install the wheel and tire assemblies.
15. Carefully lower the vehicle.

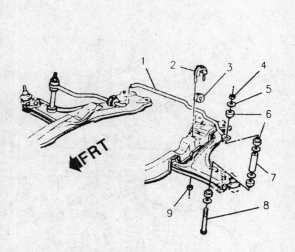

1 SHAFT, STABILIZER
2 CLAMP
3 INSULATOR, STABILIZER SHAFT
4 NUT
5 WASHER
6 INSULATOR, STABILIZER LINK
7 SPACER
8 BOLT
9 NUT

86888020

Fig. 18 Stabilizer shaft and related components — 1995 vehicle shown

Lower Control Arm/Suspension Support

REMOVAL & INSTALLATION

▶ See Figures 19 and 20

1. Raise and safely support the vehicle. Place jackstands under the suspension supports, then lower the vehicle slightly so the weight of the vehicle rests on the suspension supports, and not on the control arms.
2. Remove the tire and wheel assembly.
3. Unfasten the nut attaching the stabilizer link to the stabilizer shaft, then unfasten the nuts attaching the stabilizer shaft clamps to the suspension support. Detach the stabilizer shaft from the control arm and/or support assembly.

➡Be careful to avoid over-extending the axle shaft joints. When either end of the shaft is disconnected, over-extension of the joint could result in separation of internal com-

ponents and possible joint failure. Failure to observe this can result in interior joint or boot damage and possible joint failure.

4. Disconnect the ball joint from the steering knuckle using separator tool J-29330 or equivalent. For details, see the ball joint removal and installation procedure located in this section.
5. To remove the support assembly with the control arm attached, remove the bolts mounting the support assembly to the car. To remove the control arm only, remove the control arm to support assembly bolts.

To install:

6. Move the control arm into position, then loosely install the bolts attaching the control arm to the suspension support.
7. Place the suspension support into position, guiding the ball joint into the steering knuckle, then loosely install the retaining bolts.
8. Fasten the nuts attaching the stabilizer shaft clamps to the suspension support. Tighten to 22 ft. lbs. (30 Nm).
9. Install the nuts attaching the ball joint to the steering knuckle. Tighten to 55 ft. lbs. (75 Nm), plus a 60° rotation, then install a new cotter pin.
10. Install the stabilizer link-to-shaft nut, then tighten to 22 ft. lbs. (30 Nm).
11. Slightly raise the vehicle, then remove the jackstands from the under the suspension supports.
12. Install the tire and wheel assembly.
13. With the vehicle at ground height, tighten the suspension support bolts, as follows:
    a. Center bolts first, to 66 ft. lbs. (90 Nm) for vehicles through 1994 and to 89 ft. lbs. (120 Nm) for 1995 vehicles.
    b. Front bolts second, to 65 ft. lbs. (88 Nm) for vehicles through 1994 and to 89 ft. lbs. (120 Nm) for 1995 vehicles.
    c. Rear bolts third, to 65 ft. lbs. (88 Nm) for vehicles through 1994 and to 89 ft. lbs. (120 Nm) for 1995 vehicles.
14. With the vehicle still at curb height, tighten the control arm retaining bolts to 61 ft. lbs. (83 Nm).
15. Have the front end wheel alignment checked.

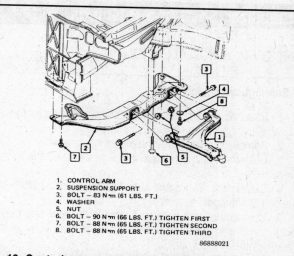

1. CONTROL ARM
2. SUSPENSION SUPPORT
3. BOLT – 83 N·m (61 LBS. FT.)
4. WASHER
5. NUT
6. BOLT – 90 N·m (66 LBS. FT.) TIGHTEN FIRST
7. BOLT – 88 N·m (65 LBS. FT.) TIGHTEN SECOND
8. BOLT – 88 N·m (65 LBS. FT.) TIGHTEN THIRD

86888021

Fig. 19 Control arm, suspension support and related components — 1989 vehicle shown

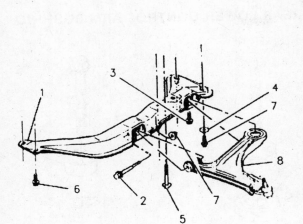

1 SUSPENSION SUPPORT
2 BOLT, FRONT CONTROL ARM
3 BOLT, CONTROL ARM REAR VERTICAL
  150 N•m (110 LBS. FT.)
4 WASHER
5 BOLT – TIGHTEN FIRST –
  120 N•m (89 LBS. FT.)
6 BOLT – TIGHTEN SECOND –
  120 N•m (89 LBS. FT.)
7 BOLT – TIGHTEN THIRD –
  120 N•m (89 LBS. FT.)
8 CONTROL ARM
9 NUTS

86888022

Fig. 20 Control arm and suspension support mounting — 1995 vehicle shown

CONTROL ARM BUSHING REPLACEMENT

▶ **See Figure 21**

1. Remove the lower control arm as outlined earlier in this section.
2. Install bushing removal tools J 29792 or equivalent.
3. Coat the threads of the tool with extreme pressure lubricant.
4. Remove the lower control arm bushings.
To install:
5. Install the bushing installation tools.
6. Coat the outer case of the bushing with a light coating of a suitable lubricant, then install the lower control arm bushings.

7. As outlined earlier, install the lower control arm.

Steering Knuckle

REMOVAL & INSTALLATION

▶ **See Figures 22, 23, 24 and 25**

1. Raise and safely support the vehicle.
2. Remove the front wheel and tire assemblies.

➡ **When drive axles are disconnected, care must be taken to avoid over-extending Tri-pot joints which could result in separation of internal joint components and possible joint failure. Also, the use of CV-joint boot protectors is recommended.**

3. Install a suitable boot protector.
4. Insert a drift punch through the rotor cooling vanes to lock the rotor in place, then remove the hub nut. Clean the drive axle threads of all dirt and grease.
5. Remove the drive shaft nut and washer.
6. Disengage the axle from the hub and bearing.
7. Disconnect the ball joint from the steering knuckle.
8. Move the axle shaft inward.
9. Remove the caliper bolts and caliper. Support the caliper using a length of wire. DO NOT allow the caliper to hang by the brake hose unsupported.
10. Remove the rotor.
11. Unfasten the hub and bearing assembly bolts, then remove the hub and bearing assembly from the knuckle.
12. Remove the strut-to-steering knuckle bolts, then remove the steering knuckle.
To install:
13. Position the steering knuckle into the strut, then install the steering knuckle-to-strut assembly bolts. Tighten to 133 ft. lbs. (180 Nm).
14. Install the hub and assembly onto the knuckle, then install the retaining bolts. Tighten to 70 ft. lbs. (95 Nm).
15. Install a new hub and bearing seal.
16. Install the rotor, then the caliper. Tighten the caliper bolts to 38 ft. lbs. (51 Nm).
17. Position the axle shaft into the hub and bearing assembly.
18. Position the ball joint into the steering knuckle, then install the ball joint nut and a new cotter pin. Tighten the ball joint-to-steering knuckle nut to 41-50 ft. lbs. (55-65 Nm). Install a new cotter pin.
19. Insert the drift through the rotor.
20. Install the washer and new drive shaft nut loosely on the drive shaft. Tighten the nut as much as possible until the axle starts to turn.
21. Remove the boot protectors.
22. Install the wheel and tire assemblies.
23. Carefully lower the vehicle.
24. Tighten the drive shaft nut to 180 ft. lbs. (260 Nm).

FRONT LOWER CONTROL ARM BUSHING

REMOVE   INSTALL

REAR LOWER CONTROL ARM BUSHING

REMOVE   INSTALL

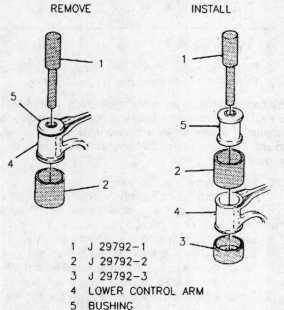

1 J 29792-1
2 J 29792-2
3 J 29792-3
4 LOWER CONTROL ARM
5 BUSHING

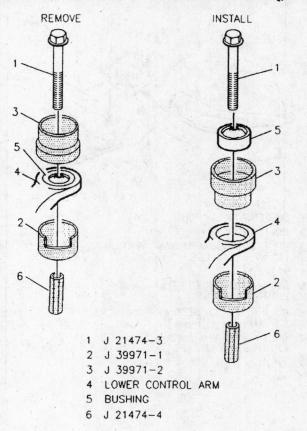

1 J 21474-3
2 J 39971-1
3 J 39971-2
4 LOWER CONTROL ARM
5 BUSHING
6 J 21474-4

86888023

Fig. 21 View of the front and rear lower control arm bushings

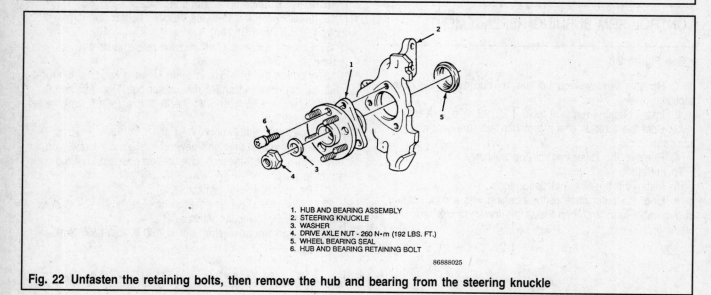

1. HUB AND BEARING ASSEMBLY
2. STEERING KNUCKLE
3. WASHER
4. DRIVE AXLE NUT - 260 N•m (192 LBS. FT.)
5. WHEEL BEARING SEAL
6. HUB AND BEARING RETAINING BOLT

86888025

Fig. 22 Unfasten the retaining bolts, then remove the hub and bearing from the steering knuckle

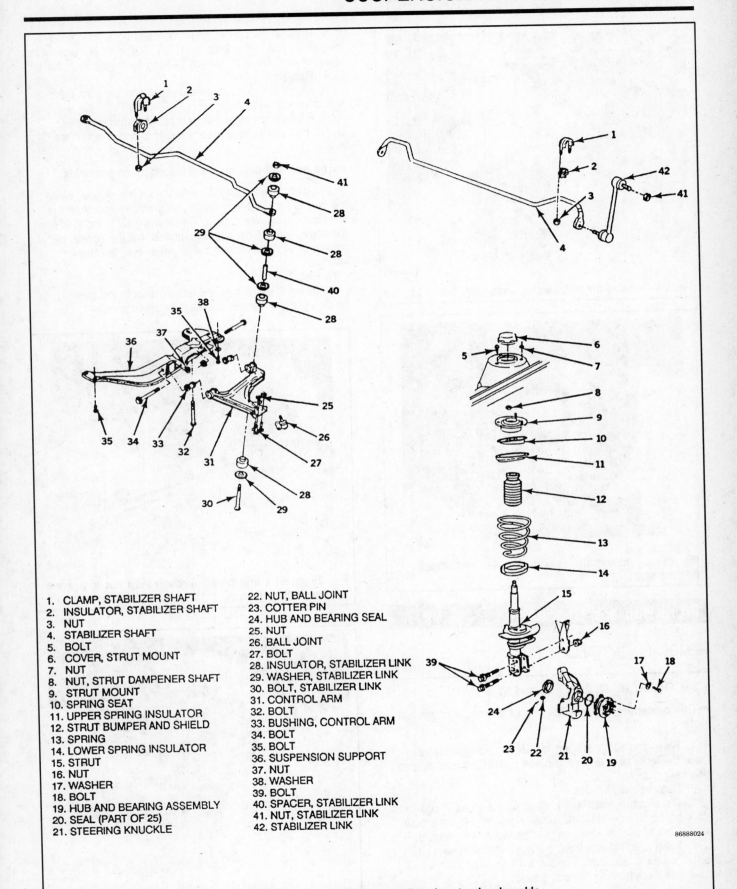

1. CLAMP, STABILIZER SHAFT
2. INSULATOR, STABILIZER SHAFT
3. NUT
4. STABILIZER SHAFT
5. BOLT
6. COVER, STRUT MOUNT
7. NUT
8. NUT, STRUT DAMPENER SHAFT
9. STRUT MOUNT
10. SPRING SEAT
11. UPPER SPRING INSULATOR
12. STRUT BUMPER AND SHIELD
13. SPRING
14. LOWER SPRING INSULATOR
15. STRUT
16. NUT
17. WASHER
18. BOLT
19. HUB AND BEARING ASSEMBLY
20. SEAL (PART OF 25)
21. STEERING KNUCKLE

22. NUT, BALL JOINT
23. COTTER PIN
24. HUB AND BEARING SEAL
25. NUT
26. BALL JOINT
27. BOLT
28. INSULATOR, STABILIZER LINK
29. WASHER, STABILIZER LINK
30. BOLT, STABILIZER LINK
31. CONTROL ARM
32. BOLT
33. BUSHING, CONTROL ARM
34. BOLT
35. BOLT
36. SUSPENSION SUPPORT
37. NUT
38. WASHER
39. BOLT
40. SPACER, STABILIZER LINK
41. NUT, STABILIZER LINK
42. STABILIZER LINK

86888024

Fig. 23 Exploded view of the front suspension components, including the steering knuckle

86888026

Fig. 24 Remove the hub/bearing assembly, then . . .

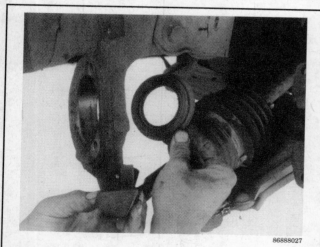

86888027

Fig. 25 . . . remove the steering knuckle and wheel bearing seal

Front Hub and Bearing

REMOVAL & INSTALLATION

◆ See Figures 26, 27, 28, 29, 30 and 31

➡This procedure requires the use of a number of special tools.

1. Raise and safely support the vehicle with jackstands. Place the jackstands under the frame so that the front suspension hangs freely.

2. Remove the front tire.

3. If a silicone (gray) boot is used on the inboard axle joint, place boot seal protector J-33162 or equivalent. If a thermoplastic (black) boot is used, no seal protector is necessary.

4. Insert a drift punch through the rotor cooling vanes to lock the rotor in place and remove the hub nut. Clean the drive axle threads of all dirt and grease.

5. Remove the brake caliper mounting bolts, then remove the caliper from the spindle assembly. Support the caliper with string or wire. Do NOT allow it to hang by the brake hose.

6. Remove the brake rotor.

7. Attach tool J-28733 or equivalent and separate the hub and drive axle/halfshaft.

8. Remove the three hub and bearing retaining bolts, shield, hub and bearing assembly and O-ring. Discard the O-ring.

➡**The hub and bearing are replaced as an assembly.**

9. Using a punch, tap the seal toward the engine. When the seal is removed from the steering knuckle, cut it off the drive axle using wire cutters. The factory seal is installed from the engine side of the steering knuckle, but the service replacement is installed from the wheel side of the steering knuckle.

To install:

10. Install the new hub and bearing seal in the steering knuckle using a suitable hub seal installer tool.

86887021

Fig. 26 Insert a drift punch through the rotor to prevent it from turning, then . . .

86887022

Fig. 27 . . . remove the hub nut and washer

Fig. 28 Unfasten the hub and bearing retaining bolts, then . . .

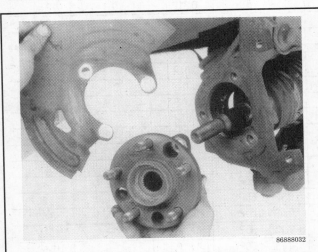

Fig. 29 . . . remove the hub/bearing and shield from the halfshaft/drive axle

Fig. 30 There is an O-ring seal on the rear of the hub and bearing assembly

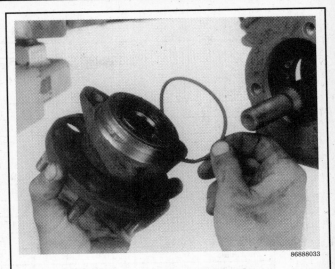

Fig. 31 Remove and discard the O-ring seal

11. The remainder of the installation is in reverse order of removal. Lubricate the hub and bearing seal with grease and install a new O-ring around the hub and bearing assembly. Tighten the hub and bearing bolts to 70 ft. lbs. (95 Nm). Tighten the hub nut to 180 ft. lbs. (260 Nm).

Front End Alignment

Front alignment refers to the angular relationship between the front wheels, the front suspension attaching parts and the ground. Camber is the tilting of the front wheels from the vertical when viewed from the front of the car. When the wheels tilt outward at the top, the camber is said to be positive (+); when the wheels tilt inward at the top, the camber is said to be negative (-). The amount of tilt is measured in degrees from the vertical and this measurement is called camber angle.

Toe-in is the turning in of the front wheels. The actual amount of toe-in is normally only a fraction of one degree. The purpose of the toe-in specification is to insure parallel rolling of the front wheels. Excessive toe-in or toe-out may increase tire wear. Toe-in also serves to offset the small deflections of the wheel support system which occur when the car is rolling forward. In other words, even when the wheels are set to toe-in slightly when the car is standing still, they tend to roll parallel on the road when the car is moving.

Toe setting is the only adjustment normally required. However, in special circumstances such as damage due to road hazard, collision, etc., camber adjustment may be required. To perform a camber adjustment, the bottom hole in the strut mounting must be slotted. Caster is not adjustable.

WHEEL ALIGNMENT

Year	Model		Caster Range (deg.)	Caster Preferred Setting (deg.)	Camber Range (deg.)	Camber Preferred Setting (deg.)	Toe-in (in.)	Steering Axis Inclination (deg.)
1985	Grand Am	F	0.69-2.69P	1.69P	0.21P-1.41P	0.81P	0.63N	13.50
	Calais	F	0.69-2.69P	1.69P	0.21P-1.41P	0.81P	0.06N	13.50
	Somerset Regal	F	1.0-3.0P	2P	0.5N-0.5P	0	0	NA
1986	Grand Am	F	0.69P-2.69P	1.69P	0.21P-1.41P	0.81P	0.63N	13.50
	Calais	F	0.69P-2.69P	0.69P-2.69P	0.21P-1.41P	0.81P	0.06P	13.50
	Somerset Regal	F	0.69P-2.69P	0.69P-2.69P	0.25P-1.25P	0.87P	0.06P	NA
1987	Grand Am [1]	F	0.69P-2.69P	1.69P	0.21P-1.41P	0.81P	0	13.50
	Grand Am [2]	F	0.69P-2.69P	1.69P	0.21P-1.41P	0.81P	0.63N	13.50
	Calais [1]	F	0.69P-2.69P	1.69P	0.21P-1.41P	0.81P	0	13.50
	Calais [2]	F	0.69P-2.69P	1.69P	0.21P-1.41P	0.81P	0.06N	13.50
	Skylark	F	0.72P-2.72P	1.72P	0.25P-1.44P	0.84P	0	13.50
1988	Grand Am	F	0.81N-4.19P	1.69P	0.19N-1.81P	0.81P	0	13.50
	Calais	F	0.81N-4.19P	1.69P	0.19N-1.81P	0.81P	0	13.50
	Skylark	F	0.81N-4.19P	1.69P	0.19N-1.81P	0.81P	0	13.50
1989	Grand Am	F	0.69P-2.69P	1.69P	0.13N-1.50P	0.81P	0	13.50
	Grand Am	R	-	-	0.75N-0.25P	0.25N	0.13P	-
	Calais [3]	F	0.69P-2.69P	1.69P	0.13P-1.50P	0.81P	0	13.50
	Calais [4]	F	0.69P-2.69P	1.69P	0.69N-0.69P	0	0	13.50
	Calais	R	-	-	0.13P-1.50P	0.81P	0.13P	-
	Skylark	F	0.69P-2.69P	1.69P	0.13N-1.50P	0.81P	0	13.50
	Skylark	R	-	-	0.75N-0.25P	0.25N	0.13P	-
1990	Grand Am [3]	F	0.69P-2.69P	1.69P	0.75N-0.25P	0.25N	0	13.50
	Grand Am [4]	F	0.69P-2.69P	1.69P	0.69N-0.69P	0	0	13.50
	Grand Am	R	-	-	0.75N-0.25P	0.25N	0.13P	-
	Calais [3]	F	0.69P-2.69P	1.69P	0.13P-1.50P	0.81P	0	13.50
	Calais [4]	F	0.69P-2.69P	1.69P	0.69N-0.69P	0	0	13.50
	Calais	R	-	-	0.13P-1.50P	0.81P	0.13P	-
	Skylark	F	0.69P-2.69P	1.69P	0.13N-1.50P	0.81P	0	13.50
	Skylark	R	-	-	0.75N-0.25P	0.25N	0.13P	-
1991	Grand Am	F	0.69P-2.69P	1.69P	0.69N-0.69P	0	0	13.50
	Grand Am	R	-	-	0.69N-0.31P	0.25N	0.13P	-
	Calais	F	0.69P-2.69P	1.69P	0.69N-0.69P	0	0	13.50
	Calais	R	-	-	0.69N-0.31P	0.25N	0.13P	-
	Skylark	F	0.69P-2.69P	1.69P	0.69N-0.69P	0	0	13.50
	Skylark	R	-	-	0.75N-0.25P	0.25N	0.13P	-
1992	Grand Am	F	0.69P-2.69P	1.69P	0.69N-0.69P	0	0	13.50
	Grand Am	R	-	-	0.69N-0.31P	0.25N	0.13P	-
	Achieva	F	0.69P-2.69P	1.69P	0.69N-0.69P	0	0	13.19
	Achieva	R	-	-	0.69N-0.31P	0.25N	0.13P	-
	Skylark	F	0.69P-2.69P	1.69P	0.69N-0.69P	0	0	13.19
	Skylark	R	-	-	0.75N-0.25P	0.25N	0.13P	-
1993	Grand Am	F	0.69P-2.69P	1.69P	0.69N-0.69P	0	0	13.19
	Grand Am	R	-	-	0.81N-0.31P	0.25N	0	-
	Achieva	F	0.44P-2.44P	1.44P	0.69N-0.69P	0	0	13.19
	Achieva	R	-	-	1.69N-.069P	0.31N	0.05P	-
	Skylark	F	0.44P-2.44P	1.44P	0.69N-0.69P	0	0	NA
	Skylark	R	-	-	0.81N-0.31P	0.25N	0	0

86888500

WHEEL ALIGNMENT

Year	Model		Caster Range (deg.)	Caster Preferred Setting (deg.)	Camber Range (deg.)	Camber Preferred Setting (deg.)	Toe-in (in.)	Steering Axis Inclination (deg.)
1994	Grand Am	F	0.44P-2.44P	1.44P	0.69N-0.69P	0	0	13.19
	Grand Am	R	-	-	0.81N-0.31P	0.25N	0	-
	Achieva	F	0.44P-2.44P	1.44P	0.69N-0.69P	0	0	NA
	Achieva	R	-	-	0.88N-0.44P	0.25N	0	-
	Skylark	F	0.44P-2.44P	1.44P	0.69N-0.69P	0	0	NA
	Skylark	R	-	-	0.81N-0.44P	.025N	0	-
1995	Grand Am	F	0.44P-2.44P	1.44P	0.69N-0.69P	0	0	13.19
	Grand Am	R	-	-	0.81N-0.31P	0.25N	0	-
	Achieva	F	0.44P-2.44P	1.44P	0.69N-0.69P	0	0	NA
	Achieva	R	-	-	0.88N-0.44P	0.25N	0	-
	Skylark	F	0.44P-2.44P	1.44P	0.69N-0.69P	0	0	NA
	Skylark	R	-	-	0.81N-0.44P	.025N	0	-

F - Front
R - Rear
1   Except P215/60R14 tires
2   With P215/60R14 tires
3   Except 16" wheels
4   With 16" wheels

86888501

REAR SUSPENSION

Coil Springs and Insulators

REMOVAL & INSTALLATION

▶ See Figures 32 and 33

✳✳CAUTION

The coil springs are under tension. To avoid personal injury, support the vehicle with jackstands under the body and allow the rear suspension to hang freely. Then, support the rear axle assembly with a floor jack. When the axle bolts have been removed, lower the jack to relax the spring tension.

1. Raise and safely support the vehicle. Remove the rear wheel and tire assemblies.
2. Using the proper equipment, support the weight of the rear axle. Unfasten the right and left brake line bracket attaching screws, then allow the brake line to hang free.

➡Do NOT suspend the rear axle by the brake hoses or damage to the hoses may result.

3. Unfasten the right and left shock absorber lower attaching bolts.
To install:

➡Prior to installing the coil springs, install the insulators in their seats using an adhesive to hold them in place.

4. Install the springs and insulators in their seats and raise the axle assembly into position. Ensure the end of the upper coil on the spring is positioned in the spring seat and within $9/16$ in. (15 mm) of the spring stop.
5. Connect the shock absorbers to the rear axle, but do not tighten the bolts to specification. The final tightening must take place with the vehicle at the proper trim height with the wheels on the ground.

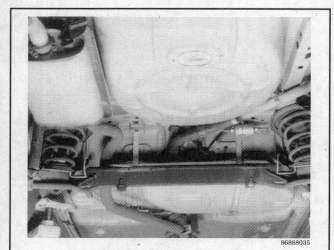

86888035

Fig. 32 Location of the coil springs — 1986 vehicle shown

6. Connect the brake lines to the body. Tighten the brake line bracket screws to 8 ft. lbs. (11 Nm).
7. Install the rear wheel and tire assemblies.
8. Remove the floor jack and jackstands.
9. Carefully lower the vehicle.
10. With all four wheels on the ground, tighten the rear axle attaching bolts to 35 ft. lbs. (47 Nm).

Shock Absorbers

REMOVAL & INSTALLATION

▶ See Figures 34, 35, 36, 37, 38 and 39

1. Disconnect the negative battery cable.
2. Open the trunk lid and remove the trim cover. If equipped, remove the nut cover.
3. Remove the upper shock attaching nut(s). If removing both shocks, remove one at a time.
4. Raise and safely support the vehicle.
5. Unfasten the lower shock absorber mounting bolt, then remove the shock from the vehicle.
To install:
6. Connect the shock absorbers at the lower attachment and install the attaching bolt.
7. Lower the vehicle enough to guide the shock absorber upper stud through the body opening, then fasten the upper shock absorber attaching nut loosely. Tighten the lower shock absorber mounting bolt to 35 ft. lbs. (47 Nm).
8. Remove the axle support, then carefully lower the vehicle. Tighten the shock absorber upper nut to 21 ft. lbs. (29 Nm).
9. If equipped, install the retaining nut cover, then install the rear trim cover. Close the trunk lid.
10. Connect the negative battery cable.

Control Arm Bushing

REMOVAL & INSTALLATION

▶ See Figure 40

➡A number of special tools are required for this procedure.

1. Raise and safely support the vehicle. Support the vehicle with jackstands under the axle.
2. Remove the rear wheel and tire assemblies.

➡Be sure to remove and install the control arm bushings one at a time.

3. If the right side bushing is being replaced, disconnect the brake lines from the body. If the left bushing is being removed, disconnect the brake line bracket from the body and parking brake cable from the hook guide on the body.
4. Remove the nut, bolt and washer from the control arm and bracket attachment, then rotate the control arm downward.

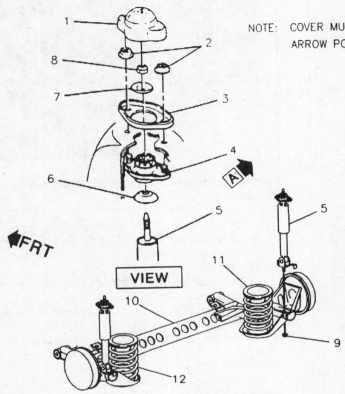

NOTE: COVER MUST BE INSTALLED SO THAT
ARROW POINTS TO LEFT SIDE OF VEHICLE

1   COVER (MUST BE INSTALLED
    WITH ARROW POINTING TO
    LEFT OF VEHICLE)
2   NUT
3   REINFORCEMENT
4   UPPER SHOCK ABSORBER
    MOUNT
5   SHOCK ABSORBER
6   WASHER
7   WASHER
8   NUT
9   NUT
10 REAR AXLE; SPRING-ON-CENTER TYPE
11 INSULATOR, COIL SPRING
12 COIL SPRING

86888034

Fig. 33 Exploded view of the rear suspension components, including the coil springs

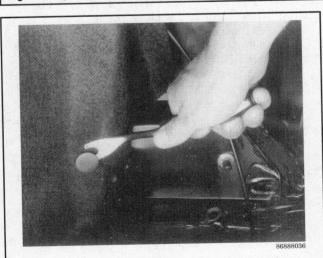

86888036

Fig. 34 After you open the trunk lid, use a suitable prytool to remove the trim cover

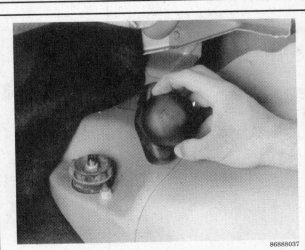

86888037

Fig. 35 Some vehicles have a cover which must be removed to access the shock retaining nuts

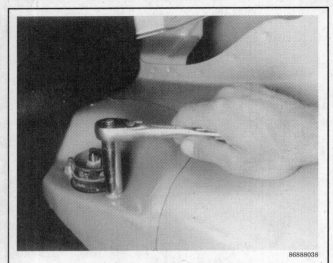

Fig. 36 Unfasten the upper shock attaching nuts

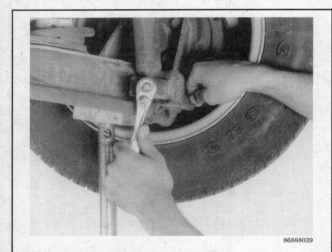

Fig. 37 After the vehicle is raised and safely supported, use a socket to unfasten the lower retaining bolt

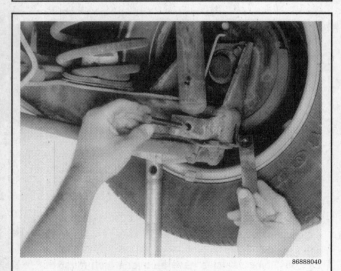

Fig. 38 Remove the retaining bolt, then . . .

Fig. 39 . . . remove the shock absorber assembly from the vehicle

5. Remove the bushing by performing the following:

a. Install receiver J-29376-1 on the control arm over the bushing and tighten the attaching nuts until the tool is securely in place.

b. Install bolt J-21474-19 through plate J-29376-7 and install into receiver J-29376-1.

c. Place remover J-29376-6 into position on the bushing and install nut J-21474-18 onto bolt J-21474-19.

d. Remove the bushing from the control arm by turning the bolt.

To install:

6. Install the bushing by performing the following:

a. Install receiver J-29376-1 onto the control arm.

b. Install bolt J-21474-19 through plate J-29376-7 and install into receiver J-29376-1.

c. Install bushing onto the bolt and position into the housing. Align bushing installer arrow with the arrow onto the receiver for proper indexing of the bushing.

d. Install nut J-21474-18 onto bolt J-21474-19.

e. Press the bushing into the control arm by turning the bolt. When the bushing is in proper position, the end flange will be flush against the face of the control arm.

7. Raise the control arm into position, then install the bolt, washer and nut. Do not tighten to specification at this time.

8. Connect the brake line bracket to the frame. Tighten to 8 ft. lbs. (11 Nm).

9. If the left side was disconnected, reconnect the brake cables to the bracket and reinstall the brake cable to the hook. Adjust the parking brake cable as necessary.

10. Install the rear wheel and tire assemblies.

11. Carefully lower the vehicle.

12. With the vehicle at proper trim height, tighten the control arm bushing bolts to 59 ft. lbs. (80 Nm), plus an additional $\frac{1}{3}$ turn (120° rotation).

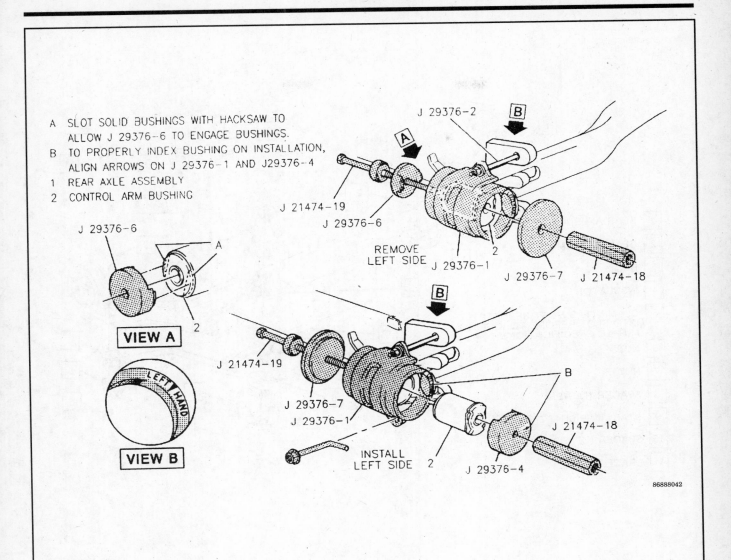

A SLOT SOLID BUSHINGS WITH HACKSAW TO
ALLOW J 29376-6 TO ENGAGE BUSHINGS.
B TO PROPERLY INDEX BUSHING ON INSTALLATION,
ALIGN ARROWS ON J 29376-1 AND J29376-4
1 REAR AXLE ASSEMBLY
2 CONTROL ARM BUSHING

J 29376-6
J 21474-19
J 29376-6
VIEW A
LEFT HAND
VIEW B
J 29376-2
J 29376-1
J 29376-7
J 21474-18
REMOVE LEFT SIDE
J 21474-19
J 29376-7
J 29376-1
INSTALL LEFT SIDE
J 29376-4
J 21474-18
86888042

Fig. 40 Control arm bushing replacement requires a variety of special tools

Stabilizer Bar

REMOVAL & INSTALLATION

▶ **See Figure 41**

1. Raise the vehicle and support it safely with jackstands.
2. Unfasten the nuts and bolts at both the axle and control arm attachments, then remove the bracket, insulator and stabilizer bar.
   To install:
3. Install the U-bolts, upper clamp, spacer and insulator in the trailing axle. Position the stabilizer bar in the insulators and loosely install the lower clamp and nuts.
4. Attach the stabilizer shaft insulator-to-control arm clamps and nuts. Tighten the stabilizer shaft insulator-to-control arm clamp nuts to 16 ft. lbs. (22 Nm). Tighten the stabilizer shaft insulator-to-axle clamp nuts to 13 ft. lbs. (18 Nm).
5. Carefully lower the vehicle.

Rear Hub and Bearing

REMOVAL & INSTALLATION

▶ **See Figure 42**

1. Raise and safely support the vehicle.
2. Remove the rear wheel and tire assemblies.

➡**Do NOT hammer on the brake drum, as this may damage the drum.**

3. Remove the brake drum. For details, please refer to Section 9 of this manual.
4. Remove the hub and bearing assembly from the axle. The top rear attaching bolt/nut will not cleaner the brake shoe when removing the hub and bearing assembly. Partially remove the hub and bearing assembly before removing this bolt.
5. If equipped, detach the rear ABS wheel speed sensor electrical connector.

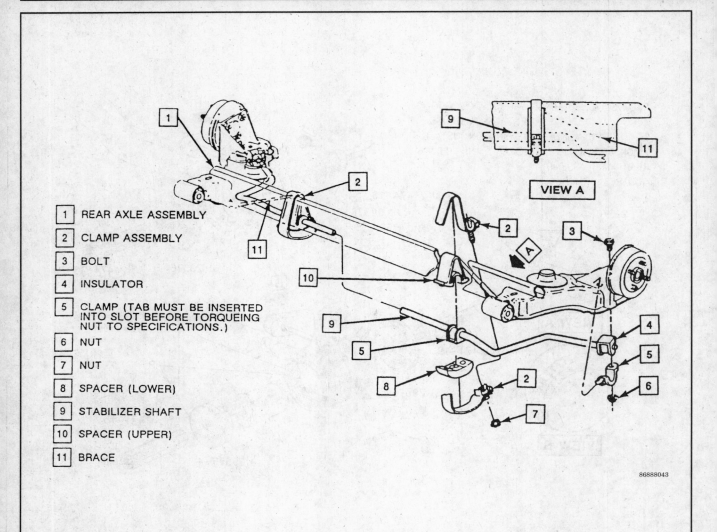

1 REAR AXLE ASSEMBLY

2 CLAMP ASSEMBLY

3 BOLT

4 INSULATOR

5 CLAMP (TAB MUST BE INSERTED INTO SLOT BEFORE TORQUEING NUT TO SPECIFICATIONS.)

6 NUT

7 NUT

8 SPACER (LOWER)

9 STABILIZER SHAFT

10 SPACER (UPPER)

11 BRACE

86888043

Fig. 41 Exploded view of the stabilizer bar — 1992 Achieva shown

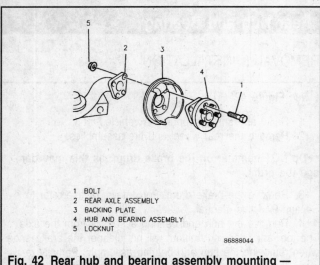

1 BOLT
2 REAR AXLE ASSEMBLY
3 BACKING PLATE
4 HUB AND BEARING ASSEMBLY
5 LOCKNUT

86888044

Fig. 42 Rear hub and bearing assembly mounting — 1995 vehicle shown

To install:

6. If equipped, attach the rear ABS wheel speed sensor electrical connector.

7. Install the hub and bearing assembly. Position the top rear attaching bolt in the hub and bearing assembly before installing it in the axle assembly. Tighten the hub and bearing-to-axle bolts to 44 ft. lbs. (60 Nm).

8. Install the brake drum, then the wheel and tire assembly.

9. Carefully lower the vehicle, then final tighten the lug nuts to 103 ft. lbs. (140 Nm).

Rear End Alignment

Rear wheel alignment is not adjustable. If a check of the rear alignment is determined to be out of specification, check for bent or broken rear suspension parts, and replace then as necessary.

STEERING

Steering Wheel

REMOVAL & INSTALLATION

▶ **See Figures 43, 44, 45, 46 and 47**

1. If equipped, disable the SIR system. For details, please refer to Section 6 of this manual.
2. Disconnect the negative battery cable, if not done already.

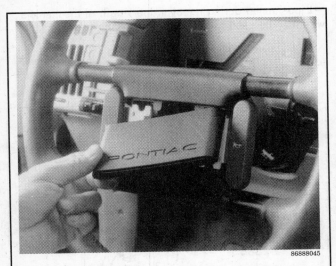

Fig. 43 Remove the steering wheel center trim piece

Fig. 44 On some earlier model vehicles, you must remove a retaining circlip

Fig. 45 Unfasten the steering wheel retaining nut

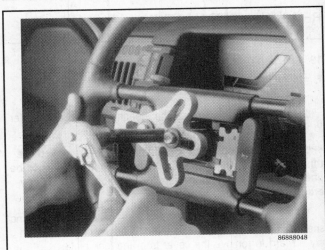

Fig. 46 Use a suitable puller to remove the steering wheel from the vehicle

3. Unfasten the screws that retain the steering pad.
4. Disconnect the horn lead, then remove the horn pad or trim cover.
5. Remove the retainer, nut and dampener, if equipped.
6. Matchmark the steering wheel to the shaft, then, using a suitable steering wheel puller, remove the steering wheel from the vehicle.

To install:

7. The installation is the reverse of the removal procedure. Tighten the attaching nut to 30 ft. lbs. (41 Nm).
8. If equipped, make sure to enable the SIR system.
9. Connect the negative battery cable.

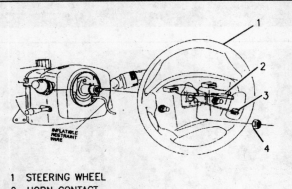

1 STEERING WHEEL
2 HORN CONTACT
3 SIR COIL ASSEMBLY PIGTAIL
4 STEERING WHEEL NUT

86888049

**Fig. 47 Exploded view of a steering wheel mounting —
1995 vehicle shown**

Turn Signal Switch

REMOVAL & INSTALLATION

1985-91 Vehicles

▶ **See Figures 48, 49, 50, 51, 52 and 53**

1. Disconnect the negative battery cable.
2. Matchmark and remove the steering wheel. Please refer to the procedure earlier in this section for details.

➡️**If necessary, the steering column may be removed for this service, but turn signal switch replacement should be possible with the column installed on most vehicles covered by this manual.**

3. Insert a small prytool into the slots between the steering shaft lock plate cover and the steering column housing, then pry upward to remove the cover from the lock plate.
4. Position a lock plate compressor tool such as J-23653-A or equivalent, by screwing the tool's center shaft onto the steering shaft (as far as it will go), then screw the center post nut clockwise until the lock plate is compressed.
5. Pry the locking plate snapring from the steering shaft slot.

➡️**If the steering column is being disassembled on a bench, the steering shaft is free to slide out of the mast jacket when the snapring is removed.**

6. Carefully release and remove the lock plate compressor tool, then remove the lock plate.
7. Loosen the retaining screw, then remove the turn signal lever.
8. Remove the hazard warning knob; press the knob inward and then unscrew it.
9. Remove the turn signal switch assembly-to-steering column retaining screws.

➡️**Whenever wiring and connectors must be pulled through the steering column, attach a length of mechanic's wire to the connector before beginning. Once**

the wiring and connector has been pulled through the column, leave the length of mechanic's wire in place (through the column) so it can be used to draw the connector back into position during installation.

10. Pull the switch connector out of the bracket on the jacket and feed the switch connector through the column support bracket. Pull the switch straight up, guiding the wiring harness through the column housing and protector.
11. If equipped with a tilt column, position the housing in the "low" position.
12. Remove the wiring protector by pulling downward and out of the column using a pair of pliers on the tab provided.
13. Remove the switch and wiring harness from the column.
To install:

➡️**If positioned during removal, the length of mechanic's wire may be used to help route the wiring harness.**

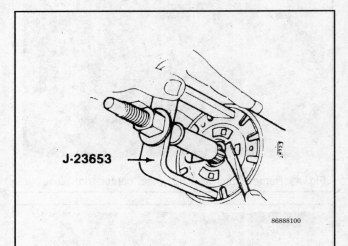

J-23653

86888100

Fig. 48 Use a suitable lock plate compressor tool when removing the shaft lock

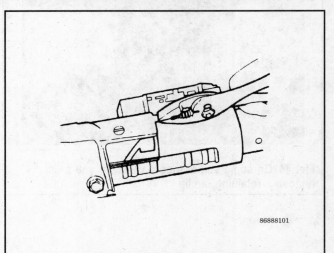

86888101

Fig. 49 Early model wiring protectors are removed by pulling downward on the tabs

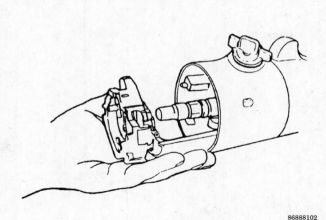

86888102

Fig. 50 Removing the turn signal switch from the steering column

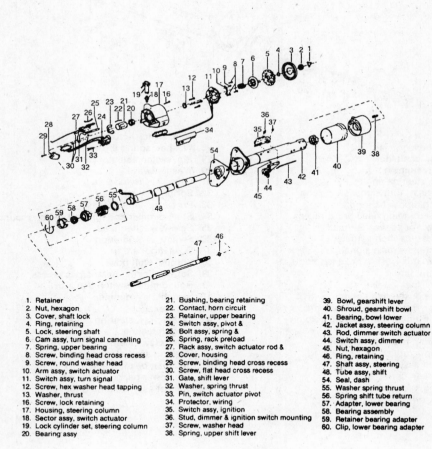

1. Retainer
2. Nut, hexagon
3. Cover, shaft lock
4. Ring, retaining
5. Lock, steering shaft
6. Cam assy, turn signal cancelling
7. Spring, upper bearing
8. Screw, binding head cross recess
9. Screw, round washer head
10. Arm assy, switch actuator
11. Switch assy, turn signal
12. Screw, hex washer head tapping
13. Washer, thrust
16. Screw, lock retaining
17. Housing, steering column
18. Sector assy, switch actuator
19. Lock cylinder set, steering column
20. Bearing assy
21. Bushing, bearing retaining
22. Contact, horn circuit
23. Retainer, upper bearing
24. Switch assy, pivot &
25. Bolt assy, spring &
26. Spring, rack preload
27. Rack assy, switch actuator rod &
28. Cover, housing
29. Screw, binding head cross recess
30. Screw, flat head cross recess
31. Gate, shift lever
32. Washer, spring thrust
33. Pin, switch actuator pivot
34. Protector, wiring
35. Switch assy, ignition
36. Stud, dimmer & ignition switch mounting
37. Screw, washer head
38. Spring, upper shift lever
39. Bowl, gearshift lever
40. Shroud, gearshift bowl
41. Bearing, bowl lower
42. Jacket assy, steering column
43. Rod, dimmer switch actuator
44. Switch assy, dimmer
45. Nut, hexagon
46. Ring, retaining
47. Shaft assy, steering
48. Tube assy, shift
54. Seal, dash
55. Washer spring thrust
56. Spring shift tube return
57. Adapter, lower bearing
58. Bearing assembly
59. Retainer bearing adapter
60. Clip, lower bearing adapter

86888103

Fig. 51 Exploded view of a common standard steering column

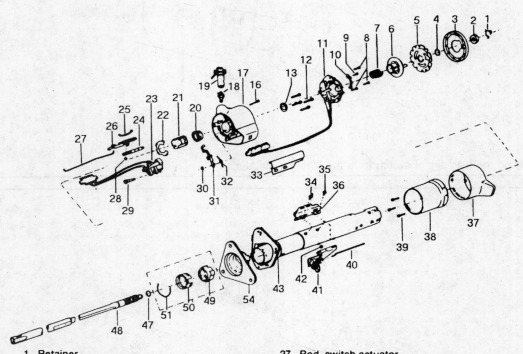

1. Retainer
2. Nut, hexagon jam
3. Cover, shaft lock
4. Ring, retaining
5. Lock, steering shaft
6. Cam assy, turn signal cancelling
7. Spring, upper bearing
8. Screw, binding head cross recess
9. Screw, round washer head
10. Arm assy, switch actuator
11. Switch assy, turn signal
12. Screw, hex washer head tapping
13. Washer, thrust
16. Screw, lock retaining
17. Housing, steering column
18. Sector assy, switch actuator
19. Lock cylinder set, steering column
20. Bearing assy
21. Bushing, bearing retaining
22. Retainer, upper bearing
23. Switch assy, pivot &
24. Bolt assy, spring &
25. Spring, rack preload
26. Rack, switch actuator

27. Rod, switch actuator
28. Washer, spring thrust
29. Pin, switch actuator pivot
30. Washer, wave
31. Lever, key release
32. Spring, key release
33. Protector, wiring
34. Stud, dimmer and ignition switch mounting
35. Screw, washer head
36. Switch assy, ignition
37. Bowl, floor shift
38. Shroud, shift bowl
39. Screw, binding head cross recess
40. Rod, dimmer switch actuator
41. Switch assy, dimmer
42. Nut, hexagon
43. Jacket assy, steering column
47. Ring, retaining
48. Shaft assy, steering
49. Bushing assy. steering shaft
50. Retainer, bearing adapter
51. Clip, lower bearing adapter
54. Bracket assy, column dash

Fig. 52 Exploded view of a common key release standard column

86888104

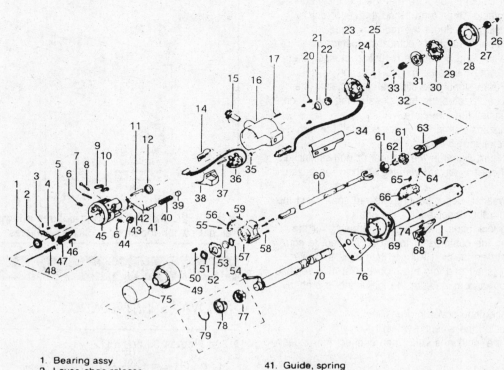

1. Bearing assy
2. Lever, shoe release
3. Pin, release lever
4. Spring, release lever
5. Spring, shoe
6. Pin, pivot
7. Pin, dowel
8. Shaft, drive
9. Shoe, steering wheel lock
10. Shoe, steering wheel lock
11. Bolt, lock
12. Bearing assy
14. Actuator, dimmer switch rod
15. Lock cylinder set, strg column
16. Cover, lock housing
17. Screw, lock retaining
20. Screw, pan head cross recess
21. Race, inner
22. Seat, upper bearing inner race
23. Switch assy, turn signal
24. Arm assy, signal switch
25. Screw, round washer head
26. Retainer
27. Nut, hex jam
28. Cover, shaft lock
29. Ring, retaining
30. Lock, shaft
31. Cam assy, turn signal cancelling
32. Spring, upper bearing
33. Screw, binding head cross recess
34. Protector, wiring
35. Spring, pin preload
36. Switch assy, pivot &
37. Pin, switch actuator pivot
38. Cap, column housing cover end
39. Retainer, spring
40. Spring, wheel tilt

41. Guide, spring
42. Spring, lock bolt
43. Screw, hex washer head
44. Sector, switch actuator
45. Housing, steering column
46. Spring, rack preload
47. Rack, switch actuator
48. Actuator assy, ignition switch
49. Bowl, gearshift lever
50. Spring, shift lever
51. Washer, wave
52. Plate, lock
53. Washer, thrust
54. Ring, shift tube retaining
55. Screw, oval head cross recess
56. Gate, shift lever
57. Support, strg column housing
58. Screw, support
59. Pin, dowel
60. Shaft assy, lower steering
61. Sphere, centering
62. Spring, joint preload
63. Shaft assy, race & upper
64. Screw, washer head
65. Stud, dimmer & ignition switch mounting
66. Switch assy, ignition
67. Rod, dimmer switch
68. Switch assy, dimmer
69. Jacket assy, steering column
70. Tube assy, shift
74. Nut, hexagon
75. Shroud, gearshift bowl
76. Seal, dash
77. Bushing assy, steering shaft
78. Retainer, bearing adapter
79. Clip, lower bearing adapter

86888105

Fig. 53 Exploded view of a common tilt steering column

14. Install the turn signal assembly to the column by first routing the connector harness:

    a. On non-tilt columns, be sure that the electrical connector is on the protector, then feed it and the cover down through the housing and under the mounting bracket.

    b. On tilt columns, feed the electrical connector down through the housing and under the mounting bracket, then install the cover onto the housing.

15. Position the turn signal and clip the connector to the bracket on the jacket. Secure the turn signal using the retaining screws, then install the trim plate.

16. Install the hazard warning knob, then install the turn signal lever and retaining screws.

17. Position the turn signal in the Neutral or non-signalling position, then pull out the hazard warning knob to the hazard On position.

18. Install the washer, upper bearing preload spring and the cancelling cam onto the upper end of the shaft.

19. Position the lock plate and a NEW snapring over the shaft, then position the compressor tool. Use the tool to compress the lock plate as far as it will go, then slide the new snapring down the shaft and into the groove. Carefully release the compressor tool and make sure the lock plate is properly positioned.

20. Snap the lock plate cover into position.

21. Align and install the steering wheel.

22. Make sure the ignition is **OFF**, then connect the negative battery cable.

1992-95 Vehicles

▶ See Figure 54

➡**This procedure covers removal and installation of the headlamp, headlamp dimmer switch, turn signal and hazard switches, as well as the cruise control switch.**

1. Disconnect the negative battery cable.

2. Unfasten the horn pad, then remove the steering wheel. For details, please refer to the procedure earlier in this section.

➡**If necessary, using locking pliers with a piece of rubber (such as a spark plug boot) between the jaws to help prevent damage to the tilt lever during removal.**

3. If equipped, remove the tilt lever from the steering column by grasping the lever firmly and twisting counterclockwise, while pulling it from the column.

4. Remove the upper and lower steering column covers.

5. Remove the dampener assembly, then unfasten and remove the switch assembly from the vehicle.

To install:

6. Position and secure the switch assembly.

7. Install the dampener and the upper and lower steering column covers.

8. If equipped, attach the tilt lever to the column.

9. Install the steering wheel, then fasten the horn pad.

10. Connect the negative battery cable.

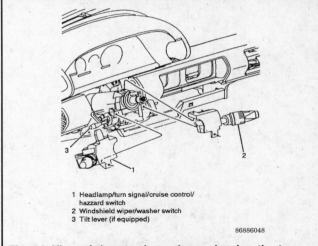

1 Headlamp/turn signal/cruise control/hazzard switch
2 Windshield wiper/washer switch
3 Tilt lever (if equipped)

86886048

Fig. 54 View of the steering column showing the turn signal switch location — 1992-95 vehicles

Ignition Switch

REMOVAL & INSTALLATION

▶ **See Figures 55 and 56**

1. Disconnect the negative battery cable.

2. If equipped, disable the SIR system. For details, please refer to the procedure located in Section 6 of this manual.

3. Detach the left instrument panel insulator.

4. Remove the left instrument panel trim pad and the steering column trim collar.

5. Unfasten the steering column upper support bracket bolts, then remove the support bracket.

6. Lower the steering column and support it safely.

7. Disconnect the wiring from the ignition switch.

8. Unfasten the ignition switch-to-steering column screws. Remove the ignition switch from the steering column.

To install:

9. Before installing, place the slider in the proper position (switch viewed with the terminals pointing up), according to the steering column and accessories:

- Standard column with key release — extreme left detent
- Standard column with PARK/LOCK — 1 detent from extreme left
- All other standard columns — 2 detents from extreme left
- Tilt column with key release — extreme right detent
- Tilt column with PARK/LOCK — 1 detent from extreme right
- All other tilt columns — 2 detents from extreme right

10. Install the activating rod into the switch and install the switch to the column. Do not use oversized screws as they could impair the collapsibility of the column.

11. Connect the wiring to the ignition switch. Adjust the switch, as required.

12. Install the steering column.

13. Fasten the steering column trim collar, instrument panel trim pad and insulator.

1. Hex locking nut
2. Retaining ring
3. Sir coil assy
4. Wave washer
5. Retaining ring
6. Shaft lock
7. T/SIG concel cam assy
8. Upper bearing spring
9. Upper bearing spacer
10. Adapter screw
11. Strg column housing assy
12. Ignition lock actuator assy

37. Shift lever spring
38. Linear shift lever assy
39. Linear shift base (NS) adapter

40. Flat hd tapping screw
41. Shift lever clip
42. Park lock cable assy
45. Support screw

13. Strg column lock cyl set
14. Lock pre-load spring
15. Interlock solenoid assy
16. Tapping screw
17. Mounting plate
18. Bearing retainer
19. Ingition switch assy
20. Tapping screw
21. Lock bolt assy
22. Lock bolt support bracket
23. Tapping screw
25. Retaining ring
26. Steering shaft assy
35. Linear shift assy
36. Shift lever pin

49. Support mounting adapter

51. Wire strap
52. Strg col jacket assy
53. Cable support bracket
54. Flng hex hd bolt
55. Column jacket bushing
56. Wire restraint clip

C/S ONLY

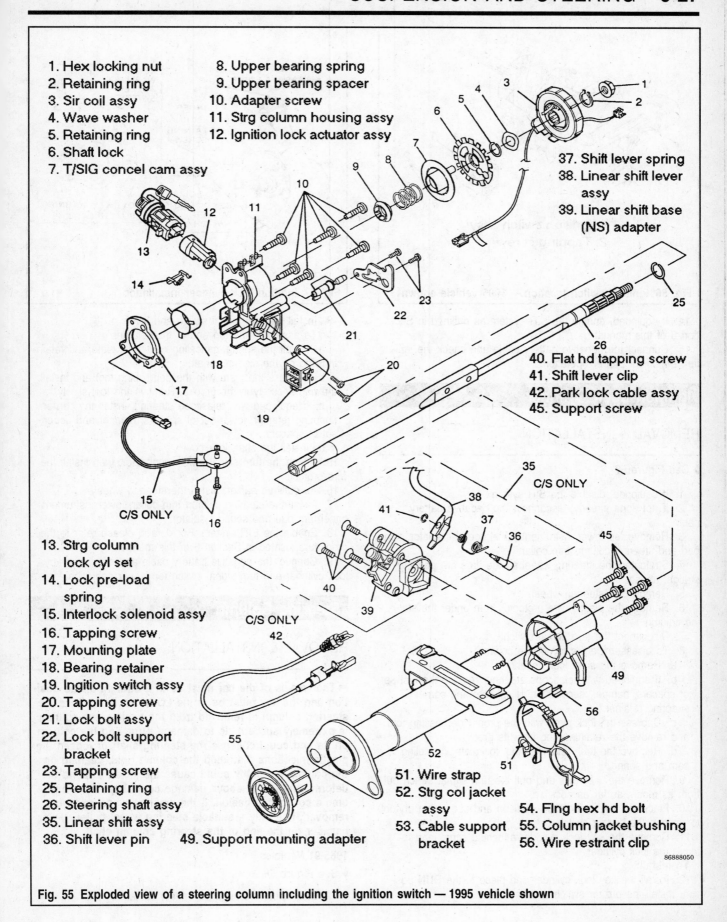

86888050

Fig. 55 Exploded view of a steering column including the ignition switch — 1995 vehicle shown

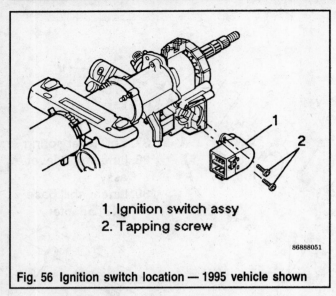

1. Ignition switch assy
2. Tapping screw

86888051

Fig. 56 Ignition switch location — 1995 vehicle shown

14. If equipped, enable the SIR system as outlined in Section 6 of this manual.

15. Connect the negative battery cable and check the ignition switch for proper operation.

Ignition Lock Cylinder

REMOVAL & INSTALLATION

▶ **See Figure 57**

1. If equipped, disable the SIR system.
2. If not done already, disconnect the negative battery cable.
3. Remove the lower instrument panel sound insulator, trim pad and steering column trim collar.
4. Straighten the steering wheel so the tires are pointing straight ahead.
5. Remove the steering wheel.
6. Remove the plastic wire protector from under the steering column.
7. Disconnect the turn signal switch.
8. To disassemble the top of the column:
   a. Remove the shaft lock cover.
   b. If equipped with telescope steering, remove the first set of spacers, bumper, second set of spacers and carrier snapring retainer.
   c. Depress the lock plate with the proper depressing tool and remove the retaining ring from its groove.
   d. Remove the tool, retaining ring, lockplate, canceling cam and spring.
9. Remove the 3 screws and pull the turn signal switch out from its mount as far as possible.
10. Place the key in the **RUN** position and use a thin prytool to remove the buzzer switch.
11. Remove the key lock cylinder attaching screw and remove the lock cylinder.
   To install:
12. Install the key lock cylinder and place in the **RUN** position. Install the buzzer switch and key light.

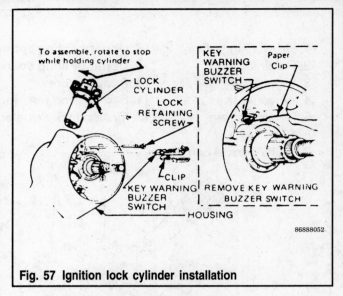

86888052

Fig. 57 Ignition lock cylinder installation

13. Install the turn signal switch and lever.
14. To assemble the top end of the column:
   a. Install the spring, canceling cam, lock plate and retaining ring on the steering shaft.
   b. Depress the plate with the depressing tool and install the ring securely in the groove. Remove the tool slowly.
   c. If equipped with telescope steering, install the carrier snapring retainer, lower set of spacers, bumper and upper set of spacers.
   d. Install the shaft lock cover.
15. Attach the turn signal switch connector, then install the wire protector.
16. As outlined earlier, install the steering wheel.
17. Install the steering column trim collar, lower instrument panel trim pad and sound insulator.
18. Enable the SIR system. For details, please refer to the procedure located in Section 6 of this manual.
19. Connect the negative battery cable and check the key lock cylinder and turn signal switch for proper operation.

Steering Column

REMOVAL & INSTALLATION

➡**The wheels of the car must be in a straight ahead position and the key must be in the LOCK position. Once the steering column is removed from the vehicle, the column is extremely susceptible to damage. Dropping the column on its end could collapse the steering shaft or loosen the plastic injections that keep the column rigid. Leaning on the column assembly could cause the jacket to bend or deform. Any of the above damage could impair the column's collapsible design. If the steering wheel must be removed, use only a suitable steering wheel puller. Never hammer on the end of the steering column shaft.**

1985-91 Vehicles
▶ **See Figure 58**

1. Disconnect the negative battery cable.

2. Detach the left instrument panel sound insulator.

3. Remove the lower steering column filler.

4. If column repairs are to be made, remove the horn pad, then the steering wheel. For details, please refer to the procedure earlier in this section.

5. Remove the steering column-to-intermediate shaft coupling pinch bolt. Remove the safety strap and bolt, if equipped.

6. Remove the upper and lower steering column trim shrouds and column covers.

7. Detach all wiring harness connectors. If equipped with column shift, disconnect the shift indicator cable. Remove the dust boot mounting screws and steering column-to-dash bracket bolts.

8. Lower the column to clear the mounting bracket and carefully remove from the vehicle.

To install:

9. Carefully, install the steering column into the vehicle.

10. If equipped with column shift, connect the shift indicator cable.

11. Attach the electrical harness connectors.

12. Install the column bracket bolts.

13. Install the flange and upper steering coupling upper pinch bolt. Tighten the column bracket support bolts to 22 ft. lbs. (30 Nm) and the upper pinch bolt to 30 ft. lbs. (41 Nm).

14. Adjust the shift indicator, if equipped.

15. If removed, install the steering wheel, then the steering wheel pad.

16. Connect the negative battery cable.

1992-95 Vehicles

▶ **See Figure 59**

1. If equipped, disable the SIR system as outlined in Section 6 of this manual.

2. Disconnect the negative battery cable, if not done already.

3. Detach the left instrument panel sound insulator.

4. Remove the lower steering column filter.

5. Unfasten the horn pad, then remove the steering wheel.

6. If equipped remove the tilt lever.

7. Remove the upper and lower steering column covers.

8. Detach the headlamp switch and windshield wiper switch electrical connections.

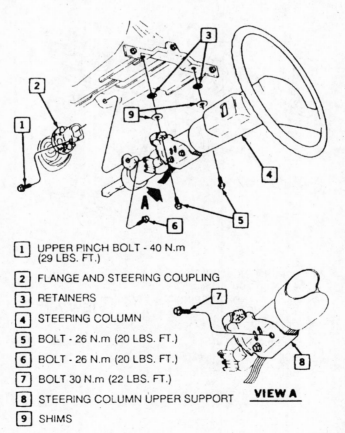

1	UPPER PINCH BOLT - 40 N.m (29 LBS. FT.)
2	FLANGE AND STEERING COUPLING
3	RETAINERS
4	STEERING COLUMN
5	BOLT - 26 N.m (20 LBS. FT.)
6	BOLT - 26 N.m (20 LBS. FT.)
7	BOLT 30 N.m (22 LBS. FT.)
8	STEERING COLUMN UPPER SUPPORT
9	SHIMS

VIEW A

86888053

Fig. 58 Steering column mounting — 1991 vehicle shown

9. If equipped, disconnect the park lock/brake transmission shift interlock cable from the ignition switch.

10. Unfasten the upper flexible column bolt.

11. Remove the column bracket support bolts, then carefully remove the steering column from the vehicle.

To install:

12. Position the steering column assembly, then install the bracket support bolts. Fasten the flexible coupling bolt. Tighten the column bracket support bolts 20 ft. lbs. (27 Nm) and the upper pinch bolt to 30 ft. lbs. (41 Nm).

13. If applicable, connect the park lock/brake transmission shift interlock cable to the ignition switch.

14. Attach the headlamp switch and the windshield wiper switch electrical connections.

15. Fasten the upper and lower steering column covers.

16. If equipped, install the tilt lever.

17. Install the steering wheel, then fasten the horn pad.

18. Install the lower steering column filler and the left instrument panel sound insulator.

19. If equipped, enable the SIR system.

20. Connect the negative battery cable.

Steering Linkage

REMOVAL & INSTALLATION

Tie Rod Ends

INNER

▶ **See Figures 60 and 61**

1. Disconnect the negative battery cable. Remove the rack and pinion gear from the vehicle.

2. Remove the lock plate from the inner tie rod bolts. Discard the lock plate.

3. If removing both tie rods, remove both bolts, the bolt support plate and one of the tie rod assemblies. Reinstall the removed tie rod's bolt to keep inner parts of the rack aligned. Remove the remaining tie rod.

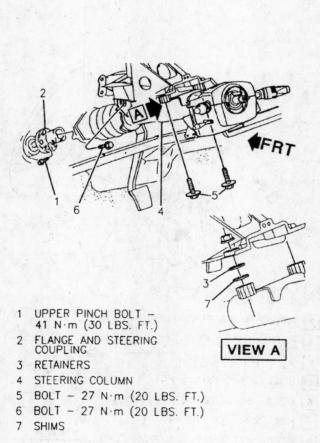

1 UPPER PINCH BOLT —
   41 N·m (30 LBS. FT.)
2 FLANGE AND STEERING
   COUPLING
3 RETAINERS
4 STEERING COLUMN
5 BOLT — 27 N·m (20 LBS. FT.)
6 BOLT — 27 N·m (20 LBS. FT.)
7 SHIMS

86888055

Fig. 59 View of the steering column assembly — 1992-95 vehicles

4. If only removing one tie rod, slide the assembly out from between the support plate and the center housing cover washer.

To install:

5. Install the center housing cover washer fitted into the rack and pinion boot.

6. Install the inner tie rod bolts through the holes in the bolt support plate, inner pivot bushing, center housing cover washer, rack housing and into the threaded holes.

7. Tighten the bolts to 65 ft. lbs. (90 Nm).

8. Install a new lock plate with its notches over the bolt flats.

9. Install the rack and pinion gear.

10. Fill the power steering pump with fluid and bleed the system.

11. Connect the negative battery cable and check the rack for proper operation and leaks.

OUTER

▶ **See Figures 61 and 62**

1. Disconnect the negative battery cable.

2. Remove the cotter pin and the nut from the tie rod ball stud at the steering knuckle. Discard the cotter pin.

3. Loosen the outer tie rod pinch bolts.

4. Using steering linkage puller J 24319-01 or equivalent, separate the tie rod taper from the steering knuckle.

5. Remove the tie rod from the adjuster.

6. Fasten the outer tie rod to the tie rod adjuster.

7. Connect the outer tie rod ball stud to the steering knuckle.

8. Fasten the hex slotted nut to the tie rod ball stud. Tighten the nut to 35 ft. lbs. (50 Nm), with a maximum torque of 50 ft. lbs. (75 Nm), then install a new cotter pin.

9. Adjust the toe by turning the tie rod adjuster. Refer to the wheel alignment chart for specifications.

10. Connect the negative battery cable, then have the front end alignment checked and adjusted as necessary.

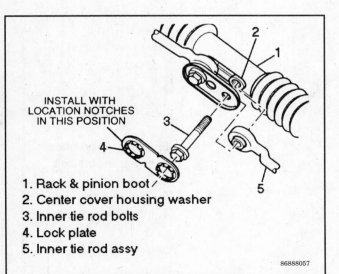

INSTALL WITH
LOCATION NOTCHES
IN THIS POSITION

1. Rack & pinion boot
2. Center cover housing washer
3. Inner tie rod bolts
4. Lock plate
5. Inner tie rod assy

86888057

Fig. 60 Inner tie rod assembly — 1995 vehicle shown

Power Steering Rack and Pinion

ADJUSTMENT

Rack Bearing Preload

▶ **See Figure 63**

1. Make the adjustment with the front wheels raised and the steering wheel centered.

2. Loosen the adjuster plug locknut, turn the adjuster plug clockwise until it bottoms in the housing, then back off about ⅛ turn (35-45°). Tighten the locknut to 50 ft. lbs. (70 Nm) while holding the position of the adjuster plug.

3. Check the steering for ability to return to center after the adjustment has been completed.

REMOVAL & INSTALLATION

▶ **See Figure 64**

1. Disconnect the negative battery cable.

2. Remove the left side sound insulator.

3. Disconnect the upper pinch bolt on the steering coupling assembly.

4. If equipped remove the line retainer.

5. Remove the power brake booster away from the cowl wall, leaving the master cylinder attached.

6. Raise and safely support the vehicle. Remove both front wheel assemblies.

7. Remove the tie rod ends from the struts using Steering Linkage Puller J 24319-01 or equivalent.

8. Carefully lower the vehicle.

9. Unfasten the left and right mounting clamps.

10. Disconnect the gear inlet and outlet hose assemblies from the pinion housing.

11. Move the rack and pinion assembly forward, then remove the lower pinch bolt from the flange on the coupling assembly.

12. Disconnect the coupling from the steering rack.

13. Remove the dash seal from the rack and pinion.

14. Remove the rack and pinion assembly through the left wheel opening.

To install:

15. If the studs were removed with the mounting clamps, reinstall the studs into the cowl. If the stud is being reused, use Loctite® to secure the threads.

16. Slide the rack and pinion assembly through the left side wheel housing opening and secure the dash seal.

17. Move the assembly forward and install the coupling.

18. Install the lower pinch bolt and tighten to 30 ft. lbs. (41 Nm).

19. Connect the gear inlet and outlet hose assemblies to pinion housing and tighten 20 ft. lbs. (27 Nm).

20. Install the clamp nuts. Tighten the left side clamp first, then tighten the right side to 22 ft. lbs. (30 Nm).

21. Raise and safely support the vehicle.

22. Connect the tie rod ends to the steering knuckle, tighten the nut to 35 ft. lbs. (47 Nm) and install a new cotter pin. Install the wheels.

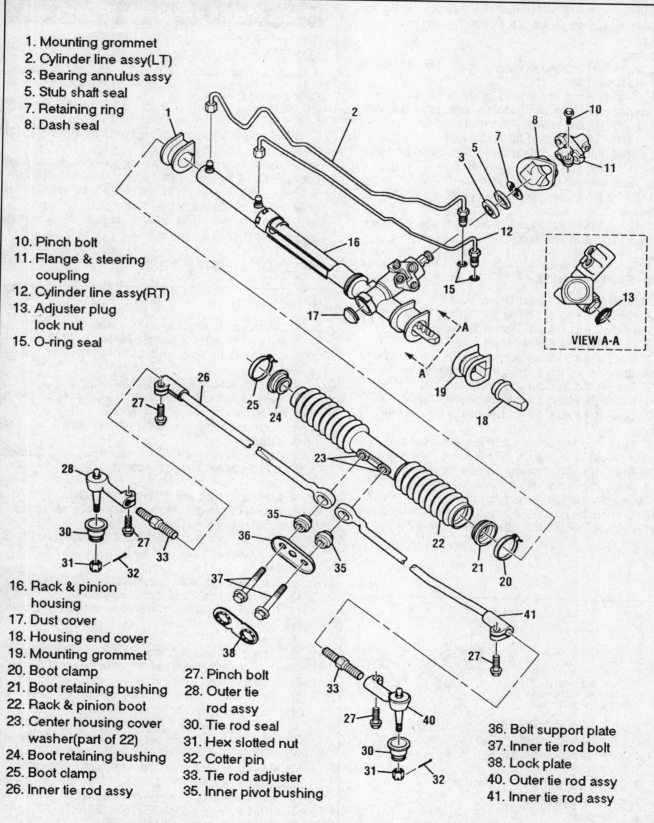

1. Mounting grommet
2. Cylinder line assy(LT)
3. Bearing annulus assy
5. Stub shaft seal
7. Retaining ring
8. Dash seal

10. Pinch bolt
11. Flange & steering coupling
12. Cylinder line assy(RT)
13. Adjuster plug lock nut
15. O-ring seal

VIEW A-A

16. Rack & pinion housing
17. Dust cover
18. Housing end cover
19. Mounting grommet
20. Boot clamp
21. Boot retaining bushing
22. Rack & pinion boot
23. Center housing cover washer(part of 22)
24. Boot retaining bushing
25. Boot clamp
26. Inner tie rod assy

27. Pinch bolt
28. Outer tie rod assy
30. Tie rod seal
31. Hex slotted nut
32. Cotter pin
33. Tie rod adjuster
35. Inner pivot bushing

36. Bolt support plate
37. Inner tie rod bolt
38. Lock plate
40. Outer tie rod assy
41. Inner tie rod assy

86888056

Fig. 61 Exploded view of the power steering rack and pinion, including the inner and outer tie rod ends

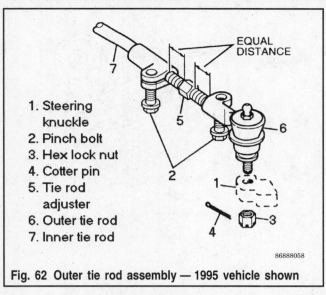

Fig. 62 Outer tie rod assembly — 1995 vehicle shown

1. Steering knuckle
2. Pinch bolt
3. Hex lock nut
4. Cotter pin
5. Tie rod adjuster
6. Outer tie rod
7. Inner tie rod

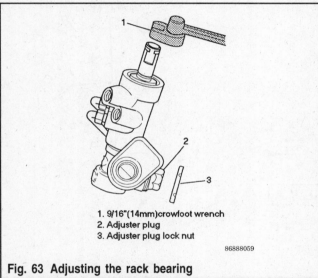

1. 9/16"(14mm)crowfoot wrench
2. Adjuster plug
3. Adjuster plug lock nut

Fig. 63 Adjusting the rack bearing

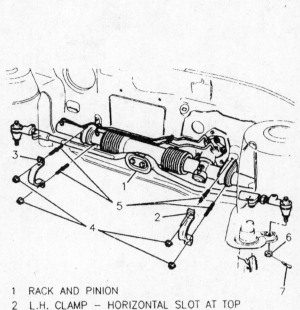

1   RACK AND PINION
2   L.H. CLAMP – HORIZONTAL SLOT AT TOP
3   R.H. CLAMP – HORIZONTAL SLOT AT TOP
4   NUT – 30 N·m (22 LBS.FT.) – HAND START ALL NUTS. TIGHTEN LEFT HAND SIDE CLAMP NUTS FIRST, THEN TIGHTEN RIGHT SIDE NUTS.
5   STUD – 18 N·m (13 LBS. FT.) – AFTER SECOND REUSE OF STUD, THREAD LOCKING KIT NO. 1052624 MUST BE USED.
6   NUT – 60 N·m (44 LBS. FT.)
7   COTTER PIN

Fig. 64 Power steering rack and pinion assembly — 1995 vehicle shown

23. Install the line retainer and lower the vehicle.
24. Install the upper pinch bolt on the coupling assembly. Tighten to 29 ft. lbs. (40 Nm).
25. Install the sound insulator.
26. Fill the power steering pump with fluid and bleed the system.
27. Connect the negative battery cable and check the rack for proper operation and leaks.
28. Check and adjust front end alignment, as required.

Power Steering Pump

REMOVAL & INSTALLATION

2.3L Engine
▶ **See Figure 65**

1. Disconnect the negative battery cable.

2. If equipped, detach the Variable Effort Steering (VES) electrical connector.
3. Disconnect the pressure and return lines from the pump.
4. Unfasten the rear bracket-to-pump bolts.
5. Remove the drive belt and position aside.
6. Unfasten the rear bracket-to-transaxle bolts.
7. Remove the front bracket-to-engine bolt.
8. Remove the pump and bracket as an assembly.
9. If installing a new pump, transfer pulley and bracket.
10. The installation is the reverse of the removal procedure.
11. Fill the power steering pump with fluid and bleed the system.
12. Connect the negative battery cable and check the pump for proper operation and leaks.

2.5L Engine
▶ **See Figure 66**

1. Disconnect the negative battery cable.
2. Remove the drive belt.
3. Disconnect and plug the pressure lines from the power steering pump.

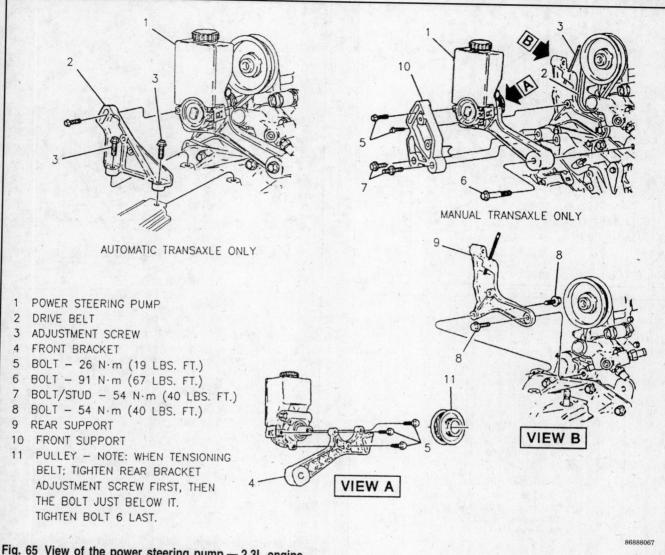

AUTOMATIC TRANSAXLE ONLY

MANUAL TRANSAXLE ONLY

VIEW A

VIEW B

1 POWER STEERING PUMP
2 DRIVE BELT
3 ADJUSTMENT SCREW
4 FRONT BRACKET
5 BOLT – 26 N·m (19 LBS. FT.)
6 BOLT – 91 N·m (67 LBS. FT.)
7 BOLT/STUD – 54 N·m (40 LBS. FT.)
8 BOLT – 54 N·m (40 LBS. FT.)
9 REAR SUPPORT
10 FRONT SUPPORT
11 PULLEY – NOTE: WHEN TENSIONING
   BELT; TIGHTEN REAR BRACKET
   ADJUSTMENT SCREW FIRST, THEN
   THE BOLT JUST BELOW IT.
   TIGHTEN BOLT 6 LAST.

86888067

Fig. 65 View of the power steering pump — 2.3L engine

4. Unfasten the front adjustment bracket-to-rear adjustment bracket bolt.

5. Remove the front adjustment bracket-to-engine bolt and spacer.

6. Remove the pump with the front adjustment bracket.

7. If installing a new pump, transfer the pulley and front adjustment bracket to the new pump.

To install:

8. Install the pump with the front adjustment bracket.

9. Fasten the front adjustment bracket-to-engine bolt and spacer, then install the front adjustment bracket-to-rear adjustment bracket bolt.

10. Unplug, then connect the lines to the pump.

11. Install the drive belt.

12. Adjust the drive belt tension.

13. Fill the power steering pump with fluid and bleed the system.

14. Connect the negative battery cable and check the pump for proper operation and leaks.

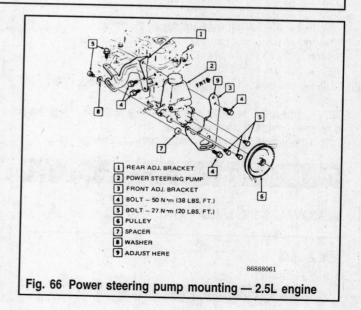

1 REAR ADJ. BRACKET
2 POWER STEERING PUMP
3 FRONT ADJ. BRACKET
4 BOLT – 50 N·m (38 LBS. FT.)
5 BOLT – 27 N·m (20 LBS. FT.)
6 PULLEY
7 SPACER
8 WASHER
9 ADJUST HERE

86888061

Fig. 66 Power steering pump mounting — 2.5L engine

2.0L, 3.0L And 3.3L Engines

▶ **See Figures 67, 68, 69 and 70**

1. Disconnect the negative battery cable.
2. If equipped, detach the Variable Effort Steering (VES) electrical connector.
3. Remove the serpentine drive belt.
4. Unfasten the power steering pump-to-engine bolts.
5. Pull the pump forward, then disconnect the pressure tubes.
6. Remove the pump and transfer the pulley, as necessary.

To install:

7. Position the pump, then connect the lines. Secure with the retaining bolts.
8. Install the serpentine belt.
9. Fill the power steering pump with fluid and bleed the system.
10. Adjust the drive belt tension.
11. If equipped attach the VES electrical connector.

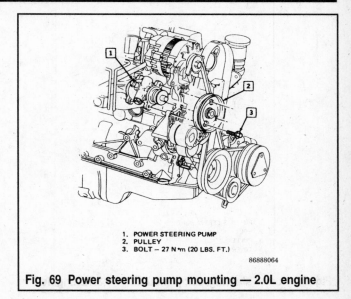

1. POWER STEERING PUMP
2. PULLEY
3. BOLT — 27 N·m (20 LBS. FT.)

86888064

Fig. 69 Power steering pump mounting — 2.0L engine

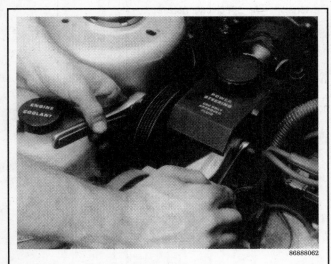

Fig. 67 Unfasten the pump retaining bolts, then . . .

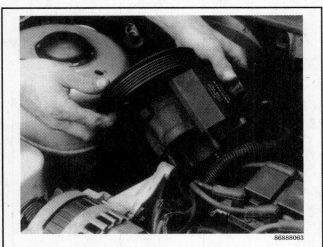

Fig. 68 . . . remove the power steering pump. Transfer the pulley, if installing a new pump

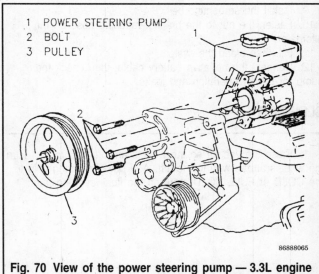

1 POWER STEERING PUMP
2 BOLT
3 PULLEY

86888065

Fig. 70 View of the power steering pump — 3.3L engine

12. Connect the negative battery cable and check the pump for proper operation and leaks.

3.1L Engine

▶ **See Figure 71**

1. Disconnect the negative battery cable.
2. Remove the serpentine belt.
3. Unfasten the nut from the bracket retaining the hose on the alternator.
4. Remove the engine mount.
5. Unfasten the pump bolts to ease pump line removal, then disconnect and plug the lines.
6. Remove the pump from the vehicle. If installing a new pump, transfer the pulley.

To install:

7. Position the pump, then uncap and connect the lines. Tighten the power steering gear inlet pipe-to-pump to 20 ft. lbs. (27 Nm).
8. Install the pump retaining bolts, then tighten to 22 ft. lbs. (30 Nm).

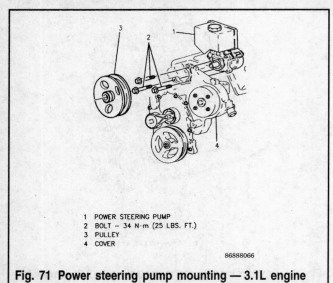

1 POWER STEERING PUMP
2 BOLT – 34 N·m (25 LBS. FT.)
3 PULLEY
4 COVER

86888066

Fig. 71 Power steering pump mounting — 3.1L engine

9. Install the serpentine belt.
10. Fasten the nut to the bracket retaining hose on the alternator.
11. Fill, then bleed the system.
12. Connect the negative battery cable, then check the pump for proper operation and leaks.

BLEEDING

1. Raise the vehicle so the wheels are off the ground. Turn the wheels all the way to the left. Add power steering fluid to the COLD or FULL COLD mark on the fluid level indicator.

2. Start the engine and check the fluid level at fast idle. Add fluid, if necessary to bring the level up to the mark.
3. Bleed air from the system by turning the wheels from side-to-side without hitting the stops. Keep the fluid level at the COLD or FULL COLD mark. Fluid with air in it has a tan appearance.
4. Return the wheels to the center position and continue running the engine for 2-3 minutes.
5. Lower the vehicle and road test to check steering function and recheck the fluid level with the system at its normal operating temperature. Fluid should be at the HOT mark when finished.

BELT ADJUSTMENT

➡**Serpentine belt driven power steering pumps do not require adjustment. If the belt is stretched beyond usable limits, replace it.**

1. Place the appropriate gauge on the belt and measure the tension. The specifications are:
   - 2.3L engine, new and used belt - 110 lbs. (50 kg)
   - 2.5L and 3.0L engine, used belt - 100 lbs. (45 kg); new belt - 180 lbs. (82 kg)
2. If the tension is not at specifications, loosen the mounting bolts and move the pump or turn the adjustment stud.
3. Tighten the mounting bolts while holding the adjusted position of the pump.
4. Run the engine for 2 minutes and recheck the tension.

ANTI-LOCK BRAKE SYSTEM (ABS)
ABS HYDRAULIC MODULATOR
  SOLENOID 9-45
ABS HYDRAULIC
  MODULATOR/MASTER CYLINDER
  ASSEMBLY 9-43
ABS SERVICE 9-43
DESCRIPTION AND
  OPERATION 9-28
DIAGNOSTIC PROCEDURES 9-29
ELECTRONIC CONTROL UNIT
  (ECU)/ELECTRONIC BRAKE
  CONTROL MODULE (EBCM) 9-43
FILLING AND BLEEDING 9-45
SPEED SENSORS 9-43
BRAKE OPERATING SYSTEM
ADJUSTMENTS 9-2
BLEEDING THE BRAKE
  SYSTEM 9-10
BRAKE HOSES AND PIPES 9-7
BRAKE LIGHT SWITCH 9-2
BRAKE PEDAL 9-2
MASTER CYLINDER 9-3
POWER BRAKE BOOSTER 9-7
PROPORTIONING VALVES 9-7
FRONT DISC BRAKES
BRAKE CALIPER 9-14
BRAKE DISC (ROTOR) 9-17
BRAKE PADS 9-12
PARKING BRAKE
CABLES 9-25
PARKING BRAKE LEVER 9-27
REAR DRUM BRAKES
BRAKE BACKING PLATE 9-24
BRAKE DRUMS 9-18
BRAKE SHOES 9-18
WHEEL CYLINDERS 9-22
SPECIFICATIONS CHARTS
BRAKE SPECIFICATIONS 9-49
TORQUE SPECIFICATIONS 9-49

9

BRAKES

ANTI-LOCK BRAKE SYSTEM (ABS) 9-28
BRAKE OPERATING SYSTEM 9-2
FRONT DISC BRAKES 9-12
PARKING BRAKE 9-25
REAR DRUM BRAKES 9-18
SPECIFICATIONS CHARTS 9-49

BRAKE OPERATING SYSTEM

Adjustments

DRUM BRAKES

▶ See Figure 1

1. Raise and safely support the vehicle.
2. Remove the rear wheel and tire assemblies. Matchmark the relationship of the wheel to the axle flange for proper balance during installation.
3. Remove the brake drum.
4. Using tool J 21177-A, or equivalent brace drum/shoe clearance gauge, measure the inside diameter of the brake drum.

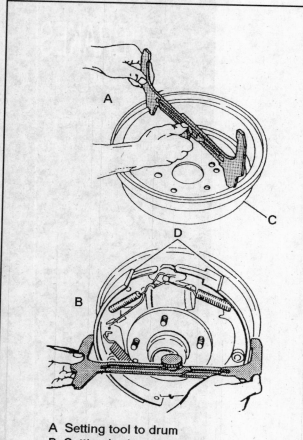

A Setting tool to drum
B Setting brake shoes to tool
C Brake drum
D Brake linings

86889001

Fig. 1 Using the proper tool to measure drum brake diameter

5. Turn the star wheel to adjust the shoe and lining diameter to be 0.030 in. (0.76mm) less than the inside diameter of the drum for each wheel.
6. Install the drums and wheels, aligning the marks made during removal. Only hand-tighten the lug nuts at this time.
7. Carefully lower the vehicle.
8. Tighten the wheel lug nuts to 103 ft. lbs. (140 Nm).
9. Make several alternate forward and reverse stops applying firm force to the brake pedal. Repeat this procedure until ample pedal reserve is built up.

Brake Light Switch

REMOVAL & INSTALLATION

▶ See Figure 2

1. Disconnect the negative battery cable.
2. Remove the left (driver's side) sound insulator.
3. Detach the switch electrical connector.
4. Remove the switch from the retainer by grasping and pulling it toward the rear of the car.
   To install:
5. Install the retainer in the bracket, at the underside of the bracket.
6. Depress the brake pedal and insert the switch into the retainer until the switch seats. Allow the pedal to return.
7. Attach the switch electrical connector.
8. To adjust the switch, pull the pedal up against the switch until no more clicks are heard. The switch will automatically move up in the retainer providing adjustment. Repeat a few times to ensure that the switch is properly adjusted.
9. Connect the negative battery cable and check the switch for proper operation.

Brake Pedal

REMOVAL & INSTALLATION

▶ See Figure 3

1. Remove the left side sound insulator/lower steering column panel.
2. Remove the brake pedal bracket.
3. Disconnect the pushrod from the brake pedal.
4. Unfasten the pivot bolt and bushing and/or retaining nut, then remove the brake pedal.
   To install:
5. Install the brake pedal, then secure with the retaining nuts and/or brake pedal bushing and pivot bolt. Tighten the bolt to 25 ft. lbs. (34 Nm) and the nut to 20 ft. lbs. (27 Nm).
6. Connect the pushrod to the brake pedal.
7. Install the brake pedal bracket.
8. Fasten the left side sound insulator/lower steering column panel.

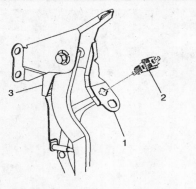

1 Brake pedal mounting bracket
2 Cruise control release switch
3 Brake pedal assembly

86889002

Fig. 2 The brake light switch is mounted on the brake pedal

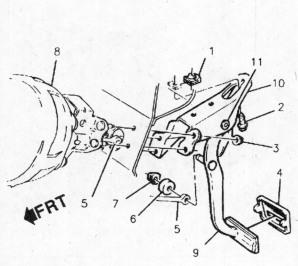

1 CLIP NUT
2 BOLT – 34 N·m (25 LBS. FT.)
3 NUT – 27 N·m (20 LBS. FT.)
4 PEDAL COVER
5 BOOSTER PUSH ROD
6 WASHER
7 RETAINER
8 VACUUM BOOSTER
9 BRAKE PEDAL
10 BRACKET
11 RIVIT

86889003

Fig. 3 Brake pedal mounting — 1995 vehicle shown

Master Cylinder

REMOVAL & INSTALLATION

Except Anti-Lock Brakes
▶ See Figures 4, 5, 6, 7, 8, 9, 10 and 11

1. Disconnect the negative battery cable.
2. Using a suitable tool, drain some of the fluid from the master cylinder.
3. Unplug the fluid level sensor connector.
4. Disconnect and plug the brake lines from the master cylinder.
5. Unfasten the nuts attaching the master cylinder to the power booster.
6. Remove the master cylinder from its mounting studs and from the vehicle.

86889004

Fig. 4 To avoid spillage, use a clean turkey baster or similar tool to drain some of the fluid from the master cylinder before removal

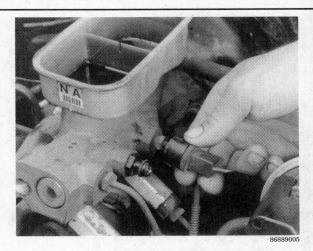

86889005

Fig. 5 Detach the master cylinder fluid level sensor electrical connector

Fig. 6 After disconnecting the brake lines, be sure to plug them to prevent contaminants from entering the brake hydraulic system

Fig. 7 Using a back-up wrench, unfasten the lines from the proportioning valve and . . .

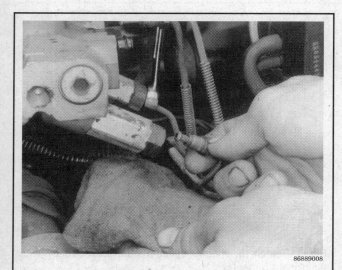

Fig. 8 . . . don't forget to plug the lines!

Fig. 9 Unfasten the master cylinder-to-power brake booster retaining nuts, then . . .

Fig. 10 . . . remove the master cylinder assembly from the engine compartment

7. If necessary, unfasten the retaining roll pins and remove the fluid reservoir from the cylinder.

To install:

8. Replace the reservoir O-rings and bench bleed the master cylinder.

9. Position the master cylinder to the booster, then install the retaining nuts.

10. Unplug and fasten the brake lines to the master cylinder.

11. Attach the brake fluid level sensor electrical connector.

12. Fill the reservoir with brake fluid, then properly bleed the hydraulic system.

13. Connect the negative battery cable, then check the brakes for proper operation.

OVERHAUL

▶ **See Figures 12, 13, 14, 15 and 16**

1. Remove the master cylinder from the car. For details, please refer to the procedure earlier in this section.

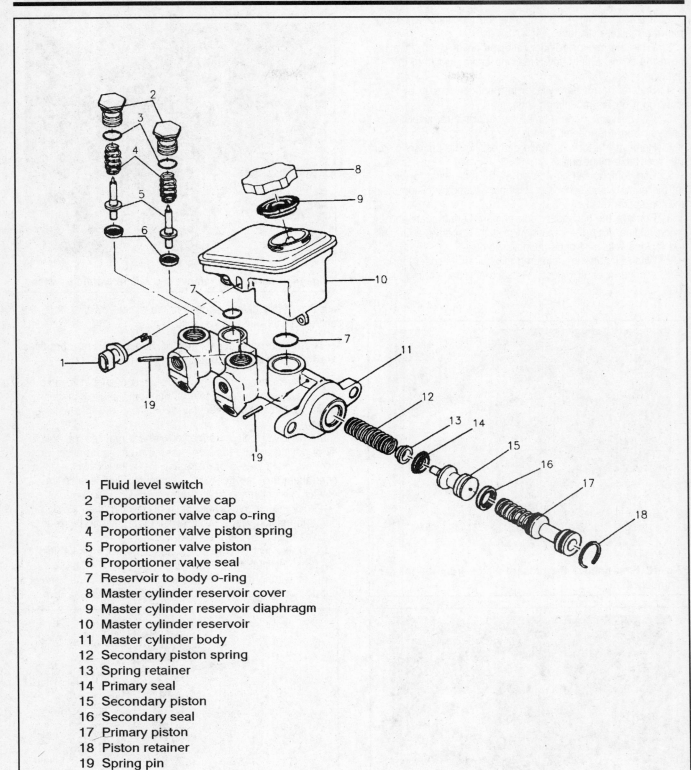

1 Fluid level switch
2 Proportioner valve cap
3 Proportioner valve cap o-ring
4 Proportioner valve piston spring
5 Proportioner valve piston
6 Proportioner valve seal
7 Reservoir to body o-ring
8 Master cylinder reservoir cover
9 Master cylinder reservoir diaphragm
10 Master cylinder reservoir
11 Master cylinder body
12 Secondary piston spring
13 Spring retainer
14 Primary seal
15 Secondary piston
16 Secondary seal
17 Primary piston
18 Piston retainer
19 Spring pin

86889011

Fig. 11 Exploded view of the master cylinder assembly — 1995 vehicle shown

2. If equipped with ABS, separate the modulator assembly from the master cylinder.

3. Wipe the master cylinder reservoir cover clean, then remove the cover. Empty any remaining brake fluid from the reservoir.

4. Secure the master cylinder in a soft-jawed vise by clamping it on the mounting flange.

5. If necessary, using a small prybar, carefully lever the reservoir from the master cylinder bore.

6. Remove the lockring while depressing the primary piston with a suitable blunt drift.

7. Use compressed air applied at the rear outlet to force out the primary and secondary pistons, secondary piston spring and the spring retainer.

8. Remove the secondary and primary O-ring seals and the spring retainer from the secondary piston. Discard the O-rings and replace with new ones during assembly.

9. Wash all parts in denatured alcohol and inspect for wear, scoring or other defects. Replace any parts found to be

Fig. 14 If necessary, remove the failure warning switch

suspect. If any defect is found in the master cylinder bore, the entire cylinder must be replaced.

➡**The master cylinder cannot be honed, and no abrasives are to be used in the bore.**

10. Assemble the master cylinder components in reverse order of disassembly. Lubricate all parts and seals with clean brake fluid. Install the reservoir by pushing in with a rocking motion.

11. Bench bleeding the master cylinder reduces the possibility of getting air into the lines when the unit is installed. Connect two short pieces of brake line to the outlet fittings, then bend them until the free end is below the fluid level in the master cylinder reservoirs.

12. Fill the reservoirs with fresh brake fluid, then slowly pump the piston with a suitable blunt drift until no more air bubbles appear in the reservoirs.

13. Disconnect the two short lines, top up the brake fluid level and install the reservoir cap.

14. Install the master cylinder on the car. Attach the lines, but do not tighten them. Force out any air that might have

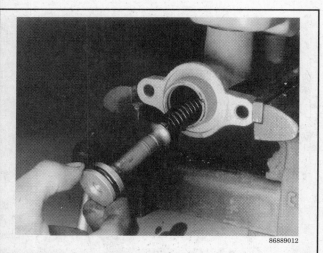

Fig. 12 First remove the primary piston from the master cylinder, then . . .

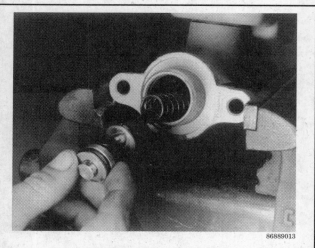

Fig. 13 . . . remove the secondary piston and spring from the master cylinder bore

Fig. 15 Exploded view of a disassembled master cylinder — 1986 model shown

Fig. 16 Remove and discard the O-ring seals from the pistons

been trapped at the connection by slowly depressing the brake pedal, then tighten the lines before releasing the pedal. Bleed the brake system as described in this section

Power Brake Booster

REMOVAL & INSTALLATION

▶ See Figures 17 and 18

1. Disconnect the negative battery cable.
2. If necessary for access to the booster, remove the battery and the air cleaner assembly.
3. Remove the master cylinder from the booster. Move the master cylinder forward just enough to clear the studs on the vacuum booster. This will flex the brake pipes slightly, so be careful not to bend or distort the pipes.
4. Disconnect the vacuum hose(s) from the booster.
5. From inside of the vehicle, remove the booster pushrod from the brake pedal.
6. Unfasten the nuts that attach the booster to the dash panel and remove it from the vehicle.
7. Transfer the necessary parts to the new booster.

To install:

8. Position the booster in the vehicle.
9. Connect the booster pushrod to the brake pedal. Tilt the entire vacuum booster slightly to work the pushrod onto the pedal clevis pin without putting unnecessary side pressure on the pushrod. Use your left hand to align the pushrod with the pedal, then push together.
10. Secure the booster using the retaining nuts. Tighten the nuts to 20 ft. lbs. (27 Nm).
11. Attach the booster vacuum hose.
12. Connect the master cylinder to the power brake booster.
13. If removed, install the air cleaner and battery.
14. Bleed the brake system, connect the negative battery cable and check the brakes for proper operation.

Proportioning Valves

REMOVAL & INSTALLATION

▶ See Figures 19, 20 and 21

1. Disconnect the negative battery cable.

➡ **On some vehicles, it may be necessary to remove the master cylinder reservoir for access to the proportioning valves.**

2. If necessary, unfasten the retaining roll pins and remove the fluid reservoir from the cylinder.
3. Detach the proportioning valve cap assemblies.
4. Remove the O-rings and the springs. Discard the O-rings.
5. Using needle-nosed pliers, carefully remove the proportioning valve pistons. Be careful not to scratch or damage the piston stems.
6. Remove the seals from the pistons.

To install:

7. Thoroughly clean and dry all parts.
8. Lubricate the new piston seals with the silicone grease included in the repair kit or brake assembly fluid. Install to the pistons with the seal lips facing upward toward the cap assembly.
9. Lubricate the stem of the pistons and install to their bores.
10. Install the springs.
11. Lubricate and install the new O-rings in their grooves in the cap assemblies.
12. Install the caps to the master cylinder and tighten to 20 ft. lbs. (27 Nm).
13. If removed, install the master cylinder reservoir.
14. Fill the reservoir with brake fluid.
15. Connect the negative battery cable and check the brakes for proper operation.

Brake Hoses and Pipes

Hydraulic brake hoses should be inspected at least twice a year. Check the hoses for:
- Road hazard damage
- Cracks and/or chafing of outer cover
- Leaks and/or blistering
- Proper routing and mounting

If you find any of these conditions, adjust or replace the necessary hose(s). A brake hose which rubs against other components will eventually fail. A light and mirror can be helpful to thoroughly inspect the hoses.

REMOVAL & INSTALLATION

1. If brake line fittings are corroded, apply a coating of penetrating oil and allow to stand before disconnecting the brake lines.
2. Use a brake line wrench to loosen the brake hose or pipe.
3. Remove the support brackets.

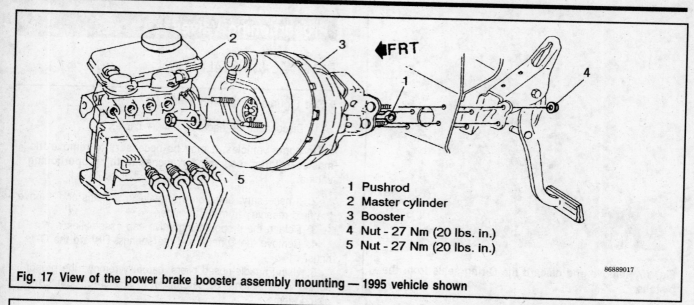

1 Pushrod
2 Master cylinder
3 Booster
4 Nut - 27 Nm (20 lbs. in.)
5 Nut - 27 Nm (20 lbs. in.)

86889017

Fig. 17 View of the power brake booster assembly mounting — 1995 vehicle shown

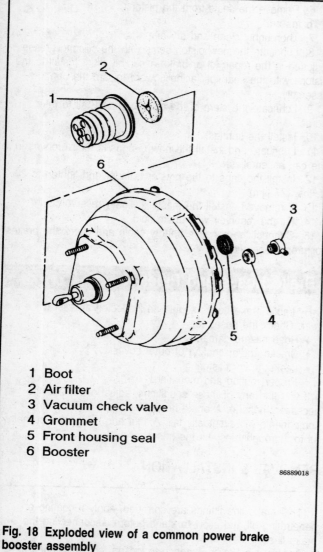

1 Boot
2 Air filter
3 Vacuum check valve
4 Grommet
5 Front housing seal
6 Booster

86889018

Fig. 18 Exploded view of a common power brake booster assembly

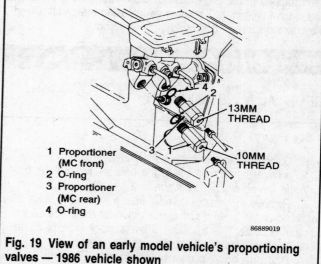

1 Proportioner (MC front)
2 O-ring
3 Proportioner (MC rear)
4 O-ring

86889019

Fig. 19 View of an early model vehicle's proportioning valves — 1986 vehicle shown

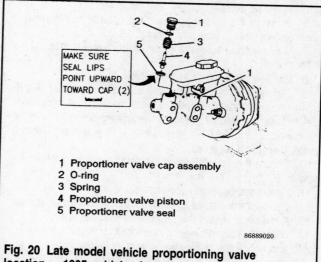

MAKE SURE SEAL LIPS POINT UPWARD TOWARD CAP (2)

1 Proportioner valve cap assembly
2 O-ring
3 Spring
4 Proportioner valve piston
5 Proportioner valve seal

86889020

Fig. 20 Late model vehicle proportioning valve location — 1995 vehicle shown

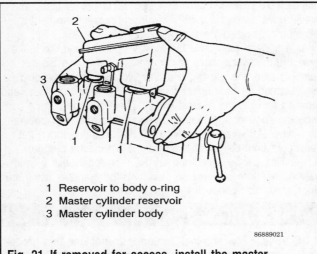

1 Reservoir to body o-ring
2 Master cylinder reservoir
3 Master cylinder body

86889021

Fig. 21 If removed for access, install the master cylinder reservoir

4. Note the location of the brake pipe before removal.
5. Remove the brake pipe or hose.
To install:
6. Install the new hose or pipe, observing the location of original installation.
7. Install the support brackets.
8. Ensure the pipes or hoses are clear of rotating parts and will not chafe on suspension parts.
9. Tighten the brake hose or pipe using a brake line wrench. Do not overtighten.
10. Properly bleed the brake hydraulic system.
11. Test drive the vehicle.

BRAKE PIPE FLARING

▶ **See Figures 22, 23 and 24**

When replacing the steel brake pipes, always use double walled steer piping which is designed to withstand high pressure and resist corrosion. Also, it is important to make sure that the pipe is of the same size to assure both a proper fit and proper brake operation.

✳✳CAUTION

Never use copper tubing. It is subject to fatigue, cracking and/or corrosion, which can result in brake line failure.

Whenever possible, try to work with brake lines that are already cut to the length needed. These lines are available at most auto parts stores and have machine made flares, the quality of which is hard to duplicate with most of the available inexpensive flaring kits.

When the brake are applied, there is a great deal of pressure developed in the hydraulic system. An improperly formed flare can leak with a resultant loss of stopping power. If you have never formed a double-flare, take time to familiarize yourself with the flaring kit; practice forming double-flares on scrap tubing until you are satisfied with the results.

Precautions:

• Always use double walled steel brake pipe.
• Carefully route and retain replacement pipes.
• Always use the correct fasteners and mount in the original location.
• Use only double lap flaring tools. The use of single lap flaring tools produces a flare which may not withstand system pressure.
1. Obtain the recommended pipe and steel fitting nut of the correct size. Use the outside diameter of the pipe to specify size.
2. Cut the pipe to the appropriate length with a pipe cutter. Do not force the cutter. Correct length of pipe is determined by measuring the old pipe using a string and adding approximately 1/8 in. (3mm) for each flare.
3. Make sure the fittings are installed before starting the flare.
4. Chamfer the inside and outside diameter of the pipe with the de-burring tool.
5. Remove all traces of lubricant from the brake pipe and flaring tool.
6. Clamp the flaring tool body in a vise.
7. Select the correct size collet and forming mandrel for the pipe size used.
8. Insert the proper forming mandrel into the tool body. While holding the forming mandrel in place with your finger, thread in the forcing screw until it makes contact and begins to move the forming mandrel. When contact is made, turn the forcing screw back 1 complete turn.
9. Slide the clamping nut over the brake pipe and insert the prepared brake pipe into the correct collet. Leave approximately 0.750 in. (19mm) of tubing extending out of the collet. Insert the assembly into the tool body. The brake pipe end must contact the face of the forming mandrel.
10. Tighten the clamping nut into the tool body very tight or the pipe may push out.
11. Wrench tighten the forcing screw in until it bottoms. Do not overtighten the forcing screw or the flare may become oversized.

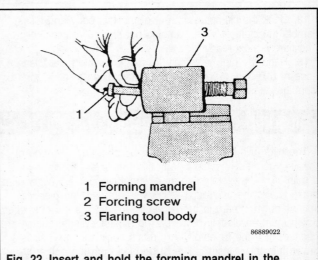

1 Forming mandrel
2 Forcing screw
3 Flaring tool body

86889022

Fig. 22 Insert and hold the forming mandrel in the flaring tool body

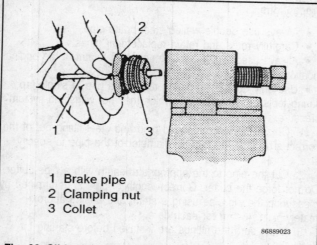

1 Brake pipe
2 Clamping nut
3 Collet

86889023

Fig. 23 Slide the clamping nut over the brake pipe before attaching the collet

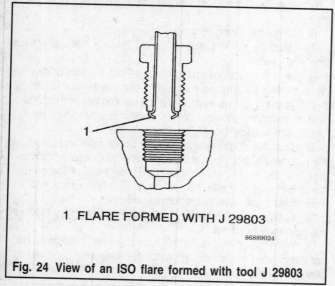

1 FLARE FORMED WITH J 29803

86889024

Fig. 24 View of an ISO flare formed with tool J 29803

12. Back the clamping nut out of the tool body and disassemble the clamping the clamping nut and collet assembly. The flare is now ready for use.

13. Bend the pipe assembly to match the old pipe. Clearance of 0.750 in. (19mm) must be maintained to all moving or vibrating parts.

Bleeding the Brake System

The hydraulic brake system must be bled any time one of the lines is disconnected or any time air enters the system. If a point in the system, such as a wheel cylinder or caliper brake line is the only point which was opened, the bleeder screws down stream in the hydraulic system are the only ones which must be bled. If however, the master cylinder fittings are opened, or if the reservoir level drops sufficiently that air is drawn into the system, air must be bled from the entire hydraulic system. If the brake pedal feels spongy upon application, and goes almost to the floor but regains height when pumped, air has entered the system. It must be bled out. If no

fittings were recently opened for service, check for leaks that would have allowed the entry of air and repair them before attempting to bleed the system.

As a general rule, once the master cylinder (and the brake pressure modulator valve or combination valve on ABS systems) is bled, the remainder of the hydraulic system should be bled starting at the furthest wheel from the master cylinder and working towards the nearest wheel. Therefore, the correct bleeding sequence is: master cylinder, modulator or combination valve (ABS vehicles only), right rear wheel cylinder, left rear, right front caliper and left front. Most master cylinder assemblies on these vehicles are NOT equipped with bleeder valves, therefore air must be bled from the cylinders using the front brake pipe connections.

✳✳CAUTION

If the vehicle has anti-lock braking, do not use this procedure without first reading the information on ABS system bleeding found later in this section. Improper service procedures on Anti-Lock Braking Systems (ABS) can cause serious personal injury. Refer to the ABS service procedures.

MANUAL BLEEDING

◆ See Figures 25 and 26

For those of us who are not fortunate enough to have access to a power bleeding tool, the manual brake bleeding procedure will quite adequately remove air from the hydraulic system. The major difference between the pressure and manual bleeding procedures is that the manual method takes more time and will require help from an assistant. One person must depress the brake pedal, while another opens and closes the bleeder screws.

➡**In addition to a length of clear neoprene bleeder hose, bleeder wrenches and a clear bleeder bottle (old plastic jar or drink bottle will suffice), bleeding late-model ABS systems may also require the use of one or more relatively inexpensive combination valve pressure bleeding tools (which are used to depress one or more valves in order to allow component/system bleeding). To fully bleed the late model ABS systems, a scan tool should also be used to run the system through functional tests.**

1. Deplete the vacuum reserve by applying the brakes several times with the ignition **OFF**.

2. Clean the top of the master cylinder, remove the cover and fill the reservoirs with clean fluid. To prevent squirting fluid, and possibly damaging painted surfaces, install the cover during the procedure, but be sure to frequently check and top off the reservoirs with fresh fluid.

✳✳WARNING

Never reuse brake fluid which has been bled from the system.

3. The master cylinder must be bled first if it is suspected to contain air. If the master cylinder was removed and bench

bled before installation it must still be bled, but it should take less time and effort. Bleed the master cylinder as follows:

a. Position a container under the master cylinder to catch the brake fluid.

❋❋WARNING

Do not allow brake fluid to spill on or come in contact with the vehicle's finish as it will remove the paint. In case of a spill, immediately flush the area with water.

b. Loosen the front brake line at the master cylinder and allow the fluid to flow from the front port.

c. Have a friend depress the brake pedal slowly and hold (air and/or fluid should be expelled from the loose fitting). Tighten the line, then release the brake pedal and wait 15 seconds. Loosen the fitting and repeat until all air is removed from the master cylinder bore.

d. When finished, tighten the line fitting to 20 ft. lbs. (27 Nm).

e. Repeat the sequence at the master cylinder rear pipe fitting.

➡**During the bleeding procedure, make sure your assistant does NOT release the brake pedal while a fitting is loosened or while a bleeder screw is opening. Air will be drawn back into the system.**

4. Check and refill the master cylinder reservoir.

➡**Remember, if the reservoir is allowed to empty of fluid during the procedure, air will be drawn into the system and the bleeding procedure must be restarted at the master cylinder assembly.**

5. On late model ABS equipped vehicles, perform the special ABS procedures as described later in this section. On 4 wheel ABS systems the Brake Pressure Modulator Valve (BPMV) must be bled (if it has been replaced or if it is suspected to contain air) and on most Rear Wheel Anti-Lock (RWAL) systems the combination valve must be held open. In both cases, special combination valve depressor tools should be used during bleeding and a scan tool must be used for ABS function tests.

6. If a single line or fitting was the only hydraulic line disconnected, then only the caliper(s) or wheel cylinder(s) affected by that line must be bled. If the master cylinder required bleeding, then all calipers and wheel cylinders must be bled in the proper sequence:

a. Right rear
b. Left rear
c. Right front
d. Left front

7. Bleed the individual calipers or wheel cylinders as follows:

a. Place a suitable wrench over the bleeder screw and attach a clear plastic hose over the screw end. Be sure the hose is seated snugly on the screw or you may be squirted with brake fluid.

➡**Be very careful when bleeding wheel cylinders and brake calipers. The bleeder screws often rust in position and may easily break off if forced. Installing a new bleeder screw will often require removal of the component and**

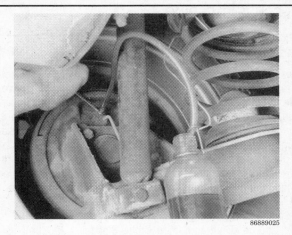

Fig. 25 Attach a clear plastic hose to the screw and submerge the other end in a transparent container of clean brake fluid

may include overhaul or replacement of the wheel cylinder/caliper. To help prevent the possibility of breaking a bleeder screw, spray it with some penetrating oil before attempting to loosen it.

b. Submerge the other end of the tube in a transparent container of clean brake fluid.

c. Loosen the bleed screw, then have a friend apply the brake pedal slowly and hold. Tighten the bleed screw to 62 inch lbs. (7 Nm), release the brake pedal and wait 15 seconds. Repeat the sequence (including the 15 second pause) until all air is expelled from the caliper or cylinder.

d. Tighten the bleeder screw to 62 inch lbs. (7 Nm) when finished.

8. Check the pedal for a hard feeling with the engine not running. If the pedal is soft, repeat the bleeding procedure until a firm pedal is obtained.

9. If the brake warning light is on, depress the brake pedal firmly. If there is no air in the system, the light will go out.

10. After bleeding, make sure that a firm pedal is achieved before attempting to move the vehicle.

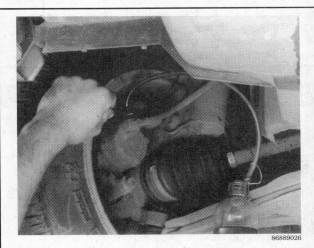

Fig. 26 It's often helpful to attach the bleeder bottle to the frame using an old coat hanger

PRESSURE BLEEDING

▶ See Figure 27

For the lucky ones with access to a pressure bleeding tool, this procedure may be used to quickly and efficiently remove air from the brake system. This procedure may be used as a guide, but be careful to follow the tool manufacturer's directions closely. Any pressure bleeding tool MUST be of the diaphragm-type. A proper pressure bleeder tool will utilize a rubber diaphragm between the air source and brake fluid in order to prevent air, moisture oil and other contaminants from entering the hydraulic system.

1. Install Pressure Bleeder Adapter Cap J 35589 or equivalent, to the master cylinder.
2. Charge Diaphragm Type Brake Bleeder J 29532 or equivalent, to 20-25 psi (140-172 kPa).
3. Connect the line to the pressure bleeder adapter cap, then open the line valve.
4. Raise and safely support the vehicle.
5. If it is necessary to bleed all of the calipers/cylinders, the following sequence should be used:
   - Right rear
   - Left rear
   - Right front
   - Left front
6. Place a proper size box end wrench (or tool J 21472) over the caliper/cylinder bleeder valve.
7. Attach a clear tube over the bleeder screw, then submerge the other end of the tube in a clear container partially filled with clean brake fluid.
8. Open the bleeder screw at least ¾ of a turn and allow flow to continue until no air is seen in the fluid.

Fig. 27 View of the pressure bleeder adapter cap installed on the master cylinder

9. Close the bleeder screw. Tighten the rear bleeder screws to 62 inch lbs. (7 Nm) and the front bleeder screws to 115 inch lbs. (13 Nm).
10. Repeat Steps 6-9 until all of the calipers and/or cylinders have been bled.
11. Carefully lower the vehicle.
12. Check the brake pedal for "sponginess". If the condition is found, the entire bleeding procedure must be repeated.
13. Remove tools J 35589 and J 29532.
14. Refill the master cylinder to the proper level with brake fluid.
15. DO NOT attempt to move the vehicle unless a firm brake pedal is obtained.

FRONT DISC BRAKES

▶ See Figure 28

❊❊CAUTION

Brake shoes may contain asbestos, which has been determined to be a cancer causing agent. Never clean the brake surfaces with compressed air! Avoid inhaling any dust from any brake surface! When cleaning brake surfaces, use a commercially available brake cleaning fluid.

Brake Pads

REMOVAL & INSTALLATION

▶ See Figures 29, 30, 31, 32 and 33

1. Using a clean turkey baster or equivalent, remove about ⅔ of the brake fluid from the master cylinder.
2. Raise and safely support the vehicle.
3. Remove the tire and wheel assembly.
4. Using a C-clamp, bottom the piston in its bore for clearance to remove it from the rotor.
5. Remove the caliper, as described later in this section.
6. Use a suitable prytool to disengage the buttons on the shoe from the holes in the caliper housing, then remove the outboard shoe and lining.
7. Remove the inboard shoe and lining.
8. Prior to installing new shoes and linings, wipe the outside surface of the boot clean with denatured alcohol.
   To install:
9. Use a large C-clamp to compress the piston back into the caliper bore. Be careful not to damage the piston or boot with the C-clamp.
10. After bottoming the piston, lift the inner edge of the boot next to the piston and press out any trapped air. The boot must lie flat.
11. Install the inboard shoe and lining by snapping the shoe retaining spring into the piston inside diameter. The shoe retainer spring is already staked to the inboard shoe. After installing the shoe and lining, make sure the boot is not touching the shoe. If there is contact, reseat or reposition the boot.
12. Install the outboard shoe and lining with the wear sensor at the trailing edge of the shoe. During forward wheel rotation, the back of the shoe must lay flat against the caliper.
13. Install caliper, as outlined later in this section.
14. Install the tire and wheel assembly.
15. Carefully lower the vehicle, then fill the master cylinder to the proper level.

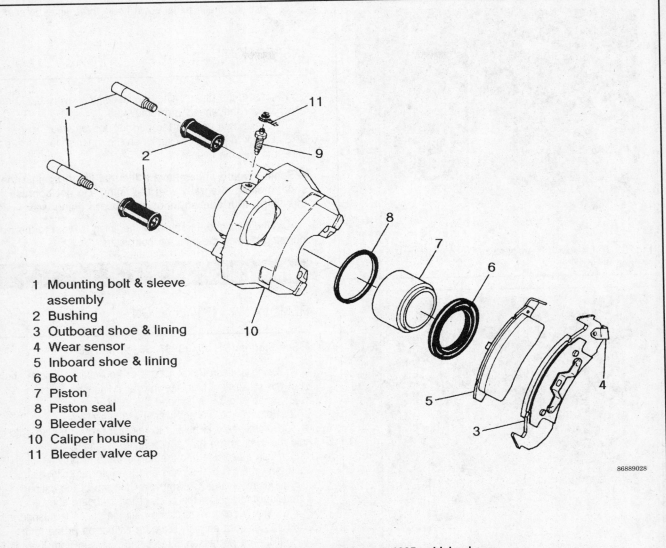

1 Mounting bolt & sleeve
   assembly
2 Bushing
3 Outboard shoe & lining
4 Wear sensor
5 Inboard shoe & lining
6 Boot
7 Piston
8 Piston seal
9 Bleeder valve
10 Caliper housing
11 Bleeder valve cap

86889028

Fig. 28 Exploded view of the front disc brake assembly components — 1995 vehicle shown

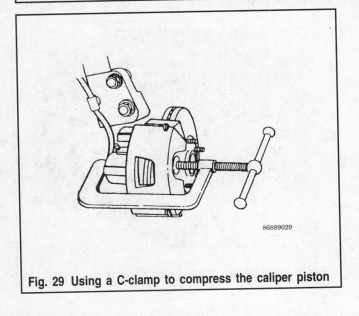

86889029

Fig. 29 Using a C-clamp to compress the caliper piston

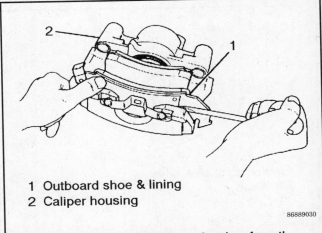

1 Outboard shoe & lining
2 Caliper housing

86889030

Fig. 30 Disengage the buttons on the shoe from the holes in the caliper housing to remove the outboard shoe and lining

Fig. 31 Remove the outboard brake pad from the caliper, then . . .

Fig. 32 . . . remove the inboard brake pad

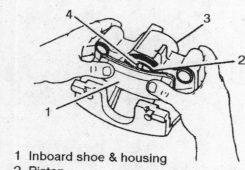

1 Inboard shoe & housing
2 Piston
3 Caliper houisng
4 Shoe retainer spring

Fig. 33 Install the inboard shoe and lining, then install the outboard shoe and lining

16. Push the brake pedal down firmly three times to seat the linings.

INSPECTION

1. Inspect the brake linings approximately every 6,000 miles or whenever the wheels are removed.
2. Check both ends of the pad for uneven wear.
3. Check the lining thickness on the inner shoe to make sure it is wearing evenly.

➡**Some inboard shoes have a thermal lining against the shoe, molded integrally with the lining. Do not confuse this lining with uneven inboard-outboard lining wear.**

4. Whenever the thickness of the lining is worn to the wear indicator, replace the pads on both sides.

Brake Caliper

REMOVAL & INSTALLATION

◆ **See Figures 34, 35, 36, 37, 38, 39 and 40**

1. Using a clean turkey baster or equivalent, remove about ⅔ of the brake fluid from the master cylinder.
2. Raise and safely support the vehicle.
3. Remove the tire and wheel assembly.
4. Sometimes it is helpful to reinstall two of the lug nuts to hold the rotor to the hub and bearing assembly.
5. Push the piston into the caliper bore to provide clearance between the brake pads and the rotor as follows:
   a. Install a large C-clamp over the top of the caliper housing and against the back of the outboard shoe.
   b. Slowly tighten the clamp until the piston is pushed into the caliper bore enough slide the caliper off of the rotor.
6. If the caliper assembly is being removed from the vehicle for overhaul, unfasten the bolt attaching the inlet fitting, then plug the exposed fitting to prevent contamination. If just

Fig. 34 View of the caliper assembly installed on the rotor

Fig. 35 Using a C-clamp, carefully bottom out the piston to provide clearance for removal

the pads are being replaced, there is no need to disconnect the inlet fitting.

7. Unfasten the caliper mounting bolt and sleeve assemblies. Some vehicles have a rubber cap over the retaining bolt which must be removed first.

8. Lift the caliper off of the rotor. If the caliper is not being removed for overhaul, suspend it from the strut with a wire hook.

9. Inspect the mounting bolts, sleeves and bushings for damage and replace as necessary.

To install:

10. Liberally coat the inside of the bushings with silicone grease.

11. Position the caliper over the rotor into the knuckle, then fasten the mounting bolt and sleeve assemblies. Tighten to 38 ft. lbs. (51 Nm).

12. If removed, connect the inlet fitting. Tighten to 32 ft. lbs. (44 Nm).

13. Remove the two nut retaining the rotor to the hub, then install the wheel and tire assembly. Only hand-tighten the lug nuts at this time.

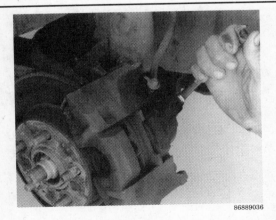

Fig. 36 If the caliper is being removed for overhaul, unfasten the bolt attaching the fluid line, then plug the line to prevent debris from entering the hydraulic system

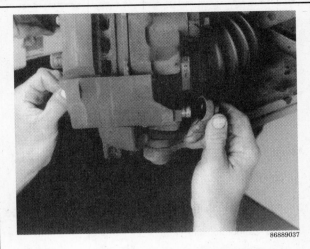

Fig. 37 Some vehicles have a cap over the retaining bolt which must be removed to access the bolt

Fig. 38 Unfasten, then remove the caliper mounting bolts and sleeves

Fig. 39 If the caliper is not being removed for overhaul, suspend it with a piece of wire (a coat hanger works well) from the strut

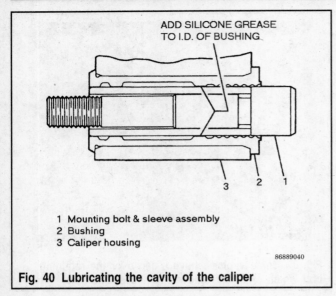

ADD SILICONE GREASE TO I.D. OF BUSHING

1 Mounting bolt & sleeve assembly
2 Bushing
3 Caliper housing

86889040

Fig. 40 Lubricating the cavity of the caliper

14. Carefully lower the vehicle, then tighten the lug nuts to 103 ft. lbs (140 Nm).

15. Fill the master cylinder to the proper level, and bleed the brakes if the inlet fitting was removed. Recheck the fluid level.

OVERHAUL

▶ **See Figures 41, 42, 43, 44 and 45**

1. Remove the caliper from the vehicle. For details, please refer to the procedure located earlier in this section. Place the caliper on a workbench.

2. Remove the bushings. Inspect for cuts and nicks. Replace as necessary.

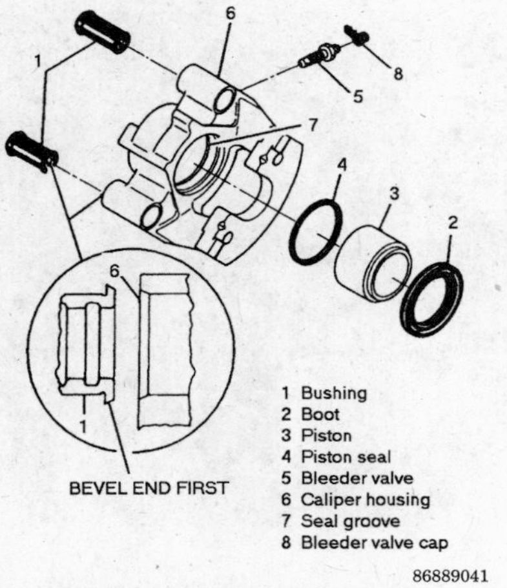

3. Stuff a shop towel or a block of wood into the caliper to catch the piston and apply compressed air to the inlet hole.

✳✳CAUTION

DO NOT apply too much air pressure to the bore, for the piston may jump out, causing damage to the piston and/or the operator. Be absolutely sure to keep your fingers away from the piston while air is being applied.

4. Remove and discard the piston boot and seal. Be careful not to scratch the bore. Use of a metal tool is NOT recommended when removing the boot and the seal because of the possibility of scoring and damaging the bore.

5. Inspect the piston for scoring, nicks, corrosion and worn chrome plating. Replace as necessary.

6. Remove the boot from the caliper housing bolt.

7. Remove the bleeder screw and its rubber cap.

8. Inspect the housing bore and seal groove for scoring, nicks, corrosion and wear. Crocus cloth can be used to polish out light corrosion.

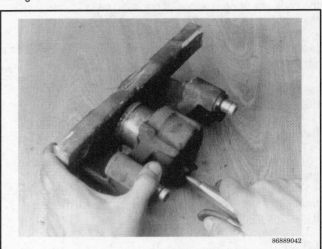

86889042

Fig. 42 Use compressed air to drive the piston out of the caliper, but make sure to keep your fingers clear!

86889043

Fig. 43 Remove the boot from the caliper housing, taking care not to score or damage the bore

6
1
7
8
5
4
3
2

6
1
BEVEL END FIRST

1 Bushing
2 Boot
3 Piston
4 Piston seal
5 Bleeder valve
6 Caliper housing
7 Seal groove
8 Bleeder valve cap

86889041

Fig. 41 Exploded view of the caliper components removed for overhaul

Fig. 44 Use extreme caution when removing the piston seal; DO NOT scratch the caliper bore

9. Remove the bleeder valve and bleeder valve cap.

To install:

10. Install the bleeder valve and bleeder valve cap into the caliper.

11. Lubricate the piston, caliper and seal with clean brake fluid.

12. Install the piston seal into the caliper seal groove. Make sure it is not twisted in the caliper bore groove.

13. Bottom the piston into the bore, then secure the boot using J 29077 or an equivalent piston seal installer tool.

14. Lubricate the bevelled end of the bushings with silicone grease. Pinch the bushing and install the bevelled end first. Push the bushing through the housing mounting bore.

15. Install the caliper assembly, then properly bleed the hydraulic brake system.

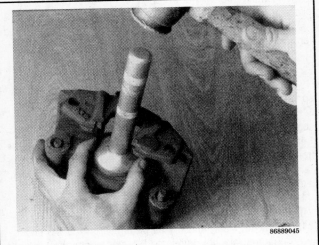

Fig. 45 During assembly, use a suitable piston boot driver to properly install the boot to the housing

Brake Disc (Rotor)

REMOVAL & INSTALLATION

♦ **See Figure 46**

1. Raise and safely support the vehicle. Remove the tire and wheel assembly.

2. Unfasten the caliper mounting bolts, then carefully remove the caliper (along with the brake pads) from the rotor. Do not disconnect the brake line; instead, wire the caliper out of the way with the line still connected.

3. Remove the rotor by simply pulling it off of the hub and bearing assembly.

4. The installation is the reverse of the removal procedure.

INSPECTION

Check the disc brake rotor for scoring, cracks or other damage. Rotor run-out should be measured while the rotor is installed, while rotor thickness/thickness variation may be checked with the rotor installed or removed. Use a dial gauge to check rotor run-out. Check the rotor thickness to make sure it is greater than minimum thickness and check for thickness variations using a caliper micrometer.

Thickness Variation

1. Measure the thickness at four or more points on the rotor. Make all measure measurements at the same distance in from the edge of the rotor. Use a micrometer calibrated in ten-thousandths of an inch.

2. A rotor that varies in thickness by more than 0.0005 in. (0.013mm) can cause pedal pulsation and/or front end vibration during brake applications. A rotor that does not meet these specifications should be resurfaced to specifications or replaced.

Fig. 46 Removing the rotor from the hub

Lateral Run-out

1. Remove the wheel and tire assembly.
2. Fasten the lug nuts to retain the rotor.
3. Secure a dial indicator to the steering knuckle so the indicator button contacts the rotor at about 0.5 in. (13mm) from the outer edge of the rotor.

REAR DRUM BRAKES

▶ See Figure 47

✳✳CAUTION

Brake shoes may contain asbestos, which has been determined to be a cancer causing agent. Never clean the brake surfaces with compressed air! Avoid inhaling any dust from any brake surface! When cleaning brake surfaces, use a commercially available brake cleaning fluid.

Brake Drums

REMOVAL & INSTALLATION

▶ **See Figures 48 and 49**

1. Raise and safely support the vehicle.

➡**Matchmark the relationship of the wheel to the axle flange and the brake drum to the axle flange to insure proper wheel balance during installation.**

2. Remove the wheel and tire assembly.
3. Remove the drum. If the drum is difficult to remove, make sure the parking brake is released, back off the parking brake cable adjustment, and/or use a rubber mallet to tap GENTLY around the inner drum diameter of the spindle. Be careful not to deform the drum by tapping too hard.
4. Inspect the drum for scoring, cracking or grooving. Replace if necessary.
To install:
5. Install the drum aligning the marks made during removal.
6. Using the marks previously made, install the tire and wheel assembly.
7. Carefully lower the vehicle, then tighten the lug nuts to 103 ft. lbs. (140 Nm).

INSPECTION

1. Inspect the brake drum for scoring, cracking or grooving. Light scoring of the drum not exceeding 0.020 in. (0.51mm) in depth will not affect brake operation.
2. Inspect the brake drum for excessive taper and out-of-round. When measuring a drum for out-of-round, taper and wear, take measurements at the open and closed edges of the machined surface and at right angles to each other.

4. Set the dial indicator to zero.
5. Turn the wheel one complete revolution and observe the total indicated run-out.
6. If the run-out exceeds 0.0031 in. (0.08mm), resurface or replace the rotor.

Brake Shoes

INSPECTION

1. Remove the wheel and drum.
2. Inspect the shoes for proper thickness. The lining should be at least 1/32 in. (0.8mm) above the rivet head for riveted brakes and 1/16 in. (1.6mm) above the mounting surface for bonded brake linings.
3. Inspect the linings for even wear, cracking and scoring. Replace as necessary.

REMOVAL & INSTALLATION

▶ **See Figures 50, 51, 52, 53, 54, 55, 56, 57, 58, 59, 60, 61 and 62**

➡**If unsure of spring positioning, finish one side before starting the other and use the untouched side as a guide.**

1. Raise and safely support the vehicle.
2. Remove the tire and wheel assemblies, then remove the brake drum.
3. Using tool J 8049, J 29840 or equivalent brake spring remover and installer, Unfasten the primary and secondary shoe return springs from the anchor pin, but leave them installed in the shoes.
4. Remove the hold-down springs, and pins using suitable pliers or brake tool.
5. While lifting up on the actuator lever, remove the actuator link, lever and lever return spring.
6. Unfasten and remove the bearing sleeve.
7. Remove the parking brake strut and spring.
8. Remove the brake shoes, held together by the lower spring, after disconnecting the parking brake cable.
9. Disconnect the adjusting screw assembly and adjusting screw spring.
10. Remove the retaining ring, pin and parking brake lever from the secondary brake shoe.
11. Lift the wheel cylinder dust boots and inspect for fluid leakage.
12. Thoroughly clean and dry the backing plate.
To install:
13. Remove, clean and dry all parts still on the old shoes with denatured alcohol. Lubricate the star wheel shaft threads and transfer all the parts to the new shoes in their proper locations.
14. To prepare the backing plate, lubricate the bosses, anchor pin and parking brake actuating lever pivot surface lightly with the brake-compatible lubricant.

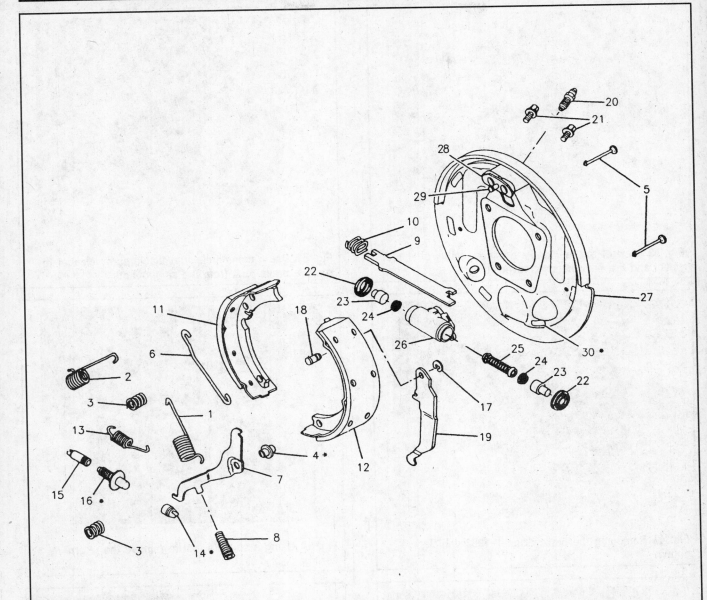

1 Return spring
2 Return spring
3 Hold down spring
4 Bearing sleeve
5 Hold-down pin
6 Actuator link
7 Actuator lever
8 Lever return spring
9 Parking brake strut
10 Strut spring

11 Primary shoe and lining
12 Secondary shoe and lining
13 Adjusting screw spring
14 Socket
15 Pivot nut
16 Adjusting screw
17 Retaining ring
18 Pin
19 Parking lever
20 Bleeder valve

21 Bolt
22 Boot
23 Piston
24 Seal
25 Spring assembly
26 Wheel cylinder
27 Backing plate
28 Shoe retainer
29 Anchor pin
30 Shoe pads (6 places)

* LUBRICATE WITH THIN COATING OF 1052196 LUBRICANT OR EQUIVALENT

86889047

Fig. 47 Exploded view of the rear drum brake system components (drum removed)

Fig. 48 View of the rear brake drum assembly after the wheel and tire have been removed

Fig. 49 Removing the brake drum — 1986 vehicle shown

Fig. 50 View of drum brake components

Fig. 51 Use a commercially available spray cleaner to remove brake dust from the components

Fig. 52 Using a suitable tool to remove the return springs

Fig. 53 Unfasten the primary return spring, then . . .

Fig. 54 . . . remove the secondary return spring

Fig. 55 Use the brake tool to compress the hold-down spring and twist the plate to free the pin

Fig. 56 Once the pin and the slot on the top of the spring plate are aligned, separate the hold-down spring and pin

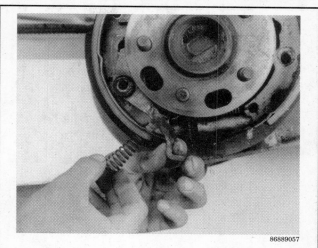

Fig. 57 Lift up on the actuator lever and remove the return spring, then . . .

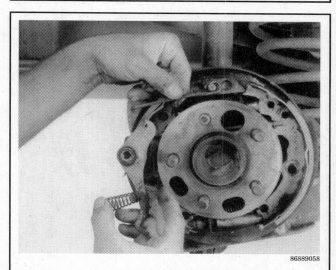

Fig. 58 . . . remove the lever and actuator link

Fig. 59 Remove the parking brake strut and spring assembly

Fig. 60 Remove the brake shoe assembly which is held together by the lower spring

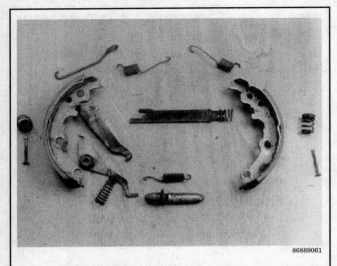

Fig. 61 Exploded view of the drum brake components

15. Install the parking brake lever on the secondary shoe with the pin and retaining ring.

16. Install the adjusting screw assembly and adjusting screw spring.

17. Position the shoe and lining assemblies after attaching the parking brake cable.

18. Spread the shoes apart, install the parking brake strut and strut spring. The end without the strut spring should engage the parking brake lever and secondary shoe and lining. The end with the strut spring should engage the primary shoe and lining.

➡**In the next step, the bearing sleeve must be installed between the secondary and lining and the actuator lever. Refer to the accompanying figure.**

19. Install the bearing sleeve, actuator lever and lever return spring.

20. Install the hold-down pins and springs.

21. Fasten the actuator link on the anchor pin. While holding up the lever, fasten the actuator link into the lever.

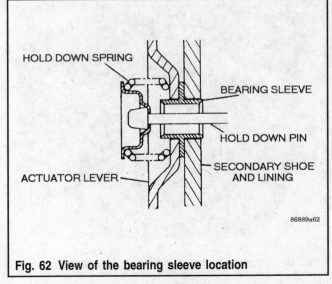

Fig. 62 View of the bearing sleeve location

22. Secure the shoe return springs, using tool J 8057 or equivalent pliers.

23. Adjust the brakes using the procedure located in this section.

24. Aligning the marks made during removal, install the brake drum.

25. Install the tire and wheel assembly.

26. Carefully lower the vehicle, then tighten the lug nuts to 103 ft. lbs. (140 Nm).

27. Adjust the parking brake, as outlined later in this section.

Wheel Cylinders

REMOVAL & INSTALLATION

▶ **See Figures 63, 64 and 65**

1. Raise and safely support the vehicle.

2. Remove the wheel and tire assembly.

3. Unfasten the inlet brake fluid line, then cap the line to prevent contamination from entering.

4. Following the procedures located in this section, remove the brake drum and brake shoes (if necessary for access).

5. If necessary for access to the cylinder, remove the hub and bearing assembly.

➡**On some vehicles, you will need a #6 Torx® bit to remove the wheel cylinder bolts.**

6. To remove the round retainer type cylinders, insert two awls or pins into the access slots between the wheel cylinder pilot and the retainer locking tabs. Bend both tabs away simultaneously. The wheel cylinder can be removed, as the retainer is released.

7. To remove the bolted wheel cylinders, unfasten the wheel cylinder bolts, then remove the cylinder from the backing plate.

To install:

8. Apply a very thin coating of silicone sealer to the cylinder mounting surface.

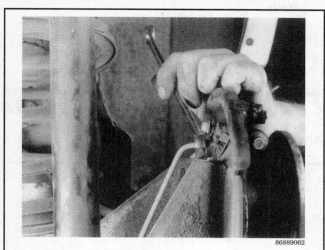

Fig. 63 Disconnect and plug the brake line from the rear of the backing plate

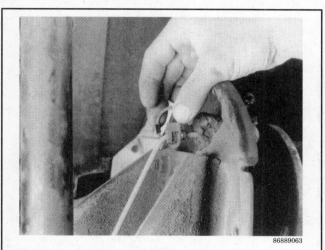

Fig. 64 Two awls may be used to bend the retainer stubs, releasing the wheel cylinder

Fig. 65 Once the cylinder is free of the backing plate, it can be removed from the vehicle

9. For round retainer type wheel cylinders, position the cylinder and hold it in place with a wooden block between the cylinder and the axle flange. Carefully seat the new retainer clip, using a 1⅛ in. 12-point socket and socket extension (to help preserve your fingers). The socket is used to assure that the retainer seats evenly.

10. For bolt type wheel cylinders, position, install the cylinder to the backing plate and fasten the attaching bolts. Tighten to 15 ft. lbs. (20 Nm).

11. If removed, install the hub and bearing assembly. Tighten to 43 ft. lbs. (58 Nm).

12. Install the brake shoes, if removed, and the brake drum.

13. Uncap, then connect the brake line to the wheel cylinder. Tighten the inlet tube nut to 17 ft. lbs. (23 Nm).

14. Install the tire and wheel assembly.

15. Carefully lower the vehicle, then tighten the lug nuts to 103 ft. lbs. (140 Nm).

16. Properly bleed the hydraulic brake system.

OVERHAUL

▶ See Figures 66, 67, 68, 69 and 70

Wheel cylinder overhaul kits may be available, but often at little or no savings over a reconditioned wheel cylinder. It often makes sense with these components to substitute a new or reconditioned part instead of attempting an overhaul.

If no replacement is available, or you would prefer to overhaul your wheel cylinders, the following procedure may be used. When rebuilding and installing wheel cylinders, avoid getting any contaminants into the system. Always install clean, new, high-quality brake fluid. If dirty or improper fluid has been used, it will be necessary to drain the entire system, flush the system with proper brake fluid, replace all rubber components, refill, and bleed the system.

1. Remove the wheel cylinder from the vehicle.

2. First remove and discard the old rubber boots, then withdraw the pistons. Piston cylinders are equipped with seals and a spring assembly, all located behind the pistons in the cylinder bore.

Fig. 66 Carefully remove the old boots from the wheel cylinder

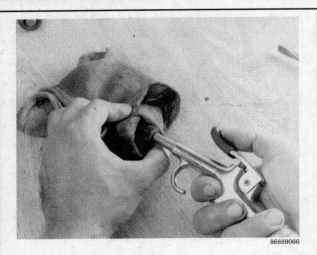

Fig. 67 A small amount of compressed air may be used to free the inner components

Fig. 68 Remove the cylinder inner components

3. Remove the remaining inner components seals and spring assembly. Compressed air may be useful in removing these components. If no compressed air is available, be VERY careful not to score the wheel cylinder bore when removing parts from it. Discard all components for which replacements were supplied in the rebuild kit.

4. Wash the cylinder and metal parts in denatured alcohol or clean brake fluid.

❋❋WARNING

Never use a mineral-based solvent such as gasoline, kerosene, or paint thinner for cleaning purposes. These solvents will swell rubber components and quickly deteriorate them.

5. Allow the parts to air dry or use compressed air. Do not use rags for cleaning since lint will remain in the cylinder bore.

6. Inspect the piston and replace it if it shows scratches.

7. Lubricate the cylinder bore and seals using clean brake fluid.

8. Position the spring assembly.

9. Install the inner seals then the pistons.

10. Insert the new boots into the counterbores by hand. Do not lubricate the boots.

11. Install the wheel cylinder to the vehicle.

Brake Backing Plate

REMOVAL & INSTALLATION

▶ **See Figures 71, 72 and 73**

1. Raise and safely support the vehicle. Remove the rear wheel(s).

2. Remove the brake components, as described earlier in this section.

3. Detach and cap the inlet tube and nut from the wheel cylinder, then remove the wheel cylinder.

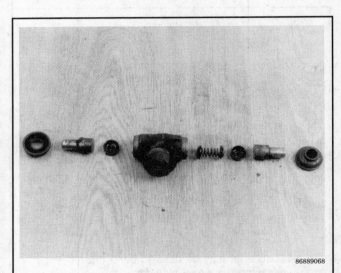

Fig. 69 View of the wheel cylinder inner components

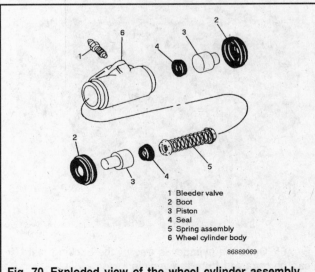

1 Bleeder valve
2 Boot
3 Piston
4 Seal
5 Spring assembly
6 Wheel cylinder body

Fig. 70 Exploded view of the wheel cylinder assembly

4. Disconnect the parking brake cable from the backing plate.

To install:

5. Install the backing plate to the axle assembly.

6. Position the wheel cylinder to the backing plate and secure with the retainers.

7. Install the hub and bearing, then secure using the assembly bolts.

8. Connect the parking brake cable to the backing plate.

9. Uncap and attach the inlet tube and nut to the wheel cylinder. Tight to 17 ft. lbs. (23 Nm).

10. Install the brake system components. Check the brake adjustment.

11. Bleed the brake system.

12. Install the rear wheel(s).

13. Carefully lower the vehicle, then tighten the lug nuts to 103 ft. lbs. (140 Nm).

14. Adjust the parking brake.

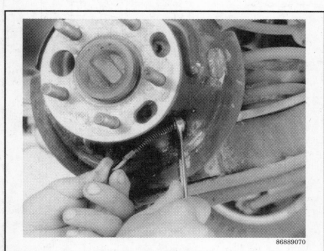

Fig. 71 Remove the parking brake cable from the backing plate

15. Unfasten the hub and bearing assembly bolts, then remove the assembly.

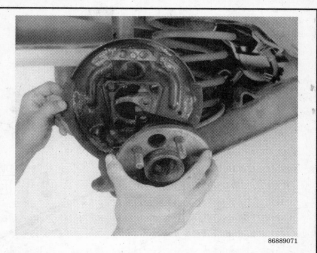

Fig. 72 Unfasten the retaining bolts, remove the hub and bearing assembly, then . . .

16. Remove the brake backing plate.

Fig. 73 . . . remove the brake backing plate from the axle

PARKING BRAKE

Cables

REMOVAL & INSTALLATION

Front Cable

CONSOLE LEVER PARKING BRAKE

▶ **See Figure 74**

1. Disconnect the negative battery cable. Raise and safely support the vehicle.

2. Loosen or remove the equalizer nut. Lower the vehicle.

3. Remove the console.

4. Disconnect the parking brake cable from the lever.

5. Remove the nut that secures the front cable to the floor pan.

6. Loosen the catalytic converter shield and the parking brake cable from the body.

7. Remove the cable from the equalizer, guide and underbody clips.

8. The installation is the reverse of the removal procedure.

9. Adjust the cable, as outlined in this section.

10. Connect the negative battery cable and check the parking brake for proper operation.

FOOT LEVER PARKING BRAKE

▶ **See Figure 75**

1. Disconnect the negative battery cable.

2. Raise and safely support the vehicle.

3. Bend the tang on the connector to allow cable removal.

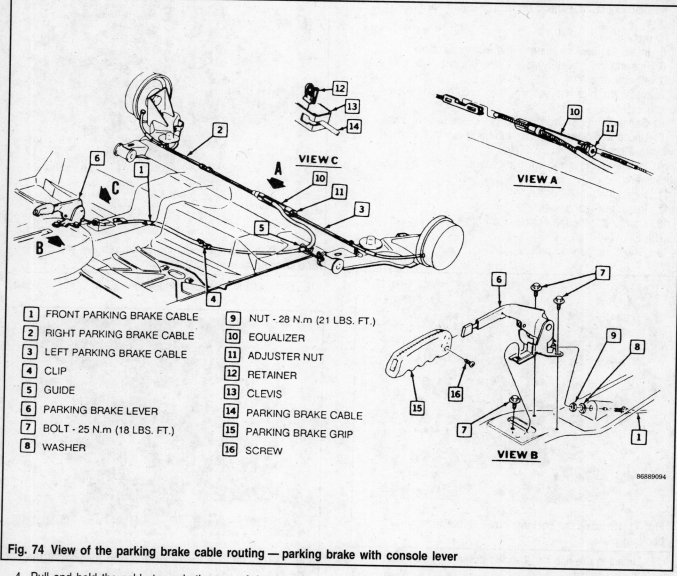

1 FRONT PARKING BRAKE CABLE
2 RIGHT PARKING BRAKE CABLE
3 LEFT PARKING BRAKE CABLE
4 CLIP
5 GUIDE
6 PARKING BRAKE LEVER
7 BOLT - 25 N.m (18 LBS. FT.)
8 WASHER
9 NUT - 28 N.m (21 LBS. FT.)
10 EQUALIZER
11 ADJUSTER NUT
12 RETAINER
13 CLEVIS
14 PARKING BRAKE CABLE
15 PARKING BRAKE GRIP
16 SCREW

86889094

Fig. 74 View of the parking brake cable routing — parking brake with console lever

4. Pull and hold the cable towards the rear of the car to create slack in the cable.

5. Detach the cable from the connector, equalizer assembly and guide.

6. Carefully lower the vehicle.

7. Remove the parking brake cable from the reel assembly.

➡**Use caution when removing the spring. This is to avoid hitting and knocking the self-adjusting spring loose.**

8. Disconnect the cable conduit fitting from the lever assembly while depressing the retaining tangs.

9. Remove the left rocker panel/door sill plate.

10. Detach the grommet from the floor pan and the cable from the center two body clips. Remove the front cable from the vehicle.

To install:

11. Connect the parking brake cable to the lever and reel assembly.

12. Install the cable conduit fitting securing the cable to the lever assembly.

13. Fasten the grommet to the floor pan, the grommet retainer and the center two body clips.

14. Install the left rocker panel/sill plate.

15. Raise and safely support the vehicle.

16. Install the cable through the guide and the equalizer to the connector.

17. Carefully lower the vehicle.

18. Fully apply and release the foot brake 4-6 times to self-adjust the braking system.

Rear Cables

1. Disconnect the negative battery cable. Raise and safely support the vehicle.

2. Loosen or remove the equalizer nut.

3. Remove the wheel(s) and drum(s).

4. Insert a suitable tool between the brake shoe and the top part of the brake adjuster bracket. Push the bracket to the front and release the top adjuster bracket rod.

5. Remove the hold-down spring, actuator lever and lever return spring.

6. Remove the adjuster spring.

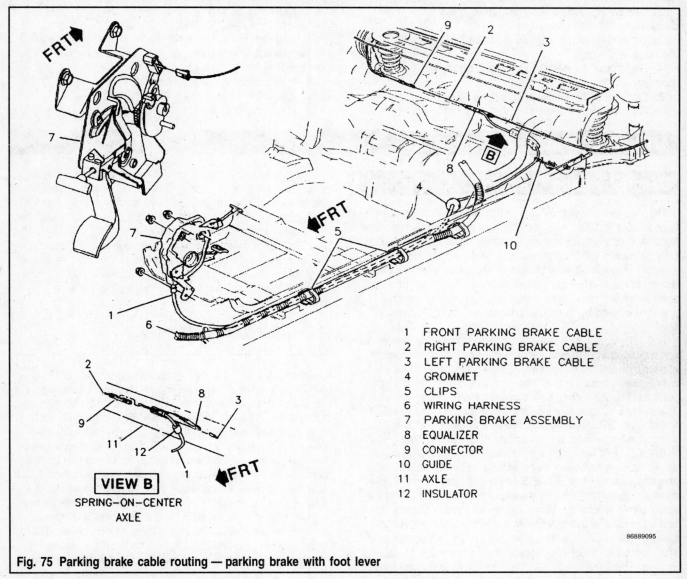

1 FRONT PARKING BRAKE CABLE
2 RIGHT PARKING BRAKE CABLE
3 LEFT PARKING BRAKE CABLE
4 GROMMET
5 CLIPS
6 WIRING HARNESS
7 PARKING BRAKE ASSEMBLY
8 EQUALIZER
9 CONNECTOR
10 GUIDE
11 AXLE
12 INSULATOR

VIEW B
SPRING-ON-CENTER
AXLE

86889095

Fig. 75 Parking brake cable routing — parking brake with foot lever

7. Remove the top rear brake shoe return spring.

8. Disconnect the parking brake cable from the actuating lever.

9. Pull the cable through the backing plate while depressing the retaining tangs.

10. On the right side, remove the cable end button from the connector.

11. Remove the conduit fitting from the axle bracket while depressing the retaining tangs.

To install:

12. Install the conduit fitting into the axle bracket, securing the retaining tangs.

13. Install the cable end button to the connector, if working on the right side.

14. Click the cable assembly into the backing plate.

15. Connect the cable to the actuating lever.

16. Assemble the rear brake components.

17. Install the drum(s) and wheel(s).

18. Adjust the rear brakes and parking brake cable.

19. Connect the negative battery cable and check the parking brakes for proper operation.

ADJUSTMENT

1. Adjust the rear brake shoes.

2. Depress the parking brake pedal exactly 3 ratchet clicks.

3. Raise and safely support the vehicle.

4. Check that the equalizer nut groove is liberally lubricated with chassis lube. Tighten the adjusting nut until the right rear wheel can just be turned to the rear with both hands, but is locked when forward rotation is attempted.

5. With the mechanism totally disengaged, both rear wheels should turn freely in either direction with no brake drag. Do not adjust the parking brake so tightly as to cause brake drag.

Parking Brake Lever

REMOVAL & INSTALLATION

1. Raise and safely support the vehicle.

2. Loosen the cable adjustment to allow the cable to be disconnected from the lever.

3. On models with a console mounted brake lever, remove the console.

4. Disconnect the parking brake cable from the lever assembly.

5. Disconnect the electrical connector.

6. Remove the bolts securing the lever to the floor pan.

7. Install the parking brake lever and attaching bolts. Tighten to 18 ft. lbs. (25 Nm).

8. Connect the parking brake cable to the lever assembly. Tighten the parking brake cable-to-lever assembly nut to 21 ft. lbs. (28 Nm).

9. If applicable, install the console.

10. Adjust the parking brake cable.

11. Lower the vehicle.

ANTI-LOCK BRAKE SYSTEM (ABS)

Description and Operation

The Anti-lock Braking System (ABS) was first introduced on N-body cars in 1991. ABS provides the driver with 3 important benefits over standard braking systems: increased vehicle stability, improved vehicle steerability, and potentially reduced stopping distances during braking. It should be noted that although the ABS-VI system offers definite advantages, the system cannot increase brake pressure above master cylinder pressure applied by the driver and cannot apply the brakes itself.

The ABS-VI Anti-lock Braking System consist of a conventional braking system with vacuum power booster, compact master cylinder, front disc brakes, rear drum brakes and interconnecting hydraulic brake lines augmented with the ABS components. The ABS-VI system consists of a hydraulic modulator assembly, Electronic Control Unit (ECU)/Electronic Brake Control Module (EBCM), a system relay, 4 wheel speed sensors, interconnecting wiring and an amber ABS warning light.

The ECU/EBCM monitors inputs from the individual wheel speed sensors and determines when a wheel or wheels is/are about to lock up. The ECU/EBCM controls the motors on the hydraulic modulator assembly to reduce brake pressure to the wheel about to lock up. When the wheel regains traction, the brake pressure is increased until the wheel again approaches lock-up. The cycle repeats until either the vehicle comes to a stop, the brake pedal is released, or no wheels are about to lock up. The ECU/EBCM also has the ability to monitor itself and can store diagnostic codes in a non-volatile (will not be erased if the battery is disconnected) memory. The ECU/EBCM is serviced as an assembly.

The ABS-VI braking system employs 2 modes: base (conventional) braking and anti-lock braking. Under normal braking, the conventional part of the system stops the vehicle. When in the ABS mode, the Electromagnetic Brakes (EMB) action of the ABS system controls the two front wheels individually and the rear wheels together. If the one rear wheel is about to lock up, the hydraulic pressure to both wheels is reduced, controlling both wheels together. Since the vast majority of the braking is controlled by the front wheels, there is no adverse effect on vehicle control during hard braking.

ONBOARD DIAGNOSTICS

The ABS-VI contains sophisticated onboard diagnostics that, when accessed with a bidirectional scan tool, are designed to identify the source of any system fault as specifically as possible, including whether or not the fault is intermittent. There are 58 diagnostic fault codes to assist the service technician with diagnosis. The last diagnostic fault code to occur is specifically identified, and specific ABS data is stored at the time of this fault, also, the first five codes set. Additionally, using a bidirectional scan tool, each input and output can be monitored, thus enabling fault confirmation and repair verification. Manual control of components and automated functional tests are also available when using a GM approved scan tool. Details of many of these functions are contained in the following sections.

ENHANCED DIAGNOSTICS

Enhanced Diagnostic Information, found in the CODE HISTORY function of the bidirectional scan tool, is designed to provide the service technician with specific fault occurrence information. For each of the first five (5) and the very last diagnostic fault codes stored, data is stored to identify the specific fault code number, the number of failure occurrences, and the number of drive cycles since the failure first and last occurred (a drive cycle occurs when the ignition is turned ON and the vehicle is driven faster than 10 mph). However, if a fault is present, the drive cycle counter will increment by turning the ignition ON and OFF. These first five (5) diagnostic fault codes are also stored in the order of occurrence. The order in which the first 5 faults occurred can be useful in determining if a previous fault is linked to the most recent faults, such as an intermittent wheel speed sensor which later becomes completely open.

During difficult diagnosis situations, this information can be used to identify fault occurrence trends. Does the fault occur more frequently now than it did during the last time when it only failed 1 out of 35 drive cycles? Did the fault only occur once over a large number of drive cycles, indication an unusual condition present when the fault occurred? Does the fault occur infrequently over a large number of drive cycles, indication special diagnosis techniques may be required to identify the source of the fault?

If a fault occurred 1 out of 20 drive cycles, the fault is intermittent and has not reoccurred for 19 drive cycles. This fault may be difficult or impossible to duplicate and may have been caused by a severe vehicle impact (large pot hole, speed bump at high speed, etc.) that momentarily opened an electrical connector or caused unusual vehicle suspension movement. Problem resolution is unlikely, and the problem may never reoccur (check diagnostic aids proved for that code). If the fault occurred 3 out of 15 drive cycles, the odds of finding the cause are still not good, but you know how often it occurs and you can determine whether or not the fault is becoming more frequent based on an additional or past occurrences visit if the source of the problem can not or could not be found. If the fault occurred 10 out of 20 drive cycles, the odds of finding the cause are very good, as the fault may be easily reproduced.

By using the additional fault data, you can also determine if a failure is randomly intermittent or if it has not reoccurred for long periods of time due to weather changes or a repair prior to this visit. Say a diagnostic fault code occurred 10 of 20 drive cycles but has not reoccurred for 10 drive cycles. This means the failure occurred 10 of 10 drive cycles but has not reoccurred since. A significant environmental change or a repair occurred 10 drive cycles ago. A repair may not be necessary if a recent repair can be confirmed. If no repair was made, the service can focus on diagnosis techniques used to locate difficult to recreate problems.

Diagnostic Procedures

▶ **See Figures 76, 77, 78, 79, 80, 81 and 82**

When servicing the ABS-VI, the following steps should be followed in order. Failure to follow these steps may result in the loss of important diagnostic data and may lead to difficult and time consuming diagnosis procedures.

1. Connect a bidirectional scan tool, as instructed by the tool manufacturer, then read all current and historical diagnostic codes. Be certain to note which codes are current diagnostic code failures. DO NOT CLEAR CODES unless directed to do so.

2. Using a bidirectional scan tool, read the CODE HISTORY data. Note the diagnostic fault codes stored and their frequency of failure. Specifically note the last failure that occurred and the conditions present when this failure occurred. This last failure should be the starting point for diagnosis and repair.

3. Perform a vehicle preliminary diagnosis inspection. This should include:

   a. Inspection of the compact master cylinder for proper brake fluid level.

   b. Inspection of the ABS hydraulic modulator for any leaks or wiring damage.

   c. Inspection of brake components at all four (4) wheels. Verify that no drag exists and that the brakes apply properly.

   d. Inspection for worn or damaged wheel bearings that allow a wheel to wobble.

   e. Inspection of the wheel speed sensors and their wiring. Verify correct air gap range, solid sensor attachment, undamaged sensor toothed ring, and undamaged wiring, especially at vehicle attachment points.

   f. Verification of proper outer CV-joint alignment and operation.

   g. Verification that tires meet legal tread depth requirements.

4. If no codes are present, or mechanical component failure codes are present, perform the automated modulator test using the Tech 1 or T-100 to isolate the cause of the problem. If the failure is intermittent and not reproducible, test drive the vehicle while using the automatic snapshot feature of the bidirectional scan tool.

Perform normal acceleration, stopping, and turning maneuvers. If this does not reproduce the failure, perform an ABS stop, on a low coefficient surface such as gravel, from approximately 30-50 mph (48-81 km/h) while triggering any ABS code. If the failure is still not reproducible, use the enhanced diagnostic information found in CODE HISTORY to determine whether or not this failure should be further diagnosed.

5. Once all system failures have been corrected, clear the ABS codes. The Tech 1 and T-100, when plugged into the ALDL connector, becomes part of the vehicle's electronic system. The Tech 1 and T-100 can also perform the following functions on components linked by the Serial Data Link (SDL):

- Display ABS data
- Display and clear ABS trouble codes
- Control ABS components
- Perform extensive ABS diagnosis
- Provide diagnostic testing for intermittent ABS conditions

Each test mode has specific diagnosis capabilities which depend upon various keystrokes. In general, five (5) keys control sequencing: "YES," "NO," "EXIT," "UP" arrow and "DOWN" arrow. The FO through F9 keys select operating modes, perform functions within an operating mode, or enter trouble code or model year designations.

In general, the Tech 1 has five (5) test modes for diagnosing the anti-lock brake system. The five (5) test modes are as follows:

MODE FO: DATA LIST — In this test mode, the Tech 1 continuously monitors wheel speed data, brake switch status and other inputs and outputs.

MODE F1: CODE HISTORY — In this mode, fault code history data is displayed. This data includes how many ignition cycles since the fault code occurred, along with other ABS information. The first five (5) and last fault codes set are included in the ABS history data.

MODE F2: TROUBLE CODES — In this test mode, trouble codes stored by the EBCM, both current ignition cycle and history, may be displayed or cleared.

MODE F3: ABS SNAPSHOT — In this test mode, the Tech 1 captures ABS data before and after a fault occurrence or a forced manual trigger.

MODE F4: ABS TESTS — In this test mode, the Tech 1 performs hydraulic modulator functional tests to assist in problem isolation during troubleshooting. Included here is manual control of the motors which is used prior to bleeding the brake system.

Press **F7** to covert from English to metric figures.

DISPLAYING CODES

▶ **See Figures 83 and 84**

Diagnostic fault codes can only be read through the use of a bidirectional scan tool. There are no provisions for "Flash Code" diagnostics.

CLEARING CODES

The trouble codes in EBCM memory are erased in one of two ways:
- Tech 1 "Clear Codes" selection
- Ignition cycle default

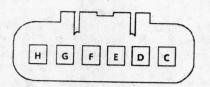

6 WAY EBCM CONNECTOR

PIN	CIRCUIT NO.	COLOR	CIRCUIT
C	1284	DK GRN	REAR MOTOR HIGH
D	1285	ORN	REAR MOTOR LOW
E	1281	PNK	L/F MOTOR LOW
F	1280	BLK	L/F MOTOR HIGH
G	1283	BLK	R/F MOTOR LOW
H	1282	PPL	R/F MOTOR HIGH

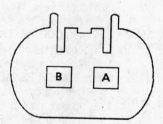

2 WAY EBCM CONNECTOR

PIN	CIRCUIT NO.	COLOR	CIRCUIT
A	1633	RED	SWITCHED BATTERY INPUT
B	250	BLK	GROUND

Fig. 76 View of the EBCM 6 and 2-way connectors

86889091

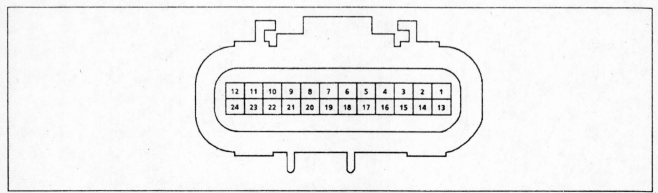

Figure 11 - EBCM Connector Face View: ABS Without VES

24-WAY EBCM HARNESS CONNECTOR (ABS WITHOUT VES)

PIN	CIRCUIT NO.	COLOR	CIRCUIT
1	OPEN		NOT USED
2	800	TAN	SERIAL DATA
3	OPEN		NOT USED
4	1289	LT BLU	R/F ABS SOLENOID CONTROL
5	830	LT BLU	L/F WHEEL SIGNAL HIGH
6	873	YEL	L/F WHEEL SIGNAL LOW
7	882	BRN	R/R WHEEL SIGNAL HIGH
8	883	WHT	R/R WHEEL SIGNAL LOW
9	872	DK GRN	R/F WHEEL SIGNAL HIGH
10	833	TAN	R/F WHEEL SIGNAL LOW
11	885	RED	L/R WHEEL SIGNAL LOW
12	884	BLK	L/R WHEEL SIGNAL HIGH
13	17	WHT	BRAKE SWITCH INPUT
14	41	BRN	SWITCHED IGNITION
15	340	ORN	BATTERY FEED
16	OPEN		NOT USED
17	OPEN		NOT USED
18	VENT TUBE	BLK	VENT TUBE
19	1286	LT GRN	L/F EMB CONTROL
20	1287	GRY	R/F EMB CONTROL
21	33	TAN/WHT	BRAKE WARNING LAMP CONTROL
22	1632	PNK	ENABLE RELAY CONTROL
23	852	WHT	ABS WARNING LAMP CONTROL
24	1288	DK GRN	L/F ABS SOLENOID CONTROL

86889092

Fig. 77 View of the EBCM 24-way electrical connector — vehicles without Variable Effort Steering (VES)

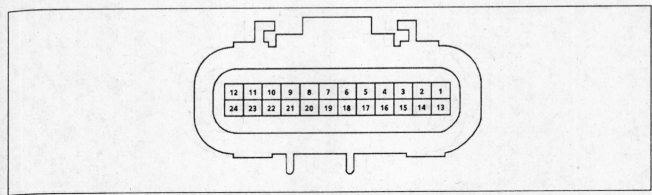

Figure 12 - EBCM Connector Face View: ABS With VES

24-WAY EBCM HARNESS CONNECTOR (ABS WITH VES)

PIN	CIRCUIT NO.	COLOR	CIRCUIT
1	800	TAN	SERIAL DATA
2	1289	LT BLU	R/F ABS SOLENOID CONTROL
3	830	LT BLU	L/F WHEEL SIGNAL HIGH
4	873	YEL	L/F WHEEL SIGNAL LOW
5	882	BRN	R/R WHEEL SIGNAL HIGH
6	883	WHT	R/R WHEEL SIGNAL LOW
7	872	DK GRN	R/F WHEEL SIGNAL HIGH
8	833	TAN	R/F WHEEL SIGNAL LOW
9	884	BLK	L/R WHEEL SIGNAL HIGH
10	885	RED	L/R WHEEL SIGNAL LOW
11	1295	BRN	EVO ACTUATOR CONTROL
12	1056	GRY	STEERING WHEEL SENSOR VCC
13	17	WHT	BRAKE SWITCH INPUT
14	41	BRN	SWITCHED IGNITION
15	340	ORN	BATTERY FEED
16	556	ORN/BLK	STEERING WHEEL SENSOR GROUND
17	1286	LT GRN	L/F EMB CONTROL
18	1287	GRY	R/F EMB CONTROL
19	33	TAN/WHT	BRAKE WARNING LAMP CONTROL
20	1632	PNK	ENABLE RELAY CONTROL
21	852	WHT	ABS WARNING LAMP CONTROL
22	1288	DK GRN	L/F ABS SOLENOID CONTROL
23	1059	LT BLU	STEERING WHEEL SENSOR INPUT
24	VENT TUBE	BLK	VENT TUBE

86889093

Fig. 78 View of the EBCM 24-way electrical connector — vehicles with Variable Effort Steering (VES)

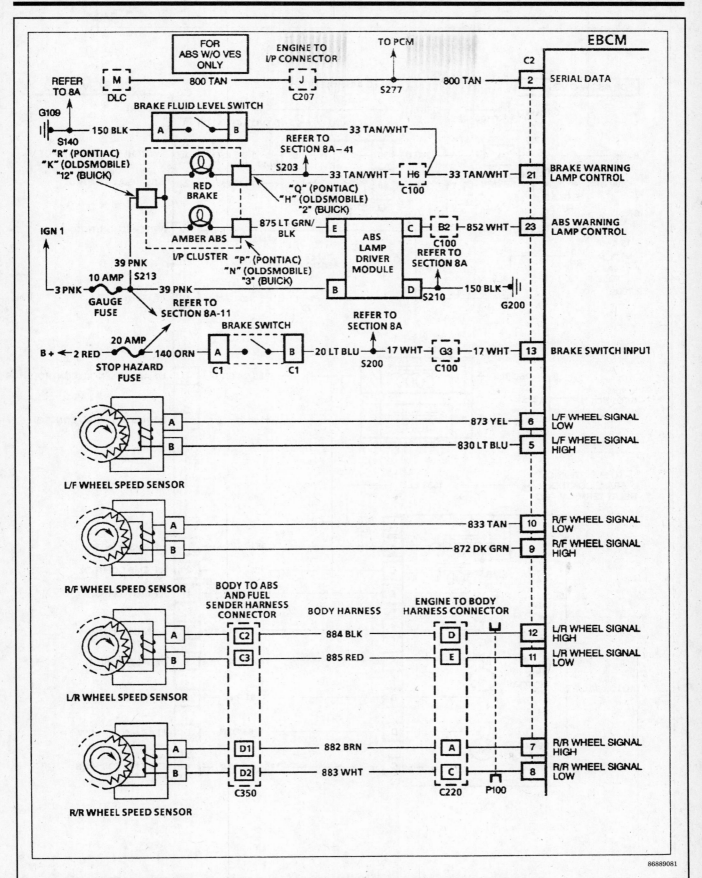

Fig. 79 ABS wiring diagram (page 1 of 2) — vehicles without Variable Effort Steering (VES)

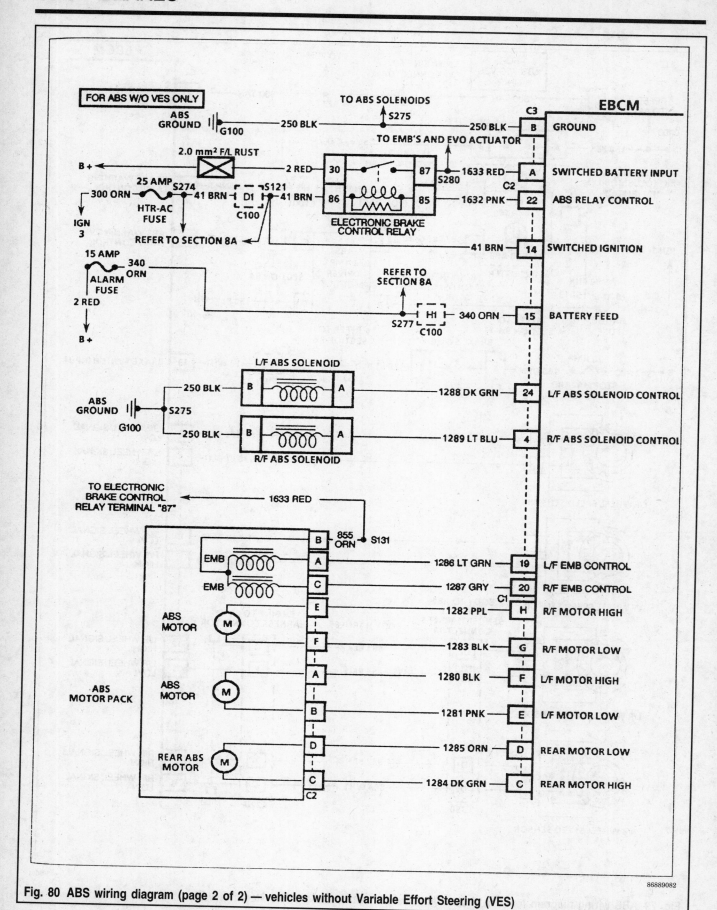

Fig. 80 ABS wiring diagram (page 2 of 2) — vehicles without Variable Effort Steering (VES)

86889082

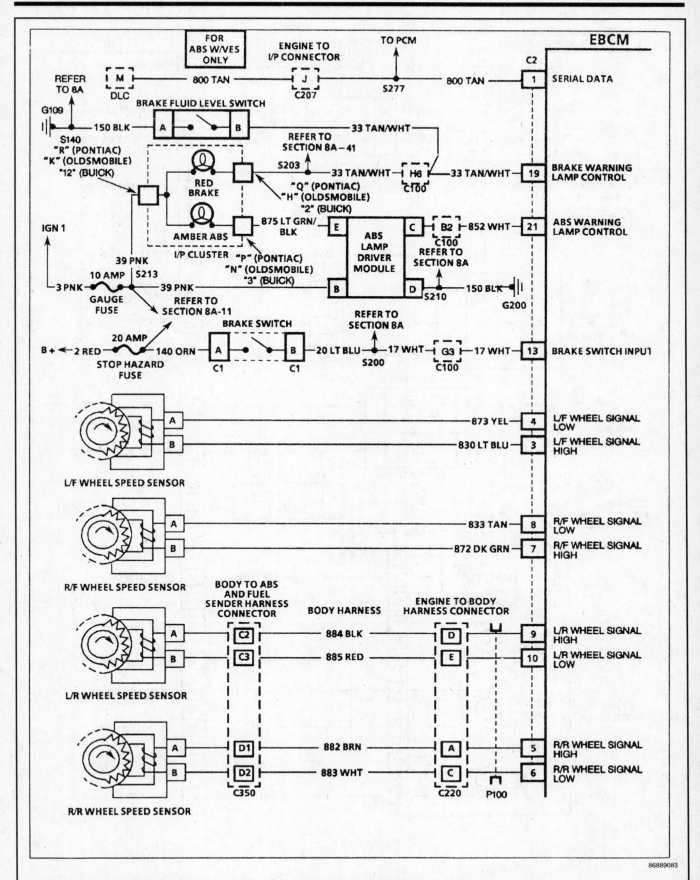

Fig. 81 ABS wiring diagram (page 1 of 2) — vehicles with Variable Effort Steering (VES)

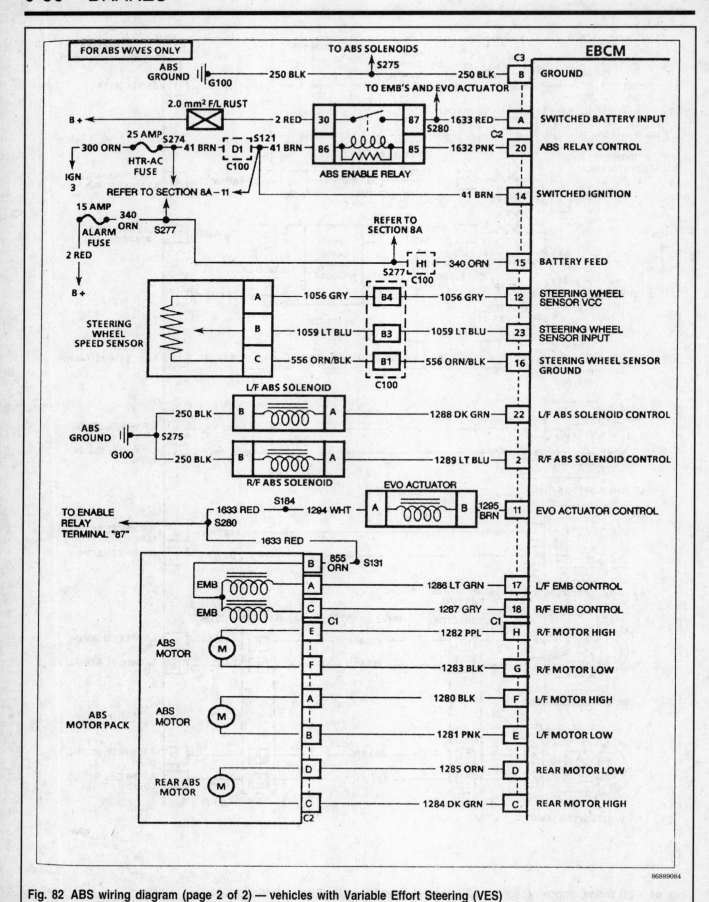

Fig. 82 ABS wiring diagram (page 2 of 2) — vehicles with Variable Effort Steering (VES)

86889084

DIAGNOSTIC TROUBLE CODE AND SYMPTOM TABLE	
CHART	**SYMPTOM**
A	ABS (Amber) Warning Lamp "ON" Constantly, No DTCs Stored
B	ABS (Amber) Warning Lamp "ON" Intermittently, No DTCs Stored (1 of 2)
C	ABS (Amber) Warning Lamp "ON" Constantly, No DTCs Stored
D	Tech 1 Displays Undefined DTCs
DIAGNOSTIC TROUBLE CODE	**DESCRIPTION**
11	ABS Warning Lamp Circuit Malfunction (1 of 2)
14	ABS Enable Relay Contact Circuit Open (1 of 3)
15	ABS Enable Relay Contact Circuit Shorted to Battery or Always Closed
16	ABS Enable Relay Coil Circuit Open
17	ABS Enable Relay Coil Circuit Shorted to Ground
18	ABS Enable Relay Coil Circuit Shorted to Battery or Coil Shorted
21	Left Front Wheel Speed = 0 or Unreasonable (For ABS W/O VES Only) (1 of 2)
21	Left Front Wheel Speed = 0 (For ABS With VES Only)
22	Right Front Wheel Speed = 0 or Unreasonable (For ABS W/O VES Only) (1 of 2)
22	Right Front Wheel Speed = 0 (For ABS With VES Only)
23	Left Rear Wheel Speed = 0 or Unreasonable (For ABS W/O VES Only) (1 of 4)
23	Left Rear Wheel Speed = 0 (For ABS With VES Only) (1 of 2)
24	Right Rear Wheel Speed = 0 or Unreasonable (For ABS W/O VES Only) (1 of 4)
24	Right Rear Wheel Speed = 0 (For ABS With VES Only) (1 of 2)
25	Left Front Excessive Wheel Speed Variation (1 of 3)
26	Right Front Excessive Wheel Speed Variation (1 of 3)
27	Left Rear Excessive Wheel Speed Variation (1 of 3)
28	Right Rear Excessive Wheel Speed Variation (1 of 3)
32	Left Front Wheel Speed Sensor Circuit Open or Shorted to Ground/Battery (For ABS With VES Only) (1 of 3)
33	Right Front Wheel Speed Sensor Circuit Open or Shorted to Ground/Battery (For ABS With VES Only) (1 of 3)
34	Left Rear Wheel Speed Sensor Circuit Open or Shorted to Ground/Battery (For ABS With VES Only) (1 of 3)
35	Right Rear Wheel Speed Sensor Circuit Open or Shorted to Ground/Battery (For ABS With VES Only) (1 of 3)
36	Low System Voltage
37	High System Voltage
38	Left Front EMB Will Not Hold Motor
41	Right Front EMB Will Not Hold Motor
42	Rear ESB Will Not Hold Motor
43	VES Steering Wheel Speed Sensor Circuit Malfunction (For ABS With VES Only) (1 of 3)
44	Left Front ABS Channel Will Not Move (1 of 2)
45	Right Front ABS Channel Will Not Move (1 of 2)
46	Rear ABS Channel Will Not Move
47	Left Front ABS Motor Free Spins (1 of 2)
48	Right Front ABS Motor Free Spins (1 of 2)
51	Rear ABS Motor Free Spins (1 of 2)
52	Left Front ABS Channel in Release Too Long

86889085

Fig. 83 List of ABS Diagnostic Trouble Codes (DTCs)

DIAGNOSTIC TROUBLE CODE AND SYMPTOM TABLE	
CHART	SYMPTOM
53	Right Front ABS Channel in Release Too Long
54	Rear ABS Channel in Release Too Long
55	EBCM Malfunction
56	Left Front ABS Motor Circuit Open
57	Left Front ABS Motor Circuit Shorted to Ground
58	Left Front ABS Motor Circuit Shorted to Battery or Motor Shorted
61	Right Front ABS Motor Circuit Open
62	Right Front ABS Motor Circuit Shorted to Ground
63	Right Front ABS Motor Circuit Shorted to Battery or Motor Shorted
64	Rear ABS Motor Circuit Open
65	Rear ABS Motor Circuit Shorted to Ground
66	Rear ABS Motor Circuit Shorted to Battery or Motor Shorted
67	Left Front EMB Circuit Open or Shorted to Ground
68	Left Front EMB Circuit Shorted to Battery or Driver Open
71	Right Front EMB Circuit Open or Shorted to Ground
72	Right Front EMB Circuit Shorted to Battery or Driver Open
73	EVO Actuator Circuit Open or Shorted to Ground (For ABS With VES Only)
74	EVO Actuator Circuit Shorted to Battery or Solenoid Shorted (For ABS With VES Only)
76	Left Front Solenoid Circuit Open or Shorted to Battery
77	Left Front Solenoid Circuit Shorted to Ground or Driver Open
78	Right Front Solenoid Circuit Open or Shorted to Battery
81	Right Front Solenoid Circuit Shorted to Ground or Driver Open
82	Calibration Malfunction
86	EBCM Turned "ON" the Red "BRAKE" Warning Lamp
87	Red "BRAKE" Warning Lamp Circuit Open
88	Red "BRAKE" Warning Lamp Circuit Shorted to Battery
91	Open Brake Switch Contacts During Deceleration
92	Open Brake Switch Contacts When ABS Was Required
93	DTCs 91 or 92 Set in Current or Previous Ignition Cycle
94	Brake Switch Contacts Always Closed
95	Brake Switch Circuit Open
96	Brake Lamp Circuit Open

86889086

Fig. 84 List of ABS Diagnostic Trouble Codes (DTCs)

These two methods are detailed below. Be sure to verify proper system operation and absence of codes when clearing procedure is completed.The EBCM will not permit code clearing until all of the codes have been displayed. Also, codes cannot be cleared by unplugging the EBCM, disconnecting the battery cables, or turning the ignition **OFF** (except on an ignition cycle default).

Tech 1 "Clear Codes" Method

Select F2 for trouble codes. After codes have been viewed completely, Tech 1 will ask, "CLEAR ABS CODES"; Answer "YES." Tech 1 will then read, "DISPLAY CODE HIST. DATA?", followed by "LOST" if the codes have been cleared or "NO" to clear the codes. Answer "NO" and the codes will be cleared.

Ignition Cycle Default

If no diagnostic fault code occurs for 100 drive cycles (a drive cycle occurs when the ignition is turned **ON** and the vehicle is driven faster than 10 mph or 16 km/h), any existing fault codes are cleared from the EBCM memory.

DIAGNOSTIC CHARTS

▶ **See Figures 85, 86, 87 and 88**

The following charts can be used to diagnose faults when no Diagnostic Trouble Codes (DTCs) or undefined DTCs are stored.

INTERMITTENT FAILURES

As with most electronic systems, intermittent failures may be difficult to accurately diagnose. The following is a method to try to isolate an intermittent failure, especially wheel speed circuitry failures.

If an ABS fault occurs, the ABS warning light indicator will be on during the ignition cycle in which the fault was detected. If it is an intermittent problem which seems to have corrected itself (ABS warning light off), a history trouble code will be stored. The history data of the code at the time the fault

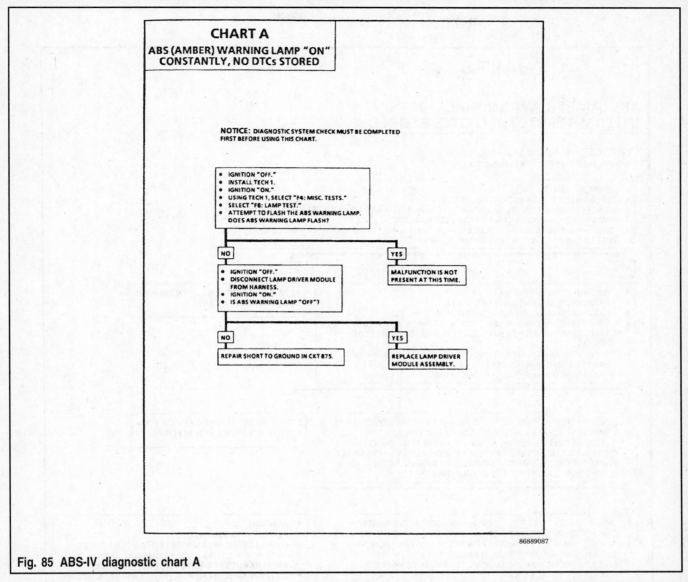

CHART A
ABS (AMBER) WARNING LAMP "ON" CONSTANTLY, NO DTCs STORED

NOTICE: DIAGNOSTIC SYSTEM CHECK MUST BE COMPLETED FIRST BEFORE USING THIS CHART.

- IGNITION "OFF."
- INSTALL TECH 1.
- IGNITION "ON."
- USING TECH 1, SELECT "F4: MISC. TESTS."
- SELECT "F8: LAMP TEST."
- ATTEMPT TO FLASH THE ABS WARNING LAMP. DOES ABS WARNING LAMP FLASH?

NO

- IGNITION "OFF."
- DISCONNECT LAMP DRIVER MODULE FROM HARNESS.
- IGNITION "ON."
- IS ABS WARNING LAMP "OFF"?

YES

MALFUNCTION IS NOT PRESENT AT THIS TIME.

NO

REPAIR SHORT TO GROUND IN CKT 875.

YES

REPLACE LAMP DRIVER MODULE ASSEMBLY.

86889087

Fig. 85 ABS-IV diagnostic chart A

occurred will also be stored. The Tech 1 must be used to read ABS history data.

INTERMITTENTS AND POOR CONNECTIONS

Most intermittents are caused by faulty electrical connections or wiring, although occasionally a sticking relay or solenoid can be a problem. Some items to check are:

1. Poor mating of connector halves, or terminals not fully seated in the connector body (backed out).

2. Dirt or corrosion on the terminals. The terminals must be clean and free of any foreign material which could impede proper terminal contact.

3. Damaged connector body, exposing the terminals to moisture and dirt, as well as not maintaining proper terminal orientation with the component or mating connector.

4. Improperly formed or damaged terminals. All connector terminals in problem circuits should be checked carefully to ensure good contact tension. Use a corresponding mating ter-minal to check for proper tension. Refer to "Checking Terminal Contact" in this section for the specific procedure.

5. The J 35616-A Connector Test Adapter Kit must be used whenever a diagnostic procedure requests checking or probing a terminal. Using the adapter will ensure that no damage to the terminal will occur, as well as giving an idea of whether contact tension is sufficient. If contact tension seems incorrect, refer to "Checking Terminal Contact" in this section for specifics.

6. Poor terminal-to-wire connection. Checking this requires removing the terminal from the connector body. Some conditions which fall under this description are poor crimps, poor solder joints, crimping over wire insulation rather than the wire itself, corrosion in the wire-to-terminal contact area, etc.

7. Wire insulation which is rubbed through, causing an intermittent short as the bare area touches other wiring or parts of the vehicle.

8. Wiring broken inside the insulation. This condition could cause a continuity check to show a good circuit, but if only 1 or 2 strands of a multi-strand-type wire are intact, resistance could be far too high.

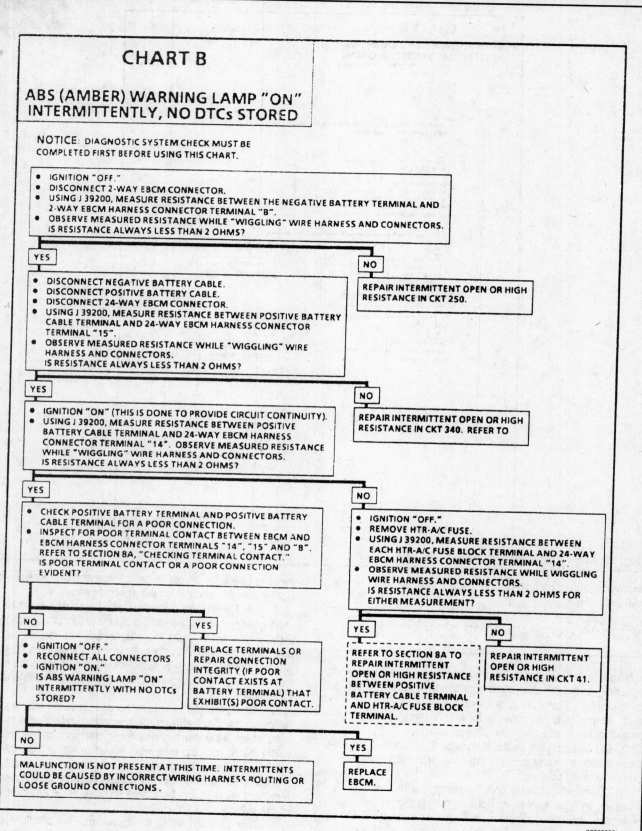

CHART B

ABS (AMBER) WARNING LAMP "ON" INTERMITTENTLY, NO DTCs STORED

NOTICE: DIAGNOSTIC SYSTEM CHECK MUST BE COMPLETED FIRST BEFORE USING THIS CHART.

- IGNITION "OFF."
- DISCONNECT 2-WAY EBCM CONNECTOR.
- USING J 39200, MEASURE RESISTANCE BETWEEN THE NEGATIVE BATTERY TERMINAL AND 2-WAY EBCM HARNESS CONNECTOR TERMINAL "B".
- OBSERVE MEASURED RESISTANCE WHILE "WIGGLING" WIRE HARNESS AND CONNECTORS. IS RESISTANCE ALWAYS LESS THAN 2 OHMS?

YES

NO → REPAIR INTERMITTENT OPEN OR HIGH RESISTANCE IN CKT 250.

- DISCONNECT NEGATIVE BATTERY CABLE.
- DISCONNECT POSITIVE BATTERY CABLE.
- DISCONNECT 24-WAY EBCM CONNECTOR.
- USING J 39200, MEASURE RESISTANCE BETWEEN POSITIVE BATTERY CABLE TERMINAL AND 24-WAY EBCM HARNESS CONNECTOR TERMINAL "15".
- OBSERVE MEASURED RESISTANCE WHILE "WIGGLING" WIRE HARNESS AND CONNECTORS. IS RESISTANCE ALWAYS LESS THAN 2 OHMS?

YES

NO → REPAIR INTERMITTENT OPEN OR HIGH RESISTANCE IN CKT 340. REFER TO

- IGNITION "ON" (THIS IS DONE TO PROVIDE CIRCUIT CONTINUITY).
- USING J 39200, MEASURE RESISTANCE BETWEEN POSITIVE BATTERY CABLE TERMINAL AND 24-WAY EBCM HARNESS CONNECTOR TERMINAL "14". OBSERVE MEASURED RESISTANCE WHILE "WIGGLING" WIRE HARNESS AND CONNECTORS. IS RESISTANCE ALWAYS LESS THAN 2 OHMS?

YES

NO

- CHECK POSITIVE BATTERY TERMINAL AND POSITIVE BATTERY CABLE TERMINAL FOR A POOR CONNECTION.
- INSPECT FOR POOR TERMINAL CONTACT BETWEEN EBCM AND EBCM HARNESS CONNECTOR TERMINALS "14", "15" AND "B". REFER TO SECTION 8A, "CHECKING TERMINAL CONTACT." IS POOR TERMINAL CONTACT OR A POOR CONNECTION EVIDENT?

- IGNITION "OFF."
- REMOVE HTR-A/C FUSE.
- USING J 39200, MEASURE RESISTANCE BETWEEN EACH HTR-A/C FUSE BLOCK TERMINAL AND 24-WAY EBCM HARNESS CONNECTOR TERMINAL "14".
- OBSERVE MEASURED RESISTANCE WHILE WIGGLING WIRE HARNESS AND CONNECTORS. IS RESISTANCE ALWAYS LESS THAN 2 OHMS FOR EITHER MEASUREMENT?

NO

- IGNITION "OFF."
- RECONNECT ALL CONNECTORS.
- IGNITION "ON."
  IS ABS WARNING LAMP "ON" INTERMITTENTLY WITH NO DTCs STORED?

YES → REPLACE TERMINALS OR REPAIR CONNECTION INTEGRITY (IF POOR CONTACT EXISTS AT BATTERY TERMINAL) THAT EXHIBIT(S) POOR CONTACT.

YES → REFER TO SECTION 8A TO REPAIR INTERMITTENT OPEN OR HIGH RESISTANCE BETWEEN POSITIVE BATTERY CABLE TERMINAL AND HTR-A/C FUSE BLOCK TERMINAL.

NO → REPAIR INTERMITTENT OPEN OR HIGH RESISTANCE IN CKT 41.

NO → MALFUNCTION IS NOT PRESENT AT THIS TIME. INTERMITTENTS COULD BE CAUSED BY INCORRECT WIRING HARNESS ROUTING OR LOOSE GROUND CONNECTIONS.

YES → REPLACE EBCM.

86889088

Fig. 86 ABS-IV diagnostic chart B

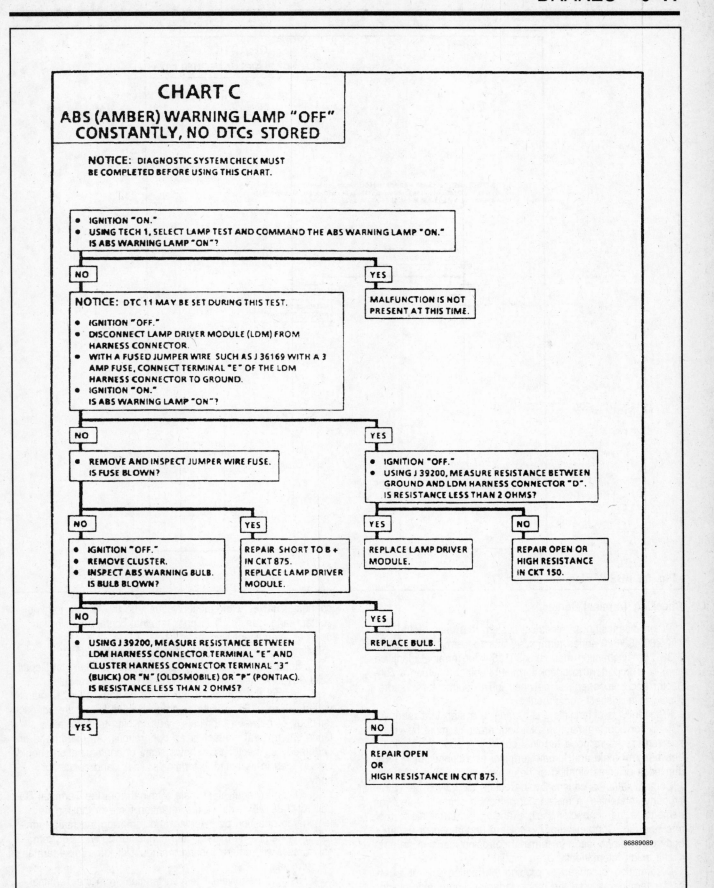

CHART C

**ABS (AMBER) WARNING LAMP "OFF"
CONSTANTLY, NO DTCs STORED**

NOTICE: DIAGNOSTIC SYSTEM CHECK MUST
BE COMPLETED BEFORE USING THIS CHART.

- IGNITION "ON."
- USING TECH 1, SELECT LAMP TEST AND COMMAND THE ABS WARNING LAMP "ON."
  IS ABS WARNING LAMP "ON"?

NO

NOTICE: DTC 11 MAY BE SET DURING THIS TEST.

- IGNITION "OFF."
- DISCONNECT LAMP DRIVER MODULE (LDM) FROM
  HARNESS CONNECTOR.
- WITH A FUSED JUMPER WIRE SUCH AS J 36169 WITH A 3
  AMP FUSE, CONNECT TERMINAL "E" OF THE LDM
  HARNESS CONNECTOR TO GROUND.
- IGNITION "ON."
  IS ABS WARNING LAMP "ON"?

YES

MALFUNCTION IS NOT
PRESENT AT THIS TIME.

NO

- REMOVE AND INSPECT JUMPER WIRE FUSE.
  IS FUSE BLOWN?

YES

- IGNITION "OFF."
- USING J 39200, MEASURE RESISTANCE BETWEEN
  GROUND AND LDM HARNESS CONNECTOR "D".
  IS RESISTANCE LESS THAN 2 OHMS?

NO

- IGNITION "OFF."
- REMOVE CLUSTER.
- INSPECT ABS WARNING BULB.
  IS BULB BLOWN?

YES

REPAIR SHORT TO B +
IN CKT 875.
REPLACE LAMP DRIVER
MODULE.

YES

REPLACE LAMP DRIVER
MODULE.

NO

REPAIR OPEN OR
HIGH RESISTANCE
IN CKT 150.

NO

- USING J 39200, MEASURE RESISTANCE BETWEEN
  LDM HARNESS CONNECTOR TERMINAL "E" AND
  CLUSTER HARNESS CONNECTOR TERMINAL "3"
  (BUICK) OR "N" (OLDSMOBILE) OR "P" (PONTIAC).
  IS RESISTANCE LESS THAN 2 OHMS?

YES

REPLACE BULB.

YES

NO

REPAIR OPEN
OR
HIGH RESISTANCE IN CKT 875.

86889089

Fig. 87 ABS-IV diagnostic chart C

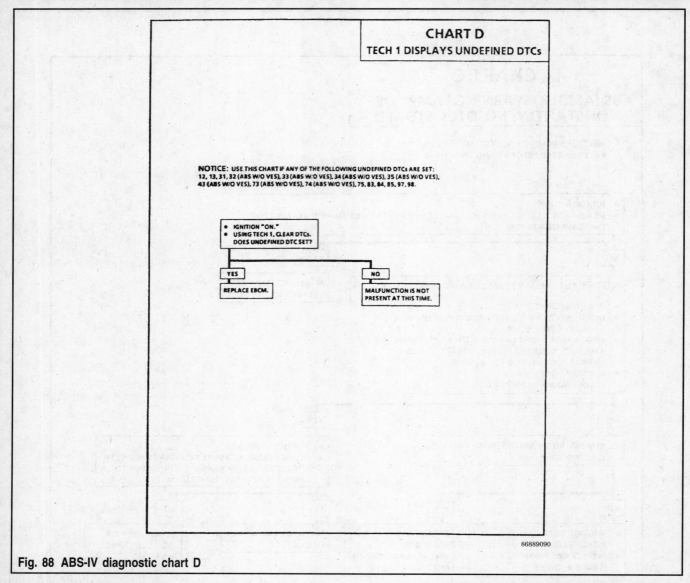

CHART D
TECH 1 DISPLAYS UNDEFINED DTCs

NOTICE: USE THIS CHART IF ANY OF THE FOLLOWING UNDEFINED DTCs ARE SET:
12, 13, 31, 32 (ABS W/O VES), 33 (ABS W/O VES), 34 (ABS W/O VES), 35 (ABS W/O VES),
43 (ABS W/O VES), 73 (ABS W/O VES), 74 (ABS W/O VES), 75, 83, 84, 85, 97, 98.

- IGNITION "ON."
- USING TECH 1, CLEAR DTCs.
  DOES UNDEFINED DTC SET?

YES

REPLACE EBCM.

NO

MALFUNCTION IS NOT
PRESENT AT THIS TIME.

86889090

Fig. 88 ABS-IV diagnostic chart D

Checking Terminal Contact

When diagnosing an electrical system that uses Metri-Pack 150/280/480/630 series terminals (refer to Terminal Repair Kit J 38125-A instruction manual J 38125-4 for terminal identification), it is important to check terminal contact between a connector and component, or between in-line connectors, before replacing a suspect component.

Frequently, a diagnostic chart leads to a step that reads "Check for poor connection". Mating terminals must be inspected to ensure good terminal contact. A poor connection between the male and female terminal at a connector may be the result of contamination or deformation.

Contamination is caused by the connector halves being improperly connected, a missing or damaged connector seal, or damage to the connector itself, exposing the terminals to moisture and dirt. Contamination, usually in underhood or underbody connectors, leads to terminal corrosion, causing an open circuit or an intermittently open circuit.

Deformation is caused by probing the mating side of a connector terminal without the proper adapter, improperly joining the connector halves or repeatedly separating and joining the connector halves. Deformation, usually to the female terminal contact tang, can result in poor terminal contact causing an open or intermittently open circuit.

Follow the procedure below to check terminal contact.

1. Separate the connector halves. Refer to Terminal Repair Kit J 38125-A instruction manual J 38125-4, if available.

2. Inspect the connector halves for contamination. Contamination will result in a white or green buildup within the connector body or between terminals, causing high terminal resistance, intermittent contact or an open circuit. An underhood or underbody connector that shows signs of contamination should be replaced in its entirety: terminals, seals, and connector body.

3. Using an equivalent male terminal from the Terminal Repair Kit J 38125-A, check the retention force of the female terminal in question by inserting and removing the male terminal to the female terminal in the connector body. Good terminal contact will require a certain amount of force to separate the terminals.

4. Using an equivalent female terminal from the Terminal Repair Kit J 38125-A, compare the retention force of this ter-

minal to the female terminal in question by joining and separating the male terminal to the female terminal in question. If the retention force is significantly different between the two female terminals, replace the female terminal in question, using a terminal from Terminal Repair Kit J 38125-A.

ABS Service

PRECAUTIONS

Failure to observe the following precautions may result in system damage.

• Performing diagnostic work on the ABS-VI requires the use of a Tech I Scan diagnostic tool or equivalent. If unavailable, please refer diagnostic work to a qualified technician.

• Before performing electric arc welding on the vehicle, disconnect the Electronic Brake Control Module (EBCM) and the hydraulic modulator connectors.

• When performing painting work on the vehicle, do not expose the Electronic Brake Control Module (EBCM) to temperatures in excess of 185°F (85°C) for longer than 2 hours. The system may be exposed to temperatures up to 200°F (95°C) for less than 15 minutes.

• Never disconnect or connect the Electronic Brake Control Module (EBCM) or hydraulic modulator connectors with the ignition switch ON.

• Never disassemble any component of the Anti-Lock Brake System (ABS) which is designated non-serviceable; the component must be replaced as an assembly.

• When filling the master cylinder, always use Delco Supreme 11 brake fluid or equivalent, which meets DOT-3 specifications; petroleum-base fluid will destroy the rubber parts.

ABS Hydraulic Modulator/Master Cylinder Assembly

REMOVAL & INSTALLATION

▶ See Figure 89

➡To avoid personal injury, use the Tech I scan tool to relieve the gear tension in the hydraulic modulator. This procedure must be performed prior to removal of the brake control and motor assembly.

1. Disconnect the negative battery cable.
2. Disengage the two solenoid electrical connectors and the fluid level sensor connector.
3. Detach the 6-pin and 3-pin motor pack electrical connectors.
4. Wrap a shop towel around the hydraulic brake lines, then disconnect the four brake lines from the modulator.

➡Cap the disconnected lines to prevent the loss of fluid and the entry of moisture and contaminants.

5. Unfasten the 2 nuts attaching the ABS hydraulic modulator/master cylinder assembly to the vacuum booster.

6. Remove the ABS hydraulic modulator assembly from the vehicle.

To install:
7. Install the ABS hydraulic modulator assembly to the vehicle. Secure using the two attaching nuts and tighten to 20 ft. lbs. (27 Nm).
8. Uncap and connect the 4 brake pipes to the modulator assembly. Tighten to 13 ft. lbs. (17 Nm).
9. Attach the 6-pin and 3-pin electrical connectors.
10. Engage the fluid level sensor connector and the two solenoid electrical connections.
11. Properly bleed the system, as outlined later in this section.
12. Connect the negative battery cable.

Electronic Control Unit (ECU)/Electronic Brake Control Module (EBCM)

REMOVAL & INSTALLATION

▶ See Figure 90

1. Disconnect the negative battery cable.
2. Detach the Electronic Control Unit (ECU)/Electronic Brake Control Module (EBCM) electrical connectors.
3. Unfasten the hex head screws attaching the ECU/EBCM to the dash panel.
4. Remove the ECU from the dash panel.

To install:
5. Ensure that the three plastic grommets are properly located.
6. Position the ECU/EBCM to the dash panel, aligning the screw holes.
7. Fasten the retaining hex head screws attaching the ECU/EBCM. Tighten the screws to 17 ft. lbs. (21 Nm).
8. Attach the electrical connectors.
9. Connect the negative battery cable.

Speed Sensors

REMOVAL & INSTALLATION

Front Wheel Speed Sensors
▶ See Figure 91

1. Disconnect the negative battery cable.
2. Raise and safely support the vehicle.
3. Detach the front sensor electrical connector.
4. Unfasten the retaining bolt, then remove the front wheel speed sensor. If the sensor will not slide out of the knuckle, remove the brake rotor and use a blunt punch or equivalent to push the sensor from the back side of the knuckle.

➡If the sensor locating pin breaks off and remains in the knuckle during removal, remove the brake rotor and remove the broken pin using a blunt punch. Clean the hole using sand paper wrapped around a screwdriver or other suitable tool. NEVER attempt to enlarge the hole.

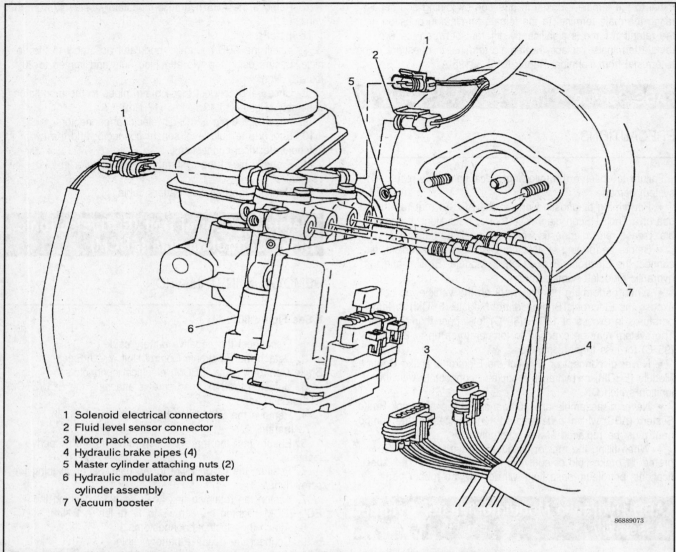

1 Solenoid electrical connectors
2 Fluid level sensor connector
3 Motor pack connectors
4 Hydraulic brake pipes (4)
5 Master cylinder attaching nuts (2)
6 Hydraulic modulator and master
  cylinder assembly
7 Vacuum booster

86889073

Fig. 89 View of the ABS hydraulic modulator/master cylinder assembly — 1995 vehicle shown

To install:

5. Position the front wheel speed sensor on the mounting bracket.

➡️**Make sure the front wheel speed sensor is properly aligned and lays flat against the bracket bosses.**

6. Install the retaining bolts. Tighten to 107 inch lbs. (12 Nm).
7. Attach the front sensor electrical connector.
8. Lower the vehicle.
9. Connect the negative battery cable.

Rear Wheel Bearing and Speed Sensor Assembly

▶ See Figure 92

➡️**The rear integral wheel bearing and sensor assembly must be replaced as a unit.**

1. Disconnect the negative battery cable.
2. Raise and safely support the vehicle.
3. Remove the rear wheel and tire assembly.
4. Remove the brake drum.

5. Detach the rear sensor electrical connector.
6. Unfasten the bolts and nuts attaching the rear wheel bearing and speed sensor assembly to the backing plate. Rotate the axle flange to align the large hole with each bolt. Remove the bolt while holding the nut.

➡️**With the rear wheel bearing and speed sensor attaching bolts and nuts removed, the drum brake assembly is supported only by the brake line connection. To avoid bending or damage to the brake line, do not bump or exert force on the assembly.**

7. Remove the rear wheel bearing and speed sensor assembly.

To install:

8. Install the rear wheel bearing and speed sensor assembly by aligning the bolt holes in the wheel bearing and speed sensor assembly, drum brake assembly and rear suspension bracket.

9. Fasten the attaching bolts and nuts. Rotate the axle flange to align the large hole with each bolt location. Install the bolt while holding the nut. Tighten to 37 ft. lbs. (50 Nm).

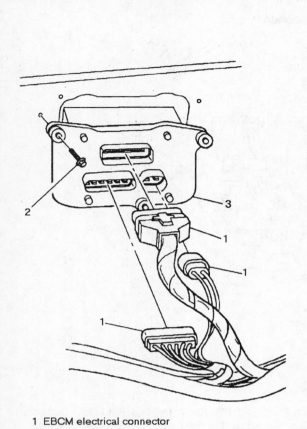

1 EBCM electrical connector
2 HEX head screws
3 EBCM

86889074

Fig. 90 Electronic Brake Control Module (EBCM) mounting

10. Attach the rear speed sensor electrical connector.
11. Install the brake drum and the rear wheel and tire assembly.
12. Carefully lower the vehicle.
13. Connect the negative battery cable.

ABS Hydraulic Modulator Solenoid

REMOVAL & INSTALLATION

▶ See Figure 93

1. Disconnect the negative battery cable.
2. Detach the solenoid electrical connector.
3. Unfasten the Torx® head bolts, then remove the solenoid assembly.

To install:

4. Lubricate the O-rings on the new solenoid with clean brake fluid.
5. Position the solenoid so the connectors face each other.

6. Press down firmly by hand until the solenoid assembly flange seats on the modulator assembly.
7. Install the Torx® head bolts. Tighten to 40 inch lbs. (4.5 Nm).
8. Attach the solenoid electrical connector. Make sure the connectors are installed on the correct solenoids.
9. Properly bleed the brake system.
10. Connect the negative battery cable.

Filling and Bleeding

❋❋WARNING

Do NOT allow brake fluid to spill on or come in contact with the vehicle's finish as it will remove the paint. In case of a spill, immediately flush the area with water.

SYSTEM FILLING

The master cylinder reservoirs must be kept properly filled to prevent air from entering the system. No special filling procedures are required because of the anti-lock system.

When adding fluid, use only DOT 3 fluid; the use of DOT 5 or silicone fluids is specifically prohibited. Use of improper or contaminated fluid may cause the fluid to boil or cause the rubber components in the system to deteriorate. Never use any fluid with a petroleum base or any fluid which has been exposed to water or moisture.

BLEEDING THE ABS HYDRAULIC SYSTEM

Before bleeding the ABS brake system, the front and rear displacement cylinder pistons must be returned to the topmost position. The preferred method uses a Tech 1 or T-100 scan tool to perform the rehoming procedure. If a Tech 1 is not available, the second procedure may be used, but it must be followed exactly.

Rehome Procedure

WITH TECH 1 OR T-100 (PREFERRED METHOD)

1. Using a Tech 1 or T-100 (CAMS), select "F5: Motor Rehome". The motor rehome function cannot be performed if current DTC's are present. If DTC's are present, the vehicle must be repaired and the codes cleared before performing the motor rehome function.
2. The entire brake system should now be bled using the pressure or manual bleeding procedures outlined later in this section.

WITHOUT TECH 1 OR T-100

➡Do not place your foot on the brake pedal through this entire procedure unless specifically instructed to do so.

This method can only be used if the ABS warning lamp is not illuminated and not DTC's are present.

1. Remove your foot from the brake pedal.
2. Start the engine and allow it to run for at least 10 seconds while observing the ABS warning lamp.

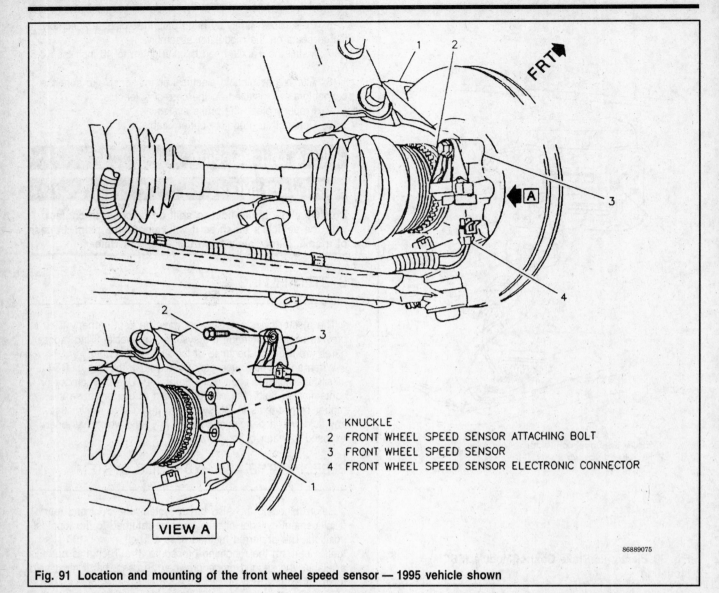

1 KNUCKLE
2 FRONT WHEEL SPEED SENSOR ATTACHING BOLT
3 FRONT WHEEL SPEED SENSOR
4 FRONT WHEEL SPEED SENSOR ELECTRONIC CONNECTOR

VIEW A

86889075

Fig. 91 Location and mounting of the front wheel speed sensor — 1995 vehicle shown

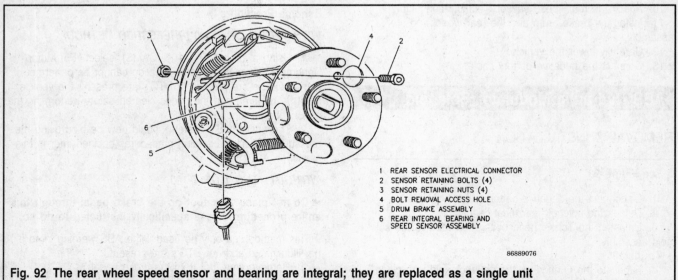

1 REAR SENSOR ELECTRICAL CONNECTOR
2 SENSOR RETAINING BOLTS (4)
3 SENSOR RETAINING NUTS (4)
4 BOLT REMOVAL ACCESS HOLE
5 DRUM BRAKE ASSEMBLY
6 REAR INTEGRAL BEARING AND
  SPEED SENSOR ASSEMBLY

86889076

Fig. 92 The rear wheel speed sensor and bearing are integral; they are replaced as a single unit

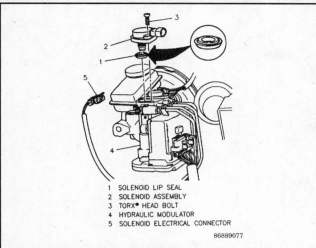

1 SOLENOID LIP SEAL
2 SOLENOID ASSEMBLY
3 TORX® HEAD BOLT
4 HYDRAULIC MODULATOR
5 SOLENOID ELECTRICAL CONNECTOR

86889077

Fig. 93 ABS modulator solenoid mounting — 1995 vehicle shown

3. If the ABS warning lamp turned "ON" and stayed "ON" after about 10 seconds, the bleeding procedure must be stopped and a Tech 1 must be used to diagnose the ABS function.

4. If the ABS warning lamp turned "ON" for about 3 seconds, then turned "OFF" and stayed "OFF", turn the ignition "OFF".

5. Repeat Steps 1-4 one more time.

6. The entire brake system should now be bled following the manual or pressure bleeding procedure.

Pressure Bleeding

◗ **See Figures 94 and 95**

➡**The pressure bleeding equipment must be of the diaphragm type. It must have a rubber diaphragm between the air supply and the brake fluid to prevent air, moisture and other contaminants from entering the hydraulic system.**

1. Clean the master cylinder fluid reservoir cover and surrounding area, then remove the cover.

2. Add fluid, if necessary to obtain a proper fluid level.

3. Connect bleeder adapter J 35589, or equivalent, to the brake fluid reservoir, then connect the bleeder adapter to the pressure bleeding equipment.

4. Adjust the pressure bleed equipment t o 5-10 psi (35-70 kPa) and wait about 30 seconds to be sure there is no leakage.

5. Adjust the pressure bleed equipment to 30-35 psi (205-240 kPa).

✳✳WARNING

Use a shop rag to catch the escaping brake fluid. Be careful not to let any fluid run down the motor pack base or into the electrical connector.

6. With the pressure bleeding equipment connected and pressurized, proceed as follows:

a. Attach a clear plastic bleeder hose to the rearward bleeder valve on the hydraulic modulator.

b. Slowly open the bleeder valve and allow fluid to flow until no air is seen in the fluid.

c. Close the valve when fluid flows out without any air bubbles.

d. Repeat Steps 6b and 6c until no air bubbles are present.

e. Relocate the bleeder hose on the forward hydraulic modulator bleed valve and repeat Steps 6a through 6d.

7. Tighten the bleeder valve to 80 inch lbs. (9 Nm).

8. Proceed to bleed the hydraulic modulator brake pipe connections as follows with the pressure bleeding equipment connected and pressurized:

a. Slowly open the forward brake pipe tube nut on the hydraulic modulator and check for air in the escaping fluid.

b. When the air flow ceases, immediately tighten the tube nut. Tighten the tube nut to 18 ft. lbs. (24 Nm).

9. Repeat Steps 8a and 8b for the remaining three brake pipe connections moving from the front to the rear.

10. Raise and safely support the vehicle.

11. Proceed, as outlined in the following steps, to bleed the wheel brakes in the following sequence: right rear, left rear, right front, then left front.

a. Attach a clear plastic bleeder hose to the bleeder valve at the wheel, then submerge the opposite hose end in a clean container partially filled with clean brake fluid.

b. Slowly open the bleeder valve and allow the fluid to flow.

c. Close the valve when fluid begins to flow without any air bubbles. Tap lightly on the caliper or backing plate to dislodge any trapped air bubbles.

12. Repeat Step 11 on the other brakes using the earlier sequence.

13. Remove the pressure bleeding equipment, including bleeder adapter J 35589.

14. Carefully lower the vehicle, then check the brake fluid and add if necessary. Don't forget to put the reservoir cap back on.

15. With the ignition turned to the RUN position, apply the brake pedal with moderate force and hold it. Note the pedal travel and feel. If the pedal feels firm and constant and the pedal travel is not excessive, start the engine. With the engine running, recheck the pedal travel. If it's still firm and constant and pedal travel is not excessive, go to Step 17.

16. If the pedal feels soft or has excessive travel either initially or after the engine is started, the following procedure may be used:

a. With the Tech 1 scan tool, "release" then "apply" each motor 2-3 times and cycle each solenoid 5-10 times. When finished, be sure to "apply" the front and rear motors to ensure the pistons are in the upmost position. DO NOT DRIVE THE VEHICLE.

b. If a Tech 1 is not available, remove your foot from the brake pedal, start the engine and allow it run for at least 10 seconds to initialize the ABS. DO NOT DRIVE THE VEHICLE. After 10 seconds, turn the ignition "OFF". The initialization procedure most be repeated 5 times to ensure any trapped air has been dislodged.

c. Repeat the bleeding procedure, starting with Step 1.

17. Road test the vehicle, and make sure the brakes are operating properly.

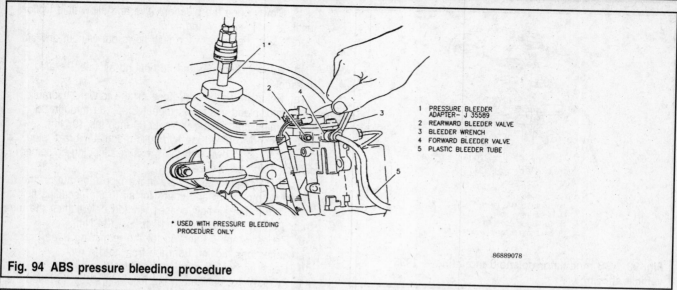

1 PRESSURE BLEEDER
  ADAPTER— J 35589
2 REARWARD BLEEDER VALVE
3 BLEEDER WRENCH
4 FORWARD BLEEDER VALVE
5 PLASTIC BLEEDER TUBE

* USED WITH PRESSURE BLEEDING
  PROCEDURE ONLY

86889078

Fig. 94 ABS pressure bleeding procedure

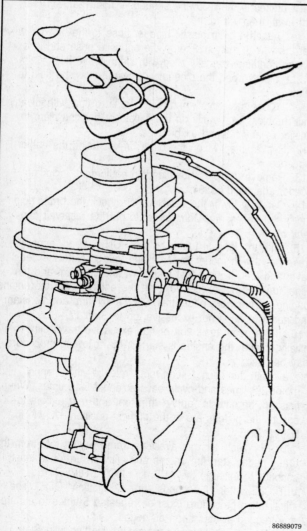

86889079

Fig. 95 Position a shop rag to catch escaping brake fluid

Manual Bleeding

♦ See Figure 96

1. Clean the master cylinder fluid reservoir cover and surrounding area, then remove the cover.

2. Add fluid, if necessary to obtain a proper fluid level, then put the reservoir cover back on.

3. Prime the ABS hydraulic modulator/master cylinder assembly as follows:

   a. Attach a bleeder hose to the rearward bleeder valve, then submerge the opposite hose end in a clean container partially filled with clean brake fluid.

   b. Slowly open the rearward bleeder valve.

   c. Depress and hold the brake pedal until the fluid begins to flow.

   d. Close the valve, then release the brake pedal.

   e. Repeat Steps 3b-3d until no air bubbles are present.

   f. Relocate the bleeder hose to the forward hydraulic modulator bleeder valve, then repeat Steps 3a-3e.

4. Once the fluid is seen to flow from both modulator bleeder valves, the ABS modulator/master cylinder assembly is sufficiently full of fluid. However, it may not be completely purged of air. At this point, move to the wheel brakes and bleed them. This ensures that the lowest points in the system are completely free of air and then the assembly can purged of any remaining air.

5. Remove the fluid reservoir cover. Fill to the correct level, if necessary, then fasten the cover.

6. Raise and safely support the vehicle.

7. Proceed, as outlined in the following steps, to bleed the wheel brakes in the following sequence: right rear, left rear, right front, then left front.

   a. Attach a clear plastic bleeder hose to the bleeder valve at the wheel, then submerge the opposite hose end in a clean container partially filled with clean brake fluid.

   b. Open the bleeder valve.

   c. Have an assistant slowly depress the brake pedal.

   d. Close the valve and slowly release the release the brake pedal.

   e. Wait 5 seconds.

   f. Repeat Steps 7a-7e until the brake pedal feels firm at half travel and no air bubbles are observed in the bleeder

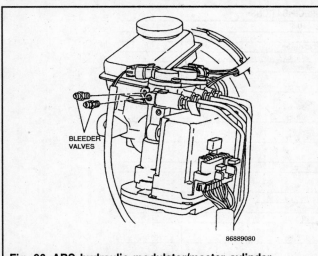

BLEEDER
VALVES

86889080

Fig. 96 ABS hydraulic modulator/master cylinder bleeder locations

hose. To assist in freeing the entrapped air, tap lightly on the caliper or braking plate to dislodge any trapped air bubbles.

8. Repeat Step 7 for the remaining brakes in the sequence given earlier.

9. Carefully lower the vehicle.

10. Remove the reservoir cover, then fill to the correct level with brake fluid and replace the cap.

11. Bleed the ABS hydraulic modulator/master cylinder assembly as follows:

   a. Attach a clear plastic bleeder hose to the rearward bleeder valve on the modulator, then submerge the opposite hose end in a clean container partially filled with clean brake fluid.

   b. Have an assistant depress the brake pedal with moderate force.

   c. Slowly open the rearward bleeder valve and allow the fluid to flow.

   d. Close the valve, then release the brake pedal.

   e. Wait 5 seconds.

   f. Repeat Steps 11a-11e until no air bubbles are present.

   g. Relocate the bleeder hose to the forward hydraulic modulator bleeder valve, then repeat Steps 11a-11f.

12. Carefully lower the vehicle, then check the brake fluid and add if necessary. Don't forget to put the reservoir cap back on.

13. With the ignition turned to the **RUN** position, apply the brake pedal with moderate force and hold it. Note the pedal travel and feel. If the pedal feels firm and constant and the pedal travel is not excessive, start the engine. With the engine running, recheck the pedal travel. If it's still firm and constant and pedal travel is not excessive, go to Step 17.

14. If the pedal feels soft or has excessive travel either initially or after the engine is started, the following procedure may be used:

   a. With the Tech 1 scan tool, "Release" then "Apply" each motor 2-3 times and cycle each solenoid 5-10 times. When finished, be sure to "Apply" the front and rear motors to ensure the pistons are in the upmost position. DO NOT DRIVE THE VEHICLE.

   b. If a Tech 1 scan tool is not available, remove your foot from the brake pedal, start the engine and allow it run for at least 10 seconds to initialize the ABS. DO NOT DRIVE THE VEHICLE. After 10 seconds, turn the ignition **OFF**. The initialization procedure most be repeated 5 times to ensure any trapped air has been dislodged.

   c. Repeat the bleeding procedure, starting with Step 1.

15. Road test the vehicle, and make sure the brakes are operating properly.

TORQUE SPECIFICATIONS

Component	U.S.	Metric
ABS Electronic Control Unit (ECU)/Electronic Brake Control Module (EBCM)	17 ft. lbs.	21 Nm
ABS Hydraulic Modulator Solenoid	40 inch lbs.	4.5 Nm
ABS Hydraulic Modulator/Master Cylinder Assembly	20 ft. lbs.	27 Nm
Bleeder Screw	62 inch lbs.	7 Nm
Brake Line Fitting		
Except ABS	20 ft. lbs.	27 Nm
Brake Pedal		
Retaining bolt	25 ft. lbs.	34 Nm
Retaining nut	20 ft. lbs.	27 Nm
Brake Pipes		
ABS equipped vehicles	13 ft. lbs.	17 Nm
Caliper		
Retaining bolts	38 ft. lbs.	51 Nm
Front Wheel Speed Sensors	107 inch lbs.	12 Nm
Hub and Bearing Assembly		
Without ABS	43 ft. lbs.	58 Nm
Parking Brake Lever	18 ft. lbs.	25 Nm
Power Brake Booster	20 ft. lbs.	27 Nm
Proportioning Valves	20 ft. lbs.	27 Nm
Rear Wheel Speed Sensors/Hub and Bearing Assembly		
ABS equipped vehicles	37 ft. lbs.	50 Nm
Wheel Cylinder		
Bolt-on type	15 ft. lbs.	20 Nm
Wheel Lug Nuts	103 ft. lbs.	140 Nm

86889501

BRAKE SPECIFICATIONS
All measurements in inches unless noted

Year	Model	Master Cylinder Bore	Brake Disc Original Thickness	Brake Disc Minimum Thickness	Brake Disc Maximum Runout	Brake Drum Diameter Original Inside Diameter	Brake Drum Diameter Max. Wear Limit	Brake Drum Diameter Maximum Machine Diameter	Minimum Lining Thickness Front	Minimum Lining Thickness Rear
1985	All	0.874	0.885	0.815	0.004	7.880	7.929	7.899	0.030	0.030 [1]
1986	All	0.874	0.885	0.815	0.004	7.880	7.929	7.899	0.030	0.030 [1]
1987	All	0.874	0.885	0.815	0.004	7.880	7.929	7.899	0.030	0.030 [1]
1988	All	0.874	0.885	0.815	0.004	7.880	7.929	7.899	0.030	0.030 [1]
1989	All	0.874	0.885	0.815	0.004	7.880	7.929	7.899	0.030	0.030 [1]
1990	All	0.874	0.885	0.815	0.004	7.880	7.929	7.899	0.030	0.030 [1]
1991	All	0.874	0.806	0.736	0.004	7.879	7.929	7.889	0.030	0.030 [1]
1992	All	0.874	0.806	0.736	0.004	7.879	7.929	7.899	0.030	0.030 [1]
1993	All	0.874	0.806	0.736	0.004	7.874	7.929	7.899	0.030	0.030 [1]
1994	All	0.874	0.806	0.736	0.004	7.874	7.929	7.899	0.030	0.030 [1]
1995	All	0.874	0.806	0.736	0.004	7.874	7.929	7.899	0.030	0.030 [1]

[1] 0.030 over rivet head. If bonded lining, use 0.062 from shoe

86889500

EXTERIOR
  ANTENNA 10-13
  BUMPERS 10-5
  DOORS 10-2
  FENDERS 10-16
  GRILLE 10-11
  HOOD 10-2
  OUTSIDE MIRRORS 10-13
  TRUNK LID 10-4
INTERIOR
  CENTER CONSOLE 10-22
  DOOR GLASS 10-38
  DOOR LOCKS 10-35
  DOOR PANELS 10-23
  ELECTRIC WINDOW MOTOR 10-39
  HEADLINER 10-31
  INSIDE REAR VIEW MIRROR 10-44
  INSTRUMENT PANEL AND
    PAD 10-18
  INTERIOR TRIM PANELS 10-27
  POWER SEAT MOTOR 10-50
  REAR QUARTER WINDOW 10-41
  SEAT BELTS 10-46
  SEATS 10-46
  WINDOW REGULATOR 10-38
  WINDSHIELD AND REAR
    WINDOW 10-40
SPECIFICATIONS CHARTS
  TORQUE SPECIFICATIONS 10-50

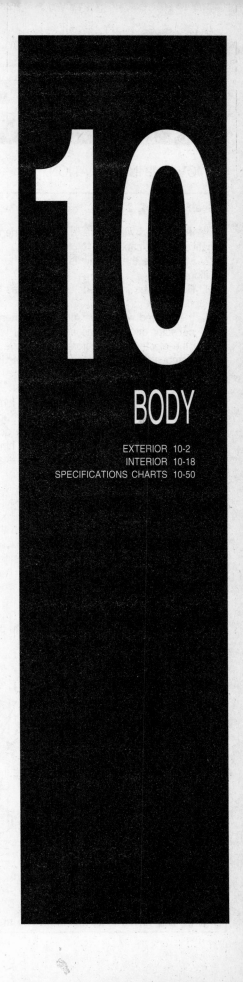

10

BODY

EXTERIOR 10-2
INTERIOR 10-18
SPECIFICATIONS CHARTS 10-50

EXTERIOR

Doors

REMOVAL & INSTALLATION

▶ See Figures 1, 2 and 3

1. If equipped with power door components, disconnect the negative battery cable.
2. Make sure the window is raised up to its fully closed position.
3. Remove the inner door trim panel, as outlined later in this section.
4. If equipped with power door components, move the water deflector enough to access the door wiring harness, then detach the electrical connectors and remove the harness.
5. Remove the rubber conduit from the door.
6. Unfasten the door hold-open bolt.
7. Have an assistant support the door.
8. Matchmark the position of the door hinge to the hinge pillar. Unfasten the lower and upper hinge bolts from the pillar.
9. With an assistant's help, detach the door from the body.
10. Matchmark the position of the door hinge to the door, then unfasten the upper and lower hinge retaining bolts. Carefully remove the door from the vehicle.

To install:

11. Snug the upper and lower hinge-to-door bolts so the door can be moved.
12. With the aid of an assistant, position the door to the body.
13. Snug the upper and lower hinge-to-pillar bolts and nuts so that the door can be moved.
14. Carefully close the door. Adjust the door for proper alignment.
15. Slowly open the door.
16. Tighten the upper and lower hinge-to-pillar bolts and nuts to 16 ft. lbs. (22 Nm).

17. Tighten the upper and lower hinge-to-door bolts to 16 ft. lbs. (22 Nm).
18. Check the door for proper alignment. If the door does not align properly, readjust.
19. Install the door detent-to-hinge pillar bolt, then tighten to 80 inch lbs. (9 Nm).
20. If so equipped, install the electrical harness through the conduit access hole and connect the electrical connectors to the power door components.
21. Fasten the rubber conduit to the door.
22. Reposition and secure the door water deflector.
23. Install the inner door trim panel, as outlined later in this section.
24. Connect the negative battery cable.

ADJUSTMENT

1. Adjust the door so that the door to body and lock to striker align properly.
2. The hinge to door bolts may need to be loosened to adjust the alignment properly.

Hood

REMOVAL & INSTALLATION

▶ See Figures 4 and 5

1. Raise the hood. Install a protective covering over the fenders to protect the paint.
2. Remove the engine compartment lamp.
3. Using a suitable tool, mark the position of the hinges in relation to the hood.
4. If equipped, disconnect the hood assist rod strut, by unfastening the retainers using a suitable prytool.

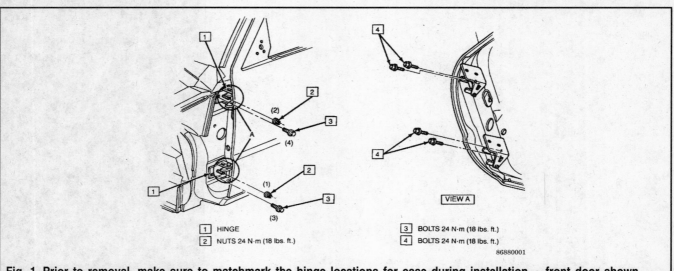

1	HINGE
2	NUTS 24 N·m (18 lbs. ft.)
3	BOLTS 24 N·m (18 lbs. ft.)
4	BOLTS 24 N·m (18 lbs. ft.)

VIEW A

86880001

Fig. 1 Prior to removal, make sure to matchmark the hinge locations for ease during installation — front door shown

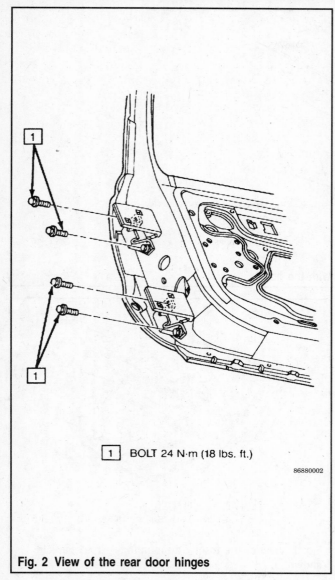

[1] BOLT 24 N·m (18 lbs. ft.)

86880002

Fig. 2 View of the rear door hinges

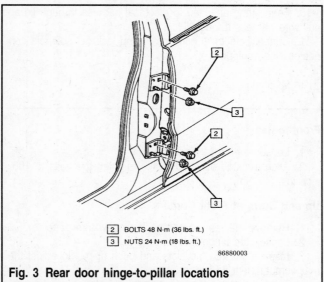

[2] BOLTS 48 N·m (36 lbs. ft.)
[3] NUTS 24 N·m (18 lbs. ft.)

86880003

Fig. 3 Rear door hinge-to-pillar locations

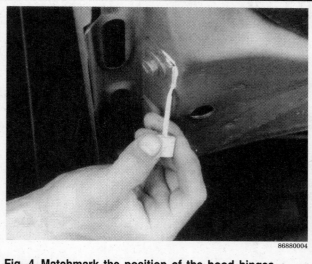

86880004

Fig. 4 Matchmark the position of the hood hinges

5. With an assistant supporting the hood, unfasten the bolts attaching the hinge to the hood and remove the hood from the vehicle.

To install:

6. With the aid of an assistant, align the hood to the hinges, then install the retaining bolts.

7. Check alignment marks and tighten the bolts to 20-22 ft. lbs. (27-30 Nm).

8. Connect the hood assist rod strut, if equipped.

9. Install the engine compartment lamp.

10. Remove the fender covers, then lower the hood.

ALIGNMENT

▶ **See Figure 6**

1. Loosen the bolts for the hood latch.

2. Adjust the front hood bumpers until the hood aligns with the front of the fenders, as follows:

   a. Turn the bolt clockwise to lower the bumper.

   b. Turn the bolt counterclockwise to raise the bumper.

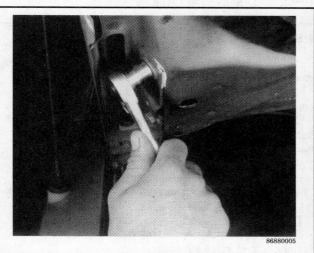

86880005

Fig. 5 Before unfastening the hood retaining bolts, have an assistant support the hood

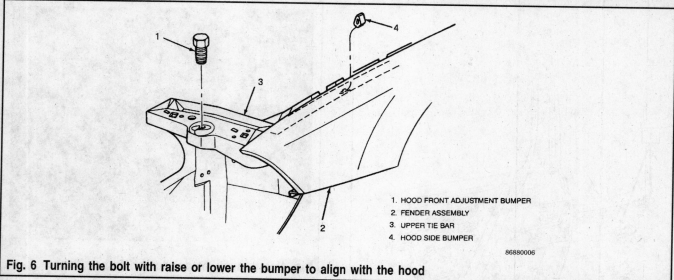

1. HOOD FRONT ADJUSTMENT BUMPER
2. FENDER ASSEMBLY
3. UPPER TIE BAR
4. HOOD SIDE BUMPER

86880006

Fig. 6 Turning the bolt with raise or lower the bumper to align with the hood

3. Measure the difference between the hood and the rear of the fender.

4. Get a shim the same thickness of the difference between the hood and the rear of the fender.

5. Loosen the hood hinge bolts.

6. Install a shim between the hood hinge and the hood.

7. Hand-tighten the hood latch bolts.

8. Position the hood latch upward.

9. Hand-tighten the hood latch bolts.

10. Carefully close the hood to engage the hood striker and the hood latch.

11. Press on the hood until it is aligned with the front of the fenders.

12. Adjust the clearance between the hood and the fender.

13. Pull on the hood release cable, then carefully open the hood. Tighten the hood hinge and latch bolts to 22 ft. lbs. (30 Nm).

Trunk Lid

REMOVAL & INSTALLATION

▶ See Figure 7

1. Open trunk lid. Place a protective covering over the adjacent body panels to protect from damage.

2. Detach all electrical connectors attached to electrical components connected to the trunk lid.

3. Tie a string to the wire harness, then pull it out of the trunk lid. Be sure to allow enough string to feed the wire harness back through the lid.

4. Remove the lock release cable.

5. If so equipped, disconnect the lock out solenoid.

6. While an assistant supports the lid, unfasten the lid to hinge bolts, then remove the lid.

To install:

7. With the aid of an assistant, reposition the trunk lid to the hinges and install the bolts.

8. Tighten retaining bolts to 106 inch lbs. (12 Nm).

9. Adjust the hood as needed.

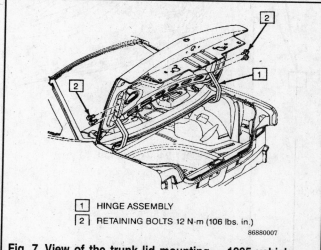

| 1 | HINGE ASSEMBLY |
| 2 | RETAINING BOLTS 12 N·m (106 lbs. in.) |

86880007

Fig. 7 View of the trunk lid mounting — 1995 vehicle shown

10. Feed string attached to electrical harness through lid and pull wire harness through lid.

11. Connect electrical connectors and lock out solenoid connector if so equipped.

ALIGNMENT

Front-to-Rear

1. Loosen the lid to hinge bolts.

2. Align trunk lid as needed, then tighten the bolts to 106 inch lbs. (12 Nm).

Up and Down at Front Corners

1. Remove the rear seat-to-back window trim panel,.

2. Loosen the hinge lock screw.

3. Insert a pin into the slots and push or pull to adjust the rear compartment lid to the quarter.

4. Tighten the screw to 44 inch lbs. (5 Nm).

Up and Down at Rear Corners
▶ See Figure 8

Additional adjustment can be made on the rear corners of the lid by rotating the bumpers clockwise to bring the corners down or counterclockwise to bring the corners up.

Bumpers

REMOVAL & INSTALLATION

Front

1985-91 VEHICLES
▶ See Figure 9

1. Raise and safely support the vehicle.
2. Unfasten the nuts, bolts and screws attaching the front fascia to the fender.
3. Detach the park/turn signal bulb connectors if necessary.
4. Unfasten the bolts attaching the bumper bar and energy absorber assembly, then remove the bumper assembly.
   To install:
5. Install the bumper unit.
6. Attach any electrical connectors that were detached.
7. Install all nuts, bolts and screws previously removed.
8. Carefully lower the vehicle.

1992-95 VEHICLES
▶ See Figures 10, 11 and 12

1. Remove the right and left wheel housing.
2. Remove the right and left fascia to fender bolts.
3. On 1992-95 Grand Ams, remove the parking lamp assemblies.

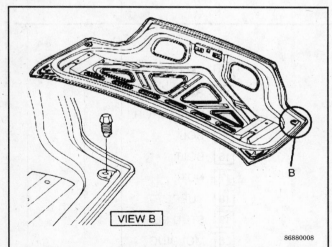

VIEW B

86880008

Fig. 8 Adjustment of the rear corners is possible by rotating the bumpers

4. Unfasten the fascia retainers and remove the fascia from the impact bar.
5. Remove the impact bar bolts and remove the front impact bar from the vehicle.
   To install:
6. Position the front impact bar to the vehicle, then secure with the retaining bolts. Tighten the bolts to 22 ft. lbs. (30 Nm).
7. Install the parking lamp assemblies on 1992-95 Grand Ams.
8. Install the energy absorber to the impact bar and connect with nine 3/16 in. rivets.
9. Fasten the front fascia to the energy absorber and install the retainers and bolts.
10. Install the right and left wheel housings. Carefully lower the vehicle.

Rear Bumpers

1985-91 VEHICLES
▶ See Figure 13

1. Remove the fascia attaching screws and bolts.
2. From inside the trunk, unfasten the bumper attaching nuts and washers.
3. Remove the bumper assembly from the vehicle.
   To install:
4. Installation is the reverse of the removal procedure. Tighten the nuts to 20 ft. lbs. (27 Nm).

1992-95 VEHICLES
▶ See Figures 14 and 15

1. Open the trunk lid.
2. Unfasten the fascia retaining screws from the inside of the trunk.
3. Remove the fascia retaining screws from inside the rear wheelhouse.
4. On 1992-95 Grand Am GT model only, remove the additional support and screw.
5. From beneath the vehicle, remove the 4 fascia retaining screws from the bracket.
6. Remove the retainers from below the fascia.
7. Detach any electrical connectors, then remove the rear fascia from the impact bar.
8. Remove the nuts that attach the rear bumper impact bar to the vehicle.
9. Remove the impact bar from the body.
   To install:
10. Connect the impact bar and energy absorber assembly to the body.
11. Install the nuts and tighten to 26 ft. lbs. (35 Nm).
12. Fasten the fascia to the impact bar.
13. Attach any electrical connectors that were disconnected.
14. Install the retainers and attaching screws in opposite order of removal.
15. Close the trunk lid.

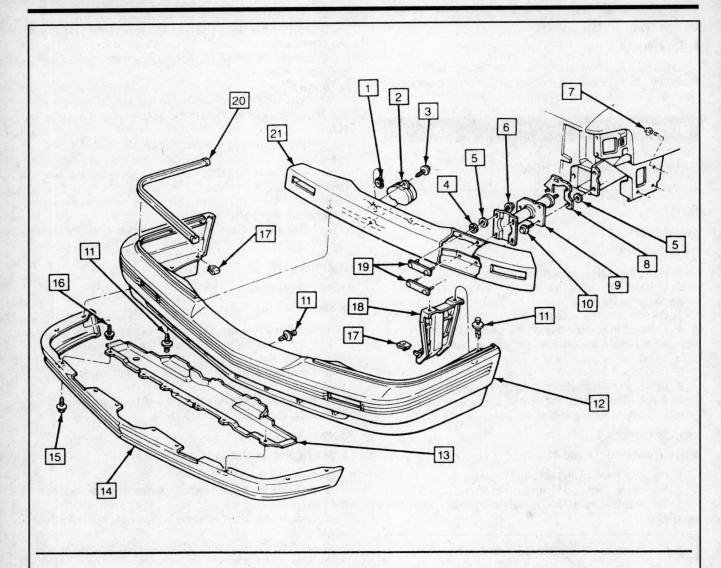

1	NUT	12	FASCIA
2	DAMPENER	13	BAR
3	BOLT	14	DEFLECTOR
4	RETAINER	15	BOLT
5	WASHER	16	BOLT
6	NUT	17	NUT
7	BOLT	18	SUPPORT
8	SHIM	19	STUD PLATE
9	ABSORBER	20	MOLDING
10	BOLT	21	IMPACT BAR
11	RETAINER		

86880009

Fig. 9 Exploded view of a bumper mounting — 1991 Grand Am shown

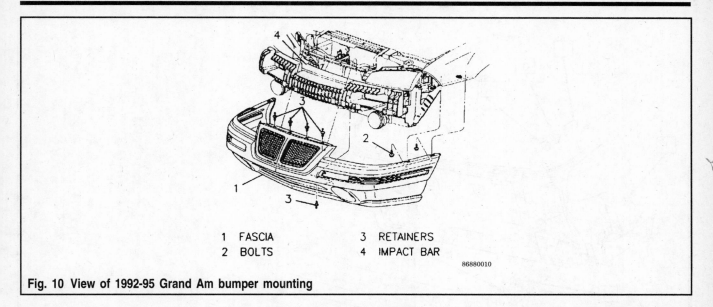

1 FASCIA
2 BOLTS
3 RETAINERS
4 IMPACT BAR

86880010

Fig. 10 View of 1992-95 Grand Am bumper mounting

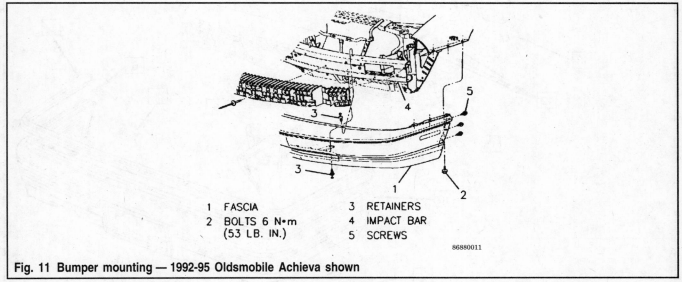

1 FASCIA
2 BOLTS 6 N•m
  (53 LB. IN.)
3 RETAINERS
4 IMPACT BAR
5 SCREWS

86880011

Fig. 11 Bumper mounting — 1992-95 Oldsmobile Achieva shown

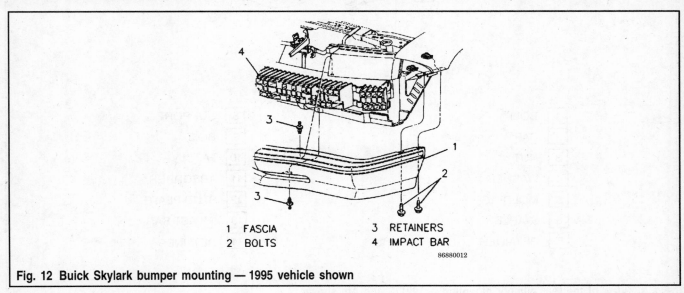

1 FASCIA
2 BOLTS
3 RETAINERS
4 IMPACT BAR

86880012

Fig. 12 Buick Skylark bumper mounting — 1995 vehicle shown

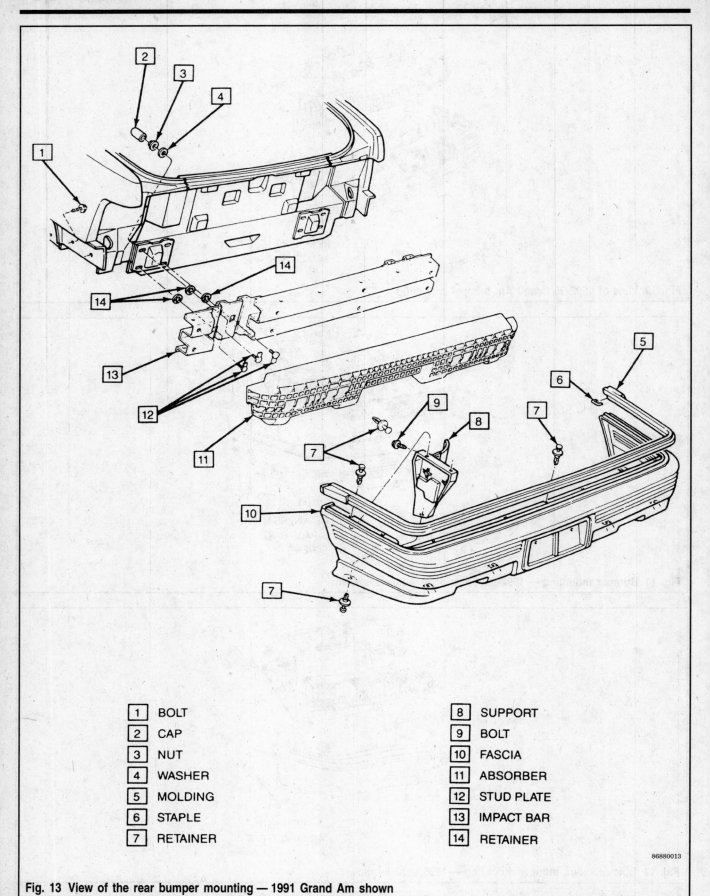

1	BOLT		**8**	SUPPORT
2	CAP		**9**	BOLT
3	NUT		**10**	FASCIA
4	WASHER		**11**	ABSORBER
5	MOLDING		**12**	STUD PLATE
6	STAPLE		**13**	IMPACT BAR
7	RETAINER		**14**	RETAINER

86880013

Fig. 13 View of the rear bumper mounting — 1991 Grand Am shown

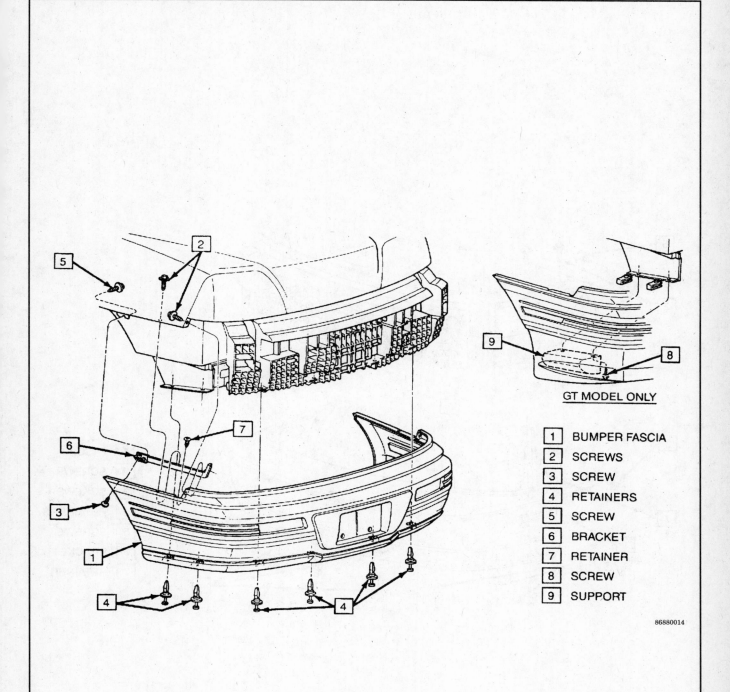

GT MODEL ONLY

1	BUMPER FASCIA
2	SCREWS
3	SCREW
4	RETAINERS
5	SCREW
6	BRACKET
7	RETAINER
8	SCREW
9	SUPPORT

86880014

Fig. 14 Rear bumper mounting — 1995 Grand Am shown

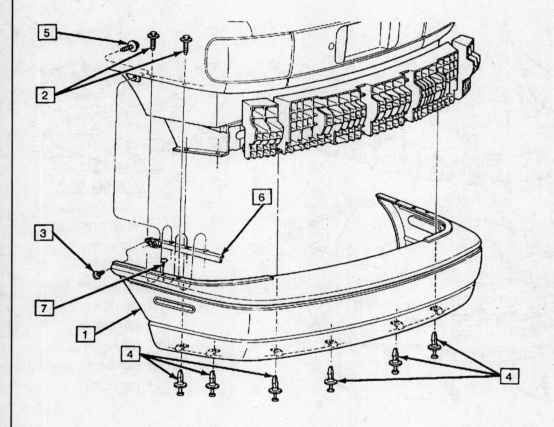

1 FASCIA
2 SCREWS
3 SCREWS
4 RETAINERS
5 SCREWS
6 BRACKET
7 RETAINER

86880015

Fig. 15 View of the rear bumper assembly — Achieva and Skylark shown

Grille

REMOVAL & INSTALLATION

1985-91 Vehicles

EXCEPT 1989-91 GRAND AM

▶ See Figures 16 and 17

1. Unfasten the retaining screws from the grille.
2. Remove the grill assembly.

To install:

3. Position the grill, then secure using the retaining screws.

1989-91 GRAND AM

▶ See Figure 18

To remove grille, just release the tabs and pull grille the outward. Installation is done by inserting grille and locking the retaining tabs.

1992-95 Vehicles

▶ See Figures 19, 20 and 21

1. Unfasten the screws along the top of the grille.
2. For Achievas, unfasten the retainers from the bottom of the grille.
3. Pull out on the grille to release the lower tabs.

To install:

4. Installation is the reverse of the removal procedure.

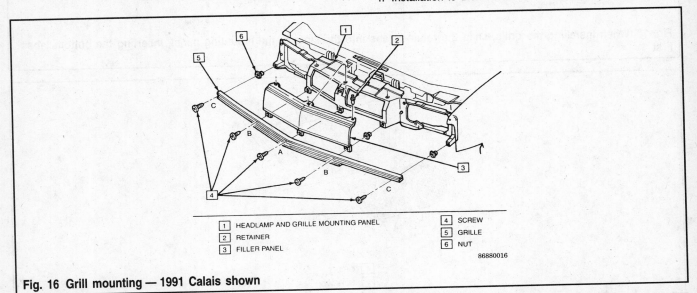

1	HEADLAMP AND GRILLE MOUNTING PANEL	4	SCREW
2	RETAINER	5	GRILLE
3	FILLER PANEL	6	NUT

86880016

Fig. 16 Grill mounting — 1991 Calais shown

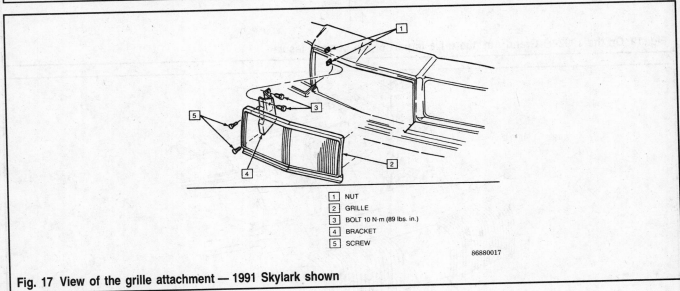

1	NUT
2	GRILLE
3	BOLT 10 N·m (89 lbs. in.)
4	BRACKET
5	SCREW

86880017

Fig. 17 View of the grille attachment — 1991 Skylark shown

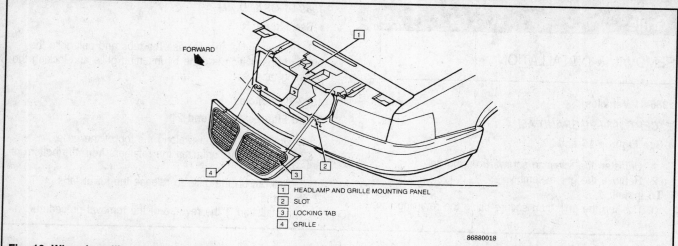

1 HEADLAMP AND GRILLE MOUNTING PANEL
2 SLOT
3 LOCKING TAB
4 GRILLE

86880018

Fig. 18 When installing the grille, snap the retainer tabs into the slots in the mounting panel, inserting the bottom tabs first

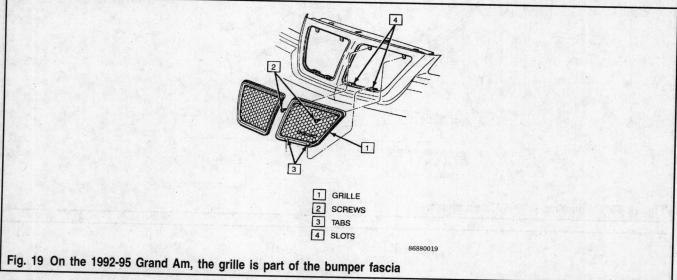

1 GRILLE
2 SCREWS
3 TABS
4 SLOTS

86880019

Fig. 19 On the 1992-95 Grand Am, the grille is part of the bumper fascia

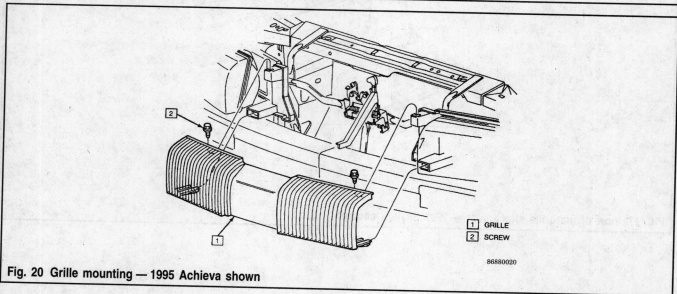

1 GRILLE
2 SCREW

86880020

Fig. 20 Grille mounting — 1995 Achieva shown

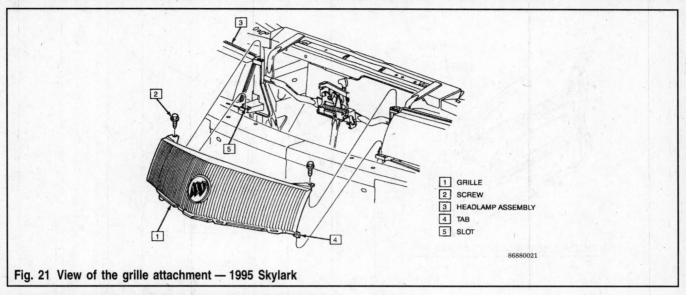

1	GRILLE
2	SCREW
3	HEADLAMP ASSEMBLY
4	TAB
5	SLOT

86880021

Fig. 21 View of the grille attachment — 1995 Skylark

Outside Mirrors

REMOVAL & INSTALLATION

▶ **See Figure 22**

1. From inside of door remove the retaining screw.
2. Remove the outside mirror escutcheon by pulling inward.
3. For manual mirrors, remove mirror control handle and remove escutcheon.
4. If equipped with power mirrors, detach the electrical connector.
5. Remove the gasket, then unfasten the retaining nuts and remove the mirror from the door.

To install:

6. Install the mirror to the door and secure with the retaining nuts. Tighten the nuts to 45 in. lbs. (5 Nm).
7. Install the gasket and, if equipped with power mirrors, attach the electrical connector.
8. Slide the escutcheon onto handle shaft and install handle onto shaft.
9. Snap escutcheon into place and install the screw.

Antenna

REPLACEMENT

Fixed Antenna

REAR FENDER MOUNT

▶ **See Figure 23**

1. Remove rear compartment trim.
2. Remove the antenna mast from the base.
3. Remove the screws that secure the antenna base to the brace.
4. Disconnect the lead-in cable from the base and remove the base from the vehicle.

To install:

5. Install the antenna base into the vehicle and connect the lead-in cable.
6. Install the base to panel screws and tighten to 18 in. lbs. (2 Nm).
7. Secure the antenna mast to the base, then install the rear compartment trim.

FRONT FENDER MOUNT

▶ **See Figure 24**

1. Disconnect the negative battery cable.
2. Remove the radio trim and the radio.
3. Disconnect the antenna cable and connect a piece of wire or string to the cable.
4. Unfasten the antenna nut and bezel.
5. Remove the wheelhouse inner shield.
6. Unfasten and remove the kick panel door sill trim screws nearest the door hinge.
7. Pull carpet away to gain access to the radio cable.
8. Remove the antenna base mounting screws and remove the assembly.

To install:

9. Install the antenna base assembly and install the mounting screws.
10. Secure the carpet to the kick panel.
11. Install the panel door sill trim screws.
12. Install the wheelhouse inner shield.
13. Fasten the antenna nut and bezel.
14. Attach the antenna cable and install the radio and radio trim.
15. Connect the negative battery cable.

Power Antenna

REAR FENDER MOUNT

▶ **See Figure 25**

1. Disconnect the negative battery cable.
2. Remove the rear compartment trim.
3. Detach the relay connector from the antenna assembly.
4. Unfasten the screws that secure the antenna assembly to the brace.

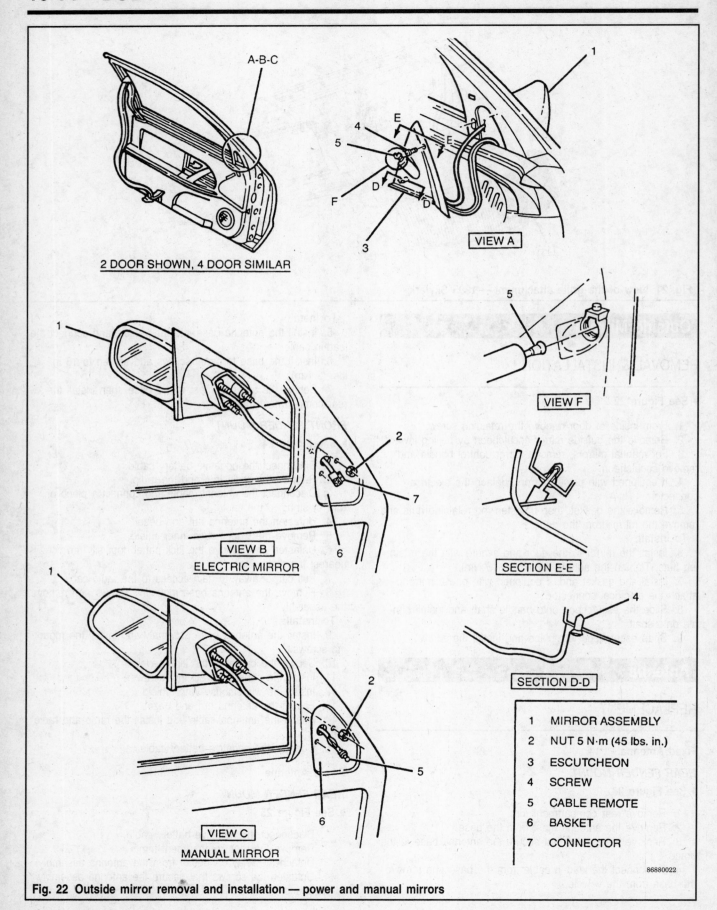

2 DOOR SHOWN, 4 DOOR SIMILAR

VIEW A

VIEW F

VIEW B
ELECTRIC MIRROR

SECTION E-E

SECTION D-D

VIEW C
MANUAL MIRROR

1	MIRROR ASSEMBLY
2	NUT 5 N·m (45 lbs. in.)
3	ESCUTCHEON
4	SCREW
5	CABLE REMOTE
6	BASKET
7	CONNECTOR

86880022

Fig. 22 Outside mirror removal and installation — power and manual mirrors

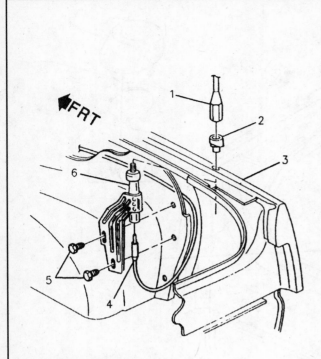

1   ANTENNA MAST
2   ANTENNA BEZEL (PRESS FIT)
3   RIGHT REAR QUARTER PANEL
4   ANTENNA LEAD IN
5   SCREWS
6   ANTENNA BASE ASSEMBLY

86880023

Fig. 23 Exploded view of a rear fender mounted fixed antenna

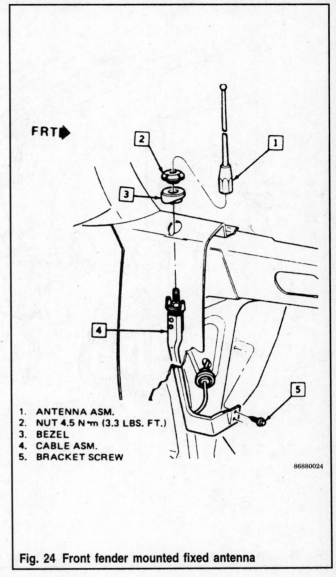

1.   ANTENNA ASM.
2.   NUT 4.5 N·m (3.3 LBS. FT.)
3.   BEZEL
4.   CABLE ASM.
5.   BRACKET SCREW

86880024

Fig. 24 Front fender mounted fixed antenna

5. Remove the antenna insulator and disconnect the lead-in cable from the antenna assembly.
6. Remove antenna assembly from the vehicle.

To install:

7. Connect the lead-in cable to the antenna assembly.
8. Install the base to panel screws and tighten to 53 inch lbs. (6 Nm).
9. Install the antenna insulator.
10. Attach the electrical connector to the antenna.
11. Install the rear compartment trim and connect the negative battery cable.

FRONT FENDER MOUNT

1. Disconnect the negative battery cable.
2. Remove the right side sound insulator.
3. Disconnect the antenna lead-in cable from extension cable.

4. Detach the antenna wiring connector.
5. Remove the grommet from the right cowl.
6. Unfasten the screws from the right inner fender splash shield.
7. Remove the screws from the antenna motor bracket.
8. Unfasten the nut and bezel holding the antenna to the fender, then remove the assembly from the vehicle.

To install:

9. Install the antenna assembly to the vehicle and fasten the nut and bezel to the antenna.
10. Install the screws to the antenna motor and bracket.
11. Attach the wiring connector.
12. Connect the antenna lead-in cable to the extension cable.
13. Install the right side sound insulator.
14. Connect the negative battery cable.

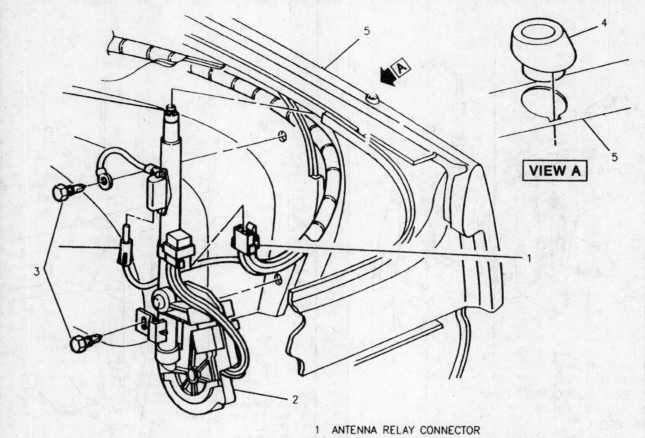

1 ANTENNA RELAY CONNECTOR
2 ANTENNA ASSEMBLY
3 SCREWS — FULLY DRIVEN, SEATED AND NOT STRIPPED
4 BEZEL (PRESS FIT)
5 REAR QUARTER PANEL
6 ANTENNA LEAD

86880025

Fig. 25 View of the power antenna mounting — rear fender mount antenna

Fenders

REMOVAL & INSTALLATION

▶ See Figures 26 and 27

➡Use masking tape and heavy rags to protect the painted surfaces around the fender area. This procedure will help avoid expensive paint damage during fender removal and installation.

1. Raise the vehicle and support safely. Remove the hood.
2. Remove the front wheel and tire assembly.
3. As outlined in this section, remove the front bumper.
4. Remove the inner fender well.
5. Detach the rocker molding, if equipped.
6. Remove the grille and headlamp mounting panel.
7. Unfasten the bolts from along the top of the fender.
8. Remove the bolts that attach the bottom of the fender to the rocker panel.
9. Unfasten the front brace attaching bolts.
10. Remove the fender from the vehicle.

To install:

11. Connect the braces and hardware to the fender.
12. Fasten the bolts along the top of the fender.
13. Install the bolts to the bottom of the fender at the rocker panel. Check the fender alignment and tighten the bolts.
14. Install the grille and headlamp mounting panel.
15. Install the front bumper and wheel well.
16. Attach all electrical connectors.
17. Install the front wheel and tire assembly.
18. Carefully lower the vehicle, then install the hood. Slowly lower the hood and check alignment. Realign if necessary.

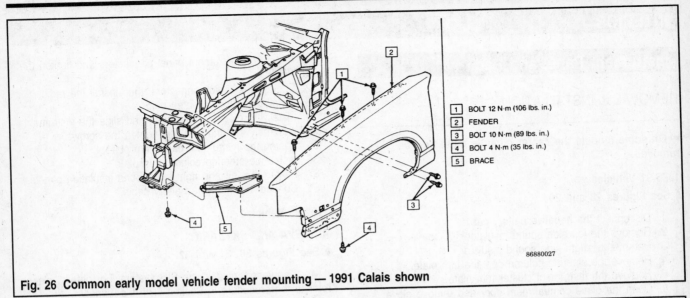

Fig. 26 Common early model vehicle fender mounting — 1991 Calais shown

1	BOLT 12 N·m (106 lbs. in.)
2	FENDER
3	BOLT 10 N·m (89 lbs. in.)
4	BOLT 4 N·m (35 lbs. in.)
5	BRACE

86880027

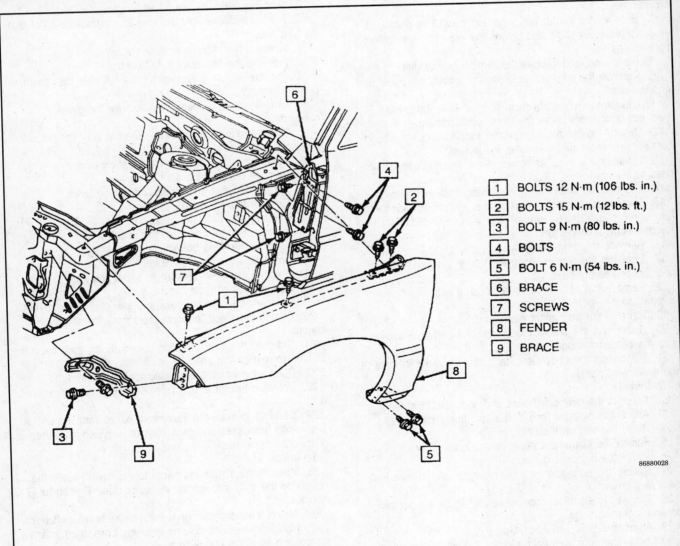

Fig. 27 View of the fender mounting — 1995 vehicle shown

1	BOLTS 12 N·m (106 lbs. in.)
2	BOLTS 15 N·m (12 lbs. ft.)
3	BOLT 9 N·m (80 lbs. in.)
4	BOLTS
5	BOLT 6 N·m (54 lbs. in.)
6	BRACE
7	SCREWS
8	FENDER
9	BRACE

86880028

INTERIOR

Instrument Panel and Pad

REMOVAL & INSTALLATION

➡**On some models the center console must first be removed.**

1985-91 Vehicles

▶ **See Figures 28 and 29**

1. Disconnect the negative battery cable.
2. Remove the left side sound insulator.
3. Remove the right side sound insulator.
4. Remove the steering column opening trim plate.
5. Remove the instrument cluster trim plate.
6. Open the glove compartment door and remove glove compartment.
7. Remove the instrument panel extension trim plate.
8. Remove the radio and detach the electrical and antenna connections.
9. Disconnect and remove the climate control unit.
10. Remove the two nuts between the instrument panel pad and the cowl.
11. Loosen the panel attaching screws, then detach the electrical connectors under the glove compartment.
12. Detach the bulkhead connector located under the hood between the wiper motor and the left fender.
13. Unfasten the nuts that connect the steering column harness to the cowl.
14. Remove the bolts from the steering column support.
15. Disconnect the high beam dimmer switch, ignition switch, turn signal switch, brake light switch, cruise and clutch start switch electrical connectors.
16. Remove the defroster grilles.
17. Unfasten the screws along the top of the pad that connect the pad to the cowl.
18. Remove the pad brace screw located near the glove compartment.
19. Remove the instrument panel pad.
20. Disconnect the antenna lead from the pad and disconnect the defroster hoses.
21. Disconnect the body electrical lead from the right side of the instrument panel.

To install:

22. Connect the defroster hoses and body electrical lead.
23. Attach the antenna lead to the instrument panel pad.
24. Place the pad on the cowl.
25. Fasten the instrument panel pad to cowl screws.
26. Install the defroster grilles.
27. Secure the nuts attaching the steering column wire harness to the cowl.
28. Fasten the electrical connectors and install the steering column mounting bolts.
29. Attach the bulkhead connector.
30. Install the nuts from each side of the instrument panel pad.

31. Attach the instrument panel connectors and tighten the bolts.
32. Engage the radio connectors, then install the radio.
33. Install the climate control unit.
34. Install the glove compartment and slide the instrument panel assembly into the pad and tighten the screws.
35. Fasten the instrument panel trim plate.
36. Install the steering column trim plate.
37. Fasten the left and right side sound insulation panels.
38. Connect the negative battery cable.

1992-95 Vehicles

ACHIEVA AND SKYLARK

▶ **See Figures 30, 31 and 32**

1. If equipped, disable the SIR system. For details, please refer to the procedure in Section 6 of this manual.
2. Disconnect the negative battery cable.
3. For the Achieva only, remove the instrument panel cluster trim plate.
4. Remove the radio from the vehicle.
5. Remove the heater and A/C control.
6. For the Skylark only, remove the left side instrument panel trim plate.
7. Unfasten the retainers, then remove the glove compartment.
8. Unfasten the screw retaining the brace in the left side of the glove compartment.
9. Detach the body 26-way electrical connector.
10. Remove the left side sound insulator.
11. For the Achieva only, remove the fuse block.
12. Remove the bulkhead.
13. Unfasten the defroster grille.
14. Remove the steering column filler.
15. Remove the knee bolster.
16. Unfasten the screw to the left brace.
17. Remove the lower instrument panel screws.
18. Remove the console assembly.
19. Unfasten the steering column upper and lower covers.
20. Detach the electrical connectors from the steering column.
21. Unfasten the three steering column bolts, then allow the column to rest on the seat.
22. Detach the brake switch electrical connectors.
23. Unfasten the remaining screws through the defroster duct.
24. Carefully remove the instrument panel from the vehicle. The wiring harnesses and ducts can be serviced from the rear of the instrument panel.

To install:

25. Position the instrument panel to the cowl. Fasten the screws to the cowl through the defroster duct. Tighten to 17 inch lbs. (2 Nm).
26. Attach the electrical connectors to the brake switches.
27. Install the steering column retaining bolts, then attach the column electrical connectors.
28. Fasten the steering column covers.
29. Install the lower instrument panel screws, then tighten to 17 inch lbs. (2 Nm).

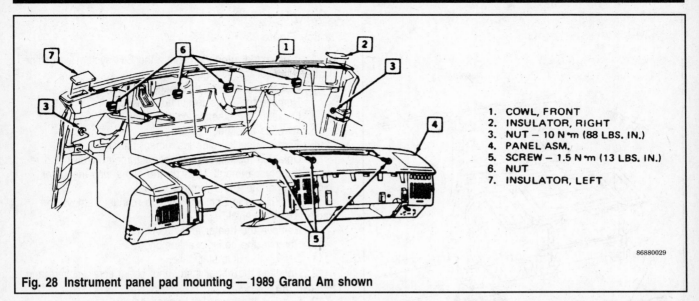

1. COWL, FRONT
2. INSULATOR, RIGHT
3. NUT — 10 N·m (88 LBS. IN.)
4. PANEL ASM.
5. SCREW — 1.5 N·m (13 LBS. IN.)
6. NUT
7. INSULATOR, LEFT

86880029

Fig. 28 Instrument panel pad mounting — 1989 Grand Am shown

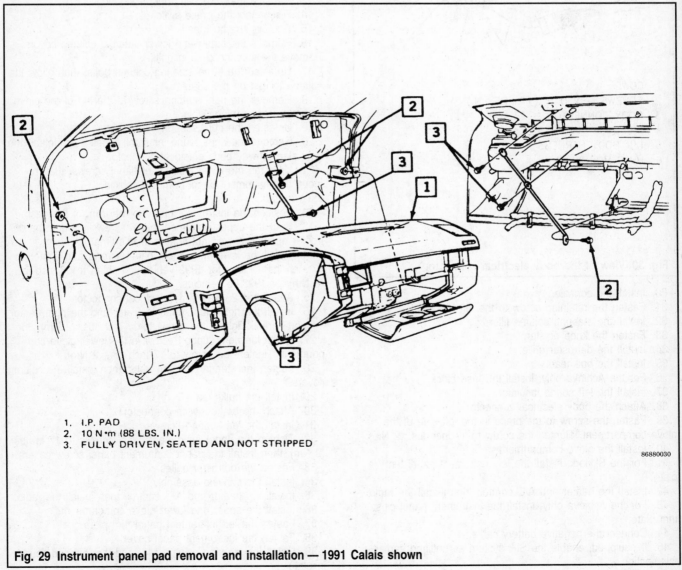

1. I.P. PAD
2. 10 N·m (88 LBS. IN.)
3. FULLY DRIVEN, SEATED AND NOT STRIPPED

86880030

Fig. 29 Instrument panel pad removal and installation — 1991 Calais shown

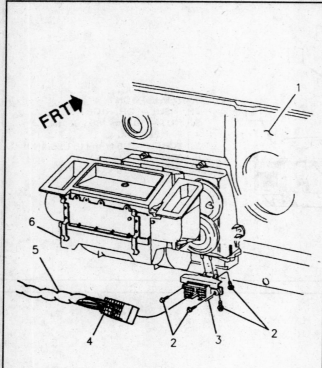

```
1  COWL
2  SCREWS – 2 N·m (17 LBS. IN.)
3  BODY CONNECTOR – 23 WAY
4  I/P BODY HARNESS
5  I/P BODY HARNESS
6  HVAC MODULE
```

86880031

Fig. 30 View of the body electrical connector

30. Install the console.
31. Fasten the retaining screw to the left brace.
32. Install the steering column filler.
33. Fasten the knee bolster.
34. Install the defroster grille.
35. Install the bulkhead.
36. For the Achieva only, install the fuse block.
37. Install the left sound insulator.
38. Attach the body electrical connector.
39. Fasten the screw to the brace in the left side of the glove compartment. Tighten the screw to 17 inch lbs. (2 Nm).
40. Install the glove compartment.
41. For the Skylark, install the left instrument panel trim plate.
42. Install the heater and A/C control, then install the radio.
43. For the Achieva only, install the instrument panel cluster trim plate.
44. Connect the negative battery cable.
45. If equipped, enable the SIR system as outlined earlier in this section.

GRAND AM

▶ **See Figure 33**

1. If equipped, properly disable the SIR system as outlined in Section 6 of this manual.
2. Disconnect the negative battery cable.
3. Remove the left side sound insulator.
4. Unfasten the steering column filler.
5. Remove the knee bolster.
6. Remove the left side instrument panel trim plate.
7. Unfasten the upper glove compartment screws and remove the compartment. Then do the same with the lower glove compartment and remove it also.
8. As outlined in Section 6 of this manual, remove the radio from the vehicle.
9. Remove the heater and A/C control.
10. Remove the console assembly.
11. Detach the defroster grille.
12. Unfasten the upper instrument panel screw covers and remove the screws.
13. Remove the lower left support screw.
14. Disconnect the brake switches.
15. Remove the bulkhead.
16. Remove the upper and lower steering column covers. Remove the steering column bolts.
17. Unfasten the three steering column bolts, then allow the column to rest on the seat.
18. Remove the right support screw at the left of the glove compartment opening.
19. Unfasten the right support screw.
20. Remove the right sound insulator panel, then detach the right side 23-way body electrical connector.
21. Unfasten the lower instrument panel screws, then remove the instrument panel from the vehicle.

To install:

22. Position the instrument panel to the front of the dash.
23. Start the upper instrument panel screws through the defroster opening but do not tighten at this time.
24. Install the lower instrument panel screws and tighten to 17 inch lbs. (2 Nm) for 1992 vehicles. Tighten to 56 inch lbs. (6 Nm) for 1993–95 vehicles.
25. Attach the 23-way body electrical connector.
26. Install the right side sound insulator and the right center support screw. Tighten the screw to 17 inch lbs. (2 Nm).
27. Install the right support screw in the lower glove compartment. Tighten the screw to 17 inch lbs. (2 Nm).
28. Fasten the steering column bolts, then install the column covers.
29. Install the bulkhead.
30. Attach the brake switch connectors.
31. Install the left support screws.
32. Tighten the upper instrument panel screws to 17 in. lbs. (2 Nm), then install the upper instrument panel screw covers.
33. Fasten the defroster grilles.
34. Install the console assembly.
35. Install the heater and A/C control, then install the radio.
36. Install the upper and lower glove compartments.
37. Fasten the left instrument panel trim plate.
38. Fasten the instrument panel cover.
39. Install the steering column filler and the left side sound insulator.
40. Connect the negative battery cable.

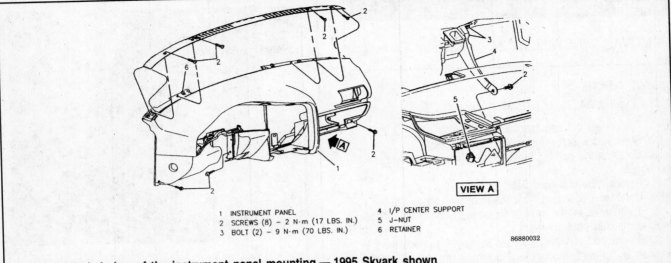

1 INSTRUMENT PANEL
2 SCREWS (8) — 2 N·m (17 LBS. IN.)
3 BOLT (2) — 9 N·m (70 LBS. IN.)
4 I/P CENTER SUPPORT
5 J-NUT
6 RETAINER

86880032

Fig. 31 Exploded view of the instrument panel mounting — 1995 Skyark shown

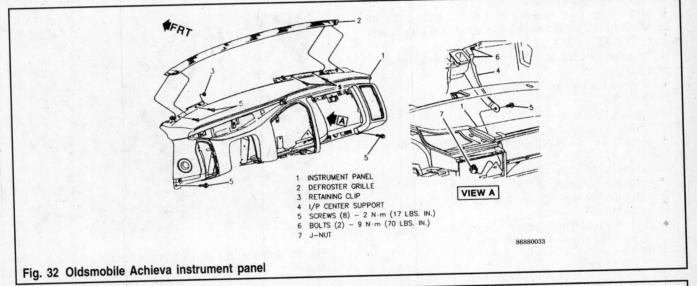

1 INSTRUMENT PANEL
2 DEFROSTER GRILLE
3 RETAINING CLIP
4 I/P CENTER SUPPORT
5 SCREWS (8) — 2 N·m (17 LBS. IN.)
6 BOLTS (2) — 9 N·m (70 LBS. IN.)
7 J-NUT

86880033

Fig. 32 Oldsmobile Achieva instrument panel

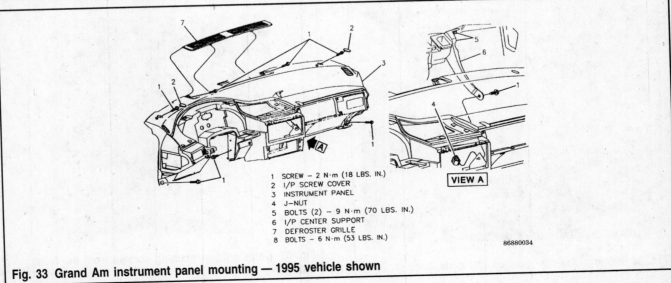

1 SCREW — 2 N·m (18 LBS. IN.)
2 I/P SCREW COVER
3 INSTRUMENT PANEL
4 J-NUT
5 BOLTS (2) — 9 N·m (70 LBS. IN.)
6 I/P CENTER SUPPORT
7 DEFROSTER GRILLE
8 BOLTS — 6 N·m (53 LBS. IN.)

86880034

Fig. 33 Grand Am instrument panel mounting — 1995 vehicle shown

Center Console

REMOVAL & INSTALLATION

1985-91 Vehicles

▶ See Figures 34, 35, 36, 37, 38, 39 and 40

1. Disconnect the negative battery cable.
2. Remove the screws from the rear trim plate.
3. Unfasten the parking brake handle screw and remove the handle.
4. Remove the rear trim plate.
5. Unfasten the screws from the front trim plate.
6. If equipped with a manual transaxle, remove the shifter knob and shifter boot screws.
7. If equipped with an automatic transaxle, remove the horseshoe clip from the handle and remove the handle.
8. Remove the ashtray/coin compartment, then unfasten the front console trim plate screw.
9. Remove the front console trim plate and radio trim plate.
10. Disconnect the radio mounting screws, then detach the radio connectors.
11. Unfasten the console mounting screws and detach the electrical connectors.
12. Remove the console from the vehicle.

To install:

13. Position the the console, then install the console mounting screws.
14. Connect the radio connectors and install the radio screws.
15. Fasten the radio trim plate.
16. Install the front console trim plate screws.
17. Install the ashtray/coin compartment.
18. Install the shifter knob.
19. Install the rear trim plate and parking brake handle.
20. Connect the negative battery cable.

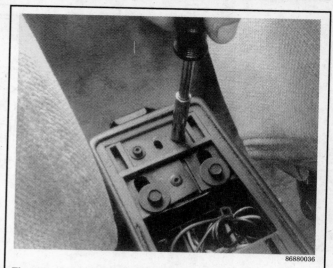

Fig. 35 . . . unfasten the retaining screws

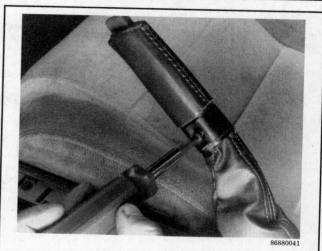

Fig. 36 Unfasten the parking brake handle retaining screw

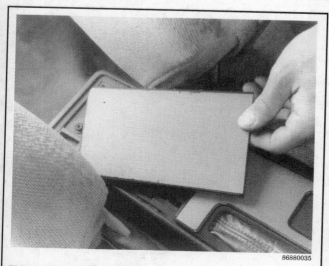

Fig. 34 Remove the rear control trim plate, then . . .

Fig. 37 Unfasten the retaining screws from the front trim plate

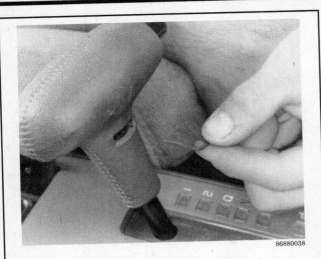

Fig. 38 If equipped with an automatic transaxle, unfasten the horseshoe clip from the shift handle

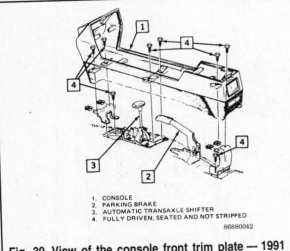

1. CONSOLE
2. PARKING BRAKE
3. AUTOMATIC TRANSAXLE SHIFTER
4. FULLY DRIVEN, SEATED AND NOT STRIPPED

86880042

Fig. 39 View of the console front trim plate — 1991 Calais shown

1992-95 Vehicles
▶ **See Figures 41, 42, 43, 44 and 45**

1. Disconnect the negative battery cable.
2. For Grand Am, remove the console trim as follows:
   a. Remove the shift control handle.
   b. Pry upward gently on the outside edges of the trim plate.
   c. Detach the electrical connectors and the ash tray lamp.
3. For the Achieva, remove the console trim as follows:
   a. Block the wheels, set the parking brake, then place the shifter lever in N.
   b. Remove the shift lever handle.
   c. Carefully pry upward on the outside edges of the trim plate.
4. For the Skylark, remove the console trim as follows:
   a. Remove the shift lever handle
   b. Carefully pry the trim plate upward to disengage the retaining clips.
5. Remove the console compartment.
6. Unfasten the screws at the rear compartment.
7. Pull console towards the rear and detach the electrical connectors.
8. Remove the console from the vehicle.
9. Installation is the reverse of the removal procedure.

Door Panels

REMOVAL & INSTALLATION

1985-91 Vehicles
▶ **See Figures 46, 47, 48, 49, 50, 51 and 52**

1. Remove the inner belt sealing strip.
2. If necessary, remove the outside mirror escutcheon and seat belt opening escutcheon.
3. Detach the escutcheon located on the top of the door panel.
4. Unfasten the side trim panel-to-door pillar retaining screw(s).

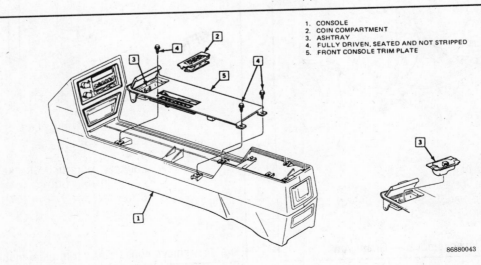

1. CONSOLE
2. COIN COMPARTMENT
3. ASHTRAY
4. FULLY DRIVEN, SEATED AND NOT STRIPPED
5. FRONT CONSOLE TRIM PLATE

86880043

Fig. 40 Console mounting — 1991 Calais shown

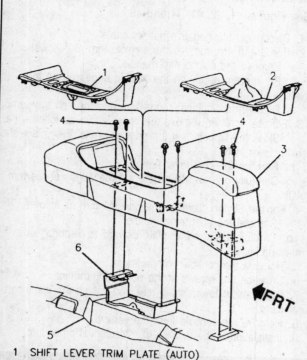

Fig. 41 Exploded view of the console mounting and trim plate — 1995 Grand Am shown

1 SHIFT LEVER TRIM PLATE (AUTO)
2 SHIFT LEVER PLATE (MANUAL)
3 CONSOLE
4 SCREWS (6) — 7 N·m (57 LBS. IN.)
5 BODY FLOOR PAN
6 CONSOLE MOUNTING BRACKET

86880044

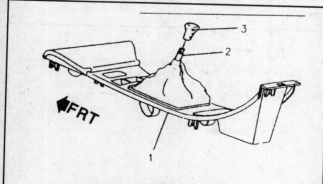

1 CONSOLE TRIM PLATE
2 SHIFT CONTROL LEVER
3 SHIFT CONTROL HANDLE — FULLY DRIVEN,
   SEATED AND NOT STRIPPED

86880047

Fig. 42 Shift control lever removal — Grand Am

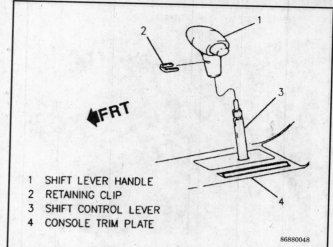

1 SHIFT LEVER HANDLE
2 RETAINING CLIP
3 SHIFT CONTROL LEVER
4 CONSOLE TRIM PLATE

86880048

Fig. 43 On the Achieva and Skylark, you must remove a retaining clip to remove the shift lever handle

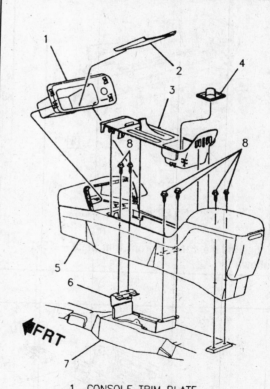

1 CONSOLE TRIM PLATE
2 CONSOLE PAD
3 SHIFT LEVER TRIM PLATE
4 CUP HOLDER
5 CONSOLE
6 CONSOLE MOUNTING BRACKET
7 FLOOR PAN — BODY
8 SCREWS (6) — 7 N·m (57 LBS. IN.)

86880045

Fig. 44 Achieva console and trim plate mounting

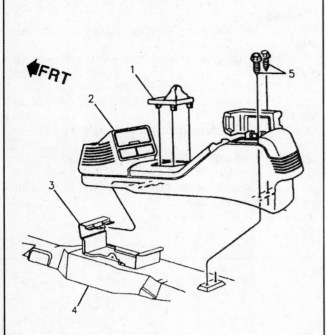

1 SHIFT LEVER TRIM PLATE
2 CONSOLE
3 CONSOLE MOUNTING BRACKET
4 BODY FLOOR PAN
5 BOLTS

86880046

Fig. 45 Buick Skylark console and shift lever trim plate — 1995 vehicle shown

5. For the Grand Am, remove the armrest.

6. Remove the two retaining screws located on the bottom of the door panel.

7. Unfasten door pull handle retaining screws, then remove the handle or escutcheon as applicable.

8. If equipped, detach window crank handle using special remover tool.

9. Detach the electrical connections to the door handle escutcheon and/or locking knob (if equipped).

10. If not already done, remove the door handle escutcheon.

11. Unfasten the retainers, then remove the retractor cover.

12. If equipped, remove the window regulator handle.

13. Separate the trim panel from the door by disengaging the fasteners on the trim panel from the holes in the door inner panel using door panel removal tool no. J 24595-C or equivalent. Pull door panel outward to separate studs from the retainers.

14. Slide seat belt through slit in bottom of trim panel.

15. Lift up on bottom of trim panel to disengage the door panel hooks from the slots.

86880050

Fig. 47 Some retaining screws are "hidden" by covers which must be removed to access the screw

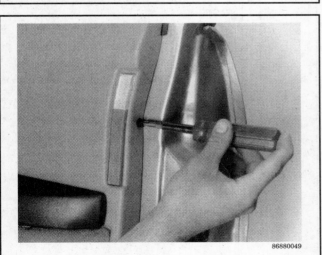

86880049

Fig. 46 Unfasten the retaining screws located on the side of the door trim panel

86880051

Fig. 48 Unfasten the door pull handle retaining screw

Fig. 49 Unfasten the armrest retaining screw, then . . .

Fig. 50 . . . remove the door inside pull handle escutcheon

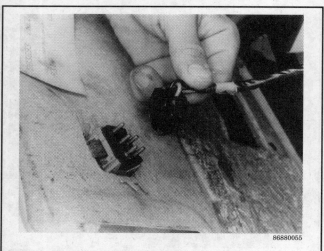

Fig. 51 Don't forget to detach any electrical connections from the trim panel

16. Detach any electrical connectors to switches on the door panel.

17. Remove the trim panel from the vehicle.

To install:

18. Attach any electrical connectors to switches on the door panel.

19. Slide the door panel hooks into the slots and push down to engage.

20. Slide the seat belt through the slits in the door panel.

21. Align the studs to the retainers and push inward so the clips engage.

22. Replace all of the screws that were removed. Install the reflector.

23. Install the inside pull handle and window crank handle.

24. For Grand Ams, install the armrest.

25. If necessary, install the outside mirror escutcheon and seat belt opening escutcheon.

26. Install the inner belt sealing strip.

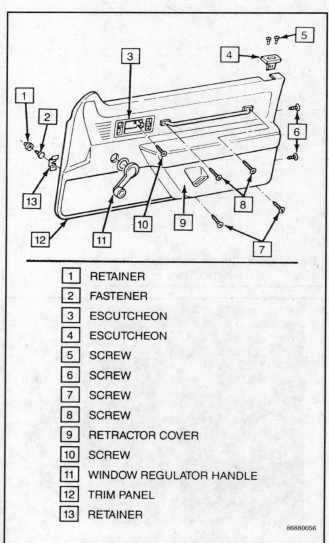

1	RETAINER
2	FASTENER
3	ESCUTCHEON
4	ESCUTCHEON
5	SCREW
6	SCREW
7	SCREW
8	SCREW
9	RETRACTOR COVER
10	SCREW
11	WINDOW REGULATOR HANDLE
12	TRIM PANEL
13	RETAINER

Fig. 52 Door trim panel retainer, fastener and related component locations — 1991 Skylark 2-door shown

1992-95 Vehicles

▶ **See Figures 53, 54, 55 and 56**

1. Disconnect the negative battery cable.
2. Unfasten the door trim panel screws.
3. For the Grand Am only, remove the manual lock rod.
4. For the Achieva and Skylark, remove the reflector using a suitable prytool the carefully detach it.
5. Remove the door inside handle escutcheon by pulling out at the bottom and disengaging the top of the escutcheon from the door inside handle. Detach the wiring harness, if necessary.
6. For the Achieva only, remove the power window switch escutcheon.
7. Remove the door lock switch and escutcheon.
8. Unfasten the door mirror escutcheon.
9. Using a suitable prytool, remove the seat belt escutcheon by carefully prying at the inboard edge.
10. If equipped, remove the window regulator handle by using tool J 9886, or equivalent, to free the spring clip.
11. Detach the door trim panel fasteners, then remove the panel hooks from the door inner panel. Detach any necessary electrical connectors.
12. Carefully remove the door trim panel from the vehicle.

To install:

13. Route the seat belts and the door lock harness through the trim panel. Attach any necessary electrical connectors.
14. Position the door trim panel to the door. Fasten the trim panel hooks to the door inner panel.
15. Install the door trim panel fasteners.
16. Fasten the door mirror escutcheon, then, if applicable, install the manual window regulator.
17. Install the door lock switch and escutcheon.
18. For the Achieva only, install the power window switch escutcheon.
19. Attach the electrical connector, then install the door inside handle escutcheon.
20. For the Achieva and the Skylark, install the reflector.
21. For the Grand Am only, install the manual lock rod knob.
22. Secure the assembly using the door trim panel retaining screws. Tighten the screws to 11.5 inch lbs. (1.3 Nm).

23. Connect the negative battery cable.

Interior Trim Panels

REMOVAL & INSTALLATION

Upper and Lower Inside Door Trim Panels

1. Remove the inside door panel as detailed earlier in this section
2. Remove the nuts securing the trim panel to the door panel.
3. Separate the trim panel from the door panel.
4. Installation is the reverse of the removal procedure.

Rear Quarter Interior Trim Panel

▶ **See Figures 57 and 58**

2-DOOR VEHICLES

1. Remove the rear seat back and rear seat cushion.
2. Disconnect the carpet retainer by removing the screws and lifting up on carpet retainer.
3. Remove windshield side upper molding by grasping molding and pulling down to disengage molding.
4. Remove the trim panel screws.
5. Pull outward on the trim panel to disengage the fasteners from the retainers.
6. Remove the seat belt from the slit in the panel and remove the panel.

To install:

7. Install the seat belt through the slit in the panel.
8. Align the fasteners to the retainers and push in on panel to engage.
9. Install the panel screw.
10. Install windshield side upper molding.
11. Install carpet retainers and install rear seat back and cushion.

4-DOOR VEHICLES

1. Remove rear seat cushion and rear seat back.

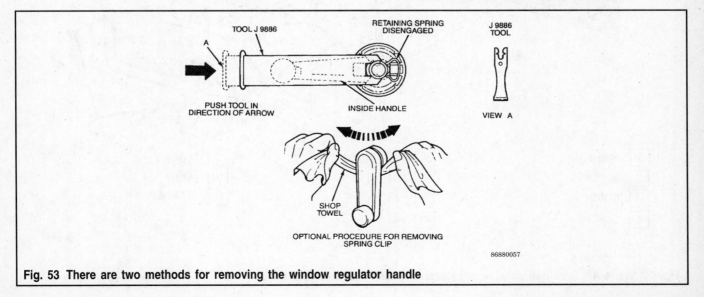

Fig. 53 There are two methods for removing the window regulator handle

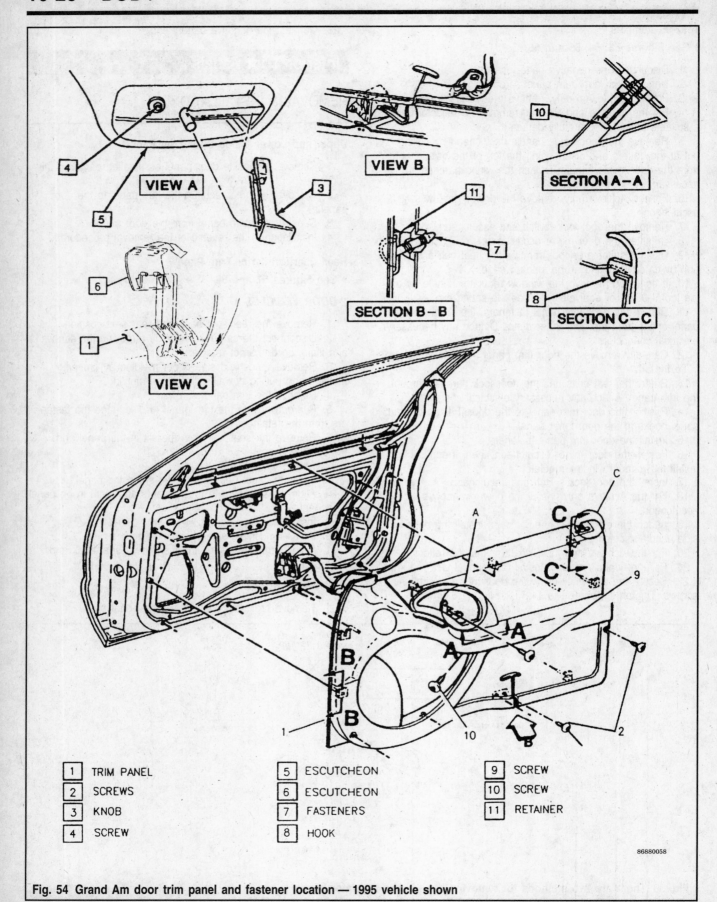

1	TRIM PANEL	5	ESCUTCHEON	9	SCREW
2	SCREWS	6	ESCUTCHEON	10	SCREW
3	KNOB	7	FASTENERS	11	RETAINER
4	SCREW	8	HOOK		

86880058

Fig. 54 Grand Am door trim panel and fastener location — 1995 vehicle shown

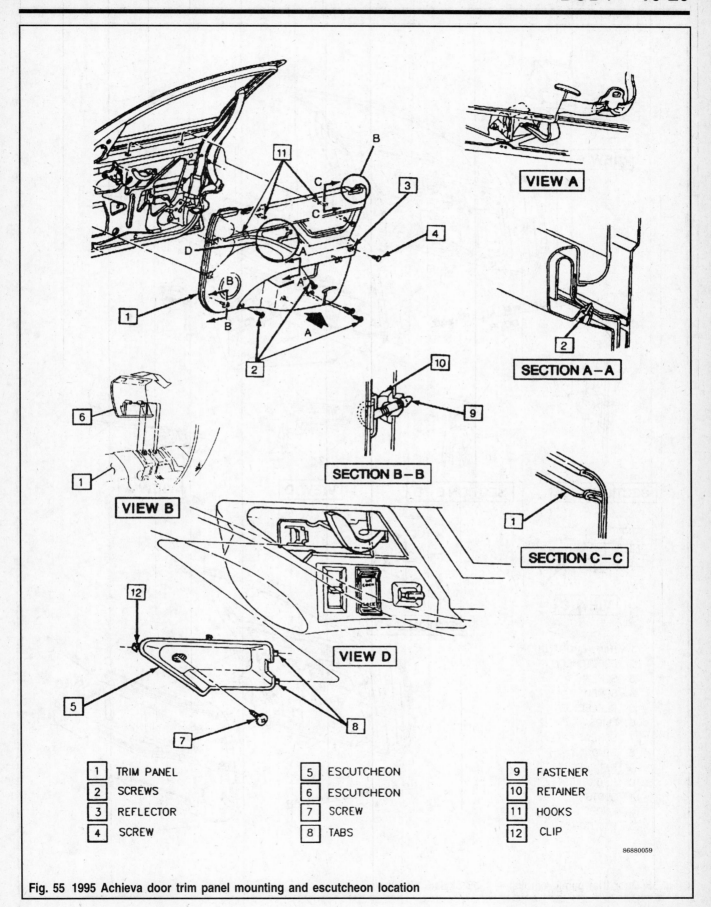

VIEW A

SECTION A–A

SECTION B–B

SECTION C–C

VIEW B

VIEW D

1	TRIM PANEL	5	ESCUTCHEON	9	FASTENER
2	SCREWS	6	ESCUTCHEON	10	RETAINER
3	REFLECTOR	7	SCREW	11	HOOKS
4	SCREW	8	TABS	12	CLIP

86880059

Fig. 55 1995 Achieva door trim panel mounting and escutcheon location

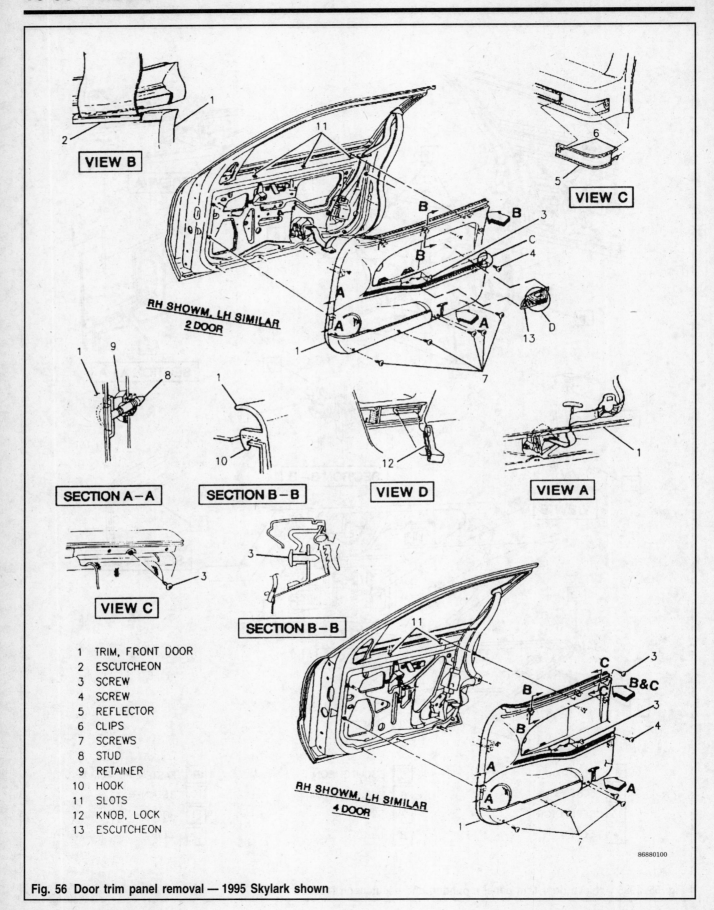

VIEW B

RH SHOWM, LH SIMILAR
2 DOOR

VIEW C

SECTION A–A

SECTION B–B

VIEW D

VIEW A

VIEW C

SECTION B–B

RH SHOWM, LH SIMILAR
4 DOOR

1 TRIM, FRONT DOOR
2 ESCUTCHEON
3 SCREW
4 SCREW
5 REFLECTOR
6 CLIPS
7 SCREWS
8 STUD
9 RETAINER
10 HOOK
11 SLOTS
12 KNOB, LOCK
13 ESCUTCHEON

86880100

Fig. 56 Door trim panel removal — 1995 Skylark shown

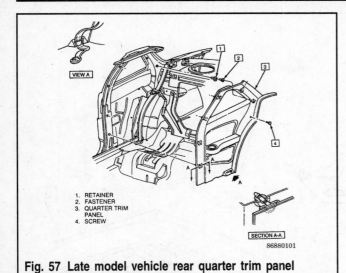

1. RETAINER
2. FASTENER
3. QUARTER TRIM PANEL
4. SCREW

SECTION A-A

86880101

Fig. 57 Late model vehicle rear quarter trim panel removal — 1992 vehicle shown

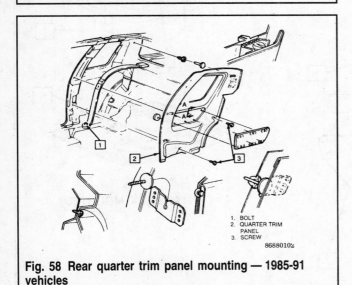

1. BOLT
2. QUARTER TRIM PANEL
3. SCREW

86880102

Fig. 58 Rear quarter trim panel mounting — 1985-91 vehicles

2. Remove the panel screws and remove trim panel by pulling downward to disengage clips.

To install:

3. Install the trim panel by aligning tabs and retainers and pressing upward until secure.

4. Install panel screws and install rear seat back and rear seat cushion.

Headliner

REMOVAL & INSTALLATION

1985-91 Vehicles

◆ See Figures 59, 60, 61, 62 and 63

1. Remove the sunshades by unfastening the screws, detaching the wiring connector (if equipped), then removing the sunshade assemblies.

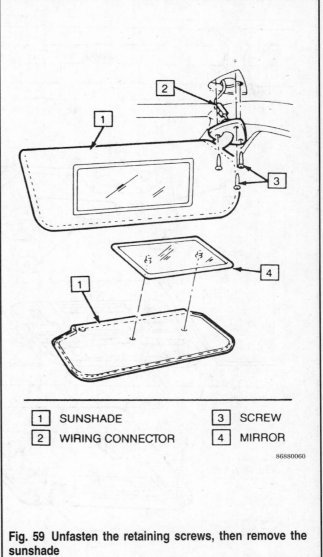

| 1 | SUNSHADE | 3 | SCREW |
| 2 | WIRING CONNECTOR | 4 | MIRROR |

86880060

Fig. 59 Unfasten the retaining screws, then remove the sunshade

2. Remove the dome lamp(s).

3. Detach the courtesy lamp coat hook assemblies or coat hooks, as applicable.

4. On 2-door vehicles, remove the windshield side upper moldings.

5. Unfasten the shoulder belt at the pillar and floor attachments as required for removal of the headliner.

6. Remove the rear seat cushion and seatback.

7. On 4-door vehicles, remove the center pillar trim panel, windshield side upper molding, side roof rail, and the lock pillar lower trim panel.

8. On 2-door vehicles, remove the carpet retainers.

9. If equipped with a sunroof, remove the vista vent finishing lace.

10. On 2-door vehicles, remove the quarter inner trim panel.

➡**Failure to follow this procedure could damage the headlining backing and require headlining replacement.**

11. Using heading removal/installation tool J 2772 or equivalent, loosen the headlining. Starting at one end of the hook and loop material, insert the tool between the hook and

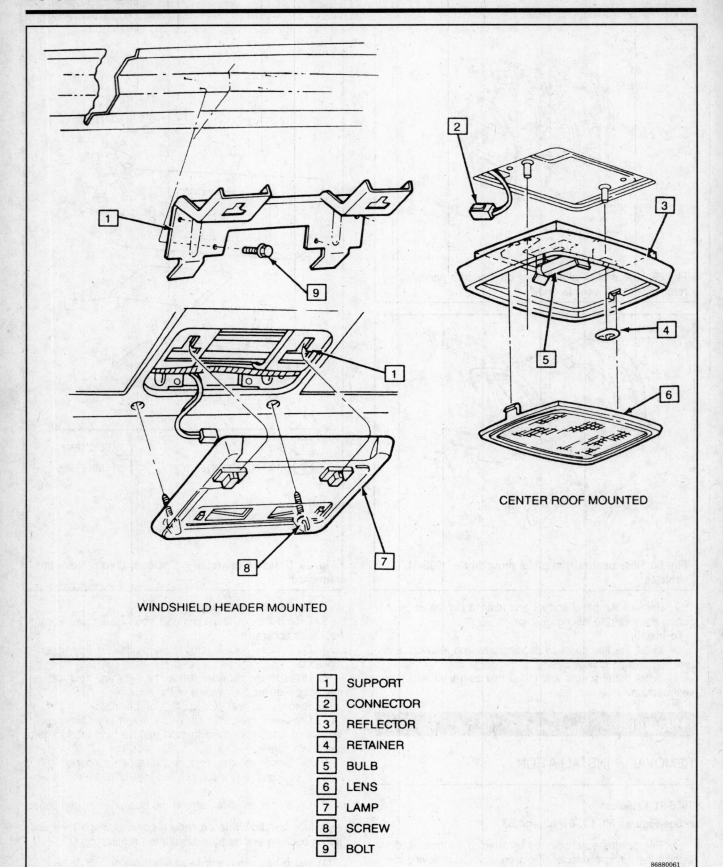

CENTER ROOF MOUNTED

WINDSHIELD HEADER MOUNTED

1	SUPPORT
2	CONNECTOR
3	REFLECTOR
4	RETAINER
5	BULB
6	LENS
7	LAMP
8	SCREW
9	BOLT

86880061

Fig. 60 Depending upon application, remove the center roof mounted or windshield header mounted dome lamp

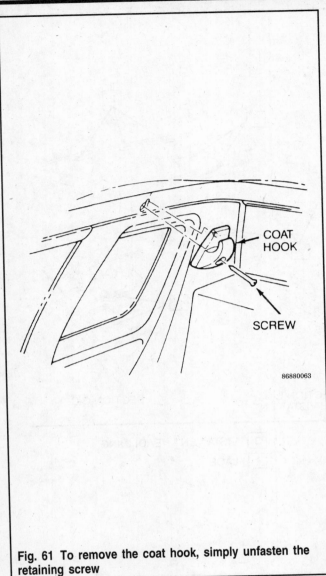

Fig. 61 To remove the coat hook, simply unfasten the retaining screw

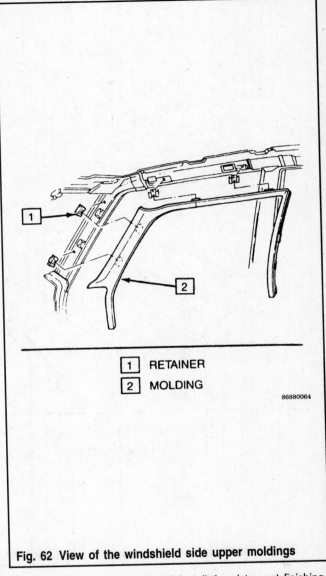

1 RETAINER
2 MOLDING

86880064

Fig. 62 View of the windshield side upper moldings

loop and carefully separate the hook portion from the loop portion of the material until the headlining is loose from the windshield header.

12. Remove the headlining assembly through the right front door.

To install:

➡ **When installing the headlining, be careful not to overflex the assembly or damage may result.**

13. Load the rear portion of the headlining diagonally through the right front door opening and position into the body.

14. Align the headlining assembly with the sunshade cutout holes to sunshade holes and apply upward pressure along the front edge of the headlining. Engage the hook and loop material on the headlining with the mating hook and loop material at the windshield inner reinforcement.

15. Position the rear of the headlining to the back window inner reinforcement. Apply upward pressure to the rear edge of the headlining at the area of the hook and loop material at the back window inner reinforcement.

16. On 2-door vehicles, fasten the quarter inner trim panel.

17. If equipped with a sunroof, install the vista vent finishing lace.

18. On 2-door vehicles, secure the carpet retainers.

19. On 4 door vehicles, install the windshield side upper molding, side roof rail and lock pillar lower trim panel. Begin at the center pillar and install the moldings by working outward.

20. Install the rear seat cushion and seatback.

21. Fasten the shoulder belt at the pillar and floor attachments.

22. On 2-door vehicles, install the windshield side upper moldings.

23. Attach the courtesy lamp coat hook assemblies or coat hooks, as applicable.

24. Install the dome lamps.

25. Install the sunshades. Position the sunshade to the headlining, attach the wiring connector (if equipped), then fasten the retaining screws.

1992-95 Vehicles

1. Disconnect the negative battery cable.

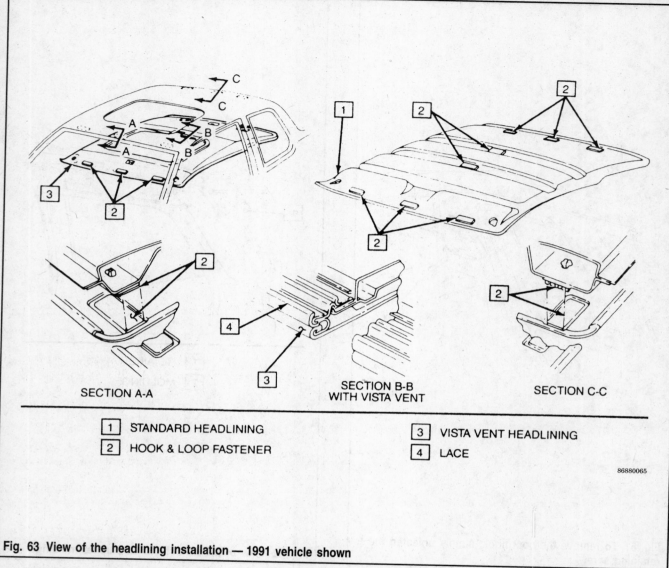

1 STANDARD HEADLINING
2 HOOK & LOOP FASTENER
3 VISTA VENT HEADLINING
4 LACE

86880065

Fig. 63 View of the headlining installation — 1991 vehicle shown

2. Pull the quarter trim panel away from the quarter inner panel. The entire panel does not need to be removed.

3. On sedans only, remove the center pillar trim panel.

4. Detach the windshield side upper garnish moldings.

5. Unfasten the left sound insulator.

6. Detach the wire harness connectors, then disconnect the harness from the pillar.

7. Remove the wire harness from around the end of the instrument panel.

8. Remove the sunshades as follows:

   a. Unfasten the sunshade retaining screws.

   b. For the lighted vanity mirror only, remove the windshield side upper garnish molding, then detach the electrical connector.

   c. Apply downward pressure on the sunshade elbow to disengage the sunshade spring clip.

9. Remove the center dome lamp cover. Pry the center dome lamp base at the "U" shape cutouts using a suitable prytool. Disconnect the lamp wiring harness.

10. Remove the front courtesy/reading lamps.

11. Unfasten the retaining screws, then remove the front assist handle.

12. Remove the rear courtesy/reading lamp and assist handle.

13. For the Grand Am and Achieva only, remove the center high mount brake light. For details, please refer to the procedure located in Section 6 of this manual.

14. Unfasten the retaining screw, then remove the coat hook.

15. Carefully pull at the rear of the headlining to disengage the rear centering clip.

16. Remove the rear view mirror assembly.

17. For vehicles equipped with a center dome lamp, using a suitable prytool, carefully pry at the top center of the storage box and headliner to the release the clip. Slide the headliner rearward to access the storage box screws. Unfasten the storage box screws.

18. Carefully remove the headliner assembly from the vehicle.

19. Remove the rear centering clip.

20. For vehicles equipped with a center dome lamp, unfasten the storage box nuts from the front header metal. The nuts will be destroyed during removal.

To install:

21. Fasten the rear centering clip to the headlining using surface activator 3M part no. 62-3874-0830-5 or equivalent, and adhesive, Loctite Quick Set® 404 or equivalent.

22. If equipped with a center dome lamp, position the storage box to the headliner, then secure with the retaining nuts and screws. Do NOT overtighten. Install the storage box clip.

23. Install the headlining module, then fasten to the rear centering clip.

24. Position the coat hooks, then secure using the retaining screws. Tighten the screws to 4.4 inch lbs. (0.5 Nm).

25. For the Grand Am and Achieva, install the center high mount brake light.

26. Install the rear courtesy/reading lamp and rear assist handle.

27. Position the front assist handle and secure with the retaining screws.

28. Install the front courtesy/reading lamp.

29. Connect the center dome lamp wiring harness, then install the dome lamp base and fasten the lamp cover.

30. Install the sunshades.

31. Fasten the wiring harness around the end of the instrument panel.

32. Secure the wiring harness the to the pillar, then attach the electrical connector.

33. Install the left sound insulator.

34. Fasten the windshield side upper garnish moldings.

35. For the sedan only, install the center pillar trim panel.

36. Install the quarter trim panels.

37. Connect the negative battery cable.

Door Locks

REMOVAL & INSTALLATION

Except 1995 Vehicles

▶ **See Figure 64**

1. Remove the inside door trim panel.

2. Detach the water deflector enough to access the lock actuator.

3. Disconnect the outside handle to lock assembly rod.

4. Disconnect the lock cylinder to lock assembly rod.

5. Disconnect the inside handle to lock assembly rod.

6. Unfasten the lock assembly screws and remove the lock from the door. If equipped, detach the electrical connectors.

To install:

7. Attach the electrical connector (if equipped), position the lock assembly to the door and install the retaining screws. Tighten the screws to 62 inch lbs. (7 Nm). Do NOT overtighten.

8. Attach the outside handle to the lock assembly rod.

9. Connect the lock cylinder to the lock assembly rod.

10. Connect the inside handle to the lock rod and inside locking rod.

11. Fasten the water deflector.

12. Install the inside door trim panel.

1995 Vehicles

▶ **See Figures 65, 66, 67 and 68**

1. Remove the door trim panel. For details, please refer to the procedure located earlier in this section.

2. Remove the seat belt retractor.

3. Unfasten the water deflector enough to access the lock actuator.

4. Remove the lower window run channel by unfastening the retaining bolt (located under the water deflector), then pulling up on the channel to detach the retainer.

5. Remove the door outside handle and lock cylinder as follows:

a. Unfasten the outside handle and lock cylinder retaining bolts.

b. Remove the outside handle and lock cylinder rods from the handle.

c. Remove the handle, then unfasten the lock cylinder nut and remove the cylinder from the handle.

6. Remove the inside door handle retaining rivet and screw, then disconnect the rod from the handle. Remove the inside door handle.

7. Unfasten the door lock actuator Torx® head retaining screws, then remove the actuator.

To install:

8. Push up on the outside lock rod lever and pull on the inside lock handle lever until the lock assembly is in the full open position.

9. Push the lock switch teeth fully towards the actuating arm so the teeth will mesh correctly with the teeth on the lock assembly when installed.

10. Make sure that the actuating arm rubber bumper is on the actuating arm. Install the actuating arm and bumper into the locking lever.

11. Align the lock switch teeth to the gear tooth forkbolt.

12. Secure the lock assembly Torx® head retaining screws.

13. Manually operate the lock assembly by pushing inward on the fork bolt until it clicks into the fully closed position. The lock must operate to the fully closed position without any interference.

14. Attach the door lock actuator wire harness, then install the actuator and secure with the Torx® retaining screws. Tighten the screws to 40 inch lbs. (4.5 Nm).

15. Test the operation of the actuator and door lock switch.

16. Install the door inside handle and lock cylinder.

17. Fasten the lower window run channel.

18. Fasten the door water deflector.

19. Install the seat belt retractor.

20. As outlined earlier in this section, install door trim panel.

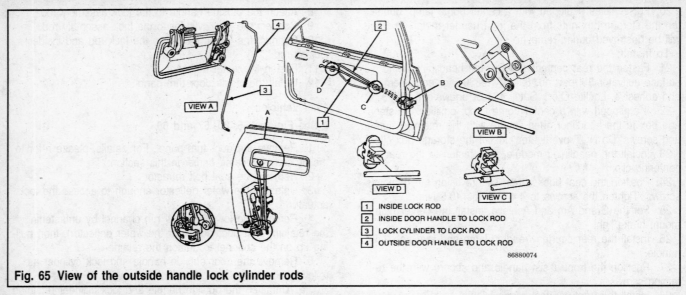

Fig. 65 View of the outside handle lock cylinder rods

1	INSIDE LOCK ROD
2	INSIDE DOOR HANDLE TO LOCK ROD
3	LOCK CYLINDER TO LOCK ROD
4	OUTSIDE DOOR HANDLE TO LOCK ROD

86880074

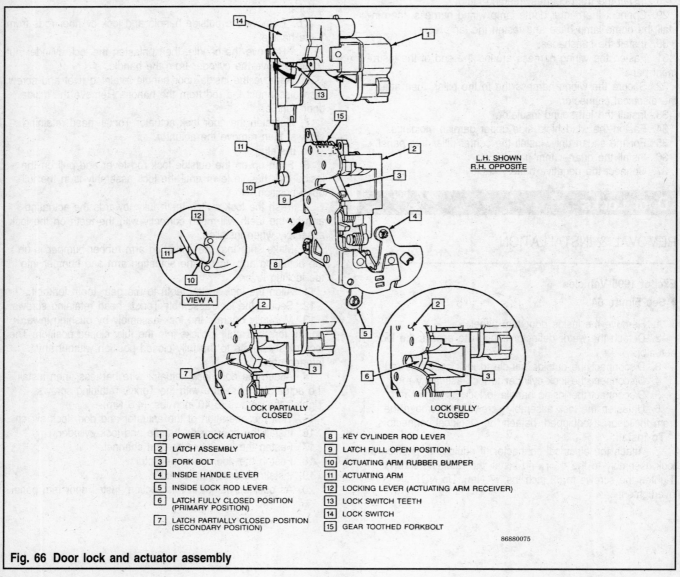

L.H. SHOWN
R.H. OPPOSITE

LOCK PARTIALLY CLOSED

LOCK FULLY CLOSED

1	POWER LOCK ACTUATOR	8	KEY CYLINDER ROD LEVER
2	LATCH ASSEMBLY	9	LATCH FULL OPEN POSITION
3	FORK BOLT	10	ACTUATING ARM RUBBER BUMPER
4	INSIDE HANDLE LEVER	11	ACTUATING ARM
5	INSIDE LOCK ROD LEVER	12	LOCKING LEVER (ACTUATING ARM RECEIVER)
6	LATCH FULLY CLOSED POSITION (PRIMARY POSITION)	13	LOCK SWITCH TEETH
7	LATCH PARTIALLY CLOSED POSITION (SECONDARY POSITION)	14	LOCK SWITCH
		15	GEAR TOOTHED FORKBOLT

86880075

Fig. 66 Door lock and actuator assembly

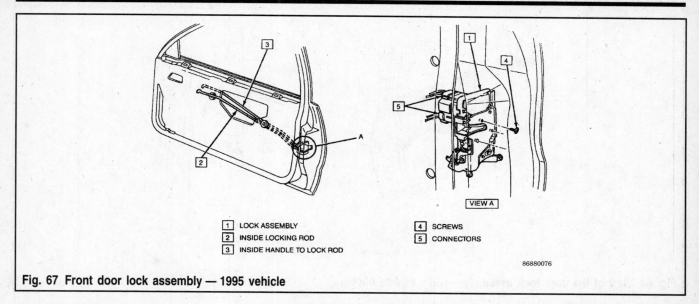

1 LOCK ASSEMBLY
2 INSIDE LOCKING ROD
3 INSIDE HANDLE TO LOCK ROD
4 SCREWS
5 CONNECTORS

86880076

Fig. 67 Front door lock assembly — 1995 vehicle

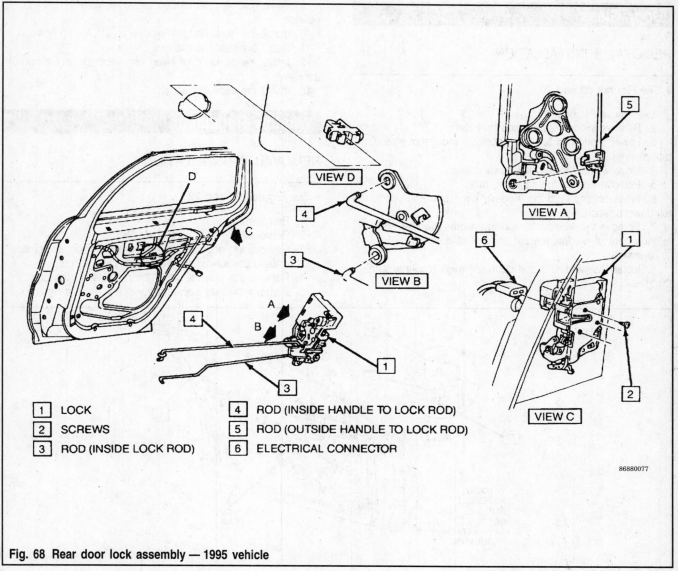

1 LOCK
2 SCREWS
3 ROD (INSIDE LOCK ROD)
4 ROD (INSIDE HANDLE TO LOCK ROD)
5 ROD (OUTSIDE HANDLE TO LOCK ROD)
6 ELECTRICAL CONNECTOR

86880077

Fig. 68 Rear door lock assembly — 1995 vehicle

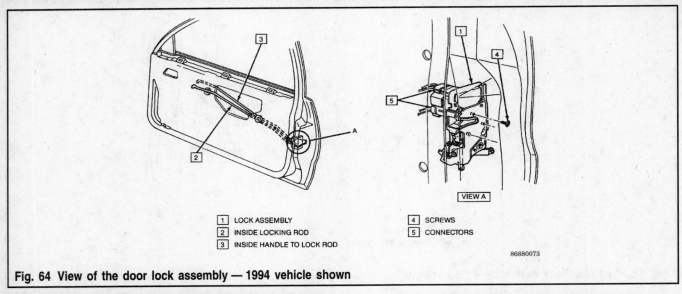

1 LOCK ASSEMBLY
2 INSIDE LOCKING ROD
3 INSIDE HANDLE TO LOCK ROD

4 SCREWS
5 CONNECTORS

86880073

Fig. 64 View of the door lock assembly — 1994 vehicle shown

Door Glass

REMOVAL & INSTALLATION

▶ See Figures 69 and 70

1. Remove the door trim panel.
2. Remove inside plastic lining from door.
3. Lower window to full down position and remove window run channel.
4. Move window to the half down position.
5. Remove the window retaining nuts.
6. While holding onto the window, lower the regulator to the full down position.
7. Remove the window by sliding towards the rear and rotating front of window upward and out of door.

To install:

8. Install the window to the door and align regulator with the glass.

9. While holding onto window move regulator to half up position.
10. Install the nuts. Roll the window to the full up position.
11. Install the rear run channel.
12. Install the plastic door lining and secure with waterproof adhesive.
13. Install the door trim panel.

Window Regulator

REMOVAL & INSTALLATION

▶ See Figures 71 and 72

1. Remove the door trim panel.
2. Remove the inside plastic door liner.
3. Remove the door window assembly. For details, please refer to the procedure located earlier in this section.
4. Remove the bolts securing the regulator to the door.
5. Remove the nuts securing the upper regulator guide.

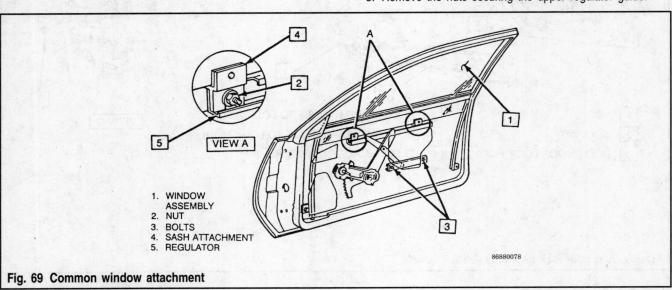

1. WINDOW ASSEMBLY
2. NUT
3. BOLTS
4. SASH ATTACHMENT
5. REGULATOR

86880078

Fig. 69 Common window attachment

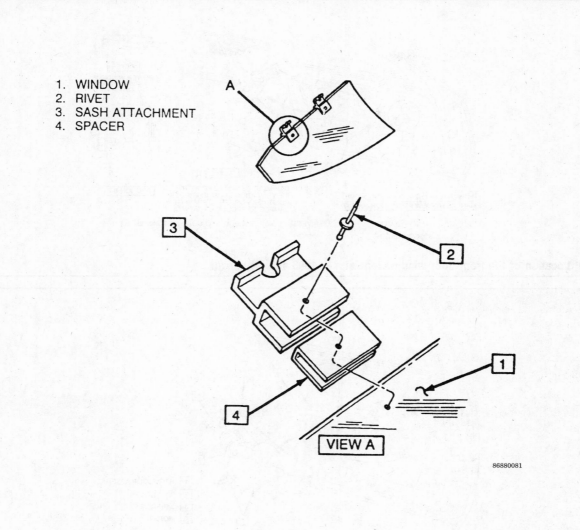

1. WINDOW
2. RIVET
3. SASH ATTACHMENT
4. SPACER

VIEW A

86880081

Fig. 70 Lower window sash attachment

6. Using a 1/4 in. drill, drill out the regulator rivets.
7. If equipped with power windows, detach the electrical connector.
8. Remove the regulator through the large access hole in door.
   To install:
9. Install the regulator to the door, and attach the electrical connector if equipped with power windows.
10. While holding the regulator to the inner door panel, insert the rivets.
11. Fasten the regulator bolts and upper guide nuts. Tighten the nuts to 44 in. lbs. (5 Nm)
12. Install the door glass, and inside door plastic panel.
13. Install the inside door trim panel.

Electric Window Motor

REMOVAL & INSTALLATION

▶ **See Figures 71 and 72**

1. Remove the window regulator assembly from the door as outlined earlier in this section.
2. Remove the motor from the regulator by drilling out the attaching rivets with a 3/16 in. drill bit.
   To install:
3. Connect the window motor to the regulator with 3/16 in. rivets.
4. Install the window regulator assembly as outlined earlier in this section.

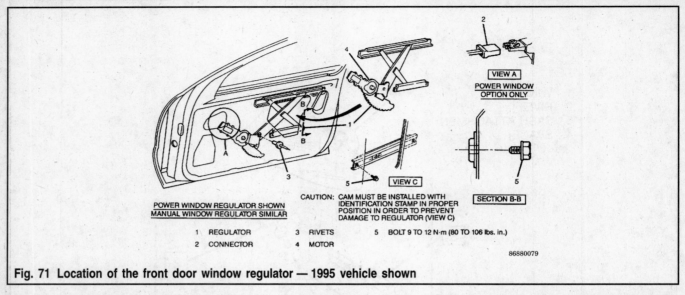

Fig. 71 Location of the front door window regulator — 1995 vehicle shown

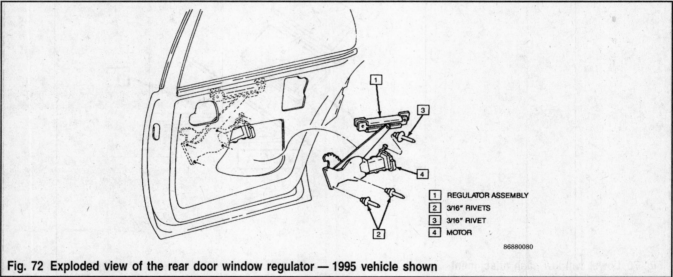

Fig. 72 Exploded view of the rear door window regulator — 1995 vehicle shown

Windshield and Rear Window

REMOVAL & INSTALLATION

◗ **See Figures 73, 74, 75, 76, 77, 78, 79 and 80**

➡ **The windshield is a very delicate and expensive piece of glass. During the procedure the glass can break very easily. Removal and installation is recommended to be performed by a qualified glass installation shop.**

1. Remove the wiper arms and the shroud top vent grille panel.

2. Remove the reveal moldings from around the glass. To do this follow the steps below:

   a. On 1992-95 models, remove the screws securing the side reveal moldings and slide the molding down to disengage it from the top molding.

   b. Grasp the end of the top molding and slowly pull away from the body.

   c. On 1991 and older models, pry the end of the molding out approximately 3 in. (8cm) and slowly pull away from around the perimeter of the windshield.

   d. Remove the glass supports on the 1991 and older models.

3. Apply masking tape around the windshield area to protect the painted areas.

4. Using tool J24402A or equivalent, and/or a power tool with a reciprocating blade, cut around the entire perimeter of the windshield. Be sure that the blade of the tool is kept as close to the windshield as is possible.

5. Carefully remove the glass from the vehicle.

To install:

6. If reusing the old glass, clean all traces of urethane and primer from the glass. Install the windshield supports, if removed.

7. Inspect window frame for any metal damage, repair if any present.

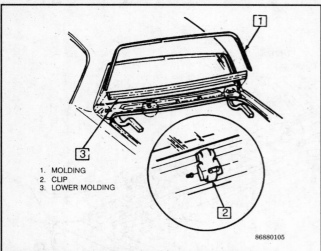

Fig. 73 There is a retaining clip holding the rear window reveal molding on 1985-91 vehicles

1. GLASS REMOVAL TOOL
2. TAPE
3. ADHESIVE
4. GLASS

Fig. 75 Use the glass sealant remover tool to carefully cut out the stationary glass

8. On 1992-95 models, insert the acoustic sealing strip around the perimeter of the windshield opening.

9. Apply the clear primer to the perimeter of the windshield, then immediately apply a smooth continuous bead of the black primer around the glass. The clear primer will dry immediately. Allow the black primer to dry for five minutes before applying the urethane.

10. Replace spacers, if removed.

11. Cut the tip of the urethane cartridge as shown in the accompanying figure. Apply a smooth and continuous bead of urethane adhesive around the primed edge of the window.

12. With the aid of an assistant, carefully install the windshield into the vehicle. On rear window installations, it will be necessary to use suction cups to position the window into the opening.

13. Check windshield alignment and reposition if needed.

14. Press firmly on the glass to set adhesive. Smooth the adhesive out around the windshield to ensure a watertight seal. If necessary, paddle in more adhesive material to fill the voids in the seal.

15. Water test the seal with soft spray. Do not direct hard spray at fresh adhesive.

16. Install all reveal moldings and vent grille panel if removed. Attach the rear window defroster connectors, if unfastened.

Rear Quarter Window

REMOVAL & INSTALLATION

✷✷CAUTION

To prevent personal injury, gloves and safety glasses must be worn when removing glass.

This procedure applies to 2-door models only.

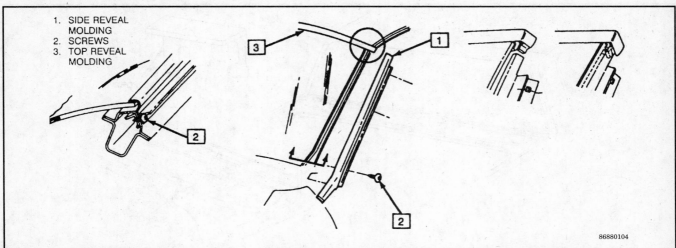

1. SIDE REVEAL MOLDING
2. SCREWS
3. TOP REVEAL MOLDING

Fig. 74 The side reveal molding on 1992-95 vehicles is removed by unfastening the screws and sliding the side moldings down and off the top molding

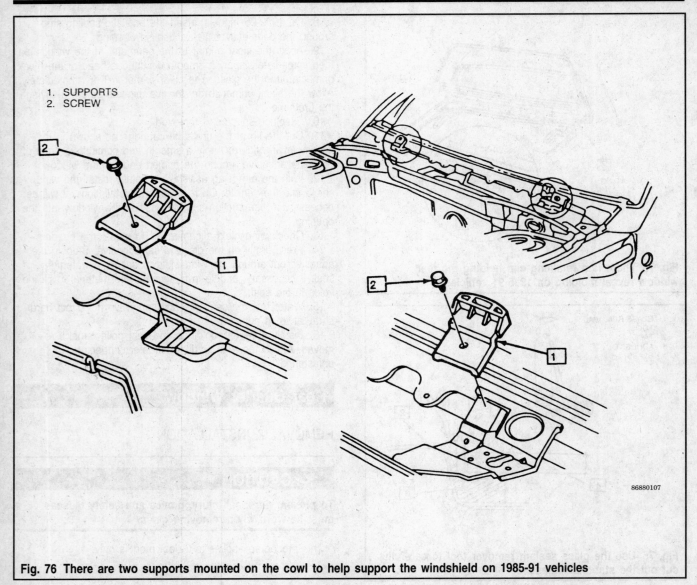

1. SUPPORTS
2. SCREW

86880107

Fig. 76 There are two supports mounted on the cowl to help support the windshield on 1985-91 vehicles

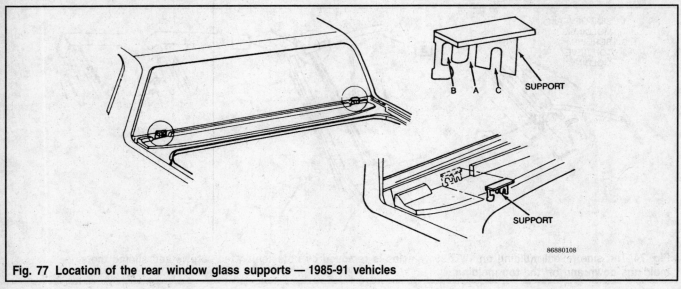

SUPPORT

B   A   C

SUPPORT

SUPPORT

86880108

Fig. 77 Location of the rear window glass supports — 1985-91 vehicles

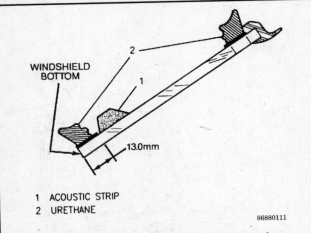

1 ACOUSTIC STRIP
2 URETHANE

86880111

Fig. 78 You must insert the acoustic sealing strip around the perimeter of the windshield opening on 1992-95 vehicles

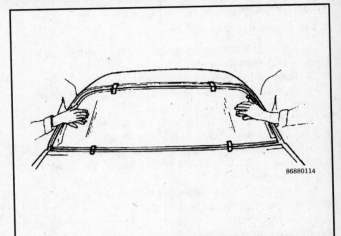

86880114

Fig. 80 ALWAYS have an assistant help you position the windshield or rear glass into the vehicle! NEVER attempt to do this by yourself

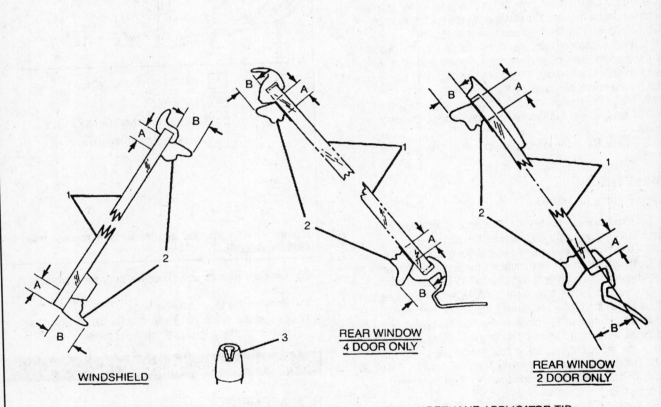

REAR WINDOW
4 DOOR ONLY

REAR WINDOW
2 DOOR ONLY

WINDSHIELD

A = 7.0mm (0.28 in.)   1 WINDOW   3   URETHANE APPLICATOR TIP

B = 14.0mm (0.55 in.)   2 BEAD OF URETHANE

86880113

Fig. 79 Cut the tip of the urethane cartridge, then carefully apply to the primed edge of the window

1985-91 Vehicles

♦ **See Figure 81**

1. Apply tape to body of vehicle around the rear quarter window to protect the body.
2. Remove the roof drip molding.
3. Unfasten the screws from the quarter window reveal molding frame, at the body lock pillar.
4. Using a putty knife, carefully release the molding from around the quarter window at the retainer clips.
5. Using a putty knife with a sharpened blade and a hammer, carefully cut the urethane bond between the reveal molding and the glass.
6. Apply tape to the inside and outside of the glass to minimize the scattering of broken glass.
7. Carefully break the glass with a hammer, then cut or pull the module from the vehicle.
8. Clean the remaining urethane from the pinch weld flange.

To install:

9. Apply black primer from the urethane adhesive kit part no. 12345633, or equivalent to the pinch weld flange.
10. Apply clear primer from the urethane kit to the quarter window module around the entire perimeter of the module. Allow the primer to dry for about five minutes.
11. With a caulking gun, insert the nozzle into the grooves of the module, then carefully apply a smooth and continuous bead of adhesive material $9/16$ in. (14mm) high into the groove around the entire perimeter of the module.
12. Place the module into the body opening and press firmly in until the clips on the module engage through the pinch weld flange.
13. Check for water leaks, then install all previously removed moldings.

1992-95 Vehicles

♦ **See Figures 82 and 83**

1. Remove the screws securing the body lock applique panel to the door frame and remove the panel.
2. Detach the upper and lower quarter trim panels.
3. Apply tape to the body around the entire perimeter of the window to help prevent damage to the vehicle's finish.
4. Using cold knife tool no. J 24402-A and/or a power tool with a oscillating blade, cut around the entire perimeter of window. Be sure that the blade of the tool is kept as close to the pinch weld flange as possible to avoid damaging any portion of the module during the cutout procedure.
5. Carefully remove the window from the vehicle. Clean all traces of adhesive from the window and from the frame.

To install:

6. Apply the black primer from the urethane adhesive kit, part no. 12345633, or equivalent around the pinch weld flange.
7. Using a caulking gun, carefully apply a smooth, continuous bead of adhesive material 0.24x0.47 in. (6x12mm) high around the entire mounting surface of the window.
8. Place the window into the opening and press firmly to set the glass.
9. Check quarter window for any water leaks by spraying water onto window area while having an assistant watching inside for leakage.

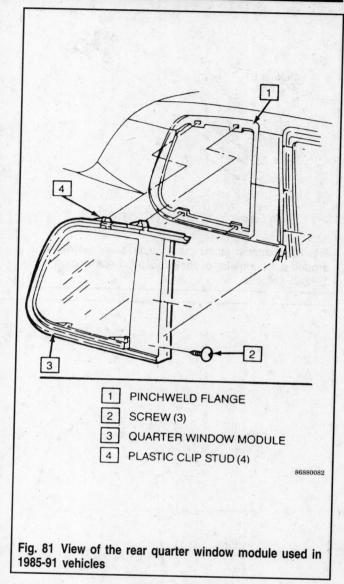

1	PINCHWELD FLANGE
2	SCREW (3)
3	QUARTER WINDOW MODULE
4	PLASTIC CLIP STUD (4)

86880082

Fig. 81 View of the rear quarter window module used in 1985-91 vehicles

10. Carefully remove any excessive urethane from around the window.
11. Remove the tape from the body.
12. Fasten the upper and lower quarter trim finish panels.
13. Install the body lock pillar applique panel.

Inside Rear View Mirror

REPLACEMENT

♦ **See Figures 84 and 85**

The rearview mirror is attached to a support with a retaining screw. The support is secured to the windshield glass by using a plastic polyvinyl butyl adhesive. A service replacement windshield support has the mirror support bonded to the assembly. To install a detached mirror support or install a new part, use the following procedure.

1. Determine the rearview mirror support position on the windshield. Refer to the accompanying figure.

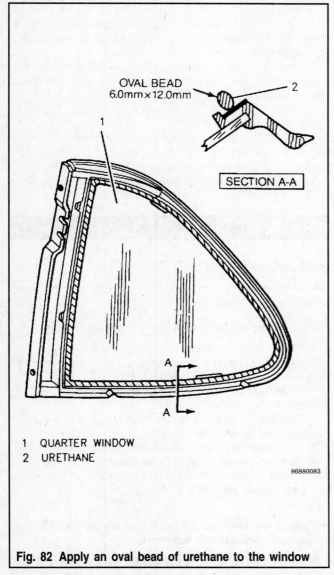

OVAL BEAD
6.0mm×12.0mm

SECTION A-A

1 QUARTER WINDOW
2 URETHANE

86880083

Fig. 82 Apply an oval bead of urethane to the window

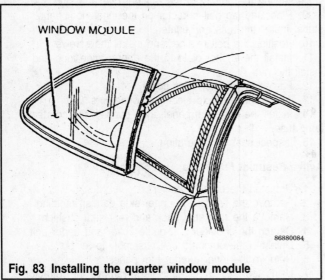

WINDOW MODULE

86880084

Fig. 83 Installing the quarter window module

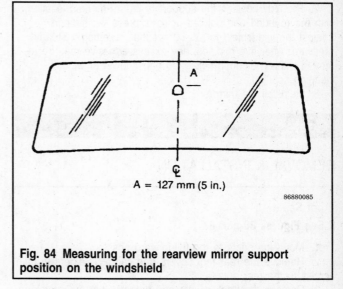

A

A = 127 mm (5 in.)

86880085

Fig. 84 Measuring for the rearview mirror support position on the windshield

2. Using a wax pencil or crayon, mark a horizontal line following dimension A (in the figure) and a vertical line following the centerline of the windshield. Also mark a 3 in. (75mm) circle around the mounting area.

3. On the inside surface of the windshield, clean a large circle with a paper towel and domestic scouring cleanser, window cleaning solution or polishing compound. Rub until area is completely clean and dry. When dry, clean the area with an alcohol saturated paper to remove any traces of scouring powder or cleaning solution from this area.

4. With a piece of 320 or 360 grit emery cloth or paper, sand the bonding surface of the new rearview mirror support or factory installed support. If the original rearview mirror support is to be reused, all traces of the factory installed adhesive must be removed prior to installation.

5. Wipe the sanded mirror support with a clean paper towel saturated with alcohol and allow it to dry.

6. Follow the directions on the manufacturer's kit to prepare the rearview mirror support before installation on the windshield.

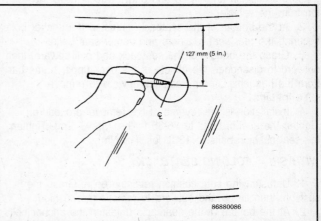

127 mm (5 in.)

86880086

Fig. 85 Using a wax pencil or crayon, mark a horizontal line following dimension A (in the figure) and a vertical line following the centerline of the windshield. Also mark a 3 in. (75mm) circle around the mounting area

7. Properly position the support to its pre-marked location, with the rounded end pointed upward; press the support against the windshield for 30-60 seconds, exerting a steady pressure. After five minutes, any excess adhesive may be removed with an alcohol moistened paper towel or window cleaning solution.

8. Reinstall the mirror.

Seats

REMOVAL & INSTALLATION

Front Seats

▶ **See Figures 86 and 87**

1. Move the seats to the full-forward position.
2. Remove the rear foot covers and carpet retainers to gain access to the rear nuts.
3. Remove the track covers and unfasten the nuts securing the adjuster to the floor.
4. Move the seat to the full-rearward position.
5. Remove the adjuster front foot covers and unfasten the adjuster-to-front floor pan nuts.
6. If equipped with power seats, tilt the seat forward and detach the electrical connectors.
7. Carefully remove the seat assembly from the vehicle.

To install:

8. Installation is the reverse of the removal procedure. Check that both seat adjusters are parallel and in phase with each other. Tighten the seat adjuster-to-floor pan nuts to 18-21 ft. lbs. (24-29 Nm). Check the operation of the seat assembly for full limit of travel.

Rear Seats

▶ **See Figures 88, 89 and 90**

WITHOUT SPLIT FOLDING SEATBACK

1. Unfasten the rear seat cushion retaining bolts, then grasp the cushion and lift up and outward to remove the cushion from the vehicle.
2. At the bottom of the seatback, unfasten the anchor bolts securing the rear seat retainers and center seat belts.
3. Grasp the bottom of the seatback and pull upward, then outward to disengage the offsets of the back upper frame bar from the hangers. Lift the seatback upward to remove.

To install:

4. Installation is the reverse of the removal procedure. Tighten the anchor bolts to 26-35 ft. lbs. (35-48 Nm). Tighten the seat cushion bolts to 13 ft. lbs. (18 Nm).

WITH SPLIT FOLDING SEATBACK

1. Unfasten the seat cushion retaining bolts. Grasp the cushion, then lift up and outward to remove the cushion.
2. At the bottom of the seatback, unfasten the anchor bolts securing the rear seat retainers and center seat belts.
3. Grasp the bottom of the seatback and swing upward to disengage the offsets on the back upper frame bar from the hangers, then lift the seatback upward to remove it.

To install:

4. Align the seatback and engage the upper retainer with a sharp downward motion until you hear an audible snap indicating engagement.
5. Install the seat belt anchors on top of the seat retainer brackets. Stack the outer belt anchor plate on top of the center belt anchor plate.
6. Install and tighten the anchor bolts to 26-35 ft. lbs. (35-48 Nm).
7. Fold the seatback down to the full horizontal position. Place the closeout flaps in position, then rub your hand over the flaps to secure the hook/loop strips to the trunk trim.
8. Install the rear seat cushion. Tighten the retaining bolts to 13 ft. lbs. (18 Nm).

Seat Belts

REMOVAL & INSTALLATION

▶ **See Figures 91 and 92**

Passive Restraint (Automatic) Front Seat Belt System

1. Detach the front courtesy lamp fuse.
2. Remove the door trim panel. For details, please refer to the procedure located in this section.
3. Disengage the solenoid connectors from the seat and shoulder belt retractor units.
4. Remove the anchor plate cover and unfasten the nut connecting the upper guide loop.
5. Disconnect the safety belt retainer from the door.
6. Remove the top screw from the shoulder belt retractor.
7. Unfasten the nuts from the seat and shoulder belt retractors, then remove the seat belt assembly.

To install:

➡ **Remove any twists in the belt assembly before securing the lap and shoulder belt retractors.**

8. Insert the belt retaining tab into the inner door panel while seating the bottom of the retainer over the stud.
9. Place the lap belt retractor on the inner door panel studs. Install the nuts and tighten.
10. Position the belt retainer and install the screws.
11. Install the anchor plate to the upper guide loop and install the nut.
12. Fasten the anchor plate cover.
13. Attach the solenoid electrical connectors.
14. Install the door trim panel, then connect the courtesy lamp fuse.
15. Inspect seat belt operation.

Active Restraint Front Seat Belt System

1. Unfasten the carpet retainer.
2. Remove the windshield upper side garnish molding.
3. Remove the rear seat back and rear seat cushion.
4. Detach the shoulder belt guide cover and upper bolt.
5. Unfasten the outboard belt assembly lower bolt.
6. Remove the inner quarter trim panel.
7. Using tool J23457 or equivalent, remove the retractor bolts and anchor bolts as required, then remove the seat belt assembly from the vehicle.

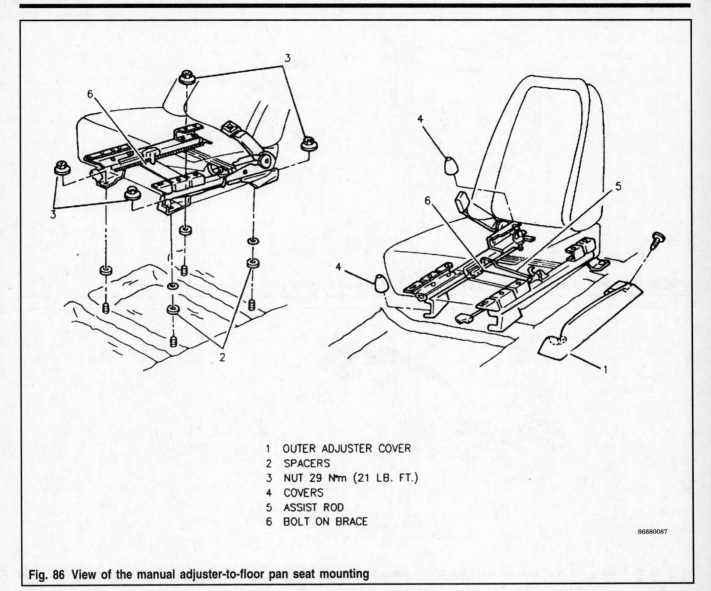

1 OUTER ADJUSTER COVER
2 SPACERS
3 NUT 29 N·m (21 LB. FT.)
4 COVERS
5 ASSIST ROD
6 BOLT ON BRACE

86880087

Fig. 86 View of the manual adjuster-to-floor pan seat mounting

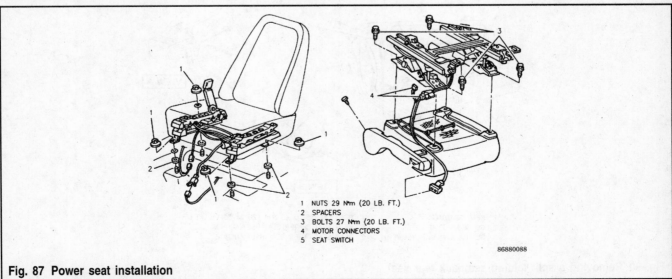

1 NUTS 29 N·m (20 LB. FT.)
2 SPACERS
3 BOLTS 27 N·m (20 LB. FT.)
4 MOTOR CONNECTORS
5 SEAT SWITCH

86880088

Fig. 87 Power seat installation

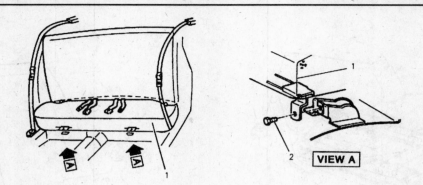

1 REAR SEAT CUSHION
2 BOLT (2) 18 N·m (13 LB. FT.)

86880089

Fig. 88 Unfasten the retaining bolts, then removed the rear seat cushion by lifting it up and outward

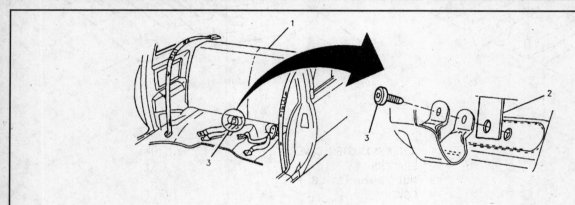

1 REAR SEATBACK
2 SEAT RETAINER BRACKET
3 ANCHOR BOLTS (2), 35 TO 48 N·m (26 TO 35 LB. FT.)

86880090

Fig. 89 Removing the rear seat (without the split folding seatback)

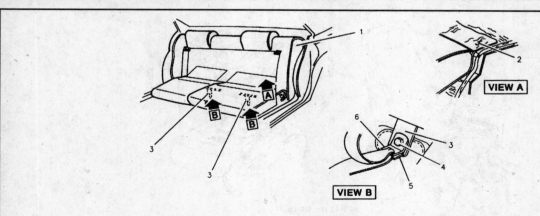

1 REAR SEATBACK   4 BOLT (2), 35 TO 48 N·m (26 TO 35 LB. FT.)
2 CLOSEOUT FLAP   5 REAR SEAT CENTER SEAT BELT ANCHOR
3 SEATBACK ANCHOR (LOWER)   6 REAR SEAT OUTER SEAT BELT ANCHOR

86880091

Fig. 90 Removing a split folding seatback rear seat

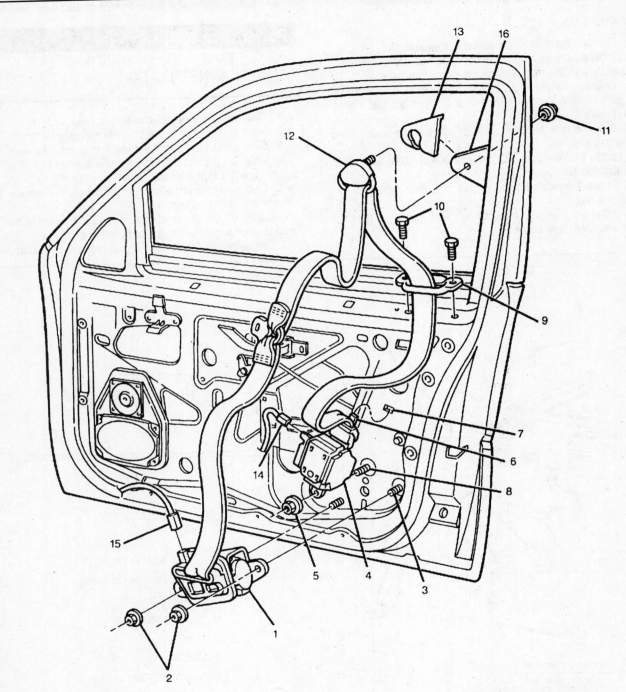

1	LAP RETRACTOR	7	SLOT	12	UPPER GUIDE LOOP
2	NUTS 28 N·m (21 lbs. ft.)	8	STUD	13	ANCHOR PLATE COVER
3	STUD	9	RETAINER	14	CONNECTOR
4	SHOULDER RETRACTOR	10	SCREWS	15	CONNECTOR
5	NUT 28 N·m (21 lbs. ft.)	11	NUT 26 N·m (19 lbs. ft.)	16	ANCHOR PLATE
6	TAB				

86880093

Fig. 91 Front seat automatic seat belt routing

8. Installation is the reverse of the removal procedure.

Rear Seat Belts

1. Remove the rear seat cushion and seat back.
2. If necessary for access, remove the upper and lower trim panels and the rear seat back window trim panel.
3. Unfasten the rear seat belt anchor bolts and retractor bolt, then remove the rear seat belt assembly from the vehicle.

To install:

4. Slide the rear seat belt retractor tab into the rear window shelf panel slot.
5. Install the rear seat belt retractor bolt. Tighten the bolt to 27 ft. lbs. (36 Nm).
6. Fasten the rear seat belt anchor bolt, then tighten to 31 ft. lbs. (42 Nm).
7. Install the rear seat back window trim panel and the upper and lower trim panels.

8. Position and install the rear seat cushion and seat back.

Power Seat Motor

REMOVAL & INSTALLATION

1. Disconnect the negative battery cable.
2. Remove the seat assembly from the vehicle.
3. Disconnect the motor feed wires from the motors.
4. Unfasten the nut that attaches the front of the motor support bracket to the inboard adjuster.
5. Disconnect the drive cables and completely remove the bracket and motor assembly.
6. Grind off the grommet that secures the motor to the bracket, then separate the motor from the bracket.
7. Installation is the reverse of the removal procedure.

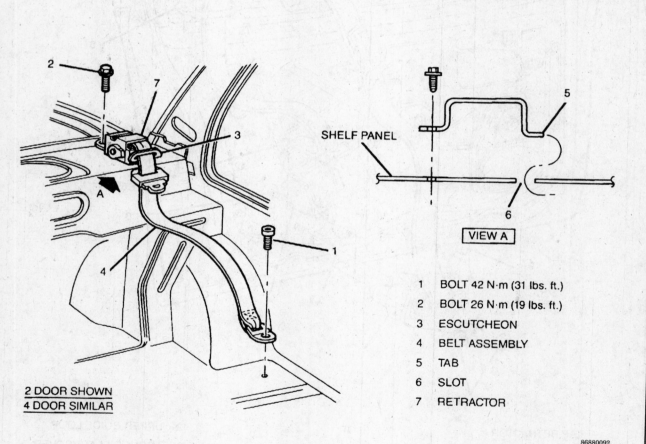

SHELF PANEL

VIEW A

1	BOLT 42 N·m (31 lbs. ft.)
2	BOLT 26 N·m (19 lbs. ft.)
3	ESCUTCHEON
4	BELT ASSEMBLY
5	TAB
6	SLOT
7	RETRACTOR

2 DOOR SHOWN
4 DOOR SIMILAR

86880092

Fig. 92 Once the seats and trim panels trim panels are removed, seat belt removal is simply a matter of unfastening the retaining bolts

TORQUE SPECIFICATIONS

Component	U.S.	Metric
Antenna		
Rear fender mount		
Fixed antenna	18 inch lbs.	2 Nm
Power antenna	53 inch lbs.	6 Nm
Bumpers		
Rear bumper retaining nuts		
1985-91 vehicles	20 ft. lbs.	27 Nm
1992-95 vehicles	26 ft. lbs.	35 Nm
Door Locks		
Lock retaining screws		
Except 1995 vehicles	62 inch lbs.	7 Nm
1995 vehicles	40 inch lbs.	4.5 Nm
Doors		
Upper and lower hinge-to-pillar and door bolts	16 ft. lbs.	22 Nm
Door detent-to-hinge pillar bolt	80 inch lbs.	9 Nm
Front Impact Bar		
1992-95 vehicles only	22 ft. lbs.	30 Nm
Front Seats		
Seat adjuster-to-floor pan bolts	18-21 ft. lbs.	24-29 Nm
Hood		
Retaining bolts	20-22 ft. lbs.	27-30 Nm
Instrument Panel and Pad		
1992-95 Skylark and Achieva	17 inch lbs.	2 Nm
1992 Grand Am	17 inch lbs.	2 Nm
1993-95 Grand Am	56 inch lbs.	6 Nm
Outside Mirror		
Mirror-to-door retaining screws/bolts	45 inch lbs.	5 Nm
Rear Seats		
Anchor bolts	26-35 ft. lbs.	35-48 Nm
Rear seat cushion bolts	13 ft. lbs.	18 Nm
Seat Belts		
Retractor bolt	27 ft. lbs.	36 Nm
Trunk Lid		
Retaining bolts	106 inch lbs.	12 Nm
Window regulator		
Retaining nuts	44 inch lbs.	5 Nm

86880500

AIR/FUEL RATIO: The ratio of air-to-gasoline by weight in the fuel mixture drawn into the engine.

AIR INJECTION: One method of reducing harmful exhaust emissions by injecting air into each of the exhaust ports of an engine. The fresh air entering the hot exhaust manifold causes any remaining fuel to be burned before it can exit the tailpipe.

ALTERNATOR: A device used for converting mechanical energy into electrical energy.

AMMETER: An instrument, calibrated in amperes, used to measure the flow of an electrical current in a circuit. Ammeters are always connected in series with the circuit being tested.

AMPERE: The rate of flow of electrical current present when one volt of electrical pressure is applied against one ohm of electrical resistance.

ANALOG COMPUTER: Any microprocessor that uses similar (analogous) electrical signals to make its calculations.

ARMATURE: A laminated, soft iron core wrapped by a wire that converts electrical energy to mechanical energy as in a motor or relay. When rotated in a magnetic field, it changes mechanical energy into electrical energy as in a generator.

ATMOSPHERIC PRESSURE: The pressure on the Earth's surface caused by the weight of the air in the atmosphere. At sea level, this pressure is 14.7 psi at 32°F (101 kPa at 0°C).

ATOMIZATION: The breaking down of a liquid into a fine mist that can be suspended in air.

AXIAL PLAY: Movement parallel to a shaft or bearing bore.

BACKFIRE: The sudden combustion of gases in the intake or exhaust system that results in a loud explosion.

BACKLASH: The clearance or play between two parts, such as meshed gears.

BACKPRESSURE: Restrictions in the exhaust system that slow the exit of exhaust gases from the combustion chamber.

BAKELITE: A heat resistant, plastic insulator material commonly used in printed circuit boards and transistorized components.

BALL BEARING: A bearing made up of hardened inner and outer races between which hardened steel balls roll.

BALLAST RESISTOR: A resistor in the primary ignition circuit that lowers voltage after the engine is started to reduce wear on ignition components.

BEARING: A friction reducing, supportive device usually located between a stationary part and a moving part.

BIMETAL TEMPERATURE SENSOR: Any sensor or switch made of two dissimilar types of metal that bend when heated or cooled due to the different expansion rates of the alloys. These types of sensors usually function as an on/off switch.

BLOWBY: Combustion gases, composed of water vapor and unburned fuel, that leak past the piston rings into the crankcase during normal engine operation. These gases are removed by the PCV system to prevent the buildup of harmful acids in the crankcase.

BRAKE PAD: A brake shoe and lining assembly used with disc brakes.

BRAKE SHOE: The backing for the brake lining. The term is, however, usually applied to the assembly of the brake backing and lining.

BUSHING: A liner, usually removable, for a bearing; an antifriction liner used in place of a bearing.

CALIPER: A hydraulically activated device in a disc brake system, which is mounted straddling the brake rotor (disc). The caliper contains at least one piston and two brake pads. Hydraulic pressure on the piston(s) forces the pads against the rotor.

CAMSHAFT: A shaft in the engine on which are the lobes (cams) which operate the valves. The camshaft is driven by the crankshaft, via a belt, chain or gears, at one half the crankshaft speed.

CAPACITOR: A device which stores an electrical charge.

CARBON MONOXIDE (CO): A colorless, odorless gas given off as a normal byproduct of combustion. It is poisonous and extremely dangerous in confined areas, building up slowly to toxic levels without warning if adequate ventilation is not available.

CARBURETOR: A device, usually mounted on the intake manifold of an engine, which mixes the air and fuel in the proper proportion to allow even combustion.

CATALYTIC CONVERTER: A device installed in the exhaust system, like a muffler, that converts harmful byproducts of combustion into carbon dioxide and water vapor by means of a heat-producing chemical reaction.

CENTRIFUGAL ADVANCE: A mechanical method of advancing the spark timing by using flyweights in the distributor that react to centrifugal force generated by the distributor shaft rotation.

CHECK VALVE: Any one-way valve installed to permit the flow of air, fuel or vacuum in one direction only.

CHOKE: A device, usually a moveable valve, placed in the intake path of a carburetor to restrict the flow of air.

CIRCUIT: Any unbroken path through which an electrical current can flow. Also used to describe fuel flow in some instances.

CIRCUIT BREAKER: A switch which protects an electrical circuit from overload by opening the circuit when the current flow exceeds a predetermined level. Some circuit breakers must be reset manually, while most reset automatically.

COIL (IGNITION): A transformer in the ignition circuit which steps up the voltage provided to the spark plugs.

COMBINATION MANIFOLD: An assembly which includes both the intake and exhaust manifolds in one casting.

COMBINATION VALVE: A device used in some fuel systems that routes fuel vapors to a charcoal storage canister instead of venting them into the atmosphere. The valve relieves fuel tank pressure and allows fresh air into the tank as the fuel level drops to prevent a vapor lock situation.

COMPRESSION RATIO: The comparison of the total volume of the cylinder and combustion chamber with the piston at BDC and the piston at TDC.

CONDENSER: 1. An electrical device which acts to store an electrical charge, preventing voltage surges. 2. A radiator-like device in the air conditioning system in which refrigerant gas condenses into a liquid, giving off heat.

CONDUCTOR: Any material through which an electrical current can be transmitted easily.

CONTINUITY: Continuous or complete circuit. Can be checked with an ohmmeter.

COUNTERSHAFT: An intermediate shaft which is rotated by a mainshaft and transmits, in turn, that rotation to a working part.

CRANKCASE: The lower part of an engine in which the crankshaft and related parts operate.

CRANKSHAFT: The main driving shaft of an engine which receives reciprocating motion from the pistons and converts it to rotary motion.

CYLINDER: In an engine, the round hole in the engine block in which the piston(s) ride.

CYLINDER BLOCK: The main structural member of an engine in which is found the cylinders, crankshaft and other principal parts.

CYLINDER HEAD: The detachable portion of the engine, usually fastened to the top of the cylinder block and containing all or most of the combustion chambers. On overhead valve engines, it contains the valves and their operating parts. On overhead cam engines, it contains the camshaft as well.

DEAD CENTER: The extreme top or bottom of the piston stroke.

DETONATION: An unwanted explosion of the air/fuel mixture in the combustion chamber caused by excess heat and compression, advanced timing, or an overly lean mixture. Also referred to as "ping".

DIAPHRAGM: A thin, flexible wall separating two cavities, such as in a vacuum advance unit.

DIESELING: A condition in which hot spots in the combustion chamber cause the engine to run on after the key is turned off.

DIFFERENTIAL: A geared assembly which allows the transmission of motion between drive axles, giving one axle the ability to turn faster than the other.

DIODE: An electrical device that will allow current to flow in one direction only.

DISC BRAKE: A hydraulic braking assembly consisting of a brake disc, or rotor, mounted on an axle, and a caliper assembly containing, usually two brake pads which are activated by hydraulic pressure. The pads are forced against the sides of the disc, creating friction which slows the vehicle.

DISTRIBUTOR: A mechanically driven device on an engine which is responsible for electrically firing the spark plug at a predetermined point of the piston stroke.

DOWEL PIN: A pin, inserted in mating holes in two different parts allowing those parts to maintain a fixed relationship.

DRUM BRAKE: A braking system which consists of two brake shoes and one or two wheel cylinders, mounted on a fixed backing plate, and a brake drum, mounted on an axle, which revolves around the assembly.

DWELL: The rate, measured in degrees of shaft rotation, at which an electrical circuit cycles on and off.

ELECTRONIC CONTROL UNIT (ECU): Ignition module, module, amplifier or igniter. See Module for definition.

ELECTRONIC IGNITION: A system in which the timing and firing of the spark plugs is controlled by an electronic control unit, usually called a module. These systems have no points or condenser.

END-PLAY: The measured amount of axial movement in a shaft.

ENGINE: A device that converts heat into mechanical energy.

EXHAUST MANIFOLD: A set of cast passages or pipes which conduct exhaust gases from the engine.

FEELER GAUGE: A blade, usually metal, of precisely predetermined thickness, used to measure the clearance between two parts.

FIRING ORDER: The order in which combustion occurs in the cylinders of an engine. Also the order in which spark is distributed to the plugs by the distributor.

FLOODING: The presence of too much fuel in the intake manifold and combustion chamber which prevents the air/fuel mixture from firing, thereby causing a no-start situation.

FLYWHEEL: A disc shaped part bolted to the rear end of the crankshaft. Around the outer perimeter is affixed the ring gear. The starter drive engages the ring gear, turning the flywheel, which rotates the crankshaft, imparting the initial starting motion to the engine.

FOOT POUND (ft. lbs. or sometimes, ft.lb.): The amount of energy or work needed to raise an item weighing one pound, a distance of one foot.

FUSE: A protective device in a circuit which prevents circuit overload by breaking the circuit when a specific amperage is present. The device is constructed around a strip or wire of a lower amperage rating than the circuit it is designed to protect. When an amperage higher than that stamped on the fuse is present in the circuit, the strip or wire melts, opening the circuit.

GEAR RATIO: The ratio between the number of teeth on meshing gears.

GENERATOR: A device which converts mechanical energy into electrical energy.

HEAT RANGE: The measure of a spark plug's ability to dissipate heat from its firing end. The higher the heat range, the hotter the plug fires.

HUB: The center part of a wheel or gear.

HYDROCARBON (HC): Any chemical compound made up of hydrogen and carbon. A major pollutant formed by the engine as a byproduct of combustion.

HYDROMETER: An instrument used to measure the specific gravity of a solution.

INCH POUND (inch lbs.; sometimes in.lb. or in. lbs.): One twelfth of a foot pound.

INDUCTION: A means of transferring electrical energy in the form of a magnetic field. Principle used in the ignition coil to increase voltage.

INJECTOR: A device which receives metered fuel under relatively low pressure and is activated to inject the fuel into the engine under relatively high pressure at a predetermined time.

INPUT SHAFT: The shaft to which torque is applied, usually carrying the driving gear or gears.

INTAKE MANIFOLD: A casting of passages or pipes used to conduct air or a fuel/air mixture to the cylinders.

JOURNAL: The bearing surface within which a shaft operates.

KEY: A small block usually fitted in a notch between a shaft and a hub to prevent slippage of the two parts.

MANIFOLD: A casting of passages or set of pipes which connect the cylinders to an inlet or outlet source.

MANIFOLD VACUUM: Low pressure in an engine intake manifold formed just below the throttle plates. Manifold vacuum is highest at idle and drops under acceleration.

MASTER CYLINDER: The primary fluid pressurizing device in a hydraulic system. In automotive use, it is found in brake and hydraulic clutch systems and is pedal activated, either directly or, in a power brake system, through the power booster.

MODULE: Electronic control unit, amplifier or igniter of solid state or integrated design which controls the current flow in the ignition primary circuit based on input from the pick-up coil. When the module opens the primary circuit, high secondary voltage is induced in the coil.

NEEDLE BEARING: A bearing which consists of a number (usually a large number) of long, thin rollers.

OHM:(Ω) The unit used to measure the resistance of conductor-to-electrical flow. One ohm is the amount of resistance that limits current flow to one ampere in a circuit with one volt of pressure.

OHMMETER: An instrument used for measuring the resistance, in ohms, in an electrical circuit.

OUTPUT SHAFT: The shaft which transmits torque from a device, such as a transmission.

OVERDRIVE: A gear assembly which produces more shaft revolutions than that transmitted to it.

OVERHEAD CAMSHAFT (OHC): An engine configuration in which the camshaft is mounted on top of the cylinder head and operates the valve either directly or by means of rocker arms.

OVERHEAD VALVE (OHV): An engine configuration in which all of the valves are located in the cylinder head and the camshaft is located in the cylinder block. The camshaft operates the valves via lifters and pushrods.

OXIDES OF NITROGEN (NOx): Chemical compounds of nitrogen produced as a byproduct of combustion. They combine with hydrocarbons to produce smog.

OXYGEN SENSOR: Used with the feedback system to sense the presence of oxygen in the exhaust gas and signal the computer which can reference the voltage signal to an air/fuel ratio.

PINION: The smaller of two meshing gears.

PISTON RING: An open-ended ring which fits into a groove on the outer diameter of the piston. Its chief function is to form a seal between the piston and cylinder wall. Most automotive pistons have three rings: two for compression sealing; one for oil sealing.

PRELOAD: A predetermined load placed on a bearing during assembly or by adjustment.

PRIMARY CIRCUIT: The low voltage side of the ignition system which consists of the ignition switch, ballast resistor or resistance wire, bypass, coil, electronic control unit and pick-up coil as well as the connecting wires and harnesses.

PRESS FIT: The mating of two parts under pressure, due to the inner diameter of one being smaller than the outer diameter of the other, or vice versa; an interference fit.

RACE: The surface on the inner or outer ring of a bearing on which the balls, needles or rollers move.

REGULATOR: A device which maintains the amperage and/or voltage levels of a circuit at predetermined values.

RELAY: A switch which automatically opens and/or closes a circuit.

RESISTANCE: The opposition to the flow of current through a circuit or electrical device, and is measured in ohms. Resistance is equal to the voltage divided by the amperage.

RESISTOR: A device, usually made of wire, which offers a preset amount of resistance in an electrical circuit.

RING GEAR: The name given to a ring-shaped gear attached to a differential case, or affixed to a flywheel or as part of a planetary gear set.

ROLLER BEARING: A bearing made up of hardened inner and outer races between which hardened steel rollers move.

ROTOR: 1. The disc-shaped part of a disc brake assembly, upon which the brake pads bear; also called, brake disc. 2. The device mounted atop the distributor shaft, which passes current to the distributor cap tower contacts.

SECONDARY CIRCUIT: The high voltage side of the ignition system, usually above 20,000 volts. The secondary includes the ignition coil, coil wire, distributor cap and rotor, spark plug wires and spark plugs.

SENDING UNIT: A mechanical, electrical, hydraulic or electromagnetic device which transmits information to a gauge.

SENSOR: Any device designed to measure engine operating conditions or ambient pressures and temperatures. Usually electronic in nature and designed to send a voltage signal to an on-board computer, some sensors may operate as a simple on/off switch or they may provide a variable voltage signal (like a potentiometer) as conditions or measured parameters change.

SHIM: Spacers of precise, predetermined thickness used between parts to establish a proper working relationship.

SLAVE CYLINDER: In automotive use, a device in the hydraulic clutch system which is activated by hydraulic force, disengaging the clutch.

SOLENOID: A coil used to produce a magnetic field, the effect of which is to produce work.

SPARK PLUG: A device screwed into the combustion chamber of a spark ignition engine. The basic construction is a conductive core inside of a ceramic insulator, mounted in an outer conductive base. An electrical charge from the spark plug wire travels along the conductive core and jumps a preset air gap to a grounding point or points at the end of the conductive base. The resultant spark ignites the fuel/air mixture in the combustion chamber.

SPLINES: Ridges machined or cast onto the outer diameter of a shaft or inner diameter of a bore to enable parts to mate without rotation.

TACHOMETER: A device used to measure the rotary speed of an engine, shaft, gear, etc., usually in rotations per minute.

THERMOSTAT: A valve, located in the cooling system of an engine, which is closed when cold and opens gradually in response to engine heating, controlling the temperature of the coolant and rate of coolant flow.

TOP DEAD CENTER (TDC): The point at which the piston reaches the top of its travel on the compression stroke.

TORQUE: The twisting force applied to an object.

TORQUE CONVERTER: A turbine used to transmit power from a driving member to a driven member via hydraulic action, providing changes in drive ratio and torque. In automotive use, it links the driveplate at the rear of the engine to the automatic transmission.

TRANSDUCER: A device used to change a force into an electrical signal.

TRANSISTOR: A semi-conductor component which can be actuated by a small voltage to perform an electrical switching function.

TUNE-UP: A regular maintenance function, usually associated with the replacement and adjustment of parts and components in the electrical and fuel systems of a vehicle for the purpose of attaining optimum performance.

TURBOCHARGER: An exhaust driven pump which compresses intake air and forces it into the combustion chambers at higher than atmospheric pressures. The increased air pressure allows more fuel to be burned and results in increased horsepower being produced.

VACUUM ADVANCE: A device which advances the ignition timing in response to increased engine vacuum.

VACUUM GAUGE: An instrument used to measure the presence of vacuum in a chamber.

VALVE: A device which control the pressure, direction of flow or rate of flow of a liquid or gas.

VALVE CLEARANCE: The measured gap between the end of the valve stem and the rocker arm, cam lobe or follower that activates the valve.

VISCOSITY: The rating of a liquid's internal resistance to flow.

VOLTMETER: An instrument used for measuring electrical force in units called volts. Voltmeters are always connected parallel with the circuit being tested.

WHEEL CYLINDER: Found in the automotive drum brake assembly, it is a device, actuated by hydraulic pressure, which, through internal pistons, pushes the brake shoes outward against the drums.

AIR CONDITIONER
  ACCUMULATOR
    REMOVAL & INSTALLATION 6-27
  COMPRESSOR
    REMOVAL & INSTALLATION 6-20
  CONDENSER
    REMOVAL & INSTALLATION 6-24
  CONTROL CABLES
    REMOVAL & INSTALLATION 6-31
  EVAPORATOR CORE
    REMOVAL & INSTALLATION 6-25
  GENERAL INFORMATION 6-20
  HEATER/AIR CONDITIONER CONTROL PANEL
    REMOVAL & INSTALLATION 6-31
  ORIFICE (EXPANSION) TUBE
    REMOVAL & INSTALLATION 6-31
  RECEIVER DEHYDRATOR
    REMOVAL & INSTALLATION 6-30
  REFRIGERANT LINES
    REMOVAL & INSTALLATION 6-30
  THERMAL EXPANSION VALVE (TXV)
    REMOVAL & INSTALLATION 6-32
  VACUUM MOTORS
    REMOVAL & INSTALLATION 6-31
AIR POLLUTION
  AUTOMOTIVE POLLUTANTS 4-2
  INDUSTRIAL POLLUTANTS 4-2
  INTERNAL COMBUSTION ENGINE POLLUTANTS
    HEAT TRANSFER 4-3
  NATURAL POLLUTANTS 4-2
  TEMPERATURE INVERSION 4-2
ANTI-LOCK BRAKE SYSTEM (ABS)
  ABS HYDRAULIC MODULATOR SOLENOID
    REMOVAL & INSTALLATION 9-45
  ABS HYDRAULIC MODULATOR/MASTER CYLINDER ASSEMBLY
    REMOVAL & INSTALLATION 9-43
  ABS SERVICE
    PRECAUTIONS 9-43
  DESCRIPTION AND OPERATION
    ENHANCED DIAGNOSTICS 9-28
    ONBOARD DIAGNOSTICS 9-28
  DIAGNOSTIC PROCEDURES
    CLEARING CODES 9-29
    DIAGNOSTIC CHARTS 9-38
    DISPLAYING CODES 9-29
    INTERMITTENT FAILURES 9-38
    INTERMITTENTS AND POOR CONNECTIONS 9-39
  ELECTRONIC CONTROL UNIT (ECU)/ELECTRONIC BRAKE
  CONTROL MODULE (EBCM)
    REMOVAL & INSTALLATION 9-43
  FILLING AND BLEEDING
    BLEEDING THE ABS HYDRAULIC SYSTEM 9-45
    SYSTEM FILLING 9-45
  SPEED SENSORS
    REMOVAL & INSTALLATION 9-43
AUTOMATIC TRANSAXLE
  ADJUSTMENTS
    SHIFT CABLE ADJUSTMENT 7-33
    TV CABLE ADJUSTMENT 7-32
  FLUID PAN
    FILTER SERVICE 7-32
    REMOVAL & INSTALLATION 7-30
  GENERAL INFORMATION 7-29
  HALFSHAFTS 7-37
  IDENTIFICATION 7-30
  NEUTRAL SAFETY AND BACK-UP SWITCH
    ADJUSTMENT 7-33
    REMOVAL & INSTALLATION 7-33
  TRANSAXLE
    REMOVAL & INSTALLATION 7-34
AUTOMOTIVE EMISSIONS
  CRANKCASE EMISSIONS 4-5

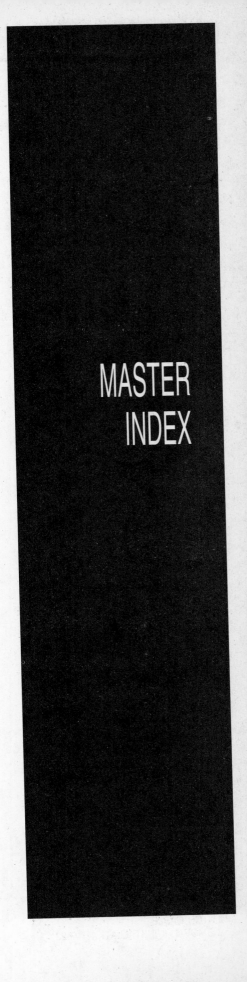

MASTER
INDEX

EVAPORATIVE EMISSIONS 4-5
EXHAUST GASES
  CARBON MONOXIDE 4-4
  HYDROCARBONS 4-3
  NITROGEN 4-4
  OXIDES OF SULFUR 4-4
  OZONE 4-4
  PARTICULATE MATTER 4-5
BASIC ELECTRICITY
BATTERY, STARTING AND CHARGING SYSTEMS
  BASIC OPERATING PRINCIPLES 3-3
  UNDERSTANDING BASIC ELECTRICITY 3-2
BASIC FUEL SYSTEM DIAGNOSIS
PRECAUTIONS 5-2
BASIC MECHANICAL TROUBLESHOOTING
BACKFIRE — EXHAUST MANIFOLD 3-123
BACKFIRE — INTAKE MANIFOLD 3-123
ENGINE DETONATION (DIESELING) 3-123
ENGINE SPEED OSCILLATES AT IDLE 3-122
EXCESSIVE OIL LEAKAGE 3-123
HEAVY OIL CONSUMPTION 3-123
HIGH OIL PRESSURE 3-124
KNOCKING CONNECTING RODS 3-124
KNOCKING MAIN BEARINGS 3-124
KNOCKING PISTONS AND RINGS 3-124
KNOCKING VALVE TRAIN 3-124
KNOCKING VALVES 3-124
LOW OIL PRESSURE 3-124
LOW POWER OUTPUT OF ENGINE 3-122
NEGATIVE OIL PRESSURE 3-123
POOR ACCELERATION 3-123
POOR HIGH SPEED OPERATION 3-123
BRAKE OPERATING SYSTEM
ADJUSTMENTS
  DRUM BRAKES 9-2
BLEEDING THE BRAKE SYSTEM
  MANUAL BLEEDING 9-10
  PRESSURE BLEEDING 9-12
BRAKE HOSES AND PIPES
  BRAKE PIPE FLARING 9-9
  REMOVAL & INSTALLATION 9-7
BRAKE LIGHT SWITCH
  REMOVAL & INSTALLATION 9-2
BRAKE PEDAL
  REMOVAL & INSTALLATION 9-2
MASTER CYLINDER
  OVERHAUL 9-4
  REMOVAL & INSTALLATION 9-3
POWER BRAKE BOOSTER
  REMOVAL & INSTALLATION 9-7
PROPORTIONING VALVES
  REMOVAL & INSTALLATION 9-7
CIRCUIT PROTECTION
CIRCUIT BREAKERS
  REPLACEMENT 6-68
FLASHERS
  REPLACEMENT 6-68
FUSE BLOCK AND FUSES
  REPLACEMENT 6-66
FUSIBLE LINKS
  REPLACEMENT 6-67
CLUTCH
ADJUSTMENTS
  CLUTCH CABLE 7-22
  HYDRAULIC CLUTCH 7-22
CLUTCH CABLE
  REMOVAL & INSTALLATION 7-22

CLUTCH MASTER AND SLAVE CYLINDER ASSEMBLY
  REMOVAL & INSTALLATION 7-26
CLUTCH PEDAL
  REMOVAL & INSTALLATION 7-22
DRIVEN DISC AND PRESSURE PLATE
  REMOVAL & INSTALLATION 7-24
HYDRAULIC CLUTCH SYSTEM BLEEDING
  WITH BLEED SCREW 7-29
  WITHOUT BLEED SCREW 7-29
COMPUTER CONTROLLED COIL IGNITION (C³I)/ELECTRONIC IGNITION (EI) SYSTEM
3.0L (VIN L), 3.1L (VIN M) AND 3.3L (VIN N) ENGINES
  COMPONENT REPLACEMENT 2-50
  DIAGNOSIS AND TESTING 2-41
  GENERAL DESCRIPTION 2-39
  SYSTEM COMPONENTS 2-39
  SYSTEM OPERATION 2-39
CRUISE CONTROL
ACTUATOR SWITCH
  REMOVAL & INSTALLATION 6-33
BRAKE/CLUTCH RELEASE SWITCHES
  ADJUSTMENT 6-35
  REMOVAL & INSTALLATION 6-35
SPEED SENSOR
  REMOVAL & INSTALLATION 6-35
VACUUM RESERVOIR/TANK
  REMOVAL & INSTALLATION 6-38
VACUUM SERVO UNIT
  REMOVAL & INSTALLATION 6-37
  VACUUM SYSTEM LINKAGE ADJUSTMENT 6-37
DIAGNOSTIC TROUBLE CODES AND CHARTS 4-27
DIRECT IGNITION SYSTEM (DIS)
1987-91 2.5L (VIN U) ENGINE
  COMPONENT REPLACEMENT 2-38
  DIAGNOSIS AND TESTING 2-33
  GENERAL DESCRIPTION 2-33
  SYSTEM COMPONENTS 2-33
  SYSTEM OPERATION 2-33
ELECTRONIC ENGINE CONTROLS
ENGINE COOLANT TEMPERATURE (ECT) SENSOR
  OPERATION 4-17
ENGINE/POWERTRAIN CONTROL MODULE (ECM/PCM)
  FUNCTIONAL CHECK 4-17
  REMOVAL & INSTALLATION 4-17
ESC KNOCK SENSOR (KS)
  OPERATION 4-23
  REMOVAL & INSTALLATION 4-23
IDLE AIR CONTROL (IAC) VALVE
  OPERATION 4-18
MANIFOLD ABSOLUTE PRESSURE (MAP) SENSOR
  OPERATION 4-20
MANIFOLD AIR TEMPERATURE (MAT)/INTAKE AIR TEMPERATURE (IAT) SENSOR
  OPERATION 4-20
MASS AIR FLOW (MAF) SENSOR
  OPERATION 4-20
  REMOVAL & INSTALLATION 4-20
OPERATION 4-16
OXYGEN (O₂) SENSOR
  OPERATION 4-20
THROTTLE POSITION SENSOR (TPS)
  OPERATION 4-22
VEHICLE SPEED SENSOR (VSS)
  OPERATION 4-23
  REMOVAL & INSTALLATION 4-23
EMISSION CONTROLS
CATALYTIC CONVERTER
  OPERATION 4-14

TESTING 4-16
CRANKCASE VENTILATION SYSTEM
  OPERATION 4-6
  TESTING 4-6
EVAPORATIVE EMISSION CONTROL SYSTEM
  OPERATION 4-7
  REMOVAL & INSTALLATION 4-8
  TESTING 4-8
EXHAUST GAS RECIRCULATION SYSTEM
  OPERATION 4-8
  REMOVAL & INSTALLATION 4-10
  TESTING 4-10
ENGINE ELECTRICAL
  ALTERNATOR
    ALTERNATOR PRECAUTIONS 3-4
    REMOVAL & INSTALLATION 3-5
  REGULATOR 3-6
  SENDING UNITS AND SENSORS
    REMOVAL & INSTALLATION 3-10
  STARTER
    REMOVAL & INSTALLATION 3-8
    SOLENOID REPLACEMENT 3-10
    TESTING 3-7
ENGINE MECHANICAL
  BLOCK HEATER
    REMOVAL & INSTALLATION 3-108
  CAMSHAFT
    BEARING REPLACEMENT 3-99
    INSPECTION 3-100
    REMOVAL & INSTALLATION 3-93
  CRANKSHAFT AND MAIN BEARINGS
    CLEANING AND INSPECTION 3-113
    CONNECTING ROD AND MAIN BEARING
    REPLACEMENT 3-114
    REMOVAL & INSTALLATION 3-112
  CRANKSHAFT DAMPENER
    REMOVAL & INSTALLATION 3-80
  CYLINDER HEAD
    CLEANING & INSPECTION 3-68
    REMOVAL & INSTALLATION 3-61
    RESURFACING 3-69
  ENGINE FAN
    REMOVAL & INSTALLATION 3-54
  ENGINE OVERHAUL TIPS
    INSPECTION TECHNIQUES 3-13
    OVERHAUL TIPS 3-13
    REPAIRING DAMAGED THREADS 3-13
    TOOLS 3-13
  ENGINE
    REMOVAL & INSTALLATION 3-23
  EXHAUST MANIFOLD
    REMOVAL & INSTALLATION 3-47
  FLYWHEEL
    REMOVAL & INSTALLATION 3-115
  FREEZE PLUGS
    REMOVAL & INSTALLATION 3-107
  FRONT COVER OIL SEAL
    REPLACEMENT 3-85
  INTAKE MANIFOLD
    REMOVAL & INSTALLATION 3-40
  OIL PAN
    REMOVAL & INSTALLATION 3-72
  OIL PUMP
    INSPECTION 3-78
    OVERHAUL 3-79
    REMOVAL & INSTALLATION 3-77
  PISTONS AND CONNECTING RODS
    CLEANING AND INSPECTION 3-102

HONING 3-104
    INSTALLATION 3-106
    PISTON PIN REPLACEMENT 3-105
    PISTON RING REPLACEMENT 3-105
    REMOVAL 3-100
  RADIATOR
    REMOVAL & INSTALLATION 3-52
  REAR MAIN SEAL
    REMOVAL & INSTALLATION 3-108
  ROCKER ARM ASSEMBLY
    REMOVAL & INSTALLATION 3-36
  ROCKER ARM/VALVE/CAMSHAFT COVER
    REMOVAL & INSTALLATION 3-30
  THERMOSTAT
    REMOVAL & INSTALLATION 3-37
  TIMING BELT AND TENSIONER
    REMOVAL & INSTALLATION 3-86
  TIMING BELT FRONT COVER
    OIL SEAL REPLACEMENT 3-80
    REMOVAL & INSTALLATION 3-80
  TIMING CHAIN AND SPROCKETS
    REMOVAL & INSTALLATION 3-88
  TIMING CHAIN FRONT COVER
    REMOVAL & INSTALLATION 3-80
  TIMING GEAR FRONT COVER
    REMOVAL & INSTALLATION 3-85
  TIMING GEARS
    REMOVAL & INSTALLATION 3-93
  TIMING SPROCKETS
    REMOVAL & INSTALLATION 3-93
  TURBOCHARGER
    REMOVAL & INSTALLATION 3-50
  VALVE GUIDE SERVICE 3-70
  VALVE LIFTERS
    OVERHAUL 3-72
    REMOVAL & INSTALLATION 3-71
  VALVE SPRINGS AND VALVE STEM SEALS
    REMOVAL & INSTALLATION 3-70
    VALVE SPRING TESTING 3-71
  VALVES
    INSPECTION 3-70
    LAPPING 3-70
    REFACING 3-70
    REMOVAL & INSTALLATION 3-69
  WATER PUMP
    REMOVAL & INSTALLATION 3-57
ENTERTAINMENT SYSTEMS
  RADIO RECEIVER/AMPLIFIER/TAPE PLAYER/COMPACT DISC
  PLAYER
    REMOVAL & INSTALLATION 6-38
  SPEAKERS
    REMOVAL & INSTALLATION 6-39
EXHAUST SYSTEM
  CATALYTIC CONVERTER
    REMOVAL & INSTALLATION 3-120
  EXHAUST CROSSOVER PIPE
    REMOVAL & INSTALLATION 3-120
  FRONT EXHAUST PIPE WITH FLANGE/THREE WAY CATALYTIC
  CONVERTER
    REMOVAL & INSTALLATION 3-118
  FRONT EXHAUST PIPE WITHOUT FLANGE
    REMOVAL & INSTALLATION 3-119
  GENERAL INFORMATION 3-117
  INTERMEDIATE PIPE
    REMOVAL & INSTALLATION 3-120
  MUFFLER AND TAILPIPE
    REMOVAL & INSTALLATION 3-121
  SAFETY PRECAUTIONS 3-117

EXTERIOR
ANTENNA
REPLACEMENT 10-13
BUMPERS
REMOVAL & INSTALLATION 10-5
DOORS
ADJUSTMENT 10-2
REMOVAL & INSTALLATION 10-2
FENDERS
REMOVAL & INSTALLATION 10-16
GRILLE
REMOVAL & INSTALLATION 10-11
HOOD
ALIGNMENT 10-3
REMOVAL & INSTALLATION 10-2
OUTSIDE MIRRORS
REMOVAL & INSTALLATION 10-13
TRUNK LID
ALIGNMENT 10-4
REMOVAL & INSTALLATION 10-4
FIRING ORDERS 2-12
FLUIDS AND LUBRICANTS
AUTOMATIC TRANSAXLE
DRAIN AND REFILL 1-36
FLUID RECOMMENDATIONS 1-35
LEVEL CHECK 1-36
PAN AND FILTER SERVICE 1-38
BODY LUBRICATION AND MAINTENANCE
BODY DRAIN HOLES 1-45
DOOR HINGES AND HINGE CHECKS 1-44
LOCK CYLINDERS 1-44
TRUNK LID OR TAILGATE 1-45
BRAKE MASTER CYLINDER
FLUID RECOMMENDATIONS 1-42
LEVEL CHECK 1-42
CHASSIS GREASING 1-44
CLUTCH MASTER CYLINDER
FLUID RECOMMENDATIONS 1-43
LEVEL CHECK 1-43
COOLING SYSTEM
COOLING SYSTEM INSPECTION 1-39
DRAIN AND REFILL 1-41
FLUID RECOMMENDATIONS 1-39
FLUSHING AND CLEANING THE SYSTEM 1-42
LEVEL CHECK 1-39
ENGINE
OIL AND FILTER CHANGE 1-34
OIL LEVEL CHECK 1-33
FLUID DISPOSAL 1-32
FUEL AND ENGINE OIL RECOMMENDATIONS
ENGINE OIL 1-32
FUEL 1-32
MANUAL TRANSAXLE
FLUID RECOMMENDATIONS 1-35
LEVEL CHECK 1-35
POWER STEERING
FLUID RECOMMENDATIONS 1-43
LEVEL CHECK 1-44
REAR WHEEL BEARINGS 1-45
FRONT DISC BRAKES
BRAKE CALIPER
OVERHAUL 9-16
REMOVAL & INSTALLATION 9-14
BRAKE DISC (ROTOR)
INSPECTION 9-17
REMOVAL & INSTALLATION 9-17
BRAKE PADS
INSPECTION 9-14

REMOVAL & INSTALLATION 9-12
FRONT SUSPENSION
FRONT END ALIGNMENT 8-13
FRONT HUB AND BEARING
REMOVAL & INSTALLATION 8-12
LOWER BALL JOINT
INSPECTION 8-6
REMOVAL & INSTALLATION 8-6
LOWER CONTROL ARM/SUSPENSION SUPPORT
CONTROL ARM BUSHING REPLACEMENT 8-9
REMOVAL & INSTALLATION 8-8
MACPHERSON STRUTS
REMOVAL & INSTALLATION 8-3
STABILIZER SHAFT AND BUSHINGS
REMOVAL & INSTALLATION 8-7
STEERING KNUCKLE
REMOVAL & INSTALLATION 8-9
FUEL LINE FITTINGS
QUICK-CONNECT FITTINGS
REMOVAL & INSTALLATION 5-38
FUEL TANK
TANK ASSEMBLY
DRAINING 5-39
REMOVAL & INSTALLATION 5-39
SENDING UNIT REPLACEMENT 5-40
HEATER
BLOWER MOTOR AND FAN
REMOVAL & INSTALLATION 6-14
BLOWER SWITCH
REMOVAL & INSTALLATION 6-19
CONTROL PANEL/HEAD
REMOVAL & INSTALLATION 6-18
GENERAL INFORMATION 6-14
HEATER CORE
REMOVAL & INSTALLATION 6-15
TEMPERATURE CONTROL CABLE
ADJUSTMENT 6-16
REMOVAL & INSTALLATION 6-16
HIGH ENERGY IGNITION (HEI) SYSTEM
2.0L (VIN M) AND 1985-86 2.5L (VIN U) ENGINES
COMPONENT REPLACEMENT 2-20
DIAGNOSIS AND TESTING 2-15
GENERAL DESCRIPTION 2-13
SYSTEM COMPONENTS 2-14
SYSTEM OPERATION 2-14
HOW TO USE THIS BOOK 1-2
IDLE SPEED AND MIXTURE ADJUSTMENTS 2-57
IGNITION TIMING
INSPECTION AND ADJUSTMENT
1985-86 2.5L (VIN U) ENGINE 2-56
2.0L (VIN M) ENGINE 2-56
INSTRUMENTS AND SWITCHES
HEADLIGHT SWITCH
REMOVAL & INSTALLATION 6-55
INSTRUMENT CLUSTER
REMOVAL & INSTALLATION 6-49
PRINTED CIRCUIT BOARD
REMOVAL & INSTALLATION 6-53
SPEEDOMETER CABLE
REMOVAL & INSTALLATION 6-53
SPEEDOMETER
REMOVAL & INSTALLATION 6-53
WINDSHIELD WIPER SWITCH
REMOVAL & INSTALLATION 6-54
**INTEGRATED DIRECT IGNITION (IDI)/ELECTRONIC IGNITION
SYSTEM**
2.3L (VIN A, D, AND 3) ENGINES
COMPONENT REPLACEMENT 2-26

DIAGNOSIS AND TESTING 2-26
GENERAL DESCRIPTION 2-23
SYSTEM COMPONENTS 2-24
SYSTEM OPERATION 2-24
INTERIOR
CENTER CONSOLE
  REMOVAL & INSTALLATION 10-22
DOOR GLASS
  REMOVAL & INSTALLATION 10-38
DOOR LOCKS
  REMOVAL & INSTALLATION 10-35
DOOR PANELS
  REMOVAL & INSTALLATION 10-23
ELECTRIC WINDOW MOTOR
  REMOVAL & INSTALLATION 10-39
HEADLINER
  REMOVAL & INSTALLATION 10-31
INSIDE REAR VIEW MIRROR
  REPLACEMENT 10-44
INSTRUMENT PANEL AND PAD
  REMOVAL & INSTALLATION 10-18
INTERIOR TRIM PANELS
  REMOVAL & INSTALLATION 10-27
POWER SEAT MOTOR
  REMOVAL & INSTALLATION 10-50
REAR QUARTER WINDOW
  REMOVAL & INSTALLATION 10-41
SEAT BELTS
  REMOVAL & INSTALLATION 10-46
SEATS
  REMOVAL & INSTALLATION 10-46
WINDOW REGULATOR
  REMOVAL & INSTALLATION 10-38
WINDSHIELD AND REAR WINDOW
  REMOVAL & INSTALLATION 10-40
JACKING
CHANGING A FLAT TIRE 1-46
JUMP STARTING 1-48
LIGHTING
FOG LIGHTS
  AIMING 6-65
  REMOVAL & INSTALLATION 6-64
HEADLIGHTS
  AIMING 6-58
  REMOVAL & INSTALLATION 6-56
SIGNAL AND MARKER LIGHTS
  REMOVAL & INSTALLATION 6-59
MANUAL TRANSAXLE
ADJUSTMENTS
  SHIFT LINKAGE 7-2
BACK-UP LIGHT SWITCH
  REMOVAL & INSTALLATION 7-2
GENERAL INFORMATION 7-2
HALFSHAFTS/DRIVE AXLES
  CV-JOINT OVERHAUL 7-17
  REMOVAL & INSTALLATION 7-14
IDENTIFICATION 7-2
METRIC FASTENERS 7-2
TRANSAXLE
  REMOVAL & INSTALLATION 7-2
MODEL IDENTIFICATION 1-7
MULTI-PORT FUEL INJECTION SYSTEM
ELECTRIC FUEL PUMP
  FUEL PRESSURE TESTING 5-15
  REMOVAL & INSTALLATION 5-13
FUEL INJECTORS
  REMOVAL & INSTALLATION 5-22

FUEL PRESSURE REGULATOR
  REMOVAL & INSTALLATION 5-23
FUEL PUMP RELAY
  REMOVAL & INSTALLATION 5-26
FUEL RAIL ASSEMBLY
  REMOVAL & INSTALLATION 5-19
IDLE AIR CONTROL (IAC) VALVE
  REMOVAL & INSTALLATION 5-25
RELIEVING FUEL SYSTEM PRESSURE
  WITH FUEL RAIL TEST FITTING 5-12
  WITHOUT FUEL RAIL TEST FITTING 5-13
SYSTEM DESCRIPTION
  OPERATING MODES 5-10
THROTTLE BODY
  REMOVAL & INSTALLATION 5-15
THROTTLE POSITION (TP) SENSOR
  ADJUSTMENT 5-25
  REMOVAL & INSTALLATION 5-24
PARKING BRAKE
CABLES
  ADJUSTMENT 9-27
  REMOVAL & INSTALLATION 9-25
PARKING BRAKE LEVER
  REMOVAL & INSTALLATION 9-27
REAR DRUM BRAKES
BRAKE BACKING PLATE
  REMOVAL & INSTALLATION 9-24
BRAKE DRUMS
  INSPECTION 9-18
  REMOVAL & INSTALLATION 9-18
BRAKE SHOES
  INSPECTION 9-18
  REMOVAL & INSTALLATION 9-18
WHEEL CYLINDERS
  OVERHAUL 9-23
  REMOVAL & INSTALLATION 9-22
REAR SUSPENSION
COIL SPRINGS AND INSULATORS
  REMOVAL & INSTALLATION 8-16
CONTROL ARM BUSHING
  REMOVAL & INSTALLATION 8-16
REAR END ALIGNMENT 8-20
REAR HUB AND BEARING
  REMOVAL & INSTALLATION 8-19
SHOCK ABSORBERS
  REMOVAL & INSTALLATION 8-16
STABILIZER BAR
  REMOVAL & INSTALLATION 8-19
ROUTINE MAINTENANCE
AIR CLEANER
  REMOVAL & INSTALLATION 1-16
AIR CONDITIONING SYSTEM
  DISCHARGING, EVACUATING AND CHARGING 1-26
  GAUGE SETS 1-26
  SAFETY PRECAUTIONS 1-25
  SYSTEM INSPECTION 1-26
BATTERY
  CABLES 1-19
  CHARGING 1-20
  FLUID LEVEL (EXCEPT MAINTENANCE-FREE
  BATTERIES) 1-18
  GENERAL MAINTENANCE 1-18
  REPLACEMENT 1-21
  SPECIFIC GRAVITY (EXCEPT MAINTENANCE-FREE
  BATTERIES) 1-19
  TESTING 1-19
BELTS
  ADJUSTING 1-22

INSPECTION 1-22
    REMOVAL & INSTALLATION 1-22
CV-BOOT
    INSPECTION 1-25
EVAPORATIVE CANISTER
    REMOVAL & INSTALLATION 1-18
FUEL FILTER
    REMOVAL & INSTALLATION 1-17
HOSES
    REMOVAL & INSTALLATION 1-24
PCV VALVE
    REMOVAL & INSTALLATION 1-17
TIMING BELT
    INSPECTION 1-24
TIRES AND WHEELS
    CARE OF SPECIAL WHEELS 1-32
    TIRE DESIGN 1-27
    TIRE INFLATION 1-31
    TIRE ROTATION 1-27
    TIRE STORAGE 1-31
WINDSHIELD WIPERS
    REMOVAL & INSTALLATION 1-27
SELF-DIAGNOSTIC SYSTEMS
DASHBOARD WARNING LAMP 4-24
DIAGNOSIS AND TESTING
    CLEARING THE TROUBLE CODES 4-26
    DIAGNOSTIC MODE 4-26
    FIELD SERVICE MODE 4-26
    TROUBLESHOOTING 4-25
GENERAL INFORMATION 4-24
INTERMITTENTS 4-24
LEARNING ABILITY 4-24
TOOLS AND EQUIPMENT
    ELECTRICAL TOOLS 4-25
    SCAN TOOLS 4-25
SEQUENTIAL FUEL INJECTION
ELECTRIC FUEL PUMP
    REMOVAL & INSTALLATION 5-31
FUEL INJECTORS
    REMOVAL & INSTALLATION 5-33
FUEL PRESSURE REGULATOR
    REMOVAL & INSTALLATION 5-36
FUEL PUMP RELAY
    REMOVAL & INSTALLATION 5-38
FUEL RAIL ASSEMBLY
    REMOVAL & INSTALLATION 5-35
IDLE AIR CONTROL (IAC) VALVE
    REMOVAL & INSTALLATION 5-37
INTAKE MANIFOLD PLENUM
    REMOVAL & INSTALLATION 5-33
RELIEVING FUEL SYSTEM PRESSURE 5-31
SYSTEM DESCRIPTION
    OPERATING MODES 5-30
THROTTLE BODY
    REMOVAL & INSTALLATION 5-33
THROTTLE POSITION (TP) SENSOR
    REMOVAL & INSTALLATION 5-37
SERIAL NUMBER IDENTIFICATION
ENGINE 1-7
TRANSAXLE 1-7
VEHICLE 1-7
SERVICING YOUR VEHICLE SAFELY
DO'S 1-5
DON'TS 1-6
SPECIFICATIONS CHARTS
ALTERNATOR SPECIFICATIONS 3-7
BRAKE SPECIFICATIONS 9-49
CAMSHAFT SPECIFICATIONS 3-18

CAPACITIES 1-48
CRANKSHAFT AND CONNECTING ROD SPECIFICATIONS 3-20
ENGINE IDENFICATION 1-7
ENGINE REBUILDING SPECIFICATIONS 3-124
GENERAL ENGINE SPECIFICATIONS 3-15
MAINTENANCE INTERVALS 1-48
PISTON AND RING SPECIFICATIONS 3-22
STARTER SPECIFICATIONS 3-10
TORQUE SPECIFICATIONS 9-49, 10-50, 3-124
TUNE-UP SPECIFICATIONS 2-58
VALVE SPECIFICATIONS 3-16
VEHICLE IDENTIFICATION 1-7
WHEEL ALIGNMENT SPECIFICATIONS 8-14
STEERING
IGNITION LOCK CYLINDER
    REMOVAL & INSTALLATION 8-28
IGNITION SWITCH
    REMOVAL & INSTALLATION 8-26
POWER STEERING PUMP
    BELT ADJUSTMENT 8-36
    BLEEDING 8-36
    REMOVAL & INSTALLATION 8-33
POWER STEERING RACK AND PINION
    ADJUSTMENT 8-31
    REMOVAL & INSTALLATION 8-31
STEERING COLUMN
    REMOVAL & INSTALLATION 8-28
STEERING LINKAGE
    REMOVAL & INSTALLATION 8-30
STEERING WHEEL
    REMOVAL & INSTALLATION 8-21
TURN SIGNAL SWITCH
    REMOVAL & INSTALLATION 8-22
SUPPLEMENTAL INFLATABLE RESTRAINT (SIR) SYSTEM
GENERAL INFORMATION
    DISABLING THE SYSTEM 6-13
    ENABLING THE SYSTEM 6-13
    SERVICE PRECAUTIONS 6-13
    SYSTEM COMPONENTS 6-10
    SYSTEM OPERATION 6-10
THROTTLE BODY FUEL INJECTION SYSTEM
ELECTRIC FUEL PUMP
    FUEL PRESSURE TESTING 5-4
    REMOVAL & INSTALLATION 5-4
FUEL METER BODY
    INJECTOR REPLACEMENT 5-6
    REMOVAL & INSTALLATION 5-6
FUEL PRESSURE REGULATOR
    REMOVAL & INSTALLATION 5-7
FUEL PUMP RELAY
    REMOVAL & INSTALLATION 5-8
IDLE AIR CONTROL (IAC) VALVE
    REMOVAL & INSTALLATION 5-8
RELIEVING FUEL SYSTEM PRESSURE 5-4
SYSTEM DESCRIPTION
    OPERATING MODES 5-2
THROTTLE BODY
    REMOVAL & INSTALLATION 5-5
THROTTLE POSITION (TP) SENSOR
    REMOVAL & INSTALLATION 5-7
TUBE MODULE
    REMOVAL & INSTALLATION 5-8
TOOLS AND EQUIPMENT
SPECIAL TOOLS 1-5
TOWING THE VEHICLE 1-46
TRAILER TOWING
GENERAL RECOMMENDATIONS 1-45
HITCH WEIGHT 1-45

TRAILER WEIGHT   1-45
WIRING   1-45
TRAILER WIRING   6-65
TUNE-UP PROCEDURES
 SPARK PLUG WIRES
  REMOVAL & INSTALLATION   2-11
  TESTING   2-11
 SPARK PLUGS
  REMOVAL & INSTALLATION   2-2
  SPARK PLUG HEAT RANGE   2-2
  SPARK PLUG INSPECTION   2-10
UNDERSTANDING AND TROUBLESHOOTING ELECTRICAL
 SYSTEMS
 MECHANICAL TEST EQUIPMENT
  HAND VACUUM PUMP   6-9
  VACUUM GAUGE   6-9
 SAFETY PRECAUTIONS
  ORGANIZED TROUBLESHOOTING   6-2
  TEST EQUIPMENT   6-3
 WIRING HARNESSES
  WIRE GAUGE   6-7
  WIRING DIAGRAMS   6-7

WIRING REPAIR   6-8
VACUUM DIAGRAMS   4-117
VALVE LASH   2-57
WHEELS
 FRONT AND REAR WHEELS
  INSPECTION   8-2
  REMOVAL & INSTALLATION   8-2
 WHEEL LUG STUDS
  REPLACEMENT   8-2
WINDSHIELD WIPERS AND WASHERS
 WINDSHIELD WASHER FLUID RESERVOIR
  REMOVAL & INSTALLATION   6-48
 WINDSHIELD WASHER MOTOR
  REMOVAL & INSTALLATION   6-48
 WINDSHIELD WIPER BLADE AND ARM
  REMOVAL & INSTALLATION   6-43
 WINDSHIELD WIPER MOTOR
  REMOVAL & INSTALLATION   6-43
 WIPER LINKAGE
  REMOVAL & INSTALLATION   6-43
WIRING DIAGRAMS   6-69